MANAGEMENT PERSPECTIVE

INTERNATIONAL PERSPECTIVE

ONLINE ACTIVITIES

Included at the end of every chapter are at least two Internet exercises that students can perform to learn more about topics covered in the chapter. These exercises, as well as a number of interactive quiz questions per chapter, are available on the *Business Law Today, Comprehensive Edition,* Seventh Edition, Web site at

http://blt.westbuslaw.com

ON THE WEB

These margin features give specific Uniform Resource Locators (URLs), or Internet addresses, concerning topics discussed in the text. You will find over one hundred such references throughout this text. Two examples are shown here.

You can find links to most uniform laws online at the Web site of the National Conference of Commissioners on Uniform State Laws. Go to

http://www.nccusl.org.

To find state compilations (codes) of statutory laws, go to

http://www.findlaw.com/casecode/state.html.

Business Law for Today's Real-World Business Environment

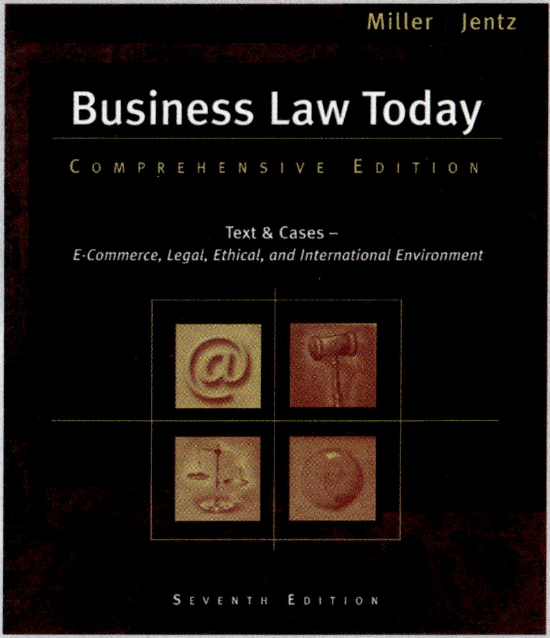

Fascinating . . .

new cases

new online tools

the latest on cyberlaw and bankruptcy

Immersing students in the excitement of intriguing new cases and the latest developments in the field, this Seventh Edition of Miller and Jentz's

***Business Law Today*, Comprehensive Edition**

brings real-world energy to the study of business law.

Students respond to each chapter's visually engaging, carefully crafted learning tools, which *illustrate* how law is applied to real-world business problems . . . *and* how landmark cases, statutes, and other laws are having significant impact on the way businesses operate in the United States and globally. Instructors praise the authors' comprehensive attention to leading-edge topics without sacrificing coverage of traditional business law.

There are many reasons why this 7th Edition of ***Business Law Today*, Comprehensive Edition** is an indispensable resource for your business law course. Here are just a few:

- **Exceptional new coverage of cyberlaw, ethics, and professional responsibility integrated throughout**
  See page two of this Preview
- **High-interest, real-world cases (more than 70 percent of the cases in this edition are new)**
  See page three of this Preview
- **Many Application features that offer practical advice on correctly applying the law**
  See page four of this Preview
- **New material in every chapter of this significant revision**
  See page five of this Preview
- **Landmark cases, insightful perspectives, essential study tools**
  See pages six and seven of this Preview

Plus many online, video, and CD-ROM tools, as well as an extensive Course Planning Guide that helps you to effectively use all these great tools for course preparation, lecture presentation, exam preparation, and more. This textbook features the most comprehensive, state-of-the-art array of ancillary materials every offered for this course!

LEADING-EDGE TOPICS

The newest developments in cyberlaw and practical, example-rich coverage of ethical responsibility

NEW! *Adapting the Law to the Online Environment*

Completely new to this edition, *Adapting the Law to the Online Environment* features cutting-edge cyberlaw issues coming before today's courts. For example, "Stalking and Internet Data Brokers" explores whether or not a Web broker who sells personal information to a stalker can be sued under tort law. Other *Adapting the Law to the Online Environment* topics include "International Jurisdiction and the Internet," "School Shootings and Strict Liability," "Who Bears the Costs of Electronic Discovery?" and many others.

ADAPTING THE LAW TO THE ONLINE ENVIRONMENT

Stalking and Internet Data Brokers

A cutting-edge issue coming before today's courts has to do with stalking and Internet data brokers—those in the business of selling personal information via the Internet. Suppose that a stalker purchases personal information (such as a home address) from a Web broker and then uses that information to commit a crime (such as murder). The stalker, of course, can be prosecuted under criminal law for the crime of murder. At issue is the broker's responsibility for the crime. Can the broker be sued under tort law (see Chapter 4) for damages?

ONE COURT WEIGHS IN

At least one court has weighed in on this issue. In ...*search, Inc.*,[a] the Supreme Court of ...

Helen Remsburg, Boyer's mother, sued Docusearch, claiming that the defendant had acted wrongfully. The federal district court referred the case to the New Hampshire Supreme Court for a determination of the parties' duties under the state's common law. The state supreme court held that an information broker who sells information about a third person to a client has a duty to exercise reasonable care in disclosing the information.

A FORESEEABLE RISK?

One of the key issues for the court was whether the crime committed by Youens was a foreseeable risk to Docusearch. Remember from Chapter 4 that under tort law, the test for proximate cause—and the extent of a defendant's duty of care—is the foreseeability of a risk of harm. If certain consequences of an action are not foreseeable, there is no proximate cause.

New coverage of Internet law integrated throughout

Leading-edge topics relating to cyberlaw in this Seventh Edition include privacy rights in the online world, jurisdictional issues that arise in cyberspace, cyber torts and cyber crimes, and online securities offerings. The Seventh Edition also includes an entire chapter devoted to e-contracts (Chapter 17).

Many new *Ethical Issue* features

Numbered for easy access, these special features address ethical dilemmas related to the chapter topic. New *Ethical Issues* include "Should Secret Settlements Be Allowed?" "How Can a Business Decide Whether a Warning Is Adequate?" "Should Insider Trading Be Legal?" and "Does an Insurance Agent Have a Duty to Advise Insurance Applicants about Coverage?"

ETHICAL ISSUE 3.2

Should "Secret" Settlements Be Allowed? Perhaps one of the greatest incentives for settling a case is to avoid the publicity of a trial. Often an individual or business defendant is willing to pay a significant amount of money in return for the plaintiff's silence about the terms of the settlement. This practice, however, is increasingly coming under fire, particularly when the lawsuit involves a potential public safety or health hazard. For example, suppose that you are seriously injured by a defective product and sue the manufacturer of that product (product liability will be discussed in Chapter 18). Rather than proceed to trial, the manufacturer offers to pay you several million dollars provided that you agree to keep the terms of the settlement confidential. Many plaintiffs would find it difficult to refuse such an offer.

CHAPTER 7

Ethics and Business Decision Making

"New occasions teach new duties."

James Russell Lowell, 1819–1891
(American editor, poet, and diplomat)

"Ethics and Business Decision Making"

Chapter 7, "Ethics and Business Decision Making," now presents a more practical approach to ethics and examines several companies that have been accused of defying their ethical obligations (including the Enron Corporation and Merck & Company), as well as a discussion of the Sarbanes-Oxley Act and the corporate scandals that led to the passage of that legislation. In addition, many of the cases in the text conclude with an "Ethical Consideration" that encourages students to probe the ethical ramifications of the court's decision.

CASE 7.1 Time Warner Entertainment Co. v. Six Flags Over Georgia, L.L.C.

Georgia Court of Appeals, 2002.
254 Ga.App. 598,
563 S.E.2d 178.
http://www.ganet.org/appeals/opinions/index.cgi[a]

BACKGROUND AND FACTS The Six Flags Over Georgia theme park in Atlanta, Georgia, was developed in 1967 as a limited partnership known as Six Flags Over Georgia, L.L.C. (Flags). The sole limited partner was Six Flags Fund, Limited (Fund). The general partner was Six Flags Over Georgia, Inc. (SFOG). In 1991, Time Warner Entertainment Company (TWE) became the majority shareholder of SFOG. The next year, TWE secretly bought 13.7 acres of land next to the park, limiting the park's expansion opportunities. Over the next couple of years, using confidential business information from the park, TWE began plans to develop a competing park. Meanwhile, TWE installed no major new attractions at the park, deferred basic maintenance, withheld financial information from Fund (the limited partner), and began signing future employment contracts with SFOG officers. TWE also charged Flags for unrelated expenses, including over $4 million for lunches in New York City and luxury automobiles for TWE officers. Flags and Fund filed a suit in a Georgia state court against TWE and SFOG, alleging, among other things, breach of fiduciary duty. A jury awarded the plaintiffs $197,296,000 in compensatory damages and $257,000,000 in punitive damages. TWE appealed to a state intermediate appellate court, alleging in part that the amount of the punitive damages was excessive.

a. At the search screen, click on "Search Court of Appeals Opinions." On the appellate court's screen, set the search year to "all." You can go to a case most directly if you use as key words the full name of a party—for example, "Time Warner Entertainment Co." This Web site is sponsored by the state of Georgia.

IN THE WORDS OF THE COURT . . .
ELLINGTON, Judge.

* * * *

We begin our analysis by examining the degree of reprehensibility [wrongfulness] of appellants' conduct in this case. *In examining the degree of reprehensibility of a defendant's conduct, [there are] a number of aggravating factors [to consider], including whether the harm was more than purely economic in nature, and whether* ...

FOR CRITICAL ANALYSIS—Ethical Consideration
If TWE had proceeded with its plans to build a competing park but had not otherwise acted "reprehensibly" toward Flags and Fund, how might the decision in this case have been different?

DECISION AND REMEDY The state intermediate appellate court affirmed the judgment of the lower court, finding that the award of punitive damages was not excessive, considering the defendants' financial status and "reprehensible" conduct toward the plaintiffs.

Setting the Right Ethical Tone

Many unethical business decisions are made simply because they *can* be ma... other words, the decision makers not only have the opportunity to make such... sions but also are not too concerned about being seriously sanctioned for their... ical actions. Perhaps one of the most difficult challenges for business leaders to... to create the right "ethical tone" in their workplaces so as to deter unethical co...

THE IMPORTANCE OF ETHICAL LEADERSHIP

Talking about ethical business decision making means nothing if managemen... not set standards. Moreover, managers must apply those standards to themselv...

Many new cases—fascinating stories that clarify legal principles and issues faced by today's businesses

No other business law text offers the quality and presentation of case material you'll find here. Relevant, engaging, and current—with nearly 70 percent new to this edition, including forty-three cases decided in 2003 and 2004—these cases were chosen specifically to reflect the most current law or represent a significant precedent in case law. After briefly outlining the background and facts of the case, the words of the court are given, followed by a section entitled "Decision and Remedy," in which the authors summarize the court's decision. Numbered sequentially for easy referencing, the cases offer excellent topics for class discussion and homework assignments.

CASE 2.3 Interactive Digital Software Association v. St. Louis County, Missouri

WHY IS THIS CASE IMPORTANT? *Even though the courts allow more regulation of commercial speech than other types of speech, the state's power to regulate such speech is still limited. Proof that the message is violent or objectionable in some way does not justify regulating commercial speech. The government must establish that it has a substantial interest in regulating the speech and that the proposed regulation advances that interest.*

NEW!
Why Is This Case Important?

One case in each chapter now includes a section titled *Why Is This Case Important?* that clearly sets forth the practical relevance of the case for businesspersons today.

Extended Case Studies
at the end of each unit—all are NEW!

These recent (2003 and 2004) court cases enrich students' understanding of a key principle or topic covered in the unit. Each begins by discussing the background and significance of the case, then presents the majority and dissenting opinions. The presentation concludes with *Questions for Analysis* that encourage students to evaluate the legal, ethical, economic, international, or general business implications of the case.

UNIT ONE Extended Case Study
Vo v. City of Garden Grove

MAJORITY OPINION
IKOLA, J. [Judge]
* * *

DISSENTING OPINION
SILLS, P.J. [Presiding Judge], * * * Dissenting.

QUESTIONS FOR ANALYSIS
1 Law. What is the significant, or substantial, governmental interest that is supported by the city ordinance in the *Vo* case?

NEW!
Case Problem with Sample Answer
at the end of every chapter!

These realistic scenarios—no more than a paragraph long—include a sample answer located on the Book Companion Website. The sample answer provides a model for students—helping them to more effectively respond to other case problems they will encounter in this book.

CASE PROBLEM WITH SAMPLE ANSWER

5–5. In 1999, Steve and Pierce Thumann and their father, Fred, created Spider Webs, Ltd., a partnership, to, according to Steve, "develop Internet address names." Spider Webs registered nearly two thousand Internet domain names for an average of $70 each, including the

Plus many new
Questions and Case Problems
for analysis at the end of each chapter

QUESTIONS AND CASE PROBLEMS

5–1. Copyright Infringement. In which of the following situations would a court likely hold Maruta liable for copyright infringement?

APPLICATIONS AND CASES THAT TEACH

Application features practical advice on how to apply the law

Typically one or two pages in length, the *Application* feature included in most chapters offers specific, practical advice on ways to navigate the legal waters of the business environment. For example, this new *Application* from Chapter 5 discusses how to protect trade secrets with specific do's and don't for developing confidentiality agreements. Other *Application* topics include "How Can You Create an Ethical Workplace?" "How Can You Prevent Problems with Oral Contracts?" "How to Negotiate a Favorable Business Lease" and many more.

APPLICATION How Can You Protect Your Trade Secrets?*

Most successful businesses have trade secrets. The law protects trade secrets indefinitely, provided that the information is not generally known, is kept a secret, and has commercial value. Sometimes, of course, a business needs to disclose secret information to a party in the course of conducting business. For example, a company may need to hire a consultant to revamp a computer system, an engineer to design a manufacturing system, or a marketing firm to implement a sales program. All of these individuals may need access to some of the company's trade secrets. One way to protect against the unauthorized disclosure of such information is through confidentiality agreements.

CONFIDENTIALITY AGREEMENTS

In a confidentiality agreement, one party promises not to divulge information about the other party to anyone else or to use the other party's confidential information for his or her own benefit. Confidentiality agreements are often included in licensing and employment contracts, but they can also be separate contracts. The key is to make sure that the agreement adequately protects the trade secrets and applies to any related transactions between the parties. For instance, if you execute a separate confidentiality agreement with a marketing firm, you need to make sure that it refers to any other contracts you have made with that firm prior to the confidentiality agreement. Also, subsequent contracts with the firm should either refer back to the confidentiality agreement or include a new confidentiality provision.

DEFINING THE SCOPE OF THE AGREEMENT

Confidentiality agreements must be reasonable. Businesspersons should consider what information needs to be protected and for how long. Make certain to define what you mean by *confidential information* in the agreement. Do you want to protect just your customer list or all financial, technical, and other business information? Think ahead, cover the bases, and be specific.

The duration of the agreement usually depends on the nature of the information. Very important secret information should remain confidential for a longer time than less important secrets. Sometimes, as with an advertising campaign, the time period for confidentiality may be self-evident (if the campaign ends in six months, for example). Tailor the agreement to your needs as much as possible. If the party to whom you are disclosing information will no longer need the information after a certain date—such as when the project is completed—include a provision requiring the return of confidential information after that date. This will alleviate concerns that your confidential trade secrets might later fall into the hands of a stranger.

CHECKLIST FOR THE OWNER OF TRADE SECRETS

1. Determine what your trade secrets are and who may need access to them.
2. Make sure that confidentiality agreements define, in an all-inclusive manner, what information should be considered confidential.
3. Specify a time period that is reasonable under the circumstances.
4. Identify the agreements to which the confidentiality provisions apply.
5. Require that the confidential materials be returned to you.

* This *Application* is not meant to substitute for the services of an attorney who is licensed to practice law in your state.

Featured Cases that test comprehension

In each of the nine units, we present one or more *Featured Cases* that do not include the usual pedagogy ("Background and Facts," "In the Words of the Court," and "Decision and Remedy"). Instead, only the words of the court are given—including a dissenting opinion—followed by a series of five questions in a section titled "Test Your Comprehension: Case Details."

Featured Case

CASE 5.3 New York Times Co. v. Tasini

Supreme Court of the United States, 2001.
533 U.S. 483,
121 S.Ct. 2381,
150 L.Ed.2d 500.
http://straylight.law.cornell.edu/supct/index.html[a]

a. In the "Search" box at the top of the page, enter "Tasini." Click on "search." On the page that opens, in the "Search for:" box, type in "Tasini." Then select "All decisions" and click on "Search." In the result, scroll to the case name and select the appropriate link to access the opinion.

MAJORITY OPINION

Justice *GINSBURG* delivered the opinion of the Court.

* * * *

Respondents Jonathan Tasini, Mary Kay Blakely, Barbara Garson, Margot Mifflin, Sonia Jaffe Robbins, and David S. Whitford are authors (Authors). Between

(Continued)

TEST YOUR COMPREHENSION: CASE DETAILS

1. What was at the center of the dispute between the parties in this case?
2. Which side do you think has the better argument in this case? Why?
3. According to the United States Supreme Court, do publishers who want to put the contents of periodicals into e-databases and onto CD-ROMs need to obtain the permission of the writers whose contributions are included?
4. The Copyright Act of 1976 was enacted before the Internet and online databases became widely used. Should the act apply to the uses of copyrighted material at issue in this case? Explain.
5. When rights such as those in this case become more valuable as a result of new technology, should the law be changed to redistribute the economic benefit of those rights? Why or why not?

Take a close look for relevant, involving, and leading-edge material throughout

- New coverage of the *Bankruptcy Reform Act of 2005*
- The most recent and significant court decisions
- The *USA Patriot Act* and its effect on constitutional rights
- New sections discussing corporate governance and the impact of the Sarbanes-Oxley Act in this area
- "Electronic Discovery"—a new section discussing electronic evidence and discovery issues
- New material on the *CAN-SPAM Act of 2003,* as well as on spamming and online defamation
- Added coverage of intellectual property rights, including recent Supreme Court decisions, file sharing, and practical advice on how to protect trade secrets
- The 2003 amendments to Article 2 and 2A—and how they alter existing law
- Completely updated discussion of e-contracts, including additional examples and expanded coverage of the *Uniform Electronic Transactions Act*
- A reorganized and streamlined unit on business organizations, including agency relationships in business, sole proprietorships, partnerships, corporate formation, corporate mergers, and more
- A new section on identity theft and the *Fair and Accurate Credit Transactions Act of 2003*
- Thoroughly updated coverage of employment law, including the latest developments and court decisions concerning such issues as telecommuting and work-place safety laws, electronic surveillance of employees and privacy rights, online harassment, and genetic testing
- "Business Activities and the Legal Environment"—a new section showing students how many different areas of law can affect a single business transaction

The Bankruptcy Reform Act of 2005

"In 2005, the United States Supreme Court held that Congress has the authority to prohibit the intrastate . . ."

"In 2005, however, the United States Supreme Court addressed this issue in *Metro-Goldwyn-Mayer Studios, Inc. v. Grokster, Ltd.* . . ."

Featured Case: *Kelo v. New London, Connecticut,* 2005

APPLICATIONS AND CASES THAT TEACH

IMPORTANT FOR UNDERSTANDING

Seminal cases and many insightful perspectives enrich understanding and promote critical thinking

Each of these features explores a landmark case, statute, or other law that has had a significant impact on business law. Each includes a brief *Application to Today's Business World* discussion, focusing students on why the case is important to businesses today. The *Landmark in the Law* features in this edition include "The Bankruptcy Reform Act of 2005," "The Digital Millennium Copyright Act of 1998," *Marbury v. Madison* (1803)," and "The Check 21 Act." To help students learn about these cases and laws, this edition also includes a new "Relevant Web Sites" section within each *Landmark in the Law*.

Landmark in the Law—pivotal cases come to life

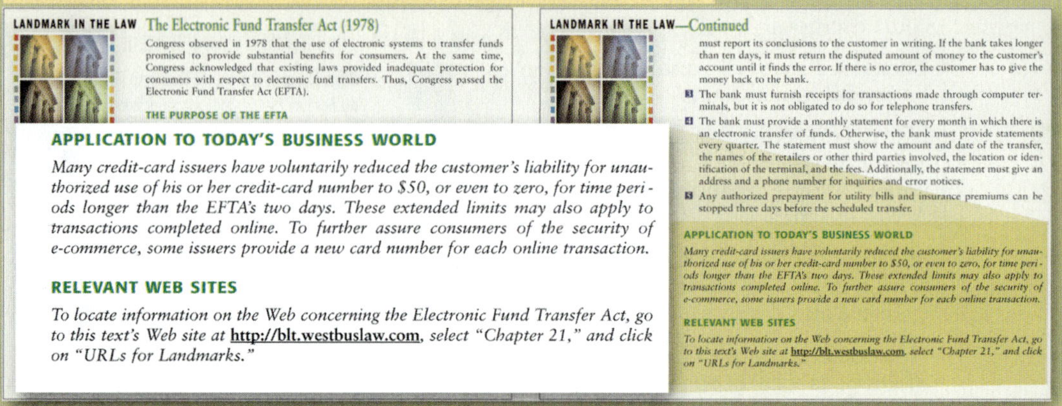

Management Perspectives

Each *Management Perspective* contains three sections: a "Management Faces a Legal Issue" section that describes a practical issue facing management; a "What the Courts Say" section that presents what the courts have concluded concerning the issue; and an "Implications for Managers" section that indicates the importance of the courts' decisions for business making and offers some practical guidance.

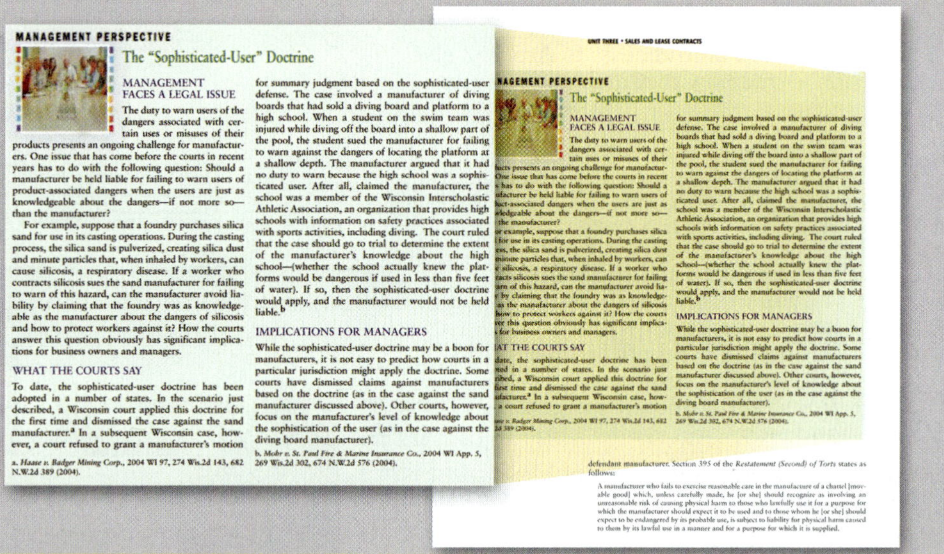

International Perspectives—the global legal environment

Expanding students' awareness of the global legal environment, these perspectives show how international law and the laws of other nations deal with specific topics or concepts being discussed.

In-chapter learning tools and other resources that help students excel in this course

STUDY FOR RESULTS

Learning Objectives linked to *For Review* questions

The numbered *Learning Objectives* located at the beginning of each chapter are presented again as *For Review* questions near the end of the chapter—giving students both a framework for reading the chapter and structured opportunities to review chapter highlights. Answers to even-numbered *For Review* questions are can be found in Appendix P, which is new to this edition.

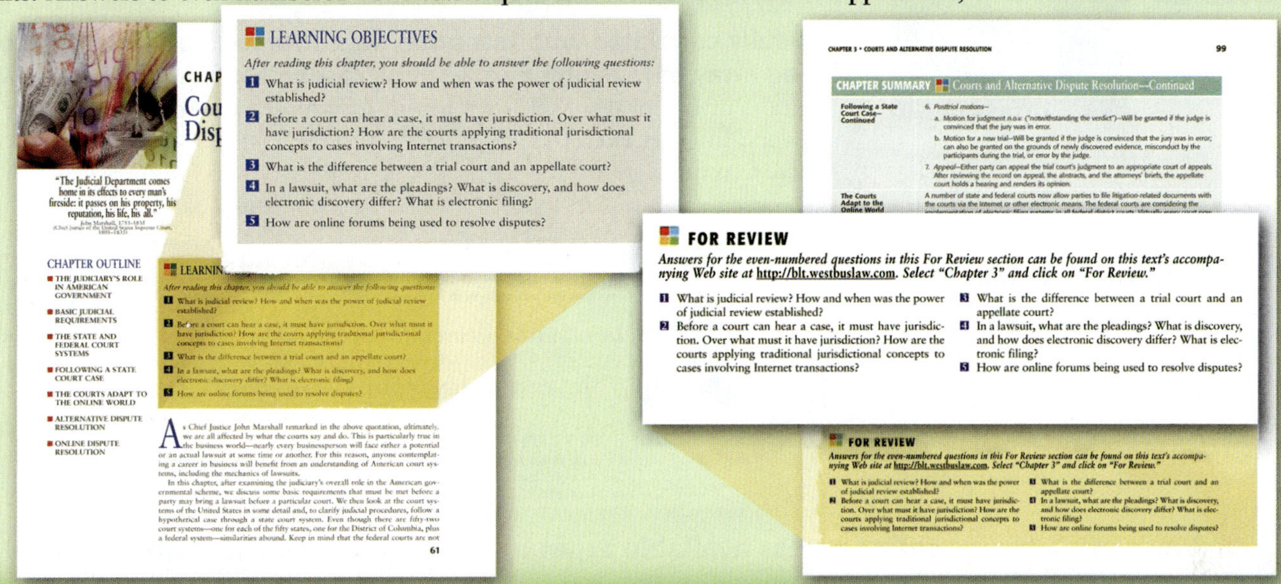

LEARNING OBJECTIVES

After reading this chapter, you should be able to answer the following questions:

1. What is judicial review? How and when was the power of judicial review established?
2. Before a court can hear a case, it must have jurisdiction. Over what must it have jurisdiction? How are the courts applying traditional jurisdictional concepts to cases involving Internet transactions?
3. What is the difference between a trial court and an appellate court?
4. In a lawsuit, what are the pleadings? What is discovery, and how does electronic discovery differ? What is electronic filing?
5. How are online forums being used to resolve disputes?

FOR REVIEW

Answers for the even-numbered questions in this For Review section can be found on this text's accompanying Web site at http://blt.westbuslaw.com. *Select "Chapter 3" and click on "For Review."*

1. What is judicial review? How and when was the power of judicial review established?
2. Before a court can hear a case, it must have jurisdiction. Over what must it have jurisdiction? How are the courts applying traditional jurisdictional concepts to cases involving Internet transactions?
3. What is the difference between a trial court and an appellate court?
4. In a lawsuit, what are the pleadings? What is discovery, and how does electronic discovery differ? What is electronic filing?
5. How are online forums being used to resolve disputes?

Concept Summaries for quick clarification

New to this edition, *Concept Summaries* found in selected chapters give students quick point-by-point clarification of complex concepts.

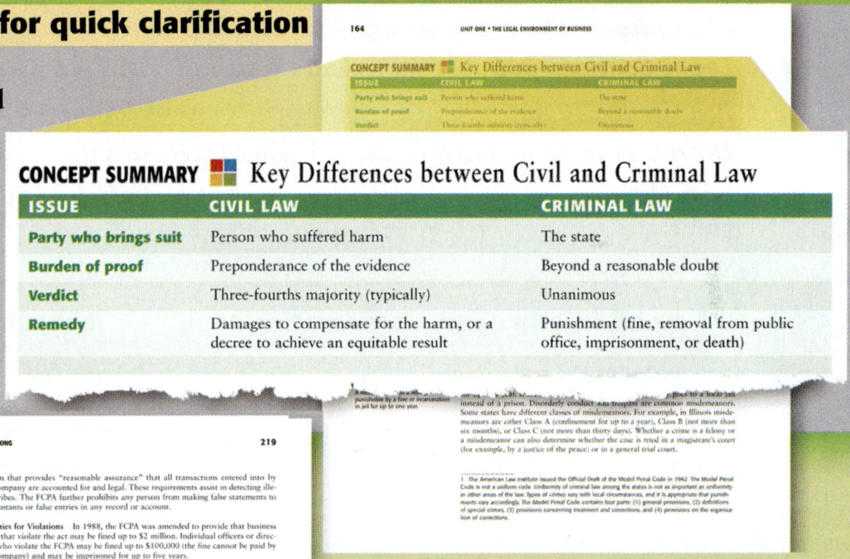

CONCEPT SUMMARY Key Differences between Civil and Criminal Law

ISSUE	CIVIL LAW	CRIMINAL LAW
Party who brings suit	Person who suffered harm	The state
Burden of proof	Preponderance of the evidence	Beyond a reasonable doubt
Verdict	Three-fourths majority (typically)	Unanimous
Remedy	Damages to compensate for the harm, or a decree to achieve an equitable result	Punishment (fine, removal from public office, imprisonment, or death)

Many opportunities to review

Located at the end of each chapter, features such as "Reviewing Ethics and Business Decision Making" from Chapter 7 help students to solidify their understanding of chapter materials. Each "Reviewing . . ." feature presents a hypothetical scenario and then asks a series of questions that require students to identify the issues and apply the legal concepts discussed.

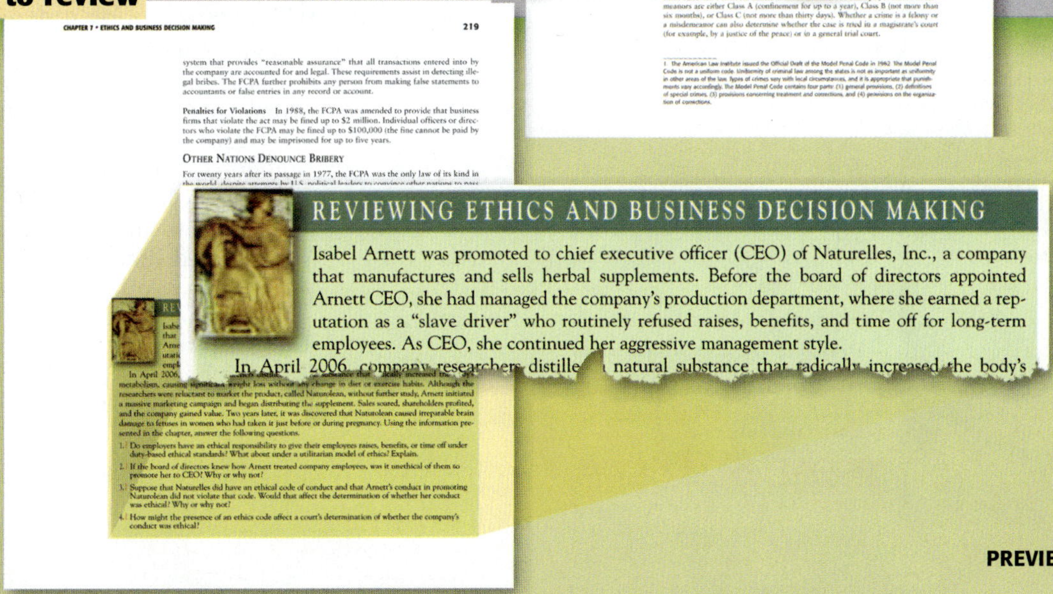

REVIEWING ETHICS AND BUSINESS DECISION MAKING

Isabel Arnett was promoted to chief executive officer (CEO) of Naturelles, Inc., a company that manufactures and sells herbal supplements. Before the board of directors appointed Arnett CEO, she had managed the company's production department, where she earned a reputation as a "slave driver" who routinely refused raises, benefits, and time off for long-term employees. As CEO, she continued her aggressive management style.

In April 2006, company researchers distille[...] natural substance that radically increased the body's

Innovative online resources for course management, preparation, testing, and more

The robust, completely updated Book Companion Web Site

http://blt.westbuslaw.com

Carefully correlated with this book, this information-packed site offers a broad array of teaching and learning resources: Video clips from West's Digital Video Library; Web sites for all *Landmark in the Law* features; sample answers; Internet exercises; interactive quizzes; court case updates; links to selected statutes.

In-text prompts and activities encourage students to visit the web site

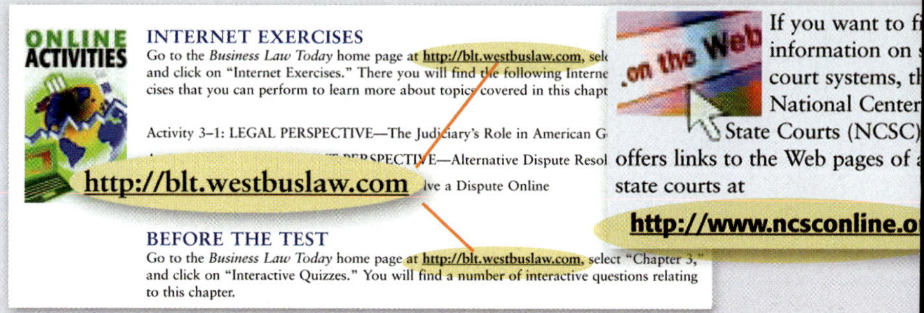

West's Digital Video Library—online access available as an *optional* package item with each new text

This dynamic video library features more than sixty video clips that spark class discussion and clarify core legal principles. The library is organized into four series:

- ***Legal Conflicts in Business*** includes specific modern business and e-commerce scenarios.
- ***Ask the Instructor*** presents clear explanations of concepts for student review.
- ***Drama of the Law*** features classic business scenarios that spark classroom participation.
- ***Law Flix*** contains clips from many popular films, including *Bowfinger, The Money Pit, Midnight Run,* and *Casino*

Instructor's Resource CD-ROM

an all-in-one course preparation tool.

Includes the following:

- *Course Planning Guide*
- *Instructor's Manual*
- *Answers Manual,*
- Case-Problems Cases
- *Test Bank*
- ExamView® Computerized Testing
- PowerPoint® slides
- *Instructor's Manual* for the *Drama of the Law* Video Series
- Lecture Outline System
- Case Printouts

0-324-30548-6

WebTutor™ ToolBox

managing your course online was never this easy.

The FREE access code is available upon request with your adoption order.

Preloaded with content and available free via access code when packaged with this text, WebTutor ToolBox pairs all the content of Miller and Jentz's web site with exceptional course management functionality (both WebCT and Blackboard versions are available).

To package WebTutor ToolBox with every student copy of this book, please contact your local representative.

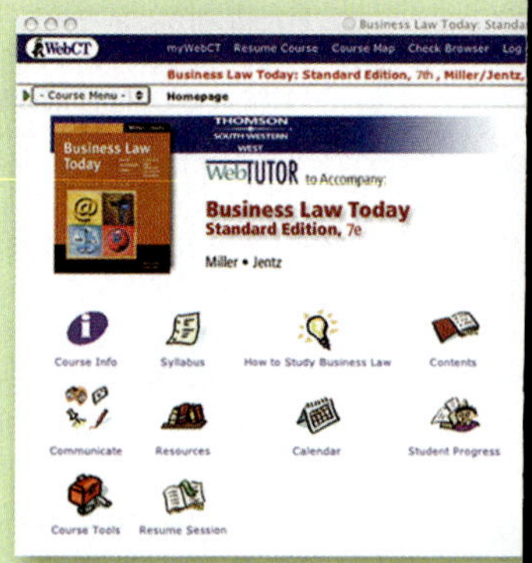

COURSE PLANNING GUIDE **available FREE to qualified adopters**

This unique supplement helps make teaching the principles of business law efficient and rewarding with an array of materials for:

- ***Organizing your lectures***
- ***Developing class assignments and discussions***
- ***Preparing examinations***

Correlated to each chapter in the textbook, the Course Planning Guide identifies parallel materials that can be drawn from the extensive set of supplements that are available with the Seventh Edition of Business Law Today: Comprehensive Edition.

Chapter 5: Intellectual Property

–MULTIMEDIA MATERIALS:

⌘ *Instructor's Resource CD-ROM (IRCD)*

The IRCD includes the following supplements:

Course Planning Guide
Instructor's Manual
Case Printouts
Answers to Questions and Case Problems
Test Bank
Lecture Outline System
ExamView Testing Software
Case-Problem Cases
PowerPoint Slides
Instructor's Manual for the Drama of the Law video series

–PRINTED SUPPLEMENTS:

➔ *Instructor's Manual*

Pages 79-100. To add to your discussion of trademark law, you might want to photocopy (or print out from the computerized version of the IM) the text of the Federal Trademark Dilution Act, which is presented in this chapter of the IM. Other items included in this chapter of the IM that might be of interest to your students are the excerpts from the Berne Convention.

Study Guide

Pages 29-35.

Transparencies

Transparency No. 17 (BLTC Chapter Summary): *Trademarks and Related Property*
Transparency No. 18 (BLTC Chapter Summary): *Cyber Marks*
Transparency No. 19 (BLTC Chapter Summary): *Patents*
Transparency No. 20 (BLTC Chapter Summary): *Copyrights*
Transparency No. 21 (BLTC Chapter Summary): *Trade Secrets*

EXCERPTED FROM THE COURSE PLANNING GUIDE

Case Printouts
See Chapter 5 for full versions of cases excerpted in this chapter.

Ω *Answers to Questions and Case Problems*
Pages 31-38.

Test Bank
Pages 55-68.

Lecture Outline System
Chapter 5 Overheads.

—SOFTWARE SUPPLEMENTS:

➔ *Instructor's Manual*
See Chapter 5 of the Instructor's Manual on the *IRCD*.

Ω *Answers to Questions and Case Problems*
See Chapter 5 of the Answers Manual on the *IRCD*.

ExamView Testing Software
IRCD: See Chapter 5.

Case-Problem Cases
See Chapter 5 of the Case-Problem Cases on the *IRCD*.

♦ *Legal Research Exercises on the Web*
For the activities that correspond to the material in BLTC Chapter 5, go to **http://blt.westbuslaw.com**, and select Chapter 5. Click on "Internet Exercises" to access the following exercises:

- **Activity 5-1: LEGAL PERSPECTIVE—Unwarranted Legal Threats**
- **Activity 5-2: TECHNOLOGICAL PERSPECTIVE—File Sharing**
- **Activity 5-3: MANAGEMENT PERSPECTIVE—Protecting Intellectual Property across Borders**

Before the Test Questions
Your students may find it helpful to take a "pre-test." For twenty interactive questions that correspond to the material in this chapter, advise them to go to **http://blt.westbuslaw.com** and select "Interactive Quizzes."

—VIDEO SUPPLEMENTS:

PowerPoint Slides

To highlight some of this chapter's key points, you might use the Lecture Review PowerPoint slides compiled for Chapter 5.

Drama of the Law II

- Intellectual Property: Trade Name

Court TV

Northside Partners v. Page and New Kids on the Block is a video that features a copyright infringement case. You may want your students to watch this video when discussing copyright infringement with your class.

—SPECIAL RESOURCES:

Business Law Today on the Web

Information valuable to instructor and student alike is available on, and will continue to be added to, our *Business Law Today* Web site at the following address:

http://blt.westbuslaw.com

Resources include:

Relevant Web sites—
⇒ *Landmark of the Law* features
⇒ *Landmark and Classic Cases* presented in BLTC
Sample Answers to the Case Problems with Sample Answers that appear at the end of every chapter
Videos referenced in the new *Video Questions* at the ends of selected chapters
Internet Exercises that familiarize students with online legal resources and additional information for every chapter in BLTC

EXCERPTED FROM THE COURSE PLANNING GUIDE

Interactive Quizzes for the *Before the Test* section at the end of every chapter in BLTC

Court case updates that summarize new cases keyed to specific chapters

A "Statutes" page that offers links to selected statutes referenced in BLTC

Links to other important legal resources on the Web

1-800-946-B-LAW

To order any of these supplements, to order additional texts, or if you have any questions, problems, or comments, you can contact a specialist in business law and the legal environment directly, toll-free.

SEVENTH EDITION

BUSINESS LAW TODAY

COMPREHENSIVE EDITION

TEXT & CASES

E-Commerce, Legal, Ethical, and International Environment

SEVENTH EDITION

BUSINESS LAW TODAY

COMPREHENSIVE EDITION

TEXT & CASES

E-Commerce, Legal, Ethical, and International Environment

ROGER LEROY MILLER
Institute for University Studies
Arlington, Texas

GAYLORD A. JENTZ
Herbert D. Kelleher
Emeritus Professor in Business Law
MSIS Department
University of Texas at Austin

THOMSON
WEST

Australia · Canada · Mexico · Singapore · Spain · United Kingdom · United States

THOMSON
WEST

SEVENTH EDITION

BUSINESS LAW TODAY

COMPREHENSIVE EDITION

TEXT & CASES

E-Commerce, Legal, Ethical, and International Environment

ROGER LEROY MILLER GAYLORD A. JENTZ

Vice President and Editorial Director:
Jack Calhoun

Publisher, Business Law and Accounting:
Rob Dewey

Acquisition Editor:
Steve Silverstein

Senior Developmental Editor:
Jan Lamar

Executive Marketing Manager:
Lisa L. Lysne

Production Manager:
Bill Stryker

Technology Project Editor:
Christine A. Wittmer

Manufacturing Coordinator:
Charlene Taylor

Compositor:
Parkwood Composition
New Richmond, WI

Printer:
RR Donnelley, Willard

Art Director:
Michelle Kunkler

Internal Designer:
Bill Stryker

Cover Designer:
Diane Gliebe/Design Matters

Web Coordinator:
Kelly Reid

Cover Images:
© Getty Images, Inc.; Gavel Illustration by Lisa Ballard/Cincinnati, OH

Printed in the United States of America
1 2 3 4 5 08 07 06

ISBN 0-324-37721-5 (Text Only)
ISBN 0-324-30392-0 (Student's Edition)
ISBN 0-324-37713-4 (Instructor's Edition)

Library of Congress Control Number:
2005933012

Thomson Higher Education
5191 Natorp Boulevard
Mason, Ohio, 45040
USA

Or you can visit our Internet site at:
http://www.westbuslaw.com

INTERNATIONAL LOCATIONS

ASIA (including India)
Thomson Learning
5 Shenton Way
#01-01 UIC Building
Singapore 068808

AUSTRALIA/NEW ZEALAND
Thomson Learning Australia
102 Dodds Street
Southbank, Victoria 3006
Australia

LATIN AMERICA
Thomson Learning
Seneca, 53
Colonia Polanco
11560 Mexico
D.F.Mexico

CANADA
Thomson Nelson
1120 Birchmount Road
Toronto, Ontario
Canada M1K 5G4

UK/EUROPE/MIDDLE EAST/AFRICA
Thomson Learning
High Holborn House
50-51 Bedford Road
London WC1R 4LR
United Kingdom

SPAIN (includes Portugal)
Thomson Paraninfo
Calle Magallanes, 25
28015 Madrid, Spain

CONTENTS IN BRIEF

APPENDICES

CONTENTS

Preface
To the Instructor

We have always felt that business law and the legal environment should be an exciting, contemporary, and interesting course. We believe that the Seventh Edition of *Business Law Today: Comprehensive Edition* imparts this excitement to your students. We have spent a great deal of effort in giving this book a visual appeal that will encourage students to learn the law. We have also worked hard to make sure that *Business Law Today: Comprehensive Edition* continues its established tradition of being the most up-to-date text on the market. The law presented in this edition includes new statutes, regulations, and cases, as well as the most recent developments in cyberlaw.

You will find that coverage of traditional business law has not been sacrificed in the process of creating this text. Additionally, *Business Law Today: Comprehensive Edition* explicitly addresses the American Assembly of Collegiate Schools of Business's (AACSB's) broad array of curriculum requirements. As you will see, many of the features and special pedagogical devices in this text focus on the global, political, ethical, social, environmental, technological, and cultural contexts of business law.

What's New in the Seventh Edition

Instructors have come to rely on the coverage, accuracy, and applicability of *Business Law Today: Comprehensive Edition*. To make sure that our text engages your students' interests, solidifies their understanding of the legal concepts presented, and provides the best teaching tools available, we now offer the following items either in the text or in conjunction with the text.

New Bankruptcy Reform Act of 2005

The chapter on bankruptcy (Chapter 27) has been significantly revamped due to the passage of the 2005 bankruptcy reform legislation. Bankruptcy reform has been a topic of major debate for many years. Now that the reform act has been enacted, we have overhauled the content of this chapter to reflect the changes.

Amendments to Articles 2 and 2A of the UCC

To ensure that our text offers the most up-to-date coverage possible, we have rewritten portions of the chapters covering sales and lease contracts (Chapters 18 through 21) to incorporate the 2003 amendments to Articles 2 and 2A of the Uniform Commercial Code (UCC). These amendments were promulgated largely to accommodate electronic commerce. At the time this book went to press, no state had as yet adopted these amendments. Thus, instead of basing the text of these chapters on the amended version of Articles 2 and 2A, we refer in footnotes to any amendments that significantly change the UCC provisions currently in effect in most states. We include excerpts from these amendments in Appendix C, which also contains the full text of several articles of the UCC.

REVIEWING FEATURES IN EVERY CHAPTER

For the Seventh Edition of *Business Law Today: Comprehensive Edition,* we have added a special new feature at the end of every chapter (except Chapter 1) entitled *Reviewing [chapter topic].* Each of these features presents a hypothetical scenario and then asks a series of questions that requires students to identify the issues and apply the legal concepts discussed in the chapter. These features are designed to help students review the chapter topics in a simple and interesting way and to see how the legal principles discussed in the chapter apply to the world in which they live. An instructor can use these features as the basis for in-class discussion or encourage students to use them for self-study prior to completing homework assignments.

WEST'S DIGITAL VIDEO LIBRARY

For this edition of *Business Law Today: Comprehensive Edition,* we have added special new *Video Questions* at the end of selected chapters. Each of these questions directs students to the text's Web site (at **http://blt.westbuslaw.com**) to view a video relevant to a topic covered in the chapter. This instruction is followed by a series of questions based on the video. The questions are again repeated on the Web site, when the student accesses the video. An access code for the videos can be packaged with each new copy of this textbook for no additional charge. If West's Digital Video Library access did not come packaged with the textbook, students can purchase it online at **http://digitalvideolibrary.westbuslaw.com**.

These videos can be used for homework assignments, discussion starters, or classroom demonstrations and are useful for generating student interest. Some of the videos are clips from actual movies, such as *The Money Pit* and *Bowfinger*. By watching a video and answering the questions, students will gain an understanding of how the legal concepts they have studied in the chapter apply to the real-life situation portrayed in the video. **Suggested answers for all of the *Video Questions* are given in both the *Instructor's Manual* and the *Answers Manual* that accompany this text.**

CORPORATE GOVERNANCE

Because today's companies are placing a greater emphasis on developing internal rules of corporate governance to prevent corporate misconduct, encourage accountability, and balance potentially conflicting interests, we have added coverage of this topic as appropriate. For example, the chapter on ethics (Chapter 7) includes a subsection discussing corporate governance principles. The chapter covering securities law (Chapter 35) now includes an entire section on corporate governance.

ETHICS AND BUSINESS DECISION MAKING

For the Seventh Edition of *Business Law Today: Comprehensive Edition,* we have included a significantly revised and updated chapter on ethics and business decision making (Chapter 7). The chapter now presents a more practical approach to this topic and examines several companies that have been accused of avoiding their ethical obligations (including, for example, the accusations against Merck & Company, which continued to market its popular painkiller Vioxx until late in 2004 despite allegedly knowing that long-term use of the drug was linked to serious health risks). The emphasis on ethics is reiterated in other materials throughout the text—in the numbered *Ethical Issue* sections that appear throughout the text, in "Ethical Considerations" ending many of the cases, and in the case problems entitled *A Question of Ethics* that appear in selected chapters.

Appendix on the Sarbanes-Oxley Act of 2002

In a number of places in this text, we refer to the Sarbanes-Oxley Act of 2002 and the corporate scandals that led to the passage of that legislation. For example, Chapter 7 contains a section examining the requirements of the Sarbanes-Oxley Act relating to confidential reporting systems. In Chapter 35, we discuss this act in the context of securities law and present an exhibit (Exhibit 35–4) containing some of the key provisions of the act relating to corporate accountability with respect to securities transactions. Finally, in Chapter 42 we again look at provisions of the Sarbanes-Oxley Act as they relate to public accounting firms and accounting practices.

Because the act is a topic of significant concern in today's business climate, for the Seventh Edition we have added **excerpts and explanatory comments on the Sarbanes-Oxley Act of 2002 as Appendix P.** Students and instructors alike will find it useful to have the provisions of the act immediately available for reference.

Emphasis on Critical Thinking and Legal Reasoning

Your students' critical-thinking and legal reasoning skills will be increased as they work through the numerous pedagogical devices within the book.

- **Case-ending questions**—Many of the cases presented in the text conclude with a section entitled "For Critical Analysis" that raises a question about some aspect of the case for the student to consider.
- **Feature-ending questions**—Concluding each boxed-in feature entitled *Adapting the Law to the Online Environment* (to be discussed shortly) is a question for critical analysis that asks the student to explore some of the implications or consequences of the court decision or other development discussed in the feature.
- **Reviewing hypotheticals**—As already discussed, this new end-of-chapter feature poses a series of questions about a hypothetical scenario that requires the student to apply legal reasoning skills to decide how the principles of law discussed in the chapter should be applied to the situation.
- **Additional *Featured Cases***—For the Seventh Edition, we have increased the number of *Featured Cases* in the text. Each of these cases is presented entirely in the words of the court so that students can learn how judges reason through legal questions. Each case concludes with a series of questions designed to help the student test his or her understanding of the case.
- **Unit-ending *Extended Case Study***—At the end of each unit is a two-page feature entitled *Extended Case Study.* This feature focuses on a recent court case relating to a topic covered in the unit. Each feature opens with an introductory section, which discusses the background and significance of the case being presented. Then we present excerpts from the court's majority opinion and from a dissenting opinion in the case as well. The feature concludes with a series of questions, under the heading *Questions for Analysis,* that prompts the student to think critically about the legal, ethical, economic, international, or general business implications of the case.

Suggested answers to all critical-thinking questions in the features and all questions in the *Featured Case* and *Extended Case Study* features can be found in both the *Instructor's Manual* and the *Answers Manual* that accompany this text.

Business Law Today on the Web

For this edition of *Business Law Today: Comprehensive Edition,* we have redesigned and streamlined the text's Web site so that users can easily locate the resources they seek. When you visit our Web site at **http://blt.westbuslaw.com**, you will find a broad array of teaching/learning resources, including the following:

- ***Relevant Web sites*** for all of the *Landmark in the Law* features and *Landmark and Classic Cases* that are presented in this text.
- ***Answers to the* For Review *questions***—For this edition, we have included on the text's Web site the answers to the even-numbered *For Review* questions that conclude each chapter.
- ***Sample answers for selected case problems***—Included on the Web site is a sample answer to each case problem entitled *Case Problem with Sample Answer.* This case problem, which is set off by a special heading and followed by instructions to the student, appears in the *Questions and Case Problems* at the end of every chapter. This problem/answer set is designed to help your students learn how to answer case problems by acquainting them with the courts' reasoning and conclusions for selected problems.
- ***Videos*** referenced in the new *Video Questions* (discussed previously) that have been added to selected chapters for this edition of *Business Law Today: Comprehensive Edition.*
- ***Internet exercises*** for every chapter in the text (at least two per chapter), many of which are new to this edition. These exercises familiarize students with online legal resources while introducing them to additional information on the topics covered in the chapters.
- ***Interactive quizzes*** for every chapter in this text.
- ***Court case updates*** that present summaries of new cases from various West legal publications. The case selection is continually updated, and the cases are specifically keyed to chapters in this text.
- ***Legal reference materials,*** including a "Statutes" page that offers links to the full text of selected statutes referenced in the text, a Spanish glossary, and links to other important legal resources available for free on the Web.
- ***Appendix A of the text***—This appendix, which is entitled "How to Brief Cases and Analyze Case Problems" is included both in the text and on the Web site.

Additional Special Features in This Text

We have included in the Seventh Edition of *Business Law Today: Comprehensive Edition* a number of pedagogical devices and special features, including those discussed here.

Adapting the Law to the Online Environment

Many chapters in the Seventh Edition contain one of these special features. As mentioned earlier, a concluding *For Critical Analysis* section asks the student to think critically about some aspect of the issue discussed in the feature. **Suggested answers to these questions are included in both the *Instructor's Manual* and the *Answers Manual* that accompany this text.**

Management Perspective

Each of these features begins with a section titled "Management Faces a Legal Issue" that describes a practical issue facing management (such as whether employees have a right to privacy in their e-mail communications). A section titled "What the Courts Say" then follows, in which we discuss what the courts have concluded with respect to this issue. The feature concludes with "Implications for Managers," a section indicating the importance of the courts' decisions for business decision making and offering some practical guidance.

Landmark in the Law

This feature, which appears in selected chapters, discusses a landmark case, statute, or other law that has had a significant effect on business law. Each of these features has a section titled *Application to Today's Business World,* which indicates how the law discussed in the feature affects the legal landscape of today's world. In addition, for the Seventh Edition we have added a *Relevant Web Sites* section that directs students to the book's companion Web site for links to additional information available online.

Application

This feature, which appears in selected chapters, presents the student with some practical advice on how to apply the law discussed in the chapter to real-world business problems. Each *Application* concludes with a "Checklist" for the future businessperson on how to avoid legal problems.

Concept Summaries

Whenever key areas of the law need additional emphasis, we provide a *Concept Summary*. These summaries, which are new to the Seventh Edition, serve as helpful reviewing tools.

Exhibits

When appropriate, we also illustrate important aspects of the law in graphic or summary form in exhibits. For the Seventh Edition of *Business Law Today: Comprehensive Edition*, we have added numerous exhibits, including ten new exhibits in the contracts unit.

An Effective Case Format

In each chapter, we present cases that illustrate the principles of law discussed in the text. The cases are numbered sequentially for easy referencing in class discussions, homework assignments, and examinations. In selecting the cases to be included in this edition, our goal has been to choose cases that reflect the most current law or that represent significant precedents in case law.

Each case is presented in a special format, beginning with the case title and citation (including parallel citations). Whenever possible, we also include a URL, just below the case citation, that can be used to access the case online (a footnote to the URL explains how to find the specific case at that Web site). We then briefly outline the background and facts of the dispute, after which the court's reasoning is presented in the words of the court. To enhance student understanding, we paraphrase the court's decision and remedy. Each case normally concludes with a *For Critical Analysis* section. For one case in each chapter, however, we have added a section titled *Why Is This Case Important?* This section clearly sets forth the importance of the court's decision for businesspersons today.

We give special emphasis to landmark and classic cases by setting them off with a special heading and logo. These cases also include a *Comments* section that stresses the significance of that particular decision for the evolution of the law in that area. For the Seventh Edition, we have added a section titled *Relevant Web Sites* at the conclusion of each landmark and classic case that directs students to additional online resources.

The Most Complete Supplements Package Available Today

This edition of *Business Law Today: Comprehensive Edition* is accompanied by a vast number of teaching and learning supplements, including those listed below. For further information on the *Business Law Today: Comprehensive Edition* teaching/learning package, contact your local West sales representative or visit the *Business Law Today* Web site.

Suggestions on how you can adapt the teaching/learning package to fit your particular teaching and learning goals are given in the *Course Planning Guide* that accompanies the text. Furthermore, each chapter of the *Instructor's Manual* contains teaching suggestions, possible discussion questions, and additional information on key statutes or other legal sources that you may wish to use in your classroom. These and numerous other supplementary materials (including printed and multimedia supplements) all contribute to the goal of making *Business Law Today* the most flexible teaching/learning package on the market today.

Printed Supplements

- ***Online Legal Research Guide***—Packaged with every new copy of the text.
- ***Course Planning Guide***—For a sample chapter from this guide, see the Visual Preface at the beginning of this book. (The *Course Planning Guide* is also available on the *Instructor's Resource CD-ROM,* or IRCD.)
- ***Instructor's Manual***—Includes additional cases on point with at least one such case summary per chapter, answers to all *For Critical Analysis* questions in the features, answers for the *Video Questions* at the end of selected chapters, and answers to the questions presented in the *Extended Case Study* feature that concludes each unit; also available on the IRCD.
- ***Study Guide.***
- A comprehensive ***Test Bank*** (also available on the IRCD).
- ***Case Printouts***—Includes printouts of cases presented in the text and referred to in selected features (also available on the IRCD).
- ***Answers Manual***—Includes answers to the *Questions and Case Problems,* answers to the *For Critical Analysis* questions in the features, and answers for the *Video Questions* that conclude selected chapters (also available on the IRCD).
- ***Instructor's Manual* for the *Drama of the Law*** video series (also available on the IRCD).
- ***Wall Street Journal***—A subscription is available at a discount to adopters and students.

Software, Video, and Multimedia Supplements

- ***Instructor's Resource CD-ROM* (IRCD)**—The IRCD includes the following supplements: *Course Planning Guide, Instructor's Manual, Answers Manual, Test*

Bank, Case-Problem Cases, Case Printouts, Lecture Outline System, PowerPoint slides, ExamView, and *Instructor's Manual* for the *Drama of the Law* video series.

- **ExamView Testing Software** (also available on the IRCD).
- **Lecture Outline System** (also available on the IRCD).
- **PowerPoint slides** (also available on the IRCD).
- **WebTutor Toolbox.**
- **Case-Problem Cases** (available only on the IRCD).
- **Transparency acetates.**
- **Westlaw®**—Ten free hours on Westlaw are available to qualified adopters.
- **West's Digital Video Library**—Provides access to over sixty-five videos, including the *Drama of the Law* videos and video clips from actual Hollywood movies. Access to West's Digital Video Library is available in an optional package with each new text at no additional cost. If West's Digital Video Library access did not come packaged with the textbook, your students can purchase it online at **http://digitalvideolibrary.westbuslaw.com**.
- **VHS Videotapes**—Qualified adopters using this text have access to the entire library of West videos in VHS format, a vast selection covering most business law issues. For more information about these videotapes, visit **http://www.swlearning.com/blaw/video_library/video_library.html**.
- ***LegalTrac*™**—Provides indexing for approximately 875 research titles (including major law reviews, legal newspapers, bar association journals, and international legal journals) and law-related articles from over 1,000 additional business and general interest titles. *LegalTrac*™ is available as an optional package with a new text.
- **Business & Company Resource Center**—Put a complete business library at your students' fingertips with the Business & Company Resource Center (BCRC). The BCRC is a premier online business research tool that allows you to seamlessly search thousands of periodicals, journals, references, financial information, industry reports, company histories, and much more. The BCRC is a powerful and time-saving research tool for business students—whether they are completing a case study analysis, preparing for a presentation or discussion, creating a business plan, or writing a reaction paper. Access to the BCRC is available as an optional package with each new text and comes with a user's guide that includes exercises to provide hands-on experience and a real-world context for using the BCRC. For more information, please visit **http://bcrc.swlearning.com**.
- ***Wall Street Journal***—Students and professors have the opportunity to subscribe to the *Wall Street Journal* and to access the *Journal*'s Web site (**http://wsj.com**) at a discount when bundled with the text. For students, the offer includes a fifteen-week subscription and access to the Web site. Qualifying professors can receive a fifty-two-week subscription, one-year access to the Web site, access to ProfessorJournal.com, and a video instructing students on how to use the *Wall Street Journal*.

Acknowledgments

Numerous careful and conscientious users of *Business Law Today* were kind enough to help us revise the book. In addition, the staff at West went out of its way to make sure that this edition came out early and in accurate form. In particular, we wish to thank Rob Dewey and Steve Silverstein for their countless new ideas, many of which have been incorporated into the Seventh Edition. Our production manager and designer, Bill Stryker, made sure that we came out with an error-free, visually attractive edition. We will always be in his debt. We also extend special thanks to Jan Lamar, our longtime developmental editor, for her many useful suggestions and for her efforts in coordinating reviews and ensuring the timely and accurate publication of all supplemental materials. We are particularly indebted to Lisa Lysne for her support and excellent marketing advice, and to Scott Cook and Christine Wittmer for their help in managing the Web site.

We must especially thank Katherine Marie Silsbee and Lavina Leed Miller, who provided expert research, editing, and proofing services for this project. We also wish to thank William Eric Hollowell, co-author of the *Instructor's Manual, Study Guide, Test Bank,* and *Online Legal Research Guide,* for his excellent research efforts. The copyediting and proofreading services of Pat Lewis and Suzie Franklin DeFazio will not go unnoticed. We also thank Roxanna Lee and Vickie Reierson for their proofreading and other assistance, which helped to ensure an error-free text. Finally, our appreciation goes to Suzanne Jasin for her many special efforts on the project.

ACKNOWLEDGMENTS FOR PREVIOUS EDITIONS

John J. Balek
Morton College, Illinois

Lorraine K. Bannai
Western Washington University

Marlene E. Barken
Ithaca College, New York

Daryl Barton
Eastern Michigan University

Merlin Bauer
Mid State Technical College, Wisconsin

Donna E. Becker
Frederick Community College, Maryland

Brad Botz
Garden City Community College, Kansas

Teresa Brady
Holy Family College, Philadelphia

Lee B. Burgunder
California Polytechnic University—San Luis Obispo

Dale Clark
Corning Community College, New York

Sandra J. Defebaugh
Eastern Michigan University

Patricia L. DeFrain
Glendale College, California

Julia G. Derrick
Brevard Community College, Florida

Joe D. Dillsaver
Northeastern State University, Oklahoma

Claude W. Dotson
Northwest College, Wyoming

Larry R. Edwards
Tarrant County Junior College, South Campus, Texas

Jacolin Eichelberger
Hillsborough Community College, Florida

George E. Eigsti
Kansas City, Kansas, Community College

Tony Enerva
Lakeland Community College, Ohio

Benjamin C. Fassberg
Prince George's Community College, Maryland

Jerry Furniss
University of Montana

Elizabeth J. Guerriero
Northeast Louisiana University

Phil Harmeson
University of South Dakota

Nancy L. Hart
Midland College, Texas

Janine S. Hiller
Virginia Polytechnic Institute & State University

Florence E. Elliott-Howard
Stephen F. Austin State University, Texas

Fred Ittner
College of Alameda, California

Susan S. Jarvis
University of Texas, Pan American, Texas

Jack E. Karns
East Carolina University, North Carolina

Sarah Weiner Keidan
Oakland Community College, Michigan

Richard N. Kleeberg
Solano Community College, California

Bradley T. Lutz
Hillsborough Community College, Florida

Darlene Mallick
Anne Arundel Community College, Maryland

John D. Mallonee
Manatee Community College, Florida

Joseph D. Marcus
Prince George's Community College, Maryland

Woodrow J. Maxwell
Hudson Valley Community College, New York

Beverly McCormick
Morehead State University, Kentucky

William J. McDevitt
Saint Joseph's University, Pennsylvania

John W. McGee
Aims Community College, Colorado

James K. Miersma
Milwaukee Area Technical Institute, Wisconsin

Susan J. Mitchell
Des Moines Area Community College, Iowa

Jim Lee Morgan
West Los Angeles College

Jack K. Morton
University of Montana

Solange North
Fox Valley Technical Institute, Wisconsin

Robert H. Orr
Florida Community College at Jacksonville

George Otto
Truman College, Illinois

Thomas L. Palmer
Northern Arizona University

Donald L. Petote
Genessee Community College, New York

Francis D. Polk
Ocean County College, New Jersey

Gregory Rabb
Jamestown Community College, New York

Hugh Rode
Utah Valley State College

William M. Rutledge
Macomb Community College, Michigan

Martha Wright Sartoris
North Hennepin Community College, Minnesota

Anne W. Schacherl
Madison Area Technical College, Wisconsin

Edward F. Shafer
Rochester Community College, Minnesota

Lou Ann Simpson
Drake University, Iowa

Denise Smith
Missouri Western State College

Hugh M. Spall
Central Washington University

James D. Van Tassel
Mission College, California

Frederick J. Walsh
Franklin Pierce College, New Hampshire

James E. Walsh, Jr.
Tidewater Community College, Virginia

Edward L. Welsh, Jr.
Phoenix College

Clark W. Wheeler
Santa Fe Community College, Florida

Kay O. Wilburn
The University of Alabama at Birmingham

James L. Wittenbach
University of Notre Dame

Joseph Zavaglia, Jr.
Brookdale Community College, New Jersey

Acknowledgments for the Seventh Edition

Marlene E. Barken
Ithaca College

Bradley D. Childs
Belmont University

Karen A. Holmes
Hudson Valley Community College

Susan J. Mitchell
Des Moines Area Community College

Jamie L. O'Brien
South Dakota State University

David W. Pan
University of Tulsa

Maurice Tonissi
Quinsigamond Community College

Randy Waterman
Richland College

Jerry Wegman
University of Idaho

Lori Whisenant
University of Houston

We know that we are not perfect. If you or your students find something you don't like or want us to change, write to us or let us know via e-mail, using the "Contact Us" feature on this text's Web site. That is how we can make *Business Law Today* an even better book in the future.

Roger LeRoy Miller
Gaylord A. Jentz

Dedication

To Serge,
Discovering the best
of the very best
riding places continues
to be a delight for me.
Thanks for your
guiding skills.

R.L.M.

To my wife, JoAnn; to my children,
Kathy, Gary, Lori, and Rory; and to
my grandchildren, Erin,
Megan, Eric, Emily, Michelle,
Javier, Carmen, and Steve.

G.A.J.

UNIT ONE

THE LEGAL ENVIRONMENT OF BUSINESS

UNIT CONTENTS

CHAPTER 1
The Legal Environment

"The law is of as much interest to the layman as it is to the lawyer."

Lord Balfour, 1848–1930
(British prime minister, 1902–1905)

CHAPTER OUTLINE

- THE NATURE OF LAW
- BUSINESS ACTIVITIES AND THE LEGAL ENVIRONMENT
- SOURCES OF AMERICAN LAW
- THE COMMON LAW TRADITION
- CLASSIFICATIONS OF LAW

LEARNING OBJECTIVES

After reading this chapter, you should be able to answer the following questions:

1. What is the Uniform Commercial Code?
2. What is the common law tradition?
3. What is a precedent? When might a court depart from precedent?
4. What is the difference between remedies at law and remedies in equity?
5. What are some important differences between civil law and criminal law?

Lord Balfour's assertion in the quotation above emphasizes the underlying theme of every page in this book—that law is of interest to all persons, not just to lawyers. Those entering the world of business will find themselves subject to numerous laws and government regulations. A basic knowledge of these laws and regulations is beneficial—if not essential—to anyone contemplating a successful career in today's business world.

In this introductory chapter, we first look at the nature of law and at some concepts that have significantly influenced how jurists (those skilled in the law, including judges, lawyers, and legal scholars) view the nature and function of law. We then look at an important question for any student reading this text: How does the legal environment affect business decision making? We next describe the basic sources of American law, the common law tradition, and the importance of the common law today. We conclude the chapter with a discussion of some general classifications of law.

The Nature of Law

LAW
A body of enforceable rules governing relationships among individuals and between individuals and their society.

There have been, and will continue to be, different definitions of law. Although the definitions vary in their particulars, they all are based on the general observation that, at a minimum, **law** consists of *enforceable rules governing relationships among individuals and between individuals and their society.* These "enforceable rules" may consist of unwritten principles of behavior established by a nomadic tribe. They may be set forth in an ancient or a contemporary law code. They may consist of written laws and court decisions created by modern legislative and judicial bodies, as in the United States. Regardless of how such rules are created, they all have one thing in common: they establish rights, duties, and privileges that are consistent with the values and beliefs of their society or its ruling group.

JURISPRUDENCE
The science or philosophy of law.

Those who embark on a study of law will find that these broad statements leave unanswered some important questions concerning the nature of law. Part of the study of law, often referred to as **jurisprudence,** involves learning about different schools of legal thought and discovering how each school's approach to law can affect judicial decision making.

You may think that legal philosophy is far removed from the practical study of business law and the legal environment. In fact, it is not. As you will learn in the chapters of this text, how judges apply the law to specific disputes, including disputes relating to the business world, depends in part on their philosophical approaches to law. We look now at some of the significant schools of legal, or jurisprudential, thought that have evolved over time.

THE NATURAL LAW TRADITION

NATURAL LAW
The belief that government and the legal system should reflect universal moral and ethical principles that are inherent in human nature. The natural law school is the oldest and one of the most significant schools of legal thought.

An age-old question about the nature of law has to do with the finality of a nation's laws, such as the laws of the United States at the present time. For example, what if a particular law is deemed to be a "bad" law by a substantial number of that nation's citizens? Must a citizen obey the law if it goes against his or her conscience to do so? Is there a higher or universal law to which individuals can appeal? One who adheres to the natural law tradition would answer this question in the affirmative. **Natural law** denotes a system of moral and ethical principles that are inherent in human nature and that people can discover through the use of their native intelligence.

The natural law tradition is one of the oldest and most significant schools of jurisprudence. It dates back to the days of the Greek philosopher Aristotle (384–322 B.C.E.), who distinguished between natural law and the laws governing a particular nation. According to Aristotle, natural law applies universally to all humankind.

The notion that people have "natural rights" stems from the natural law tradition. Those who claim that a specific foreign government is depriving certain citizens of their human rights are implicitly appealing to a higher law that has universal applicability. The question of the universality of basic human rights also comes into play in the context of international business operations. For example, U.S. companies that have operations abroad often hire foreign workers as employees. Should the same laws that protect U.S. employees apply to these foreign employees? This question is rooted implicitly in a concept of universal rights that has its origins in the natural law tradition.

POSITIVE LAW
The body of conventional, or written, law of a particular society at a particular point in time.

LEGAL POSITIVISM
A school of legal thought centered on the assumption that there is no law higher than the laws created by a national government. Laws must be obeyed, even if they are unjust, to prevent anarchy.

LEGAL POSITIVISM

In contrast, **positive law,** or national law (the written law of a given society at a particular point in time), applies only to the citizens of that nation or society. Those who adhere to **legal positivism** believe that there can be no higher law than a nation's positive law. According to the positivist school, there is no such thing as "natural rights." Rather, human rights exist solely because of laws. If the laws are not enforced, anarchy will result. Thus, whether a law is "bad" or "good" is irrelevant. The law is the law and must be obeyed until it is changed—in an orderly manner through a legitimate lawmaking process. A judge with positivist leanings probably would be more inclined to defer to an existing law than would a judge who adheres to the natural law tradition.

The Historical School

HISTORICAL SCHOOL
A school of legal thought that emphasizes the evolutionary process of law and that looks to the past to discover what the principles of contemporary law should be.

The **historical school** of legal thought emphasizes the evolutionary process of law by concentrating on the origin and history of the legal system. Thus, this school looks to the past to discover what the principles of contemporary law should be. The legal doctrines that have withstood the passage of time—those that have worked in the past—are deemed best suited for shaping present laws. Hence, law derives its legitimacy and authority from adhering to the standards that historical development has shown to be workable. Adherents of the historical school are more likely than those of other schools to strictly follow decisions made in past cases.

Legal Realism

LEGAL REALISM
A school of legal thought of the 1920s and 1930s that generally advocated a less abstract and more realistic approach to the law, an approach that takes into account customary practices and the circumstances in which transactions take place. This school left a lasting imprint on American jurisprudence.

SOCIOLOGICAL SCHOOL
A school of legal thought that views the law as a tool for promoting justice in society.

In the 1920s and 1930s, a number of jurists and scholars, known as legal realists, rebelled against the historical approach to law. **Legal realism** is based on the idea that law is just one of many institutions in society and that it is shaped by social forces and needs. The law is a human enterprise, and judges should take social and economic realities into account when deciding cases. Legal realists also believe that the law can never be applied with total uniformity. Given that judges are human beings with unique personalities, value systems, and intellects, obviously different judges will bring different reasoning processes to the same case.

Legal realism strongly influenced the growth of what is sometimes called the **sociological school** of jurisprudence. This school views law as a tool for promoting justice in society. In the 1960s, for example, the justices of the United States Supreme Court played a leading role in the civil rights movement by upholding long-neglected laws calling for equal treatment for all Americans, including African Americans and other minorities. Generally, jurists who adhere to the sociological school are more likely to depart from past decisions than are those jurists who adhere to the other schools of legal thought.

Business Activities and the Legal Environment

As those entering the world of business will learn, laws and government regulations affect virtually all business activities—from hiring and firing decisions to workplace safety, the manufacturing and marketing of products, and business financing, for example. To make good business decisions, a basic knowledge of the laws and regulations governing these activities is beneficial, if not essential. In today's world, though, a knowledge of "black-letter" law is not enough. Businesspersons are also pressured to make ethical decisions. Thus, the study of business law necessarily involves an ethical dimension.

Many Different Laws May Affect a Single Business Transaction

As you will note, each chapter in this text covers a specific area of the law and shows how the legal rules in that area affect business activities. Although compartmentalizing the law in this fashion facilitates learning, it does not indicate the extent to which many different laws may apply to just one transaction. It is important for businesspersons to be aware of this fact and to understand enough about the law to know when to hire an expert for advice. (For information on how to hire an attorney, see the *Application* feature at the end of this chapter.)

■ EXAMPLE 1.1 Suppose that you are the president of NetSys, Inc., a company that creates and maintains computer network systems for its clients, including business firms. NetSys also markets software for customers who need an internal computer network but cannot afford an individually designed intranet. One day, Janet, an operations officer for Southwest Distribution Corporation (SDC), contacts you by e-mail about a possible contract involving SDC's computer network. In deciding whether to enter into a contract with SDC, you need to consider, among other things, the legal requirements for an enforceable contract. Are the requirements different for a contract for services and a contract for products? What are your options if SDC **breaches** (breaks, or fails to perform) the contract? The answers to these questions are part of contract law and sales law.

BREACH
The failure to perform a legal obligation.

Other questions might concern payment under the contract. How can you guarantee that NetSys will be paid? For example, if SDC pays with a check that is returned for insufficient funds, what are your options? Answers to these questions can be found in the laws that relate to negotiable instruments (such as checks) and creditors' rights. Also, a dispute may occur over the rights to NetSys's software, or there may be a question of liability if the software is defective. Questions may arise as to whether you and Janet had the authority to make the deal in the first place. Resolutions of these questions may be found in areas of the law that relate to intellectual property, e-commerce, torts, product liability, agency, or business organizations. ■ Finally, if any dispute cannot be resolved amicably, then the laws and the rules concerning courts and court procedures spell out the steps of a lawsuit. Exhibit 1–1 illustrates the various areas of the law that may influence business decision making.

EXHIBIT 1–1 AREAS OF THE LAW THAT MAY AFFECT BUSINESS DECISION MAKING

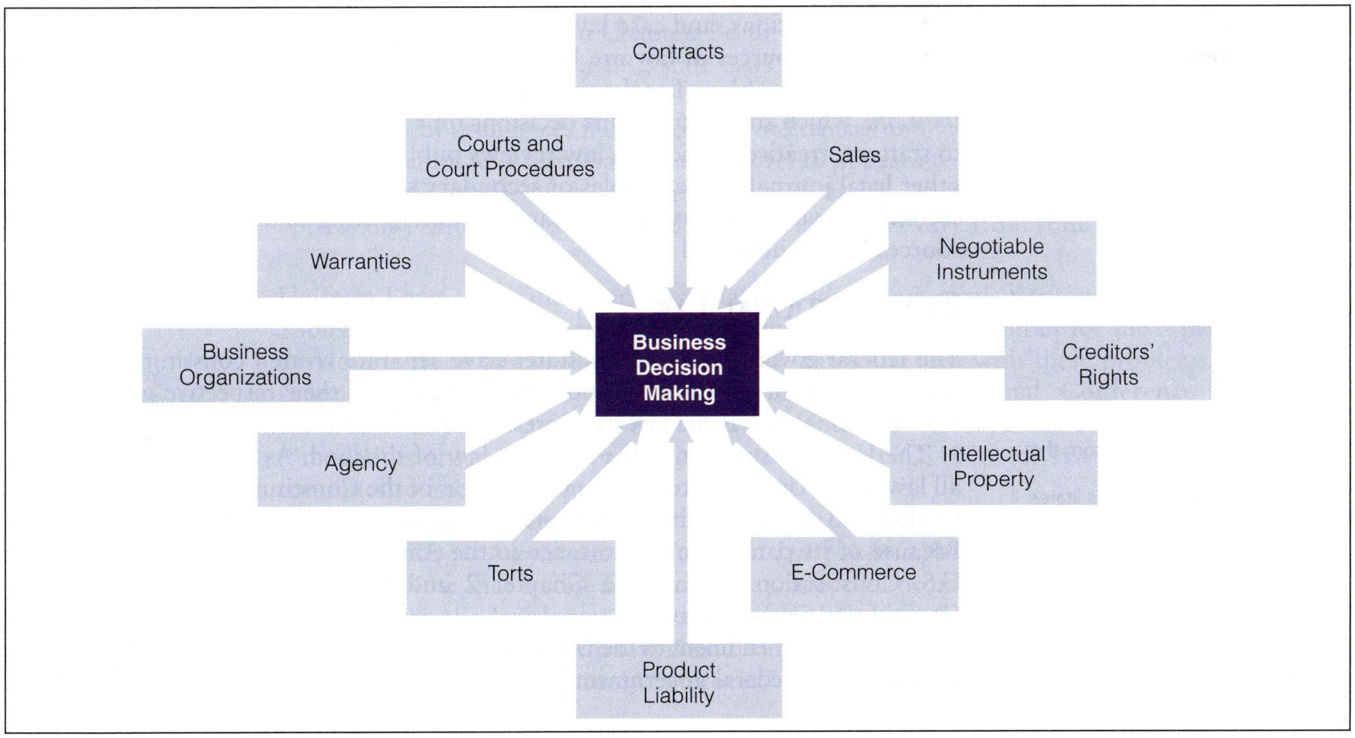

The court of chancery in the reign of King George I. Early English court decisions formed the basis of what type of law? (From a painting by Benjamin Ferrers in the National Portrait Gallery; Photo, Corbis Bettmann)

In the early years of the common law, there was no single place or publication where court opinions, or written decisions, could be found. Beginning in the late thirteenth and early fourteenth centuries, however, each year portions of significant decisions of that year were gathered together and recorded in *Year Books*. The *Year Books* were useful references for lawyers and judges. In the sixteenth century, the *Year Books* were discontinued, and other reports of cases became available. (See the appendix following this chapter for a discussion of how cases are reported, or published, in the United States today.)

STARE DECISIS

The practice of deciding new cases with reference to former decisions, or precedents, eventually became a cornerstone of the English and American judicial systems. The practice forms a doctrine called ***stare decisis***[3] ("to stand on decided cases").

STARE DECISIS
A common law doctrine under which judges are obligated to follow the precedents established in prior decisions.

The Importance of Precedents in Judicial Decision Making The doctrine of *stare decisis* means that once a court has set forth a principle of law as being applicable to a certain set of facts, that court and courts of lower rank must adhere to that principle and apply it in future cases involving similar fact patterns.

■ EXAMPLE 1.2 Suppose that the lower state courts in California have reached conflicting conclusions on whether drivers are liable for accidents they cause while merging into freeway traffic, even though the drivers looked and did not see any oncoming vehicles and even though witnesses (passengers in their cars) testified to that effect. To settle the law on this issue, the California Supreme Court decides to review a case involving this fact pattern. The court rules that in such a situation, the driver who is merging into traffic is liable for any accidents caused by the driver's failure to yield to freeway traffic—even if the driver looked carefully and did not see an approaching vehicle. The California Supreme Court's decision on the matter will influence the outcome of all future cases on this issue brought before the California state courts. ■ Similarly, a decision on a given issue by the United States Supreme Court (the nation's highest court) is binding on all other courts.

BINDING AUTHORITY
Any source of law that a court must follow when deciding a case. Binding authorities include constitutions, statutes, and regulations that govern the issue being decided, as well as court decisions that are controlling precedents within the jurisdiction.

Controlling precedents in a *jurisdiction* (an area in which a court or courts have the power to apply the law—see Chapter 3) are referred to as binding authorities. A **binding authority** is any source of law that a court must follow when deciding a case. Binding authorities include constitutions, statutes, and regulations that govern the issue being decided, as well as court decisions that are controlling precedents within the jurisdiction.

***Stare Decisis* and Legal Stability** The doctrine of *stare decisis* helps the courts to be more efficient, because if other courts have carefully reasoned through a similar case, their legal reasoning and opinions can serve as guides. *Stare decisis* also makes the law more stable and predictable. If the law on a given subject is well settled, someone bringing a case to court can usually rely on the court to make a decision based on what the law has been.

Departures from Precedent Although courts are obligated to follow precedents, sometimes a court will depart from the rule of precedent if it decides that a given precedent should no longer be followed. If a court decides that a precedent is simply incorrect or that technological or social changes have rendered the precedent

3. Pronounced *ster*-ay dih-*si*-ses.

To learn how the Supreme Court justified its departure from precedent in the 1954 *Brown* decision, you can access the Court's opinion online by going to

http://findlaw.com/casecode/supreme.html

and entering "347 U.S. 483" in the "Citation Search" box.

inapplicable, the court might rule contrary to the precedent. Cases that overturn precedent often receive a great deal of publicity.

■ EXAMPLE 1.3 In *Brown v. Board of Education of Topeka,*[4] the United States Supreme Court expressly overturned precedent when it concluded that separate educational facilities for whites and blacks, which had been upheld as constitutional in numerous previous cases,[5] were inherently unequal. The Supreme Court's departure from precedent in *Brown* received a tremendous amount of publicity as people began to realize the ramifications of this change in the law. ■

PERSUASIVE AUTHORITY
Any legal authority or source of law that a court may look to for guidance but on which it need not rely in making its decision. Persuasive authorities include cases from other jurisdictions and secondary sources of law.

When There Is No Precedent At times, courts hear cases for which there are no precedents within their jurisdictions on which to base their decisions. When hearing such cases, called "cases of first impression," courts often look to precedents set in other jurisdictions for guidance. Precedents from other jurisdictions, because they are not binding on the court, are referred to as **persuasive authorities.** A court may also consider a number of factors, including legal principles and policies underlying previous court decisions or existing statutes, fairness, social values and customs, public policy, and data and concepts drawn from the social sciences.

ETHICAL ISSUE 1.2

Should the Supreme Court look to other nations' laws for guidance? Over the last several years, justices on the United States Supreme Court have exhibited an increasing tendency to consider foreign law when deciding issues of national importance. For example, in 2003—for the first time ever—a majority opinion of the Supreme Court cited foreign law (references to foreign law have appeared in footnotes and dissents on a few occasions in the past). The citation occurred in a controversial case in which the Court struck down laws that prohibit oral and anal sex between consenting adults of the same gender. In the majority opinion (an opinion that the majority of justices have signed), Justice Anthony Kennedy mentioned that the European Court of Human Rights and other foreign courts have consistently acknowledged that homosexuals have a right "to engage in intimate, consensual conduct."[6] This comment sparked debate in legal circles over whether the Supreme Court, or other U.S. courts, should ever consider world opinion or cite foreign law as a persuasive authority. The practice has many critics, including Justice Antonin Scalia, who believes that foreign views are irrelevant to rulings on U.S. law. Other Supreme Court justices, however, including Justices Ginsburg, Breyer, and O'Connor, believe that in our increasingly global community we should not ignore the opinions of courts in the rest of the world. ■

EQUITABLE REMEDIES AND COURTS OF EQUITY

REMEDY
The relief given to an innocent party to enforce a right or compensate for the violation of a right.

A **remedy** is the means given to a party to enforce a right or to compensate for the violation of a right. ■ EXAMPLE 1.4 Suppose that Shem is injured because of Rowan's wrongdoing. A court may order Rowan to compensate Shem for the harm by paying Shem a certain amount of money. ■

In the early king's courts of England, the kinds of remedies that could be granted were severely restricted. If one person wronged another, the king's courts could

4. 347 U.S. 483, 74 S.Ct. 686, 98 L.Ed. 873 (1954). See the appendix following this chapter for an explanation of how to read legal citations.

5. See *Plessy v. Ferguson,* 163 U.S. 537, 16 S.Ct. 1138, 41 L.Ed. 256 (1896).

6. *Lawrence v. Texas,* 539 U.S. 558, 123 S.Ct. 2472, 156 L.Ed.2d 508 (2003). Other cases in which the Supreme Court has referenced foreign law include *Grutter v. Bollinger,* 539 U.S. 306, 123 S.Ct. 2325, 156 L.Ed.2d 304 (2003), in the dissent; and *Roper v. Simmons,* 538 U.S. 11, 123 S.Ct. 1183, 161 L.Ed.2d 1 (2005).

award as compensation either money or property, including land. These courts became known as *courts of law,* and the remedies were called *remedies at law.* Even though this system introduced uniformity in the settling of disputes, when plaintiffs wanted a remedy other than economic compensation, the courts of law could do nothing, so "no remedy, no right."

Remedies in Equity *Equity* refers to a branch of the law, founded in justice and fair dealing, that seeks to supply a fair and adequate remedy when no remedy is available at law. In medieval England, when individuals could not obtain an adequate remedy in a court of law, they petitioned the king for relief. Most of these petitions were decided by an adviser to the king called the *chancellor.* The chancellor was said to be the "keeper of the king's conscience." When the chancellor thought that the claim was a fair one, new and unique remedies were granted. In this way, a new body of rules and remedies came into being, and eventually formal *chancery courts,* or *courts of equity,* were established. The remedies granted by these courts were called *remedies in equity.* Thus, two distinct court systems were created, each having a different set of judges and a different set of remedies.

PLAINTIFF
One who initiates a lawsuit.

DEFENDANT
One against whom a lawsuit is brought; the accused person in a criminal proceeding.

Plaintiffs (those bringing lawsuits) had to specify whether they were bringing an "action at law" or an "action in equity," and they chose their courts accordingly. ■ EXAMPLE 1.5 A plaintiff might ask a court of equity to order a **defendant** (a person against whom a lawsuit is brought) to perform within the terms of a contract. A court of law could not issue such an order, because its remedies were limited to payment of money or property as compensation for damages. A court of equity, however, could issue a decree for *specific performance*—an order to perform what was promised. A court of equity could also issue an *injunction,* directing a party to do or refrain from doing a particular act. In certain cases, a court of equity could allow for the *rescission* (cancellation) of the contract so that the parties would be returned to the positions that they held prior to the contract's formation. ■ Equitable remedies will be discussed in greater detail in Chapter 15.

REMEMBER Even though, in most states, courts of law and equity have merged, the principles of equity still apply.

The Merging of Law and Equity Today, in most states, the courts of law and equity have merged, and thus the distinction between the two courts has largely disappeared. A plaintiff may now request both legal and equitable remedies in the same action, and the trial court judge may grant either form—or both forms—of relief. The merging of law and equity, however, does not diminish the importance of distinguishing legal remedies from equitable remedies. To request the proper remedy, a businessperson (or her or his attorney) must know what remedies are available for the specific kinds of harms suffered. Today, as a rule, courts will grant an equitable remedy only when the remedy at law (money damages) is inadequate. Exhibit 1–2 summarizes the procedural differences (applicable in most states) between an action at law and an action in equity.

EXHIBIT 1–2 PROCEDURAL DIFFERENCES BETWEEN AN ACTION AT LAW AND AN ACTION IN EQUITY

PROCEDURE	ACTION AT LAW	ACTION IN EQUITY
Initiation of lawsuit	By filing a complaint	By filing a petition
Decision	By jury or judge	By judge (no jury)
Result	Judgment	Decree
Remedy	Monetary damages	Injunction, specific performance, or rescission

LANDMARK IN THE LAW

Equitable Principles and Maxims

In medieval England, courts of equity had the responsibility of using discretion in supplementing the common law. Even today, when the same court can award both legal and equitable remedies, it must exercise discretion. Courts often invoke equitable principles and maxims when making their decisions. Here are some of the most significant equitable principles and maxims:

1. *Whoever seeks equity must do equity.* (Anyone who wishes to be treated fairly must treat others fairly.)
2. *Where there is equal equity, the law must prevail.* (The law will determine the outcome of a controversy in which the merits of both sides are equal.)
3. *One seeking the aid of an equity court must come to the court with clean hands.* (Plaintiffs must have acted fairly and honestly.)
4. *Equity will not suffer a wrong to be without a remedy.* (Equitable relief will be awarded when there is a right to relief and there is no adequate remedy at law.)
5. *Equity regards substance rather than form.* (Equity is more concerned with fairness and justice than with legal technicalities.)
6. *Equity aids the vigilant, not those who rest on their rights.* (Equity will not help those who neglect their rights for an unreasonable period of time.)

The last maxim has become known as the *equitable doctrine of laches*. The doctrine arose to encourage people to bring lawsuits while the evidence was fresh; if they failed to do so, they would not be allowed to bring a lawsuit. What constitutes a reasonable time, of course, varies according to the circumstances of the case. Time periods for different types of cases are now usually fixed by **statutes of limitations.** After the time allowed under a statute of limitations has expired, no action can be brought, no matter how strong the case was originally.

STATUTE OF LIMITATIONS
A federal or state statute setting the maximum time period during which a certain action can be brought or certain rights enforced.

APPLICATION TO TODAY'S BUSINESS WORLD

The equitable maxims listed above underlie many of the legal rules and principles that are commonly applied by the courts today—and that you will read about in this book. For example, in Chapter 10 you will read about the doctrine of promissory estoppel. *Under this doctrine, a person who has reasonably and substantially relied on the promise of another may be able to obtain some measure of recovery, even though no enforceable contract, or agreement, exists. The court will* estop *(bar, or impede) the one making the promise from asserting the lack of a valid contract as a defense. The rationale underlying the doctrine of promissory estoppel is similar to that expressed in the fourth and fifth maxims above.*

RELEVANT WEB SITES

To locate information on the Web concerning equitable principles, *go to this text's Web site at* http://blt.westbuslaw.com, *select "Chapter 1," and click on "URLs for Landmarks."*

EQUITABLE PRINCIPLES AND MAXIMS
General propositions or principles of law that have to do with fairness (equity).

Equitable Principles and Maxims Over time, a number of **equitable principles and maxims** evolved that have since guided the courts in deciding whether plaintiffs should be granted equitable relief. Because of their importance, both historically and in our judicial system today, these principles and maxims are set forth in this chapter's *Landmark in the Law* feature on the previous page.

Classifications of Law

SUBSTANTIVE LAW
Law that defines, describes, regulates, and creates legal rights and obligations.

PROCEDURAL LAW
Law that establishes the methods of enforcing the rights established by substantive law.

CYBERLAW
An informal term used to refer to all laws governing electronic communications and transactions, particularly those conducted via the Internet.

The huge body of the law may be broken down according to several classification systems. For example, one classification system divides law into **substantive law** (all laws that define, describe, regulate, and create legal rights and obligations) and **procedural law** (all laws that establish the methods of enforcing the rights established by substantive law). Other classification systems divide law into federal law and state law or private law (dealing with relationships between persons) and public law (addressing the relationship between persons and their governments).

Frequently, people use the term **cyberlaw** to refer to the emerging body of law that governs transactions conducted via the Internet. Cyberlaw is not really a classification of law, nor is it a new *type* of law. Rather, it is an informal term used to describe traditional legal principles that have been modified and adapted to fit situations that are unique to the online world. Of course, in some areas new statutes have been enacted, at both the federal and state levels, to cover specific types of problems stemming from online communications. Throughout this book, you will read how the law in a given area is evolving to govern specific legal issues that arise in the online context. We look at one important issue in this chapter's *Adapting the Law to the Online Environment* feature.

Civil Law and Criminal Law

CIVIL LAW
The branch of law dealing with the definition and enforcement of all private or public rights, as opposed to criminal matters.

Civil law spells out the rights and duties that exist between persons and between persons and their governments, and the relief available when a person's rights are violated. Typically, in a civil case, a private party sues another private party (although the government can also sue a party for a civil law violation) to make that other party comply with a duty or pay for the damage caused by the failure to comply with a duty. ■ **Example 1.6** If a seller fails to perform a contract with a buyer, the buyer may bring a lawsuit against the seller. The purpose of the lawsuit will be either to compel the seller to perform as promised or, more commonly, to obtain money damages for the seller's failure to perform. ■

Much of the law that we discuss in this text is civil law. Contract law, for example, which we discuss in Chapters 8 through 17, is civil law. The whole body of tort law (see Chapter 4) is civil law. Note that *civil law* is not the same as a *civil law system.* As you will read shortly, in the subsection discussing national law, a civil law system is a legal system based on a written code of laws.

CRIMINAL LAW
Law that defines and governs actions that constitute crimes. Generally, criminal law has to do with wrongful actions committed against society for which society demands redress.

Criminal law has to do with wrongs committed against society for which society demands redress. Criminal acts are proscribed by local, state, or federal government statutes. Thus, criminal defendants are prosecuted by public officials, such as a district attorney (D.A.), on behalf of the state, not by their victims or other private parties. Whereas in a civil case the object is to obtain remedies (such as money damages) to compensate the injured party, in a criminal case the object is to punish the wrongdoer in an attempt to deter others from similar actions. Penalties for violations of criminal statutes consist of fines and/or imprisonment—and, in some cases, death. We will discuss the differences between civil and criminal law in greater detail in Chapter 6.

ADAPTING THE LAW TO THE ONLINE ENVIRONMENT

International Jurisdiction and the Internet

As you will learn in Chapter 3, *jurisdiction* is an important legal concept that relates to the authority of a court to hear and decide a case. Within the United States, there is a federal court system, which has jurisdiction over specific types of cases. There are also fifty state court systems, each having jurisdiction over certain types of cases. In today's interconnected world, the issue of jurisdiction has become critical. Specifically, businesses using the Internet can reach individuals in any part of the world. Does that mean that every court everywhere has jurisdiction over, say, an Internet-based company in Chicago? Clearly, this question has significant implications for any business that owns or operates a Web site.

THE MINIMUM-CONTACTS REQUIREMENT

Domestically, jurisdiction over individuals and businesses is based on the requirement of minimum contacts as outlined in *International Shoe Co. v. State of Washington.*[a] Essentially, this requirement means that a business must have a minimum level of contacts with residents of a particular state for that state's courts to exercise jurisdiction over the firm. For example, suppose that a Wisconsin driver, while on vacation in California, crashes into a California resident's car. If the crash resulted from the Wisconsin driver's negligence, a *tort,* or civil wrong (see Chapter 4), will have been committed. This contact will be sufficient to allow a California court to exercise jurisdiction over a lawsuit brought by the California resident. In the international arena, other countries' courts are applying the requirement of minimum contacts as developed in the U.S. courts.

a. 326 U.S. 310, 66 S.Ct. 154, 90 L.Ed. 95 (1945).

SPECIAL INTERNATIONAL JURISDICTIONAL CHALLENGES

Suppose that a firm located in New Jersey posts a statement on its Web site that is defamatory. (As you will read in Chapter 4, *defamation* is a tort that occurs when someone publishes or publicly makes a false statement that harms another's good name, reputation, or character.) Further suppose that the person who has been defamed, or injured by the statement, lives in Australia. Can the Australian citizen sue the New Jersey firm in an Australian court? Perhaps, but at a minimum, jurisdictional authority would depend on whether the tort occurred in Australia. Thus, the question essentially is as follows: Did the tort occur when the defamatory statement was posted on the Web site (in New Jersey) or when it was downloaded and viewed (in Australia)?

To date, only one nation's highest court—that of Australia—has ruled on this issue. The case involved Joseph Gutnick, a resident of Melbourne, Australia, who sued Dow Jones & Company, the U.S. publisher of the *Wall Street Journal,* for defamation. Dow Jones argued that the Australian court could not exercise jurisdiction over its U.S. servers, which were located in New Jersey. The case ultimately reached Australia's highest court, which rejected Dow Jones's argument. The court concluded that the tort had occurred in Australia, where the article had been downloaded and viewed, and thus the Australian court had jurisdiction over the dispute.[b]

FOR CRITICAL ANALYSIS

If the opinion of the Australian high court becomes widely accepted, how might this have a "chilling effect" on Internet communications and on the dissemination of ideas?

b. *Dow Jones & Co., Inc. v. Gutnick,* HCA 56 (December 10, 2002).

.on the Web The Library of Congress offers extensive information on national and international law at **http://www.loc.gov.**

NATIONAL AND INTERNATIONAL LAW

Although the focus of this book is U.S. business law, increasingly businesspersons in this country engage in transactions that extend beyond our national borders. In these situations, the laws of other nations or the laws governing relationships among nations may come into play. For this reason, those who pursue a career in business today should have an understanding of the global legal environment.

NATIONAL LAW
Law that pertains to a particular nation (as opposed to international law).

National Law The law of a particular nation, such as the United States or Sweden, is **national law.** National law, of course, varies from country to country because each country's law reflects the interests, customs, activities, and values that are unique to that nation's culture. Even though the laws and legal systems of various countries differ substantially, broad similarities do exist.

Basically, there are two legal systems in the world today. One is the common law system of England and the United States, which we have already discussed. The other system is based on Roman civil law, or "code law." The term *civil law,* as used here, refers not to civil as opposed to criminal law but to codified law—an ordered grouping of legal principles enacted into law by a legislature or governing body. In a **civil law system,** the primary source of law is a statutory code, and case precedents are not judicially binding, as they normally are in a common law system. Although judges in a civil law system commonly refer to previous decisions as sources of legal guidance, they are not bound by precedent; in other words, the doctrine of *stare decisis* does not apply.

CIVIL LAW SYSTEM
A system of law derived from that of the Roman Empire and based on a code rather than case law; the predominant system of law in the nations of continental Europe and the nations that were once their colonies. In the United States, Louisiana, because of its historical ties to France, has in part a civil law system.

Exhibit 1–3 lists some countries that today follow either the common law system or the civil law system. Generally, those countries that were once colonies of Great Britain retained their English common law heritage after they achieved independence. Similarly, the civil law system, which is followed in most continental European countries, was retained in the Latin American, African, and Asian countries that were once colonies of those nations. Japan and South Africa also have civil law systems, and ingredients of the civil law system are found in the Islamic courts of predominantly Muslim countries. In the United States, the state of Louisiana, because of its historical ties to France, has in part a civil law system. The legal systems of Puerto Rico, Québec, and Scotland are similarly characterized as having elements of the civil law system.

International Law In contrast to national law, international law applies to more than one nation. **International law** can be defined as a body of written and unwritten laws observed by independent nations and governing the acts of individuals as well as governments. International law is an intermingling of rules and constraints derived from a variety of sources, including the laws of individual nations, the customs that have evolved among nations in their relations with one another, treaties, and international organizations. In essence, international law is the result of centuries-old attempts to reconcile the traditional need of each nation to be the final authority over its own affairs with the desire of nations to benefit economically from trade and harmonious relations with one another.

INTERNATIONAL LAW
The law that governs relations among nations. National laws, customs, treaties, and international conferences and organizations are generally considered to be the most important sources of international law.

The key difference between national law and international law is that national law can be enforced by government authorities. If a nation violates an international law, however, the most that other countries or international organizations can do

EXHIBIT 1–3 THE LEGAL SYSTEMS OF SELECTED NATIONS

CIVIL LAW		COMMON LAW	
Argentina	Indonesia	Australia	Nigeria
Austria	Iran	Bangladesh	Singapore
Brazil	Italy	Canada	United Kingdom
Chile	Japan	Ghana	United States
China	Mexico	India	Zambia
Egypt	Poland	Israel	
Finland	South Korea	Jamaica	
France	Sweden	Kenya	
Germany	Tunisia	Malaysia	
Greece	Venezuela	New Zealand	

(if persuasive tactics fail) is to resort to coercive actions against the violating nation. Coercive actions range from the severance of diplomatic relations and boycotts to, at the last resort, war. We will examine the laws governing international business transactions in later chapters (including parts of Chapters 18 through 21, which cover contracts for the sale of goods, and all of Chapter 46).

APPLICATION How Should You Choose and Use a Lawyer?*

If you are contemplating a career in the business world, sooner or later you will probably face the question, "Do I need a lawyer?" The answer to this question will likely be "Yes," at least at some time during your career. Even businesspersons who have gone to law school often hire an outside lawyer to help them with their legal problems. Today, it is virtually impossible for nonexperts to keep up with the myriad rules and regulations that govern the conduct of business in the United States. It is also increasingly possible for businesspersons to incur penalties for violating laws or regulations of which they are totally unaware.

Although lawyers may seem expensive—anywhere from $100 to $500 or more per hour—cautious businesspersons will make sure that they are not "penny wise and pound foolish." The consultation fee paid to an attorney may be insignificant compared with the potential liability facing a businessperson.

SELECTING AN ATTORNEY

In selecting an attorney, you can ask friends, relatives, or business associates to recommend someone. Alternatively, you can call the local or state bar association to obtain the names of several lawyers. West Group has an online database containing biographies of attorneys throughout the country, listed by area of specialty and by state. You can find attorneys in your area by accessing West's Legal Directory online at http://directory.findlaw.com. Some legal aid programs have staff attorneys, and others may refer you to volunteers. You might also investigate legal clinics and prepaid legal service plans.

For your initial meeting with the attorney you have selected, you should prepare a written list of your questions and perhaps a summary of the problem for which you need legal advice. Attach to your list copies of any relevant documents that you can leave with the lawyer. While at the meeting, ask about legal fees, discuss the legal problem you are facing (remember that virtually everything you say to your attorney is protected by the attorney-client privilege of confidentiality), and clarify the scope of what you want the lawyer to do for you.

EVALUATING YOUR ATTORNEY

Ask yourself the following questions after your first meeting: Did the attorney seem knowledgeable about what is needed to address your concerns? Did he or she seem willing to investigate the law and the facts further to ensure an accurate understanding of your legal situation? Did you communicate well with each other? Did the attorney perceive what issues were of foremost concern to you and address those issues to your satisfaction? Did the attorney "speak your language" when explaining the legal implications of those issues?

Continue to evaluate the relationship over time. For many businesspersons, relationships with attorneys last for decades. Make sure that your relationship with your attorney will be a fruitful one.

CHECKLIST FOR CHOOSING AND USING A LAWYER

1. If you ever think that you need legal advice, you probably do.
2. When choosing an attorney, try to get recommendations from friends, relatives, or business associates who have had long-standing relationships with their attorneys. If that fails, check with your local or state bar association or check West Group's online directory.
3. When you initially consult with an attorney, bring a written list of questions to which you want answers, perhaps a summary of your problem, and copies of relevant documents.
4. Do not hesitate to ask about the legal fees that your attorney will charge, and be sure to clarify the scope of the work to be undertaken by the attorney. Ask whatever questions are necessary to ensure that you understand what your legal options are. Do not worry about appearing foolish.

* With appreciation to James D. Van Tassel at Mission College, California, for his helpful suggestions on this topic.

KEY TERMS

administrative agency 8
administrative law 8
binding authority 10
breach 5
case law 9
citation 7
civil law 14
civil law system 16
common law 9
constitutional law 6
criminal law 14
cyberlaw 14
defendant 12
equitable principles and maxims 14
executive agency 8
historical school 4
independent regulatory agency 8
international law 16
jurisprudence 3
law 3
legal positivism 3
legal realism 4
national law 15
natural law 3
ordinance 7
persuasive authority 11
plaintiff 12
positive law 3
precedent 9
primary source of law 6
procedural law 14
remedy 11
secondary source of law 6
sociological school 4
stare decisis 10
statute of limitations 13
statutory law 7
substantive law 14

CHAPTER SUMMARY The Legal Environment

The Nature of Law
(See pages 3–4.)

Law can be defined as a body of rules of conduct with legal force and effect, prescribed by the controlling authority (the government) of a society. Four important schools of legal thought, or legal philosophies, are the following:

1. *Natural law tradition*—One of the oldest and most significant schools of legal thought. Those who believe in natural law hold that there is a universal law applicable to all human beings and that this law is of a higher order than positive, or conventional, law.
2. *Legal positivism*—A school of legal thought centered on the assumption that there is no law higher than the laws created by the government. Laws must be obeyed, even if they are unjust, to prevent anarchy.
3. *The historical school*—A school of legal thought that stresses the evolutionary nature of law and that looks to doctrines that have withstood the passage of time for guidance in shaping present laws.
4. *Legal realism*—A school of legal thought, popular during the 1920s and 1930s, that left a lasting imprint on American jurisprudence. Legal realists generally advocated a less abstract and more realistic approach to the law, an approach that would take into account customary practices and the circumstances in which transactions take place.

Sources of American Law
(See pages 6–9.)

1. *Constitutional law*—The law as expressed in the U.S. Constitution and the various state constitutions. The U.S. Constitution is the supreme law of the land. State constitutions are supreme within state borders to the extent that they do not violate the U.S. Constitution or a federal law.
2. *Statutory law*—Laws or ordinances created by federal, state, and local legislatures and governing bodies. None of these laws can violate the U.S. Constitution or the relevant state constitutions. Uniform laws, when adopted by a state legislature, become statutory law in that state.
3. *Administrative law*—The rules, orders, and decisions of federal or state government administrative agencies.

CHAPTER SUMMARY The Legal Environment—Continued

Sources of American Law—Continued	4. *Case law and common law doctrines*—Judge-made law, including interpretations of constitutional provisions, of statutes enacted by legislatures, and of regulations created by administrative agencies. The common law—the doctrines and principles embodied in case law—governs all areas not covered by statutory law (or agency regulations issued to implement various statutes).
The Common Law Tradition (See pages 9–14.)	1. *Common law*—Law that originated in medieval England with the creation of the king's courts, or *curiae regis,* and the development of a body of rules that were common to (or applied throughout) the land. 2. *Stare decisis*—A doctrine under which judges "stand on decided cases"—or follow the rule of precedent—in deciding cases. *Stare decisis* is the cornerstone of the common law tradition. 3. *Remedies*— a. Remedies at law—Money or something else of value. b. Remedies in equity—Remedies that are granted when the remedies at law are unavailable or inadequate. Equitable remedies include specific performance, an injunction, and contract rescission (cancellation).
Classifications of Law (See pages 14–17.)	The law may be broken down according to several classification systems, such as substantive or procedural law, federal or state law, and private or public law. Two broad classifications are civil and criminal law, and national and international law.

FOR REVIEW

Answers for the even-numbered questions in this For Review section can be found on this text's accompanying Web site at http://blt.westbuslaw.com. *Select "Chapter 1" and click on "For Review."*

1. What is the Uniform Commercial Code?
2. What is the common law tradition?
3. What is a precedent? When might a court depart from precedent?
4. What is the difference between remedies at law and remedies in equity?
5. What are some important differences between civil law and criminal law?

QUESTIONS AND CASE PROBLEMS

1–1. Philosophy of Law. After World War II ended in 1945, an international tribunal of judges convened at Nuremberg, Germany. The judges convicted several Nazi war criminals of "crimes against humanity." Assuming that the Nazis who were convicted had not disobeyed any law of their country and had merely been following their government's (Hitler's) orders, what law had they violated? Explain.

1–2. Legal Systems. What are the key differences between a common law system and a civil law system? Why do some countries have common law systems and others have civil law systems?

1–3. Reading Citations. Assume that you want to read the entire court opinion in the case of *Thompson v. Altheimer & Gray,* 248 F.3d 621 (7th Cir. 2001). The case deals with whether an attorney may dismiss "for cause" a prospective juror in a case involving racial discrimination. Read the section entitled "Finding Case Law" in the appendix that follows this chapter, and then explain specifically where you would find the court's opinion.

1–4. Sources of American Law. This chapter discussed a number of sources of American law. Which source of law takes priority in each of the following situations, and why?

(a) A federal statute conflicts with the U.S. Constitution.
(b) A federal statute conflicts with a state constitution.
(c) A state statute conflicts with the common law of that state.
(d) A state constitutional amendment conflicts with the U.S. Constitution.
(e) A federal administrative regulation conflicts with a state constitution.

1–5. *Stare Decisis.* In the text of this chapter, we stated that the doctrine of *stare decisis* "became a cornerstone of the English and American judicial systems." What does *stare decisis* mean, and why has this doctrine been so fundamental to the development of our legal tradition?

1–6. Court Opinions. Read through the subsection entitled "Case Titles and Terminology" in the appendix following this chapter. What is the difference between a concurring opinion and a majority opinion? Between a concurring opinion and a dissenting opinion? Why do judges and justices write concurring and dissenting opinions, given that these opinions will not affect the outcome of the case at hand, which has already been decided by majority vote?

1–7. Binding versus Persuasive Authority. A county court in Illinois is deciding a case involving an issue that has never been addressed before in that state's courts. The Iowa Supreme Court, however, recently decided a case involving a very similar fact pattern. Is the Illinois court obligated to follow the Iowa Supreme Court's decision on the issue? If the United States Supreme Court had decided a similar case, would that decision be binding on the Illinois court? Explain.

1–8. Remedies. Arthur Rabe is suing Xavier Sanchez for breaching a contract in which Sanchez promised to sell Rabe a Van Gogh painting for $150,000.

(a) In this lawsuit, who is the plaintiff and who is the defendant?
(b) If Rabe wants Sanchez to perform the contract as promised, what remedy should Rabe seek?
(c) Suppose that Rabe wants to cancel the contract because Sanchez fraudulently misrepresented the painting as an original Van Gogh when in fact it is a copy. In this situation, what remedy should Rabe seek?
(d) Will the remedy Rabe seeks in either situation be a remedy at law or a remedy in equity?
(e) Suppose that the court finds in Rabe's favor and grants one of these remedies. Sanchez then appeals the decision to a higher court. Read the subsection entitled "Appellants and Appellees" in the appendix following this chapter. On appeal, which party in the Rabe-Sanchez case will be the appellant (or petitioner), and which party will be the appellee (or respondent)?

A QUESTION OF ETHICS

1–9. On July 5, 1884, Dudley, Stephens, and Brooks—"all able-bodied English seamen"—and a teenage English boy were cast adrift in a lifeboat following a storm at sea. They had no water with them in the boat, and all they had for sustenance were two one-pound tins of turnips. On July 24, Dudley proposed that one of the four in the lifeboat be sacrificed to save the others. Stephens agreed with Dudley, but Brooks refused to consent—and the boy was never asked for his opinion. On July 25, Dudley killed the boy, and the three men then fed on the boy's body and blood. Four days later, the men were rescued by a passing vessel. They were taken to England and tried for the murder of the boy. If the men had not fed on the boy's body, they would probably have died of starvation within the four-day period. The boy, who was in a much weaker condition, would likely have died before the rest. [*Regina v. Dudley and Stephens,* 14 Q.B.D. (Queen's Bench Division, England) 273 (1884)]

1. The basic question in this case is whether the survivors should be subject to penalties under English criminal law, given the men's unusual circumstances. You be the judge and decide the issue. Give the reasons for your decision.
2. Should judges ever have the power to look beyond the written "letter of the law" in making their decisions? Why or why not?

FOR CRITICAL ANALYSIS

1–10. Courts of equity tend to follow general rules or maxims rather than common law precedents, as courts of law do. Some of these maxims were listed in this chapter's *Landmark in the Law* feature. Why would equity courts give credence to such general maxims rather than to a hard-and-fast body of law?

INTERNET EXERCISES

Go to the *Business Law Today* home page at **http://blt.westbuslaw.com**, select "Chapter 1," and click on "Internet Exercises." There you will find the following Internet research exercises that you can perform to learn more about topics covered in this chapter.

Activity 1–1: LEGAL PERSPECTIVE—Internet Sources of Law

Activity 1–2: MANAGEMENT PERSPECTIVE—Online Assistance from Government Agencies

Activity 1–3: SOCIAL PERSPECTIVE—The Case of the Speluncean Explorers

BEFORE THE TEST

Go to the *Business Law Today* home page at **http://blt.westbuslaw.com**, select "Chapter 1," and click on "Interactive Quizzes." You will find a number of interactive questions relating to this chapter.

CHAPTER 1

Appendix

The statutes, agency regulations, and case law referred to in this text establish the rights and duties of businesspersons engaged in various types of activities. The cases presented in the following chapters provide you with concise, real-life illustrations of how the courts interpret and apply these laws. Because of the importance of knowing how to find statutory, administrative, and case law, this appendix offers a brief introduction to how these laws are published and to the legal "shorthand" employed in referencing these legal sources.

Finding Statutory and Administrative Law

When Congress passes laws, they are collected in a publication titled *United States Statutes at Large*. When state legislatures pass laws, they are collected in similar state publications. Most frequently, however, laws are referred to in their codified form—that is, the form in which they appear in the federal and state codes. In these codes, laws are compiled by subject.

UNITED STATES CODE

.on the Web You can search the *United States Code* online at **http://www4.law.cornell.edu/uscode**.

The *United States Code* (U.S.C.) arranges all existing federal laws of a public and permanent nature by subject. Each of the fifty subjects into which the U.S.C. arranges the laws is given a title and a title number. For example, laws relating to commerce and trade are collected in "Title 15, Commerce and Trade." Titles are subdivided by sections. A citation to the U.S.C. includes title and section numbers. Thus, a reference to "15 U.S.C. Section 1" means that the statute can be found in Section 1 of Title 15. ("Section" may also be designated by the symbol §, and "Sections" by §§.)

Sometimes a citation includes the abbreviation *et seq.*—as in "15 U.S.C. Sections 1 *et seq.*" The term is an abbreviated form of *et sequitur,* which in Latin means "and the following"; when used in a citation, it refers to sections that concern the same subject as the numbered section and follow it in sequence.

Commercial publications of these laws and regulations are available and are widely used. For example, West Group publishes the *United States Code Annotated* (U.S.C.A.). The U.S.C.A. contains the complete text of laws included in the U.S.C., as well as notes of court decisions that interpret and apply specific sections of the statutes, plus the text of presidential proclamations and executive orders. The U.S.C.A. also includes research aids, such as cross-references to related statutes, historical notes, and library references. A citation to the U.S.C.A. is similar to a citation to the U.S.C.: "15 U.S.C.A. Section 1."

STATE CODES

State codes follow the U.S.C. pattern of arranging law by subject. The state codes may be called codes, revisions, compilations, consolidations, general statutes, or statutes, depending on the preferences of the states. In some codes, subjects are designated by number. In others, they are designated by name. For example, "13 Pennsylvania Consolidated Statutes Section 1101" means that the statute can be found in Title 13, Section 1101, of the Pennsylvania code. "California Commercial Code Section 1101" means the statute can be found under the subject heading "Commercial Code" of the California code in Section 1101. Abbreviations may be used. For example, "13 Pennsylvania Consolidated Statutes Section 1101" may be abbreviated "13 Pa. C.S. § 1101," and "California Commercial Code Section 1101" may be abbreviated "Cal. Com. Code § 1101."

Administrative Rules

.on the Web The *Code of Federal Regulations* is online at **http://www.gpoaccess.gov/cfr/index.html**.

Rules and regulations adopted by federal administrative agencies are compiled in the *Code of Federal Regulations* (C.F.R.). Like the U.S.C., the C.F.R. is divided into fifty titles. Rules within each title are assigned section numbers. A full citation to the C.F.R. includes title and section numbers. For example, a reference to "17 C.F.R. Section 230.504" means that the rule can be found in Section 230.504 of Title 17.

Finding Case Law

Before discussing the case reporting system, we need to look briefly at the court system (which will be discussed in detail in Chapter 3). There are two types of courts in the United States, federal courts and state courts. Both the federal and state court systems consist of several levels, or tiers, of courts. *Trial courts,* in which evidence is presented and testimony given, are on the bottom tier (which also includes lower courts handling specialized issues). Decisions from a trial court can be appealed to a higher court, which commonly would be an intermediate *court of appeals,* or an *appellate court.* Decisions from these intermediate courts of appeals may be appealed to an even higher court, such as a state supreme court or the United States Supreme Court.

State Court Decisions

Most state trial court decisions are not published. Except in New York and a few other states that publish selected opinions of their trial courts, decisions from state trial courts are merely filed in the office of the clerk of the court, where the decisions are available for public inspection. (Sometimes, they can be found online as well.) Written decisions of the appellate, or reviewing, courts, however, are published and distributed. As you will note, most of the state court cases presented in this book are from state appellate courts. The reported appellate decisions are published in volumes called *reports* or *reporters,* which are numbered consecutively. State appellate court decisions are found in the state reporters of that particular state.

Additionally, state court opinions appear in regional units of the *National Reporter System,* published by West Group. Most lawyers and libraries have the West reporters because they report cases more quickly and are distributed more widely than the state-published reports. In fact, many states have eliminated their own reporters in favor of West's National Reporter System. The National Reporter System divides the states into the following geographic areas: *Atlantic* (A. or A.2d), *South Eastern* (S.E. or S.E.2d), *South Western* (S.W., S.W.2d, or S.W.3d), *North Western* (N.W. or N.W.2d), *North Eastern* (N.E. or N.E.2d), *Southern* (So. or So.2d), and *Pacific* (P., P.2d, or P.3d). (The *2d* and *3d* in the abbreviations refer to *Second Series* and *Third Series,* respectively.) The states included in each of these regional divisions are indicated in Exhibit 1A–1, which illustrates West's National Reporter System.

EXHIBIT 1A–1 NATIONAL REPORTER SYSTEM—REGIONAL/FEDERAL

Regional Reporters	Coverage Beginning	Coverage
Atlantic Reporter (A. or A.2d)	1885	Connecticut, Delaware, Maine, Maryland, New Hampshire, New Jersey, Pennsylvania, Rhode Island, Vermont, and District of Columbia.
North Eastern Reporter (N.E. or N.E.2d)	1885	Illinois, Indiana, Massachusetts, New York, and Ohio.
North Western Reporter (N.W. or N.W.2d)	1879	Iowa, Michigan, Minnesota, Nebraska, North Dakota, South Dakota, and Wisconsin.
Pacific Reporter (P., P.2d, or P.3d)	1883	Alaska, Arizona, California, Colorado, Hawaii, Idaho, Kansas, Montana, Nevada, New Mexico, Oklahoma, Oregon, Utah, Washington, and Wyoming.
South Eastern Reporter (S.E. or S.E.2d)	1887	Georgia, North Carolina, South Carolina, Virginia, and West Virginia.
South Western Reporter (S.W., S.W.2d, or S.W.3d)	1886	Arkansas, Kentucky, Missouri, Tennessee, and Texas.
Southern Reporter (So. or So.2d)	1887	Alabama, Florida, Louisiana, and Mississippi.
Federal Reporters		
Federal Reporter (F., F.2d, or F.3d)	1880	U.S. Circuit Courts from 1880 to 1912; U.S. Commerce Court from 1911 to 1913; U.S. District Courts from 1880 to 1932; U.S. Court of Claims (now called U.S. Court of Federal Claims) from 1929 to 1932 and since 1960; U.S. Courts of Appeals since 1891; U.S. Court of Customs and Patent Appeals since 1929; U.S. Emergency Court of Appeals since 1943.
Federal Supplement (F.Supp. or F.Supp.2d)	1932	U.S. Court of Claims from 1932 to 1960; U.S. District Courts since 1932; U.S. Customs Court since 1956.
Federal Rules Decisions (F.R.D.)	1939	U.S. District Courts involving the Federal Rules of Civil Procedure since 1939 and Federal Rules of Criminal Procedure since 1946.
Supreme Court Reporter (S.Ct.)	1882	U.S. Supreme Court since the October term of 1882.
Bankruptcy Reporter (Bankr.)	1980	Bankruptcy decisions of U.S. Bankruptcy Courts, U.S. District Courts, U.S. Courts of Appeals, and U.S. Supreme Court.
Military Justice Reporter (M.J.)	1978	U.S. Court of Military Appeals and Courts of Military Review for the Army, Navy, Air Force, and Coast Guard.

NATIONAL REPORTER SYSTEM MAP

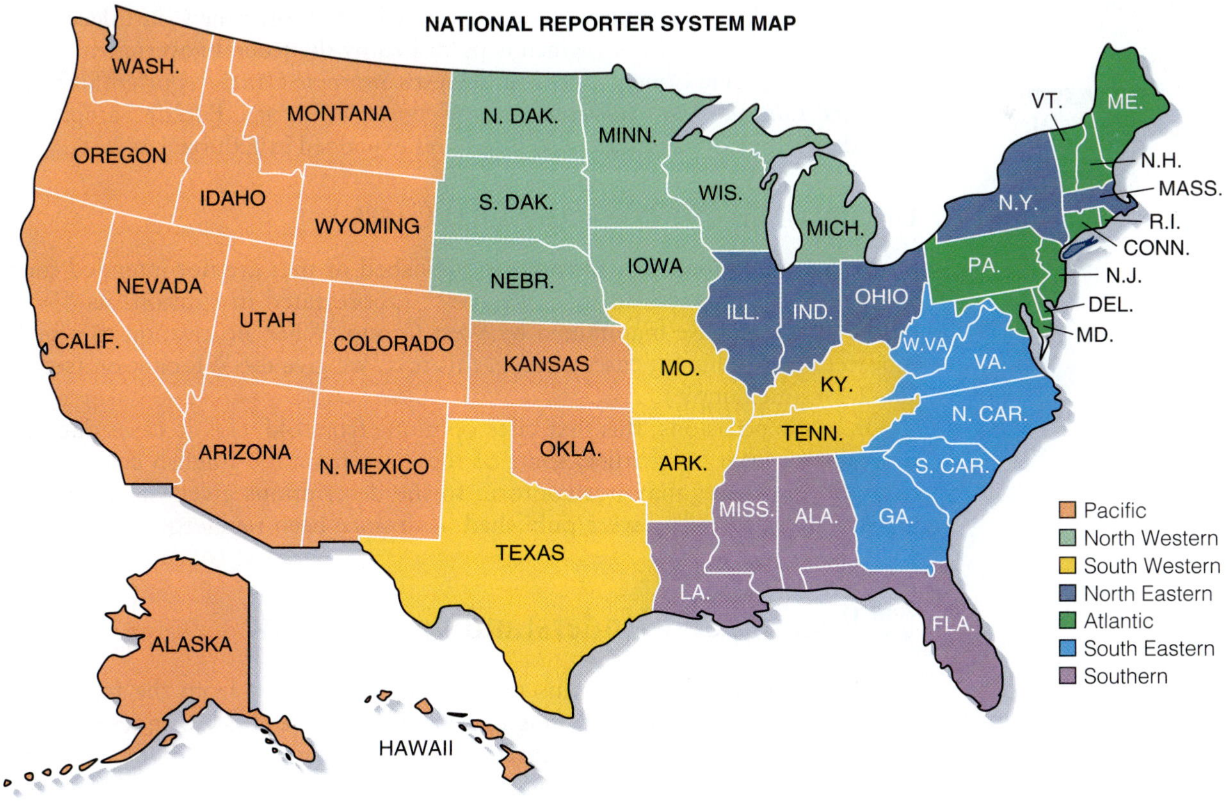

After appellate decisions have been published, they are normally referred to (cited) by the name of the case; the volume, name, and page number of the state's official reporter (if different from West's National Reporter System); the volume, name, and page number of the *National Reporter;* and the volume, name, and page number of any other selected reporter. This information is included in the *citation.* (Citing a reporter by volume number, name, and page number, in that order, is common to all citations.) When more than one reporter is cited for the same case, each reference is called a *parallel citation.* For example, consider the following case: *Yale Diagnostic Radiology v. Estate of Harun Foundation,* 267 Conn. 351, 838 A.2d 179 (2004). We see that the opinion in this case may be found in Volume 267 of the official *Connecticut Reports,* on page 351. The parallel citation is to Volume 838 of the *Atlantic Reporter, Second Series,* page 179. In presenting appellate opinions in this text, in addition to the reporter, we give the name of the court hearing the case and the year of the court's decision.

A few states—including those with intermediate appellate courts, such as California, Illinois, and New York—have more than one reporter for opinions issued by their courts. Sample citations from these courts, as well as others, are listed and explained in Exhibit 1A–2.

FEDERAL COURT DECISIONS

.on the Web To find links to Supreme Court opinions and opinions issued by the federal appellate courts, a good starting point is FindLaw's guide at **http://findlaw.com/10fedgov/judicial**.

Federal district court decisions are published unofficially in West's *Federal Supplement* (F. Supp. or F.Supp.2d), and opinions from the circuit courts of appeals (federal reviewing courts) are reported unofficially in West's *Federal Reporter* (F., F.2d, or F.3d). Cases concerning federal bankruptcy law are published unofficially in West's *Bankruptcy Reporter* (Bankr.). The official edition of United States Supreme Court decisions is the *United States Reports* (U.S.), which is published by the federal government. Unofficial editions of Supreme Court cases include West's *Supreme Court Reporter* (S.Ct.) and the *Lawyers' Edition of the Supreme Court Reports* (L.Ed. or L.Ed.2d). Sample citations for federal court decisions are also listed and explained in Exhibit 1A–2.

UNPUBLISHED OPINIONS AND OLD CASES

Many court opinions that are not yet published or that are not intended for publication can be accessed through Westlaw® (abbreviated in citations as "WL"), an online legal database maintained by West Group. When no citation to a published reporter is available for cases cited in this text, we give the WL citation (see Exhibit 1A–2 for an example).

On a few occasions, this text cites opinions from old, classic cases dating to the nineteenth century or earlier; some of these are from the English courts. The citations to these cases may not conform to the descriptions given above because the reporters in which they were published have since been replaced.

Reading and Understanding Case Law

All of the court opinions in this text consist of excerpts from the full text of the courts' opinions. For those wishing to review court cases for future research projects or to gain additional legal information, the following sections will provide useful insights into how to read and understand case law.

EXHIBIT 1A–2 HOW TO READ CITATIONS

State Courts

267 Neb. 397, 675 N.W.2d 89 (2004)[a]

N.W. is the abbreviation for West's publication of state court decisions rendered in the *North Western Reporter* of the National Reporter System. *2d* indicates that this case was included in the *Second Series* of that reporter. The number 675 refers to the volume number of the reporter; the number 89 refers to the page in that volume on which this case begins.

Neb. is an abbreviation for *Nebraska Reports*, Nebraska's official reports of the decisions of its highest court, the Nebraska Supreme Court.

115 Cal.App.4th 715,109 Cal.Rptr.3d 544 (2004)

Cal.Rptr. is the abbreviation for West's unofficial reports—titled *California Reporter*—of the decisions of California courts.

1 N.Y.3d 280, 803 N.E.2d 757, 771 N.Y.S.2d 484 (2003)

N.Y.S. is the abbreviation for West's unofficial reports—titled *New York Supplement*—of the decisions of New York courts.

N.Y. is the abbreviation for *New York Reports*, New York's official reports of the decisions of its court of appeals. The New York Court of Appeals is the state's highest court, analogous to other states' supreme courts. In New York, a supreme court is a trial court.

119 Wash.App. 582, 81 P.3d 929 (2003)

Wash.App. is the abbreviation for *Washington Appellate Reports*, Washington's official reports of the decisions of its court of appeals.

Federal Courts

538 U.S. 456, 123 S.Ct. 1667, 155 L.Ed.2d 631 (2003)

L.Ed. is an abbreviation for *Lawyers' Edition of the Supreme Court Reports*, an unofficial edition of decisions of the United States Supreme Court.

S.Ct. is the abbreviation for West's unofficial reports—titled *Supreme Court Reporter*—of decisions of the United States Supreme Court.

U.S. is the abbreviation for *United States Reports*, the official edition of the decisions of the United States Supreme Court.

a. The case names have been deleted from these citations to emphasize the publications. It should be kept in mind, however, that the name of a case is as important as the specific page numbers in the volumes in which it is found. If a citation is incorrect, the correct citation may be found in a publication's index of case names. In addition to providing a check on errors in citations, the date of a case is important because the value of a recent case as an authority is likely to be greater than that of older cases.

EXHIBIT 1A–2 HOW TO READ CITATIONS—CONTINUED

Federal Courts (continued)

354 F.3d 508 (5th Cir. 2004)

5th Cir. is an abbreviation denoting that this case was decided in the United States Court of Appeals for the Fifth Circuit.

298 F.Supp.2d 276 (D. Conn. 2004)

D. Conn. is an abbreviation indicating that the United States District Court for the District of Connecticut decided this case.

English Courts

9 Exch. 341, 156 Eng.Rep. 145 (1854)

Eng.Rep. is an abbreviation for *English Reports, Full Reprint,* a series of reports containing selected decisions made in English courts between 1378 and 1865.

Exch. is an abbreviation for *English Exchequer Reports*, which includes the original reports of cases decided in England's Court of Exchequer.

Statutory and Other Citations

18 U.S.C. Section 1961(1)(A)

U.S.C. denotes *United States Code*, the codification of *United States Statutes at Large*. The number 18 refers to the statute's U.S.C. title number and 1961 to its section number within that title. The number 1 refers to a subsection within the section and the letter A to a subdivision within the subsection.

UCC 2–206(1)(b)

UCC is an abbreviation for *Uniform Commercial Code*. The first number 2 is a reference to an article of the UCC, and 206 to a section within that article. The number 1 refers to a subsection within the section, and the letter b to a subdivision within the subsection.

Restatement (Second) of Torts, Section 568

Restatement (Second) of Torts refers to the second edition of the American Law Institute's *Restatement of the Law of Torts*. The number 568 refers to a specific section.

17 C.F.R. Section 230.505

C.F.R. is an abbreviation for *Code of Federal Regulations*, a compilation of federal administrative regulations. The number 17 designates the regulation's title number, and 230.505 designates a specific section within that title.

EXHIBIT 1A–2 HOW TO READ CITATIONS—CONTINUED

Westlaw® Citations

2004 WL 405961

WL is an abbreviation for Westlaw®. The number 2004 is the year of the document that can be found with this citation in the Westlaw® database. The number 405961 is a number assigned to a specific document. A higher number indicates that a document was added to the Westlaw® database later in the year.

Uniform Resource Locators[b]

www.westlaw.com

The suffix *com* is the top level domain (TLD) for this Web site. The TLD *com* is an abbreviation for "commercial," which usually means that a for-profit entity hosts (maintains) this Web site.

westlaw is the host name—the part of the domain name selected by the organization that registered the name. In this case, West Group registered the name. This Internet site is the Westlaw database on the Web.

www is an abbreviation for "World Wide Web." The Web is a system of Internet servers[c] that support documents formatted in *HTML* (hypertext markup language). HTML supports links to text, graphics, and audio and video files.

www.uscourts.gov

This is "The Federal Judiciary Home Page." The host is the Administrative Office of the U.S. Courts. The TLD *gov* is an abbreviation for "government." This Web site includes information and links from, and about, the federal courts.

www.law.cornell.edu/index.html

This part of a URL points to a Web page or file at a specific location within the host's domain. This page, at this Web site, is a menu with links to documents within the domain and to other Internet resources.

This is the host name for a Web site that contains the Internet publications of the Legal Information Institute (LII), which is a part of Cornell Law School. The LII site includes a variety of legal materials and links to other legal resources on the Internet. The TLD *edu* is an abbreviation for "educational institution" (a school or a university).

www.ipl.org.ref/RR

RR is an abbreviation for this Web site's "Ready Reference Collection," which contains links to a variety of Internet resources.

ref is an abbreviation for "Internet Public Library Reference Center," which is a map of the topics into which the links at this Web site have been categorized.

ipl is an abbreviation for Internet Public Library, which is an online service that provides reference resources and links to other information services on the Web. The IPL is supported chiefly by the School of Information at the University of Michigan. The TLD *org* is an abbreviation for "organization" (usually nonprofit).

b. The basic form for a URL is "service://hostname/path." The Internet service for all of the URLs in this text is *http* (hypertext transfer protocol). Most Web browsers will add this prefix automatically when a user enters a host name or a hostname/path.
c. A *server* is hardware that manages the resources on a network. For example, a network server is a computer that manages the traffic on the network, and a print server is a computer that manages several printers.

Case Titles and Terminology

The title of a case, such as *Adams v. Jones,* indicates the names of the parties to the lawsuit. The *v.* in the case title stands for *versus,* which means "against." In the trial court, Adams was the plaintiff—the person who filed the suit. Jones was the defendant. If the case is appealed, however, the appellate court will sometimes place the name of the party appealing the decision first, so the case may be called *Jones v. Adams*. Because some reviewing courts retain the trial court order of names, it is often impossible to distinguish the plaintiff from the defendant in the title of a reported appellate court decision. You must carefully read the facts of each case to identify the parties.

The following terms and phrases are frequently encountered in court opinions and legal publications. Because it is important to understand what these terms and phrases mean, we define and discuss them here.

Plaintiffs and Defendants As mentioned in Chapter 1, the plaintiff in a lawsuit is the party that initiates the action. The defendant is the party against which a lawsuit is brought. Lawsuits frequently involve more than one plaintiff and/or defendant.

Appellants and Appellees The *appellant* is the party that appeals a case to another court or jurisdiction from the court or jurisdiction in which the case was originally brought. Sometimes, an appellant is referred to as the *petitioner.* The *appellee* is the party against which the appeal is taken. Sometimes, the appellee is referred to as the *respondent.*

Judges and Justices The terms *judge* and *justice* are usually synonymous and represent two designations given to judges in various courts. All members of the United States Supreme Court, for example, are referred to as justices. And justice is the formal title usually given to judges of appellate courts, although this is not always the case. In New York, a justice is a judge of the trial court (which is called the Supreme Court), and a member of the Court of Appeals (the state's highest court) is called a judge. The term *justice* is commonly abbreviated to J., and *justices* to JJ. A Supreme Court case might refer to Justice O'Connor as O'Connor, J., or to Chief Justice Rehnquist as Rehnquist, C.J.

Decisions and Opinions Most decisions reached by reviewing, or appellate, courts are explained in written *opinions.* The opinion contains the court's reasons for its decision, the rules of law that apply, and the judgment. When all judges or justices unanimously agree on an opinion, the opinion is written for the entire court and can be deemed a *unanimous opinion.* When there is not unanimous agreement, a *majority opinion* is written, outlining the views of the majority of the judges or justices deciding the case.

Often, a judge or justice who feels strongly about making or emphasizing a point that was not made or emphasized in the unanimous or majority opinion will write a *concurring opinion.* That means the judge or justice agrees (concurs) with the judgment given in the unanimous or majority opinion but for different reasons. When there is not a unanimous opinion, a *dissenting opinion* is usually written by a judge or justice who does not agree with the majority. (See the *Extended Case Study* following Chapter 7 for an example of a dissenting opinion.) The dissenting opinion is important because it may form the basis of the arguments used years later in overruling the precedential majority opinion. Occasionally, a court issues a *per curiam* (Latin for "of the court") opinion, which does not indicate which judge or justice authored the opinion.

A Sample Court Case

Knowing how to read and analyze a court opinion is an essential step in undertaking accurate legal research. A further step involves "briefing" the case. Legal researchers routinely brief cases by summarizing and reducing the texts of the opinions to their essential elements. (For instructions on how to brief a case, go to Appendix A at the end of this text.) The cases contained within the chapters of this text have already been analyzed and partially briefed by the authors, and the essential aspects of each case are presented in a convenient format consisting of three basic sections: *Background and Facts, In the Words of the Court* (excerpts from the court's opinion), and *Decision and Remedy.*

Throughout this text, in addition to this basic format, we sometimes include a special introductory section entitled *Historical and Social [Economic, Technological, Political, or other] Setting.* In some instances, a *Company Profile* is included in place of the introductory setting. These profiles provide a background on one of the parties to the lawsuit. Each case is followed by either a brief *For Critical Analysis* section, which presents a question regarding some issue raised by the case, or a *Why Is This Case Important?* section, which explains the significance of the case.

To illustrate the elements in a court opinion, we present an annotated opinion in Exhibit 1A–3 beginning on the next page. The opinion is from an actual case that the U.S. Court of Appeals for the Sixth Circuit decided in 2005.

The Supreme Court building in Washington, D.C. In what reporters are Supreme Court opinions published? (PhotoDisc)

EXHIBIT 1A–3 A SAMPLE COURT CASE

This section contains the case citation—the name of the case, the name of the court that heard the case, the year of the court's decision, and reporters in which the court's opinion can be found.	**D.A.B.E., INC. v. CITY OF TOLEDO** United States Court of Appeals, Sixth Circuit, 2005. 393 F.3d 692.
This line gives the name of the judge who authored the opinion of the court.	BOYCE F. MARTIN, JR., Circuit Judge. * * * *
The court divides the opinion into three parts, headed by roman numerals. The first part of the opinion summarizes the factual background of the case.	I.
A law passed by a local government unit, such as a city or a county.	The City of Toledo has regulated smoking in public places since 1987 * * * . In early 2003, the City Council * * * enacted a new Clean Indoor Air **Ordinance**, No. 509-03.
Present or current.	Ordinance No. 509-03 regulates the ability to smoke in public places, such as retail stores, theaters, courtrooms, libraries, museums, health-care facilities, and—most relevant to the **instant** case—restaurants and bars. In enclosed public places, smoking is generally prohibited except in a "separate smoking lounge" that is designated for the exclusive purpose of smoking * * * . * * * *
Prevented from taking effect.	* * * Appellants * * * [challenge] the ordinance on two grounds: first, that it constitutes a * * * taking of their property in violation of the Fifth [Amendment to the U.S. Constitution] * * * ; and second, that it is **preempted** by Section 3791.031 of the Ohio Revised Code, a state law that regulates smoking in places of public assembly but that does not apply to restaurants, bowling alleys and bars. * * * *
The second major section of the opinion sets out and applies the law to the plaintiffs' arguments.	II. * * * *
The first part of this section addresses the claim that the ordinance is a taking of the plaintiffs' property.	A. * * * **Taking Claim**
Financially sustainable; capable of working, functioning, or developing adequately.	The * * * Fifth Amendment * * * provides that private property shall not "be taken for public use, without just compensation." * * * [A] statute regulating the uses that can be made of property effects a taking if it denies an owner **economically viable** use of his land. * * *
The words of a writing in their apparent or obvious meaning.	The evidence presented in this case fails to establish that, **on its face**, the Clean Indoor Air Ordinance denies appellants economically viable use of their respective properties. Appellants

EXHIBIT 1A–3 A SAMPLE COURT CASE—CONTINUED

have submitted affidavits alleging that they have lost—or fear they will lose—customers as a result of the ordinance, because smoking is an activity in which many customers wish to engage while patronizing their establishments. * * *

* * * First, there is nothing on the face of the Clean Indoor Air Ordinance that prevents the beneficial use of appellants' property. To the contrary, the ordinance has absolutely no effect on any aspect of appellants' businesses other than to restrict the areas in which appellants' patrons may smoke. Second, the ordinance does not **categorically** prohibit smoking inside appellants' establishments; it merely regulates the conditions under which smoking is permitted. We recognize that the construction of separate smoking lounges in most cases will require some financial investment, but an ordinance does not effect a taking merely because compliance with it requires the expenditure of money. Finally, for obvious reasons, the ordinance does not purport to regulate alternative uses of appellants' respective properties. Therefore, * * * it is clear that appellants have failed to establish that the Clean Indoor Air Ordinance, on its face, effects a * * * taking of their property.

> Absolutely, unqualifiedly.

> The second part of this section addresses the assertion that the city ordinance is void because a state statute already covers the subject and thus takes precedence.

B. Preemption Claim

Appellants' second argument is that the Clean Indoor Air Ordinance conflicts with—and, therefore, is preempted by—Section 3791.031(A) of the Ohio Revised Code.

A state statute takes precedence over a local ordinance when * * * the ordinance is in conflict with the statute * * *.

* * * [T]he test is whether the ordinance permits or licenses that which the statute forbids or prohibits, and vice versa. To the extent that the statute does not address or apply to an item or issue, however, an ordinance regulating the excluded item or issue does not conflict with the statute, even if it deals with the same general subject matter. * * *

In this case, Section 3791.031 of the Ohio Revised Code regulates indoor smoking throughout the State of Ohio within "places of public assembly." It explicitly provides, however, that "[r]estaurants, food service establishments, dining rooms, cafes, cafeterias, or other rooms used primarily for the service of food, as well as bowling alleys and places licensed by the division of

(Continued)

In this chapter, we first look at some basic constitutional concepts and clauses and their significance for business. Then we examine how certain fundamental freedoms guaranteed by the Constitution affect businesspersons and the workplace.

The Constitutional Powers of Government

.on the Web You can find a copy of the U.S. Constitution online, as well as information about the document, including its history, at **http://www.constitutioncenter.org**.

Following the Revolutionary War, the states created a *confederal* form of government. The Articles of Confederation, which went into effect in 1781, established a confederation of independent states and a central (national) government that could exercise only very limited powers. The sovereign power, or supreme authority to govern, rested largely with the states. The limitation on the central government's powers reflected a basic tenet of the American Revolution—that a national government should not have unlimited power that could be used tyrannically against the states.

The confederation, however, faced serious problems. For one thing, laws passed by the various states hampered national commerce and foreign trade by preventing the free movement of goods and services. By 1784, the nation faced a serious economic depression. Many who could not afford to pay their debts were thrown into "debtors' prisons." By 1786, a series of uprisings by farmer debtors were proving difficult to control because the national government did not have the authority to demand revenues (by levying taxes, for example) to support a militia.

Because of these problems, a national convention was called to amend the Articles of Confederation. Instead of amending the articles, however, the delegates to the convention, now called the Constitutional Convention, wrote the U.S. Constitution. This document, after its ratification by the states in 1789, became the basis for an entirely new form of government. Many of the provisions of the Constitution, including those discussed in the following pages, were shaped by the delegates' experiences during the confederal era (1781–1789).

A Federal Form of Government

The new government created by the Constitution reflected a series of compromises made by the convention delegates on various issues. Some delegates wanted sovereign power to remain with the states; others wanted the national government alone to exercise sovereign power. The end result was a compromise—a **federal form of government** in which the national government and the states *share* sovereign power.

FEDERAL FORM OF GOVERNMENT
A system of government in which the states form a union and the sovereign power is divided between the central government and the member states.

The Constitution sets forth specific powers that can be exercised by the national government and provides that the national government has the implied power to undertake actions necessary to carry out its expressly designated powers. All other powers are "reserved" to the states. The broad language of the Constitution, though, has left much room for debate over the specific nature and scope of these powers. Generally, it has been the task of the courts to determine where the boundary line between state and national powers should lie—and that line changes over time. For most of the twentieth century, for example, the national government met little resistance from the courts when extending its regulatory authority over broad areas of social and economic life. Today, in contrast, the courts, and particularly the United States Supreme Court, are more willing to interpret the Constitution in such a way as to curb the national government's regulatory powers.

on the Web The *Federalist Papers,* which are a series of essays by the founders explaining their views on federalism, are available online at **http://www.law.emory.edu/FEDERAL/federalist.**

CHECKS AND BALANCES The principle under which the powers of the national government are divided among three separate branches—the executive, legislative, and judicial branches—each of which exercises a check on the actions of the others.

THE SEPARATION OF POWERS

To make it difficult for the national government to use its power arbitrarily, the Constitution divided the national government's powers among the three branches of government. The legislative branch makes the laws, the executive branch enforces the laws, and the judicial branch interprets the laws. Each branch performs a separate function, and no branch may exercise the authority of another branch.

Additionally, a system of **checks and balances** allows each branch to limit the actions of the other two branches, thus preventing any one branch from exercising too much power. Some examples of these checks and balances are the following:

1. The legislative branch (Congress) can enact a law, but the executive branch (the president) has the constitutional authority to veto that law.
2. The executive branch is responsible for foreign affairs, but treaties with foreign governments require the advice and consent of the Senate.
3. Congress determines the jurisdiction of the federal courts and the president appoints federal judges, with the advice and consent of the Senate, but the judicial branch has the power to hold actions of the other two branches unconstitutional.[2]

THE COMMERCE CLAUSE

COMMERCE CLAUSE The provision in Article I, Section 8, of the U.S. Constitution that gives Congress the power to regulate interstate commerce.

To prevent states from establishing laws and regulations that would interfere with trade and commerce among the states, the Constitution expressly delegated to the national government the power to regulate interstate commerce. Article I, Section 8, of the U.S. Constitution expressly permits Congress "[t]o regulate Commerce with foreign Nations, and among the several States, and with the Indian Tribes." This clause, referred to as the **commerce clause,** has had a greater impact on business than any other provision in the Constitution.

For some time, the commerce power was interpreted as being limited to *interstate* commerce (commerce among the states) and not applicable to *intrastate* commerce (commerce within a state). In 1824, however, in *Gibbons v. Ogden* (see this chapter's *Landmark in the Law* feature on the following page, the United States Supreme Court held that commerce within a state could also be regulated by the national government as long as the commerce *substantially affected* commerce involving more than one state.

The Commerce Clause and the Expansion of National Powers In *Gibbons v. Ogden,* the commerce clause was expanded to regulate activities that "substantially affect interstate commerce." As the nation grew and faced new kinds of problems, the commerce clause became a vehicle for the additional expansion of the national government's regulatory powers. Even activities that seemed purely local came under the regulatory reach of the national government if those activities were deemed to substantially affect interstate commerce. ■ EXAMPLE 2.1 In 1942, in *Wickard v. Filburn,*[3] the Supreme Court held that wheat production by an individual farmer intended wholly for consumption on his own farm was subject to federal regulation. The Court reasoned that the home consumption of wheat reduced the demand for wheat and thus could have a substantial effect on interstate commerce. ■

2. See the *Landmark in the Law* feature in Chapter 3 on *Marbury v. Madison,* 5 U.S. (1 Cranch) 137, 2 L.Ed. 60 (1803), a case in which the doctrine of judicial review was clearly enunciated by Chief Justice John Marshall.

3. 317 U.S. 111, 63 S.Ct. 82, 87 L.Ed. 122 (1942).

LANDMARK IN THE LAW

Gibbons v. Ogden (1824)

The commerce clause, which is found in Article I, Section 8, of the U.S. Constitution, gives Congress the power "[t]o regulate Commerce with foreign Nations, and among the several States, and with the Indian Tribes." What exactly does "to regulate commerce" mean? What does "commerce" entail? These questions came before the United States Supreme Court in 1824 in the case of *Gibbons v. Ogden*.[a]

BACKGROUND In 1803, Robert Fulton, the inventor of the steamboat, and Robert Livingston, who was then American minister to France, secured a monopoly on steam navigation on the waters in the state of New York from the New York legislature. Fulton and Livingston licensed Aaron Ogden, a former governor of New Jersey and a U.S. senator, to operate steam-powered ferryboats between New York and New Jersey. Thomas Gibbons, who had obtained a license from the U.S. government to operate boats in interstate waters, competed with Ogden without New York's permission. Ogden sued Gibbons. The New York state courts granted Ogden's request for an injunction—an order prohibiting Gibbons from operating in New York waters. Gibbons appealed the decision to the United States Supreme Court.

MARSHALL'S DECISION Sitting as chief justice on the Supreme Court was John Marshall, an advocate of a strong national government. In his decision, Marshall defined the word *commerce* as used in the commerce clause to mean all commercial intercourse—that is, all business dealings that affect more than one state. The Court ruled against Ogden's monopoly, reversing the injunction against Gibbons. Marshall used this opportunity not only to expand the definition of commerce but also to validate and increase the power of the national legislature to regulate commerce. Said Marshall, "What is this power? It is the power . . . to prescribe the rule by which commerce is to be governed." Marshall held that the power to regulate interstate commerce was an exclusive power of the national government and that this power included the power to regulate any intrastate commerce that substantially affects interstate commerce.

APPLICATION TO TODAY'S BUSINESS WORLD

Marshall's broad definition of the commerce power established the foundation for the expansion of national powers in the years to come. Today, the national government continues to rely on the commerce clause for its constitutional authority to regulate business activities. Marshall's conclusion that the power to regulate interstate commerce was an exclusive power of the national government has also had significant consequences. By implication, this means that a state cannot *regulate activities that extend beyond its borders, such as out-of-state online gambling operations that affect the welfare of in-state citizens. It also means that state regulations over in-state activities normally will be invalidated if the regulations substantially burden interstate commerce.*

RELEVANT WEB SITES

To locate information on the Web concerning the Gibbons v. Ogden *decision, go to this text's Web site at* **http://blt.westbuslaw.com**, *select "Chapter 2," and click on "URLs for Landmarks."*

a. 22 U.S. (9 Wheat.) 1, 6 L.Ed. 23 (1824).

The following landmark case involved a challenge to the scope of the national government's constitutional authority to regulate local activities.

LANDMARK AND CLASSIC CASES

CASE 2.1 Heart of Atlanta Motel v. United States

Supreme Court of the United States, 1964.
379 U.S. 241,
85 S.Ct. 348,
13 L.Ed.2d 258.
http://supct.law.cornell.edu/supct/cases/name.htm[a]

HISTORICAL AND SOCIAL SETTING *In the first half of the twentieth century, state governments sanctioned segregation on the basis of race. In 1954, the United States Supreme Court decided that racially segregated school systems violated the Constitution. In the following decade, the Court ordered an end to racial segregation imposed by the states in other public facilities, such as beaches, golf courses, buses, parks, auditoriums, and courtroom seating. Privately owned facilities that excluded or segregated African Americans and others on the basis of race were not subject to the same constitutional restrictions, however. Congress passed the Civil Rights Act of 1964 to prohibit racial discrimination in "establishments affecting interstate commerce." These facilities included "places of public accommodation."*

a. This is the "Historic Supreme Court Decisions—by Party Name" page within the "Caselists" collection of the Legal Information Institute available at its site on the Web. Click on the "H" link or scroll down the list of cases to the entry for the *Heart of Atlanta* case. Click on the case name.

BACKGROUND AND FACTS The owner of the Heart of Atlanta Motel, in violation of the Civil Rights Act of 1964, refused to rent rooms to African Americans. The motel owner brought an action in a federal district court to have the Civil Rights Act declared unconstitutional, alleging that Congress had exceeded its constitutional authority to regulate commerce by enacting the act. The owner argued that his motel was not engaged in interstate commerce but was "of a purely local character." The motel, however, was accessible to state and interstate highways. The owner advertised nationally, maintained billboards throughout the state, and accepted convention trade from outside the state (75 percent of the guests were residents of other states). The court ruled that the act did not violate the Constitution and enjoined (prohibited) the owner from discriminating on the basis of race. The owner appealed. The case ultimately went to the United States Supreme Court.

IN THE WORDS OF THE COURT . . .
Mr. Justice *CLARK* delivered the opinion of the Court.

* * * *

While the Act as adopted carried no congressional findings, the record of its passage through each house is replete with evidence of the burdens that discrimination by race or color places upon interstate commerce * * * . This testimony included the fact that our people have become increasingly mobile with millions of all races traveling from State to State; that Negroes in particular have been the subject of discrimination in transient accommodations, having to travel great distances to secure the same; that often they have been unable to obtain accommodations and have had to call upon friends to put them up overnight. * * * These exclusionary practices were found to be nationwide, the Under Secretary of Commerce testifying that there is "no question that this discrimination in the North still exists to a large degree" and in the West and Midwest as well * * * . This testimony indicated a qualitative as well as quantitative effect on

(Continued)

CASE 2.1—Continued

interstate travel by Negroes. The former was the obvious impairment of the Negro traveler's pleasure and convenience that resulted when he continually was uncertain of finding lodging. As for the latter, there was evidence that this uncertainty stemming from racial discrimination had the effect of discouraging travel on the part of a substantial portion of the Negro community * * * . We shall not burden this opinion with further details since the voluminous testimony presents overwhelming evidence that discrimination by hotels and motels impedes interstate travel.

* * * *

It is said that the operation of the motel here is of a purely local character. But, assuming this to be true, "if it is interstate commerce that feels the pinch, it does not matter how local the operation that applies the squeeze." * * * Thus the power of Congress to promote interstate commerce also includes the power to regulate the local incidents thereof, including local activities in both the States of origin and destination, which might have a substantial and harmful effect upon that commerce.

DECISION AND REMEDY The United States Supreme Court upheld the constitutionality of the Civil Rights Act of 1964. The power of Congress to regulate interstate commerce permitted the enactment of legislation that could halt local discriminatory practices.

COMMENTS *If the Supreme Court had invalidated the Civil Rights Act of 1964, the legal landscape of the United States would be much different today. The act prohibited discrimination based on race, color, national origin, religion, or gender in all "public accommodations" as well as discrimination in employment based on these criteria. Although state laws now prohibit many of these forms of discrimination as well, the protections available vary from state to state—and it is not certain when (and if) such laws would have been passed had the 1964 federal Civil Rights Act been deemed unconstitutional.*

RELEVANT WEB SITES *To locate information on the Web concerning the* Heart of Atlanta Motel *case, go to this text's Web site at* **http://blt.westbuslaw.com**, *select "Chapter 2," and click on "URLs for Landmarks."*

The Commerce Power Today Today, at least theoretically, the power over commerce authorizes the national government to regulate every commercial enterprise in the United States. Federal (national) legislation governs virtually every major activity conducted by businesses—from hiring and firing decisions to workplace safety, competitive practices, and financing.

In the last decade, however, the Supreme Court has begun to curb somewhat the national government's regulatory authority under the commerce clause. In 1995, the Court held—for the first time in sixty years—that Congress had exceeded its regulatory authority under the commerce clause. The Court struck down an act that banned the possession of guns within one thousand feet of any school because the act attempted to regulate an area that had "nothing to do with commerce."[4] Subsequently, the Court invalidated key portions of two other federal acts on the ground that they exceeded Congress's commerce clause authority.[5]

The current trend of not allowing the federal government to regulate noncommercial activities that take place wholly within a state's borders has led to some controversial decisions in the lower courts. In 2003, for example, the U.S. Court of Appeals for the Ninth Circuit decided a case involving marijuana use on commerce

4. The United States Supreme Court held the Gun-Free School Zones Act of 1990 to be unconstitutional in *United States v. Lopez,* 514 U.S. 549, 115 S.Ct. 1624, 131 L.Ed.2d 626 (1995).

5. See, for example, *Printz v. United States,* 521 U.S. 898, 117 S.Ct. 2365, 138 L.Ed.2d 914 (1997), involving the Brady Handgun Violence Prevention Act of 1993; and *United States v. Morrison,* 529 U.S. 598, 120 S.Ct. 1740, 146 L.Ed.2d 658 (2000), concerning the federal Violence Against Women Act of 1994.

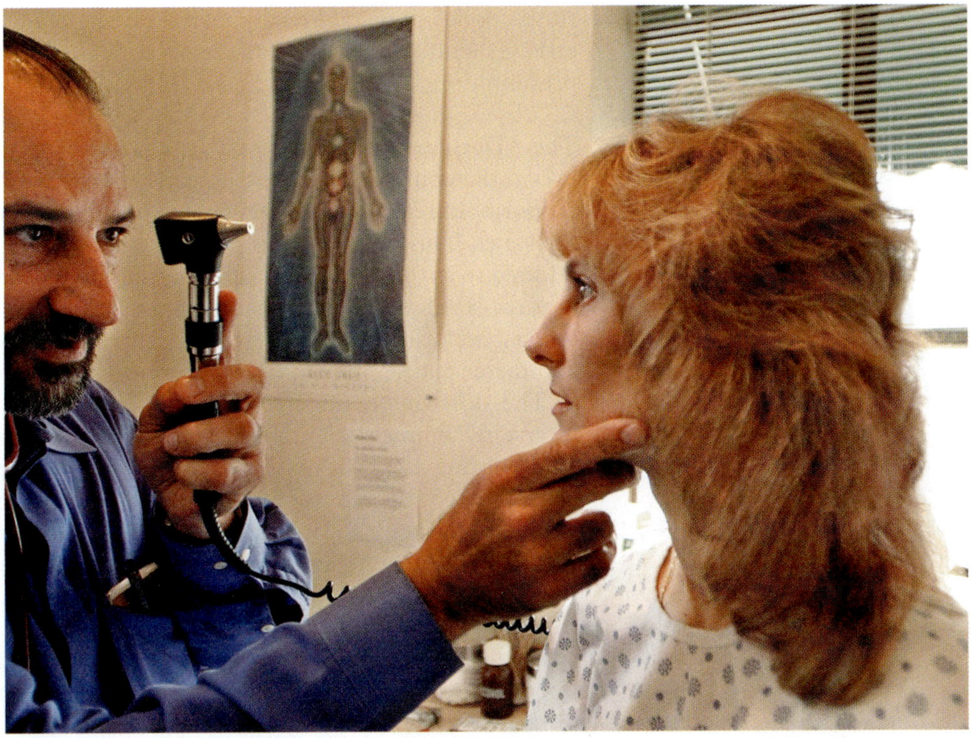

A physician examines the eyes of a woman who suffers from a brain tumor. The woman was partially paralyzed on the right side of her body until she started smoking marijuana. Although the United States Supreme Court ruled in 2005 that the federal government can use its power under the commerce clause to regulate the use of medical marijuana within a state's borders, this issue remains controversial. (AP Photo/ Ben Margot)

clause grounds. Eleven states, including California, have adopted "medical marijuana" laws that legalize marijuana for medical purposes. Marijuana possession, however, is illegal under the federal Controlled Substances Act (CSA).[6] The case arose after the federal government seized the marijuana that two seriously ill California women were using on the advice of their physicians. The women argued that it is unconstitutional for the federal act to prohibit them from using marijuana for medical purposes that are legal within the state. The federal appellate court agreed. In 2005, however, the United States Supreme Court held that Congress has the authority to prohibit the intrastate possession and noncommercial cultivation of marijuana as part of a larger regulatory scheme (the CSA).[7]

The Regulatory Powers of the States As part of their inherent sovereignty, state governments have the authority to regulate affairs within their borders. This authority stems in part from the Tenth Amendment to the Constitution, which reserves all powers not delegated to the national government to the states. State regulatory powers are often referred to as **police powers.** The term encompasses not only the enforcement of criminal law but also the right of state governments to regulate private activities to protect or promote the public order, health, safety, morals, and general welfare. Fire and building codes, antidiscrimination laws, parking regulations, zoning restrictions, licensing requirements, and thousands of other state statutes covering virtually every aspect of daily life have been enacted pursuant to a

POLICE POWERS
Powers possessed by the states as part of their inherent sovereignty. These powers may be exercised to protect or promote the public order, health, safety, morals, and general welfare.

6. 21 U.S.C. Sections 801 *et seq.*
7. *Gonzales v. Raich,* ____ U.S. ____, 125 S.Ct. 2195, 162 L.Ed.2d 1 (2005).

state's police powers. Local governments, including cities, also exercise police powers.[8] Generally, state laws enacted pursuant to a state's police powers carry a strong presumption of validity.

The "Dormant" Commerce Clause The United States Supreme Court has interpreted the commerce clause to mean that the national government has the *exclusive* authority to regulate commerce that substantially affects trade and commerce among the states. This express grant of authority to the national government, which is often referred to as the "positive" aspect of the commerce clause, implies a negative aspect—that the states do *not* have the authority to regulate interstate commerce. This negative aspect of the commerce clause is often referred to as the "dormant" (implied) commerce clause.

The dormant commerce clause comes into play when state regulations affect interstate commerce. In this situation, the courts normally weigh the state's interest in regulating a certain matter against the burden that the state's regulation places on interstate commerce. Because courts balance the interests involved, it can be extremely difficult to predict the outcome in a particular case.

■ EXAMPLE 2.2 A Michigan statute prohibited out-of-state wineries from shipping wine directly to Michigan residents but allowed in-state wineries to do so. The U.S. Court of Appeals for the Sixth Circuit ruled that the statute violated the dormant commerce clause. The court concluded that the regulations benefited in-state wineries and burdened out-of-state wineries, while failing to promote any legitimate local purpose.[9] Other federal appellate courts, however, had upheld similar statutes on the ground that a state has a legitimate interest in monitoring the flow of alcohol into the state. In 2005, the United States Supreme Court resolved this conflict by affirming the opinion of the Sixth Circuit on the issue.[10] ■

What if a state law attempts to regulate the types of materials that may be distributed to state residents via the Internet? Would such a law violate the dormant commerce clause? See this chapter's *Adapting the Law to the Online Environment* feature for a discussion of that question.

The Supremacy Clause

Article VI of the Constitution provides that the Constitution, laws, and treaties of the United States are "the supreme Law of the Land." This article, commonly referred to as the **supremacy clause,** is important in the ordering of state and federal relationships. When there is a direct conflict between a federal law and a state law, the state law is rendered invalid. Because some powers are *concurrent* (shared by the federal government and the states), however, it is necessary to determine which law governs in a particular circumstance.

SUPREMACY CLAUSE
The provision in Article VI of the Constitution that provides that the Constitution, laws, and treaties of the United States are "the supreme Law of the Land." Under this clause, state and local laws that directly conflict with federal law will be rendered invalid.

Preemption occurs when Congress chooses to act exclusively in a concurrent area. In this circumstance, a valid federal statute or regulation will take precedence over a conflicting state or local law or regulation on the same general subject. Often, it is not clear whether Congress, in passing a law, intended to preempt an entire subject area against state regulation. In these situations, it is left to the courts to deter-

PREEMPTION
A doctrine under which certain federal laws preempt, or take precedence over, conflicting state or local laws.

8. Local governments derive their authority to regulate their communities from the state, because they are creatures of the state. In other words, they cannot come into existence unless authorized by the state to do so.

9. *Heald v. Engler,* 342 F.3d 517 (6th Cir. 2003).

10. *Granholm v. Heald,* ___ U.S. ___, 125 S.Ct. 1885, 161 L.Ed.2d 796 (2005).

ADAPTING THE LAW TO THE ONLINE ENVIRONMENT

Can States Regulate Internet Commerce?

The Constitution's commerce clause—and most of the United States Supreme Court's decisions interpreting that clause—were created long before the Internet became a reality. Prior to the advent of the Internet, "interstate commerce" typically meant commerce in goods or services that extended beyond a particular state's borders. In the online environment, however, physical boundaries do not exist. Thus, one of the difficulties facing the courts in the last several years has been how to apply this traditional body of law to online transactions.

TRADITIONAL COMMERCE CLAUSE ANALYSIS

The Constitution's commerce clause, as interpreted by the United States Supreme Court, gives the national government the *exclusive* power to regulate interstate commerce. That means, in effect, that states *cannot* regulate interstate commerce. As noted elsewhere in this chapter, this limitation on state powers is referred to as the negative, or "dormant," commerce clause. If a court finds that a state law places too great a burden on interstate commerce, the law will be deemed unconstitutional on the ground that it violates the dormant commerce clause.

By and large, the courts have applied traditional commerce clause analysis in cases challenging the constitutionality of state laws regulating the Internet. As in traditional commerce clause cases, the courts tend to invalidate state laws regulating the Internet if those laws extend to activities beyond their borders and place too great a burden on interstate commerce.

CAN VERMONT LIMIT MINORS' ACCESS TO WEB MATERIAL?

Consider a case that came before a federal appellate court in *American Booksellers Foundation v. Dean.*[a] The case challenged the constitutionality of a Vermont law that prohibited the Internet distribution to minors of sexually explicit materials that are "harmful to minors."

The effect of this law on out-of-state residents was made clear in the argument put forth by one of the plaintiffs (those who brought the lawsuit), Sexual Health Network, Inc. (SHN). SHN, which was located in Connecticut, operated a Web site on which it posted information concerning a range of sex-related topics. SHN's aim was to provide access to sexuality-related information designed to assist persons with disabilities, illnesses, and changes in their lifestyles. Clearly, SHN could not prevent minors living in Vermont (or any other state—or nation) from accessing its Web site. To avoid possible prosecution for violating Vermont's law, SHN would essentially have to shut down its Web site. SHN and the other plaintiffs, including the American Civil Liberties Union, thus sought a court order barring the enforcement of the Vermont statute on the ground that, among other things, it violated the dormant commerce clause.

The court agreed with the plaintiffs. The court held that the Vermont law violated the dormant commerce clause because it "regulates Internet commerce occurring wholly outside Vermont's borders." The court noted that although Vermont aimed to protect only Vermont minors, in effect the rest of the nation was forced to comply with its regulation or risk prosecution under Vermont's law.

FOR CRITICAL ANALYSIS

In its opinion, the court pointed out that "at the same time that the Internet's geographic reach increases Vermont's interest in regulating out-of-state conduct, it makes state regulation impracticable." Analyze this statement.

a. 342 F.3d 96 (2d Cir. 2003).

mine whether Congress intended to exercise exclusive power over a given area. No single factor is decisive as to whether a court will find preemption. Generally, congressional intent to preempt will be found if a federal law regulating an activity is so pervasive, comprehensive, or detailed that the states have little or no room to regulate in that area. Also, when a federal statute creates an agency—such as the

National Labor Relations Board—to enforce the law, matters that may come within the agency's jurisdiction will likely preempt state laws.

THE TAXING AND SPENDING POWERS

Article I, Section 8, provides that Congress has the "Power to lay and collect Taxes, Duties, Imposts [taxes on imported goods], and Excises [taxes on domestic goods]." Section 8 further provides that "all Duties, Imposts and Excises shall be uniform throughout the United States." The requirement of uniformity refers to uniformity among the states; thus, Congress may not tax some states while exempting others.

Traditionally, if Congress attempted to regulate indirectly, by taxation, an area over which it had no authority, the tax would be invalidated by the courts. Today, however, if a tax measure bears some reasonable relationship to revenue production, it is generally held to be within the national taxing power. Moreover, the expansive interpretation of the commerce clause almost always provides a basis for sustaining a federal tax.

Under Article I, Section 8, Congress has the power "to pay the Debts and provide for the common Defence and general welfare of the United States." Through the spending power, Congress disposes of the revenues accumulated from the taxing power. Congress can spend revenues not only to carry out its enumerated (explicit) powers but also to promote any objective it deems worthwhile, so long as it does not violate the Constitution or its amendments. For example, Congress could not condition welfare payments on the recipients' political views. The spending power necessarily involves policy choices, with which taxpayers may disagree.

Business and the Bill of Rights

The importance of a written declaration of the rights of individuals eventually caused the first Congress of the United States to submit twelve amendments to the Constitution to the states for approval. The first ten of these amendments, commonly known as the **Bill of Rights,** were adopted in 1791 and embody a series of protections for the individual against various types of interference by the federal government.[11] Some constitutional protections apply to business entities as well. For example, corporations exist as separate legal entities, or legal persons, and enjoy many of the same rights and privileges as natural persons do. Summarized here are the protections guaranteed by these ten amendments (see the Constitution in Appendix B for the complete text of each amendment):

BILL OF RIGHTS
The first ten amendments to the U.S. Constitution.

BE CAREFUL Although most of these rights apply to actions of the states, some of them apply only to actions of the federal government.

1. The First Amendment guarantees the freedoms of religion, speech, and the press and the rights to assemble peaceably and to petition the government.
2. The Second Amendment guarantees the right to keep and bear arms.
3. The Third Amendment prohibits, in peacetime, the lodging of soldiers in any house without the owner's consent.
4. The Fourth Amendment prohibits unreasonable searches and seizures of persons or property.
5. The Fifth Amendment guarantees the rights to *indictment* (formal accusation—see Chapter 6) by grand jury, to due process of law, and to fair payment when private property is taken for public use. The Fifth Amendment also prohibits compulsory self-incrimination and double jeopardy (trial for the same crime twice).

11. One of these proposed amendments was ratified 203 years later (in 1992) and became the Twenty-seventh Amendment to the Constitution. See Appendix B.

Police search a crack house in Florida. Should the owners and occupants of such houses receive protection from unreasonable searches and seizures under the U.S. Constitution? Why or why not? (© Corbis. All rights reserved.)

6 The Sixth Amendment guarantees the accused in a criminal case the right to a speedy and public trial by an impartial jury and with counsel. The accused has the right to cross-examine witnesses against him or her and to solicit testimony from witnesses in his or her favor.

7 The Seventh Amendment guarantees the right to a trial by jury in a civil (noncriminal) case involving at least twenty dollars.[12]

8 The Eighth Amendment prohibits excessive bail and fines, as well as cruel and unusual punishment.

9 The Ninth Amendment establishes that the people have rights in addition to those specified in the Constitution.

10 The Tenth Amendment establishes that those powers neither delegated to the federal government nor denied to the states are reserved for the states.

As originally intended, the Bill of Rights limited only the powers of the national government. Over time, however, the Supreme Court "incorporated" most of these rights into the protections against state actions afforded by the Fourteenth Amendment to the Constitution. That amendment, passed in 1868 after the Civil War, provides in part that "[n]o State shall . . . deprive any person of life, liberty, or property, without due process of law." Starting in 1925, the Supreme Court began to define various rights and liberties guaranteed in the national Constitution as constituting "due process of law," which was required of state governments under the Fourteenth Amendment. Today, most of the rights and liberties set forth in the Bill of Rights apply to state governments as well as the national government.

We will look closely at several of the amendments in the above list in Chapter 6, in the context of criminal law and procedures. Here we examine two important guarantees of the First Amendment—freedom of speech and freedom of religion.

REMEMBER The First Amendment guarantee of freedom of speech applies only to *government* restrictions on speech.

12. Twenty dollars was forty days' pay for the average person when the Bill of Rights was written.

These and other First Amendment freedoms (of the press, assembly, and petition) have all been applied to the states through the due process clause of the Fourteenth Amendment. As you read through the following pages, keep in mind that none of these (or other) constitutional freedoms confers an absolute right. Ultimately, it is the United States Supreme Court, as the final interpreter of the Constitution, that gives meaning to these rights and determines their boundaries.

THE FIRST AMENDMENT—FREEDOM OF SPEECH

Freedom of speech is the most prized freedom that Americans have. Indeed, it forms the basis for our democratic form of government, which could not exist if people were not allowed to express their political opinions freely and criticize government actions or policies. Because of its importance, the courts traditionally have protected this right to the fullest extent possible.

SYMBOLIC SPEECH
Nonverbal expressions of beliefs. Symbolic speech, which includes gestures, movements, and articles of clothing, is given substantial protection by the courts.

Speech often includes not only what we say, but also what we do to express our political, social, and religious views. The courts generally protect **symbolic speech**—gestures, movements, articles of clothing, and other forms of nonverbal expressive conduct. ■ EXAMPLE 2.3 In 1989, the Supreme Court held that the burning of the American flag to protest government policies is a constitutionally protected form of expression.[13] Similarly, participating in a hunger strike or wearing a black armband would be protected as symbolic speech. ■

Expression—oral, written, or symbolized by conduct—is subject to reasonable restrictions. For example, on the campus of a public high school, certain rights may be circumscribed or denied, in part to protect minors from predatory adults and to protect adults and others from predatory minors. A balance must be struck, however, between a government's obligation to protect its citizens and those citizens' exercise of their rights. These competing interests were at issue in the following case.

13. See *Texas v. Johnson,* 491 U.S. 397, 109 S.Ct. 2533, 105 L.Ed.2d 342 (1989).

CASE 2.2 Hodgkins v. Peterson

United States Court of Appeals,
Seventh Circuit, 2004.
355 F.3d 1048.

BACKGROUND AND FACTS Shortly after 11 P.M. on August 26, 1999, sixteen-year-old Colin Hodgkins and three friends left a Steak 'n Shake restaurant in Indianapolis, Indiana, where they had stopped to eat after a school soccer game. At the time, an Indiana statute made it illegal for minors between the ages of fifteen and seventeen to be in a public place after 11 P.M. on weeknights unless accompanied by a parent or guardian, with a few exceptions. As Colin and his friends left the restaurant, police arrested and handcuffed them for violating this statute. Colin's mother, Nancy Hodgkins, and others filed a suit in a federal district court against Bart Peterson, the mayor of Indianapolis, and other local government officials, asking the court to order the defendants to stop enforcing the curfew on the ground that it violated the First Amendment. The court ruled in the defendants' favor, and the plaintiffs appealed to the U.S. Court of Appeals for the Seventh Circuit.

IN THE WORDS OF THE COURT . . .
ROVNER, Circuit Judge.

* * * *

* * * The government claims that plaintiffs cannot mount a * * * challenge to the curfew law * * * because they have not demonstrated either that the curfew law imposes a disproportionate burden on those engaged in First Amendment activities or that it regulates conduct with an expressive element.

CASE 2.2—Continued

We agree that the Indiana curfew ordinance does not disproportionately impact First Amendment rights. As Colin Hodgkins can attest, it burdens minors who want to attend soccer games as much as it burdens those who wish to speak at a political rally. On the other hand, the curfew ordinance regulates minors' abilities to engage in some of the purest and most protected forms of speech and expression. [A] wide range of First Amendment activities occur during curfew hours, including political events, death penalty protests, late night sessions of the Indiana General Assembly, and neighborhood association meetings or nighttime events. A number of religions mark particular days or events with late-night services, prayers, or other activities: many Christians, for example, commemorate the birth of Christ with a midnight service on Christmas Eve and the Last Supper with an all-night vigil on Holy Thursday; Jews observe the first night of Shavuot by studying Torah all through the night; and throughout the month of Ramadan, Muslims engage in late-evening prayer. Late-night or all-night marches, rallies, and sleep-ins are often held to protest government action or inaction. And it is not unusual for political campaigns, particularly in the whirlwind final hours before an election, to hold rallies in the middle of the night. Thus, during the last weeks of the 1960 presidential campaign, then-Senator John F. Kennedy addressed a group of University of Michigan students at 2:00 A.M. on the steps of the Michigan Union. In unprepared remarks, he asked the students whether they would be willing to devote a few years of their lives working in underdeveloped countries in order to foster better relations between the people of those nations and the United States. The students responded with a petition calling for the creation of the Peace Corps, which came into being the following year. These are but a few examples. *The curfew ordinance regulates access to almost every form of public expression during the late-night hours. The effect on the speech of the plaintiffs is significant.* [Emphasis added.]

* * * *

* * * Any juvenile who chooses to participate in a late-night religious or political activity thus runs the risk that he will be arrested if a police officer stops him en route to or from that activity and he cannot prove to the officer's satisfaction that he is out after hours in order to exercise his First Amendment rights.

* * * *

* * * The prospect of an arrest is intimidating in and of itself; but one should also have in mind what else might follow from the arrest. * * * We have no doubt that the authorities are well meaning in administering the drug and alcohol testing and in questioning the minor and his parents about his friends and family life. But these are also rather serious intrusions upon one's personal and familial privacy, and they represent a substantial price for a minor to have to pay in order to take part in a late-night political or religious event. *The chill that the prospect of arrest imposes on a minor's exercise of his or her First Amendment rights is patent [evident].* [Emphasis added.]

DECISION AND REMEDY The U.S. Court of Appeals for the Seventh Circuit reversed the lower court's judgment and ordered a permanent injunction against the enforcement of the curfew. The court held that the curfew law was not narrowly tailored to serve a significant governmental interest and failed to allow for ample alternative channels for expression. The statute restricted a minor's access to any public forum during curfew hours. The concrete possibility of arrest made clear that the statute unduly chilled the exercise of minors' First Amendment rights.

FOR CRITICAL ANALYSIS—Political Consideration *Can a curfew law be written to protect both the fundamental constitutional rights of minors and the safety of all citizens?*

Corporate Political Speech Political speech by corporations also falls within the protection of the First Amendment. ■ EXAMPLE 2.4 In *First National Bank of Boston v. Bellotti,*[14] national banking associations and business corporations sought United States Supreme Court review of a Massachusetts statute that prohibited corporations from making political contributions or expenditures that individuals were permitted to make. The Court ruled that the Massachusetts law was unconstitutional because it violated the right of corporations to freedom of speech. ■ Similarly, the Court has held that a law prohibiting a corporation from using bill inserts to express its views on controversial issues violates the First Amendment.[15] Although a more conservative Supreme Court subsequently reversed this trend somewhat,[16] corporate political speech continues to be given significant protection under the First Amendment.

Commercial Speech The courts also give substantial protection to "commercial" speech, which consists of communications—primarily advertising and marketing—made by business firms that involve only their commercial interests. The protection given to commercial speech under the First Amendment is not as extensive as that afforded to noncommercial speech, however. A state may restrict certain kinds of advertising, for example, in the interest of protecting consumers from being misled by the advertising practices. States also have a legitimate interest in the beautification of roadsides, and this interest allows states to place restraints on billboard advertising. ■ EXAMPLE 2.5 Café Erotica, a nude dancing establishment, sued the state after being denied a permit to erect a billboard along an interstate highway in Florida. The state appellate court decided that because the law directly advanced a substantial government interest in highway beautification and safety, it was not an unconstitutional restraint on commercial speech.[17] ■

.on the Web The law firm of Arent Fox offers extensive information relating to advertising law at **http://www.advertisinglaw.com**.

Generally, a restriction on commercial speech will be considered valid as long as it meets the following three criteria: (1) it must seek to implement a substantial government interest, (2) it must directly advance that interest, and (3) it must go no further than necessary to accomplish its objective. ■ EXAMPLE 2.6 The South Carolina Supreme Court held that a state statute banning ads for video gambling violated the First Amendment because the statute did not directly advance a substantial government interest. Although the court acknowledged that the state had a substantial interest in minimizing gambling, there was no evidence that a reduction in video gambling ads would result in a reduction in gambling.[18] ■

The court in the following case applied these principles to determine the constitutionality of a county ordinance that regulated video games based on their content—the ordinance applied only to "graphically violent" video games.

---

14. 435 U.S. 765, 98 S.Ct. 1407, 55 L.Ed.2d 707 (1978).

15. *Consolidated Edison Co. v. Public Service Commission,* 447 U.S. 530, 100 S.Ct. 2326, 65 L.Ed.2d 319 (1980).

16. See *Austin v. Michigan Chamber of Commerce,* 494 U.S. 652, 110 S.Ct. 1391, 108 L.Ed.2d 652 (1990), in which the Court upheld a state law prohibiting corporations from using general corporate funds for independent expenditures in state political campaigns.

17. *Café Erotica v. Florida Department of Transportation,* 830 So.2d 181 (Fla.App. 1 Dist. 2002); review denied, *Café Erotica/We Dare to Bare v. Florida Department of Transportation,* 845 So.2d 888 (2003).

18. *Evans v. State,* 344 S.C. 60, 543 S.E.2d 547 (2001).

CASE 2.3 Interactive Digital Software Association v. St. Louis County, Missouri

United States Court of Appeals,
Eighth Circuit, 2003.
329 F.3d 954.

BACKGROUND AND FACTS St. Louis County, Missouri, passed an ordinance that made it unlawful for any person knowingly to sell, rent, or make available "graphically violent" video games to minors or to "permit the free play of" such games by minors, without a parent or guardian's consent.[a] Interactive Digital Software Association, and others that create or provide the public with video games and related software, filed a suit against the county in a federal district court. The plaintiffs asserted that the ordinance violated the First Amendment. The county argued that the ordinance promoted the compelling state interest of protecting the "psychological well-being of minors" by reducing the harm suffered by children who play violent video games. A psychologist, a high school principal, and other experts offered their conclusions that playing violent video games leads to aggressive behavior, but the county did not provide proof of a link between the games and any psychological harm. The court dismissed the case. The plaintiffs appealed to the U.S. Court of Appeals for the Eighth Circuit.

a. St. Louis County Revised Ordinances Sections 602.425 through 602.460.

IN THE WORDS OF THE COURT . . .

MORRIS SHEPPARD ARNOLD, Circuit Judge.

* * * *

* * * If the First Amendment is versatile enough to shield the painting of Jackson Pollock, music of Arnold Schoenberg, or Jabberwocky verse of Lewis Carroll, we see no reason why the pictures, graphic design, concept art, sounds, music, stories, and narrative present in video games are not entitled to a similar protection. The mere fact that they appear in a novel medium is of no legal consequence. Our review of the record convinces us that these violent video games contain stories, imagery, age-old themes of literature, and messages, even an ideology, just as books and movies do. * * *

We recognize that while children have in the past experienced age-old elemental violent themes by reading a fairy tale or an epic poem, or attending a Saturday matinee, the interactive play of a video game might present different difficulties. The County suggests in fact that with video games, the story lines are incidental and players may skip the expressive parts of the game and proceed straight to the player-controlled action. But the same could be said of action-packed movies like "The Matrix" or "Charlie's Angels"; any viewer with a videocassette or DVD player could simply skip to and isolate the action sequences. * * *

We note, moreover, that *there is no justification for disqualifying video games as speech simply because they are constructed to be interactive;* indeed, literature is most successful when it draws the reader into the story, makes him identify with the characters, invites him to judge them and quarrel with them, to experience their joys and sufferings as the reader's own. In fact, some books, such as the pre-teen oriented "Choose Your Own Nightmare" series (in which the reader makes choices that determine the plot of the story, and which lead the reader to one of several endings, by following the instructions at the bottom of the page) can be every bit as interactive * * * . [Emphasis added.]

Whether we believe the advent of violent video games adds anything of value to society is irrelevant; *guided by the First Amendment, we are obliged to recognize that they are as much entitled to the protection of free speech as the best of literature.* * * * [Emphasis added.]

(Continued)

CASE 2.3—Continued

* * * *

* * * [To] constitutionally restrict the speech at issue here, the County must come forward with empirical support for its belief that violent video games cause psychological harm to minors. In this case, * * * the County has failed to present the substantial supporting evidence of harm that is required before an ordinance that threatens protected speech can be upheld. * * * [T]he County may not simply surmise that it is serving a compelling state interest because "[s]ociety in general believes that continued exposure to violence can be harmful to children." Where First Amendment rights are at stake, the Government must present more than anecdote and supposition.

DECISION AND REMEDY The U.S. Court of Appeals for the Eighth Circuit reversed the judgment of the lower court and remanded the case for the entry of an injunction against the county's enforcement of its ordinance. Video games are entitled to the same First Amendment protection as other types of speech, and the defendants failed to present the required evidence of harm to uphold a law threatening protected speech.

WHY IS THIS CASE IMPORTANT? *Even though the courts allow more regulation of commercial speech than other types of speech, the state's power to regulate such speech is still limited. Proof that the message is violent or objectionable in some way does not justify regulating commercial speech. The government must establish that it has a substantial interest in regulating the speech and that the proposed regulation advances that interest.*

Unprotected Speech The United States Supreme Court has made it clear that certain types of speech will not be given any protection under the First Amendment. Speech that harms the good reputation of another, or defamatory speech (see Chapter 4), will not be protected. Speech that violates criminal laws (such as threatening speech) is not constitutionally protected. Other unprotected speech includes "fighting words," or words that are likely to incite others to respond violently.

The Supreme Court has also held that obscene speech is not protected by the First Amendment. The Court has grappled from time to time with the problem of trying to establish an objective definition of obscene speech. In a 1973 case, *Miller v. California,*[19] the Supreme Court created a test for legal obscenity, which involved a set of requirements that must be met for material to be legally obscene. Under this test, material is obscene if (1) the average person finds that it violates contemporary community standards; (2) the work taken as a whole appeals to a prurient (arousing or obsessive) interest in sex; (3) the work shows patently offensive sexual conduct; and (4) the work lacks serious redeeming literary, artistic, political, or scientific merit.

Because community standards vary widely, the *Miller* test has had inconsistent applications, and obscenity remains a constitutionally unsettled issue. Numerous state and federal statutes make it a crime to disseminate obscene materials, however, and the Supreme Court has often upheld such laws, including laws prohibiting the sale and possession of child pornography.[20]

on the Web To learn about issues involving free speech and cyberspace, go to the Web site of the American Civil Liberties Union at **http://www.aclu.org**. Click on one of the issues listed on the right side of the screen for links to ACLU articles on that issue.

Online Obscenity Congress first attempted to protect minors from pornographic materials on the Internet by passing the Communications Decency Act (CDA) of 1996. The CDA made it a crime to make available to minors online any "obscene or indecent" message that "depicts or describes, in terms patently offensive as mea-

19. 413 U.S. 15, 93 S.Ct. 2607, 37 L.Ed.2d 419 (1973).
20. For example, see *Osborne v. Ohio,* 495 U.S. 103, 110 S.Ct. 1691, 109 L.Ed.2d 98 (1990).

sured by contemporary community standards, sexual or excretory activities or organs."[21] The act was challenged as an unconstitutional restraint on speech, and ultimately the United States Supreme Court ruled that portions of the act were unconstitutional. The Court held that the terms *indecent* and *patently offensive* covered large amounts of nonpornographic material with serious educational or other value.[22]

The Child's Online Protection Act (COPA) of 1998[23] banned material "harmful to minors" distributed without some kind of age-verification system to separate adult and minor users. Although the COPA was more narrowly tailored than its predecessor, the CDA, it still used "contemporary community standards" to define which material was obscene and harmful to minors. When the act was challenged as violating free speech, the federal court hearing the case granted an injunction suspending the COPA, and the appellate court upheld the injunction.[24] In 2002, however, the Supreme Court reversed that decision and remanded the case, concluding that the reference to contemporary community standards alone was not sufficient to render the entire act unconstitutional.[25] On remand, the appellate court again held that the COPA violated free speech guarantees.[26] In June 2004, the Supreme Court affirmed the appellate court's decision and remanded the case for trial. The Court concluded that the claim that the COPA violated the right to free speech would likely prevail and hence left the injunction in place.[27]

In 2000, Congress enacted the Children's Internet Protection Act (CIPA),[28] which requires public schools and libraries to block adult content from access by children by installing **filtering software.** Such software is designed to prevent persons from viewing certain Web sites by responding to a site's Internet address or its **meta tags,** or key words. The CIPA was also challenged on constitutional grounds, but in 2003 the Supreme Court held that the act did not violate the First Amendment. The Court concluded that because libraries can disable the filters for any patrons who ask, the system was reasonably flexible and did not burden free speech to an unconstitutional extent.[29]

FILTERING SOFTWARE
A computer program that includes a pattern through which data are passed. When designed to block access to certain Web sites, the pattern blocks the retrieval of a site whose URL or key words are on a list within the program.

META TAG
A key word in a document that can serve as an index reference to the document. On the Web, search engines return results based, in part, on the tags in Web documents.

The First Amendment—Freedom of Religion

The First Amendment states that the government may neither establish any religion nor prohibit the free exercise of religious practices. The first part of this constitutional provision is referred to as the **establishment clause,** and the second part is known as the **free exercise clause.** Government action, both federal and state, must be consistent with this constitutional mandate.

ESTABLISHMENT CLAUSE
The provision in the First Amendment to the Constitution that prohibits the government from establishing any state-sponsored religion or enacting any law that promotes religion or favors one religion over another.

FREE EXERCISE CLAUSE
The provision in the First Amendment to the Constitution that prohibits the government from interfering with people's religious practices or forms of worship.

The Establishment Clause The establishment clause prohibits the government from establishing a state-sponsored religion, as well as from passing laws that promote (aid or endorse) religion or that show a preference for one religion over another. The

21. 47 U.S.C. Section 223(a)(1)(B)(ii).
22. *Reno v. American Civil Liberties Union,* 521 U.S. 844, 117 S.Ct. 2329, 138 L.Ed.2d 874 (1997).
23. 47 U.S.C. Section 231.
24. *American Civil Liberties Union v. Reno,* 31 F.Supp.2d 473 (E.D.Pa. 1999); *aff'd,* 217 F.3d 162 (3d Cir. 2002).
25. *Ashcroft v. American Civil Liberties Union,* 535 U.S. 564, 122 S.Ct. 1700, 152 L.Ed.2d 771 (2002).
26. *American Civil Liberties Union v. Ashcroft,* 322 F.3d 240 (3d Cir. 2003).
27. *American Civil Liberties Union v. Ashcroft,* ___ U.S. ___, 124 S.Ct. 2783, 159 L.Ed.2d 690 (2004).
28. 17 U.S.C. Sections 1701–1741.
29. *United States v. American Library Association,* 539 U.S. 194, 123 S.Ct. 2297, 156 L.Ed.2d 221 (2003).

establishment clause does not require a complete separation of church and state, though. On the contrary, it requires the government to accommodate religions.[30]

The establishment clause covers all conflicts about such matters as the legality of state and local government support for a particular religion, government aid to religious organizations and schools, the government's allowing or requiring school prayers, and the teaching of evolution versus fundamentalist theories of creation. The Supreme Court has held that for a government law or policy to be constitutional, it must be secular in aim, must not have the primary effect of advancing or inhibiting religions, and must not create "an excessive government entanglement with religion."[31] Generally, federal or state regulation that does not promote religion or place a significant burden on religion is constitutional even if it has some impact on religion.

■ EXAMPLE 2.7 "Sunday closing laws" make the performance of some commercial activities on Sunday illegal. These statutes, also known as "blue laws" (from the color of the paper on which an early Sunday law was written), have been upheld on the ground that it is a legitimate function of government to provide a day of rest. The United States Supreme Court has held that the closing laws, although originally of a religious character, have taken on the secular purpose of promoting the health and welfare of workers.[32] Even though Sunday closing laws admittedly make it easier for Christians to attend religious services, the Court has viewed this effect as an incidental, not a primary, purpose of Sunday closing laws. ■

ETHICAL ISSUE 2.1

Do religious displays on public property violate the establishment clause? The thorny issue of whether religious displays on public property violate the establishment clause often arises during the holiday season. Time and again, the courts have wrestled with this issue, but it has never been resolved in a way that satisfies everyone and continues to decide such cases on a case-by-case basis. In a 1984 case, the United States Supreme Court decided that a city's official Christmas display, which included a crèche (Nativity scene), did not violate the establishment clause because it was just one part of a larger holiday display that featured secular symbols, such as reindeer and candy canes.[33] In a later case, the Court held that the presence of a crèche within a county courthouse violated the establishment clause because it was not in close proximity to nonreligious symbols, including a Christmas tree, which were located outside, on the building's steps.[34] For example, in 2005 the Supreme Court ruled that the presence of a six-foot monument in a public park in Austin, Texas, did not violate the establishment clause because it was just one of seventeen sculptures. In another ruling issued on the same day, however, the Court held that wall displays of the Ten Commandments in two county courthouses in Kentucky were so overtly religious as to be impermissible.[35] The courts continue to apply this reasoning in cases involving similar issues.■

The Free Exercise Clause The free exercise clause guarantees that a person can hold any religious belief that she or he wants; or a person can have no religious belief.

30. *Zorach v. Clauson,* 343 U.S. 306, 72 S.Ct. 679, 96 L.Ed. 954 (1952).

31. *Lemon v. Kurtzman,* 403 U.S. 602, 91 S.Ct. 2105, 29 L.Ed.2d 745 (1971).

32. *McGowan v. Maryland,* 366 U.S. 420, 81 S.Ct. 1101, 6 L.Ed.2d 393 (1961).

33. *Lynch v. Donnelly,* 465 U.S. 668, 104 S.Ct. 1355, 79 L.Ed.2d 604 (1984).

34. See, for example, *County of Allegheny v. American Civil Liberties Union,* 492 U.S. 573, 109 S.Ct. 3086, 106 L.Ed.2d 472 (1989).

35. *Van Orden v. Perry,* ___U.S.___, 125 S.Ct. 2854, ___L.Ed.2d___ (2005), and *McCreary County, Kentucky v. American Civil Liberties Union of Kentucky,* ___U.S.___, 125 S.Ct. 2722, ___L.Ed.2d___ (2005), respectively.

A woman reads from the Qur'an, the holy book of the Islamic religion, to illustrate that her religious beliefs require her to keep her head and face covered. She is testifying that it is unconstitutional for the government to force her to remove her veil and be photographed to get a driver's license in Florida. By taking a photo of an Islamic woman without her face covered, does the state violate the woman's religious freedom? Why or why not? What state interests might justify such an intrusion? (Library of Congress)

When religious *practices* work against public policy and the public welfare, however, the government can act. For example, regardless of a child's or parent's religious beliefs, the government can require certain types of vaccinations. Similarly, although children of Jehovah's Witnesses are not required to say the Pledge of Allegiance at school, their parents cannot prevent them from accepting medical treatment (such as blood transfusions) if in fact their lives are in danger. Additionally, public school students can be required to study from textbooks chosen by school authorities.

For business firms, an important issue involves the accommodation that businesses must make for the religious beliefs of their employees. For example, if an employee's religion prohibits him or her from working on a certain day of the week or at a certain type of job, the employer must make a reasonable attempt to accommodate these religious requirements. Employers must reasonably accommodate an employee's religious beliefs even if the beliefs are not based on the tenets or dogma of a particular church, sect, or denomination. The only requirement is that the belief be religious in nature and sincerely held by the employee. (We will look further at this issue in Chapter 41, in the context of employment discrimination.)

Due Process and Equal Protection

Two other constitutional guarantees of great significance to Americans are mandated by the due process clauses of the Fifth and Fourteenth Amendments and the equal protection clause of the Fourteenth Amendment.

Due Process

Both the Fifth and the Fourteenth Amendments provide that no person shall be deprived "of life, liberty, or property, without due process of law." The **due process clause** of each of these constitutional amendments has two aspects—procedural and substantive.

DUE PROCESS CLAUSE
The provisions in the Fifth and Fourteenth Amendments to the Constitution that guarantee that no person shall be deprived of life, liberty, or property without due process of law. Similar clauses are found in most state constitutions.

Procedural Due Process Procedural due process requires that any government decision to take life, liberty, or property must be made fairly. For example, fair procedures must be used in determining whether a person will be subjected to punishment or have some burden imposed on him or her. Fair procedure has been interpreted as requiring that the person have at least an opportunity to object to a proposed action before a fair, neutral decision maker (which need not be a judge). Thus, for example, if a driver's license is construed as a property interest, some sort of opportunity to object to its suspension or termination by the state must be provided.

Substantive Due Process Substantive due process focuses on the content, or substance, of legislation. If a law or other governmental action limits a *fundamental right,* it will be held to violate substantive due process unless it promotes a compelling or overriding state interest. Fundamental rights include interstate travel, privacy, voting, and all First Amendment rights. Compelling state interests could include, for example, the public's safety. ■ EXAMPLE 2.8 Laws setting speed limits may be upheld even though they affect interstate travel, if they are shown to reduce highway fatalities. The courts uphold these laws because the state has a compelling interest in protecting the lives of its citizens. ■

In situations not involving fundamental rights, a law or action does not violate substantive due process if it rationally relates to any legitimate governmental end. It is almost impossible for a law or action to fail the "rationality" test. Under this test, virtually any business regulation will be upheld as reasonable—the United States Supreme Court has sustained insurance regulations, price and wage controls, banking limitations, and restrictions of unfair competition and trade practices against substantive due process challenges.

■ EXAMPLE 2.9 If a state legislature enacted a law imposing a fifteen-year term of imprisonment without a trial on all businesspersons who appeared in their own television commercials, the law would be unconstitutional on both substantive and procedural grounds. Substantive review would invalidate the legislation because it abridges freedom of speech. Procedurally, the law is unfair because it imposes the penalty without giving the accused a chance to defend her or his actions. ■ The lack of procedural due process will cause a court to invalidate any statute or prior court decision. Similarly, the courts will overrule any state or federal law that violates the Constitution by denying substantive due process.

EQUAL PROTECTION

EQUAL PROTECTION CLAUSE
The provision in the Fourteenth Amendment to the Constitution that guarantees that no state will "deny to any person within its jurisdiction the equal protection of the laws." This clause mandates that the state governments treat similarly situated individuals in a similar manner.

Under the Fourteenth Amendment, a state may not "deny to any person within its jurisdiction the equal protection of the laws." The United States Supreme Court has used the due process clause of the Fifth Amendment to make the **equal protection clause** applicable to the federal government as well. Equal protection means that the government must treat similarly situated individuals in a similar manner.

Both substantive due process and equal protection require review of the substance of the law or other governmental action rather than review of the procedures used. When a law or action limits the liberty of all persons to do something, it may violate substantive due process; when a law or action limits the liberty of some persons but not others, it may violate the equal protection clause. ■ EXAMPLE 2.10 If a law prohibits all persons from buying contraceptive devices, it raises a substantive due process question. If a law prohibits only unmarried persons from buying the same devices, it raises an equal protection issue. ■

"When one undertakes to administer justice, . . . what is done for one, must be done for everyone in equal degree."
THOMAS JEFFERSON,
1743–1826
(Third president of the United States, 1801–1809)

Basically, in determining whether a law or action violates the equal protection clause, a court will consider questions similar to those previously noted as applicable in a substantive due process review. Under an equal protection inquiry, when a law or action distinguishes between or among individuals, the basis for the distinction—that is, the classification—is examined. Depending on the classification, the courts apply different levels of scrutiny, or "tests," to determine whether the law or action violates the equal protection clause.

Minimal Scrutiny—The "Rational Basis" Test Generally, laws regulating economic and social matters are presumed to be valid and are subject to only minimal scrutiny. A classification will be considered valid if there is any conceivable "rational basis" on which the classification might relate to any *legitimate government interest.* It is almost impossible for a law or action to fail the rational basis test. ■ EXAMPLE 2.11 A city ordinance that in effect prohibits all pushcart vendors except a specific few from operating in a particular area of the city will be upheld if the city proffers a rational basis—such as reducing the traffic in the particular area—for the ordinance. In contrast, a law that provides unemployment benefits only to people over six feet tall would clearly fail the rational basis test because it could not further any legitimate government interest. ■

Intermediate Scrutiny A harder standard to meet, that of "intermediate scrutiny," is applied in cases involving discrimination based on gender or legitimacy. Laws using these classifications must be substantially related to *important government objectives.* ■ EXAMPLE 2.12 An important government objective is preventing illegitimate teenage pregnancies. Because males and females are not similarly situated in this circumstance—only females can become pregnant—a law that punishes men but not women for statutory rape will be upheld. A state law requiring illegitimate children to bring paternity suits within six years of their births, however, will be struck down if legitimate children are allowed to seek support from their parents at any time. ■

Strict Scrutiny The most difficult standard to meet is that of "strict scrutiny." Very few cases survive strict-scrutiny analysis. Strict scrutiny is applied when a law or action inhibits some persons' exercise of a fundamental right or is based on a suspect trait (such as race, national origin, or citizenship status). Strict scrutiny means that the court will examine the law or action involved very closely, and the law or action will be allowed to stand only if it is necessary to promote a *compelling government interest.* ■ EXAMPLE 2.13 Suppose that a city gives preference to minority applicants in awarding construction contracts. Because the policy is based on suspect traits (race and national origin), it will violate the equal protection clause *unless* it is necessary to promote a compelling state interest.[36] ■

Privacy Rights

"There was, of course, no way of knowing whether you were being watched at any given moment."

GEORGE ORWELL, 1903–1950 (Author, from his famous novel *1984*)

In the past, privacy issues typically related to personal information that government agencies, including the Federal Bureau of Investigation, might obtain and keep about an individual. Later, concerns about what banks and insurance companies might know and transmit to others about individuals became an issue. Since the 1990s, one of the major concerns of individuals has been how to protect privacy rights in cyberspace and to safeguard private information that may be revealed online (including credit-card numbers and financial information). The increasing value of personal information for online marketers—who are willing to pay a high price to those who collect and sell them such information—has exacerbated the situation.

Today, individuals face additional concerns about government intrusions into their privacy. Legislation passed by Congress in the wake of the terrorist attacks of September 11, 2001, has given increased authority to government officials to monitor Internet activities (such as e-mail and Web site visits) and to gain access to personal financial data and student information.[37] Using technology, law enforcement officials can track the telephone and e-mail conversations of one party to find out the identity of the other party or parties. The government must certify that the information likely to be obtained is relevant to an ongoing criminal investigation, but it does not need to provide proof of any wrongdoing to gain access to this information. Privacy advocates argue that this law has adversely affected the constitutional rights of all Americans, and it has been widely criticized in the media, fueling the public debate over how to secure privacy rights in an electronic age.

In this section, we look at the protection of privacy rights under the U.S. Constitution and various federal statutes. Note that state constitutions and statutes

36. See, for example, *Adarand Constructors, Inc. v. Peña,* 515 U.S. 200, 115 S.Ct. 2097, 132 L.Ed.2d 158 (1995).

37. Uniting and Strengthening America by Providing Appropriate Tools Required to Intercept and Obstruct Terrorism Act of 2001, also known as the USA Patriot Act, was enacted as Pub. L. No. 107-56 (2001).

also protect individuals' privacy rights, often to a significant degree. Privacy rights are also protected under tort law (see Chapter 4). Additionally, the Federal Trade Commission has played an active role in protecting the privacy rights of online consumers (see Chapter 38). The protection of employees' privacy rights, particularly with respect to electronic monitoring practices, is another area of growing concern (see Chapter 40).

CONSTITUTIONAL PROTECTION OF PRIVACY RIGHTS

The U.S. Constitution does not explicitly mention a general right to privacy, and only relatively recently have the courts regarded the right to privacy as a constitutional right. In a 1928 Supreme Court case, *Olmstead v. United States,*[38] Justice Louis Brandeis stated in his dissent that the right to privacy is "the most comprehensive of rights and the right most valued by civilized men." At that time, the majority of the justices did not agree, and it was not until the 1960s that a majority on the Supreme Court endorsed the view that the Constitution protects individual privacy rights.

In a landmark 1965 case, *Griswold v. Connecticut,*[39] the Supreme Court invalidated a Connecticut law that effectively prohibited the use of contraceptives. The Court held that the law violated the right to privacy. Justice William O. Douglas formulated a unique way of reading this right into the Bill of Rights. He claimed that "emanations" from the rights guaranteed by the First, Third, Fourth, Fifth, and Ninth Amendments formed and gave "life and substance" to "penumbras" (partial shadows) around these guaranteed rights. These penumbras included an implied constitutional right to privacy.

When we read these amendments, we can see the foundation for Justice Douglas's reasoning. Consider the Fourth Amendment. By prohibiting unreasonable searches and seizures, the amendment effectively protects individuals' privacy. Consider also the words of the Ninth Amendment: "The enumeration in the Constitution of certain rights, shall not be construed to deny or disparage others retained by the people." In other words, just because the Constitution, including its amendments, does not specifically mention the right to privacy does not mean that this right is denied to the people. Indeed, in a recent survey of America Online subscribers, respondents ranked privacy second behind freedom of speech and ahead of freedom of religion as the most important rights guaranteed by the Constitution. A recent Harris poll showed that almost 80 percent of those questioned believed that if the framers were writing the Constitution today, they would add privacy as an important right.[40]

FEDERAL STATUTES PROTECTING PRIVACY RIGHTS

"There is nothing new in the realization that the Constitution sometimes insulates the criminality of a few in order to protect the privacy of us all."

ANTONIN SCALIA, 1936–
(United States Supreme Court justice, 1986 to present)

In the last several decades, Congress has enacted a number of statutes that protect the privacy of individuals in various areas of concern. In the 1960s, Americans were sufficiently alarmed by the accumulation of personal information in government files that they pressured Congress to pass laws permitting individuals to access their files. Congress responded in 1966 with the Freedom of Information Act, which allows any person to request copies of any information on her or him contained in federal government files. In 1974, Congress passed the Privacy Act, which also gives persons the right to access such information. These and other major federal laws protecting privacy rights are listed and described in Exhibit 2–1.

38. 277 U.S. 438, 48 S.Ct. 564, 72 L.Ed. 944 (1928).

39. 381 U.S. 479, 85 S.Ct. 1678, 14 L.Ed.2d 510 (1965).

40. *Public Perspective,* November/December 2000, p. 9.

Responding to the growing need to protect the privacy of individuals' health records—particularly computerized records—Congress passed the Health Insurance Portability and Accountability Act (HIPAA) of 1996.[41] This act, which took effect on April 14, 2003, defines and limits the circumstances in which an individual's "protected health information" may be used or disclosed.

The HIPAA requires health-care providers and health-care plans, including certain employers who sponsor health plans, to inform patients of their privacy rights and of how their personal medical information may be used. The act also generally states that a person's medical records may not be used for purposes unrelated to health care—such as marketing, for example—or disclosed to others without the individual's permission. Covered entities must formulate written privacy policies, designate privacy officials, limit access to computerized health data, physically secure medical records with lock and key, train employees and volunteers on their

41. The HIPAA was enacted as Pub. L. No. 104-191 (1996) and is codified in 29 U.S.C.A. Sections 1181 *et seq.*

EXHIBIT 2–1 FEDERAL LEGISLATION RELATING TO PRIVACY

TITLE	PROVISIONS CONCERNING PRIVACY
Freedom of Information Act (1966)	Provides that individuals have a right to obtain access to information about them collected in government files.
Family and Educational Rights and Privacy Act (1974)	Limits access to computer-stored records of education-related evaluations and grades in private and public colleges and universities.
Privacy Act (1974)	Protects the privacy of individuals about whom the federal government has information. Under this act, agencies that use or disclose personal information must make sure that the information is reliable and guard against its misuse. Individuals must be able to find out what data concerning them the agency is compiling and how the data will be used. In addition, the agency must give individuals a means to correct inaccurate data and must obtain their consent before using the data for any other purpose.
Tax Reform Act (1976)	Preserves the privacy of personal financial information.
Right to Financial Privacy Act (1978)	Prohibits financial institutions from providing the federal government with access to customers' records unless a customer authorizes the disclosure.
Electronic Communications Privacy Act (1986)	Prohibits the interception of information communicated by electronic means.
Driver's Privacy Protection Act (1994)	Prevents states from disclosing or selling a driver's personal information without the driver's consent.
Health Insurance Portability and Accountability Act (1996)	Prohibits the use of a consumer's medical information for any purpose other than that for which such information was provided, unless the consumer expressly consents to the use. Final rules became effective on April 14, 2003.
Financial Services Modernization Act (Gramm-Leach-Bliley Act) (1999)	Prohibits the disclosure of nonpublic personal information about a consumer to an unaffiliated third party unless strict disclosure and opt-out requirements are met. Final rules became mandatory on July 1, 2001.

privacy policies, and sanction those who violate those policies. These protections are intended to assure individuals that their health information, including genetic information, will be properly protected and not used for purposes that the patient did not know about or authorize.

REVIEWING CONSTITUTIONAL LAW

A state legislature enacted a statute that required any motorcycle operator or passenger on the state's highways to wear a protective helmet. Jim Alderman, a licensed motorcycle operator, sued the state to block enforcement of the law. Alderman asserted that the statute violated the equal protection clause because it placed requirements on motorcyclists that were not imposed on other motorists. Using the information presented in the chapter, answer the following questions.

1. Why does this statute raise equal protection issues instead of substantive due process concerns?
2. What are the three levels of scrutiny that the courts use in determining whether a law violates the equal protection clause?
3. What type of government interest must be served to justify discriminatory classifications under each of these three standards of scrutiny?
4. Which standard, or test, would apply to this situation? Why?
5. Applying this standard, or test, is the helmet statute constitutional? Why or why not?

APPLICATION Creating a Web Site Privacy Policy*

Firms with online business operations realize that to do business effectively with their customers, they need to have some information about those customers. Yet online consumers are often reluctant to part with personal information because they do not know how that information may be used. To allay consumer fears about the privacy of their personal data, as well as to avoid liability under existing laws, most online businesses today are taking steps to create and implement Web site privacy policies.

PRIVACY POLICY GUIDELINES

In the last several years, a number of independent, nonprofit organizations have developed model Web site privacy policies and guidelines for online businesses to use. Web site privacy guidelines are now available from a number of online privacy groups and other organizations, including the Online Privacy Alliance, the Internet Alliance, and the Direct Marketing Association. Some organizations, including the Better Business Bureau, have even developed a "seal of approval" that Web-based businesses can display at their sites if they follow the organization's privacy guidelines.

One of the best known of these organizations is TRUSTe. Web site owners that agree to TRUSTe's privacy standards are allowed to post the TRUSTe "seal of approval" on their Web sites. The idea behind the seal, which many describe as the online equivalent of the "Good Housekeeping Seal of Approval," is to allay users' fears about privacy problems.

DRAFTING A PRIVACY POLICY

Online privacy guidelines generally recommend that businesses post notices on their Web sites about the type of information being collected, how it will be used, and the parties to whom it will be disclosed. Other recommenda-

* This *Application* is not meant to substitute for the services of an attorney who is licensed to practice law in your state.

APPLICATION Creating a Web Site Privacy Policy—Continued

tions include allowing Web site visitors to access and correct or remove personal information and giving visitors an "opt-in" or "opt-out" choice. For example, if a user selects an "opt-out" policy, the personal data collected from that user would be kept private.

In the last several years, the Federal Trade Commission (FTC) has developed privacy standards that can serve as guidelines. An online business that includes these standards in its Web site privacy policy—and makes sure that they are enforced—will be in a better position to defend its policy should consumers complain about the site's practices to the FTC. The FTC standards are incorporated into the following checklist.

CHECKLIST FOR A WEB SITE PRIVACY POLICY

1. Include on your Web site a notice of your privacy policy.
2. Give consumers a choice (such as opt-in or opt-out) with respect to any information collected.
3. Outline the safeguards that you will employ to secure all consumer data.
4. Let consumers know that they can correct and update any personal information collected by your business.
5. State that parental consent is required if a child is involved.
6. Create a mechanism to enforce the policy.

KEY TERMS

Bill of Rights 42
checks and balances 35
commerce clause 35
due process clause 51
equal protection clause 52
establishment clause 49
federal form of government 34
filtering software 49
free exercise clause 49
meta tags 49
police powers 39
preemption 40
supremacy clause 40
symbolic speech 44

CHAPTER SUMMARY Constitutional Law

The Constitutional Powers of Government (See pages 34–35.)	The U.S. Constitution established a federal form of government, in which government powers are shared by the national government and the state governments. At the national level, government powers are divided among the legislative, executive, and judicial branches.
The Commerce Clause (See pages 35–40.)	1. *The expansion of national powers*—The commerce clause expressly permits Congress to regulate commerce. Over time, courts expansively interpreted this clause, thereby enabling the national government to wield extensive powers over the economic life of the nation. 2. *The commerce power today*—Today, the commerce power authorizes the national government, at least theoretically, to regulate every commercial enterprise in the United States. In recent years, the Supreme Court has reined in somewhat the national government's regulatory powers under the commerce clause. 3. *The regulatory powers of the states*—The Tenth Amendment reserves all powers not expressly delegated to the national government to the states. Under their police powers, state governments may regulate private activities to protect or promote the public order, health, safety, morals, and general welfare.

CHAPTER SUMMARY Constitutional Law—Continued

The Commerce Clause—Continued	4. *The "dormant" commerce clause*—If state regulations substantially interfere with interstate commerce, they will be held to violate the "dormant" commerce clause of the U.S. Constitution. The positive aspect of the commerce clause, which gives the national government the exclusive authority to regulate interstate commerce, implies a "dormant" aspect—that the states do *not* have this power.
The Supremacy Clause (See pages 40–42.)	The U.S. Constitution provides that the Constitution, laws, and treaties of the United States are "the supreme Law of the Land." Whenever a state law directly conflicts with a federal law, the state law is rendered invalid.
The Taxing and Spending Powers (See page 42.)	The U.S. Constitution gives Congress the power to impose uniform taxes throughout the United States and to spend revenues accumulated from the taxing power. Congress can spend revenues to promote any objective it deems worthwhile, so long as it does not violate the Bill of Rights.
Business and the Bill of Rights (See pages 42–51.)	The Bill of Rights, which consists of the first ten amendments to the U.S. Constitution, was adopted in 1791 and embodies a series of protections for individuals—and, in some instances, business entities—against various types of interference by the federal government. Freedoms guaranteed by the First Amendment that affect businesses include freedom of speech and freedom of religion.
Due Process and Equal Protection (See pages 51–53.)	1. *Due process*—Both the Fifth and the Fourteenth Amendments provide that no person shall be deprived of "life, liberty, or property, without due process of law." Procedural due process requires that any government decision to take life, liberty, or property must be made fairly, using fair procedures. Substantive due process focuses on the content of legislation. 2. *Equal protection*—Under the Fourteenth Amendment, a state may not "deny to any person within its jurisdiction the equal protection of the laws." A law or action that limits the liberty of some persons but not others may violate the equal protection clause.
Privacy Rights (See pages 53–56.)	Americans are increasingly becoming concerned over privacy issues raised by Internet-related technology. The Constitution does not contain a specific guarantee of a right to privacy, but such a right has been derived from guarantees found in several constitutional amendments. A number of federal statutes protect privacy rights. Privacy rights are also protected by many state constitutions and statutes, as well as under tort law.

FOR REVIEW

Answers for the even-numbered questions in this For Review *section can be found on this text's accompanying Web site at* http://blt.westbuslaw.com. *Select "Chapter 2" and click on "For Review."*

1. What is the basic structure of the U.S. government?
2. What constitutional clause gives the federal government the power to regulate commercial activities among the various states?
3. What constitutional clause allows laws enacted by the federal government to take priority over conflicting state laws?
4. What is the Bill of Rights? What freedoms are guaranteed by the First Amendment?
5. Where in the Constitution can the due process clause be found?

QUESTIONS AND CASE PROBLEMS

2–1. Commercial Speech. A mayoral election is about to be held in a large U.S. city. One of the candidates is Luis Delgado, and his campaign supporters wish to post campaign signs on lampposts and utility posts throughout the city. A city ordinance, however, prohibits the posting of any signs on public property. Delgado's supporters contend that the city ordinance is unconstitutional because it violates their rights to free speech. What factors might a court consider in determining the constitutionality of this ordinance?

2–2. Commerce Clause. Suppose that Georgia enacts a law requiring the use of contoured rear-fender mudguards on trucks and trailers operating within its state lines. The statute further makes it illegal for trucks and trailers to use straight mudguards. In thirty-five other states, straight mudguards are legal. Moreover, in the neighboring state of Florida, straight mudguards are explicitly required by law. There is some evidence suggesting that contoured mudguards might be a little safer than straight mudguards. Discuss whether this Georgia statute would violate the commerce clause of the U.S. Constitution.

2–3. Freedom of Religion. A business has a backlog of orders, and to meet its deadlines, management decides to run the firm seven days a week, eight hours a day. One of the employees, Marjorie Tollens, refuses to work on Saturday on religious grounds. Her refusal to work means that the firm may not meet its production deadlines and may therefore suffer a loss of future business. The firm fires Tollens and replaces her with an employee who is willing to work seven days a week. Tollens claims that her employer, in terminating her employment, violated her constitutional right to the free exercise of her religion. Do you agree? Why or why not?

2–4. Equal Protection. With the objectives of preventing crime, maintaining property values, and preserving the quality of urban life, New York City enacted an ordinance to regulate the locations of commercial establishments that featured adult entertainment. The ordinance expressly applied to female, but not male, topless entertainment. Adele Buzzetti owned the Cozy Cabin, a New York City cabaret that featured female topless dancers. Buzzetti and an anonymous dancer filed a suit in a federal district court against the city, asking the court to block the enforcement of the ordinance. The plaintiffs argued in part that the ordinance violated the equal protection clause. Under the equal protection clause, what standard applies to the court's consideration of this ordinance? Under this test, how should the court rule? Why? [*Buzzetti v. City of New York,* 140 F.3d 134 (2d Cir. 1998)]

2–5. Free Speech. The city of Tacoma, Washington, enacted an ordinance that prohibited the playing of car sound systems at a volume that would be "audible" at a distance greater than fifty feet. Dwight Holland was arrested and convicted for violating the ordinance. The conviction was later dismissed, but Holland filed a civil suit in a Washington state court against the city. He claimed in part that the ordinance violated his freedom of speech under the First Amendment. On what basis might the court conclude that this ordinance is constitutional? (Hint: In playing a sound system, was Holland actually expressing himself?) [*Holland v. City of Tacoma,* 90 Wash.App. 533, 954 P.2d 290 (1998)]

CASE PROBLEM WITH SAMPLE ANSWER

2–6. In February 1999, Carl Adler mailed a driver's license renewal application form and a check for $28 to the New York Department of Motor Vehicles (DMV). The form required Adler's Social Security number, which he intentionally omitted. The DMV returned the application and check and told Adler to supply his Social Security number or send proof that the Social Security Administration could not give him a number. Claiming a right to privacy, Adler refused to comply. The DMV responded that federal law authorizes the states to obtain Social Security numbers from individuals in the context of administering certain state programs, including driver's license programs, and that Adler's application would not be processed until he supplied the number. Adler filed a suit in a New York state court against the DMV, asserting in part that it was in violation of the federal Privacy Act of 1974. Adler asked the court to, among other things, order the DMV to renew his license. Should the court grant Adler's request? Why or why not? [*Adler v. Jackson,* 712 N.Y.S.2d 240 (Sup. 2000)]

After you have answered this problem, compare your answer with the sample answer given on the Web site that accompanies this text. Go to http://blt.westbuslaw.com, select "Chapter 2," and click on "Case Problem with Sample Answer."

2–7. Free Speech. Henry Mishkoff is a Web designer whose firm does business as "Webfeats." When Taubman Co. began building a mall called "The Shops at Willow Bend" near Mishkoff's home, Mishkoff registered the domain name "shopsatwillowbend.com" and created a Web site with that address. The site featured information about the mall, a disclaimer indicating that Mishkoff's site was unofficial, and a link to the mall's official site. Taubman discovered Mishkoff's site and filed a suit in a federal district court against him. Mishkoff then registered other names, including "taubmansucks.com," with links to a site documenting his battle with Taubman. (A Web name with a "sucks.com" moniker attached to it is known as a "complaint name," and the process of registering and using such names is known as "cybergriping.") Taubman asked the court to order Mishkoff to stop using all of these names. Should the court grant Taubman's request? On what basis might the court protect Mishkoff's use of the names? [*Taubman Co. v. Webfeats,* 319 F.3d 770 (6th Cir. 2003)]

2–8. Due Process. In 1994, the Board of County Commissioners of Yellowstone County, Montana, created Zoning District 17 in interactivity through a Web site; and (3) passive advertising. Jurisdiction is proper for the first category, improper for the third, and may or may not be appropriate for the second.[4] An Internet communication is typically considered passive if people have to voluntarily access it to read the message, and active if it is sent to specific individuals.

In certain situations, even a single contact can satisfy the minimum-contacts requirement. ■ EXAMPLE 3.4 A Texas resident, Davis, sent an unsolicited e-mail message to numerous Mississippi residents advertising a pornographic Web site. Davis falsified the "from" header in the e-mail so that it appeared that Internet Doorway had sent the mail. Internet Doorway filed a lawsuit against Davis in Mississippi claiming that its reputation and goodwill in the community had been harmed. The U.S. district court in Mississippi held that Davis's single e-mail to Mississippi residents satisfied the minimum-contacts requirement for jurisdiction. The court concluded that Davis, by sending the e-mail solicitation, should reasonably have expected that she could be "haled into court in a distant jurisdiction to answer for the ramifications."[5] ■ In the following case, the court considered whether jurisdiction could be exercised over defendants whose only contacts with the jurisdiction were through their Web site.

4. For a leading case on this issue, see *Zippo Manufacturing Co. v. Zippo Dot Com, Inc.,* 952 F.Supp. 1119 (W.D.Pa. 1997).

5. *Internet Doorway, Inc. v. Parks,* 138 F.Supp.2d 773 (S.D.Miss. 2001).

CASE 3.1 Bird v. Parsons

United States Court of Appeals,
Sixth Circuit, 2002.
289 F.3d 865.

BACKGROUND AND FACTS Darrell Bird, a citizen of Ohio, has operated Financia, Inc., a national computer software business, since 1983. Financia, Inc., owns the domain name financia.com. Dotster, Inc., a domain name registrar incorporated in Washington, operates its registry at **http://www.dotster.com**.[a] Dotster allows registrants who lack an Internet server to which a name can be assigned to park their names on Dotster's "Futurehome" page. Marshall Parsons registered the name efinancia.com on Dotster's site in 2000 and "parked" the name on the Futurehome page with the address **http://www.efinancia.com**. George DeCarlo and Steven Vincent, on behalf of Dotster, activated Parsons's site. The name efinancia.com was soon offered for sale at **http://www.afternic.com**, an auction site for the sale of domain names. Bird filed a suit against Dotster and others in a federal district court, alleging, in part, trademark infringement, copyright infringement, and cybersquatting.[b] Dotster, DeCarlo, and Vincent (the "Dotster defendants") asked the court to dismiss the complaint against them for, among other reasons, lack of personal jurisdiction. The court dismissed the suit. Alleging that Dotster sold 4,666 registrations to Ohio residents, Bird appealed to the U.S. Court of Appeals for the Sixth Circuit.

a. Dotster's registration process is in conjunction with the Domain Registration of Internet Assigned Names and Numbers, which is maintained by Network Solutions, Inc. (owned by VeriSign), and regulated by the Internet Corporation for Assigned Names and Numbers (ICANN). Dotster is an ICANN-accredited registrar.

b. *Cybersquatting* is registering another person's trademark as a domain name and offering it for sale. This is a violation of the Anticybersquatting Consumer Protection Act of 1999. Cybersquatting and trademark and copyright infringement will be discussed in more detail in Chapter 5.

CASE 3.1—Continued

IN THE WORDS OF THE COURT . . .

RONALD LEE GILMAN, Circuit Judge.

* * * *

* * * [J]urisdiction over the Dotster defendants is permissible only if their contacts with Ohio satisfy [a] three-part test * * * :

> First, the defendant must purposefully avail himself of the privilege of acting in the forum state [the state in which the lawsuit is initiated] or causing a consequence in the forum state. Second, the cause of action must arise from the defendant's activities there. Finally, the acts of the defendant or consequences caused by the defendant must have a substantial enough connection with the forum state to make the exercise of jurisdiction over the defendant reasonable.

* * * We conclude that by maintaining a website on which Ohio residents can register domain names and by allegedly accepting the business of 4,666 Ohio residents, the Dotster defendants have satisfied the *purposeful-availment requirement.* * * * [Emphasis added.]

The second requirement * * * involves an analysis of whether Bird's claims arise from the Dotster defendants' contacts with Ohio. * * *

The operative facts in the present case include Bird's allegation that the Dotster defendants committed copyright and trademark law violations by registering Parsons's domain name efinancia.com. Both the Dotster defendants' contacts with Ohio and Bird's claim of copyright and trademark violations stem from these defendants' operation of the Dotster website. As a result, the operative facts are at least marginally related to the alleged contacts between the Dotster defendants and Ohio. * * *

The final requirement * * * is that the exercise of jurisdiction be reasonable in light of the connection that allegedly exists between the Dotster defendants and Ohio. * * *

Although the Dotster defendants might face a burden in having to defend a lawsuit in Ohio, they cannot reasonably object to this burden given that Dotster has allegedly transacted business with 4,666 Ohio residents. Ohio has a legitimate interest in protecting the business interests of its citizens, *even though all of Bird's claims involve federal law.* Bird has an obvious interest in obtaining relief, and *Ohio might be the only forum where jurisdiction would exist over all of the defendants.* Although the state of Washington also has an interest in this dispute, because the claim involves its citizens, this interest does not override the other factors suggesting that personal jurisdiction in Ohio is reasonable. [Emphasis added.]

DECISION AND REMEDY The U.S. Court of Appeals for the Sixth Circuit concluded that the lower court erred in granting the Dotster defendants' motion to dismiss for lack of personal jurisdiction. Bird had established that the court's exercise of jurisdiction over the Dotster defendants was proper.

WHY IS THIS CASE IMPORTANT? *This case illustrates how defendants can be sued in states in which they may never have been physically present, provided they have had sufficient contact with that state's residents over the Internet.*

International Jurisdictional Issues As noted in Chapter 1, because the Internet is international in scope, international jurisdictional issues understandably have come to the fore. What seems to be emerging in the world's courts is a standard that echoes the "minimum-contacts" requirement applied by the U.S. courts. Most courts are indicating that minimum contacts—doing business within the jurisdiction, for example—are enough to compel a defendant to appear and that a physical presence is not necessary. The effect of this standard is that a business firm must comply with the laws in any jurisdiction in which it targets customers for its products.

VENUE

VENUE
The geographic district in which an action is tried and from which the jury is selected.

Jurisdiction has to do with whether a court has authority to hear a case involving specific persons, property, or subject matter. **Venue**[6] is concerned with the most appropriate location for a trial. Two state courts (or two federal courts) may have the authority to exercise jurisdiction over a case, but it may be more appropriate or convenient to hear the case in one court than in the other.

Basically, the concept of venue reflects the policy that a court trying a suit should be in the geographic neighborhood (usually the county) where the incident leading to the lawsuit occurred or where the parties involved in the lawsuit reside. Venue in a civil case typically is where the defendant resides, whereas venue in a criminal case is normally where the crime occurred. Pretrial publicity or other factors, though, may require a change of venue to another community, especially in criminal cases when the defendant's right to a fair and impartial jury has been impaired. ■ EXAMPLE 3.5 A change of venue from Oklahoma City to Denver, Colorado, was ordered for the trials of Timothy McVeigh and Terry Nichols, who had been indicted in connection with the 1995 bombing of the Alfred P. Murrah Federal Building in Oklahoma City. (At trial, both McVeigh and Nichols were convicted. McVeigh received the death penalty and was put to death by lethal injection in early 2001. Nichols was sentenced to life imprisonment.) ■

STANDING TO SUE

STANDING TO SUE
The requirement that an individual must have a sufficient stake in a controversy before he or she can bring a lawsuit. The plaintiff must demonstrate that he or she has been either injured or threatened with injury.

Before a person can bring a lawsuit before a court, the party must have **standing to sue,** or a sufficient "stake" in a matter to justify seeking relief through the court system. In other words, to have standing, a party must have a legally protected and tangible interest at stake in the litigation. The party bringing the lawsuit must have suffered a harm, or have been threatened by a harm, as a result of the action about which she or he has complained. At times, a person will have standing to sue on behalf of another person. ■ EXAMPLE 3.6 Suppose that a child suffered serious injuries as a result of a defectively manufactured toy. Because the child is a minor, a lawsuit could be brought on his or her behalf by another person, such as the child's parent or legal guardian. ■

JUSTICIABLE CONTROVERSY
A controversy that is not hypothetical or academic but real and substantial; a requirement that must be satisfied before a court will hear a case.

Standing to sue also requires that the controversy at issue be a **justiciable**[7] **controversy**—a controversy that is real and substantial, as opposed to hypothetical or academic. ■ EXAMPLE 3.7 In the above example, the child's parent could not sue the toy manufacturer merely on the ground that the toy was defective. The issue would become justiciable only if the child had actually been injured due to the defect in the toy as marketed. In other words, the parent normally could not ask the court to determine, for example, what damages might be obtained if the child had been injured, because this would be merely a hypothetical question. ■

6. Pronounced *ven-yoo.*

7. Pronounced jus-*tish*-uh-bul.

The State and Federal Court Systems

As mentioned earlier in this chapter, each state has its own court system. Additionally, there is a system of federal courts. Although state court systems differ, Exhibit 3–2 illustrates the basic organizational structure characteristic of the court systems in many states. The exhibit also shows how the federal court system is structured. We turn now to an examination of these court systems, beginning with the state courts.

STATE COURT SYSTEMS

Typically, a state court system will include several levels, or tiers, of courts. As indicated in Exhibit 3–2, state courts may include (1) trial courts of limited jurisdiction, (2) trial courts of general jurisdiction, (3) appellate courts, and (4) the state's highest court (often called the state supreme court). Generally, any person who is a party to a lawsuit has the opportunity to plead the case before a trial court and then, if he or she loses, before at least one level of appellate court. Finally, if a federal statute or federal constitutional issue is involved in the decision of the state supreme court, that decision may be further appealed to the United States Supreme Court.

Judges in the state court system are usually elected by the voters for a specified term. State judicial elections or appointments vary significantly, however, from state to state. For example, in Iowa the governor appoints judges, and then the general population decides whether to confirm their appointment in the next general election. The states usually specify the number of years that the judge will serve. In contrast, as you will read shortly, judges in the federal court system are appointed by the president of the United States and, if they are confirmed by the Senate, hold office for life—unless they engage in blatantly illegal conduct.

> **.on the Web** If you want to find information on state court systems, the National Center for State Courts (NCSC) offers links to the Web pages of all state courts at
> **http://www.ncsconline.org**.

Trial Courts Trial courts are exactly what their name implies—courts in which trials are held and testimony taken. State trial courts have either general or limited jurisdiction. Trial courts that have general jurisdiction as to subject matter may be

EXHIBIT 3–2 FEDERAL COURTS AND STATE COURT SYSTEMS

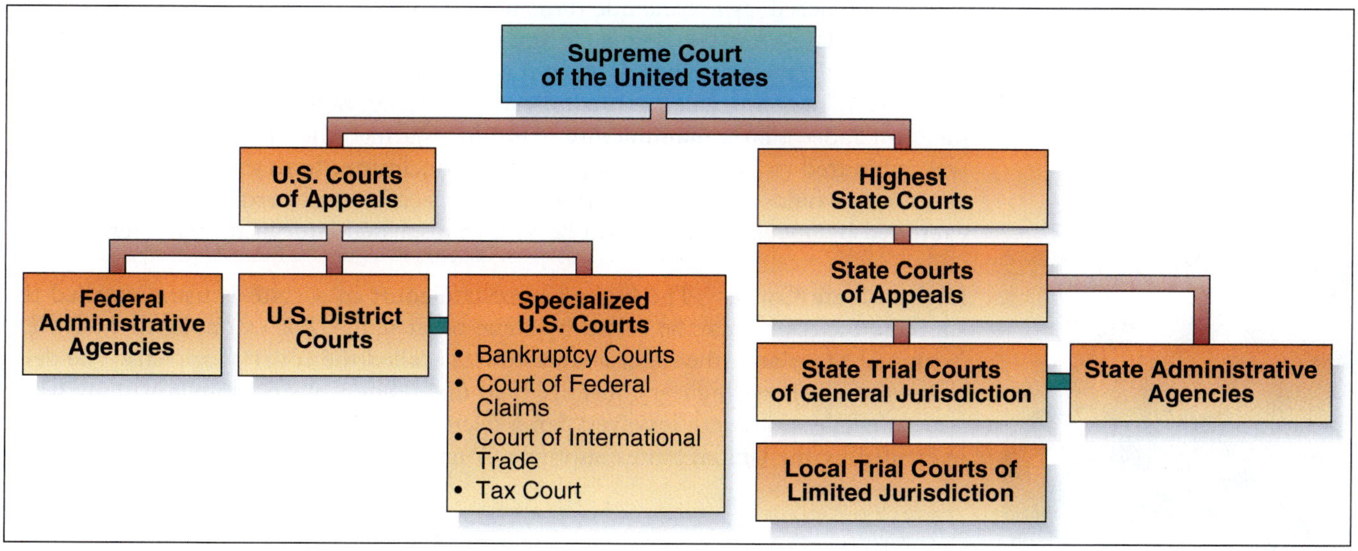

called county, district, superior, or circuit courts.[8] The jurisdiction of these courts is often determined by the size of the county in which the court sits. State trial courts of general jurisdiction have jurisdiction over a wide variety of subjects, including both civil disputes and criminal prosecutions.

SMALL CLAIMS COURT
A special court in which parties may litigate small claims (such as $5,000 or less). Attorneys are not required in small claims courts and, in some states, are not allowed to represent the parties.

Some courts of limited jurisdiction are called special inferior trial courts or minor judiciary courts. **Small claims courts** are inferior trial courts that hear only civil cases involving claims of less than a certain amount, such as $5,000 (the amount varies from state to state). Suits brought in small claims courts are generally conducted informally, and lawyers are not required. In a minority of states, lawyers are not even allowed to represent people in small claims courts for most purposes. Another example of an inferior trial court is a local municipal court that hears mainly traffic cases. Decisions of small claims courts and municipal courts may sometimes be appealed to a state trial court of general jurisdiction.

Other courts of limited jurisdiction as to subject matter include domestic relations courts, which handle primarily divorce actions and child-custody disputes, and probate courts, as mentioned earlier.

Appellate, or Reviewing, Courts Every state has at least one court of appeals (appellate court, or reviewing court), which may be an intermediate appellate court or the state's highest court. About three-fourths of the states have intermediate appellate courts. Generally, courts of appeals do not conduct new trials, in which evidence is submitted to the court and witnesses are examined. Rather, an appellate court panel of three or more judges reviews the record of the case on appeal, which includes a transcript of the trial proceedings, and determines whether the trial court committed an error.

Usually, appellate courts do not look at questions of *fact* (such as whether a party did, in fact, commit a certain action, such as burning a flag) but at questions of *law* (such as whether the act of flag-burning is a form of speech protected by the First Amendment to the Constitution). Only a judge, not a jury, can rule on questions of law. Appellate courts normally defer to a trial court's findings on questions of fact because the trial court judge and jury were in a better position to evaluate testimony—by directly observing witnesses' gestures, demeanor, and nonverbal behavior during the trial. At the appellate level, the judges review the written transcript of the trial, which does not include these nonverbal elements.

BE CAREFUL The decisions of a state's highest court are final on questions of state law.

An appellate court will challenge a trial court's finding of fact only when the finding is clearly erroneous (that is, when it is contrary to the evidence presented at trial) or when there is no evidence to support the finding. ■ EXAMPLE 3.8 Suppose that a jury concluded that a manufacturer's product harmed the plaintiff but no evidence was submitted to the court to support that conclusion. In that situation, the appellate court would hold that the trial court's decision was erroneous. (The options exercised by appellate courts will be further discussed later in this chapter.) ■

A mother talks with a social worker after a court awarded the mother custody of her child. Are child-custody matters decided by federal or state courts? (Albuquerque Journal, *Mark Holm/AP Photo)*

Highest State Courts The highest appellate court in a state is usually called the supreme court but may be called by some other name. For example, in both New York and Maryland, the highest state court is called the court of appeals. The decisions of each state's highest court are final on all questions of state law. Only when issues of federal law are involved can a decision made by a state's highest court be overruled by the United States Supreme Court.

8. The name in Ohio is court of common pleas; the name in New York is supreme court.

THE FEDERAL COURT SYSTEM

The federal court system is basically a three-tiered model consisting of (1) U.S. district courts (trial courts of general jurisdiction) and various courts of limited jurisdiction, (2) U.S. courts of appeals (intermediate courts of appeals), and (3) the United States Supreme Court.

Unlike state court judges, who are usually elected, federal court judges—including the justices of the Supreme Court—are appointed by the president of the United States and confirmed by the U.S. Senate. All federal judges receive lifetime appointments (because under Article III they "hold their offices during Good Behavior").

on the Web To find information about the federal court system and links to all federal courts, go to the home page of the federal judiciary at **http://www.uscourts.gov**.

U.S. District Courts At the federal level, the equivalent of a state trial court of general jurisdiction is the district court. There is at least one federal district court in every state. The number of judicial districts can vary over time, primarily owing to population changes and corresponding caseloads. Currently, there are ninety-four federal judicial districts.

U.S. district courts have original jurisdiction in federal matters. Federal cases typically originate in district courts. There are other courts with original, but special (or limited), jurisdiction, such as the federal bankruptcy courts and others shown in Exhibit 3–2 on page 71.

U.S. Courts of Appeals In the federal court system, there are thirteen U.S. courts of appeals—also referred to as U.S. circuit courts of appeals. The federal courts of appeals for twelve of the circuits, including the U.S. Court of Appeals for the District of Columbia Circuit, hear appeals from the federal district courts located within their respective judicial circuits. The Court of Appeals for the Thirteenth Circuit, called the Federal Circuit, has national appellate jurisdiction over certain types of cases, such as cases involving patent law and cases in which the U.S. government is a defendant.

The decisions of the circuit courts of appeals are final in most cases, but appeal to the United States Supreme Court is possible. Exhibit 3–3 on the following page shows the geographic boundaries of the U.S. circuit courts of appeals and the boundaries of the U.S. district courts within each circuit.

The United States Supreme Court The highest level of the three-tiered model of the federal court system is the United States Supreme Court. According to the language of Article III of the U.S. Constitution, there is only one national Supreme Court. All other courts in the federal system are considered "inferior." Congress is empowered to create other inferior courts as it deems necessary. The inferior courts that Congress has created include the second tier in our model—the U.S. courts of appeals—as well as the district courts and any other courts of limited, or specialized, jurisdiction.

The United States Supreme Court consists of nine justices. Although the Supreme Court has original, or trial, jurisdiction in rare instances (set forth in Article III, Section 2), most of its work is as an appeals court. The Supreme Court can review any case decided by any of the federal courts of appeals, and it also has appellate authority over some cases decided in the state courts.

WRIT OF *CERTIORARI*
A writ from a higher court asking the lower court for the record of a case.

Appeals to the Supreme Court. To bring a case before the Supreme Court, a party requests the Court to issue a writ of *certiorari.* A **writ of *certiorari***[9] is an order

9. Pronounced sur-shee-uh-*rah*-ree.

issued by the Supreme Court to a lower court requiring the latter to send it the record of the case for review. The Court will not issue a writ unless at least four of the nine justices approve of it. This is called the **rule of four.** Whether the Court will issue a writ of *certiorari* is entirely within its discretion. The Court is not required to issue one, and most petitions for writs are denied. (Thousands of cases are filed with the Supreme Court each year; yet it hears, on average, fewer than one hundred of these cases.)[10] A denial is not a decision on the merits of a case, nor does it indicate agreement with the lower court's opinion. Furthermore, a denial of the writ has no value as a precedent.

RULE OF FOUR
A rule of the United States Supreme Court under which the Court will not issue a writ of *certiorari* unless at least four justices approve of the decision to issue the writ.

on the Web To access Supreme Court opinions, as well as information about the history and function of the Court, go to the Court's official Web site at **http://supremecourtus.gov**.

Petitions Granted by the Court. Typically, the Court grants petitions when cases raise important constitutional questions or conflict with other state or federal court decisions. Similarly, if federal appellate courts are rendering inconsistent opinions on an important issue, the Supreme Court may review the case and issue a decision to define the law on the matter. The justices, however, never explain their reasons for hearing certain cases and not others, so it is difficult to predict which type of case the Court might select.

10. From the mid-1950s through the early 1990s, the Supreme Court reviewed more cases per year than it has in the last few years. In the Court's 1982–1983 term, for example, the Court issued opinions in 151 cases. In contrast, in its 2004–2005 term, the Court issued opinions in only 80 cases.

EXHIBIT 3–3 BOUNDARIES OF THE U.S. COURTS OF APPEALS AND U.S. DISTRICT COURTS

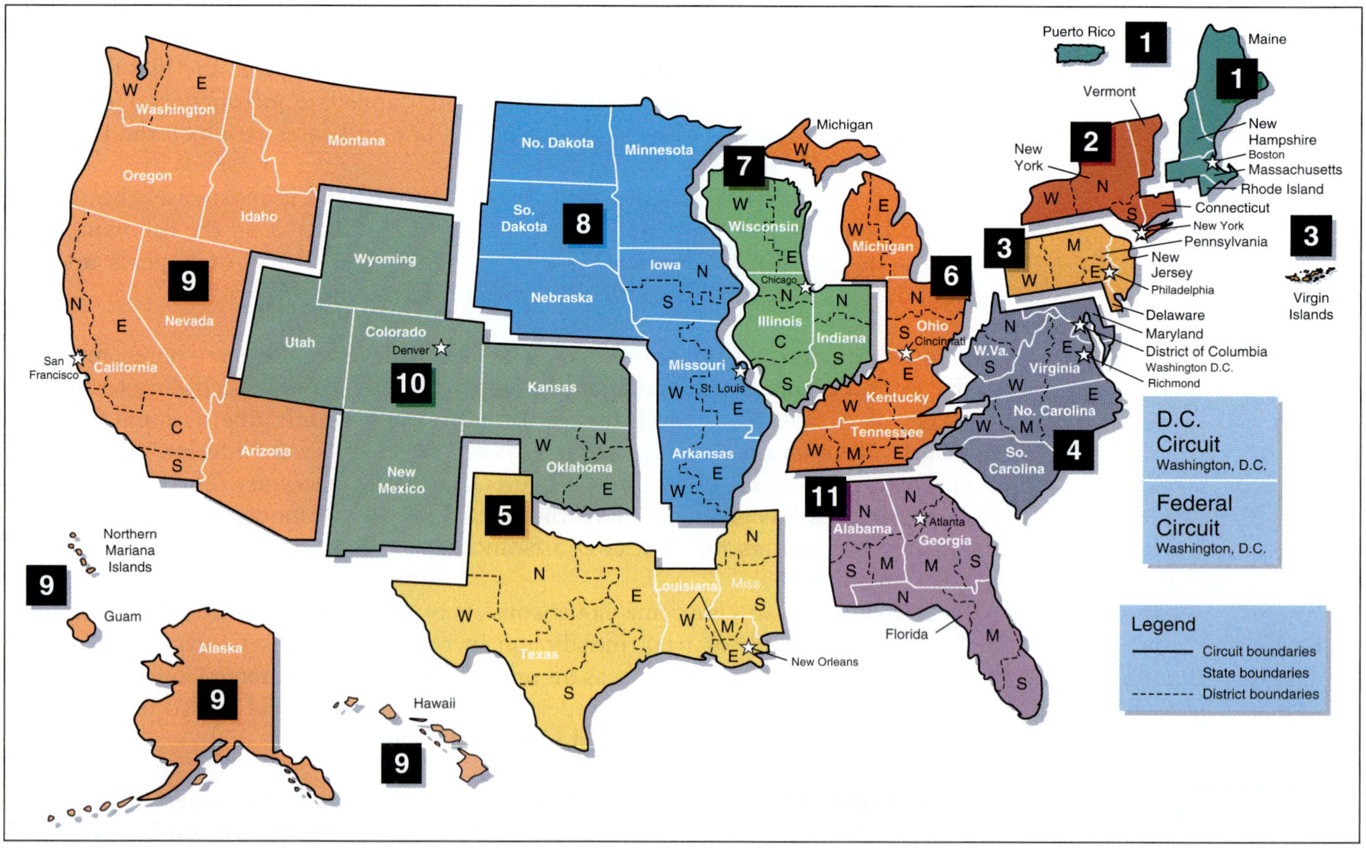

Source: Administrative Office of the United States Courts.

Following a State Court Case

To illustrate the procedures that would be followed in a civil lawsuit brought in a state court, we present a hypothetical case and follow it through the state court system. The case involves an automobile accident in which Kevin Anderson, driving a Mercedes, struck Lisa Marconi, driving a Ford Taurus. The accident occurred at the intersection of Wilshire Boulevard and Rodeo Drive in Beverly Hills, California. Marconi suffered personal injuries, incurring medical and hospital expenses as well as lost wages for four months. Anderson and Marconi are unable to agree on a settlement, and Marconi sues Anderson. Marconi is the plaintiff, and Anderson is the defendant. Both are represented by lawyers.

LITIGATION
The process of resolving a dispute through the court system.

During each phase of the **litigation** (the process of working a lawsuit through the court system), Marconi and Anderson will be required to observe strict procedural requirements. A large body of law—procedural law—establishes the rules and standards for determining disputes in courts. Procedural rules are very complex, and they vary from court to court and from state to state. There is a set of federal rules of procedure as well as various sets of rules for state courts. Additionally, the applicable procedures will depend on whether the case is a civil or criminal proceeding. Generally, the Marconi-Anderson civil lawsuit will involve the procedures discussed in the following subsections. Keep in mind that attempts to settle the case may be ongoing throughout the trial.

The Pleadings

PLEADINGS
Statements made by the plaintiff and the defendant in a lawsuit that detail the facts, charges, and defenses involved in the litigation. The complaint and answer are part of the pleadings.

COMPLAINT
The pleading made by a plaintiff alleging wrongdoing on the part of the defendant; the document that, when filed with a court, initiates a lawsuit.

SUMMONS
A document informing a defendant that a legal action has been commenced against him or her and that the defendant must appear in court on a certain date to answer the plaintiff's complaint. The document is delivered by a sheriff or any other person so authorized.

DEFAULT JUDGMENT
A judgment entered by a court against a defendant who has failed to appear in court to answer or defend against the plaintiff's claim.

ANSWER
Procedurally, a defendant's response to the plaintiff's complaint.

The complaint and answer (and the counterclaim and reply)—all of which are discussed below—taken together are called the **pleadings.** The pleadings inform each party of the other's claims and specify the issues (disputed questions) involved in the case. Because the rules of procedure vary depending on the jurisdiction of the court, the style and form of the pleadings may look quite different in different states.

The Plaintiff's Complaint Marconi's suit against Anderson commences when her lawyer files a **complaint** with the appropriate court. The complaint contains a statement alleging (asserting to the court, in a pleading) the facts necessary for the court to take jurisdiction, a brief summary of the facts necessary to show that the plaintiff is entitled to a remedy, and a statement of the remedy the plaintiff is seeking. Exhibit 3–4 on the following page illustrates how the complaint might read in the Marconi-Anderson case. Complaints may be lengthy or brief, depending on the complexity of the case and the rules of the jurisdiction.

After the complaint has been filed, the sheriff, a deputy of the county, or another *process server* (one who delivers a complaint and summons) serves a **summons** and a copy of the complaint on defendant Anderson. The summons notifies Anderson that he must file an answer to the complaint with both the court and the plaintiff's attorney within a specified time period (usually twenty to thirty days). The summons also informs Anderson that failure to answer may result in a **default judgment** for the plaintiff, meaning the plaintiff will be awarded the damages alleged in her complaint.

The Defendant's Answer The defendant's **answer** either admits the statements or allegations set forth in the complaint or denies them and outlines any defenses that the defendant may have. If Anderson admits to all of Marconi's allegations in his answer, the court will enter a judgment for Marconi. If Anderson denies any of Marconi's allegations, the litigation will go forward.

EXHIBIT 3–4 EXAMPLE OF A TYPICAL COMPLAINT

IN THE LOS ANGELES SUPERIOR COURT
COUNTY OF LOS ANGELES, STATE OF CALIFORNIA

Lisa Marconi Plaintiff, v. Kevin Anderson Defendant.	CIVIL NO. 8–1026 COMPLAINT

Comes now the plaintiff and for her cause of action against the defendant alleges and states as follows:

1. The jurisdiction of this court is based on Section 86 of the California Civil Code.
2. This action is between plaintiff, a California resident living at 1434 Palm Drive, Anaheim, California, and defendant, a California resident living at 6950 Garrison Avenue, Los Angeles, California.
3. On September 10, 2006, plaintiff, Lisa Marconi, was exercising good driving habits and reasonable care in driving her car through the intersection of Rodeo Drive and Wilshire Boulevard when defendant, Kevin Anderson, negligently drove his vehicle through a red light at the intersection and collided with plaintiff's vehicle. Defendant was negligent in the operation of the vehicle as to:
   a. Speed,
   b. Lookout,
   c. Management and control.
4. As a result of the collision, plaintiff suffered severe physical injury that prevented her from working and property damage to her car. The costs she incurred included $10,000 in medical bills, $9,000 in lost wages, and $5,000 for automobile repairs.

WHEREFORE, plaintiff demands judgment against the defendant for the sum of $24,000 plus interest at the maximum legal rate and the costs of this action.

By *Roger Harrington*
Roger Harrington
Attorney for the Plaintiff
800 Orange Avenue
Anaheim, CA 91426

COUNTERCLAIM
A claim made by a defendant in a civil lawsuit against the plaintiff. In effect, the defendant is suing the plaintiff.

REPLY
Procedurally, a plaintiff's response to a defendant's answer.

Anderson can deny Marconi's allegations and set forth his own claim that Marconi was in fact negligent and therefore owes him for the damages to his Mercedes. This is appropriately called a **counterclaim.** If Anderson files a counterclaim, Marconi will have to answer it with a pleading, normally called a **reply,** which has the same characteristics as an answer.

Anderson can also admit the truth of Marconi's complaint but raise new facts that may result in dismissal of the action. This is called *raising an affirmative defense*. For example, Anderson could assert the expiration of the time period under the relevant statute of limitations (a state or federal statute that sets the maximum time period during which a certain action can be brought or rights enforced) as an affirmative defense.

MOTION TO DISMISS
A pleading in which a defendant asserts that the plaintiff's claim fails to state a cause of action (that is, has no basis in law) or that there are other grounds on which a suit should be dismissed.

Motion to Dismiss A **motion to dismiss** requests the court to dismiss the case for stated reasons. A defendant often makes a motion to dismiss before filing an answer to the plaintiff's complaint. Grounds for dismissal of a case include improper delivery of the complaint and summons, improper venue, and the plaintiff's failure to state a claim for which a court could grant relief (a remedy). For example, if Marconi had suffered no injuries or losses as a result of Anderson's negligence, Anderson could move to have the case dismissed because Marconi had not stated a claim for which relief could be granted.

If the judge grants the motion to dismiss, the plaintiff generally is given time to file an amended complaint. If the judge denies the motion, the suit will go forward, and the defendant must then file an answer. Note that if Marconi wishes to discontinue the suit because, for example, an out-of-court settlement has been reached, she can likewise move for dismissal. The court can also dismiss the case on its own motion.

PRETRIAL MOTIONS

Either party may attempt to get the case dismissed before trial through the use of various pretrial motions. We have already mentioned the motion to dismiss. Two other important pretrial motions are the motion for judgment on the pleadings and the motion for summary judgment.

MOTION FOR JUDGMENT ON THE PLEADINGS
A motion by either party to a lawsuit at the close of the pleadings requesting the court to decide the issue solely on the pleadings without proceeding to trial. The motion will be granted only if no facts are in dispute.

MOTION FOR SUMMARY JUDGMENT
A motion requesting the court to enter a judgment without proceeding to trial. The motion can be based on evidence outside the pleadings and will be granted only if no facts are in dispute.

At the close of the pleadings, either party may make a **motion for judgment on the pleadings,** or on the merits of the case. The judge will grant the motion only when there is no dispute over the facts of the case and the sole issue to be resolved is a question of law. In deciding on the motion, the judge may consider only the evidence contained in the pleadings.

In contrast, in a **motion for summary judgment** the court may consider evidence outside the pleadings, such as sworn statements (affidavits) by parties or witnesses or other documents relating to the case. A motion for summary judgment can be made by either party. As with the motion for judgment on the pleadings, a motion for summary judgment will be granted only if there are no genuine questions of fact and the sole question is a question of law.

DISCOVERY

DISCOVERY
A phase in the litigation process during which the opposing parties may obtain information from each other and from third parties prior to trial.

Before a trial begins, each party can use a number of procedural devices to obtain information and gather evidence about the case from the other party or from third parties. The process of obtaining such information is known as **discovery.** Discovery includes gaining access to witnesses, documents, records, and other types of evidence.

The Federal Rules of Civil Procedure and similar rules in the states set forth the guidelines for discovery activity. The rules governing discovery are designed to make sure that a witness or a party is not unduly harassed, that privileged material (communications that need not be presented in court) is safeguarded, and that only matters relevant to the case at hand are discoverable.

Discovery prevents surprises at trial by giving parties access to evidence that might otherwise be hidden. This allows both parties to learn as much as they can about what to expect at a trial before they reach the courtroom. It also serves to narrow the issues so that trial time is spent on the main questions in the case.

DEPOSITION
The testimony of a party to a lawsuit or a witness taken under oath before a trial.

Depositions and Interrogatories Discovery can involve the use of depositions or interrogatories, or both. **Depositions** are sworn testimony by a party to the lawsuit or any witness. The person being deposed (the deponent) answers questions asked by the attorneys, and the questions and answers are recorded by an authorized court official and sworn to and signed by the deponent. (Occasionally, written depositions are taken when witnesses are unable to appear in person.) The answers given to depositions will, of course, help the attorneys prepare their cases. They can also be used in court to impeach (challenge the credibility of) a party or a witness who changes testimony at the trial. In addition, the answers given in a deposition can be used as testimony if the witness is not available at trial.

INTERROGATORIES
A series of written questions for which written answers are prepared, usually with the assistance of the party's attorney, and then signed under oath by a party to a lawsuit.

Interrogatories are written questions for which written answers are prepared and then signed under oath. The main difference between interrogatories and written depositions is that interrogatories are directed to a party to the lawsuit (the plaintiff or the defendant), not to a witness, and the party can prepare answers with the aid of an attorney. The scope of interrogatories is broader because parties are obligated to answer questions, even if that means disclosing information from their records and files.

Other Information A party can serve a written request on the other party for an admission of the truth of matters relating to the trial. Any matter admitted under such a request is conclusively established for the trial. For example, Marconi can ask Anderson to admit that he was driving at a speed of forty-five miles an hour. A request for admission saves time at trial because the parties will not have to spend time proving facts on which they already agree.

A party can also gain access to documents and other items not in her or his possession in order to inspect and examine them. Likewise, a party can gain "entry upon land" to inspect the premises. Anderson's attorney, for example, normally can gain permission to inspect and duplicate Marconi's car repair bills.

When the physical or mental condition of one party is in question, the opposing party can ask the court to order a physical or mental examination. If the court is willing to make the order, which it will do only if the need for the information outweighs the right to privacy of the person to be examined, the opposing party can obtain the results of the examination.

E-EVIDENCE
A type of evidence that consists of computer-generated or electronically recorded information, including e-mail, voice mail, spreadsheets, word-processing documents, and other data.

Electronic Discovery Any relevant material, including information stored electronically, can be the object of a discovery request. Electronic evidence, or **e-evidence,** consists of all types of computer-generated or electronically recorded information, including e-mail, voice mail, spreadsheets, word-processing documents, and other data. E-evidence is important because it can reveal significant facts that are not discoverable by other means. For example, whenever a person is working on a computer, information is being recorded on the hard drive disk without ever being saved by the user. This information includes the file's location, path, creator, date created, date last accessed, concealed notes, earlier versions, passwords, and formatting. It reveals information about how, when, and by whom a document was created, accessed, modified, and transmitted. This information can be obtained from the file only in its electronic format—not from printed-out versions.

The federal rules and most state rules (as well as court decisions) now specifically allow parties to obtain discovery of electronic "data compilations" (or e-evidence). Although traditional means, such as interrogatories and depositions, may still be used to find out about the e-evidence, the parties must usually hire an expert to retrieve the evidence in its electronic format. Using special software, the expert can reconstruct e-mail exchanges to establish who knew what and when they knew it. The expert can even recover files from a computer that the user thought had been deleted. Reviewing back-up copies of documents and e-mail can provide useful—and often quite damaging—information about how a particular matter progressed over several weeks or months.

Although electronic discovery has significant advantages over paper discovery, it is also time consuming and expensive. Who should pay the costs associated with electronic discovery? This chapter's *Adapting the Law to the Online Environment* feature on the next page discusses how the law is evolving to address this issue.

PRETRIAL CONFERENCE

Either party or the court can request a pretrial conference, or hearing. Usually, the hearing consists of an informal discussion between the judge and the opposing attorneys after discovery has taken place. The purpose of the hearing is to explore the possibility of a settlement without trial and, if this is not possible, to identify the matters that are in dispute and to plan the course of the trial.

JURY SELECTION

A trial can be held with or without a jury. The Seventh Amendment to the U.S. Constitution guarantees the right to a jury trial for cases in federal courts when the amount in controversy exceeds $20. Most states have similar guarantees in their own constitutions (although the threshold dollar amount is higher than $20). The right to a trial by jury does not have to be exercised, and many cases are tried without a jury. In most states and in federal courts, one of the parties must request a jury, or the right is presumed to be waived.

Before a jury trial commences, a jury must be selected. The jury selection process is known as ***voir dire.***[11] During *voir dire* in most jurisdictions, attorneys for the plaintiff and the defendant ask prospective jurors oral questions to determine whether a potential jury member is biased or has any connection with a party to the action or with a prospective witness. In some jurisdictions, the judge may do all or part of the questioning based on written questions submitted by counsel for the parties.

During *voir dire,* a party may challenge a certain number of prospective jurors *peremptorily*—that is, ask that an individual not be sworn in as a juror without providing any reason. Alternatively, a party may challenge a prospective juror *for cause*—that is, provide a reason why an individual should not be sworn in as a juror. If the judge grants the challenge, the individual is asked to step down. A prospective juror may not be excluded from the jury by the use of discriminatory challenges, however, such as those based on racial criteria[12] or gender.[13]

.on the Web Picking the "right" jury is often an important aspect of litigation strategy, and a number of firms now specialize in jury consulting services. You can learn more about these services by going to the Web site of the Jury Research Institute at **http://www.jri-inc.com**.

VOIR DIRE
An old French phrase meaning "to speak the truth." In legal language, the phrase refers to the process in which the attorneys question prospective jurors to learn about their backgrounds, attitudes, biases, and other characteristics that may affect their ability to serve as impartial jurors.

TAKE NOTE A prospective juror cannot be excluded solely on the basis of his or her race or gender.

11. Pronounced vwahr *deehr.*
12. *Batson v. Kentucky,* 476 U.S. 79, 106 S.Ct. 1712, 90 L.Ed.2d 69 (1986).
13. *J.E.B. v. Alabama ex rel. T.B.,* 511 U.S. 127, 114 S.Ct. 1419, 128 L.Ed.2d 89 (1994). (*Ex rel.* is Latin for *ex relatione.* The phrase refers to an action brought on behalf of the state, by the attorney general, at the instigation of an individual who has a private interest in the matter.)

ADAPTING THE LAW TO THE ONLINE ENVIRONMENT

Who Bears the Costs of Electronic Discovery?

Traditionally, the party responding to a discovery request must pay the expenses involved in obtaining the requested materials. If compliance would be too burdensome or too costly, however, the judge can either limit the scope of the request or shift some or all of the costs to the requesting party. How do these traditional rules governing discovery apply to requests for electronic evidence?

WHY COURTS MIGHT SHIFT THE COSTS OF ELECTRONIC DISCOVERY

Electronic discovery has dramatically increased the costs associated with complying with discovery requests. It is no longer simply a matter of photocopying paper documents. Now the responding party may need to hire computer forensics experts to make "image" copies of desktop, laptop, and server hard drives, as well as removable storage media (including CD-ROMs, DVDs, and Zip drives), back-up tapes, voice mail, cell phones, and any other device that digitally stores data.

In cases involving multiple parties or large corporations with many offices and employees, the electronic discovery process can easily run into hundreds of thousands—if not millions—of dollars. For example, in one case concert promoters alleged that thirty separate defendant companies had engaged in discriminatory practices. The federal district court hearing the case found that the complete restoration of the back-up tapes of just one of those defendants would cost $9.75 million. Acquiring 200,000 e-mail messages from another defendant would cost between $43,000 and $84,000, with an additional $247,000 to have an attorney review the retrieved documents. Restoring the 523 back-up tapes of a third defendant would cost $395,000 and another $120,000 for the attorney to review them. The judge hearing the case decided that both plaintiffs and defendants would share in these discovery costs.[a]

WHAT FACTORS DO COURTS CONSIDER IN DECIDING WHETHER TO SHIFT COSTS?

Increasingly, the courts are shifting part of the costs of obtaining electronic discovery to the party requesting it (which is usually the plaintiff). At what point, however, should this cost-shifting occur? In *Zubulake v. UBS Warburg LLC*,[b] the court identified a three-step analysis for deciding disputes over discovery costs. First, if the data are kept in an accessible format, the usual rules of discovery apply: the responding party should pay the costs of producing responsive data. A court should consider cost-shifting *only* when electronic data are in a relatively inaccessible form, such as in back-up tapes or deleted files. Second, the court should determine what data may be found on the inaccessible media. Requiring the responding party to restore and produce responsive documents from a small sample of the requested medium is a sensible approach in most cases. Third, the court should consider a series of other factors, including, for example, the availability of the information from other sources, the total cost of production compared to the amount in controversy, and each party's ability to pay these costs.

FOR CRITICAL ANALYSIS

The court in the Zubulake *case noted that "as large companies increasingly move to entirely paper-free environments, the frequent use of cost-shifting will have the effect of crippling discovery," especially in cases in which private parties are suing large corporations. Why might cost-shifting thwart discovery? Who would benefit if courts considered cost-shifting in every case involving electronic discovery?*

a. *Rowe Entertainment, Inc. v. William Morris Agency*, 2002 WL 975713 (S.D.N.Y.).

b. 2003 WL 21087884 (S.D.N.Y.).

AT THE TRIAL

At the beginning of the trial, the attorneys present their opening arguments, setting forth the facts that they expect to provide during the trial. Then the plaintiff's case is presented. In our hypothetical case, Marconi's lawyer would introduce evidence (relevant documents, exhibits, and the testimony of witnesses) to support Marconi's position. The defendant has the opportunity to challenge any evidence introduced and to cross-examine any of the plaintiff's witnesses.

At the end of the plaintiff's case, the defendant's attorney has the opportunity to ask the judge to direct a verdict for the defendant on the ground that the plaintiff has presented no evidence that would justify the granting of the plaintiff's remedy. This is called a **motion for a directed verdict** (known in federal courts as a *motion for judgment as a matter of law*). If the motion is not granted (it seldom is), the defendant's attorney then presents the evidence and witnesses for the defendant's case. At the conclusion of the defendant's case, the defendant's attorney has another opportunity to make a motion for a directed verdict. The plaintiff's attorney can challenge any evidence introduced and cross-examine the defendant's witnesses.

MOTION FOR A DIRECTED VERDICT
In a jury trial, a motion for the judge to take the decision out of the hands of the jury and to direct a verdict for the party who filed the motion on the ground that the other party has not produced sufficient evidence to support her or his claim.

After the defense concludes its presentation, the attorneys present their closing arguments, each urging a verdict in favor of her or his client. The judge instructs the jury in the law that applies to the case (these instructions are often called *charges*), and the jury retires to the jury room to deliberate a verdict. In the Marconi-Anderson case, the jury will not only decide for the plaintiff or for the defendant but, if it finds for the plaintiff, will also decide on the amount of the **award** (the money to be paid to her).

AWARD
In litigation, the amount of money awarded to a plaintiff in a civil lawsuit as damages. In the context of alternative dispute resolution, the decision rendered by an arbitrator.

POSTTRIAL MOTIONS

After the jury has rendered its verdict, either party may make a posttrial motion. If Marconi wins, and Anderson's attorney has previously moved for a directed verdict, Anderson's attorney may make a **motion for judgment *n.o.v.*** (from the Latin *non obstante veredicto,* which means "notwithstanding the verdict"—called a *motion for judgment as a matter of law* in the federal courts) in Anderson's favor on the ground that the jury's verdict in favor of Marconi was unreasonable and erroneous. If the judge decides that the jury's verdict was reasonable in light of the evidence presented at trial, the motion will be denied. If the judge agrees with Anderson's attorney, then he or she will set the jury's verdict aside and enter a judgment in favor of Anderson.

MOTION FOR JUDGMENT *N.O.V.*
A motion requesting the court to grant judgment in favor of the party making the motion on the ground that the jury's verdict against him or her was unreasonable and erroneous.

Alternatively, Anderson could make a **motion for a new trial,** requesting the judge to set aside the adverse verdict and to hold a new trial. The motion will be granted if the judge is convinced, after looking at all the evidence, that the jury was in error but does not feel it is appropriate to grant judgment for the other side. A new trial may also be granted on the ground of newly discovered evidence, misconduct by the participants or the jury during the trial, or error by the judge.

MOTION FOR A NEW TRIAL
A motion asserting that the trial was so fundamentally flawed (because of error, newly discovered evidence, prejudice, or other reason) that a new trial is necessary to prevent a miscarriage of justice.

THE APPEAL

Assume here that any posttrial motion is denied and that Anderson appeals the case. (If Marconi wins but receives a smaller money award than she sought, she can appeal also.) A notice of appeal must be filed with the clerk of the trial court within a prescribed time. Anderson now becomes the appellant, or petitioner, and Marconi becomes the appellee, or respondent.

Filing the Appeal Anderson's attorney files with the appellate court the record on appeal, which includes the pleadings, the trial transcript, the judge's rulings on motions made by the parties, and other trial-related documents. Anderson's attorney will also provide a condensation of the record, known as an *abstract,* which is filed with the reviewing court along with the brief. The **brief** is a formal legal document outlining the facts and issues of the case, the judge's rulings or jury's findings that should be reversed or modified, the applicable law, and arguments on Anderson's behalf (citing applicable statutes and relevant cases as precedents).

BRIEF
A formal legal document submitted by the attorney for the appellant or the appellee (in answer to the appellant's brief) to an appellate court when a case is appealed. The appellant's brief outlines the facts and issues of the case, the judge's rulings or jury's findings that should be reversed or modified, the applicable law, and the arguments on the client's behalf.

Marconi's attorney will file an answering brief. Anderson's attorney can file a reply to Marconi's brief, although it is not required. The reviewing court then considers the case.

Appellate Review As mentioned earlier, a court of appeals does not hear evidence. Rather, it reviews the record for errors of law. Its decision concerning a case is based on the record on appeal, the abstracts, and the attorneys' briefs. The attorneys can present oral arguments, after which the case is taken under advisement. In general, appellate courts do not reverse findings of fact unless the findings are unsupported or contradicted by the evidence.

If the reviewing court believes that an error was committed during the trial or that the jury was improperly instructed, the judgment will be *reversed*. Sometimes the case will be *remanded* (sent back to the court that originally heard the case) for a new trial. Even when a case is remanded to a trial court for further proceedings, however, the appellate court normally spells out how the relevant law should be interpreted and applied to the case.

■ EXAMPLE 3.9 A case may be remanded for several reasons. For instance, if the appellate court decides that a judge improperly granted summary judgment, the case will be remanded for a trial. If the appellate court decides that the trial judge erroneously applied the law, the case will be remanded for a new trial, with instructions to the trial court to apply the law as clarified by the appellate court. If the appellate court decides that the trial jury's award of damages was too high, the case will be remanded with instructions to reduce the damages award. ■ In most cases, the judgment of the lower court is *affirmed*, resulting in the enforcement of the court's judgment or decree.

Appeal to a Higher Appellate Court If the reviewing court is an intermediate appellate court, the losing party normally may appeal to the state supreme court (the highest state court). Such a petition corresponds to a petition for a writ of *certiorari* from the United States Supreme Court. If the petition is granted (in some states, a petition is automatically granted), new briefs must be filed before the state supreme court, and the attorneys may be allowed or requested to present oral arguments. Like the intermediate appellate court, the supreme court may reverse or affirm the appellate court's decision or remand the case. At this point, unless a federal question is at issue, the case has reached its end.

ENFORCING THE JUDGMENT

The uncertainties of the litigation process are compounded by the lack of guarantees that any judgment will be enforceable. Even if a plaintiff wins an award of damages in court, the defendant may not have sufficient assets or insurance to cover that amount. Usually, one of the factors considered before a lawsuit is initiated is whether the defendant has sufficient assets to cover the amount of damages sought, should the plaintiff win the case. What other factors should be considered when deciding whether to initiate a lawsuit? See the *Application* feature at the end of this chapter for answers to this question.

.on the Web For links to every trial-level court in the United States that has a Web site, go to the Web site of the Nation's Courts Directory at **http://www.courts.net**.

The Courts Adapt to the Online World

We have already mentioned that the courts have attempted to adapt traditional jurisdictional concepts to the online world. Not surprisingly, the Internet has also brought about changes in court procedures and practices, including new methods for filing pleadings and other documents and issuing decisions and opinions. Several courts are experimenting with electronic delivery, such as via the Internet or CD-ROM. Some jurisdictions are exploring the possibility of cyber courts, in which legal proceedings could be conducted totally online.

Electronic Filing

The federal court system first experimented with an electronic filing system in January 1996, in an asbestos case heard by the U.S. District Court for the Northern District of Ohio. Today, a number of federal courts permit attorneys to file documents electronically in certain types of cases. At last count, more than 130,000 documents in approximately 10,000 cases had been filed electronically in federal courts. The Administrative Office of the U.S. Courts is considering permitting electronic filing in all U.S. district courts nationwide.

State and local courts are also setting up electronic filing systems. Since the late 1990s, the court system in Pima County, Arizona, has been accepting pleadings via e-mail. The supreme court of the state of Washington also now accepts online filings of litigation documents. In addition, electronic filing projects are being developed in other states, including California, Idaho, Kansas, Maryland, Michigan, Texas, Utah, and Virginia. The state of Colorado implemented the first statewide court e-filing system and currently allows e-filing in over sixty courts. Generally, when electronic filing is made available, it is optional. In early 2001, however, a trial court judge in the District of Columbia launched a pilot project that *required* attorneys to use electronic filing for all documents relating to certain types of civil cases.

The expenses associated with an appeal can be considerable, and e-filing can add substantially to the cost. In some cases, appellants who successfully appeal a judgment are entitled to be awarded their costs, including an amount for printing the copies of the record on appeal and the briefs. In the following case, the appellants spent $16,112 for the paper copies and an additional $16,065 to prepare and submit briefs and other documents in an electronic format. Should the appellants be reimbursed for these expenses?

CASE 3.2 Phansalkar v. Andersen, Weinroth & Co.

United States Court of Appeals,
Second Circuit, 2004.
356 F.3d 188.

BACKGROUND AND FACTS Andersen, Weinroth & Company (AW) is a small firm that finds and creates investment opportunities for itself, its partners, and other investors. AW's income includes returns on its investments, fees paid by its investors, and the compensation and other benefits earned by its employees for their service on boards of directors of the companies with which AW does business. Some AW employees receive stock and "investment opportunities" rather than salaries. Rohit Phansalkar worked for AW from February 1998 until June 2000, when he became the chairman and chief executive officer of Osicom Technologies, Inc. After Phansalkar left, AW refused to pay him the returns on certain "investment opportunities" that he had been given while at AW. Phansalkar filed a suit in a federal district court against AW, alleging in part breach of contract. The court awarded Phansalkar more than $4.4 million. AW appealed to the U.S. Court of Appeals for the Second Circuit, which reversed this judgment on the ground that Phansalkar had acted with disloyalty during his employment with AW by failing to disclose compensation and benefits that he received for serving on various boards. AW then asked for an award of the amount that it spent to create copies of the briefs and other documents involved in the appeal in hyperlinked CD-ROM format.

(Continued)

CASE 3.2—Continued

IN THE WORDS OF THE COURT . . .

PER CURIAM: [By the whole court]

* * * *

On September 16, 2003, this Court reversed a judgment of approximately $4.4 million entered by the U.S. District Court for the Southern District of New York in favor of Phansalkar. On September 29, 2003 the AW parties submitted an itemized bill of costs. As appellants who have won a reversal, they are clearly entitled to costs for the docketing of the appeal and for printing the "necessary" copies of the regular and special appendices of appellants' main brief and reply brief, an amount totaling $16,112. That entitlement is supported by Rule 39 [of the *Federal Rules of Appellate Procedure* and] by this Court's Local Instructions for Bill of Costs * * * . In addition, the AW parties seek $16,065 in costs associated with preparing and submitting companion appendices and briefs in hyperlinked CD-ROM format.

The AW parties and Phansalkar vigorously dispute whether an agreement was ever reached over how these CD-ROM costs would be allocated between them following this appeal. There is no dispute, however, that if such an agreement was reached, it was never committed to writing * * * . The issue raised by the parties, which this Court has not yet decided, is whether Rule 39 and the rules of this Court contemplate [an award] of the costs of preparing such electronic submissions.

* * *

Under Rule 25(a)(2)(D) of the *Federal Rules of Appellate Procedure,*

> [a] court of appeals may by local rule permit papers to be filed, signed, or verified by electronic means that are consistent with technical standards, if any, that the Judicial Conference of the United States establishes.

This Court was among the first [federal courts of appeals] to promulgate such a local rule, by * * * order on October 17, 1997. That order was supplemented on January 30, 1998 with * * * Order 98-2 * * * , which states that the submission of electronic format briefs is "allowed and encouraged" as long as "[a]ll parties have consented * * * or a motion to file has been granted." Several other [federal courts of appeals] have adopted local rules that permit or even require the filing of electronic briefs, usually on companion disks. The submission of an electronic version of a paper brief very likely entails small incremental costs.

CD-ROM submissions that hyperlink briefs to relevant sections of the appellate record are more versatile, more useful, and considerably more expensive. Our January 30, 1998 order allows and encourages the use of such "interactive CD-ROM" formats. The [U.S. Court of Appeals for the] Federal Circuit also allows CD-ROM briefs to be filed with the prior consent of both the court and the opposing party. To date, only the [U.S. Court of Appeals for the] First Circuit appears to have adopted formally a local rule that applies to submission of hyperlinked CD-ROM briefs. Such submissions can assist judicial review and are welcomed, but they are not necessarily [part of an award] as costs.

We have found no local rule or holding from another circuit that allocates CD-ROM costs. No guidance can be found in the relevant text of Rule 39, which authorizes [an award] of costs incurred to produce "necessary" copies of briefs, appendices, and portions of the record relevant to an appeal and a variety of other costs of appeal, such as filing fees. * * * [I]n the absence of a specific textual reference in Rule 39, an expense can be an allowable cost of appeal when it is analogous to one of the costs specifically authorized by Rule 39(e). Citing this test, and our administrative orders encouraging the use of CD-ROM's, the AW parties argue that CD-ROM expenses are allowable costs under Rule 39.

CASE 3.2—Continued

However, * * * several other factors * * * are also important in determining if a cost is authorized by Rule 39: whether the party seeking disallowance has clearly consented to the expense; whether a court has previously approved the expense; and whether the alternative arrangement costs less than the expense specifically authorized by the Rule. None of these factors assists the AW parties. In particular, it appears that a substantial portion of the costs were duplicative. Since the AW parties incurred costs both to produce hard copies of their appellate materials *and* to produce hyperlinked CD-ROM copies, Rule 25(a)(2)(D) suggests that the CD-ROM costs in this case were duplicative rather than an analog of hard copy production costs. [Awarding] the CD-ROM costs under such circumstances is inconsistent with our past applications of Rule 39.

Finally, it is decisive that there is no written stipulation or understanding between the parties concerning the allocation of the incremental costs of this useful technology.

DECISION AND REMEDY The U.S. Court of Appeals for the Second Circuit ruled that AW could not recover the costs associated with preparing and submitting electronic copies of the appeal documents. No rule or court decision allocated CD-ROM costs, and in this case, there was no agreement between the parties to allocate the costs and no other relevant factors.

FOR CRITICAL ANALYSIS—Social Consideration *How might the result in this case have been different if the court had required, rather than merely encouraged, the submission of electronic copies of the appeal documents?*

Courts Online

Most courts today have sites on the Web. Of course, each court decides what to make available at its site. Some courts display only the names of court personnel and office phone numbers. Others add court rules and forms. Many include judicial decisions, although generally the sites do not feature archives of old decisions. Instead, decisions are usually available online only for a limited time. For example, California keeps opinions online for only sixty days. In addition, in some states, such as California and Florida, court clerks offer docket information and other searchable databases online.

Appellate court decisions are often posted online immediately after they are rendered. Recent decisions of the U.S. courts of appeals, for example, are available online at their Web sites. The United States Supreme Court also has an official Web site and publishes its opinions there immediately after they are announced to the public. (These Web sites are listed elsewhere in this chapter in the *On the Web* features.) In fact, even decisions that are designated as unpublished opinions by the appellate courts are often published online.

Cyber Courts and Proceedings

.on the Web Smith & Johnson, P.C., a Michigan law firm, offers a summary of Michigan's cyber court legislation on its Web page at **http://www.smith-johnson.com/businesslaw/cybercourt.htm**.

Someday, litigants may be able to use cyber courts, in which judicial proceedings take place only on the Internet. The parties to a case could meet online to make their arguments and present their evidence. This might be done with e-mail submissions, through video cameras, in designated "chat" rooms, at closed sites, or through the use of other Internet facilities. These courtrooms could be efficient and economical. We might also see the use of virtual lawyers, judges, and juries—and possibly the replacement of court personnel with computer software. Already the state of Michigan has passed legislation creating cyber courts that will hear cases involving technology issues and high-tech businesses. Many lawyers predict that other states will follow suit.

The courts may also use the Internet in other ways. In a groundbreaking decision in early 2001, for example, a Florida county court granted "virtual" visitation rights in a couple's divorce proceeding. Although the court granted custody of the couple's ten-year-old daughter to the father, the court also ordered each parent to buy a computer and a videoconferencing system so that the mother could "visit" with her child via the Internet at any time.[14]

ETHICAL ISSUE 3.1

How will online access to courts affect privacy? From a practical perspective, trial court records, although normally available to the public, remain obscure. Because the decisions of most state trial courts (and some federal courts) are not published, someone must be strongly motivated to go to the trouble of traveling to the relevant courthouse in person to access the documents. As online access to court records increases and electronic filing becomes the norm, this "practical obscurity," as lawyers call it, may soon disappear. Electronic filing on a nationwide basis would open up all court documents to anyone with an Internet connection and a Web browser. Utilizing special "data-mining" software, anyone could go online and within just a few minutes access information—ranging from personal health records to financial reports to criminal violations—from dozens of courts. This means that serious privacy issues are at stake. Should the courts restrict public access to certain types of documents, such as bankruptcy records or documents containing personal information that is not directly related to the legal issue being decided? Many courts are struggling with these questions and have taken a myriad of different approaches. Some courts make civil case information available, but restrict Internet access to criminal case information. Other courts, such as those in Florida, have deemed certain types of documents and court proceedings confidential and no longer post this information online. ■ [15]

Alternative Dispute Resolution

ALTERNATIVE DISPUTE RESOLUTION (ADR) The resolution of disputes in ways other than those involved in the traditional judicial process. Negotiation, mediation, and arbitration are forms of ADR.

Litigation is expensive. It is also time consuming. Because of the backlog of cases pending in many courts, several years may pass before a case is actually tried. For these and other reasons, more and more businesspersons are turning to **alternative dispute resolution (ADR)** as a means of settling their disputes.

Methods of ADR range from neighbors sitting down over a cup of coffee in an attempt to work out their differences to huge multinational corporations agreeing to resolve a dispute through a formal hearing before a panel of experts. The great advantage of ADR is its flexibility. Normally, the parties themselves can control how the dispute will be settled, what procedures will be used, and whether the decision reached (either by themselves or by a neutral third party) will be legally binding or nonbinding.

Today, approximately 95 percent of cases are settled before trial through some form of ADR. Indeed, most states either require or encourage parties to undertake ADR prior to trial. Several federal courts have instituted ADR programs as well. In the following pages, we examine various forms of ADR. Keep in mind, though, that new methods of ADR—and new combinations of existing methods—are constantly being devised and employed. In addition, ADR services are now being offered via

---

14. For a discussion of this case, see Shelley Emling, "After the Divorce, Internet Visits?" *Austin American-Statesman,* January 30, 2001, pp. A1 and A10.

15. *In re Report of Supreme Court Workgroup on Public Records,* 825 So.2d 889 (Fla. 2002).

the Internet. After looking at traditional forms of ADR, we examine some of the ways in which disputes are being resolved in various online forums.

NEGOTIATION

NEGOTIATION
A process in which parties attempt to settle their dispute informally, with or without attorneys to represent them.

One of the simplest forms of ADR is **negotiation,** a process in which the parties attempt to settle their dispute informally, with or without attorneys to represent them. Attorneys frequently advise their clients to negotiate a settlement voluntarily before they proceed to trial.

Negotiation traditionally involves just the parties themselves and (typically) their attorneys. The attorneys, though, are advocates—they are obligated to put their clients' interests first. Often parties find it helpful to have the opinion and guidance of a neutral (unbiased) third party when deciding whether or how to negotiate a settlement of their dispute. The methods of ADR discussed next all involve neutral third parties.

MEDIATION

MEDIATION
A method of settling disputes outside of court by using the services of a neutral third party, who acts as a communicating agent between the parties and assists them in negotiating a settlement.

In the **mediation** process, the parties themselves attempt to negotiate an agreement, but with the assistance of a neutral third party, a mediator. In mediation, the mediator talks with the parties separately as well as jointly. The mediator emphasizes points of agreement, helps the parties evaluate their positions, and proposes solutions. The mediator, however, does not make a decision on the matter being disputed. The mediator, who need not be a lawyer, usually charges a fee for his or her services (which can be split between the parties). States that require parties to undergo ADR before trial often offer mediation as one of the ADR options or (as in Florida) the only option.

.on the Web For a guide to alternative dispute resolution, mediation, and arbitration, go to the Web site of Hieros Gamos at **http://www.hg.org/adr.html**.

Mediation is not adversarial in nature, as lawsuits are. In litigation, the parties "do battle" with each other in the courtroom, while the judge is the neutral party. Because of its nonadversarial nature, the mediation process tends to reduce the antagonism between the disputants and to allow them to resume their former relationship. For this reason, mediation is often the preferred form of ADR for disputes involving business partners, employers and employees, or other parties involved in long-term relationships. ■ EXAMPLE 3.10 Suppose that two business partners have a dispute over how the profits of their firm should be distributed. If the dispute is litigated, the parties will be adversaries, and their respective attorneys will emphasize how the parties' positions differ, not what they have in common. In contrast, when a dispute is mediated, the mediator emphasizes the common ground shared by the parties and helps them work toward agreement. ■

Today, characteristics of mediation are being combined with those of arbitration (to be discussed next). In *binding mediation,* for example, the parties agree that if they cannot resolve the dispute, the mediator can make a legally binding decision on the issue. In *mediation-arbitration,* or "med-arb," the parties agree to first attempt to settle their dispute through mediation. If no settlement is reached, the dispute will be arbitrated.

ARBITRATION

ARBITRATION
The settling of a dispute by submitting it to a disinterested third party (other than a court), who renders a decision that is (most often) legally binding.

A more formal method of ADR is **arbitration,** in which an arbitrator (a neutral third party or a panel of experts) hears a dispute and renders a decision. The key difference between arbitration and the forms of ADR just discussed is that in arbitration, the third party hearing the dispute makes the decision for the parties. Usually, the parties in arbitration agree that the third party's decision will be *legally binding,* although the parties can also agree to *nonbinding* arbitration. Additionally, arbitration that is

KEY TERMS

alternative dispute resolution (ADR) 86
answer 75
arbitration 87
arbitration clause 88
award 81
bankruptcy court 65
brief 81
complaint 75
concurrent jurisdiction 66
counterclaim 76
default judgment 75
deposition 78
discovery 77
diversity of citizenship 66
docket 67
early neutral case evaluation 92
e-evidence 78
exclusive jurisdiction 66
federal question 66
interrogatories 78
judicial review 62
jurisdiction 63
justiciable controversy 70
litigation 75
long arm statute 63
mediation 87
mini-trial 92
motion for a directed verdict 81
motion for a new trial 81
motion for judgment *n.o.v.* 81
motion for judgment on the pleadings 77
motion for summary judgment 77
motion to dismiss 77
negotiation 87
online dispute resolution (ODR) 93
pleadings 75
probate court 65
reply 76
rule of four 74
small claims court 72
standing to sue 70
summary jury trial (SJT) 92
summons 75
venue 70
voir dire 79
writ of *certiorari* 73

CHAPTER SUMMARY Courts and Alternative Dispute Resolution

The Judiciary's Role in American Government (See pages 62–63.)	The role of the judiciary—the courts—in the American governmental system is to interpret and apply the law. Through the process of judicial review—determining the constitutionality of laws—the judicial branch acts as a check on the executive and legislative branches of government.
Basic Judicial Requirements (See pages 63–70.)	1. *Jurisdiction*—Before a court can hear a case, it must have jurisdiction over the person against whom the suit is brought or the property involved in the suit, as well as jurisdiction over the subject matter. a. Limited versus general jurisdiction—Limited jurisdiction exists when a court is limited to a specific subject matter, such as probate or divorce. General jurisdiction exists when a court can hear any kind of case. b. Original versus appellate jurisdiction—Original jurisdiction exists with courts that have authority to hear a case for the first time (trial courts). Appellate jurisdiction exists with courts of appeals, or reviewing courts; generally, appellate courts do not have original jurisdiction. c. Federal jurisdiction—Arises (1) when a federal question is involved (when the plaintiff's cause of action is based, at least in part, on the U.S. Constitution, a treaty, or a federal law) or (2) when a case involves diversity of citizenship (citizens of different states, for example) and the amount in controversy exceeds $75,000. d. Concurrent versus exclusive jurisdiction—Concurrent jurisdiction exists when two different courts have authority to hear the same case. Exclusive jurisdiction exists when only state courts or only federal courts have authority to hear a case.

CHAPTER SUMMARY Courts and Alternative Dispute Resolution—Continued

Basic Judicial Requirements—Continued	2. *Jurisdiction in cyberspace*—Because the Internet does not have physical boundaries, traditional jurisdictional concepts have been difficult to apply in cases involving activities conducted via the Web. Gradually, the courts are developing standards to use in determining when jurisdiction over a Web owner or operator in another state is proper. 3. *Venue*—Venue has to do with the most appropriate location for a trial, which is usually the geographic area where the event leading to the dispute took place or where the parties reside. 4. *Standing to sue*—A requirement that a party must have a legally protected and tangible interest at stake sufficient to justify seeking relief through the court system. The controversy at issue must also be a justiciable controversy—one that is real and substantial, as opposed to hypothetical or academic.
The State and Federal Court Systems (See pages 71–74.)	1. *Trial courts*—Courts of original jurisdiction, in which legal actions are initiated. a. State—Courts of general jurisdiction can hear any case; courts of limited jurisdiction include divorce courts, probate courts, traffic courts, small claims courts, and so on. b. Federal—The federal district court is the equivalent of the state trial court. Federal courts of limited jurisdiction include the U.S. Tax Court, the U.S. Bankruptcy Court, and the U.S. Court of Federal Claims. 2. *Intermediate appellate courts*—Courts of appeals, or reviewing courts; generally without original jurisdiction. Many states have an intermediate appellate court; in the federal court system, the U.S. circuit courts of appeals are the intermediate appellate courts. 3. *Supreme (highest) courts*—Each state has a supreme court, although it may be called by some other name; appeal from the state supreme court to the United States Supreme Court is possible only if a federal question is involved. The United States Supreme Court is the highest court in the federal court system and the final arbiter of the Constitution and federal law.
Following a State Court Case (See pages 75–82.)	Rules of procedure prescribe the way in which disputes are handled in the courts. Rules differ from court to court, and separate sets of rules exist for federal and state courts, as well as for criminal and civil cases. A sample civil court case in a state court would involve the following procedures: 1. *The pleadings*— a. Complaint—Filed by the plaintiff with the court to initiate the lawsuit; served with a summons on the defendant. b. Answer—Admits or denies allegations made by the plaintiff; may assert a counterclaim or an affirmative defense. c. Motion to dismiss—A request to the court to dismiss the case for stated reasons, such as the plaintiff's failure to state a claim for which relief can be granted. 2. *Pretrial motions (in addition to the motion to dismiss)*— a. Motion for judgment on the pleadings—May be made by either party; will be granted if the parties agree on the facts and the only question is how the law applies to the facts. The judge bases the decision solely on the pleadings. b. Motion for summary judgment—May be made by either party; will be granted if the parties agree on the facts. The judge applies the law in rendering a judgment. The judge can consider evidence outside the pleadings when evaluating the motion. 3. *Discovery*—The process of gathering evidence concerning the case. Discovery involves depositions (sworn testimony by a party to the lawsuit or any witness), interrogatories (written questions and answers to these questions made by parties to the action with the aid

(Continued)

CHAPTER SUMMARY Courts and Alternative Dispute Resolution—Continued

Following a State Court Case—Continued (See pages 75–82.)	of their attorneys), and various requests (for admissions, documents, and medical examinations, for example). Discovery may also involve electronically recorded information, such as e-mail, voice mail, word-processing documents, and other data compilations. Although electronic discovery has significant advantages over paper discovery, it is also more time consuming and expensive and often requires the parties to hire experts. 4. *Pretrial conference*—Either party or the court can request a pretrial conference to identify the matters in dispute after discovery has taken place and to plan the course of the trial. 5. *Trial*—Following jury selection *(voir dire),* the trial begins with opening statements from both parties' attorneys. The following events then occur: a. The plaintiff's introduction of evidence (including the testimony of witnesses) supporting the plaintiff's position. The defendant's attorney can challenge evidence and cross-examine witnesses. b. The defendant's introduction of evidence (including the testimony of witnesses) supporting the defendant's position. The plaintiff's attorney can challenge evidence and cross-examine witnesses. c. Closing arguments by the attorneys in favor of their respective clients, the judge's instructions to the jury, and the jury's verdict. 6. *Posttrial motions*— a. Motion for judgment *n.o.v.* ("notwithstanding the verdict")—Will be granted if the judge is convinced that the jury was in error. b. Motion for a new trial—Will be granted if the judge is convinced that the jury was in error; can also be granted on the grounds of newly discovered evidence, misconduct by the participants during the trial, or error by the judge. 7. *Appeal*—Either party can appeal the trial court's judgment to an appropriate court of appeals. After reviewing the record on appeal, the abstracts, and the attorneys' briefs, the appellate court holds a hearing and renders its opinion.
The Courts Adapt to the Online World (See pages 82–86.)	A number of state and federal courts now allow parties to file litigation-related documents with the courts via the Internet or other electronic means. The federal courts are considering the implementation of electronic filing systems in all federal district courts. Almost every court now has a Web page offering information about the court and its procedures, and increasingly courts are publishing their opinions online. In the future, we may see "cyber courts," in which all trial proceedings are conducted online.
Alternative Dispute Resolution (See pages 86–93.)	1. *Negotiation*—The parties come together, with or without attorneys to represent them, and try to reach a settlement without the involvement of a third party. 2. *Mediation*—The parties themselves reach an agreement with the help of a neutral third party, called a mediator, who proposes solutions. At the parties' request, a mediator may make a legally binding decision. 3. *Arbitration*—A more formal method of ADR in which the parties submit their dispute to a neutral third party, the arbitrator, who renders a decision. The decision may or may not be legally binding, depending on the circumstances. 4. *Other types of ADR*—These include early neutral case evaluation, mini-trials, and summary jury trials (SJTs); generally, these are forms of "assisted negotiation." 5. *Providers of ADR services*—The leading nonprofit provider of ADR services is the American Arbitration Association. Hundreds of for-profit firms also provide ADR services.

CHAPTER SUMMARY Courts and Alternative Dispute Resolution—Continued

Online Dispute Resolution (See pages 93–94.)	A number of organizations and firms are now offering negotiation, mediation, and arbitration services through online forums. To date, these forums have been a practical alternative for the resolution of domain name disputes and e-commerce disputes in which the amount in controversy is relatively small.

FOR REVIEW

Answers for the even-numbered questions in this For Review *section can be found on this text's accompanying Web site at* http://blt.westbuslaw.com. *Select "Chapter 3" and click on "For Review."*

1. What is judicial review? How and when was the power of judicial review established?
2. Before a court can hear a case, it must have jurisdiction. Over what must it have jurisdiction? How are the courts applying traditional jurisdictional concepts to cases involving Internet transactions?
3. What is the difference between a trial court and an appellate court?
4. In a lawsuit, what are the pleadings? What is discovery, and how does electronic discovery differ? What is electronic filing?
5. How are online forums being used to resolve disputes?

QUESTIONS AND CASE PROBLEMS

3–1. Arbitration. In an arbitration proceeding, the arbitrator need not be a judge or even a lawyer. How, then, can the arbitrator's decision have the force of law and be binding on the parties involved?

3–2. Jurisdiction. Marya Callais, a citizen of Florida, was walking near a busy street in Tallahassee one day when a large crate fell off a passing truck and hit her, resulting in several injuries. She incurred a great deal of pain and suffering plus numerous medical expenses, and she could not work for six months. She wishes to sue the trucking firm for $300,000 in damages. The firm's headquarters are in Georgia, although the company does business in Florida. In what court may Callais bring suit—a Florida state court, a Georgia state court, or a federal court? What factors might influence her decision?

3–3. Standing. Blue Cross and Blue Shield insurance companies (the Blues) provide 68 million Americans with health-care financing. The Blues have paid billions of dollars for care attributable to illnesses related to tobacco use. In an attempt to recover some of this amount, the Blues filed a suit in a federal district court against tobacco companies and others, alleging fraud, among other things. The Blues claimed that beginning in 1953, the defendants conspired to addict millions of Americans, including members of Blue Cross plans, to cigarettes and other tobacco products. The conspiracy involved misrepresentation about the safety of nicotine and its addictive properties, marketing efforts targeting children, and agreements not to produce or market safer cigarettes. As a result of the defendants' efforts, many tobacco users developed lung, throat, and other cancers, as well as heart disease, stroke, emphysema, and other illnesses. The defendants asked the court to dismiss the case on the ground that the plaintiffs did not have standing to sue. Do the Blues have standing in this case? Why or why not? [*Blue Cross and Blue Shield of New Jersey, Inc. v. Philip Morris, Inc.*, 36 F.Supp.2d 560 (E.D.N.Y. 1999)]

3–4. Jurisdiction. George Noonan, a Boston police detective and a devoted nonsmoker, has spent most of his career educating Bostonians about the health risks of tobacco use. In 1992, an ad for Winston cigarettes featuring Noonan's image appeared in several French magazines. Some of the magazines were on sale at newsstands in Boston. Noonan filed a suit in a federal district court against The Winston Co., Lintas:Paris (the French ad agency that created the ads), and others. Lintas:Paris and the other French defendants claimed that they did not know the magazines would be sold in Boston and filed a motion to dismiss the suit for lack of personal jurisdiction. Does the court have jurisdiction? Why or why not? [*Noonan v. The Winston Co.*, 135 F.3d 85 (1st Cir. 1998)]

CASE PROBLEM WITH SAMPLE ANSWER

3–5. Ms. Thompson filed a suit in a federal district court against her employer, Altheimer & Gray, seeking damages for alleged racial discrimination in violation of federal law. During *voir dire,* the judge asked the prospective jurors whether "there is something about this kind of lawsuit for money damages that would start any of you leaning for or against a particular party?" Ms. Leiter, one of the prospective jurors, raised her hand and explained that she had "been an owner of a couple of businesses and am currently an owner of a business, and I feel that as an employer and owner of a business that will definitely sway my judgment in this case." She explained, "I am constantly faced with people that want various benefits or different positions in the company or better contacts or, you know, a myriad of issues that employers face on a regular basis, and I have to decide whether or not that person should get them." Asked by Thompson's lawyer whether "you believe that people file lawsuits just because they don't get something they want," Leiter answered, "I believe there are some people that do." In answer to another question, she said, "I think I bring a lot of background to this case, and I can't say that it's not going to cloud my judgment. I can try to be as fair as I can, as I do every day." Thompson filed a motion to strike Leiter for cause. Should the judge grant the motion? Explain. [*Thompson v. Altheimer & Gray,* 248 F.3d 621 (7th Cir. 2001)]

After you have answered this problem, compare your answer with the sample answer given on the Web site that accompanies this text. Go to http://blt.westbuslaw.com, select "Chapter 3," and click on "Case Problem with Sample Answer."

3–6. Arbitration. Alexander Little worked for Auto Stiegler, Inc., an automobile dealership in Los Angeles County, California, eventually becoming the service manager. While employed, Little signed an arbitration agreement that required all employment-related disputes to be submitted to arbitration. The agreement also provided that any award over $50,000 could be appealed to a second arbitrator. Little was later demoted and terminated. Alleging that these actions were in retaliation for investigating and reporting warranty fraud and thus were in violation of public policy, Little filed a suit in a California state court against Auto Stiegler. The defendant filed a motion with the court to compel arbitration. Little responded that the arbitration agreement should not be enforced in part because the appeal provision was unfairly one sided. Is this provision enforceable? Should the court grant Auto Stiegler's motion? Why or why not? [*Little v. Auto Stiegler, Inc.,* 29 Cal.4th 1064, 63 P.3d 979, 130 Cal.Rptr.2d 892 (2003)]

3–7. Standing to Sue. Lamar Advertising of Penn, LLC, an outdoor advertising business, wanted to erect billboards of varying sizes in a multiphase operation throughout the town of Orchard Park, New York. An Orchard Park ordinance restricted the signs to certain sizes in certain areas, to advertising products and services available for sale only on the premises, and to other limits. Lamar asked Orchard Park for permission to build signs in some areas larger than the ordinance allowed in those locations (but not as large as allowed in other areas). When the town refused, Lamar filed a suit in a federal district court, claiming that the ordinance violated the First Amendment. Did Lamar have standing to challenge the ordinance? If the court could sever the provisions of the ordinance restricting a sign's content from the provisions limiting a sign's size, would your answer be the same? Explain. [*Lamar Advertising of Penn, LLC v. Town of Orchard Park, New York,* 356 F.3d 365 (2d Cir. 2004)]

A QUESTION OF ETHICS

3–8. Linda Bender brought an action in a federal court against her supervisor at A. G. Edwards & Sons, Inc., a stockbrokerage firm (the defendants). Bender alleged sexual harassment in violation of Title VII of the Civil Rights Act of 1964, which prohibits, among other things, employment discrimination based on gender. In her application for registration as a stockbroker, Bender had agreed to arbitrate any disputes with her employer. The defendants moved to compel arbitration. The district court judge denied the motion, holding that Bender could not be forced to waive her right to adjudicate Title VII claims in federal court. The appellate court reversed, ruling that Title VII claims are arbitrable. The court held that compelling Bender to submit her claim for arbitration did not deprive her of the right to a judicial forum, because if the arbitration proceedings were somehow legally deficient, she could still take her case to a federal court for review. [*Bender v. A. G. Edwards & Sons, Inc.,* 971 F.2d 698 (11th Cir. 1992)]

1. Does the right to a postarbitration judicial forum equate to the right to initial access to a judicial forum in employment disputes?
2. Should the fact that reviewing courts rarely set aside arbitrators' awards have any bearing on the arbitrability of certain types of claims, such as those brought under Title VII?

FOR CRITICAL ANALYSIS

3–9. American courts are forums for adversarial justice, in which attorneys defend the interests of their respective clients before the court. This means that an attorney may end up claiming in court that his or her client is innocent, even though the attorney knows that the client acted wrongfully. Is it ethical for attorneys to try to "deceive" the court in these situations? Can the adversarial system of justice really lead to "truth"?

VIDEO QUESTION

DIGITAL VIDEO LIBRARY
WEST LEGAL STUDIES IN BUSINESS

3–10. Go to this text's Web site at http://blt.westbuslaw.com and select "Chapter 3." Click on "Video Questions" and view the video titled *Jurisdiction in Cyberspace.* Then answer the following questions.

1. What standard would a court apply to determine whether it has jurisdiction over the out-of-state computer firm in the video?
2. What factors is a court likely to consider in assessing whether sufficient contacts existed when the only connection to the jurisdiction is through a Web site?
3. How do you think the court would resolve the issue in this case?

INTERNET EXERCISES

Go to the *Business Law Today* home page at http://blt.westbuslaw.com, select "Chapter 3," and click on "Internet Exercises." There you will find the following Internet research exercises that you can perform to learn more about topics covered in this chapter.

Activity 3–1: LEGAL PERSPECTIVE—The Judiciary's Role in American Government

Activity 3–2: MANAGEMENT PERSPECTIVE—Alternative Dispute Resolution

Activity 3–3: SOCIAL PERSPECTIVE—Resolve a Dispute Online

BEFORE THE TEST

Go to the *Business Law Today* home page at http://blt.westbuslaw.com, select "Chapter 3," and click on "Interactive Quizzes." You will find a number of interactive questions relating to this chapter.

CHAPTER 4

Torts and Cyber Torts

"'Tort' more or less means 'wrong' . . . . One of my friends [in law school] said that Torts is the course which proves that your mother was right."

Scott Turow, 1949–
(American lawyer and author)

CHAPTER OUTLINE

- THE BASIS OF TORT LAW
- INTENTIONAL TORTS AGAINST PERSONS
- INTENTIONAL TORTS AGAINST PROPERTY
- UNINTENTIONAL TORTS (NEGLIGENCE)
- STRICT LIABILITY
- CYBER TORTS

LEARNING OBJECTIVES

After reading this chapter, you should be able to answer the following questions:

1. What is a tort?
2. What is the purpose of tort law? What are two basic categories of torts?
3. What are the four elements of negligence?
4. What is meant by strict liability? In what circumstances is strict liability applied?
5. What is a cyber tort, and how are tort theories being applied in cyberspace?

TORT
A civil wrong not arising from a breach of contract. A breach of a legal duty that proximately causes harm or injury to another.

As Scott Turow's statement in the above quotation indicates, **torts** are wrongful actions.[1] Through tort law, society compensates those who have suffered injuries as a result of the wrongful conduct of others. Although some torts, such as assault and trespass, originated in the English common law, the field of tort law continues to expand. As new ways to commit wrongs are discovered, such as the use of the Internet to commit wrongful acts, the courts are extending tort law to cover these wrongs.

As you will see in later chapters of this book, many of the lawsuits brought by or against business firms are based on the tort theories discussed in this chapter. Some of the torts examined here can occur in any context, including the business environment.

1. The word *tort* is French for "wrong."

BUSINESS TORT
Wrongful interference with another's business rights.

Others traditionally have been referred to as **business torts,** which are defined as wrongful interferences with the business rights of others. Included in business torts are such vague concepts as *unfair competition* and *wrongfully interfering with the business relations of others.*

The Basis of Tort Law

DAMAGES
Money sought as a remedy for a breach of contract or a tortious action.

Two notions serve as the basis of all torts: wrongs and compensation. Tort law is designed to compensate those who have suffered a loss or injury due to another person's wrongful act. In a tort action, one person or group brings a personal suit against another person or group to obtain compensation (money **damages**) or other relief for the harm suffered.

THE PURPOSE OF TORT LAW

Generally, the purpose of tort law is to provide remedies for the invasion of various *protected interests.* Society recognizes an interest in personal physical safety, and tort law provides remedies for acts that cause physical injury or that interfere with physical security and freedom of movement. Society recognizes an interest in protecting real and personal property, and tort law provides remedies for acts that cause destruction or damage to property. Society also recognizes an interest in protecting certain intangible interests, such as personal privacy, family relations, reputation, and dignity, and tort law provides remedies for invasion of these protected interests.

.on the Web You can find cases and articles on torts in the tort law library at the Internet Law Library's Web site. Go to **http://www.lawguru.com/ilawlib.**

CLASSIFICATIONS OF TORTS

There are two broad classifications of torts: *intentional torts* and *unintentional torts* (torts involving negligence). The classification of a particular tort depends largely on how the tort occurs (intentionally or negligently) and the surrounding circumstances. In the following pages, you will read about these two classifications of torts.

CYBER TORT
A tort committed in cyberspace.

Torts committed via the Internet are sometimes referred to as **cyber torts.** We look at how the courts have applied traditional tort law to wrongful actions in the online environment in the concluding pages of this chapter.

Intentional Torts against Persons

INTENTIONAL TORT
A wrongful act knowingly committed.

TORTFEASOR
One who commits a tort.

An **intentional tort,** as the term implies, requires *intent.* The **tortfeasor** (the one committing the tort) must intend to commit an act, the consequences of which interfere with the personal or business interests of another in a way not permitted by law. An evil or harmful motive is not required—in fact, the actor may even have a beneficial motive for committing what turns out to be a tortious act. In tort law, intent means only that the actor intended the consequences of his or her act or knew with substantial certainty that specific consequences would result from the act. The law generally assumes that individuals intend the *normal* consequences of their actions. Thus, forcefully pushing another—even if done in jest and without any evil motive—is an intentional tort (if injury results), because the object of a strong push can ordinarily be expected to fall down.

This section discusses intentional torts against persons, which include assault and battery, false imprisonment, intentional infliction of emotional distress, defamation, invasion of the right to privacy, appropriation, misrepresentation (fraud), and wrongful interference.

Assault and Battery

ASSAULT
Any word or action intended to make another person fearful of immediate physical harm; a reasonably believable threat.

Any intentional, unexcused act that creates in another person a reasonable apprehension or fear of immediate harmful or offensive contact is an **assault.** Apprehension is not the same as fear. If a contact is such that a reasonable person would want to avoid it, and if there is a reasonable basis for believing that the contact will occur, then the plaintiff suffers apprehension whether or not he or she is afraid. The interest protected by tort law concerning assault is the freedom from having to expect harmful or offensive contact. The occurrence of apprehension is enough to justify compensation.

BATTERY
The unprivileged, intentional touching of another.

The *completion* of the act that caused the apprehension, if it results in harm to the plaintiff, is a **battery,** which is defined as an unexcused and harmful or offensive physical contact *intentionally* performed. For example, suppose that Ivan threatens Jean with a gun, then shoots her. The pointing of the gun at Jean is an assault; the firing of the gun (if the bullet hits Jean) is a battery. The interest protected by tort law concerning battery is the right to personal security and safety. The contact can be harmful, or it can be merely offensive (such as an unwelcome kiss). Physical injury need not occur. The contact can involve any part of the body or anything attached to it—for example, a hat or other item of clothing, a purse, or a chair or an automobile in which one is sitting. Whether the contact is offensive or not is determined by the *reasonable person standard.*[2] The contact can be made by the defendant or by some force the defendant sets in motion—for example, a rock thrown, food poisoned, or a stick swung.

Compensation If the plaintiff shows that there was contact, and the jury agrees that the contact was offensive, the plaintiff has a right to compensation. There is no need to show that the defendant acted out of malice; the person could have just been joking or playing around. The underlying motive does not matter, only the intent to bring about the harmful or offensive contact to the plaintiff. In fact, proving a motive is never necessary (but is sometimes relevant). A plaintiff may be compensated for the emotional harm or loss of reputation resulting from a battery, as well as for physical harm.

DEFENSE
A reason offered and alleged by a defendant in an action or suit as to why the plaintiff should not recover or establish what she or he seeks.

BE AWARE Some of these same four defenses can be raised by a defendant who is sued for other torts.

Defenses to Assault and Battery A number of legally recognized **defenses** (reasons why plaintiffs should not obtain what they are seeking) can be raised by a defendant who is sued for assault or battery, or both:

1. *Consent.* When a person consents to the act that damages her or him, there is generally no liability (legal responsibility) for the damage done.
2. *Self-defense.* An individual who is defending his or her life or physical well-being can claim self-defense. In situations of both *real* and *apparent* danger, a person may use whatever force is *reasonably* necessary to prevent harmful contact.
3. *Defense of others.* An individual can act in a reasonable manner to protect others who are in real or apparent danger.
4. *Defense of property.* Reasonable force may be used in attempting to remove intruders from one's home, although force that is likely to cause death or great bodily injury can never be used just to protect property.

2. The *reasonable person standard* is an objective test of how a reasonable person would have acted under the same circumstances. See "The Duty of Care and Its Breach" later in this chapter.

False Imprisonment

False imprisonment is the intentional confinement or restraint of another person's activities without justification. False imprisonment interferes with the freedom to move without restraint. The confinement can be accomplished through the use of physical barriers, physical restraint, or threats of physical force. Moral pressure or threats of future harm do not constitute false imprisonment. It is essential that the person being restrained not comply with the restraint willingly.

Businesspersons are often confronted with suits for false imprisonment after they have attempted to confine a suspected shoplifter for questioning. Under the "privilege to detain" granted to merchants in some states, a merchant can use the defense of *probable cause* to justify delaying a suspected shoplifter. Probable cause exists when there is sufficient evidence to support the belief that a person is guilty. Although laws governing false imprisonment vary from state to state, generally they require that any detention be conducted in a *reasonable* manner and for only a *reasonable* length of time.

Intentional Infliction of Emotional Distress

The tort of *intentional infliction of emotional distress* can be defined as an intentional act that amounts to extreme and outrageous conduct resulting in severe emotional distress to another. ■ **Example 4.1** A prankster telephones an individual and says that the individual's spouse has just been in a horrible accident. As a result, the individual suffers intense mental pain or anxiety. The caller's behavior is deemed to be extreme and outrageous conduct that exceeds the bounds of decency accepted by society and is therefore **actionable** (capable of serving as the ground for a lawsuit). ■

ACTIONABLE
Capable of serving as the basis of a lawsuit. An actionable claim can be pursued in a lawsuit or other court action.

The tort of intentional infliction of emotional distress poses several problems for the courts. One problem is the difficulty of proving the existence of emotional suffering. For this reason, courts in some jurisdictions require that the emotional distress be evidenced by some physical symptom or illness or some emotional disturbance that can be documented by a psychiatric consultant or other medical professional.

Another problem is that emotional distress claims must be subject to some limitation, or they could flood the courts with lawsuits. A society in which individuals are rewarded if they are unable to endure the normal emotional stresses of day-to-day living is obviously undesirable. Therefore, the law usually holds that indignity or annoyance alone is not enough to support a lawsuit based on the intentional infliction of emotional distress. Repeated annoyances (such as those experienced by a person who is being stalked), however, coupled with threats, are enough. In the business context, the repeated use of extreme methods to collect a delinquent account may be actionable.

Defamation

DEFAMATION
Anything published or publicly spoken that causes injury to another's good name, reputation, or character.

SLANDER
Defamation in oral form.

LIBEL
Defamation in writing or other permanent form (such as a digital recording) having the quality of permanence.

Defamation of character involves wrongfully hurting a person's good reputation. The law has imposed a general duty on all persons to refrain from making false, defamatory statements about others. Breaching this duty orally involves the tort of **slander;** breaching it in writing involves the tort of **libel.** The tort of defamation also arises when a false statement is made about a person's product, business, or title to property. We deal with these torts later in the chapter.

The Publication Requirement The basis of the tort of defamation is the publication of a statement or statements that hold an individual up to contempt, ridicule, or hatred. *Publication* here means that the defamatory statements are communicated to persons other than the defamed party. ■ EXAMPLE 4.2 If Thompson writes Andrews a private letter accusing him of embezzling funds, the action does not constitute libel. If Peters calls Gordon dishonest, unattractive, and incompetent when no one else is around, the action does not constitute slander. In neither case was the message communicated to a third party. ■

The courts have generally held that even dictating a letter to a secretary constitutes publication, although the publication may be privileged (privileged communications will be discussed shortly). Moreover, if a third party overhears defamatory statements by chance, the courts usually hold that this also constitutes publication. Defamatory statements made via the Internet are also actionable, as you will read later in this chapter. Note further that any individual who republishes or repeats defamatory statements is liable even if that person reveals the source of such statements.

Damages for Defamation Generally, in a case alleging slander, the plaintiff must prove "special damages" to establish the defendant's liability. The plaintiff must show that the slanderous statement caused her or him to suffer actual economic or monetary losses. This requirement is imposed in cases involving slander because slanderous statements have a temporary quality. In contrast, a libelous (written) statement has the quality of permanence, can be circulated widely, and usually results from some degree of deliberation on the part of the author. For that reason, a plaintiff can recover "general damages" for libel and need not prove any special damages.

Exceptions to the burden of proving special damages in cases alleging slander are made for certain types of slanderous statements. If a false statement constitutes "slander *per se,*" no proof of special damages is required for it to be actionable. The following four types of utterances are considered to be slander *per se:*

1. A statement that another has a loathsome communicable disease.
2. A statement that another has committed improprieties while engaging in a profession or trade.
3. A statement that another has committed or has been imprisoned for a serious crime.
4. A statement that a woman is unchaste or has engaged in serious sexual misconduct.

Defenses against Defamation Truth is normally an absolute defense against a defamation charge. In other words, if the defendant in a defamation suit can prove that his or her allegedly defamatory statements were true, the defendant will not be liable.

PRIVILEGE
A legal right, exemption, or immunity granted to a person or a class of persons. In the context of defamation, an absolute privilege immunizes the actor from suit, regardless of whether the actor's statements were malicious. A qualified privilege immunizes an actor from suit only when the privilege is properly exercised in the performance of a legal or moral duty.

Privileged Communications. Another defense that is sometimes raised is that the statements were **privileged** communications, and thus the defendant is immune from liability. Privileged communications are of two types: absolute and qualified. Only in judicial proceedings and certain government proceedings is *absolute* privilege granted. For example, statements made in the courtroom by attorneys and judges during a trial are absolutely privileged. So are statements made by government officials during legislative debate, even if the officials make such statements maliciously—that is, knowing them to be untrue. An absolute privilege is granted in these situations because government personnel deal with matters that are so much in the public interest that the parties involved should be able to speak out fully and freely without restriction.

A *qualified,* or *conditional,* privilege applies when a statement is related to a matter of public interest or when the statement is necessary to protect a person's private interest and is made to another person with an interest in the same subject matter. ■ EXAMPLE 4.3 Jorge applies for membership at the local country club. After the country club's board rejects his application, Jorge sues the club's office manager for making allegedly defamatory statements to the board concerning a conversation she had with Jorge. Assuming that the office manager had simply relayed what she thought was her duty to convey to the club's board, her statements would likely be protected by a qualified privilege.[3] ■

ACTUAL MALICE
In a defamation suit, a statement made about a public figure normally must be made with actual malice (with either knowledge of its falsity or a reckless disregard of the truth) for liability to be incurred.

Public Figures. In general, false and defamatory statements that are made about *public figures* (public officials who exercise substantial governmental power and any persons in the public limelight) and that are published in the press are privileged if they are made without **actual malice.**[4] To be made with actual malice, a statement must be made *with either knowledge of its falsity or a reckless disregard of the truth.* Statements made about public figures, especially when they are made via a public medium, are usually related to matters of general interest; they are made about people who substantially affect all of us. Furthermore, public figures generally have some access to a public medium for answering disparaging (belittling, discrediting) falsehoods about themselves; private individuals do not. For these reasons, public figures have a greater burden of proof in defamation cases (they must prove actual malice) than do private individuals.

INVASION OF THE RIGHT TO PRIVACY

A person has a right to solitude and freedom from prying public eyes—in other words, to privacy. As discussed in Chapter 2, the Supreme Court has held that a fundamental right to privacy is also implied by various amendments to the U.S. Constitution. Some state constitutions explicitly provide for privacy rights. In addition, a number of federal and state statutes have been enacted to protect individual rights in specific areas. Tort law also safeguards these rights through the tort of *invasion of privacy.* Four acts qualify as an invasion of privacy:

1. *The use of a person's name, picture, or other likeness for commercial purposes without permission.* This tort, which is usually referred to as the tort of appropriation, will be examined shortly.
2. *Intrusion into an individual's affairs or seclusion.* For example, invading someone's home or illegally searching someone's briefcase is an invasion of privacy. The tort has been held to extend to eavesdropping by wiretap, the unauthorized scanning of a bank account, compulsory blood testing, and window peeping.
3. *Publication of information that places a person in a false light.* This could be a story attributing to the person ideas not held or actions not taken by the person. (Publishing such a story could involve the tort of defamation as well.)
4. *Public disclosure of private facts about an individual that an ordinary person would find objectionable.* A newspaper account of a private citizen's sex life or financial affairs could be an actionable invasion of privacy.

3. For a case involving a qualified privilege, see *Hickson Corp. v. Northern Crossarm Co.,* 235 F.Supp.2d 1352 (N.D.Ga. 2002).
4. *New York Times Co. v. Sullivan,* 376 U.S. 254, 84 S.Ct. 710, 11 L.Ed.2d 686 (1964).

APPROPRIATION

The use by one person of another person's name, likeness, or other identifying characteristic, without permission and for the benefit of the user, constitutes the tort of **appropriation.** Under the law, an individual's right to privacy normally includes the right to the exclusive use of her or his identity.

APPROPRIATION
In tort law, the use by one person of another person's name, likeness, or other identifying characteristic without permission and for the benefit of the user.

■ EXAMPLE 4.4 Vanna White, the hostess of the popular television game show *Wheel of Fortune,* brought a case against Samsung Electronics America, Inc. Without White's permission, Samsung included in an advertisement for its videocassette recorders (VCRs) a depiction of a robot dressed in a wig, gown, and jewelry, posed in a scene that resembled the *Wheel of Fortune* set, in a stance for which White is famous. The court held in White's favor, holding that the tort of appropriation does not require the use of a celebrity's name or likeness. The court stated that Samsung's robot ad left "little doubt" as to the identity of the celebrity whom the ad was meant to depict.[5] ■

Cases of wrongful appropriation, or misappropriation, may also involve the rights of those who invest time and funds in the creation of a special system, such as a method of broadcasting sports events. Commercial misappropriation may also occur when a person takes and uses the property of another for the sole purpose of capitalizing unfairly on the goodwill or reputation of the property owner.

MISREPRESENTATION (FRAUD)

A misrepresentation leads another to believe in a condition that is different from the condition that actually exists. This is often accomplished through a false or incorrect statement. Misrepresentations may be innocently made by someone who is unaware of the existing facts, but the tort of **fraudulent misrepresentation,** or fraud, involves intentional deceit for personal gain. The tort includes several elements:

FRAUDULENT MISREPRESENTATION
Any misrepresentation, either by misstatement or omission of a material fact, knowingly made with the intention of deceiving another and on which a reasonable person would and does rely to his or her detriment.

1. The misrepresentation of facts or conditions with knowledge that they are false or with reckless disregard for the truth.
2. An intent to induce another to rely on the misrepresentation.
3. Justifiable reliance by the deceived party.
4. Damages suffered as a result of the reliance.
5. A causal connection between the misrepresentation and the injury suffered.

For fraud to occur, more than mere **puffery,** or *seller's talk,* must be involved. Fraud exists only when a person represents as a fact something he or she knows is untrue. For example, it is fraud to claim that a building does not leak when one knows it does. Facts are objectively ascertainable, whereas seller's talk is not. "I am the best accountant in town" is seller's talk. The speaker is not trying to represent something as fact because the term *best* is a subjective, not an objective, term.[6]

PUFFERY
A salesperson's often exaggerated claims concerning the quality of property offered for sale. Such claims involve opinions rather than facts and are not considered to be legally binding promises or warranties.

on the Web The 'Lectric Law Library's Legal Lexicon includes an informative discussion of the elements of fraud, as well as different types of fraud. To access this page, go to **http://www.lectlaw.com/def/f1079.htm.**

Normally, the tort of misrepresentation or fraud occurs only when there is reliance on a *statement of fact.* Sometimes, however, reliance on a *statement of opinion* may involve the tort of misrepresentation if the individual making the statement of opinion has a superior knowledge of the subject matter. For example, when a lawyer makes a statement of opinion about the law in a state in which the lawyer

5. *White v. Samsung Electronics America, Inc.,* 971 F.2d 1395 (9th Cir. 1992).
6. In contracts for the sale of goods, Article 2 of the Uniform Commercial Code distinguishes, for warranty purposes, between statements of opinion (*puffery*) and statements of fact. See Chapter 21 for a further discussion of this issue.

is licensed to practice, a court would construe reliance on such a statement to be equivalent to reliance on a statement of fact. We examine fraudulent misrepresentation in further detail in Chapter 12, in the context of contract law.

WRONGFUL INTERFERENCE

Business torts involving wrongful interference are generally divided into two categories: wrongful interference with a contractual relationship and wrongful interference with a business relationship.

Wrongful Interference with a Contractual Relationship The body of tort law relating to *intentional interference with a contractual relationship* has expanded greatly in recent years. A landmark case involved an opera singer, Joanna Wagner, who was under contract to sing for a man named Lumley for a specified period of years. A man named Gye, who knew of this contract, nonetheless "enticed" Wagner to refuse to carry out the agreement, and Wagner began to sing for Gye. Gye's action constituted a tort because it wrongfully interfered with the contractual relationship between Wagner and Lumley.[7] (Of course, Wagner's refusal to carry out the agreement also entitled Lumley to sue Wagner for breach of contract.)

Three elements are necessary for wrongful interference with a contractual relationship to occur:

1. A valid, enforceable contract must exist between two parties.
2. A third party must know that this contract exists.
3. The third party must *intentionally* cause either of the two parties to breach the contract.

REMEMBER It is the intent to do an act that is important in tort law, not the motive behind the intent.

The contract may be between a firm and its employees or a firm and its customers. Sometimes a competitor of a firm draws away one of the firm's key employees. If the original employer can show that the competitor induced the breach—that is, that the former employee would not otherwise have broken the contract—damages can be recovered from the competitor.

The following case illustrates the elements of the tort of wrongful interference with a contractual relationship in the context of a contract between an independent sales representative and his agent (agency relationships will be discussed in Chapter 28). The case was complicated by the existence of a second contract between the sales representative and the third party.

7. *Lumley v. Gye,* 118 Eng.Rep. 749 (1853).

CASE 4.1 Mathis v. Liu

United States Court of Appeals,
Eighth Circuit, 2002.
276 F.3d 1027.

BACKGROUND AND FACTS Ching and Alex Liu own Pacific Cornetta, Inc. In 1997, Pacific Cornetta entered into a contract with Lawrence Mathis, under which Mathis agreed to solicit orders for Pacific Cornetta's products from Kmart Corporation for a commission of 5 percent on net sales. Under the terms, either party could terminate the contract at any time. The next year, Mathis entered into a one-year contract with John Evans, under which Evans agreed to serve as Mathis's agent to solicit orders from Kmart for the product lines that Mathis represented, including Pacific Cornetta, for a commission of 1 percent on net sales. Under the terms of this contract, either party could terminate it only on written notice of six months. A few months later, Pacific Cornetta persuaded Evans to break his contract with Mathis and enter into a contract with Pacific Cornetta to be its sales representative to

(Continued)

CASE 4.1—Continued

Kmart. Evans terminated his contract with Mathis without notice. Two days later, Pacific Cornetta terminated its contract with Mathis. Mathis filed a suit in a federal district court against the Lius and Pacific Cornetta, alleging in part wrongful interference with a contractual relationship. The court issued a judgment that included a ruling in Mathis's favor on this claim, but Mathis appealed the amount of damages to the U.S. Court of Appeals for the Eighth Circuit.

IN THE WORDS OF THE COURT . . .
MORRIS SHEPHARD ARNOLD, Circuit Judge.

* * * *

* * * *[A] defendant is liable for tortious interference only if the defendant's interference with some relevant advantage was improper. [The] courts [look at several considerations] to determine whether a defendant's interference is improper.* These considerations include the nature of the actor's conduct[,] * * * the actor's motive[,] * * * the interests of the other with which the actor's conduct interferes[,] * * * the interests sought to be advanced by the actor[,] * * * the social interests in protecting the freedom of action of the actor and the contractual interests of the other[,] * * * the proximity or remoteness of the actor's conduct to the interference[,] and * * * the relations between the parties. [Emphasis added.]

We conclude that Mr. Mathis made out a * * * case on this element of his claim. If Mr. Evans's agency arrangement with Mr. Mathis had been purely at-will [a legal doctrine under which a contractual relationship can be terminated at any time by either party for any or no reason], we do not believe that Pacific Cornetta's successful effort to hire Mr. Evans * * * would have risen to the level of impropriety necessary to make out a case for tortious interference. That is because a party's interference with an at-will contract is primarily an interference with the future relation between the parties, and *when an at-will contract is terminated there is no breach of it.* In such circumstances, the interfering party is free for its own competitive advantage, to obtain the future benefits for itself by causing the termination, provided it uses suitable means. [Emphasis added.]

Mr. Evans's contract with Mr. Mathis, however, did not create a simple at-will arrangement because Mr. Evans could terminate it only after giving Mr. Mathis six months' notice of his intention to do so. In these circumstances, we think that the jury was entitled to conclude that Pacific Cornetta's blandishments [flattering statements] were improper, especially since *inducing a breach of contract absent compelling justification is, in and of itself, improper.* [Emphasis added.]

* * * *

Mr. Mathis asked for damages for the loss of anticipatory profits on his tortious interference claim. He argues that the damages that the jury awarded were supported by Mr. Evans's sales of * * * Pacific Cornetta products to Kmart [after Pacific Cornetta terminated the firm's contract with Mathis].

* * * *

We reject this theory * * * . Mr. Mathis's losses on these sales were a result of Pacific Cornetta exercising its right to terminate its contract with him at will, not Pacific Cornetta's tortious interference, and the losses were therefore not recoverable under a theory of tortious interference.

DECISION AND REMEDY The U.S. Court of Appeals for the Eighth Circuit affirmed the judgment of the lower court. The appellate court concluded that the defendants had committed wrongful interference with Mathis's contract with Evans. Evans's sales of Pacific Cornetta products after Pacific Cornetta terminated its

CASE 4.1—Continued

contract with Mathis could not furnish a basis for an award of damages on this claim, however, because the firm's contract with Mathis was terminable at will.

FOR CRITICAL ANALYSIS—Ethical Consideration

Does the ruling in this case mean that Mathis is entirely without recourse? Could he sue Evans for anything?

Wrongful Interference with a Business Relationship Businesspersons devise countless schemes to attract customers, but they are forbidden by the courts to interfere unreasonably with another's business in their attempts to gain a share of the market. There is a difference between competitive methods and **predatory behavior**—actions undertaken with the intention of unlawfully driving competitors completely out of the market.

PREDATORY BEHAVIOR
Business behavior that is undertaken with the intention of unlawfully driving competitors out of the market.

The distinction usually depends on whether a business is attempting to attract customers in general or to solicit only those customers who have shown an interest in a similar product or service of a specific competitor. If a shopping center contains two shoe stores, an employee of Store A cannot be positioned at the entrance of Store B for the purpose of diverting customers to Store A. This type of activity constitutes the tort of wrongful interference with a business relationship, which is commonly considered to be an unfair trade practice. If this type of activity were permitted, Store A would reap the benefits of Store B's advertising.

Defenses to Wrongful Interference A person will not be liable for the tort of wrongful interference with a contractual or business relationship if it can be shown that the interference was justified, or permissible. Bona fide competitive behavior is a permissible interference even if it results in the breaking of a contract. ■ EXAMPLE 4.5 If Antonio's Meats advertises so effectively that it induces Beverly's Restaurant Chain to break its contract with Otis Meat Company, Otis Meat Company will be unable to recover against Antonio's Meats on a wrongful interference theory. After all, the public policy that favors free competition in advertising outweighs any possible instability that such competitive activity might cause in contractual relations. ■

REMEMBER What society and the law consider permissible often depends on the circumstances.

Intentional Torts against Property

Intentional torts against property include trespass to land, trespass to personal property, conversion, and disparagement of property. These torts are wrongful actions that interfere with individuals' legally recognized rights with regard to their land or personal property. The law distinguishes real property from personal property (see Chapters 43 and 44). *Real property* is land and things "permanently" attached to the land. *Personal property* consists of all other items, which are basically movable. Thus, a house and lot are real property, whereas the furniture inside a house is personal property. Money and stocks and bonds are also personal property.

Trespass to Land

A **trespass to land** occurs whenever a person, without permission, enters onto, above, or below the surface of land that is owned by another; causes anything to enter onto the land; remains on the land; or permits anything to remain on it. Actual harm to the land is not an essential element of this tort because the tort is designed

TRESPASS TO LAND
The entry onto, above, or below the surface of land owned by another without the owner's permission or legal authorization.

to protect the right of an owner to exclusive possession of his or her property. Common types of trespass to land include walking or driving on someone else's land, shooting a gun over the land, throwing rocks at a building that belongs to someone else, building a dam across a river and thereby causing water to back up on someone else's land, and constructing a building so that part of it is on an adjoining landowner's property.

A sign warns trespassers. Should the law allow a trespasser to recover from a landowner for injuries sustained on the premises? Why or why not? (Frederick D. Bodling/Stock, Boston)

Trespass Criteria, Rights, and Duties Before a person can be a trespasser, the owner of the real property (or other person in actual and exclusive possession of the property) must establish that person as a trespasser. For example, "posted" trespass signs expressly establish as a trespasser a person who ignores these signs and enters onto the property. A guest in your home is not a trespasser—unless she or he has been asked to leave but refuses. Any person who enters onto your property to commit an illegal act (such as a thief entering a lumberyard at night to steal lumber) is established impliedly as a trespasser, without posted signs.

At common law, a trespasser is liable for damages caused to the property and generally cannot hold the owner liable for injuries sustained on the premises. This common law rule is being abandoned in many jurisdictions in favor of a "reasonable duty of care" rule that varies depending on the status of the parties; for example, a landowner may have a duty to post a notice that the property is patrolled by guard dogs. Furthermore, under the "attractive nuisance" doctrine, children do not assume the risks of the premises if they are attracted to the property by some object, such as a swimming pool, an abandoned building, or a sandpile. Trespassers normally can be removed from the premises through the use of reasonable force without the owner's being liable for assault and battery.

Defenses against Trespass to Land Trespass to land involves wrongful interference with another person's real property rights. One defense against a trespass claim is to show that the trespass was warranted, as when a trespasser enters to assist someone in danger. Another defense exists when the trespasser can show that he or she had a license to come onto the land. A *licensee* is one who is invited (or allowed to enter) onto the property of another for the licensee's benefit. A person who enters another's property to read an electric meter, for example, is a licensee. When you purchase a ticket to attend a movie or sporting event, you are licensed to go onto the property of another to view that movie or event. Note that licenses to enter on another's property are *revocable* by the property owner. If a property owner asks a meter reader to leave and the meter reader refuses to do so, the meter reader at that point becomes a trespasser.

Trespass to Personal Property

TRESPASS TO PERSONAL PROPERTY The unlawful taking or harming of another's personal property; interference with another's right to the exclusive possession of his or her personal property.

Whenever an individual unlawfully harms the personal property of another or otherwise interferes with the personal property owner's right to exclusive possession and enjoyment of that property, **trespass to personal property**—also called *trespass to personalty*[8]—occurs. If a student takes a classmate's business law book as a practical joke and hides it so that the owner is unable to find it for several days prior to the final examination, the student has engaged in a trespass to personal property.

If it can be shown that the trespass to personal property was warranted, then a complete defense exists. Most states, for example, allow automobile repair shops to

8. Pronounced *per*-sun-ul-tee.

hold a customer's car (under what is called an *artisan's lien,* discussed in Chapter 26) when the customer refuses to pay for repairs already completed. Trespass to personal property was one of the allegations in the following case. (For a discussion of whether spamming constitutes trespass to personal property, see the examination of cyber torts later in this chapter.)

CASE 4.2 Register.com, Inc. v. Verio, Inc.

United States Court of Appeals,
Second Circuit, 2004.
356 F.3d 393.

BACKGROUND AND FACTS The Internet Corporation for Assigned Names and Numbers (ICANN) administers the Internet domain name system. (Domain names will be discussed in detail in Chapter 5.) ICANN appoints registrars to issue the names to persons preparing to establish Web sites on the Internet. An applicant for a name must provide certain information, including an e-mail address. An agreement between ICANN and its registrars refers to this information as "WHOIS information" and requires the registrars to provide public access to it through the Internet "for any lawful purposes" except "the transmission of mass unsolicited, commercial advertising or solicitations via email (spam)." A party who wishes to obtain this information must also agree not to use it for this purpose. Register.com, Inc., is an ICANN registrar. Verio, Inc., sells Web site design and other services. Verio devised an automated software program (robot, or bot) to submit daily queries for Register's WHOIS data. Verio would then send ads by e-mail and other methods to the identified parties. Despite Register's request, Verio refused to stop. Register filed a suit in a federal district court against Verio, alleging in part trespass to personal property. The court ordered Verio to, among other things, stop accessing Register's computers by bot. Verio appealed to the U.S. Court of Appeals for the Second Circuit.

IN THE WORDS OF THE COURT . . .

LEVAL, Circuit Judge.

* * * *

* * * Register asserted, among other claims, that Verio was * * * trespassing on Register's chattels [personal property] in a manner likely to harm Register's computer systems by the use of Verio's automated robot software programs. On December 8, 2000, the district court entered a preliminary injunction. The injunction barred Verio from * * * [a]ccessing Register.com's computers and computer networks in any manner, including, but not limited to, * * * software programs performing multiple, automated, successive queries * * * .

* * * *

Verio * * * attacks the grant of the preliminary injunction against its accessing Register's computers by automated software programs performing multiple successive queries. This prong of the injunction was premised on Register's claim of trespass to chattels. Verio contends the ruling was in error because Register failed to establish that Verio's conduct resulted in harm to Register's servers and because Verio's robot access to the WHOIS database through Register was "not unauthorized." We believe the district court's findings were within the range of its permissible discretion.

A trespass to a chattel may be committed by intentionally * * * using or intermeddling with a chattel in the possession of another, where the chattel is impaired as to its condition, quality, or value.

The district court found that Verio's use of search robots, consisting of software programs performing multiple automated successive queries, consumed a significant

(Continued)

CASE 4.2—Continued

portion of the capacity of Register's computer systems. While Verio's robots alone would not incapacitate Register's systems, the court found that if Verio were permitted to continue to access Register's computers through such robots, it was "highly probable" that other Internet service providers would devise similar programs to access Register's data, and that the system would be overtaxed and would crash. We cannot say these findings were unreasonable.

Nor is there merit to Verio's contention that it cannot be engaged in trespass when Register had never instructed it not to use its robot programs. As the district court noted, Register's complaint sufficiently advised Verio that its use of robots was not authorized and, according to Register's contentions, would cause harm to Register's systems.

DECISION AND REMEDY The U.S. Court of Appeals for the Second Circuit affirmed the lower court's order. Trespass to personal property is "committed by intentionally * * * using or intermeddling with a chattel [personal property] in the possession of another, where the chattel is impaired as to its condition, quality, or value." In this case, Verio's use of search robots, "consumed a significant portion of the capacity of Register's computer systems."

FOR CRITICAL ANALYSIS—Technological Consideration *Why should the use of a bot to initiate "multiple automated successive queries" have a different legal effect than typing and submitting queries manually?*

CONVERSION

CONVERSION Wrongfully taking or retaining possession of an individual's personal property and placing it in the service of another.

KEEP IN MIND In tort law, the underlying motive for an act does not matter. What matters is the intent to do the act that results in the tort.

Whenever personal property is wrongfully taken from its rightful owner or possessor and placed in the service of another, the act of **conversion** occurs. Conversion is defined as any act depriving an owner of personal property without that owner's permission and without just cause. When conversion occurs, the lesser offense of trespass to personal property usually occurs as well. If the initial taking of the property was unlawful, there is trespass; retention of that property is conversion. If the initial taking of the property was permitted by the owner or for some other reason is not a trespass, failure to return it may still be conversion. Conversion is the civil side of crimes related to theft. A store clerk who steals merchandise from the store commits a crime and engages in the tort of conversion at the same time.

Even if a person mistakenly believed that she or he was entitled to the goods, the tort of conversion may occur. In other words, good intentions are not a defense against conversion; in fact, conversion can be an entirely innocent act. Someone who buys stolen goods, for example, is guilty of conversion even if he or she did not know that the goods were stolen. If the true owner brings a tort action against the buyer, the buyer must either return the property to the owner or pay the owner the full value of the property, despite having already paid the thief.

A successful defense against the charge of conversion is that the purported owner does not in fact own the property or does not have a right to possess it that is superior to the right of the holder. Necessity is another possible defense against conversion. ■ **EXAMPLE 4.6** If Abrams takes Mendoza's cat, Abrams is guilty of conversion. If Mendoza sues Abrams, Abrams must return the cat or pay damages. If, however, the cat has rabies and Abrams took the cat to protect the public, Abrams has a valid defense—necessity (and perhaps even self-defense, if he can prove that he was in danger because of the cat). ■

"To answer your question. Yes, if you shoot an arrow into the air and it falls to earth you should know not where, you could be liable for any damage it may cause."

DISPARAGEMENT OF PROPERTY

DISPARAGEMENT OF PROPERTY
An economically injurious falsehood made about another's product or property. A general term for torts that are more specifically referred to as slander of quality or slander of title.

Disparagement of property occurs when economically injurious falsehoods are made about another's product or property, not about another's reputation. Disparagement of property is a general term for torts that can be more specifically referred to as *slander of quality* or *slander of title.*

SLANDER OF QUALITY (TRADE LIBEL)
The publication of false information about another's product, alleging that it is not what its seller claims.

Slander of Quality Publication of false information about another's product, alleging that it is not what its seller claims, constitutes the tort of **slander of quality,** or **trade libel.** The plaintiff must prove that actual damages proximately resulted from the slander of quality. In other words, the plaintiff must show not only that a third person refrained from dealing with the plaintiff because of the improper publication but also that there were associated damages. The economic calculation of such damages—they are, after all, conjectural—is often extremely difficult.

An improper publication may be both a slander of quality and a defamation. For example, a statement that disparages the quality of a product may also, by implication, disparage the character of the person who would sell such a product.

SLANDER OF TITLE
The publication of a statement that denies or casts doubt on another's legal ownership of any property, causing financial loss to that property's owner.

Slander of Title When a publication denies or casts doubt on another's legal ownership of any property, and this results in financial loss to that property's owner, the tort of **slander of title** may exist. Usually, this is an intentional tort in which someone knowingly publishes an untrue statement about property with the intent of discouraging a third person from dealing with the person slandered. For example, it would be difficult for a car dealer to attract customers after competitors published a notice that the dealer's stock consisted of stolen autos.

Unintentional Torts (Negligence)

NEGLIGENCE
The failure to exercise the standard of care that a reasonable person would exercise in similar circumstances.

The tort of **negligence** occurs when someone suffers injury because of another's failure to live up to a required *duty of care.* In contrast to intentional torts, in torts involving negligence, the tortfeasor neither wishes to bring about the consequences of the act nor believes that they will occur. The actor's conduct merely creates a *risk* of such consequences. If no risk is created, there is no negligence.

Many of the actions discussed in the section on intentional torts constitute negligence if the element of intent is missing. ■ EXAMPLE 4.7 If Juarez intentionally shoves Natsuyo, who falls and breaks an arm as a result, Juarez will have committed the intentional tort of assault and battery. If Juarez carelessly bumps into Natsuyo, however, and she falls and breaks an arm as a result, Juarez's action will constitute negligence. In either situation, Juarez has committed a tort. ■

In examining a question of negligence, one should ask the following four questions (each of these elements of negligence will be discussed below):

1. Did the defendant owe a duty of care to the plaintiff?
2. Did the defendant breach that duty?
3. Did the plaintiff suffer a legally recognizable injury as a result of the defendant's breach of the duty of care?
4. Did the defendant's breach cause the plaintiff's injury?

THE DUTY OF CARE AND ITS BREACH

DUTY OF CARE
The duty of all persons, as established by tort law, to exercise a reasonable amount of care in their dealings with others. Failure to exercise due care, which is normally determined by the "reasonable person standard," constitutes the tort of negligence.

The concept of a **duty of care** arises from the notion that if we are to live in society with other people, some actions can be tolerated and some cannot; some actions are right and some are wrong; and some actions are reasonable and some are not. The basic principle underlying the duty of care is that people are free to act as they please so long as their actions do not infringe on the interests of others.

When someone fails to comply with the duty to exercise reasonable care, a potentially tortious act may have been committed. Failure to live up to a standard of care may be an act (setting fire to a building) or an omission (neglecting to put out a campfire). It may be a careless act or a carefully performed but nevertheless dangerous act that results in injury. Courts consider the nature of the act (whether it is outrageous or commonplace), the manner in which the act is performed (cautiously versus heedlessly), and the nature of the injury (whether it is serious or slight) in determining whether the duty of care has been breached.

REASONABLE PERSON STANDARD
The standard of behavior expected of a hypothetical "reasonable person"; the standard against which negligence is measured and that must be observed to avoid liability for negligence.

The Reasonable Person Standard Tort law measures duty by the **reasonable person standard.** In determining whether a duty of care has been breached, the courts ask how a reasonable person would have acted in the same circumstances. The reasonable person standard is said to be (though in an absolute sense it cannot be) objective. It is not necessarily how a particular person would act. It is society's judgment on how people *should* act. If the so-called reasonable person existed, he or she would be careful, conscientious, even tempered, and honest. The courts frequently use this hypothetical reasonable person in decisions relating to other areas of law as well.

That individuals are required to exercise a reasonable standard of care in their activities is a pervasive concept in business law, and many of the issues discussed in subsequent chapters of this text have to do with this duty. What constitutes reasonable care varies, of course, with the circumstances.

ETHICAL ISSUE 4.1

Does a person's duty of care include a duty to come to the aid of a stranger in peril? Suppose that you are walking down a city street and notice that a pedestrian is about to step directly in front of an oncoming bus. Do you have a legal duty to warn that individual? No. Although most people would probably concede that the observer has an *ethical* or moral duty to warn the other in this situation, tort law does not impose a general duty to rescue others in peril. People involved in special relationships, however, have been held to have a duty to rescue other parties within the relationship. A person has a duty to rescue his or her child or spouse if either is in danger, for example. Other special relationships, such as those between teachers and students or hiking and hunting partners, may also give rise to a duty to rescue. In addition, if a person who has no duty to rescue undertakes to rescue another, then the rescuer is charged with a duty to follow through with due care in the rescue attempt. ■

The Duty of Landowners Landowners are expected to exercise reasonable care to protect persons coming onto their property from harm. As mentioned earlier, in some jurisdictions, landowners are held to owe a duty to protect even trespassers against certain risks. Landowners who rent or lease premises to tenants (see Chapter 44) are expected to exercise reasonable care to ensure that the tenants and their guests are not harmed in common areas, such as stairways, entryways, laundry rooms, and the like.

Retailers and other firms that explicitly or implicitly invite persons to come onto their premises are usually charged with a duty to exercise reasonable care to protect those persons, who are considered **business invitees.** For example, if you entered a supermarket, slipped on a wet floor, and sustained injuries as a result, the owner of the supermarket would be liable for damages if when you slipped there was no sign warning that the floor was wet. A court would hold that the business owner was negligent because the owner failed to exercise a reasonable degree of care in protecting the store's customers against foreseeable risks about which the owner knew or *should have known.* That a patron might slip on the wet floor and be injured as a result was a foreseeable risk, and the owner should have taken care to avoid this risk or to warn the customer of it. The landowner also has a duty to discover and remove any hidden dangers that might injure a customer or other invitee.

BUSINESS INVITEE
A person, such as a customer or a client, who is invited onto business premises by the owner of those premises for business purposes.

Some risks, of course, are so obvious that the owner need not warn of them. For instance, a business owner does not have to warn customers to open a door before attempting to walk through it. Other risks, however, even though they may seem obvious to a business owner, may not be so in the eyes of another, such as a child. For example, a hardware store owner may not think it is necessary to warn customers not to climb a stepladder leaning against the back wall of the store. It is possible, though, that a child could climb up and tip the ladder over and be hurt as a result and that the store could be held liable.

The Duty of Professionals If an individual has knowledge, skill, or intelligence superior to that of an ordinary person, the individual's conduct must be consistent with that status. Professionals—including physicians, dentists, architects, engineers, accountants, lawyers, and others—are required to have a standard minimum level of special knowledge and ability. Therefore, in determining what constitutes reasonable care in the case of professionals, their training and expertise are taken into account. In other words, an accountant cannot defend against a lawsuit for negligence by stating, "But I was not familiar with that principle of accounting."

.on the Web You can locate the professional standards for various organizations at **http://www.lib.uwaterloo.ca/society/standards.html**.

MALPRACTICE
Professional misconduct or the lack of the requisite degree of skill as a professional. Negligence—the failure to exercise due care—on the part of a professional, such as a physician, is commonly referred to as malpractice.

If a professional violates her or his duty of care toward a client, the professional may be sued for **malpractice.** For example, a patient might sue a physician for *medical malpractice.* A client might sue an attorney for *legal malpractice.*

THE INJURY REQUIREMENT AND DAMAGES

For a tort to have been committed, the plaintiff must have suffered a *legally recognizable* injury. To recover damages (receive compensation), the plaintiff must have suffered some loss, harm, wrong, or invasion of a protected interest. Essentially, the purpose of tort law is to compensate for legally recognized injuries resulting from wrongful acts. If no harm or injury results from a given negligent action, there is nothing to compensate—and no tort exists. ■ EXAMPLE 4.8 If you carelessly bump into a passerby, who stumbles and falls as a result, you may be liable in tort if the passerby is injured in the fall. If the person is unharmed, however, there normally could be no suit for damages, because no injury was suffered. ■

COMPENSATORY DAMAGES
A money award equivalent to the actual value of injuries or damages sustained by the aggrieved party.

PUNITIVE DAMAGES
Money damages that may be awarded to a plaintiff to punish the defendant and deter future similar conduct.

As already mentioned, the purpose of tort law is not to punish people for tortious acts but to compensate the injured parties for harm suffered by awarding damages. **Compensatory damages** are intended to reimburse a plaintiff for actual losses—to make the plaintiff whole. Occasionally, **punitive damages** are also awarded to punish the wrongdoer and deter others from similar wrongdoing. Punitive damages are rarely awarded in lawsuits for ordinary negligence and usually are given only in cases involving intentional torts. They may be awarded, however, in suits involving *gross negligence,* which can be defined as an intentional failure to perform a manifest duty in reckless disregard of the consequences of such a failure for the life or property of another. (Do other nations award punitive damages in tort cases? See this chapter's *International Perspective* feature for a discussion of tort liability in other countries.)

In *State Farm Mutual Automobile Insurance Co. v. Campbell,*[9] the United States Supreme Court held that to the extent an award of punitive damages is grossly excessive, it furthers no legitimate purpose and violates due process requirements (discussed in Chapter 2). While this case dealt with intentional torts (fraud and intentional infliction of emotional distress), the Court's holding applies equally to punitive damages awards in gross negligence cases.

CAUSATION

Another element necessary to a tort is *causation.* If a person fails in a duty of care and someone suffers injury, the wrongful activity must have caused the harm for a tort to have been committed. In deciding whether there is causation, the court must address two questions:

CAUSATION IN FACT
An act or omission without which an event would not have occurred.

PROXIMATE CAUSE
Legal cause; exists when the connection between an act and an injury is strong enough to justify imposing liability.

1. *Is there causation in fact?* Did the injury occur because of the defendant's act, or would it have occurred anyway? If an injury would not have occurred without the defendant's act, then there is causation in fact. **Causation in fact** can usually be determined by the use of the *but for* test: "but for" the wrongful act, the injury would not have occurred. Theoretically, causation in fact is limitless. One could claim, for example, that "but for" the creation of the world, a particular injury would not have occurred. Thus, as a practical matter, the law has to establish limits, and it does so through the concept of proximate cause.
2. *Was the act the proximate cause of the injury?* **Proximate cause,** or legal cause, exists when the connection between an act and an injury is strong enough to jus-

9. 538 U.S. 408, 123 S.Ct. 1513, 155 L.Ed.2d 585 (2003).

INTERNATIONAL PERSPECTIVE

Tort Liability and Damages in Other Nations

In contrast to U.S. courts, courts in Europe generally limit damages to compensatory damages; punitive damages are virtually unheard of in European countries. Even when plaintiffs do win compensatory damages, they generally receive much less than would be awarded in a similar case brought in the United States. In part, this is because citizens of European countries usually receive government-provided health care and relatively generous Social Security benefits. Yet it is also because European courts tend to view the duty of care and the concept of risk differently than U.S. courts do. In the United States, if a swimmer falls off a high diving board and is injured, a court may decide that the pool owner should be held liable, given that such a fall is a foreseeable risk. If punitive damages are awarded, they could total millions of dollars. In a similar situation in Europe, a court might hold that the plaintiff, not the pool owner, was responsible for the injury.

Tort laws in other nations also differ in the way damages are calculated. For example, under Swiss law and Turkish law, a court is permitted to reduce the amount of damages if an award of full damages would cause undue hardship for a party who was found negligent. In the United States, in contrast, the courts normally do not take this factor into consideration.

FOR CRITICAL ANALYSIS

Punitive damages are a very important element in American tort litigation. Why is this? What do awards of punitive damages achieve?

tify imposing liability. ■ EXAMPLE 4.9 Ackerman carelessly leaves a campfire burning. The fire not only burns down the forest but also sets off an explosion in a nearby chemical plant that spills chemicals into a river, killing all the fish for a hundred miles downstream and ruining the economy of a tourist resort. Should Ackerman be liable to the resort owners? To the tourists whose vacations were ruined? These are questions of proximate cause that a court must decide. ■

NOTE Proximate cause can be thought of as a question of social policy. Should the defendant be made to bear the loss instead of the plaintiff?

Probably the most cited case on proximate cause is the *Palsgraf* case, discussed in this chapter's *Landmark in the Law* feature on the following page. In determining the issue of proximate cause, the court addressed the following question: Does a defendant's duty of care extend only to those who may be injured as a result of a foreseeable risk, or does it extend also to a person whose injury could not reasonably be foreseen?

DEFENSES TO NEGLIGENCE

Defendants often defend against negligence claims by asserting that the plaintiffs failed to prove the existence of one or more of the required elements for negligence. Additionally, there are three basic *affirmative* defenses in negligence cases (defenses that defendants can use to avoid liability even if the facts are as the plaintiffs state): (1) assumption of risk, (2) superseding cause, and (3) contributory and comparative negligence.

ASSUMPTION OF RISK
A doctrine under which a plaintiff may not recover for injuries or damages suffered from risks he or she knows of and has voluntarily assumed.

Assumption of Risk A plaintiff who voluntarily enters into a risky situation, knowing the risk involved, will not be allowed to recover. This is the defense of **assumption of risk.** The requirements of this defense are (1) knowledge of the risk and (2) voluntary assumption of the risk.

The risk can be assumed by express agreement, or the assumption of risk can be implied by the plaintiff's knowledge of the risk and subsequent conduct. For example,

LANDMARK IN THE LAW

Palsgraf v. Long Island Railroad Co. (1928)

In 1928, the New York Court of Appeals (that state's highest court) issued its decision in *Palsgraf v. Long Island Railroad Co.*,[a] a case that has become a landmark in negligence law with respect to proximate cause.

THE FACTS OF THE CASE The plaintiff, Palsgraf, was waiting for a train on a station platform. A man carrying a small package wrapped in newspaper was rushing to catch a train that had begun to move away from the platform. As the man attempted to jump aboard the moving train, he seemed unsteady and about to fall. A railroad guard on the train car reached forward to grab him, and another guard on the platform pushed him from behind to help him board the train. In the process, the man's package fell on the railroad tracks and exploded, because it contained fireworks. The repercussions of the explosion caused scales at the other end of the train platform to fall on Palsgraf, who was injured as a result. She sued the railroad company for damages in a New York state court.

THE QUESTION OF PROXIMATE CAUSE At the trial, the jury found that the railroad guards were negligent in their conduct. On appeal, the question before the New York Court of Appeals was whether the conduct of the railroad guards was the proximate cause of Palsgraf's injuries. In other words, did the guards' duty of care extend to Palsgraf, who was outside the zone of danger and whose injury could not reasonably have been foreseen?

The court stated that the question of whether the guards were negligent *with respect to Palsgraf* depended on whether her injury was *reasonably foreseeable* to the railroad guards. Although the guards may have acted negligently with respect to the man boarding the train, this had no bearing on the question of their negligence with respect to Palsgraf. This was not a situation in which a person committed an act so potentially harmful (for example, firing a gun at a building) that he or she would be held responsible for any harm that resulted. The court stated that here "there was nothing in the situation to suggest to the most cautious mind that the parcel wrapped in newspaper would spread wreckage through the station." The court thus concluded that the railroad guards were not negligent with respect to Palsgraf because her injury was not reasonably foreseeable.

APPLICATION TO TODAY'S BUSINESS WORLD

The Palsgraf *case established* foreseeability *as the test for proximate cause. Today, the courts continue to apply this test in determining proximate cause—and thus tort liability for injuries. Generally, if the victim of a harm or the consequences of a harm done are unforeseeable, there is no proximate cause. Note, though, that in the online environment, distinctions based on physical proximity, such as the "zone of danger" cited by the court in this case, are largely inapplicable.*

RELEVANT WEB SITES

To locate information on the Web concerning the Palsgraf *decision, go to this text's Web site at* **http://blt.westbuslaw.com**, *select "Chapter 4," and click on "URLs for Landmarks."*

a. 248 N.Y. 339, 162 N.E. 99 (1928).

a driver entering a race knows that there is a risk of being killed or injured in a crash. Of course, the plaintiff does not assume a risk different from or greater than the risk normally carried by the activity. In our example, the race driver would not assume the risk that the banking in the curves of the racetrack will give way during the race because of a construction defect.

Risks are not deemed to be assumed in situations involving emergencies. Neither are they assumed when a statute protects a class of people from harm and a member of the class is injured by the harm. For example, employees are protected by statute from harmful working conditions and therefore do not assume the risks associated with the workplace. An employee who is injured will generally be compensated regardless of fault under state workers' compensation statutes (discussed in Chapter 40).

Superseding Cause An unforeseeable intervening event may break the connection between a wrongful act and an injury to another. If so, the event acts as a *superseding cause*—that is, it relieves a defendant of liability for injuries caused by the intervening event. ■ EXAMPLE 4.10 Suppose that Derrick keeps a can of gasoline in the trunk of his car. The presence of the gasoline creates a foreseeable risk and is thus a negligent act. If Derrick's car skids and crashes into a tree, causing the gasoline can to explode, Derrick would be liable for injuries sustained by passing pedestrians because of his negligence. If the explosion had been caused by lightning striking the car, however, the lightning would supersede Derrick's original negligence as a cause of the damage, because the lightning was not foreseeable. ■

CONTRIBUTORY NEGLIGENCE
A rule in tort law that completely bars the plaintiff from recovering any damages if the damage suffered is partly the plaintiff's own fault; used in a minority of states.

COMPARATIVE NEGLIGENCE
A rule in tort law that reduces the plaintiff's recovery in proportion to the plaintiff's degree of fault, rather than barring recovery completely; used in the majority of states.

Contributory and Comparative Negligence All individuals are expected to exercise a reasonable degree of care in looking out for themselves. In the past, under the common law doctrine of **contributory negligence,** a plaintiff who was also negligent (failed to exercise a reasonable degree of care) could not recover anything from the defendant. Under this rule, no matter how insignificant the plaintiff's negligence was relative to the defendant's negligence, the plaintiff would be precluded from recovering any damages. Today, only a few jurisdictions still hold to this doctrine. In the majority of states, the doctrine of contributory negligence has been replaced by a **comparative negligence** standard.

Under the comparative negligence standard, both the plaintiff's and the defendant's negligence are computed, and the liability for damages is distributed accordingly. Some jurisdictions have adopted a "pure" form of comparative negligence that allows the plaintiff to recover, even if the extent of his or her fault is greater than that of the defendant. For example, if the plaintiff was 80 percent at fault and the defendant 20 percent at fault, the plaintiff may recover 20 percent of his or her damages. Many states' comparative negligence statutes, however, contain a "50 percent" rule that precludes the plaintiff from any recovery if she or he was more than 50 percent at fault.

A bungee jumper leaps from a platform. If the jumper is injured and sues the operator of the jump for negligence, what defenses might the operator use to avoid liability? (Paul Thompson/Image State)

Special Negligence Doctrines and Statutes

There are a number of special doctrines and statutes relating to negligence. We examine a few of them here.

Res Ipsa Loquitur Generally, in lawsuits involving negligence, the plaintiff has the burden of proving that the defendant was negligent. In certain situations, however, when negligence is very difficult or impossible to prove, the courts may infer that negligence has occurred; then the burden of proof rests on the defendant—to prove

RES IPSA LOQUITUR
A doctrine under which negligence may be inferred simply because an event occurred, if it is the type of event that would never occur in the absence of negligence. Literally, the term means "the facts speak for themselves."

he or she was *not* negligent. The inference of the defendant's negligence is known as the doctrine of ***res ipsa loquitur,***[10] which translates as "the facts speak for themselves."

This doctrine is applied only when the event creating the damage or injury is one that ordinarily would occur only as a result of negligence. ■ **EXAMPLE 4.11** If a person undergoes knee surgery and following the surgery has a severed nerve in the knee area, that person can sue the surgeon under a theory of *res ipsa loquitur.* In this instance, the injury would never have occurred in the absence of the surgeon's negligence.[11] ■ For the doctrine of *res ipsa loquitur* to apply, the event must have been within the defendant's power to control, and it must not have been due to any voluntary action or contribution on the part of the plaintiff.

NEGLIGENCE *PER SE*
An action or failure to act in violation of a statutory requirement.

Negligence *Per Se* Certain conduct, whether it consists of an action or a failure to act, may be treated as **negligence *per se*** (*per se* means "in or of itself"). Negligence *per se* may occur if an individual violates a statute or an ordinance providing for a criminal penalty and that violation causes another to be injured. The injured person must prove (1) that the statute clearly sets out what standard of conduct is expected, when and where it is expected, and of whom it is expected; (2) that he or she is in the class intended to be protected by the statute; and (3) that the statute was designed to prevent the type of injury that he or she suffered. The standard of conduct required by the statute is the duty that the defendant owes to the plaintiff, and a violation of the statute is the breach of that duty.

■ **EXAMPLE 4.12** A statute may require a landowner to maintain a building in safe condition and may also subject the owner to a criminal penalty, such as a fine, if the building is not kept safe. The statute is meant to protect those who are rightfully in the building. Thus, if the owner, without a sufficient excuse, violates the statute and a tenant is thereby injured, a majority of courts will hold that the owner's unexcused violation of the statute conclusively establishes a breach of a duty of care—that is, that the owner's violation is negligence *per se.* ■

"Danger Invites Rescue" Doctrine Typically, if an individual takes a defensive action, such as swerving to avoid an oncoming car, the original wrongdoer will not be relieved of liability even if the injury actually resulted from the attempt to escape harm. The same is true under the "danger invites rescue" doctrine. ■ **EXAMPLE 4.13** If Lemming commits an act that endangers Salter, and Yokem sustains an injury trying to protect Salter, then Lemming will be liable for Yokem's injury. Lemming will also be liable for any injuries Salter may sustain. ■ Rescuers can injure themselves, or the person rescued, or even a stranger, but the original wrongdoer will still be liable.

GOOD SAMARITAN STATUTE
A state statute stipulating that persons who provide emergency services to, or rescue, someone in peril cannot be sued for negligence, unless they act recklessly, thereby causing further harm.

Special Negligence Statutes A number of states have enacted statutes prescribing duties and responsibilities in certain circumstances. For example, most states now have what are called **Good Samaritan statutes.** Under these statutes, someone who is aided voluntarily by others cannot turn around and sue the "Good Samaritans" for negligence. These laws were passed largely to protect physicians and medical personnel who voluntarily render services in emergency situations to those in need, such as individuals hurt in car accidents.

---

10. Pronounced *rehz ihp*-suh *low*-kwuh-tuhr.
11. *Edwards v. Boland,* 41 Mass.App.Ct. 375, 670 N.E.2d 404 (1996).

DRAM SHOP ACT
A state statute that imposes liability on the owners of bars and taverns, as well as those who serve alcoholic drinks to the public, for injuries resulting from accidents caused by intoxicated persons when the sellers or servers of alcoholic drinks contributed to the intoxication.

Many states have also passed **dram shop acts,** under which a tavern owner or bartender may be held liable for injuries caused by a person who became intoxicated while drinking at the bar or who was already intoxicated when served by the bartender. In some states, statutes impose liability on *social hosts* (persons hosting parties) for injuries caused by guests who became intoxicated at the hosts' homes. Under these statutes, it is unnecessary to prove that the tavern owner, bartender, or social host was negligent.

Strict Liability

STRICT LIABILITY
Liability regardless of fault. In tort law, strict liability is imposed on a manufacturer or seller that introduces into commerce a good that is unreasonably dangerous when in a defective condition.

Another category of torts is called **strict liability,** or *liability without fault.* Intentional torts and torts of negligence involve acts that depart from a reasonable standard of care and cause injuries. Under the doctrine of strict liability, liability for injury is imposed for reasons other than fault. Strict liability for damages proximately caused by an abnormally dangerous or exceptional activity is one application of this doctrine. Courts apply the doctrine of strict liability in such cases because of the extreme risk of the activity. Even if blasting with dynamite is performed with all reasonable care, there is still a risk of injury. Balancing that risk against the potential for harm, it seems reasonable to ask the person engaged in the activity to pay for injuries caused by that activity. Although there is no fault, there is still responsibility because of the dangerous nature of the undertaking.

There are other applications of the strict liability principle. Persons who keep dangerous animals, for example, are strictly liable for any harm inflicted by the animals. A significant application of strict liability is in the area of *product liability*—liability of manufacturers and sellers for harmful or defective products. Liability here is a matter of social policy and is based on two factors: (1) the manufacturer or seller can better bear the cost of injury because it can spread the cost throughout society by increasing prices of goods and services, and (2) the manufacturer or seller is making a profit from its activities and therefore should bear the cost of injury as an operating expense. We will discuss product liability in greater detail in Chapter 21.

Cyber Torts

It should come as no surprise that torts can also be committed in the online environment. Torts committed via the Internet are often called *cyber torts.* Over the last ten years, the courts have had to decide how to apply traditional tort law to torts committed in cyberspace. Consider, for example, issues of proof. How can it be proved that an online defamatory remark was "published" (which requires that a third party see or hear it)? How can the identity of the person who made the remark be discovered? Can an Internet service provider (ISP), such as AOL, be forced to reveal the source of an anonymous comment made by one of its subscribers? We explore some of these questions in this section, as well as some of the legal issues that have arisen with respect to bulk e-mail advertising.

Defamation Online

Recall from the discussion of defamation earlier in this chapter that one who repeats or otherwise republishes a defamatory statement can be subject to liability as if he or she had originally published it. Thus, publishers generally can be held liable for

For an interesting article discussing the increasing number of online defamation cases and the associated costs, go to the Web site of *Computer Times* at

http://computertimes.asia1.com/issues/story/0,5104,1577,00.html.

defamatory contents in the books and periodicals that they publish. Now consider online forums. These forums allow anyone—customers, employees, or crackpots—to complain about a firm's personnel, policies, practices, or products. Whatever the truth of the complaint is, it might have an impact on the business of the firm. One of the early questions in the online legal arena was whether the providers of such forums could be held liable, as publishers, for defamatory statements made in those forums.

Liability of Internet Service Providers Prior to the passage of the Communications Decency Act (CDA) of 1996, the courts grappled on several occasions with the question of whether ISPs should be regarded as publishers and thus be held liable for defamatory messages made by users of their services. The CDA resolved the issue by stating that "[n]o provider or user of an interactive computer service shall be treated as the publisher or speaker of any information provided by another information content provider."[12] In a number of key cases, the ISP provisions of the CDA have been invoked to shield ISPs from liability for defamatory postings on their bulletin boards.

■ **EXAMPLE 4.14** In a leading case on this issue, decided the year after the CDA was enacted, America Online, Inc. (AOL, now part of Time Warner, Inc.), was not held liable even though it did not promptly remove defamatory messages of which it had been made aware. In upholding a U.S. district court's ruling in AOL's favor, a federal appellate court stated that the CDA "plainly immunizes computer service providers like AOL from liability for information that originates with third parties." The court explained that the purpose of the statute is "to maintain the robust nature of Internet communication and, accordingly, to keep government interference in the medium to a minimum."[13] ■

In subsequent cases, the courts have reached similar conclusions.[14] The courts have also extended the immunity to liability provided by the CDA to auction houses, such as eBay.[15] At issue in the following case was whether the CDA also shields secondary publishers, or distributors, from liability.

---

12. 47 U.S.C. Section 230.
13. *Zeran v. America Online, Inc.,* 129 F.3d 327 (4th Cir. 1997); *cert.* denied, 524 U.S. 934, 118 S.Ct. 2341, 141 L.Ed.2d 712 (1998).
14. See, for example, *Noah v. AOL Time Warner, Inc.,* 261 F.Supp.2d 532 (E.D.Va. 2003).
15. *Stoner v. eBay, Inc.,* 2000 WL 1705637 (Cal.Super.Ct. 2000).

CASE 4.3 Barrett v. Rosenthal

California Court of Appeal,
First District,
Division 2, 2004.
9 Cal.Rptr.3d 142.

BACKGROUND AND FACTS Stephen Barrett and Terry Polevoy are physicians engaged in combating illegal or unsubstantiated alternative health-care practices and products. Each maintains Web sites that expose "health frauds and quackery" and provide guides to help consumers make intelligent health-care decisions. Ilena Rosenthal directs the Humantics Foundation for Women and participates in usenet newsgroups that focus on alternative medicine. Among her postings, Rosenthal distributed an e-mail message that she received from another individual, Timothy Bolen, accusing Polevoy of stalking women. Polevoy informed Rosenthal that the message was not true and asked her to withdraw it, but she refused and reposted the message many times, referring to Barrett and Polevoy as "quacks." She also posted statements that the two physicians were "a power-hungry, misguided bunch of pseudo-scientific socialist bigots" and were "being sued by many doctors and health organizations." Barrett and Polevoy filed

CASE 4.3—Continued

a suit in a California state court against Rosenthal and others, alleging libel and other torts. The court ruled in part that under the CDA, Rosenthal was immune from liability for the reposting of Bolen's statements. The plaintiffs appealed to a state intermediate appellate court, arguing that the CDA's use of the word *publisher* does not include "secondary" publishers, or distributors.

IN THE WORDS OF THE COURT . . .

KLINE, Presiding Judge.

* * * *

* * * [S]tatutes which invade the common law * * * are to be read with a presumption favoring the retention of long-established and familiar principles, except when a statutory purpose to the contrary is evident. In such cases, Congress does not write upon a clean slate. In order to abrogate a common-law principle, the statute must speak directly to the question addressed by the common law.

* * * Section 230(c)(1) [of the CDA states] "No provider or user of an interactive computer service shall be treated as the publisher or speaker of any information provided by another information content provider." * * *

It is true that defamation requires a publication, and that every repetition is a publication, whether it is effectuated by a primary publisher or by a distributor; this is why distributors are sometimes referred to as "secondary publishers." However, * * * the common law subjects the two types of publishers to distinctly different standards of liability for the transmission of the defamation of a third person. Because primary publishers ordinarily exercise control over content, they have a duty to monitor content; distributors, who have no such control, therefore have no such duty. It is entirely reasonable to assume Congress was aware of this significant and very well-established distinction, and that if it intended Section 230 to immunize providers and users not merely from primary publisher liability but also from distributor liability it would have made this clear, as, for example, by adding the word "distributor," and not merely barring liability "as the publisher or speaker" of information provided by another. Section 230 does not explicitly absolve providers or users from all liability. The statement that they "shall not incur liability as publishers or speakers of information provided by other content providers" does not expressly or even by necessary implication foreclose the possibility of holding them liable as distributors. Indeed, one could argue from the enumeration of publisher and speaker in Section 230(c)(1) that distributor was deliberately omitted.

* * * *

Legislative use of the legally uncertain word "publisher" is simply too flimsy a basis upon which to grant providers and users of interactive computer services what amounts to an absolute protection requiring the total sacrifice of the competing value served by the law of defamation and the subordination of a concept at the root of any decent system of ordered liberty. When distinguishing the liability of publishers and distributors, eminent law professors writing scholarly articles in learned journals commonly use the word "publisher" to refer only to a primary publisher, even when their subject is the transmission of speech in cyberspace. So too do courts commonly use the word "publisher" to refer only to an original or primary publisher. * * * It is impossible to say with confidence that Congress did not also use the word "publisher" in this conventional manner. In any case, in law and as it appears in Section 230, the word "publisher" is at least capable of two reasonable

(Continued)

CASE 4.3—Continued

constructions and therefore ambiguous * * * . Where there is a limitation by statute which is capable of more than one construction the statute must be given that construction which is consistent with common law.

* * * *

The findings and declarations set forth in Section 230 applaud the "true diversity of political discourse," the "opportunities for cultural development," and the "myriad avenues for intellectual activity" provided by "the vibrant and competitive free market that presently exists for the Internet and other interactive computer services," but nowhere in the findings and declarations is there any indication that Congress considered online speech in need of protection. Nor is a general concern for the promotion of speech evident in Section 230(c), entitled "Protection for 'Good Samaritan' blocking and screening of offensive material," which we think particularly revealing. Section 230(c)(2) immunizes providers and users against liability on account of action "to restrict access to or availability of material that the provider or user considers to be * * * objectionable, whether or not such material is constitutionally protected," or to provide others "the technical means to restrict access to [such] material * * * ."

If Congress's use of the word "publisher" covers distributors as well as original publishers, and therefore reflects an intent to create an absolute immunity, it would not have been necessary for Congress to specifically protect providers and users who monitor content; Section 230(c)(2) would be mere surplusage.

DECISION AND REMEDY The state intermediate appellate court vacated the lower court's ruling on this issue and remanded the case for further proceedings. A secondary publisher, or distributor, of another's libelous statements is not immune from liability under the CDA. If Congress intended the CDA "to immunize providers and users not merely from primary publisher liability but also from distributor liability it would have made this clear."

WHY IS THIS CASE IMPORTANT? *In this case, the court refused to extend to secondary publishers (distributors) the immunity that the CDA gives to primary publishers. The court concluded that if Congress had intended to protect providers and users from distributor liability, Congress would have made that intent clear. This ruling establishes that, on some level, secondary publishers can be held responsible for the libelous materials that they distribute.*

Piercing the Veil of Anonymity A threshold barrier to anyone who seeks to bring an action for online defamation is discovering the identity of the person who posted the defamatory message online. ISPs can disclose personal information about their customers only when ordered to do so by a court. Consequently, businesses and individuals are increasingly resorting to lawsuits against "John Does." Then, using the authority of the courts, they can obtain from the ISPs the identities of the persons responsible for the messages.

■ **EXAMPLE 4.15** In one case, Eric Hvide, a former chief executive of a company called Hvide Marine, sued a number of "John Does" who had posted allegedly defamatory statements about his company on various online message boards. Hvide, who eventually lost his job, sued the John Does for libel in a Florida court. The court ruled that Yahoo and AOL had to reveal the identities of the defendant Does.[16] ■

16. *Does v. Hvide,* 770 So.2d 1237 (Fla.App.3d 2000).

In other cases, however, the courts have refused to order an ISP to disclose the identity of subscribers.[17] Generally, in these cases the courts must decide which right should take priority: the right to free (anonymous) speech under the First Amendment or the right not to be defamed.

SPAM

SPAM
Bulk, unsolicited ("junk") e-mail.

Bulk, unsolicited e-mail ("junk" e-mail) sent to all of the users on a particular e-mailing list is often called **spam.**[18] Typically, spam consists of a product ad sent to all of the users on an e-mailing list or all of the members of a newsgroup.

.on the Web The Center for Democracy and Technology conducted a study on spam. The report and the center's recommendations on how to avoid receiving spam are available online at

http://www.cdt.org/speech/spam/030319spamreport.shtml.

Spam wastes user time and network bandwidth (the amount of data that can be transmitted within a certain time). It also imposes a burden on an ISP's equipment as well as on e-mail recipients' computer systems. Does this mean that spamming may constitute a form of trespass to personal property? For a discussion of this question, see this chapter's *Adapting the Law to the Online Environment* feature on the following page.

In the last few years, the number of e-mail ads traveling through cyberspace has escalated significantly, and today spam accounts for an estimated 60 percent of all e-mail. Indeed, many contend that unwanted e-mail is threatening the viability of e-mail as a communications tool and an instrument of commerce. Because of the problems associated with spam, a majority of the states now have laws regulating spam. In 2003, the U.S. Congress also enacted a law to regulate the use of spam.

State Regulation of Spam Because of the problems associated with spam, thirty-six states have enacted laws that prohibit or regulate its use. A few states, such as Washington, prohibit unsolicited e-mail that is promoting goods, services, or real estate for sale or lease. In some other states, including Minnesota, an unsolicited e-mail ad must state in its subject line that it is an ad ("ADV:"). Many state laws regulating spam require the senders of e-mail ads to instruct the recipients on how they can "opt out" of further e-mail ads from the same sources. For instance, in some states an unsolicited e-mail ad must include a toll-free phone number or return e-mail address through which the recipient can contact the sender to request that no more ads be e-mailed.

The most stringent state law is California's antispam law, which went into effect on January 1, 2004. That law follows the "opt-in" model favored by consumer groups and antispam advocates. In other words, the law prohibits any person or business from sending e-mail ads to or from any e-mail address in California unless the recipient has expressly agreed to receive e-mails from the sender. An exemption is made for e-mail sent to consumers with whom the advertiser has a "preexisting or current business relationship."

The Federal CAN-SPAM Act In 2003, Congress enacted the Controlling the Assault of Non-Solicited Pornography and Marketing (CAN-SPAM) Act, which took effect on January 1, 2004. The legislation applies to any "commercial electronic mail messages" that are sent to promote a commercial product or service. Significantly, the statute preempts state antispam laws except for those provisions in state laws that prohibit false and deceptive e-mailing practices.

17. See, for example, *Graham v. Oppenheimer,* 2000 WL 33381418 (E.D.Va. 2000).

18. The term *spam* is said to come from a Monty Python song with the lyrics, "Spam spam spam spam, spam spam spam spam, lovely spam, wonderful spam." Like these lyrics, spam online is often considered to be a repetition of worthless text.

ADAPTING THE LAW TO THE ONLINE ENVIRONMENT

Can Spamming Constitute a Tort?

Spam-related issues are, of course, unique to the cyber age. Can traditional tort law apply to such issues? For example, when spam overloads a business's computer system or impairs its computer equipment, can the recipient of the spam bring an action under tort law? Since the latter half of the 1990s, a number of plaintiffs have done so, with some success, by claiming that spamming constitutes a trespass to personal property, or *chattels*—a term used under the common law to denote all forms of personal property. The term *trespass to chattels* is usually defined as any unauthorized interference with the use of the personal property of another.

SPAMMING AS A FORM OF TRESPASS

In a leading case on this issue, decided in 1997, Cyber Promotions, Inc., sent bulk e-mail to subscribers of CompuServe, Inc., an ISP. CompuServe subscribers complained to the service about the ads, and many canceled their subscriptions. Handling the ads also placed a tremendous burden on CompuServe's equipment.

CompuServe told Cyber Promotions to stop using CompuServe's equipment to process and store the ads—in effect, to stop sending the ads to CompuServe subscribers. Ignoring the demand, Cyber Promotions stepped up the volume of its ads. After CompuServe attempted unsuccessfully to block the flow with screening software, it filed a suit against Cyber Promotions in a federal district court, seeking an injunction on the ground that the ads constituted trespass to personal property. The court agreed and ordered Cyber Promotions to stop sending its ads to e-mail addresses maintained by CompuServe.[a]

NEW DIRECTIONS IN CALIFORNIA

A 2003 decision by the California Supreme Court may make it more difficult for plaintiffs in that state's courts to combat spammers using tort law. The case was brought by Intel Corporation against one of its former employees, Ken Hamidi. After he was fired, Hamidi sent a series of six e-mail messages to 35,000 Intel employees over a twenty-one-month period. In the messages, Hamidi criticized the company's labor practices and urged employees to leave the company.

Intel sought a court order to stop the e-mail campaign, arguing that Hamidi's actions constituted a trespass to chattels because the e-mail significantly interfered with productivity, thus causing economic damage. When the case reached the California Supreme Court, the court held that under California law, the tort of trespass to chattels requires some evidence of injury to the plaintiff's personal property. Because Hamidi's e-mail had neither damaged Intel's computer system nor impaired its functioning, Hamidi's actions did not amount to a trespass to chattels.

The court distinguished Intel's case from cases in which spamming actually interfered with a computer system or threatened to do so. The court did not reject the idea that trespass theory could apply to cyberspace. Rather, the court simply held that to succeed in a lawsuit for trespass to chattels, a plaintiff must demonstrate that some concrete harm resulted from the unwanted e-mail. Although Hamidi's e-mail messages may have diverted employees' time and attention, thereby interfering with their productivity, the e-mails did not overburden Intel's computer systems—and thus did not amount to a concrete harm in the eyes of the court.[b]

FOR CRITICAL ANALYSIS

Three dissenting justices in the California case maintained that intruding on private property, regardless of injury, should be sufficient to demonstrate trespass to chattels. Do you agree? Why or why not?

a. *CompuServe, Inc. v. Cyber Promotions, Inc.*, 962 F.Supp. 1015 (S.D. Ohio 1997).

b. *Intel Corp. v. Hamidi*, 30 Cal.4th 1342, 71 P.3d 296, 1 Cal.Rptr.3d 32 (2003).

Generally, the act permits the use of unsolicited commercial e-mail but prohibits certain types of spamming activities, including the use of a false return address and the use of false, misleading, or deceptive information when sending e-mail. The statute also prohibits the use of "dictionary attacks"—sending messages to randomly generated e-mail addresses—and the "harvesting" of e-mail addresses from Web sites through the use of specialized software. Additionally, the law requires senders of commercial e-mail to do the following:

1. Include a return address on the e-mail.
2. Include a clear notification that the message is an ad and provide a valid physical postal address.
3. Provide a mechanism that allows recipients to "opt out" of further e-mail ads from the same source.
4. Take action on a recipient's "opt-out" request within ten days.
5. Label any sexually oriented materials as such.

ETHICAL ISSUE 4.2

Who benefits from the CAN-SPAM Act? Some of the stricter state laws regulating spam, such as California's law, favor the members of the public who are not engaged in e-mail advertising. Through its "opt-in" provisions requiring e-mail advertisers to obtain the recipient's consent before sending ads, California's law would have significantly curbed Internet advertising campaigns. The federal CAN-SPAM Act, however, preempts state laws, except for certain provisions relating to deceptive e-mailing practices. This means that these stricter provisions in state laws will no longer be effective.

Clearly, the federal act reflects Congress's intent to protect the e-mail marketing industry against state laws, such as California's, that would make e-mail advertising extremely difficult. The federal government also sought to eliminate advertising by peddlers of financial scams and pornography. Yet critics point out that the new law will do little to reduce the amount of unsolicited e-mail flowing through cyberspace. For one thing, many of the Internet ads being sent today already meet the requirements of the CAN-SPAM Act. For another, because the federal act uses an "opt-out" approach, it places the burden on e-mail recipients to prevent the delivery of further ads from the same source. Additionally, the act cannot regulate spam sent from foreign servers. Indeed, a survey showed that during the first two months after the act became effective, 56 percent of the respondents saw no noticeable reduction in the amount of spam received through e-mail, and 16 percent reported that they had received more spam since the law went into effect.[19]

19. Pew Internet and American Life Project survey conducted from February 3 to March 1, 2004.

REVIEWING TORTS AND CYBER TORTS

Alaina Sweeney went to Ragged Mountain Ski Resort in New Hampshire with her friend Derrick. Alaina was snow tubing down a snow tube run designed exclusively for snow tubers. There were no Ragged Mountain employees present in the snow tube area to instruct Alaina on the proper use of a snow tube. On her fourth run down the trail, Alaina crossed over the center line between snow tube lanes, collided with another snow tuber, and was injured. Alaina filed an action against Ragged Mountain seeking compensation for the injuries that she sustained. Two years earlier, the New Hampshire state legislature had enacted a statute that prohibited a person who participates in the sport of skiing from suing a ski area operator for injuries caused by the risks inherent in skiing. Using the information presented in the chapter, answer the following questions.

1. What tort theory discussed in the chapter might provide the basis of Alaina's lawsuit?
2. What defense will Ragged Mountain probably assert?
3. The central question in this case is whether the state statute establishing that skiers assume the risks inherent in the sport bars Alaina's suit. What would your decision be on this issue? Why?
4. Suppose that the court concludes that the statute applies only to skiing and does not apply to snow tubing. Will Alaina's lawsuit be successful? Explain.
5. Now suppose that the jury concludes that Alaina was partly at fault for the accident. Under what theory might her damages be reduced in proportion to the degree to which her actions contributed to the accident and her resulting injuries?

KEY TERMS

actionable 105
actual malice 107
appropriation 108
assault 104
assumption of risk 119
battery 104
business invitee 117
business tort 103
causation in fact 118
comparative negligence 121
compensatory damages 118
contributory negligence 121
conversion 114
cyber tort 103
damages 103
defamation 105
defense 104
disparagement of property 115
dram shop act 123
duty of care 116
fraudulent misrepresentation 108
Good Samaritan statute 122
intentional tort 103
libel 105
malpractice 118
negligence 116
negligence *per se* 122
predatory behavior 111
privilege 106
proximate cause 118
puffery 108
punitive damages 118
reasonable person standard 116
res ipsa loquitur 122
slander 105
slander of quality 115
slander of title 115
spam 127
strict liability 123
tort 102
tortfeasor 103
trade libel 115
trespass to land 111
trespass to personal property 112

CHAPTER SUMMARY Torts and Cyber Torts

Intentional Torts against Persons (See pages 103–111.)	1. *Assault and battery*—An assault is an unexcused and intentional act that causes another person to be apprehensive of immediate harm. A battery is an assault that results in physical contact. 2. *False imprisonment*—The intentional confinement or restraint of another person's movement without justification. 3. *Intentional infliction of emotional distress*—An intentional act that amounts to extreme and outrageous conduct resulting in severe emotional distress to another.

CHAPTER SUMMARY Torts and Cyber Torts—Continued

Intentional Torts against Persons—Continued	4. *Defamation (libel or slander)*—A false statement of fact, not made under privilege, that is communicated to a third person and that causes damage to a person's reputation. For public figures, the plaintiff must also prove actual malice. 5. *Invasion of the right to privacy*—The use of a person's name or likeness for commercial purposes without permission, wrongful intrusion into a person's private activities, publication of information that places a person in a false light, or disclosure of private facts that an ordinary person would find objectionable. 6. *Appropriation*—The use of another person's name, likeness, or other identifying characteristic, without permission and for the benefit of the user. 7. *Misrepresentation (fraud)*—A false representation made by one party, through misstatement of facts or through conduct, with the intention of deceiving another and on which the other reasonably relies to his or her detriment. 8. *Wrongful interference*—The knowing, intentional interference by a third party with an enforceable contractual relationship or an established business relationship between other parties for the purpose of advancing the economic interests of the third party.
Intentional Torts against Property (See pages 111–116.)	1. *Trespass to land*—The invasion of another's real property without consent or privilege. Specific rights and duties apply once a person is expressly or impliedly established as a trespasser. 2. *Trespass to personal property*—Unlawfully damaging or interfering with the owner's right to use, possess, or enjoy her or his personal property. 3. *Conversion*—Wrongfully taking personal property from its rightful owner or possessor and placing it in the service of another. 4. *Disparagement of property*—Any economically injurious falsehood that is made about another's product or property; an inclusive term for the torts of *slander of quality* and *slander of title.*
Unintentional Torts (Negligence) (See pages 116–123.)	1. *Negligence*—The careless performance of a legally required duty or the failure to perform a legally required act. Elements that must be proved are that a legal duty of care exists, that the defendant breached that duty, and that the breach caused damage or injury to another. 2. *Defenses to negligence*—The basic affirmative defenses in negligence cases are (a) assumption of risk, (b) superseding cause, and (c) contributory or comparative negligence. 3. *Special negligence doctrines and statutes*— a. *Res ipsa loquitur*—A doctrine under which a plaintiff need not prove negligence on the part of the defendant because "the facts speak for themselves." b. Negligence *per se*—A type of negligence that may occur if a person violates a statute or an ordinance providing for a criminal penalty and the violation causes another to be injured. c. Special negligence statutes—State statutes that prescribe duties and responsibilities in certain circumstances, the violation of which will impose civil liability. Dram shop acts and Good Samaritan statutes are examples of special negligence statutes.
Strict Liability (See page 123.)	Under the doctrine of strict liability, a person may be held liable, regardless of the degree of care exercised, for damages or injuries caused by her or his product or activity. Strict liability includes liability for harms caused by abnormally dangerous activities, by dangerous animals, and by defective products (product liability).
Cyber Torts (See pages 123–129.)	General tort principles are being extended to cover cyber torts, or torts that occur in cyberspace, such as online defamation and spamming (which may constitute trespass to personal property). Federal and state statutes may also apply to certain forms of cyber torts. For example, under the federal Communications Decency Act of 1996, Internet service providers (ISPs) are not liable for defamatory messages posted by their subscribers. A majority of the states and the federal government now regulate unwanted e-mail ads (spam).

FOR REVIEW

Answers for the even-numbered questions in this For Review *section can be found on this text's accompanying Web site at* http://blt.westbuslaw.com*. Select "Chapter 4" and click on "For Review."*

1. What is a tort?
2. What is the purpose of tort law? What are two basic categories of torts?
3. What are the four elements of negligence?
4. What is meant by strict liability? In what circumstances is strict liability applied?
5. What is a cyber tort, and how are tort theories being applied in cyberspace?

QUESTIONS AND CASE PROBLEMS

4–1. Defenses to Negligence. Corinna was riding her bike on a city street. While she was riding, she frequently looked back to verify that the books that she had fastened to the rear part of her bike were still attached. On one occasion while she was looking behind her, she failed to notice a car that was entering an intersection just as she was crossing it. The car hit her, causing her to sustain numerous injuries. Three eyewitnesses stated that the driver of the car had failed to stop at the stop sign before entering the intersection. Corinna sued the driver of the car for negligence. What defenses might the defendant driver raise in this lawsuit? Discuss fully.

4–2. Liability to Business Invitees. Kim went to Ling's Market to pick up a few items for dinner. It was a rainy, windy day, and the wind had blown water through the door of Ling's Market each time the door opened. As Kim entered through the door, she slipped and fell in the approximately one-half inch of rainwater that had accumulated on the floor. The manager knew of the weather conditions but had not posted any sign to warn customers of the water hazard. Kim injured her back as a result of the fall and sued Ling's for damages. Can Ling's be held liable for negligence in this situation? Discuss.

4–3. Negligence. In which of the following situations will the acting party be liable for the tort of negligence? Explain fully.

(a) Mary goes to the golf course on Sunday morning, eager to try out a new set of golf clubs she has just purchased. As she tees off on the first hole, the head of her club flies off and injures a nearby golfer.

(b) Mary's doctor gives her some pain medication and tells her not to drive after she takes it, as the medication induces drowsiness. In spite of the doctor's warning, Mary decides to drive to the store while on the medication. Owing to her lack of alertness, she fails to stop at a traffic light and crashes into another vehicle, injuring a passenger.

4–4. Causation. Ruth carelessly parks her car on a steep hill, leaving the car in neutral and failing to engage the parking brake. The car rolls down the hill, knocking down an electric line. The sparks from the broken line ignite a grass fire. The fire spreads until it reaches a barn one mile away. The barn houses dynamite, and the burning barn explodes, causing part of the roof to fall on and injure a passing motorist, Jim. Can Jim recover from Ruth? Why or why not?

4–5. Duty of Care. As pedestrians exited at the close of an arts and crafts show, Jason Davis, an employee of the show's producer, stood near the exit. Suddenly and without warning, Davis turned around and collided with Yvonne Esposito, an eighty-year-old woman. Esposito was knocked to the ground, fracturing her hip. After hip-replacement surgery, she was left with a permanent physical impairment. Esposito filed a suit in a federal district court against Davis and others, alleging negligence. What are the factors that indicate whether Davis owed Esposito a duty of care? What do those factors indicate in these circumstances? [*Esposito v. Davis,* 47 F.3d 164 (5th Cir. 1995)]

CASE PROBLEM WITH SAMPLE ANSWER

4–6. During the spring and summer of 1999, Edward and Geneva Irvine received numerous "hang up" phone calls, including three calls in the middle of the night. With the help of their local phone company, the Irvines learned that many of the calls were from the telemarketing department of the *Akron Beacon Journal* in Akron, Ohio. The *Beacon*'s sales force was equipped with an automatic dialing machine. During business hours, the dialer was used to maximize productivity by calling multiple phone numbers at once and connecting a call to a sales representative only after it was answered. After business hours, the dialer was used to dial a list of disconnected numbers to determine whether they had been reconnected. If the dialer detected a ring, it recorded the information and dropped the call. If the automated dialing system crashed, which it did frequently, it redialed the entire list. The Irvines filed a suit in an Ohio state court against the *Beacon* and others, alleging in part invasion of privacy. In whose favor should the court rule, and why? [*Irvine v. Akron Beacon Journal,* 147 Ohio App.3d 428, 770 N.E.2d 1105 (9 Dist. 2002)]

After you have answered this problem, compare your answer with the sample answer given on the Web site that accompanies this text. Go to http://blt.westbuslaw.com, select "Chapter 4," and click on "Case Problem with Sample Answer."

4–7. Defamation. Lydia Hagberg went to her bank, California Federal Bank, FSB, to cash a check made out to her by Smith

Barney (SB), an investment services firm. Nolene Showalter, a bank employee, suspected that the check was counterfeit. Showalter phoned SB and was told that the check was not valid. As she phoned the police, Gary Wood, a bank security officer, contacted SB again and was told that its earlier statement was "erroneous" and that the check was valid. Meanwhile, a police officer arrived, drew Hagberg away from the teller's window, spread her legs, patted her down, and handcuffed her. The officer searched her purse, asked her whether she had any weapons or stolen property and whether she was driving a stolen vehicle, and arrested her. Hagberg filed a suit in a California state court against the bank and others, alleging, among other things, slander. Should the absolute privilege for communications made in judicial or other official proceedings apply to statements made when a citizen contacts the police to report suspected criminal activity? Why or why not? [*Hagberg v. California Federal Bank, FSB,* 32 Cal.4th 350, 81 P.3d 244, 7 Cal.Rptr.3d 803 (2004)]

A QUESTION OF ETHICS

4–8. Patsy Slone, while a guest at the Dollar Inn, a hotel, was stabbed in the thumb by a hypodermic needle concealed in the tube of a roll of toilet paper. Slone, fearing that she might have been exposed to the virus that causes acquired immune deficiency syndrome (AIDS), sued the hotel for damages to compensate her for the emotional distress she suffered after the needle stab. An Indiana trial court held for Slone and awarded her $250,000 in damages. The hotel appealed, and one of the issues before the court was whether Slone had to prove that she was actually exposed to AIDS to recover for emotional distress. The appellate court held that she did not and that her fear of getting AIDS was reasonable in these circumstances. [*Dollar Inn, Inc. v. Slone,* 695 N.E.2d 185 (Ind.App. 1998)]

1. Should the plaintiff in this case have been required to show that she was actually exposed to the AIDS virus in order to recover for emotional distress? Should she have been required to show that she actually acquired the AIDS virus as a result of the needle stab?
2. In some states, plaintiffs are barred from recovery in emotional distress cases unless the distress is evidenced by some kind of physical symptoms. Is this fair?

FOR CRITICAL ANALYSIS

4–9. What general principle underlies the common law doctrine that business owners have a duty of care toward their customers? Does the duty of care unfairly burden business owners? Why or why not?

VIDEO QUESTION

DIGITAL VIDEO LIBRARY — WEST LEGAL STUDIES IN BUSINESS

4–10. Go to this text's Web site at http://blt.westbuslaw.com and select "Chapter 4." Click on "Video Questions" and view the video titled *Jaws.* Then answer the following questions.

1. In the video, the mayor (Murray Hamilton) and a few other men try to persuade Chief Brody (Roy Scheider) not to close the town's beaches. If Brody keeps the beaches open and a swimmer is injured or killed because he failed to warn swimmers about the potential shark danger, has Brody committed a tort? If so, what kind of tort (intentional tort against persons, intentional tort against property, negligence)? Explain your answer.
2. Can Chief Brody be held liable for any injuries or deaths to swimmers under the doctrine of strict liability? Why or why not?
3. If Chief Brody goes against the mayor's instructions and warns swimmers to stay off the beach, and the town suffers economic damages as a result, has he committed the tort of disparagement of property? Why or why not?

INTERNET EXERCISES

Go to the *Business Law Today* home page at http://blt.westbuslaw.com, select "Chapter 4," and click on "Internet Exercises." There you will find the following Internet research exercises that you can perform to learn more about topics covered in this chapter.

Activity 4–1: LEGAL PERSPECTIVE—Negligence and the *Titanic*

Activity 4–2: MANAGEMENT PERSPECTIVE—Legal and Illegal Uses of Spam

BEFORE THE TEST

Go to the *Business Law Today* home page at http://blt.westbuslaw.com, select "Chapter 4," and click on "Interactive Quizzes." You will find a number of interactive questions relating to this chapter.

The purple and orange colors displayed on FedEx envelopes, packets, and delivery vehicles, including this airplane, are a distinctive feature of that company. If a start-up company specializing in courier delivery services used those same colors, would the new company be infringing on FedEx's trademark? (Photo Courtesy of Federal Express)

meaning, this issue was of no significance in this case. The court stated that it would not consider whether the mark had acquired any secondary meaning because "generic marks with secondary meaning are still not entitled to protection."[7] ■

A "UL" certification mark. How does a certification mark differ from a trademark?

SERVICE, CERTIFICATION, AND COLLECTIVE MARKS

A **service mark** is similar to a trademark but is used to distinguish the services of one person or company from those of another. For instance, each airline has a particular mark or symbol associated with its name. Titles and character names used in radio and television are frequently registered as service marks.

SERVICE MARK
A mark used in the sale or the advertising of services to distinguish the services of one person from those of others. Titles, character names, and other distinctive features of radio and television programs may be registered as service marks.

Other marks protected by law include certification marks and collective marks. A *certification mark* is used by one or more persons other than the owner to certify the region, materials, mode of manufacture, quality, or accuracy of the owner's goods or services. When used by members of a cooperative, association, or other organization, it is referred to as a *collective mark*. ■ EXAMPLE 5.3 Certification marks include such marks as "Good Housekeeping Seal of Approval" and "UL Tested." Collective marks appear at the ends of the credits of movies to indicate the various associations and organizations that participated in making the movie. The union marks found on the tags of certain products are also collective marks. ■

TRADE NAMES

TRADE NAME
A term that is used to indicate part or all of a business's name and that is directly related to the business's reputation and goodwill. Trade names are protected under the common law (and under trademark law, if the name is the same as that of the firm's trademarked property).

Trademarks apply to *products*. The term **trade name** is used to indicate part or all of a business's name, whether the business is a sole proprietorship, a partnership, or a corporation. Generally, a trade name is directly related to a business and its goodwill.

7. *America Online, Inc. v. AT&T Corp.*, 243 F.3d 812 (4th Cir. 2001).

Trade names may be protected as trademarks if the trade name is also the name of the company's trademarked product—for example, Coca-Cola. Unless also used as a trademark or service mark, a trade name cannot be registered with the federal government. Trade names are protected under the common law, however. As with trademarks, words must be unusual or fancifully used if they are to be protected as trade names. The word *Safeway,* for instance, was held by the courts to be sufficiently fanciful to obtain protection as a trade name for a grocery chain.[8]

TRADE DRESS

TRADE DRESS
The image and overall appearance of a product—for example, the distinctive decor, menu, layout, and style of service of a particular restaurant. Basically, trade dress is subject to the same protection as trademarks.

The term **trade dress** refers to the image and overall appearance of a product. Basically, trade dress is subject to the same protection as trademarks. ■ EXAMPLE 5.4 The distinctive decor, menu, layout, and style of service of a particular restaurant may be regarded as the restaurant's trade dress. Similarly, if a golf course is distinguished from other golf courses by prominent features, such as a golf hole designed to look like a lighthouse, those features may be considered the golf course's trade dress. ■ In cases involving trade dress infringement, as in trademark infringement cases, a major consideration is whether consumers are likely to be confused by the allegedly infringing use. Also, features that enhance a product's function will not be protected as trade dress.

Cyber Marks

CYBER MARK
A trademark in cyberspace.

In cyberspace, trademarks are sometimes referred to as **cyber marks.** We turn now to a discussion of trademark-related issues in cyberspace and how new laws and the courts are addressing these issues. One concern relates to the rights of a trademark's owner to use the mark as part of a domain name (Internet address). Other issues have to do with cybersquatting, meta tags, and trademark dilution on the Web. The use of licensing as a way to avoid liability for infringing on another's intellectual property rights in cyberspace will also be discussed.

DOMAIN NAMES

DOMAIN NAME
The last part of an Internet address, such as "westlaw.com." The top level (the part of the name to the right of the period) indicates the type of entity that operates the site ("com" is an abbreviation for "commercial"). The second level (the part of the name to the left of the period) is chosen by the entity.

In the real world, one business can often use the same name as another without causing any conflict, particularly if the businesses are small, their goods or services are different, and the areas where they do business are separate. In the online world, however, there is only one area of business—cyberspace. Thus, disputes between parties over which one has the right to use a particular domain name have become common. A **domain name** is part of an Internet address, such as "westlaw.com." The top level domain (TLD) is the part of the name to the right of the period and indicates the type of entity that operates the site (for example, "com" is an abbreviation for "commercial"). The second level (the part of the name to the left of the period) is chosen by the business entity or individual registering the domain name.

Conflicts over rights to domain names emerged during the 1990s as e-commerce expanded on a worldwide scale. As e-commerce grew, the *.com* TLD came to be widely used by businesses on the Web. Competition among firms with similar names and products preceding the *.com* TLD led, understandably, to numerous disputes over domain name rights. By using the same, or a similar, domain name, parties have attempted to profit from the goodwill of a competitor, to sell pornography, to

8. *Safeway Stores v. Suburban Foods,* 130 F.Supp. 249 (E.D.Va. 1955).

offer for sale another party's domain name, and to otherwise infringe on others' trademarks.

As noted in Chapter 3, the federal government set up the Internet Corporation for Assigned Names and Numbers (ICANN), a nonprofit corporation, to oversee the distribution of domain names. ICANN has also played a leading role in facilitating the settlement of domain name disputes worldwide. Since January 2000, ICANN has been operating an online arbitration system to resolve domain name disputes and approve dispute-resolution providers. By 2003, ICANN-approved online arbitration providers were handling over one thousand disputes annually.

Anticybersquatting Legislation

CYBERSQUATTING
The act of registering a domain name that is the same as, or confusingly similar to, the trademark of another and then offering to sell that domain name back to the trademark owner.

In the late 1990s, Congress passed legislation prohibiting another practice that had given rise to numerous disputes over domain names: cybersquatting. **Cybersquatting** occurs when a person registers a domain name that is the same as, or confusingly similar to, the trademark of another and then offers to sell the domain name back to the trademark owner. During the 1990s, cybersquatting became a contentious issue and led to much litigation. Although it was not always easy for the courts to separate cybersquatting from legitimate business activity, many cases held that cybersquatting violated trademark law.[9]

In 1999, Congress addressed this issue by passing the Anticybersquatting Consumer Protection Act (ACPA), which amended the Lanham Act—the federal law protecting trademarks, discussed earlier in this chapter. The ACPA makes it illegal for a person to "register, traffic in, or use" a domain name (1) if the name is identical or confusingly similar to the trademark of another and (2) if the one registering, trafficking in, or using the domain name has a "bad faith intent" to profit from that trademark. The act does not define what constitutes bad faith. Instead, it lists several factors that courts can consider in deciding whether bad faith exists. Some of these factors are the trademark rights of the other person, whether there is an intent to divert consumers in a way that could harm the goodwill represented by the trademark, whether there is an offer to transfer or sell the domain name to the trademark owner, and whether there is an intent to use the domain name to offer goods and services.

The ACPA applies to all domain name registrations of trademarks, even domain names registered before the passage of the act. Successful plaintiffs in suits brought under the act can collect actual damages and profits, or elect to receive statutory damages of from $1,000 to $100,000.

Meta Tags

Search engines compile their results by looking through a Web site's key-word field. Meta tags, or key words (see Chapter 2), may be inserted into this field to increase the site's inclusion in search engine results, even though the site may have nothing to do with the inserted words. Using this same technique, one site may appropriate the key words of other sites with more frequent hits, so that the appropriating site appears in the same search engine results as the more popular sites. Using another's trademark in a meta tag without the owner's permission, however, constitutes trademark infringement. One use of meta tags was at issue in the following case.

9. See, for example, *Panavision International, L.P. v. Toeppen,* 141 F.3d 1316 (9th Cir. 1998).

CASE 5.2 Playboy Enterprises, Inc. v. Welles

United States Court of Appeals,
Ninth Circuit, 2002.
279 F.3d 796.

BACKGROUND AND FACTS Playboy Enterprises, Inc. (PEI), maintains Web sites to promote *Playboy* magazine and PEI models. PEI's trademarks include the terms *Playboy, Playmate,* and *Playmate of the Year.* Terri Welles is a self-employed model and spokesperson who was featured as the "Playmate of the Year" in June 1981. Welles maintains a Web site titled "Terri Welles—Playmate of the Year 1981." As meta tags, Welles's site uses the terms *Playboy* and *Playmate,* among others. PEI asked Welles to stop using these terms, but she refused. PEI filed a suit in a federal district court against Welles, asking the court to order her to, among other things, stop using those terms as meta tags. On this issue, the court granted a summary judgment in Welles's favor. PEI appealed to the U.S. Court of Appeals for the Ninth Circuit.

IN THE WORDS OF THE COURT . . .

T. G. NELSON, Circuit Judge.

* * * *

* * * [The] test for nominative use [of a trademark is]:[a]

> First, the product or service in question must be one not readily identifiable without use of the trademark; second, only so much of the mark or marks may be used as is reasonably necessary to identify the product or service; and third, the user must do nothing that would, in conjunction with the mark, suggest sponsorship or endorsement by the trademark holder. * * *

* * * *

A large portion of Welles' website discusses her association with Playboy over the years. Thus, the trademarked terms accurately describe the contents of Welles' website, in addition to describing Welles. Forcing Welles and others to use absurd turns of phrase in their metatags, such as those necessary to identify Welles, would be particularly damaging in the Internet search context. *Searchers would have a much more difficult time locating relevant websites if they could do so only by correctly guessing the long phrases necessary to substitute for trademarks.* We can hardly expect someone searching for Welles' site to imagine [a] phrase * * * to describe Welles without referring to Playboy—"the nude model selected by Mr. Hefner's organization * * * ." Yet if someone could not remember her name, that is what they would have to do. Similarly, someone searching for critiques of Playboy on the Internet would have a difficult time if Internet sites could not list the object of their critique in their metatags. [Emphasis added.]

There is simply no descriptive substitute for the trademarks used in Welles' metatags. Precluding their use would have the unwanted effect of hindering the free flow of information on the Internet, something which is certainly not a goal of trademark law. Accordingly, the use of trademarked terms in the metatags meets the first part of the test for nominative use.

We conclude that the metatags satisfy the second and third elements of the test as well. The metatags use only so much of the marks as reasonably necessary and nothing is done in conjunction with them to suggest sponsorship or endorsement by the trademark holder. We note that our decision might differ if the metatags listed the trademarked term so repeatedly that Welles' site would regularly appear above PEI's in searches for one of the trademarked terms.

a. A *nominative use* of a trademark is one that does not imply sponsorship or endorsement of a product because the product's mark is used only to describe the thing, rather than to identify its source. See *New Kids on the Block v. News America Publishing, Inc.,* 971 F.2d 302 (9th Cir. 1992).

(Continued)

CASE 5.2—Continued

DECISION AND REMEDY The U.S. Court of Appeals for the Ninth Circuit concluded that Welles's use of PEI's trademarks as meta tags was a permissible, nominative use. The use implied no current sponsorship or endorsement by PEI. Instead, the meta tags identified Welles as a past PEI "Playmate of the Year."

WHY IS THIS CASE IMPORTANT? *This case illustrates how some uses of another's trademark are permissible and not infringing, provided that the user does not suggest that the trademark owner authorized or sponsored the use.*

Dilution in the Online World

As discussed earlier, trademark *dilution* occurs when a trademark is used, without authorization, in a way that diminishes the distinctive quality of the mark. Unlike trademark infringement, a dilution cause of action does not require proof that consumers are likely to be confused by a connection between the unauthorized use and the mark. For this reason, the products involved do not have to be similar. In the first case alleging dilution on the Web, a court precluded the use of "candyland.com" as the URL for an adult site. The suit was brought by the maker of the "Candyland" children's game and owner of the "Candyland" mark.[10]

In another case, a court issued an injunction on the ground that spamming under another's logo is trademark dilution. In that case, Hotmail, Inc., provided e-mail services and worked to dissociate itself from spam. Van$ Money Pie, Inc., and others spammed thousands of e-mail customers, using the free e-mail Hotmail as a return address. The court ordered the defendants to stop.[11]

Licensing

One of the ways to make use of another's trademark or other form of intellectual property, while avoiding litigation, is to obtain a license to do so. A license in this context is essentially an agreement permitting the use of a trademark, copyright, patent, or trade secret for certain purposes. For instance, a licensee (the party obtaining the license) might be allowed to use the trademark of the licensor (the party issuing the license) as part of the name of its company, or as part of its domain name, without otherwise using the mark on any products or services. Like all contracts, contracts granting licenses must be carefully drafted.

Patents

PATENT
A government grant that gives an inventor the exclusive right or privilege to make, use, or sell his or her invention for a limited time period.

A **patent** is a grant from the government that gives an inventor the exclusive right to make, use, and sell an invention for a period of twenty years from the date of filing the application for a patent. Patents for designs, as opposed to inventions, are given for a fourteen-year period. For either a regular patent or a design patent, the applicant must demonstrate to the satisfaction of the U.S. Patent and Trademark Office that the invention, discovery, process, or design is genuine, novel, useful, and not obvious in light of current technology. A patent holder gives notice to all that an article or design is patented by placing on it the word *Patent* or *Pat.* plus the patent number. In contrast to patent law in other countries, in the United States patent protection

10. *Hasbro, Inc. v. Internet Entertainment Group, Ltd.,* 1996 WL 84853 (W.D.Wash. 1996).
11. *Hotmail Corp. v. Van$ Money Pie, Inc.,* 47 U.S.P.Q.2d 1020 (N.D.Cal. 1998).

is given to the first person to invent a product or process, even though someone else may have been the first to file for a patent on that product or process.

At one time, it was difficult for developers and manufacturers of software to obtain patent protection because many software products simply automate procedures that can be performed manually. In other words, the computer programs do not meet the "novel" and "not obvious" requirements previously mentioned. Also, the basis for software is often a mathematical equation or formula, which is not patentable. In 1981, however, the United States Supreme Court held that it is possible to obtain a patent for a process that incorporates a computer program—providing, of course, that the process itself is patentable.[12] Subsequently, many patents have been issued for software-related inventions.

A significant development relating to patents is the availability online of the world's patent databases. The Web site of the U.S. Patent and Trademark Office provides searchable databases covering U.S. patents granted since 1976. The Web site of the European Patent Office maintains databases covering all patent documents in sixty-five nations and the legal status of patents in twenty-two of those countries.

Patent Infringement

If a firm makes, uses, or sells another's patented design, product, or process without the patent owner's permission, it commits the tort of patent infringement. Patent infringement may exist even though the patent owner has not put the patented product in commerce. Patent infringement may also occur even though not all features or parts of an invention are copied. (With respect to a patented process, however, all steps or their equivalent must be copied for infringement to exist.)

.on the Web A good online source for information on patents can be found at **http://www.patents.com**.

Often, litigation for patent infringement is so costly that the patent holder will instead offer to sell to the infringer a license to use the patented design, product, or process. Indeed, in many cases the costs of detection, prosecution, and monitoring are so high that patents are valueless to their owners; the owners cannot afford to protect them.

Business Process Patents

Traditionally, patents have been granted for inventions that are "new and useful processes, machines, manufactures, or compositions of matter, or any new and useful improvements thereof." The U.S. Patent and Trademark Office routinely rejected computer systems and software applications because they were deemed not to be useful processes, machines, articles of manufacture, or compositions of matter. They were simply considered to be mathematical algorithms, abstract ideas, or "methods of doing business." In a landmark 1998 case, however, *State Street Bank & Trust Co. v. Signature Financial Group, Inc.*,[13] the U.S. Court of Appeals for the Federal Circuit ruled that only three categories of subject matter will always remain unpatentable: (1) the laws of nature, (2) natural phenomena, and (3) abstract ideas. This decision meant, among other things, that business processes were patentable.

After this decision, numerous technology firms applied for business process patents. Walker Digital applied for a business process patent for its "Dutch auction" system, which allowed consumers to make offers for airline tickets on the Internet

12. *Diamond v. Diehr,* 450 U.S. 175, 101 S.Ct. 1048, 67 L.Ed.2d 155 (1981).
13. 149 F.3d 1368 (Fed. Cir. 1998).

Should a software program that allows consumers to make offers for vacation packages via the Internet be considered a "new and useful" process that can be the subject of a business process patent? Why or why not?

and led to the creation of Priceline.com. Amazon.com obtained a business process patent for its "one-click" ordering system, a method of processing credit-card orders securely. Indeed, since the *State Street* decision, the number of Internet-related patents issued by the U.S. Patent and Trademark Office has increased more than 800 percent.

Copyrights

COPYRIGHT
The exclusive right of "authors" to publish, print, or sell an intellectual production for a statutory period of time. A copyright has the same monopolistic nature as a patent or trademark, but it differs in that it applies exclusively to works of art, literature, and other works of authorship (including computer programs).

A **copyright** is an intangible property right granted by federal statute to the author or originator of certain literary or artistic productions. Copyrights are governed by the Copyright Act of 1976,[14] as amended. Works created after January 1, 1978, are automatically given statutory copyright protection for the life of the author plus 70 years. For copyrights owned by publishing houses, the copyright expires 95 years from the date of publication or 120 years from the date of creation, whichever is first. For works by more than one author, the copyright expires 70 years after the death of the last surviving author.

These time periods reflect the extensions of the length of copyright protection enacted by Congress in the Copyright Term Extension Act of 1998.[15] Critics challenged this act as overstepping the bounds of Congress's power and violating the constitutional requirement that copyrights endure for only a limited time. In 2003, however, the United States Supreme Court upheld the act in *Eldred v. Ashcroft*.[16] This ruling obviously favored copyright holders by preventing copyrighted works from the 1920s and 1930s from losing protection and falling into the public domain for an additional two decades.

Copyrights can be registered with the U.S. Copyright Office in Washington, D.C. A copyright owner no longer needs to place a © or *Copr.* or *Copyright* on the work, however, to have the work protected against infringement. Chances are that if somebody created it, somebody owns it.

on the Web For information on copyrights, go to the U.S. Copyright Office at **http://www.copyright.gov**.

What Is Protected Expression?

Works that are copyrightable include books, records, films, artworks, architectural plans, menus, music videos, product packaging, and computer software. To obtain protection under the Copyright Act, a work must be original and fall into one of the following categories: (1) literary works; (2) musical works; (3) dramatic works; (4) pantomimes and choreographic works; (5) pictorial, graphic, and sculptural works; (6) films and other audiovisual works; and (7) sound recordings. To be protected, a work must be "fixed in a durable medium" from which it can be perceived, reproduced, or communicated. Protection is automatic. Registration is not required.

Section 102 Exclusions Section 102 of the Copyright Act specifically excludes copyright protection for any "idea, procedure, process, system, method of operation, concept, principle, or discovery, regardless of the form in which it is described, explained, illustrated, or embodied." Note that it is not possible to copyright an *idea*. The underlying ideas embodied in a work may be freely used by others. What is copyrightable is the particular way in which an idea is *expressed*. Whenever an

14. 17 U.S.C. Sections 101 *et seq.*
15. 17 U.S.C.A. Section 302.
16. 537 U.S. 186, 123 S.Ct. 769, 154 L.Ed.2d 683 (2003).

idea and an expression are inseparable, the expression cannot be copyrighted. Generally, anything that is not an original expression will not qualify for copyright protection. Facts widely known to the public are not copyrightable. Page numbers are not copyrightable because they follow a sequence known to everyone. Mathematical calculations are not copyrightable.

Compilations of Facts *Compilations* of facts, however, are copyrightable. Section 103 of the Copyright Act defines a compilation as "a work formed by the collection and assembling of preexisting materials of data that are selected, coordinated, or arranged in such a way that the resulting work as a whole constitutes an original work of authorship." The key requirement for the copyrightability of a compilation is originality. ■ EXAMPLE 5.5 The white pages of a telephone directory do not qualify for copyright protection when the information that makes up the directory (names, addresses, and telephone numbers) is not selected, coordinated, or arranged in an original way.[17] In one case, even the Yellow Pages of a telephone directory did not qualify for copyright protection.[18] ■

> .on the Web You can find a host of information on copyright law, including the Copyright Act and significant United States Supreme Court cases in the area of copyright law, at
>
> **http://straylight.law.cornell.edu/supct/cases/copyrt.htm**.

COPYRIGHT INFRINGEMENT

Whenever the form or expression of an idea is copied, an infringement of copyright occurs. The reproduction does not have to be exactly the same as the original, nor does it have to reproduce the original in its entirety. If a substantial part of the original is reproduced, there is copyright infringement.

Damages for Copyright Infringement Those who infringe copyrights may be liable for damages or criminal penalties. These range from actual damages or statutory damages, imposed at the court's discretion, to criminal proceedings for willful violations. Actual damages are based on the harm caused to the copyright holder by the infringement, while statutory damages, not to exceed $150,000, are provided for under the Copyright Act. In addition, criminal proceedings may result in fines and/or imprisonment.

The "Fair Use" Exception An exception to liability for copyright infringement is made under the "fair use" doctrine. In certain circumstances, a person or organization can reproduce copyrighted material without paying royalties (fees paid to the copyright holder for the privilege of reproducing the copyrighted material). Section 107 of the Copyright Act provides as follows:

> [T]he fair use of a copyrighted work, including such use by reproduction in copies or phonorecords or by any other means specified by [Section 106 of the Copyright Act,] for purposes such as criticism, comment, news reporting, teaching (including multiple copies for classroom use), scholarship, or research, is not an infringement of copyright. In determining whether the use made of a work in any particular case is a fair use the factors to be considered shall include—
>
> (1) the purpose and character of the use, including whether such use is of a commercial nature or is for nonprofit educational purposes;
>
> (2) the nature of the copyrighted work;

---

17. *Feist Publications, Inc. v. Rural Telephone Service Co.,* 499 U.S. 340, 111 S.Ct. 1282, 113 L.Ed.2d 358 (1991).

18. *Bellsouth Advertising & Publishing Corp. v. Donnelley Information Publishing, Inc.,* 999 F.2d 1436 (11th Cir. 1993).

(3) the amount and substantiality of the portion used in relation to the copyrighted work as a whole; and

(4) the effect of the use upon the potential market for or value of the copyrighted work.

Because these guidelines are very broad, the courts determine whether a particular use is fair on a case-by-case basis. Thus, anyone reproducing copyrighted material may be committing a violation. In determining whether a use is fair, courts have often considered the fourth factor to be the most important.

Copyright Protection for Software

In 1980, Congress passed the Computer Software Copyright Act, which amended the Copyright Act of 1976 to include computer programs in the list of creative works protected by federal copyright law. The 1980 statute, which classifies computer programs as "literary works," defines a computer program as a "set of statements or instructions to be used directly or indirectly in a computer in order to bring about a certain result."

Because of the unique nature of computer programs, the courts have had many problems applying and interpreting the 1980 act. Generally, though, the courts have held that copyright protection extends not only to those parts of a computer program that can be read by humans, such as the high-level language of a source code, but also to the binary-language object code of a computer program, which is readable only by the computer.[19] Additionally, such elements as the overall structure, sequence, and organization of a program were deemed copyrightable.[20] The courts have disagreed as to whether the "look and feel"—the general appearance, command structure, video images, menus, windows, and other screen displays—of computer programs should also be protected by copyright. The courts have tended, however, not to extend copyright protection to look-and-feel aspects of computer programs.

Copyrights in Digital Information

Copyright law is probably the most important form of intellectual property protection on the Internet. This is because much of the material on the Internet consists of works of authorship (including multimedia presentations, software, and database information), which are the traditional focus of copyright law. Copyright law is also important because the nature of the Internet requires that data be "copied" to be transferred online. Copies are a significant part of the traditional controversies arising in this area of the law.

.on the Web The University of Michigan provides information on copyrights generally and copyrights in digital information at **http://www.copyright.umich.edu/law.html**.

The Copyright Act of 1976 When Congress drafted the principal U.S. law governing copyrights, the Copyright Act of 1976, cyberspace did not exist for most of us. The threat to copyright owners was posed not by computer technology but by unauthorized *tangible* copies of works and the sale of rights to movies, television, and other media.

Some issues that were unimagined when the Copyright Act was drafted have posed thorny questions for the courts. For instance, to sell a copy of a work, permission of the copyright holder is necessary. Because of the nature of cyberspace, however, one

19. See *Stern Electronics, Inc. v. Kaufman*, 669 F.2d 852 (2d Cir. 1982); and *Apple Computer, Inc. v. Franklin Computer Corp.*, 714 F.2d 1240 (3d Cir. 1983).

20. *Whelan Associates, Inc. v. Jaslow Dental Laboratory, Inc.*, 797 F.2d 1222 (3d Cir. 1986).

Reprinted with permission © Scott Stantis and Copley News Service.

of the early controversies involved determining at what point an intangible, electronic "copy" of a work has been made. The courts have held that loading a file or program into a computer's random access memory, or RAM, constitutes the making of a "copy" for purposes of copyright law.[21] RAM is a portion of a computer's memory into which a file, for instance, is loaded so that it can be accessed (read or written over). Thus, a copyright is infringed when a party downloads software into RAM without owning the software or otherwise having a right to download it.[22]

Other rights, including those relating to the revision of "collective works" such as magazines, were acknowledged thirty years ago but were considered to have only limited economic value. Today, technology has made some of those rights vastly more significant. How does the old law apply to these rights? That was one of the questions in the following case.

21. *MAI Systems Corp. v. Peak Computer, Inc.*, 991 F.2d 511 (9th Cir. 1993).
22. *DSC Communications Corp. v. Pulse Communications, Inc.*, 170 F.3d 1354 (Fed. Cir. 1999).

Featured Case

CASE 5.3 New York Times Co. v. Tasini

Supreme Court of the United States, 2001.
533 U.S. 483,
121 S.Ct. 2381,
150 L.Ed.2d 500.
http://straylight.law.cornell.edu/supct/index.html[a]

a. In the "Search" box at the top of the page, enter "Tasini." Click on "Search." On the page that opens, in the "Search for:" box, type in "Tasini." Then select "All decisions" and click on "Search." In the result, scroll to the case name and select the appropriate link to access the opinion.

MAJORITY OPINION

Justice *GINSBURG* delivered the opinion of the Court.

* * * *

Respondents Jonathan Tasini, Mary Kay Blakely, Barbara Garson, Margot Mifflin, Sonia Jaffe Robbins, and David S. Whitford are authors (Authors). Between

(Continued)

CASE 5.3—Continued

1990 and 1993, they wrote the 21 articles (Articles) on which this dispute centers. Tasini, Mifflin, and Blakely contributed 12 Articles to *The New York Times,* the daily newspaper published by petitioner The New York Times Company (Times), [and 9 articles to other periodicals]. * * * The Authors registered copyrights in each of the Articles. The Times [and the other publishers] (Print Publishers) registered collective work copyrights in each periodical edition in which an Article originally appeared. The Print Publishers engaged the Authors as independent contractors (freelancers) under contracts that in no instance secured consent from an Author to placement of an Article in an electronic database.

At the time the Articles were published, [the] Print Publishers had agreements with petitioner LEXIS/NEXIS * * * , owner and operator of NEXIS, a computerized database that stores information in a text-only format. NEXIS contains articles from hundreds of journals (newspapers and periodicals) spanning many years. The Print Publishers have licensed to LEXIS/NEXIS the text of articles appearing in [the] periodicals. The licenses authorize LEXIS/NEXIS to copy and sell any portion of those texts.

* * * *

The Times * * * also has licensing agreements with petitioner University Microfilms International (UMI). The agreements authorize reproduction of Times materials on two CD-ROM products, the *New York Times OnDisc* (NYTO) and *General Periodicals OnDisc* (GPO).

* * * *

On December 16, 1993, the Authors filed this civil action in the United States District Court for the Southern District of New York. The Authors alleged that their copyrights were infringed when, as permitted and facilitated by the Print Publishers, LEXIS/NEXIS and UMI (Electronic Publishers) placed the Articles in the NEXIS, NYTO, and GPO databases (Databases). The Authors sought declaratory and injunctive relief, and damages. In response to the Authors' complaint, the Print and Electronic Publishers raised the reproduction and distribution privilege accorded collective work copyright owners by [the Copyright Act]. * * *

The * * * Court granted summary judgment for the Publishers * * * .

The Authors appealed, and the [U.S. Court of Appeals for the] Second Circuit reversed. * * *

We granted *certiorari* to determine whether the copying of the Authors' Articles in the Databases is privileged by [the Copyright Act]. * * *

* * * *

Under the Copyright Act, as amended in 1976, "[c]*opyright protection subsists* * * * *in original works of authorship fixed in any tangible medium of expression* * * * *from which they can be perceived, reproduced, or otherwise communicated.*" When, as in this case, a freelance author has contributed an article to a "collective work" such as a newspaper or magazine, the statute recognizes two distinct copyrighted works: "Copyright in *each separate contribution to a collective work* is distinct from copyright in *the collective work as a whole* * * * " (emphasis added [by the Court]). Copyright in the separate contribution "vests initially in the author of the contribution" (here, the freelancer). Copyright in the collective work vests in the collective author (here, the newspaper or magazine publisher) and extends only to the creative material contributed by that author, not to "the preexisting material employed in the work." [Emphasis added.]

* * * *

A newspaper or magazine publisher is thus privileged to reproduce or distribute an article contributed by a freelance author, absent a contract otherwise providing, only "as part of" any (or all) of three categories of collective works: (a) "that collective work" to which the author contributed her work, (b) "any revision of that collective work," or (c) "any later collective work in the same series." In accord with Congress' prescription, a publishing company could reprint a contribution from one issue in a later issue of its magazine, and could reprint an article from a 1980 edition of an encyclopedia in a 1990 revision of it; the publisher could not revise the contribution itself or include it in a new anthology or an entirely different magazine or other collective work.

* * * *

In determining whether the Articles have been reproduced and distributed "as part of" a "revision" of the collective works in issue, we focus on the Articles as presented to, and perceptible by, the user of the Databases. In this case, the * * * Databases present articles to users clear of the context provided either by the original periodical editions or by any revision of those editions. The Databases first prompt users to search the universe of their contents: thousands or millions of files containing individual articles from thousands of collective works (*i.e.,* editions), either in one series (the *Times,* in NYTO) or in scores of series (the sundry titles in NEXIS and GPO). When the user conducts a search, each article appears as a separate item within the search result. In NEXIS and NYTO, an article appears to a user without the graphics, formatting, or other articles with which the article was initially published. In GPO, the article

CASE 5.3—Continued

appears with the other materials published on the same page or pages, but without any material published on other pages of the original periodical. In either circumstance, we cannot see how the Database perceptibly reproduces and distributes the article "as part of" either the original edition or a "revision" of that edition.

One might view the articles as parts of a new compendium—namely, the entirety of works in the Database. In that compendium, each edition of each periodical represents only a min[u]scule fraction of the ever-expanding Database. The Database no more constitutes a "revision" of each constituent edition than a 400-page novel quoting a sonnet in passing would represent a "revision" of that poem. * * *

* * * *

We conclude that the Electronic Publishers infringed the Authors' copyrights by reproducing and distributing the Articles in a manner not authorized by the Authors and not privileged by [the Copyright Act]. We further conclude that the Print Publishers infringed the Authors' copyrights by authorizing the Electronic Publishers to place the Articles in the Databases and by aiding the Electronic Publishers in that endeavor. We therefore affirm the judgment of the Court of Appeals.

It is so ordered.

DISSENTING OPINION

Justice *STEVENS* * * * dissenting.

* * * *

* * * [W]hat is sent from the New York Times to the Electronic Databases * * * is simply a collection of ASCII text files representing the editorial content of the *New York Times* for a particular day. * * *

* * * *

No one doubts that the New York Times has the right to reprint its issues in Braille, in a foreign language, or in microform, even though such revisions might look and feel quite different from the original. Such differences, however, would largely result from the different medium being employed. Similarly, the decision to convert the single collective work newspaper into a collection of individual ASCII files can be explained as little more than a decision that reflects the different nature of the electronic medium. Just as the paper version of the *New York Times* is divided into "sections" and "pages" in order to facilitate the reader's navigation and manipulation of large batches of newsprint, so too the decision to subdivide the electronic version of that collective work into individual article files facilitates the reader's use of the electronic information.

TEST YOUR COMPREHENSION: CASE DETAILS

1. What was at the center of the dispute between the parties in this case?
2. Which side do you think has the better argument in this case? Why?
3. According to the United States Supreme Court, do publishers who want to put the contents of periodicals into e-databases and onto CD-ROMs need to obtain the permission of the writers whose contributions are included?
4. The Copyright Act of 1976 was enacted before the Internet and online databases became widely used. Should the act apply to the uses of copyrighted material at issue in this case? Explain.
5. When rights such as those in this case become more valuable as a result of new technology, should the law be changed to redistribute the economic benefit of those rights? Why or why not?

Further Developments in Copyright Law In the last several years, Congress has enacted legislation designed specifically to protect copyright holders in a digital age. Prior to 1997, criminal penalties under copyright law could be imposed only if unauthorized copies were exchanged for financial gain. Yet much piracy of copyrighted materials was "altruistic" in nature; that is, unauthorized copies were made and distributed not for financial gain but simply for reasons of generosity—to share the copies with others.

To combat altruistic piracy and for other reasons, Congress passed the No Electronic Theft (NET) Act of 1997. This act extends criminal liability for the piracy of copyrighted materials to persons who exchange unauthorized copies of copyrighted

LANDMARK IN THE LAW

The Digital Millennium Copyright Act of 1998

The United States leads the world in the production of creative products, including books, films, videos, recordings, and software. In fact, as indicated earlier in this chapter, the creative industries are more important to the U.S. economy than the traditional product industries are. Exports of U.S. creative products, for example, surpass those of every other U.S. industry in value. Creative industries are growing at nearly three times the rate of the economy as a whole.

Steps have been taken, both nationally and internationally, to protect ownership rights in intellectual property, including copyrights. To curb unauthorized copying of copyrighted materials, the World Intellectual Property Organization (WIPO) of 1996, a special agreement under the Berne Convention (discussed later in this chapter), upgraded global standards of copyright protection, particularly for the Internet.

IMPLEMENTING THE WIPO TREATY In 1998, Congress implemented the provisions of the WIPO treaty by updating U.S. copyright law. The new law—the Digital Millennium Copyright Act of 1998—is a landmark step in the protection of copyright owners and, because of the leading position of the United States in the creative industries, serves as a model for other nations. Among other things, the act established civil and criminal penalties for anyone who circumvents (bypasses, or gets around—through clever maneuvering, for example) encryption software or other technological antipiracy protection. Also prohibited are the manufacture, import, sale, and distribution of devices or services for circumvention.

The act provides for exceptions to fit the needs of libraries, scientists, universities, and others. In general, the law does not restrict the "fair use" of circumvention methods for educational and other noncommercial purposes. For example, circumvention is allowed to test computer security, conduct encryption research, protect personal privacy, and enable parents to monitor their children's use of the Internet. The exceptions are to be reconsidered every three years.

works, such as software, even though they realize no profit from the exchange. The act also imposes penalties on those who make unauthorized electronic copies of books, magazines, movies, or music for *personal* use, thus altering the traditional "fair use" doctrine. The criminal penalties for violating the act are steep; they include fines as high as $250,000 and incarceration for up to five years.

In 1998, Congress passed further legislation to protect copyright holders—the Digital Millennium Copyright Act. Because of its significance in protecting against the piracy of copyrighted materials in the online environment, this act is presented as this chapter's *Landmark in the Law* feature.

MP3 AND FILE-SHARING TECHNOLOGY

At one time, music fans swapped compact discs (CDs) and recorded the songs that they liked from others' CDs onto their own cassettes. This type of "file-sharing" was awkward at best. Soon after the Internet became popular, a few enterprising programmers created software to compress large data files, particularly those associated with music. The reduced file sizes make transmitting music over the Internet feasible. The most widely known compression and decompression system is MP3,

LANDMARK IN THE LAW—Continued

LIMITING THE LIABILITY OF INTERNET SERVICE PROVIDERS The 1998 act also limited the liability of Internet service providers (ISPs). Under the act, an ISP is not liable for any copyright infringement by its customer *unless* the ISP is aware of the subscriber's violation. An ISP may be held liable only if it fails to take action to shut the subscriber down after learning of the violation. A copyright holder has to act promptly, however, by pursuing a claim in court, or the subscriber has the right to be restored to online access.

APPLICATION TO TODAY'S BUSINESS WORLD

The application of the Digital Millennium Copyright Act of 1998 to today's world is fairly self-evident. If Congress had not enacted this legislation, copyright owners would have a far more difficult time obtaining legal redress against those who, without authorization, decrypt and/or copy copyrighted materials. Of course, problems remain, particularly because of the global nature of the Internet. From a practical standpoint, the degree of protection afforded to copyright holders depends on the extent to which other nations that have signed the WIPO treaty actually implement its provisions and agree on the interpretation of terms, such as what constitutes an electronic copy, for example.

RELEVANT WEB SITES

To locate information on the Web concerning the Digital Millennium Copyright Act of 1998, go to this text's Web site at **http://blt.westbuslaw.com**, *select "Chapter 5," and click on "URLs for Landmarks."*

which enables music fans to download songs or entire CDs onto their computers or onto a portable listening device, such as Rio or iPod. The MP3 system also made it possible for music fans to access other music fans' files by engaging in file-sharing via the Internet.

Peer-to-Peer (P2P) Networking File-sharing via the Internet is accomplished through what is called **peer-to-peer (P2P) networking.** The concept is simple. Rather than going through a central Web server, P2P involves numerous personal computers (PCs) that are connected to the Internet. Files stored on one PC can be accessed by others who are members of the same network. Sometimes this is called a **distributed network.** In other words, parts of the network are distributed all over the country or the world. File-sharing offers an unlimited number of uses for distributed networks. For instance, many researchers allow their home computers' computing power to be accessed through file-sharing software so that very large mathematical problems can be solved quickly. Additionally, persons scattered throughout the country or the world can work together on the same project by using file-sharing programs.

PEER-TO-PEER (P2P) NETWORKING
The sharing of resources (such as files, hard drives, and processing styles) among multiple computers without necessarily requiring a central network server.

DISTRIBUTED NETWORK
A network that can be used by persons located (distributed) around the country or the globe to share computer files.

Cary Sherman, president of the Recording Industry Association of America (RIAA), is seen here talking with reporters after announcing that the RIAA is filing hundreds of lawsuits against individuals who shared copyrighted music files via the Internet. Under what theories can a company that distributes file-sharing software also be held liable if individuals use the software to exchange copyrighted music? (AP Photo/George Nikitin)

Sharing Stored Music Files When file-sharing is used to download others' stored music files, copyright issues arise. Recording artists and their labels stand to lose large amounts of royalties and revenues if relatively few CDs are purchased and then made available on distributed networks, from which everyone can get them for free. The issue of file-sharing infringement has been the subject of an ongoing debate over the last few years.

■ EXAMPLE 5.6 In the highly publicized case of *A&M Records, Inc. v. Napster, Inc.*,[23] several firms in the recording industry sued Napster, Inc., the owner of the then-popular Napster Web site. The Napster site provided registered users with free software that enabled them to transfer exact copies of the contents of MP3 files from one computer to another via the Internet. Napster also maintained centralized search indices so that users could locate specific titles or artists' recordings on the computers of other members. The firms argued that Napster should be liable for contributory and vicarious[24] copyright infringement because it assisted others in obtaining copies of copyrighted music without the copyright owners' permission. Both the federal district court and the U.S. Court of Appeals for the Ninth Circuit agreed and held Napster liable for violating copyright laws. ■

Since the 2001 *Napster* decision, the recording industry has filed and won numerous lawsuits against companies that distribute online file-sharing software. The courts have held these Napster-like companies liable based on two theories: contributory infringement, which applies if the company had reason to know about a user's infringement and failed to stop it; and vicarious liability, which exists if the company was able to control the users' activities and stood to benefit financially from their infringement. In the *Napster* case, the court held the company liable under both doctrines, largely because the technology that Napster had used was centralized and gave it "the ability to locate infringing material listed on its search indices, and the right to terminate users' access to the system."

New File-Sharing Technologies In the wake of the *Napster* decision, other companies developed new technologies that allow P2P network users to share stored music files, without paying a fee, more quickly and efficiently than ever. Today's file-sharing software is decentralized and does not use search indices. Thus, the companies have no ability to supervise or control which music (or other media files) their users are exchanging. Unlike the Napster system, in which the company played a role in connecting people who were downloading and uploading songs, the new systems are designed to work without the company's input.

Software such as Morpheus and KaZaA, for example, provides users with an interface that is similar to a Web browser. This technology is different from that used by Napster. Instead of the company locating songs for users on other members' computers, the software automatically annotates files with descriptive information so that the music can easily be categorized and cross-referenced (by artist and title, for instance). When a user performs a search, the software is able to locate a list of peers that have the file available for downloading. Also, to expedite

23. 239 F.3d 1004 (9th Cir. 2001).

24. Vicarious (indirect) liability exists when one person is subject to liability for another's actions. A common example occurs in the employment context, when an employer is held vicariously liable by third parties for torts committed by employees in the course of their employment.

the P2P transfer and ensure that the complete file is received, the software distributes the download task over the entire list of peers simultaneously. By downloading even one file, the user becomes a point of distribution for that file, which is then automatically shared with others on the network. How the courts have decided the legality of these new digital technologies is discussed in this chapter's *Management Perspective* feature on the following page.

Trade Secrets

TRADE SECRETS
Information or processes that give a business an advantage over competitors that do not know the information or processes.

Some business processes and information that are not or cannot be patented, copyrighted, or trademarked are nevertheless protected against appropriation by a competitor as trade secrets. **Trade secrets** consist of customer lists, plans, research and development, pricing information, marketing techniques, production methods, and generally anything that makes an individual company unique and that would have value to a competitor.

Unlike copyright and trademark protection, protection of trade secrets extends both to ideas and to their expression. (For this reason, and because a trade secret involves no registration or filing requirements, trade secret protection may be well suited for software.) Of course, the secret formula, method, or other information must be disclosed to some persons, particularly to key employees. Businesses generally attempt to protect their trade secrets by having all employees who use the process or information agree in their contracts, or in confidentiality agreements, never to divulge it.

State and Federal Law on Trade Secrets

Under Section 757 of the *Restatement of Torts,* those who disclose or use another's trade secret, without authorization, are liable to that other party if (1) they discovered the secret by improper means, or (2) their disclosure or use constitutes a breach of a duty owed to the other party. The theft of confidential business data by industrial espionage, as when a business taps into a competitor's computer, is a theft of trade secrets without any contractual violation and is actionable in itself.

Until twenty years ago, virtually all law with respect to trade secrets was common law. In an effort to reduce the unpredictability of the common law in this area, a model act, the Uniform Trade Secrets Act, was presented to the states for adoption in 1979. Parts of this act have been adopted in more than thirty states. Typically, a state that has adopted parts of the act has adopted only those parts that encompass its own existing common law. Additionally, in 1996 Congress passed the Economic Espionage Act, which made the theft of trade secrets a federal crime. We will examine the provisions and significance of this act in Chapter 6, in the context of crimes related to business.

.on the Web The Cyberspace Law Institute offers articles and information on such topics as trade secrets at **http://www.cli.org**.

Trade Secrets in Cyberspace

The nature of new computer technology undercuts a business firm's ability to protect its confidential information, including trade secrets.[25] For instance, a dishonest employee could e-mail trade secrets in a company's computer to a competitor or a future employer. If e-mail is not an option, the employee might walk out with the information on a computer disk.

25. Note that the courts have even found that customers' e-mail addresses may constitute trade secrets. See *T-N-T Motorsports, Inc. v. Hennessey Motorsports, Inc.,* 965 S.W.2d 18 (Tex.App.—Hous. [1 Dist.] 1998); rehearing overruled (1998); petition dismissed (1998).

MANAGEMENT PERSPECTIVE

File-Sharing Technology and Copyright Law

MANAGEMENT FACES A LEGAL ISSUE

Clearly, any person who downloads copyrighted music without permission from the copyright holder is liable for copyright infringement. But what about the companies that provide the software that enables users to swap copyrighted music? In what circumstances will the companies be held liable? For some time, it was difficult for the courts to apply traditional doctrines of contributory and vicarious copyright liability to new file-sharing technologies.

WHAT THE COURTS SAY

In 2005, however, the United States Supreme Court addressed this issue in *Metro-Goldwyn-Mayer Studios, Inc. v. Grokster, Ltd.*[a] In that case, organizations in the music and film industry (the plaintiffs) sued several companies that distribute file-sharing software used in P2P networks, including Grokster, Ltd., and StreamCast Networks, Inc. (the defendants). The plaintiffs claimed that the companies were contributorily and vicariously liable for the infringement of their end users.

The federal district court that initially heard the case examined the technology involved and concluded that the defendants were not liable for contributory infringement because they lacked the requisite level of knowledge. It was not enough that the defendants *generally* knew that the software they provided might be used to infringe on copyrights; they also had to have *specific knowledge* of the infringement "at a time when they can use that knowledge to stop the particular infringement." Here, the companies had merely distributed free software. They had no knowledge of whether users were swapping copyrighted files and no ability to stop users from infringing activities. Further, the two defendants could not be held vicariously liable for the infringement because it was not possible for the companies to supervise or control their users' conduct. The district court's decision was affirmed on appeal.

The United States Supreme Court reversed the lower court's decision and remanded the case for further proceedings. The Court held that "one who distributes a device [software] with the object of promoting its use to infringe the copyright, as shown by clear expression or other affirmative steps taken to foster infringement, is liable for the resulting acts of infringement by third parties." The Court did not, however, specify what kind of "affirmative steps" are necessary to establish liability and left it to the lower court on remand to determine whether the defendants had actually induced their users to commit infringement. In the Court's view, however, there was ample evidence in the record that the defendants had acted with the intent to cause copyright violations by use of their software.

IMPLICATIONS FOR MANAGERS

The Supreme Court's decision in this case shifts the focus in secondary copyright infringement cases away from specific knowledge of acts of infringement to acts that induce or promote infringement. Essentially, this means that file-sharing companies that have taken affirmative steps to promote copyright infringement can be held secondarily liable for millions of infringing acts that their users commit daily. Because the Court did not define exactly what is necessary to impose liability, however, a great deal of legal uncertainty remains concerning this issue.

a. ___ U.S. ___, 125 S.Ct. 2764, ___ L.Ed.2d ___ (2005).

ETHICAL ISSUE 5.2

Does preventing a Web site from posting computer codes that reveal trade secrets violate free speech rights? An ongoing issue with ethical dimensions is the point at which free speech rights come into conflict with the right of copyright holders to protect their property by using encryption technology. This issue came before the California Supreme Court in 2003 in the case of *DVD Copy Control Association v. Bunner.*[26] Trade associations in the movie industry (the plaintiffs) sued an Internet Web site operator (the defen-

26. 31 Cal.4th 864, 75 P.3d 1, 4 Cal.Rptr.3d 69 (2003).

dant) who had posted the code of a computer program that cracked technology used to encrypt DVDs. This posed a significant threat to the plaintiffs because, by using the code-cracking software, users would be able to duplicate the copyrighted movies stored on the DVDs. In their suit, the plaintiffs claimed that the defendant had misappropriated trade secrets. The defendant argued that software programs designed to break encryption programs were a form of constitutionally protected speech. When the case reached the California Supreme Court, the court held that although the First Amendment applies to computer code, computer code is not a form of "pure speech" and the courts can therefore protect it to a lesser extent. The court reinstated the trial court's order that enjoined (prevented) the defendant from continuing to post the code. ■

International Protection for Intellectual Property

For many years, the United States has been a party to various international agreements relating to intellectual property rights. For example, the Paris Convention of 1883, to which about ninety countries are signatory, allows parties in one country to file for patent and trademark protection in any of the other member countries. Other international agreements include the Berne Convention and the TRIPS agreement.

The Berne Convention

Under the Berne Convention of 1886, an international copyright agreement, if a U.S. author writes a book, every country that has signed the convention must recognize that author's copyright in the book. Also, if a citizen of a country that has not signed the convention first publishes a book in a country that has signed, all other countries that have signed the convention must recognize that author's copyright. Copyright notice is not needed to gain protection under the Berne Convention for works published after March 1, 1989.

This convention and other international agreements have given some protection to intellectual property on a worldwide level. None of them, however, has been as significant and far reaching in scope as the agreement on Trade-Related Aspects of Intellectual Property Rights, or, more simply, TRIPS.

.on the Web The Web site of Cornell University's Legal Information Institute includes the texts of the Berne Convention and other international treaties on copyright issues at **http://www.law.cornell.edu/topics/copyright.html**.

The TRIPS Agreement

Representatives from over one hundred nations signed the TRIPS agreement in 1994. The agreement established, for the first time, standards for the international protection of intellectual property rights, including patents, trademarks, and copyrights for movies, computer programs, books, and music. Prior to the agreement, U.S. sellers of intellectual property in the international market faced difficulties because many other countries had no laws protecting intellectual property rights or failed to enforce existing laws. To address this problem, the TRIPS agreement provides that each member country must include in its domestic laws broad intellectual property rights and effective remedies (including civil and criminal penalties) for violations of those rights.

Generally, the TRIPS agreement provides that each member nation must not discriminate (in the administration, regulation, or adjudication of intellectual property rights) against foreign owners of such rights. In other words, a member nation cannot give its own nationals (citizens) favorable treatment without offering the same treatment to nationals of all member countries. For instance, if a U.S. software manufacturer brings a suit for the infringement of intellectual property rights under a member country's national laws, the U.S. manufacturer is entitled to receive the same treatment as a domestic manufacturer. Each member nation must also ensure that legal procedures are available for parties who wish to bring actions for infringement of intellectual property rights. Additionally, a related document established a mechanism for settling disputes among member nations.

Particular provisions of the TRIPS agreement relate to patent, trademark, and copyright protection for intellectual property. The agreement specifically provides copyright protection for computer programs by stating that compilations of data, databases, and other materials are "intellectual creations" and that they are to be protected as copyrightable works. Other provisions relate to trade secrets and the rental of computer programs and cinematographic works.

The Madrid Protocol

In the past, one of the difficulties in protecting U.S. trademarks internationally was that it was time consuming and expensive to apply for trademark registration in foreign countries. The filing fees and procedures for trademark registration vary significantly among individual countries. The Madrid Protocol, however, which President George W. Bush signed into law in the fall of 2003, may help to resolve these problems. The Madrid Protocol is an international treaty that has been signed by sixty-one countries. Under its provisions, a U.S. company wishing to register its trademark abroad can submit a single application and designate other member countries in which it would like to register the mark. The treaty is designed to reduce the costs of obtaining international trademark protection by more than 60 percent, according to proponents.

Although the Madrid Protocol may simplify and reduce the cost of trademark registration in foreign nations, it remains to be seen whether it will provide significant benefits to trademark owners. Even with an easier registration process, the issue of whether member countries will enforce the law and protect the mark still remains.

REVIEWING INTELLECTUAL PROPERTY

Two computer science majors, Trent and Xavier, have an idea for a new video game, which they propose to call "Hallowed." They form a business and begin developing their idea. Several months later, Trent and Xavier run into a problem with their design and consult with a friend, Brad, who is an expert in designing computer source codes. Before Hallowed is marketed, however, the video game "Halo 2" is released for both the Xbox and Game Cube systems. Halo 2 uses the same source codes as Hallowed and imitates its overall look and feel. Using the information presented in the chapter, answer the following questions.

1. Is an idea for a video game patentable? Why or why not?
2. Suppose that Trent and Xavier did not file an application for a patent. Does that mean that they do not have a right to exclude others from making the game? Explain.
3. If Trent and Xavier did hold the patent on Hallowed, would the release of Halo 2 infringe on their patent? Why or why not?
4. Is an idea for a video game copyrightable? Is a video game copyrightable? At what point does copyright protection apply?
5. Based only the facts described above, could Trent and Xavier sue the makers of Halo 2 for copyright infringement? Why or why not?
6. Would the name "Hallowed" receive protection as a trademark or as trade dress?
7. Suppose that Trent and Xavier discover that Brad took the idea of Hallowed and sold it to the company that produced Halo 2. Which type of intellectual property issue does this raise?

APPLICATION How Can You Protect Your Trade Secrets?*

Most successful businesses have trade secrets. The law protects trade secrets indefinitely, provided that the information is not generally known, is kept a secret, and has commercial value. Sometimes, of course, a business needs to disclose secret information to a party in the course of conducting business. For example, a company may need to hire a consultant to revamp a computer system, an engineer to design a manufacturing system, or a marketing firm to implement a sales program. All of these individuals may need access to some of the company's trade secrets. One way to protect against the unauthorized disclosure of such information is through confidentiality agreements.

CONFIDENTIALITY AGREEMENTS

In a confidentiality agreement, one party promises not to divulge information about the other party to anyone else or to use the other party's confidential information for his or her own benefit. Confidentiality agreements are often included in licensing and employment contracts, but they can also be separate contracts. The key is to make sure that the agreement adequately protects the trade secrets and applies to any related transactions between the parties. For instance, if you execute a separate confidentiality agreement with a marketing firm, you need to make sure that it refers to any other contracts you have made with that firm prior to the confidentiality agreement. Also, subsequent contracts with the firm should either refer back to the confidentiality agreement or include a new confidentiality provision.

DEFINING THE SCOPE OF THE AGREEMENT

Confidentiality agreements must be reasonable. Businesspersons should consider what information needs to be protected and for how long. Make certain to define what you mean by *confidential information* in the agreement. Do you want to protect just your customer list or all financial, technical, and other business information? Think ahead, cover the bases, and be specific.

The duration of the agreement usually depends on the nature of the information. Very important secret information should remain confidential for a longer time than less important secrets. Sometimes, as with an advertising campaign, the time period for confidentiality may be self-evident (if the campaign ends in six months, for example). Tailor the agreement to your needs as much as possible. If the party to whom you are disclosing information will no longer need the information after a certain date—such as when the project is completed—include a provision requiring the return of confidential information after that date. This will alleviate concerns that your confidential trade secrets might later fall into the hands of a stranger.

CHECKLIST FOR THE OWNER OF TRADE SECRETS

1. Determine what your trade secrets are and who may need access to them.
2. Make sure that confidentiality agreements define, in an all-inclusive manner, what information should be considered confidential.
3. Specify a time period that is reasonable under the circumstances.
4. Identify the agreements to which the confidentiality provisions apply.
5. Require that the confidential materials be returned to you.

* This *Application* is not meant to substitute for the services of an attorney who is licensed to practice law in your state.

KEY TERMS

copyright 146
cyber mark 141
cybersquatting 142
distributed network 153
domain name 141
intellectual property 134
patent 144
peer-to-peer (P2P) networking 153
service mark 140
trade dress 141
trade name 140
trade secret 155
trademark 136

CHAPTER SUMMARY Intellectual Property

Trademarks and Related Property (See pages 136–141.)	1. A *trademark* is a distinctive mark, motto, device, or emblem that a manufacturer stamps, prints, or otherwise affixes to the goods it produces so that they may be identified on the market and their origin vouched for. 2. The major federal statutes protecting trademarks and related property are the Lanham Act of 1946 and the Federal Trademark Dilution Act of 1995. Generally, to be protected, a trademark must be sufficiently distinctive from all competing trademarks. 3. *Trademark infringement* occurs when one uses a mark that is the same as, or confusingly similar to, the protected trademark, service mark, trade name, or trade dress of another without permission when marketing goods or services.
Cyber Marks (See pages 141–144.)	A *cyber mark* is a trademark in cyberspace. Trademark infringement in cyberspace occurs when one person uses, in a domain name or in meta tags, a name that is the same as, or confusingly similar to, the protected mark of another.
Patents (See pages 144–146.)	1. A *patent* is a grant from the government that gives an inventor the exclusive right to make, use, and sell an invention for a period of twenty years from the date of filing the application for a patent. To be patentable, an invention (or a discovery, process, or design) must be genuine, novel, useful, and not obvious in light of current technology. Computer software may be patented. 2. *Patent infringement* occurs when one uses or sells another's patented design, product, or process without the patent owner's permission.
Copyrights (See pages 146–155.)	1. A *copyright* is an intangible property right granted by federal statute to the author or originator of certain literary or artistic productions. Computer software may be copyrighted. 2. *Copyright infringement* occurs whenever the form or expression of an idea is copied without the permission of the copyright holder. An exception applies if the copying is deemed a "fair use." 3. Copyrights are governed by the Copyright Act of 1976, as amended. To protect copyrights in digital information, Congress passed the No Electronic Theft Act of 1997 and the Digital Millennium Copyright Act of 1998. 4. Technology that allows users to share files via the Internet on distributed networks often raises copyright infringement issues. In 2005, the United States Supreme Court made it clear that software companies that have taken affirmative steps to induce or promote infringement may be held liable for their end users' infringement.
Trade Secrets (See pages 155–157.)	*Trade secrets* include customer lists, plans, research and development, and pricing information, for example. Trade secrets are protected under the common law and, in some states, under statutory law against misappropriation by competitors. The Economic Espionage Act of 1996 made the theft of trade secrets a federal crime (see Chapter 6).
International Protection for Intellectual Property (See pages 157–158.)	Various international agreements provide international protection for intellectual property. A landmark agreement is the 1994 agreement on Trade-Related Aspects of Intellectual Property Rights (TRIPS), which provides for enforcement procedures in all countries signatory to the agreement.

FOR REVIEW

Answers for the even-numbered questions in this For Review *section can be found on this text's accompanying Web site at* http://blt.westbuslaw.com. *Select "Chapter 5" and click on "For Review."*

1 What is intellectual property?
2 Why are trademarks and patents protected by the law?
3 What laws protect authors' rights in the works they generate?

4 What are trade secrets, and what laws offer protection for this form of intellectual property?

5 What steps have been taken to protect intellectual property rights in today's digital age?

QUESTIONS AND CASE PROBLEMS

5–1. Copyright Infringement. In which of the following situations would a court likely hold Maruta liable for copyright infringement?

(a) At the library, Maruta photocopies ten pages from a scholarly journal relating to a topic on which she is writing a term paper.
(b) Maruta makes leather handbags and sells them in her small leather shop. She advertises her handbags as "Vutton handbags," hoping that customers might mistakenly assume that they were made by Vuitton, the well-known maker of high-quality luggage and handbags.
(c) Maruta owns a small country store. She purchases one copy of several popular movie DVDs from various DVD distributors. Then, using blank DVDs, she makes copies to rent or sell to her customers.
(d) Maruta teaches Latin American history at a small university. She has a videocassette recorder and frequently tapes television programs relating to Latin America. She then takes the videos to her classroom so that her students can watch them.

5–2. Patent Infringement. John and Andrew Doney invented a hard-bearing device for balancing rotors. Although they registered their invention with the U.S. Patent and Trademark Office, it was never used as an automobile wheel balancer. Some time later, Exetron Corp. produced an automobile wheel balancer that used a hard-bearing device with a support plate similar to that of the Doneys. Given that the Doneys had not used their device for automobile wheel balancing, does Exetron's use of a similar hard-bearing device infringe on the Doneys' patent?

5–3. Trademark Infringement. Elvis Presley Enterprises, Inc. (EPE), owns all of the trademarks of the Elvis Presley estate. None of these marks is registered for use in the restaurant business. Barry Capece registered "The Velvet Elvis" as a service mark for a restaurant and tavern with the U.S. Patent and Trademark Office. Capece opened a nightclub called "The Velvet Elvis" with a menu, decor, advertising, and promotional events that evoked Elvis Presley and his music. EPE filed a suit in a federal district court against Capece and others, claiming, among other things, that "The Velvet Elvis" service mark infringed on EPE's trademarks. During the trial, witnesses testified that they thought the bar was associated with Elvis Presley. Should Capece be ordered to stop using "The Velvet Elvis" mark? Why or why not? [*Elvis Presley Enterprises, Inc. v. Capece,* 141 F.3d 188 (5th Cir. 1998)]

5–4. Trademark Infringement. A&H Sportswear, Inc., a swimsuit maker, obtained a trademark for its MIRACLESUIT in 1992. The MIRACLESUIT design makes the wearer appear slimmer. The MIRACLESUIT was widely advertised and discussed in the media. The MIRACLESUIT was also sold for a brief time in the Victoria's Secret (VS) catalogue, which is published by Victoria's Secret Catalogue, Inc. In 1993, Victoria's Secret Stores, Inc., began selling a cleavage-enhancing bra, which was named THE MIRACLE BRA and for which a trademark was obtained. The next year, THE MIRACLE BRA swimwear debuted in the VS catalogue and stores. A&H filed a suit in a federal district court against VS Stores and VS Catalogue, alleging in part that THE MIRACLE BRA mark, when applied to swimwear, infringed on the MIRACLESUIT mark. A&H argued that there was a "possibility of confusion" between the marks. The VS entities contended that the appropriate standard was "likelihood of confusion" and that, in this case, there was no likelihood of confusion. In whose favor will the court rule, and why? [*A&H Sportswear, Inc. v. Victoria's Secret Stores, Inc.,* 166 F.3d 197 (3d Cir. 1999)]

CASE PROBLEM WITH SAMPLE ANSWER

5–5. In 1999, Steve and Pierce Thumann and their father, Fred, created Spider Webs, Ltd., a partnership, to, according to Steve, "develop Internet address names." Spider Webs registered nearly two thousand Internet domain names for an average of $70 each, including the names of cities, the names of buildings, names related to a business or trade (such as air conditioning or plumbing), and the names of famous companies. It offered many of the names for sale on its Web site and through eBay.com. Spider Webs registered the domain name "ERNESTANDJULIOGALLO.COM" in Spider Webs' name. E. & J. Gallo Winery filed a suit against Spider Webs, alleging, in part, violations of the Anticybersquatting Consumer Protection Act. Gallo asked the court for, among other things, statutory damages. Gallo also sought to have the domain name at issue transferred to Gallo. During the suit, Spider Webs published anticorporate articles and opinions, and discussions of the suit, at the URL "ERNESTANDJULIOGALLO.COM." Should the court rule in Gallo's favor? Why or why not? [*E. & J. Gallo Winery v. Spider Webs, Ltd.,* 129 F.Supp.2d 1033 (S.D.Tex. 2001)]

After you have answered this problem, compare your answer with the sample answer given on the Web site that accompanies this text. Go to http://blt.westbuslaw.com, select "Chapter 5," and click on "Case Problem with Sample Answer."

5–6. Trade Secrets. Four Pillars Enterprise Co. is a Taiwanese company owned by Pin Yen Yang. Avery Dennison, Inc., a U.S. corporation, is one of Four Pillars' chief competitors in the manufacture of adhesives. In 1989, Victor Lee, an Avery employee, met Yang and Yang's daughter Hwei Chen. They agreed to pay

Lee $25,000 a year to serve as a consultant to Four Pillars. Over the next eight years, Lee supplied the Yangs with confidential Avery reports, including information that Four Pillars used to make a new adhesive that had been developed by Avery. The Federal Bureau of Investigation (FBI) confronted Lee, and he agreed to cooperate in an operation to catch the Yangs. When Lee next met the Yangs, he showed them documents provided by the FBI. The documents bore "confidential" stamps, and Lee said that they were Avery's confidential property. The FBI arrested the Yangs with the documents in their possession. The Yangs and Four Pillars were charged with, among other crimes, the attempted theft of trade secrets. The defendants argued in part that it was impossible for them to have committed this crime because the documents were not actually trade secrets. Should the court acquit them? Why or why not? [*United States v. Yang*, 281 F.3d 534 (6th Cir. 2002)]

5–7. Patent Infringement. As a cattle rancher in Nebraska, Gerald Gohl used handheld searchlights to find and help calving animals (animals giving birth) in harsh blizzard conditions. Gohl thought that it would be more helpful to have a portable searchlight mounted on the outside of a vehicle and remotely controlled. He and Al Gebhardt developed and patented practical applications of this idea—the Golight and the wireless, remote-controlled Radio Ray, which could rotate 360 degrees—and formed Golight, Inc., to make and market these products. In 1997, Wal-Mart Stores, Inc., began selling a portable, wireless, remote-controlled searchlight that was identical to the Radio Ray except for a stop piece that prevented the light from rotating more than 351 degrees. Golight sent Wal-Mart a letter, claiming that its device infringed Golight's patent. Wal-Mart sold its remaining inventory of the devices, and stopped carrying the product. Golight filed a suit in a federal district court against Wal-Mart, alleging patent infringement. How should the court rule? Explain. [*Golight, Inc. v. Wal-Mart Stores, Inc.*, 355 F.3d 1327 (Fed. Cir. 2004)]

FOR CRITICAL ANALYSIS

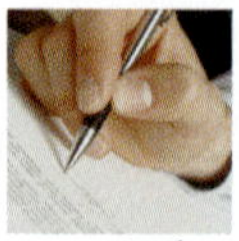

5–8. Patent protection in the United States is granted to the first person to invent a given product or process, even though another person may be the first to file for a patent on the same product or process. What are the advantages of this patenting procedure? Can you think of any disadvantages? Explain.

VIDEO QUESTION

DIGITAL VIDEO LIBRARY
WEST LEGAL STUDIES IN BUSINESS

5–9. Go to this text's Web site at http://blt.westbuslaw.com and select "Chapter 5." Click on "Video Questions" and view the video titled *Jerk*. Then answer the following questions.

1. In the video, Navin (Steve Martin) creates a special handle for Mr. Fox's (Bill Macy's) glasses. Can Navin obtain a patent or a copyright protecting his invention? Explain your answer.
2. Suppose that after Navin legally protects his idea, Fox steals it and decides to develop it for himself, without Navin's permission. Has Fox committed infringement? If so, what kind: trademark, patent, or copyright?
3. Suppose that after Navin legally protects his idea, he realizes he doesn't have the funds to mass produce the special glasses handle. Navin therefore agrees to allow Fox to manufacture the product. Has Navin granted Fox a license? Explain.
4. Assume that Navin is able to manufacture his invention. What might Navin do to ensure that his product is identifiable and can be distinguished from other products on the market?

INTERNET EXERCISES

Go to the *Business Law Today* home page at http://blt.westbuslaw.com, select "Chapter 5," and click on "Internet Exercises." There you will find the following Internet research exercises that you can perform to learn more about topics covered in this chapter.

Activity 5–1: LEGAL PERSPECTIVE—Unwarranted Legal Threats

Activity 5–2: MANAGEMENT PERSPECTIVE—Protecting Intellectual Property across Borders

BEFORE THE TEST

Go to the *Business Law Today* home page at http://blt.westbuslaw.com, select "Chapter 5," and click on "Interactive Quizzes." You will find a number of interactive questions relating to this chapter.

CHAPTER 6

Criminal Law and Cyber Crimes

"No State shall . . . deprive any person of life, liberty, or property without due process of law, nor deny to any person within its jurisdiction the equal protection of the laws."

Fourteenth Amendment to the U.S. Constitution, July 28, 1868

CHAPTER OUTLINE

LEARNING OBJECTIVES

After reading this chapter, you should be able to answer the following questions:

1. What two elements must exist before a person can be held liable for a crime? Can a corporation commit crimes?
2. What are five broad categories of crimes? What is white-collar crime?
3. What defenses might be raised by criminal defendants to avoid liability for criminal acts?
4. What constitutional safeguards exist to protect persons accused of crimes? What are the basic steps in the criminal process?
5. What is cyber crime? What laws apply to crimes committed in cyberspace?

Various sanctions are used to bring about a society in which individuals engaging in business can compete and flourish. These sanctions include damages for various types of tortious conduct (as discussed in Chapter 4), damages for breach of contract (to be discussed in Chapter 15), and the equitable remedies discussed in Chapter 1. Additional sanctions are imposed under criminal law. Many statutes regulating business provide for criminal as well as civil sanctions. Therefore, criminal law joins civil law as an important element in the legal environment of business.

In this chapter, following a brief summary of the major differences between criminal and civil law, we look at how crimes are classified and what elements must be present for criminal liability to exist. We then examine various categories of crime, the defenses that can be raised to avoid liability for criminal actions, and criminal procedural law. Criminal procedural law attempts to ensure that a criminal defendant's right to "due process of law" is enforced. This right is guaranteed by the Fourteenth Amendment to the U.S. Constitution, as stated in the chapter-opening quotation.

CYBER CRIME
A crime that occurs online, in the virtual community of the Internet, as opposed to the physical world.

Since the advent of computer networks and, more recently, the Internet, new types of crimes or new variations of traditional crimes have been committed in cyberspace. For that reason, they are often referred to as **cyber crime.** Generally, cyber crime refers more to the way particular crimes are committed than to a new category of crimes. We devote the concluding pages of this chapter to a discussion of this increasingly significant area of criminal activity.

Civil Law and Criminal Law

Remember from Chapter 1 that *civil law* spells out the duties that exist between persons or between persons and their governments, excluding the duty not to commit crimes. Contract law, for example, is part of civil law. The whole body of tort law, which deals with the infringement by one person on the legally recognized rights of another, is also an area of civil law.

CRIME
A wrong against society proclaimed in a statute and punishable by society through fines and/or imprisonment—and, in some cases, death.

Criminal law, in contrast, has to do with crime. A **crime** can be defined as a wrong against society proclaimed in a statute and punishable by society through fines and/or imprisonment—and, in some cases, death. As mentioned in Chapter 1, because crimes are *offenses against society as a whole,* they are prosecuted by a public official, such as a district attorney (D.A.), not by victims.

Key Differences between Civil Law and Criminal Law

Because the state has extensive resources at its disposal when prosecuting criminal cases, there are numerous procedural safeguards to protect the rights of defendants. One of these safeguards is the higher burden of proof that applies in a criminal case. As you can see in the *Concept Summary* on the next page, which summarizes some of the key differences between civil law and criminal law, in a civil case the plaintiff usually must prove his or her case by a *preponderance of the evidence.* Under this standard, the plaintiff must convince the court that, based on the evidence presented by both parties, it is more likely than not that the plaintiff's allegation is true.

BEYOND A REASONABLE DOUBT
The burden of proof used in criminal cases. If there is any reasonable doubt that a criminal defendant committed the crime with which she or he has been charged, then the verdict must be "not guilty."

In a criminal case, however, the state must prove its case **beyond a reasonable doubt.** In addition, the verdict normally must be unanimous. For the defendant to be convicted, then, *every* juror in a criminal case must be convinced, beyond a reasonable doubt, that the defendant has committed each essential element of the offense with which she or he is charged. In contrast, in civil cases typically only three-fourths of the jurors need to agree that it is more likely than not that the defendant caused the plaintiff's harm. The higher burden of proof in criminal cases reflects a fundamental social value—the belief that it is worse to convict an innocent individual than to let a guilty person go free. We will look at other safeguards later in the chapter, in the context of criminal procedure.

CONCEPT SUMMARY Key Differences between Civil Law and Criminal Law

ISSUE	CIVIL LAW	CRIMINAL LAW
Party who brings suit	Person who suffered harm	The state
Burden of proof	Preponderance of the evidence	Beyond a reasonable doubt
Verdict	Three-fourths majority (typically)	Unanimous
Remedy	Damages to compensate for the harm, or a decree to achieve an equitable result	Punishment (fine, imprisonment, or death)

CIVIL LIABILITY FOR CRIMINAL ACTS

Those who commit crimes may be subject to both civil and criminal liability. ■ EXAMPLE 6.1 Joe is walking down the street, minding his own business, when suddenly a person attacks him. In the ensuing struggle, the attacker stabs Joe several times, seriously injuring him. A police officer restrains and arrests the wrongdoer. In this situation, the attacker may be subject both to criminal prosecution by the state and to a tort lawsuit brought by Joe. ■ Exhibit 6–1 on the next page illustrates how the same act can result in both a tort action and a criminal action against the wrongdoer.

Classification of Crimes

FELONY
A crime—such as arson, murder, rape, or robbery—that carries the most severe sanctions, which range from more than one year in a state or federal prison to the death penalty.

MISDEMEANOR
A lesser crime than a felony, punishable by a fine or incarceration in jail for up to one year.

Depending on their degree of seriousness, crimes are classified as felonies or misdemeanors. **Felonies** are serious crimes punishable by death or by imprisonment in a federal or state penitentiary for more than a year. The Model Penal Code[1] provides for four degrees of felony: (1) capital offenses, for which the maximum penalty is death; (2) first degree felonies, punishable by a maximum penalty of life imprisonment; (3) second degree felonies, punishable by a maximum of ten years' imprisonment; and (4) third degree felonies, punishable by a maximum of five years' imprisonment.

Under federal law and in most states, any crime that is not a felony is considered a **misdemeanor.** Misdemeanors are crimes punishable by a fine or by confinement for up to a year. If incarcerated (imprisoned), the guilty party goes to a local jail instead of a prison. Disorderly conduct and trespass are common misdemeanors. Some states have different classes of misdemeanors. For example, in Illinois misdemeanors are either Class A (confinement for up to a year), Class B (not more than six months), or Class C (not more than thirty days). Whether a crime is a felony or a misdemeanor can also determine whether the case is tried in a magistrate's court (for example, by a justice of the peace) or in a general trial court.

1. The American Law Institute issued the Official Draft of the Model Penal Code in 1962. The Model Penal Code is not a uniform code. Uniformity of criminal law among the states is not as important as uniformity in other areas of the law. Types of crimes vary with local circumstances, and it is appropriate that punishments vary accordingly. The Model Penal Code contains four parts: (1) general provisions, (2) definitions of special crimes, (3) provisions concerning treatment and corrections, and (4) provisions on the organization of corrections.

EXHIBIT 6–1 TORT LAWSUIT AND CRIMINAL PROSECUTION FOR THE SAME ACT

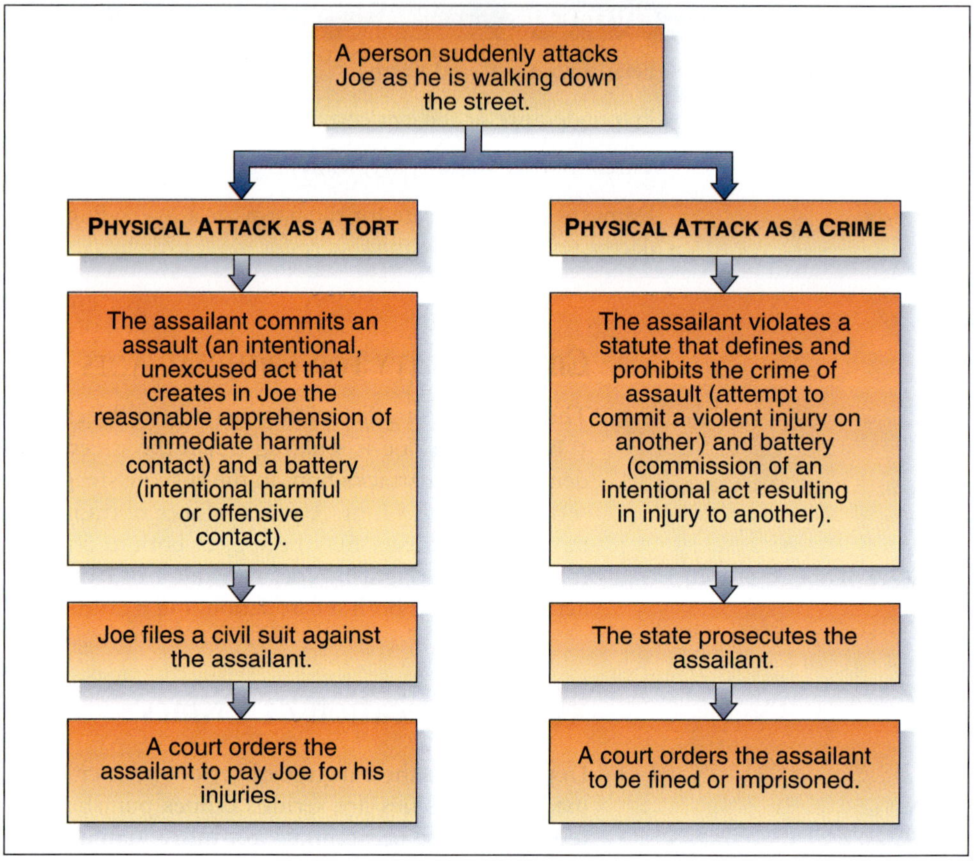

PETTY OFFENSE
In criminal law, the least serious kind of criminal offense, such as a traffic or building-code violation.

In most jurisdictions, **petty offenses** are considered to be a subset of misdemeanors. Petty offenses are minor violations, such as jaywalking or violations of building codes. Even for petty offenses, however, a guilty party can be put in jail for a few days, fined, or both, depending on state or local law.

Criminal Liability

Two elements must exist simultaneously for a person to be convicted of a crime: (1) the performance of a prohibited act and (2) a specified state of mind or intent on the part of the actor. Every criminal statute prohibits certain behavior. Most crimes require an act of *commission;* that is, a person must *do* something in order to be accused of a crime.[2] In some instances, an act of *omission* can be a crime, but only when a person has a legal duty to perform the omitted act. Failure to file a tax return is an example of an omission that is a crime.

The *guilty act* requirement is based on one of the premises of criminal law—that a person is punished for harm done to society. Thinking about killing someone or about

2. Called the *actus reus* (pronounced *ak*-tuhs *ray*-uhs), or "guilty act."

stealing a car may be wrong, but the thoughts do no harm until they are translated into action. Of course, a person can be punished for attempting murder or robbery, but normally only if he or she took substantial steps toward the criminal objective.

A *wrongful mental state*[3] is generally required to establish criminal liability. What constitutes such a mental state varies according to the wrongful action. For murder, the act is the taking of a life, and the mental state is the intent to take life. For theft, the guilty act is the taking of another person's property, and the mental state involves both the knowledge that the property belongs to another and the intent to deprive the owner of it.

Criminal liability typically arises for actions that violate state criminal statutes. Federal criminal jurisdiction is normally limited to crimes that occur outside the jurisdiction of any state, crimes involving interstate commerce or communications, crimes that interfere with the operation of the federal government or its agents, and crimes directed at citizens or property located outside the United States. Federal jurisdiction also exists if a federal law or a federal government agency (such as the U.S. Department of Justice or the federal Environmental Protection Agency) defines a certain type of action as a crime. Today, businesspersons are subject to criminal penalties under numerous federal laws and regulations. We will examine many of these laws in later chapters of this text.

.on the Web Many state criminal codes are now online. To find your state's code, go to

http://www.findlaw.com

and select "State" under the link to "US Laws: Cases and Codes."

Corporate Criminal Liability

At one time, it was thought that a corporation could not incur criminal liability because, although a corporation is a legal person, it can act only through its agents (corporate directors, officers, and employees). Therefore, the corporate entity itself could not "intend" to commit a crime. Under modern criminal law, however, a corporation may be held liable for crimes. Obviously, corporations cannot be imprisoned, but they can be fined or denied certain legal privileges (such as a license). Today, corporations are normally liable for the crimes committed by their agents and employees within the course and scope of their employment.

Corporate directors and officers are personally liable for the crimes they commit, regardless of whether the crimes were committed for their personal benefit or on the corporation's behalf. Additionally, corporate directors and officers may be held liable for the actions of employees under their supervision. Under what has become known as the "responsible corporate officer" doctrine, a court may impose criminal liability on a corporate officer regardless of whether she or he participated in, directed, or even knew about a given criminal violation.

■ **EXAMPLE 6.2** In *United States v. Park,*[4] the chief executive officer of a national supermarket chain was held personally liable for sanitation violations in corporate warehouses, in which the food was exposed to contamination by rodents. The United States Supreme Court imposed personal liability on the corporate officer not because he intended the crime or even knew about it but because he was in a "responsible relationship" to the corporation and had the power to prevent the violation. ■ Since the *Park* decision, courts have applied this "responsible corporate officer" doctrine on a number of occasions to hold corporate officers liable for their employees' statutory violations.

3. Called the *mens rea* (pronounced mehns *ray*-uh), or "evil intent."
4. 421 U.S. 658, 95 S.Ct. 1903, 44 L.Ed.2d 489 (1975).

Types of Crimes

The number of acts that are defined as criminal is nearly endless. Federal, state, and local laws provide for the classification and punishment of hundreds of thousands of different criminal acts. Traditionally, though, crimes have been grouped into five broad categories, or types: violent crime (crimes against persons), property crime, public order crime, white-collar crime, and organized crime. Cyber crime—which consists of crimes committed in cyberspace with the use of computers—is, as mentioned earlier in this chapter, less a category of crime than a new way to commit crime. We will examine cyber crime later in this chapter.

VIOLENT CRIME

Crimes against persons, because they cause others to suffer harm or death, are referred to as *violent crimes*. Murder is a violent crime. So is sexual assault, or rape. Assault and battery, which were discussed in Chapter 4 in the context of tort law, are also classified as violent crimes. **Robbery**—defined as the taking of cash, personal property, or any other article of value from a person by means of force or fear—is also a violent crime. Typically, states have more severe penalties for *aggravated robbery*—robbery with the use of a deadly weapon.

ROBBERY
The act of forcefully and unlawfully taking personal property of any value from another. Force or intimidation is usually necessary for an act of theft to be considered a robbery.

Each of these violent crimes is further classified by degree, depending on the circumstances surrounding the criminal act. These circumstances include the intent of the person committing the crime, whether a weapon was used, and (in cases other than murder) the level of pain and suffering experienced by the victim.

PROPERTY CRIME

The most common type of criminal activity is property crime—crimes in which the goal of the offender is some form of economic gain or the damaging of property. Robbery is a form of property crime, as well as a violent crime, because the offender seeks to gain the property of another. We look here at a number of other crimes that fall within the general category of property crime.

Burglary Traditionally, **burglary** was defined under the common law as breaking and entering the dwelling of another at night with the intent to commit a felony. Originally, the definition was aimed at protecting an individual's home and its occupants. Most state statutes have eliminated some of the requirements found in the common law definition. The time at which the breaking and entering occurs, for example, is usually immaterial. State statutes frequently omit the element of breaking, and some states do not require that the building be a dwelling. Aggravated burglary, which is defined as burglary with the use of a deadly weapon, burglary of a dwelling, or both, incurs a greater penalty.

BURGLARY
The unlawful entry or breaking into a building with the intent to commit a felony. (Some state statutes expand this to include the intent to commit any crime.)

Larceny Any person who wrongfully or fraudulently takes and carries away another person's personal property is guilty of **larceny.** Larceny includes the fraudulent intent to deprive an owner permanently of property. Many business-related larcenies entail fraudulent conduct. Whereas robbery involves force or fear, larceny does not. Therefore, picking pockets is larceny. Similarly, taking company products and supplies home for personal use, if one is not authorized to do so, is larceny.

LARCENY
The wrongful taking and carrying away of another person's personal property with the intent to permanently deprive the owner of the property. Some states classify larceny as either grand or petit, depending on the property's value.

In most states, the definition of property that is subject to larceny statutes has expanded. Stealing computer programs may constitute larceny even though the "property" consists of magnetic impulses. Stealing computer time can also constitute larceny. So, too, can the theft of natural gas. Trade secrets can be subject to larceny statutes. Obtaining another's phone-card number and then using that number, without authorization, to place long-distance calls is a form of property theft. These types of larceny are covered by "theft of services" statutes in many jurisdictions.

The common law distinguishes between grand and petit larceny depending on the value of the property taken. Many states have abolished this distinction, but in those that have not, grand larceny is a felony and petit larceny, a misdemeanor.

Obtaining Goods by False Pretenses It is a criminal act to obtain goods by means of false pretenses—for example, buying groceries with a check, knowing that one has insufficient funds to cover it. Statutes dealing with such illegal activities vary widely from state to state.

Receiving Stolen Goods It is a crime to receive stolen goods. The recipient of such goods need not know the true identity of the owner or the thief. All that is necessary is that the recipient knows or should have known that the goods are stolen, which implies an intent to deprive the owner of those goods.

ARSON
The intentional burning of another's dwelling. Some statutes have expanded this to include any real property regardless of ownership and the destruction of property by other means—for example, by explosion.

Arson The willful and malicious burning of a building (and in some states, personal property) owned by another is the crime of **arson.** At common law, arson traditionally applied only to burning down another person's house. The law was designed to protect human life. Today, arson statutes have been extended to cover the destruction of any building, regardless of ownership, by fire or explosion.

Every state has a special statute that covers a person's burning a building for the purpose of collecting insurance. ■ EXAMPLE 6.3 If Smith owns an insured apartment building that is falling apart and sets fire to it himself or pays someone else to do so, he is guilty not only of arson but also of defrauding insurers, which is an attempted larceny. ■ Of course, the insurer need not pay the claim when insurance fraud is proved.

FORGERY
The fraudulent making or altering of any writing in a way that changes the legal rights and liabilities of another.

Forgery The fraudulent making or altering of any writing in a way that changes the legal rights and liabilities of another is **forgery.** If, without authorization, Severson signs Bennett's name to the back of a check made out to Bennett, Severson is committing forgery. Forgery also includes changing trademarks, falsifying public records, counterfeiting, and altering a legal document.

PUBLIC ORDER CRIME

Historically, societies have always outlawed activities that are considered to be contrary to public values and morals. Today, the most common public order crimes include public drunkenness, prostitution, gambling, and illegal drug use. These crimes are sometimes referred to as *victimless crimes* because they normally harm only the offender. From a broader perspective, however, they are deemed detrimental to society as a whole because they might create an environment that gives rise to property and violent crimes.

WHITE-COLLAR CRIME

WHITE-COLLAR CRIME
Nonviolent crime committed by individuals or corporations to obtain a personal or business advantage.

Crimes that typically occur only in the business context are commonly referred to as **white-collar crimes.** Although there is no official definition of white-collar crime, the term is popularly used to mean an illegal act or series of acts committed by an individual or business entity using some nonviolent means. Usually, this kind of crime is committed in the course of a legitimate occupation. Corporate crimes fall into this category.

EMBEZZLEMENT
The fraudulent appropriation of funds or other property by a person to whom the funds or property has been entrusted.

Embezzlement When a person entrusted with another person's funds or property fraudulently appropriates the funds or property, **embezzlement** occurs. Typically, embezzlement involves an employee who steals funds. Banks face this problem, and so do a number of businesses in which corporate officers or accountants "jimmy" the books to cover up the fraudulent conversion of funds for their own benefit. Embezzlement is not larceny, because the wrongdoer does not physically take the property from the possession of another, and it is not robbery, because force or fear is not used.

It does not matter whether the accused takes the funds from the victim or from a third person. If, as the financial officer of a large corporation, Saunders pockets a certain number of checks from third parties that were given to her to deposit into the corporate account, she is embezzling.

Ordinarily, an embezzler who returns what has been taken will not be prosecuted because the owner usually will not take the time to make a complaint, give depositions, and appear in court. That the accused intended eventually to return the embezzled property, however, does not constitute a sufficient defense to the crime of embezzlement.

Mail and Wire Fraud One of the most potent weapons against white-collar criminals is the Mail Fraud Act of 1990.[5] Under this act, it is a federal crime (mail fraud) to use the mails to defraud the public. Illegal use of the mails must involve (1) mailing or causing someone else to mail a writing—something written, printed, or photocopied—for the purpose of executing a scheme to defraud and (2) a contemplated or an organized scheme to defraud by false pretenses. If, for example, Johnson advertises by mail the sale of a cure for cancer that he knows to be fraudulent because it has no medical validity, he can be prosecuted for fraudulent use of the mails.

Federal law also makes it a crime to use wire (for example, the telephone), radio, or television transmissions to defraud.[6] Violators may be fined up to $1,000, imprisoned for up to five years, or both. If the violation affects a financial institution, the violator may be fined up to $1 million, imprisoned for up to thirty years, or both.

Bribery Basically, three types of bribery are considered crimes: bribery of public officials, commercial bribery, and bribery of foreign officials. The attempt to influence a public official to act in a way that serves a private interest is a crime. As an element of this crime, intent must be present and proved. The bribe can be anything the recipient considers to be valuable. Realize that *the crime of bribery occurs when the bribe is offered.* It does not matter whether the person to whom the bribe is offered accepts the bribe or agrees to perform whatever action is desired by the person offering the bribe. *Accepting a bribe* is a separate crime.

Typically, people make commercial bribes to obtain proprietary information, cover up an inferior product, or secure new business. Industrial espionage sometimes involves commercial bribes. For example, a person in one firm may offer an employee in a competing firm some type of payoff in exchange for trade secrets or pricing schedules. So-called kickbacks, or payoffs for special favors or services, are a form of commercial bribery in some situations.

5. 18 U.S.C. Sections 1341–1342.
6. 18 U.S.C. Section 1343.

Bribing foreign officials to obtain favorable business contracts is a crime. The Foreign Corrupt Practices Act of 1977, which will be discussed in Chapter 7, was passed to curb the use of bribery by American businesspersons in securing foreign contracts.

Bankruptcy Fraud Today, federal bankruptcy law (see Chapter 27) allows individuals and businesses to be relieved of oppressive debt through bankruptcy proceedings. Numerous white-collar crimes may be committed during the many phases of a bankruptcy proceeding. A creditor, for example, may file a false claim against the debtor, which is a crime. Also, a debtor may fraudulently transfer assets to favored parties before or after the petition for bankruptcy is filed. For example, a company-owned automobile may be "sold" at a bargain price to a trusted friend or relative. Closely related to the crime of fraudulent transfer of property is the crime of fraudulent concealment of property, such as hiding gold coins.

The Theft of Trade Secrets As discussed in Chapter 5, trade secrets constitute a form of intellectual property that for many businesses can be extremely valuable. The Economic Espionage Act of 1996[7] made the theft of trade secrets a federal crime. The act also made it a federal crime to buy or possess trade secrets of another person, knowing that the trade secrets were stolen or otherwise acquired without the owner's authorization.

Violations of the act can result in steep penalties. An individual who violates the act can be imprisoned for up to ten years and fined up to $500,000. If a corporation or other organization violates the act, it can be fined up to $5 million. Additionally, the law provides that any property acquired as a result of the violation and any property used in the commission of the violation are subject to criminal *forfeiture*—meaning that the government can take the property. A theft of trade secrets conducted via the Internet, for example, could result in the forfeiture of every computer, printer, or other device used to commit or facilitate the violation.

Insider Trading An individual who obtains "inside information" about the plans of a publicly listed corporation can often make stock-trading profits by using the information to guide decisions relating to the purchase or sale of corporate securities. **Insider trading** is a violation of securities law and will be considered more fully in Chapter 35. Generally, the rule is that a person who possesses inside information and has a duty not to disclose it to outsiders may not profit from the purchase or sale of securities based on that information until the information is available to the public.

INSIDER TRADING
The purchase or sale of securities on the basis of "inside information" (information that has not been made available to the public).

ORGANIZED CRIME

As mentioned, white-collar crime takes place within the confines of the legitimate business world. *Organized crime,* in contrast, operates *illegitimately* by, among other things, providing illegal goods and services. For organized crime, the traditional preferred markets are gambling, prostitution, illegal narcotics, and loan sharking (lending money at higher-than-legal-maximum interest rates), along with more recent ventures into counterfeiting and credit-card scams.

on the Web You can find a wealth of information on famous criminal trials at a Web site maintained by the University of Missouri–Kansas City law school. Go to **http://www.law.umkc.edu/faculty/projects/ftrials/ftrials.html.**

Money Laundering The profits from illegal activities amount to billions of dollars a year, particularly the profits from illegal drug transactions and, to a lesser extent, from racketeering, prostitution, and gambling. Under federal law, banks, savings and

7. 18 U.S.C. Sections 1831–1839.

Jeffrey Skilling, former chief executive officer (CEO) of Enron Corporation, testifies before a congressional committee concerning allegations that Enron insiders profited at the company's expense while improperly concealing losses and inflating earnings. About a month after Skilling resigned as CEO, he sold nearly $60 million of his stock in Enron. This led prosecutors to believe that he sold those shares knowing of the bankruptcy that Enron was facing. Skilling was subsequently indicted on numerous counts of fraud and insider trading. If Skilling knew that the company was on the brink of bankruptcy at the time that he sold his stock, is he guilty of a crime? Explain your answer. (AP Photo/Kenneth Lambert)

loan associations, and other financial institutions are required to report currency transactions involving more than $10,000. Consequently, those who engage in illegal activities face difficulties in depositing their cash profits from illegal transactions.

As an alternative to simply storing cash from illegal transactions in a safe-deposit box, wrongdoers and racketeers have invented ways to launder "dirty" money to make it "clean." This **money laundering** is done through legitimate businesses.

MONEY LAUNDERING
Falsely reporting income that has been obtained through criminal activity as income obtained through a legitimate business enterprise—in effect, "laundering" the "dirty money."

■ **EXAMPLE 6.4** Matt, a successful drug dealer, becomes a partner with a restaurateur. Little by little, the restaurant shows an increasing profit. As a partner in the restaurant, Matt is able to report the "profits" of the restaurant as legitimate income on which he pays federal and state income taxes. He can then spend those after-tax funds without worrying that his lifestyle may exceed the level possible with his reported income. ■

The Federal Bureau of Investigation estimates that organized crime has invested tens of billions of dollars in as many as a hundred thousand business establishments in the United States for the purpose of money laundering. Globally, it is estimated that more than $500 billion in illegal money moves through the world banking system every year.

The Racketeer Influenced and Corrupt Organizations Act In 1970, in an effort to curb the apparently increasing entry of organized crime into the legitimate business world, Congress passed the Racketeer Influenced and Corrupt Organizations Act (RICO).[8] The act, which was enacted as part of the Organized Crime Control Act, makes it a federal crime to (1) use income obtained from racketeering activity to purchase any interest in an enterprise, (2) acquire or maintain an interest in an enterprise through racketeering activity, (3) conduct or participate in the affairs of

8. 18 U.S.C. Sections 1961–1968.

an enterprise through racketeering activity, or (4) conspire to do any of the preceding activities.

Racketeering activity is not a new type of substantive crime created by RICO; rather, RICO incorporates by reference twenty-six separate types of federal crimes and nine types of state felonies[9] and declares that if a person commits two of these offenses, he or she is guilty of "racketeering activity." Additionally, RICO is more often used today to attack white-collar crimes than organized crime.

In the event of a violation, the statute permits the government to seek civil penalties, including the divestiture of a defendant's interest in a business (called forfeiture) or the dissolution of the business. Perhaps the most controversial aspect of RICO is that, in some cases, private individuals are allowed to recover three times their actual losses (treble damages), plus attorneys' fees, for business injuries caused by a violation of the statute. Under criminal provisions of RICO, any individual found guilty of a violation is subject to a fine of up to $25,000 per violation, imprisonment for up to twenty years, or both. Additionally, the statute provides that those who violate RICO may be required to forfeit (give up) any assets, in the form of property or cash, that were acquired as a result of the illegal activity or that were "involved in" or an "instrumentality of" the activity. (See the *Concept Summary* on the following page for an overview of the types of crimes discussed above.)

Defenses to Criminal Liability

Among the most important defenses to criminal liability are infancy, intoxication, insanity, mistake, consent, duress, justifiable use of force, entrapment, and the statute of limitations. Many of these defenses involve assertions that the intent requirement for criminal liability is lacking. Also, in some cases, defendants are given immunity and thus relieved, at least in part, of criminal liability for crimes they committed. We look at each of these defenses here.

Note that procedural violations, such as obtaining evidence without a valid search warrant, may operate as defenses also. As you will read later in this chapter, evidence obtained in violation of a defendant's constitutional rights normally may not be admitted in court. If the evidence is suppressed, then there may be no basis for prosecuting the defendant.

.on the Web You can gain insights into criminal law and procedures, including a number of the defenses that can be raised to avoid criminal liability, by looking at some of the famous criminal law cases included on Court TV's Web site. Go to

http://www.courttv.com/index.html.

INFANCY

The term *infant,* as used in the law, refers to any person who has not yet reached the age of majority (see Chapter 11). In all states, certain courts handle cases involving children who are alleged to have violated the law. In some states, juvenile courts handle children's cases exclusively. In other states, however, courts that handle children's cases may also have jurisdiction over additional matters.

Originally, juvenile court hearings were informal, and lawyers were rarely present. Since 1967, however, when the United States Supreme Court ruled that a child charged with delinquency must be allowed to consult with an attorney before being committed to a state institution,[10] juvenile court hearings have become more formal. In some states, a child may be treated as an adult and tried in a regular court if she or he is above a certain age (usually fourteen) and is charged with a felony, such as rape or murder.

9. See 18 U.S.C. Section 1961(1)(A).
10. *In re Gault,* 387 U.S. 1, 87 S.Ct. 1428, 18 L.Ed.2d 527 (1967).

CONCEPT SUMMARY Types of Crimes

CRIME CATEGORY	DEFINITIONS AND EXAMPLES
Violent Crime	1. *Definition*—Crimes that cause others to suffer harm or death. 2. *Examples*—Murder, assault and battery, sexual assault (rape), and robbery.
Property Crime	1. *Definition*—Crimes in which the goal of the offender is some form of economic gain or the damaging of property; the most common form of crime. 2. *Examples*—Burglary, larceny, arson, receiving stolen goods, forgery, and obtaining goods by false pretenses.
Public Order Crime	1. *Definition*—Crimes contrary to public values and morals. 2. *Examples*—Public drunkenness, prostitution, gambling, and illegal drug use.
White-Collar Crime	1. *Definition*—An illegal act or series of acts committed by an individual or business entity using some nonviolent means to obtain a personal or business advantage; usually committed in the course of a legitimate occupation. 2. *Examples*—Embezzlement, mail and wire fraud, bribery, bankruptcy fraud, theft of trade secrets, and insider trading.
Organized Crime	1. *Definition*—A form of crime conducted by groups operating illegitimately to provide the public with illegal goods and services (such as gambling or illegal narcotics). 2. *Money laundering*—The establishment of legitimate enterprises through which "dirty" money (obtained through criminal activities, such as organized crime) can be "laundered" (made to appear to be legitimate income). 3. *RICO*—The Racketeer Influenced and Corrupt Organizations Act (RICO) of 1970 makes it a federal crime to (a) use income obtained from racketeering activity to purchase any interest in an enterprise, (b) acquire or maintain an interest in an enterprise through racketeering activity, (c) conduct or participate in the affairs of an enterprise through racketeering activity, or (d) conspire to do any of the preceding activities. RICO provides for both civil and criminal liability.

INTOXICATION

The law recognizes two types of intoxication, whether from drugs or from alcohol: *involuntary* and *voluntary*. Involuntary intoxication occurs when a person either is physically forced to ingest or inject an intoxicating substance or is unaware that a substance contains drugs or alcohol. Involuntary intoxication is a defense to a crime if its effect was to make a person incapable of obeying the law or incapable of understanding that the act committed was wrong. Voluntary intoxication is rarely a defense, but it may be effective in cases in which the defendant was *extremely* intoxicated when committing the wrong.

INSANITY

Someone suffering from a mental illness may be judged incapable of having the state of mind required to commit a crime. Thus, insanity may be a defense to a criminal charge. The courts have had difficulty deciding what the test for legal insanity should be, however, and psychiatrists as well as lawyers are critical of the tests used. Almost all federal courts and some states use the relatively liberal standard set forth in the Model Penal Code:

Three suspects were charged with assaulting Matthew Shepard, a gay University of Wyoming student. Shepard was beaten, burned, and tied to a fence like a scarecrow. Should the court allow the defendants to claim that they were temporarily insane because of "homosexual rage"? Why or why not? (AP Photo/Ed Andrieski)

> A person is not responsible for criminal conduct if at the time of such conduct as a result of mental disease or defect he [or she] lacks substantial capacity either to appreciate the wrongfulness of his [or her] conduct or to conform his [or her] conduct to the requirements of the law.

Some states use the *M'Naghten* test,[11] under which a criminal defendant is not responsible if, at the time of the offense, he or she did not know the nature and quality of the act or did not know that the act was wrong. Other states use the irresistible-impulse test. A person operating under an irresistible impulse may know an act is wrong but cannot refrain from doing it.

MISTAKE

Everyone has heard the saying, "Ignorance of the law is no excuse." Ordinarily, ignorance of the law or a mistaken idea about what the law requires is not a valid defense. In some states, however, that rule has been modified. Criminal defendants who claim that they honestly did not know that they were breaking a law may have a valid defense if (1) the law was not published or reasonably made known to the public or (2) the defendant relied on an official statement of the law that was erroneous.

COMPARE "Ignorance" is a lack of information. "Mistake" is a confusion of information.

A *mistake of fact,* as opposed to a *mistake of law,* operates as a defense if it negates the mental state necessary to commit a crime. ■ **EXAMPLE 6.5** If Oliver Wheaton mistakenly walks off with Julie Cabrera's briefcase because he thinks it is his, there is no theft. Theft requires knowledge that the property belongs to another. (If Wheaton's act causes Cabrera to incur damages, however, Wheaton may be subject to liability for trespass to personal property or conversion, torts that were discussed in Chapter 4.) ■

11. A rule derived from *M'Naghten's Case,* 8 Eng.Rep. 718 (1843).

CONSENT

CONSENT
The voluntary agreement to a proposition or an act of another; a concurrence of wills.

What if a victim consents to a crime or even encourages the person intending a criminal act to commit it? Ordinarily, **consent** does not operate as a bar to criminal liability. In some rare circumstances, however, the law may allow consent to be used as a defense. In each case, the question is whether the law forbids an act that was committed against the victim's will or forbids the act without regard to the victim's wish. The law forbids murder, prostitution, and drug use regardless of whether the victim consents to it. Also, if the act causes harm to a third person who has not consented, there is no escape from criminal liability. Consent or forgiveness given after a crime has been committed is not really a defense, though it can affect the likelihood of prosecution or the severity of the sentence. Consent operates most successfully as a defense in crimes against property.

■ EXAMPLE 6.6 Barry gives Phong permission to hunt for deer on Barry's land while staying in Barry's lakeside cabin. After observing Phong carrying a gun into the cabin at night, a neighbor calls the police, and an officer subsequently arrests Phong. If charged with burglary (or aggravated burglary, because he had a weapon), Phong can assert the defense of consent. He had obtained Barry's consent to enter the premises. ■

DURESS

DURESS
Unlawful pressure brought to bear on a person, causing the person to perform an act that she or he would not otherwise perform.

Duress exists when the *wrongful threat* of one person induces another person to perform an act that she or he would not otherwise perform. In such a situation, duress is said to negate the mental state necessary to commit a crime. For duress to qualify as a defense, the following requirements must be met:

1. The threat must be of serious bodily harm or death.
2. The harm threatened must be greater than the harm caused by the crime.
3. The threat must be immediate and inescapable.
4. The defendant must have been involved in the situation through no fault of his or her own.

JUSTIFIABLE USE OF FORCE

SELF-DEFENSE
The legally recognized privilege to protect oneself or one's property against injury by another. The privilege of self-defense protects only acts that are reasonably necessary to protect oneself, one's property, or another person.

Probably the best-known defense to criminal liability is **self-defense.** Other situations, however, also justify the use of force: the defense of one's dwelling, the defense of other property, and the prevention of a crime. In all of these situations, it is important to distinguish between deadly and nondeadly force. *Deadly force* is likely to result in death or serious bodily harm. *Nondeadly force* is force that reasonably appears necessary to prevent the imminent use of criminal force.

Generally speaking, people can use the amount of nondeadly force that seems necessary to protect themselves, their dwellings, or other property or to prevent the commission of a crime. Deadly force can be used in self-defense if there is a *reasonable belief* that imminent death or grievous bodily harm will otherwise result, if the attacker is using unlawful force (an example of lawful force is that exerted by a police officer), and if the defender has not initiated or provoked the attack. Deadly force normally can be used to defend a dwelling only if the unlawful entry is violent and the person believes deadly force is necessary to prevent imminent death or great bodily harm or—in some jurisdictions—if the person believes deadly force is necessary to prevent the commission of a felony (such as arson) in the dwelling.

ENTRAPMENT

ENTRAPMENT
In criminal law, a defense in which the defendant claims that he or she was induced by a public official—usually an undercover agent or police officer—to commit a crime that he or she would otherwise not have committed.

Entrapment is a defense designed to prevent police officers or other government agents from encouraging crimes in order to apprehend persons wanted for criminal acts. In the typical entrapment case, an undercover agent *suggests* that a crime be committed and somehow pressures or induces an individual to commit it. The agent then arrests the individual for the crime.

For entrapment to be considered a defense, both the suggestion and the inducement must take place. The defense is intended not to prevent law enforcement agents from setting a trap for an unwary criminal but rather to prevent them from pushing the individual into it. The crucial issue is whether the person who committed a crime was predisposed to do so or acted because the agent induced it.

STATUTE OF LIMITATIONS

With some exceptions, such as for the crime of murder, statutes of limitations apply to crimes just as they do to civil wrongs. In other words, criminal cases must be prosecuted within a certain number of years. If a criminal action is brought after the statutory time period has expired, the accused person can raise the statute of limitations as a defense.

IMMUNITY

At times, the state may wish to obtain information from a person accused of a crime. Accused persons are understandably reluctant to give information if it will be used to prosecute them, and they cannot be forced to do so. The privilege against self-incrimination is granted by the Fifth Amendment to the Constitution, which reads, in part, "nor shall [any person] be compelled in any criminal case to be a witness against himself." In cases in which the state wishes to obtain information from a person accused of a crime, the state can grant *immunity* from prosecution or agree to prosecute for a less serious offense in exchange for the information. Once immunity is given, the person can no longer refuse to testify on Fifth Amendment grounds, because he or she now has an absolute privilege against self-incrimination.

Often, a grant of immunity from prosecution for a serious crime is part of the **plea bargaining** between the defendant and the prosecuting attorney. The defendant may be convicted of a lesser offense, while the state uses the defendant's testimony to prosecute accomplices for serious crimes carrying heavy penalties.

PLEA BARGAINING
The process by which a defendant and the prosecutor in a criminal case work out a mutually satisfactory disposition of the case, subject to court approval; usually involves the defendant's pleading guilty to a lesser offense in return for a lighter sentence.

Constitutional Safeguards and Criminal Procedures

Criminal law brings the power of the state, with all its resources, to bear against the individual. Criminal procedures are designed to protect the constitutional rights of individuals and to prevent the arbitrary use of power on the part of the government.

The U.S. Constitution provides specific safeguards for those accused of crimes. Most of these safeguards protect individuals against state government actions, as well as federal government actions, by virtue of the due process clause of the Fourteenth Amendment. These safeguards are set forth in the Fourth, Fifth, Sixth, and Eighth Amendments.

FOURTH AMENDMENT PROTECTIONS

The Fourth Amendment protects the "right of the people to be secure in their persons, houses, papers, and effects." Before searching or seizing private property, law enforcement officers must obtain a **search warrant**—an order from a judge or other public official authorizing the search or seizure.

SEARCH WARRANT
An order granted by a public authority, such as a judge, that authorizes law enforcement personnel to search particular premises or property.

PROBABLE CAUSE
Reasonable grounds for believing that a person should be arrested or searched.

Search Warrants and Probable Cause To obtain a search warrant, the officers must convince a judge that they have reasonable grounds, or **probable cause,** to believe a search will reveal a specific illegality. Probable cause requires law enforcement officials to have trustworthy evidence that would convince a reasonable person that the proposed search or seizure is more likely justified than not. Furthermore, the Fourth Amendment prohibits general warrants. It requires a particular description of what is to be searched or seized. General searches through a person's belongings are impermissible. The search cannot extend beyond what is described in the warrant.

There are exceptions to the requirement of a search warrant, as when it is likely that the items sought will be removed before a warrant can be obtained. For example, if a police officer has probable cause to believe an automobile contains evidence of a crime and the vehicle is likely to be unavailable by the time a warrant is obtained, the officer can search the vehicle without a warrant.

.on the Web You can learn about some of the constitutional questions raised by various criminal laws and procedures by going to the Web site of the American Civil Liberties Union at

http://www.aclu.org.

Searches and Seizures in the Business Context Constitutional protection against unreasonable searches and seizures is important to businesses and professionals. As federal and state regulation of commercial activities increased, frequent and unannounced government inspections were conducted to ensure compliance with the regulations. Such inspections were extremely disruptive at times. In *Marshall v. Barlow's, Inc.*,[12] the United States Supreme Court held that government inspectors do not have the right to enter business premises without a warrant, although the standard of probable cause is not the same as that required in nonbusiness contexts. The existence of a general and neutral enforcement plan will justify issuance of the warrant.

Lawyers and accountants frequently possess the business records of their clients, and inspecting these documents while they are out of the hands of their true owners also requires a warrant. No warrant is required, however, for seizures of spoiled or contaminated food. Nor are warrants required for searches of businesses in such highly regulated industries as liquor, guns, and strip mining. General manufacturing is not considered to be one of these highly regulated industries, however.

Of increasing concern to many employers is how to maintain a safe and efficient workplace without jeopardizing the Fourth Amendment rights of employees "to be secure in their persons." Requiring employees to undergo random drug tests, for example, may be held to violate the Fourth Amendment. In Chapter 40, we will discuss Fourth Amendment issues in the employment context, as well as the privacy rights of employees in general, in detail.

FIFTH AMENDMENT PROTECTIONS

The Fifth Amendment offers significant protections for accused persons. One is the guarantee that no one can be deprived of "life, liberty, or property without due process of law." Two other important Fifth Amendment provisions protect persons against double jeopardy and self-incrimination.

12. 436 U.S. 307, 98 S.Ct. 1816, 56 L.Ed.2d 305 (1978).

Due Process of Law Remember from Chapter 2 that *due process of law* has both procedural and substantive aspects. Procedural due process requirements underlie criminal procedures. Basically, the law must be carried out in a fair and orderly way. In criminal cases, due process means that defendants should have an opportunity to object to the charges against them before a fair, neutral decision maker, such as a judge. Defendants must also be given the opportunity to confront and cross-examine witnesses and accusers and to present their own witnesses.

DOUBLE JEOPARDY
A situation occurring when a person is tried twice for the same criminal offense; prohibited by the Fifth Amendment to the Constitution.

Double Jeopardy The Fifth Amendment also protects persons from **double jeopardy** (being tried twice for the same criminal offense). The prohibition against double jeopardy means that once a criminal defendant is acquitted (found "not guilty") of a particular crime, the government may not reindict the person and retry him or her for the same crime.

The prohibition against double jeopardy does not preclude the crime victim from bringing a civil suit against the same person to recover damages, however. Additionally, a state's prosecution of a crime will not prevent a separate federal prosecution relating to the same activity, and vice versa. ■ EXAMPLE 6.7 A person found "not guilty" of assault and battery in a criminal case may be sued by the victim in a civil tort case for damages. A person who is prosecuted for assault and battery in a state court may be prosecuted in a federal court for civil rights violations resulting from the same action. ■

BE AWARE The Fifth Amendment protection against self-incrimination does not cover partnerships or corporations.

Self-Incrimination The Fifth Amendment guarantees that no person "shall be compelled in any criminal case to be a witness against himself." Thus, in any criminal proceeding, an accused person cannot be compelled to give testimony that might subject her or him to any criminal prosecution.

SELF-INCRIMINATION
The giving of testimony that may subject the testifier to criminal prosecution. The Fifth Amendment to the Constitution protects against self-incrimination by providing that no person "shall be compelled in any criminal case to be a witness against himself."

The Fifth Amendment's guarantee against **self-incrimination** extends only to natural persons. Because a corporation is a legal entity and not a natural person, the privilege against self-incrimination does not apply to it. Similarly, the business records of a partnership do not receive Fifth Amendment protection.[13] When a partnership is required to produce these records, it must do so even if the information incriminates the persons who constitute the business entity. Sole proprietors and sole practitioners (those who fully own their businesses) who have not incorporated normally cannot be compelled to produce their business records. These individuals have full protection against self-incrimination because they function in only one capacity; there is no separate business entity (see Chapter 29).

Protections under the Sixth and Eighth Amendments

The Sixth Amendment guarantees several important rights for criminal defendants: the right to a speedy trial, the right to a jury trial, the right to a public trial, the right to confront witnesses, and the right to counsel. The Eighth Amendment prohibits excessive bail and fines, as well as cruel and unusual punishment.

The Sixth Amendment right to counsel is one of the rights of which a suspect must be advised when he or she is arrested under the *Miranda* rule (discussed later in this chapter). In many cases, a statement that a criminal suspect makes in the absence of counsel is not admissible at trial unless the suspect has knowingly and voluntarily waived this right. Is the right to counsel triggered when judicial proceedings are initiated through any preliminary step? Or is this right triggered only when a suspect is "interrogated" by the police? In the following case, the Supreme Court considered these questions.

13. The privilege has been applied to some small family partnerships. See *United States v. Slutsky,* 352 F.Supp. 1105 (S.D.N.Y. 1972).

CASE 6.1 Fellers v. United States

Supreme Court of the United States, 2004.
540 U.S. 519,
124 S.Ct. 1019,
157 L.Ed.2d 1016.
http://straylight.law.cornell.edu/supct/index.html[a]

BACKGROUND AND FACTS In February 2000, an indictment was issued charging John Fellers, a resident of Lincoln, Nebraska, with conspiracy to distribute methamphetamine. Police officers Michael Garnett and Jeff Bliemeister went to Fellers's home to arrest him. They told Fellers that the purpose of their visit was to discuss his use and distribution of methamphetamine. They said that they had a warrant for his arrest and that the charges referred to his involvement with four individuals. Fellers responded that he knew the persons and had used methamphetamine with them. The officers took Fellers to jail and advised him for the first time of his right to counsel. He waived this right and repeated his earlier statements. Before Fellers's trial, the court ruled that his "jailhouse statements" could be admitted at his trial because he had waived his right to counsel before making them. After Fellers's conviction, he appealed to the U.S. Court of Appeals for the Eighth Circuit, arguing that the officers had elicited his incriminating "home statements" without advising him of his right to counsel and that his "jailhouse statements" should thus have been excluded from his trial as "fruits" of his earlier statements. The appellate court affirmed the lower court's judgment, holding that Fellers had not had a right to counsel at his home because he had not been subject to police "interrogation." Fellers appealed to the United States Supreme Court.

a. In the "Search" box, type "Fellers," select "Current decisions only," and click on "submit." In the result, scroll to the name of the case, and click on it to access the opinion. The Legal Information Institute of Cornell Law School in Ithaca, New York, maintains this Web site.

IN THE WORDS OF THE COURT . . .

Justice *O'CONNOR* delivered the opinion of the Court.

* * * *

The Sixth Amendment right to counsel is triggered at or after the time that judicial proceedings have been initiated * * * whether by way of formal charge, preliminary hearing, indictment, information, or arraignment. We have held that an accused is denied the basic protections of the Sixth Amendment when there is used against him at his trial evidence of his own incriminating words, which federal agents * * * deliberately elicited from him after he had been indicted and in the absence of his counsel.

We have consistently applied the deliberate-elicitation standard in * * * Sixth Amendment cases * * *.

The Court of Appeals erred in holding that the absence of an "interrogation" foreclosed petitioner's claim that the jailhouse statements should have been suppressed as fruits of the statements taken from petitioner [Fellers] at his home. First, there is no question that the officers in this case deliberately elicited information from petitioner. Indeed, the officers, upon arriving at petitioner's house, informed him that their purpose in coming was to discuss his involvement in the distribution of methamphetamine and his association with certain charged co-conspirators. Because the ensuing discussion took place after petitioner had been indicted, outside the presence of counsel, and in the absence of any waiver of petitioner's Sixth Amendment rights, the Court of Appeals erred in holding that the officers' actions did not violate the Sixth Amendment standards * * *.

Second, because of its erroneous determination that petitioner was not questioned in violation of Sixth Amendment standards, the Court of Appeals improperly conducted its "fruits" analysis * * *. Specifically, it * * * [held] that the admissibility of the jailhouse statements turns solely on whether the statements were knowingly and voluntarily made. The Court of Appeals did not reach the question whether the Sixth Amendment requires suppression of petitioner's jailhouse state-

CASE 6.1—Continued

ments on the ground that they were the fruits of previous questioning conducted in violation of the Sixth Amendment deliberate-elicitation standard. We have not had occasion to decide whether [such statements should be excluded from trial] when a suspect makes incriminating statements after a knowing and voluntary waiver of his right to counsel notwithstanding earlier police questioning in violation of Sixth Amendment standards. We therefore remand to the Court of Appeals to address this issue in the first instance.

Accordingly, the judgment of the Court of Appeals is reversed, and the case is remanded for further proceedings consistent with this opinion.

DECISION AND REMEDY The United States Supreme Court reversed the lower court's decision and remanded the case for the determination of a different issue. The Supreme Court held that the Sixth Amendment bars the use at trial of a suspect's incriminating words, deliberately elicited by police after an indictment, in the absence of either counsel or a waiver of the right to counsel, regardless of whether police conduct constitutes an "interrogation."

FOR CRITICAL ANALYSIS—Social Consideration *Should Fellers's "jailhouse statements" also have been excluded from his trial? Why or why not?*

THE EXCLUSIONARY RULE AND THE *MIRANDA* RULE

Two other procedural protections for criminal defendants are the exclusionary rule and the *Miranda* rule.

EXCLUSIONARY RULE
In criminal procedure, a rule under which any evidence that is obtained in violation of the accused's constitutional rights guaranteed by the Fourth, Fifth, and Sixth Amendments, as well as any evidence derived from illegally obtained evidence, will not be admissible in court.

The Exclusionary Rule Under what is known as the **exclusionary rule,** all evidence obtained in violation of the constitutional rights spelled out in the Fourth, Fifth, and Sixth Amendments, as well as all evidence derived from the illegally obtained evidence, normally must be excluded from the trial. Evidence derived from illegally obtained evidence is known as the "fruit of the poisonous tree." For example, if a confession is obtained after an illegal arrest, the arrest is "the poisonous tree," and the confession, if "tainted" by the arrest, is the "fruit."

The purpose of the exclusionary rule is to deter police from conducting warrantless searches and from engaging in other misconduct. The rule is sometimes criticized because it can lead to injustice. Many a defendant has "gotten off on a technicality" because law enforcement personnel failed to observe procedural requirements. Even though a defendant may be obviously guilty, if the evidence of that guilt was obtained improperly (without a valid search warrant, for example), it normally cannot be used against the defendant in court. In the following case, the court had to decide whether a lost computer printout should cause evidence to be excluded.

CASE 6.2 People v. McFarlan

New York Supreme Court, 2002.[a]
191 Misc.2d 531,
744 N.Y.S.2d 287.

BACKGROUND AND FACTS In May 2001, Lisa Kordes saw two men picking pockets on a Lexington Avenue bus in Manhattan, in New York City. Based on Kordes's description of the men, a police department computer produced a six-photo array of possible suspects. Kordes selected a photo of Kevin McFarlan as one of the men she had seen. Five days later, on a bus, Neal Ariano, a police officer, arrested McFarlan after seeing him bump an elderly woman while placing his hand near her pocketbook. At the police station, Kordes viewed a lineup including McFarlan and identified him as the man she had seen on the Lexington Avenue bus. McFarlan was charged in a New York state court with various crimes. The printout

a. In New York, a supreme court is a trial court.

(Continued)

CASE 6.2—Continued

of the computer-generated photo array that Kordes had been shown was lost, but the "People" (the state of New York) introduced into evidence a second printout to show what Kordes had seen. McFarlan argued, among other things, that the first printout was the original photo array and that because that printout had been lost, the court should presume the photo-array procedure had been illegal. Thus, McFarlan's arrest and Kordes's identification of him in the lineup should be excluded as "fruit of the poisonous tree."

IN THE WORDS OF THE COURT . . .

LEWIS BART STONE, J. [Judge]

* * * *

Since the advent of the computer and the growth of the electronic storage of information, there has been a growing appreciation of the need to rearticulate rules of law relating to what is a writing, and in such context, what is an original document. There now seems a consensus embodied in recent proposed and enacted legislation [the Electronic Signatures and Records Act, or ESRA, a New York statute] that *for the pre-computer concept of "writing" the term "record" should now be substituted to accommodate this new reality.* * * * [Emphasis added.]

Under this concept, the record is electronic information which is retrievable in usable form. As no reported New York decision has yet cited or construed ESRA * * *, this is generally a case of first impression [a case presenting a legal issue that has not been addressed by the court's jurisdiction], and especially as to whether such law applies in the context of a criminal proceeding or trial. ESRA itself makes no distinction between civil and criminal proceedings, and was designed to be generally applicable and to change prior ways of doing business, superseding all other statutes, cases and rules. The only reason that a criminal or civil context might lead to a different result is, if in some way, an important constitutional protection of a criminal defendant would be lost by applying ESRA in a criminal proceeding. Thus, the issue here is whether the maintenance of a record in electronic form, and the use of a manifestation of the record, either as a printout or as a screen or other display, in connection with the arrest, prosecution and possible conviction of a criminal defendant, could violate constitutional rules.

Here, as both printouts were generated in the same format, there can be no prejudice from the fact that the defendant was selected from the first printout and that a second identical printout was later [introduced into evidence]. Each is identical and conveys the full recoverable information. To decide * * * to the contrary * * * is absurd. Where, for example, a witness is shown only the screen display, what must the People [public prosecutor] keep? For on such an analysis the printout of the screen could not be the "original." The purpose of requiring the preservation of a record is clear. Concern for the integrity of information has always led the Courts to prefer the original, and have led to many rules to bar or limit the use of non-"original" material. Here the original array was in electronic form in the computer memory, the testimony was unequivocal that [both] printout[s] * * * were generated in the same manner. * * * [A]s a result, defendant's argument crumbles.

DECISION AND REMEDY The New York state court held that the second printout of the photo array was identical to the first and thus could be properly admitted into evidence. While acknowledging that the first printout was lost, the court reasoned that this did not indicate the photo-array procedure had been illegal because the first printout was not the original photo array. The original photo array was the electronic record in the computer.

FOR CRITICAL ANALYSIS—Technological Consideration *When a record is stored on a computer, which should be considered the "original" record—the version on the computer or a printout of the computer version? Why?*

REMEMBER Once a suspect has been informed of his or her rights, anything that person says can be used as evidence in a trial.

The *Miranda* Rule In *Miranda v. Arizona,* a case decided in 1966, the United States Supreme Court established the rule that individuals who are arrested must be informed of certain constitutional rights, including their Fifth Amendment right to remain silent and their Sixth Amendment right to counsel. If the arresting officers fail to inform a criminal suspect of these constitutional rights, any statements the suspect makes normally will not be admissible in court. Because of its importance in criminal procedure, the *Miranda* case is presented as this chapter's *Landmark in the Law* feature on the next page.

The Supreme Court's *Miranda* decision was controversial, and Congress subsequently attempted to overrule it by enacting Section 3501 of the Omnibus Crime Control Act[14] of 1968. Essentially, Section 3501 reinstated the rule that had been in effect for 180 years before *Miranda*—namely, that statements by defendants can be used against them as long as the statements are made voluntarily. The U.S. Justice Department immediately refused to enforce Section 3501, however. Although the U.S. Court of Appeals for the Fourth Circuit attempted to enforce the provision in 1999, its decision was reversed by the United States Supreme Court in 2000. The Supreme Court held that the *Miranda* rights enunciated by the Court in the 1966 case were constitutionally based and thus could not be overruled by a legislative act.[15]

.on the Web If you are interested in reading the Supreme Court's opinion in *Miranda v. Arizona,* go to **http://straylight.law.cornell.edu/supct/cases/name.htm**. Select "M" from the menu at the top of the page, and scroll down the page that opens to the *Miranda v. Arizona* case.

Exceptions to the *Miranda* Rule Over time, as part of a continuing attempt to balance the rights of accused persons against the rights of society, the United States Supreme Court has carved out numerous exceptions to the *Miranda* rule. In 1984, for example, the Court recognized a "public safety" exception to the *Miranda* rule. The need to protect the public warranted the admissibility of statements made by the defendant (in this case, indicating where he placed the gun) as evidence at trial, even though the defendant had not been informed of his *Miranda* rights.[16]

In 1986, the Supreme Court further held that a confession need not be excluded even though the police failed to inform a suspect in custody that his attorney had tried to reach him by telephone.[17] In an important 1991 decision, the Court stated that a suspect's conviction will not be automatically overturned if the suspect was coerced into making a confession. If other, legally obtained evidence admitted at trial is strong enough to justify the conviction without the confession, then the fact that the confession was obtained illegally can, in effect, be ignored.[18]

In yet another case, in 1994, the Supreme Court ruled that a suspect must unequivocally and assertively request to exercise his or her right to counsel in order to stop police questioning. Saying, "Maybe I should talk to a lawyer" during an interrogation after being taken into custody is not enough. The Court held that police officers are not required to decipher the suspect's intentions in such situations.[19]

Criminal Process

As mentioned, a criminal prosecution differs significantly from a civil case in several respects. These differences reflect the desire to safeguard the rights of the individual

14. 42 U.S.C. Section 3789d.
15. *Dickerson v. United States,* 530 U.S. 428, 120 S.Ct. 2326, 147 L.Ed.2d 405 (2000).
16. *New York v. Quarles,* 467 U.S. 649, 104 S.Ct. 2626, 81 L.Ed.2d 550 (1984).
17. *Moran v. Burbine,* 475 U.S. 412, 106 S.Ct. 1135, 89 L.Ed.2d 410 (1986).
18. *Arizona v. Fulminante,* 499 U.S. 279, 111 S.Ct. 1246, 113 L.Ed.2d 302 (1991).
19. *Davis v. United States,* 512 U.S. 452, 114 S.Ct. 2350, 129 L.Ed.2d 362 (1994).

LANDMARK IN THE LAW

Miranda v. Arizona (1966)

The United States Supreme Court's decision in *Miranda v. Arizona*[a] has been cited in more court decisions than any other case in the history of American law. Through television shows and other media, the case has also become familiar to most of the adult population in the United States.

The case arose after Ernesto Miranda was arrested in his home, on March 13, 1963, for the kidnapping and rape of an eighteen-year-old woman. Miranda was taken to a Phoenix, Arizona, police station and questioned by two police officers. Two hours later, the officers emerged from the interrogation room with a written confession signed by Miranda.

RULINGS BY THE LOWER COURTS The confession was admitted into evidence at the trial, and Miranda was convicted and sentenced to prison for twenty to thirty years. Miranda appealed the decision, claiming that he had not been informed of his constitutional rights. He did not claim that he was innocent of the crime or that his confession was false or made under duress. He claimed only that he would not have confessed to the crime if he had been advised of his right to remain silent and to have an attorney. The Supreme Court of Arizona held that Miranda's constitutional rights had not been violated and affirmed his conviction. In forming its decision, the court emphasized that Miranda had not specifically requested an attorney.

THE SUPREME COURT'S DECISION The *Miranda* case was subsequently consolidated with three other cases involving similar issues and reviewed by the United States Supreme Court. In its decision, the Supreme Court stated that whenever an individual is taken into custody, "the following measures are required: He must be warned prior to any questioning that he has the right to remain silent, that anything he says can be used against him in a court of law, that he has the right to the presence of an attorney, and that if he cannot afford an attorney one will be appointed for him prior to any questioning if he so desires." If the accused waives his or her rights to remain silent and to have counsel present, the government must be able to demonstrate that the waiver was made knowingly, intelligently, and voluntarily.

APPLICATION TO TODAY'S BUSINESS WORLD

*Today, both on television and in the real world, police officers routinely advise suspects of their "*Miranda *rights" on arrest. When Ernesto Miranda himself was later murdered, the suspected murderer was "read his* Miranda *rights." Despite Congress's attempt to overrule the* Miranda *requirements through legislation in 1968, the decision continues to protect the rights of criminal defendants and, as noted in the text, was affirmed by the Supreme Court in 2000 as constitutional.*

RELEVANT WEB SITES

To locate information on the Web concerning the Miranda *decision, go to this text's Web site at* **http://blt.westbuslaw.com**, *select "Chapter 6," and click on "URLs for Landmarks."*

a. 384 U.S. 436, 86 S.Ct. 1602, 16 L.Ed.2d 694 (1966).

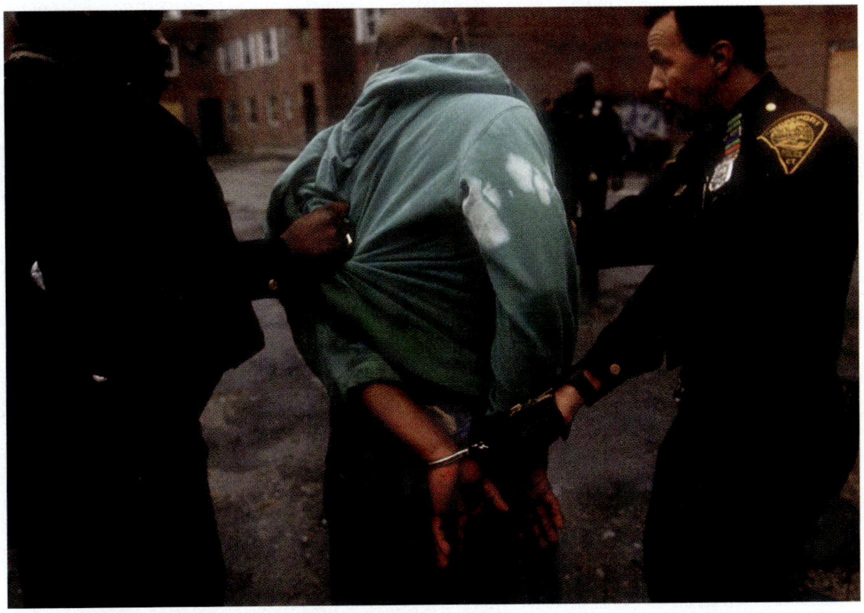

Police officers take a suspect into custody. Why must a criminal suspect be informed of his or her legal rights? (© Corbis. All rights reserved.)

against the state. Exhibit 6–2 on the next page summarizes the major procedural steps in processing a criminal case. We discuss three phases of the criminal process—arrest, indictment or information, and trial—in more detail below.

> **.on the Web** To learn more about criminal procedures, access the following site and select "Anatomy of a Murder: A Trip through Our Nation's Legal Justice System":
>
> **http://library.thinkquest.org/2760/home.htm**.

ARREST

Before a warrant for arrest can be issued, there must be probable cause for believing that the individual in question has committed a crime. As discussed earlier, *probable cause* can be defined as a substantial likelihood that the person has committed or is about to commit a crime. Note that probable cause involves a likelihood, not just a possibility. Arrests may sometimes be made without a warrant if there is no time to get one, as when a police officer observes a crime taking place, but the action of the arresting officer is still judged by the standard of probable cause.

INDICTMENT OR INFORMATION

INDICTMENT
A charge by a grand jury that a named person has committed a crime.

GRAND JURY
A group of citizens called to decide, after hearing the state's evidence, whether a reasonable basis (probable cause) exists for believing that a crime has been committed and whether a trial ought to be held.

INFORMATION
A formal accusation or complaint (without an indictment) issued in certain types of actions (usually criminal actions involving lesser crimes) by a law officer, such as a magistrate.

Individuals must be formally charged with having committed specific crimes before they can be brought to trial. If issued by a grand jury, this charge is called an **indictment.**[20] A **grand jury** usually consists of more jurors than the ordinary trial jury. A grand jury does not determine the guilt or innocence of an accused party; rather, its function is to determine, after hearing the state's evidence, whether a reasonable basis (probable cause) exists for believing that a crime has been committed and whether a trial ought to be held.

Usually, grand juries are used in cases involving serious crimes, such as murder. For lesser crimes, an individual may be formally charged with a crime by what is called an **information,** or criminal complaint. An information will be issued by a government prosecutor if the prosecutor determines that there is sufficient evidence to justify bringing the individual to trial.

20. Pronounced in-*dyte*-ment.

EXHIBIT 6–2 MAJOR PROCEDURAL STEPS IN A CRIMINAL CASE

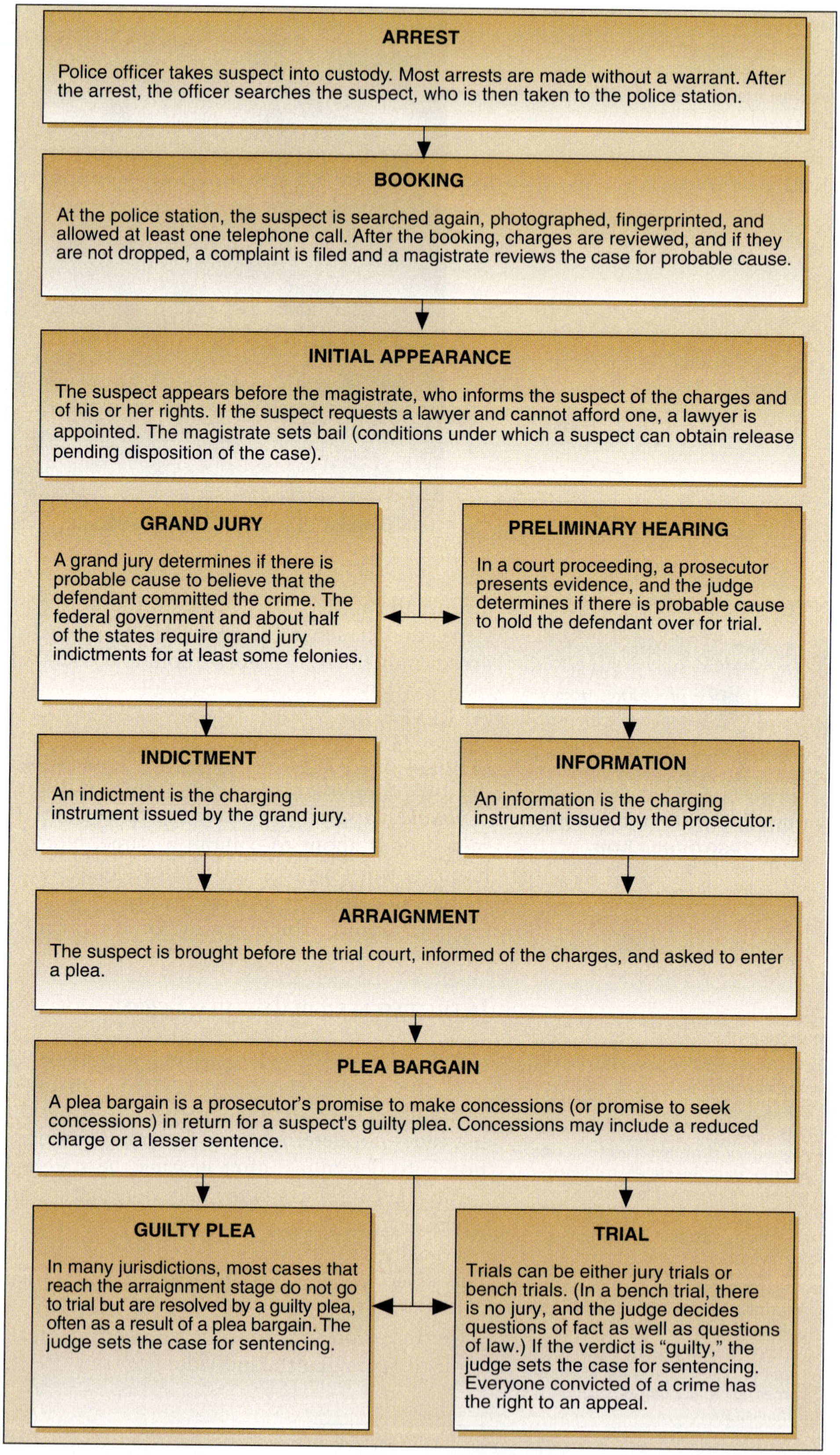

TRIAL

At a criminal trial, the accused person does not have to prove anything; the entire burden of proof is on the prosecutor (the state). As mentioned earlier, the prosecution must show that, based on all the evidence presented, the defendant's guilt is established *beyond a reasonable doubt.* If there is any reasonable doubt as to whether a criminal defendant did, in fact, commit the crime with which she or he has been charged, then the verdict must be "not guilty." Note that giving a verdict of "not guilty" is not the same as stating that the defendant is innocent; it merely means that not enough evidence was properly presented to the court to prove guilt beyond a reasonable doubt.

Courts have complex rules about what types of evidence may be presented and how the evidence may be brought out in criminal cases, especially in jury trials. These rules are designed to ensure that evidence presented at trials is relevant, reliable, and not prejudicial toward the defendant. For example, under the Sixth Amendment, persons accused of a crime have the right to confront, in open court, the witnesses against them. Is a defendant's Sixth Amendment right to confront witnesses violated when, in a jury trial, witnesses who are reluctant to travel consequently testify by way of two-way video teleconferencing? That was the question in the following case.

CASE 6.3 United States v. Yates

United States Court of Appeals,
Eleventh Circuit, 2004.
391 F.3d 1182.

BACKGROUND AND FACTS Anton Pusztai and Anita Yates were involved in operating an Internet pharmacy based in Clanton, Alabama, called the Norfolk Men's Clinic. They were charged in a federal district court with mail fraud and other crimes, including prescription drug–related offenses, in connection with the pharmacy. The government asked the court to allow two witnesses in Australia to testify at Pusztai and Yates's trial by means of a two-way video teleconference. The witnesses—Paul Christian, who allegedly processed customers' Internet payments for Pusztai and Yates, and Dr. Tibor Konkoly, whose name was allegedly used on Internet drug prescriptions—were "essential witnesses," according to the government. But "they are unwilling to travel to the United States" and "they are beyond the government's subpoena powers." Pusztai and Yates argued that allowing the testimony would violate their Sixth Amendment right to confront witnesses. The court allowed the witnesses to testify. A jury found Pusztai and Yates guilty. The defendants appealed to the U.S. Court of Appeals for the Eleventh Circuit.

IN THE WORDS OF THE COURT . . .
COX, Circuit Judge.

* * * *

Pusztai and Yates contend that their Sixth Amendment confrontation rights were violated by the admission of testimony by two-way live video teleconference with the witnesses in Australia because it was not necessary to further an important public policy * * * .

* * * *

The Sixth Amendment provides: "In all criminal prosecutions, the accused shall enjoy the right * * * to be confronted with the witnesses against him." This clause, known as the Confrontation Clause, guarantees the defendant a face-to-face meeting with witnesses appearing before the trier of fact. But this guarantee is not without exception.

* * * [A] Maryland rule of criminal procedure * * * allows child victims of abuse to testify by one-way closed circuit television from outside the courtroom. In

(Continued)

CASE 6.3—Continued

such a scenario, the defendant [can] see the testifying child witness on a video monitor, but the child witness [can]not see the defendant. * * * *[A] defendant's right to confront accusatory witnesses may be satisfied absent a physical, face-to-face confrontation at trial only where denial of such confrontation is necessary to further an important public policy* * * * . [Emphasis added.]

* * * *

In its order, the district court * * * permit[ted] the Australian witnesses to testify by two-way video teleconference before the court in the United States Attorney's Office in Montgomery, Alabama.

* * * [T]he district court ruled that the testimony was necessary to further an important public policy. The court accepted the Government's contention that the testimony would serve the "important public policy of providing the fact-finder with crucial evidence," and found that "the Government also has an interest in expeditiously and justly resolving the case."

We accept the district court's rationale that the witnesses were necessary to the prosecution's case on at least some of the charges, as the record supports the Government's assertion that the testimony was crucial to a successful prosecution of the Defendants and aided expeditious resolution of the case. * * *

But the prosecutor's need for the testimony in order to make a case and expeditiously resolve it are not public policies that are important enough to outweigh a defendant's right to confront an accuser face-to-face. Comparing the public policy behind Maryland's rule—protection of certain children from trauma caused by confronting their attacker—with the policies offered in this case—providing the fact-finder with crucial prosecution evidence and expeditious resolution of the case—leaves us unconvinced that the policy justification in this case meets [the] standard for an important public policy.

The district court made no findings of fact that would support a conclusion that this case is different from any other criminal prosecution in which the Government would find it convenient to present testimony by two-way video teleconference. All criminal prosecutions include at least some evidence crucial to the Government's case, and there is no doubt that many criminal cases could be more expeditiously resolved were it not necessary for witnesses to appear at trial. If we were to approve introduction of testimony in this manner, on this record, every prosecutor could argue that providing crucial prosecution evidence and expeditious resolution of the case are important public policies that support the admission of testimony by two-way video teleconference.

The Sixth Amendment demands more. *The text of the Sixth Amendment does not suggest any open-ended exceptions from the confrontation requirement to be developed by the courts.* We therefore hold that providing the fact-finder with crucial prosecution evidence and expeditious resolution of the case, on the record before us, are not important public policies that justify the denial of actual confrontation between witness and defendant. [Emphasis added.]

DECISION AND REMEDY The U.S Court of Appeals for the Eleventh Circuit reversed the decision of the lower court to allow the overseas witnesses to testify electronically and remanded the case for a new trial. The appellate court reasoned that the admission of the testimony via a live, two-way video teleconference violated the defendants' Sixth Amendment right to confront witnesses.

FOR CRITICAL ANALYSIS—Social Consideration *Suppose that there was only one essential witness in Australia, Paul Christian, who was asked to attend the trial in the United States. Further suppose that Christian was undergoing an intensive course of chemotherapy and was too sick to travel. How might the fact that a witness is unable (as opposed to unwilling) to attend the trial affect the court's opinion on teleconferencing and the Sixth Amendment?*

SENTENCING GUIDELINES

Traditionally, persons who committed the same crime might receive very different sentences, depending on the judge hearing the case, the jurisdiction in which it was heard, and many other factors. Today, however, court judges typically must follow state or federal guidelines when sentencing convicted persons.

At the federal level, the Sentencing Reform Act created the U.S. Sentencing Commission, which was charged with the task of standardizing sentences for federal crimes. The commission fulfilled its task, and since 1987 its sentencing guidelines for all federal crimes have been applied by federal court judges. The guidelines establish a range of possible penalties for each federal crime. Depending on the defendant's criminal record, the seriousness of the offense, and other factors specified in the guidelines, federal judges must select a sentence from within this range.

.on the Web The U.S. Sentencing Guidelines can be found online at **http://www.ussc.gov**.

The commission also created specific guidelines for the punishment of crimes committed by corporate employees (white-collar crimes). These guidelines established stiffer penalties for criminal violations of securities laws (see Chapter 35), antitrust laws (see Chapter 37), employment laws (see Chapters 40 and 41), mail and wire fraud, commercial bribery, and kickbacks and money laundering.[21] The guidelines allow federal judges to take into consideration a number of factors when selecting from the range of possible penalties for a specified crime. These factors include the defendant company's history of past violations, the scope of management's cooperation with federal investigators, and the extent to which the firm has undertaken specific programs and procedures to prevent criminal activities by its employees.

Cyber Crimes

COMPUTER CRIME
Any act that is directed against computers and computer parts, that uses computers as instruments of crime, or that involves computers and constitutes abuse.

Some years ago, the American Bar Association defined **computer crime** as any act that is directed against computers and computer parts, that uses computers as instruments of crime, or that involves computers and constitutes abuse. Today, because much of the crime committed with the use of computers occurs in cyberspace, many computer crimes fall under the broad label of cyber crime.

As we mentioned earlier, most cyber crimes are not "new" crimes. Rather, they are existing crimes in which the Internet is the instrument of wrongdoing. The challenge for law enforcement is to apply traditional laws—which were designed to protect persons from physical harm or to safeguard their physical property—to crimes committed in cyberspace. Here we look at several types of activity that constitute cyber crimes against persons or property. Other cyber crimes will be discussed in later chapters of this text as they relate to particular topics, such as banking or consumer law.

BE AWARE Technological change is one of the primary factors that lead to new types of crime.

CYBER THEFT

In cyberspace, thieves are not subject to the physical limitations of the "real" world. A thief can steal data stored in a networked computer with dial-in access from anywhere on the globe. Only the speed of the connection and the thief's computer equipment limit the quantity of data that can be stolen.

Financial Crimes Computer networks also provide opportunities for employees to commit crimes that can involve serious economic losses. For example, employees of a

21. The sentencing guidelines were amended in 2003, as required under the Sarbanes-Oxley Act of 2002, to impose stiffer penalties for corporate securities fraud—see Chapter 35.

company's accounting department can transfer funds among accounts with little effort and often with less risk than would be involved in transactions evidenced by paperwork.

Generally, the dependence of businesses on computer operations has left firms vulnerable to sabotage, fraud, embezzlement, and the theft of proprietary data, such as trade secrets or other intellectual property. As noted in Chapter 5, the piracy of intellectual property via the Internet is one of the most serious legal challenges facing lawmakers and the courts today.

on the Web The U.S. Department of Justice offers an impressive collection of statistics on crime, including cyber crime, at the following Web site:

http://www.ojp.usdoj.gov/bjs.

Identity Theft A form of cyber theft that has become particularly troublesome in recent years is **identity theft.** Identity theft occurs when the wrongdoer steals a form of identification—such as a name, date of birth, or Social Security number—and uses the information to access the victim's financial resources. This crime existed to a certain extent before the widespread use of the Internet. Thieves would "steal" calling-card numbers by watching people using public telephones, or they would rifle through garbage to find bank account or credit-card numbers. The identity thieves would then use the calling-card or credit-card numbers or would withdraw funds from the victims' accounts.

IDENTITY THEFT
The act of stealing another's identifying information—such as a name, date of birth, or Social Security number—and using that information to access the victim's financial resources.

The Internet, however, has turned identity theft into perhaps the fastest-growing financial crime in the United States. From the identity thief's perspective, the Internet provides those who steal information offline with an easy medium for using items such as stolen credit-card numbers or e-mail addresses while protected by anonymity. An estimated 10 million Americans are victims of identity theft each year, and annual losses are estimated to exceed $50 billion.

CYBERSTALKING

California enacted the first stalking law in 1990, in response to the murders of six women—including Rebecca Schaeffer, a television star—by men who had harassed them. The law made it a crime to harass or follow a person while making a "credible

An Arkansas man holds a picture of his thirteen-year-old daughter, who was kidnapped and murdered by a man she met through an Internet chat room. How do cyberstalking laws differ from traditional stalking laws? (AP Photo/Mike Wintroath)

threat" that puts that person in reasonable fear for his or her safety or the safety of the person's immediate family.[22] Since then, all other states have enacted some form of stalking laws. In about half of the states, these laws require a physical act such as following the victim.

CYBERSTALKER
A person who commits the crime of stalking in cyberspace. Generally, stalking consists of harassing a person and putting that person in reasonable fear for his or her safety or the safety of the person's immediate family.

Cyberstalkers (stalkers who commit their crimes in cyberspace), however, find their victims through Internet chat rooms, Usenet newsgroups or other bulletin boards, or e-mail. To close this "loophole" in existing stalking laws, more than three-fourths of the states now have laws specifically designed to combat cyberstalking and other forms of online harassment.

Note that cyberstalking can be even more threatening than physical stalking in some respects. While it takes a great deal of effort to physically stalk someone, it is relatively easy to harass a victim with electronic messages. Furthermore, the possibility of personal confrontation may discourage a stalker from actually following a victim. This disincentive is removed in cyberspace. Also, there is always the possibility that a cyberstalker will eventually pose a physical threat to her or his target. Finally, the Internet makes it easier to obtain information about the victim, such as where he or she lives or works. (Can Internet sellers of personal information be held responsible for crimes by stalkers who use that information to locate their victims? For a discussion of this issue, see this chapter's *Adapting the Law to the Online Environment* feature on the following page.)

Hacking and Cyberterrorism

HACKER
A person who uses one computer to break into another. Professional computer programmers refer to such persons as "crackers."

CYBERTERRORIST
A hacker whose purpose is to exploit a target computer for a serious impact, such as corrupting a program to sabotage a business.

Persons who use one computer to break into another are sometimes referred to as **hackers.** Hackers who break into computers without authorization often commit cyber theft. Sometimes, however, their principal aim is to prove how smart they are by gaining access to others' password-protected computers and causing random data errors or making unpaid-for telephone calls.[23] **Cyberterrorists** are hackers who, rather than trying to attract attention, strive to remain undetected so that they can exploit computers for a serious impact. Just as "real" terrorists destroyed the World Trade Center towers and a portion of the Pentagon in September 2001, cyberterrorists might explode "logic bombs" to shut down central computers. Such activities can pose a danger to national security.

Businesses may be targeted by cyberterrorists as well as hackers. The goals of a hacking operation might include a wholesale theft of data, such as a merchant's customer files, or the monitoring of a computer to discover a business firm's plans and transactions. A cyberterrorist might also want to insert false codes or data. For example, the processing control system of a food manufacturer could be changed to alter the levels of ingredients so that consumers of the food would become ill.

on the Web The Computer Crime Research Center is a non-profit organization that provides up-to-date information and articles on cyber crime and cyberterrorism at **http://www.crime-research.org**.

A cyberterrorist attack on a major financial institution such as the New York Stock Exchange or a large bank could leave securities or money markets in flux and seriously affect the daily lives of millions of citizens. Similarly, any prolonged disruption of computer, cable, satellite, or telecommunications systems due to the actions of expert hackers would have serious repercussions on business operations—and national security—on a global level. Computer viruses are another tool that can be used by cyberterrorists to cripple communications networks.

---

22. See, for example, Cal. Penal Code Section 646.9.

23. The total cost of crime on the Internet is estimated to be several billion dollars annually, but two-thirds of that total is said to consist of unpaid-for toll calls.

ADAPTING THE LAW TO THE ONLINE ENVIRONMENT

Stalking and Internet Data Brokers

A cutting-edge issue coming before today's courts has to do with stalking and Internet data brokers—those in the business of selling personal information via the Internet. Suppose that a stalker purchases personal information (such as a home address) from a Web broker and then uses that information to commit a crime (such as murder). The stalker, of course, can be prosecuted under criminal law for the crime of murder. At issue is the broker's responsibility for the crime. Can the broker be sued under tort law (see Chapter 4) for damages?

ONE COURT WEIGHS IN

At least one court has weighed in on this issue. In *Remsburg v. Docusearch, Inc.,*[a] the Supreme Court of New Hampshire concluded that an Internet data broker had a duty to exercise reasonable care when selling personal information online. The case involved Liam Youens, a New Hampshire resident, and Docusearch, Inc., an Internet-based investigation and information service. Youens contacted Docusearch through its Web site and requested information about Amy Boyer. Youens provided his name, address, and phone number and paid Docusearch's fee by credit card. In return, Docusearch provided Boyer's home address, birth date, and Social Security number. Youens also asked for Boyer's workplace address, which Docusearch obtained for him. After Youens had obtained the address of Boyer's place of employment, he drove to the workplace, fatally shot her, and then shot and killed himself.

a. 149 N.H. 148, 816 A.2d 1001 (2003).

Helen Remsburg, Boyer's mother, sued Docusearch, claiming that the defendant had acted wrongfully. The federal district court referred the case to the New Hampshire Supreme Court for a determination of the parties' duties under the state's common law. The state supreme court held that an information broker who sells information about a third person to a client has a duty to exercise reasonable care in disclosing the information.

A FORESEEABLE RISK?

One of the key issues for the court was whether the crime committed by Youens was a foreseeable risk to Docusearch. Remember from Chapter 4 that under tort law, the test for proximate cause—and the extent of a defendant's duty of care—is the foreseeability of a risk of harm. If certain consequences of an action are not foreseeable, there is no proximate cause.

In determining whether a risk of criminal misconduct was foreseeable to Docusearch, the Supreme Court of New Hampshire found that Docusearch's information disclosure presented two foreseeable risks: stalking and identity theft. Therefore, the company had a duty to exercise reasonable care in disclosing personal information about Boyer to Youens. Because Docusearch had not exercised reasonable care (taken steps to find out if Youens's requests were for a legitimate purpose), Docusearch could be sued for damages for breaching this duty.

FOR CRITICAL ANALYSIS

What other crimes can you think of, in addition to stalking and identity theft, that might qualify as "foreseeable risks" created by the online sale of personal data by information brokers?

ETHICAL ISSUE 6.1

Is it possible to control cyber crime without sacrificing some civil liberties? Governments in some countries, such as China, have succeeded in controlling Internet crime to a certain extent by monitoring the e-mail and other electronic transmissions of users of specific Internet service providers. In the United States, however, Americans have been reluctant to allow the government to monitor Internet use to detect criminal conspiracies or terrorist activities. The traditional attitude has been that civil liberties must be safeguarded to the greatest extent feasible.

As noted in Chapter 1, however, after the terrorist attacks on the World Trade Center and the Pentagon in September 2001, Congress enacted legislation, including the USA Patriot Act, to give law enforcement personnel more authority to conduct electronic surveillance, such as monitoring Web sites and e-mail exchanges. For a time, it seemed that the terrorist attacks might have made Americans more willing to trade off some of their civil liberties for greater national security. Today, however, many complain that this legislation has gone too far in curbing traditional civil liberties guaranteed by the U.S. Constitution. ■

PROSECUTING CYBER CRIMES

The "location" of cyber crime (cyberspace) has raised new issues in the investigation of crimes and the prosecution of offenders. A threshold issue is, of course, jurisdiction. A person who commits an act against a business in California, where the act is a cyber crime, might never have set foot in California but might instead reside in New York, or even in Canada, where the act may not be a crime. If the crime was committed via e-mail, the question arises as to whether the e-mail would constitute sufficient "minimum contacts" (see Chapter 3) for the victim's state to exercise jurisdiction over the perpetrator.

Identifying the wrongdoers can also be difficult. Cyber criminals do not leave physical traces, such as fingerprints or DNA samples, as evidence of their crimes. Even electronic "footprints" can be hard to find and follow. For example, e-mail may be sent through a remailer, an online service that guarantees that a message cannot be traced to its source.

For these reasons, laws written to protect physical property are difficult to apply in cyberspace. Nonetheless, governments at both the state and federal levels have taken significant steps toward controlling cyber crime, both by applying existing criminal statutes and by enacting new laws that specifically address wrongs committed in cyberspace. For suggestions on how to protect your business from losses caused by cyber crime, see the *Application* feature at the end of this chapter.

> **.on the Web** Professor Susan Brenner at the University of Dayton Law School posts numerous articles on combating cyber crime, as well as information and links to the relevant laws of other nations, the policies of the European Council, and the United Nations' approach. You can access the site at
>
> **http://www.cybercrimes.net/International/IntLinks.html**.
>
> The U.S. Department of Justice maintains a site dedicated to cyber crime at
>
> **http://www.usdoj.gov/criminal/cybercrime**.

The Computer Fraud and Abuse Act Perhaps the most significant federal statute specifically addressing cyber crime is the Counterfeit Access Device and Computer Fraud and Abuse Act of 1984 (commonly known as the Computer Fraud and Abuse Act, or CFAA). This act, as amended by the National Information Infrastructure Protection Act of 1996,[24] provides, among other things, that a person who accesses a computer online, without authority, to obtain classified, restricted, or protected data, or attempts to do so, is subject to criminal prosecution. Such data could include financial and credit records, medical records, legal files, military and national security files, and other confidential information in government or private computers. The crime has two elements: accessing a computer without authority and taking the data.

This theft is a felony if it is committed for a commercial purpose or for private financial gain, or if the value of the stolen data (or computer time) exceeds $5,000. Penalties include fines and imprisonment for up to twenty years. A victim of computer theft can also bring a civil suit against the violator to obtain damages, an injunction, and other relief.

Other Federal Statutes The federal wire fraud statute, the Economic Espionage Act of 1996, and RICO, all of which were discussed earlier in this chapter, extend to crimes committed in cyberspace as well. Other federal statutes that may apply include the Electronic Fund Transfer Act of 1978, which makes unauthorized access to an electronic fund transfer system a crime; the Anticounterfeiting Consumer Protection Act of 1996, which increased penalties for stealing copyrighted or trademarked

---

24. 18 U.S.C. Section 1030.

property; and the National Stolen Property Act of 1988, which concerns the interstate transport of stolen property. Recall from Chapter 2 that the federal government has also enacted laws (many of which have been challenged on constitutional grounds) to protect minors from online pornographic materials. In later chapters of this text, you will read about other federal statutes and regulations that are designed to address wrongs committed in cyberspace in specific areas of the law.

REVIEWING CRIMINAL LAW AND CYBER CRIMES

Edward Hanousek worked for Pacific & Arctic Railway and Navigation Company (P&A) as a roadmaster of the White Pass & Yukon Railroad in Alaska. Hanousek was responsible "for every detail of the safe and efficient maintenance and construction of track, structures and marine facilities of the entire railroad," including special projects. One project was a rock quarry, known as "6-mile," above the Skagway River. Next to the quarry, and just beneath the surface, ran a high-pressure oil pipeline owned by Pacific & Arctic Pipeline, Inc., P&A's sister company. When the quarry's backhoe operator punctured the pipeline, an estimated 1,000 to 5,000 gallons of oil were discharged into the river. Hanousek was charged with negligently discharging a harmful quantity of oil into a navigable water of the United States in violation of the criminal provisions of the Clean Water Act. Using the information presented in the chapter, answer the following questions.

1. What are the two elements of criminal liability? Are both elements present in this case? Explain.
2. Under which theory discussed in the chapter might Hanousek be found guilty of a crime?
3. Could the quarry's backhoe operator who punctured the pipeline also be charged with a crime in this situation? Why or why not?
4. Suppose that at trial, Hanousek argued that he could not be convicted because he was not aware of the requirements of the Clean Water Act. Would this defense be successful? Why or why not?
5. If corporate actors were able to avoid responsibility for violations of environmental statutes of which they were unaware, what might result?
6. Based solely on the facts given, are there any defenses to criminal liability that Hanousek could assert? Explain.

APPLICATION How Can You Protect against Cyber Crime?*

In addition to protecting their physical property, business owners today also are concerned about protecting their intangible property—such as computer data or files—from unauthorized access. U.S. business firms lose millions of dollars to industrial espionage and sabotage every year. Once a computer system has been corrupted, it can be difficult to recover. To prevent losses through computer systems, some firms hire experts to improve the security of the systems.

* This *Application* is not meant to substitute for the services of an attorney who is licensed to practice law in your state.

COMPUTER SYSTEM SAFEGUARDS

Many sources of software offer security programs that can easily be used to protect computers that are connected to an internal network or to the Internet. For example, most word-processing programs include a "password" function. To gain access to information within the program, a user must know the password. A document that can be unlocked only with the password can be e-mailed as an attachment, providing some security.

Cryptography also provides increased protection for computer data and files. Encryption hardware is available

APPLICATION How Can You Protect against Cyber Crime?—Continued

in the form of computer chips and is commonly used in automated teller machines. These chips quickly encrypt or decrypt information. The same results can be achieved using encryption software.

Additionally, effective "firewalls" can be installed at the interface between computers and the Internet to protect against unwanted intruders. Firewall software can also be used to keep internal network segments secure.

EMPLOYMENT POLICIES

Although outside hackers are a threat, employees, former employees, and other "insiders" are responsible for most computer abuse, including breaches of information security. Generally, employees should be given access only to information that they need to know. Additionally, employees and other insiders should be instructed in what constitutes proper and improper use of your company's computer systems. They should also be told that any form of computer abuse is against company policy, is illegal, and will be the basis for termination of employment and even criminal prosecution.

Another safeguard is to have employees agree, in a written confidentiality agreement (see the *Application* feature in Chapter 5), not to disclose confidential information during or after employment without the employer's consent. Monitoring certain computer-related employee activities may be appropriate, but if monitoring is to take place, employees should be informed (see Chapter 40). Still other security measures include the use of digital signatures (see Chapter 17), facility lockups, visitor screenings, and announced briefcase checks.

CHECKLIST FOR THE BUSINESS OWNER

1. Consider protecting your computer security and documents through the use of passwords, encryption, and firewalls.
2. Instruct your employees in how computers and computer information are to be used and not used.
3. Consider using confidentiality agreements, monitoring, and digital signatures to protect your computer system and data against unauthorized use.

KEY TERMS

arson 169
beyond a reasonable doubt 164
burglary 168
computer crime 189
consent 176
crime 164
cyber crime 164
cyberstalker 191
cyberterrorist 191
double jeopardy 179
duress 176
embezzlement 170
entrapment 177
exclusionary rule 181
felony 165
forgery 169
grand jury 185
hacker 191
identity theft 190
indictment 185
information 185
insider trading 171
larceny 168
misdemeanor 165
money laundering 172
petty offense 166
plea bargaining 177
probable cause 178
robbery 168
search warrant 178
self-defense 176
self-incrimination 179
white-collar crime 169

CHAPTER SUMMARY Criminal Law and Cyber Crimes

Civil Law and Criminal Law (See pages 164–165.)	1. *Civil law*—Spells out the duties that exist between persons or between citizens and their governments, excluding the duty not to commit crimes.

(Continued)

CHAPTER SUMMARY Criminal Law and Cyber Crimes—Continued

Civil Law and Criminal Law—continued (See pages 164–165.)	2. *Criminal law*—Has to do with crimes, which are defined as wrongs against society proclaimed in statutes and punishable by society through fines and/or imprisonment—and, in some cases, death. Because crimes are *offenses against society as a whole,* they are prosecuted by a public official, not by victims. 3. *Key differences*—An important difference between civil and criminal law is that the burden of proof is higher in criminal cases (see the *Concept Summary* on page 165 for other differences between criminal and civil law). 4. *Civil liability for criminal acts*—A criminal act may give rise to both criminal liability and tort liability (see Exhibit 6–1 for an example of criminal and tort liability for the same act).
Classification of Crimes (See pages 165–166.)	1. *Felonies*—Serious crimes punishable by death or by imprisonment in a penitentiary for more than one year. 2. *Misdemeanors*—Under federal law and in most states, any crimes that are not felonies.
Criminal Liability (See pages 166–167.)	1. *Guilty act*—In general, some form of harmful act must be committed for a crime to exist. 2. *Intent*—An intent to commit a crime, or a wrongful mental state, is generally required for a crime to exist.
Corporate Criminal Liability (See page 167.)	1. *Liability of corporations*—Corporations normally are liable for the crimes committed by their agents and employees within the course and scope of their employment. Corporations cannot be imprisoned, but they can be fined or denied certain legal privileges. 2. *Liability of corporate officers and directors*—Corporate directors and officers are personally liable for the crimes they commit and may be held liable for the actions of employees under their supervision.
Types of Crimes (See pages 168–173.)	Crimes fall into five general categories: violent crime, property crime, public order crime, white-collar crime, and organized crime. See the *Concept Summary* on page 174 for definitions and examples of these types of crimes.
Defenses to Criminal Liability (See pages 173–177.)	Defenses to criminal liability include infancy, intoxication, insanity, mistake, consent, duress, justifiable use of force, entrapment, and the statute of limitations. Also, in some cases defendants may be relieved of criminal liability, at least in part, if they are given immunity.
Constitutional Safeguards and Criminal Procedures (See pages 177–183.)	1. *Fourth Amendment*—Provides protection against unreasonable searches and seizures and requires that probable cause exist before a warrant for a search or an arrest can be issued. 2. *Fifth Amendment*—Requires due process of law, prohibits double jeopardy, and protects against self-incrimination. 3. *Sixth Amendment*—Provides guarantees of a speedy trial, a trial by jury, a public trial, the right to confront witnesses, and the right to counsel. 4. *Eighth Amendment*—Prohibits excessive bail and fines, as well as cruel and unusual punishment. 5. *Exclusionary rule*—A criminal procedural rule that prohibits the introduction at trial of all evidence obtained in violation of constitutional rights, as well as any evidence derived from the illegally obtained evidence. 6. *Miranda rule*—A rule set forth by the Supreme Court in *Miranda v. Arizona* that individuals who are arrested must be informed of certain constitutional rights, including their right to counsel.
Criminal Process (See pages 183–189.)	1. *Arrest, indictment, and trial*—Procedures governing arrest, indictment, and trial for a crime are designed to safeguard the rights of the individual against the state. See Exhibit 6–2 on page 186 for a summary of the procedural steps involved in prosecuting a criminal case.

CHAPTER SUMMARY Criminal Law and Cyber Crimes—Continued

Criminal Process—Continued	2. *Sentencing guidelines*—Both the federal government and the states have established sentencing laws or guidelines. The federal sentencing guidelines indicate a range of penalties for each federal crime; federal judges must abide by these guidelines when imposing sentences on those convicted of federal crimes.
Cyber Crimes (See pages 189–194.)	Cyber crime is any crime that occurs in cyberspace. Examples include cyber theft (financial crimes committed with the aid of computers, as well as identity theft), cyberstalking, hacking, and cyberterrorism. Significant federal statutes addressing cyber crimes include the Electronic Fund Transfer Act of 1978 and the Counterfeit Access Device and Computer Fraud and Abuse Act of 1984, as amended by the National Information Infrastructure Protection Act of 1996.

FOR REVIEW

Answers for the even-numbered questions in this For Review *section can be found on this text's accompanying Web site at* http://blt.westbuslaw.com. *Select "Chapter 6" and click on "For Review."*

1. What two elements must exist before a person can be held liable for a crime? Can a corporation commit crimes?
2. What are five broad categories of crimes? What is white-collar crime?
3. What defenses might be raised by criminal defendants to avoid liability for criminal acts?
4. What constitutional safeguards exist to protect persons accused of crimes? What are the basic steps in the criminal process?
5. What is cyber crime? What laws apply to crimes committed in cyberspace?

QUESTIONS AND CASE PROBLEMS

6–1. Criminal versus Civil Trials. In criminal trials, the defendant must be proved guilty beyond a reasonable doubt, whereas in civil trials, the defendant need only be proved guilty by a preponderance of the evidence. Discuss why a higher burden of proof is required in criminal trials.

6–2. Types of Crimes. The following situations are similar (all involve the theft of Makoto's television set), yet they represent three different crimes. Identify the three crimes, noting the differences among them.

(a) While passing Makoto's house one night, Sarah sees a portable television set left unattended on Makoto's lawn. Sarah takes the television set, carries it home, and tells everyone she owns it.

(b) While passing Makoto's house one night, Sarah sees Makoto outside with a portable television set. Holding Makoto at gunpoint, Sarah forces him to give up the set. Then Sarah runs away with it.

(c) While passing Makoto's house one night, Sarah sees a portable television set in a window. Sarah breaks the front-door lock, enters, and leaves with the set.

6–3. Types of Crimes. Which, if any, of the following crimes necessarily involve illegal activity on the part of more than one person?

(a) Bribery.
(b) Forgery.
(c) Embezzlement.
(d) Larceny.
(e) Receiving stolen property.

6–4. Double Jeopardy. Armington, while robbing a drugstore, shot and seriously injured Jennings, a drugstore clerk. Armington was subsequently convicted in a criminal trial of armed robbery and assault and battery. Jennings later brought a civil tort suit against Armington for damages. Armington contended that he could not be tried again for the same crime, as that would constitute double jeopardy, which is prohibited by the Fifth Amendment to the Constitution. Is Armington correct? Explain.

6–5. Fifth Amendment. The federal government was investigating a corporation and its employees. The alleged criminal wrongdoing, which included the falsification of corporate books and records, occurred between 1993 and 1996 in one division of the corporation. In 1999, the corporation pleaded guilty and agreed to cooperate in an investigation of the individuals who might have been involved in the improper corporate activities. "Doe I," "Doe II," and "Doe III" were officers of the corporation during the period when the illegal activities occurred and worked in the division where the wrongdoing took place. They were no longer working for the corporation, however, when, as part of the subsequent investigation, the government asked them to provide specific corporate documents in their possession. All three asserted the Fifth Amendment privilege against self-incrimination. The government asked a federal district court to order the three to produce the records. Corporate employees can be compelled to produce corporate records in a criminal proceeding because they hold the records as representatives of the corporation, to which the Fifth Amendment privilege against self-incrimination does not apply. Should *former* employees also be compelled to produce corporate records in their possession? Why or why not? [*In re Three Grand Jury Subpoenas* Duces Tecum *Dated January 29, 1999,* 191 F.3d 173 (2d Cir. 1999)]

CASE PROBLEM WITH SAMPLE ANSWER

6–6. The District of Columbia Lottery Board licensed Soo Young Bae, a Washington, D.C., merchant, to operate a terminal that prints and dispenses lottery tickets for sale. Bae used the terminal to generate tickets with a face value of $525,586, for which he did not pay. The winning tickets among these had a total redemption value of $296,153, of which Bae successfully obtained all but $72,000. Bae pleaded guilty to computer fraud, and the court sentenced him to eighteen months in prison. In sentencing a defendant for fraud, a federal court must make a reasonable estimate of the victim's loss. The court determined that the value of the loss due to the fraud was $503,650—the market value of the tickets less the commission Bae would have received from the lottery board had he sold those tickets. Bae appealed, arguing that "[a]t the instant any lottery ticket is printed," it is worth whatever value the lottery drawing later assigns to it; that is, losing tickets have no value. Bae thus calculated the loss at $296,153, the value of his winning tickets. Should the U.S. Court of Appeals for the District of Columbia Circuit affirm or reverse Bae's sentence? Why? [*United States v. Bae,* 250 F.3d 774 (C.A.D.C. 2001)]

After you have answered this problem, compare your answer with the sample answer given on the Web site that accompanies this text. Go to http://blt.westbuslaw.com, select "Chapter 6," and click on "Case Problem with Sample Answer."

6–7. Larceny. In February 2001, a homeowner hired Jimmy Smith, a contractor claiming to employ a crew of thirty workers, to build a garage. The homeowner paid Smith $7,950 and agreed to make additional payments as needed to complete the project, up to $15,900. Smith promised to start the next day and finish within eight weeks. Nearly a month passed with no work, while Smith lied to the homeowner that materials were on "back order." During a second month, footings were created for the foundation, and a subcontractor poured the concrete slab, but Smith did not return the homeowner's phone calls. After eight weeks, the homeowner confronted Smith, who promised to complete the job, worked on the site that day until lunch, and never returned. Three months later, the homeowner again confronted Smith, who promised to "pay [him] off" later that day but did not do so. In March 2002, the state of Georgia filed criminal charges against Smith. While his trial was pending, he promised to pay the homeowner "next week" but again failed to refund any money. The value of the labor performed before Smith abandoned the project was between $800 and $1,000, the value of the materials was $367, and the subcontractor was paid $2,270. Did Smith commit larceny? Explain. [*Smith v. State of Georgia,* __ S.E.2d __ (Ga.App. 2004)]

A QUESTION OF ETHICS

6–8. A troublesome issue concerning the constitutional privilege against self-incrimination has to do with "jail plants"—that is, undercover police officers placed in cells with criminal suspects to gain information from the suspects. For example, in one case the police placed an undercover agent, Parisi, in a jail cell block with Lloyd Perkins, who had been imprisoned on charges unrelated to the murder that Parisi was investigating. When Parisi asked Perkins if he had ever killed anyone, Perkins made statements implicating himself in the murder. Perkins was then charged with the murder. [*Illinois v. Perkins,* 496 U.S. 292, 110 S.Ct. 2394, 110 L.Ed.2d 243 (1990)]

1. Review the discussion of *Miranda v. Arizona* in this chapter's *Landmark in the Law* feature. Should Perkins's statements be suppressed—that is, not be admissible as evidence at trial—because he was not "read his rights," as required by the *Miranda* decision, prior to making his self-incriminating statements? Does *Miranda* apply to Perkins's situation?
2. Do you think that it is fair for the police to resort to trickery and deception to bring those who have committed crimes to justice? Why or why not? What rights or public policies must be balanced in deciding this issue?

FOR CRITICAL ANALYSIS

6–9. Do you think that criminal procedure in this country is weighted too heavily in favor of accused persons? Can you think of a fairer way to balance the constitutional rights of accused persons against the right of society to be protected against criminal behavior? Should different criminal procedures be used when terrorism is involved? Explain.

VIDEO QUESTION

6–10. Go to this text's Web site at **http://blt.westbuslaw.com** and select "Chapter 6." Click on "Video Questions" and view the video titled *Casino*. Then answer the following questions.

1. In the video, a casino manager, Ace (Robert DeNiro), discusses how politicians "won their 'comp life' when they got elected." "Comps" are the free gifts that casinos give to high-stakes gamblers to keep their business. If an elected official accepts comps, is he or she committing a crime? If so, what type of crime? Explain your answers.
2. Assume that Ace committed a crime by giving politicians comps. Can the casino, Tangiers Corp., be held liable for that crime? Why or why not? How could a court punish the corporation?
3. Suppose that the Federal Bureau of Investigation wants to search the premises of Tangiers for evidence of criminal activity. If casino management refuses to consent to the search, what constitutional safeguards and criminal procedures, if any, protect Tangiers?

INTERNET EXERCISES

Go to the *Business Law Today* home page at **http://blt.westbuslaw.com**, select "Chapter 6," and click on "Internet Exercises." There you will find the following Internet research exercises that you can perform to learn more about topics covered in this chapter.

Activity 6–1: LEGAL PERSPECTIVE—Revisiting *Miranda*

Activity 6–2: MANAGEMENT PERSPECTIVE—Hackers

Activity 6–3: INTERNATIONAL PERSPECTIVE—Fighting Cyber Crime Worldwide

BEFORE THE TEST

Go to the *Business Law Today* home page at **http://blt.westbuslaw.com**, select "Chapter 6," and click on "Interactive Quizzes." You will find a number of interactive questions relating to this chapter.

CHAPTER 7

Ethics and Business Decision Making

"New occasions teach new duties."

James Russell Lowell, 1819–1891
(American editor, poet, and diplomat)

CHAPTER OUTLINE

- BUSINESS ETHICS
- SETTING THE RIGHT ETHICAL TONE
- COMPANIES THAT DEFY THE RULES
- BUSINESS ETHICS AND THE LAW
- APPROACHES TO ETHICAL REASONING
- BUSINESS ETHICS ON A GLOBAL LEVEL

LEARNING OBJECTIVES

After reading this chapter, you should be able to answer the following questions:

1. What is ethics? What is business ethics? Why is business ethics important?
2. How can business leaders encourage their companies to act ethically?
3. What are corporate compliance programs?
4. How do duty-based ethical standards differ from outcome-based ethical standards?
5. What types of ethical issues might arise in the context of international business transactions?

During the early part of the 2000s, the American public was shocked as one business ethics scandal after another became headline news. Each scandal involved serious consequences. Certainly, those responsible for grossly inflating the reported profits at WorldCom, Inc., ended up not only destroying shareholder value in a great company but also facing possible prison terms. Those officers and directors at Enron Corporation who utilized a system of complicated off-the-books transactions to inflate current earnings saw their company go bankrupt—one of the largest bankruptcies in U.S. history. They harmed not only their employees and shareholders but also the communities in which they worked—and themselves (some of them have since received prison sentences, and others have been indicted). The officers and directors of Tyco International who used corporate funds to pay for lavish personal lifestyles also ended up in court. The shareholders of that company suffered dearly, too.

In response to the public's outrage over these scandals, Congress passed the Sarbanes-Oxley Act of 2002, which will be discussed in detail in Chapters 35 and 42.

This act imposed requirements on corporations that are designed to deter similar unethical and illegal business behavior in the future. As the chapter-opening quotation states, "New occasions teach new duties." Indeed, the ethics scandals of the early 2000s taught businesses throughout the country that corporate governance is not to be taken lightly. Nevertheless, new allegations of unethical business conduct continue to surface.

Business ethics, the focus of this chapter, is not just theory. It is practical, useful, and essential. Although a good understanding of business law and the legal environment is critical, it is not enough. Understanding how one should act in her or his business dealings is equally—if not more—important in today's business arena.

Business Ethics

ETHICS
Moral principles and values applied to social behavior.

Before we look at business ethics, we need to discuss what is meant by ethics generally. **Ethics** can be defined as the study of what constitutes right or wrong behavior. It is the branch of philosophy that focuses on morality and the way in which moral principles are derived or the way in which a given set of moral principles applies to one's conduct in daily life. Ethics has to do with questions relating to the fairness, justness, rightness, or wrongness of an action. What is fair? What is just? What is the right thing to do in this situation? These are essentially ethical questions.

What Is Business Ethics?

BUSINESS ETHICS
Ethics in a business context; a consensus of what constitutes right or wrong behavior in the world of business and the application of moral principles to situations that arise in a business setting.

Business ethics focuses on what constitutes right or wrong behavior in the business world and on how moral and ethical principles are applied by businesspersons to situations that arise in their daily activities in the workplace. Note that business ethics is not a separate *kind* of ethics. The ethical standards that guide our behavior as, say, mothers, fathers, or students apply equally well to our activities as businesspersons. Business decision makers, though, must often address more complex ethical issues and conflicts in the workplace than they face in their personal lives.

Why Is Business Ethics Important?

Why is business ethics important? The answer to this question is clear from this chapter's introduction. A keen and in-depth understanding of business ethics is important to the long-run viability of a corporation. A thorough knowledge of business ethics is also important to the well-being of the individual officers and directors of the corporation, as well as to the welfare of the firm's employees and various "stakeholders" in the entity's well-being. Certainly, corporate decisions and activities can significantly affect not only those who own, operate, or work for the company but also such groups as suppliers, the community, and society as a whole.

Note that questions concerning ethical and responsible behavior are not confined to the corporate context. Business ethics applies to *all* businesses, regardless of their organizational forms. In a business partnership, for example, partners owe a *fiduciary duty* (a duty of trust and loyalty) to each other and to their firm. This duty can sometimes conflict with what a partner sees as his or her own best interest. Partners who act solely in their own interests may violate their duties to the other partners and the firm, however. By violating this duty, they may end up paying steep penalties—as the following case illustrates.

A potential dilemma for those who support rights theory, however, is that they may disagree on which rights are most important. When considering all those affected by a business decision, for example, how much weight should be given to employees relative to shareholders, customers relative to the community, or employees relative to society as a whole?

In general, rights theorists believe that whichever right is stronger in a particular circumstance takes precedence. ■ EXAMPLE 7.10 Suppose that a firm can shut down a plant to avoid dumping pollutants into a river, which would negatively affect the health of thousands of people. Alternatively, the firm could keep the plant open (and pollute the river) but save the jobs of the twelve workers in the plant. In this situation, a rights theorist can easily choose which group to favor. (Not all choices are so clear-cut, however.) ■

OUTCOME-BASED ETHICS: UTILITARIANISM

"Thou shalt act so as to generate the greatest good for the greatest number." This is a paraphrase of the major premise of the utilitarian approach to ethics. **Utilitarianism** is a philosophical theory developed by Jeremy Bentham (1748–1832) and then advanced, with some modifications, by John Stuart Mill (1806–1873)—both British philosophers. In contrast to duty-based ethics, utilitarianism is outcome oriented. It focuses on the consequences of an action, not on the nature of the action itself or on any set of preestablished moral values or religious beliefs.

UTILITARIANISM
An approach to ethical reasoning that evaluates behavior not on the basis of any absolute ethical or moral values but on the consequences of that behavior for those who will be affected by it. In utilitarian reasoning, a "good" decision is one that results in the greatest good for the greatest number of people affected by the decision.

COST-BENEFIT ANALYSIS
A decision-making technique that involves weighing the costs of a given action against the benefits of that action.

Under a utilitarian model of ethics, an action is morally correct, or "right," when, among the people it affects, it produces the greatest amount of good for the greatest number. When an action affects the majority adversely, it is morally wrong. Applying the utilitarian theory thus requires (1) a determination of which individuals will be affected by the action in question; (2) a **cost-benefit analysis,** which involves an assessment of the negative and positive effects of alternative actions on these individuals; and (3) a choice among alternative actions that will produce maximum societal utility (the greatest positive net benefits for the greatest number of individuals).

The utilitarian approach to decision making commonly is employed by businesses, as well as by individuals. Weighing the consequences of a decision in terms of its costs and benefits for everyone affected by it is a useful analytical tool in the decision-making process. At the same time, utilitarianism is often criticized because its objective, calculated approach to problems tends to reduce the welfare of human beings to plus and minus signs on a cost-benefit worksheet and to "justify" human costs that many find totally unacceptable.

Business Ethics on a Global Level

Given the various cultures and religions throughout the world, it is not surprising that conflicts in ethics frequently arise between foreign and U.S. businesspersons. ■ EXAMPLE 7.11 In certain countries, the consumption of alcohol and specific foods is forbidden for religious reasons. Under such circumstances, it would be thoughtless and imprudent for a U.S. businessperson to invite a local business contact out for a drink. ■

The role played by women in other countries may also present some difficult ethical problems for firms doing business internationally. Equal employment opportunity is a fundamental public policy in the United States, and Title VII of the Civil

Costco Background

Costco Wholesale Corporation operates a chain of cash-and-carry membership warehouses that sell high-quality, nationally branded, and selected private-label merchandise at low prices. Its target markets include both businesses that buy goods for commercial use or resale and individuals who are employees or members of specific organizations and associations. The company tries to reach high sales volume and fast inventory turnover by offering a limited choice of merchandise in many product groups at competitive prices.

The company takes a strong position on behaving ethically in all transactions and relationships. It expects employees to behave ethically. For example, no one can accept gratuities from vendors. The company also expects employees to behave ethically, according to domestic ethical standards, in any country in which it operates.

COSTCO™

CODE OF ETHICS

By Jim Sinegal

OBEY THE LAW

The law is irrefutable! Absent a moral imperative to challenge a law, we must conduct our business in total compliance with the laws of every community where we do business.

- Comply with all statutes.
- Cooperate with authorities.

TAKE CARE OF OUR EMPLOYEES

To claim "people are our most important asset" is true and an understatement. Each employee has been hired for a very important job. Jobs such as stocking the shelves, ringing members' orders, buying products, and paying our bills are jobs we would all choose to perform because of their importance. The employees hired to perform these jobs are performing as management's "alter egos." Every employee, whether they are in a Costco warehouse, or whether they work in the regional or corporate offices, is a Costco ambassador trained to give our members professional, courteous treatment.

A lab worker conducts research for the development of a drug. If the drug proves beneficial to most people but adverse to a few, would it, under a utilitarian model of ethics, be marketed? Why or why not? (© Ted Horowitz, Getty Images)

.on the Web Global Exchange offers information on global business activities, including some of the ethical issues stemming from those activities, at **http://www.globalexchange.org**.

Rights Act of 1964 prohibits discrimination against women in the employment context (see Chapter 41). Some other countries, however, offer little protection for women against gender discrimination in the workplace, including sexual harassment.

Laws governing workers in other countries have created some especially difficult ethical problems for U.S. sellers of goods manufactured in foreign countries. For example, what if a foreign company exploits its workers—by hiring women and children at below-minimum-wage rates or by requiring its employees to work long hours in a workplace full of health hazards? Given today's global communications network, few companies can assume that their actions in other nations will go unnoticed by "corporate watch" groups that discover and publicize unethical corporate behavior. As a result, U.S. businesses today usually take steps to avoid such adverse publicity—either by refusing to deal with certain suppliers or by arranging to monitor their suppliers' workplaces to make sure that the employees are not being mistreated.

The Foreign Corrupt Practices Act

"Never doubt that a small group of committed citizens can change the world; indeed, it is the only thing that ever has."

Margaret Mead, 1901–1978 (American anthropologist)

Another ethical problem in international business dealings has to do with the legitimacy of certain side payments to government officials. In the United States, the majority of contracts are formed within the private sector. In many foreign countries, however, decisions on most major construction and manufacturing contracts are made by government officials because of extensive government regulation and control over trade and industry. Side payments to government officials in exchange for favorable business contracts are not unusual in such countries, nor are they considered to be unethical. In the past, U.S. corporations doing business in these countries largely followed the dictum, "When in Rome, do as the Romans do."

Workers at their sewing machines in a garment plant in Micronesia. How might cultural differences affect what businesspersons consider ethical conduct? If, for example, employees in a particular region typically work fifteen-hour days, is it unethical for an American business operating in that region to require the same number of hours? Why or why not? Would it be any more ethical if the American company subcontracted with another company whose employees were required to work fifteen-hour days? (AP Photo/Charles Hanley)

In the 1970s, however, the U.S. press, and government officials as well, uncovered a number of business scandals involving large side payments by U.S. corporations—such as Lockheed Aircraft—to foreign representatives for the purpose of securing advantageous international trade contracts. In response to this unethical behavior, in 1977 Congress passed the Foreign Corrupt Practices Act (FCPA), which prohibits U.S. businesspersons from bribing foreign officials to secure advantageous contracts.

Prohibition against the Bribery of Foreign Officials The first part of the FCPA applies to all U.S. companies and their directors, officers, shareholders, employees, and agents. This part prohibits the bribery of most officials of foreign governments if the purpose of the payment is to get the officials to act in their official capacity to provide business opportunities.

The FCPA does not prohibit payment of substantial sums to minor officials whose duties are ministerial. These payments are often referred to as "grease," or facilitating payments. They are meant to accelerate the performance of administrative services that might otherwise be carried out at a slow pace. Thus, for example, if a firm makes a payment to a minor official to speed up an import licensing process, the firm has not violated the FCPA.

Generally, the act, as amended, permits payments to foreign officials if such payments are lawful within the foreign country. The act also does not prohibit payments to private foreign companies or other third parties unless the U.S. firm knows that the payments will be passed on to a foreign government in violation of the FCPA.

Accounting Requirements In the past, bribes were often concealed in corporate financial records. Thus, the second part of the FCPA is directed toward accountants. All companies must keep detailed records that "accurately and fairly" reflect the company's financial activities. In addition, all companies must have an accounting system that provides "reasonable assurance" that all transactions entered into by the company are accounted for and legal. These requirements assist in detecting illegal bribes. The FCPA further prohibits any person from making false statements to accountants or false entries in any record or account.

Penalties for Violations In 1988, the FCPA was amended to provide that business firms that violate the act may be fined up to $2 million. Individual officers or directors who violate the FCPA may be fined up to $100,000 (the fine cannot be paid by the company) and may be imprisoned for up to five years.

Other Nations Denounce Bribery

For twenty years after its passage in 1977, the FCPA was the only law of its kind in the world, despite attempts by U.S. political leaders to convince other nations to pass similar legislation. That situation is now changing. In 1997, the Organization for Economic Cooperation and Development created a convention (treaty) that made the bribery of foreign public officials a serious crime. By 2005, at least thirty-five countries had adopted the convention, which obligates them to enact legislation within their nations in accordance with the treaty. In addition, other international institutions, including the European Union, the Organization of American States, and the United Nations, have either passed or are in the process of negotiating rules against bribery in business transactions.

REVIEWING ETHICS AND BUSINESS DECISION MAKING

Isabel Arnett was promoted to chief executive officer (CEO) of Naturelles, Inc., a company that manufactures and sells herbal supplements. Before the board of directors appointed Arnett CEO, she had managed the company's production department, where she earned a reputation as a "slave driver" who routinely refused raises, benefits, and time off for long-term employees. As CEO, she continued her aggressive management style.

In April 2006, company researchers distilled a natural substance that radically increased the body's metabolism, causing significant weight loss without any change in diet or exercise habits. Although the researchers were reluctant to market the product, called Naturolean, without further study, Arnett initiated a massive marketing campaign and began distributing the supplement. Sales soared, shareholders profited, and the company gained value. Two years later, it was discovered that Naturolean caused irreparable brain damage to fetuses in women who had taken it just before or during pregnancy. Using the information presented in the chapter, answer the following questions.

1. Do employers have an ethical responsibility to give their employees raises, benefits, or time off under duty-based ethical standards? What about under a utilitarian model of ethics? Explain.
2. If the board of directors knew how Arnett treated company employees, was it unethical of them to promote her to CEO? Why or why not?
3. Suppose that Naturelles did have an ethical code of conduct and that Arnett's conduct in promoting Naturolean did not violate that code. Would that affect the determination of whether her conduct was ethical? Why or why not?
4. How might the presence of an ethics code affect a court's determination of whether the company's conduct was ethical?

APPLICATION How Can You Create an Ethical Workplace?*

If you are a manager, rest assured that unless you are totally committed to the goal of creating and maintaining an ethical workplace, you will not succeed in achieving it. In addition to your attitude toward ethics and your conduct, two other factors help to create an ethical workplace environment: a written code of ethics, or policy statement, and the effective communication of the firm's ethical policies to employees. Finally, you should provide employees with a means by which they can anonymously complain about unethical behavior on the part of their co-workers or supervisors.

THE ROLE OF MANAGEMENT

As mentioned in this chapter, management's behavior is crucial in establishing the ethical tone of a firm. Managers must make it clear, both in their words and by their conduct, that unethical behavior is not acceptable. If an employee persists in unethical behavior, you should consider discharging the employee as a clear example to other employees that you will not tolerate unethical actions. Studies have shown that employees quickly adapt to the "rules" of their workplace environments, but it is up to the company managers to let employees know what those rules are—and to enforce them.

INSTRUCT EMPLOYEES IN ETHICAL STANDARDS

A written ethics code or policy statement helps to make clear to employees how they are expected to relate to their supervisors or managers, to consumers, to suppliers, and to other employees. Above all, it is important to state explicitly what your firm's ethical priorities are and make sure that the firm's employees are aware of those priorities.

A good way to communicate these priorities to employees is by implementing an ethics training program, in which managers discuss with employees—face to face—the firm's policies and the importance of ethical conduct. Ethics seminars should be held at routine intervals so that employees have an opportunity to discuss ethical problems as they arise. Another effective technique is to evaluate periodically the ethical performance of each employee.

Employees should also be instructed in how they can anonymously report unethical behavior. For publicly traded companies, federal law now requires the establishment of confidential reporting systems for this purpose. This can be accomplished through a Web-based reporting system, as described earlier in this chapter, or a special company "hot line."

CHECKLIST FOR THE BUSINESS MANAGER

1. Make sure that management is committed to ethical behavior and sets an ethical example.
2. Create, print, and distribute an ethical code clearly stating your firm's ethical goals and priorities, as well as what behavior is expected of employees in their areas of responsibility.
3. Implement an ethics training program to communicate your firm's ethical policies to employees.
4. Devise a method, such as an ethical checklist, for evaluating the ethical performance of each individual employee.
5. Provide a mechanism through which employees can anonymously complain about unethical behavior in the workplace.

* This *Application* is not meant to substitute for the services of an attorney who is licensed to practice law in your state.

KEY TERMS

business ethics 201
categorical imperative 215
cost-benefit analysis 216
ethical reasoning 214
ethics 201
moral minimum 210
principle of rights 215
utilitarianism 216

CHAPTER SUMMARY Ethics and Business Decision Making

Business Ethics (See pages 201–203.)	Ethics can be defined as the study of what constitutes right or wrong behavior. Business ethics focuses on how moral and ethical principles are applied in the business context.
Setting the Right Ethical Tone (See pages 203–208.)	1. *Role of management*—Management's commitment and behavior are essential in creating an ethical workplace. Most large firms have ethical codes or policies and corporate compliance programs to help employees determine whether certain actions are ethical. 2. *Ethical trade-offs*—Management constantly faces ethical trade-offs because firms have ethical and legal duties to a number of groups, including shareholders and employees.
Business Ethics and the Law (See pages 210–214.)	1. *The moral minimum*—Lawful behavior is a moral minimum. The law has its limits, though, and some actions may be legal but not ethical. 2. *Legal uncertainties*—It may be difficult to predict with certainty whether particular actions are legal given the numerous and frequent changes in the laws regulating business and the "gray areas" in the law. 3. *Technological developments and legal uncertainties*—Technological developments can also lead to legal uncertainties until it is clear how the law will be applied to the questions raised by these developments.
Approaches to Ethical Reasoning (See pages 214–216.)	1. *Duty-based ethics*—Ethics based on religious beliefs; philosophical reasoning, such as that of Immanuel Kant; and the basic rights of human beings (the principle of rights). 2. *Outcome-based ethics (utilitarianism)*—Ethics based on philosophical reasoning, such as that of John Stuart Mill, and focusing on the consequences of actions rather than the actions themselves.
Business Ethics on a Global Level (See pages 216–219.)	Businesses must take account of the many cultural, religious, and legal differences among nations. Notable differences relate to the role of women in society, employment laws governing workplace conditions, and the practice of giving side payments to foreign officials to secure favorable contracts.

FOR REVIEW

Answers for the even-numbered questions in this For Review *section can be found on this text's accompanying Web site at* http://blt.westbuslaw.com. *Select "Chapter 7" and click on "For Review."*

1. What is ethics? What is business ethics? Why is business ethics important?
2. How can business leaders encourage their companies to act ethically?
3. What are corporate compliance programs?
4. How do duty-based ethical standards differ from outcome-based ethical standards?
5. What types of ethical issues might arise in the context of international business transactions?

QUESTIONS AND CASE PROBLEMS

7–1. Business Ethics. Some business ethicists maintain that whereas personal ethics has to do with right or wrong behavior, business ethics is concerned with appropriate behavior. In other words, ethical behavior in business has less to do with moral principles than with what society deems to be appropriate behavior in the business context. Do you agree with this distinction? Do personal and business ethics ever overlap? Should personal ethics play any role in business ethical decision making?

7–2. Business Ethics and Public Opinion. Assume that you are a high-level manager for a shoe manufacturer. You know that your firm could increase its profit margin by producing shoes in Indonesia, where you could hire women for $100 a month to assemble them. You also know, however, that a competing shoe manufacturer recently was accused by human rights advocates of engaging in exploitative labor practices because the manufacturer sold shoes made by Indonesian women for similarly low wages. You personally do not believe that paying $100 a month to Indonesian women is unethical because you know that in their country, $100 a month is a better-than-average wage rate. Assuming that the decision is yours to make, should you have the shoes manufactured in Indonesia and make higher profits for your company? Should you instead avoid the risk of negative publicity and the consequences of that publicity for the firm's reputation and subsequent profits? Are there other alternatives? Discuss fully.

7–3. Business Ethics and Public Opinion. Human rights groups, environmental activists, and other interest groups concerned with unethical business practices have often conducted publicity campaigns against various corporations that those groups feel have engaged in unethical practices. Do you believe that a small group of well-organized activists should dictate how a major corporation conducts its affairs? Discuss fully.

7–4. Ethical Decision Making. Shokun Steel Co. owns many steel plants. One of its plants is much older than the others. Equipment at that plant is outdated and inefficient, and the costs of production at that plant are now twice as high as at any of Shokun's other plants. The company cannot raise the price of steel because of competition, both domestic and international. The plant is located in Twin Firs, Pennsylvania, which has a population of about 45,000, and employs over a thousand workers. Shokun is contemplating whether to close the plant. What factors should the firm consider in making its decision? Will the firm violate any ethical duties if it closes the plant? Analyze these questions from the two basic perspectives on ethical reasoning discussed in this chapter.

7–5. Ethical Conduct. Richard and Suzanne Weinstein owned Elm City Cheese Co. Elm City sold its products to three major customers that used the cheese as a "filler" to blend into their cheeses. In 1982, Mark Federico, a certified public accountant, became Elm City's accountant and the Weinsteins' personal accountant. The Weinsteins had known Federico since he was seven years old, and even before he became their accountant, he knew the details of Elm City's business. Federico's duties went beyond typical accounting work, and when the Weinsteins were absent, Federico was put in charge of operations. In 1992, Federico was made a vice president of the company, and a year later he was placed in charge of day-to-day operations. He also continued to serve as Elm City's accountant. The relationship between Federico and the Weinsteins deteriorated, and in 1995, he resigned as Elm City's employee and as its accountant. Less than two years later, Federico opened Lomar Foods, Inc., to make the same products as Elm City by the same process and to sell the products to the same customers. Federico located Lomar closer to Elm City's suppliers. Elm City filed a suit in a Connecticut state court against Federico and Lomar, alleging, among other things, misappropriation of trade secrets. Elm City argued that it was entitled to punitive damages because Federico's conduct was "willful and malicious." Federico responded in part that he did not act willfully and maliciously because he did not know that Elm City's business details were trade secrets. Were Federico's actions "willful and malicious"? Were they ethical? Explain. [*Elm City Cheese Co. v. Federico*, 251 Conn. 59, 752 A.2d 1037 (1999)]

CASE PROBLEM WITH SAMPLE ANSWER

7–6. Richard Fraser was an "exclusive career insurance agent" under a contract with Nationwide Mutual Insurance Co. Fraser leased computer hardware and software from Nationwide for his business. During a dispute between Nationwide and the Nationwide Insurance Independent Contractors Association, an organization representing Fraser and other exclusive career agents, Fraser prepared a letter to Nationwide's competitors asking whether they were interested in acquiring the represented agents' policyholders. Nationwide obtained a copy of the letter and searched its electronic file server for e-mail indicating that the letter had been sent. It found a stored e-mail that Fraser had sent to a co-worker indicating that the letter had been sent to at least one competitor. The e-mail was retrieved from the co-worker's file of already received and discarded messages stored on the server. When Nationwide canceled its contract with Fraser, he filed a suit in a federal district court against the firm, alleging, among other things, violations of various federal laws that prohibit the interception of electronic communications during transmission. In whose favor should the court rule, and why? Did Nationwide act ethically in retrieving the e-mail? Explain. [*Fraser v. Nationwide Mutual Insurance Co.*, 352 F.3d 107 (3d Cir. 2004)]

After you have answered this problem, compare your answer with the sample answer given on the Web site that accompanies this text. Go to http://blt.westbuslaw.com, select "Chapter 7," and click on "Case Problem with Sample Answer."

7–7. Ethical Conduct. Unable to pay more than $1.2 billion in debt, Big Rivers Electric Corp. filed a petition to declare bankruptcy in a federal bankruptcy court in September 1996. Big Rivers' creditors included Bank of New York (BONY), Chase Manhattan Bank, Mapco Equities, and others. The court appointed J. Baxter Schilling to work as a "disinterested" (neutral) party with Big Rivers and the creditors to resolve their disputes; the court set an hourly fee as Schilling's compensation. Schilling told Chase, BONY, and Mapco that he wanted them to pay him an additional percentage fee based on the "success" he attained in finding "new value" to pay Big Rivers' debts. He said that without such a deal, he would not perform his mediation duties. Chase agreed; the others disputed the deal, but no one told the court. In October 1998, Schilling asked the court for nearly $4.5 million in compensation, including the hourly fees, which totaled about $531,000, and the percentage fees. Big Rivers and others asked the court to deny Schilling any fees on the basis that he had improperly negotiated "secret side agreements." How did Schilling violate his duties as a "disinterested" party? Should he be denied compensation? Why or why not? [*In re Big Rivers Electric Corp.*, 355 F.3d 415 (6th Cir. 2004)]

7–8. Ethical Conduct. Eden Electrical, Ltd., owned twenty-five appliance stores throughout Israel, at least some of which sold refrigerators made by Amana Co. Eden bought the appliances from Amana's Israeli distributor, Pan El A/Yesh Shem, which approached Eden about taking over the distributorship. Eden representatives met with Amana executives. The executives made assurances about Amana's good faith, its hope of having a long-term business relationship with Eden, and its willingness to have Eden become its exclusive distributor in Israel. Eden signed a distributorship agreement and paid Amana $2.4 million. Amana failed to deliver this amount in inventory to Eden, continued selling refrigerators to other entities for the Israeli market, and represented to others that it was still looking for a long-term distributor. Less than three months after signing the agreement with Eden, Amana terminated it, without explanation. Eden filed a suit in a federal district court against Amana, alleging fraud. The court awarded Eden $12.1 million in damages. Is this amount warranted? Why or why not? How does this case illustrate why business ethics is important? [*Eden Electrical, Ltd. v. Amana Co.*, 370 F.3d 824 (8th Cir. 2004)]

FOR CRITICAL ANALYSIS

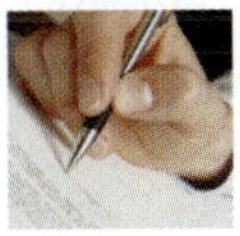

7–9. If a firm engages in "ethically responsible" behavior solely for the purpose of gaining profits from the goodwill it generates, the "ethical" behavior is essentially a means toward a self-serving end (profits and the accumulation of wealth). In this situation, is the firm acting unethically in any way? Should motive or conduct carry greater weight on the ethical scales in this situation?

VIDEO QUESTION

7–10. Go to this text's Web site at **http://blt.westbuslaw.com** and select "Chapter 7." Click on "Video Questions" and view the video titled *Ethics: Business Ethics an Oxymoron?* Then answer the following questions.

1. According to the instructor in the video, what is the primary reason why businesses act ethically?
2. Which of the two approaches to ethical reasoning that were discussed in the chapter seems to have had more influence on the instructor in the discussion of how business activities are related to societies? Explain your answer.
3. The instructor asserts that "[i]n the end, it is the unethical behavior that becomes costly, and conversely ethical behavior creates its own competitive advantage." Do you agree with this statement? Why or why not?

INTERNET EXERCISES

Go to the *Business Law Today* home page at **http://blt.westbuslaw.com**, select "Chapter 7," and click on "Internet Exercises." There you will find the following Internet research exercises that you can perform to learn more about topics covered in this chapter.

Activity 7–1: LEGAL PERSPECTIVE—Ethics in Business

Activity 7–2: MANAGEMENT PERSPECTIVE—Environmental Self-Audits

BEFORE THE TEST

Go to the *Business Law Today* home page at **http://blt.westbuslaw.com**, select "Chapter 7," and click on "Interactive Quizzes." You will find a number of interactive questions relating to this chapter.

UNIT ONE Extended Case Study

Vo v. City of Garden Grove

As explained in Chapter 2, the First Amendment protects the freedom of speech. This protection is not unlimited. Expression—oral, written, or symbolized by conduct—is subject to reasonable restrictions on time, place, and manner. A restriction is valid if it can be justified without reference to the content of the regulated speech. It also must be narrowly tailored (go no further than necessary) to serve a significant governmental interest and leave open ample alternative channels for communication of information. The requirement of narrow tailoring is satisfied as long as the regulation promotes a substantial governmental interest that would be achieved less effectively without the regulation. In this extended case study, we examine Vo v. City of Garden Grove,[1] *a decision in which these principles were applied.*

CASE BACKGROUND

On December 30, 2001, Phong Ly, a minor, was stabbed to death with a screwdriver while standing outside PC Café, a cybercafé in the city of Garden Grove, California.

1. 115 Cal.App.4th 425, 9 Cal.Rptr.3d 257 (4 Dist. 2004).

A *cybercafé* is an establishment that provides Internet access to customers for a fee. The number of cybercafés in Garden Grove rose from three to twenty-two between 2000 and 2002. Over the same period, gang-related activities, including violent crime, increased near some of the cybercafés. Within a few days of Ly's murder, on the basis of a report from Joseph Polisar, the city's chief of police, who detailed the accelerating criminal activity, the city enacted a temporary ordinance to halt the establishment of new cybercafés.

In July 2002, on the strength of an updated report from Polisar, the city enacted a permanent ordinance that, as amended the following December, required cybercafé owners to provide security guards and install video surveillance systems, among other things. Minors were prohibited from visiting the cybercafés during school hours unless accompanied by a parent or guardian. Thanh Thuy Vo and four other owners filed a suit in a California state court against the city, alleging in part that the ordinance violated their right to freedom of speech. The court agreed with the owners and enjoined the city from enforcing the ordinance. The city appealed to a state intermediate appellate court.

MAJORITY OPINION

IKOLA, J. [Judge]

* * * *

From the information provided [by Chief Polisar], the city concluded that excluding minors from Cybercafes during school hours would advance its significant public interest in their protection and safety. That conclusion is reasonable. Although parents presumably believe their minor children are in school while it is in session, they are not in a position to assert direct supervision and control during school hours. As noted by the chief of police, if Cybercafes allow minor children on the premises during school hours, the potential that gang members will recruit minors is increased, as well as the potential that minors will become witnesses or victims of gang violence. *Thus, the regulation promotes a substantial government interest that would be achieved less effectively absent the regulation.* This is all that is required to meet the narrow tailoring requirement. [Emphasis added.]

Further, the means chosen to advance the city's interest are not substantially broader than necessary. The city perceived that danger to minors existed in the risky environment of the Cybercafes. The daytime curfew is limited to Cybercafes with their risky environment, and to those times when the students are not under the presumed direct control and supervision of their parents. * * *

Finally, plaintiffs presented no evidence to establish the lack of open ample alternative channels for communication. It is common knowledge that alternative channels for communication over the Internet are abundant. Many have Internet access at home. Schools (where the minors should be in any event) commonly provide Internet access, as do public libraries. And, of course, the Cybercafes themselves are open to minors, even without parental supervision, for seven hours each day.

* * * *

* * * [T]he staffing requirements make no reference to the content of any communication and are thus content neutral. And, as with the daytime curfew, ample alternative channels for communication are available. The remaining question is whether the staffing requirements are narrowly tailored to advance the city's substantial interest in public safety.

* * * *

Given the well-demonstrated criminal activity observed at Cybercafes, and their tendency to attract gang members, the * * * staffing requirements are * * * narrowly tailored to serve a significant governmental interest. Ample alternative means of communication remain open, and the requirements are not substantially broader than necessary. * * *

* * * *

* * * [W]e are not persuaded the video surveillance system affects First Amendment activity any more than does the presence of an adult employee and/or security guard. The ordinance does not require video surveillance of e-mail or images from the Internet appearing on the customer's computer screens. The ordinance requires only that the system be capable of showing "the activity and physical features of persons or areas within the premises." This is no more than can be observed by employees, security guards, or indeed, other customers. * * * For the reasons discussed * * * in connection with the employee and security guard requirements, the video surveillance requirement is a content-neutral manner restriction, narrowly tailored to advance the city's legitimate interest in public safety and deterrence of gang violence. * * *

* * * *

* * * The court's order * * * enjoining [preventing] the enforcement of * * * [the cybercafé ordinance is] reversed.

DISSENTING OPINION

SILLS, P.J. [Presiding Judge], * * * Dissenting.

I respectfully dissent to the most important part of the majority opinion, in which it holds that Garden Grove may *require* video surveillance in *every* cybercafe in the city, regardless of whether that cybercafe has experienced any gang-related violence, or, indeed, even any problems of the most minor nature.

* * * [O]nly 3 of 22 cybercafes have experienced "gang-related" violence, only 2 more have experienced serious crime of any kind (one of the two was a drug deal), * * * [and] the city's own evidence concerning cybercafes in other cities showed *no* gang-related crimes at cybercafes outside of Garden Grove. That leaves 17 cybercafes which have experienced no serious problems, a fact which should be enough to require this court to affirm the trial court's injunction * * *.

It is the video surveillance issue, though, that is the most problematic[.] * * *

* * * *

* * * There are any number of substantial means by which the city's interest in protecting against gang violence could be realized without video surveillance. Police patrols could be increased. Owners could be supplied with a list of gang-members who could be refused service. Security guards could be posted at those cybercafes which have already experienced gang-related violence. Yet the majority steadfastly refuse to confront such possibilities, all in the name of deference to " * * * facts" found by the city council. Whatever that is, it isn't trying to minimize any burden on * * * speech to what is reasonably necessary.

* * * *

* * * This is the way Constitutional rights are lost. Not in the thunder of a tyrant's edict, but in the soft judicial whispers of deference.

QUESTIONS FOR ANALYSIS

1 Law. What is the significant, or substantial, governmental interest that is supported by the city ordinance in the *Vo* case?

2 Law. How exactly does this ordinance implicate First Amendment activities involving "speech"?

3 Ethics. Would an ordinance that allowed city officials to deny a business license to a cybercafé whose "operation does not comport with good morals" be constitutional under the First Amendment?

4 Technological Dimensions. Why might a cybercafé attract more criminal activity and gang-related violence than other business establishments?

5 Implications for the Business Manager. Before installing a video surveillance system, should a business consider any other legal issues besides those relating to freedom of speech?

UNIT TWO

CONTRACTS

UNIT CONTENTS

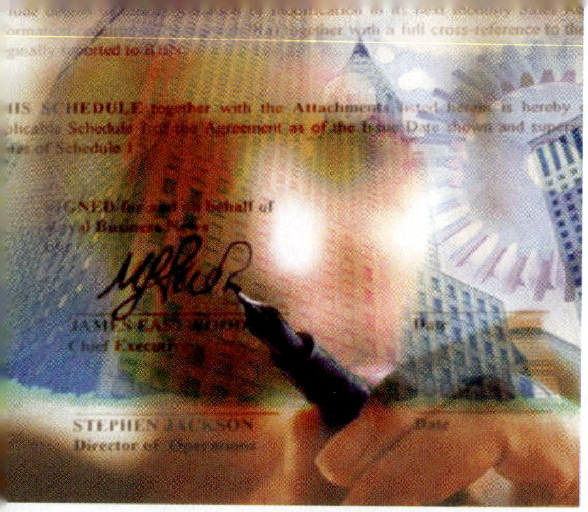

CHAPTER 8

Nature and Classification

"The social order rests upon the stability and predictability of conduct, of which keeping promises is a large item."

Roscoe Pound, 1870–1964
(American jurist)

CHAPTER OUTLINE

- THE FUNCTION OF CONTRACTS
- DEFINITION OF A CONTRACT
- REQUIREMENTS OF A CONTRACT
- FREEDOM OF CONTRACT AND FREEDOM FROM CONTRACT
- TYPES OF CONTRACTS
- QUASI CONTRACTS
- INTERPRETATION OF CONTRACTS

LEARNING OBJECTIVES

After reading this chapter, you should be able to answer the following questions:

1. What is a contract? What is the objective theory of contracts?
2. What are the four basic elements necessary to the formation of a valid contract?
3. What is the difference between an implied-in-fact contract and an implied-in-law contract (quasi contract)?
4. How does a void contract differ from a voidable contract? What is an unenforceable contract?
5. Why have plain language laws been enacted? What rules guide the courts in interpreting contracts?

PROMISE
An assertion that something either will or will not happen in the future.

As Roscoe Pound—an eminent jurist—observed in the above quotation, "keeping promises" is important to a stable social order. Contract law deals with, among other things, the formation and keeping of promises. A **promise** is an assertion that something either will or will not happen in the future.

Like other types of law, contract law reflects our social values, interests, and expectations at a given point in time. It shows, for example, what kinds of promises our society thinks should be legally binding. It shows what excuses our society accepts for breaking such promises. Additionally, it shows what promises are considered to be contrary to public policy, or against the interests of society, and therefore legally void. If a promise goes against the interests of society as a whole, it will be invalid. Also, if it was made by a child or a mentally incompetent person, or on the basis of false information, a question will arise as to whether the promise should be enforced. Resolving such questions is the essence of contract law.

In the business world, questions and disputes concerning contracts arise daily. Although aspects of contract law vary from state to state, much of it is based on the common law. In 1932, the American Law Institute compiled the *Restatement of the Law of Contracts*. This work is a nonstatutory, authoritative exposition of the present law on the subject of contracts and is now in its second edition (a third edition is in the process of being drafted). Throughout the following chapters on contracts, we will refer to the second edition of the *Restatement of the Law of Contracts* as simply the *Restatement (Second) of Contracts*.

.on the Web You can keep abreast of recent and planned revisions of the *Restatements of the Law* by accessing the American Law Institute's Web site at **http://www.ali.org**.

The Uniform Commercial Code (UCC), which governs contracts and other transactions relating to the sale and lease of goods, occasionally departs from common law contract rules. Generally, the different treatment of contracts falling under the UCC stems from the general policy of encouraging commerce. The ways in which the UCC changes common law contract rules will be discussed extensively in later chapters. In this unit covering the common law of contracts (Chapters 8 through 17), we only indicate briefly or in footnotes those common law rules that have been altered significantly by the UCC for sales and lease contracts.[1]

The Function of Contracts

No aspect of modern life is entirely free of contractual relationships. You acquire rights and obligations, for example, when you borrow funds, when you buy or lease a house, when you procure insurance, when you form a business, and when you purchase goods or services. Contract law is designed to provide stability and predictability for both buyers and sellers in the marketplace.

Contract law assures the parties to private agreements that the promises they make will be enforceable. Clearly, many promises are kept because the parties involved feel a moral obligation to do so or because keeping a promise is in their mutual self-interest, not because the **promisor** (the person making the promise) or the **promisee** (the person to whom the promise is made) is conscious of the rules of contract law. Nevertheless, the rules of contract law are often followed in business agreements to avoid potential problems.

PROMISOR
A person who makes a promise.

PROMISEE
A person to whom a promise is made.

By supplying procedures for enforcing private agreements, contract law provides an essential condition for the existence of a market economy. Without a legal framework of reasonably assured expectations within which to plan and venture, businesspersons would be able to rely only on the good faith of others. Duty and good faith are usually sufficient, but when dramatic price changes or adverse economic conditions make it costly to comply with a promise, these elements may not be enough. Contract law is necessary to ensure compliance with a promise or to entitle the innocent party to some form of relief.

Definition of a Contract

CONTRACT
An agreement that can be enforced in court; formed by two or more competent parties who agree, for consideration, to perform or to refrain from performing some legal act now or in the future.

A **contract** is an agreement that can be enforced in court. It is formed by two or more parties who agree to perform or to refrain from performing some act now or in the future. Generally, contract disputes arise when there is a promise of future

1. Note that throughout the chapters on the common law of contracts, we cite in the footnotes the section numbers of the UCC that are used in the UCC version that is currently in effect in most states. As you will read in later chapters covering sales contracts, the UCC was amended in 2003, and thus some of the section numbers may have been changed by those amendments.

performance. If the contractual promise is not fulfilled, the party who made it is subject to the sanctions of a court (see Chapter 15). That party may be required to pay money damages for failing to perform the contractual promise; in limited instances, the party may be required to perform the promised act.

OBJECTIVE THEORY OF CONTRACTS A theory under which the intent to form a contract will be judged by outward, objective facts (what the party said when entering into the contract, how the party acted or appeared, and the circumstances surrounding the transaction) as interpreted by a reasonable person, rather than by the party's own secret, subjective intentions.

In determining whether a contract has been formed, the element of intent is of prime importance. In contract law, intent is determined by what is referred to as the **objective theory of contracts,** not by the personal or subjective intent, or belief, of a party. The theory is that a party's intention to enter into a contract is judged by outward, objective facts as interpreted by a reasonable person, rather than by the party's own secret, subjective intentions. Objective facts include (1) what the party said when entering into the contract, (2) how the party acted or appeared, and (3) the circumstances surrounding the transaction. As will be discussed later in this chapter, in the subsection on express versus implied contracts, intent to form a contract may be manifested not only in words, oral or written, but also by conduct.

Requirements of a Contract

on the Web An extensive definition of the term *contract* is offered by the 'Lectric Law Library at **http://www.lectlaw.com/def/c123.htm**.

The following list describes the four requirements that must be met for a valid contract to exist. Each item will be explained more fully in the chapter indicated. Although we pair two of these requirements (capacity and legality) in a subsequent chapter, it is important to stress that each requirement is separate and independent. Capacity and legality are paired merely for reasons of space.

1. *Agreement.* An agreement includes an offer and an acceptance. One party must offer to enter into a legal agreement, and another party must accept the terms of the offer (Chapter 9).
2. *Consideration.* Any promises made by parties must be supported by legally sufficient and bargained-for consideration (something of value received or promised, to convince a person to make a deal) (Chapter 10).
3. *Contractual capacity.* Both parties entering into the contract must have the contractual capacity to do so; the law must recognize them as possessing characteristics that qualify them as competent parties (Chapter 11).
4. *Legality.* The contract's purpose must be to accomplish some goal that is legal and not against public policy (Chapter 11).

If any of these four elements is lacking, no contract will have been formed. Even if all of these elements exist, however, a contract may be unenforceable if the following requirements are not met. These requirements typically are raised as *defenses* to the enforceability of an otherwise valid contract.

1. *Genuineness of assent.* The apparent consent of both parties must be genuine (Chapter 12).
2. *Form.* The contract must be in whatever form the law requires; for example, some contracts must be in writing to be enforceable (Chapter 13).

Freedom of Contract and Freedom from Contract

As a general rule, the law recognizes everyone's ability to enter freely into contractual arrangements. This recognition is called *freedom of contract,* a freedom protected by the U.S. Constitution in Article I, Section 10. Because freedom of contract is a fundamental public policy of the United States, courts rarely interfere with contracts that have been voluntarily made.

Of course, as in other areas of the law, there are many exceptions to the general rule that contracts voluntarily negotiated will be enforced. For example, illegal bargains, agreements that unreasonably restrain trade, and certain unfair contracts made between one party with a great amount of bargaining power and another with little power are generally not enforced. In addition, as you will read in Chapter 11, certain contracts and clauses may not be enforceable if they are contrary to public policy, fairness, and justice. These exceptions provide *freedom from contract* for persons who may have been forced into making contracts unfavorable to themselves.

.on the Web For an excellent overview of the basic principles of contract law, go to **http://profs.lp.findlaw.com/contracts/index.html**.

Types of Contracts

There are numerous types of contracts. They are categorized based on legal distinctions as to their formation, performance, and enforceability.

CONTRACT FORMATION

As you can see in Exhibit 8–1, three classifications, or categories, of contracts are based on how and when a contract is formed. The best way to explain each type of contract is to compare one type with another, as we do in the following pages.

Bilateral versus Unilateral Contracts Every contract involves at least two parties. The **offeror** is the party making the offer. The **offeree** is the party to whom the offer is made. The offeror always promises to do or not to do something and thus is also a promisor. Whether the contract is classified as *bilateral* or *unilateral* depends on what the offeree must do to accept the offer and bind the offeror to a contract.

OFFEROR
A person who makes an offer.

OFFEREE
A person to whom an offer is made.

Bilateral Contracts. If to accept the offer the offeree must only promise to perform, the contract is a **bilateral contract.** Hence, a bilateral contract is a "promise for a promise." An example of a bilateral contract is a contract in which one person agrees to buy another person's automobile for a specified price. No performance, such as the payment of money or delivery of goods, need take place for a

BILATERAL CONTRACT
A type of contract that arises when a promise is given in exchange for a return promise.

EXHIBIT 8–1 CLASSIFICATIONS BASED ON CONTRACT FORMATION

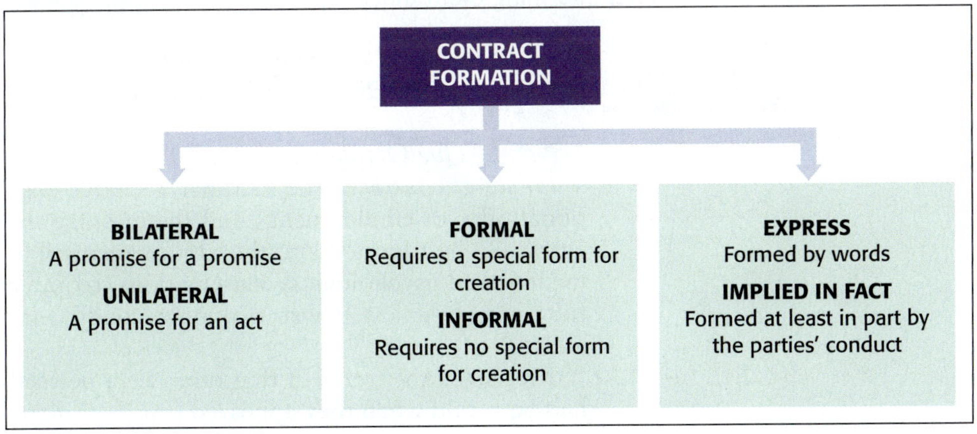

bilateral contract to be formed. The contract comes into existence at the moment the promises are exchanged.

UNILATERAL CONTRACT
A contract that results when an offer can be accepted only by the offeree's performance.

Unilateral Contracts. If the offer is phrased so that the offeree can accept only by completing the contract performance, the contract is a **unilateral contract.** Hence, a unilateral contract is a "promise for an act." In other words, the contract is formed not at the moment when promises are exchanged but rather when the contract is *performed.* ■ EXAMPLE 8.1 Joe says to Celia, "If you drive my car from New York to Los Angeles, I'll give you $1,000." Only on Celia's completion of the act—bringing the car to Los Angeles—does she fully accept Joe's offer to pay $1,000. If she chooses not to accept the offer to drive the car to Los Angeles, there are no legal consequences. ■

Contests, lotteries, and other competitions offering prizes are also examples of offers for unilateral contracts. If a person complies with the rules of the contest—such as by submitting the right lottery number at the right place and time—a unilateral contract is formed, binding the organization offering the prize to a contract to perform as promised in the offer.

Can a school's, or an employer's, letter of tentative acceptance to a prospective student, or a possible employee, qualify as a unilateral contract? That was the question in the following case.

CASE 8.1 Ardito v. City of Providence

United States District Court,
District of Rhode Island, 2003.
263 F.Supp.2d 358.

BACKGROUND AND FACTS In 2001, the city of Providence, Rhode Island, decided to begin hiring police officers to fill vacancies in its police department. Because only individuals who had graduated from the Providence Police Academy were eligible, the city also decided to conduct two training sessions, the "60th and 61st Police Academies." To be admitted, an applicant had to pass a series of tests and be deemed qualified by members of the department after an interview. The applicants judged most qualified were sent a letter informing them that they had been selected to attend the academy if they successfully completed a medical checkup and a psychological examination. The letter for the applicants to the 61st Academy, dated October 15, stated that it was "a conditional offer of employment." Meanwhile, a new chief of police, Dean Esserman, decided to revise the selection process, which caused some of those who had received the letter to be rejected. Derek Ardito and thirteen other newly rejected applicants filed a suit in a federal district court against the city, seeking a halt to the 61st Academy unless they were allowed to attend. They alleged in part that the city was in breach of contract.

IN THE WORDS OF THE COURT . . .
ERNEST C. TORRES, Chief District Judge.

* * * *

* * * *[T]he October 15 letter* * * * *is a classic example of an offer to enter into a unilateral contract.* The October 15 letter expressly stated that it was a "conditional offer of employment" and the message that it conveyed was that the recipient would be admitted into the 61st Academy if he or she successfully completed the medical and psychological examinations, requirements that the City could not lawfully impose unless it was making a conditional offer of employment. [Emphasis added.]

Moreover, the terms of that offer were perfectly consistent with what applicants had been told when they appeared [for their interviews]. At that time, [Police Major

CASE 8.1—Continued

Dennis] Simoneau informed them that, if they "passed" the [interviews], they would be offered a place in the Academy provided that they also passed medical and psychological examinations.

The October 15 letter also was in marked contrast to notices sent to applicants by the City at earlier stages of the selection process. Those notices merely informed applicants that they had completed a step in the process and remained eligible to be considered for admission into the Academy. Unlike the October 15 letter, the prior notices did not purport to extend a "conditional offer" of admission.

The plaintiffs accepted the City's offer of admission into the Academy by satisfying the specified conditions. Each of the plaintiffs submitted to and passed lengthy and intrusive medical and psychological examinations. In addition, many of the plaintiffs, in reliance on the City's offer, jeopardized their standing with their existing employers by notifying the employers of their anticipated departure, and some plaintiffs passed up opportunities for other employment.

* * * *

The City argues that there is no contract between the parties because the plaintiffs have no legally enforceable right to employment. The City correctly points out that, even if the plaintiffs graduate from the Academy and there are existing vacancies in the Department, they would be required to serve a one-year probationary period during which they could be terminated without cause * * * . That argument misses the point. The contract that the plaintiffs seek to enforce is not a contract that they will be appointed as permanent Providence police officers; rather, it is a contract that they would be admitted to the Academy if they passed the medical and psychological examinations.

DECISION AND REMEDY The court issued an injunction to prohibit the city from conducting the 61st Police Academy unless the plaintiffs were included. The October 15 letter was a unilateral offer that the plaintiffs had accepted by passing the required medical and psychological examinations.

FOR CRITICAL ANALYSIS—Social Consideration *How might the city have phrased the October 15 letter to avoid its being considered a unilateral contract?*

Revocation of Offers for Unilateral Contracts. A problem arises in unilateral contracts when the promisor attempts to *revoke* (cancel) the offer after the promisee has begun performance but before the act has been completed. ■ EXAMPLE 8.2 Suppose that Roberta offers to buy Ed's sailboat, moored in San Francisco, on delivery of the boat to Roberta's dock in Newport Beach, three hundred miles south of San Francisco. Ed rigs the boat and sets sail. Shortly before his arrival at Newport Beach, Ed receives a radio message from Roberta withdrawing her offer. Roberta's offer is an offer for a unilateral contract, and only Ed's delivery of the sailboat at her dock is an acceptance. ■

> **on the Web** For easy-to-understand definitions of legal terms and concepts, including terms and concepts relating to contract law, go to
> **http://dictionary.law.com**
> and key in a term, such as *contract* or *consideration.*

In contract law, offers are normally *revocable* (capable of being taken back, or canceled) until accepted. Under the traditional view of unilateral contracts, Roberta's revocation would terminate the offer. Because of the harsh effect on the offeree of the revocation of an offer to form a unilateral contract, the modern-day view is that once performance has been *substantially* undertaken, the offeror cannot revoke the offer. Thus, in our example, even though Ed has not yet accepted the offer by complete performance, Roberta is prohibited from revoking it. Ed can deliver the boat and bind Roberta to the contract.

FORMAL CONTRACT
A contract that by law requires a specific form, such as being executed under seal, to be valid.

Formal versus Informal Contracts Contracts that require a special form or method of creation (formation) to be enforceable are known as **formal contracts.** Formal contracts include (1) contracts under seal, (2) recognizances, (3) negotiable instruments, and (4) letters of credit.[2]

Contracts under seal are formalized writings with a special seal attached.[3] The significance of the seal has lessened, although about ten states require no consideration for formation of a valid contract when a contract is under seal. A *recognizance* is an acknowledgment in court by a person that he or she will perform some specified obligation or pay a certain sum if he or she fails to perform. One form of recognizance is the surety bond.[4] Another is the personal recognizance bond used as bail in a criminal matter. As will be discussed at length in subsequent chapters, *negotiable instruments* include checks, notes, drafts, and certificates of deposit; letters of credit are agreements to pay contingent on the purchaser's receipt of invoices and bills of lading (documents evidencing receipt of, and title to, goods shipped).

KEEP IN MIND Not every contract is a document with "Contract" printed in block letters at the top. A contract can be expressed in a letter, a memo, or another document.

INFORMAL CONTRACT
A contract that does not require a specified form or formality to be valid.

Informal contracts (also called *simple contracts*) include all other contracts. No special form is required (except for certain types of contracts that must be in writing), as the contracts are usually based on their substance rather than their form. Typically, businesspersons put their contracts in writing to ensure that there is some proof of a contract's existence should problems arise.

Express versus Implied Contracts Contracts may also be formed and categorized as express or implied by the conduct of the parties. We look here at the differences between these two types of contracts.

2. *Restatement (Second) of Contracts,* Section 6.
3. A seal may be actual (made of wax or some other durable substance), impressed on the paper, or indicated simply by the word *seal* or the letters *L.S.* at the end of the document. *L.S.* stands for *locus sigilli,* which means "the place for the seal."
4. An obligation of a party who guarantees that he or she will pay a second party if a third party does not perform.

What determines whether a contract for accounting, tax preparation, or any other service is an express contract or an implied-in-fact contract? (© Getty Images)

EXPRESS CONTRACT
A contract in which the terms of the agreement are stated in words, oral or written.

Express Contracts. An **express contract** is one in which the terms of the agreement are fully and explicitly stated in words, oral or written. A signed lease for an apartment or a house is an express written contract. If a classmate accepts your offer to sell your textbooks from last semester for $75, an express oral contract has been made.

IMPLIED-IN-FACT CONTRACT
A contract formed in whole or in part from the conduct of the parties (as opposed to an express contract).

Implied Contracts. A contract that is implied from the conduct of the parties is called an **implied-in-fact contract,** or an implied contract. This type of contract differs from an express contract in that the *conduct* of the parties, rather than their words, creates and defines at least some of the terms of the contract.

■ EXAMPLE 8.3 Suppose that you need an accountant to fill out your tax return this year. You look through the Yellow Pages and find an accounting firm located in your neighborhood. You drop by the firm's office, explain your problem to an accountant, and learn what fees will be charged. The next day you return and give the receptionist all of the necessary information and documents, such as canceled checks, W-2 forms, and so on. Then you walk out the door without saying anything expressly to the receptionist. In this situation, you have entered into an implied-in-fact contract to pay the accountant the usual and reasonable fees for the accounting services. The contract is implied by your conduct. The accountant expects to be paid for completing your tax return. By bringing in the records the accountant will need to do the work, you have implied an intent to pay for the services. ■ (For another example of how an implied-in-fact contract can arise, see this chapter's *Management Perspective* feature on the following page.)

Requirements for an Implied-in-Fact Contract. For an implied-in-fact contract to arise, certain requirements must be met. Normally, if the following conditions exist, a court will hold that an implied contract was formed:

1. The plaintiff furnished some service or property.
2. The plaintiff expected to be paid for that service or property, and the defendant knew or should have known that payment was expected (by using the objective-theory-of-contracts test, discussed previously).
3. The defendant had a chance to reject the services or property and did not.

CONTRACT PERFORMANCE

EXECUTED CONTRACT
A contract that has been completely performed by both parties.

EXECUTORY CONTRACT
A contract that has not yet been fully performed.

Contracts are also classified according to their state of performance. A contract that has been fully performed on both sides is called an **executed contract.** A contract that has not been fully performed is called an **executory contract.** If one party has fully performed but the other has not, the contract is said to be executed on the one side and executory on the other, but the contract is still classified as executory.

■ EXAMPLE 8.4 Assume that you agree to buy ten tons of coal from Western Coal Company. Further assume that Western has delivered the coal to your steel mill, where it is now being burned. At this point, the contract is an executory contract—it is executed on the part of Western and executory on your part. After you pay Western for the coal, the contract will be executed on both sides. ■

CONTRACT ENFORCEABILITY

VALID CONTRACT
A contract that results when the elements necessary for contract formation (agreement, consideration, legal purpose, and contractual capacity) are present.

A **valid contract** has the four elements necessary for contract formation: (1) an agreement (offer and acceptance) (2) supported by legally sufficient consideration (3) for a legal purpose and (4) made by parties who have the legal capacity to enter

MANAGEMENT PERSPECTIVE

Employment Manuals and Implied Contracts

MANAGEMENT FACES A LEGAL ISSUE

It is a common practice today for large companies or other organizations to create and distribute to their employees an employment manual, or handbook, setting forth the conditions of employment. Yet when drafting and distributing such manuals to employees, business owners and managers must consider the following question: Will statements made in an employee handbook constitute "promises" in an implied-in-fact employment contract?

WHAT THE COURTS SAY

Increasingly, courts are holding that promises made in an employment manual may create an implied-in-fact employment contract. For example, if an employment handbook states that employees will only be fired for "good cause," the employer may be held to that promise.

This is possible even if, under state law, employment is "at will." Under the employment-at-will doctrine, employers may hire and terminate employees at will, with or without cause. The at-will doctrine will not apply, however, if the terms of employment are subject to a contract between the employer and the employee. If a court holds that an implied employment contract exists, on the basis of promises made in an employment manual, the employer will be bound by the contract and liable for damages for breaching the contract.[a]

IMPLICATIONS FOR MANAGERS

To avoid being contractually bound by terms in an employment manual, you should avoid making definite statements (such as "employees will only be terminated for good cause") that would cause employees to reasonably believe that those statements are contractual promises. You should also inform employees, when initially giving them the handbook or discussing its contents with them, that it is not intended as a contract. A conspicuous written disclaimer to this effect should also be included in the employment manual. The disclaimer might read as follows: "This policy manual describes the basic personnel policies and practices of our Company. You should understand that the manual does not modify our Company's 'at will' employment doctrine or provide employees with any kind of contractual rights."

a. See, for example, *Cisco v. King,* ___ S.W.3d ___ (Ark.App. 2005).

into the contract. As mentioned, we will discuss each of these elements in the following chapters. As you can see in Exhibit 8–2, valid contracts may be enforceable, voidable, or unenforceable. Additionally, a contract may be referred to as a *void contract.* We look next at the meaning of the terms *voidable, unenforceable,* and *void* in relation to contract enforceability.

VOIDABLE CONTRACT
A contract that may be legally avoided (canceled, or annulled) at the option of one or both of the parties.

Voidable Contracts A **voidable contract** is a *valid* contract but one that can be avoided at the option of one or both of the parties. The party having the option can elect either to avoid any duty to perform or to *ratify* (make valid) the contract. If the contract is avoided, both parties are released from it. If it is ratified, both parties must fully perform their respective legal obligations.

As you will read in Chapter 11, contracts made by minors, insane persons, and intoxicated persons may be voidable. As a general rule, for example, contracts made by minors are voidable at the option of the minor. Additionally, contracts entered into under fraudulent conditions are voidable at the option of the defrauded party.

EXHIBIT 8–2 ENFORCEABLE, VOID, VOIDABLE, AND UNENFORCEABLE CONTRACTS

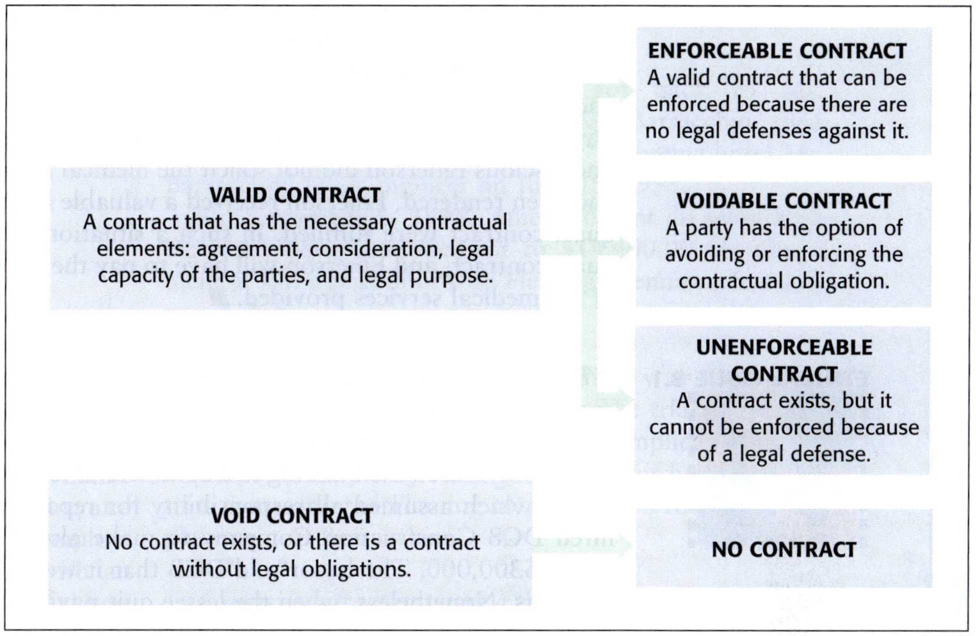

Contracts entered into under legally defined duress or undue influence are voidable (see Chapter 12).

UNENFORCEABLE CONTRACT
A valid contract rendered unenforceable by some statute or law.

Unenforceable Contracts An **unenforceable contract** is one that cannot be enforced because of certain legal defenses against it. It is not unenforceable because a party failed to satisfy a legal requirement of the contract; rather, it is a valid contract rendered unenforceable by some statute or law. For example, some contracts must be in writing (see Chapter 13), and if they are not, they will not be enforceable except in certain exceptional circumstances.

VOID CONTRACT
A contract having no legal force or binding effect.

Void Contracts A **void contract** is no contract at all. The terms *void* and *contract* are contradictory. None of the parties has any legal obligations if a contract is void. A contract can be void because, for example, one of the parties was previously determined by a court to be legally insane (and thus lacked the legal capacity to enter into a contract) or because the purpose of the contract was illegal.

Quasi Contracts

QUASI CONTRACT
A fictional contract imposed on parties by a court in the interests of fairness and justice; usually imposed to avoid the unjust enrichment of one party at the expense of another.

Quasi contracts, or contracts *implied in law,* are wholly different from actual contracts. Express contracts and implied-in-fact contracts are actual, or true, contracts. The word *quasi* is Latin for "as if" or "analogous to." Quasi contracts are thus not true contracts. They do not arise from any agreement, express or implied, between the parties themselves. Rather, quasi contracts are fictional contracts imposed on parties by courts writing. Judges and clients are also pressuring lawyers to make legal concepts and documents more comprehensible. At times, judges have refused to accept motions that are incoherent due to their highly technical legal language.

In some jurisdictions, judges themselves are being asked to write their opinions more clearly. For example, the chief judge of New York's highest court has encouraged judges in the New York court system to issue clearly written rulings so that other judges, lawyers, lawmakers, and everyone affected by the decisions will know what they mean.

The Plain Meaning Rule

When the terms of a written contract are clear and unequivocal, a court will enforce the contract according to its plain terms (what is clearly stated in the contract), and there is no need for the court to interpret the language of the contract. The meaning of the terms must be determined from *the face of the instrument*—from the written document alone. This is sometimes referred to as the *plain meaning rule.*

NOTE No one can avoid contractual obligations by claiming that she or he did not read the contract. A contract is interpreted as if each party read every word carefully.

Under the plain meaning rule, if a contract's words appear to be clear and unambiguous, a court cannot consider *extrinsic evidence,* which is any evidence not contained in the document itself. Admissibility of extrinsic evidence can significantly affect how a court interprets ambiguous contractual provisions and thus can affect the outcome of litigation.

Other Rules of Interpretation

When a court finds that there is a need to determine the parties' intentions from the terms of the contract, it will interpret the language to give effect to the parties' intent as *expressed in their contract.* This is the primary purpose of the rules of interpretation—to determine the parties' intent from the language used in their agreement and to give effect to that intent. A court normally will not make or remake a contract, nor will it normally interpret the language according to what the parties *claim* their intent was when they made the contract.[8] The courts use the following rules in interpreting contractual terms:

1. Insofar as possible, a reasonable, lawful, and effective meaning will be given to all of a contract's terms.
2. A contract will be interpreted as a whole; individual, specific clauses will be considered subordinate to the contract's general intent. All writings that are a part of the same transaction will be interpreted together.
3. Terms that were the subject of separate negotiation will be given greater consideration than standardized terms and terms that were not negotiated separately.
4. A word will be given its ordinary, commonly accepted meaning, and a technical word or term will be given its technical meaning, unless the parties clearly intended something else.
5. Specific and exact wording will be given greater consideration than general language.
6. Written or typewritten terms prevail over preprinted terms.

"How many a dispute could have been deflated into a single paragraph if the disputants had dared define their terms."

ARISTOTLE,
384–322 B.C.E.
(Greek philosopher)

8. Nevertheless, if a court finds that even after applying the rules of interpretation the terms are susceptible to more than one meaning, the court may permit extrinsic evidence to prove what the parties intended. See, for example, *Langdon v. United Restaurants, Inc.,* 105 S.W.3d 882 (Mo.Ct.App. 2003).

7 Because a contract should be drafted in clear and unambiguous language, a party that uses ambiguous expressions is held to be responsible for the ambiguities. Thus, when the language has more than one meaning, it will be interpreted *against* the party that drafted the contract.

8 Evidence of *usage of trade, course of dealing,* and *course of performance* may be admitted to clarify the meaning of an ambiguously worded contract. (We define and discuss these terms in Chapter 18.) What each of the parties does pursuant to the contract will be interpreted as consistent with what the other does and with any relevant usage of trade and course of dealing or performance. Express terms (terms expressly stated in the contract) are given the greatest weight, followed by course of performance, course of dealing, and custom and usage of trade—in that order. When considering custom and usage, a court will look at the trade customs and usage common to the particular business or industry and to the locale in which the contract was made or is to be performed.

In the following case, the ordinary meaning of a word was at the heart of a significant dispute.

CASE 8.3 Citizens Communications Co. v. Trustmark Insurance

United States District Court,
District of Connecticut, 2004.
303 F.Supp.2d 197.

BACKGROUND AND FACTS Citizens Communications Company is the seventh largest telephone company in the United States, with assets of nearly $7 billion. Citizens provides health insurance to its nearly five thousand employees under a self-funded health plan. Under such a plan, a company normally buys an insurance policy to cover claims that exceed a certain amount. Citizens bought a policy from Trustmark Insurance to cover claims that exceeded $100,000, subject to a $1 million maximum benefit per employee. In November 1999, Garry Lonquist, a Citizens employee, experienced complications from heart surgery that required intensive care. By January, Lonquist's medical bills exceeded $1 million. Trustmark refused to renew Citizens' policy unless, among other things, it included an amendment providing a separate $1 million deductible for Lonquist, effectively removing him from coverage. This amendment was referred to as the "Lonquist Laser." Citizens accepted this offer in a letter dated March 6, 2000. Later, Citizens filed a suit in a federal district court against Trustmark and others, seeking damages and other relief for an alleged breach of contract. Citizens claimed in part that the "Lonquist Laser" was not valid. Both parties filed motions for summary judgment.

(Continued)

CASE 8.3—Continued

IN THE WORDS OF THE COURT . . .
KRAVITZ, D.J. [District Judge]

* * * *

There seems to be no dispute that the March 6 agreement between Citizens and Trustmark, in which the parties agreed upon the premium for the policy renewal and also agreed upon the Lonquist Laser, ordinarily would constitute a valid contract. The standard for creating a contract is well settled. *To form a valid and binding contract in Connecticut, there must be a mutual understanding of the terms that are definite and certain between the parties.* * * * *If the minds of the parties have not truly met, no enforceable contract exists.* Here, there was an offer by Trustmark, an acceptance by Citizens, intent by the parties to form a contract, a meeting of the minds about its terms, definite terms, and consideration. Under traditional contract principles, therefore, the March 6 agreement unquestionably would qualify as a valid amendment to the existing insurance contract between the parties. [Emphasis added.]

* * * *

* * * Both sides agree that an agreement was reached and what that agreement specifies. The sole point of contention is whether the agreement constitutes a valid amendment under the terms of the insurance policy. * * * Although the policy defines many of its terms, it does not define the term "amendment"; nor does anything in the policy specify precisely what an amendment must look like, other than that it must be approved by Trustmark and signed by Citizens, both of which occurred here.

DECISION AND REMEDY The court granted Trustmark's motion for summary judgment. The insurance policy did not define *amendment* specifically, so the court referred to a dictionary's definition of the word: "a change made by correction, addition, or deletion." Both parties signed and approved the "Lonquist Laser" change, and under the plain language of the contract, it was a valid and enforceable amendment.

FOR CRITICAL ANALYSIS—Social Consideration *What might the parties have done to avoid this litigation?*

REVIEWING NATURE AND CLASSIFICATION

Grant Borman, who was engaged in a construction project, leased a crane from Allied Equipment and hired Crosstown Trucking Company to deliver the crane to the construction site. Crosstown, while the crane was in its possession and without permission from either Borman or Allied Equipment, used the crane to install a transformer for a utility company, which paid Crosstown for the job. Crosstown then delivered the crane to Borman's construction site at the appointed time of delivery. When Allied Equipment learned of the unauthorized use of the crane by Crosstown, it sued Crosstown for damages, seeking to recover the rental value of Crosstown's use of the crane. Using the information presented in the chapter, answer the following questions.

1. What are the four requirements of a valid contract?
2. Did Crosstown have a valid contract with Borman concerning the use of the crane? If so, was it a bilateral or a unilateral contract? Explain.
3. What are the requirements of an implied-in-fact contract? Can Allied Equipment obtain damages from Crosstown based on an implied-in-fact contract? Explain.
4. Should a court impose a quasi contract on the parties in this situation to allow Allied to recover damages from Crosstown? Why or why not?

KEY TERMS

bilateral contract 231
contract 229
executed contract 235
executory contract 235
express contract 235
formal contract 234
implied-in-fact contract 235
informal contract 234
objective theory of contracts 230
offeree 231
offeror 231
promise 228
promisee 229
promisor 229
quasi contract 237
unenforceable contract 237
unilateral contract 232
valid contract 235
void contract 237
voidable contract 236

CHAPTER SUMMARY Nature and Classification

The Function of Contracts (See page 229.)	Contract law establishes what kinds of promises will be legally binding and supplies procedures for enforcing legally binding promises, or agreements.
Definition of a Contract (See pages 229–230.)	A contract is an agreement that can be enforced in court. It is formed by two or more competent parties who agree to perform or to refrain from performing some act now or in the future.
Requirements of a Contract (See page 230.)	1. *Elements of a valid contract*—Agreement, consideration, contractual capacity, and legality. 2. *Possible defenses to the enforcement of a contract*—Genuineness of assent and form.
Types of Contracts (See pages 231–237.)	1. *Bilateral*—A promise for a promise. 2. *Unilateral*—A promise for an act (acceptance is the completed—or substantial—performance of the contract by the offeree). 3. *Formal*—Requires a special form for contract formation. 4. *Informal*—Requires no special form for contract formation. 5. *Express*—Formed by words (oral, written, or a combination). 6. *Implied in fact*—Formed at least in part by the conduct of the parties. 7. *Executed*—A fully performed contract. 8. *Executory*—A contract not yet fully performed. 9. *Valid*—A contract that has the necessary contractual elements of offer and acceptance, consideration, parties with legal capacity, and having been made for a legal purpose. 10. *Voidable*—A contract in which a party has the option of avoiding or enforcing the contractual obligation. 11. *Unenforceable*—A valid contract that cannot be enforced because of a legal defense. 12. *Void*—No contract exists, or there is a contract without legal obligations.
Quasi Contracts (See pages 237–240.)	A quasi contract, or a contract implied in law, is a contract that is imposed by law to prevent unjust enrichment.
Interpretation of Contracts (See pages 240–244.)	Increasingly, plain language laws are requiring private contracts to be written in plain language so that the terms are clear and understandable to the parties. Under the plain meaning rule, a court will enforce the contract according to its plain terms, the meaning of which must be determined from the written document alone. Other rules applied by the court when interpreting contracts include the following: 1. A reasonable, lawful, and effective meaning will be given to all contract terms.

(Continued)

CHAPTER SUMMARY Nature and Classification—Continued

Interpretation of Contracts—Continued (See pages 240–244.)	2. A contract will be interpreted as a whole, specific clauses will be considered subordinate to the contract's general intent, and all writings that are a part of the same transaction will be interpreted together. 3. Terms that were negotiated separately will be given greater consideration than standardized terms and terms not negotiated separately. 4. Words will be given their commonly accepted meanings and technical words their technical meanings, unless the parties clearly intended otherwise. 5. Specific wording will be given greater consideration than general language. 6. Written or typewritten terms prevail over preprinted terms. 7. A party that uses ambiguous expressions is held to be responsible for the ambiguities. 8. Evidence of course of dealing, course of performance, or usage of trade is admissible to clarify an ambiguously worded contract. In these circumstances, express terms are given the greatest weight, followed by course of performance, course of dealing, and custom and usage of trade—in that order.

FOR REVIEW

Answers for the even-numbered questions in this For Review *section can be found on this text's accompanying Web site at* http://blt.westbuslaw.com. *Select "Chapter 8" and click on "For Review."*

1 What is a contract? What is the objective theory of contracts?

2 What are the four basic elements necessary to the formation of a valid contract?

3 What is the difference between an implied-in-fact contract and an implied-in-law contract (quasi contract)?

4 How does a void contract differ from a voidable contract? What is an unenforceable contract?

5 Why have plain language laws been enacted? What rules guide the courts in interpreting contracts?

QUESTIONS AND CASE PROBLEMS

8–1. Express versus Implied Contracts. Suppose that a local businessperson, McDougal, is a good friend of Krunch, the owner of a local candy store. Every day on his lunch hour McDougal goes into Krunch's candy store and spends about five minutes looking at the candy. After examining Krunch's candy and talking with Krunch, McDougal usually buys one or two candy bars. One afternoon, McDougal goes into Krunch's candy shop, looks at the candy, and picks up a $1 candy bar. Seeing that Krunch is very busy, he catches Krunch's eye, waves the candy bar at Krunch without saying a word, and walks out. Is there a contract? If so, classify it within the categories presented in this chapter.

8–2. Contractual Promises. Rosalie, a wealthy widow, invited an acquaintance, Jonathan, to her home for dinner. Jonathan accepted the offer and, eager to please her, spent lavishly in preparing for the evening. His purchases included a new blazer, new shoes, an expensive floral arrangement, and champagne. At the appointed time, Jonathan arrived at Rosalie's house only to find that she had left for the evening. Jonathan wants to sue Rosalie to recover some of his expenses. Can he? Why or why not?

8–3. Contract Classification. High-Flying Advertising, Inc., contracted with Big Burger Restaurants to fly an advertisement above the Connecticut beaches. The advertisement offered $5,000 to any person who could swim from the Connecticut beaches to Long Island across Long Island Sound in less than a day. McElfresh saw the streamer and accepted the challenge. He started his marathon swim that same day at 10 A.M. After he had been swimming for four hours and was about halfway across the sound, McElfresh saw another plane pulling a streamer that read, "Big Burger revokes." Is there a contract between McElfresh and Big Burger? If there is a contract, what type(s) of contract is (are) formed?

8–4. Implied Contract. Thomas Rinks and Joseph Shields developed Psycho Chihuahua, a caricature of a Chihuahua dog with a "do-not-back-down" attitude. They promoted and marketed the character through their company, Wrench, L.L.C. Ed Alfaro and Rudy Pollak, representatives of Taco Bell Corp., learned of Psycho Chihuahua and met with Rinks and Shields to talk about using the character as a Taco Bell "icon." Wrench sent artwork, merchandise, and marketing ideas to Alfaro, who promoted the character within Taco Bell. Alfaro asked Wrench to propose terms for Taco Bell's use of Psycho Chihuahua. Taco Bell did not accept Wrench's terms, but Alfaro continued to promote the character within the company. Meanwhile, Taco Bell hired a new advertising agency, which proposed an advertising campaign involving a Chihuahua. When Alfaro learned of this proposal, he sent the Psycho Chihuahua materials to the agency. Taco Bell made a Chihuahua the focus of its marketing but paid nothing to Wrench. Wrench filed a suit against Taco Bell in a federal district court, claiming in part that it had an implied contract with Taco Bell, which the latter breached. Do these facts satisfy the requirements for an implied contract? Why or why not? [*Wrench L.L.C. v. Taco Bell Corp.*, 256 F.3d 446 (6th Cir. 2001)]

CASE PROBLEM WITH SAMPLE ANSWER

8–5. Professor Dixon was an adjunct professor at Tulsa Community College (TCC) in Tulsa, Oklahoma. Each semester, near the beginning of the term, the parties executed a written contract that always included the following provision: "It is agreed that this agreement may be cancelled by the Administration or the instructor at anytime before the first class session." In the spring semester of Dixon's seventh year, he filed a complaint with TCC alleging that one of his students, Meredith Bhuiyan, had engaged in disruptive classroom conduct. He gave her an incomplete grade and asked TCC to require her to apologize as a condition of receiving a final grade. TCC later claimed, and Dixon denied, that he was told to assign Bhuiyan a grade if he wanted to teach in the fall. Toward the end of the semester, Dixon was told which classes he would teach in the fall, but the parties did not sign a written contract. The Friday before classes began, TCC terminated him. Dixon filed a suit in an Oklahoma state court against TCC and others, alleging breach of contract. Did the parties have a contract? If so, did TCC breach it? Explain. [*Dixon v. Bhuiyan*, 10 P.3d 888 (Okla. 2000)]

After you have answered this problem, compare your answer with the sample answer given on the Web site that accompanies this text. Go to http://blt.westbuslaw.com, select "Chapter 8," and click on "Case Problem with Sample Answer."

8–6. Bilateral versus Unilateral Contracts. D.L. Peoples Group (D.L.) placed an ad in a Missouri newspaper to recruit admissions representatives, who were hired to recruit Missouri residents to attend D.L.'s college in Florida. Donald Hawley responded to the ad, his interviewer recommended him for the job, and he signed, in Missouri, an "Admissions Representative Agreement," which was mailed to D.L.'s president, who signed it in his office in Florida. The agreement provided in part that Hawley would devote exclusive time and effort to the business in his assigned territory in Missouri and that D.L. would pay Hawley a commission if he successfully recruited students for the school. While attempting to make one of his first calls on his new job, Hawley was accidentally shot and killed. On the basis of his death, a claim was filed in Florida for workers' compensation. (Under Florida law, when an accident occurs outside Florida, workers' compensation benefits are payable only if the employment contract was made in Florida.) Is this admissions representative agreement a bilateral or a unilateral contract? What are the consequences of the distinction in this case? Explain. [*D.L. Peoples Group, Inc. v. Hawley*, 804 So.2d 561 (Fla.App. 1 Dist. 2002)]

8–7. Interpretation of Contracts. East Mill Associates (EMA) was developing residential "units" in East Brunswick, New Jersey, within the service area of the East Brunswick Sewerage Authority (EBSA). The sewer system required an upgrade to the Ryder's Lane Pumping Station to accommodate the new units. EMA agreed to pay "fifty-five percent (55%) of the total cost" of the upgrade. At the time, the estimated cost to EMA was $150,000 to $200,000. Impediments to the project arose, however, substantially increasing the cost. Among other things, the pumping station had to be moved to accommodate a widened road nearby. The upgrade was delayed for almost three years. When it was completed, EBSA asked EMA for $340,022.12, which represented 55 percent of the total cost. EMA did not pay. EBSA filed a suit in a New Jersey state court against EMA for breach of contract. What rule should the court apply to interpret the parties' contract? How should that rule be applied? Why? [*East Brunswick Sewerage Authority v. East Mill Associates, Inc.*, 365 N.J.Super. 120, 838 A.2d 494 (A.D. 2004)]

FOR CRITICAL ANALYSIS

8–8. Review the list of basic requirements for contract formation given at the beginning of this chapter. In view of those requirements, analyze the relationship entered into when a student enrolls in a college or university. Has a contract been formed? If so, is it a bilateral contract or a unilateral contract? Discuss.

VIDEO QUESTION

8–9. Go to this text's Web site at http://blt.westbuslaw.com and select "Chapter 8." Click on "Video Questions" and view the video titled *Bowfinger.* Then answer the following questions.

1. In the video, Renfro (Robert Downey, Jr.) says to Bowfinger (Steve Martin), "You bring me this script and Kit Ramsey and you've got yourself a 'go' picture."

Assume for the purposes of this question that their agreement is a contract. Is the contract bilateral or unilateral? Is it express or implied? Is it formal or informal? Is it executed or executory? Explain your answers.

2. What criteria would a court rely on to interpret the terms of the contract?
3. Recall from the video that the contract between Bowfinger and the producer was oral. Suppose that a statute requires contracts of this type to be in writing. In that situation, would the contract be void, voidable, or unenforceable? Explain.

INTERNET EXERCISES

Go to the *Business Law Today* home page at **http://blt.westbuslaw.com**, select "Chapter 8," and click on "Internet Exercises." There you will find the following Internet research exercises that you can perform to learn more about topics covered in this chapter.

Activity 8–1: LEGAL PERSPECTIVE—Contracts and Contract Provisions

Activity 8–2: MANAGEMENT PERSPECTIVE—Implied Employment Contracts

Activity 8–3: HISTORICAL PERSPECTIVE—Contracts in Ancient Mesopotamia

BEFORE THE TEST

Go to the *Business Law Today* home page at **http://blt.westbuslaw.com**, select "Chapter 8," and click on "Interactive Quizzes." You will find a number of interactive questions relating to this chapter.

CHAPTER 9

Agreement

"It is necessity that makes laws."

Voltaire, 1694–1778
(French philosopher and writer)

CHAPTER OUTLINE

- REQUIREMENTS OF THE OFFER
- TERMINATION OF THE OFFER
- ACCEPTANCE

LEARNING OBJECTIVES

After reading this chapter, you should be able to answer the following questions:

1. What elements are necessary for an effective offer?
2. What are some examples of nonoffers?
3. In what circumstances will an offer be irrevocable?
4. What elements are necessary for an effective acceptance?
5. Can silence ever operate as an acceptance?

Voltaire's statement that it is "necessity that makes laws" is certainly true in regard to contracts. In Chapter 8, we pointed out that promises and agreements, and the knowledge that some of those promises and agreements will be legally enforced, are essential to civilized society. The homes we live in, the food we eat, the clothes we wear, the cars we drive, the books we read, the videos and recordings we watch and listen to—all of these have been purchased through contractual agreements. Contract law developed over time, through the common law tradition, to meet society's need to know with certainty what kinds of promises, or contracts, will be enforced and the point at which a valid and binding contract is formed.

AGREEMENT
A meeting of two or more minds in regard to the terms of a contract; usually broken down into two events—an offer by one party to form a contract, and an acceptance of the offer by the person to whom the offer is made.

For a contract to be considered valid and enforceable, the requirements listed in Chapter 8 must be met. In this chapter, we look closely at one of these requirements, *agreement*. **Agreement** is an essential element for contract formation. The parties must agree on the terms of the contract. Ordinarily, agreement is evidenced by two events: an *offer* and an *acceptance*. One party offers a certain bargain to another party, who then accepts that bargain. Because words often fail to convey the precise meaning intended, the law of contracts generally adheres to the *objective theory of contracts,* as discussed in Chapter 8. Under this theory, a party's words and conduct are held to mean whatever a reasonable person in the offeree's position would think they meant. The court will give words their usual meanings even if "it were proved by twenty bishops that [the] party . . . intended something else."[1]

As you read through this chapter, keep in mind that the requirement of agreement applies to all contracts, regardless of how they are formed. Many contracts continue to be formed in the traditional way—through the exchange of paper documents. Increasingly, contracts are also being formed online—through the exchange of electronic messages or documents. Although we discuss online contracts to a limited extent in this chapter, we will look at them more closely in Chapter 17.

Requirements of the Offer

OFFER
A promise or commitment to perform or refrain from performing some specified act in the future.

An **offer** is a promise or commitment to perform or refrain from performing some specified act in the future. As discussed in Chapter 8, the party making an offer is called the *offeror,* and the party to whom the offer is made is called the *offeree.*

Three elements are necessary for an offer to be effective:

1. There must be a serious, objective intention by the offeror.
2. The terms of the offer must be reasonably certain, or definite, so that the parties and the court can ascertain the terms of the contract.
3. The offer must be communicated to the offeree.

Essentially, the requirements for traditional offers apply to online offers as well, as you will read in Chapter 17. Once an effective offer has been made, the offeree's acceptance of that offer creates a legally binding contract (providing the other essential elements for a valid and enforceable contract are present).

Intention

The first requirement for an effective offer to exist is a serious, objective intention on the part of the offeror. Intent is not determined by the *subjective* intentions, beliefs, or assumptions of the offeror. Rather, it is determined by what a reasonable person in the offeree's position would conclude the offeror's words and actions meant. Offers made in obvious anger, jest, or undue excitement do not meet the serious-and-objective-intent test. Because these offers are not effective, an offeree's acceptance does not create an agreement.

■ **Example 9.1** You and three classmates ride to school each day in Julio's new automobile, which has a market value of $18,000. One cold morning the four of you get into the car, but Julio cannot get it started. He yells in anger, "I'll sell this car to anyone for $500!" You drop $500 in his lap. A reasonable person, taking into consideration Julio's frustration and the obvious difference in value between the car's market price and the purchase price, would declare that Julio's offer was not made with serious and objective intent and that you do not have an agreement. ■

1. Judge Learned Hand in *Hotchkiss v. National City Bank of New York,* 200 F. 287 (2d Cir. 1911); aff'd 231 U.S. 50, 34 S.Ct. 20, 58 L.Ed. 115 (1913). (The term *aff'd* is an abbreviation for *affirmed;* an appellate court can affirm a lower court's judgment, decree, or order, thereby declaring that it is valid and must stand as rendered.)

In the subsections that follow, we examine the concept of intention further as we look at the distinctions between offers and nonoffers. *Lucy v. Zehmer,* presented below, is a classic case in the area of contractual agreement. The case involved a business transaction in which boasts, brags, and dares "after a few drinks" resulted in a contract to sell certain property. The sellers claimed that the offer had been made in jest and that, in any event, the contract was voidable at their option because they were intoxicated when the offer was made and thus lacked contractual capacity (see Chapter 11). The court, however, looked to the words and actions of the parties—not their secret intentions—to determine whether a contract had been formed.

LANDMARK AND CLASSIC CASES

CASE 9.1 Lucy v. Zehmer

Supreme Court of Appeals of Virginia, 1954.
196 Va. 493,
84 S.E.2d 516.

BACKGROUND AND FACTS Lucy and Zehmer had known each other for fifteen to twenty years. For some time, Lucy had been wanting to buy Zehmer's farm. Zehmer had always told Lucy that he was not interested in selling. One night, Lucy stopped in to visit with the Zehmers at a restaurant they operated. Lucy said to Zehmer, "I bet you wouldn't take $50,000 for that place." Zehmer replied, "Yes, I would, too; you wouldn't give fifty." Throughout the evening, the conversation returned to the sale of the farm. At the same time, the parties were drinking whiskey. Eventually, Zehmer wrote up an agreement, on the back of a restaurant check, for the sale of the farm, and he asked his wife to sign it—which she did. When Lucy brought an action in a Virginia state court to enforce the agreement, Zehmer argued that he had been "high as a Georgia pine" at the time and that the offer had been made in jest: "two doggoned drunks bluffing to see who could talk the biggest and say the most." Lucy claimed that he had not been intoxicated and did not think Zehmer had been, either, given the way Zehmer handled the transaction. The trial court ruled in favor of the Zehmers, and Lucy appealed.

IN THE WORDS OF THE COURT . . .

BUCHANAN, J. [Justice] delivered the opinion of the court.

* * * *

The appearance of the contract, the fact that it was under discussion for forty minutes or more before it was signed; Lucy's objection to the first draft because it was written in the singular, and he wanted Mrs. Zehmer to sign it also; the rewriting to meet that objection and the signing by Mrs. Zehmer; the discussion of what was to be included in the sale, the provision for the examination of the title, the completeness of the instrument that was executed, the taking possession of it by Lucy with no request or suggestion by either of the defendants that he give it back, are facts which furnish persuasive evidence that the execution of the contract was a serious business transaction rather than a casual, jesting matter as defendants now contend.

* * * *

In the field of contracts, as generally elsewhere, "*We must look to the outward expression of a person as manifesting his intention rather than to his secret and unexpressed intention.* 'The law imputes to a person an intention corresponding to the reasonable meaning of his words and acts.' " [Emphasis added.]

DECISION AND REMEDY The Supreme Court of Virginia determined that the writing was an enforceable contract and reversed the ruling of the lower court. The Zehmers were required by court order to carry through with the sale of the farm to Lucy.

(Continued)

CASE 9.1—Continued

COMMENTS *This is a classic case in contract law because it illustrates so clearly the objective theory of contracts with respect to determining whether an offer was intended. Today, the objective theory of contracts continues to be applied by the courts, and* Lucy v. Zehmer *is routinely cited as a significant precedent in this area. Note that in cases involving contracts formed online, the issue of contractual intent rarely arises. Perhaps this is because an online offer is, by definition, "objective" in the sense that it consists of words only—the offeror's physical actions and behavior are not evidenced.*

RELEVANT WEB SITES *To locate information on the Web concerning* Lucy v. Zehmer, *go to this text's Web site at* **http://blt.westbuslaw.com**, *select "Chapter 9," and click on "URLs for Landmarks."*

BE CAREFUL An opinion is not an offer and not a contract term. Goods or services can be "perfect" in one party's opinion and "poor" in another's.

Expressions of Opinion An expression of opinion is not an offer. It does not evidence an intention to enter into a binding agreement. ■ EXAMPLE 9.2 In *Hawkins v. McGee,*[2] Hawkins took his son to McGee, a doctor, and asked McGee to operate on the son's hand. McGee said that the boy would be in the hospital three or four days and that the hand would *probably* heal a few days later. The son's hand did not heal for a month, but nonetheless the father did not win a suit for breach of contract. The court held that McGee did not make an offer to heal the son's hand in three or four days. He merely expressed an opinion as to when the hand would heal. ■

Statements of Intention A statement of an *intention* to do something in the future is not an offer. ■ EXAMPLE 9.3 If Ari says, "I *plan* to sell my stock in Novation, Inc., for $150 per share," a contract is not created if John "accepts" and tenders $150 per share for the stock. Ari has merely expressed his intention to enter into a future contract for the sale of the stock. If John accepts and tenders the $150 per share, no contract is formed because a reasonable person would conclude that Ari was only *thinking about* selling his stock, not promising to sell it. ■

Preliminary Negotiations A request or invitation to negotiate is not an offer; it only expresses a willingness to discuss the possibility of entering into a contract. Examples are statements such as "Will you sell Forest Acres?" and "I wouldn't sell my car for less than $5,000." A reasonable person in the offeree's position would not conclude that such a statement evidenced an intention to enter into a binding obligation. Likewise, when the government and private firms need to have construction work done, contractors are invited to submit bids. The *invitation* to submit bids is not an offer, and a contractor does not bind the government or private firm by submitting a bid. (The bids that the contractors submit are offers, however, and the government or private firm can bind the contractor by accepting the bid.)

KEEP IN MIND Advertisements are not binding, but they cannot be deceptive.

Advertisements, Catalogues, and Circulars In general, advertisements, mail-order catalogues, price lists, and circular letters (meant for the general public) are treated as invitations to negotiate, not as offers to form a contract.[3] ■ EXAMPLE 9.4 Suppose that you put an ad in the classified section of your local newspaper offering to sell your guitar for $75. Seven people call and "accept" your "offer" before you can remove the ad from the newspaper. If the ad were truly an offer, you would be bound by seven contracts to sell your guitar. Because *initial* advertisements are treated as *invitations* to make offers rather than offers, however, you will have seven offers to choose from, and you can accept the best one without incurring any lia-

2. 84 N.H. 114, 146 A. 641 (1929).
3. *Restatement (Second) of Contracts,* Section 26, Comment b.

bility for the six you reject. ■ On some occasions, though, courts have construed advertisements to be offers because the ads contained definite terms that invited acceptance (such as an ad offering a reward for the return of a lost dog).[4]

Price lists are another form of invitation to negotiate or trade. A seller's price list is not an offer to sell at that price; it merely invites the buyer to offer to buy at that price. In fact, the seller usually puts "prices subject to change" on the price list. Only in rare circumstances will a price quotation be construed as an offer.[5]

ETHICAL ISSUE 9.1

Should promises of prizes made in ads and circulars always be enforced? Businesses and other organizations commonly promote their products or services by offering prizes, rewards, and the like for certain performance. Ordinarily, these ads for prizes present few problems. At times, though, people perform whatever is necessary to win advertised prizes only to learn that the offers were made in jest—that is, the ads' sponsors had no real intention of giving anyone the prizes. Consider an example. PepsiCo launched an ad campaign in which consumers could use "Pepsi Points"—which could be found on specially marked packages of Pepsi or purchased for ten cents each—to obtain T-shirts and other merchandise with the Pepsi logo. One of the ads featured a Harrier fighter jet, which was listed at 7,000,000 Pepsi Points. When a consumer, John Leonard, raised $700,000, purchased 7,000,000 Pepsi Points, and laid claim to the prize, however, PepsiCo contended that the Harrier jet in the commercial was "fanciful" and that the offer was made in jest.

In the lawsuit that followed, the court agreed, stating that "no objective person could reasonably have concluded that the commercial actually offered consumers a Harrier jet."[6] Yet Leonard obviously did draw that conclusion, and in a number of other cases, individuals have undertaken serious efforts to win nonexistent prizes. Some claim that not enforcing such promises is unfair to individuals who rely on the promises, as John Leonard did in the *PepsiCo* case. ■

Auctions In an auction, a seller "offers" goods for sale through an auctioneer. This is not, however, an offer to form a contract. Rather, it is an invitation asking bidders to submit offers. In the context of an auction, a bidder is the offeror, and the auctioneer is the offeree. The offer is accepted when the auctioneer strikes the hammer. Before the fall of the hammer, a bidder may revoke (take back) her or his bid, or the auctioneer may reject that bid or all bids. Typically, an auctioneer will reject a bid that is below the price the seller is willing to accept.

When the auctioneer accepts a higher bid, he or she rejects all previous bids. Because rejection terminates an offer (as will be discussed later), those bids represent offers that have been terminated. Thus, if the highest bidder withdraws his or her bid before the hammer falls, none of the previous bids is reinstated. If the bid is not withdrawn or rejected, the contract is formed when the auctioneer announces, "Going once, going twice, sold!" (or something similar) and lets the hammer fall.

Traditionally, auctions have been either "with reserve" or "without reserve." In an auction with reserve, the seller (through the auctioneer) may withdraw the goods at any time before the auctioneer closes the sale by announcement or by the fall of the hammer. All auctions are assumed to be auctions with reserve unless the terms of the auction are explicitly stated to be *without reserve*. In an auction without

4. The classic example is *Lefkowitz v. Great Minneapolis Surplus Store, Inc.,* 251 Minn. 188, 86 N.W.2d 689 (1957).
5. See, for example, *Fairmount Glass Works v. Grunden-Martin Woodenware Co.,* 106 Ky. 659, 51 S.W. 196 (1899).
6. *Leonard v. PepsiCo,* 88 F.Supp.2d 116 (S.D.N.Y. 1999); aff'd 210 F.3d 88 (2d Cir. 2000).

In an auction, such as this one in Boonville, Missouri, is the party selling the goods the "offeror" for purposes of contract law? Why or why not? (AP Photo/L. G. Patterson)

reserve, the goods cannot be withdrawn by the seller and must be sold to the highest bidder. In auctions with reserve, the seller may reserve the right to confirm or reject the sale even after "the hammer has fallen." In this situation, the seller is obligated to notify those attending the auction that sales of goods made during the auction are not final until confirmed by the seller.[7]

How do these rules apply to an online auction of rights to a domain name? For a discussion of a case involving this issue, see this chapter's *Adapting the Law to the Online Environment* feature.

Agreements to Agree Traditionally, agreements to agree—that is, agreements to agree to the material terms of a contract at some future date—were not considered to be binding contracts. The modern view, however, is that agreements to agree may be enforceable agreements (contracts) if it is clear that the parties intend to be bound by the agreements. In other words, under the modern view the emphasis is on the parties' intent rather than on form.

■ EXAMPLE 9.5 When the Pennzoil Company discussed with the Getty Oil Company the possible purchase of Getty's stock, a memorandum of agreement was drafted to reflect the terms of the conversations. After more negotiations over the price, both companies issued press releases announcing an agreement in principle on the terms of the memorandum. The next day, Texaco, Inc., offered to buy all of Getty's stock at a higher price. The day after that, Getty's board of directors voted to accept Texaco's offer, and Texaco and Getty signed a merger agreement. When Pennzoil sued Texaco for tortious interference with its "contractual" relationship with Getty, a jury concluded that Getty and Pennzoil had intended to form a binding contract, with only the details left to be worked out, before Texaco made its offer. Texaco was held liable for wrongfully interfering with this contract.[8] ■

on the Web To view the terms of a sample contract, go to the "forms" pages of the 'Lectric Law Library at **http://www.lectlaw.com/formb.htm** and select one of the types of contracts listed there to review.

7. These rules apply under both the common law of contracts and the Uniform Commercial Code, or UCC. See UCC 2–328.

8. *Texaco, Inc. v. Pennzoil Co.,* 729 S.W.2d 768 (Tex.App.—Houston [1st Dist.] 1987, writ ref'd n.r.e.). (Generally, a complete Texas Court of Appeals citation includes the writ-of-error history showing the Texas Supreme Court's disposition of the case. In this case, *writ ref'd n.r.e.* is an abbreviation for "writ refused, no reversible error," which means that Texas's highest court refused to grant the appellant's request to review the case, because the court did not think there was any reversible error.)

ADAPTING THE LAW TO THE ONLINE ENVIRONMENT

Can an Online Bid Constitute an Acceptance?

Under the Uniform Commercial Code, or UCC (see Chapter 18), a bid at an auction constitutes an offer. The offer (the highest bid) is accepted when the auctioneer's hammer falls. The UCC also states that auctions are "with reserve" unless the seller specifies otherwise. As just noted, in an auction with reserve, the seller reserves the right not to sell the goods to the highest bidder. Hence, even after the hammer falls, the contract for sale remains conditioned on the seller's approval. The question of how these rules should be applied to an online auction of a domain name, in which no hammer falls, came before a California court.

THE BID (OR OFFER?)

The case involved an online auction conducted by The.TV Corporation International (DotTV) on its Web site. DotTV posted an announcement on its Web site asking for bids for rights to the "Golf.tv" domain name and stating that the name would go to the highest bidder. Je Ho Lim submitted a bid for $1,010 and authorized DotTV to charge that amount to his credit card if his bid was the highest. Later, DotTV sent Lim an e-mail message stating that he had "won the auction" and charged the bid price of $1,010 to Lim's credit card. When DotTV subsequently refused to transfer the name, Lim sued DotTV for, among other things, breach of contract. Lim argued that his bid constituted an acceptance of DotTV's offer to sell the name. DotTV contended that Lim's bid was an offer, which it had not accepted. Furthermore, even if it had accepted Lim's offer, because the auction was "with reserve," DotTV could withdraw the domain name from the auction even after acceptance. The trial court held for DotTV, and Lim appealed.

THE COURT'S ANALYSIS

The appellate court first looked at the UCC's provisions concerning auctions, but noted that the UCC did not apply in this case because the UCC applies only to "goods" and domain names are not goods. The court then looked at common law principles as codified in the *Restatement (Second) of Contracts*. The rules under the *Restatement* are similar to those of the UCC: a bid in an auction is an offer that is accepted when the "hammer falls," and an auction is with reserve unless otherwise specified by the seller.

The court also pointed out, however, that DotTV's charging of the bid price to Lim's credit card was inconsistent with DotTV's claim that it could withdraw the domain name from the bidding because the auction was with reserve. Furthermore, stated the court, even if it concluded that Lim's bid was an offer and not an acceptance, DotTV had accepted the offer by its e-mail to Lim stating that he had won the auction. In all, held the court, there was no evidence that a contract between DotTV and Lim had *not* been formed, and Lim had stated a valid claim against DotTV for breach of contract. The court thus reversed the lower court's decision and remanded the case for further deliberation consistent with the appellate court's opinion.[a]

FOR CRITICAL ANALYSIS

Should the UCC rules governing auctions apply to items sold on online auction sites, such as eBay? Why or why not? How can you know whether eBay's auctions are "with reserve" or "without reserve"?

a. *Lim v. The.TV Corp. International,* 99 Cal.App.4th 684, 121 Cal.Rptr.2d 333 (2d Dist. 2002).

Suppose that two parties draw up a brief, handwritten memorandum of agreement, intending to create a more formal document later. If the arrangements are never formalized, can the memorandum constitute a binding contract? See this chapter's *Management Perspective* feature on the next page for a discussion of this question.

DEFINITENESS

The second requirement for an effective offer involves the definiteness of its terms. An offer must have reasonably definite terms so that a court can determine if a breach has occurred and provide an appropriate remedy.[9]

9. *Restatement (Second) of Contracts,* Section 33. The UCC has relaxed the requirements regarding the definiteness of terms in contracts for the sale of goods. See UCC 2–204(3).

MANAGEMENT PERSPECTIVE

The Enforcement of Preliminary Agreements

MANAGEMENT FACES A LEGAL ISSUE

Suppose that at some point during contract negotiations, the parties proclaim that they have "made a deal." Does their agreement mean that an enforceable contract has been formed even though the parties have not signed a formal contract? Or does their agreement simply mean that they have "agreed to agree" to a contract in the future? How the courts interpret such situations can, of course, have significant consequences for business owners and managers.

WHAT THE COURTS SAY

Increasingly, the courts are holding that a preliminary agreement constitutes a binding contract if all essential terms have been agreed on and no disputed issues remain to be resolved. In contrast, if the parties agree on certain major terms but leave other terms open for further negotiation, a preliminary agreement is binding only in the sense that the parties have committed themselves to negotiate the undecided terms in good faith in an effort to reach a final agreement.

Fluorogas, Ltd., learned about this distinction to its dismay when a federal district court in Texas held that a preliminary agreement that it had formed with Fluorine On Call, Ltd., was a binding contract. After executives of the two companies had enjoyed a weekend of yachting in the Florida Keys, the executives drew up a brief handwritten document stating that Fluorogas would sell to Fluorine the exclusive rights to a technology to build and sell sophisticated semiconductor equipment. When Fluorogas refused to transfer the patents and intellectual property at issue to Fluorine, Fluorine sued for breach of contract. Was there a contract? Yes, according to the court. Because the handwritten document included the essential terms of the agreement, the document constituted a contract, not an agreement to agree to form a contract at some point in the future.[a]

IMPLICATIONS FOR MANAGERS

Business owners and managers should exercise care when forming preliminary agreements. When engaging in preliminary negotiations, managers should be aware that if all material terms are agreed on, they may be bound in contract even though they have not yet drawn up a formal contract.

a. *Fluorine On Call, Ltd. v. Fluorogas Limited,* No. 01-CV-186 (W.D.Tex. 2002). This decision is not published in the *Federal Supplement.*

An offer may invite an acceptance to be worded in such specific terms that the contract is made definite. ■ EXAMPLE 9.6 Suppose that Marcus Business Machines contacts your corporation and offers to sell "from one to ten MacCool copying machines for $1,600 each; state number desired in acceptance." Your corporation agrees to buy two copiers. Because the quantity is specified in the acceptance, the terms are definite, and the contract is enforceable. ■

In the following case, the court had to decide whether the terms of an agreement were sufficiently definite to create an enforceable contract.

CASE 9.2 Satellite Entertainment Center, Inc. v. Keaton

Superior Court of New Jersey,
Appellate Division, 2002.
347 N.J.Super. 268,
789 A.2d 662.

BACKGROUND AND FACTS In 1993, John Keaton decided to open a barbecue restaurant in Jersey City, New Jersey, and entered into a six-year lease with George Williams to occupy a portion of Williams's building. After Williams died, Morris Winograd, the owner of Satellite Entertainment Center, Inc., bought the building that included Keaton's restaurant. Winograd planned to renovate the entire premises to open a new restaurant and bar. In September 1995, Winograd asked Keaton how much it would cost to buy his business. Keaton named a price of $175,000. Keaton later claimed, as corroborated by witnesses, that Winograd said he would pay that

CASE 9.2—Continued

amount, that he wanted Keaton out by the end of the year, and that he wanted Keaton to manage the new enterprise. Keaton vacated the premises by December. In January, Winograd began paying Keaton a salary, but did not pay him the $175,000, despite repeated requests. In April 1997, Winograd terminated Keaton. In a subsequent claim in a New Jersey state court against Satellite and Winograd, Keaton sought the $175,000. Winograd denied agreeing to pay Keaton anything. The court ruled in Keaton's favor. Winograd appealed to a state intermediate appellate court, claiming in part that the alleged agreement should not be enforced because it did not include the essential terms of an enforceable contract.

IN THE WORDS OF THE COURT . . .
LESEMANN, J.A.D. [Judge, Appellate Division]

* * * *

We * * * reject the claim that Winograd's contractual undertaking to pay $175,000 to Keaton should be invalidated for lack of specificity concerning the terms of the contract. The basic terms of this very simple agreement were clear.

First, the price was firm: it was $175,000. So too was the description of what Winograd was purchasing. He was buying all of Keaton's business, including whatever tangible assets, inventory or "good will" might be involved. However, * * * none of those assets were particularly significant to Winograd. Thus, it is not surprising that the parties did not, for example, itemize with specificity the inventory or the furniture of Keaton's business which was to be turned over to Winograd. To Winograd, those details were unimportant. The critical point, and the real reason for Winograd's payment of $175,000, was Keaton's agreement to vacate the property by the end of 1995, which he did.

Winograd also argues that the contract was too vague for enforcement because there was no description of the interest rate or the due date of the * * * payment for the business. * * *

It is a settled principle that when the essential parts of a contract are spelled out, a court will not refuse to enforce that contract because some of its less critical terms have not been articulated. * * * And that is particularly true when there has been part performance of the contract, or—as here—where one of the parties (Keaton) has fully performed his part of the bargain. [Emphasis added.]

* * * Here, * * * the heart of the contract is the dollar amount to be paid to Keaton and Keaton's obligation to vacate the premises for Winograd's use. The incidental terms of the [interest and the date for] payment were just that: incidental terms, which do not bar enforcement of the essential agreement between the parties.

DECISION AND REMEDY The state intermediate appellate court affirmed the judgment of the lower court on Keaton's claim for $175,000. The essential terms of the agreement for the sale of Keaton's business could be determined, and thus there was an enforceable contract between the parties.

FOR CRITICAL ANALYSIS—Economic Consideration *Suppose that the assets, inventory, and "goodwill" belonging to Keaton's business had been important to Winograd. In this situation, would the court have held that an enforceable contract existed? Why or why not?*

COMMUNICATION

A third requirement for an effective offer is communication—the offer must be communicated to the offeree. ■ **EXAMPLE 9.7** Suppose that Tolson advertises a reward for the return of her lost cat. Dirlik, not knowing of the reward, finds the cat and returns it to Tolson. Ordinarily, Dirlik cannot recover the reward because an essential element of a reward contract is that the one who claims the reward must have known it was offered. A few states would allow recovery of the reward, but not on contract principles—Dirlik would be allowed to recover on the basis that it would be unfair to deny him the reward just because he did not know about it. ■

Termination of the Offer

The communication of an effective offer to an offeree gives the offeree the power to transform the offer into a binding, legal obligation (a contract) by an acceptance. This power of acceptance, however, does not continue forever. It can be terminated by action of the parties or by operation of law.

TERMINATION BY ACTION OF THE PARTIES

An offer can be terminated by the action of the parties in any of three ways: by revocation, by rejection, or by counteroffer.

REVOCATION
In contract law, the withdrawal of an offer by an offeror. Unless the offer is irrevocable, it can be revoked at any time prior to acceptance without liability.

Revocation of the Offer The offeror's act of withdrawing an offer is referred to as **revocation.** Unless an offer is irrevocable, the offeror usually can revoke the offer (even if he or she has promised to keep the offer open), as long as the revocation is communicated to the offeree before the offeree accepts. Revocation may be accomplished by an express repudiation of the offer (for example, with a statement such as "I withdraw my previous offer of October 17") or by the performance of acts that are inconsistent with the existence of the offer and that are made known to the offeree.

■ EXAMPLE 9.8 Geraldine offers to sell some land to Gary. A week passes, and Gary, who has not yet accepted the offer, learns from his friend Konstantine that Geraldine has in the meantime sold the property to Nunan. Gary's knowledge of Geraldine's sale of the land to Nunan, even though he learned of it through a third party, effectively revokes Geraldine's offer to sell the land to Gary. Geraldine's sale of the land to Nunan is inconsistent with the continued existence of the offer to Gary, and thus the offer to Gary is revoked. ■

The general rule followed by most states is that a revocation becomes effective when the offeree or the offeree's agent (a person who acts on behalf of another) actually receives it. Therefore, a letter of revocation mailed on April 1 and delivered at the offeree's residence or place of business on April 3 becomes effective on April 3.

An offer made to the general public can be revoked in the same manner in which the offer was originally communicated. ■ EXAMPLE 9.9 Suppose that a department store offers a $10,000 reward to anyone giving information leading to the apprehension of the persons who burglarized its downtown store. The offer is published in three local papers and in four papers in neighboring communities. To revoke the offer, the store must publish the revocation in all seven papers for the same number of days it published the offer. The revocation is then accessible to the general public, and the offer is revoked even if some particular offeree does not know about the revocation. ■

Irrevocable Offers Although most offers are revocable, some can be made irrevocable. Increasingly, courts refuse to allow an offeror to revoke an offer when the offeree has changed position because of justifiable reliance on the offer (under the doctrine of detrimental reliance, or promissory estoppel, which will be discussed in Chapter 10). In some circumstances, "firm offers" made by merchants may also be considered irrevocable. We will discuss these offers in Chapter 18.

A poster offers a reward for a missing seven-year-old girl. How can this offer be revoked? (AP Photo/Denis Poroy)

OPTION CONTRACT
A contract under which the offeror cannot revoke his or her offer for a stipulated time period, and the offeree can accept or reject the offer during this period without fear that the offer will be made to another person. The offeree must give consideration for the option (the irrevocable offer) to be enforceable.

Another form of irrevocable offer is an option contract. An **option contract** is created when an offeror promises to hold an offer open for a specified period of time in return for a payment (consideration) given by the offeree. An option contract takes away the offeror's power to revoke an offer for the period of time specified in the option. If no time is specified, then a reasonable period of time is implied. ■ EXAMPLE 9.10 Suppose that you are in the business of writing movie scripts. Your agent contacts the head of development at New Line Cinema and offers to sell New Line your new movie script. New Line likes your script and agrees to pay you $5,000 for a six-month option. In this situation, you (through your agent) are the offeror, and New Line is the offeree. You cannot revoke your offer to sell New Line your script for the next six months. If after six months no contract has been formed, however, New Line loses the $5,000, and you are free to sell your movie script to another firm. ■

Option contracts are also frequently used in conjunction with the sale of real estate. ■ EXAMPLE 9.11 You might agree with a landowner to lease a home and include in the lease contract a clause stating that you will pay $2,000 for an option to purchase the home within a specified period of time. If you decide not to purchase the home after the specified period has lapsed, you lose the $2,000, and the landlord is free to sell the property to another buyer. ■

BE CAREFUL The way in which a response to an offer is phrased can determine whether the offer is accepted or rejected.

Rejection of the Offer by the Offeree If the offeree rejects the offer, the offer is terminated. Any subsequent attempt by the offeree to accept will be construed as a new offer, giving the original offeror (now the offeree) the power of acceptance. A rejection is ordinarily accomplished by words or by conduct evidencing an intent not to accept the offer.

As with revocation, rejection of an offer is effective only when it is actually received by the offeror or the offeror's agent. ■ EXAMPLE 9.12 Suppose that Growgood Farms mails a letter to Campbell Soup Company offering to sell carrots at ten cents a pound. (Of course, today, such offers tend to be sent electronically rather than by mail, as will be discussed in Chapter 17.) Campbell Soup Company could reject the offer by sending or faxing a letter to Growgood Farms expressly rejecting the offer or by mailing the offer to Growgood, evidencing an intent to reject it. Alternatively, Campbell could offer to buy the carrots at eight cents per pound (a counteroffer), necessarily rejecting the original offer. ■

Merely inquiring about an offer does not constitute rejection. ■ EXAMPLE 9.13 A friend offers to buy your CD-ROM library for $300. You respond, "Is this your best offer?" or "Will you pay me $375 for it?" A reasonable person would conclude that you did not reject the offer but merely made an inquiry for further consideration of the offer. You can still accept and bind your friend to the $300 purchase price. When the offeree merely inquires as to the firmness of the offer, there is no reason to presume that she or he intends to reject it. ■

COUNTEROFFER
An offeree's response to an offer in which the offeree rejects the original offer and at the same time makes a new offer.

Counteroffer by the Offeree A **counteroffer** is a rejection of the original offer and the simultaneous making of a new offer. ■ EXAMPLE 9.14 Suppose that Burke offers to sell his home to Lang for $170,000. Lang responds, "Your price is too high. I'll offer to purchase your house for $165,000." Lang's response is called a counteroffer because it rejects Burke's offer to sell at $170,000 and creates a new offer by Lang to purchase the home at a price of $165,000. ■

MIRROR IMAGE RULE
A common law rule that requires that the terms of the offeree's acceptance adhere exactly to the terms of the offeror's offer for a valid contract to be formed.

At common law, the **mirror image rule** requires that the offeree's acceptance match the offeror's offer exactly. In other words, the terms of the acceptance must "mirror" those of the offer. If the acceptance materially changes or adds to the terms of the original offer, it will be considered not an acceptance but a counteroffer—which, of course, need not be accepted. The original offeror can, however, accept the terms of the counteroffer and create a valid contract.[10]

TERMINATION BY OPERATION OF LAW

The offeree's power to transform an offer into a binding, legal obligation can be terminated by operation of law if any of four conditions occur: lapse of time, destruction of the specific subject matter, death or incompetence of the offeror or offeree, or supervening illegality of the proposed contract.

Lapse of Time An offer terminates automatically by law when the period of time *specified in the offer* has passed. If the offer states that it will be left open until a particular date, then the offer will terminate at midnight on that day. If the offer states that it will be left open for a number of days, such as ten days, this time period normally begins to run when the offer is actually received by the offeree, not when it is formed or sent. When the offer is delayed (through the misdelivery of mail, for example), the period begins to run from the date the offeree would have received the offer, but only if the offeree knows or should know that the offer is delayed.[11]

.on the Web For answers to some common questions about contract law, go to the Web site of the Legal Information Network, Inc., at **http://www.contract-law.com/TheLaw.htm**.

■ EXAMPLE 9.15 Suppose that Beth offers to sell her boat to Jonah, stating that the offer will remain open until May 20. Unless Jonah accepts the offer by midnight on May 20, the offer will lapse (terminate). Now suppose that Beth writes a letter to Jonah, offering to sell him her boat if Jonah accepts the offer within twenty days of

10. The mirror image rule has been greatly modified in regard to sales contracts. Section 2–207 [Section 2–206(3) in the 2003 amendments] of the UCC provides that a contract is formed if the offeree makes a definite expression of acceptance (such as signing the form in the appropriate location), even though the terms of the acceptance modify or add to the terms of the original offer (see Chapter 18).
11. *Restatement (Second) of Contracts,* Section 49.

the letter's date, which is May 1. Jonah must accept within twenty days after May 1, or the offer will terminate. The same rule would apply even if Beth had used improper postage when mailing the offer, and Jonah received the letter ten days after May 1, not knowing of the improper mailing. If, however, Jonah knew about the improper mailing, the offer would lapse twenty days after the day Jonah ordinarily would have received the offer had Beth used proper postage. ■

If the offer does not specify a time for acceptance, the offer terminates at the end of a *reasonable* period of time. A reasonable period of time is determined by the subject matter of the contract, business and market conditions, and other relevant circumstances. An offer to sell farm produce, for example, will terminate sooner than an offer to sell farm equipment because farm produce is perishable and subject to greater fluctuations in market value.

Destruction of the Subject Matter An offer is automatically terminated if the specific subject matter of the offer is destroyed before the offer is accepted. For example, if Martin offers to sell his prize cow to Yatsen, but the cow is struck by lightning and dies before Yatsen can accept, the offer is automatically terminated. (Note that if Yatsen accepted the offer just before lightning struck the cow, a contract would have been formed, but, because of the cow's death, a court would likely excuse Martin's obligation to perform the contract on the basis of impossibility of performance—see Chapter 14.)

Death or Incompetence of the Offeror or Offeree An offeree's power of acceptance is terminated when the offeror or offeree dies or is deprived of legal capacity to enter into the proposed contract, *unless the offer is irrevocable.*[12] An offer is personal to both parties and normally cannot pass to the decedent's heirs, guardian, or estate. This rule applies whether or not one party had notice of the death or incompetence of the other party. ■ EXAMPLE 9.16 Kapola, who is quite ill, writes to her friend Amanda, offering to sell Amanda her grand piano for only $400. That night, Kapola dies. The next day, Amanda, not knowing of Kapola's death, writes a letter to Kapola accepting the offer and enclosing a check for $400. Is there a contract? No. There is no contract because the offer automatically terminated on Kapola's death. ■

Supervening Illegality of the Proposed Contract A statute or court decision that makes an offer illegal automatically terminates the offer. ■ EXAMPLE 9.17 If Acme Finance Corporation offers to lend Jack $20,000 at 15 percent annually, and the state legislature enacts a statute prohibiting loans at interest rates greater than 12 percent before Jack can accept, the offer is automatically terminated. (If the statute is enacted after Jack accepts the offer, a valid contract is formed, but the contract may still be unenforceable—see Chapter 11.) ■

Acceptance

ACCEPTANCE
A voluntary act by the offeree that shows assent, or agreement, to the terms of an offer; may consist of words or conduct.

An **acceptance** is a voluntary act by the offeree that shows assent, or agreement, to the terms of an offer. The offeree's act may consist of words or conduct. The acceptance must be unequivocal and must be communicated to the offeror.

12. *Restatement (Second) of Contracts,* Section 48. If the offer is irrevocable, it is not terminated when the offeror dies. Also, if the offer is such that it can be accepted by the performance of a series of acts, and those acts began before the offeror died, the offeree's power of acceptance is not terminated.

Who Can Accept?

Generally, a third person cannot substitute for the offeree and effectively accept the offer. After all, the identity of the offeree is as much a condition of a bargaining offer as any other term contained therein. Thus, except in special circumstances, only the person to whom the offer is made or that person's agent can accept the offer and create a binding contract. For example, Lottie makes an offer to Paul. Paul is not interested, but Paul's friend José accepts the offer. No contract is formed.

Unequivocal Acceptance

To exercise the power of acceptance effectively, the offeree must accept unequivocally. This is the *mirror image rule* previously discussed. If the acceptance is subject to new conditions or if the terms of the acceptance materially change the original offer, the acceptance may be deemed a counteroffer that implicitly rejects the original offer.

DON'T FORGET When an offer is rejected, it is terminated.

Certain terms, when added to an acceptance, will not qualify the acceptance sufficiently to constitute rejection of the offer. ■ **Example 9.18** Suppose that in response to a person offering to sell a painting by a well-known artist, the offeree replies, "I accept; please send a written contract." The offeree is requesting a written contract but is not making it a condition for acceptance. Therefore, the acceptance is effective without the written contract. If the offeree replies, "I accept *if* you send a written contract," however, the acceptance is expressly conditioned on the request for a writing, and the statement is not an acceptance but a counteroffer. (Notice how important each word is!)[13] ■

13. As noted in footnote 10, in regard to sales contracts, the UCC provides that an acceptance may still be effective even if some terms are added. The new terms are simply treated as proposals for additions to the contract, unless both parties are merchants—in which case the additional terms (with some exceptions) become part of the contract [UCC 2–207(2)].

"It's a deal, but just to be on the safe side let's have our lawyers look at this handshake."

SILENCE AS ACCEPTANCE

Ordinarily, silence cannot constitute acceptance, even if the offeror states, "By your silence and inaction, you will be deemed to have accepted this offer." This general rule applies because an offeree should not be put under a burden of liability to act affirmatively in order to reject an offer. No consideration—that is, nothing of value—has passed to the offeree to impose such a liability.

In some instances, however, the offeree does have a duty to speak; if so, his or her silence or inaction will operate as an acceptance. Silence may be an acceptance when an offeree takes the benefit of offered services even though he or she had an opportunity to reject them and knew that they were offered with the expectation of compensation. ■ **EXAMPLE 9.19** Suppose that John, a college student who earns extra income by washing store windows, taps on the window of a store and catches the attention of the store's manager. John points to the window and raises his cleaner, signaling that he will be washing the window. The manager does nothing to stop him. Here, the store manager's silence constitutes an acceptance, and an implied-in-fact contract is created. The store is bound to pay a reasonable value for John's work. ■

Silence can also operate as an acceptance when the offeree has had prior dealings with the offeror. If a merchant, for example, routinely receives shipments from a supplier and in the past has always notified the supplier when defective goods are rejected, then silence constitutes acceptance. Also, if a buyer solicits an offer specifying that certain terms and conditions are acceptable, and the seller makes the offer in response to the solicitation, the buyer has a duty to reject—that is, a duty to tell the seller that the offer is not acceptable. Failure to reject (silence) would operate as an acceptance.

COMMUNICATION OF ACCEPTANCE

REMEMBER A bilateral contract is a promise for a promise, and a unilateral contract is performance for a promise.

Whether the offeror must be notified of the acceptance depends on the nature of the contract. In a bilateral contract, communication of acceptance is necessary because acceptance is in the form of a promise (not performance), and the contract is formed when the promise is made (rather than when the act is performed). Communication of acceptance is not necessary, however, if the offer dispenses with the requirement. Also, if the offer can be accepted by silence, no communication is necessary.[14]

In a unilateral contract, the full performance of some act is called for; therefore, acceptance is usually evident, and notification is unnecessary. Exceptions do exist, however. When the offeror requests notice of acceptance or has no adequate means of determining whether the requested act has been performed, or when the law (such as Article 2 of the UCC) requires notice of acceptance, then notice is necessary.[15]

MODE AND TIMELINESS OF ACCEPTANCE

The general rule is that acceptance in a bilateral contract is timely if it is effected within the duration of the offer. Problems arise, however, when the parties involved are not dealing face to face. In such situations, the offeree may use an authorized mode of communication.

The Mailbox Rule Acceptance takes effect, thus completing formation of the contract, at the time the offeree sends or delivers the communication via the mode expressly or impliedly authorized by the offeror. This is the so-called **mailbox rule,**

MAILBOX RULE
A rule providing that an acceptance of an offer becomes effective on dispatch (on being placed in an official mailbox), if mail is, expressly or impliedly, an authorized means of communication of acceptance to the offeror.

14. Under the UCC, an order or other offer to buy goods that are to be promptly shipped may be treated as either a bilateral or a unilateral offer and can be accepted by a promise to ship or by actual shipment. See UCC 2–206(1)(b).

15. UCC 2–206(2).

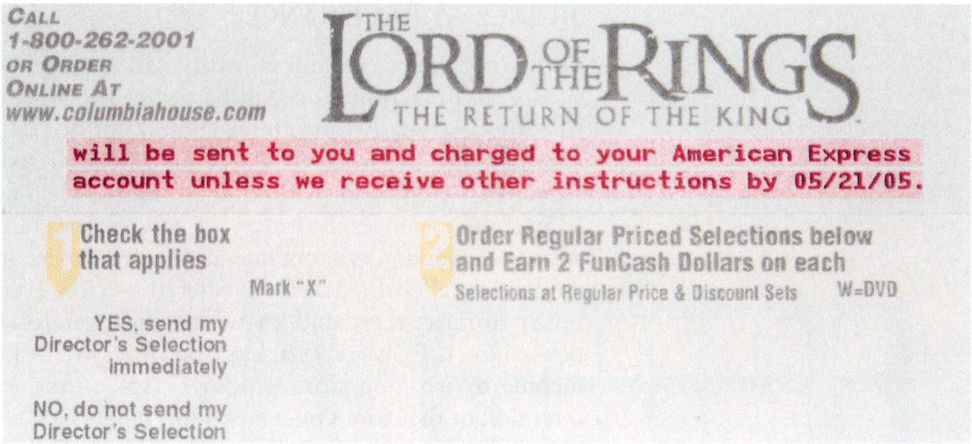

This photo shows a letter from a DVD club that was sent to a club member. If the recipient (offeree) does nothing, has he or she accepted the offer? Why or why not?

also called the "deposited acceptance rule," which the majority of courts uphold. Under this rule, if the authorized mode of communication is the mail, then an acceptance becomes valid when it is dispatched (placed in the control of the U.S. Postal Service)—*not* when it is received by the offeror.

The mailbox rule was formed to prevent the confusion that arises when an offeror sends a letter of revocation but, before it arrives, the offeree sends a letter of acceptance. Thus, whereas a revocation becomes effective only when it is *received* by the offeree, an acceptance becomes effective on *dispatch* (even if it is never received), provided that an *authorized* means of communication is used.

Authorized Means of Communication Authorized means of communicating an acceptance can be either expressly authorized—that is, expressly stipulated in the offer—or impliedly authorized by facts or law.[16] An acceptance sent by means not expressly or impliedly authorized is normally not effective until it is received by the offeror.

When an offeror specifies how acceptance should be made (for example, by first class mail or express delivery), *express authorization* is said to exist. Moreover, both the offeror and the offeree are bound in contract the moment that such means of acceptance are employed. Most offerors do not expressly specify the means by which the offeree is to accept. Thus, the common law recognizes the following implied authorized means of acceptance:[17]

1. The offeror's choice of a particular means in making the offer implies that the offeree is authorized to use the same *or a faster* means for acceptance.
2. When two parties are at a distance, mailing is impliedly authorized.

At issue in the following case was whether a notice of intent to renew a lease contract had been sent by authorized means.

16. *Restatement (Second) of Contracts,* Section 30, provides that an offer invites acceptance "by any medium reasonable in the circumstances," unless the offer is specific about the means of acceptance. Under Section 65, a medium is reasonable if it is one used by the offeror or one customary in similar transactions, unless the offeree knows of circumstances that would argue against the reasonableness of a particular medium (the need for speed because of rapid price changes, for example).

17. Note that UCC 2–206(1)(a) states specifically that an acceptance of an offer for the sale of goods can be made by any medium that is *reasonable* under the circumstances.

CASE 9.3 Osprey L.L.C. v. Kelly-Moore Paint Co.

Supreme Court of Oklahoma, 1999.
984 P.2d 194.

BACKGROUND AND FACTS Kelly-Moore Paint Company leased a store in Edmond, Oklahoma, from Osprey L.L.C. The parties signed a fifteen-year lease with two five-year renewal options. The lease required Kelly-Moore to give Osprey written notice of the lessee's intent to renew at least six months before the lease expired. The notice "may be delivered either personally or by depositing the same in United States mail, first class postage prepaid, registered or certified mail, return receipt requested." Six months before the end of the fifteen-year term, Kelly-Moore sent the required notice by certified mail. Five years later, however, at the end of the first five-year term, on the last day of the six-month notification deadline, at 5:28 P.M., Kelly-Moore sent the notice by fax. Phone company records indicated that the fax was transmitted correctly, but Osprey denied receiving it. Osprey filed a suit in an Oklahoma state court to evict Kelly-Moore. Osprey argued that the lease specifically prescribed delivery of the notice personally or by mail. Kelly-Moore countered that the lease's use of the word *may* permitted other means of delivery. The court granted a judgment in favor of Kelly-Moore, and Osprey appealed. The state intermediate appellate court reversed this judgment, and Kelly-Moore appealed to the Oklahoma Supreme Court.

IN THE WORDS OF THE COURT . . .

KAUGER, J. [Justice]

* * * *

* * * Although the question tendered is novel in Oklahoma, the sufficiency of the notice given when exercising an option contract or an option to renew or extend a lease has been considered by several jurisdictions. A few have found that delivery of notice by means other than hand delivery or by certified or registered mail was insufficient if the terms of the contract specifically referred to the method of delivery. However, the majority have reached the opposite conclusion. These courts generally recognize that, despite the contention that there must be strict compliance with the notice terms of a lease option agreement, *use of an alternative method does not render the notice defective if the substituted method performed the same function or served the same purpose as the authorized method.* [Emphasis added.]

* * * *

* * * The lease does not appear to be ambiguous. "Shall" is ordinarily construed as mandatory and "may" is ordinarily construed as permissive. * * * The provision for delivery, either personally or by certified or registered mail, uses the permissive "may" and it does not bar other modes of transmission which are just as effective.

* * * The purpose of providing notice by personal delivery or registered mail is to insure the delivery of the notice, and to settle any dispute which might arise between the parties concerning whether the notice was received. A substituted method of notice which performs the same function and serves the same purpose as an authorized method of notice is not defective. Here, the contract provided that time was of the essence. Although Osprey denies that it ever received the fax, the fax activity report and telephone company records confirm that the fax was transmitted successfully, and that it was sent to Osprey's correct facsimile number on the last day of the deadline to extend the lease. The fax provided immediate written communication similar to personal delivery and, like a telegram, would be timely if it were properly transmitted before the expiration of the deadline to renew. Kelly-Moore's use of the fax served the same function and the same purpose as the two methods suggested by the lease and it was transmitted before the expiration of the deadline to renew. Under these facts, we hold that the faxed or facsimile delivery of

(Continued)

CASE 9.3—Continued the written notice to renew the commercial lease was sufficient to exercise timely the renewal option of the lease.

DECISION AND REMEDY The Oklahoma Supreme Court vacated the decision of the state intermediate appellate court. The state supreme court held that the use of an alternative method to exercise a lease option does not render the notice defective if the alternative method accomplishes the same objective as the authorized method.

FOR CRITICAL ANALYSIS—Social Consideration *How would you have drafted the lease term regarding notice of renewal in order to prevent this lawsuit (and the costs associated with it for both parties)?*

If an offer expressly authorizes acceptance of the offer by first class mail or express delivery, can the offeree accept by a faster means, such as by fax or e-mail? Why or why not? (© Michael Newman/ PhotoEdit)

Exceptions There are three basic exceptions to the rule that a contract is formed when acceptance is sent by authorized means:

1. If the acceptance is not properly dispatched (if a letter is incorrectly addressed, for example, or lacks the proper postage), in most states it will not be effective until it is received by the offeror.
2. The offeror can stipulate in the offer that an acceptance will not be effective until it is received (usually by a specified time) by the offeror.
3. Sometimes an offeree sends a rejection first, then later changes his or her mind and sends an acceptance. Obviously, this chain of events could cause confusion and even detriment to the offeror, depending on whether the rejection or the acceptance arrives first. In such situations, the law cancels the rule of acceptance on dispatch, and the first communication received by the offeror determines whether a contract is formed. If the rejection arrives first, there is no contract.[18]

TECHNOLOGY AND ACCEPTANCES

Technology, and particularly the Internet, has all but eliminated the need for the mailbox rule because online acceptances typically are communicated instantaneously to the offeror. As you will learn in Chapter 17, while online offers are not significantly different from traditional offers contained in paper documents, online acceptances have posed some unusual problems.

18. *Restatement (Second) of Contracts,* Section 40.

REVIEWING AGREEMENT

Shane Durbin wanted to have a recording studio custom-built in his home. He sent invitations to a number of local contractors to submit bids on the project. Rory Johnson submitted the lowest bid, which was $20,000 less than any of the other bids Durbin received. Durbin called Johnson to find out the type and quality of the materials that were included in the bid and ask if he could substitute a superior brand of acoustic tiles for the same bid price. Johnson said he

REVIEWING AGREEMENT—Continued

would have to check into the price difference. The parties also discussed a possible start date for construction. Two weeks later, Durbin changed his mind and decided not to go forward with his plan to build a recording studio. Johnson filed a suit against Durbin for breach of contract. Using the information presented in the chapter, answer the following questions.

1. Who is the offeror, and who is the offeree in this scenario?
2. Did Johnson's bid meet the requirements of an offer? Explain.
3. Was there an acceptance of the offer? Why or why not?
4. How is an offer terminated? Assuming that Durbin did not inform Johnson that he was rejecting the offer, was the offer terminated at any time described here? Explain.

APPLICATION Controlling the Terms of the Offer*

The courts normally attempt to "save" contracts whenever possible, but sometimes it is simply impossible to do so. Two common reasons why contracts fail are that (1) the terms of the offer were too unclear or indefinite to constitute a binding contract on the offer's acceptance and (2) the acceptance was not timely. If you are an offeror, you can control both of these factors: you can determine what the terms of the future contract will be, as well as the time and mode of acceptance.

Include Clear and Definite Terms

If a contract's terms are too unclear or indefinite, the contract will fail. Unless a court can ascertain exactly what the rights and duties of the parties are under a particular contract, the court cannot enforce those rights and duties. Therefore, as an offeror, make sure that the terms of your offer are sufficiently definite to constitute a binding contract if the offer is accepted. A statement such as "Quantity to be determined later" may allow the offeree, after acceptance, to claim that no contract was ever formed because no quantity term was specified.

Another reason why an offeror should make sure that the offer's terms are clear and definite is that if a contract results, any ambiguous provision may be interpreted against the party that drafted the contract (see Chapter 8).

* This *Application* is not meant to substitute for the services of an attorney who is licensed to practice law in your state.

Specify the Time and Mode of Acceptance

Problems concerning contract formation also arise when it is unclear whether an acceptance is effective. To avoid such problems, you should take some precautions when phrasing the offer. Whether your offer is made via the Internet, fax, express delivery, or mail, you can specify that the offer must be accepted (or even that the acceptance must be received by you) by a certain time and that if it is not, the offer will terminate. Similarly, you can specify the mode of acceptance. In online offers, you can indicate that to accept the offer, the user must click on a certain box on the screen. If you make an offer and want the acceptance to be faxed to you, make sure that you clearly indicate that the acceptance must be faxed to you at a given fax number by a specific time or it will not be effective.

Checklist for the Offeror

1. **Make sure that the terms of the offer are sufficiently clear and definite to allow both the parties and a court to determine the specific rights and obligations of the parties. Otherwise, the contract may fail for indefiniteness.**
2. **Specify in the offer the date on which the offer will terminate and the authorized mode of acceptance. For example, you can indicate that an acceptance, to be effective, must be faxed to you at a specific fax number by a specific time or date.**

9–7. Intention. Music that is distributed on compact discs and similar media generates income in the form of "mechanical" royalties. Music that is publicly performed, such as when a song is played on the radio, included in a movie or commercial, or sampled in another song, produces "performance" royalties. Both types of royalties are divided between the songwriter and the song's publisher. Vincent Cusano is a musician and songwriter who performed under the name "Vinnie Vincent" as a guitarist with the group KISS in the early 1980s. Cusano co-wrote three songs entitled "Killer," "I Love It Loud," and "I Still Love You," which KISS recorded and released in 1982 on an album titled *Creatures of the Night.* Cusano left KISS in 1984. Eight years later, Cusano sold to Horipro Entertainment Group "one hundred (100%) percent undivided interest" of his rights in the songs "other than Songwriter's share of performance income." Later, Cusano filed a suit in a federal district court against Horipro, claiming in part that he never intended to sell the writer's share of the mechanical royalties. Horipro filed a motion for summary judgment. Should the court grant the motion? Explain. [*Cusano v. Horipro Entertainment Group,* 301 F.Supp.2d 272 (S.D.N.Y. 2004)]

A QUESTION OF ETHICS

9–8. The parents of a newborn baby who sustained brain damage during birth sued the attending physician and the hospital for medical malpractice. After eight days of trial and while the jury was still deliberating, the attorneys for the parties orally agreed to a "high-low" settlement. The defendants (the physician and hospital) would pay damages in an amount that depended on the amount of the jury's verdict, but the total would not exceed the limits of insurance coverage ($1 million for the physician and $8 million for the hospital). The hospital's attorney announced the settlement agreement on the record but did not specify how much each of the defendants would contribute to the total. A few minutes later, the hospital's attorney told the judge that the hospital had only intended to agree to pay for its percentage of fault. The jury came back moments later with a verdict stating that the physician was 100 percent at fault and awarding nearly $1.35 million to the plaintiffs. The trial court refused to enforce the settlement agreement, concluding, as the hospital had argued, that there had been no true meeting of the minds. The appellate court reversed, noting that the agreement had been announced on behalf of all the defendants and therefore all were liable regardless of the jury's finding of fault. Given these facts, consider the following questions. [*Fiegener v. Freeman-Oak Hill Health System,* 996 S.W.2d 767 (Mo.App. 1999)]

1. Should the appellate court have considered what the hospital said about its intentions *after* the agreement had been entered into the record?
2. Generally, is it fair to hold the hospital liable for damages under the contract even though the jury determined that the hospital was not at fault for the plaintiff's injuries? Why or why not?

FOR CRITICAL ANALYSIS

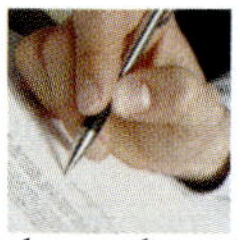

9–9. Review the ways to terminate an offer listed earlier in this chapter. If a defendant offers to settle a case for a specific amount of money, and the plaintiff asks if the defendant would offer more, does that mean the plaintiff cannot now accept the original offer? What do you think?

VIDEO QUESTION

9–10. Go to this text's Web site at http://blt.westbuslaw.com and select "Chapter 9." Click on "Video Questions" and view the video titled *Offer and Acceptance.* Then answer the following questions.

1. On the video, Vinny indicates that he can't sell his car to Oscar for four thousand dollars; then he says, "maybe five . . . ." Discuss whether Vinny has made an offer or a counteroffer.
2. Oscar then says to Vinny, "Okay, I'll take it. But you gotta let me pay you four thousand now and the other thousand in two weeks." According to the chapter, do Oscar and Vinny have an agreement? Why or why not?
3. When Maria later says to Vinny, "I'll take it," has she accepted an offer? Why or why not?

INTERNET EXERCISES

Go to the *Business Law Today* home page at http://blt.westbuslaw.com, select "Chapter 9," and click on "Internet Exercises." There you will find the following Internet research exercises that you can perform to learn more about topics covered in this chapter.

Activity 9–1: LEGAL PERSPECTIVE—Contract Terms

Activity 9–2: ETHICAL PERSPECTIVE—Offers and Advertisements

Activity 9–3: MANAGEMENT PERSPECTIVE—Sample Contracts

BEFORE THE TEST

Go to the *Business Law Today* home page at http://blt.westbuslaw.com, select "Chapter 9," and click on "Interactive Quizzes." You will find a number of interactive questions relating to this chapter.

CHAPTER 10
Consideration

"No cause of action arises from a bare promise."
Legal Maxim

CHAPTER OUTLINE

- ELEMENTS OF CONSIDERATION
- LEGAL SUFFICIENCY AND ADEQUACY OF CONSIDERATION
- CONTRACTS THAT LACK CONSIDERATION
- SETTLEMENT OF CLAIMS
- PROMISSORY ESTOPPEL

LEARNING OBJECTIVES

After reading this chapter, you should be able to answer the following questions:

1. What is consideration?
2. What is required for consideration to be legally sufficient?
3. What are some examples of contracts that lack consideration?
4. What is an accord and satisfaction?
5. In what circumstances might a promise be enforced despite a lack of consideration?

In every legal system, some promises will be enforced, and some promises will not be enforced. As the chapter-opening quotation suggests, the simple fact that a party has made a promise does not mean that the promise is enforceable. Under Roman law, a promise was not enforceable without some sort of *causa*—that is, a reason for making the promise that was also deemed to be a sufficient reason for enforcing it. Under the common law, a primary basis for the enforcement of promises is **consideration,** which is usually defined as the value given in return for a promise.

CONSIDERATION
Generally, the value given in return for a promise. The consideration must be something of legally sufficient value, and there must be a bargained-for exchange.

In this chapter, we first examine the basic elements of consideration and the requirement that consideration be legally sufficient. We then describe certain types of contracts in which consideration is lacking. Next, we discuss the requirement of consideration with respect to the settlement of claims. The chapter concludes with a discussion of a doctrine under which promises may be enforceable despite the lack of consideration.

fairness of the bargain. On the surface, fairness would appear to be an issue when the items exchanged are of unequal value. In general, however, courts do not question the adequacy of consideration if the consideration is legally sufficient. Under the doctrine of freedom of contract, parties are usually free to bargain as they wish. If people could sue merely because they had entered into an unwise contract, the courts would be overloaded with frivolous suits.

In extreme cases, however, a court of law may look to the amount or value (the adequacy) of the consideration because apparently inadequate consideration can indicate that fraud, duress, or undue influence was involved or that a gift was made (if a father "sells" a $100,000 house to his daughter for only $1, for example). Additionally, when the consideration is grossly inadequate, the courts may declare the contract unenforceable on the ground that it is unconscionable,[2] meaning that, generally speaking, it is so one sided under the circumstances as to be clearly unfair. (Unconscionability will be discussed further in Chapter 11.)

BE AWARE A consumer's signature on a contract does not always guarantee that the contract will be enforced. Ultimately, the terms must be fair.

In the following case, the issue was whether consideration existed in a contract to accept lower payments for medical services than the maximum fees allowed under state regulations.

2. Pronounced un-*kon*-shun-uh-bul.

CASE 10.1 Seaview Orthopaedics v. National Healthcare Resources, Inc.

Superior Court of New Jersey,
Appellate Division, 2004.
366 N.J.Super. 501,
841 A.2d 917.
http://lawlibrary.rutgers.edu/search.shtml[a]

BACKGROUND AND FACTS Consumer Health Network (CHN) is a large health-insurance preferred provider organization (PPO) in New Jersey. CHN provides medical services providers (its clients) with a PPO network in three distinct areas: workers' compensation, group health benefits, and auto insurance. The network includes over 11,000 physicians and nearly 14,000 medical services providers (which include physicians, laboratories, and hospitals). By entering into a contract with CHN, a medical services provider gains potential access to 950,000 enrollees in exchange for accepting reimbursement at rates lower than the maximum rates permitted by New Jersey state regulations. Seaview Orthopaedics is a CHN client that renders services to auto accident victims insured by Allstate Indemnity Company. Allstate pays the CHN rates for Seaview's services through Allstate's claims administrator, National Healthcare Resources (NHR). Seaview and others filed a suit in a New Jersey state court against NHR and others to recover the difference between the CHN rates and the state's maximum rates. The court issued a summary judgment in favor of the defendants. The plaintiffs appealed to a state intermediate appellate court, claiming that the CHN contract was not enforceable, in part because it lacked consideration.

a. Click on "Search by Party Name." On that page, select "Appellate Division" as the court, and type "Seaview Orthopaedics" in the "First Name" box. Click on "Submit Form" to view a synopsis of the case, and then "click here to get this case" to read the opinion. Rutgers University School of Law in Camden, New Jersey, maintains this Web site.

IN THE WORDS OF THE COURT . . .
FISHER, J.A.D. [Judge, Appellate Division]

* * * *

Plaintiffs * * * argue that their agreement to be bound to the CHN rates for auto accident victims is not supported by consideration. It is well-settled that contracts are not enforceable in the absence of consideration, [that is,] both sides must get something out of the exchange. Consideration may take many forms and may be based upon either a detriment incurred by the promisee or a benefit received by the promisor. Courts, however, do not inquire into the adequacy of consideration in determining whether to enforce a contract. Any inquiry into the presence of consideration does not depend upon the comparative value of the things exchanged. Instead, when we speak of the need for an exchange of valuable consideration what

CASE 10.1—Continued

is meant is that the consideration must merely be valuable in the sense that it is something that is bargained for in fact.

Here, the contract provided benefits to plaintiffs in a variety of ways which either collectively or separately constituted valuable consideration for plaintiffs' promise to accept the CHN rates for reimbursement from auto accident victims (and other types of patients) and not the maximum rate permitted by the [state's] fee schedule. Plaintiffs, for example, obtained the benefit of marketing their businesses in a directory of providers utilized by numerous payors in the workers' compensation and health benefits markets and many thousands of potential patients. Payors make the list available to the largest PPO membership network in New Jersey and, in the health and workers' compensation settings, are generally offered substantial financial incentives when those patients use the providers on the list.

Plaintiffs argue that the likelihood of a provider receiving a referral from the CHN network of an auto accident victim "is practically nil." Defendants dispute this, contending that an auto accident victim, who is in a health benefits or workers' compensation plan that utilized the CHN network, may likely use the same provider that was engaged for these other purposes. This point is, perhaps, debatable. But even if plaintiffs' argument is accurate and the actual benefits received by them in the auto insurance area are illusory, plaintiffs received valuable consideration by being in the network and by obtaining or at least gaining access to patients in the workers' compensation and health benefits areas. That the predominant (or even exclusive) benefits for providers may come from workers' compensation or health benefit sources does not render the contract unenforceable for lack of consideration when services provided for auto accident victims are reimbursed at a lesser rate. We need not, as plaintiffs argue, find some specific monetary benefit for plaintiffs when called upon to provide services for auto accident victims so long as the other aspects of the contract provide, or have the potential to provide, a benefit to plaintiffs. It is the totality of the exchange of promises and benefits that is considered and, in this case, this exchange was sufficient to create an enforceable contract.

* * * *

* * * [W]e reject plaintiffs' contentions in their entirety and affirm the entry of summary judgment dismissing the complaints in these * * * actions. We * * * also affirm the order imposing costs in favor of defendants and against plaintiffs in each action.

DECISION AND REMEDY The state intermediate appellate court affirmed the lower court's summary judgment. The CHN contract did not lack consideration. "Here, the contract provided benefits to plaintiffs in a variety of ways which either collectively or separately constituted valuable consideration for plaintiffs' promise to accept the CHN rates for reimbursement from auto accident victims (and other types of patients) and not the maximum rate permitted by the [state's] schedule."

WHY IS THIS CASE IMPORTANT? *As this case illustrates, something need not be of direct economic or financial value to be considered legally sufficient consideration. In many situations, as here, the exchange of promises and potential benefits is deemed sufficient as consideration.*

Contracts That Lack Consideration

Sometimes, one or both of the parties to a contract may think that they have exchanged consideration when in fact they have not. Here we look at some situations in which the parties' promises or actions do not qualify as contractual consideration.

PREEXISTING DUTY

To learn more about how the courts decide such issues as whether consideration was lacking for a particular contract, look at relevant case law, which can be accessed through the Web site of Cornell University's School of Law at

http://www.law.cornell.edu/topics/contracts.html.

Under most circumstances, a promise to do what one already has a legal duty to do does not constitute legally sufficient consideration because no legal detriment is incurred.[3] The preexisting legal duty may be imposed by law or may arise out of a previous contract. A sheriff, for example, cannot collect a reward for information leading to the capture of a criminal if the sheriff already has a legal duty to capture the criminal. Likewise, if a party is already bound by contract to perform a certain duty, that duty cannot serve as consideration for a second contract.

■ EXAMPLE 10.4 Suppose that Bauman-Bache, Inc., begins construction on a seven-story office building and after three months demands an extra $75,000 on its contract. If the extra $75,000 is not paid, it will stop working. The owner of the land, having no one else to complete construction, agrees to pay the extra $75,000. The agreement is not enforceable because it is not supported by legally sufficient consideration; Bauman-Bache had a preexisting contractual duty to complete the building. ■

Unforeseen Difficulties The rule regarding preexisting duty is meant to prevent extortion and the so-called holdup game. What happens, though, when an honest contractor, who has contracted with a landowner to build a house, runs into extraordinary difficulties that were totally unforeseen at the time the contract was formed? In the interests of fairness and equity, the courts sometimes allow exceptions to the preexisting duty rule. In the example just mentioned, if the landowner agrees to pay extra compensation to the contractor for overcoming the unforeseen difficulties (such as having to use dynamite and special equipment to remove an unexpected rock formation to excavate for a basement), the court may refrain from applying the preexisting duty rule and enforce the agreement. When the "unforeseen difficulties" that give rise to a contract modification are the types of risks ordinarily assumed in business, however, the courts will usually assert the preexisting duty rule.[4]

RESCISSION
A remedy whereby a contract is canceled and the parties are returned to the positions they occupied before the contract was made; may be effected through the mutual consent of the parties, by the parties' conduct, or by court decree.

Rescission and New Contract The law recognizes that two parties can mutually agree to rescind their contract, at least to the extent that it is executory (still to be carried out). **Rescission**[5] is defined as the unmaking of a contract so as to return the parties to the positions they occupied before the contract was made. When rescission and the making of a new contract take place at the same time, the courts frequently are given a choice of applying the preexisting duty rule or allowing rescission and letting the new contract stand.

PAST CONSIDERATION

PAST CONSIDERATION
An act that takes place before the contract is made and that ordinarily, by itself, cannot be consideration for a later promise to pay for the act.

Promises made in return for actions or events that have already taken place are unenforceable. These promises lack consideration in that the element of bargained-for exchange is missing. In short, you can bargain for something to take place now or in the future but not for something that has already taken place. Therefore, **past consideration** is no consideration.

■ EXAMPLE 10.5 Suppose that Elsie, a real estate agent, does her friend Judy a favor by selling Judy's house and not charging any commission. Later, Judy says to Elsie, "In return for your generous act, I will pay you $3,000." This promise is made

3. See *Foakes v. Beer*, 9 App.Cas. 605 (1884).

4. Note that under the Uniform Commercial Code (UCC), any agreement modifying a contract within Article 2 on Sales needs no consideration to be binding. See UCC 2–209(1).

5. Pronounced reh-*sih*-zhen.

in return for past consideration and is thus unenforceable; in effect, Judy is stating her intention to give Elsie a gift. ■

ILLUSORY PROMISES

If the terms of the contract express such uncertainty of performance that the promisor has not definitely promised to do anything, the promise is said to be *illusory*—without consideration and unenforceable. ■ **EXAMPLE 10.6** The president of Tuscan Corporation says to his employees, "All of you have worked hard, and if profits remain high, a 10 percent bonus at the end of the year will be given—if management thinks it is warranted." This is an *illusory promise,* or no promise at all, because performance depends solely on the discretion of the president (the management). There is no bargained-for consideration. The statement declares merely that management may or may not do something in the future. ■

Option-to-cancel clauses in contracts for specified time periods sometimes present problems in regard to consideration. ■ **EXAMPLE 10.7** Abe contracts to hire Chris for one year at $5,000 per month, reserving the right to cancel the contract at any time. On close examination of these words, you can see that Abe has not actually agreed to hire Chris, as Abe could cancel without liability before Chris started performance. Abe has not given up the opportunity of hiring someone else. This contract is therefore illusory. Now suppose that Abe contracts to hire Chris for a one-year period at $5,000 per month, reserving the right to cancel the contract at any time after Chris has begun performance by giving Chris thirty days' notice. Abe, by saying that he will give Chris thirty days' notice, is relinquishing the opportunity (legal right) to hire someone else instead of Chris for a thirty-day period. If Chris works for one month, at the end of which Abe gives him thirty days' notice, Chris has a valid and enforceable contractual claim for $10,000 in salary. ■

Settlement of Claims

Businesspersons or others can settle legal claims in several ways. It is important to understand the nature of the consideration given in these settlement agreements, or contracts. Claims are commonly settled through an *accord and satisfaction,* in which a debtor offers to pay a lesser amount than the creditor purports to be owed. Two other methods that are also often used to settle claims are the *release* and the *covenant not to sue.*

ACCORD AND SATISFACTION

ACCORD AND SATISFACTION
A common means of settling a disputed claim, in which a debtor offers to pay a lesser amount than the creditor purports to be owed. The creditor's acceptance of the offer creates an accord (agreement), and when the accord is executed, satisfaction occurs.

In an **accord and satisfaction,** a debtor offers to pay, and a creditor accepts, a lesser amount than the creditor originally claimed was owed. Thus, in an accord and satisfaction, the debtor attempts to terminate an existing obligation. The *accord* is the settlement agreement. In an accord, the debtor offers to give or perform something less than the parties originally agreed on, and the creditor accepts that offer in satisfaction of the claim. *Satisfaction* is the performance (usually payment), which takes place after the accord is executed. A basic rule is that there can be no satisfaction unless there is first an accord.

For accord and satisfaction to occur, the amount of the debt *must be in dispute.* If a debt is *liquidated,* accord and satisfaction cannot take place. A debt is liquidated if its amount has been ascertained, fixed, agreed on, settled, or exactly determined. An example of a liquidated debt is a loan contract in which the borrower agrees to

REMEMBER Businesspersons should consider settling potential legal disputes to save both their own time and resources and those of the courts.

pay a stipulated amount every month until the amount of the loan is paid. In the majority of states, acceptance of (an accord for) a lesser sum than the entire amount of a liquidated debt is not satisfaction, and the balance of the debt is still legally owed. The rationale for this rule is that the debtor has given no consideration to satisfy the obligation of paying the balance to the creditor—because the debtor has a preexisting legal obligation to pay the entire debt.

An *unliquidated debt* is the opposite of a liquidated debt. Here, reasonable persons may differ over the amount owed. It is not settled, fixed, agreed on, ascertained, or determined. In these circumstances, acceptance of payment of the lesser sum operates as a satisfaction, or discharge, of the debt. One argument to support this rule is that the parties give up a legal right to contest the amount in dispute, and thus consideration is given.

Release

RELEASE
A contract in which one party forfeits the right to pursue a legal claim against the other party.

A **release** is a contract in which one party forfeits the right to pursue a legal claim against the other party. Releases will generally be binding if they are (1) given in good faith, (2) stated in a signed writing (required by many states), and (3) accompanied by consideration.[6] Clearly, parties are better off if they know the extent of their injuries or damages before signing releases.

On the Web: You can find a copy of a release form and the information that should be included in a release by going to **http://www.nolo.com/category/cm_home.html** and typing "Release from Legal Claims" in the "Search" box, and hitting "Search."

■ EXAMPLE 10.8 Suppose that you are involved in an automobile accident caused by Raoul's negligence. Raoul offers to give you $1,000 if you will release him from further liability resulting from the accident. You believe that this amount will cover your damages, so you agree to and sign the release. Later you discover that the repairs to your car will cost $1,200. Can you collect the balance from Raoul? The answer is normally no; you are limited to the $1,000 in the release. Why? The reason is that a valid contract existed. You and Raoul both assented to the bargain (hence, agreement existed), and sufficient consideration was present. Your consideration for the contract was the legal detriment you suffered (by releasing Raoul from liability, you forfeited your right to sue to recover damages, should they be more than $1,000). This legal detriment was induced by Raoul's promise to give you the $1,000. Raoul's promise was, in turn, induced by your promise not to pursue your legal right to sue him for damages. ■

The following case illustrates how important it is to understand the effect of a release.

6. Under the UCC, a written, signed waiver or renunciation by an aggrieved party discharges any further liability for a breach, even without consideration [UCC 1–107].

CASE 10.2 Mills v. Berlex Laboratories, Inc.

Court of Appeals of Georgia, 1999.
235 Ga.App. 873,
510 S.E.2d 621.

BACKGROUND AND FACTS William Mills was a pharmaceutical sales representative for Berlex Laboratories, Inc. On February 15, Berlex told Mills that his position was being eliminated and that he would be terminated effective February 28. Berlex gave Mills a proposed separation agreement and release. Mills hired Samuel Cruse, an attorney, to review the release. The same week, Mills injured his back while boxing up Berlex supplies in his home office. Within a few days, Mills signed a revised separation agreement and release. This release provided that "as of the day following the Termination Date, [Mills] will not be eligible to participate in any of Berlex's benefits plans" and released Berlex from "any claims arising out of or in any way related to Employee's employment with Berlex and the conclusion

CASE 10.2—Continued

thereof." In exchange, Berlex paid Mills one year's salary as severance pay, a $5,388 bonus, and five days' vacation pay. Berlex also paid to continue Mills's health insurance for eighteen months and provided him with unlimited outplacement services for one year. On March 3, Mills filed a disability claim with Berlex for his back injury. Berlex refused to pay. Mills filed a suit in a Georgia state court against Berlex, seeking disability benefits. When the court ruled in Berlex's favor, Mills appealed to a state intermediate appellate court.

IN THE WORDS OF THE COURT . . .
McMURRAY, Presiding Judge.

* * * *

Mills contends the trial court erred when it found his civil action was barred because the parties did not contemplate that Berlex would deny his short-term disability claim at the time they entered into the general release. * * * The scope of a release is determined by the intention of the parties as expressed in the terms of the particular instrument, considered in the light of all the facts and circumstances. *A general release, not restricted by its terms to particular claims or demands, ordinarily covers all claims and demands due at the time of its execution and within the contemplation of the parties.* [Emphasis added.]

We find the evidence authorized the trial court's conclusion that Mills' claim for short-term disability benefits fell within the scope of the release. By its terms, the release applies to all claims "arising out of or in any way related to [Mills'] employment with Berlex and the conclusion thereof * * * ." It also specifically provided that Mills "will not be eligible to participate in any of Berlex's benefit plans" as of the day following his termination date (February 28 * * *). This language is sufficient to include Mills' claim for short-term disability benefits.

Mills' contention that the parties did not contemplate a release of his claim for short-term disability benefits when they entered into the general release is without merit. Mills retained counsel to review the release, and the record shows that both Mills and his attorney were aware of his short-term disability claim before Mills signed the Separation Agreement and General Release. These facts and circumstances, taken together with the plain language of the release, support the conclusion that Mills' short-term disability claim was within the contemplation of the parties at the time they entered into the release.

DECISION AND REMEDY The state intermediate appellate court affirmed the judgment of the trial court. The release barred Mills's claim for short-term disability benefits from Berlex.

FOR CRITICAL ANALYSIS—Social Consideration *Would the outcome of this case have been different if the employee had not been given severance pay in exchange for signing the release? Why or why not?*

Covenant Not to Sue

COVENANT NOT TO SUE
An agreement to substitute a contractual obligation for some other type of legal action based on a valid claim.

Unlike a release, a **covenant not to sue** does not always bar further recovery. The parties simply substitute a contractual obligation for some other type of legal action based on a valid claim. Suppose (following the earlier example) that you agree with Raoul not to sue for damages in a tort action if he will pay for the damage to your car. If Raoul fails to pay, you can bring an action for breach of contract.

Promissory Estoppel

PROMISSORY ESTOPPEL A doctrine that applies when a promisor makes a clear and definite promise on which the promisee justifiably relies; such a promise is binding if justice will be better served by the enforcement of the promise.

ESTOPPED Barred, impeded, or precluded.

Sometimes individuals rely on promises, and such reliance may form a basis for contract rights and duties. Under the doctrine of **promissory estoppel** (also called *detrimental reliance*), a person who has reasonably relied on the promise of another can often obtain some measure of recovery. When the doctrine of promissory estoppel is applied, the promisor (the offeror) is **estopped** (barred, or impeded) from revoking the promise. For the doctrine of promissory estoppel to be applied, the following elements are required:

1. There must be a clear and definite promise.
2. The promisee must justifiably rely on the promise.
3. The reliance normally must be of a substantial and definite character.
4. Justice will be better served by the enforcement of the promise.

■ EXAMPLE 10.9 Your uncle tells you, "I'll pay you $150 a week so you won't have to work anymore." In reliance on your uncle's promise, you quit your job, but your uncle refuses to pay you. Under the doctrine of promissory estoppel, you may be able to enforce his promise.[7] Now your uncle makes a promise to give you $10,000 to buy a car. If you buy the car with your own funds and he does not pay you, you may once again be able to enforce the promise under this doctrine. ■

ETHICAL ISSUE 10.1

Should the doctrine of promissory estoppel be applied to promises of employment? A number of cases have come before the courts in which the story is strikingly similar: in reliance on an offer of employment, a person has left a job, sold her or his home, and moved to another location—only to learn that the offer has been revoked. In those jurisdictions that are governed by the common law doctrine of employment at will,[8] these persons often have little recourse. Courts in these jurisdictions often hold that even though an employer has made an offer of employment to a particular job candidate, under the at-will doctrine the employer need not hire that person.

Occasionally, however, a court will apply the doctrine of promissory estoppel in such circumstances. For example, in one case, Julie Goff-Hamel, who had worked for a family planning clinic for eleven years and who enjoyed an excellent benefits package, left her job in reliance on a job offer from a group of obstetricians and gynecologists. The day before she was to begin her new job, one of the obstetricians told her that they were hiring someone else for the position. Goff-Hamel sued the group for damages on the basis of detrimental reliance (promissory estoppel). Although the trial court granted summary judgment in favor of the group, concluding that the doctrine of promissory estoppel did not apply because the employment was at will, the appellate court reversed. The case was remanded to the trial court for a determination of the amount of damages to be awarded to Goff-Hamel.[9] ■

7. A classic example is *Ricketts v. Scothorn,* 57 Neb. 51, 77 N.W. 365 (1898).
8. *Employment at will* is an employment relationship that either party may terminate at any time for any reason—see Chapter 40 for a further discussion of this doctrine.
9. *Goff-Hamel v. Obstetricians & Gynecologists, P.C.,* 256 Neb. 19, 588 N.W.2d 798 (1999).

REVIEWING CONSIDERATION

Blair is a college freshman whose uncle is paying her tuition. Toward the end of the second semester, Blair's uncle tells her that if she earns straight As, he will continue paying her tuition, and as a reward, will give her a new Mercedes when she graduates. Blair earns straight As for three years, but gets two Bs in her senior year. Her uncle sends her a bill for the entire amount spent on tuition for all four years. Using the information presented in the chapter, answer the following questions.

1. What are the basic elements of consideration? Are these elements present in Blair's uncle's promise to pay her tuition? Why or why not?
2. Did Blair's uncle have a preexisting duty to pay her tuition?
3. Was there adequate consideration to support the uncle's promise of a Mercedes? Why or why not? What is this type of promise called?
4. What principle discussed in the chapter might lead a court to conclude that this agreement lacked consideration?
5. Should a court require Blair to refund all or part of the tuition paid by her uncle? Explain.
6. If Blair had actually received straight As throughout college, would she be entitled to enforce her uncle's promises?

KEY TERMS

accord and satisfaction 277
consideration 271
covenant not to sue 279
estopped 280
forbearance 272
past consideration 276
promissory estoppel 280
release 278
rescission 276

CHAPTER SUMMARY Consideration

Elements of Consideration (See page 272.)	Consideration is broken down into two parts: (1) something of *legally sufficient value* must be given in exchange for the promise, and (2) there must be a *bargained-for exchange.*
Legal Sufficiency and Adequacy of Consideration (See pages 272–275.)	Legal sufficiency of consideration relates to the first element of consideration just mentioned—something of legal value must be given in exchange for a promise. Adequacy of consideration relates to how much consideration is given and whether a fair bargain was reached. Courts will inquire into the adequacy of consideration (if the consideration is legally sufficient) only when fraud, undue influence, duress, or unconscionability may be involved.
Contracts That Lack Consideration (See pages 275–277.)	Consideration is lacking in the following situations: 1. *Preexisting duty*—Consideration is not legally sufficient if one is either by law or by contract under a *preexisting duty* to perform the action being offered as consideration for a new contract. 2. *Past consideration*—Actions or events that have already taken place do not constitute legally sufficient consideration. 3. *Illusory promises*—When the nature or extent of performance is too uncertain, the promise is rendered illusory (without consideration and unenforceable).

(Continued)

CHAPTER SUMMARY Consideration—Continued

Settlement of Claims (See pages 277–279.)	1. *Accord and satisfaction*—An *accord* is an agreement in which a debtor offers to pay a lesser amount than the creditor purports to be owed. *Satisfaction* may take place when the accord is executed. 2. *Release*—An agreement by which, for consideration, a party is barred from further recovery beyond the terms specified in the release. 3. *Covenant not to sue*—An agreement not to sue on a present, valid claim.
Promissory Estoppel (See page 280.)	The equitable doctrine of promissory estoppel applies when a promisor makes a clear and definite promise on which the promisee reasonably relies, and the promise substantially alters the promisee's actions. The court will enforce such promises only in situations where an injustice would occur otherwise. Also known as the doctrine of detrimental reliance.

FOR REVIEW

Answers for the even-numbered questions in this For Review *section can be found on this text's accompanying Web site at* http://blt.westbuslaw.com. *Select "Chapter 10" and click on "For Review."*

1. What is consideration?
2. What is required for consideration to be legally sufficient?
3. What are some examples of contracts that lack consideration?
4. What is an accord and satisfaction?
5. In what circumstances might a promise be enforced despite a lack of consideration?

QUESTIONS AND CASE PROBLEMS

10–1. Contract Modification. Tabor is a buyer of file cabinets manufactured by Martin. Martin's contract with Tabor calls for delivery of fifty file cabinets at $40 per cabinet in five equal installments. After delivery of two installments (twenty cabinets), Martin informs Tabor that because of inflation, Martin is losing money and will promise to deliver the remaining thirty cabinets only if Tabor will pay $50 per cabinet. Tabor agrees in writing to do so. Discuss whether Martin can legally collect the additional $100 on delivery to Tabor of the next installment of ten cabinets.

10–2. Contract Modification. Bernstein owns a lot and wants to build a house according to a particular set of plans and specifications. She solicits bids from building contractors and receives three bids: one from Carlton for $60,000, one from Friend for $58,000, and one from Shade for $53,000. She accepts Shade's bid. One month after construction of the house has begun, Shade contacts Bernstein and informs her that because of inflation and a recent price hike in materials, he will not finish the house unless Bernstein agrees to pay an extra $3,000. Bernstein reluctantly agrees to pay the additional sum. After the house is finished, however, Bernstein refuses to pay the extra $3,000. Discuss whether Bernstein is legally required to pay this additional amount.

10–3. Payment for Services to Another. Daniel, a recent college graduate, is on his way home for the Christmas holidays from his new job. Daniel gets caught in a snowstorm and is taken in by an elderly couple, who provide him with food and shelter. After the snowplows have cleared the road, Daniel proceeds home. Daniel's father, Fred, is most appreciative of the elderly couple's action and in a letter promises to pay them $500. The elderly couple, in need of money, accepts Fred's offer. Then, because of a dispute between Daniel and Fred, Fred refuses to pay the elderly couple the $500. Discuss whether the couple can hold Fred in contract for the services rendered to Daniel.

10–4. Consideration. Ben hired Lewis to drive his racing car in a race. Tuan, a friend of Lewis, promised to pay Lewis $3,000 if he won the race. Lewis won the race, but Tuan refused to pay the $3,000. Tuan contended that no legally binding contract had been formed because he had received no consideration from Lewis for his promise to pay the $3,000. Lewis sued Tuan for breach of contract, arguing that winning the race was the consideration given in exchange for Tuan's promise to pay the $3,000. What rule of law discussed in this chapter supports Tuan's claim? Explain.

10–5. Past Consideration. Rivendell Forest Products, Ltd., had a computer program—the *Quote Screen* system—that allowed it to quote prices to its customers many times faster than its competitors. To keep the *Quote Screen* system a secret, Rivendell insisted that all of its employees, including Timothy Cornwell, sign a confidentiality agreement in 1988. Cornwell was employed by Rivendell from 1987 to 1990, when he left Rivendell to work as a marketing manager for the Georgia-Pacific Corp., a competitor. Cornwell introduced Georgia-Pacific to Rivendell's *Quote Screen* system. Rivendell sued Cornwell for, among other things, breach of the confidentiality agreement. The trial court held that the confidentiality agreement was not a valid contract because Rivendell had failed to provide consideration, such as a salary increase or a promotion, in exchange for Cornwell's promise to keep the *Quote Screen* system a secret. If Cornwell had signed the confidentiality agreement when he was first hired, would the result have been the same? Explain. [*Rivendell Forest Products, Ltd. v. Georgia-Pacific Corp.*, 824 F.Supp. 961 (D.Colo. 1993)]

10–6. Preexisting Duty. New England Rock Services, Inc., agreed to work as a subcontractor on a sewer project on which Empire Paving, Inc., was the general contractor. For drilling and blasting a certain amount of rock, Rock Services was to be paid $29 per cubic yard or on a time-and-materials basis, whichever was less. From the beginning, Rock Services experienced problems. The primary obstacle was a heavy concentration of water, which, according to the custom in the industry, Empire should have controlled but did not. Rock Services was compelled to use more costly and time-consuming methods than anticipated, and it was unable to complete the work on time. The subcontractor asked Empire to pay for the rest of the project on a time-and-materials basis. Empire signed a modification of the original agreement. On completion of the work, Empire refused to pay Rock Services the balance due under the modification. Rock Services filed a suit in a Connecticut state court against Empire. Empire claimed that the modification lacked consideration and was thus not valid and enforceable. Is Empire right? Why or why not? [*New England Rock Services, Inc. v. Empire Paving, Inc.*, 53 Conn.App. 771, 731 A.2d 784 (1999)]

CASE PROBLEM WITH SAMPLE ANSWER

10–7. In 1995, Helikon Furniture Co. appointed Gaede as its independent sales agent for the sale of its products in parts of Texas. The parties signed a one-year contract that specified, among other things, the commissions that Gaede would receive. Over a year later, although the parties had not signed a new contract, Gaede was still representing Helikon when it was acquired by a third party. Helikon's new management allowed Gaede to continue to receive the same commissions and sent him a letter stating that it would make no changes in its sales representatives "for at least the next year." Three months later, in December 1996, the new managers sent Gaede a letter proposing new terms for a contract. Gaede continued to sell Helikon products until May 1997 when he received a letter effectively reducing the amount of his commissions. Gaede filed a suit in a Texas state court against Helikon, alleging breach of contract. Helikon argued in part that there was no contract because there was no consideration. In whose favor should the court rule, and why? [*Gaede v. SK Investments, Inc.*, 38 S.W.3d 753 (Tex.App.—Houston [14 Dist.] 2001)]

After you have answered this problem, compare your answer with the sample answer given on the Web site that accompanies this text. Go to http://blt.westbuslaw.com, select "Chapter 10," and click on "Case Problem with Sample Answer."

10–8. Settlement of Claims. Shoreline Towers Condominium Owners Association in Gulf Shores, Alabama, authorized Resort Development, Inc. (RDI), to manage Shoreline's property. On Shoreline's behalf, RDI obtained a property insurance policy from Zurich American Insurance Co. In October 1995, Hurricane Opal struck Gulf Shores. RDI filed claims with Zurich regarding damage to Shoreline's property. Zurich determined that the cost of the damage was $334,901. Zurich then subtracted an applicable $40,000 deductible and sent checks totaling $294,901 to RDI. RDI disputed the amount. Zurich eventually agreed to issue a check for an additional $86,000 in return for RDI's signing a "Release of All Claims." Later, contending that the deductible had been incorrectly applied and that this was a breach of contract, among other things, Shoreline filed a suit against Zurich in a federal district court. How, if at all, should the agreement reached by RDI and Zurich affect Shoreline's claim? Explain. [*Shoreline Towers Condominium Owners Association, Inc. v. Zurich American Insurance Co.*, 196 F.Supp.2d 1210 (S.D.Ala. 2002)]

A QUESTION OF ETHICS

10–9. E. S. Herrick Co. grows and sells blueberries. Maine Wild Blueberry Co. agreed to buy all of Herrick's 1990 crop under a contract that left the price unliquidated. Herrick delivered the berries, but a dispute arose over the price. Maine Wild sent Herrick a check with a letter stating that the check was the "final settlement." Herrick cashed the check but filed a suit in a Maine state court against Maine Wild, on the ground of breach of contract, alleging that the buyer owed more. Given these facts, consider the following questions. [*E. S. Herrick Co. v. Maine Wild Blueberry Co.*, 670 A.2d 944 (Me. 1996)]

1. What will the court likely decide in this case? Why?
2. Generally, what are the ethical underpinnings of the legal concept of accord and satisfaction? Why does this concept apply only to unliquidated debts?

FOR CRITICAL ANALYSIS

10–10. Under what circumstances should courts examine the adequacy of consideration?

INTERNET EXERCISES

Go to the *Business Law Today* home page at **http://blt.westbuslaw.com**, select "Chapter 10," and click on "Internet Exercises." There you will find the following Internet research exercises that you can perform to learn more about topics covered in this chapter.

Activity 10–1: LEGAL PERSPECTIVE—Consideration

Activity 10–2: INTERNATIONAL PERSPECTIVE—Contract Consideration in Canada

Activity 10–3: MANAGEMENT PERSPECTIVE—Promissory Estoppel

BEFORE THE TEST

Go to the *Business Law Today* home page at **http://blt.westbuslaw.com**, select "Chapter 10," and click on "Interactive Quizzes." You will find a number of interactive questions relating to this chapter.

"Liberty of contract is not an absolute concept. It is relative to many conditions of time and place and circumstance."

Benjamin Cardozo, 1870–1938
(Associate justice of the United States Supreme Court, 1932–1938)

CHAPTER 11

Capacity and Legality

CHAPTER OUTLINE

- CONTRACTUAL CAPACITY
- LEGALITY
- THE EFFECT OF ILLEGALITY

LEARNING OBJECTIVES

After reading this chapter, you should be able to answer the following questions:

1. What are some exceptions to the rule that a minor can disaffirm (avoid) any contract?
2. Does an intoxicated person have the capacity to enter into an enforceable contract?
3. Does the mental incompetence of one party necessarily make a contract void?
4. Under what circumstances will a covenant not to compete be enforceable? When will such covenants not be enforced?
5. What is an exculpatory clause? In what circumstances might exculpatory clauses be enforced? When will they not be enforced?

Courts generally want contracts to be enforceable, and much of the law is devoted to aiding the enforceability of contracts. Nonetheless, as indicated in the chapter-opening quotation, "liberty of contract" is not absolute. In other words, not all people can make legally binding contracts at all times. Contracts entered into by persons lacking the capacity to do so may be voidable. Similarly, contracts calling for the performance of an illegal act are illegal and thus void—they are not contracts at all. In this chapter, we examine contractual capacity and some aspects of illegal bargains.

Contractual Capacity

CONTRACTUAL CAPACITY
The threshold mental capacity required by law for a party who enters into a contract to be bound by that contract.

Contractual capacity is the legal ability to enter into a contractual relationship. Courts generally presume the existence of contractual capacity, but in some situations, capacity is lacking or may be questionable. A person *adjudged by a court* to be mentally incompetent, for example, cannot form a legally binding contract with another party. In other situations, a party may have the capacity to enter into a valid contract but also have the right to avoid liability under it. For example, minors—or *infants,* as they are commonly referred to in legal parlance—usually are not legally bound by contracts. In this section, we look at the effects of youth, intoxication, and mental incompetence on contractual capacity.

MINORS

Today, in virtually all states, the *age of majority* (when a person is no longer a minor) for contractual purposes is eighteen years—the so-called coming of age. (The age of majority may still be twenty-one for other purposes, however, such as the purchase and consumption of alcohol.) In addition, some states provide for the termination of minority on marriage. Subject to certain exceptions, the contracts entered into by a minor are voidable at the option of that minor.

The general rule is that a minor can enter into any contract an adult can, provided that the contract is not one prohibited by law for minors (for example, the sale of alcoholic beverages or tobacco). Although minors have the right to avoid their contracts, there are exceptions (to be discussed shortly).

DISAFFIRMANCE
The legal avoidance, or setting aside, of a contractual obligation.

Disaffirmance The legal avoidance, or setting aside, of a contractual obligation is referred to as **disaffirmance.** To disaffirm, a minor must express his or her intent, through words or conduct, not to be bound to the contract. The minor must disaffirm the entire contract, not merely a portion of it. For instance, a minor cannot decide to keep part of the goods purchased under a contract and return the remaining goods. When a minor disaffirms a contract, the minor can recover any property that he or she transferred to the adult as consideration for the contract, even if it is then in the possession of a third party.[1]

A contract can ordinarily be disaffirmed at any time during minority[2] or for a reasonable time after the minor comes of age. While two months would probably be considered reasonable, a court may not consider it reasonable to wait a year or more after coming of age to disaffirm, depending on the circumstances. If an individual fails to disaffirm an executed contract within a reasonable time after reaching the age of majority, a court will likely hold that the contract has been ratified (*ratification* will be discussed shortly).

Note that an adult who enters into a contract with a minor cannot avoid his or her contractual duties on the ground that the minor can do so. Unless the minor exercises the option to disaffirm the contract, the adult party normally is bound by it.

---

1. The Uniform Commercial Code, in Section 2–403(1), allows an exception if the third party is a "good faith purchaser for value." See Chapter 19.
2. In some states, however, a minor who enters into a contract for the sale of land cannot disaffirm the contract until she or he reaches the age of majority.

Two young men discuss the sale of a car. When a minor disaffirms a contract, such as a contract to buy a car, most states require the minor to return whatever he or she purchased, if it is within his or her control. Why do some states require more? (© Michael Newman/PhotoEdit)

A Minor's Obligations on Disaffirmance. Although all states' laws permit minors to disaffirm contracts (with certain exceptions), including executed contracts, state laws differ on the extent of a minor's obligations on disaffirmance. Courts in a majority of states hold that the minor need only return the goods (or other consideration) subject to the contract, provided the goods are in the minor's possession or control. ■ EXAMPLE 11.1 Jim Garrison, a seventeen-year-old, purchases a computer from Radio Shack. While transporting the computer to his home, Garrison, through no fault of his own, is involved in a car accident. As a result of the accident, the plastic casing of the computer is broken. The next day, he returns the computer to Radio Shack and disaffirms the contract. Under the majority view, this return fulfills Garrison's duty even though the computer is now damaged. Garrison is entitled to receive a refund of the purchase price (if paid in cash) or to be relieved of any further obligations under an agreement to purchase the computer on credit. ■

A growing number of states, either by statute or by court decision, place an additional duty on the minor—the duty to restore the adult party to the position she or he held before the contract was made.

In the following case, the Tennessee Supreme Court faced the issue of whether a minor should be held responsible for damage, ordinary wear and tear, and depreciation of goods used by the minor prior to his disaffirmance of the contract. The case illustrates the trend among today's courts in regard to this issue.

CASE 11.1 Dodson v. Shrader

Supreme Court of Tennessee, 1992.
824 S.W.2d 545.

BACKGROUND AND FACTS When Joseph Dodson was sixteen years old, he bought a used pickup truck for $4,900 from Shrader's Auto, which was owned by Burns and Mary Shrader. Nine months later, the truck developed mechanical problems. A mechanic informed Dodson that

(Continued)

CASE 11.1—Continued
the problem might be a burnt valve. Without having the truck repaired, Dodson continued to drive it. One month later, the truck's engine "blew up," and the truck was rendered inoperable. Dodson disaffirmed the contract and sought to return the truck to the Shraders and obtain a full refund of the purchase price. The Shraders refused to refund the purchase price and would not accept possession of the truck. Later, while parked in Dodson's front yard, the pickup was hit by an unknown driver. Dodson filed suit against the Shraders to compel a refund of the purchase price. Although the Shraders claimed that the truck's value had been reduced to $500, the trial court granted rescission and ordered the Shraders to refund the full $4,900 purchase price to Dodson on Dodson's delivery of the truck to them. The Shraders appealed.

IN THE WORDS OF THE COURT . . .
O'BRIEN, Justice.

* * * *

* * * If the minor has not been overreached [taken advantage of] in any way, and there has been no undue influence, and the contract is a fair and reasonable one, and the minor has actually paid money on the purchase price, and taken and used the article purchased, [then] he ought not to be permitted to recover the amount actually paid, without allowing the vendor of the goods reasonable compensation for the use of, depreciation, and willful or negligent damage to the article purchased, while in his hands. * * *

* * * Minors are permitted to, and do in fact, transact a great deal of business for themselves, long before they have reached the age of legal majority. * * * Further, it does not appear consistent with * * * proper moral influence upon young people * * * if they are taught that they can make purchases with their own money, for their own benefit, and after paying for them, and using them until they are worn out and destroyed, go back and compel the vendor to return to them what they have paid upon the purchase price. *Such a doctrine can only lead to the corruption of principles and encourage young people in habits of trickery and dishonesty.* [Emphasis added.]

DECISION AND REMEDY The Supreme Court of Tennessee adopted a rule that required the seller to be compensated for the depreciated value—not the purchase price—of the pickup and remanded the case for a determination of the fairness of the contract and the fair market value of the vehicle.

FOR CRITICAL ANALYSIS—Ethical Consideration
Do you believe that the goal of protecting minors from the consequences of unwise contracts should ever outweigh the goal of encouraging minors to behave in a responsible manner?

Misrepresentation of Age. Suppose that a minor tells a seller she is twenty-one years old when she is really seventeen. Ordinarily, the minor can disaffirm the contract even though she has misrepresented her age. Moreover, in some jurisdictions the minor is not liable for the tort of fraudulent misrepresentation, the rationale being that such a tort judgment might indirectly force the minor to perform the contract.

In many jurisdictions, however, a minor who has misrepresented his or her age can be bound by a contract under certain circumstances. First, several states have enacted statutes for precisely this purpose. In these states, misrepresentation of age is enough to prohibit disaffirmance. Other statutes prohibit disaffirmance by a minor who has engaged in business as an adult. Second, some courts refuse to allow minors to disaffirm executed (fully performed) contracts unless they can return the consideration received. The combination of the minors' misrepresentations and their unjust enrichment has persuaded these courts to *estop* (prevent) the minors from asserting contractual incapacity.

Finally, some courts allow a misrepresenting minor to disaffirm the contract, but they hold the minor liable for damages in tort. Here, the defrauded party may sue the minor for misrepresentation or fraud. Authority is split on this point because some courts, as previously noted, have recognized that allowing a suit in tort is equivalent to indirectly enforcing the minor's contract.

NECESSARIES
Necessities required for life, such as food, shelter, clothing, and medical attention; may include whatever is believed to be necessary to maintain a person's standard of living or financial and social status.

Contracts for Necessaries, Insurance, and Loans. A minor who enters into a contract for necessaries may disaffirm the contract but remains liable for the reasonable value of the goods used. **Necessaries** are basic needs, such as food, clothing, shelter, and medical services, at a level of value required to maintain the minor's standard of living or financial and social status. Thus, what will be considered a necessary for one person may be a luxury for another. Additionally, what is considered a necessary depends on whether the minor is under the care or control of his or her parents, who are required by law to provide necessaries for the minor. If a minor's parents provide the minor with shelter, for example, then a contract to lease shelter (such as an apartment) normally will not be considered a contract for necessaries.

Generally, then, to qualify as a contract for necessaries, (1) the item contracted for must be necessary to the minor's existence, (2) the value of the necessary item may be up to a level required to maintain the minor's standard of living or financial and social status, and (3) the minor must not be under the care of a parent or guardian who is required to supply this item. Unless these three criteria are met, the minor can normally disaffirm the contract *without* being liable for the reasonable value of the goods used.

BE AWARE A minor's station in life (including financial and social status and lifestyle) is important in determining whether an item is a necessary or a luxury. For example, clothing is a necessary, but if a minor from a low-income family contracts for the purchase of a $2,000 leather coat, a court may deem the coat a luxury. In this situation, the contract would not be for "necessaries."

Traditionally, insurance has not been viewed as a necessary, so minors can ordinarily disaffirm their insurance contracts and recover all premiums paid. Some jurisdictions, however, prohibit the disaffirmance of insurance contracts—for example, when minors contract for life insurance on their own lives. Financial loans are seldom considered to be necessaries, even if the minor spends the money borrowed on necessaries. If, however, a lender makes a loan to a minor for the express purpose of enabling the minor to purchase necessaries, and the lender personally makes sure the money is so spent, the minor normally is obligated to repay the loan. The issue in the following case was whether a medical services provider could collect from a minor the cost of emergency services rendered to the minor when his mother did not pay.

CASE 11.2 Yale Diagnostic Radiology v. Estate of Harun Fountain

Supreme Court of Connecticut, 2004.
267 Conn. 351,
838 A.2d 179.

BACKGROUND AND FACTS In March 1996, Harun Fountain was shot in the back of the head at point-blank range by a playmate. Fountain required extensive lifesaving medical services from a variety of providers, including Yale Diagnostic Radiology. Yale billed Fountain's mother, Vernetta Turner-Tucker, for the cost of its services,

(Continued)

CASE 11.2—Continued

$17,694, but she did not pay. Instead, in January 2001, Turner-Tucker filed for bankruptcy (see Chapter 27), and all of her debts, including the amount owed to Yale, were discharged. Meanwhile, she filed a suit in a Connecticut state court against the boy who shot Fountain and obtained money for Fountain's medical care. These funds were deposited in an account—sometimes referred to as an "estate"—established on Fountain's behalf. Yale filed a suit against Fountain's estate, asking the court to order the estate to pay Yale's bill, but the court refused to grant the order. Yale appealed to a state intermediate appellate court, which reversed this ruling and ordered the payment. The estate appealed to the state supreme court.

IN THE WORDS OF THE COURT . . .

BORDEN, J. [Justice]

* * * *

Connecticut has long recognized the common-law rule that a minor child's contracts are voidable. Under this rule, *a minor may, upon reaching majority, choose either to ratify or to avoid contractual obligations entered into during his minority.* The traditional reasoning behind this rule is based on the well established common-law principles that the law should protect children from the detrimental consequences of their youthful and improvident acts, and that children should be able to emerge into adulthood unencumbered by financial obligations incurred during the course of their minority. The rule is further supported by a policy of protecting children from unscrupulous individuals seeking to profit from their youth and inexperience. [Emphasis added.]

The rule that a minor's contracts are voidable, however, is not absolute. An exception to this rule, eponymously known as the doctrine of necessaries, is that a minor may not avoid a contract for goods or services necessary for his health and sustenance. Such contracts are binding even if entered into during minority, and *a minor, upon reaching majority, may not, as a matter of law, disaffirm them.* [Emphasis added.]

* * * *

We have not heretofore articulated the particular legal theory underlying the doctrine of necessaries. We therefore take this occasion to do so, and we conclude that the most apt theory is that of an implied in law contract, also sometimes referred to as a quasi-contract. * * *

In distinction to an implied in fact contract, a quasi or implied in law contract is not a contract, but an obligation which the law creates out of the circumstances present, even though a party did not assume the obligation. * * * It is based on equitable principles to operate whenever justice requires compensation to be made * * * . With no other test than what, under a given set of circumstances, is just or unjust, equitable or inequitable, conscionable or unconscionable, it becomes necessary * * * to examine the circumstances and the conduct of the parties and apply this standard. [Emphasis added.]

Thus, when a medical services provider renders necessary medical care to an injured minor, two contracts arise: the primary contract between the provider and the minor's parents; and an implied in law contract between the provider and the minor himself. The primary contract between the provider and the parents is based on the parents' duty to pay for their children's necessary expenses * * * . Such contracts, where not express, may be implied in fact and generally arise both from the parties' conduct and their reasonable expectations. The primacy of this contract means that the provider of necessaries must make all reasonable efforts to collect from the parents before resorting to the secondary, implied in law contract with the minor.

The secondary implied in law contract between the medical services provider and the minor arises from equitable considerations, including the law's disfavor of

CASE 11.2—Continued

unjust enrichment. Therefore, where necessary medical services are rendered to a minor whose parents do not pay for them, equity and justice demand that a secondary implied in law contract arise between the medical services provider and the minor who has received the benefits of those services. These principles compel the conclusion that, in the circumstances of the present case, the [defendant is] liable to the plaintiff, under the common-law doctrine of necessaries, for the services rendered by the plaintiff to Fountain.

* * * *

The judgment is affirmed.

DECISION AND REMEDY The Connecticut Supreme Court affirmed the judgment of the lower court. A party who provides emergency medical services to a minor can collect for those services from the minor if his or her parents do not pay. Thus, Yale could collect from Fountain's estate for the cost of its services under the doctrine of necessaries.

FOR CRITICAL ANALYSIS—Social Consideration *What might have happened in future cases if the court had held that there was no implied-in-law contract between Fountain and Yale?*

RATIFICATION
The act of accepting and giving legal force to an obligation that previously was not enforceable.

Ratification In contract law, **ratification** is the act of accepting and giving legal force to an obligation that previously was not enforceable. A minor who has reached the age of majority can ratify a contract expressly or impliedly. Express ratification occurs when the minor expressly states, orally or in writing, that she or he intends to be bound by the contract. Implied ratification exists when the conduct of the minor indicates an intention to be bound by the contract. Ratification will be implied if the minor's conduct is inconsistent with disaffirmance (as when the minor enjoys the benefits of the contract) or if the minor fails to disaffirm an executed (fully performed) contract within a reasonable time after reaching the age of majority. If the contract is still executory (not yet performed or only partially performed), however, failure to disaffirm the contract will not necessarily imply ratification.

■ EXAMPLE 11.2 Lin enters a contract to sell her laptop to Arturo, a minor. If Arturo does not disaffirm the contract and, on reaching the age of majority, writes a letter to Lin stating that he still agrees to buy the laptop, he has expressly ratified the contract. If, instead, Arturo takes possession of the laptop as a minor and continues to use it well after reaching the age of majority, he has impliedly ratified the contract. ■

In determining whether implied ratification has occurred, the courts generally look at whether the minor, after reaching the age of majority, has had ample opportunity to consider the nature of the contractual obligations he or she entered into as a minor and at the extent to which the adult party to the contract has performed.

Parents' Liability As a general rule, parents are not liable for the contracts made by minor children acting on their own, except contracts for necessaries, which the parents are legally required to provide. This is why businesses ordinarily require parents to cosign any contract made with a minor. The parents then become personally obligated to perform the conditions of the contract, even if their child avoids liability.

Generally, minors are personally liable for their own torts. The parents of the minor can *also* be held liable in certain situations. In some states, parents may be

.on the Web ...y provisions ...nancipation of ... view Wyoming's statutory provisions on this topic at **http://legisweb.state.wy.us/statutes/sub14.htm**.

liable if they failed to exercise proper parental control when they knew or should have known that this lack of control posed an unreasonable risk of harm to others. ■ EXAMPLE 11.3 Suppose that parents allow their eleven-year-old child to drive a car on public roads. If the child drives negligently and causes someone else to be injured, the parents may be held liable for the minor's tort (negligence). ■ Other states have enacted statutes that impose liability on parents for certain kinds of tortious acts committed by their children, such as those that are willful and malicious.

The *Concept Summary* on this page summarizes the rules relating to contracts by minors.

Emancipation Minority status may be terminated through **emancipation,** which occurs when a child's parent or legal guardian gives up the legal right to exercise control over the child. Normally, a minor who leaves home to support himself or herself is considered emancipated. In many states, marriage terminates the status of minority. A number of jurisdictions permit minors to petition a court for emancipation. In addition, a minor may petition a court to be treated as an adult for business purposes. If the court grants the minor's request, it removes the minor's lack of contractual capacity, and the minor no longer has the right to disaffirm business contracts.

EMANCIPATION
In regard to minors, the act of being freed from parental control; occurs when a child's parent or legal guardian relinquishes the legal right to exercise control over the child. Normally, a minor who leaves home to support himself or herself is considered emancipated.

INTOXICATED PERSONS

Contractual capacity also becomes an issue when a party to a contract was intoxicated at the time the contract was made. Intoxication is a condition in which a person's normal capacity to act or think is inhibited by alcohol or some other drug. If the person was sufficiently intoxicated to lack mental capacity, the contract may be voidable even if the intoxication was purely voluntary. For the contract to be voidable, however, the person must prove that the intoxication impaired her or his reason and judgment so severely that she or he did not comprehend the legal consequences of entering into the contract. In addition, to avoid the contract in the majority of states, the person claiming intoxication must be able to return all consideration received.

If, despite intoxication, the person understood the legal consequences of the agreement, the contract is enforceable. The fact that the terms of the contract are

CONCEPT SUMMARY Contracts by Minors

General Rule	Contracts entered into by minors are voidable at the option of the minor.
Rules of Disaffirmance	A minor may disaffirm a contract at any time while still a minor and within a reasonable time after reaching the age of majority. Most states do not require restitution.
Exceptions to Basic Rules of Disaffirmance	1. *Necessaries*—Minors may disaffirm contracts for necessaries but remain liable for the reasonable value of the goods or services. 2. *Ratification*—After reaching the age of majority, a person can ratify a contract that he or she formed as a minor, becoming fully liable thereon. 3. *Fraud or misrepresentation*—In many jurisdictions, a minor who misrepresents her or his age is denied the right of disaffirmance.

foolish or obviously favor the other party does not make the contract voidable (unless the other party fraudulently induced the person to become intoxicated). As a practical matter, courts rarely permit contracts to be avoided on the ground of intoxication because it is difficult to determine whether a party was sufficiently intoxicated to avoid legal duties. Rather than inquire into the intoxicated person's mental state, many courts instead focus on objective indications of capacity to determine whether the contract is voidable.[3]

Mentally Incompetent Persons

Contracts made by mentally incompetent persons can be void, voidable, or valid. We look here at the circumstances that determine when these classifications apply.

.on the Web For a brief covering contractual capacity and mentally incompetent persons, go to **http://www.zlawyer2b.com/Contract-4-brief.html**.

When the Contract Will Be Void If a court has previously determined that a person is mentally incompetent and has appointed a guardian to represent the person, any contract made by that mentally incompetent person is *void*—no contract exists. Only the guardian can enter into a binding contract on behalf of the mentally incompetent person.

When the Contract Will Be Voidable If a court has not previously judged a person to be mentally incompetent but in fact the person was incompetent at the time, the contract may be *voidable*. A contract is voidable if the person did not know he or she was entering into the contract or lacked the mental capacity to comprehend its nature, purpose, and consequences. In such situations, the contract is voidable at the option of the mentally incompetent person but not the other party. The contract may then be disaffirmed or ratified (if the person regains mental competence). Like intoxicated persons, mentally incompetent persons must return any consideration and pay for the reasonable value of any necessaries they receive.

■ Example 11.4 Milo, a mentally incompetent man who had not been previously declared incompetent by a judge, agrees to sell twenty lots in a prime residential neighborhood to Anastof. At the time he enters into the contract, Milo is confused over which lots he is selling and how much they are worth. As a result, he contracts to sell the properties for substantially less than their value. If the court finds that Milo was unable to understand the nature and consequences of the contract, the contract is voidable. Milo can avoid the sale, provided that he returns any consideration he received. ■

When the Contract Will Be Valid A contract entered into by a mentally incompetent person (whom a court has not previously declared incompetent) may also be deemed *valid* if the person had capacity *at the time the contract was formed*. For instance, a person may be able to understand the nature and effect of entering into a certain contract yet simultaneously lack capacity to engage in other activities. In such cases, the contract ordinarily will be valid because the person is not legally mentally incompetent for contractual purposes.[4] Similarly, an otherwise mentally incompetent person may have a *lucid interval*—a temporary restoration of sufficient

3. See, for example, the court's decision in *Lucy v. Zehmer,* presented as Case 9.1 in Chapter 9.

4. Modern courts no longer require a person to be completely irrational to disaffirm contracts on the basis of mental incompetence. A contract may be voidable if, by reason of a mental illness or defect, an individual was unable to act reasonably with respect to the transaction and the other party had reason to know of the condition.

intelligence, judgment, and will to enter into contracts—during which he or she will be considered to have full legal capacity.

Legality

To this point, we have discussed three of the requirements for a valid contract to exist—agreement, consideration, and contractual capacity. Now we examine a fourth—legality. For a contract to be valid and enforceable, it must be formed for a legal purpose. A contract to do something that is prohibited by federal or state statutory law is illegal and, as such, void from the outset and thus unenforceable. Additionally, a contract to commit a tortious act or to commit an action that is contrary to public policy is illegal and unenforceable.

CONTRACTS CONTRARY TO STATUTE

Statutes often set forth rules specifying which terms and clauses may be included in contracts and which are prohibited. We examine here several ways in which contracts may be contrary to a statute and thus illegal.

Usury Virtually every state has a statute that sets the maximum rate of interest that can be charged for different types of transactions, including ordinary loans. A lender who makes a loan at an interest rate above the lawful maximum commits **usury.** The maximum rate of interest varies from state to state.

USURY
Charging an illegal rate of interest.

Although usury statutes place a ceiling on allowable rates of interest, exceptions are made to facilitate business transactions. For example, many states exempt corporate loans from the usury laws. In addition, almost all states have special statutes allowing much higher interest rates on small loans to help those borrowers who need funds and could not otherwise obtain loans.

The consequences for lenders who make usurious loans vary from state to state. A number of states allow the lender to recover only the principal of a loan along with interest up to the legal maximum. In effect, the lender is denied recovery of the excess interest. In other states, the lender can recover the principal amount of the loan but no interest. In a few states, a usurious loan is a void transaction, and the lender cannot recover either the principal or the interest.

Gambling All states have statutes that regulate gambling—defined as any scheme that involves the distribution of property by chance among persons who have paid valuable consideration for the opportunity (chance) to receive the property.[5] Gambling is the creation of risk for the purpose of assuming it. Traditionally, the states have deemed gambling contracts illegal and thus void.

In several states, however, including Louisiana, Nevada, and New Jersey, casino gambling is legal. In other states, certain other forms of gambling are legal. California, for example, has not defined draw poker as a crime, although criminal statutes prohibit numerous other types of gambling games. A number of states allow gambling on horse races, and the majority of states have legalized state-operated lotteries, as well as lotteries (such as bingo) conducted for charitable purposes. Many states also allow gambling on Native American reservations.

---

5. See *Wishing Well Club v. Akron,* 66 Ohio Law Abs. 406, 112 N.E.2d 41 (1951).

Sometimes it is difficult to distinguish a gambling contract from the risk sharing inherent in almost all contracts. ■ EXAMPLE 11.5 In one case, five co-workers each received a free lottery ticket from a customer and agreed to split the winnings if one of the tickets turned out to be the winning one. At first glance, this may seem entirely legal. The court, however, noted that the oral contract in this case "was an exchange of promises to share winnings from the parties' individually owned lottery tickets upon the happening of the uncertain event" that one of the tickets would win. Consequently, concluded the court, the agreement at issue was "founded on a gambling consideration" and therefore was void.[6] ■

.on the Web ...sted in reading the ...n regulating ... Sabbath in colonial ... out some of the punishments meted out for failing to obey these regulations), go to

http://www.natreformassn.org/statesman/99/charactr.html.

Sabbath (Sunday) Laws Statutes referred to as Sabbath (Sunday) laws prohibit the formation or performance of certain contracts on a Sunday. Under the common law, such contracts are legal in the absence of this statutory prohibition. According to some state and local laws, all contracts entered into on a Sunday are illegal. Laws in other states or municipalities prohibit only the sale of certain types of merchandise, such as alcoholic beverages, on a Sunday.

BLUE LAWS
State or local laws that prohibit the performance of certain types of commercial activities on Sunday.

As noted in Chapter 2, these laws, which date back to colonial times, are often called **blue laws.** Blue laws get their name from the blue paper on which New Haven, Connecticut, printed its new town ordinance in 1781. The ordinance prohibited all work on Sunday and required all shops to close on the "Lord's Day." A number of states and municipalities enacted laws forbidding the carrying on of "all secular labor and business on the Lord's Day." Exceptions to Sunday laws permit contracts for necessities (such as food) and works of charity. Additionally, a fully performed (executed) contract that was entered into on a Sunday normally cannot be rescinded (canceled).

6. *Dickerson v. Deno,* 770 So.2d 63 (Ala. 2000).

Adults gamble at a casino. Would this same activity be illegal if it were conducted online? If so, could it be prevented? How? (© M. Borchi/Photo Researchers)

Sunday laws are often not enforced, and some of these laws have been held to be unconstitutional on the ground that they are contrary to the freedom of religion. Nonetheless, as a precaution, business owners contemplating doing business in a particular locality should check to see if any Sunday statutes or ordinances will affect their business activities.

Licensing Statutes All states require that members of certain professions obtain licenses allowing them to practice. Physicians, lawyers, real estate brokers, architects, electricians, and stockbrokers are but a few of the people who must be licensed. Some licenses are obtained only after extensive schooling and examinations, which indicate to the public that a special skill has been acquired. Others require only that the particular person be of good moral character and pay a fee.

The Purpose of Licensing Statutes. Generally, business licenses provide a means of regulating and taxing certain businesses and protecting the public against actions that could threaten the general welfare. For example, in nearly all states, a stockbroker must be licensed and must file a bond with the state to protect the public from fraudulent transactions in stock. Similarly, a plumber must be licensed and bonded to protect the public against incompetent plumbers and to protect the public health. Only persons or businesses possessing the qualifications and complying with the conditions required by statute are entitled to licenses. For instance, the owner of a tavern can be required to sell food as a condition of obtaining a license to serve liquor.

Contracts with Unlicensed Practitioners. A contract with an unlicensed practitioner may still be enforceable, depending on the nature of the licensing statute. Some states expressly provide that the lack of a license in certain occupations bars the enforcement of work-related contracts. If the statute does not expressly state this, one must look to the underlying purpose of the licensing requirements for a particular occupation. If the purpose is to protect the public from unauthorized practitioners, a contract involving an unlicensed individual is illegal and unenforceable. If, however, the underlying purpose of the statute is to raise government revenues, a contract with an unlicensed practitioner is enforceable—although the unlicensed person is usually fined.

At issue in the following case was whether a contract entered into with an unlicensed contractor could serve as the basis for an action for wrongful interference with a contractual relationship.

CASE 11.3 RCDI Construction, Inc. v. Spaceplan/Architecture, Planning & Interiors, P.A.[a]

United States District Court,
Western District of North Carolina, 2001.
148 F.Supp.2d 607.

BACKGROUND AND FACTS RCDI Construction Management, Inc. (RCDI-CM), signed a contract with Dr. Anjil Patel for the construction of a hotel in North Carolina. At the time, RCDI-CM was a licensed contractor in West Virginia but not in North Carolina. The contract was assigned to RCDI Construction, Inc. (RCDI), a wholly owned subsidiary of RCDI-CM that did have a North Carolina contractor's license. RCDI began to build the hotel. When construction was nearly complete, a discharge of water damaged the hotel. On behalf of Patel,

a. *P.A.* is an abbreviation for "Professional Association," a form of business organization.

CASE 11.3—Continued

Spaceplan/Architecture, Planning & Interiors, P.A. (SAPI), assessed the condition of the building. SAPI recommended that Patel terminate the contract with RCDI, gut the building, and reconstruct the hotel. Following its termination, RCDI agreed to forfeit to Patel $421,000 owed under the construction contract and to pay Patel $6.7 million. RCDI then filed a suit in a federal district court against SAPI, alleging, among other things, wrongful interference with a contractual relationship (see Chapter 4). SAPI filed a motion for a judgment on the pleadings.[b]

b. Recall from Chapter 3 that in a motion for judgment on the pleadings, a party asks the court to decide the issue based only on the pleadings (complaint, answer, and other documents) and no additional evidence or testimony. The motion will be granted only if no facts are in dispute and the sole issue is how the law applies to the facts.

IN THE WORDS OF THE COURT . . .

THORNBURG, District Court J. [Judge]

* * * *

* * * [T]o establish a cause of action for tortious interference with a contract * * * the plaintiff must allege and prove these essential elements: First, that a valid contract existed between the plaintiff and a third person, conferring upon the plaintiff some contractual right against the third person. Second, that the outsider had knowledge of the plaintiff's contract with the third person. Third, that the outsider intentionally induced the third person not to perform his contract with the plaintiff. Fourth, that in so doing the outsider acted without justification. Fifth, that the outsider's act caused the plaintiff actual damages. * * *

Here, [RCDI and RCDI-CM's] claim fails because they cannot satisfy the first element of the offense. While there is no question that a contract for the construction of a hotel was signed by RCDI-CM and Dr. Patel, it is equally uncontested that Plaintiff RCDI-CM was not a contractor licensed by the State of North Carolina at the time of the signing of the contract. * * * [C]ontracts entered into by unlicensed construction contractors, in violation of a statute passed for the protection of the public are unenforceable by the contractor. The unenforceability of such contracts by the contractor stems directly from their conception in the contractor's illegal act. Thus, because Plaintiffs possessed no contractual rights to enforce against the other party to the contract (Dr. Patel), a related claim for tortious interference with a contract will not be recognized by the courts.

Though this result is harsh, * * * it is consistent with the position taken by the courts that despite possible injustice resulting between the parties, they will not lend their assistance to a party who seeks compensation [stemming from] an illegal act. * * * This rule is consistent with the well founded policy of law that *no person be permitted to acquire a right of action from their own unlawful act and one who participates in an unlawful act cannot recover damages for the consequences of that act.* * * * The authorities from the earliest time to the present unanimously hold that no court will lend its assistance in any way towards carrying out the terms of an illegal contract. In case any action is brought which it is necessary to prove the illegal contract in order to maintain the action, courts will not enforce it, nor will they enforce any alleged rights directly springing from such contract. [Emphasis added.]

DECISION AND REMEDY The federal district court held that no valid contract existed because the plaintiff was an unlicensed contractor in the state of North Carolina. Therefore, the plaintiff could not sue SAPI for wrongful interference with the contract. The court granted SAPI's motion and dismissed RCDI's complaint.

FOR CRITICAL ANALYSIS—Social Consideration *Considering the amount of money involved, does it seem harsh to apply the illegality doctrine to contracts such as the one in the* RCDI *case? Should it matter that the party performing the work was licensed in the state? Why or why not?*

CONTRACTS CONTRARY TO PUBLIC POLICY

Although contracts involve private parties, some are not enforceable because of the negative impact they would have on society. These contracts are said to be *contrary to public policy.* Examples include a contract to commit an immoral act, such as selling a child, and a contract that prohibits marriage. ■ EXAMPLE 11.6 Everett offers a young man $10,000 if he refrains from marrying Everett's daughter. If the young man accepts, no contract is formed (the contract is void) because it is contrary to public policy. Thus, if the man marries Everett's daughter, Everett cannot sue him for breach of contract. ■ Business contracts that may be contrary to public policy include contracts in restraint of trade and unconscionable contracts or clauses.

Contracts in Restraint of Trade Contracts in restraint of trade (anticompetitive agreements) usually adversely affect the public policy that favors competition in the economy. Typically, such contracts also violate one or more federal or state statutes.[7] An exception is recognized when the restraint is reasonable and is part of, or supplemental to, a contract for the sale of a business or an **employment contract** (a contract stating the terms and conditions of employment). Many such exceptions involve a type of restraint called a **covenant not to compete,** or a restrictive covenant.

EMPLOYMENT CONTRACT
A contract between an employer and an employee in which the terms and conditions of employment are stated.

COVENANT NOT TO COMPETE
A contractual promise of one party to refrain from conducting business similar to that of another party for a certain period of time and within a specified geographic area. Courts commonly enforce such covenants if they are reasonable in terms of time and geographic area and part of, or supplemental to, an employment contract or a contract for the sale of a business.

Covenants Not to Compete and the Sale of an Ongoing Business. Covenants not to compete are often contained in contracts concerning the sale of an ongoing business. A covenant not to compete is created when a seller agrees not to open a new store in a certain geographic area surrounding the old store. Such an agreement, when it is ancillary to a sales contract and reasonable in terms of time and geographic area, enables the seller to sell, and the purchaser to buy, the "goodwill" and "reputation" of an ongoing business. If, for example, a well-known merchant sells his or her store and opens a competing business a block away, many of the merchant's customers will likely do business at the new store. This renders valueless the good name and reputation sold to the other merchant for a price. If a covenant not to compete is not ancillary to a sales agreement, however, it will be void because it unreasonably restrains trade and is contrary to public policy.

Covenants Not to Compete in Employment Contracts. Agreements not to compete can also be included in employment contracts. People in middle-level and upper-level management positions commonly agree not to work for competitors or not to start a competing business for a specified period of time after terminating employment. Such agreements are generally legal so long as the specified period of time is not excessive in duration and the geographic restriction is reasonable. Basically, the restriction on competition must be reasonable—that is, not any greater than necessary to protect a legitimate business interest. While a time restriction of one year may be upheld by a court as reasonable, a time restriction of two, three, or five years may not be.

on the Web
nation on restrictive ployment contracts, n article written by se Brown & Associates, P.C., at **http://www.loosebrown.com/articles/art009.pdf**.

Determining what should be considered "reasonable" time and geographic restrictions in the online environment is a more difficult issue being addressed by the courts. The Internet environment has no physical borders, so geographic restrictions are no longer relevant. Also, a reasonable time period in the online environment may be less than what is reasonable in conventional employment contracts because the restrictions would apply worldwide. (For a further discussion of this issue, see this chapter's *Management Perspective* feature.)

7. Federal statutes prohibiting anticompetitive agreements include the Sherman Antitrust Act, the Clayton Act, and the Federal Trade Commission Act (see Chapter 37).

MANAGEMENT PERSPECTIVE

Covenants Not to Compete in the Internet Context

MANAGEMENT FACES A LEGAL ISSUE

For some companies today, particularly those in high-tech industries, trade secrets are their most valuable assets. Often, to prevent departing employees from disclosing trade secrets to competing employers, business owners and managers have their key employees sign covenants not to compete. In such a covenant, the employee typically agrees not to set up a competing business or work for a competitor in a specified geographic area for a certain period of time. Generally, the time and geographic restrictions must be reasonable. A serious issue facing management today is whether time and space restrictions that have been deemed reasonable in the past serve as a guide to what might constitute reasonable restrictions in today's changing legal landscape, which includes the Internet environment.

WHAT THE COURTS SAY

There is little case law to guide management on this issue. One case involved Mark Schlack, who worked as a Web site manager for EarthWeb, Inc., in New York. Schlack signed a covenant stating that, on termination of his employment, he would not work for any competing company for one year. When he resigned and accepted an offer from a company in Massachusetts to design a Web site, EarthWeb sued to enforce the covenant not to compete. The court refused to enforce the covenant, in part because there was no evidence that Schlack had misappropriated any of EarthWeb's trade secrets or clients. The court also stated that because the Internet lacks physical borders, a covenant prohibiting an employee from working for a competitor anywhere in the world for one year is excessive in duration.[a]

In a later case, a federal district court enforced a one-year noncompete agreement against the founder of a law-related Web site business even though no geographic restriction was included in the agreement. According to the court, "Although there is no geographic limitation on the provision, this is nonetheless reasonable in light of the national, and indeed international, nature of Internet business."[b]

IMPLICATIONS FOR MANAGERS

Management in high-tech companies should avoid overreaching in terms of time and geographic restrictions in noncompete agreements. Additionally, when considering the reasonability of time and place restrictions, the courts tend to balance time restrictions against other factors, such as geographic restrictions. Because for Web-based work the geographic restriction can be worldwide in scope, the time restriction should be narrowed considerably to compensate for the extensive geographic restriction.

a. *EarthWeb, Inc. v. Schlack*, 71 F.Supp.2d 299 (S.D.N.Y. 1999).
b. *West Publishing Corp. v. Stanley*, 2004 WL 73590 (D.N.D. 2004).

Enforcement Problems. The laws governing the enforceability of covenants not to compete vary significantly from state to state. In some states, such as Texas, such a covenant will not be enforced unless the employee has received some benefit in return for signing the noncompete agreement. This is true even if the covenant is reasonable as to time and area. If the employee receives no benefit, the covenant will be deemed void. California prohibits the enforcement of covenants not to compete altogether.

Occasionally, depending on the jurisdiction, courts will *reform* covenants not to compete. If a covenant is found to be unreasonable in time or geographic area, the court may convert the terms into reasonable ones and then enforce the reformed covenant. This presents a problem, however, in that the judge, implicitly, has become a party to the contract. Consequently, courts usually resort to contract **reformation** only when necessary to prevent undue burdens or hardships.

REFORMATION
A court-ordered correction of a written contract so that it reflects the true intentions of the parties or prevents undue burdens or hardships.

Unconscionable Contracts or Clauses Ordinarily, a court does not look at the fairness or equity of a contract; for example, a court normally will not inquire into the adequacy of consideration. Persons are assumed to be reasonably intelligent, and the court does not come to their aid just because they have made unwise or foolish bargains. In certain circumstances, however, bargains are so oppressive that the courts relieve innocent parties of part or all of their duties. Such a bargain is called an **unconscionable contract** (or **unconscionable clause**). Both the Uniform Commercial Code (UCC) and the Uniform Consumer Credit Code (UCCC) embody the unconscionability concept—the former with regard to the sale of goods and the latter with regard to consumer loans and the waiver of rights.[8] A contract can be unconscionable on either procedural or substantive grounds, as discussed in the following subsections and illustrated graphically in Exhibit 11–1.

UNCONSCIONABLE CONTRACT (OR UNCONSCIONABLE CLAUSE)
A contract or clause that is void on the basis of public policy because one party, as a result of disproportionate bargaining power, is forced to accept terms that are unfairly burdensome and that unfairly benefit the dominating party.

Procedural Unconscionability. Procedural unconscionability may exist when a term that one of the parties does not understand becomes part of a contract. The party may not understand the term because of inconspicuous print, unintelligible language ("legalese"), lack of opportunity to read the contract, lack of opportunity to ask questions about the contract's meaning, and other factors. Procedural unconscionability sometimes relates to purported lack of voluntariness because of a disparity in bargaining power between the two parties. Contracts entered into because of one party's vastly superior bargaining power may be deemed unconscionable. These situations usually involve an **adhesion contract,** which is a contract drafted by the dominant party and then presented to the other—the adhering party—on a "take-it-or-leave-it" basis.[9]

ADHESION CONTRACT
A "standard-form" contract, such as that between a large retailer and a consumer, in which the stronger party dictates the terms.

8. See, for example, UCC Sections 2–302 and 2–719.
9. See, for example, *Henningsen v. Bloomfield Motors, Inc.,* 32 N.J. 358, 161 A.2d 69 (1960).

EXHIBIT 11–1 UNCONSCIONABILITY

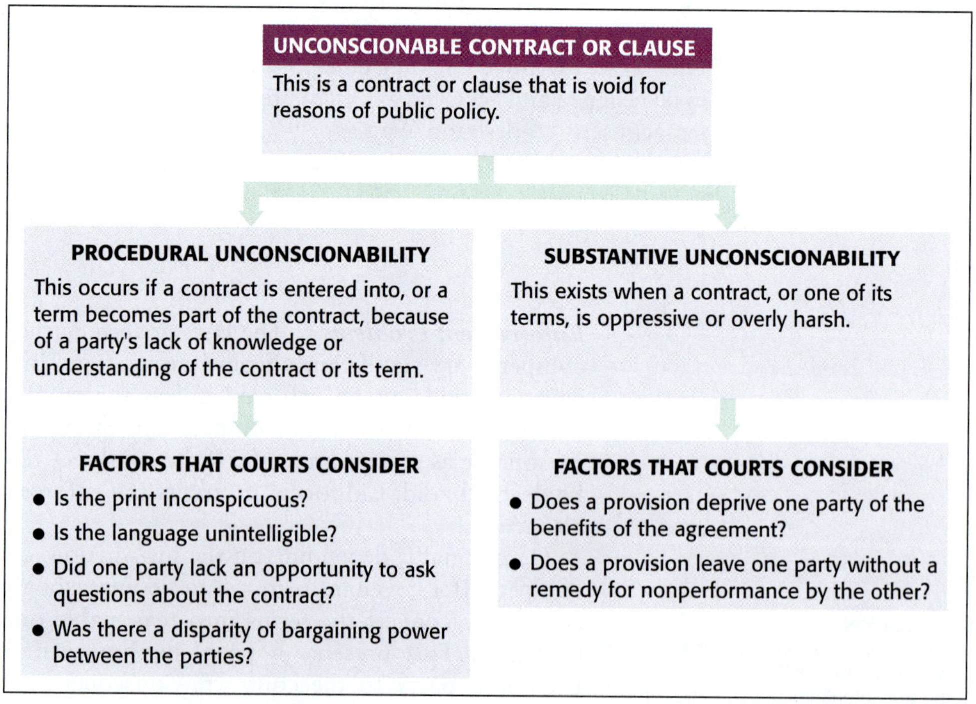

Substantive Unconscionability. Substantive unconscionability characterizes those contracts, or portions of contracts, that are oppressive or overly harsh. Courts generally focus on provisions that deprive one party of the benefits of the agreement or leave that party without remedy for nonperformance by the other. For example, suppose that a person with little income and only a fourth-grade education agrees to purchase a refrigerator for $3,000 and signs a two-year installment contract. The same type of refrigerator usually sells for $600 on the market. Despite the general rule that the courts will not inquire into the adequacy of the consideration, some courts hold that this type of contract is unconscionable because the contract terms are so oppressive as to "shock the conscience" of the court.[10] Is a contract to prescribe medications via the Internet unconscionable? For a discussion of this issue, see the *Adapting the Law to the Online Environment* feature on the next page.

EXCULPATORY CLAUSE
A clause that releases a contractual party from liability in the event of monetary or physical injury, no matter who is at fault.

Exculpatory Clauses Sometimes closely related to the concept of unconscionability are **exculpatory clauses,** which release a party from liability in the event of monetary or physical injury, *no matter who is at fault.* Indeed, some courts refer to such clauses in terms of unconscionability. ■ EXAMPLE 11.7 Suppose, for example, that Madison Manufacturing Company hires a laborer and has him sign a contract containing the following clause:

> Said employee hereby agrees with employer, in consideration of such employment, that he will take upon himself all risks incident to his position and will in no case hold the company liable for any injury or damage he may sustain, in his person or otherwise, by accidents or injuries in the factory, or which may result from defective machinery or carelessness or misconduct of himself or any other employee in service of the employer.

This contract provision attempts to remove Madison's potential liability for injuries occurring to the employee, and it would usually be held contrary to public policy.[11] ■ Additionally, exculpatory clauses found in agreements to lease commercial property are normally held to be contrary to public policy. Such clauses are almost universally held to be illegal and unenforceable when they are included in residential property leases.

REMEMBER Virtually everyone is liable for her or his own torts, and this responsibility cannot be contracted away.

Exculpatory clauses may be enforced, however, when the parties seeking their enforcement are not involved in businesses considered important to the public interest. Businesses such as health clubs, amusement parks, horse-rental concessions, golf-cart concessions, and skydiving organizations frequently use exculpatory clauses to limit their liability for patrons' injuries. Because these services are not essential, the firms offering them are sometimes considered to have no relative advantage in bargaining strength, and anyone contracting for their services is considered to do so voluntarily.

The Effect of Illegality

In general, an illegal contract is void; that is, the contract is deemed never to have existed, and the courts will not aid either party. In most illegal contracts, both parties are considered to be equally at fault—*in pari delicto*. If the contract is executory

10. See, for example, *Jones v. Star Credit Corp.,* 59 Misc.2d 189, 298 N.Y.S.2d 264 (1969). This case is presented in Chapter 18 as Case 18.3.
11. For a case with similar facts, see *Little Rock & Fort Smith Railway Co. v. Eubanks,* 48 Ark. 460, 3 S.W. 808 (1887). In such a case, the exculpatory clause may also be illegal because it violates a state workers' compensation law.

ADAPTING THE LAW TO THE ONLINE ENVIRONMENT

Is It Unconscionable for Physicians to Prescribe Medication Online?

Anyone with an e-mail address has undoubtedly received scores of messages offering to sell prescription medications, such as Viagra, online. In the past, someone who wanted a prescription for a certain medication—whether it was for allergies, weight loss, or sexual enhancement—had to see a physician and, normally, undergo a physical examination to see if that medication was appropriate. Today, however, it is possible to enter into a contract to obtain a prescription for, and order, many medications via the Internet without ever setting foot in a physician's office. Contracting with a physician online to receive prescription drugs may be ill advised, but are such contracts unconscionable?

A VIRTUAL DIAGNOSIS

The hallmark of an unconscionable contract is that its terms are so oppressive, one sided, or unfair as to "shock the conscience" of the court. Thus, the issue is whether Internet prescription contracts are so unfair that they "shock the conscience" of the court. After all, physicians are trained to examine patients, diagnose medical conditions, and evaluate possible treatments. A physician who is prescribing medication for a person online, however, has no objective way to determine the person's health status or whether the person understands the risks involved. For example, in the online context, a physician cannot tell if a person is truthfully reporting his or her age and weight, which can significantly affect whether a medication is recommended. In addition, physicians who prescribe drugs online cannot monitor the use of these drugs and evaluate their effectiveness.

AN EMERGING ISSUE

To date, only a few courts have addressed this issue, and no court as yet has held that prescribing drugs online is unconscionable. For example, in 2003, in a case before the Kansas Supreme Court, the state attorney general claimed that it was unconscionable for an out-of-state physician to contract with residents to prescribe drugs via the Internet. The case involved three Kansas residents, including a minor, who entered into contracts on the Web to obtain prescription weight-loss drugs (Meridia and phentermine).[a]

The court held that the physician's conduct and the resulting contracts were not unconscionable because there was no evidence that the physician had deceived, oppressed, or misused superior bargaining power. The Web site used by the physician had included a great deal of general information about the specific drugs and their side effects, online questionnaires to obtain medical histories, and waivers of the physician's liability for the prescriptions. The Web site had also provided an online calculator for body weight so that a person could determine if she or he was twenty-five pounds overweight, as required to obtain a prescription for Meridia. Because the court found that the individuals had gotten exactly what they bargained for—the prescription medications they sought—the court refused to step in and declare the contracts unconscionable.

FOR CRITICAL ANALYSIS

If the physicians are not deceptive, should the courts allow all types of medications to be prescribed over the Internet? Why or why not? Explain whether the practice of prescribing medications via the Internet might reach the point at which it "shocks the conscience" of the court.

a. *State ex rel. Stovall v. DVM Enterprises, Inc.*, 275 Kan. 243, 62 P.3d 653 (2003); see also *State ex rel. Stovall v. Confimed.com, L.L.C.*, 272 Kan. 1313, 38 P.3d 707 (2002). (The Latin phrase *ex rel.* means "by or on the relation of" and is used in case names when the suit is brought by the government on the application of a private party who is interested in the matter.)

(not yet fulfilled), neither party can enforce it. If it has been executed, there can be neither contractual nor quasi-contractual recovery.

That one wrongdoer in an illegal contract is unjustly enriched at the expense of the other is of no concern to the law—except under certain circumstances (to be discussed shortly). The major justification for this hands-off attitude is that it is improper to place the machinery of justice at the disposal of a plaintiff who has broken the law by entering into an illegal bargain. Another justification is the hoped-for deterrent effect of this general rule. A plaintiff who suffers a loss because of an illegal bargain will presumably be deterred from entering into similar illegal bargains in the future.

There are exceptions to the general rule that neither party to an illegal bargain can sue for breach and neither party can recover for performance rendered. We look at these exceptions here.

JUSTIFIABLE IGNORANCE OF THE FACTS

When one of the parties to a contract is relatively innocent (has no reason to know that the contract is illegal), that party can often recover any benefits conferred in a partially executed contract. In this situation, the courts will not enforce the contract but will allow the parties to return to their original positions.

A court may sometimes permit an innocent party who has fully performed under a contract to enforce the contract against the guilty party. ■ **EXAMPLE 11.8** A trucking company contracts with Gillespie to carry crated goods to a specific destination for a normal fee of $500. The trucker delivers the crates and later finds out that they contained illegal goods. Although the shipment, use, and sale of the goods are illegal under the law, the trucker, being an innocent party, can normally still legally collect the $500 from Gillespie. ■

MEMBERS OF PROTECTED CLASSES

When a statute protects a certain class of people, a member of that class can enforce an illegal contract even though the other party cannot. ■ **EXAMPLE 11.9** Statutes prohibit certain employees (such as flight attendants) from working more than a specified number of hours per month. These employees thus constitute a class protected by statute. An employee who is required to work more than the maximum can recover for those extra hours of service. ■

BLUE SKY LAWS
State laws that regulate the offer and sale of securities.

Other examples of statutes designed to protect a particular class of people are **blue sky laws**—state laws that regulate and supervise investment companies for the protection of the public (see Chapter 35)—and state statutes regulating the sale of insurance. If an insurance company violates a statute when selling insurance, the purchaser can nevertheless enforce the policy and recover from the insurer.

WITHDRAWAL FROM AN ILLEGAL AGREEMENT

If the illegal part of a bargain has not yet been performed, the party rendering performance can withdraw from the contract and recover the performance or its value. ■ **EXAMPLE 11.10** Suppose that Marta and Amil decide to wager (illegally) on the outcome of a boxing match. Each deposits money with a stakeholder, who agrees to pay the winner of the bet. At this point, each party has performed part of the agreement, but the illegal part of the agreement will not occur until the money is paid to the winner. Before such payment occurs, either party is entitled to withdraw from the agreement by giving notice to the stakeholder of his or her withdrawal. ■

SEVERABLE, OR DIVISIBLE, CONTRACTS

A contract that is *severable,* or divisible, consists of distinct parts that can be performed separately, with separate consideration provided for each part. With an *indivisible* contract, in contrast, the parties intended that complete performance by each party would be essential, even if the contract contains a number of seemingly separate provisions.

If a contract is divisible into legal and illegal portions, a court may enforce the legal portion but not the illegal one, so long as the illegal portion does not affect the essence of the bargain. This approach is consistent with the basic policy of enforcing the legal intentions of the contracting parties whenever possible. ■ **EXAMPLE 11.11** If an employment contract includes an overly broad and thus illegal covenant not to compete, the court might allow the employment contract to be enforceable but reform the unreasonably broad covenant by converting its terms into reasonable ones. Alternatively, the court could declare the covenant illegal (and thus void) and enforce the remaining employment terms. ■

ETHICAL ISSUE 11.1

How do courts decide when a contract is severable? Severability frequently arises in cases involving arbitration clauses. Should a court strike out illegal portions of an arbitration clause and enforce the remaining provisions? That is the fairest solution, according to the U.S. Court of Appeals for the Third Circuit in *Spinetti v. Service Corp. International.*[12] In that case, a woman sued her former employer for age and gender discrimination (see Chapter 41). The woman had signed a contract in which she agreed to arbitrate any disputes with the employer. Part of the arbitration clause required the employee to pay a substantial amount in fees for the arbitration ($500 plus $3,750 in filing fees, $150 per day, and half of the arbitrator's hourly fee of $250). Because these provisions would make arbitration prohibitively expensive for employees, the court held that they were unenforceable and illegal. The court noted that two competing public policies were involved here: first, the policy of protecting employees' ability to enforce their statutory rights against workplace discrimination; and second, the strong policy favoring arbitration agreements. By striking out the illegal portions of the arbitration clause but still requiring the dispute to be arbitrated, the court reasoned that it could further both goals. ■

Contracts Illegal through Fraud, Duress, or Undue Influence

Often, one party to an illegal contract is more at fault than the other. When a party has been induced to enter into an illegal bargain through fraud, duress, or undue influence on the part of the other party to the agreement, the first party will be allowed to recover for the performance or its value.

12. 324 F.3d 212 (3d Cir. 2003).

REVIEWING CAPACITY AND LEGALITY

Renee Beaver started racing go-karts competitively in 1997, when she was fourteen. Many of the races required her to sign an exculpatory clause to participate, which she or her parents regularly signed. In 2000, she participated in the annual Elkhart Grand Prix, a series of races in Elkhart, Indiana. During the event in which she drove, a piece of foam padding used as a course barrier was torn from its base and ended up on the track. A portion of the padding struck Beaver in the head, and another portion was thrown into oncoming traffic, causing a multikart collision during which she sustained severe injuries. Beaver filed an action against the race organizers for negligence. The organizers could not locate the exculpatory clause that Beaver was supposed to have signed.

REVIEWING CAPACITY AND LEGALITY—Continued

Race organizers argued that she must have signed one to enter the race, but even if she had not signed one, her actions showed her intent to be bound by its terms. Using the information presented in the chapter, answer the following questions.

1. Did Beaver have the contractual capacity to enter a contract with an exculpatory clause? Why or why not?
2. Assuming that Beaver did, in fact, sign the exculpatory clause, did she later disaffirm or ratify the contract? Explain.
3. Now assume that Beaver had stated that she was eighteen years old at the time that she signed the exculpatory clause. How might this affect Beaver's ability to disaffirm or ratify the contract?
4. If Beaver did not actually sign the exculpatory clause, could a court conclude that she impliedly accepted its terms by participating in the race? Why or why not?
5. Discuss whether it is likely that a court would conclude that the exculpatory clause that Beaver signed was contrary to public policy.

APPLICATION Should Retailers Enter into Contracts with Minors and Intoxicated Persons?*

Sales personnel, particularly those who are paid on a commission basis, are often eager to make contracts. Sometimes, however, these salespersons must deal with minors and intoxicated persons, both of whom have limited contractual capacity. Therefore, if you are a retailer, you should make sure that your employees are acquainted with the law governing contracts with minors and intoxicated persons.

CONTRACTS WITH MINORS

If your business involves selling consumer durables, such as furniture or automobiles, your sales personnel must be careful in forming contracts with minors and should heed the adage, "When in doubt, check." Remember that a contract signed by a minor (unless it is for necessaries) normally is voidable, and the minor may exercise the option to disaffirm the contract. Employees should demand proof of legal age when they have any doubt about whether a customer is a minor.

In addition, because the law governing minors' rights varies substantially from state to state, you should check with your attorney concerning the laws governing disaffirmance in your state. You and those you hire to sell your products should know, for example, what the consequences will be if a minor has misrepresented his or her age when forming a sales contract. Similarly, you need to find out whether and in what circumstances a minor, on disaffirming a contract, can be required to pay for damage to goods sold under the contract.

DEALING WITH INTOXICATED PERSONS

Little need be said about a salesperson's dealings with obviously intoxicated persons. If the customer, despite intoxication, understands the legal consequences of the contract being signed, the contract is enforceable. Nonetheless, it may be extremely difficult to establish that the intoxicated customer understood the consequences of entering into the contract if the customer claims that she or he did not understand. Therefore, the best advice is, "When in doubt, don't." In other words, if you suspect a customer may be intoxicated, do not sign a contract with that customer.

CHECKLIST FOR THE RETAILER

1. When in doubt about the age of a customer to whom you are about to sell major consumer durable goods or anything other than necessaries, require proof of legal age.
2. If such proof is not forthcoming, require that a parent or guardian sign the contract.
3. Check with an attorney about the laws governing minors' contracts in your state.
4. Do not sign contracts with intoxicated customers.

* This *Application* is not meant to substitute for the services of an attorney who is licensed to practice law in your state.

KEY TERMS

adhesion contract 300
blue laws 295
blue sky laws 303
contractual capacity 286
covenant not to compete 298
disaffirmance 286
emancipation 292
employment contract 298
exculpatory clause 301
necessaries 289
ratification 291
reformation 299
unconscionable contract or unconscionable clause 300
usury 294

CHAPTER SUMMARY Capacity and Legality

CONTRACTUAL CAPACITY	
Minors (See pages 286–292.)	A minor is a person who has not yet reached the age of majority. In most states, the age of majority is eighteen for contract purposes. Contracts with minors are voidable at the option of the minor. 1. *Disaffirmance*—The legal avoidance of a contractual obligation. a. Disaffirmance can take place (in most states) at any time during minority and within a reasonable time after the minor has reached the age of majority. b. If a minor disaffirms part of a contract, the entire contract must be disaffirmed. c. When disaffirming executed contracts, the minor has a duty to return received goods if they are still in the minor's control or (in some states) to pay their reasonable value. d. A minor who has committed an act of fraud (such as misrepresentation of age) will be denied the right to disaffirm by some courts. e. A minor may disaffirm a contract for necessaries but remains liable for the reasonable value of the goods. 2. *Ratification*—The acceptance, or affirmation, of a legal obligation; may be express or implied. a. *Express ratification*—Exists when the minor, through a writing or an oral agreement, explicitly assumes the obligations imposed by the contract. b. *Implied ratification*—Exists when the conduct of the minor is inconsistent with disaffirmance or when the minor fails to disaffirm an executed contract within a reasonable time after reaching the age of majority. 3. *Parents' liability*—Generally, except for contracts for necessaries, parents are not liable for the contracts made by minor children acting on their own, nor are parents liable for minors' torts except in certain circumstances. 4. *Emancipation*—Occurs when a child's parent or legal guardian relinquishes the legal right to exercise control over the child. Normally, a minor who leaves home to support himself or herself is considered emancipated. In some jurisdictions, minors themselves are permitted to petition for emancipation for limited purposes.
Intoxicated Persons (See pages 292–293.)	1. A contract entered into by an intoxicated person is voidable at the option of the intoxicated person if the person was sufficiently intoxicated to lack mental capacity, even if the intoxication was voluntary. 2. A contract with an intoxicated person is enforceable if, despite being intoxicated, the person understood the legal consequences of entering into the contract.
Mentally Incompetent Persons (See pages 293–294.)	1. A contract made by a person adjudged by a court to be mentally incompetent is void. 2. A contract made by a mentally incompetent person not adjudged by a court to be mentally incompetent is voidable at the option of the mentally incompetent person.

CHAPTER SUMMARY Capacity and Legality—Continued

LEGALITY	
Contracts Contrary to Statute (See pages 294–297.)	1. *Usury*—Usury occurs when a lender makes a loan at an interest rate above the lawful maximum. The maximum rate of interest varies from state to state. 2. *Gambling*—Gambling contracts that contravene (go against) state statutes are deemed illegal and thus void. 3. *Sabbath (Sunday) laws*—These laws prohibit the formation or the performance of certain contracts on Sunday. Such laws vary widely from state to state, and many states do not enforce them. 4. *Licensing statutes*—Contracts entered into by persons who do not have a license, when one is required by statute, will not be enforceable *unless* the underlying purpose of the statute is to raise government revenues (and not to protect the public from unauthorized practitioners).
Contracts Contrary to Public Policy (See pages 298–301.)	1. *Contracts in restraint of trade*—Contracts to reduce or restrain free competition are illegal. Most such contracts are now prohibited by statutes. An exception is a *covenant not to compete.* It is usually enforced by the courts if the terms are ancillary to a contract (such as a contract for the sale of a business or an employment contract) and are reasonable as to time and area of restraint. Courts tend to scrutinize covenants not to compete closely. If a covenant is overbroad, a court may either reform the covenant to make the constraints more reasonable and then enforce the reformed contract or declare the covenant void and thus unenforceable. 2. *Unconscionable contracts and clauses*—When a contract or contract clause is so unfair that it is oppressive to one party, it can be deemed unconscionable; as such, it is illegal and cannot be enforced. 3. *Exculpatory clauses*—An exculpatory clause is a clause that releases a party from liability in the event of monetary or physical injury, no matter who is at fault. In certain situations, exculpatory clauses may be contrary to public policy and thus unenforceable.
EFFECT OF ILLEGALITY	
General Rule (See pages 301–303.)	In general, an illegal contract is void, and the courts will not aid either party when both parties are considered to be equally at fault *(in pari delicto).* If the contract is executory, neither party can enforce it. If the contract is executed, there can be neither contractual nor quasi-contractual recovery.
Exceptions (See pages 303–304.)	Several exceptions exist to the general rule that neither party to an illegal bargain will be able to recover. In the following situations, the court may grant recovery: 1. *Justifiable ignorance of the facts*—When one party to the contract is relatively innocent. 2. *Members of protected classes*—When one party to the contract is a member of a group of persons protected by statute, such as employees. 3. *Withdrawal from an illegal agreement*—When either party seeks to recover consideration given for an illegal contract before the illegal act is performed. 4. *Severable, or divisible, contracts*—When the court can divide the contract into illegal and legal portions and the illegal portion is not essential to the bargain. 5. *Fraud, duress, or undue influence*—When one party was induced to enter into an illegal bargain through fraud, duress, or undue influence.

FOR REVIEW

Answers for the even-numbered questions in this For Review *section can be found on this text's accompanying Web site at* http://blt.westbuslaw.com. *Select "Chapter 11" and click on "For Review."*

1. What are some exceptions to the rule that a minor can disaffirm (avoid) any contract?
2. Does an intoxicated person have the capacity to enter into an enforceable contract?
3. Does the mental incompetence of one party necessarily make a contract void?
4. Under what circumstances will a covenant not to compete be enforceable? When will such covenants not be enforced?
5. What is an exculpatory clause? In what circumstances might exculpatory clauses be enforced? When will they not be enforced?

QUESTIONS AND CASE PROBLEMS

11–1. Contracts by Minors. Kalen is a seventeen-year-old minor who has just graduated from high school. He is attending a university two hundred miles from home and has contracted to rent an apartment near the university for one year at $500 per month. He is working at a convenience store to earn enough income to be self-supporting. After living in the apartment and paying monthly rent for four months, he becomes involved in a dispute with his landlord. Kalen, still a minor, moves out and returns the key to the landlord. The landlord wants to hold Kalen liable for the balance of the payments due under the lease. Discuss fully Kalen's liability in this situation.

11–2. Mental Incompetence. Jermal has been the owner of a car dealership for a number of years. One day, Jermal sold one of his most expensive cars to Kessler. At the time of the sale, Jermal thought Kessler acted in a peculiar manner, but he gave the matter no further thought until four months later, when Kessler's court-appointed guardian appeared at Jermal's office, returned the car, and demanded Kessler's money back. The guardian informed Jermal that Kessler had been adjudicated mentally incompetent two months earlier by a proper court.

(a) Discuss the rights of the parties in this situation.
(b) If Kessler had been adjudicated mentally incompetent before the contract was formed, what would be the legal effect of the contract?

11–3. Licensing Statutes. State X requires that persons who prepare and serve liquor in the form of drinks at commercial establishments be licensed by the state to do so. The only requirement for obtaining a yearly license is that the person be at least twenty-one years old. Mickey, aged thirty-five, is hired as a bartender for the Southtown Restaurant. Gerald, a staunch alumnus of a nearby university, brings twenty of his friends to the restaurant to celebrate a football victory one afternoon. Gerald orders four rounds of drinks, and the bill is nearly $200. On learning that Mickey has failed to renew his bartender's license, Gerald refuses to pay, claiming that the contract is unenforceable. Discuss whether Gerald is correct.

11–4. Minority. In the 1990s, Sergei Samsonov, a Russian, was one of the top hockey players in the world. When Samsonov was seventeen years old, he signed a contract to play hockey for two seasons with the Central Sports Army Club, a Russian club known by the abbreviation CSKA. Before the start of the second season, Samsonov learned that because of a dispute between CSKA coaches, he would not be playing in Russia's premier hockey league. Samsonov hired Athletes and Artists, Inc. (A&A), an American sports agency, to make a deal with a U.S. hockey team. Samsonov signed a contract to play for the Detroit Vipers (whose corporate name was, at the time, Arena Associates, Inc.). Neither A&A nor Arena knew about the CSKA contract. CSKA filed a suit in a federal district court against Arena and others, alleging, among other things, wrongful interference with a contractual relationship. What effect will Samsonov's age have on the outcome of this suit? [*Central Sports Army Club v. Arena Associates, Inc.*, 952 F.Supp. 181 (S.D.N.Y. 1997)]

11–5. Exculpatory Clause. Norbert Eelbode applied for a job with Travelers Inn in the state of Washington. As part of the application process, Eelbode was sent to Laura Grothe, a physical therapist at Chec Medical Centers, Inc., for a preemployment physical exam. Before the exam, Eelbode signed a document that stated in part, "I hereby release Chec and the Washington Readicare Medical Group and its physicians from all liability arising from any injury to me resulting from my participation in the exam." During the exam, Grothe asked Eelbode to lift an item while bending from the waist using only his back with his knees locked. Eelbode experienced immediate sharp and burning pain in his lower back and down the back of his right leg. Eelbode filed a suit in a Washington state court against Grothe and Chec, claiming that he was injured because of an improperly administered back torso strength test. Citing the document that Eelbode signed, Grothe and Chec filed a motion for summary judgment. Should the court grant the motion? Why or why not? [*Eelbode v. Chec Medical Centers, Inc.*, 984 P.2d 436 (Wash.App. 1999)]

CASE PROBLEM WITH SAMPLE ANSWER

11–6. In 1993, Mutual Service Casualty Insurance Co. and its affiliates (collectively, MSI) hired Thomas Brass as an insurance agent. Three years later, Brass entered into a career agent's contract with MSI. This contract contained provisions regarding Brass's activities after termination. These provisions stated that, for a period of not less than one year, Brass could not solicit any MSI customers to "lapse, cancel, or replace" any insurance contract in force with MSI in an effort to take that business to a competitor. If he did, MSI could at any time refuse to pay the commissions that it otherwise owed him. The contract also restricted Brass from working for American National Insurance Co. for three years after termination. In 1998, Brass quit MSI and immediately went to work for American National, soliciting MSI customers. MSI filed a suit in a Wisconsin state court against Brass, claiming that he had violated the noncompete terms of his MSI contract. Should the court enforce the covenant not to compete? Why or why not? [*Mutual Service Casualty Insurance Co. v. Brass,* 625 N.W.2d 648 (Wis.App. 2001)]

After you have answered this problem, compare your answer with the sample answer given on the Web site that accompanies this text. Go to http://blt.westbuslaw.com, select "Chapter 11," and click on "Case Problem with Sample Answer."

11–7. Covenant Not to Compete. Gary Forsee was an executive officer with responsibility for the U.S. operations of BellSouth Corp., a company providing global telecommunications services. Under a covenant not to compete, Forsee agreed that for a period of eighteen months after termination from employment, he would not "provide services * * * in competition with [BellSouth] * * * to any person or entity which provides products or services identical or similar to products and services provided by [BellSouth] * * * within the territory." *Territory* was defined to include the geographic area in which Forsee provided services to BellSouth. The *services* included "management, strategic planning, business planning, administration, or other participation in or providing advice with respect to the communications services business." Forsee announced his intent to resign and accept a position as chief executive officer of Sprint Corp., a competitor of BellSouth. BellSouth filed a suit in a Georgia state court against Forsee, claiming in part that his acceptance of employment with Sprint would violate the covenant not to compete. Is the covenant legal? Should it be enforced? Why or why not? [*BellSouth Corp. v. Forsee,* 595 S.E.2d 99 (Ga.App. 2004)]

A QUESTION OF ETHICS

11–8. Nancy Levy worked for Health Care Financial Enterprises, Inc., and signed a noncompete agreement in June 1992. When Levy left Health Care and opened her own similar business in 1993, Health Care brought a court action in a Florida state court to enforce the covenant not to compete. The trial court concluded that the noncompete agreement prevented Levy from working in too broad a geographic area and thus refused to enforce the agreement. A Florida appellate court, however, reversed the trial court's ruling and remanded the case with instructions that the trial court modify the geographic area to make it reasonable and then enforce the covenant. [*Health Care Financial Enterprises, Inc. v. Levy,* 715 So.2d 341 (Fla.App.4th 1998)]

1. At one time in Florida, under the common law, noncompete covenants were illegal, although modern Florida statutory law now allows such covenants to be enforced. Generally, what interests are served by refusing to enforce covenants not to compete? What interests are served by allowing them to be enforced?
2. What argument could be made in support of reforming (and then enforcing) illegal covenants not to compete? What argument could be made against this practice?

FOR CRITICAL ANALYSIS

11–9. Do you think that the advent of legalized forms of gambling, such as state-operated lotteries, is consistent with a continued public policy against the enforcement of gambling contracts? Why or why not?

VIDEO QUESTION

11–10. Go to this text's Web site at http://blt.westbuslaw.com and select "Chapter 11." Click on "Video Questions" and view the video titled *Money Pit.* Then answer the following questions.

1. Assume that a valid contract exists between Walter (Tom Hanks) and the plumber. Recall from the video that the plumber had at least two drinks before agreeing to take on the plumbing job. If the plumber was intoxicated, is the contract voidable? Why or why not?
2. Suppose that state law requires plumbers in Walter's state to have a plumber's license and that this plumber does not have a license. Would the contract be enforceable? Why or why not?
3. In the video, the plumber suggests that Walter has been "turned down by every other plumber in the valley." Although the plumber does not even look at the house's plumbing, he agrees to do the repairs if Walter gives him a check for $5,000 right now "before he changes his mind." If Walter later seeks to void the contract because it is contrary to public policy, what should he argue?

INTERNET EXERCISES

Go to the *Business Law Today* home page at **http://blt.westbuslaw.com**, select "Chapter 11," and click on "Internet Exercises." There you will find the following Internet research exercises that you can perform to learn more about topics covered in this chapter.

Activity 11–1: MANAGEMENT PERSPECTIVE—Minors and the Law

Activity 11–2: SOCIAL PERSPECTIVE—Online Gambling

Activity 11–3: LEGAL PERSPECTIVE—Covenants Not to Compete

BEFORE THE TEST

Go to the *Business Law Today* home page at **http://blt.westbuslaw.com**, select "Chapter 11," and click on "Interactive Quizzes." You will find a number of interactive questions relating to this chapter.

“Law is a pledge that the citizens of a state will do justice to one another.”

Aristotle, 384–322 B.C.E.
(Greek philosopher)

CHAPTER 12
Genuineness of Assent

CHAPTER OUTLINE

- MISTAKES
- FRAUDULENT MISREPRESENTATION
- NONFRAUDULENT MISREPRESENTATION
- UNDUE INFLUENCE AND DURESS

LEARNING OBJECTIVES

After reading this chapter, you should be able to answer the following questions:

1. In what types of situations might genuineness of assent to a contract's terms be lacking?
2. What is the difference between a mistake of value or quality and a mistake of fact?
3. What elements must exist for fraudulent misrepresentation to occur?
4. Does a party to a contract ever have a duty to disclose information to the other party?
5. What happens if a person misrepresents a fact unintentionally?

An otherwise valid contract may be unenforceable if the parties have not genuinely assented to its terms. As mentioned in Chapter 8, lack of genuine assent is a *defense* to the enforcement of a contract. As Aristotle states in the chapter-opening quotation, the law seeks to ensure that “the citizens of a state will do justice to one another.” If the law were to enforce contracts not genuinely assented to by the contracting parties, injustice would result. This chapter focuses on the kinds of factors that indicate that genuineness of assent to a contract may be lacking.

Genuineness of assent may be lacking because of mistake, fraud, misrepresentation, undue influence, or duress. Generally, a party who demonstrates that he or she did not genuinely assent to the terms of a contract can choose either to carry out the contract or to rescind (cancel) it and thus avoid the entire transaction.

Mistakes

"Mistakes are the inevitable lot of mankind."

SIR GEORGE JESSEL, 1824–1883 (English jurist)

We all make mistakes, so it is not surprising that mistakes are made when contracts are created. In certain circumstances, contract law allows a contract to be avoided on the basis of mistake. Realize, though, that the concept of mistake in contract law has to do with mistaken assumptions relating to contract formation. For example, the error you make when you send your monthly bank loan payment to your plumber "by mistake" is totally different from the kind of mistake that we are discussing here. In contract law, a mistake may be a defense to the enforcement of a contract if it can be proved that the parties entered into the contract, each having different assumptions relating to the subject matter of the contract.

Courts have considerable difficulty in specifying the circumstances that justify allowing a mistake to invalidate a contract. Generally, though, courts distinguish between *mistakes as to judgment of market value or conditions* and *mistakes as to fact.* Only the latter normally have legal significance.

■ EXAMPLE 12.1 Jud Wheeler contracts to buy ten acres of land because he believes that he can resell the land at a profit to Bart. Can Jud escape his contractual obligations if it later turns out that he was mistaken? Not likely. Jud's overestimation of the value of the land or of Bart's interest in it is an ordinary risk of business for which a court normally will not provide relief. Now suppose that Jud purchases a painting of a landscape from Roth's Gallery. Both Jud and Roth believe that the painting is by the artist Vincent van Gogh. Jud later discovers that the painting is a very clever fake. Because neither Jud nor Roth was aware of this fact when they made their deal, Jud can normally rescind the contract and recover the purchase price of the painting. ■

Mistakes occur in two forms—*unilateral* and *bilateral (mutual).* A unilateral mistake is made by only one of the contracting parties; a mutual mistake is made by both. In either situation, the mistake must concern a **material fact** (a fact that is important to the subject matter of the contract). We look next at these two types of mistakes and illustrate them graphically in Exhibit 12–1.

MATERIAL FACT
A fact to which a reasonable person would attach importance in determining his or her course of action.

UNILATERAL MISTAKES

UNILATERAL MISTAKE
Mistake that occurs when one party to a contract is mistaken as to a material fact; the contract normally is enforceable.

A **unilateral mistake** occurs when only one party is mistaken as to a *material fact.* Generally, a unilateral mistake does not give the mistaken party any right to relief from the contract. In other words, the contract normally is enforceable against the mistaken party. ■ EXAMPLE 12.2 Elena intends to sell her motor home for $17,500. When she learns that Chin is interested in buying a used motor home, she types a letter offering to sell her vehicle to him. When typing the letter, however, she mistakenly keys in the price of $15,700. Chin writes back, accepting Elena's offer. Even though Elena intended to sell her motor home for $17,500, she has made a unilateral mistake and is bound by contract to sell the vehicle to Chin for $15,700. ■

BE CAREFUL What a party to a contract knows or should know can determine whether the contract is enforceable.

There are at least two exceptions to this rule.[1] First, if the *other* party to the contract knows or should have known that a mistake of fact was made, the contract may not be enforceable. In the above example, if Chin knew that Elena intended to sell her motor home for $17,500, then Elena's unilateral mistake (stating $15,700 in her offer) may render the resulting contract unenforceable. The second exception arises when a unilateral mistake of fact was due to a mathematical error in addition,

1. The *Restatement (Second) of Contracts,* Section 153, liberalizes the general rule to take into account the modern trend of allowing avoidance in some circumstances even though only one party has been mistaken.

EXHIBIT 12–1 MISTAKES OF FACT

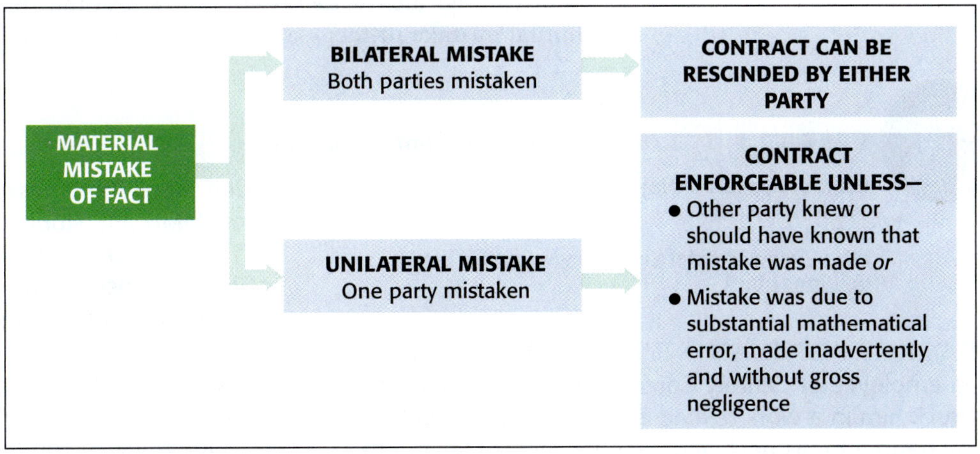

subtraction, division, or multiplication and was made inadvertently and without gross (extreme) negligence. If a contractor's bid was significantly low because he or she made a mistake in addition when totaling the estimated costs, any contract resulting from the bid normally may be rescinded. Of course, in both situations, the mistake must still involve some *material fact.*

Bilateral (Mutual) Mistakes

BILATERAL MISTAKE
Mistake that occurs when both parties to a contract are mistaken about the same material fact and the mistake is one that a reasonable person would make; either party can rescind the contract.

When both parties are mistaken about the same material fact, a **bilateral mistake** occurs, and the contract can be rescinded by either party.[2] Note that, as with unilateral mistakes, the mistake must be about a *material fact* (one that is important and central to the contract—as was the Van Gogh painting in Example 12.1). If, instead, a mutual mistake concerns the future market value or quality of the object of the contract, the contract normally can be enforced by either party. This rule is based on the theory that both parties assume certain risks when they enter into a contract. Without this rule, almost any party who did not receive what she or he considered a fair bargain could argue bilateral mistake.

A word or term in a contract may be subject to more than one reasonable interpretation. In that situation, if the parties to the contract attach materially different meanings to the term, their mutual misunderstanding may allow the contract to be rescinded.

■ EXAMPLE 12.3 In *Raffles v. Wichelhaus,*[3] a classic case involving a mutual mistake, Wichelhaus purchased a shipment of cotton from Raffles to arrive on a ship called the *Peerless* from Bombay, India. Wichelhaus meant a ship called the *Peerless* sailing from Bombay in October; Raffles meant another ship called the *Peerless* sailing from Bombay in December. When the goods arrived on the December *Peerless,* Raffles delivered them to Wichelhaus. By that time, however, Wichelhaus was no longer willing to accept them. The British court hearing the case stated, "There is nothing on the face of the contract to show that any particular ship called the 'Peerless' was meant; but the moment it appears that two ships called the 'Peerless' were about to sail from Bombay there is a latent ambiguity. . . . That being so, there was no consensus . . . and therefore no binding contract." ■

2. *Restatement (Second) of Contracts,* Section 152.
3. 159 Eng.Rep. 375 (1864).

In the following case, an injured worker sought to set aside a settlement agreement entered into with his employer, arguing that the agreement was based on a mutual mistake of fact—a physician's mistaken diagnosis of the worker's injury.

CASE 12.1 Roberts v. Century Contractors, Inc.

Court of Appeals of North Carolina, 2004.
162 N.C.App. 688,
592 S.E.2d 215.
http://www.aoc.state.nc.us/www/public/html/opinions.htm[a]

BACKGROUND AND FACTS Bobby Roberts was an employee of Century Contractors, Inc., when a pipe struck him in a work-related accident in July 1993, causing trauma to his neck and back. Dr. James Markworth of Southeastern Orthopaedic Clinic diagnosed Roberts's injuries. After surgery and treatment, Markworth concluded that Roberts was at maximum medical improvement (MMI) and stopped treating him. Roberts agreed with Century to accept $125,000 and payment of related medical expenses, and to waive any right to make further claims in regard to his injury. In June 1998, still experiencing pain, Roberts saw Dr. Allen Friedman, who determined that Roberts was not at MMI. Markworth then admitted that his diagnosis was a mistake. Roberts filed a claim for workers' compensation (see Chapter 40), seeking compensation and medical benefits for his injury. He alleged that his agreement with Century should be set aside due to a mutual mistake of fact. The North Carolina state administrative agency authorized to rule on workers' compensation claims awarded Roberts what he sought. Century appealed to a state intermediate appellate court.

a. Click on "2004" under "Court of Appeals Opinions." In the result, scroll down to "17 February 2004" and click on the name of the case to access the opinion. The North Carolina Administrative Office of the Courts maintains this Web site.

IN THE WORDS OF THE COURT . . .
LEVINSON, Judge.

* * * *

* * * Compromise settlement agreements, including mediated settlement agreements in Workers' Compensation cases, are governed by general principles of contract law.

It is a well-settled principle of contract law that a valid contract exists only where there has been a meeting of the minds as to all essential terms of the agreement. Therefore, where a mistake is common to both parties and concerns a material past or presently existing fact, such that there is no meeting of the minds, a contract may be avoided. [Emphasis added.]

To afford relief, the mistake must be of a certain nature. The fact about which the parties are mistaken must be an existing or past fact. The mistaken fact must also be material * * * . It must be as to a fact which enters into and forms the basis of the contract, or in other words it must be of the essence of the agreement, the *sine qua non,* or, as is sometimes said, the efficient cause of the agreement, and must be such that it animates and controls the conduct of the parties.

Additionally, relief from a contract due to mistake of fact will be had only where *both* parties to an agreement are mistaken. Thus, as a general rule relief will be denied where the party against whom it is sought was ignorant that the other party was acting under a mistake and the former's conduct in no way contributed thereto. Likewise, a party who assumed the risk of a mistaken fact cannot avoid a contract.

A party bears the risk of a mistake when

(a) the risk is allocated to him by agreement of the parties, or
(b) he is aware, at the time the contract is made that he has only limited knowledge with respect to the facts to which the mistake relates but treats his limited knowledge as sufficient, or

CASE 12.1—Continued

(c) the risk is allocated to him by the court on the ground that it is reasonable in the circumstances to do so.

* * * *

* * * The x-rays [examined by Dr. Friedman] after Dr. Markworth or Southern Orthopaedic Clinic had last treated plaintiff [Roberts], indicated Dr. Markworth's diagnosis of maximum medical improvement * * * was a mistake. Dr. Markworth testified * * * that advising plaintiff that he was at maximum medical improvement at that time was a mistake.

* * * *

* * * [T]he finding of maximum medical improvement and the impairment rating given by Dr. Markworth were material to the settlement of this claim and * * * both parties relied on this information in entering into settlement negotiations.

* * * *

* * * [T]he parties believed that plaintiff had reached maximum medical improvement and, further, * * * they materially relied upon this fact in reaching a settlement. Defendants' essential argument on appeal is that because plaintiff either knew that there was a possibility that [he had not reached MMI] or was negligent in not declining to sign the settlement agreement, mutual mistake is a legal impossibility in this case. As the facts * * * support a contrary conclusion, we do not agree.

* * * The plaintiff testified that he based his decision to sign the settlement agreement on Dr. Markworth's diagnosis and that he would not have settled his case if Dr. Friedman had told him that [he had not reached MMI]. Thus, there is competent record evidence to support the * * * findings that the parties were mistaken as to whether plaintiff had reached maximum medical improvement and that this mistaken fact was material. * * *

DECISION AND REMEDY The state intermediate appellate court affirmed the award of compensation and medical benefits to Roberts. The agreement between Roberts and Century was set aside on the basis of a mutual mistake of fact. Markworth's MMI diagnosis was "material to the settlement of this claim and * * * both parties relied on this information." In fact, however, "plaintiff was not at maximum medical improvement."

FOR CRITICAL ANALYSIS—Social Consideration *Why did the court consider Markworth's misdiagnosis a bilateral mistake rather than a unilateral mistake?*

Fraudulent Misrepresentation

Although fraud is a tort, the presence of fraud also affects the genuineness of the innocent party's consent to a contract. When an innocent party consents to a contract with fraudulent terms, the contract usually can be avoided because he or she has not *voluntarily* consented to the terms.[4] Normally, the innocent party can either rescind (cancel) the contract and be restored to his or her original position or enforce the contract and seek damages for injuries resulting from the fraud.

Typically, fraud involves three elements:

REMEMBER To collect damages in almost any lawsuit, there must be some sort of injury.

1. A misrepresentation of a material fact must occur.
2. There must be an intent to deceive.
3. The innocent party must justifiably rely on the misrepresentation.

4. *Restatement (Second) of Contracts,* Sections 163 and 164.

Additionally, to collect damages, a party must have been injured as a result of the misrepresentation.

"It was beautiful and simple as all truly great swindles are."
O. HENRY,
1862–1910
(American author)

Fraudulent misrepresentation can also occur in the online environment. Indeed, a major challenge today is how to curb Internet fraud—a topic that will be explored further in Chapter 38, in the context of consumer law.

MISREPRESENTATION MUST OCCUR

The first element of proving fraud is to show that misrepresentation of a material fact has occurred. This misrepresentation can take the form of words or actions. For example, an art gallery owner's statement, "This painting is a Picasso" is a misrepresentation of fact if the painting was done by another artist.

A statement of opinion is generally not subject to a claim of fraud. For example, claims such as "This computer will never break down" and "This car will last for years and years" are statements of opinion, not fact, and contracting parties should recognize them as such and not rely on them. A fact is objective and verifiable; an opinion is usually subject to debate. Therefore, a seller is allowed to "huff and puff his [or her] wares" without being liable for fraud. In certain cases, however, particularly when a naïve purchaser relies on an expert's opinion, the innocent party may be entitled to rescission or reformation (an equitable remedy granted by a court in which the terms of a contract are altered to reflect the true intentions of the parties).

Misrepresentation by Conduct Misrepresentation can occur by conduct, as well as through express oral or written statements. For example, if a seller, by her or his actions, prevents a buyer from learning of some fact that is material to the contract, such behavior constitutes misrepresentation by conduct.[5] ■ EXAMPLE 12.4 Cummings contracts to purchase a racehorse from Garner. The horse is blind in one eye, but when Garner shows the horse, he skillfully conceals this fact by keeping the horse's head turned so that Cummings does not see the defect. The concealment constitutes fraud. ■ Another example of misrepresentation by conduct is the untruthful denial of knowledge or information concerning facts that are material to the contract when such knowledge or information is requested.

Misrepresentation of Law Misrepresentation of law does not *ordinarily* entitle a party to be relieved of a contract. ■ EXAMPLE 12.5 Debbie has a parcel of property that she is trying to sell to Barry. Debbie knows that a local ordinance prohibits building anything higher than three stories on the property. Nonetheless, she tells Barry, "You can build a condominium fifty stories high if you want to do so." Barry buys the land and later discovers that Debbie's statement is false. Normally, Barry cannot avoid the contract because under the common law, people are assumed to know state and local laws. ■ Exceptions to this rule occur, however, when the misrepresenting party is in a profession known to require greater knowledge of the law than the average citizen possesses.

Misrepresentation by Silence Ordinarily, neither party to a contract has a duty to come forward and disclose facts, and a contract normally will not be set aside because certain pertinent information has not been volunteered. ■ EXAMPLE 12.6 Suppose that you are selling a car that has been in an accident and has been repaired. You do not need to volunteer this information to a potential buyer. If,

5. *Restatement (Second) of Contracts,* Section 160.

Workers excavate a site and bury a sewer line. Would the party who contracted for this work be liable for fraud if the party knew, or should have known, that subsoil conditions could greatly increase the expense of the work and failed to disclose this to the bidders? Why or why not? (© Mark Mellett/Stock Boston)

however, the purchaser asks you if the car has had extensive bodywork and you lie, you have committed a fraudulent misrepresentation. ■

Generally, if the seller knows of a serious defect or a serious potential problem about which the buyer cannot reasonably be expected to know, the seller may have a duty to speak. Normally, the seller must disclose only "latent" defects—that is, defects that could not readily be discovered. Thus, termites in a house may not be a latent defect because a buyer could normally discover their presence through a termite inspection. Also, when the parties are in a *fiduciary relationship* (one of trust, such as partners, physician and patient, or attorney and client), there is a duty to disclose material facts; failure to do so may constitute fraud.

Intent to Deceive

SCIENTER
Knowledge by the misrepresenting party that material facts have been falsely represented or omitted with an intent to deceive.

The second element of fraud is knowledge on the part of the misrepresenting party that facts have been misrepresented. This element, normally called ***scienter***,[6] or "guilty knowledge," generally signifies that there was an intent to deceive. *Scienter* clearly exists if a party knows that a fact is not as stated. *Scienter* also exists if a party makes a statement that he or she believes not to be true or makes a statement recklessly, without regard to whether it is true or false. Finally, this element is met if a party says or implies that a statement is made on some basis, such as personal knowledge or personal investigation, when it is not.

■ Example 12.7 Suppose that Alicia Rolando, when selling a house to Cariton, tells Cariton that the plumbing pipe is of a certain quality. Rolando knows nothing about the quality of the pipe but does not believe it to be what she is representing it to be (and in fact it is not what she says it is). Rolando's statement induces Cariton to buy the house. Rolando's statement is a fraudulent misrepresentation because she does not believe that what she says is true and because she knows that she does not have any basis for making the statement. Cariton can avoid the contract. ■

6. Pronounced sy-*en*-ter.

Can an employer avoid liability for the breach of a contract that was induced by an employee's fraud during the hiring process? That was the question in the following case.

CASE 12.2 Sarvis v. Vermont State Colleges

Supreme Court of Vermont, 2001.
172 Vt. 76,
772 A.2d 494.

BACKGROUND AND FACTS In 1995, Robert Sarvis was convicted of bank fraud, ordered to pay more than $12 million in restitution, and sentenced to forty-six months in prison. While incarcerated, he worked in the prison's electrical department. Two weeks after his release in 1998, he applied for an adjunct professor position at Community College of Vermont (CCV). On his résumé, he stated that during "1984–1998" he was "President and Chairman of the Board" of "CMI International Inc., Boston, Massachusetts," where he was "[r]esponsible for all operations and financial matters." For a position as CCV's Coordinator of Academic Services, he submitted a second résumé, on which he added, "1998–present. Semi-retired. Adjunct Instructor of Business at Colby-Sawyer College and Franklin Pierce College." He stated that he was "well equipped to teach" business law and business ethics, that he had "a great interest and knowledge of business law," and that he believed he would do "an excellent job" teaching a business ethics class because this subject was "of particular concern" to him. CCV hired him as academic coordinator, teacher, and independent studies instructor. After he began work, his probation officer alerted CCV to Sarvis's criminal history, and CCV terminated his employment. Sarvis filed a suit in a Vermont state court against CCV, alleging, among other things, breach of contract. CCV filed a motion for summary judgment, in part on the ground of fraud, seeking rescission. The court granted CCV's motion, and Sarvis appealed to the Vermont Supreme Court.

IN THE WORDS OF THE COURT . . .

SKOGLUND, J. [Justice]

* * * *

It is well established that a party induced into a contract by fraud or misrepresentation can rescind the contract and avoid liability for any breach thereon. A misrepresentation is fraudulent when made with knowledge of its falsity. * * *

* * * *

* * * [M]isrepresentation during the hiring process can be a basis for rescission of an employment contract. Further, we hold as a matter of law, such misrepresentation can constitute misconduct sufficient to support a just cause dismissal.

* * * *

Where one has full information and represents that he has, if he discloses a part of his information only, and by words or conduct leads the one with whom he contracts to believe that he has made a full disclosure and does this with intent to deceive and overreach and to prevent investigation, he is guilty of fraud * * *, *if his words and conduct in consequence of reliance upon them bring about the result which he desires.* [Emphasis added.]

The misrepresentation in this case occurred through plaintiff's partial disclosure of his past work history and references and his effort to limit defendant's inquiry into his past. Plaintiff was not silent; he carefully drafted his résumés and supplemental materials to lead defendant to believe he had made a full disclosure about his past and his qualifications. He listed classes in business ethics and law in which he claimed he had the highest level of capability and knowledge but failed to mention his felony bank fraud conviction. Plaintiff assured defendant that making additional inquiries into his background would have revealed "more of the same" type of information * * *. This was not true. Contact with plaintiff's probation officer or supervisor at the * * * prison would have notified defendant of plaintiff's fraud convictions, period of incarceration, and work history at the prison.

CASE 12.2—Continued

DECISION AND REMEDY The Vermont Supreme Court affirmed the lower court's judgment and rescinded the contract between Sarvis and CCV.

WHY IS THIS CASE IMPORTANT? *This case illustrates the long-applied legal principle that when a contract is formed as a result of fraudulent misrepresentation, the defrauded party can avoid the contract. From the facts in this case, CCV clearly would not have hired Sarvis had he fully disclosed information about his past and his qualifications.*

Reliance on the Misrepresentation

The third element of fraud is *justifiable reliance* on the misrepresentation of fact. The deceived party must have a justifiable reason for relying on the misrepresentation, and the misrepresentation must be an important factor (but not necessarily the sole factor) in inducing the party to enter into the contract.

Reliance is not justified if the innocent party knows the true facts or relies on obviously extravagant statements. ■ **EXAMPLE 12.8** If a used-car dealer tells you, "This old Cadillac will get over sixty miles to the gallon," you normally would not be justified in relying on this statement. Suppose, however, that Merkel, a bank director, induces O'Connell, a co-director, to sign a statement that the bank's assets will satisfy its liabilities by telling O'Connell, "We have plenty of assets to satisfy our creditors." This statement is false. If O'Connell knows the true facts or, as a bank director, should know the true facts, he is not justified in relying on Merkel's statement. If O'Connell does not know the true facts, however, *and has no way of finding them out,* he may be justified in relying on the statement. ■

REMEMBER An opinion is not a contract offer, nor a contract term, nor fraud.

ETHICAL ISSUE 12.1

How much information must employers disclose to prospective employees? One of the problems employers face is that it is not always clear what information they should disclose to prospective employees. To lure qualified workers, employers are often tempted to "promise the moon" to prospective employees and paint their companies' prospects as bright. Employers must be careful, though, to avoid any conduct that could be interpreted by a court as intentionally deceptive. In particular, they must avoid making any statements about their companies' future prospects or financial health that they know to be false. If they do make a false statement on which a prospective employee relies to her or his detriment, they may be sued for fraudulent misrepresentation.

In one case, for example, an employee accepted a job with a brokerage firm, relying on assurances that the firm was not about to be sold. In fact, as the employee was able to prove in his later lawsuit against the firm for fraud, negotiations to sell the firm were under way at the time he was hired. The trial court awarded the employee over $6 million in damages, a decision that was affirmed on appeal.[7] Generally, employers must be truthful in their hiring to avoid possible lawsuits for fraudulent misrepresentation. ■

Injury to the Innocent Party

Most courts do not require a showing of injury when the action is to *rescind* (cancel) the contract—these courts hold that because rescission returns the parties

---

7. *McConkey v. AON Corp.,* 354 N.J.Super. 25, 804 A.2d 572 (2002).

to the positions they held before the contract was made, a showing of injury to the innocent party is unnecessary.[8]

To recover damages caused by fraud, however, proof of an injury is universally required. The measure of damages is ordinarily equal to the property's value had it been delivered as represented, less the actual price paid for the property. In actions based on fraud, courts often award *punitive,* or *exemplary, damages,* which are granted to a plaintiff over and above the compensation for the actual loss. As pointed out in Chapter 4, punitive damages are based on the public-policy consideration of punishing the defendant or setting an example to deter similar wrongdoing by others.

Nonfraudulent Misrepresentation

If a plaintiff seeks to rescind a contract because of *fraudulent* misrepresentation, the plaintiff must prove that the defendant had the intent to deceive. Most courts also allow rescission in cases involving *nonfraudulent* misrepresentation—that is, innocent or negligent misrepresentation—if all of the other elements of misrepresentation exist.

Innocent Misrepresentation

If a person makes a statement that he or she believes to be true but that actually misrepresents material facts, the person is guilty only of an *innocent misrepresentation,* not of fraud. If an innocent misrepresentation occurs, the aggrieved party can rescind the contract but usually cannot seek damages. ■ **Example 12.9** Parris tells Roberta that a tract contains 250 acres. Parris is mistaken—the tract contains only 215 acres—but Parris does not know that. Roberta is induced by the statement to make a contract to buy the land. Even though the misrepresentation is innocent, Roberta can avoid the contract if the misrepresentation is material. ■

Negligent Misrepresentation

Sometimes a party makes a misrepresentation through carelessness, believing the statement is true. This misrepresentation is negligent if he or she fails to exercise reasonable care in uncovering or disclosing the facts or does not use the skill and competence that his or her business or profession requires. ■ **Example 12.10** An operator of a weight scale certifies the weight of Sneed's commodity, even though the scale's accuracy has not been checked in more than a year. In this situation, the scale operator's action could constitute negligent misrepresentation. ■ In virtually all states, such *negligent misrepresentation* is equal to *scienter*, or to knowingly making a misrepresentation. In effect, negligent misrepresentation is treated as fraudulent misrepresentation, even though the misrepresentation was not purposeful. In negligent misrepresentation, culpable ignorance of the truth supplies the intention to mislead, even if the defendant can claim, "I didn't know."

Undue Influence and Duress

Undue influence arises from relationships in which one party can greatly influence another party, thus overcoming that party's free will. Minors and elderly people, for example, are often under the influence of guardians. If a guardian induces a young

8. For a leading case on this issue, see *Kaufman v. Jaffe,* 244 App.Div. 344, 279 N.Y.S. 392 (1935).

To read more about contesting contracts on the grounds of fraud and duress, go to

http://www.lawyers.com/lawyers/A~1001073~LDC/CONTESTING+CONTRACT.html.

or elderly ward (a person placed by a court under the care of a guardian) to enter into a contract that benefits the guardian, the guardian may have exerted undue influence. Undue influence can also arise from certain confidential or fiduciary relationships, including attorney-client, physician-patient, guardian-ward, parent-child, husband-wife, and trustee-beneficiary relationships. A contract entered into under excessive or undue influence lacks genuine assent and is therefore voidable.[9]

Assent to the terms of a contract is also not genuine if one of the parties is forced into the agreement. Forcing a party to enter into a contract because of the fear created by threats is referred to as *duress.*[10] Inducing consent to a contract through blackmail or extortion also constitutes duress. Duress is both a defense to the enforcement of a contract and a ground for rescission, or cancellation, of a contract. Therefore, a party who signs a contract under duress can choose to carry out the contract or to avoid the entire transaction. (The wronged party usually has this choice in cases in which assent is not real or genuine.)

Economic need is generally not sufficient to constitute duress, even when one party exacts a very high price for an item the other party needs. If the party exacting the price also creates the need, however, economic duress may be found. ■ **EXAMPLE 12.11** The Internal Revenue Service (IRS) assessed a large tax and penalty against Weller. Weller retained Eyman to contest the assessment. Two days before the deadline for filing a reply with the IRS, Eyman declined to represent Weller unless he agreed to pay a very high fee for Eyman's services. The agreement was held to be unenforceable.[11] Although Eyman had threatened only to withdraw his services, something that he was legally entitled to do, he was responsible for delaying his withdrawal until the last two days. Because Weller was forced into either signing the contract or losing his right to challenge the IRS assessment, the agreement was secured under duress. ■

9. *Restatement (Second) of Contracts,* Section 177.
10. *Restatement (Second) of Contracts,* Sections 174 and 175.
11. *Thompson Crane & Trucking Co. v. Eyman,* 123 Cal.App.2d 904, 267 P.2d 1043 (1954).

REVIEWING GENUINENESS OF ASSENT

Chelene had been a caregiver for Marta's eighty-year-old mother, Janis, for nine years. Shortly before Janis passed away, Chelene convinced her to buy Chelene's house for her daughter, Marta. The elderly woman died before the papers were signed, however. Four months later, Marta used her inheritance to buy Chelene's house without having it inspected. The house was built in the 1950s, and Chelene said it was in "perfect condition." Nevertheless, one year after the purchase, the basement started leaking. Marta had the paneling removed from the basement walls and discovered that the walls were bowed inward and cracked. Marta then had a civil engineer inspect the basement walls, and he found that the cracks had been caulked and painted over before the paneling was installed. He concluded that the "wall failure" had existed "for at least thirty years" and that the basement walls were "structurally unsound." Using the information presented in the chapter, answer the following questions.

1. Can Marta obtain rescission of the contract based on undue influence? If the sale to Janis had been completed before her death, could Janis have obtained rescission based on undue influence? Explain.
2. Can Marta avoid the contract on the ground that both parties made a mistake about the condition of the house? Explain.

(Continued)

REVIEWING GENUINENESS OF ASSENT—Continued

3. Can Marta sue Chelene for fraudulent misrepresentation? Why or why not? What element(s) might be lacking?
4. Now assume that Chelene knew that the basement walls were cracked and bowed and that she had hired someone to install paneling prior to offering to sell the house. Did she have a duty to disclose this defect to Marta? Could a court find that Chelene's silence in this situation constituted misrepresentation? Explain.
5. If Chelene knew about the problem with the walls but did not know that the house was structurally unsound, could she be liable for negligent misrepresentation? Why or why not?

KEY TERMS

bilateral mistake 313
material fact 312
scienter 317
unilateral mistake 312

CHAPTER SUMMARY Genuineness of Assent

Mistakes (See pages 312–315.)	1. *Unilateral*—Generally, the mistaken party is bound by the contract *unless* (a) the other party knows or should have known of the mistake or (b) the mistake is an inadvertent mathematical error—such as an error in addition or subtraction—committed without gross negligence. 2. *Bilateral (mutual)*—When both parties are mistaken about the same material fact, such as identity, either party can avoid the contract. If the mistake concerns value or quality, either party can enforce the contract.
Fraudulent Misrepresentation (See pages 315–320.)	When fraud occurs, usually the innocent party can enforce or avoid the contract. The elements necessary to establish fraud are as follows: 1. A misrepresentation of a material fact must occur. 2. There must be an intent to deceive. 3. The innocent party must justifiably rely on the misrepresentation.
Nonfraudulent Misrepresentation (See page 320.)	1. *Innocent misrepresentation*—Occurs when a person makes a statement that he or she believes to be true but that actually misrepresents material facts. The aggrieved party can rescind the contract but usually cannot seek damages. 2. *Negligent misrepresentation*—Occurs when a person makes an untrue statement but, through carelessness, believes the statement to be true. Negligent misrepresentation has the same legal effect as fraudulent misrepresentation in virtually all states.
Undue Influence and Duress (See pages 320–321.)	Undue influence arises from special relationships, such as fiduciary or confidential relationships, in which one party's free will has been overcome by the undue influence exerted by the other party. A contract entered into under undue influence is voidable. Duress is defined as forcing a party to enter a contract under the fear of a threat—for example, the threat of violence or, in some situations, serious economic loss. The party forced to enter the contract can rescind the contract or enforce it.

FOR REVIEW

Answers for the even-numbered questions in this For Review *section can be found on this text's accompanying Web site at* http://blt.westbuslaw.com. *Select "Chapter 12" and click on "For Review."*

1. In what types of situations might genuineness of assent to a contract's terms be lacking?
2. What is the difference between a mistake of value or quality and a mistake of fact?
3. What elements must exist for fraudulent misrepresentation to occur?
4. Does a party to a contract ever have a duty to disclose information to the other party?
5. What happens if a person misrepresents a fact unintentionally?

QUESTIONS AND CASE PROBLEMS

12–1. Genuineness of Assent. Jerome is an elderly man who lives with his nephew, Philip. Jerome is totally dependent on Philip's support. Philip tells Jerome that unless Jerome transfers a tract of land he owns to Philip for a price 30 percent below market value, Philip will no longer support and take care of him. Jerome enters into the contract. Discuss fully whether Jerome can set aside this contract.

12–2. Assent. Grano owns a forty-room motel on Highway 100. Tanner is interested in purchasing the motel. During the course of negotiations, Grano tells Tanner that the motel netted $30,000 last year and that it will net at least $45,000 next year. The motel books, which Grano turns over to Tanner before the purchase, clearly show that Grano's motel netted only $15,000 last year. Also, Grano fails to tell Tanner that a bypass to Highway 100 is being planned that will redirect most traffic away from the front of the motel. Tanner purchases the motel. During the first year under Tanner's operation, the motel nets only $18,000. It is at this time that Tanner learns of the previous low profitability of the motel and the planned bypass. Tanner wants his money back from Grano. Discuss fully Tanner's probable success in getting his money back.

12–3. Fraudulent Misrepresentation. Larry offered to sell Stanley his car and told Stanley that the car had been driven only 25,000 miles and had never been in an accident. Stanley hired Cohen, a mechanic, to appraise the condition of the car, and Cohen said that the car probably had at least 50,000 miles on it and probably had been in an accident. In spite of this information, Stanley thought the car would be a good buy for the price, so he purchased it. Later, when the car developed numerous mechanical problems, Stanley sought to rescind the contract on the basis of Larry's fraudulent misrepresentation of the auto's condition. Will Stanley be able to rescind his contract? Discuss.

12–4. Assent. Discuss whether either of the following contracts will be unenforceable on the ground that genuineness of assent is lacking.

(a) Simmons finds a stone in his pasture that he believes to be quartz. Jenson, who also believes that the stone is quartz, contracts to purchase it for $10. Just before delivery, the stone is discovered to be a diamond worth $1,000.

(b) Jacoby's barn is burned to the ground. He accuses Goldman's son of arson and threatens to bring a criminal action unless Goldman agrees to pay him $5,000. Goldman agrees to pay.

12–5. Mistake. Steven Lanci was involved in an automobile accident with an uninsured motorist. Lanci was insured with Metropolitan Insurance Co., although he did not have a copy of the insurance policy. Lanci and Metropolitan entered settlement negotiations, during which Lanci told Metropolitan that he did not have a copy of his policy. Ultimately, Lanci agreed to settle all claims for $15,000, noting in a letter to Metropolitan that $15,000 was the "sum you have represented to be the . . . policy limits applicable to this claim." After signing a release, Lanci learned that the policy limits were actually $250,000, and he refused to accept the settlement proceeds. When Metropolitan sued to enforce the settlement agreement, Lanci argued that the release had been signed as the result of a mistake and therefore was unenforceable. Should the court enforce the contract? Explain. [*Lanci v. Metropolitan Insurance Co.*, 388 Pa.Super. 1, 564 A.2d 972 (1989)]

12–6. Fraudulent Misrepresentation. In 1987, UPS (the collective name for United Parcel Service Co. and United Parcel Service of America, Inc.) decided to change its parcel delivery business from relying on contract carriers to establishing its own airline. During the transition, which took sixteen months, UPS hired 811 pilots. At the same time, UPS expressed a desire to hire pilots who remained with its contract carriers, which included Orion Air. A UPS representative met with more than fifty Orion pilots and made promises of future employment. John Rickert, a captain with Orion, was one of the pilots. Orion ceased operation after the UPS transition, and UPS did not hire Rickert, who obtained employment about six months later as a second officer with American Airlines at a lower salary. Rickert filed a suit in a Kentucky state court against UPS, claiming, in part, fraud based on the promises made by the UPS representative. UPS filed a motion for a directed verdict. What are the elements for a cause of action based on fraudulent misrepresentation? In whose favor should the court rule in this case, and why? [*United Parcel Service, Inc. v. Rickert*, 996 S.W.2d 464 (Ky. 1999)]

12–7. Fraudulent Misrepresentation. Nosrat, a citizen of Iran, owned a hardware store with his brother-in-law, Edwin. Edwin induced Nosrat to sign a promissory note for $11,400, payable to a third party, telling Nosrat that the document was a credit application for the hardware store. Although Nosrat could read and write English, he failed to read the note or to notice that the document was clearly entitled "PROMISSORY NOTE (SECURED) and Security Agreement." The funds received from the third party in exchange for the note were spent by Edwin and others. When the third party sued for payment, Nosrat sought to void the note on the basis of Edwin's fraudulent inducement. Will Nosrat succeed in his attempt? Discuss. [*Waldrep v. Nosrat,* 426 So.2d 822 (Ala. 1983)]

CASE PROBLEM WITH SAMPLE ANSWER

12–8. Tar-Bac, Inc., leased a restaurant from Lawrence Kent. When Tar-Bac failed to pay the rent and vacated the premises, Kent attempted to obtain, in satisfaction, the restaurant equipment that Tar-Bac had left behind. Meanwhile, Robert and Cynthia Sullivan asked Kent about leasing the vacant property. Kent told them that he owned the equipment in the restaurant and, in reliance on that representation, the Sullivans entered into a lease with Kent and paid him $25,000 for the equipment, which had a rental value of $9,000 per year. The Sullivans opened their restaurant and, a year later, agreed to sell the business, including the equipment, to Mama Mia's Pizzeria and Seafood, Inc., which paid them $16,699.76. Mama Mia discovered the question about the ownership of the equipment but, after a nine-day delay, went through with the deal. The Sullivans, however, filed a suit in a Florida state court against Kent, alleging, in part, fraudulent misrepresentation and seeking damages for the delayed closing of the Mama Mia sale. What are the elements of fraud? Were they satisfied in this case? Explain. [*Kent v. Sullivan,* 793 So.2d 1027 (Fla.App., 5 Dist. 2001)]

After you have answered this problem, compare your answer with the sample answer given on the Web site that accompanies this text. Go to http://blt.westbuslaw.com, select "Chapter 12," and click on "Case Problem with Sample Answer."

FOR CRITICAL ANALYSIS

12–9. Describe the types of individuals who might be in a position to exert undue influence on others.

VIDEO QUESTION

DIGITAL VIDEO LIBRARY — WEST LEGAL STUDIES IN BUSINESS

12–10. Go to this text's Web site at http://blt.westbuslaw.com and select "Chapter 12." Click on "Video Questions" and view the video titled *Mistake.* Then answer the following questions.

1. What kind of mistake is involved in the dispute shown on the video (mutual or unilateral, mistake of fact or mistake of value)?
2. According to the chapter, in what two situations would the supermarket be able to rescind a contract to sell peppers to Melnick at the incorrectly advertised price?
3. Does it matter if the price that was advertised was a reasonable price for the peppers? Why or why not?

ONLINE ACTIVITIES

INTERNET EXERCISES

Go to the *Business Law Today* home page at http://blt.westbuslaw.com, select "Chapter 12," and click on "Internet Exercises." There you will find the following Internet research exercises that you can perform to learn more about topics covered in this chapter.

Activity 12–1: LEGAL PERSPECTIVE—Negligent Misrepresentation and *Scienter*

Activity 12–2: MANAGEMENT PERSPECTIVE—Fraudulent Misrepresentation

Activity 12–3: ECONOMIC PERSPECTIVE—Economic Duress

BEFORE THE TEST

Go to the *Business Law Today* home page at http://blt.westbuslaw.com, select "Chapter 12," and click on "Interactive Quizzes." You will find a number of interactive questions relating to this chapter.

CHAPTER 13

The Statute of Frauds

"I would sooner trust the smallest slip of paper for truth, than the strongest and most retentive memory, ever bestowed on mortal man."

Joseph Henry Lumpkin, 1799–1867
(American jurist)

CHAPTER OUTLINE

- THE REQUIREMENT OF A WRITING
- SUFFICIENCY OF THE WRITING
- THE PAROL EVIDENCE RULE

LEARNING OBJECTIVES

After reading this chapter, you should be able to answer the following questions:

1. What contracts must be in writing to be enforceable?
2. If it is possible for a contract to be performed within one year, must it be in writing?
3. When will an oral promise to pay another person's debt be enforced?
4. If a written contract is required, what terms are considered essential and must be contained in the written document?
5. What is parol evidence? When is parol evidence admissible to clarify the terms of a written contract?

A contract that is otherwise valid may still be unenforceable if it is not in the proper form. As the judge states in the chapter-opening quotation, most people trust a written document more than an individual's memory of the terms of an agreement into which they entered. For this reason, the law requires certain types of contracts to be in writing. If a contract is required by law to be in writing and there is no written evidence of the contract, it may not be enforceable.

In this chapter, we examine the kinds of contracts that require a writing under what is called the *Statute of Frauds* and what must be contained in the writing. The chapter concludes with a discussion of the parol evidence rule, under which courts determine the admissibility at trial of evidence extraneous (external) to written contracts.

The Requirement of a Writing

STATUTE OF FRAUDS
A state statute under which certain types of contracts must be in writing to be enforceable.

Today, every state has a statute that stipulates what types of contracts must be in writing. In this text, we refer to such statutes as the **Statute of Frauds.** The primary purpose of the statute is to ensure that, for certain types of contracts, there is reliable evidence of the contracts and their terms. These types of contracts are those deemed historically to be important or complex. Although the statutes vary slightly from state to state, the following types of contracts are normally required to be in writing or evidenced by a written memorandum:

1. Contracts involving interests in land.
2. Contracts that cannot by their terms be performed within one year from the date of formation.
3. Collateral contracts, such as promises to answer for the debt or duty of another.
4. Promises made in consideration of marriage.
5. Contracts for the sale of goods priced at $500 or more ($5,000 or more under the 2003 amendments to the Uniform Commercial Code, or UCC—see Chapter 18).

KEEP IN MIND Although only certain types of contracts must be in writing to be enforceable, it is good practice to put other contracts in writing as well to prevent disputes over contract terms.

Agreements or promises that fit into one or more of these categories are said to "fall under" or "fall within" the Statute of Frauds. (Certain exceptions are made to the applicability of the Statute of Frauds in some circumstances, however, as you will read later in this section.)

The actual name of the Statute of Frauds is misleading because it does not apply to fraud. Rather, the statute denies enforceability to certain contracts that do not comply with its requirements. The name derives from an English act passed in 1677, which is presented as this chapter's *Landmark in the Law* feature.

CONTRACTS INVOLVING INTERESTS IN LAND

Land is a form of *real property,* or real estate, which includes not only land but all physical objects that are permanently attached to the soil, such as buildings, plants, trees, and the soil itself. Under the Statute of Frauds, a contract involving an interest in land must be evidenced by a writing to be enforceable.[1] If Carol, for example, contracts orally to sell Seaside Shelter to Axel but later decides not to sell, Axel cannot enforce the contract. Similarly, if Axel refuses to close the deal, Carol cannot force Axel to pay for the land by bringing a lawsuit. The Statute of Frauds is a *defense* to the enforcement of this type of oral contract.

on the Web Professor Eric Talley of the University of Southern California provides an interesting discussion of the history and current applicability of the Statute of Frauds, both internationally and in the United States, at **http://www-bcf.usc.edu/~etalley/frauds.html.**

A contract for the sale of land ordinarily involves the entire interest in the real property, including buildings, growing crops, vegetation, minerals, timber, and anything else affixed to the land. Therefore, a *fixture* (personal property so affixed or so used as to become a part of the realty—see Chapter 44) is treated as real property.

The Statute of Frauds requires written contracts not just for the sale of land but also for the transfer of other interests in land, such as mortgages and leases. We describe these other interests in Chapter 44.

1. In some states, the contract will be enforced, however, if each party admits to the existence of the oral contract in court or admits to its existence during discovery before trial (see Chapter 3).

LANDMARK IN THE LAW

The Statute of Frauds

On April 12, 1677, the English Parliament passed "An Act for the Prevention of Frauds and Perjuries." Four days later, the act was signed by King Charles II and became the law of the land. The act contained twenty-five sections and stipulated that if certain types of contracts were to be enforceable by the courts, they would henceforth have to be in writing or evidenced by a written memorandum.[a]

ENFORCEMENT OF ORAL PROMISES The English act was enacted specifically to prevent the many frauds that were being perpetrated through the perjured testimony of witnesses in cases involving breached oral agreements, for which no written evidence existed. During the early history of the common law in England, oral contracts were generally not enforced by the courts, but in the fourteenth century, they began to be enforced in certain *assumpsit* actions.[b] These actions, to which the origins of modern contract law are traced, allowed a party to sue and obtain relief when a promise or contract had been breached. During the next two centuries, the king's courts commonly enforced oral promises in actions in *assumpsit.*

PROBLEMS WITH ORAL CONTRACTS Because the courts enforced oral contracts on the strength of oral testimony by witnesses, it was not too difficult to evade justice by alleging that a contract had been breached and then procuring "convincing" witnesses to support the claim. The possibility of fraud in such actions was enhanced by the fact that seventeenth-century English courts did not allow oral testimony to be given by the parties to a lawsuit—or by any parties with an interest in the litigation, such as husbands or wives. Defense against actions for breach of contract was thus limited to written evidence and the testimony of third parties. The Statute of Frauds was enacted to minimize the possibility of fraud in oral contracts relating to certain types of transactions.

APPLICATION TO TODAY'S BUSINESS WORLD

Essentially, the Statute of Frauds offers a defense against contracts that fall under the statute. Indeed, the statute has been criticized by some because, although it was created to protect the innocent, it can also be used as a technical defense by a party who has breached a genuine, mutually agreed-on oral contract—if the contract falls within the Statute of Frauds. For this reason, some legal scholars believe the act has caused more fraud than it has prevented. Nonetheless, U.S. courts continue to apply the Statute of Frauds to disputes involving oral contracts. The definitions of such terms as writing *and* signature, *however, are changing as we move further into an electronic age—as you will read in Chapter 17, which covers e-contracts.*

RELEVANT WEB SITES

To locate information on the Web concerning the Statute of Frauds, go to this text's Web site at **http://blt.westbuslaw.com**, *select "Chapter 13," and click on "URLs for Landmarks."*

a. These contracts are discussed in the text of this chapter.

b. *Assumpsit* is Latin for "he undertook" or "she promised." The emergence of remedies given on the basis of breached promises and duties dates to these actions. One of the earliest occurred in 1370, when the court allowed an individual to sue a person who, in trying to cure the plaintiff's horse, had acted so negligently that the horse died. Another such action was permitted in 1375, when a plaintiff obtained relief for having been maimed by a surgeon hired to cure him.

In the following case, the court was asked to enforce a purported purchase clause in an agreement for a lease of commercial property. There was only one problem: no one could provide a copy of the lease.

CASE 13.1 Michel v. Bush

Court of Appeals of Ohio,
Ninth District, 2001.
146 Ohio App.3d 208
765 N.E.2d 911.

BACKGROUND AND FACTS Betty and Frank Bush owned two commercial structures in Doylestown, Ohio: an office building and an unoccupied building. In 1989, Donald Michel, on behalf of himself and Amanda Enterprises, Inc., agreed to lease the unoccupied building to operate a video store and tanning salon. In 1993, Michel asked the Bushes about buying the property, and they discussed financing arrangements, but Michel failed to present an offer. Three years later, Michel again spoke with the Bushes about the possibility of a sale, but the next year, the Bushes sold the property to a third party, the B&S Group. Michel and Amanda Enterprises filed a suit in an Ohio state court against the Bushes, claiming, among other things, breach of contract. Michel alleged that the lease agreement contained an option to buy the leased property. He testified that the option read, "First right of refusal on purchase of said property." The Bushes denied this allegation. Everyone agreed that the lease agreement had been in writing, but no one could provide a copy of it. The court granted a summary judgment in the Bushes' favor, in part on the ground that the Statute of Frauds barred Michel's claim. Michel appealed to a state intermediate appellate court.

IN THE WORDS OF THE COURT . . .
WHITMORE, Judge.

* * * *

* * * Michel has claimed that the trial court incorrectly determined that the Statute of Frauds barred the prosecution of his claim. Specifically, he has argued that the Statute of Frauds bars claims based only upon oral agreements regarding the sale of a property interest, and, because the Agreement herein was admittedly in writing, the trial court's determination to that end was in error. This court disagrees.

Ohio's Statute of Frauds is found at [Revised Code Section] 1335.05. That statute provides:

> "No action shall be brought whereby to charge the defendant, * * * upon a contract or sale of lands, * * * or interest in or concerning them, * * * unless the agreement upon which such action is brought, or some memorandum or note thereof, is in writing and signed by the party to be charged therewith[.]"

Taking the plain language of the statute, it is clear that a claim regarding any interest in land, [for example,] a right of first refusal, cannot be brought, as a matter of law, unless the agreement pertaining thereto was reduced to writing, signed by the party to be charged, and produced.

Moreover, it is important to note * * * [t]his statute serves to ensure that transactions involving a transfer of realty interests are commemorated with sufficient solemnity. *A signed writing provides greater assurance that the parties and the public can reliably know when such a transaction occurs.* It supports the public policy favoring clarity in determining real estate interests and discourages indefinite or fraudulent claims about such interests. [Emphasis added.]

In this case, there is no dispute that an agreement regarding a mere leasehold interest was in writing. However, the present dispute is not over the lease agreement; rather, the issue is whether an interest, * * * the alleged option/right of first refusal, was reduced to writing. Michel has alleged and sworn that the alleged option/right of first refusal was written in the margins of the Agreement. The Bushes, on the

CASE 13.1—Continued

other hand, have argued that no such option/right of first refusal interest was ever created or given in the first place. None of the parties has produced a copy of the Agreement. Without the document or other written evidence, Michel cannot bring a claim to enforce an alleged interest in realty. To hold otherwise would be to defeat the very purpose of the Statute of Frauds.

DECISION AND REMEDY The state intermediate appellate court affirmed the judgment of the lower court. The appellate court held that when a written agreement relating to an interest in land cannot be produced, an action to enforce a purported term in the agreement cannot be sustained.

FOR CRITICAL ANALYSIS—Social Consideration *If the Statute of Frauds had not applied in this case, is there another basis on which a judgment could have been granted in the Bushes' favor?*

THE ONE-YEAR RULE

Contracts that cannot, *by their own terms,* be performed within one year *from the day after* the contract is formed must be in writing to be enforceable. Because disputes over such contracts are unlikely to occur until some time after the contracts are made, resolution of these disputes is difficult unless the contract terms have been put in writing. The one-year period begins to run *the day after the contract is made.*

■ **EXAMPLE 13.1** Suppose that Superior University forms a contract with Kimi San, stating that San will teach three courses in history during the coming academic year (September 15 through June 15). If the contract is formed in March, it must be in writing to be enforceable—because it cannot be performed within one year. If the contract is not formed until July, however, it will not have to be in writing to be enforceable—because it can be performed within one year. ■ Exhibit 13–1 graphically illustrates the one-year rule.

Normally, the test for determining whether an oral contract is enforceable under the one-year rule of the Statute of Frauds is not whether the agreement is *likely* to be performed within one year from the day after the date of contract formation but whether

EXHIBIT 13–1 THE ONE-YEAR RULE

Under the Statute of Frauds, contracts that by their terms are impossible to perform within one year from the day after the date of contract formation must be in writing to be enforceable. Put another way, if it is at all possible to perform an oral contract within one year from the day after the contract is made, the contract will fall outside the Statute of Frauds and be enforceable.

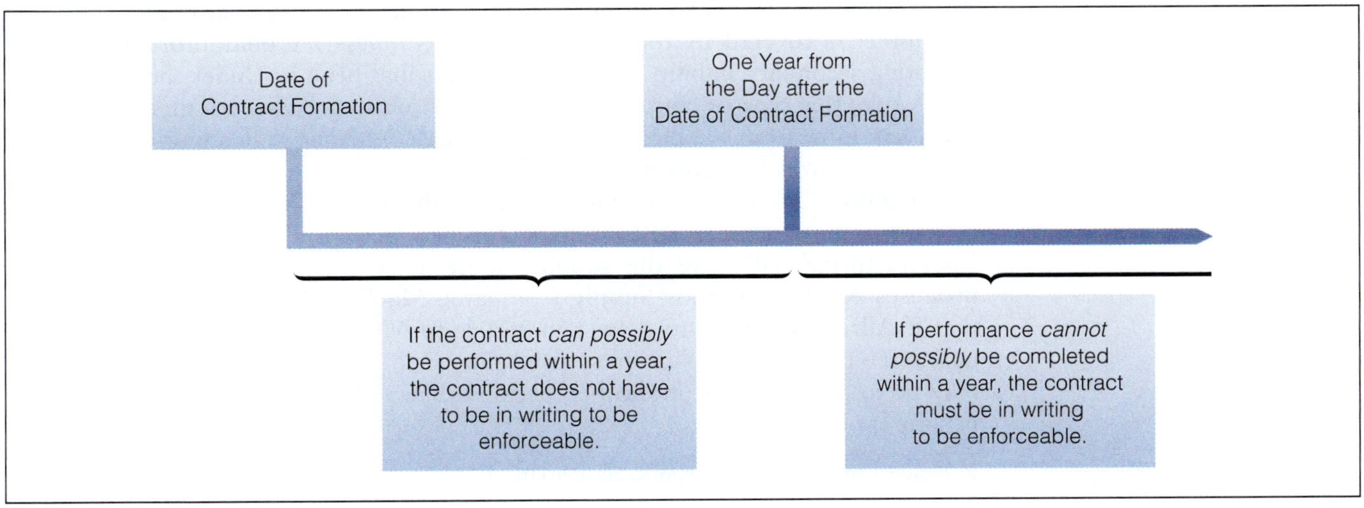

performance within a year is *possible.* When performance of a contract is objectively impossible during the one-year period, the oral contract will be unenforceable.

COLLATERAL PROMISES

COLLATERAL PROMISE
A secondary promise that is ancillary (subsidiary) to a principal transaction or primary contractual relationship, such as a promise made by one person to pay the debts of another if the latter fails to perform. A collateral promise normally must be in writing to be enforceable.

A **collateral promise,** or secondary promise, is one that is ancillary (subsidiary) to a principal transaction or primary contractual relationship. In other words, a collateral promise is one made by a third party to assume the debts or obligations of a primary party to a contract if that party does not perform. Any collateral promise of this nature falls under the Statute of Frauds and therefore must be in writing to be enforceable. To understand this concept, it is important to distinguish between primary and secondary promises and obligations.

Primary versus Secondary Obligations As a general rule, a contract in which a party assumes a primary obligation does not need to be in writing to be enforceable. ■ EXAMPLE 13.2 Suppose that Kenneth orally contracts with Joanne's Floral Boutique to send his mother a dozen roses for Mother's Day. Kenneth promises to pay the boutique when he receives the bill for the flowers. Kenneth is a direct party to this contract and has incurred a *primary* obligation under the contract. Because he is a party to the contract and has a primary obligation to Joanne's Floral Boutique, this contract does not fall under the Statute of Frauds and does not have to be in writing to be enforceable. If Kenneth fails to pay the florist and the florist sues him for payment, Kenneth cannot raise the Statute of Frauds as a defense. He cannot claim that the contract is unenforceable because it was not in writing. ■

In contrast, a contract in which a party assumes a secondary obligation does have to be in writing to be enforceable. ■ EXAMPLE 13.3 Suppose that Kenneth's mother borrows $1,000 from the Medford Trust Company on a promissory note payable six months later. Kenneth promises the bank officer handling the loan that he will pay the $1,000 *if his mother does not pay the loan on time.* Kenneth, in this situation, becomes what is known as a *guarantor* on the loan; that is, he is guaranteeing to the bank (the creditor) that he will pay the loan if his mother fails to do so. This kind of collateral promise, in which the guarantor states that he or she will become responsible only if the primary party does not perform, must be in writing to be enforceable. ■ We return to the concept of guaranty and the distinction between primary and secondary obligations in Chapter 26, in the context of creditors' rights.

An Exception—The "Main Purpose" Rule An oral promise to answer for the debt of another is covered by the Statute of Frauds *unless* the guarantor's purpose in accepting secondary liability is to secure a personal benefit. Under the "main purpose" rule, this type of contract need not be in writing.[2] The assumption is that a court can infer from the circumstances of a case whether a "leading objective" of the promisor was to secure a personal benefit.

■ EXAMPLE 13.4 Carrie Oswald contracts with Machine Manufacturing Company to have some machines custom-made for her factory. To ensure that Machine Manufacturing will have the supplies it needs to make the machines, Oswald promises Allrite Materials Supply Company, Machine Manufacturing's supplier, that if Allrite continues to deliver materials to Machine Manufacturing, she will guarantee payment. This promise need not be in writing, even though the effect may be to pay the debt of another, because Oswald's main purpose is to secure a benefit for herself. ■

2. *Restatement (Second) of Contracts,* Section 116.

Drawing by Bruce Eric Kaplan © 1993 The New Yorker Magazine, Inc.

"Now, according to this agreement, his problems will be your problems, and your problems will be your problems."

Another typical application of the so-called main purpose doctrine occurs when one creditor guarantees the debtor's debt to another creditor to forestall litigation. This allows the debtor to remain in business long enough to generate profits sufficient to pay *both* creditors. In this situation, the guaranty does not need to be in writing to be enforceable.

Promises Made in Consideration of Marriage

A unilateral promise to pay a monetary amount or to give property in consideration of marriage must be in writing. If Mr. Baumann promises to pay Joe Villard $10,000 if Villard marries Baumann's daughter, the promise must be in writing to be enforceable. The same rule applies to **prenuptial agreements**—agreements made before marriage (also called *antenuptial agreements*) that define each partner's ownership rights in the other partner's property. For example, a prospective wife or husband may wish to limit the amount the prospective spouse can obtain if the marriage ends in divorce. Prenuptial agreements made in consideration of marriage must be in writing to be enforceable.

PRENUPTIAL AGREEMENT
An agreement made before marriage that defines each partner's ownership rights in the other partner's property. Prenuptial agreements must be in writing to be enforceable.

Generally, courts tend to give more credence to prenuptial agreements that are accompanied by consideration. ■ EXAMPLE 13.5 Maureen, who is not wealthy, marries Kaiser, who has a net worth of $300 million. Kaiser has several children, and he wants them to receive most of his wealth on his death. Prior to their marriage, Maureen and Kaiser draft and sign a prenuptial agreement in which Kaiser promises to give Maureen $100,000 per year for the rest of her life if they divorce. As consideration for consenting to this amount, Kaiser offers Maureen $1 million. If Maureen consents to the agreement and accepts the $1 million, very likely a court would hold that this prenuptial agreement is valid, should it ever be contested. ■

ETHICAL ISSUE 13.1

What happens to the prenuptial agreement when an engagement is broken? Sometimes, parties include in their prenuptial agreements terms that have to do with premarital activities. For example, in one case a couple agreed that the bride-to-be (Virginia DeFina) would pay for all expenses relating to the wedding. In return, the groom-to-be (Stephen Scott) promised to transfer a one-half interest in the real property that was to be the marital abode. Then the couple broke their engagement, and the wedding was canceled. By this time, DeFina had already incurred $16,000 in wedding expenses. Given that the wedding was canceled, did DeFina have any claim on Scott's property? Scott claimed that she did not because their agreement assumed that they would marry. Furthermore, Scott maintained that traditionally the bride and/or her family pay the wedding expenses anyway.

When this question came before a New York court, the court first noted that women are usually the economic losers in broken engagements. Not only have they traditionally had to bear the wedding expenses, but under the laws of some states, they are also required to return the engagement ring. The court, referring to this "regime" as "both unequal and unjustified," decided that contract principles should apply. The court pointed out that Scott and DeFina were "well-established professional adults" who formed clear plans regarding their engagement and their eventual marriage. Indeed, Scott was an attorney who had been married twice before. Thus, the court concluded that DeFina had a lien (a claim—see Chapter 26) on Scott's property in the amount of $16,000.[3] ■

CONTRACTS FOR THE SALE OF GOODS

The Uniform Commercial Code (UCC) contains Statute of Frauds provisions that require written evidence of a contract. Section 2–201 contains the major provision, which generally requires a writing or memorandum for the sale of goods priced at $500 or more ($5,000 or more under the 2003 amendments to the UCC—see Chapter 18). A writing that will satisfy the UCC requirement need only state the quantity term; other terms agreed on need not be stated "accurately" in the writing, as long as they adequately reflect both parties' intentions. The contract will not be enforceable, however, for any quantity greater than that set forth in the writing. In addition, the writing must be signed by the person against whom enforcement is sought. Beyond these two requirements, the writing need not designate the buyer or the seller, the terms of payment, or the price.

.on the Web The online version of UCC Section 2–201 on the Statute of Frauds includes links to definitions of certain terms used in the section. To access this site, go to **http://www.law.cornell.edu/ucc/2/2-201.html**.

EXCEPTIONS TO THE STATUTE OF FRAUDS

Exceptions to the applicability of the Statute of Frauds are made in certain situations. We describe those situations here.

Partial Performance In cases involving oral contracts for the transfer of interests in land, if the purchaser has paid part of the price, taken possession, and made valuable improvements to the property, and if the parties cannot be returned to their status quo prior to the contract, a court may grant *specific performance* (performance of the contract according to its precise terms). Whether a court will enforce an oral contract for an interest in land when partial performance has taken place is usually

3. *DeFina v. Scott,* 195 Misc.2d 75, 755 N.Y.S.2d 587 (N.Y.Sup. 2003).

INTERNATIONAL PERSPECTIVE

The Statute of Frauds and International Sales Contracts

As you will read in Chapter 18, the Convention on Contracts for the International Sale of Goods (CISG) provides rules that govern international sales contracts between citizens of countries that have ratified the convention (agreement). Article 11 of the CISG does not incorporate any Statute of Frauds provisions. Rather, it states that a "contract for sale need not be concluded in or evidenced by writing and is not subject to any other requirements as to form."

Article 11 accords with the legal customs of most nations, which no longer require contracts to meet certain formal or writing requirements to be enforceable. Ironically, even England, the nation that enacted the original Statute of Frauds in 1677, has repealed all of it except the provisions relating to collateral promises and to transfers of interests in land. Many other countries that once had such statutes have also repealed all or parts of them. Civil law countries, such as France, have never required certain types of contracts to be in writing.

FOR CRITICAL ANALYSIS

If there were no Statute of Frauds and a dispute arose concerning an oral agreement, how would the parties substantiate their respective positions?

determined by the degree of injury that would be suffered if the court chose *not* to enforce the oral contract. In some states, mere reliance on certain types of oral contracts is enough to remove them from the Statute of Frauds.

Under the UCC, an oral contract for goods priced at $500 or more ($5,000 or more under the 2003 amendments) is enforceable to the extent that a seller accepts payment or a buyer accepts delivery of the goods.[4] For example, if Ajax Corporation orders by telephone twenty crates of bleach from Cloney, Inc., and repudiates the contract after ten crates have been delivered and accepted, Cloney can enforce the contract to the extent of the ten crates accepted by Ajax.

Admissions In some states, if a party against whom enforcement of an oral contract is sought admits in pleadings, testimony, or otherwise in court proceedings that a contract for sale was made, the contract will be enforceable.[5] A contract subject to the UCC will be enforceable, but only to the extent of the quantity admitted.[6] Thus, if the president of Ajax Corporation admits under oath that an oral agreement was made with Cloney, Inc., for the twenty crates of bleach, the agreement will be enforceable to that extent.

Promissory Estoppel In some states, an oral contract that would otherwise be unenforceable under the Statute of Frauds may be enforced under the doctrine of promissory estoppel, or detrimental reliance. Recall from Chapter 10 that if a promisor makes a promise on which the promisee justifiably relies to her or his detriment, a court may *estop* (prevent) the promisor from denying that a contract exists. Section 139 of the *Restatement (Second) of Contracts* provides that in these circumstances, an oral promise can be enforceable, notwithstanding the Statute of Frauds, if the reliance was foreseeable to the person making the promise and if injustice can be avoided only by enforcing the promise.

.on the Web For information on the *Restatements of the Law,* including the *Restatement (Second) of Contracts,* go to the American Law Institute's Web site at

http://www.ali.org.

Special Exceptions under the UCC Special exceptions to the applicability of the Statute of Frauds exist for sales contracts. Oral contracts for customized goods may be enforced in certain circumstances. Another exception has to do with oral contracts between merchants that have been confirmed in writing. We will examine these exceptions in Chapter 18. Exhibit 13–2 on the next page graphically summarizes the types of contracts that fall under the Statute of Frauds and the exceptions that apply.

Sufficiency of the Writing

A written contract will satisfy the writing requirement of the Statute of Frauds. A *written memorandum* (written evidence of the oral contract) signed by the party against whom enforcement is sought will also satisfy the writing requirement.[7] The signature need not be placed at the end of the document but can be anywhere in the writing; it can even be initials rather than the full name. (See the *Application*

4. UCC 2–201(3)(c). See Chapter 18.
5. *Restatement (Second) of Contracts,* Section 133.
6. UCC 2–201(3)(b). See Chapter 18.
7. As mentioned earlier, under the UCC Statute of Frauds, a writing is required only for contracts for the sale of goods priced at $500 or more ($5,000 or more under the 2003 amendments to UCC Article 2). See Chapter 18.

EXHIBIT 13–2 CONTRACTS SUBJECT TO THE STATUTE OF FRAUDS

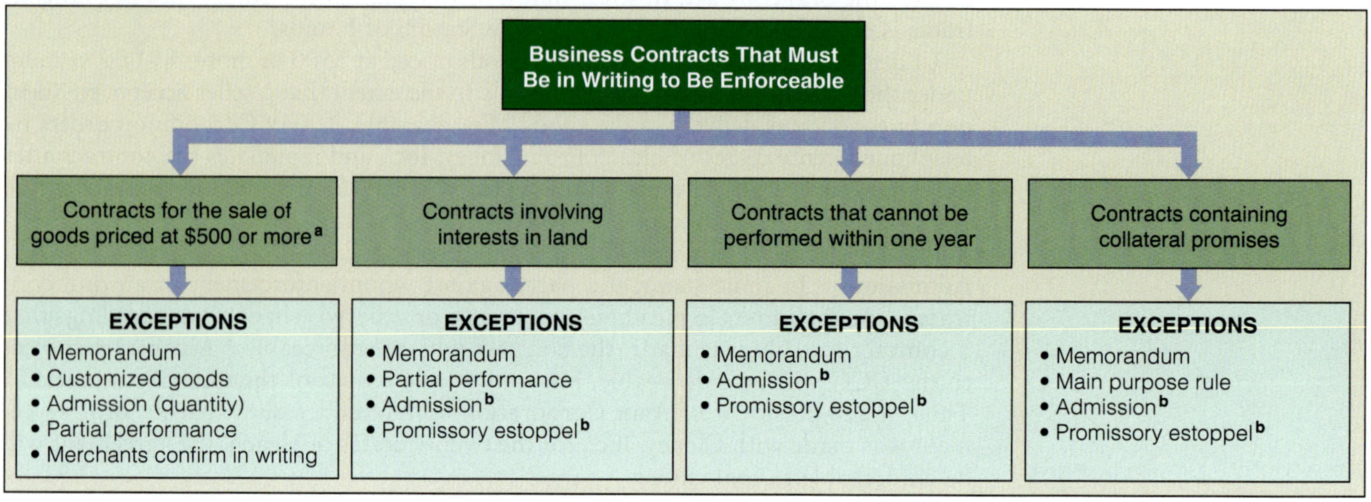

a. Under a 2003 amendment to the UCC, a contract for a sale of goods must involve goods priced at $5,000 or more to be subject to the writing requirement of the Statute of Frauds (see Chapter 18). This amendment also exempts contracts for the sale of goods from the one-year rule.
b. Some states follow Section 133 (on admissions) and Section 139 (on promissory estoppel) of the *Restatement (Second) of Contracts.*

feature at the end of this chapter for suggestions on how to prevent problems with oral contracts.)

A significant issue in today's business world has to do with how "signatures" can be created and verified on electronic contracts and other documents. We will examine electronic signatures in Chapter 17.

What Constitutes a Writing?

A writing can consist of any confirmation, invoice, sales slip, check, or fax—or such items in combination. The written contract need not consist of a single document to constitute an enforceable contract. One document may incorporate another document by expressly referring to it. Several documents may form a single contract if they are physically attached, such as by staple, paper clip, or glue. Several documents may form a single contract even if they are only placed in the same envelope.

■ **Example 13.6** Sam orally agrees to sell some land next to a shopping mall to Terry. Sam gives Terry an unsigned memo that contains a legal description of the property, and Terry gives Sam an unsigned first draft of their contract. Sam sends Terry a signed letter that refers to the memo and to the first and final drafts of the contract. Terry sends Sam an unsigned copy of the final draft of the contract with a signed check stapled to it. Together, the documents can constitute a writing sufficient to satisfy the Statute of Frauds and bind both parties to the terms of the contract as evidenced by the writings. ■

What Must Be Contained in the Writing?

A memorandum evidencing the oral contract need only contain the essential terms of the contract. Under most provisions of the Statute of Frauds, the writing must name the parties, subject matter, consideration, and quantity. With respect to contracts for the sale of land, some states require that the memorandum also set forth the essential terms of the contract, such as location and price, with sufficient clarity to allow the terms to be determined from the memo itself, without reference to any outside sources.[8] Under the UCC, in regard to the sale of goods, the writing need only name the quantity term and be signed by the party against whom enforcement is sought.

Because only the party against whom enforcement is sought need have signed the writing, a contract may be enforceable by one of its parties but not by the other. ■ EXAMPLE 13.7 Rock orally agrees to buy Betty Devlin's lake house and lot for $150,000. Devlin writes Rock a letter confirming the sale by identifying the parties and the essential terms of the sales contract—price, method of payment, and legal address—and signs the letter. Devlin has made a written memorandum of the oral land contract. Because she signed the letter, she normally can be held to the oral contract by Rock. Rock, however, because he has not signed or entered into a written contract or memorandum, can plead the Statute of Frauds as a defense, and Devlin cannot enforce the contract against him. ■

Whether a proposal to buy a pair of printing presses contained the essential terms of the contract and satisfied the Statute of Frauds was at issue in the following case.

8. *Rhodes v. Wilkins,* 83 N.M. 782, 498 P.2d 311 (1972).

CASE 13.2 Interstate Litho Corp. v. Brown

United States Court of Appeals,
First Circuit, 2001.
255 F.3d 19.

BACKGROUND AND FACTS In 1995, Interstate Litho Corporation negotiated with Marc Brown, a broker in used printing equipment, and his company, Integra Technical Services, concerning Interstate's acquisition of two used printing presses. Freidel's Manufacturing, Inc., in Illinois owned one of the presses, and Graphic Engineering in Malaysia owned the other. Both were to be refurbished before they were delivered to Interstate. Interstate's president, Henry Becker, signed a proposal reflecting a $2.6 million price. Interstate advanced $75,000, of which $50,000 was wired to Freidel's. Freidel's pulled its press off the market, and Brown signed a contract to buy it. Brown never bought the press, however, because the deal with Interstate fell apart. Freidel's kept the deposit and sold the press for less than it would have received from Brown. Interstate filed a suit in a federal district court against Brown and others, seeking the return of its $75,000. Brown counterclaimed for his lost profit, asserting in part breach of contract. After a trial, the jury rejected Interstate's claim and awarded Brown $187,500 on his counterclaim. Interstate appealed to the U.S. Court of Appeals for the First Circuit, arguing that, among other things, there was no enforceable contract because the proposal signed by Becker lacked the essential terms and failed to comply with the Statute of Frauds.

IN THE WORDS OF THE COURT . . .
LYNCH, Circuit Judge.

* * * *

The evidence was such that whether the * * * proposal contained the essential terms of a contract was an issue of fact for the jury. The writing between the parties identified in detail the two presses being purchased, identified a total price for purchasing and reworking the presses ($2.6 million, with $900,000 of this amount allocated to acquiring the two presses), and set forth a detailed delivery and payment schedule.

Interstate argues * * * that the proposal neither states that it is a final agreement for purchase of the two presses by Interstate from Integra nor provides in specific

(Continued)

CASE 13.2—Continued

terms the completion date for refurbishment of the presses. However, it is not required that all terms of the agreement be precisely specified, and the presence of undefined or unspecified terms will not necessarily preclude the formation of a binding contract. Here, the terms of the proposal—which include nine pages of nitty-gritty detail on matters such as rollers and hangers, plate and blanket cylinders, and ink fountains—were sufficient for the jury to find that Interstate had agreed to purchase the two presses. That Interstate wired $75,000 * * * to hold the presses * * * just a few days after signing the proposal, further supports the existence of a firm agreement between the parties. We cannot conclude as a matter of law that this contract lacked essential terms.

* * * *

Interstate [also] argues that the proposal does not satisfy the * * * Statute of Frauds, because the * * * proposal, though a writing, describes only the remanufacturing portion of the deal, and not the terms of the actual purchase of the two presses by Integra, for subsequent sale to Interstate. There was, however, no reason the proposal had to describe the details of Brown's own purchase of the eight-color press from Freidel's or the four-color press from Malaysia. Indeed, the important questions for a buyer like Interstate would, presumably, have centered on whether the refurbished presses met its needs and specifications, and not on the background details of how the broker (Brown) obtained those presses from third parties. As Brown himself testified, his initial acquisition of the presses was accomplished through transactions separate and distinct from the sale of the refurbished presses to Interstate. Thus the issue, properly presented to the jury, was whether the * * * proposal constituted an agreement by Interstate to purchase the two presses from Brown. The jury found that it did, and so the proposal was a writing in satisfaction of the Statute of Frauds.

DECISION AND REMEDY The U.S. Court of Appeals for the First Circuit affirmed the judgment of the lower court. The appellate court upheld the jury's finding that the proposal contained the essential terms of the contract and constituted Interstate's agreement to buy the presses. The proposal set out the details of the deal from Interstate's point of view.

FOR CRITICAL ANALYSIS—Economic Consideration *In this case, what should have formed the basis for the amount of Brown's damages?*

The Parol Evidence Rule

PAROL EVIDENCE RULE
A substantive rule of contracts, as well as a procedural rule of evidence, under which a court will not receive into evidence the parties' prior negotiations, prior agreements, or contemporaneous oral agreements if that evidence contradicts or varies the terms of the parties' written contract.

The **parol evidence rule** prohibits the introduction at trial of evidence of the parties' prior negotiations, prior agreements, or contemporaneous oral agreements if that evidence contradicts or varies the terms of the parties' written contract. The written contract is ordinarily assumed to be the final statement of the parties' agreement.

Exceptions to the Parol Evidence Rule

Because of the rigidity of the parol evidence rule, the courts make several exceptions. These exceptions include the following:

1. Evidence of a *subsequent modification* of a written contract can be introduced in court. Keep in mind that the oral modifications may not be enforceable if they come under the Statute of Frauds—for example, if they increase the price of the goods for sale to $500 or more ($5,000 or more under the 2003 amendments)

or increase the term for performance to more than one year. Also, oral modifications will not be enforceable if the original contract provides that any modification must be in writing.[9]

2 Oral evidence can be introduced in all cases to show that the contract was voidable or void (for example, induced by mistake, fraud, or misrepresentation). In this situation, if deception led one of the parties to agree to the terms of a written contract, oral evidence indicating fraud should not be excluded. Courts frown on bad faith and are quick to allow the introduction at trial of parol evidence when it establishes fraud.

NOTE The parol evidence rule and its exceptions relate to the rules concerning the *interpretation* of contracts.

3 When the terms of a written contract are ambiguous, evidence is admissible to show the meaning of the terms.

4 Evidence is admissible when the written contract is incomplete in that it lacks one or more of the essential terms. The courts allow evidence to "fill in the gaps" in the contract.

5 Under the UCC, evidence can be introduced to explain or supplement a written contract by showing a prior dealing, course of performance, or usage of trade.[10] We discuss these terms in further detail in Chapter 18, in the context of sales contracts. Here, it is sufficient to say that when buyers and sellers deal with each other over extended periods of time, certain customary practices develop. These practices are often overlooked in the writing of the contract, so courts allow the introduction of evidence to show how the parties have acted in the past. Usage of trade—practices and customs generally followed in a particular industry—can also shed light on the meaning of certain contract provisions, and thus evidence of trade usage may be admissible. Can usage of trade be considered in determining the meaning of the term *registration* in the context of domain name registration? For a discussion of this issue, see this chapter's *Adapting the Law to the Online Environment* feature on the following page.

6 The parol evidence rule does not apply if the existence of the entire written contract is subject to an orally agreed-on condition. Proof of the condition does not alter or modify the written terms but affects the *enforceability* of the written contract. ■ **EXAMPLE 13.8** Jelek agrees to purchase Armand's car for $8,000, but only if Jelek's mechanic, Frank, inspects the car and approves of the purchase. Armand agrees to this condition, but because he is leaving town for the weekend and Jelek wants to use the car (if he buys it) before Armand returns, Jelek drafts a contract of sale, and they both sign it. Frank, the mechanic, does not approve of the purchase, and when Jelek does not buy the car, Armand sues him, alleging that he breached the contract. In this case, Jelek's oral agreement did not alter or modify the terms of the written agreement but concerned whether the contract existed at all. Therefore, the parol evidence rule does not apply. ■

7 When an *obvious* or *gross* clerical (or typographic) error exists that clearly would not represent the agreement of the parties, parol evidence is admissible to correct the error. ■ **EXAMPLE 13.9** Sem Yo agrees to lease 1,000 square feet of office space at the current monthly rate of $3 per square foot from Stone Enterprises. The signed written lease provides for a monthly lease payment of $300 rather than the $3,000 agreed on by the parties. Because the error is obvious, Stone Enterprises would be allowed to admit parol evidence to correct the mistake. ■

9. UCC 2–209(2), (3). See Chapter 18.
10. UCC 1–205, 2–202. See Chapter 18.

ADAPTING THE LAW TO THE ONLINE ENVIRONMENT

What Does "Registration" Mean in the Domain Name Context?

Article 2 of the Uniform Commercial Code (UCC) specifically allows evidence of trade usage to be introduced in court to explain or supplement the written terms of a contract. As mentioned elsewhere, this is one of the exceptions to the parol evidence rule. Article 2, however, applies to sales of *goods*. Does this mean that trade usage *cannot* be admitted to explain the meaning of terms in contracts governed by the common law—that is, contracts that do not involve sales of "goods"? Specifically, can a court consider usage of trade in determining what the term *registration* means in a contract to register a domain name?

THE QUESTION OF "EXCLUSIVE USE"

Typically, when a person or business entity registers an Internet domain name as the address for a Web site, that person or entity expects to have the exclusive right to use that name. Certainly, this was Michael Zurakov's expectation when he registered the domain name "Laborzionist.org" with Register.com, Inc., a business that provides Internet services, including the registration of domain names. Register.com established a "Coming Soon" page for Zurakov's Web site. The page, which would be accessed by anyone keying in Zurakov's domain name, contained banner ads for Register.com and other organizations, as well as a list of "Additional Services." It appeared that the ads were in some way endorsed by Zurakov and that he was the provider of the additional services.

Zurakov sued Register.com, alleging that by registering the domain name, he had obtained the exclusive right to use the name and the corresponding Web page. He claimed that Register.com's use of the page interfered with this right. Register.com asked the court to dismiss the case because, among other things, nothing in the contract stated that Zurakov would have the exclusive use of the domain name. The trial court dismissed the case after concluding that Zurakov had received "everything he bargained for" in the contract—because Register.com had indeed "registered" the domain name. Zurakov appealed.

THE MEANING OF "REGISTRATION"

In arriving at its decision, the trial court had looked at the ordinary meaning of the term *register,* which is "to make a record of." The appellate court, however, stated that "the custom and usage of 'registration' of a domain name in the Internet context is certainly more relevant than the literal definition of 'registration' found in the dictionary." According to custom and usage, the registration of a domain name conferred on the person registering the name the *exclusive* right to use that name. The court also stated that the exclusiveness of the use of a registered domain name "is already a familiar concept in the law" and cited a number of cases that illustrated this concept. In sum, concluded the appellate court, Zurakov had stated a valid claim against Register.com, and the case should go to trial.[a]

FOR CRITICAL ANALYSIS

The court also noted that if Zurakov could not have the exclusive use of the domain name, the registration contract would be "rendered illusory." What did the court mean by this statement?

a. *Zurakov v. Register.com, Inc.*, 304 A.D.2d 176, 760 N.Y.S.2d 13 (1 Dept. 2003).

INTEGRATED CONTRACTS

INTEGRATED CONTRACT
A written contract that constitutes the final expression of the parties' agreement. If a contract is integrated, evidence extraneous to the contract that contradicts or alters the meaning of the contract in any way is inadmissible.

The determination of whether evidence will be allowed basically depends on whether the written contract is intended to be a complete and final embodiment of the terms of the agreement. If it is so intended, it is referred to as an **integrated contract**, and extraneous evidence is excluded. If the contract is only partially integrated, evidence of consistent additional terms is admissible to supplement the written agreement.[11]

11. *Restatement (Second) of Contracts,* Section 216.

REVIEWING THE STATUTE OF FRAUDS

Charter Golf, Inc., manufactures and sells golf apparel and supplies. Ken Odin had worked as a Charter sales representative for six months when he was offered a position with a competing firm. Charter's president, Jerry Montieth, offered Odin a 10 percent commission "for the rest of his life" if Ken would turn down the offer and stay on with Charter. He also promised that Odin would not be fired unless he was dishonest. Odin turned down the competitor's offer and stayed with Charter. Three years later, Charter fired Odin for no reason. Odin sued, alleging breach of contract. Using the information presented in the chapter, answer the following questions.

1. Discuss whether this contract falls within the Statute of Frauds.
2. Is an "employment-for-life" contract *capable* of being performed within one year? What if the employee dies within one year of making the agreement? Explain.
3. Suppose that Montieth admits that he orally promised Odin a 10 percent commission for the rest of his life. Will a court enforce Montieth's promise under the doctrine of promissory estoppel? Why or why not? Name any other exceptions discussed in the chapter that might apply.
4. Now suppose that Montieth had taken out a pencil and written on the back of a register receipt, "10 percent for life." Would this satisfy the requirements of the Statute of Frauds? Why or why not?

APPLICATION How Can You Prevent Problems with Oral Contracts?*

As a general rule, most business contracts should be in writing even when they fall outside the Statute of Frauds. Businesspersons frequently make oral contracts over the telephone, however, particularly when the parties have done business with each other in the past.

Confirm the Agreement in Writing

Any time an oral contract is made, it is advisable for one of the parties to send either a written memorandum or a confirmation of the oral agreement by fax or e-mail to the other party. This accomplishes two purposes: (1) it demonstrates the party's clear intention to form a contract, and (2) it provides the terms of the contract as that party understood them. If the party receiving the memorandum or confirmation then disagrees with the terms as described, the issue can be addressed before performance begins.

Special Rules for Contracts between Merchants

What about the sale of goods between merchants? Under the UCC, written confirmation received by one merchant removes the Statute of Frauds requirement of a writing unless the merchant receiving the confirmation objects in writing within ten days of its receipt. This law (discussed in Chapter 18) clearly points out the need for the merchant receiving the confirmation to review it carefully to ascertain that the confirmation conforms to the oral contract. If the writing does not so conform, the merchant can object in writing (the Statute of Frauds still applies), and the parties can resolve misunderstandings without legal liability. If the merchant fails to object, the written confirmation can be used as evidence to prove the terms of the oral contract. Note, however, that this ten-day rule does not apply to contracts for interests in realty or for services, to which the UCC does not apply.

Checklist for the Businessperson

1. When feasible, use written contracts.
2. If you enter into an oral contract over the telephone, fax or e-mail a written confirmation outlining your understanding of the oral contract.
3. If you receive the other party's written confirmation, read it carefully to make sure that it states the terms already agreed to in the oral contract, as you understand them.
4. If you have any objections, notify the other party of these objections, in writing, within ten days.

* This *Application* is not meant to substitute for the services of an attorney who is licensed to practice law in your state.

KEY TERMS

collateral promise	330
integrated contract	338
parol evidence rule	336
prenuptial agreement	331
Statute of Frauds	326

CHAPTER SUMMARY The Statute of Frauds

The Requirement of a Writing (See pages 326–333.)	*Applicability*—The following types of contracts fall under the Statute of Frauds and must be in writing to be enforceable: 1. *Contracts involving interests in land*—The statute applies to any contract for an interest in realty, such as a sale, a lease, or a mortgage. 2. *Contracts whose terms cannot be performed within one year*—The statute applies only to contracts objectively impossible to perform fully within one year from the day after the contract's formation. 3. *Collateral promises*—The statute applies only to promises made by a third party to become secondarily liable for the debts of a primary party to the contract. *Exception:* the "main purpose" rule. 4. *Promises made in consideration of marriage*—The statute applies to promises to pay money or give property in consideration of a promise to marry and to prenuptial agreements made in consideration of marriage. 5. *Contracts for the sale of goods priced at $500 or more*—Under the UCC Statute of Frauds provision in UCC 2–201. (Under a 2003 amendment to that UCC section, the threshold amount is raised from $500 to $5,000.) *Exceptions*—Partial performance, admissions, and promissory estoppel.
Sufficiency of the Writing (See pages 333–336.)	To constitute an enforceable contract under the Statute of Frauds, a writing must be signed by the party against whom enforcement is sought, must name the parties, must identify the subject matter, and must state with reasonable certainty the essential terms of the contract. Contracts for the sale of land may need to state the price and describe the property with sufficient clarity to allow them to be determined without reference to outside sources. Under the UCC, a contract for a sale of goods is not enforceable beyond the quantity of goods shown in the contract.
The Parol Evidence Rule (See pages 336–338.)	The parol evidence rule prohibits the introduction at trial of evidence of the parties' prior negotiations, prior agreements, or contemporaneous oral agreements that contradicts or varies the terms of the parties' written contract. The written contract is assumed to be the complete embodiment of the parties' agreement. Exceptions are made in the following circumstances: 1. To show that the contract was subsequently modified. 2. To show that the contract was voidable or void. 3. To clarify the meaning of ambiguous terms. 4. To clarify the terms of the contract when the written contract lacks one or more of its essential terms. 5. Under the UCC, to explain the meaning of contract terms in light of a prior dealing, course of performance, or usage of trade. 6. To show that the entire contract is subject to an orally agreed-on condition. 7. When an obvious clerical or typographic error was made.

FOR REVIEW

Answers for the even-numbered questions in this For Review *section can be found on this text's accompanying Web site at* http://blt.westbuslaw.com. *Select "Chapter 13" and click on "For Review."*

1. What contracts must be in writing to be enforceable?
2. If it is possible for a contract to be performed within one year, must it be in writing?
3. When will an oral promise to pay another person's debt be enforced?
4. If a written contract is required, what terms are considered essential and must be contained in the written document?
5. What is parol evidence? When is parol evidence admissible to clarify the terms of a written contract?

QUESTIONS AND CASE PROBLEMS

13–1. The One-Year Rule. On May 1, by telephone, Yu offers to hire Benson to perform personal services. On May 5, Benson returns Yu's call and accepts the offer. Discuss fully whether this contract falls under the Statute of Frauds under the following circumstances:

(a) The contract calls for Benson to be employed for one year, with the right to begin performance immediately.
(b) The contract calls for Benson to be employed for nine months, with performance of services to begin on September 1.
(c) The contract calls for Benson to submit a written research report, with a deadline of two years for submission.

13–2. Collateral Promises. Gemma promises a local hardware store that she will pay for a lawn mower that her brother is purchasing on credit if the brother fails to pay the debt. Must this promise be in writing to be enforceable? Why or why not?

13–3. Oral Contracts. Frances had lived in an apartment for ten years when she decided to buy a house. Her one-year lease would end on May 1. On April 15, she orally contracted to buy Smith's house for $100,000, with the closing (transfer of the deed) to take place on June 1. Smith's lawyer, who was out of town on vacation, would draft a written contract of sale on his return to his office on May 15. Because Frances's lease was terminating, Smith agreed to let her take possession of the house if Frances would give him a "down payment" on the house of $5,000. Frances agreed and gave Smith the $5,000. She moved into the house on May 2 and the following weekend planted trees in the backyard. On May 10, Smith received a written offer from Green to purchase Smith's house for $120,000. Smith accepted Green's offer, asked Frances to move out of the house, and tried to return the $5,000 to Frances. Frances claimed that her oral contract was enforceable. Smith claimed that it was not because the contract was required to be in writing under the Statute of Frauds. Discuss fully who is correct, and why.

13–4. Collateral Promises. Jeffrey took his mother on a special holiday to Mountain Air Resort. Jeffrey was a frequent patron of the resort and was well known by its manager. The resort required each of its patrons to make a large deposit to ensure payment for the room. Jeffrey asked the manager to waive the requirement for his mother and told the manager that if his mother for any reason failed to pay the resort for her stay there, he would cover the bill. Relying on Jeffrey's promise, the manager waived the deposit requirement for Jeffrey's mother. After she returned home from her holiday, Jeffrey's mother refused to pay the resort bill. The resort manager tried to collect the sum from Jeffrey, but Jeffrey also refused to pay, stating that his promise was not enforceable under the Statute of Frauds. Is Jeffrey correct? Explain.

13–5. The One-Year Rule. On January 1, Damon, for consideration, orally promised to pay Gary $300 a month for as long as Gary lived, with the payments to be made on the first day of every month. Damon made the payments regularly for nine months and then made no further payments. Gary claimed that Damon had breached the oral contract and sued Damon for damages. Damon contended that the contract was unenforceable because, under the Statute of Frauds, contracts that cannot be performed within one year must be in writing. Discuss whether Damon will succeed in this defense.

13–6. Oral Contracts. Samuel DaGrossa and others were planning to open a restaurant. At some point prior to August 1985, DaGrossa orally agreed with Philippe LaJaunie that LaJaunie, in exchange for his contribution in designing, renovating, and managing the restaurant, could purchase a one-third interest in the restaurant's stock if the restaurant was profitable in its first year of operations. The restaurant opened in March 1986, and a few weeks later, LaJaunie's employment was terminated. LaJaunie brought an action to enforce the stock-purchase agreement. Is the agreement enforceable? Why or why not? [*LaJaunie v. DaGrossa,* 159 A.D.2d 349, 552 N.Y.S.2d 628 (1990)]

13–7. The Parol Evidence Rule. Glenn Grove bought a 1936 Pontiac from Bernard Stanfield. Stanfield signed the certificate of title, which stated that the car was sold for $1,000. No other terms of sale were mentioned in the certificate, and none were incorporated by reference. Three years later, Stanfield filed a suit against Grove in a Missouri state court, claiming that Grove still owed $9,000 on the price of the car. At the trial, Stanfield testified that he and Grove had an oral agreement by which Grove was to pay $1,000 for the "title document" and $9,000 for the actual car.

The court entered a judgment in Stanfield's favor. What will happen on appeal? Explain. [*Stanfield v. Grove,* 924 S.W.2d 611 (Mo.App.Div. 4 1996)]

CASE PROBLEM WITH SAMPLE ANSWER

13–8. Robert Pinto, doing business as Pinto Associates, hired Richard MacDonald as an independent contractor in March 1992. The parties orally agreed on the terms of employment, including payment to MacDonald of a share of the company's income, but they did not put anything in writing. In March 1995, MacDonald quit. Pinto then told MacDonald that he was entitled to $9,602.17—25 percent of the difference between the accounts receivable and the accounts payable as of MacDonald's last day. MacDonald disagreed and demanded more than $83,500—25 percent of the revenue from all invoices, less the cost of materials and outside processing, for each of the years that he worked for Pinto. Pinto refused. MacDonald filed a suit in a Connecticut state court against Pinto, alleging breach of contract. In Pinto's response and at the trial, he testified that the parties had an oral contract under which MacDonald was entitled to 25 percent of the difference between accounts receivable and payable as of the date of MacDonald's termination. Did the parties have an enforceable contract? How should the court rule, and why? [*MacDonald v. Pinto,* 62 Conn.App. 317, 771 A.2d 156 (2001)]

After you have answered this problem, compare your answer with the sample answer given on the Web site that accompanies this text. Go to http://blt.westbuslaw.com, select "Chapter 13," and click on "Case Problem with Sample Answer."

13–9. The Parol Evidence Rule. Carlin Krieg owned a dairy farm in St. Joe, Indiana, appraised at $154,000 in December 1997. In August 1999, Krieg told Donald Hieber that he intended to sell the farm for $106,000. Hieber offered to buy it. Krieg also told Hieber that he wanted to retain a "right of residency" for life in the farm. In October, Krieg and Hieber executed a "Purchase Agreement" that provided Krieg "shall transfer full and complete possession" of the farm "subject to [his] right of residency." The agreement also contained an integration clause that stated "there are no conditions, representations, warranties, or agreements not stated in this instrument." In November 2000, the house was burned in a fire, rendering it unlivable. Hieber filed an insurance claim for the damage and received the proceeds, but he did not fix the house. Krieg filed a suit in an Indiana state court against Hieber, alleging breach of contract. Is there any basis on which the court can consider evidence regarding the parties' negotiations prior to their agreement for the sale of the farm? Explain. [*Krieg v. Hieber,* 802 N.E.2d 938 (Ind.App. 2004)]

FOR CRITICAL ANALYSIS

13–10. As discussed elsewhere in this chapter, the Statute of Frauds was originally designed to protect innocent persons from the perjury of others with respect to oral contracts. Many legal scholars now believe that the act has caused more fraud than it has prevented. What do you think? Should the Statute of Frauds be repealed by state governments? If not, should it be changed in some way?

INTERNET EXERCISES

Go to the *Business Law Today* home page at http://blt.westbuslaw.com, select "Chapter 13," and click on "Internet Exercises." There you will find the following Internet research exercises that you can perform to learn more about topics covered in this chapter.

Activity 13–1: LEGAL PERSPECTIVE—Promissory Estoppel and the Statute of Frauds

Activity 13–2: MANAGEMENT PERSPECTIVE—"Get It in Writing"

Activity 13–3: HISTORICAL PERSPECTIVE—The English Act for the Prevention of Frauds and Perjuries

BEFORE THE TEST

Go to the *Business Law Today* home page at http://blt.westbuslaw.com, select "Chapter 13," and click on "Interactive Quizzes." You will find a number of interactive questions relating to this chapter.

CHAPTER 14

Performance and Discharge

"There are occasions and causes and why and wherefore in all things."

William Shakespeare, 1564–1616
(English dramatist and poet)

CHAPTER OUTLINE

- CONDITIONS OF PERFORMANCE
- DISCHARGE BY PERFORMANCE
- DISCHARGE BY AGREEMENT
- DISCHARGE BY OPERATION OF LAW

LEARNING OBJECTIVES

After reading this chapter, you should be able to answer the following questions:

1. What is a condition precedent, and how does it affect a party's duty to perform a contract?
2. How are most contracts discharged?
3. What is substantial performance?
4. When is a breach considered material, and what effect does that have on the other party's obligation to perform?
5. Will the courts allow parties to avoid performing their contractual duties when performance becomes extremely difficult or expensive?

DISCHARGE
The termination of an obligation. In contract law, discharge occurs when the parties have fully performed their contractual obligations or when events, conduct of the parties, or operation of law releases the parties from performance.

PERFORMANCE
In contract law, the fulfillment of one's duties arising under a contract with another; the normal way of discharging one's contractual obligations.

In a perfect world, every party who signed a contract would perform his or her duties completely and in a timely fashion, thereby discharging (terminating) the contract. In the real world, however, as William Shakespeare suggests in the chapter-opening quotation, things frequently become complicated. Certainly, events often occur that may affect our performance or our ability to perform contractual duties.

In this chapter, we examine how a contract is discharged. The most common way to **discharge**, or terminate, one's contractual duties is by the **performance** of those duties. The duty to perform under a contract may be *conditioned* on the occurrence or nonoccurrence of a certain event, or the duty may be *absolute*. As you can see in Exhibit 14–1 on the next page, in addition to performance, a contract can be discharged in numerous other ways, including discharge by agreement of the parties and discharge by operation of law.

reasonable person, but some courts hold that the personal satisfaction of the third party designated in the contract (Robert Ames, in this example) must be met. Again, the personal judgment must be made honestly, or the condition will be excused.

Material Breach of Contract

When a breach of contract is *material*[3]—that is, when performance is not deemed substantial—the nonbreaching party is excused from the performance of contractual duties and has a cause of action to sue for damages caused by the breach. If the breach is *minor* (not material), the nonbreaching party's duty to perform may sometimes be suspended until the breach is remedied, but the duty is not entirely excused. Once the minor breach is cured, the nonbreaching party must resume performance of the contractual obligations that had been undertaken.

A breach entitles the nonbreaching party to sue for damages, but only a material breach discharges the nonbreaching party from the contract. The policy underlying these rules is that contracts should go forward when only minor problems occur, but contracts should be terminated if major problems arise.[4]

Did a seller's failure to repair the plumbing in an apartment building within the eight-month period specified in a contract with the buyers constitute a material breach of the parties' contract? That was the issue in the following case.

3. *Restatement (Second) of Contracts,* Section 241.

4. See Section 2–612, of the Uniform Commerical Code (UCC), which deals with installment contracts for the sale of goods.

CASE 14.2 Kim v. Park

Court of Appeals of Oregon, 2004.
192 Or.App. 365,
86 P.3d 63.
http://www.publications.ojd.state.or.us/appeals.htm[a]

BACKGROUND AND FACTS Su Yong Kim sold an apartment building in Portland, Oregon, to Chon Sik Park, Bok Soon Park, Johan Cen, William Itzineag, Johnny Perea, and Patricia Maldonado. At the time, the building's plumbing violated the Portland Housing Code. The contract provided the following: "Seller shall correct the plumbing code violation * * * within eight months * * * . Buyer shall cooperate with seller in * * * providing access to the premises to complete repairs." Kim did not make the repairs within eight months, but twelve months after the date of the contract, Kim cut holes in the walls of the apartments to expose the plumbing. Seven weeks later, early one morning, Kim sent plumbers to the building without notice to the owners, apparently in an attempt to make repairs. The owners ordered the plumbers to leave, refused to allow Kim to send others, and stopped making payments under the contract. Kim filed a suit in an Oregon state court against the buyers, seeking the amount due. The buyers asserted that Kim's failure to repair the plumbing was a material breach that excused the performance of their obligations and counterclaimed for damages for the breach. The court concluded that Kim's breach was not material and ordered relief in his favor. The buyers appealed to a state intermediate appellate court.

a. Click on "March" under "Cases decided in 2004." In the result, scroll to the name of the case under 3/3/04 and click on it to access the opinion. The state of Oregon's Judicial Branch maintains this Web site.

IN THE WORDS OF THE COURT . . .
EDMONDS, P.J. [Presiding Judge]

* * * *

Generally, a vendor [seller] is entitled to [relief] when the vendee [buyer] fails to comply with the contract terms in paying the purchase price. However, in some cir-

CASE 14.2—Continued

cumstances, an award * * * may be inequitable even when the vendee has not complied with the terms of the contract. Moreover, a party who seeks to recover damages on a contract must plead and prove its own performance or a valid excuse for its failure to perform. * * * With regard to those principles, a material breach of a land sale contract by a party will prevent that party from obtaining [relief under] the contract and excuse the other party's obligation to perform. Here, plaintiff is not entitled to [relief under] the contract if his failure to repair the plumbing was an unjustified material breach of the parties' agreement.

Plaintiff contends that, but for defendants' refusal to allow his plumbers to repair the plumbing, he would have satisfied his contractual obligation to do so. However, plaintiff made no effort to repair the plumbing until almost four months after the contractually required period and he waited another seven weeks before sending plumbers to do a partial repair. In order to make the partial repairs in the way that plaintiff intended, the plumbers would have had to shut off water to defendants' tenants for an extended period during each stage of the repairs. Given plaintiff's failure to make any effort to repair the plumbing within the eight-month period specified in the contract and the likely adverse impact of piecemeal repairs on their tenants, defendants' refusal to allow plaintiff to make partial repairs to the plumbing at that late date was reasonable. We conclude that plaintiff does not have a valid excuse for his failure to perform under the contract.

The next issue is whether plaintiff's failure to perform the plumbing repairs was a *material* breach of the parties' agreement. * * * A breach is material if it goes to the very substance of the contract and defeats the object of the parties entering into the contract. The evidence shows that, as a result of the code violations, the City of Portland continued to assess fines against defendants and defendants lost some tenants. * * * [T]he requirement that plaintiff repair the plumbing within eight months was intended to insure that the building's plumbing satisfy the city code within a reasonable time after the sale. Defendants purchased the building from plaintiff so that they could rent out the apartments in it. Although the repairs to the plumbing in the building would have caused some temporary inconvenience to the tenants, the failure of plaintiff to make the repairs in accordance with the contract ultimately prevented defendants from using the building as intended by the parties' agreement. In light of that evidence, we hold that as a matter of law the plaintiff's failure to perform as promised was a material breach of the contract.

DECISION AND REMEDY The state intermediate appellate court held that the seller's failure to repair the plumbing according to the parties' contract was a material breach excusing the buyers' performance. The court reversed the decision of the lower court and remanded the case for a determination of the amount of damages.[b]

b. The lower court's decision on remand was not available at the time this book went to press, but it may be by the time you read this. You may be able to locate the remanded decision online. See this text's inside front cover for URLs for online court decisions.

WHY IS THIS CASE IMPORTANT? *This case emphasizes that when one party's failure to perform a contractual obligation causes another to suffer significant harm, the other party normally is entitled to a remedy. Recall from Chapters 8 and 10 that even when no contract exists, if a party justifiably relies to his or her detriment on the promise of another, the party may be able to obtain relief under the doctrine of quasi contract or promissory estoppel.*

Anticipatory Repudiation of a Contract

ANTICIPATORY REPUDIATION An assertion or action by a party indicating that he or she will not perform an obligation that the party is contractually obligated to perform at a future time.

Before either party to a contract has a duty to perform, one of the parties may refuse to perform her or his contractual obligations. This is called **anticipatory repudiation.**[5] When anticipatory repudiation occurs, it is treated as a material breach of contract, and the nonbreaching party is permitted to bring an action for damages immediately, even though the scheduled time for performance under the contract may still be in the future.[6] Until the nonbreaching party treats this early repudiation as a breach, however, the breaching party can retract the anticipatory repudiation by proper notice and restore the parties to their original obligations.[7]

An anticipatory repudiation is treated as a present, material breach for two reasons. First, the nonbreaching party should not be required to remain ready and willing to perform when the other party has already repudiated the contract. Second, the nonbreaching party should have the opportunity to seek a similar contract elsewhere and may have the duty to do so to minimize his or her loss.

REMEMBER The risks that prices will fluctuate and values will change are ordinary business risks for which the law does not provide relief.

Quite often, an anticipatory repudiation occurs when a sharp fluctuation in market prices creates a situation in which performance of the contract would be extremely unfavorable to one of the parties. ■ **EXAMPLE 14.7** Shasta Manufacturing Company contracts to manufacture and sell 100,000 personal computers to New Age, Inc., a computer retailer with 500 outlet stores. Delivery is to be made two months from the date of the contract. One month later, three suppliers of computer parts raise their prices to Shasta. Because of these higher prices, Shasta stands to lose $500,000 if it sells the computers to New Age at the contract price. Shasta writes to New Age, stating that it cannot deliver the 100,000 computers at the agreed-on contract price. Even though you might sympathize with Shasta, its letter is an anticipatory repudiation of the contract, allowing New Age the option of treating the repudiation as a material breach and proceeding immediately to pursue remedies, even though the contract delivery date is still a month away. ■

Discharge by Agreement

Any contract can be discharged by agreement of the parties. The agreement can be contained in the original contract, or the parties can form a new contract for the express purpose of discharging the original contract.

Discharge by Rescission

As discussed in Chapter 10, rescission is the process in which the parties cancel the contract and are returned to the positions they occupied prior to the contract's formation. For *mutual rescission* to take place, the parties must make another agreement that also satisfies the legal requirements for a contract—there must be an *offer,* an *acceptance,* and *consideration.* Ordinarily, if the parties agree to rescind the original contract, their promises not to perform those acts promised in the original contract will be legal consideration for the second contract.

---

5. *Restatement (Second) of Contracts,* Section 253, and UCC 2–610.
6. The doctrine of anticipatory repudiation first arose in the landmark case of *Hochster v. De La Tour,* 2 Ellis and Blackburn Reports 678 (1853), when the English court recognized the delay and expense inherent in a rule requiring a nonbreaching party to wait until the time of performance before suing on an anticipatory repudiation.
7. See UCC 2–611.

Mutual rescission can occur in this manner when the original contract is executory on both sides (that is, neither party has completed performance). The agreement to rescind an executory contract is generally enforceable, even if it is made orally and even if the original agreement was in writing.[8] When one party has fully performed, however, an agreement to rescind the original contract usually is not enforceable unless additional consideration or restitution is made.[9]

DISCHARGE BY NOVATION

NOVATION The substitution, by agreement, of a new contract for an old one, with the rights under the old one being terminated. Typically, novation involves the substitution of a new person who is responsible for the contract and the removal of the original party's rights and duties under the contract.

The process of **novation** substitutes a third party for one of the original parties. Essentially, the parties to the original contract and one or more new parties all get together and agree to the substitution. The requirements of a novation are as follows:

1. The existence of a previous, valid obligation.
2. Agreement by all of the parties to a new contract.
3. The extinguishing of the old obligation (discharge of the prior party).
4. A new, valid contract.

A novation may appear similar to an assignment or delegation. There is an important distinction, however: a novation involves a new contract, and an assignment or delegation involves the old contract.

■ EXAMPLE 14.8 Suppose that you contract with Logan Enterprises to sell it your office equipment business. Logan later learns that it should not expand at this time but knows of another party, MBI Corporation, that is interested in purchasing your business. All three of you get together and agree to a novation. As long as the new contract is supported by consideration, the novation discharges the original contract between you and Logan and replaces it with the new contract between you and MBI Corporation. Logan prefers the novation because it discharges its liabilities under the contract with you. If the original contract had been an installment sales contract requiring twelve monthly payments, and Logan had merely assigned the contract (assigned its rights and delegated its duties under the contract) to MBI Corporation, Logan would have remained liable to you for the payments if MBI Corporation defaulted. ■

DISCHARGE BY ACCORD AND SATISFACTION

As discussed in Chapter 10, in an *accord and satisfaction,* the parties agree to accept performance different from the performance originally promised. An *accord* is an executory contract (one that has not yet been performed) to perform some act in order to satisfy an existing contractual duty that is not yet discharged.[10] A *satisfaction* is the performance of the accord agreement. An *accord* and its *satisfaction* discharge the original contractual obligation.

Once the accord has been made, the original obligation is merely suspended until the accord agreement is fully performed. If it is not performed, the party to whom performance is owed can bring an action on the original obligation or for breach of the accord. ■ EXAMPLE 14.9 Shea obtains a judgment against Marla for $4,000.

8. Agreements to rescind contracts involving transfers of realty, however, must be evidenced by a writing. Another exception has to do with the sale of goods under the UCC, when the sales contract requires written rescission.

9. Under UCC 2–209(1), however, no consideration is needed to modify a contract for a sale of goods. See Chapter 18. Also see UCC 1–107.

10. *Restatement (Second) of Contracts,* Section 281.

Later, both parties agree that the judgment can be satisfied by Marla's transfer of her automobile to Shea. This agreement to accept the auto in lieu of $4,000 in cash is the accord. If Marla transfers her automobile to Shea, the accord agreement is fully performed, and the $4,000 debt is discharged. If Marla refuses to transfer her car, the accord is breached. Because the original obligation is merely suspended, Shea can bring an action to enforce the judgment for $4,000 in cash or bring an action for breach of the accord. ■

Discharge by Operation of Law

"Law is a practical matter."
ROSCOE POUND, 1870–1964 (American jurist)

Under some circumstances, contractual duties may be discharged by operation of law. These circumstances include material alteration of the contract, the running of the relevant statute of limitations, bankruptcy, and impossibility of performance.

CONTRACT ALTERATION

To discourage parties from altering written contracts, the law allows an innocent party to be discharged when one party has materially altered a written contract without the knowledge or consent of the other party. For example, if a party alters a material term of the contract—such as the quantity term or the price term—without the knowledge or consent of the other party, the party who was unaware of the alteration can treat the contract as discharged or terminated.

STATUTES OF LIMITATIONS

As mentioned earlier in this text, statutes of limitations limit the period during which a party can sue on a particular cause of action. After the applicable limitations period has passed, a suit can no longer be brought. For example, the limitations period for bringing suits for breach of oral contracts is usually two to three years; for written contracts, four to five years; and for recovery of amounts awarded in judgment, ten to twenty years, depending on state law. Suits for breach of a contract for the sale of goods must be brought within four years after the cause of action has accrued. By original agreement, the parties can reduce this four-year period to a one-year period. They cannot, however, extend it beyond the four-year limitations period.

BANKRUPTCY

A proceeding in bankruptcy attempts to allocate the debtor's assets to the creditors in a fair and equitable fashion. Once the assets have been allocated, the debtor receives a *discharge in bankruptcy* (see Chapter 27). A discharge in bankruptcy ordinarily bars enforcement of most of a debtor's contracts by the creditors.

WHEN PERFORMANCE IS IMPOSSIBLE

After a contract has been made, performance may become impossible in an objective sense. This is known as **impossibility of performance** and may discharge the contract.[11]

IMPOSSIBILITY OF PERFORMANCE
A doctrine under which a party to a contract is relieved of his or her duty to perform when performance becomes objectively impossible or totally impracticable (through no fault of either party).

Objective Impossibility *Objective impossibility* ("It can't be done") must be distinguished from subjective impossibility ("I'm sorry, I simply can't do it"). An example of subjective impossibility is the inability to pay funds on time because the

11. *Restatement (Second) of Contracts,* Section 261.

A production line in a commercial bakery. If a fire incapacitated the bakery's oven, would the bakery be excused from performing its contracts until the oven was fixed? If a contract involved a special holiday order and the oven could not be fixed until after the holiday, would the contract be discharged? Why or why not? (© Dick Luria/Getty Images)

bank is closed.[12] In effect, the nonperforming party is saying, "It is impossible for *me* to perform," rather than "It is impossible for *anyone* to perform." Accordingly, such excuses do not discharge a contract, and the nonperforming party is normally held in breach of contract. Four basic types of situations will generally qualify as grounds for the discharge of contractual obligations based on impossibility of performance:[13]

1. *When a party whose personal performance is essential to the completion of the contract dies or becomes incapacitated prior to performance.* ■ **EXAMPLE 14.10** Fred, a famous dancer, contracts with Ethereal Dancing Guild to play a leading role in its new ballet. Before the ballet can be performed, Fred becomes ill and dies. His personal performance was essential to the completion of the contract. Thus, his death discharges the contract and his estate's liability for his nonperformance. ■
2. *When the specific subject matter of the contract is destroyed.* ■ **EXAMPLE 14.11** A-1 Farm Equipment agrees to sell Gudgel the green tractor on its lot and promises to have the tractor ready for Gudgel to pick up on Saturday. On Friday night, however, a truck veers off the nearby highway and smashes into the tractor, destroying it beyond repair. Because the contract was for this specific tractor, A-1's performance is rendered impossible owing to the accident. ■
3. *When a change in the law renders performance illegal.* An example is a contract to build an apartment building, when the zoning laws are changed to prohibit the construction of residential rental property at this location. This change renders the contract impossible to perform.
4. *When performance becomes commercially impracticable.* The inclusion of this type of "impossibility" as a basis for contract discharge results from a growing trend to allow parties to discharge contracts when the originally contemplated performance turns out to be much more difficult or expensive than anticipated. In such situations, courts may excuse parties from their performance obligations under the doctrine of *commercial impracticability.* For example, in one case, a court held that a contract could be discharged because a party would have to pay ten times more than the original estimate to excavate a certain amount of gravel.[14]

In the following case, a party to a contract for a sale of land argued that the contract should be rescinded because a possible spread of pollution and the potential liability involved made the sale impossible or impracticable.

12. *Ingham Lumber Co. v. Ingersoll & Co.,* 93 Ark. 447, 125 S.W. 139 (1910).
13. *Restatement (Second) of Contracts,* Sections 262–266, and UCC 2–615.
14. *Mineral Park Land Co. v. Howard,* 172 Cal. 289, 156 P. 458 (1916).

CASE 14.3 Cape-France Enterprises v. Estate of Peed

Supreme Court of Montana, 2001.
305 Mont. 513,
29 P.3d 1011,
2001 MT 139.

BACKGROUND AND FACTS Cape-France Enterprises owns real property in Bozeman, Montana. In 1994, Lola Peed and her granddaughter Marthe Moore entered into an agreement with Cape-France to buy five acres of the land on which to build a motel or hotel. To complete the sale, the state required the land to be surveyed, subdivided, and rezoned. To subdivide the property, the state required a well to be drilled and the water to be tested. The parties were aware of underground pollution in Bozeman but believed Cape-France's property to be unaffected. Montana's Department of Environmental Quality, Water Quality Division (DEQ), however, feared that the water under the land was contaminated. The DEQ warned in letters to Cape-France that if there was pollution, drilling a well could exacerbate the problem,

(Continued)

CASE 14.3—Continued

treatment of the water would be extensive, and Cape-France would be liable for the cost. When Peed and Moore would not agree to share the risk, Cape-France filed a suit in a Montana state court against Moore and Peed's estate (Peed had since died), seeking to rescind their contract in part on the ground of impossibility or impracticability. The court granted a summary judgment in Cape-France's favor. The defendants appealed to the Montana Supreme Court.

IN THE WORDS OF THE COURT . . .

Justice *JAMES C. NELSON* delivered the Opinion of the Court.

* * * *

* * * [T]he doctrine of impossibility is a valid defense not only when performance is impossible, but also when supervening circumstances make performance impracticable. * * *

* * * [A]n act is impracticable when it can only be done at an excessive, unreasonable and unbargained-for cost. *While the doctrine of impossibility or impracticability is not set in stone, it is applied by courts where, aside from the object of the contract being unlawful, the public policy underlying the strict enforcement of contracts is outweighed by the senselessness of requiring performance.* [Emphasis added.]

The doctrine is applicable under the facts in the case at bar. * * * It is undisputed that after the agreement was executed, the state and local regulatory authorities required the completion of water drilling and testing. The parties discussed the situation. Cape-France was unwilling to assume large risks related to this new, unknown and unexpected situation. Peed-Moore was unwilling to [share the risks to a degree] satisfactory to Cape-France. Contamination, if it exists or occurs by reason of well-drilling, could expose Cape-France as landowners to financial liability of an unquantifiable nature. * * *

Peed and Moore argue that the contract should not be rescinded on the basis of impossibility because it is not impossible to drill the well. They point to the [DEQ] letters as evidence that the well could be drilled and that there is no proof that there would be actual groundwater contamination where they would drill. However, Peed and Moore do not argue, and cannot argue, that there is no groundwater contamination, nor can they say that there will not be any in the future. Unfortunately, the only way to determine whether there is and, if so, the extent of groundwater contamination is to drill a well. And that is the precise activity that may exacerbate the contamination problem, to both parties' substantial and unbargained-for economic detriment. Indeed, it is clear that Peed and Moore are unwilling or unable to share in these economic risks.

Moreover, as already noted, while impossibility or impracticability is a high standard, the application of this doctrine is not limited to cases of literal impossibility. Here, the potential for substantial and unbargained-for damage involved in performing the contract is not only of an economic nature. Just as importantly, environmental degradation with consequences extending well beyond the parties' land sale is also a real possibility.

DECISION AND REMEDY The Montana Supreme Court affirmed the judgment of the lower court. The state supreme court agreed that rescission of this contract was appropriate, on the ground of impossibility or impracticability, because Cape-France would otherwise be forced to expose itself to substantial and unbargained-for economic risks, to expose the public to potential health risks, and to expose the environment to possible degradation.

FOR CRITICAL ANALYSIS—Social Consideration *The Montana state constitution requires that "the State and each person shall maintain and improve a clean and healthful environment in Montana." In light of this clause, what is another basis on which the contract in this case might be rescinded?*

ETHICAL ISSUE 14.1 ***Should the courts allow the defense of impossibility of performance to be used more often?*** The doctrine of impossibility is applied only when the parties could not have reasonably foreseen, at the time the contract was formed, the event or events that rendered performance impossible. In some cases, the courts may seem to go too far in holding that the parties should have foreseen certain events or conditions, thus precluding the parties from avoiding contractual obligations under the doctrine of impossibility of performance. Yet though the courts rarely excuse parties from performance under the doctrine of impossibility, they allow parties to raise this defense more often than they once did. Indeed, until the latter part of the nineteenth century, courts were reluctant to discharge a contract even when performance appeared to be literally impossible. Generally, the courts must balance the freedom of parties to contract (and assume the risks involved) against the injustice that may result when certain contractual obligations are enforced. If the courts allowed parties to raise impossibility of performance as a defense to contractual obligations more often, freedom of contract would suffer. ■

Temporary Impossibility An occurrence or event that makes performance temporarily impossible operates to suspend performance until the impossibility ceases. Then, ordinarily, the parties must perform the contract as originally planned. If, however, the lapse of time and the change in circumstances make it substantially more burdensome for the parties to perform as promised, the contract is discharged.

NOTE The doctrine of commercial impracticability does not provide relief from such events as ordinary price increases or easily predictable changes in the weather.

■ EXAMPLE 14.12 The leading case on the subject, *Autry v. Republic Productions,*[15] involved an actor who was drafted into the army in 1942. Being drafted rendered the actor's contract temporarily impossible to perform, and it was suspended until the end of the war. When the actor got out of the army, the purchasing power of the dollar had so changed that performance of the contract would have been substantially burdensome to him. Therefore, the contract was discharged. ■

15. 30 Cal.2d 144, 180 P.2d 888 (1947).

REVIEWING PERFORMANCE AND DISCHARGE

Val's Foods signs a contract to buy 1,500 pounds of basil from Sun Farms, a small organic herb grower, as long as an independent organization inspects and certifies that the crop contains no pesticide or herbicide residue. Val's has a number of contracts with different restaurant chains to supply pesto and intends to use Sun Farms' basil in its pesto to fulfill these contracts. While Sun Farms is preparing to harvest the basil, an unexpected hailstorm destroys half the crop. Sun Farms attempts to purchase additional basil from other farms, but it is late in the season and the price is twice the normal market price. Sun Farms is too small to absorb this cost and immediately notifies Val's that it will not fulfill the contract. Using the information presented in the chapter, answer the following questions.

1. Suppose that the basil does not pass the chemical-residue inspection. Which concept discussed in the chapter might allow Val's to refuse to perform the contract in this situation?
2. Does the notice that Sun Farms sent to Val's constitute an anticipatory repudiation? Why or why not? What rights does this notification give to Val's?
3. Under which legal theory or theories might Sun Farms claim that its obligation under the contract has been discharged by operation of law? Discuss fully.
4. Suppose that Sun Farms contacts every basil grower in the country and buys the last remaining chemical-free basil anywhere. Nevertheless, Sun Farms is only able to ship 1,475 pounds to Val's. Would this fulfill Sun Farms' obligations to Val's? Why or why not?
5. Now suppose that Sun Farms sells its operations to Happy Valley Farms. As a part of the sale, all three parties agree that Happy Valley will provide the basil as stated under the original contract. What is this type of agreement called? Does it discharge the obligations of any of the parties? Explain.

KEY TERMS

anticipatory repudiation 352
breach of contract 346
concurrent conditions 345
condition 344
condition precedent 345
condition subsequent 345
discharge 343
impossibility of performance 354
novation 353
performance 343
tender 346

CHAPTER SUMMARY Performance and Discharge

Conditions of Performance (See pages 344–345.)	Contract obligations may be subject to the following types of conditions: 1. *Condition precedent*—A condition that must be fulfilled before a party's promise becomes absolute. 2. *Condition subsequent*—A condition that operates to terminate a party's absolute promise to perform. 3. *Concurrent conditions*—Conditions that must be performed simultaneously. Each party's absolute duty to perform is conditioned on the other party's absolute duty to perform.
Discharge by Performance (See pages 346–352.)	A contract may be discharged by complete (strict) performance or by substantial performance. In some cases, performance must be to the satisfaction of another. Totally inadequate performance constitutes a material breach of contract. An anticipatory repudiation of a contract allows the other party to sue immediately for breach of contract.
Discharge by Agreement (See pages 352–354.)	Parties may agree to discharge their contractual obligations in several ways: 1. *By rescission*—The parties mutually agree to rescind (cancel) the contract. 2. *By novation*—A new party is substituted for one of the primary parties to a contract. 3. *By accord and satisfaction*—The parties agree to render and accept performance different from that on which they originally agreed.
Discharge by Operation of Law (See pages 354–357.)	Parties' obligations under contracts may be discharged by operation of law owing to one of the following: 1. Contract alteration. 2. Statutes of limitations. 3. Bankruptcy. 4. Impossibility of performance.

FOR REVIEW

Answers for the even-numbered questions in this For Review *section can be found on this text's accompanying Web site at* http://blt.westbuslaw.com. *Select "Chapter 14" and click on "For Review."*

1 What is a condition precedent, and how does it affect a party's duty to perform a contract?
2 How are most contracts discharged?
3 What is substantial performance?
4 When is a breach considered material, and what effect does that have on the other party's obligation to perform?
5 Will the courts allow parties to avoid performing their contractual duties when performance becomes extremely difficult or expensive?

QUESTIONS AND CASE PROBLEMS

14–1. Substantial Performance. Complete performance is full performance according to the terms of a contract. Discuss the effect on the parties if there is less than full performance.

14–2. Breach. ABC Clothiers, Inc., has a contract with Taylor & Sons, a retailer, to deliver 1,000 summer suits to Taylor's place of business on or before May 1. On April 1, Taylor Senior receives a letter from ABC informing him that ABC will not be able to make the delivery as scheduled. Taylor is very upset, as he had planned a big ad campaign. He wants to file suit against ABC immediately (April 2). Taylor's son, Tom, tells his father that filing a lawsuit is not proper until ABC actually fails to deliver the suits on May 1. Discuss fully who is correct, Taylor or his son.

14–3. Impossibility of Performance. In the following situations, certain events take place after the formation of contracts. Are any of these contracts discharged because the events render the contracts impossible to perform? Discuss.

(a) Jimenez, a famous singer, contracts to perform in your nightclub. He dies prior to performance.

(b) Raglione contracts to sell you her land. Just before title is to be transferred, she dies.

(c) Oppenheim contracts to sell you 1,000 bushels of apples from her orchard in the state of Washington. Because of a severe frost, she is unable to deliver the apples.

(d) Maxwell contracts to lease a service station for ten years. His principal income is from the sale of gasoline. Because of an oil embargo by foreign oil-producing nations, gasoline is rationed, cutting sharply into Maxwell's gasoline sales. He cannot make his lease payments.

14–4. Novation versus Accord and Satisfaction. Doug owes creditor Cartwright $1,000, which is due and payable on June 1. Doug has a car accident, misses several months of work, and consequently does not have the funds to pay Cartwright on June 1. Doug's father, Bert, offers to pay Cartwright $1,100 in four equal installments if Cartwright will discharge Doug from any further liability on the debt. Cartwright accepts. Is the transaction a novation or an accord and satisfaction? Explain.

14–5. Impossibility of Performance. Millie contracted to sell Frank 1,000 bushels of corn to be grown on Millie's farm. Owing to a drought during the growing season, Millie's yield was much less than anticipated, and she could deliver only 250 bushels to Frank. Frank accepted the lesser amount but sued Millie for breach of contract. Can Millie defend successfully on the basis of objective impossibility of performance? Explain.

14–6. Performance. Steven McPheters, a house builder and developer, hired Terry Tentinger, who did business as New Horizon Construction, to do some touching up and repainting on one of McPheters's new houses. Tentinger worked two days, billed McPheters $420 (a three-man crew for fourteen hours at $30 per hour), and offered to return to the house to remedy any defects in his work at no cost. McPheters objected to the number of hours on the bill—although he did not express dissatisfaction with the work—and offered Tentinger $250. Tentinger refused to accept this amount and filed a suit in an Idaho state court to collect the full amount. McPheters filed a counterclaim, alleging that Tentinger had failed to perform the job in a skilled manner, resulting in $2,500 in damages, which would cost $500 to repair. Tentinger's witnesses testified that although some touch-up work was needed, the job had been performed in a skilled manner. McPheters presented testimony indicating that the work was so defective as to render it commercially unreasonable. On what basis could the court rule in Tentinger's favor? Explain fully. [*Tentinger v. McPheters,* 132 Idaho 620, 977 P.2d 234 (Idaho App. 1999)]

CASE PROBLEM WITH SAMPLE ANSWER

14–7. In May 1996, O'Brien-Shiepe Funeral Home, Inc., in Hempstead, New York, hired Teramo & Co. to build an addition to O'Brien's funeral home. The parties' contract did not specify a date for the completion of the work. The city of Hempstead issued a building permit for the project on June 14, and Teramo began work about two weeks later. There was some delay in construction because O'Brien asked that no work be done during funeral services, but by the end of March 1997, the work was substantially complete. The city of Hempstead issued a "Certificate of Completion" on April 15. During the construction, O'Brien made periodic payments to Teramo, but there was a balance due of $17,950, which O'Brien did not pay. To recover this amount, Teramo filed a suit in a New York state court against O'Brien. O'Brien filed a counterclaim to recover lost profits for business allegedly lost due to the time Teramo took to build the addition, and for $6,180 spent to correct problems caused by poor workmanship. Which, if any, party is entitled to an award in this case? Explain. [*Teramo & Co. v. O'Brien-Shiepe Funeral Home, Inc.,* 725 N.Y.S.2d 87 (A.D. 2 Dept. 2001)]

After you have answered this problem, compare your answer with the sample answer given on the Web site that accompanies this text. Go to http://blt.westbuslaw.com, select "Chapter 14," and click on "Case Problem with Sample Answer."

14–8. Substantial Performance. Adolf and Ida Krueger contracted with Pisani Construction, Inc., to erect a metal building as an addition to an existing structure. The two structures were to share a common wall, and the frames and panel heights of the new building were to match those of the existing structure. Shortly before completion of the project, however, it was apparent that the roofline of the new building was approximately three inches higher than that of the existing structure. Pisani modified the ridge caps of the buildings to blend the rooflines. The discrepancy had other consequences, however, including misalignment of the gutters and windows of the two buildings, which resulted in an icing problem in the winter. The Kruegers occupied the new structure, but refused to make the last payment under the contract. Pisani filed a suit in a Connecticut state court to collect. Did Pisani substantially perform its obligations? Should the Kruegers be ordered to pay? Why or why not? [*Pisani Construction, Inc. v. Krueger,* 68 Conn.App. 361, 791 A.2d 634 (2002)]

A QUESTION OF ETHICS

14–9. Treasure Coast, Inc., a hazardous waste-removal company, had removed petroleum contamination at a job site for Ludlum Construction Co., Inc., and not been paid. At mediation, the parties entered into a settlement agreement in which Ludlum agreed to pay Treasure Coast a total of $37,000—$4,000 right away, and payments of $5,000 due on the first of each month until the balance was paid off. The settlement contract expressly stated that "[i]f any payment is more than ten days late then the Plaintiff will be entitled to a judgment upon Affidavit against the Defendant for $65,000, less payments made." Ludlum paid the $4,000 and made the first two payments on time. The third payment was received by Treasure Coast via Federal Express on August 17, seven days past the ten-day grace period. Because Ludlum was in breach of the settlement contract, Treasure Coast filed a motion requesting the court to enter a judgment against the construction company in the amount of $51,000 ($65,000 less the $14,000 that Ludlum had paid). Ludlum opposed the motion, claiming that the payment was late due to a clerical error and that the late payment was not a material breach of the contract. Given these facts, answer the following questions. [*Treasure Coast, Inc. v. Ludlum Construction Co., Inc.,* 760 So.2d 232 (2000)]

1. Do you think that Ludlum Construction substantially performed the settlement contract even though the payment was late? Why or why not? How do you think the court will decide this issue? Should the fact that this was a settlement agreement enter into the court's analysis?
2. If you were the judge in this case, would you grant Treasure Coast's motion and enter judgment for $51,000 against Ludlum? After all, the parties explicitly agreed that if the payment was not received by the tenth day of the month, the deal was off and Ludlum would have to pay the original amount of the debt ($65,000) to Treasure Coast.
3. Generally, do you think that the doctrine of substantial performance should apply in situations where the performance required is the payment of money? Would your decision be different if one of the parties was an individual rather than a commercial enterprise?

FOR CRITICAL ANALYSIS

14–10. The concept of substantial performance permits a party to be discharged from a contract even though the party has not fully performed his or her obligations according to the contract's terms. Is this fair? What policy interests are at issue here?

INTERNET EXERCISES

Go to the *Business Law Today* home page at **http://blt.westbuslaw.com**, select "Chapter 14," and click on "Internet Exercises." There you will find the following Internet research exercises that you can perform to learn more about topics covered in this chapter.

Activity 14–1: LEGAL PERSPECTIVE—Anticipatory Repudiation

Activity 14–2: MANAGEMENT PERSPECTIVE—Commercial Impracticability

BEFORE THE TEST

Go to the *Business Law Today* home page at **http://blt.westbuslaw.com**, select "Chapter 14," and click on "Interactive Quizzes." You will find a number of interactive questions relating to this chapter.

“Men keep their engagements when it is to the advantage of both not to break them.”

Solon, sixth century B.C.E.
(Athenian legal reformer)

CHAPTER 15

Breach and Remedies

CHAPTER OUTLINE

- DAMAGES
- EQUITABLE REMEDIES
- RECOVERY BASED ON QUASI CONTRACT
- CONTRACT PROVISIONS LIMITING REMEDIES
- ELECTION OF REMEDIES

LEARNING OBJECTIVES

After reading this chapter, you should be able to answer the following questions:

1. What is the difference between compensatory damages and consequential damages? What are nominal damages, and when do courts award nominal damages?
2. What is the standard measure of compensatory damages when a contract is breached? How are damages computed differently in construction contracts?
3. Under what circumstances is the remedy of rescission and restitution available?
4. When do courts grant specific performance as a remedy?
5. What is the rationale underlying the doctrine of election of remedies?

As the Athenian political leader Solon instructed centuries ago in the chapter-opening quotation, a contract will not be broken as long as “it is to the advantage of both” parties to fulfill their contractual obligations. Normally, a person enters into a contract with another to secure an advantage. When it is no longer advantageous for a party to fulfill her or his contractual obligations, that party may breach the contract. As discussed in Chapter 14, a *breach of contract* occurs when a party fails to perform part or all of the required duties under a contract.[1] Once a party fails to perform or performs inadequately, the other party—the nonbreaching party—can choose one or more of several remedies.

1. *Restatement (Second) of Contracts,* Section 235(2).

The most common remedies available to a nonbreaching party under contract law include damages, rescission and restitution, specific performance, and reformation. As discussed in Chapter 1, courts distinguish between *remedies at law* and *remedies in equity.* Today, the remedy at law is normally money damages. We discuss this remedy in the first part of this chapter. Equitable remedies include rescission and restitution, specific performance, and reformation, all of which we examine later in the chapter. Usually, a court will not award an equitable remedy unless the remedy at law is inadequate. In the final pages of this chapter, we look at some special legal doctrines and concepts relating to remedies.

Damages

A breach of contract entitles the nonbreaching party to sue for money damages. As you read in Chapter 4, damages are designed to compensate a party for harm suffered as a result of another's wrongful act. In the context of contract law, damages are designed to compensate the nonbreaching party for the loss of the bargain. Often, courts say that innocent parties are to be placed in the position they would have occupied had the contract been fully performed.[2]

REMEMBER The terms of a contract must be sufficiently definite for a court to determine the amount of damages to award.

TYPES OF DAMAGES

There are basically four broad categories of damages:

1. Compensatory (to cover direct losses and costs).
2. Consequential (to cover indirect and foreseeable losses).
3. Punitive (to punish and deter wrongdoing).
4. Nominal (to recognize wrongdoing when no monetary loss is shown).

Compensatory and punitive damages were discussed in Chapter 4 in the context of tort law. Here, we look at these types of damages, as well as consequential and nominal damages, in the context of contract law.

Compensatory Damages Damages compensating the nonbreaching party for the *loss of the bargain* are known as *compensatory damages*. These damages compensate the injured party only for damages actually sustained and proved to have arisen directly from the loss of the bargain caused by the breach of contract. They simply replace what was lost because of the wrong or damage.

The standard measure of compensatory damages is the difference between the value of the breaching party's promised performance under the contract and the value of her or his actual performance. This amount is reduced by any loss that the injured party has avoided, however.

■ **EXAMPLE 15.1** You contract with Marinot Industries to perform certain personal services exclusively for Marinot during August for a payment of $3,500. Marinot cancels the contract and is in breach. You are able to find another job during August but can earn only $1,000. You normally can sue Marinot for breach and recover $2,500 as compensatory damages. You may also recover from Marinot the amount

2. *Restatement (Second) of Contracts,* Section 347; and Section 1–106(1) of the Uniform Commercial Code (UCC).

that you spent to find the other job. ■ Expenses that are directly incurred because of a breach of contract—such as those incurred to obtain performance from another source—are called *incidental damages.*

The measurement of compensatory damages varies by type of contract. Certain types of contracts deserve special mention—contracts for the sale of goods, contracts for the sale of land, and construction contracts.

Sale of Goods. In a contract for the sale of goods, the usual measure of compensatory damages is the difference between the contract price and the market price.[3] ■ EXAMPLE 15.2 MediQuick Laboratories contracts with Cal Computer Industries to purchase ten model UTS 400 network servers for $8,000 each. If Cal Computer fails to deliver the ten servers, and the current market price of the servers is $8,150, MediQuick's measure of damages is $1,500 (10 × $150) plus any incidental damages (expenses) caused by the breach. ■ If the buyer breaches and the seller has not yet produced the goods, compensatory damages normally equal the seller's lost profits on the sale rather than the difference between the contract price and the market price.

.on the Web For a summary of how contracts may be breached and other information on contract law, go to **http://www.lawyers.com/lawyers/A~1001075~LDC/TERMINATING+A+CONTRACT.html.**

Sale of Land. Ordinarily, because each parcel of land is unique, the remedy for a seller's breach of a contract for a sale of real estate is specific performance—that is, the buyer is awarded the parcel of property for which he or she bargained (specific performance is discussed more fully later in this chapter). When this remedy is unavailable (because the property has been sold, for example) or when the buyer is the party in breach, the measure of damages is typically the difference between the contract price and the market price of the land. The majority of states follow this rule.

Construction Contracts. The measure of damages in a building or construction contract varies depending on which party breaches and when the breach occurs. The owner can breach at three different stages of the construction:

1. Before performance has begun.
2. During performance.
3. After performance has been completed.

If the owner breaches *before performance has begun,* the contractor can recover only the profits that would have been made on the contract (that is, the total contract price less the cost of materials and labor). If the owner breaches *during performance,* the contractor can recover the profits plus the costs incurred in partially constructing the building. If the owner breaches *after the construction has been completed,* the contractor can recover the entire contract price plus interest.

When the contractor breaches the construction contract—either by failing to begin construction or by stopping work partway through the project—the measure of damages is the cost of completion, which includes reasonable compensation for any delay in performance. If the contractor finishes late, the measure of damages is the loss of use. The *Concept Summary* on the next page summarizes the rules concerning the measurement of damages in breached construction contracts.

3. That is, the difference between the contract price and the market price at the time and place at which the goods were to be delivered or tendered. [See UCC 2–708, 2–713, and 2–715(1), to be discussed in Chapter 19.]

CONCEPT SUMMARY Measurement of Damages— Breach of Construction Contracts

PARTY IN BREACH	TIME OF BREACH	MEASUREMENT OF DAMAGES
Owner	Before construction has begun	Profits (contract price less cost of materials and labor)
Owner	During construction	Profits plus costs incurred up to time of breach
Owner	After construction is completed	Contract price plus interest
Contractor	Before construction has begun	Cost above contract price to complete work
Contractor	Before construction is completed	Generally, all costs incurred by owner to complete

CONSEQUENTIAL DAMAGES Special damages that compensate for a loss that does not directly or immediately result from the breach (for example, lost profits). For the plaintiff to collect consequential damages, they must have been reasonably foreseeable at the time the breach or injury occurred.

Consequential Damages Foreseeable damages that result from a party's breach of contract are referred to as **consequential damages,** or *special damages.* Consequential damages differ from compensatory damages in that they are caused by special circumstances beyond the contract itself. They flow from the consequences, or results, of a breach. When a seller fails to deliver goods, knowing that the buyer is planning to use or resell those goods immediately, consequential damages are awarded for the loss of profits from the planned resale.

■ EXAMPLE 15.3 Gilmore contracts to have a specific item shipped to her—one that she desperately needs to repair her printing press. In her contract with the shipper, Gilmore states that she must receive the item by Monday or she will not be able to print her paper and will lose $950. If the shipper is late, Gilmore normally can recover the consequential damages caused by the delay (that is, the $950 in losses). ■

To recover consequential damages, the breaching party must know (or have reason to know) that special circumstances will cause the nonbreaching party to suffer an additional loss.[4] When was this rule first enunciated? See this chapter's *Landmark in the Law* feature beginning on page 366 for a discussion of *Hadley v. Baxendale,* a case decided in England in 1854.

NOTE A seller who does not wish to take on the risk of consequential damages can limit the buyer's remedies via contract.

Punitive Damages Recall from Chapter 4 that punitive damages are designed to punish a wrongdoer and set an example to deter similar conduct in the future. Punitive damages, or *exemplary damages,* are generally not awarded in an action for breach of contract. Such damages have no legitimate place in contract law because they are, in essence, penalties, and a breach of contract is not unlawful in a criminal sense. A contract is simply a civil relationship between the parties. The law may compensate one party for the loss of the bargain—no more and no less.

In a few situations, a person's actions can cause both a breach of contract and a tort. ■ EXAMPLE 15.4 Two parties establish by contract a certain reasonable standard or duty of care. Failure to live up to that standard is a breach of the contract. The same act that breached the contract may also constitute negligence, or it may be an

4. UCC 2–715(2). See Chapter 20.

intentional tort if, for example, the breaching party committed fraud. In such a situation, it is possible for the nonbreaching party to recover punitive damages for the tort in addition to compensatory and consequential damages for the breach of contract. ■

NOMINAL DAMAGES
A small monetary award (often one dollar) granted to a plaintiff when no actual damage was suffered.

Nominal Damages When no actual damage or financial loss results from a breach of contract and only a technical injury is involved, the court may award **nominal damages** to the innocent party. Nominal damage awards are often small, such as one dollar, but they do establish that the defendant acted wrongfully. Most lawsuits for nominal damages are brought as a matter of principle under the theory that a breach has occurred and some damages must be imposed regardless of actual loss.

■ EXAMPLE 15.5 Hernandez contracts to buy potatoes at fifty cents a pound from Lentz. Lentz breaches the contract and does not deliver the potatoes. Meanwhile, the price of potatoes falls. Hernandez is able to buy them in the open market at half the price he agreed to pay Lentz. Hernandez is clearly better off because of Lentz's breach. Thus, in a suit for breach of contract, Hernandez may be awarded only nominal damages for the technical injury he sustained, as no monetary loss was involved. ■

(Note that nominal damages may take on greater significance in tort cases involving defamation or trade libel. If a false statement made by a competing firm calls into question a business's integrity or good reputation, the business may find it desirable to establish the falsity of the statement in public court proceedings. If the business wins in court, the court may award nominal damages because actual damages in such cases are difficult to estimate.)

MITIGATION OF DAMAGES

MITIGATION OF DAMAGES
A rule requiring a plaintiff to do whatever is reasonable to minimize the damages caused by the defendant.

In most situations, when a breach of contract occurs, the injured party is held to a duty to mitigate, or reduce, the damages that he or she suffers. Under this doctrine of **mitigation of damages,** the required action depends on the nature of the situation.

■ EXAMPLE 15.6 Some states require a landlord to use reasonable means to find a new tenant if a tenant abandons the premises and fails to pay rent. If an acceptable tenant becomes available, the landlord is required to lease the premises to this tenant to mitigate the damages recoverable from the former tenant. The former tenant is still liable for the difference between the amount of the rent under the original lease and the rent received from the new tenant. If the landlord has not used the reasonable means necessary to find a new tenant, a court will likely reduce any award by the amount of rent the landlord could have received had such reasonable means been used. ■

In the majority of states, a person whose employment has been wrongfully terminated has a duty to mitigate damages incurred because of the employer's breach of the employment contract. In other words, wrongfully terminated employees have a duty to take similar jobs if they are available. If the employees fail to do this, the damages they receive will be equivalent to their salaries less the incomes they would have received in similar jobs obtained by reasonable means. The employer has the burden of proving that such jobs existed and that the employee could have been hired. Normally, the employee is under no duty to take a job that is not of the same type and rank.

LANDMARK IN THE LAW *Hadley v. Baxendale* (1854)

The rule that notice of special ("consequential") circumstances must be given if consequential damages are to be recovered was first enunciated in *Hadley v. Baxendale,*[a] a landmark case decided in 1854.

CASE BACKGROUND This case involved a broken crankshaft used in a flour mill run by the Hadley family in Gloucester, England. The crankshaft attached to the steam engine in the mill broke, and the shaft had to be sent to a foundry located in Greenwich so that a new shaft could be made to fit the other parts of the engine.

The Hadleys hired Baxendale, a common carrier, to transport the shaft from Gloucester to Greenwich. Baxendale received payment in advance and promised to deliver the shaft the following day. It was not delivered for several days, however. As a consequence, the mill was closed during those days because the Hadleys had no extra crankshaft on hand to use. The Hadleys sued Baxendale to recover the profits they lost during that time. Baxendale contended that the loss of profits was "too remote."

In the mid-1800s, it was common knowledge that large mills, such as that run by the Hadleys, normally had more than one crankshaft in case the main one broke and had to be repaired, as happened in this case. It is against this background that the parties argued their respective positions on whether the damages resulting from loss of profits while the crankshaft was out for repair were "too remote" to be recoverable.

THE ISSUE BEFORE THE COURT AND THE COURT'S RULING The crucial issue before the court was whether the Hadleys had informed the carrier, Baxendale, of the special circumstances surrounding the crankshaft's repair, particularly that the mill would have to shut down while the crankshaft was being repaired. If Baxendale had been notified of this circumstance at the time the contract was formed, then the remedy for breaching the contract would have been the amount of damages that would reasonably follow from the breach—including the Hadleys' lost profits.

In the court's opinion, however, the only circumstances communicated by the Hadleys to Baxendale at the time the contract was made were that the item to be transported was a broken crankshaft of a mill and that the Hadleys were the owners and operators of that mill. The court concluded that these circumstances did not reasonably indicate that the mill would have to stop operations if the delivery of the crankshaft was delayed.

APPLICATION TO TODAY'S BUSINESS WORLD

Today, the rule enunciated by the court in this case still applies. When damages are awarded, compensation is given only for those injuries that the defendant could reasonably have foreseen as a probable result of the usual course of events following a breach. If the injury complained of is outside the usual and foreseeable course of events, the plaintiff must show specifically that the defendant had reason to know the facts and foresee the injury. This rule applies to contracts in the online environment as well. For example, suppose that a Web merchant loses business (and profits) due to a computer system's failure. If the failure was caused by malfunctioning soft-

a. 9 Exch. 341, 156 Eng.Rep. 145 (1854).

LANDMARK IN THE LAW —Continued

ware, the merchant normally may recover the lost profits from the software maker if these consequential damages were foreseeable.

RELEVANT WEB SITES

To locate information on the Web concerning Hadley v. Baxendale, *go to this text's Web site at* **http://blt.westbuslaw.com**, *select "Chapter 15," and click on "URLs for Landmarks."*

Whether a business firm failed to mitigate its damages was at issue in the following case.

CASE 15.1 Fujitsu, Ltd. v. Federal Express Corp.

United States Court of Appeals,
Second Circuit, 2001.
247 F.3d 423.

BACKGROUND AND FACTS On May 30, 1996, Fujitsu, Ltd., shipped a container of silicon wafers (computer chips) from Narita, Japan, to Ross Technologies, Inc., in Austin, Texas, using Federal Express (FedEx) as the carrier. The next day, the container arrived in Austin and was held for clearance by the U.S. Customs Service. (FedEx cannot release imported goods until the Customs Service has approved delivery and all applicable taxes have been paid.) Meanwhile, Ross decided to reject the shipment and paid for FedEx to ship the goods back to Fujitsu.[a] The goods left Austin in good condition, but when they arrived in Japan, Fujitsu found the outer container broken and covered with an oily substance that had permeated some of the interior boxes and coated the sealed aluminum bags containing the wafers. Fujitsu reported the damage, which FedEx acknowledged. On the instructions of Fujitsu's insurance company, Fujitsu then disposed of the container and the wafers without opening any of the bags. Fujitsu filed a suit in a federal district court against FedEx, alleging, in part, breach of contract. The court found FedEx liable for damages in the amount of $726,640. FedEx appealed to the U.S. Court of Appeals for the Second Circuit, arguing that Fujitsu failed to mitigate its damages.

a. Under the Warsaw Convention (an international treaty), if the shipment of goods had been a return shipment, paid for by Fujitsu, FedEx might have had a defense to liability. The court, however, found that this was a separate contract to ship the goods, paid for by Ross, and not a return shipment of goods.

IN THE WORDS OF THE COURT . . .

SPATT, District Judge:

* * * *

* * * FedEx challenges the court's findings on the mitigation of damages by Fujitsu.

* * * *

While FedEx is correct that the record contains no evidence that the wafers themselves were damaged, there was sufficient evidence adduced to support a finding by the court that the shipment was a total loss because the residue on the outer packaging made it impossible to access the wafers. According to the

(Continued)

CASE 15.1—Continued

testimony, the bags containing the wafers could only be opened in a specially designed and maintained "clean room" so as to prevent dust contamination. However, because the bags themselves were coated with the oily residue, they could not be brought into a clean room for inspection, as the residue itself would contaminate the clean room. Consequently, the trial court found that even if the wafers were undamaged, Fujitsu was unable to extract them from the bags in an operable condition. *This Court can discern no difference between damage rendering the wafers inoperable and damage that prevents otherwise operable wafers from being used or salvaged.* [Emphasis added.]

* * * *

In addition, with regard to mitigation, the trial court's factual finding that efforts to salvage the wafers would have been prohibitively expensive also suffices to reject FedEx's argument that Fujitsu failed to mitigate its damages.

DECISION AND REMEDY The U.S. Court of Appeals for the Second Circuit affirmed the judgment of the lower court. Fujitsu was not required to attempt to mitigate its damages under the circumstances.

WHY IS THIS CASE IMPORTANT? *Injured parties have an absolute duty to mitigate their damages. As this case illustrates, however, that duty is tempered by what actions the court considers to be reasonable under the circumstances.*

Liquidated Damages versus Penalties

LIQUIDATED DAMAGES
An amount, stipulated in a contract, that the parties to the contract believe to be a reasonable estimation of the damages that will occur in the event of a breach.

PENALTY
A contractual clause that states that a certain amount of money damages will be paid in the event of a future default or breach of contract. The damages are not a measure of compensation for the contract's breach but rather a punishment for a default. The agreement as to the amount will not be enforced, and recovery will be limited to actual damages.

A **liquidated damages** provision in a contract specifies that a certain dollar amount is to be paid in the event of a future default or breach of contract. (*Liquidated* means determined, settled, or fixed.) Liquidated damages differ from penalties. A **penalty** specifies a certain amount to be paid in the event of a default or breach of contract and is designed to penalize the breaching party. Liquidated damages provisions normally are enforceable. In contrast, if a court finds that a provision calls for a penalty, the agreement as to the amount will not be enforced, and recovery will be limited to actual damages.[5]

To determine whether a particular provision is for liquidated damages or for a penalty, the court must answer two questions:

1. At the time the contract was formed, was it apparent that damages would be difficult to estimate in the event of a breach?
2. Was the amount set as damages a reasonable estimate of those potential damages and not excessive?[6]

If the answers to both questions are yes, the provision normally will be enforced. If either answer is no, the provision will normally not be enforced. In a construction contract, it is difficult to estimate the amount of damages that might be caused by a delay in completing construction, so liquidated damages clauses are often used.

The court in the following case addressed the liquidated damages questions just referred to in evaluating a provision in an agreement for the lease of a hotel.

---

5. This is also the rule under the UCC. See UCC 2–718(1).
6. *Restatement (Second) of Contracts,* Section 356(1).

CASE 15.2 Green Park Inn, Inc. v. Moore

North Carolina Court of Appeals, 2002.
562 S.E.2d 53.
http://www.nccourts.org[a]

COMPANY PROFILE *Green Park Inn (**http://www.greenparkinn.com**) is one of the oldest hotels in the United States. Established in 1882 and listed on the National Register of Historic Places, it is located in the Blue Ridge Mountains near Blowing Rock, North Carolina. Eminent guests have included Annie Oakley, Herbert Hoover, Eleanor Roosevelt, Margaret Mitchell, Calvin Coolidge, and John D. Rockefeller. Green Park Inn is a full-service, first class hotel and restaurant.*

BACKGROUND AND FACTS Allen and Pat McCain own Green Park Inn, Inc., which operates the Green Park Inn. In 1996, they leased the Inn to GMAFCO, LLC, which is owned by Gary and Gail Moore. The lease agreement provided that, in case of a default by GMAFCO, Green Park Inn, Inc., would be entitled to $500,000 as "liquidated damages." GMAFCO defaulted on the February 2000 rent. Green Park Inn, Inc., gave GMAFCO an opportunity to cure the default, but GMAFCO made no further payments and returned possession of the property to the lessor. When Green Park Inn, Inc., sought the "liquidated damages," the Moores refused to pay. Green Park Inn, Inc., filed a suit in a North Carolina state court against the Moores, GMAFCO, and their bank to obtain the $500,000. The defendants contended in part that the lease clause requiring payment of "liquidated damages" was an unenforceable penalty provision. The court ordered the defendants to pay Green Park Inn, Inc. The defendants appealed to a state intermediate appellate court.

a. Select the link to "Court Opinions," enter "Green Park" in the box labeled "Keywords," and click on "Search." Select the name of the case from the resulting list to access the opinion. The North Carolina Appellate Division Reporter maintains this Web site.

IN THE WORDS OF THE COURT . . .

HUDSON, Judge.

* * * *

The parties agreed to the following in the liquidated damages clause of the Lease Agreement:

> Allen and Pat McCain, the only two shareholders of lessor, have actively worked in the day to day operation of the hotel for the past fourteen years, and have steadily built up the clientele, reputation and physical plant of the hotel, and, correspondingly, the revenues/profits of the hotel. In addition, Allen and Pat McCain are 64 and 55 years old respectively, and that both retired from the business after this lease was agreed to. The McCains have retired to Florida, and would have to relocate back to Blowing Rock for extended periods of time if they are forced out of retirement to take over operation of the hotel. The parties agree to the following items which will be included in lessor's damages:
>
> (a) restoration of the physical plant;
> (b) lost lease payments owed to lessor which will not be paid because of lessee's breach with due consideration having been given to lessor's obligation to mitigate damages;
> (c) harm to the reputation of the hotel, which will have to be remedied by lessor;
> (d) interruption of business damages caused by the necessity of lessor having to hire new employees to recommence operations.

While some of the items listed in the liquidated damages provision are not indefinite or uncertain, others, such as the harm to the hotel's reputation or the cost to the McCains of being forced out of retirement, clearly would have been difficult to ascertain at the time the Lease Agreement was signed. * * *

Whether a liquidated damages amount is a reasonable estimate of the damages that would likely result from a default is a question of fact. * * * [McCain] stated that, after he and his wife were forced out of retirement and back to Blowing Rock to operate the hotel, "[t]he estimate of $500,000.00 as the fair and reasonable estimate to measure the damages suffered by us in the event of default has proven to be just that

(Continued)

CASE 15.2—Continued

fair and reasonable." Additionally, the Lease Agreement states that "[t]he parties have agreed that the sum of Five Hundred Thousand Dollars ($500,000.00) represents a fair and reasonable estimate and measure of the damages to be suffered by lessor in the event of default by lessee." Defendants have proffered [offered] no evidence to show the liquidated damages amount was unreasonable. [Emphasis added.]

DECISION AND REMEDY The state intermediate appellate court affirmed the decision of the lower court. The lease provision satisfied the two-part test for liquidated damages. The amount of the damages would have been difficult to determine at the time that the lease was signed, and the estimate of the damages was reasonable.

FOR CRITICAL ANALYSIS—Economic Consideration *If the lease had specified $3 million in damages, would the result in this case have been different? If so, why?*

ETHICAL ISSUE 15.1 ***Should liquidated damages clauses be enforced when no actual damages are incurred?*** An issue involving liquidated damages clauses that occasionally comes before the courts has to do with deposits on the purchase price of a home or other real estate. For example, in one case a couple signed a contract to buy a home and paid a nonrefundable deposit of $18,000 toward the purchase price. The full agreement was contingent on the buyers' sale of their current home. Because the couple was unable to sell their existing home, they had to back out of the agreement. Shortly thereafter, another buyer agreed to purchase the home for a higher price than the initial buyers had agreed to pay. Thus, the seller incurred no actual damages and, in fact, reaped higher profits as a result of the buyers' inability to perform. In such situations, does a clause requiring the buyers to forgo their deposit constitute a penalty clause rather than a liquidated damages clause?

Not in most cases. The courts routinely hold that such clauses are enforceable liquidated damages clauses. Although this may seem unfair to home buyers who cannot perform due to events beyond their control, consider the alternative: if the courts refused to enforce liquidated damages clauses in these circumstances, it would, in the words of one court, undermine "the peace of mind and certainty of result the parties sought when they contracted for liquidated damages."[7] ■

The *Concept Summary* on the following page summarizes the rules on the availability of the different types of damages.

Equitable Remedies

In some situations, damages are an inadequate remedy for a breach of contract. In these cases, the nonbreaching party may ask the court for an equitable remedy. Equitable remedies include rescission and restitution, specific performance, and reformation.

Rescission and Restitution

As discussed in Chapter 14, *rescission* is essentially an action to undo, or cancel, a contract—to return nonbreaching parties to the positions that they occupied prior to the transaction. When fraud, mistake, duress, or failure of consideration is present, rescission is available. The failure of one party to perform under a contract enti-

7. *Kelly v. Marx,* 705 N.E.2d 1114 (Mass. 1999).

CONCEPT SUMMARY Damages

REMEDY	AVAILABILITY	RESULT
Compensatory Damages	A party sustains and proves an injury arising directly from the loss of the bargain.	The injured party is compensated for the loss of the bargain.
Consequential Damages	Special circumstances, of which the breaching party is aware or should be aware, cause the injured party additional loss.	The injured party is given the entire *benefit* of the bargain, such as forgone profits.
Punitive Damages	Damages are normally available only when a tort is also involved.	The wrongdoer is punished, and others are deterred from committing similar acts.
Nominal Damages	There is no financial loss.	Wrongdoing is established without actual damages being suffered. The plaintiff is awarded a nominal amount (such as $1) in damages.
Liquidated Damages	A contract provides a specific amount to be paid as damages in the event that the contract is later breached.	The nonbreaching party is paid the amount stipulated in the contract for the breach, unless the amount is construed as a penalty.

tles the other party to rescind the contract.[8] The rescinding party must give prompt notice to the breaching party.

RESTITUTION
An equitable remedy under which a person is restored to his or her original position prior to loss or injury, or placed in the position he or she would have been in had the breach not occurred.

Restitution To rescind a contract, both parties generally must make **restitution** to each other by returning goods, property, or money previously conveyed.[9] If the physical property or goods can be returned, they must be. If the property or goods have been consumed, restitution must be made in an equivalent dollar amount.

Essentially, restitution involves the recapture of a benefit conferred on the defendant that has unjustly enriched her or him. ■ **EXAMPLE 15.7** Andrea pays $12,000 to Myles in return for his promise to design a house for her. The next day, Myles calls Andrea and tells her that he has taken a position with a large architectural firm in another state and cannot design the house. Andrea decides to hire another architect that afternoon. Andrea can require restitution of $12,000 because Myles has received an unjust benefit of $12,000. ■

CONTRAST Restitution offers several advantages over traditional damages. First, restitution may be available in situations when damages cannot be proved or are difficult to prove. Second, restitution can be used to recover specific property. Third, restitution sometimes results in a greater overall award.

Restitution Is Not Limited to Rescission Cases Restitution may be required when a contract is rescinded, but the right to restitution is not limited to rescission cases. Restitution may be sought in actions for breach of contract, tort actions, and other actions at law or in equity. Usually, restitution can be obtained when funds or property has been transferred by mistake or because of fraud. An award in a case may include restitution of cash or property obtained through embezzlement, conversion, theft, copyright infringement, or misconduct by a party in a confidential or other special relationship.

8. The rescission discussed here refers to *unilateral* rescission, in which only one party wants to undo the contract. In *mutual* rescission, both parties agree to undo the contract. Mutual rescission discharges the contract; unilateral rescission is generally available as a remedy for breach of contract.

9. *Restatement (Second) of Contracts,* Section 370.

Suppose that a seller contracts to sell some valuable coins to a buyer. If the seller breaches the contract, would specific performance be an appropriate remedy for the buyer to seek? Why or why not? (Elizabeth Simpson/Getty Images)

Specific Performance

SPECIFIC PERFORMANCE An equitable remedy requiring exactly the performance that was specified in a contract; usually granted only when money damages would be an inadequate remedy and the subject matter of the contract is unique (for example, real property).

The equitable remedy of **specific performance** calls for the performance of the act promised in the contract. This remedy is often attractive to a nonbreaching party because it provides the exact bargain promised in the contract. It also avoids some of the problems inherent in a suit for money damages. First, the nonbreaching party need not worry about collecting the judgment.[10] Second, the nonbreaching party need not look around for another contract. Third, the actual performance may be more valuable than the money damages.

Normally, however, specific performance will not be granted unless the party's legal remedy (money damages) is inadequate.[11] For this reason, contracts for the sale of goods rarely qualify for specific performance. Money damages ordinarily are adequate in such situations because substantially identical goods can be bought or sold in the market. Only if the goods are unique will a court of equity grant specific performance. For instance, paintings, sculptures, and rare books and coins are often unique, and money damages will not enable a buyer to obtain substantially identical substitutes in the market.

Sale of Land A court will grant specific performance to a buyer in a contract for the sale of land. The legal remedy for breach of a land sales contract is inadequate because every parcel of land is considered to be unique. Money damages will not compensate a buyer adequately because the same land in the same location obviously cannot be obtained elsewhere. Only when specific performance is unavailable (for example, when the seller has sold the property to someone else) will money damages be awarded instead.

---

10. Courts dispose of cases, after trials, by entering judgments. A judgment may order the losing party to pay money damages to the winning party. Collecting a judgment, however, can pose problems. For example, the judgment debtor may be insolvent (cannot pay his or her bills when they come due) or have only a small net worth, or exemption laws may prevent a creditor from seizing the debtor's assets to satisfy a debt (see Chapter 26).

11. *Restatement (Second) of Contracts,* Section 359.

Contracts for Personal Services Personal-service contracts require one party to work personally for another party. Courts normally refuse to grant specific performance of contracts for personal services. This is because to order a party to perform personal services against his or her will amounts to a type of involuntary servitude, which is contrary to the public policy expressed in the Thirteenth Amendment to the Constitution. Moreover, the courts do not want to monitor contracts for personal services.

■ EXAMPLE 15.8 If you contract with a brain surgeon to perform brain surgery on you and the surgeon refuses to perform, the court will not compel (and you certainly would not want) the surgeon to perform under these circumstances. There is no way the court can assure meaningful performance in such a situation.[12] ■

REFORMATION

Reformation is an equitable remedy used when the parties have *imperfectly* expressed their agreement in writing. Reformation allows the contract to be rewritten to reflect the parties' true intentions. It applies most often when fraud or mutual mistake is present. ■ EXAMPLE 15.9 If Keshan contracts to buy a forklift from Shelley but the written contract refers to a crane, a mutual mistake has occurred. Accordingly, a court could reform the contract so that the writing conforms to the parties' original intention as to which piece of equipment is being sold. ■

Courts frequently reform contracts in two other situations. The first occurs when two parties who have made a binding oral contract agree to put the oral contract in writing but, in doing so, make an error in stating the terms. Universally, the courts allow into evidence the correct terms of the oral contract, thereby reforming the written contract. The second situation occurs when the parties have executed a written covenant not to compete (see Chapter 11). If the covenant not to compete is for a valid and legitimate purpose (such as the sale of a business) but the area or time restraints are unreasonable, some courts will reform the restraints by making them reasonable and will enforce the entire contract as reformed. Other courts, however, will throw the entire restrictive covenant out as illegal. Exhibit 15–1 summarizes the remedies, including reformation, that are available to the nonbreaching party.

12. Similarly, courts often refuse to order specific performance of construction contracts because courts are not set up to operate as construction supervisors or engineers.

EXHIBIT 15–1 REMEDIES FOR BREACH OF CONTRACT

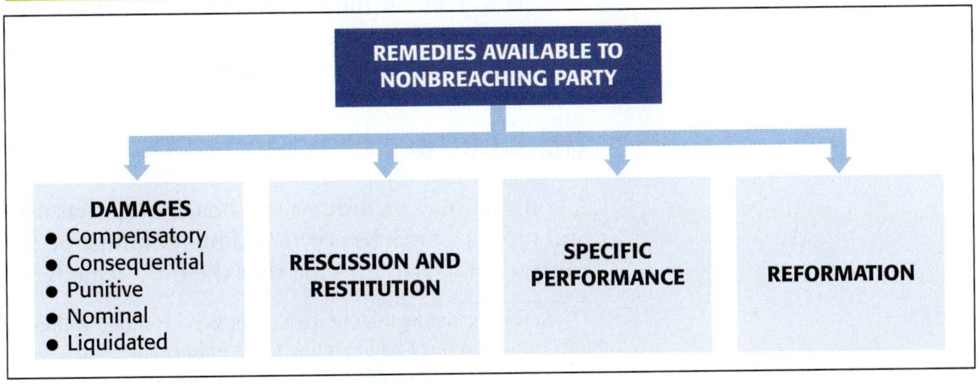

Recovery Based on Quasi Contract

DON'T FORGET The function of a quasi contract is to impose a legal obligation on a party who made no actual promise.

Recall from Chapter 8 that a quasi contract is not a true contract but rather a fictional contract that is imposed on the parties to prevent unjust enrichment. Hence, quasi contract provides a basis for relief when no enforceable contract exists. The legal obligation arises because the law considers that a promise to pay for benefits received is implied by the party accepting the benefits. Generally, when one party confers a benefit on another party, justice requires that the party receiving the benefit pay a reasonable value for it.

When Quasi Contracts Are Used

Quasi contract is a legal theory under which an obligation is imposed in the absence of an agreement. It allows the courts to act as if a contract exists when there is no actual contract or agreement between the parties. The courts can also use this theory when the parties have a contract, but it is unenforceable for some reason.

Quasi-contractual recovery is often granted when one party has partially performed under a contract that is unenforceable. It provides an alternative to suing for damages and allows the party to recover the reasonable value of the partial performance. ■ EXAMPLE 15.10 Ericson contracts to build two oil derricks for Petro Industries. The derricks are to be built over a period of three years, but the parties do not create a written contract. Therefore, the Statute of Frauds will bar the enforcement of the contract.[13] After Ericson completes one derrick, Petro Industries informs him that it will not pay for the derrick. Ericson can sue Petro Industries under the theory of quasi contract. ■

The Requirements of Quasi Contract

To recover in quasi contract, the party seeking recovery must show the following:

1. The party conferred a benefit on the other party.
2. The party conferred the benefit with the reasonable expectation of being paid.
3. The party did not act as a volunteer in conferring the benefit.
4. The party receiving the benefit would be unjustly enriched by retaining the benefit without paying for it.

In the example just given, Ericson can sue in quasi contract because all of the conditions for quasi-contractual recovery have been fulfilled. Ericson built the oil derrick with the expectation of being paid. The derrick conferred an obvious benefit on Petro Industries, and Petro Industries would be unjustly enriched if it was allowed to keep the derrick without paying Ericson for the work. Therefore, Ericson should be able to recover the reasonable value of the oil derrick that was built (under the theory of *quantum meruit*[14]—"as much as he deserves"). The reasonable value is ordinarily equal to the fair market value.

Contract Provisions Limiting Remedies

A contract may include provisions stating that no damages can be recovered for certain types of breaches or that damages must be limited to a maximum amount. The contract may also provide that the only remedy for breach is replacement, repair, or

13. Contracts that by their terms cannot be performed within one year from the day after the date of contract formation must be in writing to be enforceable. See Chapter 13. (Under the 2003 amendments to the UCC, the one-year rule will no longer apply to sales contracts. See Chapter 18.)
14. Pronounced *kwahn*-tuhm *mehr*-oo-wuht.

RECALL Exculpatory clauses may be held unconscionable, depending on the relative bargaining positions of the parties and the importance to the public interest of the business seeking to enforce the clause.

refund of the purchase price. Provisions stating that no damages can be recovered are called *exculpatory clauses* (see Chapter 11). Provisions that affect the availability of certain remedies are called *limitation-of-liability clauses.*

Whether these contract provisions and clauses will be enforced depends on the type of breach that is excused by the provision. For example, a clause excluding liability for negligence may be enforced in some cases. When an exculpatory clause for negligence is contained in a contract made between parties who have roughly equal bargaining positions, the clause usually will be enforced. The Uniform Commercial Code (UCC) specifically allows limitation-of-liability clauses to be included in contracts for the sale of goods, as will be discussed in detail in Chapter 20.[15] A provision excluding liability for fraudulent or intentional injury, however, will not be enforced. Likewise, a clause excluding liability for illegal acts or violations of the law will not be enforced.

At issue in the following case was the enforceability of a limitation-of-liability clause in a home-inspection contract.

15. UCC 2–719.

CASE 15.3 Lucier v. Williams

Superior Court of New Jersey,
Appellate Division, 2004.
366 N.J.Super. 485,
841 A.2d 907.
http://lawlibrary.rutgers.edu/search.shtml[a]

BACKGROUND AND FACTS Eric Lucier and Karen Haley, first-time home buyers, contracted to buy a single-family home for $128,500 from James and Angela Williams in Berlin Township, New Jersey. The buyers asked Cambridge Associates, Limited (CAL), to perform a home inspection. CAL presented the buyers with a contract that limited CAL's liability to "$500, or 50% of fees actually paid to CAL by Client, whichever sum is smaller. Such causes include, but are not limited to, CAL's negligence, errors, omissions, * * * [or] breach of contract." Lucier reluctantly signed the contract. On CAL's behalf, Al Vasys performed the inspection and issued a report. The buyers paid CAL $385. Shortly after Lucier and Haley moved into the house, they noticed leaks, which required roof repairs estimated to cost $8,000 to $10,000. They filed a suit in a New Jersey state court against CAL and others, seeking damages for the loss. CAL filed a motion for summary judgment, claiming that under the limitation-of-liability clause, its liability, if any, was one-half the contract price, or $192.50. The court granted the motion. The plaintiffs appealed to a state intermediate appellate court.

a. In the "Search the N.J. Courts Decisions" section, type "Lucier" in the box. In the result, click on the first link to access the opinion. Rutgers Law School in Camden, New Jersey, maintains this Web site.

IN THE WORDS OF THE COURT . . .
LISA, J.A.D. [Judge, Appellate Division]

* * * *

We begin our analysis of the enforceability of the limitation of liability clause with the fundamental proposition that contracts will be enforced as written. Ordinarily, courts will not rewrite contracts to favor a party, for the purpose of giving that party a better bargain. However, courts have not hesitated to strike limited liability clauses that are unconscionable or in violation of public policy.

There is no hard and fast definition of unconscionability. * * * *[U]nconscionability is an amorphous concept obviously designed to establish a broad business ethic. The standard of conduct that the term implies is a lack of good faith, honesty in fact and observance of fair dealing.* [Emphasis added.]

(Continued)

CASE 15.3—Continued

In determining whether to enforce the terms of a contract, we look not only to its adhesive nature, but also to the subject matter of the contract, the parties' relative bargaining positions, the degree of economic compulsion motivating the adhering party, and the public interests affected by the contract. Where the provision limits a party's liability, we pay particular attention to any inequality in the bargaining power and status of the parties, as well as the substance of the contract.

* * * *

We also focus our inquiry on whether the limitation is a reasonable allocation of risk between the parties or whether it runs afoul of the public policy disfavoring clauses which effectively immunize parties from liability for their own negligent actions. To be enforceable, the amount of the cap on a party's liability must be sufficient to provide a realistic incentive to act diligently.

Applying these principles to the home inspection contract before us, we find the limitation of liability provision unconscionable. We do not hesitate to hold it unenforceable for the following reasons: (1) the contract, prepared by the home inspector, is one of adhesion; (2) the parties, one a consumer and the other a professional expert, have grossly unequal bargaining status; and (3) the substance of the provision eviscerates the contract and its fundamental purpose because the potential damage level is so nominal that it has the practical effect of avoiding almost all responsibility for the professional's negligence. Additionally, the provision is contrary to our state's public policy of effectuating the purpose of a home inspection contract to render reliable evaluation of a home's fitness for purchase and holding professionals to certain industry standards.

* * * *

The foisting of a contract of this type in this setting on an inexperienced consumer clearly demonstrates a lack of fair dealing by the professional. * * *

* * * If, upon the occasional dereliction, the home inspector's only consequence is the obligation to refund a few hundred dollars (the smaller of fifty percent of the inspection contract price or $500), there is no meaningful incentive to act diligently in the performance of home inspection contracts. To compound the problem, such excessively restricted damage allowance is grossly disproportionate to the potential loss to the homebuyer if a substantial defect is negligently overlooked. The impact upon the homebuyer can be indeed monumental, considering issues such as habitability, health and safety, and financing obligations.

* * * *

Of course, we express no comment on whether or not Vasys or CAL breached any duty to Lucier and Haley under their agreement. Our holding here is only that if they are liable, the extent of any damages for which they should be liable is not limited by the terms of the contract.

DECISION AND REMEDY The state intermediate appellate court held that the provision was unenforceable. The limitation-of-liability clause in the CAL contract did not limit the plaintiffs' recovery. The court reversed the ruling of the lower court and remanded the case for further proceedings.[b]

b. The lower court's decision on remand was not available at the time this book went to press, but it may be by the time you read this. You may be able to locate the remanded decision online. See this text's inside front cover for URLs for online court decisions.

FOR CRITICAL ANALYSIS—Social Consideration *What is the difference between the limitation-of-liability clause in this case and an exculpatory clause (discussed in Chapter 11)?*

Election of Remedies

BE AWARE Which remedy a plaintiff elects depends on the subject of the contract, the defenses of the breaching party, the advantages that might be gained in terms of tactics against the defendant, and what the plaintiff can prove with respect to the remedy sought.

In many cases, a nonbreaching party has several remedies available. Because the remedies may be inconsistent with one another, the common law of contracts requires the party to choose which remedy to pursue. This is called *election of remedies*. The purpose of the doctrine of election of remedies is to prevent double recovery. ■ **EXAMPLE 15.11** Suppose that Jefferson agrees to sell his land to Adams. Then Jefferson changes his mind and repudiates the contract. Adams can sue for compensatory damages or for specific performance. If Adams receives damages as a result of the breach, she should not also be granted specific performance of the sales contract because that would mean she would unfairly end up with both the land and the damages. The doctrine of election of remedies requires Adams to choose the remedy she wants, and it eliminates any possibility of double recovery. ■

In contrast, remedies under the UCC are cumulative. They include all of the remedies available under the UCC for breach of a sales or lease contract.[16] We will examine the UCC provisions on limited remedies in Chapter 20, in the context of the remedies available on the breach of a contract for the sale or lease of goods.

16. See UCC 2–703 and 2–711.

REVIEWING BREACH AND REMEDIES

Suppose that Kyle Bruno enters into a contract with X Entertainment to be a stuntman in a movie that is being produced. Bruno is widely known as the best motorcycle stuntman in the business, and the movie to be produced, *Xtreme Riders*, has numerous scenes involving high-speed freestyle street-bike stunts. Filming is set to begin August 1 and end by December 1 so that the film can be released the following summer. Both parties to the contract have stipulated that the filming must end on time to capture the profits from the summer movie market. The contract states that Bruno will be paid 10 percent of the royalties from the movie for his stunts. The contract also includes a liquidated damages provision, which specifies that if Bruno breaches the contract, he will owe X Entertainment $1 million. In addition, the contract includes a limitation-of-liability clause stating that if Bruno is injured during filming, X Entertainment's liability is limited to nominal damages. Using the information presented in the chapter, answer the following questions.

1. One day, while Bruno is preparing for a difficult maneuver, he gets into an argument with the director and refuses to perform any stunts at all. Can X Entertainment seek specific performance of the contract? Why or why not?
2. Suppose that while performing a high-speed wheelie on a motorcycle, Bruno is injured by the intentionally reckless act of an X Entertainment employee. Will a court be likely to enforce the limitation-of-liability clause? Why or why not? If the court allows Bruno to seek damages, what types of damages would he be able to obtain?
3. What factors would a court consider to determine whether the $1 million liquidated damages provision is valid or constitutes a penalty?
4. Suppose that there was no liquidated damages provision (or the court refused to enforce it) and X Entertainment breached the contract. The breach caused the release of the film to be delayed until the fall. Could Bruno seek consequential (special) damages for lost profits in that situation? Explain.

APPLICATION What Do You Do When You Cannot Perform?*

Not every contract can be performed. If you are a contractor, you may take on a job that, for one reason or another, you cannot or do not wish to perform. Simply walking away from the job and hoping for the best normally is not the most effective way to avoid litigation—which can be costly, time consuming, and emotionally draining. Instead, you should consider different options that may reduce the likelihood of litigation.

For example, suppose that you are a building contractor and you sign a contract to build a home for the Andersons. Performance is to begin on June 15. On June 1, Central Enterprises offers you a position that will yield you two and a half times the amount of net income you could earn as an independent builder. To take the job, you have to start on June 15. You cannot be in two places at the same time, so to accept the new position, you must breach the contract with the Andersons.

Consider Your Options

What can you do in this situation? One option is to subcontract the work to another builder and oversee the work yourself to make sure it conforms to the contract. Another option is to negotiate with the Andersons for a release. You can offer to find another qualified builder who will build a house of the same quality at the same price. Alternatively, you can offer to pay any additional costs if another builder takes the job and is more expensive. In any event, this additional cost would be the measure of damages that a court would impose on you if the Andersons prevailed in a suit for breach of contract. Thus, by making the offer, you might be able to avoid the expense of litigation—if the Andersons accept your offer.

Settlement Offers

Often, parties are reluctant to propose compromise settlements because they fear that what they say will be used against them in court if litigation ensues. The general rule, however, is that offers for settlement cannot be used in court to prove that you are liable for a breach of contract.

Checklist for the Contractor Who Cannot Perform

1. Consider a compromise.
2. Subcontract out the work and oversee it.
3. Offer to find an alternative contractor to fulfill your obligation.
4. Make a cash offer to "buy" a release from your contract. If anything other than an insignificant amount of money is involved, however, work with an attorney in making the offer.

* This *Application* is not meant to substitute for the services of an attorney who is licensed to practice law in your state.

KEY TERMS

CHAPTER SUMMARY Breach and Remedies

	COMMON REMEDIES AVAILABLE TO NONBREACHING PARTY
Damages (See pages 362–370.)	The legal remedy designed to compensate the nonbreaching party for the loss of the bargain. By awarding money damages, the court tries to place the parties in the positions that they would have occupied had the contract been fully performed. The nonbreaching party frequently has a duty to *mitigate* (lessen or reduce) the damages incurred as a result of the contract's breach. There are five broad categories of damages: 1. *Compensatory damages*—Damages that compensate the nonbreaching party for injuries actually sustained and proved to have arisen directly from the loss of the bargain resulting from the breach of contract. a. In breached contracts for the sale of goods, the usual measure of compensatory damages is the difference between the contract price and the market price. b. In breached contracts for the sale of land, the measure of damages is ordinarily the same as in contracts for the sale of goods. c. In breached construction contracts, the measure of damages depends on which party breaches and at what stage of construction the breach occurs. 2. *Consequential damages*—Damages resulting from special circumstances beyond the contract itself; the damages flow only from the consequences of a breach. For a party to recover consequential damages, the damages must be the foreseeable result of a breach of contract, and the breaching party must have known at the time the contract was formed that special circumstances existed that would cause the nonbreaching party to incur additional loss on breach of the contract. Also called *special damages.* 3. *Punitive damages*—Damages awarded to punish the breaching party. Usually not awarded in an action for breach of contract unless a tort is involved. 4. *Nominal damages*—Damages small in amount (such as one dollar) that are awarded when a breach has occurred but no actual damages have been suffered. Awarded only to establish that the defendant acted wrongfully. 5. *Liquidated damages*—Damages that may be specified in a contract as the amount to be paid to the nonbreaching party in the event the contract is breached in the future. Clauses providing for liquidated damages are enforced if the damages were difficult to estimate at the time the contract was formed and if the amount stipulated is reasonable. If the amount is construed to be a penalty, the clause will not be enforced.
Rescission and Restitution (See pages 370–371.)	1. *Rescission*—A remedy whereby a contract is canceled and the parties are restored to the original positions that they occupied prior to the transaction. Available when fraud, a mistake, duress, or failure of consideration is present. The rescinding party must give prompt notice of the rescission to the breaching party. 2. *Restitution*—When a contract is rescinded, both parties must make restitution to each other by returning the goods, property, or funds previously conveyed. Restitution prevents the unjust enrichment of the parties.
Specific Performance (See pages 372–373.)	An equitable remedy calling for the performance of the act promised in the contract. This remedy is available only in special situations—such as those involving contracts for the sale of unique goods or land—and when monetary damages would be an inadequate remedy. Specific performance is not available as a remedy in breached contracts for personal services.
Reformation (See page 373.)	An equitable remedy allowing a contract to be "reformed," or rewritten, to reflect the parties' true intentions. Available when an agreement is imperfectly expressed in writing.

(Continued)

rule regarding assessment of the fee be enforced? Explain. [*Gaddis v. Stardust Hills Owners Association, Inc.,* 804 N.E.2d 231 (Ind.App. 2004)]

A QUESTION OF ETHICS

15–8. Julio Garza was employed by the Texas Animal Health Commission (TAHC) as a health inspector in 1981. His responsibilities included bleeding and tagging cattle, vaccinating and tattooing calves, and working livestock markets. Garza was injured on the job in 1988 and underwent surgery in January 1989. When his paid leave was exhausted, he asked TAHC for light-duty work, specifically the job of tick inspector, but his supervisor refused the request. In September, TAHC notified Garza that he was fired. Garza sued TAHC and others, alleging in part wrongful termination, and an important issue before the court was whether Garza had mitigated his damages. The court found that in the seven years between his termination and his trial date, Garza had held only one job—an unpaid job on his parents' ranch. When asked how often he looked for work during that time, Garza responded that he did not know, but he had looked in "several" places. The last time he looked for work was three or four months before the trial. That effort was merely an informal inquiry to his neighbors about working on their ranch. In view of these facts, consider the following questions. [*Texas Animal Health Commission v. Garza,* 27 S.W.3d 54 (Tex.App.—San Antonio 2000)]

1. The court in this case stated that the "general rule as to mitigation of damages in breach of employment suits is that the discharged employee must use reasonable diligence to mitigate damages by seeking other employment." In your opinion, did Garza fulfill this requirement? If you were the judge, how would you rule in this case?
2. Assume for the moment that Garza had indeed been wrongfully terminated. In this situation, would it be fair to Garza to require him to mitigate his damages? Why or why not?
3. Generally, what are the ethical underpinnings of the rule that employees seeking damages for breach of employment contracts must mitigate their damages?

FOR CRITICAL ANALYSIS

15–9. Review the discussion of the doctrine of election of remedies in this chapter. What are some of the advantages and disadvantages of this doctrine?

VIDEO QUESTION

15–10. Go to this text's Web site at **http://blt.westbuslaw.com** and select "Chapter 15." Click on "Video Questions" and view the video titled *Midnight Run.* Then answer the following questions.

1. In the video, Eddie (Joe Pantoliano) and Jack (Robert DeNiro) negotiate a contract for Jack to find the Duke, a mob accountant who embezzled funds, and bring him back for trial. Assume that the contract is valid. If Jack breaches the contract by failing to bring in the Duke, what kinds of remedies, if any, can Eddie seek? Explain your answer.
2. Would the equitable remedy of specific performance be available to either Jack or Eddie in the event of a breach? Why or why not?
3. Now assume the contract between Eddie and Jack is unenforceable. Nevertheless, Jack performs his side of the bargain (brings in the Duke). Is any remedy available to him? Why or why not?

INTERNET EXERCISES

Go to the *Business Law Today* home page at **http://blt.westbuslaw.com**, select "Chapter 15," and click on "Internet Exercises." There you will find the following Internet research exercises that you can perform to learn more about topics covered in this chapter.

Activity 15–1: LEGAL PERSPECTIVE—Contract Damages and Contract Theory

Activity 15–2: MANAGEMENT PERSPECTIVE—The Duty to Mitigate

BEFORE THE TEST

Go to the *Business Law Today* home page at **http://blt.westbuslaw.com**, select "Chapter 15," and click on "Interactive Quizzes." You will find a number of interactive questions relating to this chapter.

"The laws of a state change with the changing times."

Aeschylus, 525–456 B.C.E.
(Greek dramatist)

CHAPTER 16
Third Party Rights

CHAPTER OUTLINE

- ASSIGNMENTS
- DELEGATIONS
- THIRD PARTY BENEFICIARIES

LEARNING OBJECTIVES

After reading this chapter, you should be able to answer the following questions:

1. What is the difference between an assignment and a delegation?
2. If a contract requires a party to perform personal services, can the right to receive those services be assigned?
3. What rights can be assigned despite a contract clause expressly prohibiting assignment?
4. What factors indicate that a third party beneficiary is an intended beneficiary?
5. How do a third party beneficiary's rights become vested so that this party can sue to enforce the contract?

PRIVITY OF CONTRACT
The relationship that exists between the promisor and the promisee of a contract.

Because a contract is a private agreement between the parties who have entered into it, it is fitting that these parties alone should have rights and liabilities under the contract. This concept is referred to as **privity of contract,** and it establishes the basic principle that third parties have no rights in contracts to which they are not parties.

You are probably convinced by now that for every rule of contract law there seems to be an exception. As times change, so must the laws, as the chapter-opening quotation indicates. When justice cannot be served by adherence to a rule of law, exceptions to the rule must be made. In this chapter, we look at two exceptions to the rule of privity of contract. One exception allows a party to a contract to transfer the rights or duties arising from the contract to another person through an *assignment* (of rights) or a *delegation* (of duties). The other exception involves a *third party beneficiary contract*—a contract in which the parties to the contract intend that the contract benefit a third party.

Assignments

ASSIGNMENT
The act of transferring to another all or part of one's rights arising under a contract.

ASSIGNOR
A party who transfers (assigns) his or her rights under a contract to another party (called the assignee).

ASSIGNEE
A party to whom the rights under a contract are transferred, or assigned.

OBLIGEE
One to whom an obligation is owed.

OBLIGOR
One who owes an obligation to another.

In a bilateral contract, normally one party has a right to require the other to perform some task, and the other has a duty to perform it. The transfer of contract *rights* to a third person is known as an **assignment.** The party assigning the rights to a third party is known as the **assignor,**[1] and the party receiving the rights is the **assignee.** Other traditional terminology used to describe the parties in assignment relationships are the **obligee**[2] (the person to whom a duty, or obligation, is owed) and the **obligor** (the person who is obligated to perform the duty).

When rights under a contract are assigned unconditionally, the rights of the *assignor* (the party making the assignment) are extinguished. The third party (the *assignee,* or the party receiving the assignment) has a right to demand performance from the other original party to the contract (the *obligor,* the person who is obligated to perform). ■ **EXAMPLE 16.1** Brent owes Alex $1,000, and Alex, the assignor, assigns to Carmen the right to receive the $1,000. Here, a valid assignment of a debt exists. Carmen, the assignee, can enforce the contract against Brent, the obligor, if Brent fails to perform. ■ Exhibit 16–1 illustrates assignment relationships.

The assignee takes only those rights that the assignor originally had. Furthermore, the assignee's rights are subject to the defenses that the obligor has against the assignor. ■ **EXAMPLE 16.2** Brent owes Alex $1,000 under a contract in which Brent agreed to buy Alex's computer work station. Alex assigns his right to

1. Pronounced uh-*sye*-nore.
2. Pronounced ob-lih-*gee* (with a hard g).

EXHIBIT 16–1 ASSIGNMENT RELATIONSHIPS

In the assignment relationship illustrated here, Alex assigns his *rights* under a contract that he made with Brent to a third party, Carmen. Alex thus becomes the *assignor* and Carmen the *assignee* of the contractual rights. Brent, the *obligor* (the party owing performance under the contract), now owes performance to Carmen instead of Alex. Alex's original contract rights are extinguished after assignment.

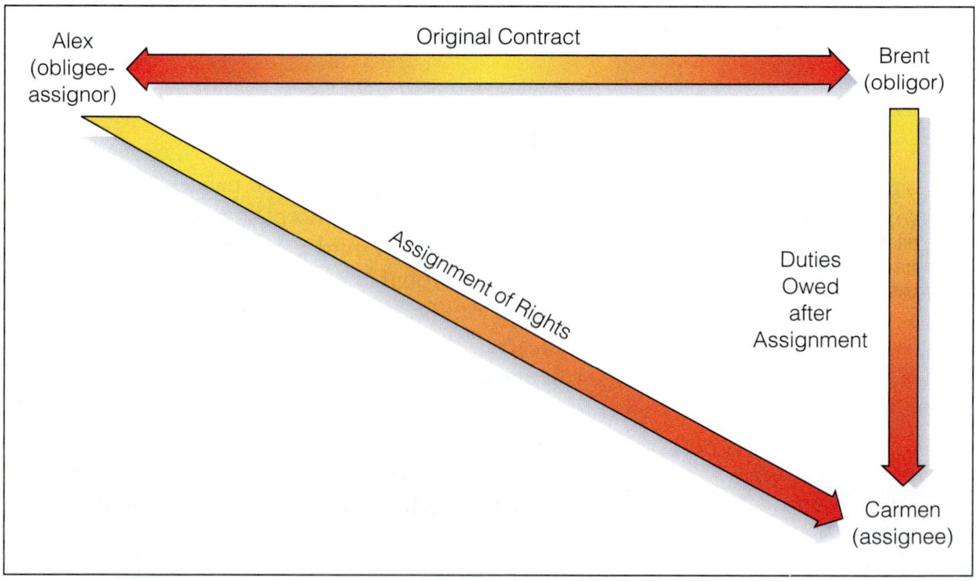

receive the $1,000 to Carmen. Brent, in deciding to purchase the work station, relied on Alex's fraudulent misrepresentation that the computer's hard drive had a storage capacity of 120 gigabytes. When Brent discovers that the computer can store only 20 gigabytes, he tells Alex that he is going to return the work station and cancel the contract. Even though Alex has assigned his "right" to receive the $1,000 to Carmen, Brent need not pay Carmen the $1,000—Brent can raise the defense of Alex's fraudulent misrepresentation to avoid payment. ■

.on the Web You can find a number of forms that can be used in the assignment of different types of contracts, at **http://www.ilrg.com/forms/#transfers**. This site is maintained by the Internet Legal Research Group.

The Importance of Assignments in the Business Context

Assignments are important because they are utilized in much business financing. Lending institutions, such as banks, frequently assign the rights to receive payments under their loan contracts to other firms, which pay for those rights. If you obtain a loan from your local bank to purchase a car, you may later receive in the mail a notice stating that your bank has transferred (assigned) its rights to receive payments on the loan to another firm and that, when the time comes to repay your loan, you must make the payments to that other firm.

Lenders that make *mortgage loans* (loans to allow prospective home buyers to purchase land or a home) often assign their rights to collect the mortgage payments to a third party, such as GMAC Mortgage Corporation. Following an assignment, the home buyer is notified that future payments must be made not to the lender that loaned the funds but to the third party. Millions of dollars change hands daily in the business world in the form of assignments of rights in contracts. If it were not possible to transfer (assign) contractual rights, many businesses could not continue to operate.

Rights That Cannot Be Assigned

As a general rule, all rights can be assigned. Exceptions are made, however, in the following special circumstances.

When a Statute Expressly Prohibits Assignment If a statute expressly prohibits assignment, the particular right in question cannot be assigned. ■ Example 16.3 Marn is a new employee of CompuFuture, Inc. CompuFuture is an employer under workers' compensation statutes (see Chapter 40) in this state, and thus Marn is a covered employee. Marn has a relatively high-risk job. In need of a loan, she borrows some money from Stark, assigning to Stark all workers' compensation benefits due her should she be injured on the job. A state statute prohibits the assignment of *future* workers' compensation benefits, and thus such rights cannot be assigned. ■

When a Contract Is Personal in Nature When a contract is for personal services, the rights under the contract normally cannot be assigned unless all that remains is a money payment. ■ Example 16.4 Brent signs a contract to be a tutor for Alex's children. Alex then attempts to assign to Carmen his right to Brent's services. Carmen cannot enforce the contract against Brent. Brent may not like Carmen's children or may for some other reason not want to tutor them. Because personal services are unique to the person rendering them, rights to receive personal services cannot be assigned. ■

When an Assignment Will Increase or Alter the Risk or Duties of the Obligor A right cannot be assigned if assignment will materially increase or alter the risk or duties of the obligor.[3] ■ Example 16.5 Alex has a hotel, and to insure it, he takes out

3. See Section 2–210(2) of the Uniform Commercial Code (UCC).

CYBERNOTARY A legally recognized authority that can certify the validity of digital signatures.

document using a private key, or code. The key has a publicly available counterpart. Anyone with the appropriate software can use the public key to verify that the digital signature was made using the private key. A **cybernotary**, or legally recognized certification authority, issues the key pair, identifies the owner of the keys, and certifies the validity of the public key. The cybernotary also serves as a repository for public keys.

Signature Dynamics With another type of signature technology, known as *signature dynamics,* a sender's signature is captured using a stylus and an electronic digitizer pad. A computer program takes the signature's measurements, the sender's identity, the time and date of the signature, and the identity of the hardware. This information is then placed in an encrypted *biometric token* attached to the document being transmitted. To verify the authenticity of the signature, the recipient of the document compares the measurements of the signature with the measurements in the token. When this type of e-signature is used, it is not necessary to have a third party verify the signatory's identity.

Other E-Signature Forms Other forms of e-signatures have been—or are now being—developed as well. ■ EXAMPLE 17.4 Some e-signatures use "smart cards." As you will read in Chapter 24, a smart card is a device the size of a credit card that is embedded with code and other data. Like credit and debit cards, a smart card can be inserted into computers to transfer information. Unlike those other cards, however, a smart card can be used to establish a person's identity as validly as a signature on a piece of paper. ■ In addition, technological innovations now under way will allow an e-signature to be evidenced by an image of a person's retina, fingerprint, or face that is scanned by a computer and then matched to a numeric code. The scanned image and the numeric code are registered with security companies that maintain files on an accessible server that can be used to authenticate a transaction.

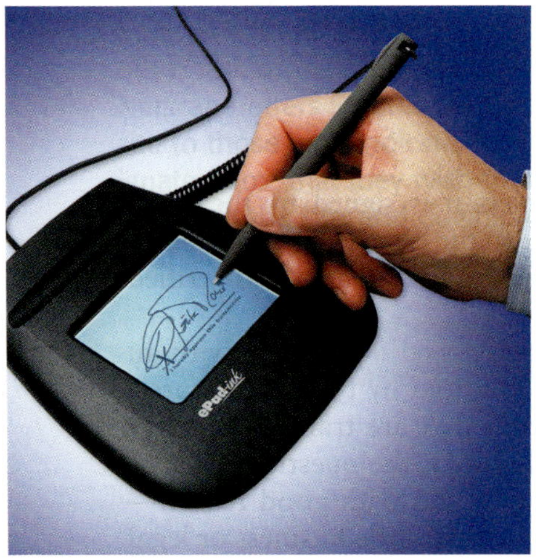

The ePad-Ink is an electronic signature pad that can be used to insert handwritten signatures into electronic documents. What type of e-signature technology does this device utilize? What procedure is used to verify the authenticity of a signature created using this ePad? (Photo Courtesy of Interlink Electronics)

STATE LAWS GOVERNING E-SIGNATURES

Most states have laws governing e-signatures. The problem is that the state e-signature laws are not uniform. Some states—California is a notable example—provide that many types of documents cannot be signed with e-signatures, while other states are more permissive. Additionally, some states recognize only digital signatures as valid, while others permit other types of e-signatures.

The National Conference of Commissioners on Uniform State Laws, in an attempt to create more uniformity among the states, promulgated the Uniform Electronic Transactions Act (UETA) in 1999. To date, the UETA has been adopted, at least in part, by more than forty states. The UETA provides, among other things, that a signature may not be denied legal effect or enforceability solely because it is in electronic form. (Other aspects of the UETA will be discussed shortly.)

FEDERAL LAW ON E-SIGNATURES AND E-DOCUMENTS

In 2000, Congress enacted the Electronic Signatures in Global and National Commerce Act (E-SIGN Act) to provide that no contract, record, or signature may be "denied legal effect" solely because it is in an electronic form. In other words, under this law, an electronic signature is as valid as a signature on paper, and an electronic document can be as enforceable as a paper one.

> **.on the Web** You can find many good resources online about the E-SIGN Act of 2000, including articles available at
> **http://archives.cnn.com/2000/ALLPOLITICS/stories/06/30/clinton.e.signatures.04/index.html**
> and
> **http://www.bizjournals.com/albany/stories/2000/09/11/editorial5.html**.

For an electronic signature to be enforceable, the contracting parties must have agreed to use electronic signatures. For an electronic document to be valid, it must be in a form that can be retained and accurately reproduced.

The E-SIGN Act does not apply to all types of documents, however. Contracts and documents that are exempt include court papers, divorce decrees, evictions, foreclosures, health-insurance terminations, prenuptial agreements, and wills. Also, the only agreements governed by the UCC that fall under this law are those covered by Articles 2 and 2A and UCC 1–107 and 1–206.

Despite these limitations, the E-SIGN Act greatly expands the possibilities for contracting online. ■ EXAMPLE 17.5 From a remote location, a businessperson can now open an account with a financial institution, obtain a mortgage or other loan, buy insurance, and purchase real estate over the Internet. Payments and transfers of funds can be done entirely online. Thus, using e-contracts can avoid the time and costs associated with producing, delivering, signing, and returning paper documents. ■

At issue in the following case was whether an exchange of e-mail between the representatives of a seller and its buyers constituted a "writing."

CASE 17.3 In re Cafeteria Operators, L.P.[a]

United States Bankruptcy Court,
Northern District of Texas, 2003.
299 Bankr. 411.

BACKGROUND AND FACTS Under the Perishable Agricultural Commodities Act (PACA) of 1930, a seller of fruits and vegetables has a right to the proceeds from their sale but loses this right if he or she agrees *in writing* to extend the time for payment beyond thirty days. Cafeteria Operators, L.P., operates cafeterias primarily in the Southwest. In 2002, Cafeteria Operators and other buyers ordered cherries from Cherrco, Inc., a wholesale food distributor, through Tim Dent of George E. Dent Sales, Inc. Cherrco bought the fruit from Peterson Farms, Inc., and others and delivered it as specified in invoices that required payment within thirty days. When the buyers failed to pay, Dent and Gene Baldwin, the buyers' representative, tried to negotiate a new payment schedule via e-mail. In January 2003, with $25,269.12 still owed, the buyers filed a petition in a federal bankruptcy court, seeking permission to pay less than this amount. Cherrco objected, asserting that it had a right to the full amount under PACA. The buyers claimed that Cherrco had waived this right in the e-mail exchanged between Dent and Baldwin. Cherrco argued in part that this e-mail was not a "writing."

a. *L.P.* is an abbreviation for *limited partnership,* a type of business organization that will be discussed in Chapter 30.

IN THE WORDS OF THE COURT . . .
HARLIN D. HALE, Bankruptcy Judge.

* * * *

* * * The Debtor argues * * * that a post-default series of e-mails between Dent and Baldwin, the representative of the Debtor, constituted a "written agreement" extending the original payment terms beyond thirty days such that Cherrco lost its ability to assert its PACA rights against the Debtor. Apparently, after the Debtor defaulted in the payment of the amounts due Cherrco, * * * Baldwin and Dent, as agent for Cherrco, began negotiating a payment schedule that would satisfy Cherrco so that Cherrco would defer enforcement of its PACA rights. A payment schedule was sent to Dent, who then forwarded the payment schedule * * * to Sarah Peterson-Schlukebir, a representative of Peterson Farms, Inc. In an e-mail dated October 10, 2002, Ms. Peterson-Schlukebir wrote to * * * Dent the following:

> * * * As discussed verbally on 10/10/02, both Peterson Farms and Cherrco are not willing to sign the * * * Release dated 10/4/02 from Gene Baldwin * * * . If we sign the release, we are no longer covered by PACA. * * *

(Continued)

CASE 17.3—Continued

On that same day, Dent sent an e-mail to Baldwin, with the above e-mail as an attachment * * * .

* * * *

On October 11, 2002, Baldwin wrote an e-mail to Dent in which he stated:

> * * * [W]e do not need a formal [contract]. We will just start making the payments starting today. All we really want is the agreement from them that the payment plan is ok. We don't want to lose them as a supplier. We know we will have to pay up front for our orders until we get thru this situation. Thanks for all your help.

* * * *

This Court rejects Cherrco's argument that the e-mails do not constitute a "writing" because this issue was resolved by Congress with the passage, in June, 2000, of the Electronic Signatures in Global and National Commerce Act (the "E-Sign Act"). The E-Sign Act, which had an effective date of October 1, 2000, provides, in pertinent part, at Section 7001:

> (a) In general
> Notwithstanding any statute, regulation, or other rule of law * * * , with respect to any transaction in or affecting interstate or foreign commerce—
> *(1) a signature, contract, or other record relating to such transaction may not be denied legal effect, validity, or enforceability solely because it is in electronic form; and*
> (2) a contract relating to such transaction may not be denied legal effect, validity, or enforceability solely because an electronic signature or electronic record was used in its formation. * * *

Thus, in transactions involving interstate commerce, e-mails constitute "writings." The transactions between Cherrco and the Debtor occurred in 2002, and clearly qualify for the requirement in Section 7001(a) that the transaction is in or affects interstate commerce. Thus, the e-mails between the parties satisfy the writing requirement, to the extent that one is required under PACA.

* * * *

For [other] reasons, [however,] the Court grants Cherrco's motion to compel the payment of its PACA * * * claim.

DECISION AND REMEDY The court rejected Cherrco's argument, holding that the e-mail exchanged between Dent and Baldwin constituted a "writing" under the E-SIGN Act. The court also held, however, that Cherrco had not waived its PACA right and awarded the seller the full amount of its claim.

FOR CRITICAL ANALYSIS—Social Consideration *Did the e-mail between Dent and Baldwin constitute an agreement between the parties to extend the original payment terms beyond thirty days? Why or why not?*

Partnering Agreements

PARTNERING AGREEMENT An agreement between a seller and a buyer who frequently do business with each other concerning the terms and conditions that will apply to all subsequently formed electronic contracts.

One way that online sellers and buyers can prevent disputes over signatures in their e-contracts, as well as disputes over the terms and conditions of those contracts, is to form partnering agreements. In a **partnering agreement,** a seller and a buyer who frequently do business with each other agree in advance on the terms and conditions that will apply to all transactions subsequently conducted electronically. The partnering agreement can also establish special access and identification codes to be used by the parties when transacting business electronically.

A partnering agreement reduces the likelihood that disputes will arise under the contract because the buyer and the seller have agreed in advance to the terms and conditions that will accompany each sale. Furthermore, if a dispute does arise, a court or arbitration forum will be able to refer to the partnering agreement when determining the parties' intent with respect to subsequent contracts. Of course, even with a partnering agreement fraud remains a possibility. If an unauthorized person uses a purchaser's designated access number and identification code, it may be some time before the problem is discovered.

The Uniform Electronic Transactions Act

As noted earlier, the Uniform Electronic Transactions Act (UETA) was promulgated in 1999. The UETA represents one of the first comprehensive efforts to create uniform laws pertaining to e-commerce.

The primary purpose of the UETA is to remove barriers to e-commerce by giving the same legal effect to electronic records and signatures as is given to paper documents and signatures. The UETA broadly defines an *e-signature* as "an electronic sound, symbol, or process attached to or logically associated with a record and executed or adopted by a person with the intent to sign the record."[5] An *e-signature* includes encrypted digital signatures, names (intended as signatures) at the ends of e-mail messages, and "clicks" on a Web page if the click includes the identification of the person. A **record** is "information that is inscribed on a tangible medium or that is stored in an electronic or other medium and is retrievable in perceivable [visual] form."[6]

RECORD
According to the Uniform Electronic Transactions Act, information that is either inscribed on a tangible medium or stored in an electronic or other media and that is retrievable. The Uniform Computer Information Transactions Act also uses the term *record* instead of *writing.*

THE SCOPE AND APPLICABILITY OF THE UETA

The UETA does not create new rules for electronic contracts but rather establishes that records, signatures, and contracts may not be denied enforceability solely due to their electronic form. The UETA does not apply to all writings and signatures but only to electronic records and electronic signatures *relating to a transaction.* A *transaction* is defined as an interaction between two or more people relating to business, commercial, or governmental activities.[7]

The act specifically does not apply to laws governing wills or testamentary trusts, to the UCC (other than Articles 2 and 2A), or to the Uniform Computer Information Transactions Act (discussed later in this chapter).[8] In addition, the provisions of the UETA allow the states to exclude its application to other areas of law.

As described earlier, Congress passed the E-SIGN Act in 2000, a year after the UETA was presented to the states for adoption. Thus, a significant issue is whether and to what extent the federal E-SIGN Act preempts the UETA as adopted by the states.

.on the Web The Web site of the National Conference of Commissioners on Uniform State Laws includes an update of the list of states that have adopted the UETA or considered it for adoption. The site also contains a summary of the act and "Question and Answer" sections concerning this law. Go to

http://www.nccusl.org.

THE FEDERAL E-SIGN ACT AND THE UETA

The E-SIGN Act refers explicitly to the UETA and provides that if a state has enacted the uniform version of the UETA, it is not preempted by the E-SIGN Act.[9] In other words, if the state has enacted the UETA *without modification,* state law will govern. The problem is that many states have enacted nonuniform (modified)

5. UETA 102(8).
6. UETA 102(15).
7. UETA 2(12) and 3.
8. UETA 3(b).
9. 15 U.S.C. Section 7002(2)(A)(i).

versions of the UETA, largely for the purpose of excluding other areas of state law from the UETA's terms. The E-SIGN Act specifies that those exclusions will be preempted to the extent that they are inconsistent with the E-SIGN Act's provisions.

The E-SIGN Act, however, explicitly allows the states to enact alternative requirements for the use of electronic records or electronic signatures. Generally, however, the requirements must be consistent with the provisions of the E-SIGN Act, and the state must not give greater legal status or effect to one specific type of technology. Additionally, if a state has enacted alternative requirements *after* the E-SIGN Act was adopted, the state law must specifically refer to the E-SIGN Act. The relationship between the UETA and the E-SIGN Act is illustrated in Exhibit 17–2.

HIGHLIGHTS OF THE UETA

We look next at selected provisions of the UETA. Our discussion is, of course, based on the act's uniform provisions. Keep in mind that the states that have enacted the UETA may have adopted slightly different versions.

The Parties Must Agree to Conduct Transactions Electronically The UETA will not apply to a transaction unless each of the parties has previously agreed to conduct transactions by electronic means. The agreement need not be explicit, however, and it may be implied by the conduct of the parties and the surrounding circumstances.[10] In the comments that accompany the UETA, the drafters stated that it may be reasonable to infer that a person who gives out a business card with an e-mail address on it has consented to transact business electronically.[11] The parties'

10. UETA 5(b).
11. UETA 5, Comment 4B.

EXHIBIT 17–2 THE E-SIGN ACT AND THE UETA

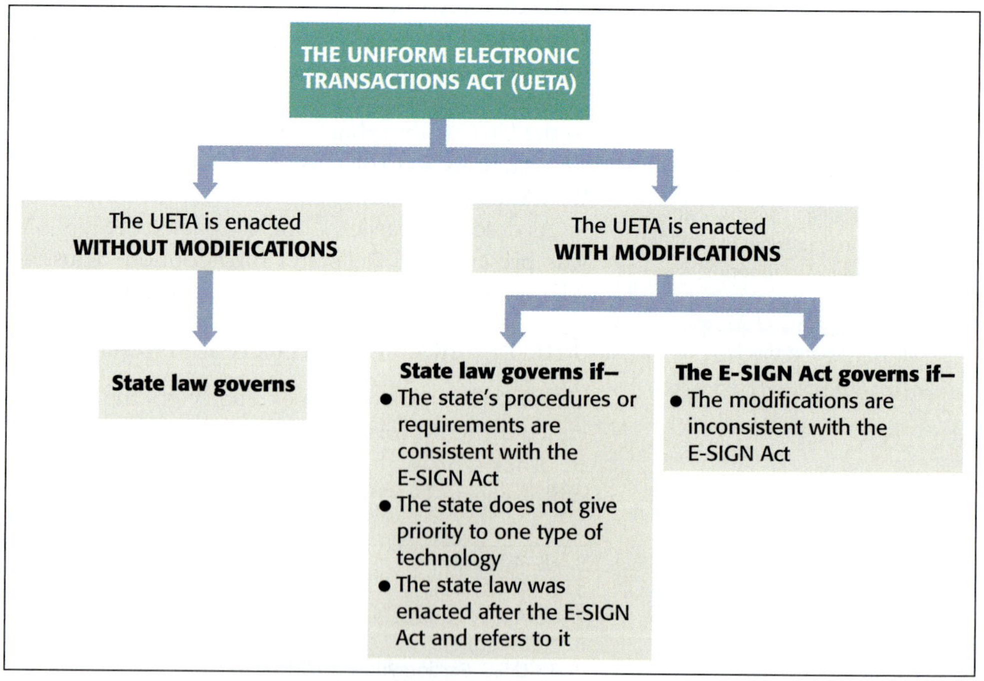

agreement may also be inferred from a letter or other writing, as well as from some verbal communications.

A person who has previously agreed to an electronic transaction can also withdraw his or her consent and refuse to conduct further business electronically. Additionally, the act expressly gives parties the power to vary the UETA's provisions by contract. In other words, *parties can opt out of all or some of the terms of the UETA*. If the parties do not opt out of the terms of the UETA, however, the UETA will govern their electronic transactions.

Attribution In the context of electronic transactions, the term *attribution* refers to the procedures that may be used to ensure that the person sending an electronic record is the same person whose e-signature accompanies the record. Under the UETA, if an electronic record or signature is the act of a particular person, the record or signature may be attributed to that person. If a person types her or his name at the bottom of an e-mail purchase order, that name would qualify as a "signature" and be attributed to the person whose name appeared. Just as in paper contracts, one may use any relevant evidence to prove that the record or signature is or is not the act of the person.[12]

Note that even if an individual's name does not appear on a record, the UETA states that the effect of the record is to be determined from the context and surrounding circumstances. In other words, a record may have legal effect even if no one has signed it. ■ **EXAMPLE 17.6** Suppose that Darby sends a fax to Corina. The fax contains a letterhead identifying Darby as the sender, but the document is not signed by Darby. Depending on the circumstances, the fax may be attributed to Darby. ■

The UETA does not contain any express provisions about what constitutes fraud or whether an agent (a person who acts on behalf of another—see Chapter 28) is authorized to enter into a contract. Under the UETA, other state laws control if any issues relating to agency, authority, forgery, or contract formation arise.

Notarization If a document is required to be notarized under existing state law, the UETA provides that this requirement is satisfied by the electronic signature of a notary public or other person authorized to verify signatures. ■ **EXAMPLE 17.7** Suppose that Joel intends to accept an offer to purchase real estate via e-mail. Under the UETA, the requirement is satisfied if a notary public is present to verify Joel's identity and affix an electronic signature to the e-mail acceptance. ■

on the Web At the Web site of the Consumers Union, you can read an article discussing some concerns that consumer groups have about many of the provisions in the UETA. Go to **http://www.consumersunion.org/finance/899nclcwc.htm**.

The Effect of Errors The UETA encourages, but does not require, the use of security procedures (such as encryption) to verify changes to electronic documents and to correct errors. Section 10 of the UETA provides that if the parties have agreed to a security procedure and one party does not detect an error because he or she did not follow the procedure, the conforming party can legally avoid the effect of the change or error. If the parties have not agreed to use a security procedure, then other state laws (including contract law governing mistakes—see Chapter 12) will determine the effect of the error on the parties' agreement.

To avoid the effect of errors, a party must take certain steps. First, the party must promptly notify the other party of the error and of her or his intent not to be bound by the error. Second, the party must take reasonable steps to return any benefit or consideration received. Parties cannot avoid a transaction from which they have benefited. ■ **EXAMPLE 17.8** Suppose that Marissa, as the result of an error, received

12. UETA 9.

access to valuable information. Because she cannot "give back" or make restitution for the valuable information she now knows, the transaction may be unavoidable. ■ In all other situations in which a change or error occurs in an electronic record (and the parties' agreement does not specifically address errors), the UETA states that the traditional law governing mistakes will govern.

Timing Section 15 of the UETA sets forth provisions relating to the sending and receiving of electronic records. These provisions apply unless the parties agree to different terms. Under Section 15, an electronic record is considered *sent* when it is properly directed to the intended recipient in a form readable by the recipient's computer system. Once the electronic record leaves the control of the sender or comes under the control of the recipient, the UETA deems it to have been sent. An electronic record is considered *received* when it enters the recipient's processing system in a readable form—*even if no individual is aware of its receipt.*

Additionally, the UETA provides that, unless otherwise agreed, an electronic record is to be sent from or received at the party's principal place of business. If a party has no place of business, the provision then authorizes the place of sending or receipt to be the party's residence. If a party has multiple places of business, the record should be sent from or received at the location that has the closest relationship to the underlying transaction.

The Uniform Computer Information Transactions Act

The National Conference of Commissioners on Uniform State Laws (NCCUSL) promulgated the Uniform Computer Information Transactions Act (UCITA) in 1999. The primary purpose of the UCITA is to validate e-contracts to license or purchase software, or contracts that give access to—or allow the distribution of—**computer information.** The UCITA is controversial, and only two states (Maryland and Virginia) have adopted it, while four states (Iowa, North Carolina, Vermont, and West Virginia) have passed anti-UCITA provisions. In 2003, the NCCUSL withdrew its support of the UCITA. Although the UCITA remains a legal resource, the NCCUSL will no longer seek its adoption by the states, which are thus unlikely to consider it further.

COMPUTER INFORMATION
As defined by the Uniform Computer Information Transactions Act, "information in an electronic form obtained from or through use of a computer, or that is in digital or an equivalent form capable of being processed by a computer."

REVIEWING E-CONTRACTS

Ted and Betty Hyatt live in California, a state that has extensive statutory protection for consumers. The Hyatts decided to buy a computer so that they could use e-mail to stay in touch with their grandchildren, who live in another state. Over the phone, they ordered a computer from CompuEdge, Inc. When the box arrived, it was sealed with a brightly colored sticker warning that the terms enclosed within the box would govern the sale unless the customer returned the computer within thirty days. Among those terms was a clause that required any disputes to be resolved in a Tennessee state court. The Hyatts then signed up for Internet service through CyberTool, an Internet service provider. They downloaded CyberTool's software and clicked on the "quick install" button that allowed them to bypass CyberTool's "Terms of Service" page. It was possible to read this page by scrolling to the next screen, but the Hyatts did not realize this. The terms included a clause that stated that

REVIEWING E-CONTRACTS—Continued

all disputes were to be submitted to a Virginia state court. As soon as the Hyatts attempted to e-mail their grandchildren, they experienced problems using CyberTool's e-mail service, which continually stated that the network was busy. They also were unable to receive the photos sent by their grandchildren. Using the information presented in the chapter, answer the following questions.

1. Did the list of contract terms included in the computer box constitute an offer that the Hyatts could accept or reject? Did the Hyatts accept the terms? If so, at what point did acceptance occur?
2. What legal term used in the chapter describes the type of agreement the Hyatts formed with CompuEdge? How does the UCC describe the way acceptance can occur in such contracts?
3. Suppose that the Hyatts experienced trouble with the computer's components after they had used the computer for two months. What factors will a court consider in deciding whether to enforce the forum-selection clause? Would a court be likely to enforce the clause in this contract? Why or why not?
4. Are the Hyatts bound by the contract terms specified on CyberTool's "Terms of Service" page that they had not read? Which of the required elements for contract formation might the Hyatts claim was lacking? How might a court rule on this issue?

APPLICATION How Can You Find and Use Online Contract Forms?*

Before the printing press, every contract form had to be handwritten. Since the advent of printing, however, most standard contract forms have been readily available at low cost. Now the Internet has made available an even larger variety of contract forms, as well as other legal and business forms.

WHERE TO OBTAIN ONLINE CONTRACT FORMS

The 'Lectric Law Library has a collection of forms at http://www.lectlaw.com/form.html. The site includes forms for the assignment of a contract, a contract for the sale of a motor vehicle, and many others. In addition to actual forms, there are comments on how the forms should be used and filled out. Another excellent online resource for various types of forms is FindForms, at http://www.findforms.com.

Other online forms collections can be found at LegalWiz.com (go to http://www.legalwiz.com/forms.htm), a Web site that provides free legal forms, including a form that can be used to sell personal property. At http://www.legaldocs.com, you will find an electronic forms book that offers hundreds of standardized legal forms, some of which are free. Washburn University School of Law has a Web page containing links to an extensive number of forms archives at http://www.washlaw.edu/legalforms.

A special Web site for small-business owners is http://www.lawvantage.com/index.shtml. Some documents are free; others require a fee or an annual subscription. Many law firms post legal forms, including contract forms, on their Web sites. See, for example, the Web site of Bornstein & Naylor (at http://lbnlaw.com/Freedownload.htm).

Finally, a number of forms are available from FindLaw (now a part of West Group). Go to http://forms.lp.findlaw.com and scroll down the screen to "Other Form Resources."

CHECKLIST FOR THE ONLINE SELLER

1. When looking for a contract form appropriate to your business, "shop around" for a form that most closely meets your needs.
2. Consider customizing any standardized contract form that you use to ensure that it will cover all of the contingencies that you deem important.
3. When using a standardized contract form, make sure that you provide for a means of acceptance—for example, by including a box stating "I accept" or "I agree."
4. Consider posting your own customized contract forms on your Web site for prospective customers or others to use.

* This *Application* is not meant to substitute for the services of an attorney who is licensed to practice law in your state.

KEY TERMS

CHAPTER SUMMARY E-Contracts

Online Offers (See pages 402–404.)	Businesspersons who present contract offers via the Internet should keep in mind that the terms of the offer should be just as inclusive as the terms in an offer made in a written (paper) document. All possible contingencies should be anticipated and provided for in the offer. Because jurisdictional issues frequently arise with online transactions, it is particularly important to include dispute-settlement provisions in the offer, as well as a forum-selection clause. The offer should be displayed in an easily readable and clear format. An online offer should also include some mechanism, such as an "I agree" or "I accept" box, by which the customer may accept the offer.
Online Acceptances (See pages 404–409.)	1. *Shrink-wrap agreement*– a. Definition–An agreement whose terms are expressed inside a box in which the goods are packaged. The party who opens the box is informed that, by keeping the goods that are in the box, he or she agrees to the terms of the shrink-wrap agreement. b. Enforceability–The courts have often enforced shrink-wrap agreements, even if the purchaser-user of the goods did not read the terms of the agreement. A court may deem a shrink-wrap agreement unenforceable, however, if the buyer learns of the shrink-wrap terms *after* the parties entered into the agreement. 2. *Click-on agreement*– a. Definition–An agreement created when a buyer, completing a transaction on a computer, is required to indicate her or his assent to be bound by the terms of an offer by clicking on a button that says, for example, "I agree." The terms of the agreement may appear on the Web site through which the buyer is obtaining goods or services, or they may appear on a computer screen when software is downloaded. b. Enforceability–The courts have enforced click-on agreements, holding that by clicking "I agree," the offeree has indicated acceptance by conduct. Browse-wrap terms, however (terms in a license that an Internet user does not have to read prior to downloading the product, such as software), may not be enforced on the ground that the user is not made aware that he or she is entering into a contract.
E-Signatures (See pages 409–412.)	1. *Definition*–The Uniform Electronic Transactions Act (UETA) defines the term *e-signature* as "an electronic sound, symbol, or process attached to or logically associated with a record and executed or adopted by a person with the intent to sign the record." 2. *E-signature technologies*–These include the *asymmetric cryptosystem* (which creates a digital signature using two different cryptographic "keys"); *signature dynamics* (which involves capturing a sender's signature using a stylus and an electronic digitizer pad); a *smart card* (a device the size of a credit card that is embedded with code and other data); and, probably in the near future, scanned images of retinas, fingerprints, or other physical characteristics that are linked to numeric codes.

CHAPTER SUMMARY E-Contracts—Continued

E-Signatures—Continued	3. *State laws governing e-signatures*—Although most states have laws governing e-signatures, these laws are not uniform. The UETA provides for the validity of e-signatures and may ultimately create more uniformity among the states in this respect. 4. *Federal law on e-signatures and e-documents*—The Electronic Signatures in Global and National Commerce Act (E-SIGN Act) of 2000 gave validity to e-signatures by providing that no contract, record, or signature may be "denied legal effect" solely because it is in an electronic form.
Partnering Agreements (See pages 412–413.)	To reduce the likelihood that disputes will arise under their e-contracts, parties who frequently do business with each other may form a *partnering agreement.* In effect, the parties agree in advance on the terms and conditions that will apply to all transactions subsequently conducted electronically. The agreement can also establish access and identification codes to be used by the parties when transacting business electronically.
The Uniform Electronic Transactions Act (UETA) (See pages 413–416.)	1. *Definition*—A uniform act submitted to the states for adoption by the National Conference of Commissioners on Uniform State Laws (NCCUSL). 2. *Purpose*—To create rules to support the enforcement of e-contracts. Under the UETA, contracts entered into online, as well as other documents, are presumed to be valid. The UETA does not apply to transactions governed by the UCC or to wills or testamentary trusts.
The Uniform Computer Information Transactions Act (See page 416.)	1. *Definition*—A uniform act previously submitted to the states for adoption by the NCCUSL. The NCCUSL withdrew its support in 2003. 2. *Purpose*—To validate e-contracts to license or purchase software, or contracts that give access to—or allow the distribution of—computer information.

FOR REVIEW

Answers for the even-numbered questions in this For Review *section can be found on this text's accompanying Web site at* http://blt.westbuslaw.com. *Select "Chapter 17" and click on "For Review."*

1. What are some important clauses to include when making offers to form electronic contracts, or e-contracts?
2. How do shrink-wrap and click-on agreements differ from other contracts? How have traditional laws been applied to these agreements?
3. What is an electronic signature? Are electronic signatures valid?
4. What is a partnering agreement? What purpose does it serve?
5. What is the Uniform Electronic Transactions Act (UETA)? What are some of the major provisions of this act?

QUESTIONS AND CASE PROBLEMS

17–1. Click-On Agreements. Paul is a financial analyst for King Investments, Inc., a brokerage firm. He uses the Internet to investigate the background and activities of companies that might be good investments for King's customers. While visiting the Web site of Business Research, Inc., Paul sees on his screen a message that reads, "Welcome to businessresearch.com. By visiting our site, you have been entered as a subscriber to our e-publication, *Companies Unlimited*. This publication will be sent to you daily at a cost of $7.50 per week. An invoice will be included with *Companies Unlimited* every four weeks. You may cancel your subscription at any time." Has Paul entered into an enforceable contract to pay for *Companies Unlimited?* Why or why not?

17–2. Click-On Agreements. Anne is a reporter for *Daily Business Journal*, a print publication consulted by investors and other businesspersons. She often uses the Internet to perform research for the articles that she writes for the publication. While visiting the Web site of Cyberspace Investments Corp., Anne reads a pop-up window that states, "Our business newsletter, *E-Commerce Weekly*, is available at a one-year subscription rate of $5 per issue. To subscribe, enter your e-mail address below and click 'SUBSCRIBE.' By subscribing, you agree to the terms of the subscriber's agreement. To read this agreement, click 'AGREEMENT.' " Anne enters her e-mail address, but does not click on "AGREEMENT" to read the terms. Has Anne entered into an enforceable contract to pay for *E-Commerce Weekly?* Explain.

17–3. Online Acceptance. Bob, a sales representative for Central Computer Co., occasionally uses the Internet to obtain information about his customers and to look for new sales leads. While visiting the Web site of Marketing World, Inc., Bob is presented with an on-screen message that offers, "To improve your ability to make deals, read our monthly online magazine, *Sales Genius,* available at a subscription rate of $15 a month. To subscribe, fill in your name, company name, and e-mail address below, and click 'YES!' By clicking 'YES!' you agree to the terms of the subscription contract. To read this contract, click 'TERMS.'" Among those terms is a clause that allows Marketing World to charge interest for subscription bills not paid within a certain time. The terms also prohibit subscribers from copying or distributing part or all of *Sales Genius* in any form. Bob subscribes without reading the terms. Marketing World later files a suit against Bob, based on his failure to pay for his subscription. Should the court hold that Bob is obligated to pay interest on the amount? Explain.

17–4. Shrink-Wrap/Click-On Agreements. 1-A Equipment Co. signed a sales order to lease Accware 10 User NT software, which is made and marketed by ICode, Inc. Just above the signature line, the order stated: "Thank you for your order. No returns or refunds will be issued for software license and/or services. All sales are final. Please read the End User License and Service Agreement." The software was delivered in a sealed envelope inside a box. On the outside of the envelope, an "End User Agreement" provided in part, "BY OPENING THIS PACKAGING, CLICKING YOUR ACCEPTANCE OF THE AGREEMENT DURING DOWNLOAD OR INSTALLATION OF THIS PRODUCT, OR BY USING ANY PART OF THIS PRODUCT, YOU AGREE TO BE LEGALLY BOUND BY THE TERMS OF THE AGREEMENT. . . . This agreement will be governed by the laws in force in the Commonwealth of Virginia . . . and exclusive venue for any litigation shall be in Virginia." Later, dissatisfied with the software, 1-A filed a suit in a Massachusetts state court against ICode, alleging breach of contract and misrepresentation. ICode asked the court to dismiss the case on the basis of the "End User Agreement." Is the agreement enforceable? Should the court dismiss the suit? Why or why not? [*1-A Equipment Co. v. ICode, Inc.,* 43 UCC Rep.Serv.2d 807 (Mass.Dist. 2000)]

CASE PROBLEM WITH SAMPLE ANSWER

17–5. Peerless Wall & Window Coverings, Inc., is a small business in Pennsylvania. To run the cash registers in its stores, manage inventory, and link the stores electronically, in 1994 Peerless installed Point of Sale V6.5 software produced by Synchronics, Inc., a small corporation in Tennessee that develops and markets business software. Point of Sale V6.5 was written with code that used only a two-digit year field—for example, 1999 was stored as "99." This meant that all dates were interpreted as falling within the twentieth century (2001, stored as "01," would be mistaken for 1901). In other words, Point of Sale V6.5 was not "Year 2000" (Y2K) compliant. The software was licensed under a shrink-wrap agreement printed on the envelopes containing the disks. The agreement included a clause that, among other things, limited remedies to replacement within ninety days if there was a defect in the disks and stated, "The entire risk as to the quality and performance of the Software is with you." In 1995, Synchronics stopped selling and supporting Point of Sale V6.5. Two years later, Synchronics told Peerless that the software was not Y2K compliant and should be replaced. Peerless sued Synchronics in a federal district court, alleging, in part, breach of contract. Synchronics filed a motion for summary judgment. Who is more likely to bear the cost of replacing the software? Why? [*Peerless Wall & Window Coverings, Inc. v. Synchronics, Inc.,* 85 F.Supp.2d 519 (W.D.Pa. 2000), *aff'd* 234 F.3d 1265 (3d Cir. 2000)]

After you have answered this problem, compare your answer with the sample answer given on the Web site that accompanies this text. Go to http://blt.westbuslaw.com, select "Chapter 17," and click on "Case Problem with Sample Answer."

17–6. Click-On Agreements. America Online, Inc. (AOL), provided e-mail service to Walter Hughes and other members under a click-on agreement titled "Terms of Service." This agreement consisted of three parts: a "Member Agreement," "Community Guidelines," and a "Privacy Policy." The "Member Agreement" included a forum-selection clause that read, "You expressly agree that exclusive jurisdiction for any claim or dispute with AOL or relating in any way to your membership or your use of AOL resides in the courts of Virginia." When Officer Thomas McMenamon of the Methuen, Massachusetts, Police Department received threatening e-mail sent from an AOL account, he requested and obtained from AOL Hughes's name and other personal information. Hughes filed a suit in a federal district court against AOL, which filed a motion to dismiss on the basis of the forum-selection clause. Considering that the clause was a click-on provision, is it enforceable? Explain. [*Hughes v. McMenamon,* 204 F.Supp.2d 178 (D.Mass. 2002)]

17–7. Shrink-Wrap Agreements/Browse-Wrap Terms. Mary DeFontes bought a computer and a service contract from Dell Computers Corp. DeFontes was charged $950.51, of which $13.51 was identified on the invoice as "tax." This amount was paid to the state of Rhode Island. DeFontes and other Dell customers filed a suit in a Rhode Island state court against Dell, claiming that Dell was overcharging its customers by collecting a tax on service contracts and transportation costs. Dell asked the court to order DeFontes to submit the dispute to arbitration. Dell cited its "Terms and Conditions Agreement," which provides in part that by accepting delivery of Dell's products or services, a customer agrees to submit any dispute to arbitration. Customers can view this agreement through an inconspicuous link at the bottom of Dell's Web site, and Dell encloses a copy with an order when it is shipped. Dell argued that DeFontes accepted these terms by failing to return her purchase within thirty days, although the agreement did not state this. Is DeFontes bound to the "Terms and Conditions Agreement"? Should the court grant Dell's request? Why or why not? [*DeFontes v. Dell Computers Corp.*, __ A.2d __ (R.I. 2004)]

FOR CRITICAL ANALYSIS

17–8. Would you say that, on balance, most of the legal issues presented by e-commerce and e-contracting are unique to the cyber age, or are they simply old legal issues in a new form?

VIDEO QUESTION

17–9. Go to this text's Web site at http://blt.westbuslaw.com and select "Chapter 17." Click on "Video Questions" and view the video titled *E-Contracts: Agreeing Online*. Then answer the following questions.

1. According to the instructor in the video, what is the key factor in determining whether a particular term in an online agreement is enforceable?
2. Suppose that you click on "I accept" in order to download software from the Internet. You do not read the terms of the agreement before accepting it, even though you know that such agreements often contain forum-selection and arbitration clauses. The software later causes irreparable harm to your computer system, and you want to sue. When you go to the Web site and view the agreement, however, you discover that a choice-of-law clause in the contract specified that the law of Nigeria controls. Is this term enforceable? Is it a term that should reasonably be expected in an online contract?
3. Does it matter what the term actually says if it is a type of term that one could reasonably expect to be in the contract? What arguments can be made for and against enforcing a choice-of-law clause in an online contract?

INTERNET EXERCISES

Go to the *Business Law Today* home page at http://blt.westbuslaw.com, select "Chapter 17," and click on "Internet Exercises." There you will find the following Internet research exercises that you can perform to learn more about topics covered in this chapter.

Activity 17–1: LEGAL PERSPECTIVE—E-Contract Formation

Activity 17–2: MANAGEMENT PERSPECTIVE—E-Signatures

BEFORE THE TEST

Go to the *Business Law Today* home page at http://blt.westbuslaw.com, select "Chapter 17," and click on "Interactive Quizzes." You will find a number of interactive questions relating to this chapter.

MPACT Construction Group, LLC v. Superior Concrete Constructors, Inc.

We set out, in Chapter 8, some of the common law rules governing the interpretation of contracts. According to these principles, when the language of a written contract is clear, a court will enforce the terms without interpreting them further. If the writing is unclear or ambiguous, however, a court will apply the rules of interpretation to give effect to the parties' intent as expressed in their contract. Among these rules is the tenet that a contract will be interpreted as a whole. Also, a term that reasonably has more than one meaning will be interpreted against the party who drafted the contract. In this extended case study, we examine MPACT Construction Group, LLC v. Superior Concrete Constructors, Inc.,[1] *a recent decision in which these principles were applied.*

CASE BACKGROUND

MPACT Construction Group, Limited Liability Company (a *limited liability company* is a special form of business organization discussed in Chapter 31), entered into a contract with Flying J, Inc., to build a travel plaza in Gibson County, Indiana. The contract was an American Institute of Architects (AIA) "Standard Form Agreement Between Owner and Contractor." The form incorporated by reference the AIA "General Conditions of the Contract for Construction," which included an arbitration clause. To complete the project, MPACT entered into several contracts with subcontractors, including Superior Concrete Constructors, Inc. The subcontracts were not AIA forms but contracts that MPACT drafted.

When Flying J did not pay for all of the work, MPACT and some of the subcontractors filed mechanic's liens against Flying J. A *mechanic's lien* is a claim on real property that ensures payment for materials and work supplied to improve the property (see Chapter 26). Superior filed a suit based on its lien in an Indiana state court to collect the amount that it was owed. MPACT and others added claims based on their liens and on allegations of breach of contract. MPACT asked the court to order the parties to submit to arbitration under the clause referenced in the contract with Flying J. The court denied the request. MPACT appealed to a state intermediate appellate court, which affirmed the decision as to the subcontractors. MPACT appealed to the Indiana Supreme Court.

1. 802 N.E.2d 901 (Ind. 2004). This opinion may be accessed online at http://www.findlaw.com/11stategov/in/inca.html. On that page, in the "Supreme Court" section, in the "2004" row, click on "February." On the resulting page, click on the appropriate link accompanying the name of the case to access the opinion.

MAJORITY OPINION

SULLIVAN, Justice

* * * *

Whether MPACT and the Subcontractors agreed to arbitrate their disputes depends on whether the arbitration clause in the General Conditions of the General Contract was incorporated by reference into the subcontracts. * * *

* * * *

MPACT argues that [certain] provisions, and particularly the sentence, "The contract documents are complementary and what is required by any one shall be as binding as if required by all," [in the subcontracts' Article VI(b)] show that the General Conditions, which were incorporated into the General Contract between MPACT and Flying J, were incorporated into the subcontracts. The Subcontractors respond, and the Court of Appeals agreed, that provisions of the General Contract were incorporated for the limited purpose of governing the work to be performed. They emphasize that the sentence MPACT relies on is preceded and followed by sentences pertaining specifically to work, and that this limits the effect of that sentence.

* * * *

Courts are required to give effect to parties' contracts and to do so, courts look to the words of a contract. *In contracting, clarity of language is key.* * * * *When there is ambiguity in a contract, it is construed against its drafter.* In this instance, the AIA Standard Form of Agreement Between Contractor and Subcontractor was not used. MPACT instead drafted its own subcontracts. It was therefore MPACT's responsibility to ensure that its subcontracts * * * incorporated the arbitration clause. MPACT did not do so. [Emphasis added.]

The problem in this case seems to have resulted from poor contract drafting and inadequate contract negotiations. Each side believed at the time of contract execution that the contract provided for what it wanted—in MPACT's case, for arbitration, and in the Subcontractors' case, not for arbitration. *Regardless, it is clear that arbitration was not sufficiently discussed by the parties. This leads to one conclusion, that there was no meeting of the minds between the parties on the issue of arbitration.* Consequently, we find that there was no agreement to arbitrate between MPACT and the Subcontractors and the Subcontractors are not required to arbitrate their disputes with MPACT. [Emphasis added.]

MPACT also sought arbitration of its disputes with Flying J. The Court of Appeals found that the disputes were governed by the arbitration provision in the General Conditions of the General Contract, and held that MPACT was entitled to arbitration with Flying J. We summarily affirm the Court of Appeals on this point.

* * * *

We * * * affirm the trial court's denial of MPACT's motion as to the Subcontractors. This case is remanded to the trial court for further proceedings consistent with this opinion.[2]

2. The lower court's decision on remand was not yet available at the time this book went to press, but it may be by the time you read this. You may be able to locate the remanded decision online. See this text's inside front cover for URLs for online court decisions.

DISSENTING OPINION

BOEHM, J. [Justice], dissenting.

I respectfully dissent. * * * I believe * * * that these agreements do call for arbitration of the entire multiparty dispute among the owner, the general contractor, and these several subcontractors.

The agreement between the general contractor and the owner is a standard printed form AIA construction agreement. All agree that that contract includes an enforceable arbitration clause, and an undertaking to bind subcontractors to the same terms that obligate the general. The general's agreements with the subs provide that each sub acknowledges the principal agreement and agrees to be bound by it. The principal agreement provides [among other things] that the general will impose conforming conditions on all subs. These agreements are among businesses fully familiar with this sort of arrangement, and fully cognizant that the last thing either the general or the owner wants is piecemeal litigation with different subs. The result the majority reaches produces * * * arbitration between the owner and the general and litigation with one or more subs in a separate forum. The majority concedes that the general intended to bind the subs to arbitration, but points to imprecision in the language used to accomplish that. It seems to me that the subs did understand, or should have, that arbitration was intended. They should be held to have accepted arbitration when they accepted these agreements. Accordingly, I would require arbitration of this entire dispute in one proceeding.

* * * Particularly in an industry where arbitration is widely used, ambiguity does not necessarily lead to the conclusion that no meeting of the minds occurred. Rather, I would conclude that ambiguity should be construed in favor of finding an agreement to arbitrate where that is commonplace in the industry.

QUESTIONS FOR ANALYSIS

1 Law. What was the plaintiff's major argument? Why did the court conclude that this argument was invalid?

2 Law. Why did the dissent disagree with the majority's decision? What would have been the result if the dissent's opinion had prevailed in this case?

3 Ethics. What is an ethical basis for the majority's holding in this case? What is an ethical basis for the dissent's position?

4 Social Dimensions. Could the outcome in this case have a practical effect in the construction industry? If so, what are some of the possible advantages and disadvantages?

5 Implications for the Business Manager. How might the contracts in this case have been drafted to bind the subcontractors to arbitration?

UNIT THREE

SALES AND LEASE CONTRACTS

UNIT CONTENTS

CHAPTER 18

The Formation of Sales and Lease Contracts

"The great object of the law is to encourage commerce."

J. Chambre, 1739–1823
(British jurist)

CHAPTER OUTLINE

- THE SCOPE OF THE UCC
- THE SCOPE OF ARTICLE 2—SALES
- THE SCOPE OF ARTICLE 2A—LEASES
- THE FORMATION OF SALES AND LEASE CONTRACTS
- CONTRACTS FOR THE INTERNATIONAL SALE OF GOODS

LEARNING OBJECTIVES

After reading this chapter, you should be able to answer the following questions:

1. How do Article 2 and Article 2A of the UCC differ? What types of transactions does each article cover?
2. What is a merchant's firm offer?
3. If an offeree includes additional or different terms in an acceptance, will a contract result? If so, what happens to these terms?
4. Article 2 and Article 2A of the UCC both define several exceptions to the writing requirements of the Statute of Frauds. What are these exceptions?
5. What law governs contracts for the international sale of goods?

The opening quotation states that the object of the law is to encourage commerce. This is particularly true with respect to the Uniform Commercial Code (UCC). The UCC facilitates commercial transactions by making the laws governing sales and lease contracts uniform, clearer, simpler, and more readily applicable to the numerous difficulties that can arise during such transactions. Recall from Chapter 1 that the UCC is one of many uniform (model) acts drafted by the National Conference of Commissioners on Uniform State Laws and submitted to the states for adoption.[1] Once a state legislature has adopted a uniform act, the act becomes statutory law in that state. Thus, when we turn to sales and lease contracts, we move away from common law principles and into the area of statutory law.

We open this chapter with a discussion of the scope of the UCC's Article 2 (on sales) and Article 2A (on leases) as a background to the focus of this chapter, which

1. The UCC has been adopted in whole or in part by all of the states. Louisiana, however, has not adopted Articles 2 and 2A.

is the formation of contracts for the sale and lease of goods. Because international sales transactions are increasingly commonplace in the business world, we conclude this chapter with an examination of the United Nations Convention on Contracts for the International Sale of Goods (CISG), which governs international sales contracts.

The UCC was amended in 2003 to update its provisions to accommodate electronic commerce. As of 2005, the amendments to Articles 2 and 2A had not been adopted by any state. Throughout this chapter and the chapters that follow, however, any amendments that significantly change the UCC provisions now in effect in most states will be discussed in footnotes. Note, though, that even when the changes are not substantive, some of the section and subsection numbers may be slightly different under the amended Article 2 due to the addition of new provisions. (Excerpts from the 2003 amendments appear in Appendix C.)

The Scope of the UCC

The UCC attempts to provide a consistent and integrated framework of rules to deal with all phases ordinarily arising in a commercial sales transaction from start to finish. For example, consider the following events, all of which occur during a single sales transaction:

.on the Web To view the text of the UCC—and keep up to date on its various revisions—go to the Web site of the National Conference of Commissioners on Uniform State Laws (NCCUSL) at **http://www.nccusl.org**. Cornell University's Legal Information Institute also offers the full text of the UCC at **http://www.law.cornell.edu/uniform/ucc.html**.

1. *A contract for the sale or lease of goods is formed and executed.* Article 2 and Article 2A of the UCC provide rules governing all facets of this transaction.
2. *The transaction may involve a payment—by check, electronic fund transfer, or other means.* Article 3 (on negotiable instruments), Article 4 (on bank deposits and collections), Article 4A (on fund transfers), and Article 5 (on letters of credit) cover this part of the transaction.
3. *The transaction may involve a bill of lading or a warehouse receipt that covers goods when they are shipped or stored.* Article 7 (on documents of title) deals with this subject.
4. *The transaction may involve the demand by a seller or lender for some form of security for a remaining balance owed.* Article 9 (on secured transactions) covers this part of the transaction.

BE CAREFUL Although the UCC has been widely adopted without many changes, states have modified some of the details to suit their particular needs.

Two articles of the UCC seemingly do not address the "ordinary" commercial sales transaction. Article 6, on bulk transfers, has to do with merchants who sell off the major part of their inventory. Such bulk sales are not part of the ordinary course of business. Article 8, which covers investment securities, deals with transactions involving negotiable securities (stocks and bonds)—transactions that do not involve the sale of goods. The UCC's drafters, however, considered the subject matter of Articles 6 and 8 to be *sufficiently* related to commercial transactions to warrant its inclusion in the UCC. Excerpts from the most recent version of the UCC are included as Appendix C in this text.

The Scope of Article 2—Sales

SALES CONTRACT
A contract for the sale of goods under which the ownership of goods is transferred from a seller to a buyer for a price.

Article 2 of the UCC governs **sales contracts,** or contracts for the sale of goods. To facilitate commercial transactions, Article 2 modifies some of the common law contract requirements that were summarized in Chapter 8 and discussed in detail in

Chapters 9 through 15. To the extent that it has not been modified by the UCC, however, the common law of contracts also applies to sales contracts. In general, the rule is that when a UCC provision addresses a certain issue, the UCC governs; when the UCC is silent, the common law governs.

In regard to Article 2, you should keep in mind two things. First, Article 2 deals with the sale of *goods;* it does not deal with real property (real estate), services, or intangible property such as stocks and bonds. Thus, if the subject matter of a dispute is goods, the UCC governs. If it is real estate or services, the common law applies. The relationship between general contract law and the law governing sales of goods is illustrated in Exhibit 18–1. Second, in some cases, the rules may vary quite a bit, depending on whether the buyer or the seller is a merchant. We look now at how the UCC defines three important terms: *sale, goods,* and *merchant status.*

WHAT IS A SALE?

SALE
The passing of title to property from the seller to the buyer for a price.

TANGIBLE PROPERTY
Property that has physical existence and can be distinguished by the senses of touch, sight, and so on. A car is tangible property; a patent right is intangible property.

The UCC defines a **sale** as "the passing of title from the seller to the buyer for a price" [UCC 2–106(1)]. The price may be payable in money or in other goods or services.

WHAT ARE GOODS?

To be characterized as a *good,* the item of property must be *tangible,* and it must be *movable.*[2] **Tangible property** has physical existence—it can be touched or seen.

2. The 2003 amendments to Article 2 change the phrasing of this section slightly. The new section states that "goods must be both *existing* and *identified* before any interest in them may pass" [Amended UCC 2–105(1)].

EXHIBIT 18–1 LAW GOVERNING CONTRACTS

This exhibit graphically illustrates the relationship between general contract law and the law governing contracts for the sale of goods. Contracts for the sale of goods are not governed exclusively by Article 2 of the Uniform Commercial Code but are also governed by general contract law whenever it is relevant and has not been modified by the UCC.

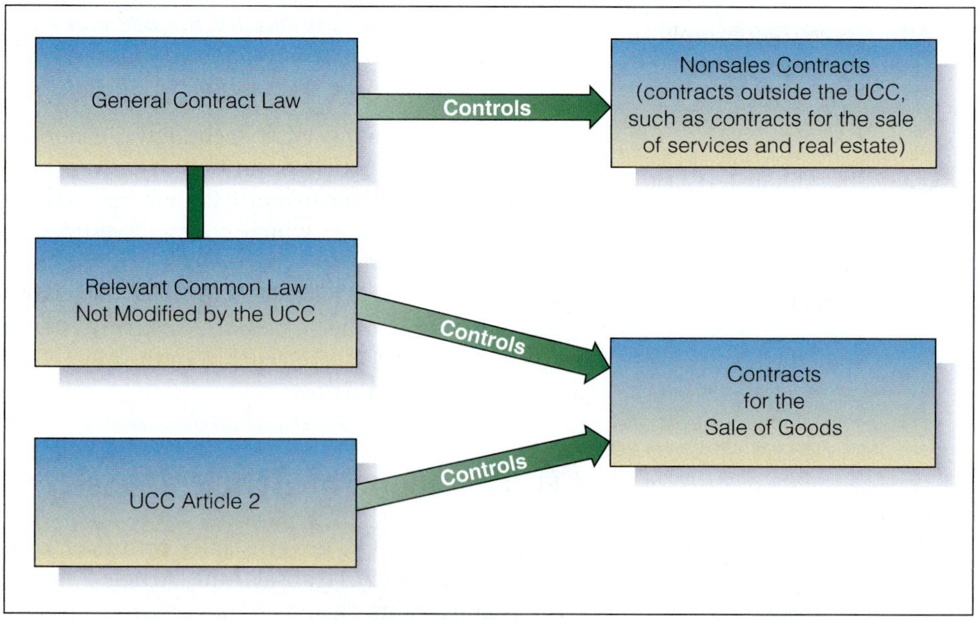

INTANGIBLE PROPERTY
Property that cannot be seen or touched but exists only conceptually, such as corporate stocks and bonds, patents and copyrights, and ordinary contract rights. Article 2 of the UCC does not govern intangible property.

Intangible property—such as corporate stocks and bonds, patents and copyrights, and ordinary contract rights—has only conceptual existence and thus does not come under Article 2.[3] A movable item can be carried from place to place. Hence, real estate is excluded from Article 2.

Two areas of dispute arise in determining whether the object of a contract is goods and thus whether Article 2 is applicable. One problem has to do with *goods associated with real estate,* such as crops or timber, and the other concerns contracts involving a *combination of goods and services.*

Goods Associated with Real Estate Goods associated with real estate often fall within the scope of Article 2. Section 2–107 provides the following rules:

1. A contract for the sale of minerals or the like (including oil and gas) or a structure (such as a building) is a contract for the sale of goods if *severance,* or *separation,* is to be made by the *seller.* If the *buyer* is to sever (separate) the minerals or structure from the land, the contract is considered to be a sale of real estate governed by the principles of real property law, not the UCC.
2. A sale of growing crops[4] (such as potatoes, carrots, wheat, and the like) or timber to be cut is considered to be a contract for the sale of goods *regardless of who severs them.*
3. Other "things attached" to realty but capable of severance without material harm to the land are considered goods *regardless of who severs them.*[5] "Things attached" that are severable without harm to realty could include such items as a heater, a window air conditioner in a house, and stools in a restaurant. Thus, removal of one of these things would be considered a sale of goods. The test is whether removal will cause substantial harm to the real property to which the item is attached.

Goods and Services Combined In cases in which goods and services are combined, courts disagree. For instance, is the blood furnished to a patient during an operation a "sale of goods" or the "performance of a medical service"? Some courts say it is a good; others say it is a service. Because the UCC does not provide the answers to such questions, the courts generally try to determine which factor is predominant—the good or the service. The UCC does stipulate, however, that serving food or drink to be consumed either on or off restaurant premises is a "sale of goods," at least for the purpose of an implied warranty of merchantability (to be explained in Chapter 21) [UCC 2–314(1)]. Other special transactions, including sales of unborn animals and rare coins, are also explicitly characterized as sales of goods by the UCC.

Whether the transaction in question involves the sale of goods or services is important because the majority of courts treat services as being excluded by the UCC. If the transaction is not covered by the UCC, then UCC provisions, including

---

3. The 2003 amendments to Article 2 specifically exclude "information" that is not associated with goods [Amended UCC 2–103(1)(k)]. Nevertheless, Article 2 *may* apply to transactions involving both goods and information when a sale involves "smart goods" (for example, a toy or automobile that contains computer programs). It is up to the courts to determine whether and to what extent the article should be applied to such transactions.
4. Note that the 2003 amendments moved the definition of goods to UCC 2–103(k), but growing crops are expressly included within the definition of *goods.* Contracts to sell timber, minerals, or structures to be removed from the land will continue to be controlled by UCC 2–107(1).
5. The UCC avoids the term *fixtures* here because of the numerous definitions of the word. A fixture is anything so firmly or permanently attached to land or to a building as to become a part of it. Once personal property becomes a fixture, it is governed by real estate law. See Chapter 44.

Sunflowers in bloom. Does Article 2 apply to the sale of sunflower seeds to a snack-foods company? Why or why not? (Telegraph Colour Library/Getty Images)

those relating to implied warranties, will not apply. ■ EXAMPLE 18.1 An Indiana company contracts to purchase customized software from Dharma Systems. The contract states that half of the purchase price is for Dharma Systems' professional services and the other half is for the goods (the software). If the court determines that the contract is predominantly for the software, rather than the services to customize the software, the court will hold that the transaction falls under Article 2.[6] ■

PREDOMINANT-FACTOR TEST
A test courts use to determine whether a contract is primarily for the sale of goods or for the sale of services.

The court in the following case applied the **predominant-factor test** to determine whether Article 2 applied to a contract that involved goods and services.

6. See *Micro Data Base Systems, Inc. v. Dharma Systems, Inc.*, 148 F.3d 649 (7th Cir. 1998).

CASE 18.1 Mécanique C.N.C., Inc. v. Durr Environmental, Inc.

United States District Court,
Southern District of Ohio, 2004.
304 F.Supp.2d 971.

BACKGROUND AND FACTS Durr Environmental, Inc., contracted with GE Quartz, Inc. (GE), to design, make, install, and test a selective catalytic reduction system at GE's plant in Hebron, Ohio. The system was to control the emission of nitrogen oxides. On August 3, 2000, Mécanique C.N.C., Inc. (CNC), sent a bid to Durr offering to make and install the ductwork necessary for the system and itemizing the price. Durr responded with a signed contract. CNC also signed the contract, added three handwritten terms in an attempt to avoid certain costs, and returned it. Durr revised the contract to include only one of the terms and sent it back to CNC. Durr also sent the project's specifications, which CNC met. When problems with the ductwork developed at GE's site, Durr submitted new specifications, which CNC also met, though at substantial added expense and with some delay. Nevertheless, CNC was on schedule to complete the work when, in March 2001, Durr terminated CNC. CNC filed a suit in a federal district court against Durr and others (the defendants), alleging in part breach of contract. One of the questions was whether Article 2 applied to the CNC contract. The defendants filed a motion for summary judgment on this point.

CASE 18.1—Continued

IN THE WORDS OF THE COURT . . .

MARBLEY, District Judge.

* * * *

* * * Article 2 of the UCC applies only to transactions in goods. Defendants contend that Article 2 applies here because the contract between Durr and CNC was predominantly a contract for the sale of goods. Plaintiff, on the other hand, asserts that the agreement was primarily a services contract.

* * * *[T]he test for the inclusion in or the exclusion from sales provisions is whether the predominant factor and purpose of the contract is the rendition of service, with goods incidentally involved, or whether the contract is for the sale of goods, with labor incidentally involved.* * * * [Emphasis added.]

* * * *

The Court concludes that the contract here was predominantly for the sale of goods, with services only incidentally involved. * * * [V]irtually all commercial goods involve some type of service, whether design, assembly, installation, or manufacture. Plaintiff's primary argument—that it devoted significant time and effort, both on and off of the Job Site, to providing fabrication and coating, as well as installation, services—thus is similar to an argument that could be made by virtually any manufacturer. Such an argument, of course, does not transform every contract for goods into a contract for services. The mere fact that a manufacturer utilizes its effort and expertise in producing a good does not mean that the buyer is purchasing those services instead of the good itself. *The question is whether the purchaser's ultimate goal is to acquire a product or procure a service.* At oral argument, Plaintiff's counsel conceded that, "at the end of the day," the purchaser's predominant purpose was to acquire an "operating good." The Court agrees. The installation service provided by Plaintiff, though extensive, was merely incidental to Durr's purpose of procuring the necessary ductwork. [Emphasis added.]

* * * *

Here, Plaintiff's compensation was tied to the goods produced rather than the labor provided. There was no separate price for installation. Though the good produced was a unique product created in accordance with specifications, CNC played no role in the design of the product. Even more significantly, the parties did not contemplate that CNC would be involved in any ongoing servicing or testing of the ductwork once it was installed. CNC's job was to provide a product in accordance with certain specifications. Once that product was created and installed, CNC had no further role. Durr's contract with GE might have been a contract for the provision of services, since Durr was involved in the design of the system and in coordinating the various pieces. What Durr sought to obtain from CNC, however, was primarily a good, with installation services being incidental.

For the foregoing reasons, Defendants have established that the UCC applies to the transaction between Durr and CNC.

DECISION AND REMEDY The court held that the contract between Durr and CNC was predominantly for a sale of goods, with services only incidentally involved. The court granted the defendants' motion for summary judgment.

WHY IS THIS CASE IMPORTANT? *This case illustrates how important it is to anticipate the factors that courts consider in determining whether Article 2 of the UCC applies. For example, even though the purchase of a product may appear to be a purchase of goods, if the contract also provides for installing and modifying the product, a court might construe the contract as predominantly for services. For the buyer, this would mean that the UCC does not apply, which may be a very important consideration in some transactions.*

Cornell University's Legal Information Institute offers online access to the UCC as enacted in several of the states at **http://www.law.cornell.edu/statutes.html#state**.

WHO IS A MERCHANT?

Article 2 governs the sale of goods in general. It applies to sales transactions between all buyers and sellers. In a limited number of instances, however, the UCC presumes that certain special business standards ought to be imposed on merchants because they possess a relatively high degree of commercial expertise.[7] Such standards do not apply to the casual or inexperienced seller or buyer ("consumer"). Section 2–104 defines three ways in which merchant status can arise:

1. A merchant is a person who *deals in goods of the kind* involved in the sales contract. Thus, a retailer, a wholesaler, or a manufacturer is a merchant of those goods sold in the business. A merchant for one type of goods is not necessarily a merchant for another type. For example, a sporting equipment retailer is a merchant when selling tennis equipment but not when selling a used computer.
2. A merchant is a person who, by occupation, holds himself or herself out as having knowledge and skill unique to the practices or goods involved in the transaction. Note that this broad definition may include banks or universities as merchants.
3. A person who *employs a merchant as a broker, agent, or other intermediary* has the status of merchant in that transaction. Hence, if a "gentleman farmer" who ordinarily does not run the farm hires a broker to purchase or sell livestock, the farmer is considered a merchant in the transaction.

MERCHANT
A person who is engaged in the purchase and sale of goods. Under the UCC, a person who deals in goods of the kind involved in the sales contract or who holds herself or himself out as having skill or knowledge peculiar to the practices or use of the goods being purchased or sold. For definitions, see UCC 2–104.

In summary, a person is a **merchant** when she or he, acting in a mercantile capacity, possesses or uses an expertise specifically related to the goods being sold. This basic distinction is not always clear-cut. For example, courts in most states have determined that farmers may be merchants if they sell products or livestock on a regular basis, but courts in other states have held that the drafters of the UCC did not intend to include farmers as merchants.

The Scope of Article 2A—Leases

In the past few decades, leases of personal property (goods) have become increasingly common. Article 2A of the UCC was created to fill the need for uniform guidelines in this area. Article 2A covers any transaction that creates a lease of goods, as well as subleases of goods [UCC 2A–102, 2A–103(1)(k)]. Except that it applies to leases of goods, rather than sales of goods, Article 2A is essentially a repetition of Article 2 and varies only to reflect differences between sale and lease transactions. (Note that Article 2A is not concerned with leases of real property, such as land or buildings. The laws governing these types of transactions will be examined in Chapter 44.) As previously mentioned, Article 2A was also amended in 2003, and these amendments have been recommended to the states for adoption.

DEFINITION OF A LEASE

LEASE AGREEMENT
In regard to the lease of goods, an agreement in which one person (the lessor) agrees to transfer the right to the possession and use of property to another person (the lessee) in exchange for rental payments.

Article 2A defines a **lease agreement** as a lessor and lessee's bargain with respect to the lease of goods, as found in their language and as implied by other circumstances, including course of dealing and usage of trade or course of performance [UCC

7. The provisions that apply only to merchants deal principally with the Statute of Frauds, firm offers, confirmatory memoranda, warranties, and contract modification. These special rules reflect expedient business practices commonly known to merchants in the commercial setting. They will be discussed later in this chapter.

Ho
sto

roa
the
vis
In
abl
to s
sha

our
cor
$1(
one
Sta
we
onl

cof
cre

eve

Pho

LESSOR
A person who sells the right to the possession and use of goods to another in exchange for rental payments.

LESSEE
A person who acquires the right to the possession and use of another's goods in exchange for rental payments.

2A–103(1)(k)]. A **lessor** is one who sells the right to the possession and use of goods under a lease [UCC 2A–103(1)(p)]. A **lessee** is one who acquires the right to the temporary possession and use of goods under a lease [UCC 2A–103(1)(o)]. In other words, the lessee is the party who is leasing the goods from the lessor. Article 2A applies to all types of leases of goods, including commercial leases and consumer leases. Special rules apply to certain types of leases, however, including consumer leases and finance leases.

CONSUMER LEASES

A *consumer lease* involves three elements: (1) a lessor who regularly engages in the business of leasing or selling; (2) a lessee (except an organization) who leases the goods "primarily for a personal, family, or household purpose"; and (3) total lease payments that are less than a dollar amount set by state statute [UCC 2A–103(1)(e)].[8] In the interest of providing special protection for consumers, certain provisions of Article 2A apply only to consumer leases. For example, one provision states that a consumer may recover attorneys' fees if a court finds that a term in a consumer lease contract is unconscionable [UCC 2A–108(4)(a)].

FINANCE LEASES

A *finance lease* involves a lessor, a lessee, and a supplier. The lessor buys or leases goods from a supplier and leases or subleases them to the lessee [UCC 2A–103(1)(g)].[9] Typically, in a finance lease, the lessor is simply financing the transaction. ■ EXAMPLE 18.2 Suppose that Marlin Corporation wants to lease a crane for use in its construction business. Marlin's bank agrees to purchase the equipment from Jennco, Inc., and lease the equipment to Marlin. In this situation, the bank is the lessor-financer, Marlin is the lessee, and Jennco is the supplier. ■

Article 2A, unlike ordinary contract law, makes the lessee's obligations under a commercial finance lease irrevocable and independent from the financer's obligations [UCC 2A–407]. In other words, the lessee must perform and continue to make lease payments even if the leased equipment turns out to be defective. The lessee must look almost entirely to the supplier for warranties.

The Formation of Sales and Lease Contracts

In regard to the formation of sales and lease contracts, the UCC modifies the common law in several ways. We look here at how Article 2 and Article 2A of the UCC modify common law contract rules. Remember, though, that parties to sales contracts are free to establish whatever terms they wish. The UCC comes into play only when the parties have failed to provide in their contract for a contingency that later gives rise to a dispute. The UCC makes this clear time and again by using such phrases as "unless the parties otherwise agree" or "absent a contrary agreement by the parties."

OFFER

In general contract law, the moment a definite offer is met by an unqualified acceptance, a binding contract is formed. In commercial sales transactions, the verbal

8. The 2003 amendments to Article 2A define a consumer lease in UCC 2A–103(1)(f). The amended section leaves it up to the states to decide whether to place a dollar limitation on the total lease payments.
9. Finance leases are defined in UCC 2A–103(1)(g) of the amended Article 2A.

NOTE Under the UCC, it is the actions of the parties that determine whether they intended to form a contract.

exchanges, correspondence, and actions of the parties may not reveal exactly when a binding contractual obligation arises. The UCC states that an agreement sufficient to constitute a contract can exist even if the moment of its making is undetermined [UCC 2–204(2), 2A–204(2)].

Open Terms Remember from Chapter 9 that under the common law of contracts, an offer must be definite enough for the parties (and the courts) to ascertain its essential terms when it is accepted. In contrast, the UCC states that a sales or lease contract will not fail for indefiniteness even if one or more terms are left open as long as (1) the parties intended to make a contract and (2) there is a reasonably certain basis for the court to grant an appropriate remedy [UCC 2–204(3), 2A–204(3)].

■ EXAMPLE 18.3 Mike agrees to lease from CompuQuik a highly specialized computer work station. Mike and one of CompuQuik's sales representatives sign a lease agreement that leaves some of the details blank, to be "worked out" the following week, when the leasing manager will be back from her vacation. In the meantime, CompuQuik obtains the necessary equipment from one of its suppliers and spends several days modifying the equipment to suit Mike's needs. When the leasing manager returns, she calls Mike and tells him that his work station is ready. Mike says he is no longer interested in the work station, as he has arranged to lease the same type of equipment for a lower price from another firm. CompuQuik sues Mike to recover its costs in obtaining and modifying the equipment, and one of the issues before the court is whether the parties had an enforceable contract. The court will likely hold that they did, based on their intent and conduct, despite the "blanks" in their written agreement. ■

Relative to the common law of contracts, the UCC has radically lessened the requirement of definiteness of terms. Keep in mind, though, that the more terms left open, the less likely it is that a court will find that the parties intended to form a contract.

Open Price Term. If the parties have not agreed on a price, the court will determine a "reasonable price at the time for delivery" [UCC 2–305(1)]. If either the buyer or the seller is to determine the price, the price is to be fixed (set) in good faith [UCC 2–305(2)]. Under the UCC, good faith means honesty in fact and the observance of reasonable commercial standards of fair dealing in the trade [UCC 2–103(1)(b)]. The concepts of *good faith* and *commercial reasonableness* permeate the UCC.

CONTRAST The common law requires that the parties make their terms definite before they have a contract. The UCC applies general commercial standards to make the terms of a contract definite.

Sometimes the price fails to be fixed through the fault of one of the parties. In that situation, the other party can treat the contract as canceled or fix a reasonable price. ■ EXAMPLE 18.4 Perez and Merrick enter into a contract for the sale of unfinished doors and agree that Perez will determine the price. Perez refuses to fix the price. Merrick can either treat the contract as canceled or set a reasonable price [UCC 2–305(3)]. ■

Open Payment Term. When parties do not specify payment terms, payment is due at the time and place at which the buyer is to receive the goods [UCC 2–310(a)]. The buyer can tender payment using any commercially normal or acceptable means, such as a check or credit card. If the seller demands payment in cash, however, the buyer must be given a reasonable time to obtain it [UCC 2–511(2)]. This is especially important when the contract states a definite and final time for performance.

ETHICAL ISSUE 18.1

Is it fair for the UCC to impose payment terms when the parties did not agree to these terms? Many people buy and sell goods all the time in their daily lives without knowing what the UCC is or how it may apply to their transactions. Is it fair for the UCC to impose terms that the parties never discussed when forming their contract?

Consider, for example, a simple transaction that took place on a farm. Max Alexander agreed to purchase hay from Wagner's farm. Alexander left his truck and trailer at the farm for the seller to load the hay. Nothing was said about when payment was due, and the parties were unaware of the UCC's rules. When Alexander came back to get the hay, a dispute broke out. Alexander claimed that he was not given the quantity of hay that he had ordered and argued that he did not have to pay at that time. Wagner refused to release the hay (or the vehicles on which the hay was loaded) until Alexander paid for it.

Eventually, Alexander jumped into his truck and drove off without paying for the hay. When Alexander was later prosecuted for the crime of theft (see Chapter 6), he claimed that he could not be guilty of taking the property of another because he had bought the hay and was the rightful owner. The court, however, disagreed. Because the parties had failed to specify when payment was due, the court held that UCC 2–310(a) controlled: payment was due at the time Alexander picked up the hay. Thus, Alexander's theft conviction was affirmed.[10] ■

Open Delivery Term. When no delivery terms are specified, the buyer normally takes delivery at the seller's place of business [UCC 2–308(a)]. If the seller has no place of business, the seller's residence is used. When goods are located in some other place and both parties know it, delivery is made there. If the time for shipment or delivery is not clearly specified in the sales contract, the court will infer a "reasonable" time for performance [UCC 2–309(1)].

Duration of an Ongoing Contract. A single contract might specify successive performances but not indicate how long the parties are required to deal with each other. In this situation, either party may terminate the ongoing contractual relationship. Principles of good faith and sound commercial practice call for reasonable notification before termination, however, to give the other party reasonable time to seek a substitute arrangement [UCC 2–309(2), (3)].

Options and Cooperation regarding Performance. When the contract contemplates shipment of the goods but does not specify the shipping arrangements, the *seller* has the right to make these arrangements in good faith, using commercial reasonableness in the situation [UCC 2–311].

When a sales contract omits terms relating to the assortment of goods, the *buyer* can specify the assortment. ■ EXAMPLE 18.5 Petry Drugs, Inc., agrees to purchase one thousand toothbrushes from Marconi's Dental Supply. The toothbrushes come in a variety of colors, but the contract does not specify color. Petry, the buyer, has the right to take six hundred blue toothbrushes and four hundred green ones if it wishes. Petry, however, must exercise good faith and commercial reasonableness in making its selection [UCC 2–311]. ■

10. *State v. Alexander,* 186 Or.App. 600, 64 P.3d 1148 (2003).

Open Quantity Term. Normally, if the parties do not specify a quantity, a court will have no basis for determining a remedy. The UCC recognizes two exceptions, however, in requirements and output contracts [UCC 2–306(1)].

REQUIREMENTS CONTRACT
An agreement in which a buyer agrees to purchase and the seller agrees to sell all or up to a stated amount of what the buyer needs or requires.

In a **requirements contract,** the buyer agrees to purchase and the seller agrees to sell all or up to a stated amount of what the buyer *needs* or *requires.* ■ EXAMPLE 18.6 Umpqua Cannery forms a contract with Al Garcia. The cannery agrees to purchase from Garcia, and Garcia agrees to sell to the cannery, all of the green beans that the cannery needs or requires during the summer of 2007. ■ There is implicit consideration in a requirements contract because the buyer (the cannery, in this situation) gives up the right to buy green beans from any other seller, and this forfeited right creates a legal detriment (that is, consideration). Requirements contracts are common in the business world and are normally enforceable. If, however, the buyer promises to purchase only if the buyer *wishes* to do so, or if the buyer reserves the right to buy the goods from someone other than the seller, the promise is illusory (without consideration) and unenforceable by either party.

OUTPUT CONTRACT
An agreement in which a seller agrees to sell and a buyer agrees to buy all or up to a stated amount of what the seller produces.

In an **output contract,** the seller agrees to sell and the buyer agrees to buy all or up to a stated amount of what the seller *produces.* ■ EXAMPLE 18.7 Al Garcia forms a contract with Umpqua Cannery. Garcia agrees to sell to the cannery, and the cannery agrees to purchase from Garcia, all of the beans that Garcia produces on his farm during the summer of 2007. ■ Again, because the seller essentially forfeits the right to sell goods to another buyer, there is implicit consideration in an output contract.

The UCC imposes a *good faith limitation* on requirements and output contracts. The quantity under such contracts is the amount of requirements or the amount of output that occurs during a *normal* production year. The actual quantity purchased or sold cannot be unreasonably disproportionate to normal or comparable prior requirements or output [UCC 2–306].

Merchant's Firm Offer Under regular contract principles, an offer can be revoked at any time before acceptance. The major common law exception is an *option contract* (discussed in Chapter 9), in which the offeree pays consideration for the offeror's irrevocable promise to keep the offer open for a stated period. The UCC creates a second exception for firm offers made by a merchant to sell, buy, or lease goods.

FIRM OFFER
An offer (by a merchant) that is irrevocable without consideration for a stated period of time or, if no definite period is stated, for a reasonable time (neither period to exceed three months). A firm offer by a merchant must be in writing and must be signed by the offeror.

A **firm offer** arises when a merchant-offeror gives *assurances* in a *signed writing* that the offer will remain open. The merchant's firm offer is irrevocable without the necessity of consideration[11] for the stated period or, if no definite period is stated, a reasonable period (neither period to exceed three months) [UCC 2–205, 2A–205]. ■ EXAMPLE 18.8 Osaka, a used-car dealer, writes a letter to Saucedo on January 1 stating, "I have a 2004 Pontiac on the lot that I'll sell you for $8,500 any time between now and January 31." This writing creates a firm offer, and Osaka will be liable for breach if he sells the Pontiac to someone other than Saucedo before January 31. ■

It is necessary that the offer be both *written* and *signed* by the offeror.[12] When a firm offer is contained in a form contract prepared by the offeree, the offeror must also sign a separate firm offer assurance. This requirement ensures that the offeror is aware of the offer. If the firm offer is buried amid copious language in one of the

11. If the offeree pays consideration, then an option contract (not a merchant's firm offer) is formed.
12. "Signed" includes any symbol executed or adopted by a party with a present intention to authenticate a writing [UCC 1–201(39)]. A complete signature is not required. Therefore, initials, a thumbprint, a trade name, or any mark used in lieu of a written signature will suffice, regardless of its location on the document.

pages of the offeree's form contract, the offeror may inadvertently sign the contract without realizing that it contains a firm offer, thus defeating the purpose of the rule—which is to give effect to a merchant's deliberate intent to be bound to a firm offer.

Acceptance

BE AWARE The UCC's rules on means of acceptance illustrate the UCC's flexibility. The rules have been adapted to new forms of communication, such as faxes and online communications.

The following subsections examine the UCC's provisions governing acceptance. As you will see, acceptance of an offer to buy, sell, or lease goods generally may be made in any reasonable manner and by any reasonable means.

Methods of Acceptance The general common law rule is that an offeror can specify, or authorize, a particular means of acceptance, making that means the only one effective for contract formation. Even an unauthorized means of communication is effective, however, as long as the acceptance is received by the specified deadline. ■ **Example 18.9** Janel offers to sell her Humvee to Arik for $48,000. The offer states, "Answer by fax within five days." If Arik sends a letter, and Janel receives it within five days, a valid contract is formed, nonetheless. ■

Any Reasonable Means. When the offeror does not specify a means of acceptance, the UCC provides that acceptance can be made by any means of communication reasonable under the circumstances [UCC 2–206(1), 2A–206(1)]. This broadens the common law rules concerning authorized means of acceptance. (For a review of the requirements relating to mode and timeliness of acceptance, see Chapter 9.)

■ **Example 18.10** Anodyne Corporation writes Bethlehem Industries a letter offering to lease $1,000 worth of postage meters. The offer states that Anodyne will keep the offer open for only ten days from the date of the letter. Before the ten days elapse, Bethlehem sends Anodyne an acceptance by fax. Is a valid contract formed? The answer is yes, because acceptance by fax is a commercially reasonable medium of acceptance under the circumstances. Acceptance is effective on Bethlehem's transmission of the fax, which occurred before the offer lapsed. ■

Promise to Ship or Prompt Shipment. The UCC permits a seller to accept an offer to buy goods "either by a prompt *promise* to ship or by the prompt or current shipment of conforming or nonconforming goods" [UCC 2–206(1)(b)]. *Conforming* goods are goods that accord with the contract's terms; *nonconforming* goods do not. The seller's prompt shipment of *nonconforming goods* in response to the offer constitutes both an acceptance (a contract) and a *breach* of that contract.

SEASONABLY
Within a specified time period or, if no period is specified, within a reasonable time.

This rule does not apply if the seller **seasonably** (within a reasonable amount of time) notifies the buyer that the nonconforming shipment is offered only as an *accommodation,* or as a favor. The notice of accommodation must clearly indicate to the buyer that the shipment does not constitute an acceptance and that, therefore, no contract has been formed.

■ **Example 18.11** McFarrell Pharmacy orders five cases of Johnson & Johnson 3-by-5-inch gauze pads from Halderson Medical Supply, Inc. If Halderson ships five cases of Xeroform 3-by-5-inch gauze pads instead, the shipment acts as both an acceptance of McFarrell's offer and a *breach* of the resulting contract. McFarrell may sue Halderson for any appropriate damages. If, however, Halderson notifies McFarrell that the Xeroform gauze pads are being shipped *as an accommodation*—because Halderson has only Xeroform pads in stock—the shipment will constitute a counteroffer, not an acceptance. A contract will be formed only if McFarrell accepts the Xeroform gauze pads. ■

Communication of Acceptance Under the common law, because acceptance of a unilateral contract is usually evident by performance, the offeree normally is not required to notify the offeror of the acceptance (see Chapter 9). The UCC changes this common law rule. According to the UCC, when "the beginning of requested performance is a reasonable mode of acceptance, an offeror who is not notified of acceptance within a reasonable time may treat the offer as having lapsed before acceptance" [UCC 2–206(2), 2A–206(2)].

■ EXAMPLE 18.12 Lee writes to Pickwick Bookstore on Monday, "Please send me a copy of *Webster's New College Dictionary* for $25.55, C.O.D.," and signs it, "Lee." Pickwick receives the request but does not ship the book for four weeks. When the book arrives, Lee rejects it, claiming that it has arrived too late to be of value. In this situation, because Lee had heard nothing from Pickwick for a month, he was justified in assuming that the store did not intend to deliver the book. Lee could consider that the offer had lapsed because of the length of time Pickwick delayed shipment. ■

Additional Terms Under the common law, if Alderman makes an offer to Beale, and Beale in turn accepts but in the acceptance makes some slight modification to the terms of the offer, there is no contract. Recall from Chapter 9 that the so-called *mirror image rule* requires that the terms of the acceptance exactly match those of the offer. The UCC, however, dispenses with the mirror image rule. The UCC generally takes the position that if the offeree's response indicates a *definite* acceptance of the offer, a contract is formed even if the acceptance includes additional or different terms from those contained in the offer [UCC 2–207(1)]. What happens to these additional terms? The answer to this question depends, in part, on whether the parties are nonmerchants or merchants.[13]

Rules When One Party or Both Parties Are Nonmerchants. If one (or both) of the parties is a *nonmerchant,* the contract is formed according to the terms of the original offer submitted by the original offeror and not according to the additional terms of the acceptance [UCC 2–207(2)]. ■ EXAMPLE 18.13 Tolsen offers in writing to sell his personal computer, printer, and scanner to Valdez for $1,500. Valdez faxes a reply to Tolsen stating, "I accept your offer to purchase your computer, printer, and scanner for $1,500. I would like a box of laser printer paper and two extra toner cartridges to be included in the purchase price." Valdez has given Tolsen a definite expression of acceptance (creating a contract), even though the acceptance also suggests an added term for the offer. Because Tolsen is not a merchant, the additional term is merely a proposal (suggestion), and Tolsen is not legally obligated to comply with that term. ■

DON'T FORGET The UCC recognizes that a proposed deal is a contract if, in commercial understanding, the deal has been closed.

Rules When Both Parties Are Merchants. In contracts *between merchants,* the additional terms automatically become part of the contract unless (1) the original offer expressly limits acceptance to the terms of the offer, (2) the new or changed terms *materially* alter the contract, or (3) the offeror objects to the new or changed terms within a reasonable period of time [UCC 2–207(2)].

13. The 2003 amendments to Article 2 do not distinguish between merchants and others in setting out rules for the effect of additional terms in sales contracts. Instead, a court is directed to determine whether (1) the terms appear in the records of both parties, (2) both parties agree to the terms even if they are not in a record, or (3) the terms are supplied or incorporated under another provision of Article 2 [Amended UCC 2–207]. Basically, the amendments give the courts more discretion to include or exclude certain additional terms.

What constitutes a material alteration is frequently a question that only a court can decide. Generally, if the modification involves no unreasonable element of surprise or hardship for the offeror, the court will hold that the modification did not materially alter the contract. The issue in the following case concerned whether an additional term in the acceptance (subjecting any disputes to arbitration) constituted a material alteration of the contract terms.

Featured Case

CASE 18.2 Wilson Fertilizer & Grain, Inc. v. ADM Milling Co.

Court of Appeals of Indiana, 1995.
654 N.E.2d 848.

MAJORITY OPINION

***BARTEAU,* Judge.**

FACTS

Wilson [Fertilizer & Grain, Inc.] and ADM [Milling Company] entered into a contract under which Wilson shipped grain to ADM. A broker facilitated the deal between Wilson and ADM, and sent each party a confirmation of trade. The confirmation of trade did not contain an arbitration provision. ADM sent a purchase confirmation to Wilson that contained boiler plate language which states: "This contract is also subject to the Trade Rules of the National Grain and Feed Association currently in effect." Wilson did not object to this language and did not respond to ADM's purchase confirmation.

A dispute arose under the contract and Wilson filed suit against ADM in [an Indiana state court]. ADM moved to dismiss the action, claiming that the Trade Rules of the National Grain and Feed Association require the parties to arbitrate the dispute. Wilson argued that the arbitration provisions were not included within the terms of its agreement with ADM. The trial court granted ADM's motion and ordered the parties to arbitration.

DISCUSSION

A party seeking to compel arbitration must satisfy a two-prong burden of proof. First, the party must demonstrate an enforceable agreement to arbitrate the dispute. Second, the party must prove that the disputed matter is the type of claim that the parties agreed to arbitrate. In this case, the second prong of our analysis is not in dispute, since neither party contends that the arbitration provisions do not encompass Wilson's claim. The only question presented herein is under the first prong: whether the additional terms are included in the contract between Wilson and ADM.

Whether the additional provisions are part of the contract is controlled by [Indiana Code Section 26-1-2-207, Indiana's version of UCC 2–207], which provides in part:

> (1) A definite and seasonable expression of acceptance or a written confirmation which is sent within a reasonable time operates as an acceptance even though it states terms additional to or different from those offered or agreed upon, unless acceptance is expressly made conditional on assent to the additional or different terms.
> (2) The additional terms are to be construed as proposals for addition to the contract. Between merchants such terms become part of the contract unless:
> (a) the offer expressly limits acceptance to the terms of the offer;
> (b) they materially alter it; or
> (c) notification of objection to them has already been given or is given within a reasonable time after notice of them is received.

* * * *

The test for whether additional terms materially alter an agreement is whether their incorporation into the contract without express awareness by the other party would result in surprise or hardship. * * *

Some jurisdictions that have considered this issue have adopted the "New York rule" holding that additional arbitration provisions create a material alteration *per se.* This rule is based on New York's well-established law that parties will not be compelled to arbitrate in the absence of an express, unequivocal agreement to that effect; absent such an explicit commitment neither party may be compelled to arbitrate. * * *

* * * Wilson argues that we should follow the New York rule and find that * * * ADM's additional arbitration provisions materially alter the agreement as a matter of law.

* * * *

(Continued)

CASE 18.2—Continued

* * * [W]e reject Wilson's argument * * * and decline to adopt the New York rule. Instead, whether included arbitration provisions result in hardship or surprise depends upon the facts and circumstances of each case. * * *

* * * *

* * * [R]equiring a party to arbitrate a dispute does not *necessarily* place a hardship on the party. To the contrary, arbitration may work to the party's benefit by facilitating an efficient and potentially favorable resolution to a dispute. Many trades employ arbitration as a usual and customary dispute resolution mechanism. In light of this, even New York courts have deviated from their *per se* rule and have held that *an additional arbitration clause is not a material alteration if the party had reason to know that such a clause was customarily used in the trade.* [Emphasis added.]

* * * *

Turning to the facts presented, Wilson argues that the trial court erroneously determined that the additional provisions did not materially alter its agreement with ADM because the evidence conclusively shows that inclusion of the provisions imposes hardship on Wilson. Specifically, Wilson argues that the National Grain and Feed Association Rules of Arbitration significantly reduce the time period during which it may file its complaint against ADM from Indiana's six-year statute of limitation to one year. Wilson argues that this results in hardship because, now that its claim has been dismissed * * *, time has run for Wilson to file its claim under the arbitration rules. We disagree for two reasons.

First of all, contractually reducing the time period during which parties may bring complaints is permitted under the Uniform Commercial Code. * * * [The UCC] specifically permits parties to a contract for sale to reduce the time for filing claims to one year, and Wilson has not shown that the one-year limitation is not within the customary limits of the trade.

Second, and even more significantly, we are persuaded by Wilson's apparent ability to have submitted its claim for arbitration within the one-year limit. The contract between Wilson and ADM was formed on October 20, 1992. There is nothing in the record indicating when Wilson delivered its grain to ADM, or when ADM's alleged breach occurred. However, Wilson filed its complaint for damages in * * * on September 24, 1993, within one year after the contract was formed. Thus, Wilson filed its complaint within one year after the cause of action accrued because, as a matter of logic, an action for breach of contract can only accrue after the contract was formed. If Wilson was able to file its complaint in court within one year after the cause of action accrued, we fail to see how a contract provision requiring Wilson to submit its claim for arbitration in the same time period imposes a hardship.

* * * *

The trial court's finding that the additional term in ADM's purchase confirmation did not materially alter the agreement is supported by the evidence and is not clearly erroneous.

AFFIRMED.

DISSENTING OPINION

***KIRSCH*, Judge, * * * dissenting.**

I fully concur with the rule of law set forth in the majority opinion. From its application to the facts of this case, however, I respectfully dissent.

* * * *

* * * [T]here are two factual issues which should be determined by the trial court: The first issue is whether ADM's confirmation even constituted an acceptance within the meaning of UCC [Section] 2–207. If the confirmation sent by the broker to Wilson was sent prior to ADM's confirmation, it constitutes the acceptance of the offer; the contract was fully formed by that confirmation. The later confirmation sent by ADM would only be a proposal to modify the contract as formed and UCC [Section] 2–207 would not apply. Second, even if ADM's confirmation constitutes the acceptance and [Section] 2–207 does apply, there is an unresolved question of fact as to whether the additional term contained in such confirmation results in hardship or surprise and thus constitutes a material alteration. In either event, these unresolved factual issues make the dismissal of this case inappropriate.

ADM Milling Company played the latest version of "Legal Gotcha." And it won. It has received the grain which it ordered and escaped paying for it.

I would reverse the dismissal and remand to the trial court to conduct an evidentiary hearing.

TEST YOUR COMPREHENSION: CASE DETAILS

1. What was the issue that the Indiana state intermediate appellate court was asked to decide in this case?
2. Did the court rule in favor of the plaintiff or the defendant? Why?
3. What was the dissent's view on the central issue in this case?
4. Why does it matter whether the arbitration clause in ADM's confirmation "materially altered" the contract with Wilson?
5. How does a court determine when an additional term in an acceptance "materially alters" the contract?

Conditioned on Offeror's Assent. Regardless of merchant status, the UCC provides that the offeree's expression cannot be construed as an acceptance if it contains additional or different terms that are explicitly conditioned on the offeror's assent to those terms [UCC 2–207(1)]. ■ EXAMPLE 18.14 Philips offers to sell Hundert 650 pounds of turkey thighs at a specified price and with specified delivery terms. Hundert responds, "I accept your offer for 650 pounds of turkey thighs *on the condition that you give me ninety days to pay for them.*" Hundert's response will be construed not as an acceptance but as a counteroffer, which Philips may or may not accept. ■

Additional Terms May Be Stricken. The UCC provides yet another option for dealing with conflicting terms in the parties' writings. Section 2–207(3) states that conduct by both parties that recognizes the existence of a contract is sufficient to establish a contract for the sale of goods even though the writings of the parties do not otherwise establish a contract. In this situation, "the terms of the particular contract will consist of those terms on which the writings of the parties agree, together with any supplementary terms incorporated under any other provisions of this Act." In a dispute over contract terms, this provision allows a court simply to strike from the contract those terms on which the parties do not agree.

■ EXAMPLE 18.15 AAA Marketing orders goods over the phone from Brigg Sales, Inc., which ships the goods with an acknowledgment form (confirming the order) to AAA. AAA accepts and pays for the goods. The parties' writings do not establish a contract, but there is no question that a contract exists. If a dispute arises over the terms, such as the extent of any warranties, UCC 2–207(3) provides the governing rule. ■

CONSIDERATION

The common law rule that a contract requires consideration also applies to sales and lease contracts. Unlike the common law, however, the UCC does not require a contract modification to be supported by new consideration. An agreement modifying a contract for the sale or lease of goods "needs no consideration to be binding" [UCC 2–209(1), 2A–208(1)].

Modifications Must Be Made in Good Faith Of course, contract modification must be sought in good faith [UCC 1–203]. ■ EXAMPLE 18.16 Allied, Inc., agrees to lease a new recreational vehicle (RV) to Louise for a stated monthly payment. Subsequently, a sudden shift in the market makes it difficult for Allied to lease the new RV to Louise at the contract price without suffering a loss. Allied tells Louise of the situation, and she agrees to pay an additional sum for the lease of the RV. Later Louise reconsiders and refuses to pay more than the original price. Under the UCC, Louise's promise to modify the contract needs no consideration to be binding. Hence, she is bound by the modified contract. ■

In this example, a shift in the market is a *good faith* reason for contract modification. What if there really was no shift in the market, however, and Allied knew that Louise needed to lease the new RV immediately but refused to deliver it unless she agreed to pay an additional sum of money? This attempt at extortion through modification without a legitimate commercial reason would be ineffective because it would violate the duty of good faith. Allied would not be permitted to enforce the higher price.

When Modification without Consideration Requires a Writing In some situations, modification of a sales or lease contract without consideration must be in writing to be enforceable. If the contract itself prohibits any changes to the contract unless they are in a signed writing, for instance, then only those changes agreed to in a signed writing are enforceable. If a consumer (nonmerchant buyer) is dealing with a merchant and the merchant supplies the form that contains a prohibition against oral modification, the consumer must sign a separate acknowledgment of such a clause [UCC 2–209(2), 2A–208(2)].

Also, under Article 2, any modification that brings a sales contract under the Statute of Frauds must usually be in writing to be enforceable. Thus, if an oral contract for the sale of goods priced at $400 is modified so that the contract goods are now priced at $600, the modification must be in writing—because sales contracts for goods priced at $500 or more must be in writing to be enforceable, as you will read shortly [UCC 2–209(3)]. If, however, the buyer accepts delivery of the goods after the modification, he or she is bound to the $600 price [UCC 2–201(3)(c)]. (Unlike Article 2, Article 2A does not say whether a lease as modified needs to satisfy the Statute of Frauds.)

STATUTE OF FRAUDS

BE AWARE It has been proposed that the UCC be revised to eliminate the Statute of Frauds.

The UCC contains Statute of Frauds provisions covering sales and lease contracts. Under these provisions, sales contracts for goods priced at $500 or more and lease contracts requiring payments of $1,000 or more must be in writing to be enforceable [UCC 2–201(1), 2A–201(1)].[14]

Sufficiency of the Writing The UCC has greatly relaxed the requirements for the sufficiency of a writing to satisfy the Statute of Frauds. A writing or a memorandum will be sufficient as long as it indicates that the parties intended to form a contract and as long as it is signed by the party (or agent of the party) against whom enforcement is sought. The contract normally will not be enforceable beyond the quantity of goods shown in the writing, however. All other terms can be proved in court by oral testimony. For leases, the writing must reasonably identify and describe the goods leased and the lease term.

Special Rules for Contracts between Merchants Once again, the UCC provides a special rule for merchants. Merchants can satisfy the requirements of a writing for the Statute of Frauds if, after the parties have agreed orally, one of the merchants sends a signed written confirmation to the other merchant within a reasonable time after the oral agreement was reached. The communication must indicate the terms of the agreement, and the merchant receiving the confirmation must have reason to know of its contents. Unless the merchant who receives the confirmation gives written notice of objection to its contents within ten days after receipt, the writing is sufficient against the receiving merchant, even though she or he has not signed anything [UCC 2–201(2)].[15] What happens if a merchant sends a written confirmation of an order that was never placed? For a discussion of this issue, see this chapter's *Adapting the Law to the Online Environment* feature.

---

14. Note that a 2003 amendment significantly increased the price of goods that will cause a sales contract to fall under the Statute of Frauds. Under Amended UCC 2–201(1), goods must be priced at $5,000 or more for a sales contract to be subject to the record (writing) requirement.

15. According to the comments accompanying UCC 2A–201 (Article 2A's Statute of Frauds), the "between merchants" provision was not included because the number of such transactions involving leases, as opposed to sales, was thought to be modest.

ADAPTING THE LAW TO THE ONLINE ENVIRONMENT

Can an Employee's E-Mail Constitute a Waiver of Contract Terms?

Under UCC 2–209, an agreement that excludes modification except by a signed writing cannot be otherwise modified. If the written-modification requirement is contained in a form supplied by one merchant to another, the other party must separately sign the form for it to be binding. This rule has an exception, though, which can be significant in the online environment. Under the UCC, *an attempt at modification that does not meet the writing requirement may operate as a waiver* [UCC 2–209(4)]. In other words, the parties can waive, or give up, the right to require that contract modifications be in a signed writing. Can an employee's e-mail communications form a waiver of a contract's written-modification requirement? This issue arose in *Cloud Corp. v. Hasbro, Inc.*[a]

THE CONTRACT TERMS AND THE PARTIES' RELATIONSHIP

Cloud Corporation contracted to supply packets of a special powder to Hasbro, Inc., for use in Hasbro's new "Wonder World Aquarium." At the time of their initial agreement, Hasbro sent a letter to Cloud containing a "terms and conditions" form, which stated that Cloud, the supplier, could not deviate from a purchase order without Hasbro's written consent. Cloud signed and returned that form to Hasbro as requested, and Hasbro began placing orders. Each time Hasbro ordered packets, Cloud sent back an "order acknowledgment" form confirming the quantity ordered.

After placing several orders, Hasbro told Cloud to change the formula in the packets. As a result, Cloud was able to produce three times as many packets using the same amount of material that it already had on hand to fill Hasbro's previous orders. Although Hasbro had not ordered any additional packets, Cloud sent Hasbro an order acknowledgment for extra packets at a lower price. Hasbro did not explicitly respond to Cloud's acknowledgment form. One of Hasbro's employees, however, referred to the additional quantities of packets at some point in her e-mail exchanges with Cloud. Several months later, after Cloud had produced the additional packets, Hasbro quit making the Wonder World Aquarium and refused to pay for the packets that it did not order. Cloud then sued Hasbro for breach of contract.

WAS THE EMPLOYEE'S E-MAIL A WAIVER?

Ultimately, a federal appellate court held that because Hasbro's employee had referred to the additional packets in at least one e-mail, Hasbro must pay for them. According to the court, the employee's e-mail alone could be sufficient to satisfy the requirement of written consent to modify the contract. Even if it did not, however, the court held that it operated as a waiver. The court stated that for the e-mail to operate as a waiver, Cloud "must show either that it reasonably relied on the other party's having waived the requirement of a writing, or that the waiver was clear and unequivocal." Here, the employee's e-mail had not clearly waived the writing requirement but there was *reasonable reliance.* According to the court, Hasbro should have advised Cloud if it did not want to be committed to buying the additional quantity rather than "leading Cloud down the primrose path."

FOR CRITICAL ANALYSIS

How might the parties to a sales contract prevent their subsequent e-mail communications from waiving the contract's explicit modification requirements? (Hint: How can the parties prevent contract disputes generally?)

a. 314 F.3d 289 (7th Cir. 2002).

■ EXAMPLE 18.17 Alfonso is a merchant-buyer in Cleveland. He contracts over the telephone to purchase $4,000 worth of spare aircraft parts from Goldstein, a New York City merchant-seller. Two days later, Goldstein sends written confirmation detailing the terms of the oral contract, and Alfonso subsequently receives it. If Alfonso does not notify Goldstein in writing of his objection to the contents of the confirmation within ten days of receipt, Alfonso cannot raise the Statute of Frauds as a defense against the enforcement of the oral contract. ■

Exceptions In addition to the special rules for merchants, the UCC defines three exceptions to the writing requirements of the Statute of Frauds. An oral contract for

CONCEPT SUMMARY Major Differences between Contract Law and Sales Law

	CONTRACT LAW	SALES LAW
Contract Terms	Contract must contain all material terms.	Open terms are acceptable, if parties intended to form a contract, but contract is not enforceable beyond quantity term.
Acceptance	Mirror image rule applies. If additional terms are added in acceptance, counteroffer is created.	Additional terms will not negate acceptance unless acceptance is made expressly conditional on assent to the additional terms.
Contract Modification	Modification requires consideration.	Modification does not require consideration.
Irrevocable Offers	Option contracts (with consideration).	Merchants' firm offers (without consideration).
Statute of Frauds Requirements	All material terms must be included in the writing.	Writing is required only for the sale of goods of $500[a] or more, but contract is not enforceable beyond quantity specified. *Exceptions:* 1. Contracts for specially manufactured goods are enforceable. 2. Contracts admitted to under oath by the party against whom enforcement is sought are enforceable. 3. Contracts will be enforced to the extent goods are delivered or paid for. 4. Confirmatory memorandum (between merchants): Contract is enforceable if the merchant fails to object in writing to confirming memorandum within ten days of its receipt.

a. Under a 2003 amendment to the UCC, a writing (record) is required only for the sale of goods priced at $5,000 or more.

the sale of goods priced at $500 or more or the lease of goods involving total payments of $1,000 or more will be enforceable despite the absence of a writing in the circumstances discussed in the following subsections [UCC 2–201(3), 2A–201(4)]. These exceptions and other ways in which sales law differs from general contract law are summarized in the *Concept Summary* on this page.

Specially Manufactured Goods. An oral contract is enforceable if (1) it is for goods that are specially manufactured for a particular buyer or specially manufactured or obtained for a particular lessee, (2) these goods are not suitable for resale or lease to others in the ordinary course of the seller's or lessor's business, and (3) the seller or lessor has substantially started to manufacture the goods or has made commitments for their manufacture or procurement. In this situation, once the seller or lessor has taken action, the buyer or lessee cannot repudiate the agreement claiming the Statute of Frauds as a defense.

An artisan creates a specially designed "bowl within a bowl" out of one piece of clay. If a restaurant orally contracted with the artisan to create twenty of the specially designed bowls for use in its business, at a price of $800, would the contract have to be in writing to be enforceable? Why or why not? (AP/Wide World Photos)

REMEMBER An admission can be made in documents, including internal memos and employee reports, that may be obtained during discovery prior to trial.

■ EXAMPLE 18.18 Womach orders custom-made draperies for her new boutique. The price is $1,000, and the contract is oral. When the merchant-seller manufactures the draperies and tenders delivery to Womach, she refuses to pay for them even though the job has been completed on time. Womach claims that she is not liable because the contract was oral. Clearly, if the unique style and color of the draperies make it improbable that the seller can find another buyer, Womach is liable to the seller. Note that the seller must have made a substantial beginning in manufacturing the specialized item prior to the buyer's repudiation. (Here, the manufacture was completed.) Of course, the court must still be convinced by evidence of the terms of the oral contract. ■

Admissions. An oral contract for the sale or lease of goods is enforceable if the party against whom enforcement of the contract is sought admits in pleadings, testimony, or other court proceedings that a contract for sale was made.[16] In this situation, the contract will be enforceable even though it was oral, but enforceability will be limited to the quantity of goods admitted.

■ EXAMPLE 18.19 Lane and Byron negotiate an agreement over the telephone. During the negotiations, Lane requests a delivery price for five hundred gallons of gasoline and a separate price for seven hundred gallons of gasoline. Byron replies that the price would be the same, $2.10 per gallon. Lane orally orders five hundred gallons. Byron honestly believes that Lane ordered seven hundred gallons and tenders that amount. Lane refuses the shipment of seven hundred gallons, and Byron sues for breach. In his pleadings and testimony, Lane admits that an oral contract was made, but only for five hundred gallons. Because Lane admits the existence of the oral contract, Lane cannot plead the Statute of Frauds as a defense. The contract is enforceable, however, only to the extent of the quantity admitted (five hundred gallons). ■

Partial Performance. An oral contract for the sale or lease of goods is enforceable if payment has been made and accepted or goods have been received and accepted. This is the "partial performance" exception. The oral contract will be enforced at least to the extent that performance *actually* took place.

■ EXAMPLE 18.20 Allan orally contracts to lease to Opus Enterprises a thousand chairs at $2 each to be used during a one-day concert. Before delivery, Opus sends Allan a check for $1,000, which Allan cashes. Later, when Allan attempts to deliver the chairs, Opus refuses delivery, claiming the Statute of Frauds as a defense, and demands the return of its $1,000. Under the UCC's partial performance rule, Allan can enforce the oral contract by tender of delivery of five hundred chairs for the $1,000 accepted. Similarly, if Opus had made no payment but had accepted the delivery of five hundred chairs from Allan, the oral contract would have been enforceable against Opus for $1,000, the lease payment due for the five hundred chairs delivered. ■

PAROL EVIDENCE

If the parties to a contract set forth its terms in a confirmatory memorandum (a writing expressing offer and acceptance of the deal) or in a writing intended as their final expression, the terms of the contract cannot be contradicted by evidence of any

16. Any admission made under oath, including one not made in a court, satisfies UCC 2–201(3)(b) and 2A–201(4)(b) under the 2003 amendments to Articles 2 and 2A.

prior agreements or contemporaneous oral agreements. The terms of the contract may, however, be explained or supplemented by *consistent additional terms* or by *course of dealing, usage of trade,* or *course of performance* [UCC 2–202, 2A–202].[17]

Ambiguous Terms If the court finds an ambiguity in a writing that is supposed to be a complete and exclusive statement of the agreement between the parties, it may accept evidence of consistent additional terms to clarify or remove the ambiguity. The court will not, however, accept evidence of contradictory terms. This is also the rule under the common law of contracts.

Course of Dealing and Usage of Trade Under the UCC, the meaning of any agreement, evidenced by the language of the parties and by their actions, must be interpreted in light of commercial practices and other surrounding circumstances. In interpreting a commercial agreement, the court will assume that the course of prior dealing between the parties and the usage of trade were taken into account when the agreement was phrased.

COURSE OF DEALING
Prior conduct between the parties to a contract that establishes a common basis for their understanding.

A **course of dealing** is a sequence of previous actions and communications between the parties to a particular transaction that establishes a common basis for their understanding [UCC 1–205(1)]. A course of dealing is restricted to the sequence of actions and communications between the parties that has occurred prior to the agreement in question. The UCC states, "A course of dealing between the parties and any usage of trade in the vocation or trade in which they are engaged or of which they are or should be aware give particular meaning to [the terms of the agreement] and supplement or qualify the terms of [the] agreement" [UCC 1–205(3)].

USAGE OF TRADE
Any practice or method of dealing having such regularity of observance in a place, vocation, or trade as to justify an expectation that it will be observed with respect to the transaction in question.

Usage of trade is any practice or method of dealing having such regularity of observance in a place, vocation, or trade as to justify an expectation that it will be observed with respect to the transaction in question [UCC 1–205(2)]. Further, the express terms of an agreement and an applicable course of dealing or usage of trade will be construed to be consistent with each other whenever reasonable. When such a construction is *unreasonable,* however, the express terms in the agreement will prevail [UCC 1–205(4)].

COURSE OF PERFORMANCE
The conduct that occurs under the terms of a particular agreement. Such conduct indicates what the parties to an agreement intended it to mean.

Course of Performance A **course of performance** is the conduct that occurs under the terms of a particular agreement. Presumably, the parties themselves know best what they meant by their words, and the course of performance actually undertaken under their agreement is the best indication of what they meant [UCC 2–208(1), 2A–207(1)].[18]

■ **EXAMPLE 18.21** Janson's Lumber Company contracts with Barrymore to sell Barrymore a specified number of "two-by-fours." The lumber in fact does not measure 2 inches by 4 inches but rather 1⅞ inches by 3¾ inches. Janson's agrees to deliver the lumber in five deliveries, and Barrymore, without objection, accepts the lumber in the first three deliveries. On the fourth delivery, however, Barrymore

17. The 2003 amendments to this section substitute the word *record* for *writing* and add the stipulation that the "terms in a record may be explained by evidence of course of performance, course of dealing, or usage of trade without a preliminary determination by the court that the language used is ambiguous" [Amended UCC 2–202(2)].

18. UCC 2–208 and UCC 2A–207 were deleted from the UCC in the 2003 amendments. Course of performance is, however, expressly mentioned in UCC 2–202.

objects that the two-by-fours do not measure 2 inches by 4 inches. The course of performance in this transaction—that is, the fact that Barrymore accepted three deliveries without objection under the agreement—is relevant in determining that here the term "two-by-four" actually means "1⅞ by 3¾." Janson's can also prove that two-by-fours need not be exactly 2 inches by 4 inches by applying usage of trade, course of prior dealing, or both. Janson's can, for example, show that in previous transactions, Barrymore took 1⅞-by-3¾-inch lumber without objection. In addition, Janson's can show that in the lumber trade, two-by-fours are commonly 1⅞ inches by 3¾ inches. ■

Rules of Construction The UCC provides *rules of construction* for interpreting contracts. Express terms, course of performance, course of dealing, and usage of trade are to be construed together when they do not contradict one another. When such a construction is unreasonable, however, the following order of priority controls: (1) express terms, (2) course of performance, (3) course of dealing, and (4) usage of trade [UCC 1–205(4), 2–208(2), 2A–207(2)].

UNCONSCIONABILITY

As discussed in Chapter 11, an unconscionable contract is one that is so unfair and one sided that it would be unreasonable to enforce it. The UCC allows the court to evaluate a contract or any clause in a contract, and if the court deems it to have been unconscionable at the time it was made, the court can (1) refuse to enforce the contract, (2) enforce the remainder of the contract without the unconscionable clause, or (3) limit the application of any unconscionable clauses to avoid an unconscionable result [UCC 2–302, 2A–108].[19] The following landmark case illustrates an early application of the UCC's unconscionability provisions.

19. The 2003 amendments to this section changed the word *clause* to *term,* recognizing that even a single term (word) in a contract can be unconscionable and authorizing the court to strike any single term that it finds unconscionable.

LANDMARK AND CLASSIC CASES

CASE 18.3 Jones v. Star Credit Corp.

Supreme Court of New York, Nassau County, 1969.
59 Misc.2d 189,
298 N.Y.S.2d 264.

HISTORICAL AND ECONOMIC SETTING *In the sixth century, Roman civil law allowed the courts to rescind a contract if the market value of the goods that were the subject of the contract equaled less than half the contract price. This same ratio has appeared over the last forty years in many cases in which courts have found contract clauses to be unconscionable under UCC 2–302 on the ground that the price was excessive. In a Connecticut case, for example, the court held that a contract requiring a person who was poor to make payments totaling $1,248 for a television set that retailed for $499 was unconscionable.*[a] *The seller had not told the buyer the full purchase price. Most of the litigants who have used UCC 2–302 successfully have been consumers who are poor or otherwise at a disadvantage. In one New York case, for example, the court held that a contract requiring a Spanish-speaking consumer to make payments totaling nearly $1,150 for a freezer that wholesaled for less than $350 was unconscionable.*[b] *The contract was in English, and the salesperson did not translate or explain it.*

a. *Murphy v. McNamara,* 36 Conn.Supp. 183, 416 A.2d 170 (1979).
b. *Frostifresh Corp. v. Reynoso,* 52 Misc.2d 26, 274 N.Y.S.2d 757 (1966); rev'd on issue of damages, 54 Misc.2d 119, 281 N.Y.S.2d 946 (1967).

(Continued)

CASE 18.3—Continued

BACKGROUND AND FACTS The Joneses, the plaintiffs, agreed to purchase a freezer for $900 as the result of a salesperson's visit to their home. Tax and financing charges raised the total price to $1,439.69. At trial, the freezer was found to have a maximum retail value of approximately $300. The plaintiffs, who had made payments totaling $619.88, brought a suit in a New York state court to have the purchase contract declared unconscionable under the UCC.

IN THE WORDS OF THE COURT . . .
Sol WACHTLER, Justice.

* * * *

* * * [Section 2–302 of the UCC] authorizes the court to find, as a matter of law, that a contract or a clause of a contract was "unconscionable at the time it was made," and upon so finding the court may refuse to enforce the contract, excise the objectionable clause or limit the application of the clause to avoid an unconscionable result. * * *

* * * *

* * * The question which presents itself is whether or not, under the circumstances of this case, the sale of a freezer unit having a retail value of $300 for $900 ($1,439.69 including credit charges and $18 sales tax) is unconscionable as a matter of law. * * *

* * * [T]he mathematical disparity between $300, which presumably includes a reasonable profit margin, and $900, which is exorbitant on its face, carries the greatest weight. Credit charges alone exceed by more than $100 the retail value of the freezer. * * * The very limited financial resources of the purchaser, known to the sellers at the time of the sale, is entitled to weight in the balance. * * *

* * * *

* * * [T]he defendant has already been amply compensated. In accordance with the statute, the application of the payment provision should be limited to amounts already paid by the plaintiffs and the contract be reformed and amended by changing the payments called for therein to equal the amount of payment actually so paid by the plaintiffs.

DECISION AND REMEDY The court held that the contract was not enforceable and reformed the contract so that no further payments were required.

COMMENTS *Classical contract theory holds that a contract is a bargain in which the terms have been worked out freely between the parties. In many modern commercial transactions, this may not be the case. For example, standard-form contracts and leases are often signed by consumer-buyers who understand few of the terms used and who often do not even read them. The inclusion of Sections 2–302 and 2A–108 in the UCC gave the courts a means of policing such transactions, and the courts continue to use this means to prevent injustice.*

RELEVANT WEB SITES *To locate information on the Web concerning* Jones v. Star Credit Corp., *go to this text's Web site at* **http://blt.westbuslaw.com**, *select "Chapter 18," and click on "URLs for Landmarks."*

Contracts for the International Sale of Goods

International sales contracts between firms or individuals located in different countries are governed by the 1980 United Nations Convention on Contracts for the International Sale of Goods (CISG). The CISG governs international contracts only if the countries of the parties to the contract have ratified the CISG and if the parties have not agreed that some other law will govern their contract. As of 2005, sixty-two countries had adopted the CISG, including the United States, Canada, Mexico, some Central and South American countries, and most European nations.

.on the Web The full text of the CISG is available online at the Pace University School of Law's Institute of International Commercial Law. Go to **http://cisgw3.law.pace.edu/cisg/text/treaty.html**.

APPLICABILITY OF THE CISG

Essentially, the CISG is to international sales contracts what Article 2 of the UCC is to domestic sales contracts. As discussed in this chapter, in domestic transactions the UCC applies when the parties to a contract for a sale of goods have failed to specify in writing some important term concerning price, delivery, or the like. Similarly, whenever the parties subject to the CISG have failed to specify in writing the precise terms of a contract for the international sale of goods, the CISG will be applied. Unlike the UCC, the CISG does not apply to consumer sales, and neither the UCC nor the CISG applies to contracts for services.

Businesspersons must take special care when drafting international sales contracts to avoid problems caused by distance, including language differences and varying national laws. The foldout exhibit contained within this chapter, which shows an actual international sales contract used by Starbucks Coffee Company, illustrates many of the special terms and clauses that are typically contained in international contracts for the sale of goods. Annotations in the exhibit explain the meaning and significance of specific clauses in the contract. (See Chapter 46 for a discussion of other laws that frame global business transactions.)

A COMPARISON OF CISG AND UCC PROVISIONS

The provisions of the CISG, although similar for the most part to those of the UCC, differ from them in certain respects. We have already mentioned some of these differences. In the *International Perspective* feature in Chapter 13, for example, we pointed out that the CISG does not include any Statute of Frauds provisions. Under

Suppose that the owner of this factory, a U.S. firm, offers to sell a German company a certain number of boxes for a set price. The parties discuss the offer on the phone, and the U.S. firm orally agrees to keep the offer open for a period of time but fails to send written assurances of the offer. Would the offer be revocable under the UCC? Would it be revocable under the CISG? Explain the different approaches. (Bloomberg News/Landov)

Article 11 of the CISG, an international sales contract does not need to be evidenced by a writing nor must it be in any particular form.

We look here at some differences between the UCC and the CISG with respect to contract formation. In the following chapters, we will continue to point out differences between the CISG and the UCC as they relate to the topics covered. These topics include risk of loss, performance, remedies, and warranties.

.on the Web To read an in-depth article comparing the provisions of the CISG and the UCC, go to **http://cisgw3.law.pace.edu/cisg/thesis/Oberman.html**.

Offers Some differences between the UCC and the CISG concern offers. For instance, the UCC provides that a merchant's firm offer is irrevocable, even without consideration, if the merchant gives assurances in a signed writing. In contrast, under the CISG, an offer can become irrevocable without a signed writing. Article 16(2) of the CISG provides that an offer will be irrevocable if the merchant-offeror simply states orally that the offer is irrevocable or if the offeree reasonably relies on the offer as being irrevocable. In both of these situations, the offer will be irrevocable even without a writing and without consideration.

Another difference is that, under the UCC, if the price term is left open, the court will determine "a reasonable price at the time for delivery" [UCC 2–305(1)]. Under the CISG, however, the price term must be specified, or at least provisions for its specification must be included in the agreement; otherwise, normally no contract will exist.

Acceptances Like UCC 2–207, the CISG provides that a contract can be formed even though the acceptance contains additional terms, unless the additional terms materially alter the contract. Under the CISG, however, the definition of a "material alteration" includes virtually any change in the terms. If an additional term relates to payment, quality, quantity, price, time and place of delivery, extent of one party's liability to the other, or the settlement of disputes, the CISG considers the added term a "material alteration." In effect, then, the CISG requires that the terms of the acceptance mirror those of the offer.

Additionally, under the UCC, an acceptance is effective on dispatch. Under the CISG, however, a contract is not created until the acceptance is received by the offeror. (The offer becomes irrevocable, however, when the acceptance is sent.) Additionally, in contrast to the UCC, the CISG provides that acceptance by performance does not require that the offeror be notified of the performance.

REVIEWING THE FORMATION OF SALES AND LEASE CONTRACTS

Guy Holcomb owns and operates Oasis Goodtime Emporium, an adult entertainment establishment. Holcomb wanted to create an adult Internet system for Oasis that would offer customers adult theme videos and "live" chat room programs using performers at the club. On May 10, Holcomb signed a work order authorizing Thomas Consulting Group (TCG) "to deliver a working prototype of a customer chat system, demonstrating the integration of live video and chatting in a Web browser." In exchange for creating the prototype, Holcomb agreed to pay TCG $64,697. On May 20, Holcomb signed an additional work order in the amount of $12,943 for TCG to install a customized firewall system. The work orders stated that Holcomb would make monthly installment payments to TCG, and both parties expected the work would be finished by September. Due to unforeseen problems largely attributable to system configuration and software incompatibility, completion of the project required more time than anticipated. By the end of the summer, the Web site was still not ready, and Holcomb had

REVIEWING THE FORMATION OF SALES AND LEASE CONTRACTS—Continued

fallen behind in his payments to TCG. TCG was threatening to cease work and file suit for breach of contract unless the bill was paid. Rather than making further payments, Holcomb wanted to abandon the Web site project. Using the information presented in the chapter, answer the following questions.

1. Is the transaction between Holcomb and TCG covered by the Uniform Commercial Code (UCC)? Why or why not? Discuss whether the predominant purpose of the contract in this scenario involved goods or services. What is the significance of this distinction?
2. Would a court be likely to consider Holcomb a merchant under the UCC? Why or why not?
3. Did the parties have a valid contract under the UCC? Were any terms left open in the contract? If so, which terms? How would a court deal with open terms?
4. Suppose that Holcomb and TCG meet in October in an attempt to resolve their problems. At that time, the parties reach an oral agreement that TCG will continue to work without demanding full payment of the past-due amounts and Holcomb will pay TCG $5,000 per week. Assuming the contract falls under the UCC, is the oral agreement enforceable? Why or why not? If TCG continues to work and completes the prototype, can TCG enforce the agreement?
5. If the parties end up taking their dispute before a court, will they be allowed to present parol evidence of their course of dealing and course of performance? Explain.

KEY TERMS

course of dealing 446
course of performance 446
firm offer 436
intangible property 429
lease agreement 432
lessee 433
lessor 433
merchant 432
output contract 436
predominant-factor test 430
requirements contract 436
sale 428
sales contract 427
seasonably 437
tangible property 428
usage of trade 446

CHAPTER SUMMARY The Formation of Sales and Lease Contracts*

The Scope of the UCC (See page 427.)	The UCC attempts to provide a consistent, uniform, and integrated framework of rules to deal with all phases *ordinarily arising* in a commercial sales or lease transaction, including contract formation, passage of title and risk of loss, performance, remedies, payment for goods, warehoused goods, and secured transactions.
The Scope of Article 2—Sales (See pages 427–432.)	Article 2 governs contracts for the sale of goods (tangible, movable personal property). The common law of contracts also applies to sales contracts to the extent that the common law has not been modified by the UCC. If there is a conflict between a common law rule and the UCC, the UCC controls.
The Scope of Article 2A—Leases (See pages 432–433.)	Article 2A governs contracts for the lease of goods. Except that it applies to leases, instead of sales, of goods, Article 2A is essentially a repetition of Article 2 and varies only to reflect differences between sale and lease transactions.

* Although we have referenced the 2003 amendments to Articles 2 and 2A of the UCC within the text of this chapter, we do not do so in this summary—because the amendments have not as yet become law in any state.

(Continued)

CHAPTER SUMMARY The Formation of Sales and Lease Contracts—Continued

Offer and Acceptance (See pages 433–441.)	1. *Offer—* a. Not all terms have to be included for a contract to be formed (only the subject matter and quantity term must be specified). b. The price need not be included for a contract to be formed. c. Particulars of performance can be left open. d. A written and signed offer by a *merchant,* covering a period of three months or less, is irrevocable without payment of consideration. 2. *Acceptance—* a. Acceptance may be made by any reasonable means of communication; it is effective when dispatched. b. The acceptance of a unilateral offer can be made by a promise to ship or by prompt shipment of conforming goods, or by prompt shipment of nonconforming goods if not accompanied by a notice of accommodation. c. Acceptance by performance requires notice within a reasonable time; otherwise, the offer can be treated as lapsed. d. A definite expression of acceptance creates a contract even if the terms of the acceptance vary from those of the offer unless the new or different terms in the acceptance are expressly conditioned on the offeror's assent to those terms.
Consideration (See pages 441–442.)	A modification of a contract for the sale of goods does not require consideration.
Statute of Frauds (See pages 442–445.)	1. All contracts for the sale of goods priced at $500 or more must be in writing. A writing is sufficient as long as it indicates a contract between the parties and is signed by the party against whom enforcement is sought. A contract is not enforceable beyond the quantity shown in the writing. 2. When written confirmation of an oral contract *between merchants* is not objected to in writing by the receiver within ten days, the contract is enforceable. 3. Exceptions to the requirement of a writing exist in the following situations: a. When the oral contract is for specially manufactured goods not suitable for resale to others, and the seller has substantially started to manufacture the goods. b. When the defendant admits in pleadings, testimony, or other court proceedings that an oral contract for the sale of goods was made. In this case, the contract will be enforceable to the extent of the quantity of goods admitted. c. The oral agreement will be enforceable to the extent that payment has been received and accepted by the seller or to the extent that the goods have been received and accepted by the buyer.
Parol Evidence Rule (See pages 445–447.)	1. The terms of a clearly and completely worded written contract cannot be contradicted by evidence of prior agreements or contemporaneous oral agreements. 2. Evidence is admissible to clarify the terms of a writing in the following situations: a. If the contract terms are ambiguous. b. If evidence of course of dealing, usage of trade, or course of performance is necessary to learn or to clarify the intentions of the parties to the contract.
Unconscionability (See pages 447–448.)	An unconscionable contract is one that is so unfair and one sided that it would be unreasonable to enforce it. If the court deems a contract to have been unconscionable at the time it was

CHAPTER SUMMARY The Formation of Sales and Lease Contracts—Continued

Unconscionability—Continued	made, the court can (1) refuse to enforce the contract, (2) refuse to enforce the unconscionable clause of the contract, or (3) limit the application of any unconscionable clauses to avoid an unconscionable result.
Contracts for the International Sale of Goods (See pages 448–450.)	International sales contracts are governed by the United Nations Convention on Contracts for the International Sale of Goods (CISG)—if the countries of the parties to the contract have ratified the CISG (and if the parties have not agreed that some other law will govern their contract). Essentially, the CISG is to international sales contracts what Article 2 of the UCC is to domestic sales contracts. Whenever parties who are subject to the CISG have failed to specify in writing the precise terms of a contract for the international sale of goods, the CISG will be applied.

FOR REVIEW

Answers for the even-numbered questions in this For Review *section can be found on this text's accompanying Web site at* http://blt.westbuslaw.com. *Select "Chapter 18" and click on "For Review."*

1. How do Article 2 and Article 2A of the UCC differ? What types of transactions does each article cover?
2. What is a merchant's firm offer?
3. If an offeree includes additional or different terms in an acceptance, will a contract result? If so, what happens to these terms?
4. Article 2 and Article 2A of the UCC both define several exceptions to the writing requirements of the Statute of Frauds. What are these exceptions?
5. What law governs contracts for the international sale of goods?

QUESTIONS AND CASE PROBLEMS

18–1. Statute of Frauds. Fresher Foods, Inc., orally agreed to purchase from Dale Vernon, a farmer, one thousand bushels of corn for $1.25 per bushel. Fresher Foods paid $125 down and agreed to pay the remainder of the purchase price on delivery, which was scheduled for one week later. When Fresher Foods tendered the balance of $1,125 on the scheduled day of delivery and requested the corn, Vernon refused to deliver it. Fresher Foods sued Vernon for damages, claiming that Vernon had breached their oral contract. Can Fresher Foods recover? If so, to what extent?

18–2. Merchant's Firm Offer. On September 1, Jennings, a used-car dealer, wrote a letter to Wheeler in which he stated, "I have a 1955 Thunderbird convertible in mint condition that I will sell you for $13,500 at any time before October 9. [signed] Peter Jennings." By September 15, having heard nothing from Wheeler, Jennings sold the Thunderbird to another party. On September 29, Wheeler accepted Jennings's offer and tendered the $13,500. When Jennings told Wheeler he had sold the car to another party, Wheeler claimed Jennings had breached their contract. Is Jennings in breach? Explain.

18–3. Accommodation Shipments. M. M. Salinger, Inc., a retailer of television sets, orders one hundred model Color-X sets from manufacturer Fulsom. The order specifies the price and that the television sets are to be shipped via Interamerican Freightways on or before October 30. Fulsom receives the order on October 5. On October 8, Fulsom writes Salinger a letter indicating that it has received the order and that it will ship the sets as directed, at the specified price. Salinger receives this letter on October 10. On October 28, Fulsom, in preparing the shipment, discovers it has only ninety Color-X sets in stock. Fulsom ships the ninety Color-X sets and ten television sets of a different model, stating clearly on the invoice that the ten sets are being shipped only as an accommodation. Salinger claims that Fulsom is in breach of contract. Fulsom claims that there was not an acceptance, and therefore no contract was formed. Explain who is correct, and why.

18–4. Statute of Frauds. SNK, Inc., makes video arcade games and sells them to distributors, including Entertainment Sales, Inc. (ESI). Most sales between SNK and ESI were phone orders. Over one four-month period, ESI phoned in several orders for "Samurai Showdown" games. SNK did not fill the orders. ESI filed a suit against SNK and others, alleging, among other things, breach of contract. There was no written contract covering the orders. ESI claimed that it had faxed purchase orders for the games to SNK but did not offer proof that the faxes had been sent or received. SNK filed a motion for summary judgment. In whose favor will the court rule, and why? [*Entertainment Sales Co. v. SNK, Inc.*, 232 Ga.App. 669, 502 S.E.2d 263 (1998)]

18–5. Goods and Services Combined. Dennis Dahlmann and Dahlmann Apartments, Ltd., entered into contracts with Sulchus Hospitality Technologies Corp. and Hospitality Management Systems, Inc. (HMS), to buy property management systems. The systems included computer hardware and software, as well as installation, training, and support services, for the Bell Tower Hotel and the Campus Inn in Ann Arbor, Michigan. The software controlled the central reservations systems at both hotels. When Dahlmann learned that the software was not Y2K compliant—that it could not be used to post reservations beyond December 31, 1999—he filed a suit against Sulchus and HMS, alleging in part breach of contract. The defendants filed a motion for summary judgment. One of the issues was whether the contracts were subject to Article 2 of the Uniform Commercial Code. Were they? Why or why not? Explain fully. [*Dahlmann v. Sulchus Hospitality Technologies Corp.*, 63 F.Supp.2d 772 (E.D.Mich. 1999)]

CASE PROBLEM WITH SAMPLE ANSWER

18–6. In 1988, International Business Machines Corp. (IBM) and American Shizuki Corp. (ASC) signed an agreement for "future purchase by IBM" of plastic film capacitors made by ASC to be used in IBM computers. The agreement stated that IBM was not obligated to buy from ASC and that future purchase orders "shall be [ASC]'s only authorization to manufacture Items." In February 1989, IBM wrote to ASC about "the possibility of IBM purchasing 15,000,000 Plastic Capacitors per two consecutive twelve (12) month periods. . . . This quantity is a forecast only, and represents no commitment by IBM to purchase these quantities during or after this time period." ASC said that it wanted greater assurances. In a second letter, IBM reexpressed its "intent to order" from ASC 30 million capacitors over a minimum period of two years, contingent on the condition "[t]hat IBM's requirements for these capacitors continue." ASC spent about $2.6 million on equipment to make the capacitors. By 1997, the need for plastic capacitors had dissipated with the advent of new technology, and IBM told ASC that it would no longer buy them. ASC filed a suit in a federal district court against IBM, seeking $8.5 million in damages. On what basis might the court rule in favor of IBM? Explain fully. [*American Shizuki Corp. v. International Business Machines Corp.*, 251 F.3d 1206 (8th Cir. 2001)]

After you have answered this problem, compare your answer with the sample answer given on the Web site that accompanies this text. Go to http://blt.westbuslaw.com, select "Chapter 18," and click on "Case Problem with Sample Answer."

18–7. Statute of Frauds. Quality Pork International is a Nebraska firm that makes and sells custom pork products. Rupari Food Services, Inc., buys and sells food products to retail operations and food brokers. In November 1999, Midwest Brokerage arranged an oral contract between Quality and Rupari, under which Quality would ship three orders to Star Food Processing, Inc., and Rupari would pay for the products. Quality shipped the goods to Star and sent invoices to Rupari. In turn, Rupari billed Star for all three orders, but paid Quality only for the first two (for $43,736.84 and $47,467.80, respectively), not for the third. Quality filed a suit in a Nebraska state court against Rupari, alleging breach of contract, to recover $44,051.98, the cost of the third order. Rupari argued that there was nothing in writing, as required by Section 2–201 of the Uniform Commercial Code (UCC), and thus there was no contract. What are the exceptions to the UCC's writing requirement? Do any of those exceptions apply here? Explain. [*Quality Pork International v. Rupari Food Services, Inc.*, 267 Neb. 474, 675 N.W.2d 642 (2004)]

A QUESTION OF ETHICS

18–8. John Schwanbeck entered into negotiations with Federal-Mogul Corp. to purchase Federal-Mogul's Vellumoid Division. The two parties drew up a letter of intent stating that "[n]o further obligation will arise until a definitive agreement is reduced to writing" and that it was the parties' intention "to proceed in good faith in the negotiation of such binding definitive agreement." At another place in the letter of intent were the following words: "Of course, this letter is not intended to create, nor do you or we presently have any binding legal obligation whatever in any way relating to such sale and purchase." Federal-Mogul eventually sold the Vellumoid Division to another party. Schwanbeck sued Federal-Mogul, alleging, among other things, that Federal-Mogul had breached an agreement to negotiate in good faith the proposed contract with Schwanbeck. Given these facts, consider the following questions. [*Schwanbeck v. Federal-Mogul Corp.*, 412 Mass. 703, 592 N.E.2d 1289 (1992)]

1. Did the letter of intent create a legally binding obligation, or was the letter merely an "agreement to agree" in the future? (You may wish to review the subsection on "Agreements to Agree" in Chapter 9 before you answer this question.)
2. Regardless of its legal duties, did Federal-Mogul have an ethical duty to proceed in negotiating a contract with Schwanbeck? Discuss.

FOR CRITICAL ANALYSIS

18–9. Why is the designation "merchant" or "nonmerchant" important?

VIDEO QUESTION

18–10. Go to this text's Web site at http://blt.westbuslaw.com and select "Chapter 18." Click on "Video Questions" and view the video titled *Sales and Lease Contracts: Price as a Term.* Then answer the following questions.

1. Is Anna correct in assuming that a contract can exist even though the sales price for the computer equipment was not specified? Explain.
2. According to the Uniform Commercial Code (UCC), what conditions must be satisfied in order for a contract to be formed when certain terms are left open? What terms (in addition to price) can be left open?
3. Are the e-mail messages that Anna refers to sufficient proof of the contract? Would parol evidence be admissible?
4. How do the 2003 amendments to Article 2 of the UCC improve Anna's position?

INTERNET EXERCISES

Go to the *Business Law Today* home page at **http://blt.westbuslaw.com**, select "Chapter 18," and click on "Internet Exercises." There you will find the following Internet research exercises that you can perform to learn more about topics covered in this chapter.

Activity 18–1: LEGAL PERSPECTIVE—Is It a Contract?

Activity 18–2: MANAGEMENT PERSPECTIVE—A Checklist for Sales Contracts

BEFORE THE TEST

Go to the *Business Law Today* home page at **http://blt.westbuslaw.com**, select "Chapter 18," and click on "Interactive Quizzes." You will find a number of interactive questions relating to this chapter.

CHAPTER 19

Title and Risk of Loss

"Now, it is of great moment that well-drawn laws should themselves define all the points they possibly can and leave as few as may be to the decision of the judges."

Aristotle, 384–322 B.C.E.
(Greek philosopher)

CHAPTER OUTLINE

- IDENTIFICATION
- PASSAGE OF TITLE
- RISK OF LOSS
- INSURABLE INTEREST
- BULK TRANSFERS

LEARNING OBJECTIVES

After reading this chapter, you should be able to answer the following questions:

1. What is the significance of identifying goods to a contract?
2. If the parties to a contract do not expressly agree on when title to goods passes, what determines when title passes?
3. Risk of loss does not necessarily pass with title. If the parties to a contract do not expressly agree when risk passes and the goods are to be delivered without movement by the seller, when does risk pass?
4. Under what circumstances will the seller's title to goods being sold be void? Under what circumstances will a seller have voidable title? What is the legal effect on a good faith purchaser of the goods of the seller's having a void title versus a voidable title?
5. At what point does the buyer acquire an insurable interest in goods subject to a sales contract? Can both the buyer and the seller have an insurable interest in the goods simultaneously?

A sale of goods transfers ownership rights in (title to) the goods from the seller to the buyer. Often, a sales contract is signed before the actual goods are available. For example, a sales contract for oranges might be signed in May, but the oranges may not be ready for picking and shipment until October. Any number of things can happen between the time the sales contract is signed and the time the goods are actually transferred into the buyer's possession. Fire, flood, or frost may destroy the orange groves, or the oranges may be lost or damaged in transit. The same problems may occur under a lease contract. Because of these possibilities, it is important to know the rights and liabilities of the parties between the time the contract is formed and the time the goods are actually received by the buyer or lessee.

Before the creation of the Uniform Commercial Code (UCC), *title*—the right of ownership—was the central concept in sales law, controlling all issues of rights and remedies of the parties to a sales contract. In some situations, title is still relevant under the UCC, and the UCC has special rules for determining who has title. These rules will be discussed in the sections that follow. In most situations, however, the UCC has replaced the concept of title with three other concepts: (1) identification, (2) risk of loss, and (3) insurable interest. By breaking down the transfer of ownership into these three components, the drafters of the UCC have essentially followed Aristotle's advice in the chapter-opening quotation and created greater precision in the law governing sales—leaving as few points of law as possible "to the decision of the judges."

In lease contracts, of course, title to the goods is retained by the lessor-owner of the goods. Hence, the UCC's provisions relating to passage of title do not apply to leased goods. Other concepts discussed in this chapter, though, including identification, risk of loss, and insurable interest, relate to lease contracts as well as to sales contracts.

Identification

Before any interest in specific goods can pass from the seller or lessor to the buyer or lessee, two conditions must prevail: (1) the goods must be in existence, and (2) they must be identified as the specific goods designated in the contract. **Identification** takes place when specific goods are designated as the subject matter of a sales or lease contract. Title and risk of loss cannot pass from seller to buyer unless the goods are identified to the contract. (As mentioned, title to leased goods remains with the lessor—or, if the owner is a third party, with that party. The lessee does not acquire title to leased goods.) Identification is significant because it gives the buyer or lessee the right to insure (or to have an insurable interest in) the goods and the right to recover from third parties who damage the goods.

IDENTIFICATION
In a sale of goods, the express designation of the goods provided for in the contract.

In their contract, the parties can agree on when identification will take place, but identification is effective to pass title and risk of loss to the buyer only after the goods are considered to be in existence. If the parties do not so specify, however, the UCC provisions discussed here determine when identification takes place [UCC 2–501(1), 2A–217].

Existing Goods

If the contract calls for the sale or lease of specific and ascertained goods that are already in existence, identification takes place at the time the contract is made. For example, you contract to purchase or lease a fleet of five cars by the serial numbers listed for the cars.

Future Goods

If a sale involves unborn animals to be born within twelve months after contracting, identification takes place when the animals are conceived. If a lease involves any unborn animals, identification occurs when the animals are conceived. If a sale involves crops that are to be harvested within twelve months (or the next harvest season occurring after contracting, whichever is longer), identification takes place when the crops are planted or begin to grow. In a sale or lease of any other future goods, identification occurs when the goods are shipped, marked, or otherwise designated by the seller or lessor as the goods to which the contract refers.

GOODS THAT ARE PART OF A LARGER MASS

As a general rule, goods that are part of a larger mass are identified when the goods are marked, shipped, or somehow designated by the seller or lessor as the particular goods that are the subject of the contract. ■ EXAMPLE 19.1 A buyer orders 1,000 cases of beans from a 10,000-case lot. Until the seller separates the 1,000 cases of beans from the 10,000-case lot, title and risk of loss remain with the seller. ■

FUNGIBLE GOODS
Goods that are alike by physical nature, by agreement, or by trade usage. Examples of fungible goods are wheat, oil, and wine that are identical in type and quality. When owners of fungible goods hold the goods as tenants in common, title and risk can pass without actually separating the goods being sold from the mass of fungible goods.

A common exception to this rule involves fungible goods. **Fungible goods** are goods that are alike by physical nature, by agreement, or by trade usage. Typical examples are specific grades or types of wheat, oil, and wine, usually stored in large containers. If these goods are held or intended to be held by owners as tenants in common (owners having shares undivided from the entire mass), a seller-owner can pass title and risk of loss to the buyer without an actual separation. The buyer replaces the seller as an owner in common [UCC 2–105(4)].

■ EXAMPLE 19.2 Alvarez, Braudel, and Carpenter are farmers. They deposit, respectively, 5,000 bushels, 3,000 bushels, and 2,000 bushels of grain of the same grade and quality in a bin. The three become owners in common, with Alvarez owning 50 percent of the 10,000 bushels, Braudel 30 percent, and Carpenter 20 percent. Alvarez contracts to sell her 5,000 bushels of grain to Tamur; because the goods are fungible, she can pass title and risk of loss to Tamur without physically separating the 5,000 bushels. Tamur now becomes an owner in common with Braudel and Carpenter. ■

Passage of Title

Once goods exist and are identified, the provisions of UCC 2–401 apply to the passage of title. In virtually all subsections of UCC 2–401, the words "unless otherwise explicitly agreed" appear, meaning that any explicit understanding between the buyer and the seller determines when title passes. Without an explicit agreement to the contrary, title passes to the buyer at the time and the place the seller performs by delivering the goods [UCC 2–401(2)]. The following case illustrates the significance of this event.

CASE 19.1 In re Stewart

United States Bankruptcy Court,
Western District of Arkansas, 2002.
274 Bankr. 503.

BACKGROUND AND FACTS In July 1997, Gary Stewart began to buy, and occasionally sell, cattle through Barry County Livestock Auction, Inc., in Exeter, Missouri. On January 29 and February 19, 2000, Stewart bought $46,749.55 worth of cattle through Barry County, but the checks he gave in payment were returned by the bank because his account did not have sufficient funds. By March 4, Stewart had given cashier's checks to Barry County to pay for the cattle.[a] Less than forty days later, on April 11, Stewart filed for bankruptcy in a federal bankruptcy court. Some payments made to creditors within ninety days of the filing of a petition in bankruptcy (called

a. A cashier's check is considered nearly the equivalent of cash.

CASE 19.1—Continued

preferences) can be recovered so that their amounts can be distributed more equitably among a debtor's creditors.[b] Stewart asked the court to recover his payments to Barry County. Barry County claimed that the payments were "contemporaneous exchanges for new value," which are not a preference and cannot be recovered. The question on which this issue turned was whether title to the cattle passed on the day of the sale or on the day of the payment.

b. Bankruptcy law will be discussed more fully in Chapter 27.

IN THE WORDS OF THE COURT . . .

ROBERT F. FUSSELL, Bankruptcy Judge.

* * * *

In this case, Barry County Livestock Auction printed on the face of each bill of sale language dealing with the transfer of title:

> ALL SALES ARE MADE, AND TITLE IS TRANSFERRED, SUBJECT TO FINAL PAYMENT * * * . IF ANY CHECK * * * TENDERED IN PAYMENT IS NOT PAID PROMPTLY ON PRESENTATION, THIS BILL OF SALE DOES NOT TRANSFER TITLE AND SHALL BE NULL AND VOID, AND OF NO EFFECT.

The first sentence states that the sale is voidable—all sales are made subject to final payment. Based on this sentence, the transfer occurred on the date of the sale. The second sentence states that the sale is void if a check is not paid upon [its presentation to the bank for payment]. Based on this sentence, it appears that Barry County Livestock Auction was attempting to retain title to the cattle in the event the debtor's personal checks were not honored [paid]. According to the UCC, any attempt to retain title to the cattle pending the debtor's personal checks being honored by the bank is ineffective. * * * [UCC] 2–401(2) states the time at which title to the goods passes to the buyer: "*Unless otherwise explicitly agreed title passes to the buyer at the time and place at which the seller completes his performance with reference to the physical delivery of the goods* * * * ." Although [UCC] 2–401(2) begins with the phrase "[u]nless otherwise explicitly agreed," the prior subsection places limits on the parties' contractual freedom. Specifically, *[UCC] 2–401(1) negates any attempt to forestall passage of title beyond the moment of final delivery* * * * . Similarly, [UCC] 2–401(1) prohibits the passage of title prior to the identification of the goods in question to the contract. In between these extremes, however, the parties may by contract specify the point at which title passes. * * * Under subsection (1), by agreement of the parties, title to goods can pass from the time the goods are identified in the contract up to the time the goods are delivered. Subsection (2) deals with fact patterns in the absence of an agreement to the contrary pursuant to subsection (1). The Court finds that under the UCC, title to the cattle passed upon delivery of the cattle on the day of the respective sales. [Emphasis added.]

DECISION AND REMEDY The court held that the transfer of title to the cattle occurred on the dates of the sales when the cattle were physically delivered. Thus, Stewart's payments with the cashier's checks were not part of a "contemporaneous exchange"—the payments occurred after the bank returned his personal checks for insufficient funds, more than two weeks after the transfer of title.

FOR CRITICAL ANALYSIS—Ethical Consideration *Often, by explicit agreement, the parties to a transaction can establish terms that differ from those provided by the UCC. In this case, why weren't the words on Barry County's bill of sale, "SUBJECT TO FINAL PAYMENT," effective in establishing the terms of the sale?*

Sometimes, circumstances make it difficult for a person to carry out the promised performance, in which case the contract may be breached. When breach occurs, the aggrieved party looks for remedies—which we deal with in the second half of the chapter.

Performance Obligations

As discussed in previous chapters and stressed in the opening quotation to this chapter, the standards of good faith and commercial reasonableness are read into every contract. These standards provide a framework in which the parties can specify particulars of performance. Thus, when one party delays specifying particulars of performance for an unreasonable period of time or fails to cooperate with the other party, the innocent party is excused from any resulting delay in performance. The innocent party can proceed to perform in any reasonable manner, and the other party's failure to specify particulars or to cooperate can be treated as a breach of contract. Good faith is a question of fact for the jury. For a discussion of the importance of good faith in the performance of contracts, see this chapter's *Management Perspective* feature.

In the performance of a sales or lease contract, the basic obligation of the seller or lessor is to *transfer and deliver conforming goods*. The basic obligation of the buyer or lessee is to *accept and pay for conforming goods* in accordance with the contract [UCC 2–301, 2A–516(1)]. Overall performance of a sales or lease contract is controlled by the agreement between the parties. When the contract is unclear and disputes arise, the courts look to the UCC.

Obligations of the Seller or Lessor

The major obligation of the seller or lessor under a sales or lease contract is to tender conforming goods to the buyer or lessee.

Tender of Delivery

Tender of delivery requires that the seller or lessor have and hold *conforming goods* at the disposal of the buyer or lessee and give the buyer or lessee whatever notification is reasonably necessary to enable the buyer or lessee to take delivery [UCC 2–503(1), 2A–508(1)].

Tender must occur at a *reasonable hour* and in a *reasonable manner.* In other words, a seller cannot call the buyer at 2:00 A.M. and say, "The goods are ready. I'll give you twenty minutes to get them." Unless the parties have agreed otherwise, the goods must be tendered for delivery at a reasonable time and kept available for a reasonable period of time to enable the buyer to take possession of them [UCC 2–503(1)(a)].

All goods called for by a contract must be tendered in a single delivery unless the parties agree otherwise or the circumstances are such that either party can rightfully request delivery in lots [UCC 2–307, 2–612, 2A–510]. Hence, an order for 1,000 shirts cannot be delivered 2 shirts at a time. If, however, the seller and the buyer contemplate that the shirts will be delivered in four orders of 250 each, as they are produced (for summer, fall, winter, and spring stock), and the price can be apportioned accordingly, it may be commercially reasonable to deliver the shirts in this way.

MANAGEMENT PERSPECTIVE

Good Faith and Fair Dealing

MANAGEMENT FACES A LEGAL ISSUE

As discussed elsewhere, all contracts governed by the Uniform Commercial Code (UCC) must meet the requirements of good faith and fair dealing. Yet do these requirements supersede the written terms of a contract? In other words, if a party adheres strictly to the express, written terms of a contract, can the party nonetheless face liability for breaching the UCC's good faith requirements?

WHAT THE COURTS SAY

Generally, the courts take the good faith provisions of the UCC very seriously. Indeed, in one case the court stated that "a party can violate the implied covenant of good faith and fair dealing without violating the express term of a contract." The issue of whether a party had breached an express provision of the contract was, in this court's view, separate and distinct from the issue of whether the implied covenant of good faith had been breached. In reaching its conclusion, the court emphasized the fact that one of the parties had superior bargaining power over the other and used this power to "prey" on the other party's lack of sophistication and financial strength.[a]

Other courts have held that good faith can be breached even when the parties have equal bargaining power. In one case, for example, the court held that although the plaintiffs were sophisticated businesspersons who had the assistance of highly competent counsel, they could still maintain an action for breach of good faith and fair dealing. The court reasoned that "the presence of bad faith is to be found in the eye of the beholder or, more to the point, in the eye of the trier of fact," indicating that it was up to a jury to determine whether the parties had performed in good faith.[b] In another case, the court held that a contract provision that gave a telephone company the right to reject potential cellular subscribers must be exercised in good faith and not selectively against the customers who were solicited by an electronics store.[c]

IMPLICATIONS FOR MANAGERS

The message for business owners and managers involved in sales contracts is clear: compliance with the literal terms of a contract is not enough—the standards of good faith and fair dealing must also be met. While the specific standards of good faith performance are still evolving, the overriding principle is that the parties to a contract should do nothing to injure or destroy the rights of the other party to receive the fruits of the contract.

a. *Sons of Thunder, Inc. v. Borden, Inc.*, 148 N.J. 396, 690 A.2d 575 (1997).

b. *Seidenberg v. Summit Bank*, 2002 WL 276149 (N.J.Super. 2002).

c. *Electronics Store, Inc. v. Cellco Partnership*, 127 Md.App. 385, 732 A.2d 980 (1999).

Place of Delivery

The UCC provides for the place of delivery pursuant to a contract if the contract does not. Of course, the parties may agree on a particular destination, or their contract's terms or the circumstances may indicate the place of delivery.

Noncarrier Cases If the contract does not designate the place of delivery for the goods, and the buyer is expected to pick them up, the place of delivery is the *seller's place of business* or, if the seller has none, the seller's residence [UCC 2–308]. If the contract involves the sale of *identified goods,* and the parties know when they enter into the contract that these goods are located somewhere other than at the seller's place of business (such as at a warehouse), then the *location of the goods* is the place for their delivery [UCC 2–308].

■ EXAMPLE 20.1 Rogers and Aguirre live in San Francisco. In San Francisco, Rogers contracts to sell Aguirre five used trucks, which both parties know are located in a Chicago warehouse. If nothing more is specified in the contract, the place of delivery for the trucks is Chicago. ■ The seller may tender delivery either by giving the buyer a *negotiable or nonnegotiable document of title* or by obtaining the *bailee's (warehouser's) acknowledgment* that the buyer is entitled to possession.[1]

Carrier Cases In many instances, attendant circumstances or delivery terms in the contract make it apparent that the parties intend that a carrier be used to move the goods. In carrier cases, a seller can complete performance of the obligation to deliver the goods in two ways—through a shipment contract or through a destination contract.

KEEP IN MIND If goods never arrive, the buyer or seller usually has at least some recourse against the carrier. Also, a buyer normally insures the goods from the time they leave the seller's possession.

Shipment Contracts. Recall from Chapter 19 that a shipment contract requires or authorizes the seller to ship goods by a carrier. The contract does not require that the seller deliver the goods at a particular destination [UCC 2–319, 2–509].[2] Under a shipment contract, unless otherwise agreed, the seller must do the following:

1. Put the goods into the hands of the carrier.
2. Make a contract for their transportation that is reasonable according to the nature of the goods and their value. (For example, certain types of goods need refrigeration in transit.)
3. Obtain and promptly deliver or tender to the buyer any documents necessary to enable the buyer to obtain possession of the goods from the carrier.
4. Promptly notify the buyer that shipment has been made [UCC 2–504].

If the seller fails to notify the buyer that shipment has been made or fails to make a proper contract for transportation, the buyer can treat the contract as breached and reject the goods, but only if a *material loss* of the goods or a significant *delay* results. Of course, the parties can agree that a lesser amount of loss or any delay will be grounds for rejection.

Destination Contracts. Under a *destination contract,* the seller agrees to see that conforming goods will be duly tendered to the buyer at a particular destination. The goods must be tendered at a reasonable hour and held at the buyer's disposal for a reasonable length of time. The seller must also give the buyer any appropriate notice that is necessary to enable the buyer to take delivery. In addition, the seller must provide the buyer with any documents of title necessary to enable the buyer to obtain delivery from the carrier [UCC 2–503].

DON'T FORGET Documents of title include bills of lading, warehouse receipts, and any other documents that, in the regular course of business, entitle a person holding these documents to obtain possession of, and title to, the goods covered.

THE PERFECT TENDER RULE

As previously noted, the seller or lessor has an obligation to ship or tender *conforming goods,* and the buyer or lessee is required to accept and pay for the goods according to the terms of the contract. Under the common law, the seller was obligated to deliver goods in conformity with the terms of the contract in every detail. This was called the *perfect tender* doctrine. The UCC preserves the perfect tender

1. If the seller delivers a nonnegotiable document of title or merely writes instructions to the bailee to release the goods to the buyer without the bailee's *acknowledgment* of the buyer's rights, this is also a sufficient tender, unless the buyer objects [UCC 2–503(4)]. Risk of loss, however, does not pass until the buyer has a reasonable amount of time in which to present the document or to give the bailee instructions for delivery.

2. As mentioned in Chapter 19, UCC 2–319 was omitted from the 2003 amendments to Article 2.

doctrine by stating that if goods or tender of delivery fail *in any respect* to conform to the contract, the buyer or lessee has the right to accept the goods, reject the entire shipment, or accept part and reject part [UCC 2–601, 2A–509].

■ EXAMPLE 20.2 A lessor contracts to lease fifty Vericlear monitors to be delivered at the lessee's place of business on or before October 1. On September 28, the lessor discovers that it has only thirty Vericlear monitors in inventory, but that it will have another forty Vericlear monitors within the next two weeks. The lessor tenders delivery of the thirty Vericlear monitors on October 1, with the promise that the other monitors will be delivered within three weeks. Because the lessor failed to make a perfect tender of fifty Vericlear monitors, the lessee has the right to reject the entire shipment and hold the lessor in breach. ■

.on the Web To view the UCC provisions discussed in this chapter, go to **http://www.law.cornell.edu/ucc/ucc.table.html**.

EXCEPTIONS TO PERFECT TENDER

Because of the rigidity of the perfect tender rule, several exceptions to the rule have been created, some of which are discussed here.

Agreement of the Parties Exceptions to the perfect tender rule may be established by agreement. If the parties have agreed, for example, that defective goods or parts will not be rejected if the seller or lessor is able to repair or replace them within a reasonable period of time, the perfect tender rule does not apply.

Cure The UCC does not specifically define the term *cure,* but it refers to the right of the seller or lessor to repair, adjust, or replace defective or nonconforming goods [UCC 2–508, 2A–513]. When any tender of delivery is rejected because of nonconforming goods and the time for performance has not yet expired, the seller or lessor can notify the buyer or lessee promptly of the intention to cure and can then do so *within the contract time for performance* [UCC 2–508(1), 2A–513(1)]. Once the time for performance has expired, the seller or lessor can still, for a reasonable time, exercise the right to cure with respect to the rejected goods if he or she had, at the time of delivery, *reasonable grounds to believe that the nonconforming tender would be acceptable to the buyer or lessee* [UCC 2–508(2), 2A–513(2)].[3]

Sometimes, a seller or lessor will tender nonconforming goods with some type of price allowance. The allowance serves as the "reasonable grounds" for the seller or lessor to believe that the nonconforming tender will be acceptable to the buyer or lessee. A seller or lessor might also have other reasons for assuming that a buyer or lessee will accept a nonconforming tender. ■ EXAMPLE 20.3 Suppose that in the past the buyer, an office supply store, frequently accepted blue pens when the seller did not have black pens in stock. In this context, the seller has reasonable grounds to believe the store will again accept such a substitute. If the store rejects the substituted goods (blue pens) on a particular occasion, the seller nonetheless had reasonable grounds to believe that the blue pens would be acceptable. Therefore, the seller can cure within a reasonable time, even though the delivery of black pens will occur after the time limit for performance allowed under the contract. ■

The right to cure means that, to reject goods, the buyer or lessee must give notice to the seller or lessor of a particular defect. For example, if a lessee refuses a tender

3. The 2003 amendments to UCC Articles 2 and 2A expressly exempt "consumer contracts" and "consumer leases" from these provisions [Amended UCC 2–508, 2A–508]. In other words, cure is not available as a matter of right after a justifiable revocation of acceptance under a consumer contract or lease. Also, the new provisions abandon the "reasonable grounds to believe" test, thus expanding the seller's right to cure after the time for performance has expired. Although this test has been abandoned, the requirement that the initial tender be made in good faith prevents a seller from deliberately tendering goods that the seller knows the buyer cannot use.

of goods as nonconforming but does not disclose the nature of the defect to the lessor, the lessee cannot later assert the defect as a defense if the defect is one that the lessor could have cured. Generally, buyers and lessees must act in good faith and state specific reasons for refusing to accept goods [UCC 2–605, 2A–514].[4]

Substitution of Carriers When an agreed-on manner of delivery (such as which carrier will be used to transport the goods) becomes impracticable or unavailable through no fault of either party, but a commercially reasonable substitute is available, the seller must use this substitute performance, which is sufficient tender to the buyer [UCC 2–614(1)]. ■ EXAMPLE 20.4 A sales contract calls for the delivery of a large generator to be shipped by Roadway Trucking Corporation on or before June 1. The contract terms clearly state the importance of the delivery date. The employees of Roadway Trucking go on strike. The seller is required to make a reasonable substitute tender, perhaps by rail if that is available. Note that the seller will normally be responsible for any additional shipping costs, unless other arrangements have been made in the sales contract. ■

INSTALLMENT CONTRACT
Under the UCC, a contract that requires or authorizes delivery in two or more separate lots to be accepted and paid for separately.

Installment Contracts An **installment contract** is a single contract that requires or authorizes delivery in two or more separate lots to be accepted and paid for separately. In an installment contract, a buyer or lessee can reject an installment *only if the nonconformity substantially impairs the value* of the installment and cannot be cured [UCC 2–612(2), 2–307, 2A–510(1)].[5]

4. The 2003 amendments to UCC 2–605 and 2A–514 change this restriction in three ways. First, a buyer's or lessee's failure to disclose the nature of the defect affects only the right to reject or revoke acceptance, not the right to establish a breach of contract. Second, the new sections expressly require that the seller or lessor must have had a right to cure, as well as the ability to cure. Finally, these sections extend to include not only rejection but also revocation of acceptance.

5. The 2003 amendments to Articles 2 and 2A make it clear that the buyer's or lessee's right to reject an installment depends on whether the value of the installment to the buyer or lessee is substantially impaired and not on whether the seller or lessor is able to cure [Amended UCC 2–612(2), 2A–510(2)].

*Competitors' trucks travel the same route. When is it acceptable to substitute one carrier for another specified in a contract? (Sandy Huffaker/*Bloomberg News/*Landov)*

Unless the contract provides otherwise, the entire installment contract is breached only when one or more nonconforming installments *substantially* impair the value of the *whole contract.* If the buyer or lessee subsequently accepts a nonconforming installment and fails to notify the seller or lessor of cancellation, however, the contract is reinstated [UCC 2–612(3), 2A–510(2)].

A major issue to be determined is what constitutes substantial impairment of the "value of the whole contract." ■ EXAMPLE 20.5 Consider an installment contract for the sale of twenty carloads of plywood. The first carload does not conform to the contract because 9 percent of the plywood deviates from the thickness specifications. The buyer cancels the contract, and immediately thereafter the second and third carloads of conforming plywood arrive at the buyer's place of business. If a lawsuit ensues, the court will have to grapple with the question of whether the 9 percent of nonconforming plywood substantially impaired the value of the whole. ■

The point to remember is that the UCC significantly alters the right of the buyer or lessee to reject the entire contract if the contract requires delivery to be made in several installments. The UCC strictly limits rejection to cases of *substantial* nonconformity.

Commercial Impracticability As mentioned in Chapter 14, occurrences that were not foreseeable by either party when a contract was made may make performance commercially impracticable. When this occurs, the rule of perfect tender no longer holds. According to UCC 2–615(a) and 2A–405(a), delay in delivery or nondelivery in whole or in part is not a breach when performance has been made impracticable "by the occurrence of a contingency the nonoccurrence of which was a basic assumption on which the contract was made." The seller or lessor must, however, notify the buyer or lessee as soon as practicable that there will be a delay or nondelivery.

Foreseeable versus Unforeseeable Contingencies. An increase in cost resulting from inflation does not in itself excuse performance, as a seller or lessor ordinarily assumes this kind of risk when conducting business. The unforeseen contingency must be one that would have been impossible to contemplate in a given business situation. ■ EXAMPLE 20.6 A major oil company that receives its supplies from the Middle East has a contract to supply a buyer with 100,000 gallons of oil. Because of an oil embargo by the Organization of Petroleum Exporting Countries (OPEC), the seller is prevented from securing oil supplies to meet the terms of the contract. Because of the same embargo, the seller cannot secure oil from any other source. This situation comes fully under the commercial impracticability exception to the perfect tender doctrine. ■

Can unanticipated increases in a seller's costs, which make performance "impracticable," constitute a valid defense to performance on the basis of commercial impracticability? The court dealt with this question in the following case.

LANDMARK AND CLASSIC CASES

CASE 20.1 Maple Farms, Inc. v. City School District of Elmira

Supreme Court of New York, 1974.
76 Misc.2d 1080,
352 N.Y.S.2d 784.

BACKGROUND AND FACTS On June 15, 1973, Maple Farms, Inc., formed an agreement with the city school district of Elmira, New York, to supply the school district with milk for the 1973–1974 school year. The agreement was in the form of a requirements contract, under which Maple Farms would sell to the school district all the milk the district required at a fixed price—which was the June market price of milk. By December 1973,

(Continued)

CASE 20.1—Continued

the price of raw milk had increased by 23 percent over the price specified in the contract. This meant that if the terms of the contract were fulfilled, Maple Farms would lose $7,350. Because it had similar contracts with other school districts, Maple Farms stood to lose a great deal if it was held to the price stated in the contracts. When the school district would not agree to release Maple Farms from its contract, Maple Farms brought an action in a New York state court for a declaratory judgment (a determination of the parties' rights under a contract). Maple Farms contended that the substantial increase in the price of raw milk was an event not contemplated by the parties when the contract was formed and that, given the increased price, performance of the contract was commercially impracticable.

IN THE WORDS OF THE COURT . . .
CHARLES B. SWARTWOOD, Justice.

* * * *

* * * [The doctrine of commercial impracticability requires that] a contingency—something unexpected—must have occurred. Second, the risk of the unexpected occurrence must not have been allocated either by agreement or by custom. * * *

* * * [H]ere we find that the contingency causing the increase of the price of raw milk was not totally unexpected. The price from the low point in the year 1972 to the price on the date of the award of the contract in June 1973 had risen nearly 10%. And *any businessman should have been aware of the general inflation in this country during the previous years* * * * . [Emphasis added.]

* * * Here the very purpose of the contract was to guard against fluctuation of price of half pints of milk as a basis for the school budget. Surely had the price of raw milk fallen substantially, the defendant could not be excused from performance. We can reasonably assume that the plaintiff had to be aware of escalating inflation. It is chargeable with knowledge of the substantial increase of the price of raw milk from the previous year's low. * * * It nevertheless entered into this agreement with that knowledge. It did not provide in the contract any exculpatory clause to excuse it from performance in the event of a substantial rise in the price of raw milk. On these facts the risk of a substantial or abnormal increase in the price of raw milk can be allocated to the plaintiff.

DECISION AND REMEDY The New York trial court ruled that performance in this case was not impracticable and granted summary judgment in favor of the school district.

COMMENTS *This case is a classic illustration of the UCC's commercial impracticability doctrine. Under this doctrine, parties who freely enter into contracts normally will not be excused from their contractual obligations simply because changed circumstances make performance difficult or very costly. Rather, to be excused from performance, a party must show that the changed circumstances were impossible to foresee at the time the contract was formed. This principle continues to be applied today.*

RELEVANT WEB SITES *To locate information on the Web concerning* Maple Farms, Inc. v. City School District of Elmira, *go to this text's Web site at* **http://blt.westbuslaw.com**, *select "Chapter 20," and click on "URLs for Landmarks."*

Partial Performance. Sometimes, an unforeseen event only *partially* affects the capacity of the seller or lessor to perform, and the seller or lessor is thus able to fulfill the contract *partially* but cannot tender total performance. In this event, the seller or lessor is required to allocate in a fair and reasonable manner any remaining production and deliveries among those to whom it is contractually obligated to deliver the goods, and this allocation may take into account its regular customers

[UCC 2–615(b), 2A–405(b)]. The buyer or lessee must receive notice of the allocation and has the right to accept or reject the allocation [UCC 2–615(c), 2A–405(c)].

■ EXAMPLE 20.7 A Florida orange grower, Best Citrus, Inc., contracts to sell this season's crop to a number of customers, including Martin's grocery chain. Martin's contracts to purchase two thousand crates of oranges. Best Citrus has sprayed some of its orange groves with a chemical called Karmoxin. The Department of Agriculture discovers that persons who eat products sprayed with Karmoxin may develop cancer. The department issues an order prohibiting the sale of these products. Best Citrus picks all of the oranges not sprayed with Karmoxin, but the quantity does not fully meet all the contracted-for deliveries. In this situation, Best Citrus is required to allocate its production, and it notifies Martin's that it cannot deliver the full quantity agreed on in the contract and specifies the amount it will be able to deliver under the circumstances. Martin's can either accept or reject the allocation, but Best Citrus has no further contractual liability. ■

Destruction of Identified Goods The UCC provides that when an unexpected event, such as a fire, totally destroys *goods identified at the time the contract is formed* through no fault of either party and *before risk passes to the buyer or lessee,* the parties are excused from performance [UCC 2–613, 2A–221]. If the goods are only partially destroyed, however, the buyer or lessee can inspect them and either treat the contract as void or accept the goods with a reduction of the contract price.

■ EXAMPLE 20.8 Atlas Sporting Equipment agrees to lease to River Bicycles sixty bicycles of a particular model that has been discontinued. No other bicycles of that model are available. River specifies that it needs the bicycles to rent to tourists. Before Atlas can deliver the bikes, they are destroyed by a fire. In this situation,

If a fire destroys warehoused goods that have been identified to a sales contract before risk of loss has passed to the buyer, will the seller be held liable for breach of contract? Why or why not? (Yakima Herald-Republic/*Gordon King, AP/Wide World Photos)*

Atlas is not liable to River for failing to deliver the bikes. The goods were destroyed through no fault of either party, before the risk of loss passed to the lessee. The loss was total, so the contract is avoided. Clearly, Atlas has no obligation to tender the bicycles, and River has no obligation to pay for them. ■

Assurance and Cooperation Two other exceptions to the perfect tender doctrine apply equally to parties to sales and lease contracts: the right of assurance and the duty of cooperation.

The Right of Assurance. The UCC provides that if one party to a contract has "reasonable grounds" to believe that the other party will not perform as contracted, he or she may *in writing* "demand adequate assurance of due performance" from the other party. Until such assurance is received, he or she may "suspend" further performance (such as payments due under the contract) without liability. What constitutes "reasonable grounds" is determined by commercial standards. If such assurances are not forthcoming within a reasonable time (not to exceed thirty days), the failure to respond may be treated as a *repudiation* of the contract [UCC 2–609, 2A–401]. The following case illustrates this principle.

CASE 20.2 Koch Materials Co. v. Shore Slurry Seal, Inc.

United States District Court,
District of New Jersey, 2002.
205 F.Supp.2d 324.
http://lawlibrary.rutgers.edu/fed/search.html[a]

BACKGROUND AND FACTS Koch Materials Company is a manufacturer of road surfacing materials. In February 1998, Koch agreed to pay $5 million, payable in three installments, to Shore Slurry Seal, Inc., for an asphalt plant in New Jersey and the rights to license a specialty road surfacing substance, known as Novachip. Shore also agreed that for seven years following the sale, it would buy all of its asphalt requirements from Koch, or at least 2 million gallons of asphalt per year (the Exclusive Supply Agreement). Shore promised to use at least 2.5 million square yards of Novachip annually and to pay royalties to Koch accordingly (the Sublicense Agreement). Midway through the term of the contract, Shore told Koch that it planned to sell its assets to Asphalt Paving Systems, Inc. Koch sought assurances that Asphalt Paving would continue the original deal. Shore refused to provide any more information. Koch filed a suit in a federal district court against Shore, asking in part for the right to treat Shore's failure to give assurances as a repudiation of their contract. Koch filed a motion for summary judgment on this issue.

a. In the "Find Decisions by Docket Number" section, select "Civil Case," type "01-2059" in the "Enter Docket Number" box, and click on "Submit Form." From the results, click on "ca01-2059-1.html" to access the opinion. Rutgers University School of Law in Camden, New Jersey, maintains this Web site.

IN THE WORDS OF THE COURT . . .
ORLOFSKY, District Judge.

* * * *

* * * Koch had a commercially reasonable basis for demanding assurances on both the Exclusive Supply and Sublicense Agreements. The Sublicense Agreement analysis is straightforward. Shore reported that it planned to sell all of its " * * * assets," but retain * * * the Sublicense Agreement. Even assuming that historically, Shore had met most of its Novachip obligations by selling sublicenses to third parties, rather than laying its own road surfacing, any reasonable person would wonder how Shore planned to sell *anything* with no telephones, no computers, and no office furniture. That Shore might well have leased these items only prompts further questions: Would Shore have had the financial capacity to obtain leases and hire a sales staff? Or were the proceeds of the sale going directly to [Shore's president]?

CASE 20.2—Continued

The Exclusive Supply Agreement [ESA] is a bit more complex, but no less certain. * * * Shore promised Koch not only a minimum annual purchase, but also all of the potential upside of Shore's requirements over and above the minimum should Shore's demand for asphalt grow over time. Thus, the identity of the purchaser, its future business plans, and its anticipated need for Koch's product could all affect significantly the amount of money that Koch would realize under the ESA, not only from the two million gallon minimum, but also from the potential upside. [Shore], it is true, promised that Shore's contracts, presumably including the ESA, would be assigned to the purchaser. *Start-up construction businesses, however, begin unbonded, unable to win any bid for their first year and unable to secure sufficient bonding for large construction bids for several years.*[b] Koch had no way of knowing whether Asphalt was already a going business, and, if not, whether it would be able to win sufficient sub-contracting bids even to meet the minimum requirements, let alone approach the potential upside of an established enterprise like Shore. [Emphasis added.]

* * * *

The remaining question, then, is whether [Shore provided those assurances]. * * * Far from assuring Koch that Shore would secure Koch's permission before assigning the ESA, [Shore's president] asserted that "I am not aware of provisions within our agreements requiring me to notify Koch of any business negotiations that I may be involved in." This evasive answer not only failed to give Koch any information about the potential successor party to the contract, but also raised a new inference that Shore might be actively planning to evade the exclusive supply aspects of the ESA. It was, furthermore, close to a vow to breach * * * the ESA. Nor did Shore give any indication about its ability to meet the Sublicense Agreement volume requirements.

b. In this context, a *bond* is a guaranty to complete or to pay the cost of a construction contract if the contractor defaults.

DECISION AND REMEDY The court issued a summary judgment in Koch's favor. The court concluded that Shore's failure to provide assurances to Koch constituted a repudiation of their contract, authorizing Koch to terminate the contract and seek damages.

WHY IS THIS CASE IMPORTANT? *This case clearly illustrates how the UCC comes to the aid of a party who has reasonable grounds to suspect that the other party to a contract will not perform as promised. Rather than having to "wait and see" (and possibly incur significant losses as a result), the party with such suspicions may seek adequate assurance of performance from the other party. The failure to give such assurance can be treated as an anticipatory repudiation (breach) of the contract, thus entitling the nonbreaching party to seek damages.*

The Duty of Cooperation. Sometimes, the performance of one party depends on the cooperation of the other. The UCC provides that when such cooperation is not forthcoming, the other party can suspend her or his own performance without liability and hold the uncooperative party in breach or proceed to perform the contract in any reasonable manner [UCC 2–311(3)(b)].

Obligations of the Buyer or Lessee

Once the seller or lessor has adequately tendered delivery, the buyer or lessee is obligated to accept the goods and pay for them according to the terms of the contract. In the absence of any specific agreements, the buyer or lessee must make payment at the time and place the goods are received [UCC 2–310(a), 2A–516(1)].

When the Goods Are in the Possession of the Seller or Lessor

Under the UCC, if the buyer or lessee breaches the contract before the goods have been delivered to her or him, the seller or lessor has the right to pursue the remedies discussed here.

NOTE A buyer or lessee breaches a contract by wrongfully rejecting the goods, wrongfully revoking acceptance, refusing to pay, or repudiating the contract.

The Right to Cancel the Contract One of the options available to a seller or lessor when the buyer or lessee breaches the contract is simply to cancel (rescind) the contract [UCC 2–703(f), 2A–523(1)(a)]. The seller or lessor must notify the buyer or lessee of the cancellation, and at that point all remaining obligations of the seller or lessor are discharged. The buyer or lessee is not discharged from all remaining obligations, however; he or she is in breach, and the seller or lessor can pursue remedies available under the UCC for breach.

The Right to Withhold Delivery In general, sellers and lessors can withhold or discontinue performance of their obligations under sales or lease contracts when the buyers or lessees are in breach. If a buyer or lessee has wrongfully rejected or revoked acceptance of contract goods (rejection and revocation of acceptance will be discussed later), failed to make proper and timely payment, or repudiated a part of the contract, the seller or lessor can withhold delivery of the goods in question [UCC 2–703(a), 2A–523(1)(c)]. If the breach results from the buyer's or the lessee's insolvency (inability to pay debts as they become due), the seller or lessor can refuse to deliver the goods unless the buyer or lessee pays in cash [UCC 2–702(1), 2A–525(1)].

The Right to Resell or Dispose of the Goods When a buyer or lessee breaches or repudiates a sales contract while the seller or lessor is still in possession of the goods, the seller or lessor can resell or dispose of the goods. The seller can retain any profits made as a result of the sale and can hold the buyer or lessee liable for any loss [UCC 2–703(d), 2–706(1), 2A–523(1)(e), 2A–527(1)].[8]

When the goods contracted for are unfinished at the time of breach, the seller or lessor can do one of two things: (1) cease manufacturing the goods and resell them for scrap or salvage value or (2) complete the manufacture and resell or dispose of them, holding the buyer or lessee liable for any deficiency. In choosing between these two alternatives, the seller or lessor must exercise reasonable commercial judgment to mitigate the loss and obtain maximum value from the unfinished goods [UCC 2–704(2), 2A–524(2)]. Any resale of the goods must be made in good faith and in a commercially reasonable manner.

INCIDENTAL DAMAGES
All costs resulting from a breach of contract, including all reasonable expenses incurred because of the breach.

In sales transactions, the seller can recover any deficiency between the resale price and the contract price, along with **incidental damages,** defined as those costs to the seller resulting from the breach [UCC 2–706(1), 2–710]. The resale can be private or public, and the goods can be sold as a unit or in parcels. The seller must give the original buyer reasonable notice of the resale, unless the goods are perishable or will

8. Under the 2003 amendments to UCC Articles 2 and 2A, this loss includes consequential damages, except that a seller or lessor cannot recover consequential damages from a consumer under a consumer contract or lease [Amended UCC 2–706(1), 2–710, 2A–527(2), 2A–530]. Consequential damages may also be recovered, except from a consumer under a consumer contract or lease, when a seller or lessor has a right to recover the purchase price or lease payments due or to recover other damages [Amended UCC 2–708(1), 2–709(1), 2–710, 2A–528(1), 2A–529(1), 2A–530]. Subtracted from these amounts, of course, would be any expenses saved as a consequence of the buyer's or lessee's breach.

rapidly decline in value [UCC 2–706(2), (3)]. A good faith purchaser in a resale takes the goods free of any of the rights of the original buyer, even if the seller fails to comply with these requirements of the UCC [UCC 2–706(5)].

In lease transactions, the lessor may lease the goods to another party and recover from the original lessee, as damages, any unpaid lease payments up to the beginning date of the lease term under the new lease. The lessor can also recover any deficiency between the lease payments due under the original lease contract and under the new lease contract, along with incidental damages [UCC 2A–527(2)].

The Right to Recover the Purchase Price or the Lease Payments Due Under the UCC, an unpaid seller or lessor can bring an action to recover the purchase price or payments due under the lease contract, plus incidental damages, if the seller or lessor is unable to resell or dispose of the goods [UCC 2–709(1), 2A–529(1)].

■ EXAMPLE 20.9 Suppose that Southern Realty contracts with Gem Point, Inc., to purchase one thousand pens with Southern Realty's name inscribed on them. Gem Point tenders delivery of the one thousand pens, but Southern Realty wrongfully refuses to accept them. In this situation, Gem Point has, as a proper remedy, an action for the purchase price. Gem Point tendered delivery of conforming goods, and Southern Realty, by failing to accept the goods, is in breach. Gem Point obviously cannot sell to anyone else the pens inscribed with the buyer's business name, so this situation falls under UCC 2–709. ■

If a seller or lessor is unable to resell or dispose of goods and sues for the contract price or lease payments due, the goods must be held for the buyer or lessee. The seller or lessor can resell or dispose of the goods at any time prior to collection (of the judgment) from the buyer or lessee but must credit the net proceeds from the sale to the buyer or lessee. This is an example of the duty to mitigate damages.

The Right to Recover Damages If a buyer or lessee repudiates a contract or wrongfully refuses to accept the goods, a seller or lessor can maintain an action to recover the damages that were sustained. Ordinarily, the amount of damages equals the difference between the contract price or lease payments and the market price or lease payments (at the time and place of tender of the goods), plus incidental damages [UCC 2–708(1), 2A–528(1)]. The time and place of tender are frequently given by such terms as F.O.B., F.A.S., C.I.F., and the like, which determine whether there is a shipment or destination contract.[9]

In the following case, the court had to determine the proper measure of damages after a buyer breached a sales contract.

9. See Exhibit 19–1 on page 464 for a definition of these contract terms, which are omitted from the 2003 amendments to Article 2 [Amended UCC 2–319 through 2–324].

CASE 20.3 Utica Alloys, Inc. v. Alcoa, Inc.

United States District Court,
Northern District of New York, 2004.
303 F.Supp.2d 247.

BACKGROUND AND FACTS Alcoa, Inc., through its business, generates scrap metal. Utica Alloys, Inc., buys and processes this type of scrap and sells it to its only user, General Electric Company (GE), which uses it in land-based power turbines. In July 2001, Utica agreed to buy all of Alcoa's scrap through August 2003. Their contract indexed the monthly price of the scrap to the monthly market price of nickel, but contemplated that the parties would review this price semiannually. In November 2001, GE reduced its production of turbines,

(Continued)

CASE 20.3—Continued

which lowered the market value of the scrap. This change was not reflected in Alcoa's arrangement with Utica, however, because the price in their contract was based on the market value of nickel. In January 2002, the opportunity arose to review the price of the scrap, and the parties began to negotiate while they continued to ship and process the scrap. In May, when the parties were unable to agree on a price, Alcoa stated that the contract was over, retrieved the scrap processed after January, and sold it to another party. Utica filed a suit in a federal district court against Alcoa, alleging in part unjust enrichment. Alcoa counterclaimed for breach of contract. The court entered a judgment in Alcoa's favor, holding that Utica breached the agreement by failing to pay for the scrap received after January. Alcoa asked for damages based on the difference between the contract price for the *unprocessed* scrap and the price at which the *processed* scrap sold after it was retrieved.

IN THE WORDS OF THE COURT . . .

HURD, District Judge.

* * * *

* * * Defendant claims its measure of damages is the difference between the purchase agreement price of the scrap and the price for which it sold the processed scrap it retrieved from plaintiff.

This, however, would serve as a double penalty to Utica Alloys, Inc., for processing the scrap. Absent the purchase agreement, Alcoa, Inc., would have sold the scrap at the unprocessed market price. Because of the purchase agreement, it is entitled to the higher purchase agreement price. The processed feature of the scrap, as Alcoa, Inc., points out numerous times, was not part of the agreement between the parties and actually decreased its value because of the demand reduction in the market for such scrap. However, Alcoa, Inc., accepted return of the processed scrap from Utica Alloys, Inc., when it elected to terminate the purchase agreement in May 2002. It has also refused to pay plaintiff for processing the scrap. Defendant cannot be permitted in one breath to denounce processing as irrelevant to the contractual relationship, while in another embrace the market change of processed scrap as the yardstick for measuring its damages under the contract.

Therefore, *the proper measure of damages is the difference between the purchase price of the unprocessed scrap, as such is calculated under the purchase agreement, and the market value of unprocessed scrap.* The market value of unprocessed scrap is not to be determined solely from the amount for which Alcoa, Inc., was able to sell the scrap in May of 2002. *Rather, because the purchase agreement called for monthly shipments and prices, damages will have to be ascertained for three different time periods.* The following determinations will therefore need to be made, for each of the months from February to April of 2002, before the proper amount of total damages can be calculated: (1) the amount, *in pounds,* of scrap shipped during each of the relevant months; (2) the per pound purchase agreement price, calculated *using the formula in the agreement,* for each of the relevant months; and (3) the per pound *fair market value of unprocessed scrap* for each of the three months. The damages will be calculated for each of the three months, and will then be added together to determine defendant's total damages for plaintiff's failure to pay for the scrap it was shipped. The parties will be permitted to submit * * * *only* the three *figures,* as well as any facts/figures supporting the same, required *for each month.* [Emphasis added.]

* * * *

* * * Defendant is * * * entitled to judgment on its counterclaim, and may receive as damages for plaintiff's failure to pay for scrap shipped and received under the purchase agreement the difference between the monthly purchase agreement price for such scrap and the monthly fair market value of unprocessed scrap. * * *

CASE 20.3—Continued

DECISION AND REMEDY The federal district court entered a judgment for the defendant and awarded damages based on the difference between the contract's monthly price for the unprocessed scrap and the monthly fair market value of unprocessed scrap.

FOR CRITICAL ANALYSIS—Economic Consideration *How, specifically, should the amount of damages in this case be determined, considering that the contract called for monthly shipments and prices?*

WHEN THE GOODS ARE IN TRANSIT

If the seller or lessor has delivered the goods to a carrier or a bailee but the buyer or lessee has not as yet received them, the goods are said to be in transit. If, while the goods are in transit, the seller or lessor learns that the buyer or lessee is insolvent, the seller or lessor can stop the carrier or bailee from delivering the goods, regardless of the quantity of goods shipped.

■ EXAMPLE 20.10 Suppose that Arturo Ortega orders a truckload of lumber from Timber Products, Inc., to be shipped to Ortega six weeks later. Ortega, who owes Timber Products for a past shipment, promises to pay the debt immediately and to pay for the current shipment as soon as it is received. After the lumber has been shipped, Timber Products is notified by a bankruptcy court judge that Ortega has filed a petition in bankruptcy and listed Timber Products as one of his creditors (see Chapter 27). If the goods are still in transit, Timber Products can stop the carrier from delivering the lumber to Ortega. ■ If the buyer or lessee is in breach but is not insolvent, the seller or lessor can stop the goods in transit only if the quantity shipped is at least a carload, a truckload, a planeload, or a larger shipment [UCC 2–705(1), 2A–526(1)].[10]

Requirements for Stopping Delivery To stop delivery, the seller or lessor must *timely notify* the carrier or other bailee that the goods are to be returned or held for the seller or lessor. If the carrier has sufficient time to stop delivery, it must hold and deliver the goods according to the instructions of the seller or lessor, who is liable to the carrier for any additional costs incurred [UCC 2–705(3), 2A–526(3)].

Exceptions UCC 2–705(2) and 2A–526(2) provide that the seller or lessor loses the right to stop delivery of goods in transit when any of the following events occur:

1. The buyer or lessee obtains possession of the goods.
2. The carrier acknowledges the rights of the buyer or lessee by reshipping or storing the goods for the buyer or lessee.
3. A bailee of the goods other than a carrier acknowledges that he or she is holding the goods for the buyer or lessee.

Additionally, in sales transactions, the seller loses the right to stop delivery of goods in transit when a negotiable document of title covering the goods has been negotiated (properly transferred, giving the buyer ownership rights in the goods) to the buyer [UCC 2–705(2)].

10. The 2003 amendments to UCC Articles 2 and 2A omit the restriction that prohibited the stoppage of less than "a carload, truckload, planeload, or larger shipment" because carriers can now identify a shipment as small as a single package [Amended UCC 2–705(1), 2A–526(1)].

Once the seller or lessor reclaims the goods in transit, she or he can pursue the remedies allowed to sellers and lessors when the goods are in their possession. In other words, the seller or lessor who has reclaimed goods may do the following:

1. Cancel (rescind) the contract.
2. Resell the goods and recover any deficiency.
3. Sue for any deficiency between the contract price (or lease payments due) and the market price (or market lease payments), plus incidental damages.
4. Sue to recover the purchase price or lease payments due if the goods cannot be resold, plus incidental damages.
5. Sue to recover damages.

WHEN THE GOODS ARE IN THE POSSESSION OF THE BUYER OR LESSEE

When the buyer or lessee breaches a sales or lease contract and the goods are in the buyer's or lessee's possession, the UCC gives the seller or lessor the following limited remedies.

RECALL Incidental damages include all reasonable expenses incurred because of a breach of contract.

The Right to Recover the Purchase Price or Payments Due under the Lease Contract If the buyer or lessee has accepted the goods but refuses to pay for them, the seller or lessor can sue for the purchase price of the goods or the lease payments due, plus incidental damages [UCC 2–709(1), 2A–529(1)].

The Right to Reclaim the Goods In regard to sales contracts, if the buyer has received goods on credit and the seller discovers that the buyer is insolvent, the seller can demand return of the goods if the demand is made within ten days of the buyer's receipt of the goods. The seller can demand and reclaim the goods at any time if the buyer misrepresented his or her solvency in writing within three months prior to the delivery of the goods [UCC 2–702(2)].[11] The seller's right to reclaim the goods, however, is subject to the rights of a good faith purchaser or other subsequent buyer in the ordinary course of business who purchases the goods from the buyer before the seller reclaims them.

Under the UCC, a seller seeking to exercise the right to reclaim goods receives preferential treatment over the buyer's other creditors—the seller need only demand the return of the goods within ten days after the buyer has received them.[12] Because of this preferential treatment, the UCC provides that reclamation *bars* the seller from pursuing any other remedy as to these goods [UCC 2–702(3)].

In regard to lease contracts, if the lessee defaults (fails to make payments that are due, for example), the lessor may reclaim the leased goods that are in the lessee's possession [UCC 2A–525(2)].

NOTE A seller or lessor breaches a contract by wrongfully failing to deliver the goods, delivering nonconforming goods, making an improper tender of the goods, or repudiating the contract.

Remedies of the Buyer or Lessee

When the seller or lessor breaches the contract, the buyer or lessee has numerous remedies available under the UCC in addition to recovery of as much of the price as has been paid. Like the remedies available to sellers and lessors, the remedies of buyers and lessees depend on the circumstances existing at the time of the breach.

11. The 2003 amendments to UCC Article 2 omit the ten-day limitation and the three-month exception to the ten-day limitation, referring instead to "a reasonable time" [Amended UCC 2–702(2)].

12. A seller who has delivered goods to an insolvent buyer also receives preferential treatment if the buyer enters into bankruptcy proceedings (discussed in Chapter 27).

When the Seller or Lessor Refuses to Deliver the Goods

If the seller or lessor refuses to deliver the goods or the buyer or lessee has rejected the goods, the remedies available to the buyer or lessee include those discussed here.

The Right to Cancel the Contract When a seller or lessor fails to make proper delivery or repudiates the contract, the buyer or lessee can cancel, or rescind, the contract. On notice of cancellation, the buyer or lessee is relieved of any further obligations under the contract but retains all rights to other remedies against the seller [UCC 2–711(1), 2A–508(1)(a)].

The Right to Recover the Goods If a buyer or lessee has made a partial or full payment for goods that remain in the possession of the seller or lessor, the buyer or lessee can recover the goods if the seller or lessor is insolvent or becomes insolvent within ten days after receiving the first payment and if the goods are identified to the contract.[13] To exercise this right, the buyer or lessee must tender to the seller or lessor any unpaid balance of the purchase price (or lease payment) [UCC 2–502, 2A–522].

The Right to Obtain Specific Performance A buyer or lessee can obtain specific performance when the goods are unique and the remedy at law is inadequate [UCC 2–716(1), 2A–521(1)]. Ordinarily, a successful suit for money damages is sufficient to place a buyer or lessee in the position he or she would have occupied if the seller or lessor had fully performed. When the contract is for the purchase of a particular work of art or a similarly unique item, however, money damages may not be sufficient. Under these circumstances, equity will require that the seller or lessor perform exactly by delivering the particular goods identified to the contract (a remedy of specific performance).

COVER
Under the UCC, a remedy that allows the buyer or lessee, on the seller's or lessor's breach, to purchase the goods, in good faith and within a reasonable time, from another seller or lessor and substitute them for the goods due under the contract. If the cost of cover exceeds the cost of the contract goods, the breaching seller or lessor will be liable to the buyer or lessee for the difference, plus incidental and consequential damages.

The Right of Cover In certain situations, buyers and lessees can protect themselves by obtaining **cover**—that is, by purchasing or leasing other goods to substitute for those due under the contract. This option is available when the seller or lessor repudiates the contract or fails to deliver the goods, or when a buyer or lessee has rightfully rejected goods or revoked acceptance.

In obtaining cover, the buyer or lessee must act in good faith and without unreasonable delay [UCC 2–712, 2A–518]. After purchasing or leasing substitute goods, the buyer or lessee can recover from the seller or lessor the difference between the cost of cover and the contract price (or lease payments), plus incidental and consequential damages, less the expenses (such as delivery costs) that were saved as a result of the breach [UCC 2–712, 2–715, 2A–518]. Consequential damages are any losses suffered by the buyer or lessee that the seller or lessor could have foreseen (had reason to know about) at the time of contract formation and any injury to the buyer's or lessee's person or property proximately resulting from the contract's breach [UCC 2–715(2), 2A–520(2)].

Buyers and lessees are not required to cover, and failure to do so will not bar them from using any other remedies available under the UCC. A buyer or lessee who

13. The 2003 amendments to UCC Articles 2 and 2A create a new right to recover goods identified to a contract when a consumer buyer or lessee makes a down payment and the seller or lessor then repudiates the contract or lease or fails to deliver the goods [Amended UCC 2–502, 2A–522].

fails to cover, however, may *not* be able to collect consequential damages that could have been avoided by purchasing or leasing substitute goods.

REPLEVIN
An action to recover identified goods in the hands of a party who is wrongfully withholding them from the other party. Under the UCC, this remedy is usually available only if the buyer or lessee is unable to cover.

The Right to Replevy Goods Buyers and lessees also have the right to replevy goods. **Replevin**[14] is an action to recover specific goods in the hands of a party who is wrongfully withholding them from the other party. Outside the UCC, the term *replevin* refers to a *prejudgment process* (a proceeding that takes place prior to a court's judgment) that permits the seizure of specific personal property in which a party claims a right or an interest. Under the UCC, the buyer or lessee can replevy goods subject to the contract if the seller or lessor has repudiated or breached the contract. To maintain an action to replevy goods, usually buyers and lessees must show that they are unable to cover for the goods after a reasonable effort [UCC 2–716(3), 2A–521(3)].

RECALL Consequential damages compensate for a loss (such as lost profits) that is not direct but was reasonably foreseeable at the time of the breach.

The Right to Recover Damages If a seller or lessor repudiates the sales contract or fails to deliver the goods, or the buyer or lessee has rightfully rejected or revoked acceptance of the goods, the buyer or lessee can sue for damages. The measure of recovery is the difference between the contract price (or lease payments) and the market price of (or lease payments that could be obtained for) the goods at the time the buyer (or lessee) *learned* of the breach.[15] The market price or market lease payments are determined at the place where the seller or lessor was supposed to deliver the goods. The buyer or lessee can also recover incidental and consequential damages, less the expenses that were saved as a result of the breach [UCC 2–713, 2A–519].

■ EXAMPLE 20.11 Schilling orders ten thousand bushels of wheat from Valdone for \$5 a bushel, with delivery due on June 14 and payment due on June 20. Valdone does not deliver on June 14. On June 14, the market price of wheat is \$5.50 per bushel. Schilling chooses to do without the wheat. He sues Valdone for damages for nondelivery. Schilling can recover \$0.50 × 10,000, or \$5,000, plus any expenses the breach may have caused him. The measure of damages is the market price less the contract price on the day Schilling was to have received delivery. Any expenses Schilling saved by the breach would be deducted from the damages. ■

WHEN THE SELLER OR LESSOR DELIVERS NONCONFORMING GOODS

When the seller or lessor delivers nonconforming goods, the buyer or lessee has several remedies available under the UCC.

on the Web Professor Cooper at the University of Missouri Law School posts a "quick and dirty" review of the remedies available under the UCC at **http://www1.law.umkc.edu/faculty/cooper/listfaq.htm#UCC%20Remedies**.

The Right to Reject the Goods If either the goods or the tender of the goods by the seller or lessor fails to conform to the contract *in any respect,* the buyer or lessee can reject the goods. If some of the goods conform to the contract, the buyer or lessee can keep the conforming goods and reject the rest [UCC 2–601, 2A–509]. If the buyer or lessee rejects the goods, she or he may then obtain cover, cancel the contract, or sue for damages for breach of contract, just as if the seller or lessor had refused to deliver the goods (see the earlier discussion of these remedies).

Timeliness and Reason for Rejection Required. The buyer or lessee must reject the goods within a reasonable amount of time and must notify the seller or lessor seasonably—that is, in a timely fashion or at the proper time [UCC 2–602(1),

14. Pronounced ruh-*pleh*-vun.

15. The 2003 amendments to UCC Article 2 change the rule that the time for measuring damages is the time the buyer learned of the breach. Unless repudiation is involved, the buyer's damages will be based on the market price at the time for tender [Amended UCC 2–713(1)(a)].

2A–509(2)]. If the buyer or lessee fails to reject the goods within a reasonable amount of time, acceptance will be presumed.

Note that when rejecting goods, the buyer or lessee must designate defects that would have been apparent to the seller or lessor on reasonable inspection. Failure to do so precludes the buyer or lessee from using such defects to justify rejection or to establish breach when the seller or lessor could have cured the defects if they had been stated seasonably [UCC 2–605, 2A–514].[16]

Employees at a retail establishment sort through boxes of nonconforming goods that will be returned to the manufacturer. If the merchant buyer is following the seller's instructions for rejecting the goods, who should bear the cost of having the employees perform this task? (AP Photo/Douglas C. Pizac)

Duties of Merchant Buyers and Lessees When Goods Are Rejected. If a merchant buyer or lessee rightfully rejects goods, and the seller or lessor has no agent or business at the place of rejection, the buyer or lessee is required to follow any reasonable instructions received from the seller or lessor with respect to the goods controlled by the buyer or lessee. The buyer or lessee is entitled to reimbursement for the care and cost entailed in following the instructions [UCC 2–603, 2A–511]. The same requirements hold if the buyer or lessee rightfully revokes his or her acceptance of the goods at some later time [UCC 2–608(3), 2A–517(5)]. (Revocation of acceptance will be discussed shortly.)

If no instructions are forthcoming and the goods are perishable or threaten to decline in value quickly, the buyer can resell the goods in good faith, taking the appropriate reimbursement from the proceeds. In addition, the buyer is entitled to a selling commission (not to exceed 10 percent of the gross proceeds) [UCC 2–603(1), (2); 2A–511(1)]. If the goods are not perishable, the buyer or lessee may store them for the seller or lessor or reship them to the seller or lessor [UCC 2–604, 2A–512].

Buyers who rightfully reject goods that remain in their possession or control have a *security interest* in the goods (basically, a legal claim to the goods to the extent necessary to recover expenses, costs, and the like—see Chapter 25). The security interest encompasses any payments the buyer has made for the goods, as well as any expenses incurred with regard to inspection, receipt, transportation, care, and custody of the goods [UCC 2–711(3)]. A buyer with a security interest in the goods is a "person in the position of a seller." This gives the buyer the same rights as an unpaid seller. Thus, the buyer can resell, withhold delivery of, or stop delivery of the goods. A buyer who chooses to resell must account to the seller for any amounts received in excess of the security interest [UCC 2–706(6), 2–711].

Revocation of Acceptance Acceptance of the goods precludes the buyer or lessee from exercising the right of rejection, but it does not necessarily preclude the buyer or lessee from pursuing other remedies. In certain circumstances, a buyer or lessee is permitted to *revoke* her or his acceptance of the goods. Acceptance of a lot or a commercial unit can be revoked if the nonconformity *substantially* impairs the value of the lot or unit and if one of the following factors is present:

1. If acceptance was predicated on the reasonable assumption that the nonconformity would be cured, and it has not been cured within a reasonable period of time [UCC 2–608(1)(a), 2A–517(1)(a)].[17]

16. The 2003 amendments to UCC 2–605 and 2A–514 change this restriction. Under the amendments, a buyer's or lessee's failure to disclose the nature of the defect affects only the right to reject or revoke acceptance, not the right to establish a breach. The new sections expressly require that the seller or lessor has had a right to cure, as well as the ability to cure.

17. Under the 2003 amendments to UCC 2–508 and 2A–513, after a justifiable revocation of acceptance cure is not available as a matter of right in a consumer contract or lease.

2 If the buyer or lessee did not discover the nonconformity before acceptance, either because it was difficult to discover before acceptance or because assurances made by the seller or lessor that the goods were conforming kept the buyer or lessee from inspecting the goods [UCC 2–608(1)(b), 2A–517(1)(b)].

Revocation of acceptance is not effective until the seller or lessor is notified, which must occur within a reasonable time after the buyer or lessee either discovers *or should have discovered* the grounds for revocation. Additionally, revocation must occur before the goods have undergone any substantial change (such as spoilage) not caused by their own defects [UCC 2–608(2), 2A–517(4)].

The Right to Recover Damages for Accepted Goods A buyer or lessee who has accepted nonconforming goods may also keep the goods and recover damages caused by the breach. The buyer or lessee, however, must notify the seller or lessor of the breach within a reasonable time after the defect was or should have been discovered. Failure to give notice of the defects (breach) to the seller or lessor bars the buyer or lessee from pursuing any remedy [UCC 2–607(3), 2A–516(3)].[18] In addition, the parties to a sales or lease contract can insert a provision requiring that the buyer or lessee give notice of any defects in the goods within a set period.

When the goods delivered and accepted are not as warranted, the measure of damages equals the difference between the value of the goods as accepted and their value if they had been delivered as warranted, plus incidental and consequential damages if appropriate [UCC 2–714(2), 2A–519(4)]. For this and other types of breaches in which the buyer or lessee has accepted the goods, the buyer or lessee is entitled to recover for any loss "resulting in the ordinary course of events . . . as determined in any manner which is reasonable" [UCC 2–714(1), 2A–519(3)]. The UCC also permits the buyer or lessee, with proper notice to the seller or lessor, to deduct all or any part of the damages from the price or lease payments still due and payable to the seller or lessor [UCC 2–717, 2A–516(1)].

Containers sit on ships as they wait to be unloaded at a port in the United States. If the buyer discovers that some of the goods are defective, what remedies under the UCC are available to the buyer? (Susan Goldman/ Bloomberg News/*Landov)*

Limitation of Remedies

The parties to a sales or lease contract can vary their respective rights and obligations by contractual agreement. For example, a seller and buyer can expressly provide for remedies in addition to those provided in the UCC. They can also provide remedies in lieu of those provided in the UCC, or they can change the measure of damages. The seller can provide that the buyer's only remedy on breach of warranty will be repair or replacement of the item, or the seller can limit the buyer's remedy to return of the goods and refund of the purchase price. In sales and lease contracts, an agreed-on remedy is in addition to those provided in the UCC unless the parties expressly agree that the remedy is exclusive of all others [UCC 2–719(1), 2A–503(1)].

When an Exclusive Remedy Fails in Its Essential Purpose

If the parties state that a remedy is exclusive, then it is the sole remedy. When circumstances cause an exclusive remedy to fail in its essential purpose, however, it is no longer considered exclusive, and the buyer or lessee may pursue other remedies

18. Under the 2003 amendments to UCC Articles 2 and 2A, a buyer or lessee who fails to give timely notice is barred from a remedy for the breach but *only* "to the extent that the seller is prejudiced by the failure." In other words, if the seller is not harmed by the buyer's failure to notify, the buyer may still recover. See Amended UCC 2–607(3)(a), 2A–516(3)(a).

INTERNATIONAL PERSPECTIVE

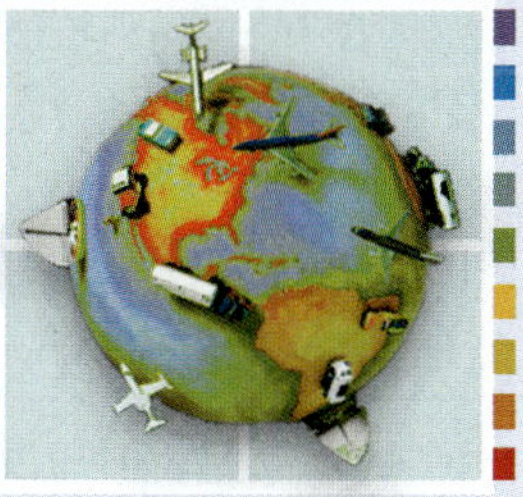

The CISG's Approach to Revocation of Acceptance

Under the UCC, a buyer or lessee who has accepted goods may be able to revoke acceptance under the circumstances just mentioned. Provisions of the United Nations Convention on Contracts for the International Sale of Goods (CISG) similarly allow buyers to rescind their contracts after they have accepted the goods.

The CISG, however, takes a somewhat different—and more direct—approach to the problem than the UCC does. In the same circumstances that permit a buyer to revoke acceptance under the UCC, under the CISG the buyer can simply declare that the seller has *fundamentally* breached the contract and proceed to sue the seller for the breach. Article 25 of the CISG states that a "breach of contract committed by one of the parties is fundamental if it results in such detriment to the other party as substantially to deprive him [or her] of what he [or she] is entitled to expect under the contract."

FOR CRITICAL ANALYSIS

What is the essential difference between revoking acceptance and bringing a suit for breach of contract?

available under the UCC [UCC 2–719(2), 2A–503(2)]. ■ EXAMPLE 20.12 Suppose that a sales contract limits the buyer's remedy to repair or replacement. If the goods at issue cannot be repaired and no replacements are available, the exclusive remedy has failed in its essential purpose. In this situation, the buyer normally is entitled to seek other remedies provided to a buyer by the UCC. ■

.on the Web For an example of a contract providing for an exclusive remedy, see the "Warranty and Limited Remedy" of 3M Company, which is online at **http://www.mmm.com/promote/warranty.htm**.

LIMITATIONS ON CONSEQUENTIAL DAMAGES

A contract can limit or exclude consequential damages, provided the limitation is not unconscionable. When the buyer or lessee is a consumer, the limitation of consequential damages for personal injuries resulting from nonconforming goods is *prima facie* (on its face) unconscionable. The limitation of consequential damages is not necessarily unconscionable, however, when the loss is commercial in nature—for example, if the loss consists of lost profits and property damage [UCC 2–719(3), 2A–503(3)].

ETHICAL ISSUE 20.1

When an exclusive remedy fails in its essential purpose, should a clause limiting consequential damages be enforced? The UCC makes it clear that a contract clause providing for an exclusive remedy is enforceable—*unless* the exclusive remedy fails in its essential purpose. If the exclusive remedy fails in its essential purpose, then the buyer can pursue the full panoply of remedies available under the UCC. One of the remedies available to the buyer is to sue for damages, including consequential damages. Yet what if the contract, in addition to providing for an exclusive remedy, also excludes consequential damages? In this situation, does the failure of the exclusive remedy effectively eliminate the clause limiting consequential damages?

The courts have reached different conclusions on this issue, as noted by the U.S. Court of Appeals for the Eighth Circuit in a case involving just this question. In that court's eyes, however, it was clear that when an exclusive remedy fails of its essential purpose, the aggrieved buyer should be able to "invoke any remedies available under the Uniform Commercial Code"—including "provable consequential damages"—even though the contract had specifically excluded consequential damages. According to the court, "To find otherwise would, in our opinion, undermine the protections afforded to parties under Section 2–719(2) and deprive [the buyer] of the substantial value of the bargain.”[19] ■

Statute of Limitations

An action for breach of contract under the UCC must be commenced *within four years after the cause of action accrues*—that is, within four years after the breach occurs. In addition to filing suit within the four-year period, a buyer or lessee who has accepted nonconforming goods usually must notify the breaching party of the breach within a reasonable time, or the aggrieved party is barred from pursuing any remedy [UCC 2–607(3)(a), 2A–516(3)]. The parties can agree in their contract to reduce this period to not less than one year, but cannot extend it beyond four years [UCC 2–725(1), 2A–506(1)]. A cause of action accrues for breach of warranty when the seller or lessor tenders delivery. This is the rule even if the aggrieved party is unaware that the cause of action has accrued [UCC 2–725(2), 2A–506(2)].[20]

19. *Arabian Agriculture Services Co. v. Chief Industries, Inc.,* 309 F.3d 479 (8th Cir. 2002).

20. The 2003 amendments to UCC 2–725 adjust this time limit. A cause of action may be brought within the later of four years after the right of action accrues or one year after a breach is, or should have been, discovered, but no later than five years after the time that the right has accrued. Specific rules are included for determining when rights of action accrue. In addition, the four-year limitation period cannot be reduced in a consumer contract or lease [Amended UCC 2–725, 2A–506(1)].

Reviewing Performance and Breach of Sales and Lease Contracts

GFI, Inc., a Hong Kong company, makes audio decoder chips, one of the essential components used in the manufacture of MP3 players. Egan Electronics contracts with GFI to buy 10,000 chips on an installment contract, with 2,500 chips to be shipped every three months, F.O.B. Hong Kong via Air Express. At the time for the first delivery, GFI delivers only 2,400 chips but explains to Egan that while the shipment is less than 5 percent short, the chips are of a higher quality than those specified in the contract and are worth 5 percent more than the contract price. Egan accepts the shipment and pays GFI the contract price. At the time for the second shipment, GFI makes a shipment identical to the first. Egan again accepts and pays for the chips. At the time for the third shipment, GFI ships 2,400 of the same chips, but this time GFI sends them via Hong Kong Air instead of Air Express. While in transit, the chips are destroyed. When it is time for the fourth shipment, GFI again sends 2,400 chips, but this time Egan rejects the chips without explanation. Using the information presented in the chapter, answer the following questions.

1. Based on Egan's acceptance of the first short shipment, does GFI have a legitimate reason to expect that Egan will accept the subsequent short shipments? Why or why not?
2. How does the substitution of carriers in the third shipment affect the contract between Egan and GFI? Does the substitution of carriers constitute a breach of the contract by GFI?
3. Suppose that the silicon used for the chips becomes unavailable for a period of time and that GFI cannot manufacture enough chips to fulfill the contract. Does this lack of availability of silicon release GFI from its obligations under the contract? Explain.
4. Suppose that Egan knows that silicon is not available but hears nothing from GFI. Does Egan have a right to ask GFI about its intentions to fulfill the contract? If so, does GFI have an obligation to respond? Explain.
5. Under the UCC, does Egan have a right to reject the fourth shipment? Why or why not?

KEY TERMS

CHAPTER SUMMARY Performance and Breach of Sales and Lease Contracts*

	REQUIREMENTS OF PERFORMANCE
Obligations of the Seller or Lessor (See pages 478–487.)	1. The seller or lessor must tender *conforming* goods to the buyer. Tender must take place at a *reasonable hour* and in a *reasonable manner.* Under the perfect tender doctrine, the seller or lessor must tender goods that conform exactly to the terms of the contract [UCC 2–503(1), 2A–508(1)]. 2. If the seller or lessor tenders nonconforming goods prior to the performance date and the buyer or lessee rejects them, the seller or lessor may *cure* (repair or replace the goods) within the contract time for performance [UCC 2–508(1), 2A–513(1)]. If the seller or lessor had reasonable grounds to believe the buyer or lessee would accept the tendered goods, on the buyer's or lessee's rejection the seller or lessor has a reasonable time to substitute conforming goods without liability [UCC 2–508(2), 2A–513(2)]. 3. If the agreed-on means of delivery becomes impracticable or unavailable, the seller must substitute an alternative means (such as a different carrier) if one is available [UCC 2–614(1)]. 4. If a seller or lessor tenders nonconforming goods in any one installment under an installment contract, the buyer or lessee may reject the installment only if its value is substantially impaired and cannot be cured. The entire installment contract is breached when one or more nonconforming installments *substantially* impair the value of the *whole* contract [UCC 2–612, 2A–510]. 5. When performance becomes commercially impracticable owing to circumstances that were not foreseeable when the contract was formed, the perfect tender rule no longer holds [UCC 2–615, 2A–405].
Obligations of the Buyer or Lessee (See pages 487–489.)	1. On tender of delivery by the seller or lessor, the buyer or lessee must pay for the goods at the time and place the buyer or lessee *receives* the goods, even if the place of shipment is the place of delivery, unless the sale is made on credit. Payment may be made by any method generally acceptable in the commercial world unless the seller demands cash [UCC 2–310, 2–511]. In lease contracts, the lessee must make lease payments in accordance with the contract [UCC 2A–516(1)]. 2. Unless otherwise agreed, the buyer or lessee has an absolute right to inspect the goods before acceptance [UCC 2–513(1), 2A–515(1)]. 3. The buyer or lessee can manifest acceptance of delivered goods expressly in words or by conduct or by failing to reject the goods after a reasonable period of time following inspection or after having had a reasonable opportunity to inspect them [UCC 2–606(1), 2A–515(1)]. A buyer will be deemed to have accepted goods if he or she performs any act inconsistent with the seller's ownership [UCC 2–606(1)(c)]. 4. Following the acceptance of delivered goods, the buyer or lessee may revoke acceptance only if the nonconformity *substantially* impairs the value of the unit or lot and if one of the following factors is present: a. Acceptance was predicated on the reasonable assumption that the nonconformity would be cured and it was not cured within a reasonable time [UCC 2–608(1)(a), 2A–517(1)(a)]. * Although we have referenced the 2003 amendments to Articles 2 and 2A of the UCC within the text of this chapter, we do not do so in this summary—because the amendments have not as yet become law in any state.

(Continued)

CHAPTER SUMMARY Performance and Breach of Sales and Lease Contracts—Continued

Obligations of the Buyer or Lessee—Continued (See pages 487–489.)	b. The buyer or lessee did not discover the nonconformity before acceptance, either because it was difficult to discover before acceptance or because the seller's or lessor's assurance that the goods were conforming kept the buyer or lessee from inspecting the goods [UCC 2–608(1)(b), 2A–517(1)(b)].
Anticipatory Repudiation (See page 489.)	If, before the time for performance, either party clearly indicates to the other an intention not to perform, under UCC 2–610 and 2A–402 the aggrieved party may do the following: 1. Await performance by the repudiating party for a commercially reasonable time. 2. Resort to any remedy for breach. 3. In either situation, suspend performance.
	REMEDIES FOR BREACH OF CONTRACT
Remedies of the Seller or Lessor (See pages 489–494.)	1. *When the goods are in the possession of the seller or lessor*—The seller or lessor may do the following: a. Cancel the contract [UCC 2–703(f), 2A–523(1)(a)]. b. Withhold delivery [UCC 2–703(a), 2A–523(1)(c)]. c. Resell or dispose of the goods [UCC 2–703(d), 2–706(1), 2A–523(1)(e), 2A–527(1)]. d. Sue to recover the purchase price or lease payments due [UCC 2–703(e), 2–709(1), 2A–529(1)]. e. Sue to recover damages [UCC 2–703(e), 2–708, 2A–528]. 2. *When the goods are in transit*—The seller or lessor may stop the carrier or bailee from delivering the goods [UCC 2–705, 2A–526]. 3. *When the goods are in the possession of the buyer or lessee*—The seller or lessor may do the following: a. Sue to recover the purchase price or lease payments due [UCC 2–709(1), 2A–529(1)]. b. Reclaim the goods. A seller may reclaim goods received by an insolvent buyer if the demand is made within ten days of receipt (reclaiming goods excludes all other remedies) [UCC 2–702]; a lessor may repossess goods if the lessee is in default [UCC 2A–525(2)].
Remedies of the Buyer or Lessee (See pages 494–498.)	1. *When the seller or lessor refuses to deliver the goods*—The buyer or lessee may do the following: a. Cancel the contract [UCC 2–711(1), 2A–508(1)(a)]. b. Recover the goods if the seller or lessor becomes insolvent within ten days after receiving the first payment and the goods are identified to the contract [UCC 2–502, 2A–522]. c. Obtain specific performance (when the goods are unique and when the remedy at law is inadequate) [UCC 2–716(1), 2A–521(1)]. d. Obtain cover [UCC 2–712, 2A–518]. e. Replevy the goods (if cover is unavailable) [UCC 2–716(3), 2A–521(3)]. f. Sue to recover damages [UCC 2–713, 2A–519]. 2. *When the seller or lessor delivers or tenders delivery of nonconforming goods*—The buyer or lessee may do the following: a. Reject the goods [UCC 2–601, 2A–509].

CHAPTER SUMMARY Performance and Breach of Sales and Lease Contracts—Continued

Remedies of the Buyer or Lessee—Continued	b. Revoke acceptance (in certain circumstances) [UCC 2–608, 2A–517]. c. Accept the goods and recover damages [UCC 2–607, 2–714, 2–717, 2A–519].
Limitation of Remedies (See pages 498–500.)	Remedies may be limited in sales or lease contracts by agreement of the parties. If the contract states that a remedy is exclusive, then that is the sole remedy unless the remedy fails in its essential purpose. Sellers and lessors can also limit the rights of buyers and lessees to consequential damages unless the limitation is unconscionable [UCC 2–719, 2A–503].
Statute of Limitations (See page 500.)	The UCC has a four-year statute of limitations for actions involving breach of contract. By agreement, the parties to a sales or lease contract can reduce this period to not less than one year, but they cannot extend it beyond four years [UCC 2–725(1), 2A–506(1)].

FOR REVIEW

Answers for the even-numbered questions in this For Review *section can be found on this text's accompanying Web site at* http://blt.westbuslaw.com. *Select "Chapter 20" and click on "For Review."*

1. What are the respective obligations of the parties under a contract for the sale or lease of goods?
2. What is the perfect tender rule? What are some important exceptions to this rule that apply to sales and lease contracts?
3. What options are available to the nonbreaching party when the other party to a sales or lease contract repudiates the contract prior to the time for performance?
4. What remedies are available to a seller or lessor when the buyer or lessee breaches the contract? What remedies are available to a buyer or lessee if the seller or lessor breaches the contract?
5. In contracts subject to the UCC, are parties free to limit the remedies available to the nonbreaching party on a breach of contract? If so, in what ways?

QUESTIONS AND CASE PROBLEMS

20–1. Remedies. Genix, Inc., has contracted to sell Larson five hundred washing machines of a certain model at list price. Genix is to ship the goods on or before December 1. Genix produces one thousand washing machines of this model but has not yet prepared Larson's shipment. On November 1, Larson repudiates the contract. Discuss the remedies available to Genix in this situation.

20–2. Right of Inspection. Cummings ordered two model X Super Fidelity speakers from Jamestown Wholesale Electronics, Inc. Jamestown shipped the speakers via United Parcel Service, C.O.D. (collect on delivery), although Cummings had not requested or agreed to a C.O.D. shipment of the goods. When the speakers were delivered, Cummings refused to accept them because he would not be able to inspect them before payment. Jamestown claimed that it had shipped conforming goods and that Cummings had breached their contract. Had Cummings breached the contract? Explain.

20–3. Anticipatory Repudiation. Moore contracted in writing to sell her 1996 Ford Taurus to Hammer for $8,500. Moore agreed to deliver the car on Wednesday, and Hammer promised to pay the $8,500 on the following Friday. On Tuesday, Hammer informed Moore that he would not be buying the car after all. By Friday, Hammer had changed his mind again and tendered $8,500 to Moore. Moore, although she had not sold the car to another party, refused the tender and refused to deliver. Hammer claimed that Moore had breached their contract. Moore contended that Hammer's repudiation released her from her duty to perform under the contract. Who is correct, and why?

20–4. Remedies. Rodriguez is a collector of antique cars. He contracts to purchase spare parts for a 1938 engine from Gerrard. These parts are not made anymore and are scarce. To get the contract with Gerrard, Rodriguez has to pay 50 percent of the purchase price in advance. On May 1, Rodriguez sends the required payment, which is received on May 2. On May 3,

Gerrard, having found another buyer willing to pay substantially more for the parts, informs Rodriguez that he will not deliver as contracted. That same day, Rodriguez learns that Gerrard is insolvent. Gerrard has the parts, and Rodriguez wants them. Discuss fully any remedies available to Rodriguez.

20–5. Limitation of Remedies. Destileria Serralles, Inc., a distributor of rum and other products, operates a rum-bottling plant in Puerto Rico. Figgie International, Inc., contracted with Serralles to provide bottle-labeling equipment capable of placing a clear label on a clear bottle of "Cristal" rum within a raised glass oval. The contract stated that Serralles's remedy, in case of a breach of contract, was limited to repair, replacement, or refund. When the equipment was installed in the Serralles plant, problems arose immediately. Figgie attempted to repair the equipment, but when it still did not work properly several months later, Figgie refunded the purchase price and Serralles returned the equipment. Serralles asked Figgie to pay for Serralles's losses caused by the failure of the equipment and by the delay in obtaining alternative machinery. Figgie filed a suit in a federal district court, asserting that it owed nothing to Serralles because the remedy for breach was limited to repair, replacement, or refund. Serralles responded that the limitation had failed in its essential purpose. In whose favor will the court resolve this dispute? Why? [*Figgie International, Inc. v. Destileria Serralles, Inc.*, 190 F.3d 252 (4th Cir. 1999)]

CASE PROBLEM WITH SAMPLE ANSWER

20–6. Metro-North Commuter Railroad Co. decided to install a fall-protection system for elevated walkways, roof areas, and interior catwalks in Grand Central Terminal, in New York City. The system was needed to ensure the safety of Metro-North employees when they worked at great heights on the interior and exterior of the terminal. Sinco, Inc., proposed a system called "Sayfglida," which involved a harness worn by the worker, a network of cables, and metal clips or sleeves called "Sayflinks" that connected the harness to the cables. Metro-North agreed to pay $197,325 for the installation of this system by June 26, 1999. Because the system's reliability was crucial, the contract required certain quality control processes. During a training session for Metro-North employees on June 29, the Sayflink sleeves fell apart. Within two days, Sinco manufactured and delivered two different types of replacement clips without subjecting them to the contract's quality control process, but Metro-North rejected them. Sinco suggested other possible solutions, which Metro-North did not accept. In September, Metro-North terminated its contract with Sinco and awarded the work to Surety, Inc., at a price of about $348,000. Sinco filed a suit in a federal district court, alleging breach of contract. Metro-North counterclaimed for its cost of cover. In whose favor should the court rule, and why? [*Sinco, Inc. v. Metro-North Commuter Railroad Co.*, 133 F.Supp.2d 308 (S.D.N.Y. 2001)]

After you have answered this problem, compare your answer with the sample answer given on the Web site that accompanies this text. Go to http://blt.westbuslaw.com, select "Chapter 20," and click on "Case Problem with Sample Answer."

20–7. Acceptance. In April 1996, Excalibur Oil Group, Inc., applied for credit and opened an account with Standard Distributors, Inc., to obtain snack foods and other items for Excalibur's convenience stores. For three months, Standard delivered the goods and Excalibur paid the invoices. In July, Standard was dissolved and its assets were distributed to J. F. Walker Co. Walker continued to deliver the goods to Excalibur, which continued to pay the invoices until November, when the firm began to experience financial difficulties. By January 1997, Excalibur owed Walker $54,241.77. Walker then dealt with Excalibur only on a collect-on-delivery basis until Excalibur's stores closed in 1998. Walker filed a suit in a Pennsylvania state court against Excalibur and its owner to recover amounts due on unpaid invoices. To successfully plead its case, Walker had to show that there was a contract between the parties. One question was whether Excalibur had manifested acceptance of the goods delivered by Walker. How does a buyer manifest acceptance? Was there an acceptance in this case? In whose favor should the court rule, and why? [*J. F. Walker Co. v. Excalibur Oil Group, Inc.*, 792 A.2d 1269 (Pa.Super. 2002)]

20–8. Right of Assurance. Advanced Polymer Sciences, Inc. (APS), based in Ohio, makes polymers and resins for use as protective coatings in industrial applications. APS also owns the technology for equipment used to make certain composite fibers. *SAVA gumarska in kemijska industria d.d.* (SAVA), based in Slovenia, makes rubber goods. In 1999, SAVA and APS contracted to form *SAVA Advanced Polymers proizvodno podjetje d.o.o.* (SAVA AP) to make and distribute APS products in Eastern Europe. Their contract provided for, among other things, the alteration of a facility to make the products using specially made equipment to be sold by APS to SAVA. Disputes arose between the parties, and in August 2000, SAVA stopped work on the new facility. APS then notified SAVA that it was stopping the manufacture of the equipment and "insist[ed] on knowing what is SAVA's intention towards this venture." In October, SAVA told APS that it was canceling their contract. In subsequent litigation, SAVA claimed that APS had repudiated the contract when it stopped making the equipment. What might APS assert in its defense? How should the court rule? Explain. [*SAVA gumarska in kemijska industria d.d. v. Advanced Polymer Sciences, Inc.*, 128 S.W.3d 304 (Tex.App.—Dallas 2004)]

A QUESTION OF ETHICS

20–9. Bobby Murray Chevrolet, Inc., contracted to supply 1,200 school bus chassis to local school boards. The contract stated that "products of any manufacturer may be offered," but Bobby Murray submitted its orders exclusively to General Motors Corp. (GMC). When a shortage in automatic transmissions occurred, GMC informed the dealer that it could not fill the orders. Bobby Murray told the school boards, which then bought the chassis from another dealer. The boards sued Bobby Murray for breach of contract. The dealer responded that its obligation to perform was excused under the doctrine of commercial impracticability, in part because of GMC's failure to fill its orders. Given these facts, answer the following questions. [*Alamance County Board of Education v. Bobby Murray Chevrolet, Inc.*, 121 N.C.App. 222, 465 S.E.2d 306 (1996)]

1. How will the court likely decide this issue? What factors will the court consider in making its decision? Discuss fully.
2. If the decision were yours to make, would you excuse Bobby Murray from its performance obligations in these circumstances? Would your decision be any different if Bobby Murray had specified in its contract that GMC would be the exclusive source of supply instead of stating that "products of any manufacturer may be offered"?
3. Generally, how does the doctrine of commercial impracticability attempt to balance the rights of both parties to a contract?

FOR CRITICAL ANALYSIS

20–10. Under what circumstances should courts not allow fully informed contracting parties to agree to limit remedies?

INTERNET EXERCISES

Go to the *Business Law Today* home page at **http://blt.westbuslaw.com**, select "Chapter 20," and click on "Internet Exercises." There you will find the following Internet research exercises that you can perform to learn more about topics covered in this chapter.

Activity 20–1: LEGAL PERSPECTIVE—The Right to Reject Goods

Activity 20–2: MANAGEMENT PERSPECTIVE—Good Faith and Fair Dealing

BEFORE THE TEST

Go to the *Business Law Today* home page at **http://blt.westbuslaw.com**, select "Chapter 20," and click on "Interactive Quizzes." You will find a number of interactive questions relating to this chapter.

CHAPTER 21

Warranties and Product Liability

"I'll warrant him heart-whole."

William Shakespeare, 1564–1616
(English dramatist and poet)

CHAPTER OUTLINE

- WARRANTIES
- LEMON LAWS
- PRODUCT LIABILITY
- STRICT PRODUCT LIABILITY
- DEFENSES TO PRODUCT LIABILITY

LEARNING OBJECTIVES

After reading this chapter, you should be able to answer the following questions:

1. What factors determine whether a seller's or lessor's statement constitutes an express warranty or mere "puffing"?
2. What implied warranties arise under the UCC?
3. Can a manufacturer be held liable to any person who suffers an injury proximately caused by the manufacturer's negligently made product?
4. What are the elements of a cause of action in strict product liability?
5. What defenses to liability can be raised in a product liability lawsuit?

Warranty is an age-old concept. In sales and lease law, a warranty is an assurance by one party of the existence of a fact on which the other party can rely. Just as William Shakespeare's character warranted his friend "heart-whole" in the quotation above from the play *As You Like It,* so sellers and lessors warrant to those who purchase or lease their goods that the goods are as represented or will be as promised.

The Uniform Commercial Code (UCC) has numerous rules governing product warranties as they occur in sales and lease contracts. That is the subject matter of the first part of this chapter. A natural addition to the discussion is *product liability:* Who is liable to consumers, users, and bystanders for physical harm and property damage caused by a particular good or the use thereof? Product liability encompasses the contract theory of warranty, as well as the tort theories of negligence and strict liability (discussed in Chapter 4).

Warranties

Article 2 (on sales) and Article 2A (on leases) of the UCC designate several types of warranties that can arise in a sales or lease contract, including warranties of title, express warranties, and implied warranties.

WARRANTIES OF TITLE

Title warranty arises automatically in most sales contracts. The UCC imposes three types of warranties of title.

Good Title In most instances, sellers warrant that they have good and valid title to the goods sold and that transfer of the title is rightful [UCC 2–312(1)(a)].[1] ■ **EXAMPLE 21.1** Sharon steals goods from Miguel and sells them to Carrie, who does not know that the goods are stolen. If Miguel reclaims the goods from Carrie, which he has a right to do, Carrie can then sue Sharon for breach of warranty. When Sharon sold Carrie the goods, Sharon *automatically* warranted to her that the title conveyed was valid and that its transfer was rightful. Because this was not in fact the case, Sharon breached the warranty of title imposed by UCC 2–312(1)(a) and became liable to the buyer for the appropriate damages. ■

LIEN
An encumbrance on a property to satisfy a debt or protect a claim for payment of a debt.

No Liens A second warranty of title provided by the UCC protects buyers who are *unaware* of any encumbrances, or **liens** (see Chapter 26)—claims, charges, or liabilities against goods at the time the contract is made [UCC 2–312(1)(b)]. This warranty protects buyers who, for example, unknowingly purchase goods that are subject to a creditor's security interest (see Chapter 25). If a creditor legally repossesses the goods from a buyer *who had no actual knowledge of the security interest,* the buyer can recover from the seller for breach of warranty.

Article 2A affords similar protection for lessees. Section 2A–211(1) provides that during the term of the lease, no claim of any third party will interfere with the lessee's enjoyment of the leasehold interest.

No Infringements A merchant-seller is also deemed to warrant that the goods delivered are free from any copyright, trademark, or patent claims of a third person[2] [UCC 2–312(3), 2A–211(2)]. If this warranty is breached and the buyer is sued by the party holding copyright, trademark, or patent rights in the goods, the buyer must notify the seller of the litigation within a reasonable time to enable the seller to decide whether to defend the lawsuit. If the seller states in writing that she or he has decided to defend and agrees to bear all expenses, including that of an adverse judgment, then the buyer must let the seller undertake the litigation; otherwise, the

1. Under the 2003 amendments to UCC 2–312(1)(a), good title also includes the warranty that the sale "shall not unreasonably expose the buyer to litigation because of any colorable [legitimate or reasonable] claim to or interest in the goods." Thus, the buyer is entitled not only to a good title, but also to a marketable title that is free of "colorable claims."

2. Recall from Chapter 18 that a *merchant* is defined in UCC 2–104(1) as a person who deals in goods of the kind involved in the sales contract or who, by occupation, presents himself or herself as having knowledge or skill peculiar to the goods involved in the transaction.

buyer loses all rights against the seller if any infringement liability is established [UCC 2–607(3)(b), 2–607(5)(b)].

Article 2A provides for the same notice of litigation in situations that involve leases rather than sales [UCC 2A–516(3)(b), 2A–516(4)(b)]. There is an exception for leases to individual consumers for personal, family, or household purposes. A consumer who fails to notify the lessor within a reasonable time does not lose his or her remedy against the lessor for any liability established in the litigation [UCC 2A–516(3)(b)].

Disclaimer of Title Warranty In an ordinary sales transaction, the title warranty can be disclaimed or modified only by *specific language* in the contract [UCC 2–312(2)]. For example, sellers can assert that they are transferring only such rights, title, and interest as they have in the goods. In a lease transaction, the disclaimer must "be specific, be by a writing, and be conspicuous" [UCC 2A–214(4)].

EXPRESS WARRANTIES

EXPRESS WARRANTY
A seller's or lessor's oral or written promise or affirmation of fact ancillary to an underlying sales or lease agreement, as to the quality, description, or performance of the goods being sold or leased.

A seller or lessor can create an **express warranty** by making representations concerning the quality, condition, description, or performance potential of the goods. Under UCC 2–313 and 2A–210, express warranties arise when a seller or lessor indicates any of the following:

1. That the goods conform to any affirmation (declaration that something is true) or promise of fact that the seller or lessor makes to the buyer or lessee about the goods. Such affirmations or promises are usually made during the bargaining

A woman tries on a fur sweater in a New York fur company. If the salesperson represents that the fur is mink, would that be enough to create an express warranty? Why or why not? (AP Photo/Tina Fineberg)

process. Statements such as "these drill bits will penetrate stainless steel—and without dulling" are express warranties.[3]

2 That the goods conform to any description of them. For example, a label that reads "Crate contains one 150-horsepower diesel engine" or a contract that calls for the delivery of a "camel's-hair coat" creates an express warranty.

3 That the goods conform to any sample or model of the goods shown to the buyer or lessee.[4]

Basis of the Bargain To create an express warranty, a seller or lessor does not have to use formal words such as *warrant* or *guarantee* [UCC 2–313(2), 2A–210(2)]. The UCC requires that for an express warranty to be created, the affirmation, promise, description, or sample must become part of the "basis of the bargain" [UCC 2–313(1), 2A–210(1)]. Just what constitutes the basis of the bargain is hard to say. The UCC does not define the concept, and it is a question of fact in each case whether a representation was made at such a time and in such a way that it induced the buyer or lessee to enter into the contract. (For more information on how sellers can create—or avoid creating—warranties, see the *Application* feature at the end of this chapter.)

Statements of Opinion Statements of fact create express warranties. If the seller or lessor merely makes a statement that relates to the supposed value or worth of the goods, or makes a statement of opinion or recommendation about the goods, however, the seller or lessor is not creating an express warranty [UCC 2–313(2), 2A–210(2)].

■ EXAMPLE 21.2 A seller claims that "this is the best used car to come along in years; it has four new tires and a 250-horsepower engine just rebuilt this year." The seller has made several *affirmations of fact* that can create a warranty: the automobile has an engine; it has a 250-horsepower engine; it was rebuilt this year; there are four tires on the automobile; and the tires are new. The seller's *opinion* that the vehicle is "the best used car to come along in years," however, is known as "puffing" and creates no warranty. (*Puffing* is the expression of opinion by a seller or lessor that is not made as a representation of fact.) ■

A statement relating to the value of the goods, such as "it's worth a fortune" or "anywhere else you'd pay $10,000 for it," usually does not create a warranty. If the seller or lessor is an expert and gives an opinion as an expert to a layperson, though, then a warranty may be created.

It is not always easy to determine whether a statement constitutes an express warranty or puffing. The reasonableness of the buyer's or lessee's reliance appears to be the controlling criterion in many cases. For example, a salesperson's statements that a ladder "will never break" and will "last a lifetime" are so clearly improbable that no reasonable buyer should rely on them. Additionally, the context in which a statement

3. The 2003 amendments to UCC Article 2 introduce the term *remedial promise,* which is "a promise by the seller to repair or replace the goods or to refund all or part of the price of the goods on the happening of a specified event" [Amended UCC 2–103(1)(n), 2–313(4)]. A remedial promise is not an express warranty, so a right of action for its breach accrues not at the time of tender, as with warranties, but if the promise is not performed when due [Amended UCC 2–725(2)(c)].

4. The 2003 amendments to the UCC distinguish between immediate buyers (those who enter into contracts with seller) and remote purchasers (those who buy or lease goods from immediate buyers) and extend sellers' obligations regarding new goods to remote purchasers. For example, suppose that a manufacturer sells packaged goods to a retailer, who resells the goods to a consumer. If a reasonable person in the position of the consumer would believe that a description on the package creates an obligation, the manufacturer is liable for its breach. [See Amended UCC 2–313, 2–313A, and 2–313B.]

*Cartons of Marlboro Light cigarettes, made by Philip Morris, sit on a shelf in a retail store. Suppose that the store clerk tells a customer that these cigarettes "are the best," and the customer buys three cartons. The customer later develops lung cancer from smoking and sues the seller. In this situation, would the seller's statements be enough to create an express warranty? Why or why not? (Nell Redmond/*Bloomberg News)

is made might be relevant in determining the reasonableness of the buyer's or lessee's reliance. For example, a reasonable person is more likely to rely on a written statement made in an advertisement than on a statement made orally by a salesperson.

ETHICAL ISSUE 21.1 ***Should sellers be held accountable for promises made to customers?*** The law assumes that most buyers know, or should know, that sellers commonly "huff and puff" their wares and that certain types of statements are not binding promises but mere puffery. Some customers, however, including persons who do not have a complete command of the English language, can easily be "taken in" by fast-talking salespersons. Also, even the courts have found it difficult at times to distinguish between statements that create guaranties and statements that amount to puffery. Because of the legal problems created by puffery, some scholars suggest that sellers should be held accountable for *all* of the promises that they make to customers, including the types of promises that traditionally have been regarded as puffery. Others, though, point out that changing the law relating to puffery could lead to further problems. Almost any innocent remark made by a sales representative could conceivably become the basis for litigation. For this reason, the National Conference of Commissioners on Uniform State Laws has not opted to change the UCC provisions on puffery. ■

Implied Warranties

IMPLIED WARRANTY
A warranty that arises by law because of the circumstances of a sale, rather than by the seller's express promise.

An **implied warranty** is one that *the law derives* by implication or inference because of the circumstances of a sale, rather than by the seller's express promise. In an action based on breach of implied warranty, it is necessary to show that an implied warranty existed and that the breach of the warranty proximately caused[5] the damage sustained. We look here at some of the implied warranties that arise under the UCC.

5. *Proximate cause,* or legal cause, exists when the connection between an act and an injury is strong enough to justify imposing liability—see Chapter 4.

IMPLIED WARRANTY OF MERCHANTABILITY
A warranty that goods being sold or leased are reasonably fit for the general purpose for which they are sold or leased, are properly packaged and labeled, and are of proper quality. The warranty automatically arises in every sale or lease of goods made by a merchant who deals in goods of the kind sold or leased.

Implied Warranty of Merchantability Every sale or lease of goods made *by a merchant* who deals in goods of the kind sold or leased automatically gives rise to an **implied warranty of merchantability** [UCC 2–314, 2A–212]. Thus, a merchant who is in the business of selling ski equipment makes an implied warranty of merchantability every time the merchant sells a pair of skis, but a neighbor selling his or her skis at a garage sale does not.

Merchantable Goods. Goods that are *merchantable* are "reasonably fit for the ordinary purposes for which such goods are used." They must be of at least average, fair, or medium-grade quality. The quality must be comparable to a level that will pass without objection in the trade or market for goods of the same description. To be merchantable, the goods must also be adequately packaged and labeled as provided by the agreement, and they must conform to the promises or affirmations of fact made on the container or label, if any.

It makes no difference whether the merchant knew or could have discovered that a product was defective (not merchantable). Of course, merchants are not absolute insurers against all accidents arising in connection with the goods. For example, a bar of soap is not unmerchantable merely because a user could slip and fall by stepping on it.

Merchantable Food. The UCC recognizes the serving of food or drink to be consumed on or off the premises as a sale of goods subject to the implied warranty of merchantability [UCC 2–314(1)]. "Merchantable" food means food that is fit to eat. Courts generally determine whether food is fit to eat on the basis of consumer expectations. For example, the courts assume that consumers should reasonably expect on occasion to find bones in fish fillets, cherry pits in cherry pie, a nutshell in a package of shelled nuts, and so on—because such substances are natural incidents of the food. In contrast, consumers would not reasonably expect to find an inchworm in a can of peas or a piece of glass in a soft drink—because these substances are not natural to the food product.[6] In the following classic case, the court had to determine whether a fish bone was a substance that one should reasonably expect to find in fish chowder.

6. See, for example, *Ruvolo v. Homovich,* 149 Ohio App.3d 701, 778 N.E.2d 661 (2002).

LANDMARK AND CLASSIC CASES

CASE 21.1 Webster v. Blue Ship Tea Room, Inc.

Supreme Judicial Court of Massachusetts, 1964.
347 Mass. 421,
198 N.E.2d 309.

HISTORICAL AND CULTURAL SETTING

Chowder, a soup or stew made with fresh fish, possibly originated in the fishing villages of Brittany (a French province to the west of Paris) and was probably carried to Canada and New England by Breton fishermen. In the nineteenth century and earlier, recipes for chowder did not call for the removal of the fish bones. Chowder recipes in the first half of the twentieth century were the same as in previous centuries, sometimes specifying that the fish head, tail, and backbone were to be broken in pieces and boiled, with the "liquor thus produced . . . added to the balance of the chowder."[a] *By the middle of the twentieth century, there was a considerable body of case law concerning implied warranties and foreign and natural substances in food. It was perhaps inevitable that sooner or later, a consumer injured by a fish bone in chowder would challenge the merchantability of chowder containing fish bones.*

a. Fannie Farmer, *The Boston Cooking School Cook Book* (Boston: Little, Brown, 1937), p. 166.

(Continued)

CASE 21.1—Continued

BACKGROUND AND FACTS Blue Ship Tea Room, Inc., was located in Boston in an old building overlooking the ocean. Priscilla Webster, who had been born and raised in New England, went to the restaurant and ordered fish chowder. The chowder was milky in color. After three or four spoonfuls, she felt something lodged in her throat. As a result, she underwent two esophagoscopies; in the second esophagoscopy, a fish bone was found and removed. Webster filed suit against the restaurant in a Massachusetts state court for breach of the implied warranty of merchantability. The jury rendered a verdict for Webster, and the restaurant appealed to the state's highest court.

IN THE WORDS OF THE COURT . . .
REARDON, Justice.

* * * *

We must decide whether a fish bone lurking in a fish chowder * * * constitutes a breach of implied warranty under applicable provisions of the Uniform Commercial Code * * * .

* * * [T]he joys of life in New England include the ready availability of fresh fish chowder. We should be prepared to cope with the hazards of fish bones, the occasional presence of which in chowders is, it seems to us, to be anticipated, and which, in the light of a hallowed tradition, do not impair their fitness or merchantability.

DECISION AND REMEDY The Supreme Judicial Court of Massachusetts held that Webster could not recover against Blue Ship Tea Room because no breach of warranty had occurred.

COMMENTS *This classic case, phrased in memorable language, was an early application of the UCC's implied warranty of merchantability to food products. The case established the rule that consumers should expect to find, on occasion, elements of food products that are natural to the product (such as fish bones in fish chowder). In such cases, the food preparers or packagers will not normally be liable. This rule continues to be applied today in cases involving similar issues.*

RELEVANT WEB SITES *To locate information on the Web concerning* Webster v. Blue Ship Tea Room, Inc., *go to this text's Web site at* **http://blt.westbuslaw.com**, *select "Chapter 21," and click on "URLs for Landmarks."*

IMPLIED WARRANTY OF FITNESS FOR A PARTICULAR PURPOSE
A warranty that goods sold or leased are fit for a particular purpose. The warranty arises when any seller or lessor knows the particular purpose for which a buyer or lessee will use the goods and knows that the buyer or lessee is relying on the skill and judgment of the seller or lessor to select suitable goods.

Implied Warranty of Fitness for a Particular Purpose The **implied warranty of fitness for a particular purpose** arises when any seller or lessor (merchant or nonmerchant) knows the particular purpose for which a buyer or lessee will use the goods and knows that the buyer or lessee is relying on the skill and judgment of the seller or lessor to select suitable goods [UCC 2–315, 2A–213].

A "particular purpose" of the buyer or lessee differs from the "ordinary purpose for which goods are used" (merchantability). Goods can be merchantable but unfit for a particular purpose. ■ EXAMPLE 21.3 Suppose that you need a gallon of paint to match the color of your living room walls—a light shade somewhere between coral and peach. You take a sample to your local hardware store and request a gallon of paint of that color. Instead, you are given a gallon of bright blue paint. Here, the salesperson has not breached any warranty of implied merchantability—the bright blue paint is of high quality and suitable for interior walls—but he or she has breached an implied warranty of fitness for a particular purpose. ■

A seller or lessor does not need to have actual knowledge of the buyer's or lessee's particular purpose. It is sufficient if a seller or lessor "has reason to know" the purpose. The buyer or lessee, however, must have *relied* on the skill or judgment of the seller or lessor in selecting or furnishing suitable goods for an implied warranty to be created.

EXAMPLE 21.4 Bloomberg leases a computer from Future Tech, a lessor of technical business equipment. Bloomberg tells the clerk that she wants a computer that will run a complicated new engineering graphics program at a realistic speed. Future Tech leases Bloomberg an Architex One computer with a CPU speed of only 2 gigahertz, even though a speed of at least 3.2 gigahertz would be required to run Bloomberg's graphics program at a "realistic speed." Bloomberg, after discovering that it takes forever to run her program, wants her money back. Here, because Future Tech has breached the implied warranty of fitness for a particular purpose, Bloomberg normally will be able to recover. The clerk knew specifically that Bloomberg wanted a computer with enough speed to run certain software. Furthermore, Bloomberg relied on the clerk to furnish a computer that would fulfill this purpose. Because Future Tech did not do so, the warranty was breached. ■

Other Implied Warranties Implied warranties can also arise (or be excluded or modified) as a result of course of dealing or usage of trade [UCC 2–314(3), 2A–212(3)]. In the absence of evidence to the contrary, when both parties to a sales or lease contract have knowledge of a well-recognized trade custom, the courts will infer that both parties intended for that trade custom to apply to their contract. For example, if an industry-wide custom is to lubricate a new car before it is delivered and a dealer fails to do so, the dealer can be held liable to a buyer for damages resulting from the breach of an implied warranty. This, of course, would also be negligence on the part of the dealer.

OVERLAPPING WARRANTIES

BE AWARE Express and implied warranties do not necessarily displace each other. More than one warranty can cover the same goods in the same transaction.

Sometimes, two or more warranties are made in a single transaction. An implied warranty of merchantability, an implied warranty of fitness for a particular purpose, or both can exist in addition to an express warranty. For example, when a sales contract for a new car states that "this car engine is warranted to be free from defects for 36,000 miles or thirty-six months, whichever occurs first," there is an express warranty against all defects and an implied warranty that the car will be fit for normal use.

The rule under the UCC is that express and implied warranties are construed as *cumulative* if they are consistent with one another [UCC 2–317, 2A–215]. If the warranties are inconsistent, the courts usually hold as follows:

1. *Express* warranties displace inconsistent *implied* warranties, except for implied warranties of fitness for a particular purpose.
2. Samples take precedence over inconsistent general descriptions.
3. Technical specifications displace inconsistent samples or general descriptions.

In Example 21.4 presented earlier, suppose that when Bloomberg leases the computer from Future Tech, the contract contains an express warranty concerning the speed of the CPU and the application programs that the computer is capable of running. Bloomberg does not realize that the speed expressly warranted in the contract is insufficient for her needs. Bloomberg later claims that Future Tech has breached the implied warranty of fitness for a particular purpose. Here, although the express warranty would take precedence over any implied warranty of merchantability, it normally would not take precedence over an implied warranty of fitness for a particular purpose. Bloomberg therefore has a good claim for the breach of implied warranty of fitness for a particular purpose, because she made it clear that she was leasing the computer to perform certain tasks.

Third Party Beneficiaries of Warranties

One of the general principles of contract law is that unless you are one of the parties to a contract, you have no rights under the contract. In other words, *privity of contract* must exist between a plaintiff and a defendant before any action based on a contract can be maintained. Two notable exceptions to the rule of privity are assignments and third party beneficiary contracts (these topics were discussed in Chapter 16). Another exception is made under warranty laws so that third parties can recover for harms suffered as a result of breached warranties.

There has been sharp disagreement among state courts as to how far warranty liability should extend, however. In view of this disagreement, the UCC offers three alternatives for liability to third parties [UCC 2–318, 2A–216].[7] All three alternatives are intended to eliminate the privity requirement with respect to certain enumerated types of injuries (personal versus property) for certain beneficiaries (for example, household members or bystanders).

Warranty Disclaimers

Because each type of warranty is created in a special way, the manner in which warranties can be disclaimed or qualified by a seller or lessor varies depending on the type of warranty.

WATCH OUT Courts generally view warranty disclaimers unfavorably, especially when consumers are involved.

Express Warranties As already stated, any affirmation of fact or promise, description of the goods, or use of samples or models by a seller or lessor creates an express warranty. Obviously, then, express warranties can be excluded if the seller or lessor carefully refrains from making any promise or affirmation of fact relating to the goods, describing the goods, or using a sample or model.

The UCC does permit express warranties to be negated or limited by specific and unambiguous language, provided that this is done in a manner that protects the buyer or lessee from surprise. Therefore, a written disclaimer in language that is clear and conspicuous, and called to a buyer's or lessee's attention, could negate all oral express warranties not included in the written sales contract [UCC 2–316(1), 2A–214(1)]. This allows the seller or lessor to avoid false allegations that oral warranties were made, and it ensures that only representations made by properly authorized individuals are included in the bargain.

Note, however, that a buyer or lessee must be made aware of any warranty disclaimers or modifications *at the time the contract is formed*. In other words, any oral or written warranties—or disclaimers—made during the bargaining process as part of a contract's formation cannot be modified at a later time by the seller or lessor.

.on the Web For an example of a warranty disclaimer, go to **http://www.bizguardian.com/terms.php**.

Implied Warranties Generally speaking, unless circumstances indicate otherwise, the implied warranties of merchantability and fitness are disclaimed by the expressions "as is," "with all faults," and other similar expressions that in common understanding call the buyer's or lessee's attention to the fact that there are no implied warranties [UCC 2–316(3)(a), 2A–214(3)(a)]. The UCC also permits a seller or lessor to specifically disclaim an implied warranty of either merchantability or fitness [UCC 2–316(2), 2A–214(2)].[8]

---

7. Under the 2003 amendments to the UCC, each alternative is expanded to cover remedial promises, as well as obligation to immediate buyers and remote purchasers [see Amended UCC 2–313, 2–313A, 2–313B, and 2–318].

8. The 2003 amendments to the UCC require more informative language for disclaimers of implied warranties [Amended UCC 2–316(2), 2A–214(2)].

Disclaimer of the Implied Warranty of Merchantability. A merchantability disclaimer must specifically mention the word *merchantability.* The disclaimer need not be written, but if it is, the writing must be conspicuous [UCC 2–316(2), 2A–214(4)].[9] According to UCC 1–201(10),

> [a] term or clause is conspicuous when it is so written that a reasonable person against whom it is to operate ought to have noticed it. A printed heading in capitals . . . is conspicuous. Language in the body of a form is conspicuous if it is in larger or other contrasting type or color.[10]

■ EXAMPLE 21.5 Forbes, a merchant, sells Maves a particular lawn mower selected by Forbes with the characteristics clearly requested by Maves. At the time of the sale, Forbes orally tells Maves that he does not warrant the merchantability of the mower, as it is last year's model and has been used as a demonstrator. If the mower proves to be defective and does not work, Maves can hold Forbes liable for breach of the warranty of fitness for a particular purpose but not for breach of the warranty of merchantability. Forbes's oral disclaimer mentioning the word *merchantability* is a proper disclaimer. ■

Disclaimer of the Implied Warranty of Fitness. To disclaim an implied warranty of fitness for a particular purpose, the disclaimer *must* be in writing and be conspicuous. The word *fitness* does not have to be mentioned in the writing; it is sufficient if, for example, the disclaimer states, "THERE ARE NO WARRANTIES THAT EXTEND BEYOND THE DESCRIPTION ON THE FACE HEREOF." Thus, in Example 21.5 above, for Forbes to have disclaimed the implied warranty of fitness for a particular purpose, a conspicuous writing would have been required. Although Forbes could not be held liable for breaching the implied warranty of merchantability, he could be held liable for breaching the warranty of fitness—because he made no *written* disclaimer with respect to that warranty.

At the center of the dispute in the following case was a disclaimer of all warranties accompanying a lease transaction. In defense against a suit for amounts due under the lease, the lessee contended that the leased goods were defective when delivered and not fit for the purpose intended and that, for this reason, the consideration for the contract failed. What was the effect of the disclaimer in this situation?

9. Under the 2003 amendments to UCC Articles 2 and 2A, if a consumer contract or lease is set forth in a writing—physical or electronic—the implied warranty of merchantability can be disclaimed only by language also set forth in a writing [Amended UCC 2–316(3), 2A–214(3)].

10. The 2003 amendments to UCC Articles 2 and 2A expand the concept to include terms in electronic records [Amended UCC 2–103(1)(b), 2A–103(1)(d)]. These sections also add a special rule for the situation in which a sender of an e-record intends to evoke a response from an e-agent.

CASE 21.2 International Turbine Services, Inc. v. VASP Brazilian Airlines

United States Court of Appeals,
Fifth Circuit, 2002.
278 F.3d 494.
http://www.ca5.uscourts.gov/opinions.aspx[a]

a. Under the heading "Search for opinions where:" in the box labeled "and/or Title contains text:" enter "VASP" and click on "Search." In the results, scroll to the name of the case and click on the docket number to access the opinion. The Clerk's Office of the U.S. Court of Appeals for the Fifth Circuit maintains this Web site.

BACKGROUND AND FACTS On October 1, 1997, International Turbine Services, Inc. (ITS), leased an aircraft turbine engine to VASP Brazilian Airlines. The lease required ITS to deliver the engine with a Federal Aviation Administration (FAA)–approved service tag. VASP otherwise leased the engine in "'AS IS, WHERE IS' condition and with all faults." VASP bore "the risk of loss and damage to the Engine and all component parts from any and

(Continued)

CASE 21.2—Continued

every cause whatsoever" with one exception: ITS agreed to overhaul and repair "time controlled" and "on-condition" parts.[b] At the end of the term—which the parties extended through August 18, 1998—VASP was to return the engine in operable condition to ITS's facility in Dallas. On June 15, the pilot of a VASP plane on which the engine was mounted aborted takeoff due to strong vibrations in the engine. VASP discovered that a high-pressure turbine (HPT) blade had failed, causing severe damage to the engine. VASP disputed responsibility for the repair cost and stopped making payments under the lease. ITS filed a suit against VASP, alleging breach of contract. A federal district court awarded ITS $8,825,000 in damages, including the cost to repair the engine and the past-due lease payments. On appeal to the U.S. Court of Appeals for the Fifth Circuit, VASP argued, in part, that it had not bargained for a defective engine.

b. A time-controlled part must be replaced or repaired after a specified number of hours or cycles. An on-condition part must be replaced or repaired whenever, on inspection, it does not comply with relevant FAA specifications.

IN THE WORDS OF THE COURT . . .
BOBBY R. BALDOCK, Circuit Judge.

* * * *

VASP * * * asserts a genuine issue of material fact exists as to whether VASP received the bargained-for consideration. * * * The Texas Business and Commercial Code [Texas's version of the Uniform Commercial Code] expressly authorizes the exclusion of warranties in lease agreements where the requisite language is present. The Code also provides that all implied warranties are excluded by the language "as is" or "with all faults."

The Lease provides:

> On the Delivery Date, Lessor will ensure that each Engine will have a Federal Aviation Administration ("FAA") approved return to service tag affixed to it. * * * [Aside from the FAA tag], the Equipment is leased and accepted by Lessee in "AS IS, WHERE IS" condition and with all faults. Lessor makes no warranties whatsoever with respect to any Equipment, express or implied, except [the warranty of title].

The Lease also expressly excludes any implied warranties of merchantability or fitness for a particular purpose. The language of these provisions tracks the language authorized by the Code. *The Lease validly excludes all warranties with the exception of title and requires only delivery of an engine with an FAA approved return to service tag.* [Emphasis added.]

VASP acknowledges the engine arrived with the appropriate FAA tag. According to VASP, however, the FAA tag constitutes an implied representation that all applicable maintenance regulations and manufacturers' recommendations have been followed, including the manufacturer's recommendations regarding HPT blades. Yet, this is precisely the type of implied representation or warranty the Lease expressly excludes. Under the express terms of the Lease, VASP waived the right to complain about the condition of the engine upon receipt.

VASP's failure of consideration claim also wants for lack of any competent * * * proof. VASP representatives signed an Equipment Delivery Receipt acknowledging the engine's compliance with the terms and conditions of the Lease. VASP also was sufficiently satisfied with the engine's performance to execute a series of extensions and amendments to the original two-month lease term.

DECISION AND REMEDY The U.S. Court of Appeals for the Fifth Circuit affirmed the judgment of the lower court. The appellate court held that VASP could not successfully assert the defense of a failure of consideration because the lease excluded all warranties (except the warranty of title and the FAA return-to-service approval tag), which meant that VASP could not legitimately complain about the condition of the leased goods.

CASE 21.2—Continued

FOR CRITICAL ANALYSIS—Social Consideration

Suppose that the lease in this case had not contained a disclaimer and that the HPT blade had been defective when VASP received it. Further suppose that during a take-off attempt by a VASP pilot with the defective HPT blade, the plane dropped suddenly and violently, causing injury to a passenger who was onboard. Can the VASP passenger who was not a party to the contract sue ITS based on the implied warranty of fitness? Why or why not?

Buyer's or Lessee's Examination or Refusal to Inspect If a buyer or lessee actually examines the goods (or a sample or model) as fully as desired before entering into a contract, or if the buyer or lessee refuses to examine the goods on the seller's or lessor's demand that he or she do so, *there is no implied warranty with respect to defects that a reasonable examination would reveal or defects that are actually found* [UCC 2–316(3)(b), 2A–214(2)(b)].

■ EXAMPLE 21.6 Suppose that Joplin buys an ax at Gershwin's Hardware Store. No express warranties are made. Gershwin requests that Joplin inspect the ax before buying it, but she refuses. Had she inspected the ax, she would have noticed that its handle was obviously cracked. If Joplin is later injured by the defective ax, she normally will not be able to hold Gershwin liable for breach of the warranty of merchantability because she would have spotted the defect during an inspection. ■

Warranty Disclaimers and Unconscionability The UCC sections dealing with warranty disclaimers do not refer specifically to unconscionability as a factor. Ultimately, however, the courts will test warranty disclaimers with reference to the UCC's unconscionability standards [UCC 2–302, 2A–108]. Such things as lack of bargaining position, "take-it-or-leave-it" choices, and a buyer's or lessee's failure to understand or know of a warranty disclaimer will become relevant to the issue of unconscionability.

MAGNUSON-MOSS WARRANTY ACT

The Magnuson-Moss Warranty Act of 1975[11] was designed to prevent deception in warranties by making them easier to understand. The act is mainly enforced by the Federal Trade Commission (FTC). Additionally, the attorney general or a consumer who has been injured can enforce the act if informal procedures for settling disputes prove to be ineffective. The act modifies UCC warranty rules to some extent when consumer transactions are involved. The UCC, however, remains the primary codification of warranty rules for industrial and commercial transactions.

Under the Magnuson-Moss Act, no seller or lessor is required to give an express written warranty for consumer goods sold. If a seller or lessor chooses to make an express written warranty, however, and the cost of the consumer goods is more than $10, the warranty must be labeled as "full" or "limited." In addition, if the cost of the goods is more than $15, by FTC regulation, the warrantor must make certain disclosures fully and conspicuously in a single document in "readily understood language." This disclosure must state the names and addresses of the warrantor(s), what specifically is warranted, procedures for enforcing the warranty, any limitations on warranty relief, and that the buyer has legal rights.

Full Warranty Although a *full warranty* may not cover every aspect of the consumer product sold, what it does cover ensures some type of consumer satisfaction

---

11. 15 U.S.C. Sections 2301–2312.

in the event that the product is defective. A full warranty requires free repair or replacement of any defective part; if the product cannot be repaired within a reasonable time, the consumer has the choice of a refund or a replacement without charge. A full warranty frequently does not have a time limit on it. Any limitation on consequential damages must be *conspicuously* stated. Additionally, the warrantor need not perform warranty services if the problem with the product was caused by the consumer's unreasonable use of the product.

REMEMBER When a buyer or lessee is a consumer, a limitation on consequential damages for personal injuries resulting from nonconforming goods is *prima facie* unconscionable.

Limited Warranty A *limited warranty* arises when the written warranty fails to meet one of the minimum requirements of a full warranty. The fact that only a limited warranty is being given must be conspicuously stated. If the only distinction between a limited warranty and a full warranty is a time limitation, the Magnuson-Moss Warranty Act allows the warrantor to identify the warranty as a full warranty by such language as "full twelve-month warranty."

Implied Warranties Implied warranties do not arise under the Magnuson-Moss Warranty Act; they continue to be created according to UCC provisions. Implied warranties may not be disclaimed under the Magnuson-Moss Warranty Act, however. Although a warrantor can impose a time limit on the duration of an implied warranty, it must correspond to the duration of the express warranty.[12]

Lemon Laws

Some purchasers of defective automobiles—called "lemons"—found that the remedies provided by the UCC were inadequate due to limitations imposed by the seller. In response to the frustrations of these buyers, all of the states have enacted *lemon laws*. Basically, lemon laws provide that if an automobile under warranty possesses a defect that significantly affects the vehicle's value or use, and the seller fails to remedy the defect within a specified number of opportunities (usually four), the buyer is entitled to a new car, replacement of defective parts, or return of all consideration paid.

The "Lemon Law Office" provides a variety of information on lemon laws at its Web site. Take a look at the "Hot Lemon Tips" and "Lemon Wisdom" pages. Go to **http://www.lemonlawoffice.com**.

In most states, lemon laws require an aggrieved new-car owner to notify the dealer or manufacturer of the problem and to provide the dealer or manufacturer with an opportunity to solve it. If the problem persists, the owner must then submit complaints to the arbitration program specified in the manufacturer's warranty before taking the case to court. Decisions by arbitration panels are binding on the manufacturer (that is, cannot be appealed by the manufacturer to the courts) but usually are not binding on the purchaser.

Most major automobile companies use their own arbitration panels. Some companies, however, subscribe to independent arbitration services, such as those provided by the Better Business Bureau. Although arbitration boards must meet state and/or federal standards of impartiality, industry-sponsored arbitration boards have been criticized for not being truly impartial. In response to this criticism, some states have established mandatory, government-sponsored arbitration programs for lemon-law disputes.

12. The time limit on an implied warranty occurring by virtue of the warrantor's express warranty must, of course, be reasonable, conscionable, and set forth in clear and conspicuous language on the face of the warranty.

A man contemplates purchasing a BMW 530. If the man buys the car and it turns out to be defective, what rights does the man have under most lemon laws? Can he immediately file suit in court against the manufacturer? Why or why not? (Sandy Huffaker/ Bloomberg News*)*

Product Liability

PRODUCT LIABILITY The legal liability of manufacturers, sellers, and lessors of goods to consumers, users, and bystanders for injuries or damages that are caused by the goods.

Manufacturers, sellers, and lessors of goods can be held liable to consumers, users, and bystanders for physical harm or property damage that is caused by the goods. This is called **product liability.** Product liability may be based on the warranty theories just discussed, as well as on the theories of negligence, misrepresentation, and strict liability. We look here at product liability based on negligence and misrepresentation.

NEGLIGENCE

Chapter 4 defined *negligence* as the failure to exercise the degree of care that a reasonable, prudent person would have exercised under the circumstances. If a manufacturer fails to exercise "due care" to make a product safe, a person who is injured by the product may sue the manufacturer for negligence.

RECALL The elements of negligence include a duty of care, a breach of the duty, and an injury to the plaintiff proximately caused by the breach.

Due Care Must Be Exercised The manufacturer must exercise due care in designing the product, selecting the materials, using the appropriate production process, assembling the product, and inspecting and testing any purchased products that are used in the final product sold by the manufacturer. The duty of care also extends to the placement of adequate warnings on the label informing the user of dangers of which an ordinary person might not be aware. (For a discussion of whether manufacturers have a duty to warn sophisticated and knowledgeable users of the dangers associated with the manufacturers' products, see this chapter's *Management Perspective* feature on the following page.)

Privity of Contract Not Required A product liability action based on negligence does not require privity of contract between the injured plaintiff and the negligent

CHAPTER SUMMARY Warranties and Product Liability—Continued

Warranties of Title—Continued (See pages 507–508.)	3. *No infringements*—A merchant-seller warrants that the goods are free of infringement claims (claims that a patent, trademark, or copyright has been infringed) by third parties. Lessors make similar warranties.
Express Warranties (See pages 508–510.)	1. *Under the UCC*—An express warranty arises under the UCC when a seller or lessor indicates, as part of the basis of the bargain, any of the following: a. An affirmation or promise of fact. b. A description of the goods. c. A sample shown as conforming to the contract goods [UCC 2–313, 2A–210]. 2. Under the *Magnuson-Moss Warranty Act*—Express written warranties covering consumer goods priced at more than $10, *if made,* must be labeled as one of the following: a. Full warranty—Free repair or replacement of defective parts; refund or replacement for goods if they cannot be repaired in a reasonable time. b. Limited warranty—When less than a full warranty is being offered.
Implied Warranty of Merchantability (See pages 511–512.)	When a seller or lessor is a merchant who deals in goods of the kind sold or leased, the seller or lessor warrants that the goods sold or leased are properly packaged and labeled, are of proper quality, and are reasonably fit for the ordinary purposes for which such goods are used [UCC 2–314, 2A–212].
Implied Warranty of Fitness for a Particular Purpose (See pages 512–513.)	Arises when the buyer's or lessee's purpose or use is expressly or impliedly known by the seller or lessor, and the buyer or lessee purchases or leases the goods in reliance on the seller's or lessor's selection [UCC 2–315, 2A–213].
Other Implied Warranties (See page 513.)	Other implied warranties can arise as a result of course of dealing or usage of trade [UCC 2–314(3), 2A–212(3)].
	PRODUCT LIABILITY
Liability Based on Negligence (See pages 519–521.)	1. The manufacturer must use due care in designing the product, selecting materials, using the appropriate production process, assembling and testing the product, and placing adequate warnings on the label or product. 2. Privity of contract is not required. A manufacturer is liable for failure to exercise due care to any person who sustains an injury proximately caused by a negligently made (defective) product.
Liability Based on Misrepresentation (See page 521.)	Fraudulent misrepresentation of a product may result in product liability based on the tort of fraud.
Strict Liability—Requirements (See pages 523–524.)	1. The defendant must sell the product in a defective condition. 2. The defendant must normally be engaged in the business of selling that product. 3. The product must be unreasonably dangerous to the user or consumer because of its defective condition (in most states). 4. The plaintiff must incur physical harm to self or property by use or consumption of the product. (Courts will also extend strict liability to include injured bystanders.) 5. The defective condition must be the proximate cause of the injury or damage. 6. The goods must not have been substantially changed from the time the product was sold to the time the injury was sustained.

CHAPTER SUMMARY Warranties and Product Liability—Continued

Product Defects (See pages 524–525.)	A product may be defective in three basic ways: 1. In its manufacture. 2. In its design. 3. In the instructions or warnings that come with it.
Market-Share Liability (See pages 525–527.)	When plaintiffs cannot prove which of many distributors of a defective product supplied the particular product that caused the plaintiffs' injuries, some courts apply market-share liability. All firms that manufactured and distributed the harmful product during the period in question are then held liable for the plaintiffs' injuries in proportion to the firms' respective shares of the market, as directed by the court.
Other Applications of Strict Liability (See page 527.)	1. Manufacturers and other sellers are liable for harms suffered by bystanders as a result of defective products. 2. Suppliers of component parts are strictly liable for defective parts that, when incorporated into a product, cause injuries to users.
Defenses to Product Liability (See pages 527–530.)	1. *Assumption of risk*—The user or consumer knew of the risk of harm and voluntarily assumed it. 2. *Product misuse*—The user or consumer misused the product in a way unforeseeable by the manufacturer. 3. *Comparative negligence and liability*—Liability may be distributed between the plaintiff and the defendant under the doctrine of comparative negligence if the plaintiff's misuse of the product contributed to the risk of injury. 4. *Commonly known dangers*—If a defendant succeeds in convincing the court that a plaintiff's injury resulted from a commonly known danger, such as the danger associated with using a sharp knife, the defendant will not be liable. 5. *Other defenses*—A defendant can also defend against a product liability claim by showing that there is no basis for the plaintiff's claim (that the plaintiff has not met the requirements for an action in negligence or strict liability, for example).

FOR REVIEW

Answers for the even-numbered questions in this For Review *section can be found on this text's accompanying Web site at* http://blt.westbuslaw.com. *Select "Chapter 21" and click on "For Review."*

1. What factors determine whether a seller's or lessor's statement constitutes an express warranty or mere "puffing"?
2. What implied warranties arise under the UCC?
3. Can a manufacturer be held liable to any person who suffers an injury proximately caused by the manufacturer's negligently made product?
4. What are the elements of a cause of action in strict product liability?
5. What defenses to liability can be raised in a product liability lawsuit?

QUESTIONS AND CASE PROBLEMS

21–1. Product Liability. Under what contract theory can a seller be held liable to a consumer for physical harm or property damage that is caused by the goods sold? Under what tort theories can the seller be held liable?

21–2. Product Liability. Carmen buys a television set manufactured by AKI Electronics. She is going on vacation, so she takes the set to her mother's house for her mother to use. Because the set is defective, it explodes, causing considerable damage to her mother's house. Carmen's mother sues AKI for the damages to her house. Discuss the theories under which Carmen's mother can recover from AKI.

21–3. Warranty Disclaimers. Tandy purchased a washing machine from Marshall Appliances. The sales contract included a provision explicitly disclaiming all express or implied warranties, including the implied warranty of merchantability. The disclaimer was printed in the same size and color as the rest of the contract. The machine turned out to be a "lemon" and never functioned properly. Tandy sought a refund of the purchase price, claiming that Marshall had breached the implied warranty of merchantability. Can Tandy recover her money, notwithstanding the warranty disclaimer in the contract? Explain.

21–4. Implied Warranties. Sam, a farmer, needs to install a two-thousand-pound piece of equipment in his barn. The equipment must be lifted thirty feet into a hayloft. Sam goes to Durham Hardware and tells Durham that he needs some heavy-duty rope to be used on his farm. Durham recommends a one-inch-thick nylon rope, and Sam purchases two hundred feet of it. Sam ties the rope around the piece of equipment, puts the rope through a pulley, and with the aid of a tractor lifts the equipment off the ground. Suddenly, the rope breaks. The equipment crashes to the ground and is extensively damaged. Sam files suit against Durham for breach of the implied warranty of fitness for a particular purpose. Discuss how successful Sam will be with his suit.

CASE PROBLEM WITH SAMPLE ANSWER

21–5. In May 1995, Ms. McCathern and her daughter, together with McCathern's cousin, Ms. Sanders, and her daughter, were riding in Sanders's 1994 Toyota 4Runner. Sanders was driving, McCathern was in the front passenger seat, and the children were in the backseat. Everyone was wearing a seat belt. While the group was traveling south on Oregon State Highway 395 at a speed of approximately 50 miles per hour, an oncoming vehicle veered into Sanders's lane of travel. When Sanders tried to steer clear, the 4Runner rolled over and landed upright on its four wheels. During the rollover, the roof over the front passenger seat collapsed, and as a result, McCathern sustained serious, permanent injuries. McCathern filed a suit in an Oregon state court against Toyota Motor Corp. and others, alleging in part that the 1994 4Runner "was dangerously defective and unreasonably dangerous in that the vehicle, as designed and sold, was unstable and prone to rollover." What is the test for product liability based on a design defect? What would McCathern have to prove to succeed under that test? [*McCathern v. Toyota Motor Corp.*, 332 Or. 59, 23 P.3d 320 (2001)]

After you have answered this problem, compare your answer with the sample answer given on the Web site that accompanies this text. Go to http://blt.westbuslaw.com, select "Chapter 21," and click on "Case Problem with Sample Answer."

21–6. Implied Warranties. Shalom Malul contracted with Capital Cabinets, Inc., in August 1999 for new kitchen cabinets made by Holiday Kitchens. The price was $10,900. On Capital's recommendation, Malul hired Barry Burger to install the cabinets for $1,600. Burger finished the job in March 2000, and Malul contracted for more cabinets at a price of $2,300, which Burger installed in April. Within a couple of weeks, the doors on several of the cabinets began to "melt"—the laminate (surface covering) began to pull away from the substrate (the material underneath the surface). Capital replaced several of the doors, but the problem occurred again, affecting a total of six of thirty doors. A Holiday Kitchens representative inspected the cabinets and concluded that the melting was due to excessive heat, the result of the doors being placed too close to the stove. Malul filed a suit in a New York state court against Capital, alleging, among other things, a breach of the implied warranty of merchantability. Were these goods "merchantable"? Why or why not? [*Malul v. Capital Cabinets, Inc.*, 191 Misc.2d 399, 740 N.Y.S.2d 828 (N.Y.City Civ.Ct. 2002)]

21–7. Product Liability. In January 1999, John Clark of Clarksdale, Mississippi, bought a paintball gun. Clark practiced with the gun and knew how to screw in the carbon dioxide cartridge, pump the gun, and use its safety and trigger. He hunted and had taken a course in hunter safety education. He was aware that protective eyewear was available for purchase, but he chose not to buy it. Clark also understood that it was "common sense" not to shoot anyone in the face. Chris Rico, another Clarksdale resident, owned a paintball gun made by Brass Eagle, Inc. Rico was similarly familiar with the gun's use and its risks. Clark, Rico, and their friends played a game that involved shooting paintballs at cars whose occupants also had the guns. One night, while Clark and Rico were cruising with their guns, Rico shot at Clark's car, but hit Clark in the eye. Clark filed a suit in a Mississippi state court against Brass Eagle to recover for the injury, alleging in part that its gun was defectively designed. During the trial, Rico testified that his gun "never malfunctioned." In whose favor should the court rule? Why? [*Clark v. Brass Eagle, Inc.*, 866 So.2d 456 (Miss. 2004)]

A QUESTION OF ETHICS

21–8. On July 1, 1993, Gian Luigi Ferri entered the offices of a law firm against which he had a grudge. Using two semiautomatic assault weapons (TEC-9 and TEC-DC9) manufactured and distributed by Navegar, Inc., he killed eight persons and wounded six others before killing himself. The survivors and the families of some of those who had died sued Navegar, based in part on negligence. They claimed that Navegar had a duty not to create risks to the public beyond those inherent in the lawful use of firearms. They offered evidence that Navegar knew or should have known that the assault guns had "no legitimate sporting or self-defense purpose" and that the guns were "particularly well adapted to military-style assault on large numbers of people." They also claimed that the TEC-DC9 advertising "targets a criminal clientele," further increasing the risk of harm. A California trial court granted summary judgment in Navegar's favor. The appellate court reversed, ruling that the case should go to trial. The court stated that "the likelihood that a third person would make use of the TEC-DC9 in the kind of criminal rampage Ferri perpetrated is precisely the hazard that would support a determination that Navegar's conduct was negligent." Navegar appealed the decision to the California Supreme Court. In view of these facts, consider the following questions. [*Merrill v. Navegar, Inc.*, 26 Cal.4th 465, 28 P.3d 116, 110 Cal.Rptr.2d 370 (2001)]

1. Do you agree with the appellate court that Navegar could be held negligent in marketing the TEC-DC9? What should the California Supreme Court decide? (Before answering this question, you may wish to review the elements of negligence in Chapter 4.)
2. Should gun manufacturers ever be held liable for deaths caused by nondefective guns? Why or why not?
3. Generally, do you believe that policy decisions regarding the liability of gun manufacturers should be made by the courts, whose job is to interpret the law, or by Congress and state legislatures, whose job is to make the law?
4. In your opinion, have Congress and state legislatures gone far enough in regulating the use of firearms, or have they gone too far? Explain.

FOR CRITICAL ANALYSIS

21–9. The United States has the strictest product liability laws in the world today. Why do you think many other countries, particularly developing countries, are more lax with respect to holding manufacturers liable for product defects?

VIDEO QUESTION

21–10. Go to this text's Web site at http://blt.westbuslaw.com and select "Chapter 21." Click on "Video Questions" and view the video titled *Warranties*. Then answer the following questions.

1. Discuss whether the grocery store's label of a "Party Platter for Twenty" creates an express warranty under the Uniform Commercial Code that the platter will actually serve twenty people.
2. List and describe any implied warranties discussed in the chapter that apply to this scenario.
3. How would a court determine whether Oscar had breached any express or implied warranties concerning the quantity of food on the platter?

INTERNET EXERCISES

Go to the *Business Law Today* home page at http://blt.westbuslaw.com, select "Chapter 21," and click on "Internet Exercises." There you will find the following Internet research exercises that you can perform to learn more about topics covered in this chapter.

Activity 21–1: LEGAL PERSPECTIVE—Remedial Promises

Activity 21–2: MANAGEMENT PERSPECTIVE—Warranties

Activity 21–3: SOCIAL PERSPECTIVE—Lemon Laws

BEFORE THE TEST

Go to the *Business Law Today* home page at http://blt.westbuslaw.com, select "Chapter 21," and click on "Interactive Quizzes." You will find a number of interactive questions relating to this chapter.

Mangold v. Nissan North America, Inc.

In Chapter 21, we discussed the Magnuson-Moss Warranty Act, which covers express warranties made in connection with sales of consumer goods costing more than $10. The act permits "a consumer who is damaged by the failure of a supplier, warrantor, or service contractor to comply with any obligation under this [statute], or under a written warranty, implied warranty, or service contract" to, among other things, elect repair, replacement, or refund of defective parts. Some—but not all—courts extend the protections of the act to leases. In this extended case study, we examine Mangold v. Nissan North America, Inc.,[1] *a decision considering whether leases generally fall under the act, and specifically, whether a lessee of an automobile can maintain a cause of action for breach of warranty under the act.*

CASE BACKGROUND

Nissan North America, Inc., makes Infiniti automobiles. Christopher and Erynn Mangold leased a new 2001 Infiniti I30 at Infiniti of Orland Park in Illinois. The dealer sold the vehicle to Debis Financial Services, Inc., which leased it to the Mangolds. Nissan provided a written warranty that covered the vehicle against factory defects for four years or 60,000 miles. The warranty was issued to Debis. As part of the lease, Debis assigned its rights under the warranty to the Mangolds.

Immediately after leasing the car, the Mangolds noticed excessive wind noise and brought the vehicle back to the dealership. The dealer made several attempts, which the warranty covered, to correct the problem. When these attempts proved unsuccessful, the Mangolds filed a suit in an Illinois state court against Nissan to revoke their acceptance of the car, alleging breach of warranty under the Magnuson-Moss Warranty Act.

Nissan filed a motion to dismiss, arguing that the act provides protection only in connection with a *sale* to a *consumer.* Nissan asserted that this transaction involved a *lease* and that *lessees* are not consumers. The court denied the motion. Nissan appealed to a state intermediate appellate court.

1. 347 Ill.App.3d 1008, 809 N.E.2d 251, 284 Ill.Dec. 129 (2004). This opinion may be accessed online at **http://www.state.il.us/court/Opinions/Search.htm**. On that page, in the "Appellate Court" section, click on "2004." On the resulting page, in the "Third District" section, click on "April." On the next page, click on the name of the case to access the opinion.

MAJORITY OPINION

Justice *LYTTON* delivered the opinion of the court.

* * * *

* * * The Act defines "consumer" as:

> [1] a buyer (other than for purposes of resale) of any consumer product, [2] any person to whom such product is transferred during the duration of an implied or written warranty (or service contract) applicable to the product, and [3] any other person who is entitled by the terms of such warranty (or service contract) * * * to enforce against the warrantor (or service contractor) the obligations of the warranty (or service contract).

* * * *

A person need only meet one of the three criteria to qualify as a consumer. Plaintiffs claim that they are consumers under both the second and third prongs of the Act. The second prong defines a consumer as any person to whom a product is transferred during a warranty's duration. The majority of courts have held that the lessees do not qualify as transferees, citing the Uniform Commercial Code's definition of transfer, which includes the "passing of title." Under this interpretation, lessees would not qualify because in a lease title does not pass to them.

Other courts have determined that the language of the Act is clear and that references to the UCC are unnecessary. Thus, when buyers transfer warranty rights to lessees, the lessees become entitled to enforce the warranty against the warrantor and therefore become "consumers."

We agree with the line of cases that finds that the Act contains sufficient language to define transfer without looking to the UCC for assistance. Since Debis transferred all its warranty rights to the plaintiffs during the duration of the warranty, plaintiffs were entitled to enforce the warranty. *Nothing in the language of the statute suggests that title must pass, and we will not add such a requirement upon review. Therefore, we find that plaintiffs are consumers under the second prong* * * * . [Emphasis added.]

* * * *

Plaintiffs also qualify as consumers under the broader third criterion in the Act * * * . To facilitate the lease,

Debis assigned its warranty rights to plaintiffs. Since the warranty does not prohibit an assignment of rights, plaintiffs were entitled to enforce them to their fullest extent, including vehicle repair and replacement.

Moreover, in this case, the dealership actually serviced plaintiffs' vehicle numerous times, and each time the repairs were covered by the warranty. We find no merit in allowing plaintiffs to enforce the warranty for repairs, but denying warranty rights when a violation under the Act is asserted. *Since plaintiffs were entitled to enforce the warranty when the vehicle required repair, they qualified as consumers under the third prong.* [Emphasis added.]

* * * *

Defendants argue that even if plaintiffs qualify as consumers, the Act does not apply to them because the warranty was not part of a "sale." The Act's definitions of implied and written warranty both include the language "made in connection with [a] sale."

Defendant looks to legislative intent in arguing that Congress did not intend to cover leases * * * .

* * * [I]f legislative intent can be ascertained from the statute's plain language, that intent prevails over any other interpretive aid. Thus, we need not examine legislative intent in reviewing the Act if the plain language of the statute sufficiently represents the legislative intent.

The plain language of the statute simply requires that warranties under the Act be issued "in connection with the sale" of a consumer product. It does not require a sale to be made to the ultimate consumer with a passage of title to that party and does not forbid the subsequent assignment of the warranty. Given the plain language of the statute, "in connection with [a] sale" means the sale between the dealership and Debis Financial.

Since the vehicle was sold to the lessor with a manufacturer's written warranty, the warranty was made "in connection with" the sale, and plaintiffs, as assignees, must be allowed to enforce it. * * *

* * * [T]he cause [is] remanded for further proceedings.

DISSENTING OPINION

Presiding Justice *HOLDRIDGE,* dissenting.

I respectfully dissent. * * * Here, we are asked to determine whether the Magnuson-Moss Warranty Act applies to lessees. In order to answer that question we must, of course, look to the statute itself. Does the Act clearly and unambiguously, *i.e.* expressly, apply to lessees? A review of the Act shows that it is silent as to lessees. * * *

* * * *

* * * I would then resort to standard rules of statutory construction in order to determine the intent of Congress on this issue. One such rule of statutory construction permits us to look to compare statutes that concern the same subject matter and to consider statutes on related subjects. Here, we have another consumer protection statute for comparison, the Truth in Lending Act, enacted seven years prior to Magnuson-Moss.[2] In that statute, Congress expressly included lessees as consumers protected by that Act. One would reasonably assume that, had Congress similarly intended Magnuson-Moss to protect lessees, it would certainly have included express language as contained in the Truth in Lending Act.

I also note that when statutory language is ambiguous, it is appropriate to resort to extrinsic aids of construction such as an examination of legislative history. Here, when we consider legislative history, it is clear that Congress was warned * * * that lessees were not covered under the language as ultimately passed in the Act. Still Congress chose not to change the language of the Act in order to make it clear that lessees were covered under the Act. I would find this to be clear evidence of Congress' intent NOT to include lessees within the protections of Magnuson-Moss.

2. The Truth-in-Lending Act will be discussed in detail in Chapter 38.

QUESTIONS FOR ANALYSIS

1 Law. What did the majority hold in this case? What was the reasoning supporting this decision?

2 Law. What was the dissent's position on the issue before the court? How did the dissent arrive at this conclusion?

3 Ethics. Is it fair for the court to treat *lessees* the same as it would treat *buyers* in enforcing express warranties? Why or why not?

4 Political Dimensions. Should there be different rules for sellers and lessors regarding warranties? If so, who should prescribe those rules?

5 Implications for the Manufacturer. What should a manufacturer do if it wishes to retain an express warranty in connection with a sale but avoid its application on a lease?

UNIT FOUR

NEGOTIABLE INSTRUMENTS

UNIT CONTENTS

CHAPTER 22

Negotiability and Transferability

"It took many generations for people to feel comfortable accepting paper in lieu of gold or silver."

Alan Greenspan, 1926–
(Chairman of the Board of Governors of the Federal Reserve System, 1987–)

CHAPTER OUTLINE

- ARTICLES 3 AND 4 OF THE UCC
- TYPES OF INSTRUMENTS
- REQUIREMENTS FOR NEGOTIABILITY
- TRANSFER OF INSTRUMENTS
- INDORSEMENTS

LEARNING OBJECTIVES

After reading this chapter, you should be able to answer the following questions:

1. What are the four types of negotiable instruments with which Article 3 of the UCC is concerned? Which of these instruments are *orders* to pay, and which are *promises* to pay?
2. What requirements must an instrument meet to be negotiable?
3. To whom is a bearer instrument payable?
4. What is the difference between an indorsement in blank and a special indorsement?
5. What is a restrictive indorsement? Does a restrictive indorsement prohibit further negotiation of the instrument?

NEGOTIABLE INSTRUMENT
A signed writing (record) that contains an unconditional promise or order to pay an exact sum of money on demand or at an exact future time to a specific person or order, or to bearer.

Most modern commercial transactions would be inconceivable without negotiable instruments. A **negotiable instrument** is a signed writing (record) that contains an unconditional promise or order to pay an exact sum of money on demand or at a specified future time to a specific person or order, or to bearer. The checks you write to pay for groceries and other items are negotiable instruments.

A negotiable instrument can function as a substitute for money or as an extension of credit. When a buyer writes a check to pay for goods, the check serves as a substitute for money. When a buyer gives a seller a promissory note in which the buyer promises to pay the seller the purchase price within sixty days, the seller has essentially extended credit to the buyer for a sixty-day period. For a negotiable instrument to operate *practically* as either a substitute for cash or a credit device, or both, it is essential that the instrument be easily transferable without danger of being uncollectible. Each rule described in the following pages can be examined in light of this essential function of negotiable instruments.

As the chapter-opening quotation indicates, it took "many generations" before paper became an acceptable substitute for gold or silver. In the medieval world, merchants engaging in foreign trade used negotiable instruments to finance and conduct their affairs. They did this largely because of the hazards of transporting and safekeeping gold or coins. The English king's courts of those times did not recognize the validity of negotiable instruments, however, so the merchants had to develop their own rules governing the use of these instruments. These rules were enforced by "fair" or "borough" courts. Eventually, the decisions of these courts formed a distinct set of laws that became known as the *Lex Mercatoria* (Law Merchant).

The Law Merchant was codified in England in the Bills of Exchange Act of 1882. In 1896, in the United States, the National Conference of Commissioners on Uniform State Laws (NCCUSL) drafted the Uniform Negotiable Instruments Law. This law, which had been adopted by all of the states by 1920, was the forerunner of Article 3 of the Uniform Commercial Code (UCC).

Articles 3 and 4 of the UCC

.on the Web To find Article 3 of the UCC as adopted by a particular state, go to the Web site of Cornell University's Law School at **http://www.law.cornell.edu/ucc/ucc.table.html**.

Negotiable instruments must meet special requirements relating to form and content. These requirements, which are imposed by Article 3 of the UCC, will be discussed at length in this chapter. Article 3 also governs the process of negotiation (transferring an instrument from one party to another), as will be discussed. Note that UCC 3–104(b) defines *instrument* as a "negotiable instrument." For that reason, whenever the term *instrument* is used in this book, it refers to a negotiable instrument.

The 1990 Revision of Articles 3 and 4

In 1990, a revised version of Article 3 was issued for adoption by the states. Many of the changes to Article 3 simply clarified old sections, but some significantly altered the former provisions. As of this writing, all of the states except New York and South Carolina have adopted the revised article. Therefore, all references to Article 3 in this chapter and in the following two chapters are to the *revised* Article 3.

Article 4 of the UCC, which governs bank deposits and collections (discussed in Chapter 24), was also revised in 1990. In part, these changes were necessary to reflect changes in Article 3 that affect Article 4 provisions. The revised Articles 3 and 4 are included in Appendix C.

The 2002 Amendments to Articles 3 and 4

In 2002, the NCCUSL and the American Law Institute approved a number of amendments to Articles 3 and 4 of the UCC. One of the purposes of these amendments was to update the law with respect to e-commerce. For example, the amended versions of the articles implement the policy of the Uniform Electronic Transactions Act (see Chapter 17) by removing unnecessary obstacles to electronic communications. Additionally, the word *writing* has been replaced by the term *record* throughout the articles. Other amendments relate to such topics as telephone-generated checks and the payment and discharge of negotiable instruments.

To date, only a few states have adopted these amendments. Therefore, in this chapter and in the chapters that follow, we will indicate in footnotes whenever the amendments significantly alter existing law. Keep in mind, however, that even when the changes are not substantive, some of the section numbers may change slightly once a state has adopted the amendments to Article 3 (subpart 9 may become subpart 12, for example).

Types of Instruments

The UCC specifies four types of negotiable instruments: *drafts, checks, promissory notes,* and *certificates of deposit (CDs).* These instruments are frequently divided into the two classifications that we will discuss in the following subsections: *orders to pay* (drafts and checks) and *promises to pay* (promissory notes and CDs).

Negotiable instruments may also be classified as either demand instruments or time instruments. A *demand instrument* is payable on demand; that is, it is payable immediately after it is issued and thereafter for a reasonable period of time. All checks are demand instruments because, by definition, they must be payable on demand. A *time instrument* is payable at a future date.

Drafts and Checks (Orders to Pay)

DRAFT
Any instrument drawn on a drawee that orders the drawee to pay a certain sum of money, usually to a third party (the payee), on demand or at a definite future time.

DRAWER
The party that initiates a draft (such as a check), thereby ordering the drawee to pay.

DRAWEE
The party that is ordered to pay a draft or check. With a check, a bank or a financial institution is always the drawee.

PAYEE
A person to whom an instrument is made payable.

ACCEPTANCE
In negotiable instruments law, the drawee's signed agreement to pay a draft when presented.

A **draft** (bill of exchange) is an unconditional written order that involves three parties. The party creating the draft (the **drawer**) orders another party (the **drawee**) to pay money, usually to a third party (the **payee**).

Time Drafts and Sight Drafts A *time draft* is payable at a definite future time. A *sight draft* (or demand draft) is payable on sight—that is, when it is presented to the drawee (usually a bank or financial institution) for payment. A draft can be both a time and a sight draft; such a draft is payable at a stated time after sight. A sight draft may be payable on acceptance. **Acceptance** is the drawee's written promise to pay the draft when it comes due. The usual manner of accepting an instrument is by writing the word *accepted* across the face of the instrument, followed by the date of acceptance and the signature of the drawee.

Exhibit 22–1 shows a typical time draft. For the drawee to be obligated to honor the order, the drawee must be obligated to the drawer either by agreement or through a debtor-creditor relationship. ■ EXAMPLE 22.1 On January 16, Ourtown Real Estate Company orders $1,000 worth of office supplies from Eastman Supply Company, with payment due April 16. Also on January 16, Ourtown sends Eastman a draft drawn on its account with the First National Bank of Whiteacre as payment. In this scenario, the drawer is Ourtown, the drawee is Ourtown's bank (First National Bank of Whiteacre), and the payee is Eastman Supply Company. ■

TRADE ACCEPTANCE
A draft that is drawn by a seller of goods ordering the buyer to pay a specified sum of money to the seller, usually at a stated time in the future. The buyer accepts the draft by signing the face of the draft, thus creating an enforceable obligation to pay the draft when it comes due. On a trade acceptance, the seller is both the drawer and the payee.

Trade Acceptances A trade acceptance is a type of draft that is frequently used in the sale of goods. In a **trade acceptance,** the seller is both the drawer and the payee on this draft. Essentially, the draft orders the buyer to pay a specified sum of money to the seller, usually at a stated time in the future. (If the draft orders the buyer's bank to pay, it is called a *banker's acceptance.*)

■ EXAMPLE 22.2 Each year Jackson River Fabrics sells fabric priced at $50,000 to Comfort Creations, Inc., on terms requiring payment to be made in ninety days. One year Jackson River needs cash, so it draws a *trade acceptance* (see Exhibit 22–2) that orders Comfort Creations to pay $50,000 to the order of Jackson River Fabrics ninety days hence. Jackson River presents the paper to Comfort Creations. Comfort Creations *accepts* the draft, by signing the face of the draft, and returns it to Jackson

EXHIBIT 22–1 A TYPICAL TIME DRAFT

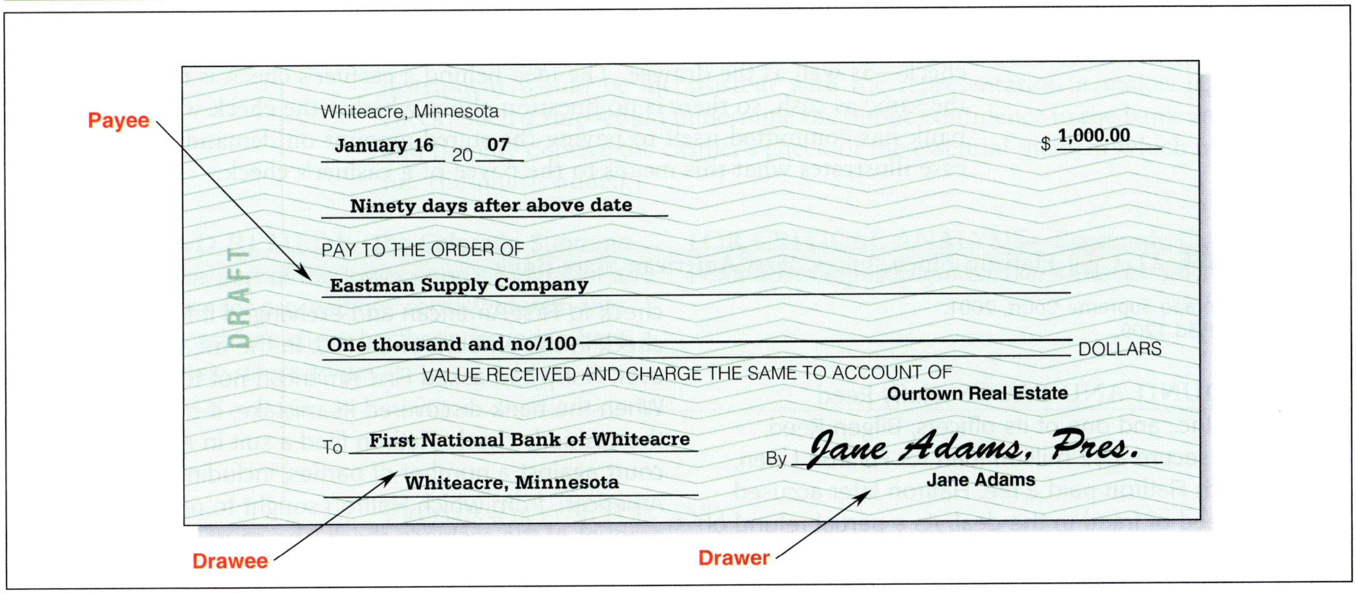

River Fabrics. The acceptance by Comfort Creations gives rise to an enforceable obligation to pay the draft when it comes due in ninety days. Jackson River can then immediately sell the trade acceptance in the commercial money market for cash. ■

CHECK
A draft drawn by a drawer ordering the drawee bank or financial institution to pay a certain amount of money to the holder on demand.

Checks The most commonly used type of draft is a **check.** The writer of the check is the drawer, the bank on which the check is drawn is the drawee, and the person to whom the check is payable is the payee. As mentioned earlier, checks are demand instruments because they are payable on demand.

Checks will be discussed more fully in Chapter 24, but it should be noted here that with certain types of checks, such as *cashier's checks,* the bank is both the

EXHIBIT 22–2 A TYPICAL TRADE ACCEPTANCE

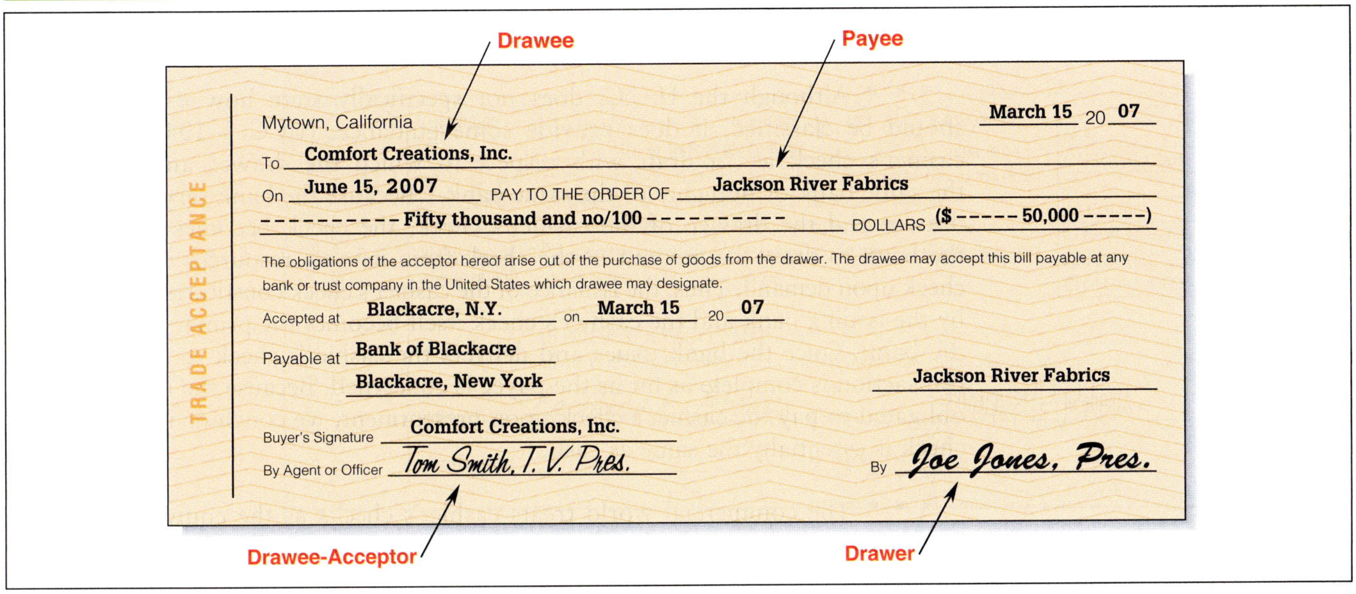

order are stated in another writing. A mere reference to another writing, however, does not of itself make the promise or order conditional [UCC 3–106(a)]. For example, the words "As per contract" or "This debt arises from the sale of goods X and Y" do not render an instrument nonnegotiable.

Payment Out of a Particular Fund. Similarly, a statement in the instrument that payment can be made only out of a particular fund or source will not render the instrument nonnegotiable [UCC 3–106(b)(ii)]. ■ EXAMPLE 22.6 Suppose that the terms in a note include the statement that payment will be made out of the proceeds of next year's cotton crop. This will not make the note nonnegotiable—although the payee of such a note may find the note commercially unacceptable and refuse to take it. ■

Note Secured by a Mortgage. Finally, a simple statement in an otherwise negotiable note indicating that the note is secured by a mortgage does not destroy its negotiability [UCC 3–106(b)(i)]. Actually, such a statement might even make the note more acceptable in commerce. Realize, though, that the statement that a note is secured by a mortgage must not stipulate that the maker's promise to pay is *subject* to the terms and conditions of the mortgage.

A Fixed Amount of Money

Negotiable instruments must state with certainty a fixed amount of money to be paid at any time the instrument is payable [UCC 3–104(a)]. This requirement ensures that the value of the instrument can be determined with clarity and certainty.

Fixed Amount The term *fixed amount* means an amount that is ascertainable from the face of the instrument. A demand note payable with 8 percent interest meets the requirement of a fixed amount because its amount can be determined at the time it is payable or at any time thereafter [UCC 3–104(a)].

The rate of interest may also be determined with reference to information that is not contained in the instrument if that information is readily ascertainable by reference to a formula or a source described in the instrument [UCC 3–112(b)]. For instance, an instrument that is payable at the *legal rate of interest* (a rate of interest fixed by statute) is negotiable. Mortgage notes tied to a variable rate of interest (a rate that fluctuates as a result of market conditions) are also negotiable.

BE AWARE Interest payable on an instrument normally cannot exceed the maximum limit on interest under a state's usury statute.

Payable in Money UCC 3–104(a) provides that a fixed amount is to be *payable in money.* The UCC defines money as "a medium of exchange authorized or adopted by a domestic or foreign government as a part of its currency" [UCC 1–201(24)].

■ EXAMPLE 22.7 Suppose that the maker of a note promises "to pay on demand $1,000 in U.S. gold." Because gold is not a medium of exchange adopted by the U.S. government, the note is not payable in money. The same result would occur if the maker promises "to pay $1,000 and fifty bottles of 1990 Château Lafite-Rothschild wine," because the instrument is not payable *entirely* in money. An instrument payable in government bonds or in shares of IBM stock is not negotiable because neither is a medium of exchange recognized by the U.S. government. ■

The statement "Payable in $1,000 U.S. currency or an equivalent value in gold" would render the instrument nonnegotiable if the maker reserved the option of paying in money *or* gold. If the option were left to the payee, some legal scholars argue that the instrument would be negotiable. Any instrument payable in the United States with a face amount stated in a foreign currency is negotiable and can be paid in the foreign money or in the equivalent in U.S. dollars [UCC 3–107].

PAYABLE ON DEMAND OR AT A DEFINITE TIME

ACCEPTOR
A drawee that is legally obligated to pay an instrument when the instrument is presented later for payment.

A negotiable instrument must "be payable on demand or at a definite time" [UCC 3–104(a)(2)]. Clearly, to ascertain the value of a negotiable instrument, it is necessary to know when the maker, drawee, or acceptor (an **acceptor** is a drawee that promises to pay an instrument when it is presented later for payment) is required to pay. It is also necessary to know when the obligations of secondary parties, such as indorsers[1] (to be discussed later in this chapter), will arise. Furthermore, it is necessary to know when an instrument is due to calculate when the statute of limitations may apply [UCC 3–118(a)]. Finally, to determine the present value of an interest-bearing instrument, it is necessary to know the exact interval during which the interest will accrue.

PRESENTMENT
The act of presenting an instrument to the party liable on the instrument to collect payment. Presentment also occurs when a person presents an instrument to a drawee for a required acceptance.

Payable on Demand Instruments that are payable on demand include those that contain the words "Payable at sight" or "Payable upon presentment." **Presentment** occurs when a person presents an instrument to the party liable on the instrument to collect payment; presentment also occurs when a person presents an instrument to a drawee for acceptance (see the discussion of trade acceptances earlier in this chapter).

The very nature of the instrument may indicate that it is payable on demand. For example, a check, by definition, is payable on demand [UCC 3–104(f)]. If no time for payment is specified and the person responsible for payment must pay on the instrument's presentment, the instrument is payable on demand [UCC 3–108(a)].

Payable at a Definite Time If an instrument is not payable on demand, to be negotiable it must be payable at a definite time. An instrument is payable at a definite time if it states that it is payable (1) on a specified date, (2) within a definite period of time (such as thirty days) after being presented for payment, or (3) on a date or time readily ascertainable at the time the promise or order is issued [UCC 3–108(b)]. The maker or drawee in a time draft, for example, is under no obligation to pay until the specified time.

■ EXAMPLE 22.8 Suppose that an instrument dated June 1, 2006, states, "One year after the death of my grandfather, Henry Adams, I promise to pay to the order of James Harmon $5,000. [Signed] Jacqueline Wells." This instrument is nonnegotiable. Because the date of the grandfather's death is uncertain, the instrument is not payable at a definite time. ■

When an instrument is payable by the maker or drawer on or before a stated date, it is clearly payable at a definite time. The maker or drawer, however, has the option of paying before the stated maturity date. If the maker or drawer does not pay early, the holder can still rely on payment being made by the maturity date. Thus, the option to pay early does not violate the definite-time requirement. ■ EXAMPLE 22.9 Suppose that Levine gives Hirsch an instrument dated November 1, 2006, that indicates on its face that it is payable on or before November 1, 2007. This instrument satisfies the requirement. ■ In contrast, an instrument that is undated and made payable "one month after date" is clearly nonnegotiable. There is no way to determine the maturity date from the face of the instrument.

ACCELERATION CLAUSE
A clause that allows a payee or other holder of a time instrument to demand payment of the entire amount due, with interest, if a certain event occurs, such as a default in the payment of an installment when due.

Acceleration Clause An **acceleration clause** allows a payee or other holder of a time instrument to demand payment of the entire amount due, with interest, if a certain event occurs, such as a default in the payment of an installment when due. (A

1. We should note here that because the UCC uses the spelling *indorse* (*indorsement,* and so forth), rather than *endorse* (*endorsement,* and so forth), we adopt that spelling here and in other chapters in the text.

HOLDER
Any person in possession of an instrument drawn, issued, or indorsed to him or her, to his or her order, to bearer, or in blank.

holder is any person in possession of an instrument drawn, issued, or indorsed to him or her, to his or her order, to bearer, or in blank [see UCC 1–201(20)]. The terms *indorse, bearer,* and *in blank* will be explained later in the chapter.) Reasons for acceleration that are stated in the instrument do not affect the instrument's negotiability. For an acceleration clause to be enforced, however, the holder must have a good faith belief that payment will not be made when she or he invokes the acceleration clause.

■ EXAMPLE 22.10 Assume that Martin lends $1,000 to Rhianna. Rhianna makes a negotiable note promising to pay $100 per month for eleven months. The note contains an acceleration provision that permits Martin or any holder to demand at once all of the remaining payments plus the interest owed to date if Rhianna fails to pay an installment in any given month. If, for example, Rhianna fails to make the third payment, the note will be due and payable in full. If Martin accelerates the unpaid balance, Rhianna will owe Martin the remaining principal plus any unpaid interest. ■

Under the UCC, instruments that include acceleration clauses are negotiable because (1) the exact value of the instrument can be ascertained and (2) the instrument will be payable on a specified date if the event allowing acceleration does not occur [UCC 3–108(b)(ii)]. Thus, the specified date is the outside limit used to determine the value and negotiability of the instrument.

EXTENSION CLAUSE
A clause in a time instrument that allows the instrument's date of maturity to be extended into the future.

Extension Clause The reverse of an acceleration clause is an **extension clause,** which allows the date of maturity to be extended into the future [UCC 3–108(b)(iii), (iv)]. To keep the instrument negotiable, the interval of the extension must be specified if the maker of the instrument has the right to extend it. If, however, the holder of the instrument can extend it, the extended maturity date does not have to be specified.

■ EXAMPLE 22.11 Alek executes a note that reads, "The maker has the right to postpone the time of payment of this note beyond its definite maturity date of January 1, 2007. This extension, however, shall be for no more than a reasonable time." A note with this language is not negotiable because it does not satisfy the definite-time requirement. The right to extend is the maker's, and Alek has not indicated when the note will become due after the extension. In contrast, if Alek's note reads, "The holder of this note at the date of maturity, January 1, 2007, can extend the time of payment until the following June 1 or later, if the holder so wishes," it is a negotiable instrument. The length of the extension does not have to be specified because the option to extend is solely that of the holder. After January 1, 2007, the note is, in effect, a demand instrument. ■

PAYABLE TO ORDER OR TO BEARER

Because one of the functions of a negotiable instrument is to serve as a substitute for cash, freedom to transfer an instrument to another person is an essential requirement. To assure a proper transfer, the instrument must be "payable to order or to bearer" at the time it is issued or first comes into the possession of the holder [UCC 3–104(a)(1)]. This is no longer required for a check to be negotiable, however [UCC 3–104(c)]. Thus, a bank could eliminate the words "the order of" in the familiar phrase "Pay to the order of," and the check would still be negotiable. All other instruments, however, will not be negotiable unless they meet this requirement. The *Concept Summary* on the facing page reiterates all of the requirements for an instrument to be negotiable.

ORDER INSTRUMENT
A negotiable instrument that is payable "to the order of an identified person" or "to an identified person or order."

Order Instruments An **order instrument** is an instrument that is payable (1) "to the order of an identified person" or (2) "to an identified person or order" [UCC 3–109(b)]. An identified person is the person "to whom the instrument is initially

CONCEPT SUMMARY Requirements for Negotiability

REQUIREMENTS	BASIC RULES
Must Be in Writing UCC 3–103(a)(6), (9)	A writing can be on anything that is readily transferable and has a degree of permanence. [See also UCC 1–201(46).]
Must Be Signed by the Maker or Drawer UCC 1–201(39) UCC 3–103(a)(3), (5) UCC 3–401(b) UCC 3–402	1. The signature can be anyplace on the face of the instrument. 2. It can be in any form (such as a word, mark, or rubber stamp) that purports to be a signature and authenticates the writing. 3. A signature may be made in a representative capacity.
Must Be a Definite Promise or Order UCC 3–103(a)(6), (9) UCC 3–104(a)	1. A promise must be more than a mere acknowledgment of a debt. 2. The words "I/We promise" or "Pay" meet this criterion.
Must Be Unconditional UCC 3–106	1. Payment cannot be expressly conditional on the occurrence of an event. 2. Payment cannot be made subject to or governed by another agreement.
Must Be an Order or Promise to Pay a Fixed Amount UCC 3–104(a) UCC 3–112(b)	An amount may be considered a fixed sum even if payable in installments, with a fixed or variable rate of interest, at a stated discount, or at an exchange rate.
Must Be Payable in Money UCC 3–104(a)(3) UCC 3–107	1. Any medium of exchange recognized as the currency of a government is money. 2. The maker or drawer cannot retain the option to pay the instrument in money *or* something else.
Must Be Payable on Demand or at a Definite Time UCC 3–104(a)(2) UCC 3–108(a), (b), (c)	1. Any instrument that is payable on demand or at sight, or otherwise indicates that it is payable at the will of the holder or does not state any time for payment, is a demand instrument. 2. An instrument is still payable at a definite time, even if it is payable on or before a stated date or within a fixed period after sight or if the drawer or maker has an option to extend the time for a definite period. 3. Acceleration clauses do not affect the negotiability of the instrument.
Must Be Payable to Order or Bearer UCC 3–104(a)(1), (c) UCC 3–109 UCC 3–110(a)	1. An order instrument must identify the payee with reasonable certainty. 2. An instrument that indicates it is not payable to an identified person is payable to bearer. 3. Checks are not required to be payable to order or bearer.

payable" as determined by the intent of the maker or drawer [UCC 3–110(a)]. The identified person, in turn, may transfer the instrument to whomever he or she wishes. Thus, the maker or drawer is agreeing to pay either the person specified on the instrument or whomever that person might designate. In this way, the instrument retains its transferability. ■ EXAMPLE 22.12 Suppose an instrument states, "Payable to the order of Kako Yung" or "Pay to Kako Yung or order." Clearly, the maker or drawer has indicated that a payment will be made to Yung or to whomever Yung designates. The instrument is negotiable. ■

Except for bearer instruments (explained in the following subsection), the person specified must be named with *certainty* because the transfer of an order instrument requires an indorsement. An **indorsement** is a signature placed on an instrument, such as on the back of a check, for the purpose of transferring one's ownership rights in the instrument. ■ EXAMPLE 22.13 If an instrument states, "Payable to the order of my kissing cousin," the instrument is nonnegotiable. This is because a holder could not be sure that the person who indorsed the instrument was actually the "kissing cousin" who was supposed to have indorsed it. ■

INDORSEMENT
A signature placed on an instrument for the purpose of transferring one's ownership rights in the instrument.

Bearer Instruments A **bearer instrument** is an instrument that does not designate a specific payee [UCC 3–109(a)]. The term **bearer** refers to a person in possession of an instrument that is payable to bearer or indorsed in blank (with a signature only, as will be discussed shortly) [UCC 1–201(5), 3–109(a), 3–109(c)]. This means that the maker or drawer agrees to pay anyone who presents the instrument for payment. An instrument containing any of the following terms is a bearer instrument:

BEARER INSTRUMENT
Any instrument that is not payable to a specific person, including instruments payable to the bearer or to "cash."

BEARER
A person in possession of an instrument payable to bearer or indorsed in blank.

1. "Payable to the order of bearer."
2. "Payable to Kathy Esposito or bearer."
3. "Payable to bearer."
4. "Pay cash."
5. "Pay to the order of cash."

NOTE An instrument that purports to be payable both to order and to bearer is a contradiction in terms. Such an instrument is a bearer instrument.

In addition, an instrument that "indicates that it is not payable to an identified person" is a bearer instrument [UCC 3–109(a)(3)]. Thus, an instrument "payable to X" or "payable to Batman" can be negotiated as a bearer instrument, as though it were payable to cash. The UCC does not accept an instrument issued to a nonexistent organization as payable to bearer, however [UCC 3–109, Comment 2]. An instrument "payable to the order of the Camrod Company," if no such company exists, therefore would not be a bearer instrument.

FACTORS THAT DO NOT AFFECT NEGOTIABILITY

Certain ambiguities or omissions will not affect the negotiability of an instrument. The UCC provides the following rules for clearing up ambiguous terms:

1. Unless the date of an instrument is necessary to determine a definite time for payment, the fact that an instrument is undated does not affect its negotiability. A typical example is an undated check [UCC 3–113(b)].
2. Antedating or postdating an instrument does not affect the instrument's negotiability [UCC 3–113(a)]. *Antedating* occurs when a party puts a date on the instrument that is before the actual date; *postdating* occurs when a party puts a date on an instrument that is after the actual date. ■ EXAMPLE 22.14 On May 1, Avery draws a check on her account with First State Bank made payable to Consumer Credit Corporation. Avery postdates the check "May 15." Consumer Credit can negotiate the check, and, unless Avery tells First State otherwise, the bank can charge the amount of the check to Avery's account before May 15 [UCC 4–401(c)]. ■

3 Handwritten terms outweigh typewritten and printed terms (preprinted terms on forms, for example), and typewritten terms outweigh printed terms [UCC 3–114]. ■ EXAMPLE 22.15 Suppose that your check, like most checks, is printed "Pay to the order of" with a blank next to it. In handwriting, you insert in the blank, "Anita Delgado or bearer." The check would be a bearer instrument. ■

4 Words outweigh figures unless the words are ambiguous [UCC 3–114]. This rule is important when the numerical amount and the written amount on a check differ. ■ EXAMPLE 22.16 Rob issues a check payable to Standard Appliance Company. For the amount, he fills in the numbers "$100" and writes in the words "One thousand and 00/100" dollars. The check is payable in the amount of $1,000. ■

5 When an instrument does not specify a particular interest rate but simply states "with interest," the interest rate is the *judgment rate of interest* (a rate of interest fixed by statute that is applied to a monetary judgment awarded by a court until the judgment is paid or terminated) [UCC 3–112(b)].

6 A check is negotiable even if there is a notation on it stating that it is "nonnegotiable" or "not governed by Article 3." Any other instrument, however, can be made nonnegotiable by the maker's or drawer's conspicuously noting on it that it is "nonnegotiable" or "not governed by Article 3" [UCC 3–104(d)].[2]

Transfer of Instruments

Once issued, a negotiable instrument can be transferred by *assignment* or by *negotiation.*

TRANSFER BY ASSIGNMENT

Recall from Chapter 16 that an assignment is a transfer of rights under a contract. Under general contract principles, a transfer by assignment to an assignee gives the assignee only those rights that the assignor possessed. Any defenses that can be raised against an assignor can normally be raised against the assignee. This same principle applies when an instrument, such as a promissory note, is transferred by assignment. The transferee is then an *assignee* rather than a *holder.* Sometimes, a transfer fails to qualify as a negotiation because it fails to meet one or more of the requirements of a negotiable instrument, discussed above. When this occurs, the transfer becomes an assignment.

TRANSFER BY NEGOTIATION

NEGOTIATION
The transfer of an instrument in such form that the transferee (the person to whom the instrument is transferred) becomes a holder.

Negotiation is the transfer of an instrument in such form that the transferee (the person to whom the instrument is transferred) becomes a holder [UCC 3–201(a)]. Under UCC principles, a transfer by negotiation creates a holder who, at the very least, receives the rights of the previous possessor [UCC 3–203(b)]. Unlike an assignment, a transfer by negotiation can make it possible for a holder to receive more rights in the instrument than the prior possessor had [UCC 3–202(b), 3–305, 3–306]. A holder who receives greater rights is known as a *holder in due course,* a concept we will discuss in Chapter 23.

2. This is not true under the unrevised Article 3.

There are two methods of negotiating an instrument so that the receiver becomes a holder. The method used depends on whether the instrument is order paper or bearer paper.

Negotiating Order Instruments An order instrument contains the name of a payee capable of indorsing it, as in "Pay to the order of Lloyd Sorenson." If the instrument is an order instrument, it is negotiated by delivery with any necessary indorsements. ■ EXAMPLE 22.17 National Express Corporation issues a payroll check "to the order of Lloyd Sorenson." Sorenson takes the check to the supermarket, signs his name on the back (an indorsement), gives it to the cashier (a delivery), and receives cash. Sorenson has *negotiated* the check to the supermarket [UCC 3–201(b)]. ■

Negotiating Bearer Instruments If an instrument is payable to bearer, it is negotiated by delivery—that is, by transfer into another person's possession. Indorsement is not necessary [UCC 2–301(b)]. The use of bearer instruments thus involves more risk through loss or theft than the use of order instruments.

■ EXAMPLE 22.18 Assume that Richard Kray writes a check "payable to cash" and hands it to Jessie Arnold (a delivery). Kray has issued the check (a bearer instrument) to Arnold. Arnold places the check in her wallet, which is subsequently stolen. The thief has possession of the check. At this point, the thief has no rights to the check. If the thief "delivers" the check to an innocent third person, however, negotiation will be complete. All rights to the check will be passed absolutely to that third person, and Arnold will lose all rights to recover the proceeds of the check from that person [UCC 3–306]. Of course, Arnold could attempt to recover the money from the thief if the thief can be found. ■

"Money has little value to its possessor unless it also has value to others."

LELAND STANFORD, 1824–1893 (U.S. senator and founder of Stanford University)

Indorsements

Indorsements are required whenever the instrument being negotiated is classified as an order instrument. An *indorsement* is a signature with or without additional words or statements. It is most often written on the back of the instrument itself. If there is no room on the instrument, indorsements can be written on a separate piece of paper, called an **allonge.**[3] The allonge must be so firmly affixed to the instrument as to become a part of it [UCC 3–204(a)]. Pins or paper clips will not suffice. Most courts hold that staples are sufficient.

A person who transfers an instrument by signing (indorsing) it and delivering it to another person is an **indorser.** The person to whom the check is indorsed and delivered is the **indorsee.** ■ EXAMPLE 22.19 Luisa Parks receives a graduation check for $500. She can transfer the check to her mother (or to anyone) by signing it on the back and delivering it. Luisa is an indorser. If Luisa indorses the check by writing "Pay to Aretha Parks," Aretha Parks is the indorsee. ■

We examine here four categories of indorsements: blank indorsements, special indorsements, qualified indorsements, and restrictive indorsements.

ALLONGE
A piece of paper firmly attached to a negotiable instrument, on which transferees can make indorsements if there is no room left on the instrument itself.

INDORSER
A person who transfers an instrument by signing (indorsing) it and delivering it to another person.

INDORSEE
The person to whom a negotiable instrument is transferred by indorsement.

BLANK INDORSEMENTS

A **blank indorsement** specifies no particular indorsee and can consist of a mere signature [UCC 3–205(b)]. Hence, a check payable "to the order of Alan Luberda" is indorsed in blank if Luberda simply writes his signature on the back of the check.

BLANK INDORSEMENT
An indorsement that specifies no particular indorsee and can consist of a mere signature. An order instrument that is indorsed in blank becomes a bearer instrument.

3. Pronounced uh-*lohnj.*

An instrument payable to order and indorsed in blank becomes a bearer instrument and can be negotiated by delivery alone, as already discussed. Exhibit 22–5 shows a blank indorsement.

EXHIBIT 22–5 A BLANK INDORSEMENT

SPECIAL INDORSEMENTS

SPECIAL INDORSEMENT An indorsement on an instrument that indicates the specific person to whom the indorser intends to make the instrument payable; that is, it names the indorsee.

A **special indorsement** identifies the person to whom the indorser intends to make the instrument payable; that is, it names the indorsee [UCC 3–205(a)]. For example, words such as "Pay to the order of Clay" or "Pay to Clay," followed by the signature of the indorser, create a special indorsement. When an instrument is indorsed in this way, it is an order instrument.

To avoid the risk of loss from theft, a holder may convert a blank indorsement to a special indorsement. This changes the bearer instrument back to an order instrument. A holder may "convert a blank indorsement that consists only of a signature into a special indorsement by writing, above the signature of the indorser, words identifying the person to whom the instrument is made payable" [UCC 3–205(c)].

■ EXAMPLE 22.20 A check is made payable to Peter Rabe. He indorses the check in blank by simply signing his name on the back and delivers the check to Anthony Bartomo. Anthony is unable to cash the check immediately and wants to avoid any risk should he lose the check. He therefore prints "Pay to Anthony Bartomo" above Peter's blank indorsement (see Exhibit 22–6). In this manner, Anthony has converted Peter's blank indorsement into a special indorsement. Further negotiation now requires Anthony Bartomo's indorsement plus delivery. ■

EXHIBIT 22–6 A SPECIAL INDORSEMENT

QUALIFIED INDORSEMENTS

Generally, an indorser, *merely by indorsing,* impliedly promises to pay the holder, or any subsequent indorser, the amount of the instrument in the event that the drawer or maker defaults on the payment [UCC 3–415(a)]. Usually, then, indorsements are *unqualified indorsements;* that is, the indorser is guaranteeing payment of the instrument in addition to transferring title to it. An indorser who does not wish to

QUALIFIED INDORSEMENT
An indorsement on a negotiable instrument in which the indorser disclaims any contract liability on the instrument. The notation "without recourse" is commonly used to create a qualified indorsement.

be liable on an instrument can use a **qualified indorsement** to disclaim this liability [UCC 3–415(b)]. The notation "without recourse" is commonly used to create a qualified indorsement, such as the one shown in Exhibit 22–7.

EXHIBIT 22–7 A QUALIFIED INDORSEMENT

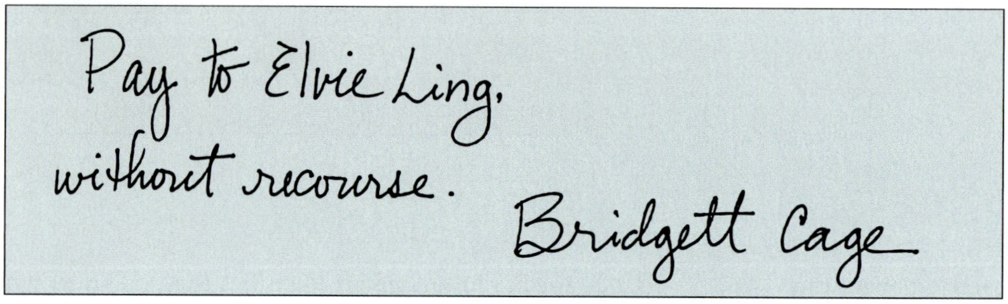
Pay to Elvie Ling, without recourse. Bridgett Cage

Qualified indorsements are often used by persons acting in a representative capacity. ■ EXAMPLE 22.21 Insurance agents sometimes receive checks payable to them that are really intended as payment to the insurance company. The agent is merely indorsing the payment through to the insurance company and should not be required to make good on the check if it is later dishonored. The "without recourse" indorsement relieves the agent from any liability on a check. If the instrument is dishonored, the holder cannot obtain recovery from the agent who indorsed "without recourse" unless the indorser has breached one of the transfer warranties discussed in Chapter 23. These warranties relate to good title, authorized signature, no material alteration, and other requirements. ■

A qualified indorsement is accompanied by either a special indorsement or a blank indorsement, which determines further negotiation. A special qualified indorsement makes the instrument an order instrument, and it requires an indorsement plus delivery for negotiation. A blank qualified indorsement makes the instrument a bearer instrument, and only delivery is required for negotiation. In either situation, the instrument still transfers title to the indorsee and can be further negotiated.

■ EXAMPLE 22.22 Assume that a check is made payable to the order of Bridgett Cage and that Bridgett wants to negotiate the check specifically to Elvie Ling with a qualified indorsement. Bridgett would indorse the check as follows: "Pay to Elvie Ling, without recourse. [Signed] Bridgett Cage." For Elvie to negotiate the check further to Joe Nantz, Elvie would have to indorse the check and deliver it to Joe. ■ The qualified indorsement shown earlier in Exhibit 22–7 is an example of a special qualified indorsement.

RESTRICTIVE INDORSEMENTS

RESTRICTIVE INDORSEMENT
Any indorsement on a negotiable instrument that requires the indorsee to comply with certain instructions regarding the funds involved. A restrictive indorsement does not prohibit the further negotiation of the instrument.

A **restrictive indorsement** requires the indorsee to comply with certain instructions regarding the funds involved. A restrictive indorsement does not prohibit the further negotiation of an instrument [UCC 3–206(a)]. Restrictive indorsements come in many forms, some of which we discuss here.

Conditional Indorsements When payment depends on the occurrence of some event specified in the indorsement, the instrument has a conditional indorsement. For example, if Ken Barton indorses a check, "Pay to Lars Johansen if he completes the renovation of my kitchen by June 1, 2006. [Signed] Ken Barton," Barton has created a conditional indorsement. Article 3, however, states that an indorsement conditioning the right to receive payment "does not affect the right of the indorsee to enforce the instrument" [UCC 3–206(b)]. A person paying or taking for value (the concept of taking for value will be discussed fully in Chapter 23) an instrument can disregard the condition without liability.

A conditional indorsement does not prevent further negotiation of the instrument. If conditional language appears on the *face* of an instrument, however, the instrument is not negotiable because it does not contain an unconditional promise to pay.

Indorsements Prohibiting Further Indorsement An indorsement such as "Pay to Makoto Chi only. [Signed] Jerome Edelman" does not destroy transfer by negotiation. Chi can negotiate the instrument to a holder just as if it had read "Pay to Makoto Chi. [Signed] Jerome Edelman" [UCC 3–206(a)]. If the holder gives value to Chi, this type of restrictive indorsement has the same legal effect as a special indorsement.

Indorsements for Deposit or Collection A common type of restrictive indorsement is one that makes the indorsee (almost always a bank) a collecting agent of the indorser [UCC 3–206(c)]. For example, if Stephanie Mallak wants to deposit a check she has received into her checking account at the bank, she can indorse the check "For deposit only. [Signed] Stephanie Mallak." (See Exhibit 22–8.) A "Pay any bank or banker" or "For deposit" indorsement has the effect of locking the instrument into the bank collection process and thus prohibits further negotiation except by a bank. Following this indorsement, only a bank can acquire the rights of a holder.

EXHIBIT 22–8 FOR DEPOSIT/FOR COLLECTION INDORSEMENTS

TRUST INDORSEMENT
An indorsement for the benefit of the indorser or a third person; also known as an agency indorsement. The indorsement results in legal title vesting in the original indorsee.

Trust Indorsements An indorsement to a person who is to hold or use the funds for the benefit of the indorser or a third party is called a **trust indorsement** (also known as an *agency indorsement*) [UCC 3–206(d)]. ■ EXAMPLE 22.23 Assume that Robert Emerson asks his accountant, Ada Johnson, to pay some bills for his invalid wife, Sarah, while he is out of the country. He indorses a check as follows: "Pay to Ada Johnson as Agent for Sarah Emerson." This agency indorsement obligates Johnson to use the funds only for the benefit of Sarah Emerson. ■ The fiduciary restrictions (restrictions mandated by a relationship involving trust and loyalty) on the instrument do not reach beyond the original indorsee [UCC 3–206(d), (e)]. Exhibit 22–9 shows sample trust indorsements.

EXHIBIT 22–9 TRUST INDORSEMENTS

or

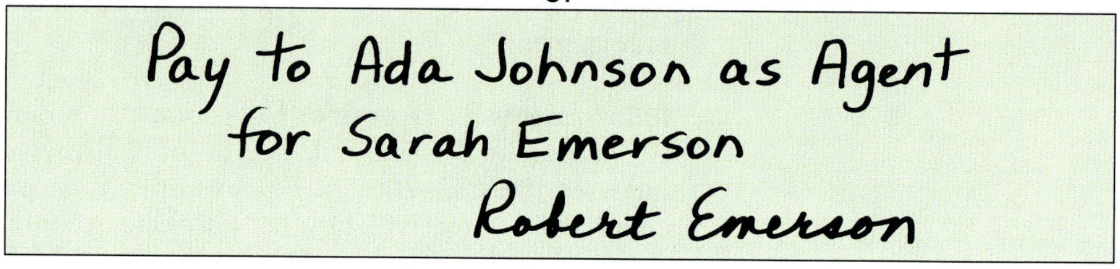

The result of a trust indorsement is that legal rights in the instrument are transferred to the original indorsee (Ada Johnson, in the example just given). To the extent that the original indorsee pays or applies the proceeds consistently with the indorsement (for example, "in trust for Sarah Emerson"), the indorsee is a holder and can become a holder in due course (described in Chapter 23).

ETHICAL ISSUE 22.1

Why should fiduciary restrictions on an instrument apply only to the original indorsee? Article 3 gives the force of law to the ethical duties of an indorsee on a trust instrument to use the funds in accordance with the wishes of the indorser. Yet what if the original indorsee disregards the fiduciary restrictions on a trust instrument and then transfers it to another person? In this situation, according to Article 3, the subsequent purchaser has no obligation to verify that the original indorsee fulfilled the fiduciary requirements. Although this may seem unfair, consider the alternative. If all subsequent holders were obligated to verify that the terms of the trust indorsement were fulfilled, it would impair the ease with which instruments could be transferred—and thus impair their function as substitutes for cash. By holding only the original indorsee to the fiduciary restrictions on an instrument with a trust indorsement, the UCC furthers one of its basic goals—to encourage the free flow of commerce by making the laws practical and reasonable. Article 3's provisions relating to trust indorsements provide just one example of the many ways in which the UCC balances this goal against other ethical principles. ■

How Indorsements Can Convert Order Instruments to Bearer Instruments and Vice Versa

As mentioned previously, order instruments and bearer instruments are negotiated differently. Nevertheless, an indorsement can convert a bearer instrument into an order instrument. ■ EXAMPLE 22.24 Suppose that a check that was originally payable to "cash" is subsequently indorsed with the words "Pay to Jessie Arnold." This instrument must be negotiated as an order instrument (by indorsement and delivery), even though it was previously a bearer instrument [UCC 3–205(a)]. ■

As mentioned earlier, an instrument payable to the order of a named payee and indorsed in blank becomes a bearer instrument [UCC 3–205(b)]. ■ EXAMPLE 22.25 A check made payable to the order of Jessie Arnold is issued to Arnold, and she indorses it by signing her name on the back. The instrument is now a bearer instrument, and Arnold can negotiate the check to whomever she wishes merely by delivery. If Arnold loses the check after she indorses it, then the finder can negotiate it further. ■

Similarly, a bearer instrument can be converted into an order instrument through indorsement. ■ EXAMPLE 22.26 Suppose that Arnold negotiates, by delivery, the check that she indorsed in blank (now a bearer instrument) to Jonas Tolling. Tolling indorses the check "Pay to Mark Hyatt, Jonas Tolling." By adding this special indorsement, Tolling has converted the check into an order instrument. The check can be further negotiated only by indorsement (by Mark Hyatt) and delivery [UCC 3–205(b)]. ■ Exhibit 22–10 illustrates how an indorsement can convert an order instrument into a bearer instrument and vice versa.

MISCELLANEOUS INDORSEMENT PROBLEMS

Of course, a significant problem occurs when an indorsement is forged or unauthorized. The UCC's rules concerning unauthorized or forged signatures and indorsements will be discussed in Chapter 23, in the context of signature liability, and again in Chapter 24, in the context of the bank's liability for payment of an instrument over an unauthorized signature. Two other problems that may arise with indorsements concern misspelled names and multiple payees.

An indorsement should be identical to the name that appears on the instrument. A payee or indorsee whose name is misspelled can indorse with the misspelled name, the correct name, or both [UCC 3–204(d)]. For example, if Sheryl Kruger receives a

EXHIBIT 22–10 CONVERTING AN ORDER INSTRUMENT TO A BEARER INSTRUMENT AND VICE VERSA

Indorsement Converting an Order Instrument to a Bearer Instrument

A check payable to the order of Jessie Arnold is an order instrument. Arnold indorses the check in blank (by simply signing her name), thus converting the instrument to a bearer instrument, and delivers the check to Jonas Tolling.

Indorsement Converting a Bearer Instrument to an Order Instrument

Jonas Tolling adds a special indorsement and negotiates the check to Mark Hyatt. The special indorsement, because it makes the instrument payable to a specific indorsee (Mark Hyatt), converts the bearer instrument back into an order instrument. To negotiate the instrument further, Mark Hyatt must indorse and deliver the instrument.

check payable to the order of Sherrill Krooger, she can indorse the check either "Sheryl Kruger" or "Sherrill Krooger," or both. The usual practice is to indorse the name as it appears on the instrument and follow it by the correct name.

An instrument payable to two or more persons *in the alternative* (for example, "Pay to the order of Tuan or Johnson") requires the indorsement of only one of the payees. If, however, an instrument is made payable to two or more persons *jointly* (for example, "Pay to the order of Sharrie and Bob Covington"), all of the payees' indorsements are necessary for negotiation. If an instrument payable to two or more persons does not clearly indicate whether it is payable in the alternative or jointly (for example, "Pay to the order of John and/or Sara Fitzgerald"), then the instrument is payable to the persons alternatively [UCC 3–110(d)]. The same principles apply to special indorsements that indicate more than one identified person to whom the indorser intends to make the instrument payable [UCC 3–205(a)]. These principles were applied in the following case.

CASE 22.3 Hyatt Corp. v. Palm Beach National Bank

District Court of Appeal of Florida,
Third District, 2003.
840 So.2d 300.

BACKGROUND AND FACTS Skyscraper Building Maintenance, LLC (limited liability company—see Chapter 31), contracted with Hyatt Corporation to perform maintenance services for certain hotels owned and operated by Hyatt in Florida. Under an agreement with Skyscraper, J & D Financial Corporation asked Hyatt to make checks for the services payable to Skyscraper and J & D. Of the many checks issued by Hyatt to the two payees, Palm Beach National Bank negotiated two that were indorsed only by Skyscraper. These two checks were made payable to "J & D Financial Corp. Skyscraper Building Maint." Parties listed in this manner are referred to as "stacked payees." J & D filed a suit in a Florida state court against the bank and others for negotiating the two checks. J & D and Hyatt asserted that the checks were payable *jointly,* requiring indorsement by both payees. The bank argued that the checks were payable to J & D and Skyscraper *alternatively* and thus negotiable on only one payee's indorsement. The court issued a summary judgment in the bank's favor. J & D and Hyatt appealed to a state intermediate appellate court.

IN THE WORDS OF THE COURT . . .

LEVY, Judge.

* * * *

In 1990, Article 3 of the UCC was revised, and the language of UCC Section 3–116 was added to UCC Section 3–110 and became subsection (d). Revised UCC Section 3–110(d), which added language to follow former 3–116(a) and (b), states, "If an instrument payable to two or more persons is ambiguous as to whether it is payable to the persons alternatively, the instrument is payable to the persons alternatively." The net effect of the amendment was to change the presumption. What was unambiguous before is now ambiguous.

Turning to our jurisdiction, Florida has adopted the statutory revision to UCC 3–110, with its enactment of Section 673.1101, Florida Statutes. Section 673.1101(4) now provides the following:

> (4) If an instrument is payable to two or more persons alternatively, it is payable to any of them and may be negotiated, discharged, or enforced by any or all of them in possession of the instrument. If an instrument is payable to two or more persons not alternatively, it is payable to all of them and may be negotiated, discharged, or enforced only by all of them. If an instrument payable to two or more persons is ambiguous as to whether it is payable to the persons alternatively, the instrument is payable to the persons alternatively.

* * * *

CASE 22.3—Continued

* * * [T]he predecessor statute provided that if an ambiguity existed as to whether multiple payees were intended as joint or alternative payees, they were deemed joint payees, while the amended statute applicable to this case reverses the prior rule.

* * * *

We conclude that based on the 1990 amendment to the Uniform Commercial Code, when a check lists two payees without the use of the word "and" or "or," the nature of the payee is ambiguous as to whether they are alternative payees or joint payees. Therefore, the UCC amendment prevails and they are to be treated as alternative payees, thus requiring only one of the payees' signatures. Consequently, the bank could negotiate the check when it was endorsed by only one of the two payees, thereby escaping liability.

* * * As the parties correctly point out, this is a case of first impression in Florida appellate courts. * * *

* * * [W]e hold that the trial court was correct in granting the Summary Final Judgment.

DECISION AND REMEDY The court affirmed the lower court's judgment on this issue, determining that the bank properly negotiated the checks even though they were indorsed by only one of the two payees. The state intermediate appellate court held that a check payable to stacked payees is payable alternatively.

WHY IS THIS CASE IMPORTANT? *This case illustrates that when drafting negotiable instruments with multiple payees, the language needs to be specific as to whether the payees are intended to be joint or alternative payees. If joint payees are intended, the instrument must clearly indicate that intent—by using the word* and *between the payees' names, for example. Otherwise, the court will find that the payees are alternative payees under UCC 3–110.*

REVIEWING NEGOTIABILITY AND TRANSFERABILITY

Regent Corporation, U.S.A., an import company in New York, contracted with Azmat Bangladesh, Ltd., a textile firm in Bangladesh, for the purchase of bedsheets and pillowcases for import and resale in the United States. An essential condition of the sale was that the goods be manufactured in Bangladesh. The contract required payment by Regent within ninety days of the date on the bill of lading (a document indicating the receipt of goods for shipment), and Regent issued promissory notes that indicated this term. After the goods were shipped, Azmat's bank presented drafts drawn against Regent to Regent's banks. Like the notes, each draft indicated that payment was to be made "at 90 days deferred from bill of lading date." The drafts were accompanied by dated bills of lading. On delivery of the goods, U.S. Customs refused to allow their entry because they had been partially manufactured in Pakistan. Regent filed a suit in a New York state court against its banks, and Azmat, to stop payment on the drafts. Using the information presented in the chapter, answer the following questions.

1. Describe what type of instruments the promissory notes and drafts are, using the categories discussed in this chapter.
2. Review the requirements for negotiability. Were the promissory notes and drafts in this case unconditional? Why or why not?
3. One of the questions here is whether the notes and drafts were "payable at a definite time." How should the court rule on this issue? Explain fully.
4. Suppose that on the original promissory notes, Regent had included handwritten notations that the notes were "not subject to Article 3." What would be the legal significance of this notation?

APPLICATION How Can You Avoid Pitfalls When Writing and Indorsing Checks?*

As a businessperson (or as a consumer), you will certainly be writing and receiving checks. Both activities can involve pitfalls.

CHECKS DRAWN IN BLANK

The danger in signing a blank check is clear. Anyone can write in an unauthorized amount and cash the check. Although you may be able to assert lack of authorization against the person who filled in the unauthorized amount, subsequent holders of the properly indorsed check may be able to enforce the check as completed. While you are haggling with the person who inserted the unauthorized figure and who may not be able to repay the amount, you will also have to honor the check for the unauthorized amount to a subsequent holder in due course (see Chapter 23).

CHECKS PAYABLE TO "CASH"

It is equally dangerous to write out and sign a check payable to "cash" until you are actually at the bank. Remember that checks payable to "cash" are bearer instruments. This means that if you lose or misplace the check, anybody who finds it can present it to the bank for payment.

CHECKS INDORSED IN BLANK

Just as a check signed in blank or payable to "cash" may be dangerous, a negotiable instrument with a blank indorsement also has dangers; as a bearer instrument, it is as easily transferred as cash. When you make a bank deposit, therefore, you should sign (indorse) the back of the check in blank only in the presence of a teller. If you choose to sign it ahead of time, make sure you insert the words "For deposit only" before you sign your name. As a precaution, you should consider obtaining an indorsement stamp from your bank. Then, when a check is received payable to your business, you can indorse it immediately. The stamped indorsement will indicate that the check is for deposit only to your business account specified by the number.

* This *Application* is not meant to substitute for the services of an attorney who is licensed to practice law in your state.

CHECKLIST FOR THE USE OF NEGOTIABLE INSTRUMENTS

1. A good rule of thumb is never to sign a blank check.
2. Another good rule of thumb is never to write and sign a check payable to "cash" until you are actually at the bank.
3. Be wary of indorsing a check in blank unless a bank teller is simultaneously giving you a receipt for your deposit.
4. Consider obtaining an indorsement stamp from your bank so that when you receive checks you can immediately indorse them "for deposit only" to your account.

KEY TERMS

acceleration clause 551
acceptance 542
acceptor 551
allonge 556
bearer 554
bearer instrument 554
blank indorsement 556
certificate of deposit (CD) 547
check 543
draft 542
drawee 542
drawer 542
extension clause 552
holder 552
indorsee 556
indorsement 554
indorser 556
maker 545
negotiable instrument 540
negotiation 555
order instrument 552
payee 542
presentment 551
promissory note 545
qualified indorsement 558
restrictive indorsement 558
signature 548
special indorsement 557
trade acceptance 542
trust indorsement 559

CHAPTER SUMMARY Negotiability and Transferability

Articles 3 and 4 of the UCC (See pages 541–542.)	Articles 3 and 4 of the Uniform Commercial Code govern the negotiability and transferability of negotiable instruments. Article 3 was significantly revised in 1990. Almost all of the states have adopted the revised article.
Types of Instruments (See pages 542–547.)	The UCC specifies four types of negotiable instruments: drafts, checks, promissory notes, and certificates of deposit (CDs). These instruments fall into two basic classifications: 1. *Demand instruments versus time instruments*—A demand instrument is payable on demand (when the holder presents it to the maker or drawer). A time instrument is payable at a future date. 2. *Orders to pay versus promises to pay*—Checks and drafts are *orders* to pay. Promissory notes and CDs are *promises* to pay.
Requirements for Negotiability (See pages 547–554.)	To be negotiable, an instrument must meet the requirements stated below, which were explained in greater detail in the *Concept Summary* on page 553. 1. Be in writing. 2. Be signed by the maker or drawer. 3. Be an unconditional promise or order to pay. 4. State a fixed amount of money. 5. Be payable on demand or at a definite time. 6. Be payable to order or bearer.
Factors That Do Not Affect Negotiability (See pages 554–555.)	1. The fact that an instrument is undated does not affect its negotiability unless the date is necessary to determine a definite time for payment. 2. Postdating or antedating an instrument does not affect its negotiability. 3. Handwritten terms take priority over typewritten and printed terms. 4. Words outweigh figures unless the words are ambiguous. 5. An instrument that states "with interest" but does not state the interest rate is payable at the judgment rate of interest. 6. A check is negotiable even if there is a notation on it stating that it is "nonnegotiable" or "not governed by Article 3."
Transfer of Instruments (See pages 555–556.)	1. *Transfer by assignment*—A transfer by assignment to an assignee gives the assignee only those rights that the assignor possessed. Any defenses against payment that can be raised against an assignor can normally be raised against the assignee. 2. *Transfer by negotiation*—An order instrument is negotiated by indorsement and delivery; a bearer instrument is negotiated by delivery only.
Indorsements (See pages 556–561.)	1. *Blank* (for example, "Alan Luberda"). 2. *Special* (for example, "Pay to Anthony Bartomo. [Signed] Peter Rabe"). 3. *Qualified* (for example, "Without recourse. [Signed] Bridgett Cage"). 4. *Restrictive* (for example, "For deposit only. [Signed] Stephanie Mallak" or "Pay to Ada Johnson in trust for Sarah Emerson. [Signed] Robert Emerson").
Miscellaneous Indorsement Problems (See pages 561–563.)	1. A payee or indorsee whose name is misspelled can indorse with the misspelled name, the correct name, or both. 2. An instrument payable to two or more persons in the alternative requires the indorsement of only one of the payees. 3. An instrument payable to two or more persons jointly requires all of the payees' indorsements for negotiation.

(Continued)

CHAPTER SUMMARY Negotiability and Transferability—Continued

Miscellaneous Indorsement Problems—Continued (See pages 561–563.)	4. If an instrument payable to two or more persons does not clearly indicate whether it is payable in the alternative or jointly, it is payable to the persons alternatively. The same principle applies to special indorsements that contain multiple indorsees.

FOR REVIEW

Answers for the even-numbered questions in this For Review *section can be found on this text's accompanying Web site at* http://blt.westbuslaw.com. *Select "Chapter 22" and click on "For Review."*

1. What are the four types of negotiable instruments with which Article 3 of the UCC is concerned? Which of these instruments are *orders* to pay, and which are *promises* to pay?
2. What requirements must an instrument meet to be negotiable?
3. To whom is a bearer instrument payable?
4. What is the difference between an indorsement in blank and a special indorsement?
5. What is a restrictive indorsement? Does a restrictive indorsement prohibit further negotiation of the instrument?

QUESTIONS AND CASE PROBLEMS

22–1. Indorsements. Bertram writes a check for $200, payable to "cash." He puts the check in his pocket and drives to the bank to cash the check. As he gets out of his car in the bank's parking lot, the check slips out of his pocket and falls to the pavement. Jerrod walks by moments later, picks up the check, and later that day delivers it to Amber, to whom he owes $200. Amber indorses the check "For deposit only. [Signed] Amber Dowel" and deposits it into her checking account. In light of these circumstances, answer the following questions.

(a) Is the check a bearer instrument or an order instrument?
(b) Did Jerrod's delivery of the check to Amber constitute a valid negotiation? Why or why not?
(c) What type of indorsement did Amber make?
(d) Does Bertram have a right to recover the $200 from Amber? Explain.

22–2. Requirements for Negotiability. Muriel Evans writes the following note on the back of an envelope: "I, Muriel Evans, promise to pay Karen Marvin or bearer $100 on demand." Is this a negotiable instrument? Discuss fully.

22–3. Indorsements. A check drawn by David for $500 is made payable to the order of Matthew and issued to Matthew. Matthew owes his landlord $500 in rent and transfers the check to his landlord with the following indorsement: "For rent paid. [Signed] Matthew." Matthew's landlord has contracted to have Juarez do some landscaping on the property. When Juarez insists on immediate payment, the landlord transfers the check to Juarez without indorsement. Later, to pay for some palm trees purchased from Green's Nursery, Juarez transfers the check with the following indorsement: "Pay to Green's Nursery, without recourse. [Signed] Juarez." Green's Nursery sends the check to its bank indorsed "For deposit only. [Signed] Green's Nursery."

(a) Classify each of these indorsements.
(b) Was the transfer from Matthew's landlord to Juarez, without indorsement, an assignment or a negotiation? Explain.

22–4. Bearer Instruments. Adam's checks are imprinted with the words "Pay to the order of" followed by a blank. Adam fills in an amount on one of the checks and signs it, but he does not write anything in the blank following the "Pay to the order of" language. Adam gives this check to Beth. On another of the checks, Adam writes in the blank "Carl or bearer." Is either of these checks a bearer instrument? Why or why not?

CASE PROBLEM WITH SAMPLE ANSWER

22–5. In October 1998, Somerset Valley Bank notified Alfred Hauser, president of Hauser Co., that the bank had begun to receive what appeared to be Hauser Co. payroll checks. None of the payees were Hauser Co. employees, however, and Hauser had not written the checks or authorized anyone to sign them on his behalf. Automatic Data Processing, Inc., provided payroll services for Hauser Co. and used a facsimile signature on all its payroll checks. Hauser told the bank not to cash the checks. In early 1999, Robert Triffin, who deals in negotiable instruments, bought eighteen of the checks, totaling more than $8,800, from various check-cashing agencies. The agencies stated that they had cashed the checks expecting the bank to pay them. Each check was payable to a bearer for a fixed amount, on demand, and did not state any undertaking by the person promising payment other than the payment of money. Each check bore a facsimile drawer's signature stamp identical to Hauser Co.'s authorized stamp. Each check had been returned to an agency marked "stolen check" and stamped "do not present again." When the bank refused to cash the checks, Triffin filed a suit in a New Jersey state court against Hauser Co. Were the checks negotiable instruments? Why or why not? [*Triffin v. Somerset Valley Bank*, 777 A.2d 993 (N.J.Super.App.Div. 2001)]

After you have answered this problem, compare your answer with the sample answer given on the Web site that accompanies this text. Go to http://blt.westbuslaw.com, select "Chapter 22," and click on "Case Problem with Sample Answer."

22–6. Negotiability. In October 1996, Robert Hildebrandt contracted with Harvey and Nancy Anderson to find a tenant for the Andersons' used-car lot. The Andersons agreed to pay Hildebrandt "a commission equal in amount to five percent up to first three years of lease." On December 12, Paramount Automotive, Inc., agreed to lease the premises for three years at $7,500 per month, and the Andersons signed a promissory note, which stated that they would pay Hildebrandt $13,500, plus interest, in consecutive monthly installments of $485, until the total sum was paid. The note contained an acceleration clause. In a separate agreement, Paramount promised to pay $485 of its monthly rent directly to Hildebrandt. Less than a year later, Paramount stopped making payments to all parties. To enforce the note, Hildebrandt filed a suit in an Oregon state court against the Andersons. One issue was whether the note was a negotiable instrument. The Andersons claimed that it was not because it was not "unconditional." They argued that their obligation to make payments on the note was conditioned on their receipt of rent from Paramount. Are the Andersons correct? Explain. [*Hildebrandt v. Anderson*, 180 Or.App. 192, 42 P.3d 355 (2002)]

22–7. Transfer of Instruments. In July 1988, Chester Crow executed a promissory note payable "to the order of THE FIRST NATIONAL BANK OF SHREVEPORT or BEARER" in the amount of $21,578.42 at an interest rate of 3 percent per year above the "prime rate in effect at The First National Bank of Shreveport" in Shreveport, Louisiana, until paid. The note was a standard preprinted promissory note. In 1999, Credit Recoveries, Inc., filed a suit in a Louisiana state court against Crow, alleging that he owed $7,222.57 on the note, plus interest. Crow responded that the debt represented by the note had been canceled by the bank in September 1994. He further contended that in any event, to collect on the note, Credit Recoveries had to prove its legitimate ownership of it. When no evidence of ownership was forthcoming, Crow filed a motion to dismiss the suit. Is the note an order instrument or a bearer instrument? How might it have been transferred to Credit Recoveries? With this in mind, should the court dismiss the suit on the basis of Crow's contention? [*Credit Recoveries, Inc. v. Crow*, 862 So.2d 1146 (La.App. 2d Cir. 2003)]

A QUESTION OF ETHICS

22–8. Richard Caliendo, an accountant, prepared tax returns for various clients. To satisfy their tax liabilities, the clients issued checks payable to various state taxing entities and gave them to Caliendo. Between 1977 and 1979, Caliendo forged indorsements on these checks, deposited them in his own bank account, and subsequently withdrew the proceeds. In 1983, after learning of these events and after Caliendo's death, the state brought an action against Barclays Bank of New York, N.A., the successor to Caliendo's bank, to recover the amount of the checks. Barclays moved for dismissal on the ground that because the checks had never been delivered to the state, the state never acquired the status of holder and therefore never acquired any rights in the instruments. The trial court held for the state, but the appellate court reversed. The state then appealed the case to the state's highest court. That court ruled that the state could not recover the amount of the checks from the bank because, although the state was the named payee on the checks, the checks had never been delivered to the payee. [*State v. Barclays Bank of New York, N.A.*, 76 N.Y.2d 533, 563 N.E.2d 11, 561 N.Y.S.2d 697 (1990)]

1. If you were deciding this case, would you make an exception to the rule and let the state collect the funds from Barclays Bank? Why or why not? What ethical policies must be balanced in this situation?
2. Under agency law, which will be discussed in Chapter 28, delivery to the agent of a given individual or entity constitutes delivery to that person or entity. The court deemed that Caliendo was not an agent of the state but an agent of the taxpayers. Does it matter that the taxpayers may not have known this principle of agency law and might have thought that, by delivering their checks to Caliendo, they were delivering them to the state?

FOR CRITICAL ANALYSIS

22–9. The Uniform Commercial Code (UCC) generally sets forth strict requirements for negotiable instruments. In regard to what constitutes a signature on an instrument, however, the UCC grants extreme latitude—X marks, initials, and rubber-stamped signatures are all permitted. Given the potential for forgery of these kinds of signatures, why does the UCC permit them?

VIDEO QUESTION

22–10. Go to this text's Web site at http://blt.westbuslaw.com and select "Chapter 22." Click on "Video Questions" and view the video titled *Negotiable Instruments*. Then answer the following questions.

1. Who is the maker of the promissory note discussed in the video?
2. Is the note in the video payable on demand or at a definite time?
3. Does the note contain an unconditional promise or order to pay?
4. If the note does not meet the requirements of negotiability, can Onyx assign the note (assignment was discussed in Chapter 16) to the bank in exchange for cash?

INTERNET EXERCISES

Go to the *Business Law Today* home page at **http://blt.westbuslaw.com**, select "Chapter 22," and click on "Internet Exercises." There you will find the following Internet research exercises that you can perform to learn more about topics covered in this chapter.

Activity 22–1: LEGAL PERSPECTIVE—Overview of Negotiable Instruments

Activity 22–2: MANAGEMENT PERSPECTIVE—Banks and Bank Accounts

Activity 22–3: TECHNOLOGICAL PERSPECTIVE—Electronic Negotiable Instruments

BEFORE THE TEST

Go to the *Business Law Today* home page at **http://blt.westbuslaw.com**, select "Chapter 22," and click on "Interactive Quizzes." You will find a number of interactive questions relating to this chapter.

CHAPTER 23

Rights and Liabilities of Parties

"Wealth, in a commercial age, is made up largely of promises."

Roscoe Pound, 1870–1964
(American jurist)

CHAPTER OUTLINE

- HOLDER VERSUS HOLDER IN DUE COURSE (HDC)
- REQUIREMENTS FOR HDC STATUS
- HOLDER THROUGH AN HDC
- SIGNATURE LIABILITY
- WARRANTY LIABILITY
- DEFENSES, LIMITATIONS, AND DISCHARGE

LEARNING OBJECTIVES

After reading this chapter, you should be able to answer the following questions:

1. What are the requirements for attaining HDC status?
2. How can a person who does not qualify as an HDC acquire the rights and privileges of an HDC?
3. What is the key to liability on a negotiable instrument? What is the difference between signature liability and warranty liability?
4. Certain defenses are valid against all holders, including HDCs. What are these defenses called? Name four defenses that fall within this category.
5. Certain defenses can be used against an ordinary holder but are not effective against an HDC. What are these defenses called? Name four defenses that fall within this category.

As pointed out in Chapter 22, negotiable instruments function as substitutes for money; they also function as extensions of credit. Any note in which a person promises to pay another a sum of money creates a debtor (the one promising) and a creditor (the one to be paid). As the eminent jurist Roscoe Pound indicated in this chapter's opening quotation, wealth "is made up largely of promises." The extensive exchange of negotiable instruments that takes place daily in the United States is predicated, ultimately, on the existence of law and a government capable of enforcing the promises made by parties to negotiable instruments.

The outcome of litigation concerning negotiable instruments usually turns on whether a holder is entitled to obtain payment on an instrument when it is due.

Often, whether a holder is entitled to obtain payment will depend on whether the holder is a *holder in due course (HDC)*, a concept we examine in the following sections of this chapter. We then discuss the liability of the parties to negotiable instruments. In the remainder of the chapter, we consider the defenses available for avoiding liability and, briefly, the ways in which a person can be discharged from an obligation on a negotiable instrument.

Holder versus Holder in Due Course (HDC)

The rules contained in Article 3 of the Uniform Commercial Code (UCC) govern a party's right to payment of a check, draft, note, or certificate of deposit.[1] Problems arise when a holder seeking payment of a negotiable instrument learns that a defense to payment exists or that another party has a prior claim to the instrument. In such situations, for the person seeking payment, it becomes important to have the rights of a *holder in due course (HDC)*. An HDC takes a negotiable instrument free of all claims and most defenses of other parties.

Status of an Ordinary Holder

As pointed out in Chapter 22, the UCC defines a *holder* as a person in the possession of an instrument drawn, issued, or indorsed to him or her, to his or her order, to bearer, or in blank [UCC 1–201(20)]. An ordinary holder obtains only those rights that the transferor had in the instrument. In this respect, a holder has the same status as an assignee (see Chapter 16). Like an assignee, a holder normally is subject to the same defenses that could be asserted against the transferor.

Status of a Holder in Due Course (HDC)

HOLDER IN DUE COURSE (HDC)
A holder who acquires a negotiable instrument for value; in good faith; and without notice that the instrument is overdue, that it has been dishonored, that any person has a defense against it or a claim to it, or that the instrument contains unauthorized signatures, has been altered, or is so irregular or incomplete as to call into question its authenticity.

In contrast, a **holder in due course** (HDC) is a holder who, by meeting certain acquisition requirements (to be discussed shortly), takes the instrument *free* of most of the defenses and claims that could be asserted against the transferor. Stated another way, an HDC can normally acquire a higher level of immunity than can an ordinary holder in regard to defenses against payment on the instrument or ownership claims to the instrument by other parties.

■ EXAMPLE 23.1 Marcia Cambry signs a $1,000 note payable to Alex Jerrod in payment for some ancient Roman coins. Jerrod negotiates the note to Alicia Larson, who promises to pay Jerrod for it in thirty days. During the next month, Larson learns that Jerrod has breached his contract with Cambry by delivering coins that were not from the Roman era, as promised, and that for this reason Cambry will not honor the $1,000 note. Whether Larson can hold Cambry liable on the note depends on whether Larson has met the requirements for HDC status. If Larson has met these requirements and thus has HDC status, Larson is entitled to payment on the note. If Larson has not met these requirements, she has the status of an ordinary holder, and Cambry's defense of breach of contract against payment to Jerrod will also be effective against Larson. ■

1. The rights and liabilities on checks, drafts, notes, and certificates of deposit are determined under Article 3 of the UCC. Certain kinds of documents, such as stock certificates, bills of lading, and other documents of title, meet the requirements of negotiable instruments, but the rights and liabilities of the parties on these documents are covered by Articles 7 and 8 of the UCC. See Chapter 43, on bailments, for information on Article 7.

Requirements for HDC Status

The basic requirements for attaining HDC status are set forth in UCC 3–302. A holder of a negotiable instrument is an HDC if she or he takes the instrument (1) for value; (2) in good faith; and (3) without notice that it is overdue, that it has been dishonored, that any person has a defense against it or a claim to it, or that the instrument contains unauthorized signatures, contains alterations, or is so irregular or incomplete as to call into question its authenticity. We now examine each of these requirements.

Taking for Value

An HDC must have given *value* for the instrument [UCC 3–302(a)(2)(i)]. A person who receives an instrument as a gift or inherits it has not met the requirement of value. In these situations, the person becomes an ordinary holder and does not possess the rights of an HDC.

How an Instrument Is Taken for Value Under UCC 3–303(a), a holder can take an instrument for value in one of five ways:

.on the Web To find Article 3 of the UCC as adopted by a particular state, go to the Web site of Cornell University's Law School at **http://www.law.cornell.edu/ucc/ucc.table.html**.

1. By performing the promise for which the instrument was issued or transferred.
2. By acquiring a security interest or other lien in the instrument, excluding a lien obtained by a judicial proceeding. (Security interests and liens will be discussed in Chapters 25 and 26.)
3. By taking an instrument in payment of, or as security for, a preexisting claim. ■ EXAMPLE 23.2 Zon owes Dwyer $2,000 on a past-due account. If Zon negotiates a $2,000 note signed by Gordon to Dwyer and Dwyer accepts it to discharge the overdue account balance, Dwyer has given value for the instrument. ■
4. By giving a negotiable instrument as payment. ■ EXAMPLE 23.3 Martin has issued a $500 negotiable promissory note to Paulene. The note is due six months from the date issued. Paulene needs money and does not want to wait for the maturity date to collect. She negotiates the note to her friend Kristen, who pays her $200 in cash and writes her a check—a negotiable instrument—for the balance of $300. Kristen has given full value for the note by paying $200 in cash and issuing Paulene the check for $300. ■
5. By giving an irrevocable commitment as payment.

The Concept of Value in Negotiable Instruments Law The concept of value in the law of negotiable instruments is not the same as the concept of *consideration* in the law of contracts. A promise to give value in the future is clearly sufficient consideration to support a contract [UCC 1–201(44)]. A promise to give value in the future, however, normally does not constitute value sufficient to make one an HDC. A holder takes an instrument for value only to the extent that the promise has been performed [UCC 3–303(a)(1)]. Therefore, if the holder plans to pay for the instrument later or plans to perform the required services at some future date, the holder has not yet given value. In that situation, the holder is not yet an HDC.

In the Larson-Cambry example presented earlier, Larson is not an HDC because she did not take the instrument (Cambry's note) for value—she has not yet paid Jerrod for the note. Thus, Cambry's defense of breach of contract is valid not only against Jerrod but also against Larson. If Larson had paid Jerrod for the note at the

EXHIBIT 23–1 TAKING FOR VALUE

By exchanging defective goods for the note, Jerrod breached his contract with Cambry. Cambry could assert this defense if Jerrod presented the note to her for payment. Jerrod exchanged the note for Larson's promise to pay in thirty days, however. Because Larson did not take the note for value, she is not a holder in due course. Thus, Cambry can assert against Larson the defense of Jerrod's breach when Larson submits the note to Cambry for payment. If Larson had taken the note for value, Cambry could not assert that defense and would be liable to pay the note.

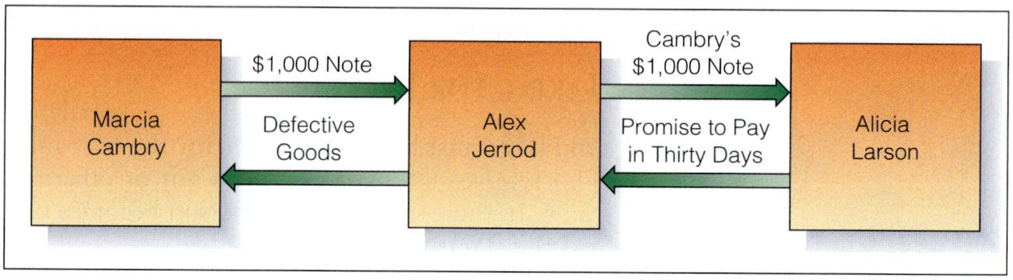

time of transfer (which would mean she had given value for the instrument), she would be an HDC. As an HDC, she could hold Cambry liable on the note even though Cambry has a valid defense against Jerrod on the basis of breach of contract. Exhibit 23–1 illustrates these concepts.

TAKING IN GOOD FAITH

The second requirement for HDC status is that the holder take the instrument in *good faith* [UCC 3–302(a)(2)(ii)]. This means that the holder must have acted honestly in the process of acquiring the instrument. UCC 3–103(a)(4) defines *good faith* as "honesty in fact and the observance of reasonable commercial standards of fair dealing." The good faith requirement applies only to the *holder.* It is immaterial whether the transferor acted in good faith. Thus, even a person who takes a negotiable instrument from a thief may become an HDC if the person acquires the instrument in good faith.

Because of the good faith requirement, one must ask whether the purchaser, when acquiring the instrument, honestly believed that the instrument was not defective. If a person purchases a $10,000 note for $300 from a stranger on a street corner, the issue of good faith can be raised on the grounds of both the suspicious circumstances and the grossly inadequate consideration (value).

In the following case, the court considered whether a bank observed "reasonable commercial standards of fair dealing" to fulfill the good faith requirement and become an HDC.

CASE 23.1 Mid Wisconsin Bank v. Forsgard Trading, Inc.

Wisconsin Court of Appeals, 2003.
2003 WI App. 186,
266 Wis.2d 685,
668 N.W.2d 830.
http://www.wisbar.org/WisCtApp/index.html[a]

a. Click on "Simple Search" and then type the docket number "03-0123" in the "Keywords" box. The State Bar of Wisconsin maintains this Web site.

BACKGROUND AND FACTS Forsgard Trading, Inc., opened an account at Mid Wisconsin Bank in July 1999. The account agreement stated, "Any items, other than cash, accepted for deposit . . . will be given provisional credit only until collection is final." Mid Wisconsin's practice is to give immediate credit on deposits, but an employee may place a hold on a check if, for example,

CASE 23.1—Continued

there is reasonable doubt about it. On May 7, 2001, Lakeshore Truck and Equipment Sales, Inc., wrote a check payable to Forsgard in the amount of $18,500. On May 8, Forsgard deposited the check in its account at Mid Wisconsin, which gave Forsgard immediate credit. The same day, Lakeshore issued a stop-payment order (an order to its bank not to pay the check—see Chapter 24). When Mid Wisconsin received notice on May 16 that payment had been stopped, it deducted the $18,500 from Forsgard's account. Because of transfers from the account between May 8 and May 16, the deduction resulted in a negative balance. Before this incident, Forsgard had overdrawn the account twenty-four times but, on each occasion, had deposited money to cover the overdraft. Forsgard did not do so this time. Mid Wisconsin filed a suit in a Wisconsin state court against Forsgard, Lakeshore, and others to recover the loss. The court issued a summary judgment in Mid Wisconsin's favor. Lakeshore appealed to a state intermediate appellate court.

IN THE WORDS OF THE COURT . . .

PETERSON, J. [Judge]

* * * *

Lakeshore claims Mid Wisconsin was not a holder in due course of the check Forsgard deposited. *Wisconsin Statutes Section 403.305 [Wisconsin's version of UCC 3–305] gives a holder in due course the right to recover from a drawer who places a stop-payment order on a check.* According to Wis. Stat. Sec. 403.302(1) [UCC 3–302(a)], a holder in due course is one who takes an instrument for value and in good faith. There is no dispute Mid Wisconsin took the check for value. Lakeshore argues, however, that Mid Wisconsin did not take the check in good faith. Wis. Stat. Sec. 403.103(1)(d) [UCC 3–103(a)(4)] defines good faith as "honesty in fact and the observance of reasonable commercial standards of fair dealing." Lakeshore concedes that Mid Wisconsin took the check with honesty in fact, but contends Mid Wisconsin did not observe reasonable commercial standards of fair dealing. [Emphasis added.]

First, Lakeshore contends that Mid Wisconsin's banking agreement with Forsgard did not allow it to give immediate credit, so that the Bank was not observing reasonable commercial standards when it granted the credit. The banking agreement states, "Any items, other than cash, accepted for deposit (including items drawn 'on us') will be given provisional credit only until collection is final * * * ." Lakeshore contends that this means Mid Wisconsin could not grant immediate credit. Lakeshore misinterprets the agreement. In fact, Mid Wisconsin complied with the agreement. Mid Wisconsin gave Forsgard provisional credit, which the agreement allows. When Lakeshore stopped payment on the check, the Bank deducted the amount of the check from Forsgard's account. This also was in accordance with the agreement. However, Forsgard did not cover the negative balance that resulted from the deduction.

Next, Lakeshore maintains that under the circumstances, reasonable commercial standards of fair dealing should have led Mid Wisconsin to place a hold on the check instead of giving immediate credit. Lakeshore notes that * * * Forsgard's account had been overdrawn many times in the past.

To begin with, Wisconsin courts have approved of the practice of extending immediate credit on deposited checks. * * * *[E]xtending immediate credit is consistent with reasonable banking standards.* * * * [Emphasis added.]

* * * *It would hinder commercial transactions if depository banks refused to permit the withdrawal prior to the clearance of checks.* * * * [B]anking practice is to the

(Continued)

CASE 23.1—Continued

contrary. It is clear that the Uniform Commercial Code was intended to permit the continuation of this practice and to protect banks who have given credit on deposited items prior to notice of a stop payment order * * * . [Emphasis added.]

DECISION AND REMEDY The state appellate court affirmed the lower court's judgment that Mid Wisconsin had observed reasonable commercial standards of fair dealing and was an HDC of the check.

FOR CRITICAL ANALYSIS—Social Consideration *What might have been the result in this case if the account had been overdrawn when the check was deposited?*

TAKING WITHOUT NOTICE

The final requirement for HDC status involves *notice* [UCC 3–302]. A person will not be afforded HDC protection if he or she acquires an instrument and is *on notice* (knows or has reason to know) that it is defective in any one of the following ways [UCC 3–302(a)]:

1. It is overdue.
2. It has been dishonored.
3. There is an uncured (uncorrected) default with respect to another instrument issued as part of the same series.
4. The instrument contains an unauthorized signature or has been altered.
5. There is a defense against the instrument or a claim to the instrument.
6. The instrument is so irregular or incomplete as to call into question its authenticity.

What Constitutes Notice? Notice of a defective instrument is given whenever the holder (1) has actual knowledge of the defect; (2) has received a notice of the defect (such as a bank's receipt of a letter listing the serial numbers of stolen bearer instruments); or (3) has reason to know that a defect exists, given all the facts and circumstances known at the time in question [UCC 1–201(25)]. The holder must also have received the notice "at a time and in a manner that gives a reasonable opportunity to act on it" [UCC 3–302(f)]. A purchaser's knowledge of certain facts, such as insolvency proceedings against the maker or drawer of the instrument, does not constitute notice that the instrument is defective [UCC 3–302(b)].

Overdue Instruments What constitutes notice that an instrument is overdue depends on whether it is a demand instrument (payable on demand) or a time instrument (payable at a definite time). As you will read in the *Application* feature at the end of this chapter, notice is one of the requirements to which you will need to pay close attention when purchasing negotiable instruments.

REMEMBER Demand instruments are payable immediately. Time instruments are payable at a future date.

Demand Instruments. A purchaser has notice that a *demand instrument* is overdue if she or he either takes the instrument knowing that demand has been made or takes the instrument an unreasonable length of time after its issue. For a check, a "reasonable time" is ninety days after the date of the check. For all other demand instruments, what will be considered a reasonable time depends on the circumstances [UCC 3–304(a)].

Time Instruments. A holder of a *time instrument* who takes the instrument at any time after its expressed due date is on notice that it is overdue [UCC 3–304(b)(2)]. Nonpayment by the due date should indicate to any purchaser that the instrument may be defective. Thus, a promissory note due on May 15 must be acquired before midnight on May 15. If it is purchased on May 16, the purchaser will be an ordinary holder, not an HDC. Sometimes, an instrument reads, "Payable in thirty days." To count thirty days, you exclude the first day and count the last day. Thus, a note dated December 1 that is payable in thirty days is due by midnight on December 31. If the payment date falls on a Sunday or holiday, the instrument is payable on the next business day.

If a debt is to be paid in installments or through a series of notes, the maker's default on any installment of principal or on any one note of the series will constitute notice to the purchaser that the instrument is overdue [UCC 3–304(b)(1)]. An instrument does not become overdue if there is a default on a payment of interest only [UCC 3–304(c)].

Dishonored Instruments An instrument is *dishonored* when the party to which the instrument is presented refuses to pay it. If a holder has actual knowledge that an instrument has been dishonored or has knowledge of facts that would lead him or her to suspect that an instrument has been dishonored, the holder is on notice [UCC 3–302(a)(2)].

■ EXAMPLE 23.4 Gonzalez holds a demand note dated September 1 made by JWB Enterprises, Inc., a local business firm. On September 17, Gonzalez demands payment, and JWB refuses to pay (that is, JWB dishonors the instrument). On September 22, Gonzalez negotiates the note to Bream, a purchaser who lives in another state. Bream does not know, and has no reason to know, that the note has been dishonored, so Bream is *not* put on notice and therefore can become an HDC. ■

Notice of Claims or Defenses A holder cannot become an HDC if she or he has notice of any claim to the instrument or any defense against it [UCC 3–302(a)(2)]. Knowledge of claims or defenses can be imputed (attributed) to the purchaser if these claims or defenses are apparent on the face of the instrument or if the purchaser otherwise had reason to know of them from facts surrounding the transaction.

Incomplete Instruments. A purchaser cannot expect to become an HDC of an instrument so incomplete on its face that an element of negotiability is lacking (for example, the amount is not filled in). Minor omissions (such as the omission of the date—see Chapter 22) are permissible because these do not call into question the validity of the instrument. Similarly, when a person accepts an instrument that has been completed without knowing that it was incomplete when issued, that person can take it as an HDC.

NOTE A difference between the handwriting in the body of a check and the handwriting in the signature does not affect the validity of the check.

■ EXAMPLE 23.5 Syd asks Brendon to buy a textbook for her at the campus bookstore. Syd writes a check payable to the bookstore, leaves the amount blank, and tells Brendon to fill in the price of the textbook. The cost of the textbook is $85. If Brendon fills in the check for $115 before he gets to the bookstore, the bookstore cashier sees only a properly completed instrument. Therefore, because the bookstore had no notice that the check was incomplete when it was issued, the bookstore can take the check for $115 and become an HDC. ■

Irregular Instruments. Any irregularity on the face of an instrument (such as an obvious forgery or alteration) that calls into question its validity or terms of ownership, or that creates an ambiguity as to the party to pay, will bar HDC status. A careful forgery of a signature or the careful alteration of an instrument, however, can go undetected by reasonable examination; therefore, the purchaser can qualify as an HDC.

ETHICAL ISSUE 23.1

Should a postdated corporate check constitute notice of a defense? What makes a check so irregular that a court will infer that the payor had notice of a defense? The answer varies depending on the court. As you learned in the previous chapter (Chapter 22), postdating an instrument normally does not affect its negotiability. In some circumstances, however, the postdating of a check may raise suspicions about its authenticity, particularly if it is a commercial check. Is it fair for a court to apply a different standard to commercial checks than it applies to checks of individuals?

Consider, for example, the court's decision in *Bay Shore Check Cashing Corp. v. Landscapes by North East Construction Corp.*[2] In August 2003, several blank checks were stolen from the defendant corporation, which promptly notified its bank of the theft. One of the checks was negotiated to the plaintiff's check-cashing business a few months later. The check was dated August 8, 2004 (that is, many months in the future), and signed illegibly by a signatory who was not an authorized corporate signatory. The plaintiff cashed the check without taking any steps to verify its authenticity, in part because the plaintiff's business had had prior dealings with the individual who cashed the check. When the defendant's bank refused to pay the check, the plaintiff filed suit, claiming to be an HDC.

The New York district court determined that receiving "a postdated commercial check, even if for value, in good faith and without actual knowledge of defect" is not enough to confer HDC status. Because the corporate check was dated eight months in the future and was not clearly authorized by the corporation, the court held that the check was so irregular as to give the plaintiff notice of a defense. ■

Holder through an HDC

A person who does not qualify as an HDC but who derives his or her title through an HDC can acquire the rights and privileges of an HDC. This rule is sometimes called the **shelter principle.** According to UCC 3–203(b),

SHELTER PRINCIPLE
The principle that the holder of a negotiable instrument who cannot qualify as a holder in due course (HDC), but who derives his or her title through an HDC, acquires the rights of an HDC.

> Transfer of an instrument, whether or not the transfer is a negotiation, vests in the transferee any right of the transferor to enforce the instrument, including any right as a holder in due course, but the transferee cannot acquire rights of a holder in due course by a transfer, directly or indirectly, from a holder in due course if the transferee engaged in fraud or illegality affecting the instrument.

Under this rule, anyone—no matter how far removed from an HDC—who can trace his or her title ultimately back to an HDC may acquire the rights of an HDC. By extending the benefits of HDC status, the shelter principle promotes the marketability and free transferability of negotiable instruments.

There are some limitations on the shelter principle, however. Certain persons who formerly held instruments cannot improve their positions by later reacquiring the instruments from HDCs [UCC 3–203(b)]. If a holder participated in fraud or illegality affecting the instrument, or had notice of a claim or defense against an instrument, that holder is not allowed to improve her or his status by repurchasing from a later HDC.

2. 776 N.Y.S.2d 742 (N.Y.Dist. 2004).

INTERNATIONAL PERSPECTIVE

"Protected Holder" Status

Good faith is an issue not only in domestic transactions involving negotiable instruments but also internationally. Under the United Nations Convention on International Bills of Exchange and International Promissory Notes (CIBN), the equivalent of a holder in due course is known as a "protected holder." As under the UCC, a protected holder is afforded greater protection than an ordinary holder. Unlike the UCC, however, the CIBN does not provide an objective test by which to measure good faith. Article 3 of the UCC, as revised in 1990, defines *good faith* as "honesty in fact and the observance of reasonable commercial standards of fair dealing." By including the phrase "the observance of reasonable commercial standards of fair dealing" in the definition, the UCC gives courts some objective guidelines as to what constitutes good faith. The CIBN, in contrast, qualifies someone as a protected holder if she or he was merely "without knowledge" of a fraud or other defense against the instrument. Generally, the CIBN's test for protected-holder status is easily passed. In fact, every holder is presumed to be a protected holder unless there is proof to the contrary.

FOR CRITICAL ANALYSIS

What might be a reason that the CIBN contains only a very broad and subjective definition of good faith?

■ EXAMPLE 23.6 Matt and Carla collaborate to defraud Lorena. Lorena is induced to give Carla a negotiable note payable to Carla's order. Carla then specially indorses the note for value to Larry, an HDC. Matt and Carla split the proceeds. Larry negotiates the note to Stuart, another HDC. Stuart then negotiates the note for value to Matt. Even though Matt obtained the note through an HDC, he does not have the rights of an HDC—and can never acquire HDC rights in this note—because he participated in the original fraud. ■

Signature Liability

"Most men are admirers of justice—when justice happens to be on their side."

RICHARD WHATELY, 1787–1863 (English theologian and logician)

The key to liability on a negotiable instrument is a *signature*.[3] The general rule is as follows: every party, except a qualified indorser,[4] who signs a negotiable instrument is either primarily or secondarily liable for payment of that instrument when it comes due. The following subsections discuss these two types of liability, as well as the conditions that must be met before liability can arise.

PRIMARY LIABILITY

A person who is primarily liable on a negotiable instrument is absolutely required to pay the instrument—unless, of course, he or she has a valid defense to payment [UCC 3–305]. Only *makers* and *acceptors* of instruments are primarily liable.

Makers The maker of a promissory note promises to pay the note. It is the maker's promise to pay that makes the note a negotiable instrument. The words "I promise

3. See Chapter 22 for a discussion of how the UCC defines a *signature*.

4. A qualified indorser—one who indorses "without recourse"—undertakes no contractual obligation to pay. A qualified indorser merely assumes warranty liability, which will be discussed later in this chapter.

to pay" embody the maker's obligation to pay the instrument according to the terms as written at the time of the signing. If the instrument was incomplete when the maker signed it, the maker is obligated to pay it according to its stated terms or according to terms that were agreed on and later filled in to complete the instrument [UCC 3–115, 3–407(a), 3–412].

■ EXAMPLE 23.7 Tristan executes a preprinted promissory note to Sharon, without filling in the blank for a due date. If Sharon does not complete the form by adding the date, the note will be payable on demand. If Sharon subsequently fills in a due date that Tristan authorized, the note is payable on the stated due date. In either situation, Tristan (the maker) is obligated to pay the note. ■

RECALL A drawee is the party ordered to pay a draft or check, such as a bank or financial institution, for example.

Acceptors An *acceptor* is a drawee that promises to pay an instrument when it is presented for payment, as mentioned in Chapter 22. Once a drawee indicates acceptance by signing the draft, the drawee becomes an acceptor and is obligated to pay the draft when it is presented for payment [UCC 3–409(a)]. A drawee that refuses to accept a draft that *requires* the drawee's acceptance (such as a trade acceptance) has dishonored the instrument.

Acceptance of a check is called *certification* (certified checks will be discussed in Chapter 24). Certification is not necessary on checks, and a bank is under no obligation to certify checks. On certification, however, the drawee bank occupies the position of an acceptor and is primarily liable on the check to any holder [UCC 3–409(d)].

SECONDARY LIABILITY

Drawers and *indorsers* are secondarily liable. On a negotiable instrument, secondary liability is similar to the liability of a guarantor in a simple contract (described in Chapter 16) in the sense that it is *contingent liability.* In other words, a drawer or an indorser will be liable only if the party that is responsible for paying the instrument refuses to do so (dishonors the instrument). In regard to drafts and checks, the drawer's secondary liability does not arise until the drawee fails to pay or to accept the instrument, whichever is required [UCC 3–412, 3–415].

RECALL A guarantor is liable on a contract to pay the debt of another only if the party who is primarily liable fails to pay.

Dishonor of an instrument thus triggers the liability of parties who are secondarily liable on the instrument—that is, the drawer and *unqualified* indorsers. ■ EXAMPLE 23.8 Nina Lee writes a check on her account at Universal Bank payable to the order of Stephen Miller. Universal Bank refuses to pay the check when Miller presents it for payment, thus dishonoring the check. In this situation, Lee will be liable to Miller on the basis of her secondary liability. ■ Drawers are secondarily liable on drafts unless they disclaim their liability by drawing the instruments "without recourse" (if the draft is a check, however, a drawer cannot disclaim liability) [UCC 3–414(e)].

Parties who are secondarily liable on a negotiable instrument promise to pay on that instrument only if the following events occur:[5]

1. The instrument is properly and timely presented.
2. The instrument is dishonored.
3. Timely notice of dishonor is given to the secondarily liable party.

5. These requirements are necessary for a secondarily liable party to have signature liability on a negotiable instrument, but they are not necessary for a secondarily liable party to have warranty liability (to be discussed later in this chapter).

EXHIBIT 23–2 TIME FOR PROPER PRESENTMENT

TYPE OF INSTRUMENT	FOR ACCEPTANCE	FOR PAYMENT
Time	On or before due date.	On due date.
Demand	Within a reasonable time (after date or issue or after secondary party becomes liable on the instrument).	
Check	Not applicable.	Within thirty days of its date, to hold drawer secondarily liable. Within thirty days of indorsement, to hold indorser secondarily liable.

Proper and Timely Presentment As noted in Chapter 22, presentment is the formal production of a negotiable instrument for acceptance, or payment. The UCC requires that a holder present the instrument to the appropriate party, in a timely fashion, and give reasonable identification if demanded [UCC 3–414(f), 3–415(e), 3–501]. The party to whom the instrument must be presented depends on the type of instrument involved. A note or certificate of deposit (CD) must be presented to the maker for payment. A draft is presented to the drawee for acceptance, payment, or both. A check is presented to the drawee for payment [UCC 3–501(a), 3–502(b)].

Presentment can be made by any commercially reasonable means, including oral, written, or electronic communication [UCC 3–501(b)]. It is effective when the demand for payment or acceptance is received, although banks can treat a presentment that takes place after an established cutoff hour (such as 2 P.M.) as occurring the next business day.

One of the most crucial criteria for proper presentment is timeliness [UCC 3–414(f), 3–415(e), 3–501(b)(4)]. Failure to present an instrument on time is the most common reason that unqualified indorsers are discharged from secondary liability. The time for proper presentment for different types of instruments is shown in Exhibit 23–2.

Dishonor An instrument is dishonored when the required acceptance or payment is refused or cannot be obtained within the prescribed time. An instrument is also dishonored when required presentment is excused (as it would be, for example, if the maker had died) and the instrument is not properly accepted or paid [UCC 3–502(e), 3–504].

In some situations, a postponement of payment or a refusal to pay an instrument will *not* dishonor the instrument. When presentment is made after an established cutoff hour, for instance, a bank can postpone payment until the following business day without dishonoring the instrument. In addition, when the holder refuses to exhibit the instrument, to give reasonable identification, or to sign a receipt on the instrument for payment, a bank's refusal to pay does not dishonor the instrument. ■ EXAMPLE 23.9 Suppose that Deere, instead of depositing Lamar's check into his bank account, demands payment from Universal Bank in cash. The bank requests identification, which Deere refuses to provide. In this situation, the bank would be within its rights to refuse payment to Deere, and the bank's refusal to pay would not dishonor the check. ■

Some banks require a check holder who does not have an account at the bank to provide a thumbprint before the bank will honor the check. The issue in the following case was whether this practice was a reasonable identification requirement.

Featured Case

CASE 23.2 Messing v. Bank of America, N.A.[a]

Maryland Court of Appeals, 2003.
373 Md. 672,
821 A.2d 22.

MAJORITY OPINION

HARRELL, Judge.

* * * *

At some point in time prior to 3 August 2000, [Jeff Messing] came into possession of a check in the amount of Nine Hundred Seventy-Six Dollars ($976.00) (the check) from Toyson J. Burruss, the drawer, doing business as Prestige Auto Detail Center. * * * Petitioner elected to present the check for payment at a branch of Mr. Burruss' bank, Bank of America, the drawee. On 3 August 2000, Petitioner [Messing] approached a teller * * * and asked to cash the check. * * *

* * * She asked if the Petitioner was a customer of Bank of America. The Petitioner stated that he was not. The teller returned the check to Petitioner and requested, consistent with bank policy when cashing checks for non-customers, that Petitioner place his thumbprint on the check. Petitioner refused and the teller informed him that she would be unable to complete the transaction without his thumbprint.

Petitioner requested, and was referred to, the branch manager. * * * The branch manager examined the check and returned it to the Petitioner, informing him that, because Petitioner was a non-customer, Bank of America would not cash the check without Petitioner's thumbprint * * *.

* * * Petitioner * * * filed a declaratory judgment action against Bank of America (the Bank) in [a Maryland state court]. * * * Petitioner asked the trial court to declare [in part] that * * * under [Maryland Code Section] 3–501(b)(2) of the state's Commercial Law Article [Maryland's version of UCC 3–501(b)(2)] a thumbprint is not reasonable identification * * *.

* * * [The court] entered [a] judgment in favor of the Bank * * *.

Petitioner appealed [to a state intermediate appellate court, which] concluded that the * * * decision in favor of the Bank was * * * correct * * *.

Petitioner [appealed to the Maryland Court of Appeals, the state's highest court] * * *.

a. *N.A.* stands for "National Association."

* * * *

The question is whether requiring a thumbprint constitutes a request for "reasonable identification" under Section 3–501(b)(2)(ii). If it is "reasonable," then under Section 3–501(b)(3)(ii), the refusal of the Bank to accept the check from Petitioner did not constitute dishonor. If, however, requiring a thumbprint is not "reasonable" under Section 3–501(b)(2)(ii), then the refusal to accept the check may constitute dishonor under Section 3–501(b)(2). The issue of dishonor is arguably relevant because Petitioner [Messing] has no cause of action against any party, including the drawer, until the check is dishonored.

* * * *

* * * According to Petitioner, the purpose of requiring "reasonable identification" is to allow the drawee bank to determine that the presenter is the proper person to be paid on the instrument. Because a thumbprint does not provide that information at the time presentment and payment are made, Petitioner argues that a thumbprint cannot be read to fall within the meaning of "reasonable identification" for the purposes of Section 3–501(b)(2)(ii).

Bank of America argues that the requirement of a thumbprint * * * is a reasonable and necessary industry response to the growing problem of check fraud. * * *

* * * We agree with Petitioner that a thumbprint cannot be used, in most instances, to confirm the identity of a non-account checkholder at the time that the check is presented for cashing, as his or her thumbprint is usually not on file with the drawee at that time. We disagree, however, with Petitioner's conclusion that a thumbprint signature is therefore not "reasonable identification" for purposes of Section 3–501(b)(2).

Nowhere does the language of Section 3–501(b)(2) suggest that "reasonable identification" is limited to information Respondent can authenticate *at the time presentment is made.* Rather, all that is required is that the person making presentment must * * * give reasonable identification. While providing a thumbprint signature does not necessarily confirm identification of the checkholder at presentment—unless of course the drawee bank has a duplicate thumbprint signature on file—it does assist in the identification of the checkholder should the check later prove to be bad. It therefore serves as a powerful deterrent to those who might otherwise attempt

CASE 23.2—Continued

to pass a bad check. That one method provides identification at the time of presentment and the other identification after the check may have been honored does not prevent the latter from being "reasonable identification" for purposes of Section 3–501(b)(2). * * * [Emphasis added.]

The reason has to do with warranties. The transfer of a check for consideration creates both transfer warranties and presentment warranties * * * . The warranties include, for example, that the payee is entitled to enforce the instrument and that there are no alterations on the check. The risk to banks is that these contractual warranties may be breached, exposing the accepting bank to a loss because the bank paid over the counter on an item which was not properly payable. In such an event, the bank would then incur the expense to find the presenter, to demand repayment, and legal expenses to pursue the presenter for breach of his warranties.

In short, when a bank cashes a check over the counter, it assumes the risk that it may suffer losses for counterfeit documents, forged endorsements, or forged or altered checks. Nothing in the [UCC] forces a bank to assume such risks. To the extent that banks are willing to cash checks over the counter, with reasonable identification, such willingness expands and facilitates the commercial activities within the State. * * * Section 1–102 * * * states in relevant part: * * *

> (2) Underlying purposes and policies of Titles 1 through 10 of this article are * * *
> (b) to permit the continued expansion of commercial practices through custom, usage and agreement of the parties * * * .

Because the reduction of risk promotes the expansion of commercial practices, we believe that the direction of Section 1–102(2)(b) requires that we conclude that a bank's requirement of a thumbprint placed upon a check presented over the counter by a non-customer is reasonable. * * * [T]he Thumbprint Program is part of an industry-wide response to the growing threat of check fraud. Prohibiting banks from taking reasonable steps to protect themselves from losses could result in banks refusing to cash checks of non-customers presented over the counter at all, a result which would be counter to the direction of Section 1–102(2)(b).

As a result of this conclusion, Bank of America in the present case did not dishonor the check when it refused to accept it over the counter. Under Section 3–501(b)(3)(ii), Bank of America "refused payment or acceptance for failure of the presentment to comply with * * * other applicable law or rule." The rule not complied with by the Petitioner-presenter was Section 3–501(b)(2)(ii) in that he refused to give what we have determined to be reasonable identification. Therefore, there was no dishonor of the check by Bank of America's refusal to accept it. * * *

* * * *

JUDGMENT OF THE COURT OF SPECIAL APPEALS AFFIRMED.

DISSENTING OPINION

***ELDRIDGE,* Judge, * * * dissenting in part.**

* * * I cannot agree with the majority's holding that, after the petitioner presented his driver's license and a major credit card, it was "reasonable" to require the petitioner's thumbprint as identification.

Today, honest citizens attempting to cope in this world are constantly being required to show or give drivers' licenses, photo identification cards, Social Security numbers, the last four digits of Social Security numbers, mothers' "maiden names," sixteen-digit account numbers, etc. Now, the majority takes the position that it is "reasonable" for banks and other establishments to require, in addition, thumbprints and fingerprints. Enough is enough. The most reasonable thing in this case was petitioner's "irritation with the Bank of America's Thumbprint Signature Program."

TEST YOUR COMPREHENSION: CASE DETAILS

1. What was the issue in this case on which the Maryland Court of Appeals, the state's highest court, was asked to focus?
2. Did the court rule in favor of the plaintiff or the defendant? Why?
3. How did the dissent view the bank's thumbprint requirement?
4. Why might a customer be reluctant to provide a thumbprint to a bank, even if he or she is presenting a valid check?
5. Could the thumbprint requirement in this case be considered an invasion of the customer's privacy? Explain your answer.

Proper Notice Once an instrument has been dishonored, proper notice must be given to secondary parties (drawers and indorsers) for them to be held contractually liable. Notice may be given in any reasonable manner, including an oral, written, or electronic communication, as well as notice written or stamped on the instrument itself. The bank must give any necessary notice before its midnight deadline (midnight of the next banking day after receipt). Notice by any party other than a bank must be given within thirty days following the day of dishonor or the day on which the person who is secondarily liable receives notice of dishonor [UCC 3–503].

ACCOMMODATION PARTIES

ACCOMMODATION PARTY
A person who signs an instrument for the purpose of lending his or her name as credit to another party on the instrument.

An **accommodation party** is one who signs an instrument for the purpose of lending his or her name as credit to another party on the instrument [UCC 3–419(a)]. Accommodation parties are one form of security against nonpayment on a negotiable instrument. ■ EXAMPLE 23.10 Frank Huston applies to Northeast Bank for a $1,000 loan. The bank wants some reasonable assurance that if it loans Huston the funds, the debt will be paid. If Huston's financial condition is uncertain, the bank may be reluctant to rely solely on his ability to pay. To reduce the risk of nonpayment, the bank can require that a third person sign Huston's promissory note as an accommodation party. ■ When one person (such as a parent) cosigns a promissory note with the maker (such as the parent's son or daughter), the cosigner is an accommodation party.

If the accommodation party signs on behalf of the *maker*, he or she becomes an *accommodation maker* and is primarily liable on the instrument. If the accommodation party indorses an instrument on behalf of a *payee or other holder* (usually to make the instrument more marketable), he or she is an *accommodation indorser* and, as an indorser, is secondarily liable. If the accommodation party pays the instrument, she or he has a right of recourse against the party accommodated [UCC 3–419(e)].[6]

AGENTS' SIGNATURES

AGENT
A person who agrees to represent or act for another, called the principal.

PRINCIPAL
In agency law, a person who agrees to have another, called the agent, act on her or his behalf.

The general law of agency, covered in Chapter 28, applies to negotiable instruments. An **agent** is a person who agrees to represent or act for another, called the **principal.** Agents can sign negotiable instruments, just as they can sign contracts, and thereby bind their principals [UCC 3–401(a)(ii), 3–402(a)]. Without such a rule, all corporate commercial business would stop—as every corporation can and must act through its agents.

Liability of the Principal Generally, an agent must be *authorized* to sign the instrument on the principal's behalf. Even an authorized agent, however, does not bind a principal on an instrument unless the agent's signature *clearly names* the principal. The agent may or may not add his or her own name, but if the signature shows clearly that it is made on behalf of the principal, the agent is not liable on the instrument.

■ EXAMPLE 23.11 Either of the following two signatures by Joan Collingsworth as agent for Brian Peterson will bind Peterson on the instrument, and Collingsworth will not be personally liable for payment on it:

1. Peterson, by Collingsworth, agent.
2. Peterson.

6. The 2002 amendments to UCC Article 3 expressly provide that an accommodation party is primarily liable if the party indicates on the instrument that he or she guarantees payment or does not clearly state the intent to guarantee collection rather than payment [Amended UCC 3–419(e)].

If Collingsworth (the agent) signs just her own name, however, she will be personally liable to an HDC who has no notice of her agency status. An agent can escape liability to ordinary holders if the agent proves that the original parties did not intend the agent to be liable on the instrument [UCC 3–402(a), 3–402(b)(2)]. In either situation, the principal is bound if the party entitled to enforce the instrument can prove the agency relationship. ■

Liability of the Agent Authorized agents may be held personally liable on the instruments they sign in several situations. As noted in the previous example, agents may be liable when they sign their own name and do not name the principal or indicate they are acting as an agent. An agent can also be personally liable when the instrument is signed in both the agent's name and the principal's name (for example, "Collingsworth, Peterson"), but nothing on the instrument indicates the agency relationship (so the agent cannot be distinguished from the principal). When the agent indicates agency status in signing a negotiable instrument but fails to name the principal (for example, "Joan Collingsworth, agent"), the agent may also be liable [UCC 3–402(b)(2)].

An important exception to the rules on agent liability is made for checks that are signed by agents. If an agent signs her or his own name on a check that is *payable from the account of the principal,* and the principal is identified on the check, the agent will not be personally liable on the check [UCC 3–402(c)]. ■ EXAMPLE 23.12 Suppose that Collingsworth, who is authorized to draw checks on Peterson Company's account, signs a check that is preprinted with Peterson Company's name. The signature reads simply "Joan Collingsworth." In this situation, Collingsworth will not be personally liable on the check. ■

The following case involved a question about the liability on a note that a corporate officer claimed to have signed in a representative capacity.

CASE 23.3 Caraway v. Land Design Studio

Texas Court of Appeals—Austin, 2001.
47 S.W.3d 696.

BACKGROUND AND FACTS Hugh Caraway was the president of Internacional Realty, Inc., when Realty hired Land Design Studio to landscape the Deerfield Project, an apartment-complex development. After Land Design completed the work, the parties executed a promissory note. The note stated, "In consideration of design services rendered, I(We) *Hugh Carraway* [sic], *Internacional Realty, Inc.* * * * do hereby promise to pay *Land Design Studio* * * *, the amount of $42,639.82." The note was signed by Caraway. Payment in full was to be made in less than seven months, but no payment was received. Land Design filed a suit in a Texas state court against Caraway to collect the amount due. Caraway denied that he was personally liable on the note, arguing in part that he had intended to sign it in a representative capacity. The court granted Land Design's motion for summary judgment. Caraway appealed to a state intermediate appellate court.

IN THE WORDS OF THE COURT . . .

PURYEAR, Justice.

* * * *

* * * We do not have the instance of a note reflecting the name of the principal only, followed by the signature of a purported representative, but rather we have a note bearing the name of the signing party, Caraway, as one of the principals. In addition, the language of the instrument reflects that payment was promised from

(Continued)

CASE 23.3—Continued

more than one source * * * . Either "We" refers to both Caraway and Realty, or exclusively to Realty, which leaves "I" to refer only to Caraway. In either event, Caraway has assumed liability. The note then bears the signature of "Hugh L. Caraway, Debtor." Given the language of the instrument, we find that the note, on its face, clearly obligates Caraway as the maker, or debtor.

Caraway would be in no different a position if the note did not bear his name as a principal. * * * Caraway's signature on the note bears no indication of his representative capacity. According to [UCC 3–402(b)], an authorized representative who signs his name to an instrument "is liable on the instrument to a holder in due course that took the instrument without notice that the representative was not intended to be liable on the instrument if * * * the form of the signature does not show unambiguously that the signature is made in a representative capacity." Accordingly, a person signing a promissory note is presumed to be personally liable unless he presents a defense.

* * * [Caraway's] assertion of his subjective intent alone is not sufficient * * * . The intent must be disclosed or communicated to the other party. * * *

* * * *

* * * *The note itself is the best indicator of intent.* * * * [Emphasis added.]

We conclude that the note identifies Caraway as a maker of the note. Moreover, because the note does not indicate that Caraway signed only in his representative capacity and because Caraway presents no other evidence that he disclosed his intent to Land Design to sign the note solely as an agent of Realty, we conclude that no factual question exists as to Caraway's capacity at the time he signed the note.

DECISION AND REMEDY The state intermediate appellate court affirmed the judgment of the lower court. The note did not indicate, and Caraway did not otherwise disclose, that he signed only as an agent of Realty.

WHY IS THIS CASE IMPORTANT? *As this case illustrates, the objective theory of contracts also applies to negotiable instruments. When deciding whether to enforce a negotiable instrument, the courts focus on the objective indications of a party's intent rather than on a party's own secret, subjective intentions.*

Unauthorized Signatures

People normally are not liable to pay on negotiable instruments unless their signatures appear on the instruments. What happens, however, if the signature is unauthorized, as occurs when a signature is forged?

The General Rule As stated previously, the general rule is that an unauthorized signature is wholly inoperative and will not bind the person whose name is forged. ■ **Example 23.13** Parra finds Dolby's checkbook lying in the street, writes out a check to himself, and forges Dolby's signature. If a bank fails to ascertain that Dolby's signature is not genuine (which banks normally have a duty to do) and cashes the check for Parra, the bank will generally be liable to Dolby for the amount. ■ (The liability of banks for paying over forged signatures will be discussed further in Chapter 24.)

Similarly, if an agent has no authority to sign the principal's name, the "unauthorized signature is ineffective except as the signature of the unauthorized signer" [UCC 3–403(a)]. ■ **Example 23.14** Maya Campbell is the principal and Lena Shem is her agent. Shem, without authority, signs a promissory note as follows: "Maya Campbell, by Lena Shem, agent." Because Maya Campbell's "signature" is unauthorized, Campbell cannot be held liable, but Shem is liable to a holder of the note. This would be true even if Shem had signed the note "Maya Campbell," without indicating any agency relationship. In either situation, the unauthorized signer, Shem, is liable on the instrument. ■

Exceptions to the General Rule There are two exceptions to the general rule that an unauthorized signature will not bind the person whose name is signed:

1. An exception is made when the person whose name is signed ratifies (affirms) the signature [UCC 3–403(a)]. A principal can ratify an unauthorized signature made by an agent, either expressly, by affirming the validity of the signature, or impliedly, by other conduct, such as keeping any benefits received in the transaction or failing to repudiate the signature. The parties involved need not be principal and agent. ■ EXAMPLE 23.15 Allison Malone steals several checks from her mother, Brenda Malone, makes them out to herself, and signs "Brenda Malone." Brenda, the mother, may ratify her daughter's forgery so that her daughter will not be prosecuted for forgery. ■
2. A person whose name is forged may be precluded from denying the effectiveness of an unauthorized signature if the person's own negligence substantially contributed to the forgery [UCC 3–115, 3–401, 3–403, 3–406]. ■ EXAMPLE 23.16 Suppose that the owner of a business, Rob, leaves his signature stamp and a blank check on an office counter. An employee, using the stamp, fills in and cashes the check. Rob can be estopped (prevented), on the basis of negligence, from denying liability for payment of the check. Whatever loss occurs may be allocated, however, between certain parties on the basis of comparative negligence [UCC 3–406(b)]. For example, if Rob can demonstrate that the bank was negligent in paying the check, the bank may bear a portion of the loss. ■

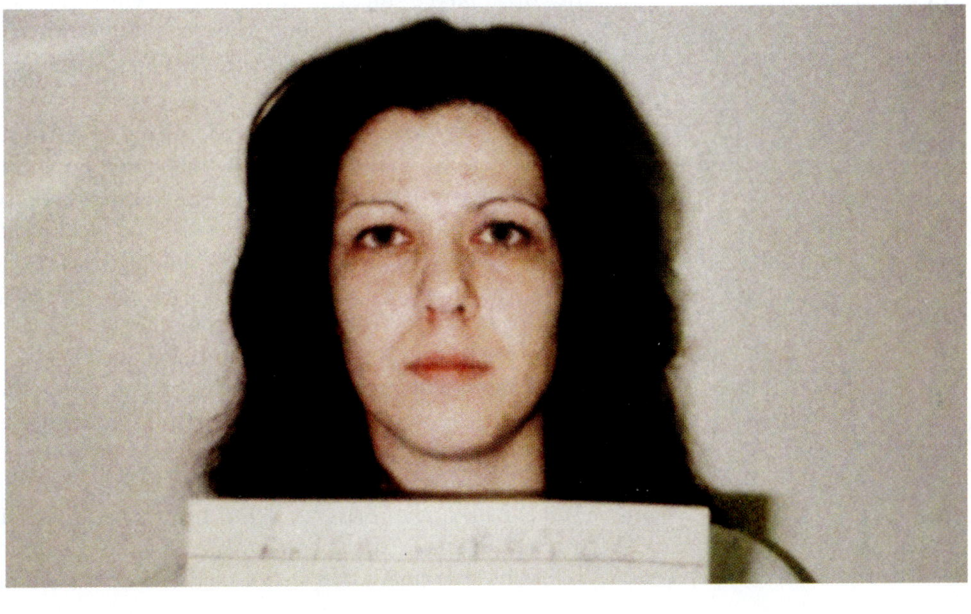

This woman was arrested for forging a series of checks. Seven of the checks were drawn on the account of Mary Smithson. If Smithson did not authorize the checks, can the bank debit her account for the amount of the checks? Why or why not? (AP Photo/Police)

An unauthorized signature operates as the signature of the unauthorized signer in favor of an HDC. A person who forges a check, for instance, can be held personally liable for payment by an HDC [UCC 3–403(a)].

Special Rules for Unauthorized Indorsements

Generally, when an indorsement is forged or unauthorized, the burden of loss falls on the first party to take the instrument with the forged or unauthorized indorsement. If the indorsement was made by an imposter or by a fictitious payee, however, the loss falls on the maker or drawer. We look at these two situations here.

IMPOSTER
One who, by use of the mails, Internet, telephone, or personal appearance, induces a maker or drawer to issue an instrument in the name of an impersonated payee. Indorsements by imposters are treated as authorized indorsements under Article 3 of the UCC.

Imposters An **imposter** is one who, by her or his personal appearance or use of the mails, Internet, telephone, or other communication, induces a maker or drawer to issue an instrument in the name of an impersonated payee. If the maker or drawer believes the imposter to be the named payee at the time of issue, the indorsement by the imposter is not treated as unauthorized when the instrument is transferred to an innocent party. This is because the maker or drawer intended the imposter to receive the instrument. In this situation, under the UCC's *imposter rule,* the imposter's indorsement will be effective—that is, not considered a forgery—insofar as the drawer or maker is concerned [UCC 3–404(a)]. ■ EXAMPLE 23.17 Carol impersonates Donna and induces Edward to write a check payable to the order of Donna. Carol, continuing to impersonate Donna, negotiates the check to First National Bank as payment on her loan there. As the drawer of the check, Edward is liable for its amount to First National. ■

FICTITIOUS PAYEE
A payee on a negotiable instrument whom the maker or drawer does not intend to have an interest in the instrument. Indorsements by fictitious payees are treated as authorized indorsements under Article 3 of the UCC.

Fictitious Payees An unauthorized indorsement will also be effective when a person causes an instrument to be issued to a payee who will have *no interest* in the instrument [UCC 3–404(b), 3–405]. In this situation, the payee is referred to as a **fictitious payee.** Situations involving fictitious payees most often arise when (1) a dishonest employee deceives the employer into signing an instrument payable to a party with no right to receive payment on the instrument or (2) a dishonest employee or agent has the authority to issue an instrument on behalf of the employer. Under the UCC's *fictitious payee rule,* the payee's indorsement is not treated as a forgery, and an innocent holder or an innocent party (such as a bank that pays the instrument in good faith) can hold the employer liable on the instrument.

"Life is unfair."
MILTON FRIEDMAN, 1912–
(American economist)

How a Fictitious Payee Can Be Created—An Example. ■ EXAMPLE 23.18 Blair Industries, Inc., gives its bookkeeper, Axel Ford, general authority to issue checks in the company name drawn on First State Bank so that Ford can pay employees' wages and other corporate bills. Ford decides to cheat Blair Industries out of $10,000 by issuing a check payable to Erica Nied, an old acquaintance. Neither Blair nor Ford intends Nied to receive any of the money, and Nied is not an employee or creditor of the company. Ford indorses the check in Nied's name, naming himself as indorsee. He then cashes the check at a local bank, which collects payment from the drawee bank, First State Bank. First State Bank charges the Blair Industries account $10,000. Blair Industries discovers the fraud and demands that the account be recredited. ■

Who Bears the Loss? Who bears the loss? UCC 3–404(b)(2) provides the answer. Neither the local bank that first accepted the check nor First State Bank is liable. Because Ford's indorsement in the name of a payee with no interest in

MANAGEMENT PERSPECTIVE

Banks Must Act in Good Faith

MANAGEMENT FACES A LEGAL ISSUE

Remember from previous chapters that the requirement of good faith underlies all transactions governed by the Uniform Commercial Code. Does this mean that a bank, to avoid liability for paying instruments with forged indorsements involving fictitious payees, must have acted in good faith when accepting the deposits? How the courts answer this question has, of course, significant implications for business owners and managers.

WHAT THE COURTS SAY

According to a number of courts, if a bank acts in bad faith in paying instruments with forged indorsements involving fictitious payees, the bank itself will end up bearing the loss. For example, in one case a Pennsylvania appellate court held that to assert the fictitious payee rule, "the bank must have acted in good faith when paying the instrument." The bank in this case had accepted 882 payroll checks generated and indorsed by Dorothy Heck, a payroll clerk employed by Pavex, Inc. The checks were made payable to various current and former Pavex employees, indorsed by Heck with the payees' names, and deposited into Heck's personal checking account at her bank.

In spite of the bank's policy that indorsements on checks must match exactly the names of the payees, the bank continued to accept Heck's deposited checks even when the indorsements did not match the payees' names. Furthermore, even though bank personnel discussed Heck's check-depositing activities on more than one occasion, they never contacted her employer to verify Heck's authority to deposit third party payroll checks. Given the bank's pattern of ignoring perceived irregularities in Heck's transactions, the trial court jury concluded that the bank had acted in bad faith and was therefore liable for approximately $170,000 of the $250,000 loss suffered by Pavex. The appellate court affirmed the trial court's decision.[a]

IMPLICATIONS FOR MANAGERS

Business owners and managers should realize that all may not always be lost when they are the victims of employees who indorse checks to fictitious payees. They should consider the possibility that the bank into which the checks were deposited may also be liable, at least in part, by failing to comply with its policies that require employees to examine the indorsements on deposited checks.

a. *Pavex, Inc. v. York Federal Savings and Loan Association,* 716 A.2d 640 (Pa.Super.Ct. 1998).

the instrument is "effective," there is no "forgery." Hence, the collecting bank is protected in paying on the check, and the drawee bank is protected in charging Blair's account. Thus, the employer-drawer, Blair Industries, will bear the loss. Of course, Blair Industries has recourse against Axel Ford, if Ford has not absconded with the funds.

Regardless of whether a dishonest employee actually signs the check or merely supplies his or her employer with names of fictitious creditors (or with true names of creditors having fictitious debts), the result is the same under the UCC. ■ **EXAMPLE 23.19** Nathan Holtz draws up the payroll list from which employees' salary checks are written. He fraudulently adds the name Sally Vix (a fictitious person) to the payroll, and the employer signs checks to be issued to her. Again, it is the employer-drawer who bears the loss. ■ (For a possible defense that an employer-drawer can use to defend against liability under the fictitious payee rule, see this chapter's *Management Perspective* feature.)

to the holder the amount due in full [UCC 3–602, 3–603]. Payment by any other party discharges only the liability of that party and subsequent parties.

Intentional cancellation of an instrument discharges the liability of all parties [UCC 3–604]. Intentionally writing "Paid" across the face of an instrument cancels it. Intentionally tearing up an instrument cancels it. If a holder intentionally crosses out a party's signature, that party's liability and the liability of subsequent indorsers who have already indorsed the instrument are discharged. Materially altering an instrument may discharge the liability of any party affected by the alteration, as previously discussed [UCC 3–407(b)]. (An HDC may be able to enforce a materially altered instrument against its maker or drawer according to the instrument's original terms, however.)

Discharge of liability can also occur when a party's right of recourse is impaired [UCC 3–605]. A *right of recourse* is a right to seek reimbursement. Ordinarily, when a holder collects the amount of an instrument from an indorser, the indorser has a right of recourse against prior indorsers, the maker or drawer, and accommodation parties. If the holder has adversely affected the indorser's right to seek reimbursement from these other parties, however, the indorser is not liable on the instrument. This occurs when, for example, the holder releases or agrees not to sue a party against whom the indorser has a right of recourse.

REVIEWING RIGHTS AND LIABILITIES OF PARTIES

Nancy Mahar was the office manager at Golden Years Nursing Home, Inc. She was given a signature stamp to issue checks to the nursing home's employees for up to $100 as advances on their pay. The checks were drawn on Golden Years' account at the First National Bank. Over a seven-year period, Mahar wrote a number of checks to employees exclusively for the purpose of embezzling funds for herself. She forged the employees' indorsements on the checks, signed her name as a second indorser, and deposited the checks in her personal account at Star Bank. The employees whose names were on the checks never actually requested them. When the scheme was uncovered, Golden Years filed a suit against Mahar, Star Bank, and others to recover the funds. Using the information presented in the chapter, answer the following questions.

1. With regard to signature liability, which UCC provision discussed in this chapter applies to this scenario?
2. What is the rule set forth by that provision?
3. Under the UCC, which party, Golden Years or Star Bank, must bear the loss in this situation? Why?
4. Describe any transfer or presentment warranties that Mahar might have violated based on these facts.

APPLICATION How to Purchase Negotiable Instruments*

Negotiable instruments are transferred every business day of the year. Most purchasers of negotiable instruments do not encounter any problems in further negotiating and transferring the instruments or in collecting payment on them if they are time instruments. Nevertheless, potential problems do exist, and purchasers should take precautions against them.

* This *Application* is not meant to substitute for the services of an attorney who is licensed to practice law in your state.

OVERDUE INSTRUMENTS

Suppose that you wish to purchase a demand instrument as a holder in due course (HDC). By definition, such an instrument has no stated time for payment and therefore

APPLICATION How to Purchase Negotiable Instruments—Continued

may be overdue—that is, the payee may have demanded payment but not received it, or a reasonable amount of time may have passed. (With checks, a reasonable amount of time is presumed to be ninety days from the date on the check.) If you have any doubt about whether a demand instrument is overdue, you should investigate.

NOTICE OF DEFECTS

As a prospective holder, you cannot afford to ignore a defect in any negotiable instrument. A four-month-old date on a check, for example, constitutes notice that the instrument is overdue. Generally, whenever an instrument has a defect, you will not qualify as an HDC, and you may be unable to obtain payment. In other words, it is prudent to determine whether the instrument is complete and, in some situations, whether the transfer will qualify you for HDC status.

CHECKLIST FOR THE PURCHASER OF NEGOTIABLE INSTRUMENTS

1. Make sure that a demand instrument is not overdue before purchasing it.
2. Make sure that the negotiable instrument has no obvious defects—that is, look for indications that the maker or drawer of the instrument might have a valid reason for refusing to pay.

KEY TERMS

CHAPTER SUMMARY Rights and Liabilities of Parties

Holder versus Holder in Due Course (HDC) (See page 570.)	1. *Holder*—A person in the possession of an instrument drawn, issued, or indorsed to him or her, to his or her order, to bearer, or in blank. A holder obtains only those rights that the transferor had in the instrument. 2. *Holder in due course (HDC)*—A holder who, by meeting certain acquisition requirements (summarized next), takes the instrument free of most defenses and claims to which the transferor was subject.
Requirements for HDC Status (See pages 571–576.)	To be an HDC, a holder must take the instrument: 1. *For value*—A holder can take an instrument for value in one of five ways [UCC 3–303]: a. By the complete or partial performance of the promise for which the instrument was issued or transferred. b. By acquiring a security interest or other lien in the instrument, excluding a lien obtained by a judicial proceeding. c. By taking an instrument in payment of (or as security for) a preexisting debt. d. By giving a negotiable instrument as payment. e. By giving an irrevocable commitment as payment. 2. *In good faith*—Good faith is defined as "honesty in fact and the observance of reasonable commercial standards of fair dealing" [UCC 3–103(a)(4)].

(Continued)

CHAPTER SUMMARY Rights and Liabilities of Parties—Continued

Requirements for HDC Status—Continued (See pages 571–576.)	3. *Without notice*—To be an HDC, a holder must not be on notice that the instrument is defective in any of the following ways [UCC 3–302, 3–304]: a. The instrument is overdue. b. The instrument has been dishonored. c. There is an uncured (uncorrected) default with respect to another instrument issued as part of the same series. d. The instrument contains an unauthorized signature or has been altered. e. There is a defense against the instrument or a claim to the instrument. f. The instrument is so irregular or incomplete as to call into question its authenticity.
Holder through an HDC (See pages 576–577.)	A holder who cannot qualify as an HDC has the *rights* of an HDC if he or she derives title through an HDC unless the holder engaged in fraud or illegality affecting the instrument [UCC 3–203(b)]. This is known as the shelter principle.
Signature Liability (See pages 577–587.)	Every party (except a qualified indorser) who signs a negotiable instrument is either primarily or secondarily liable for payment of the instrument when it comes due. 1. *Primary liability*—Makers and acceptors are primarily liable (an acceptor is a drawee that promises in writing to pay an instrument when it is presented for payment at a later time) [UCC 3–115, 3–407, 3–409, 3–412]. 2. *Secondary liability*—Drawers and indorsers are secondarily liable [UCC 3–412, 3–414, 3–415, 3–501, 3–502, 3–503]. Parties who are secondarily liable on an instrument promise to pay on that instrument if the following events occur: a. The instrument is properly and timely presented. b. The instrument is dishonored. c. Timely notice of dishonor is given to the secondarily liable party. 3. *Accommodation parties*—An accommodation party is one who signs her or his name as credit to another party on an instrument [UCC 3–419]. Accommodation *makers* are primarily liable; accommodation *indorsers* are secondarily liable. 4. *Agents' signatures*—An *agent* is a person who agrees to represent or act for another, called the *principal.* Agents can sign negotiable instruments and thereby bind their principals. Liability on an instrument signed by an agent depends on whether the agent is authorized and on whether the agent's representative capacity and the principal's identity are both indicated on the instrument [UCC 3–401, 3–402, 3–403]. Agents need not indicate their representative capacity on *checks*—provided the checks clearly identify the principal and are drawn on the principal's account. 5. *Unauthorized signatures*—An unauthorized signature is wholly inoperative *unless:* a. The person whose name is signed ratifies (affirms) it or is precluded from denying it [UCC 3–115, 3–401, 3–403, 3–406]. b. The instrument has been negotiated to an HDC [UCC 3–403]. 6. *Special rules for unauthorized indorsements*—An unauthorized indorsement will not bind the maker or drawer except in the following circumstances: a. When an imposter induces the maker or drawer of an instrument to issue it to the imposter (imposter rule) [UCC 3–404(a)].

CHAPTER SUMMARY Rights and Liabilities of Parties—Continued

Signature Liability—Continued	b. When a person signs as or on behalf of a maker or drawer, intending that the payee will have no interest in the instrument, or when an agent or employee of the maker or drawer has supplied him or her with the name of the payee, also intending the payee to have no such interest (fictitious payee rule) [UCC 3–404(b), 3–405].
Warranty Liability (See pages 588–589.)	1. *Transfer warranties*—Any person who transfers an instrument for consideration makes the following warranties to all subsequent transferees and holders who take the instrument in good faith (but when a bearer instrument is transferred by delivery only, the transferor's warranties extend only to the immediate transferee) [UCC 3–416]: a. The transferor is entitled to enforce the instrument. b. All signatures are authentic and authorized. c. The instrument has not been altered. d. The instrument is not subject to a defense or claim of any party that can be asserted against the transferor. e. The transferor has no knowledge of any insolvency proceedings against the maker, the acceptor, or the drawer of the instrument. 2. *Presentment warranties*—Any person who presents an instrument for payment or acceptance makes the following warranties to any other person who in good faith pays or accepts the instrument [UCC 3–417(a), (d)]: a. The person obtaining payment or acceptance is entitled to enforce the instrument or is authorized to obtain payment or acceptance on behalf of a person who is entitled to enforce the instrument. (This is, in effect, a warranty that there are no missing or unauthorized indorsements.) b. The instrument has not been altered. c. The person obtaining payment or acceptance has no knowledge that the signature of the drawer of the instrument is unauthorized.
Defenses, Limitations, and Discharge (See pages 589–592.)	1. *Universal (real) defenses*—The following defenses are valid against all holders, including HDCs and holders with the rights of HDCs [UCC 3–305, 3–401, 3–403, 3–407]: a. Forgery. b. Fraud in the execution. c. Material alteration. d. Discharge in bankruptcy. e. Minority—if the contract is voidable under state law. f. Illegality, mental incapacity, or extreme duress—if the contract is void under state law. 2. *Personal (limited) defenses*—The following defenses are valid against ordinary holders but not against HDCs or holders with the rights of HDCs [UCC 3–105, 3–115, 3–302, 3–305, 3–306, 3–407, 3–601, 3–602, 3–603, 3–604, 4–401]: a. Breach of contract or breach of warranty. b. Lack or failure of consideration (value). c. Fraud in the inducement. d. Illegality and mental incapacity—if the contract is voidable. e. Previous payment of the instrument.

(Continued)

CHAPTER SUMMARY Rights and Liabilities of Parties—Continued

Defenses, Limitations, and Discharge—Continued (See pages 589–592.)	f. Unauthorized completion of the instrument. g. Nondelivery of the instrument. h. Ordinary duress or undue influence that renders the contract voidable.
Federal Limitations on the Rights of HDCs (See page 593.)	Rule 433 of the Federal Trade Commission, issued in 1976, limits the rights of HDCs who purchase instruments arising out of consumer credit transactions. Under the rule, a consumer who is a party to a consumer credit transaction is permitted to bring any defense he or she has against the seller against a subsequent holder as well, even if the subsequent holder is an HDC.
Discharge from Liability (See pages 593–594.)	All parties to a negotiable instrument will be discharged when the party primarily liable on it pays to a holder the amount due in full. Discharge can also occur in other circumstances (if the instrument has been canceled or materially altered, for example) [UCC 3–601 through 3–606].

FOR REVIEW

Answers for the even-numbered questions in this For Review *section can be found on this text's accompanying Web site at* http://blt.westbuslaw.com. *Select "Chapter 23" and click on "For Review."*

1. What are the requirements for attaining HDC status?
2. How can a person who does not qualify as an HDC acquire the rights and privileges of an HDC?
3. What is the key to liability on a negotiable instrument? What is the difference between signature liability and warranty liability?
4. Certain defenses are valid against all holders, including HDCs. What are these defenses called? Name four defenses that fall within this category.
5. Certain defenses can be used against an ordinary holder but are not effective against an HDC. What are these defenses called? Name four defenses that fall within this category.

QUESTIONS AND CASE PROBLEMS

23–1. Unauthorized Indorsements. What are the exceptions to the rule that a bank will be liable for paying a check over an unauthorized indorsement?

23–2. Agents' Signatures. Karen Thorpe is a purchasing agent for GymNast, Inc., a manufacturer of sports equipment. Karen has authority to sign checks in payment for purchases made by GymNast. Karen makes out three checks to suppliers and signs each one differently, as follows:

(a) GymNast, Inc., by Karen Thorpe, purchasing agent.
(b) Karen Thorpe, purchasing agent.
(c) Karen Thorpe.

Discuss briefly whether Karen is personally liable on each signature and whether parol evidence is admissible to hold GymNast, Inc., liable.

23–3. Signature Liability. Marion makes a promissory note payable to the order of Perry. Perry indorses the note by writing "without recourse, Perry" and transfers the note for value to Steven. Steven, in need of cash, negotiates the note to Harriet by indorsing it with the words "Pay to Harriet. [Signed] Steven." On the due date, Harriet presents the note to Marion for payment, only to learn that Marion has filed for bankruptcy and will have all debts (including the note) discharged in bankruptcy. Discuss fully whether Harriet can hold Marion, Perry, or Steven liable on the note.

23–4. Unauthorized Indorsements. Telemedia Publications, Inc., publishes *Cablecast Magazine,* a weekly guide for the listings of the cable television programming in Baton Rouge, Louisiana. Cablecast hired Jennifer Pennington as a temporary employee. Pennington's duties included indorsing subscription checks received in the mail with the Cablecast deposit stamp, preparing the deposit slip, and taking the checks to be deposited to City National Bank. John McGregor, the manager of Cablecast, soon noticed shortages in revenue coming into Cablecast. When he learned that Pennington had taken checks payable to Cablecast and deposited them in her personal account at Premier Bank, N.A., he confronted her. She admitted to taking $7,913.04 in Cablecast checks. Cablecast filed a suit in a

Louisiana state court against Premier Bank. The bank responded in part that Cablecast was solely responsible for losses caused by the fraudulent indorsements of its employees. At trial, Cablecast failed to prove that Premier Bank had not acted in good faith or that it had not exercised ordinary care in its handling of the checks. What rule should the court apply here? Why? [*Cablecast Magazine v. Premier Bank, N.A.*, 729 So.2d 1165 (La.App. 1 Cir. 1999)]

CASE PROBLEM WITH SAMPLE ANSWER

23–5. Robert Helmer and Percy Helmer, Jr., were authorized signatories on the corporate checking account of Event Marketing, Inc. The Helmers signed a check drawn on Event Marketing's account and issued to Rumarson Technologies, Inc. (RTI), in the amount of $24,965. The check was signed on July 13, 1998, but dated August 14. When RTI presented the check for payment, it was dishonored due to insufficient funds. RTI filed a suit in a Georgia state court against the Helmers to collect the amount of the check. Claiming that the Helmers were personally liable on Event Marketing's check, RTI filed a motion for summary judgment. Can an authorized signatory on a corporate account be held personally liable for corporate checks returned for insufficient funds? Are the Helmers liable in this case? Discuss. [*Helmer v. Rumarson Technologies, Inc.*, 538 S.E.2d 504 (Ga.App. 2000)]

After you have answered this problem, compare your answer with the sample answer given on the Web site that accompanies this text. Go to http://blt.westbuslaw.com, select "Chapter 23," and click on "Case Problem with Sample Answer."

23–6. Defenses. On September 13, 1979, Barbara Shearer and Barbara Couvion signed a note for $22,500, with interest at 11 percent, payable in monthly installments of $232.25 to Edgar House and Paul Cook. House and Cook assigned the note to Southside Bank in Kansas City, Missouri. In 1997, the note was assigned to Midstates Resources Corp., which assigned the note to The Cadle Co. in 2000. According to the payment history that Midstates gave to Cadle, the interest rate on the note was 12 percent. A Cadle employee noticed the discrepancy and recalculated the payments at 11 percent. When Shearer and Couvion refused to make further payments on the note, Cadle filed a suit in a Missouri state court against them to collect. Couvion and Shearer responded that they had made timely payments on the note, that Cadle and the previous holders had failed to accurately apply the payments to the reduction of principal and interest, and that the note "is either paid in full and satisfied or very close to being paid in full and satisfied." Is the makers' answer sufficient to support a verdict in their favor? If so, on what ground? If not, why not? [*The Cadle Co. v. Shearer*, 69 S.W.3d 122 (Mo.App. W.D. 2002)]

23–7. Holder in Due Course. The Brown family owns several companies, including J. H. Stevedoring Co. and Penn Warehousing and Distribution, Inc. Many aspects of the companies' operations and management are intertwined. Dennis Bishop began working for J. H. and Penn in 1984. By 1997, Bishop was financial controller at J. H. where he was responsible for approving invoices for payment and reconciling the corporate checkbook. In December, Bishop began stealing from Penn and J. H. by writing checks on their accounts and usually having one of the Browns sign the checks. Over the next two years, Bishop embezzled $1,209,436. He used $370,632 of the funds to buy horses from Fasig-Tipton Co. and Fasig-Tipton Midlantic, Inc., with Penn or J. H. checks made payable to those firms. When Bishop's fraud was revealed, J. H. and Penn filed a suit in a federal district court against the Fasig-Tipton firms to recover the amounts of the checks made payable to them. In whose favor should the court rule? Why? [*J. H. Stevedoring Co. v. Fasig-Tipton Co.*, 275 F.Supp.2d 644 (E.D.Pa. 2003)]

A QUESTION OF ETHICS

23–8. One day, while Ort, a farmer, was working alone in his field, a stranger approached him. The stranger said he was the state agent for a manufacturer of iron posts and wire fence. Eventually, the stranger persuaded Ort to accept a townshipwide agency for the same manufacturer. The stranger then asked Ort to sign a document that purportedly was an agency agreement. Because Ort did not have his glasses with him and could read only with great difficulty, he asked the stranger to read what the document said. The stranger then pretended to read the document to Ort, not mentioning that it was a promissory note. Both men signed the note, and Ort assumed that he was signing a document of agency. The stranger later negotiated the note to a good faith purchaser for value. When that person sued Ort, Ort attempted to defend on the basis of fraud in the execution. In view of these facts, consider the following questions. [*Ort v. Fowler*, 31 Kan. 478, 2 P. 580 (1884)]

1. Although this classic case was decided long before the UCC was drafted, the court applied essentially the same rule that would apply under Article 3. What is this rule, and how would it be applied to Ort's attempted defense on the ground of fraud in the execution?
2. This case provides a clear example of a situation in which one of two innocent parties (Ort and the purchaser of the note) must bear the loss caused by a third party (the stranger, who was the perpetrator of the fraud). Under Article 3, which party should bear the loss, and why?

FOR CRITICAL ANALYSIS

23–9. How does the concept of holder in due course further Article 3's general goal of encouraging the negotiability of instruments? How does it further Article 3's goal of balancing the rights of parties to negotiable instruments?

VIDEO QUESTION

23–10. Go to this text's Web site at **http://blt.westbuslaw.com** and select "Chapter 23." Click on "Video Questions" and view the video titled *Negotiability & Transferability: Indorsing Checks.* Then answer the following questions.

1. According to the instructor in the video, what are the two reasons why banks generally require a person to indorse a check that is made out to cash (a bearer instrument), even when the check is signed in the presence of the teller?
2. Suppose that your friend makes out a check payable to cash, signs it, and hands it to you. You take the check to your bank and indorse the check with your name and the words "without recourse." What type of indorsement is this? How does this indorsement affect the bank's rights?
3. Now suppose that you go to your bank and write a check on your account payable to cash for $500. The teller gives you the cash *without* asking you to indorse the check. After you leave, the teller slips the check into his pocket. Later, the teller delivers it (without an indorsement) to his friend Carol in payment for a gambling debt. Carol takes your check to her bank, indorses it, and deposits the money. Discuss whether Carol is a holder in due course.

INTERNET EXERCISES

Go to the *Business Law Today* home page at **http://blt.westbuslaw.com**, select "Chapter 23," and click on "Internet Exercises." There you will find the following Internet research exercises that you can perform to learn more about topics covered in this chapter.

Activity 23–1: LEGAL PERSPECTIVE—Fictitious Payees

Activity 23–2: MANAGEMENT PERSPECTIVE—Holder in Due Course

BEFORE THE TEST

Go to the *Business Law Today* home page at **http://blt.westbuslaw.com**, select "Chapter 23," and click on "Interactive Quizzes." You will find a number of interactive questions relating to this chapter.

CHAPTER 24

Checks, the Banking System, and E-Money

"Money is just what we use to keep tally."

Henry Ford, 1863–1947
(American automobile manufacturer)

CHAPTER OUTLINE

- CHECKS
- THE BANK-CUSTOMER RELATIONSHIP
- BANK'S DUTY TO HONOR CHECKS
- BANK'S DUTY TO ACCEPT DEPOSITS
- ELECTRONIC FUND TRANSFERS
- E-MONEY AND ONLINE BANKING
- THE UNIFORM MONEY SERVICES ACT

LEARNING OBJECTIVES

After reading this chapter, you should be able to answer the following questions:

1. On what types of checks does a bank serve as both the drawer and the drawee? What type of check does a bank agree in advance to accept when the check is presented for payment?
2. When may a bank properly dishonor a customer's check without liability to the customer? What happens if a bank wrongfully dishonors a customer's check?
3. What duties does the Uniform Commercial Code impose on a bank's customers with regard to forged and altered checks? What are the consequences of a customer's negligence in performing those duties?
4. What are the four most common types of electronic fund transfers? What is the basic purpose of the Electronic Fund Transfer Act, and how does it benefit consumers?
5. What is e-money? How is e-money stored and used? What laws apply to e-money transactions and online banking services?

Checks are the most common type of negotiable instruments regulated by the Uniform Commercial Code (UCC). It is estimated that over sixty-five billion personal and commercial checks are written each year in the United States. Checks are more than a daily convenience; they are an integral part of the American economic system. They serve as substitutes for money and thus, as Henry Ford said in the chapter-opening quotation, help us to "keep tally."

Issues relating to checks are governed by Articles 3 and 4 of the UCC. Recall from Chapters 22 and 23 that Article 3 establishes the requirements that all negotiable instruments, including checks, must meet. Article 3 also sets forth the rights and liabilities of parties to negotiable instruments. Article 4 of the UCC governs bank deposits and collections as well as bank-customer relationships. Article 4 regulates the relationships of banks with one another as they process checks for payment, and it establishes a framework for deposit and checking agreements between a bank and its customers. A check therefore may fall within the scope of Article 3 and yet be subject to the provisions of Article 4 while in the course of collection. If a conflict between Article 3 and Article 4 arises, Article 4 controls [UCC 4–102(a)].

In this chapter, we first identify the legal characteristics of checks and the legal duties and liabilities that arise when a check is issued. Then we examine the collection process—that is, the actual procedure by which the checks deposited into bank accounts move through banking channels, causing the underlying funds to be shifted from one bank account to another. Increasingly, credit cards, debit cards, and other devices and methods to transfer funds electronically are being used to pay for goods and services. In the latter part of this chapter, we look at the law governing electronic fund transfers.

Checks

CHECK
A draft drawn by a drawer ordering the drawee bank or financial institution to pay a fixed amount of money to the holder on demand.

A **check** is a special type of draft that is drawn on a bank, ordering the bank to pay a fixed amount of money on demand [UCC 3–104(f)]. Article 4 defines a bank as "a person engaged in the business of banking, including a savings bank, savings and loan association, credit union or trust company" [UCC 4–105(1)]. If any other institution (such as a brokerage firm) handles a check for payment or for collection, the check is not covered by Article 4.

Recall from the discussion of negotiable instruments in Chapters 22 and 23 that a person who writes a check is called the *drawer.* The drawer is a depositor in the bank on which the check is drawn. The person to whom the check is payable is the *payee.* The bank or financial institution on which the check is drawn is the *drawee.* If Anita Cruzak writes a check from her checking account to pay her college tuition, she is the drawer, her bank is the drawee, and her college is the payee. We now look at some special types of checks.

Cashier's Checks

CASHIER'S CHECK
A check drawn by a bank on itself.

Checks are usually three-party instruments, but on certain types of checks, the bank can serve as both the drawer and the drawee. For example, when a bank draws a check on itself, the check is called a **cashier's check** and is a negotiable instrument on issue (see Exhibit 24–1) [UCC 3–104(g)]. Normally, a cashier's check indicates a specific payee. In effect, with a cashier's check, the bank assumes responsibility for paying the check, thus making the check more readily acceptable as a substitute for cash.

■ EXAMPLE 24.1 Kramer needs to pay a moving company $8,000 for moving his household goods to a new home in another state. The moving company requests payment in the form of a cashier's check. Kramer goes to a bank (he need not have an account at the bank) and purchases a cashier's check, payable to the moving company, in the amount of $8,000. Kramer has to pay the bank the $8,000 for the check, plus a small service fee. He then gives the check to the moving company. ■

Cashier's checks are sometimes used in the business community as nearly the equivalent of cash. Except in very limited circumstances, the issuing bank must

EXHIBIT 24–1 A CASHIER'S CHECK

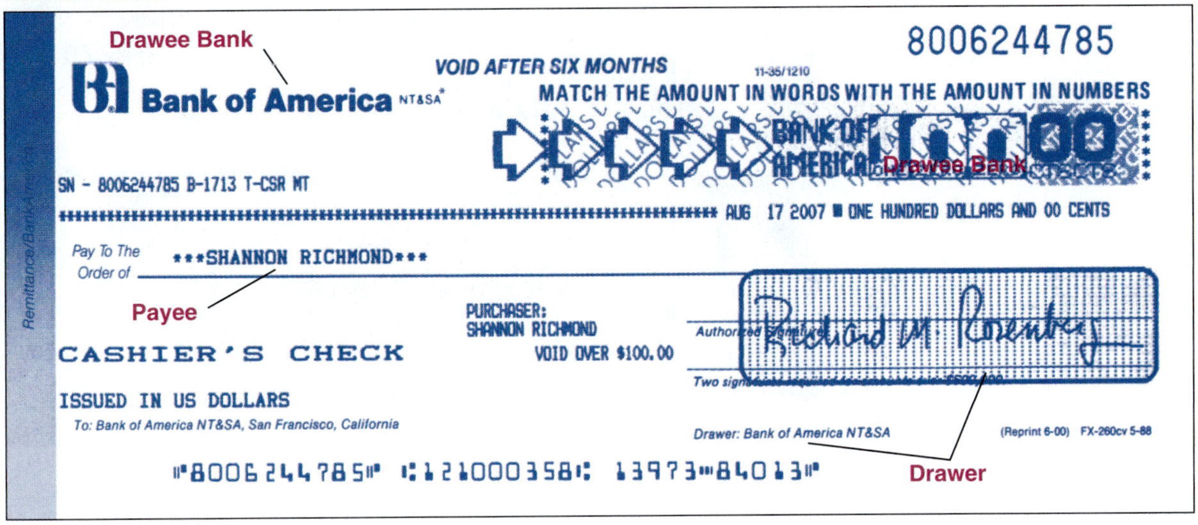

*The abbreviation *NT&SA* stands for National Trust and Savings Association.

honor its cashier's checks when they are presented for payment. If a bank wrongfully dishonors a cashier's check, a holder can recover from the bank all expenses incurred, interest, and consequential damages [UCC 3–411]. This same rule applies if a bank wrongfully dishonors a certified check (to be discussed shortly) or a teller's check. (A *teller's check* is a check drawn by a bank on another bank or, when drawn on a nonbank, payable at or through a bank [UCC 3–104(h)].)

Traveler's Checks

TRAVELER'S CHECK
A check that is payable on demand, drawn on or payable through a financial institution (bank), and designated as a traveler's check.

A **traveler's check** is an instrument that is payable on demand, drawn on or payable at or through a financial institution (such as a bank), and designated as a traveler's check. The institution is directly obligated to accept and pay its traveler's check according to the check's terms. The purchaser is required to sign the check at the time it is bought and again at the time it is used [UCC 3–104(i)]. Exhibit 24–2 on the following page shows an example of a traveler's check.

Certified Checks

CERTIFIED CHECK
A check that has been accepted in writing by the bank on which it is drawn. Essentially, the bank, by certifying (accepting) the check, promises to pay the check at the time the check is presented.

A **certified check** is a check that has been *accepted* in writing by the bank on which it is drawn [UCC 3–409(d)]. When a drawee bank *certifies* (accepts) a check, it immediately charges the drawer's account with the amount of the check and transfers those funds to its own certified check account. In effect, the bank is agreeing in advance to accept that check when it is presented for payment and to make payment from those funds reserved in the certified check account. Essentially, certification prevents the bank from denying liability. It is a promise that sufficient funds are on deposit *and have been set aside* to cover the check.

A drawee bank is not obligated to certify a check, and failure to do so is not a dishonor of the check [UCC 3–409(d)]. If a bank does certify a check, however, the bank should write on the check the amount that it will pay. If the certification does

EXHIBIT 24–2 A TRAVELER'S CHECK

not state an amount, and the amount is later increased and the instrument negotiated to a holder in due course (HDC), the obligation of the certifying bank is the amount of the instrument when it was taken by the HDC [UCC 3–413(b)].

Certification may be requested by a holder (to ensure that the check will not be dishonored for insufficient funds) or by the drawer. In either circumstance, once the check is certified, the drawer and any prior indorsers are completely discharged from liability [UCC 3–414(c), 3–415(d)].

The Bank-Customer Relationship

The bank-customer relationship begins when the customer opens a checking account and deposits funds that the bank will use to pay for checks written by the customer. Essentially, three types of relationships come into being, as discussed next.

CREDITOR-DEBTOR RELATIONSHIP

A creditor-debtor relationship is created between a customer and a bank when, for example, the customer makes cash deposits into a checking account. When a customer makes a deposit, the customer becomes a creditor, and the bank a debtor, for the amount deposited.

> **.on the Web** Cornell University's Legal Information Institute provides an overview of banking, as well as a "menu of sources" of federal and state statutes and court decisions relating to banking transactions. To access this information, go to
>
> **http://www.law.cornell.edu/topics/banking.html**.

AGENCY RELATIONSHIP

An agency relationship also arises between the customer and the bank when the customer writes a check on his or her account. In effect, the customer is ordering the bank to pay the amount specified on the check to the holder when the holder presents the check to the bank for payment. In this situation, the bank becomes the customer's agent and is obligated to honor the customer's request. Similarly, if the customer deposits a check into her or his account, the bank, as the customer's agent, is obligated to collect payment on the check from the bank on which the check was drawn. To transfer checkbook funds among different banks, each bank acts as the agent of collection for its customer [UCC 4–201(a)].

CONTRACTUAL RELATIONSHIP

Whenever a bank-customer relationship is established, certain contractual rights and duties arise. The specific rights and duties of the bank and its customer depend on the nature of the transaction. The respective rights and duties of banks and their customers are discussed in detail in the following pages.

Bank's Duty to Honor Checks

When a banking institution provides checking services, it agrees to honor the checks written by its customers, with the usual stipulation that the account must have sufficient funds available to pay each check [UCC 4–401(a)]. When a drawee bank *wrongfully* fails to honor a check, it is liable to its customer for damages resulting from its refusal to pay. The UCC does not attempt to specify the theory under which the customer may recover for wrongful dishonor; it merely states that the drawee (bank) is liable.

The customer's agreement with the bank includes a general obligation to keep sufficient funds on deposit to cover all checks written. The customer is liable to the payee or to the holder of a check in a civil suit if a check is dishonored for insufficient funds. If intent to defraud can be proved, the customer can also be subject to criminal prosecution for writing a bad check.

When the bank properly dishonors a check for insufficient funds, it has no liability to the customer. The bank may rightfully refuse payment on a customer's check in other circumstances as well. We look here at the rights and duties of both the bank and its customers in relation to specific situations.

OVERDRAFTS

OVERDRAFT
A check that is paid by the bank when the checking account on which the check is written contains insufficient funds to cover the check.

When the bank receives an item properly payable from its customer's checking account but the account contains insufficient funds to cover the amount of the check, the bank has two options. It can either (1) dishonor the item or (2) pay the item and charge the customer's account, thus creating an **overdraft,** providing that the customer has authorized the payment and the payment does not violate any bank-customer agreement [UCC 4–401(a)].[1] The bank can subtract the difference (plus a service charge) from the customer's next deposit or other customer funds because the check carries with it an enforceable implied promise to reimburse the bank.

A bank can expressly agree with a customer to accept overdrafts through what is sometimes called an "overdraft protection agreement." If such an agreement is formed, any failure of the bank to honor a check because it would create an overdraft breaches this agreement and is treated as wrongful dishonor [UCC 4–402(a)].

When a check "bounces," a holder can resubmit the check, hoping that at a later date sufficient funds will be available to pay it. The holder must notify any indorsers on the check of the first dishonor, however; otherwise, they will be discharged from their signature liability.

POSTDATED CHECKS

A bank may also charge a postdated check against a customer's account, unless the customer notifies the bank, in a timely manner, not to pay the check until the stated date. The notice of postdating must be given in time to allow the bank to act on the

1. With a joint account, the bank cannot hold the nonsigning customer liable for payment of an overdraft unless that person benefited from its proceeds [UCC 4–401(b)].

notice before committing itself to pay on the check. The UCC states that the bank should treat a notice of postdating the same as a stop-payment order—to be discussed shortly. If the bank fails to act on the customer's notice and charges the customer's account before the date on the postdated check, the bank may be liable for any damages incurred by the customer [UCC 4–401(c)].[2]

Stale Checks

STALE CHECK
A check, other than a certified check, that is presented for payment more than six months after its date.

Commercial banking practice regards a check that is presented for payment more than six months from its date as a **stale check.** A bank is not obligated to pay an uncertified check presented more than six months from its date [UCC 4–404]. When receiving a stale check for payment, the bank has the option of paying or not paying the check. The bank may consult the customer before paying the check. If a bank pays a stale check in good faith without consulting the customer, however, the bank has the right to charge the customer's account for the amount of the check.

Stop-Payment Orders

STOP-PAYMENT ORDER
An order by a bank customer to his or her bank not to pay or certify a certain check.

A **stop-payment order** is an order by a customer to his or her bank not to pay or certify a certain check. Only a customer or a person authorized to draw on the account can order the bank not to pay the check when it is presented for payment [UCC 4–403(a)].[3] A customer has no right to stop payment on a check that has been certified or accepted by a bank, however. The customer must issue the stop-payment order within a reasonable time and in a reasonable manner to permit the bank to act on it [UCC 4–403(a)]. Although a stop-payment order can be given orally, usually by phone, it is binding on the bank for only fourteen calendar days unless confirmed in writing.[4] A written stop-payment order (see Exhibit 24–3) or an oral order confirmed in writing is effective for six months, at which time it must be renewed in writing [UCC 4–403(b)].

Bank's Liability for Wrongful Payment If the bank pays the check over the customer's properly instituted stop-payment order, the bank will be obligated to recredit the customer's account—but only for the amount of the actual loss suffered by the drawer because of the wrongful payment [UCC 4–403(c)]. ■ **EXAMPLE 24.2** Toshio Murano orders six bamboo palms from a local nursery at $50 each and gives the nursery a check for $300. Later that day, the nursery tells Murano that it will not deliver the palms as arranged. Murano immediately calls his bank and stops payment on the check. If the bank nonetheless honors the check, the bank will be liable to Murano for the full $300. The result would be different, however, if the nursery had delivered five palms. In that situation, Murano would owe the nursery $250 for the delivered palms, and his actual losses would be only $50. Consequently, the bank would be liable to Murano for only $50. ■

2. Under the UCC, postdating does not affect the negotiability of a check. In the past, instead of treating postdated checks as checks payable on demand, some courts treated them as time drafts. Thus, regardless of whether the customer notified the bank of the postdating, a bank could not charge a customer's account for a postdated check without facing potential liability for the payment of later checks. Under the automated check-collection system now in use, however, a check is usually paid without respect to its date. Thus, today the bank can ignore the postdate on the check (treat it as a demand instrument) unless it has received notice from the customer that the check was postdated.

3. For a deceased customer, any person claiming a legitimate interest in the account may issue a stop-payment order [UCC 4–405].

4. Some states do not recognize oral stop-payment orders; they must be in writing.

EXHIBIT 24–3 A STOP-PAYMENT ORDER

Bank of America

Checking Account
Stop Payment Order

To: Bank of America NT&SA
I want to stop payment on the following check(s).

ACCOUNT NUMBER: ______ – ______

SPECIFIC STOP

*ENTER DOLLAR AMOUNT: ______ *CHECK NUMBER: ______

THE CHECK WAS SIGNED BY: ______

THE CHECK IS PAYABLE TO: ______

THE REASON FOR THIS STOP PAYMENT IS: ______

STOP RANGE (Use for lost or stolen check(s) only.)

DOLLAR AMOUNT: 000

*ENTER STARTING CHECK NUMBER: ______ *END CHECK NUMBER: ______

THE REASON FOR THIS STOP PAYMENT IS: ______

BANK USE ONLY

TRANCODE:

☐ 21—ENTER STOP PAYMENT (SEE OTHER SIDE TO REMOVE)

NON READS: ______
UNPROC. STMT HIST: ______
PRIOR STMT CYCLE: ______
HOLDS ON COOLS: ______
REJECTED CHKS: ______
LARGE ITEMS: ______
FEE COLLECTED: ______
DATE ACCEPTED: ______
TIME ACCEPTED: ______

I agree that this order (1) is effective only if the above check(s) has (have) not yet been cashed or paid against my account, (2) will end six months from the date it is delivered to you unless I renew it in writing, and (3) is not valid if the check(s) was (were) accepted on the strength of my Bank of America courtesy-check guarantee card by a merchant participating in that program. I also agree (1) to notify you immediately to cancel this order if the reason for the stop payment no longer exists or (2) that closing the account on which the check(s) is (are) drawn automatically cancels this order.

IF ANOTHER BRANCH OF THIS BANK OR ANOTHER PERSON OR ENTITY BECOMES A "HOLDER IN DUE COURSE" OF THE ABOVE CHECK, I UNDERSTAND THAT PAYMENT MAY BE ENFORCED AGINST THE CHECK'S MAKER (SIGNER).

*I CERTIFY THE AMOUNT AND CHECK NUMBER(S) ABOVE ARE CORRECT.

☐ I have written a replacement check (number and date of check).

(Optional—please circle one: Mr., Ms., Mrs., Miss) CUSTOMER'S SIGNATURE **X** ______ DATE ______

Customer's Liability for Wrongful Stop-Payment Order A stop-payment order has its risks for a customer. The customer-drawer must have a *valid legal ground* for issuing such an order; otherwise, the holder can sue the drawer for payment. Moreover, defenses sufficient to refuse payment against a payee may not be valid grounds to prevent payment against a subsequent holder in due course [UCC 3–305, 3–306]. A person who wrongfully stops payment on a check not only will be liable to the payee for the amount of the check but also may be liable for consequential damages incurred by the payee as a result of the wrongful stop-payment order. See the *Application* feature at the end of this chapter for guidelines on how and when to use stop-payment orders.

Death or Incompetence of a Customer

Neither the death nor the incompetence of a customer revokes a bank's authority to pay an item until the bank is informed of the situation and has had reasonable time to act on the notice. Thus, if, at the time a check is issued or its collection has been undertaken, a bank does not know of an adjudication of incompetence against the customer who wrote the check, the bank can pay the item without incurring liability [UCC 4–405]. Even when a bank knows of the death of its customer, for ten days after the *date of death,* it can pay or certify checks drawn on or before the date of death. An exception to this rule is made if a person claiming an interest in that account, such as an heir, orders the bank to stop payment. Without this provision, banks would constantly be required to verify the continued life and competence of their drawers.

Checks Bearing Forged Drawers' Signatures

When a bank pays a check on which the drawer's signature is forged, generally the bank is liable. A bank may be able to recover at least some of the loss, however, from the customer (if the customer's negligence contributed to the making of the forgery), from the forger of the check (if he or she can be found), or from the holder who presented the check for payment (if the holder knew that the signature was forged).

The General Rule A forged signature on a check has no legal effect as the signature of a drawer [UCC 3–403(a)]. For this reason, banks require signature cards from each customer who opens a checking account. Signature cards allow the bank to verify whether the signatures on their customers' checks are genuine. The general rule is that the bank must recredit the customer's account when it pays a check with a forged signature. (Note that banks today normally verify signatures only on checks that exceed a certain threshold, such as $1,000, $2,500, or some higher amount. Even though a bank sometimes incurs liability costs when it has paid forged checks, the costs involved in verifying every check's signature would be much higher.)

Customer Negligence When the customer's negligence substantially contributes to the forgery, the bank normally will not be obligated to recredit the customer's account for the amount of the check [UCC 3–406].[5] The customer's liability may be reduced, however, by the amount of loss caused by negligence on the part of the bank (or other "person") paying the instrument or taking it for value if the negligence substantially contributed to the loss [UCC 3–406(b)].

■ EXAMPLE 24.3 Gemco Corporation uses special check-writing equipment to write its payroll and business checks. Gemco discovers that one of its employees used the equipment to write himself a check for $10,000 and that the bank subsequently honored it. Gemco asks the bank to recredit $10,000 to its account for improperly paying the forged check. If the bank can show that Gemco failed to take reasonable care in controlling access to the check-writing equipment, the bank will not be required to recredit Gemco's account for the amount of the forged check. If Gemco can show that negligence on the part of the bank contributed substantially to the loss, however, then Gemco's liability may be reduced proportionately. ■

In the following case, a bank that had paid a forged check claimed that the account holder's negligence had contributed to the forgery. Specifically, the bank alleged that the account holder had failed to exercise ordinary care to prevent his wife from forging a check on the account.

5. Note that banks can shift some of the risk of forged checks to the customer by contract, such as the risk of forged signatures created by the use of facsimile or other nonmanual signature devices.

CASE 24.1 Nesper v. Bank of America

Court of Appeals of Ohio, Sixth District, Ottawa County, 2004. __ Ohio App.3d __, __ N.E.2d __.

BACKGROUND AND FACTS Robert Nesper knew his wife, Patricia Nesper, had engaged in financial misconduct both before and during their marriage. The misconduct included forging Robert's name on applications for credit cards and a contract to buy a vehicle. The couple continued to live together, but Robert kept a bank account solely in his name at Bank of America. He kept the unused checks for the account hidden in their house in a room that could be locked, although the room was not kept locked all of the time. In early 2002, he became aware that Patricia had forged his name to the account's check number 275 in the amount of $2,000. Robert filed a suit in an Ohio state court against the bank, seeking the return of the $2,000 to his account. Robert argued that banks have a responsibility to refuse to honor forged checks, regardless of the marital status of the forger. The court ruled in Robert's favor. The bank appealed to a state intermediate appellate court.

CASE 24.1—Continued

IN THE WORDS OF THE COURT . . .
KNEPPER, J. [Judge]

* * * *

* * * Bank of America argues that the trial court ignored evidence of appellee's [Robert's] negligence, as well as evidence that appellee ratified his wife's forgery. Bank of America further argues that * * * allowing appellee to recover in this case would cause banks to be reluctant to cash any checks between a husband and wife "because of the potential problem of abuse."

* * * *

* * * [A] check that bears a forged drawer's signature is not properly payable and, if the bank pays a check under such circumstances, the bank is generally liable to its customer. Nevertheless, Bank of America seeks to show that appellee should be held responsible for his wife's forgery pursuant to [Revised Code (R.C.)] Section 1303.49 [Ohio's version of UCC 3–406(a)] which states, in relevant part, that:

> (A) A person whose failure to exercise ordinary care substantially contributes to an alteration of an instrument or to the making of a forged signature on an instrument is precluded from asserting the alteration or the forgery against a person who, in good faith, pays the instrument or takes it for value or for collection.
> * * *

* * * *

The relationship between a bank and its customer is based on both statutory and contractual principles. The definition of "ordinary care" on the part of a bank is statutorily defined in R.C. Section 1303.01(A)(9) [UCC 3–103(7)] as the observance of "reasonable commercial standards that are prevailing in the area * * * ." In contrast, "ordinary care" on the part of a bank's customer, while not statutorily defined, has been described by Ohio courts as the duty of the customer to perform his or her obligations to the bank with care, skill, reasonable expedience, and faithfulness * * * . This duty has been applied in cases where a party who has notice that his signature has been forged in the past is negligent in failing to prevent further forgeries by the same person.

In addition to its statutory remedies, Bank of America seeks to invoke the common-law defense of ratification. *Ratification occurs when a party, by his conduct, affirms a prior act which did not bind him but which was done or professedly done on his account whereby the act, * * * is given effect as if it was originally authorized by him.* Affirmance can be established by showing that the party had knowledge of the facts and manifested his intent to approve the transaction. [Emphasis added.]

As to the issue of ordinary care, the record demonstrates that appellee knew his wife was capable of financial misconduct, including forgery. The record also shows that appellee attempted to keep his wife from having access to his checkbooks by keeping them hidden in a room that was usually, although not always, locked. * * * Mrs. Nesper refused to respond when she was confronted * * * about the forgery. The record contains no evidence as to how Mrs. Nesper actually obtained the blank checks.

As to the issue of ratification, Bank of America directs our attention to that portion of the record which shows that appellee unsuccessfully attempted to discuss the forgery with his wife. The rest of the record shows that appellee notified [the bank] and the police of his wife's actions, filled out police reports, and filed the complaint herein seeking return of his funds. * * *

(Continued)

its image or description is presented for payment under an electronic presentment agreement [UCC 4–110].[12]

A person who encodes information on an item warrants to any subsequent bank or payor that the encoded information is correct [UCC 4–209]. This is also true for a person who retains an item while transmitting its image or information describing it as presentation for payment. This person warrants that the retention and presentment of the item comply with the electronic presentment agreement.

Regulation CC provides that a returned check must be encoded with the routing number of the depositary bank, the amount of the check, and other information and adds that this "does not affect a paying bank's responsibility to return a check within the deadlines required by the U.C.C." Under UCC 4–301(d)(2), an item is returned "when it is sent or delivered to the bank's customer or transferor or pursuant to his [or her] instructions." The question in the following case was whether an item that was not correctly encoded could be considered properly returned by its midnight deadline.

12. This section of the UCC assumes that no bank will participate in an electronic presentment program without an agreement. See Comment 2 to UCC 4–110. For example, two banks that frequently do business with each other might enter an agreement allowing the depositary bank to retain the physical check and send an electronic image to the other bank for presentment.

CASE 24.3 NBT Bank, N.A. v. First National Community Bank

United States Court of Appeals,
Third Circuit, 2004.
393 F.3d 404.

BACKGROUND AND FACTS Human Services Consultants, Inc. (HSC), had a checking account at First National Community Bank (FNCB) in Pennsylvania. A related firm, Human Services Consultants Management, Inc., had two checking accounts at NBT Bank, N.A., in New York, one of which was under the name PA Health. On March 8, 2001, PA Health presented a check in the amount of $706,000 for deposit in its NBT account. The check was drawn on HSC's account at FNCB. NBT credited $706,000 to PA Health's account as a provisional credit and transmitted the check to the Federal Reserve Bank of Philadelphia for presentment to FNCB, which received the check on March 12. The next morning, FNCB dishonored the check because HSC's account contained insufficient funds, encoded the check for return to NBT, and sent it back to the Federal Reserve bank before 11:59 P.M. Later, on the morning of March 14, FNCB phoned NBT and also sent a letter by fax, informing it of the item's dishonor. The check's encoding was in error, however, and it was wrongly routed to another bank; as a result, NBT did not receive the physical check until March 16. Ultimately, the check was revealed to be part of a fraudulent scheme that caused NBT more than $1 million in losses. NBT filed a suit in a federal district court against FNCB, asserting that FNCB's encoding error rendered FNCB's "return" of the check ineffective. The court granted FNCB's motion for summary judgment, and NBT appealed.

IN THE WORDS OF THE COURT . . .

SMITH, Circuit Judge.

* * * *

* * * Federal law forms part of the legal framework within which check-processing activities take place. Of particular relevance to this appeal are the 1988 regulations adopted by the Federal Reserve implementing the Expedited Funds Availability Act. These regulations, referred to collectively as "Regulation CC," complement but do not necessarily replace the requirements of Article 4 of the UCC.

* * * *

* * * Regulation CC indisputably binds the parties, pursuant to both its own terms, as well as 13 Pennsylvania Consolidated Statutes Annotated Section 4103

CASE 24.3—Continued

[Pennsylvania's version of UCC 4-103], which indicates that "Federal Reserve regulations" are to be treated as agreements that may vary the terms of the UCC. * * *

Because Regulation CC * * * is binding on the parties, and because Regulation CC is the source of encoding requirement invoked by NBT, the extend of FNCB's liability for its encoding error must be measured by the standards set forth in Regulation CC. Regulation CC states that a bank that fails to exercise ordinary care in complying with the [encoding] provisions of * * * Regulation CC * * * "may be liable" to the depository bank. Then, in broad, unrestricted language, Regulation CC states:

> The measure of damages for failure to exercise ordinary care is the amount of the loss incurred, up to the amount of the check, reduced by the amount of the loss that the [plaintiff bank] would have incurred even if the [defendant] bank had exercised ordinary care.

This provision does not provide an exception to this standard for measuring damages in instances where noncompliance with Regulation CC is alleged to have resulted in noncompliance with the UCC's midnight deadline rule. Here, the parties have stipulated that NBT suffered no loss as a result of FNCB's encoding error. Thus, under the plain language of Regulation CC, NBT may not recover from FNCB for the amount of the Disputed Check.

DECISION AND REMEDY The U.S. Court of Appeals for the Third Circuit affirmed the lower court's judgment. Under Regulation CC, the amount of damages for failure to exercise ordinary care in complying with the encoding provisions is "reduced by the amount of the loss that the [plaintiff] would have incurred even if the [defendant] bank had exercised ordinary care." Here, the parties agreed that NBT suffered no loss as a result of FNCB's encoding error. Thus, NBT could not recover the amount of the check from FNCB.

FOR CRITICAL ANALYSIS—Social Consideration *How might the result in this case have been different if NBT had committed the encoding error and FNCB had suffered the loss?*

Electronic Fund Transfers

ELECTRONIC FUND TRANSFER (EFT) A transfer of funds through the use of an electronic terminal, a telephone, a computer, or magnetic tape.

The application of computer technology to banking, in the form of electronic fund transfer systems, has helped to relieve banking institutions of the burden of having to move mountains of paperwork to process fund transfers. An **electronic fund transfer (EFT)** is a transfer of funds through the use of an electronic terminal, a telephone, a computer, or magnetic tape. The law governing EFTs depends on the type of transfer involved. Consumer fund transfers are governed by the Electronic Fund Transfer Act (EFTA) of 1978.[13] Commercial fund transfers are governed by Article 4A of the UCC.

The benefits of electronic banking are obvious. Automatic payments, direct deposits, and other fund transfers are now made electronically; no physical transfers of cash, checks, or other negotiable instruments are involved.

Not surprisingly, though, electronic banking also poses difficulties on occasion. It is difficult to issue stop-payment orders with electronic banking. Also, fewer records are available to prove or disprove that a transaction took place. The possibilities for tampering with a person's private banking information have increased. Finally, customers can no longer rely on having time between the writing of a check and its deduction from an account (float time).

13. 15 U.S.C. Sections 1693–1693r. The EFTA amended Title IX of the Consumer Credit Protection Act.

TYPES OF EFT SYSTEMS

Most banks today offer EFT services to their customers. The four most common types of EFT systems used by bank customers are listed below.

1. *Automated teller machines (ATMs)*—Machines connected online to the bank's computers. Customers insert a plastic card issued by the bank and key in a personal identification number (PIN) to access their accounts and conduct banking transactions.
2. *Point-of-sale systems*—Online terminals that allow consumers to transfer funds to merchants to pay for purchases using a debit card.
3. *Direct deposits and withdrawals*—Customers can authorize the bank to allow another party—such as the government or an employer—to make direct deposits into their accounts. Similarly, customers can request the bank to make automatic payments to a third party at regular, recurrent intervals from the customer's funds (insurance premiums or loan payments, for example).
4. *Pay-by-Internet systems*—Some financial institutions permit their customers to access the institution's computer system via the Internet and direct a transfer of funds between accounts or pay a particular bill, such as a utility bill, for example.

CONSUMER FUND TRANSFERS

The Electronic Fund Transfer Act (EFTA) provides a basic framework for the rights, liabilities, and responsibilities of users of EFT systems. Additionally, the act gave the Federal Reserve Board authority to issue rules and regulations to help implement the act's provisions. The Federal Reserve Board's implemental regulation is called **Regulation E.**

REGULATION E
A set of rules issued by the Federal Reserve System's Board of Governors to protect users of elecronic fund transfer systems.

The EFTA governs financial institutions that offer electronic fund transfers involving consumer accounts. The types of accounts covered include checking accounts, savings accounts, and any other asset accounts established for personal, family, or household purposes. Note that telephone transfers are covered by the EFTA only if they are made in accordance with a prearranged plan under which periodic or recurring transfers are contemplated.[14] In the subsections that follow, we look closely at some of the act's provisions concerning consumers' rights and responsibilities under the act, including those related to unauthorized transfers and error resolution.

Consumers' Rights and Responsibilities under the EFTA The EFTA is essentially a disclosure law benefiting consumers. The act requires financial institutions to inform consumers of their rights and responsibilities, including those listed here, with respect to EFT systems.

1. If a customer's debit card is lost or stolen and used without his or her permission, the customer may be required to pay no more than $50. The customer, however, must notify the bank of the loss or theft within two days of learning about it. Otherwise, the liability increases to $500. The customer may be liable for more than $500 if he or she does not report the unauthorized use within sixty days after it appears on the customer's statement. (If a customer voluntarily gives her or his debit card to another, who then uses it improperly, the protections just mentioned do not apply.)

14. *Kashanchi v. Texas Commerce Medical Bank, N.A.,* 703 F.2d 936 (5th Cir. 1983).

2. The customer must discover any error on the monthly statement within sixty days and must notify the bank. The bank then has ten days to investigate and must report its conclusions to the customer in writing. If the bank takes longer than ten days, it must return the disputed amount of money to the customer's account until it finds the error. If there is no error, the customer has to give the money back to the bank.
3. The bank must furnish receipts for transactions made through computer terminals, but it is not obligated to do so for telephone transfers.
4. The bank must provide a monthly statement for every month in which there is an electronic transfer of funds. Otherwise, the bank must provide statements every quarter. The statement must show the amount and date of the transfer, the names of the retailers or other third parties involved, the location or identification of the terminal, and the fees. Additionally, the statement must give an address and a phone number for inquiries and error notices.
5. Any authorized prepayment for utility bills and insurance premiums can be stopped three days before the scheduled transfer.

BE CAREFUL The EFTA does not provide for the reversal of an electronic transfer of funds once it has occurred.

Unauthorized Electronic Fund Transfers Unauthorized electronic fund transfers are one of the hazards of electronic banking. A paper check leaves visible evidence of a transaction, and a customer can easily detect a forgery or an alteration on a check with ordinary vigilance. Evidence of an electronic transfer, however, is often only an entry in a computer printout of the various debits and credits made to a particular account during a specified time period.

Because of the vulnerability of EFT systems to fraudulent activities, the EFTA of 1978 clearly defined what constitutes an unauthorized transfer. Under the act, a transfer is unauthorized if (1) it is initiated by a person other than the consumer who has no actual authority to initiate the transfer; (2) the consumer receives no benefit from it; and (3) the consumer did not furnish the person "with the card, code, or other means of access" to her or his account. Unauthorized access to an EFT system constitutes a federal felony, and those convicted may be sentenced to a fine of up to $10,000 and up to ten years' imprisonment.

Violations and Damages Banks must strictly comply with the terms of the EFTA, or they will be held liable. For a bank's violation of the EFTA, a consumer may recover both actual damages (including attorneys' fees and costs) and punitive damages of not less than $100 and not more than $1,000. (Unlike actual damages, punitive damages are assessed to punish a defendant or to set an example for similar wrongdoers.) Failure to investigate an error in good faith makes the bank liable for treble damages (three times the amount of damages). Even when a customer has sustained no actual damage, the bank may be liable for legal costs and punitive damages if it fails to follow the proper procedures outlined by the EFTA in regard to error resolution.

Commercial Transfers

NOTE If any part of an electronic fund transfer is covered by the EFTA, the entire transfer is excluded from UCC Article 4A.

Funds are also transferred electronically "by wire" between commercial parties. In fact, the dollar volume of payments by wire transfer is more than $1 trillion a day—an amount that far exceeds the dollar volume of payments made by other means. The two major wire payment systems are the Federal Reserve's wire transfer network (Fedwire) and the New York Clearing House Interbank Payments Systems (CHIPS).

Commercial wire transfers are governed by Article 4A of the UCC, which has been adopted by most states. The following example illustrates the type of fund transfer covered by Article 4A. ■ EXAMPLE 24.10 Jellux, Inc., owes $5 million to Perot Corporation. Instead of sending Perot a check or some other instrument that would enable Perot to obtain payment, Jellux tells its bank, East Bank, to credit $5 million to Perot's account in West Bank. East Bank debits Jellux's East Bank account and wires $5 million to Perot's West Bank account. In more complex transactions, additional banks would be involved. ■

In these and similar circumstances, ordinarily a financial institution's instruction is transmitted electronically. Any means may be used, however, including first-class mail. To reflect this fact, Article 4A uses the term *funds transfer* rather than wire transfer to describe the overall payment transaction. The full text of Article 4A is included in Appendix C, following Article 4 of the UCC.

E-Money and Online Banking

New forms of electronic payments (e-payments) have the potential to replace *physical* cash—coins and paper currency—with *virtual* cash in the form of electronic impulses. This is the unique promise of **digital cash,** which consists of funds stored on microchips and other computer devices. Online banking has also become a reality in today's world. In a few minutes, anybody with the proper software can access his or her account, transfer money, write "checks," pay bills, monitor investments, and often even buy and sell stocks.

DIGITAL CASH
Funds contained on computer software, in the form of secure programs stored on microchips and other computer devices.

E-MONEY
Prepaid funds recorded on a computer or a card (such as a smart card or a stored-value card).

STORED-VALUE CARD
A card bearing magnetic strips that hold magnetically encoded data, providing access to stored funds.

SMART CARD
A card containing a microprocessor that permits storage of funds via security programming, can communicate with other computers, and does not require online authorization for fund transfers.

Various forms of electronic money, or **e-money,** are emerging. The simplest kind of e-money system uses **stored-value cards.** These are plastic cards embossed with magnetic strips containing magnetically encoded data. A person can use a stored-value card to purchase specific goods and services offered by the card issuer. For example, university libraries typically have copy machines that students operate by inserting a stored-value card. Each time a student makes copies, the machine deducts the per-copy fee from the card.

Another form of e-money is the smart card. **Smart cards** are plastic cards containing computer microchips that can hold more information than a magnetic strip. A smart card carries and processes security programming. This capability gives smart cards a technical advantage over stored-value cards. The microprocessors on smart cards can also authenticate the validity of transactions. Retailers can program electronic cash registers to confirm the authenticity of a smart card by examining a unique digital signature stored on its microchip. (Digital signatures were discussed in Chapter 17.)

.on the Web You can find a series of articles on smart cards at the following Web site: **http://users.aol.com/pjsmart/index.htm**.

ONLINE BANKING SERVICES

Most online bank customers use three kinds of services. One of the most popular is bill consolidation and payment. Another is transferring funds among accounts. These online services are now offered via the Internet as well as by phone. The third is applying for loans, which many banks permit customers to do via the Internet. Customers typically have to appear in person to finalize the terms of a loan.

Two important banking activities generally are not yet available online: depositing and withdrawing funds. With smart cards, people could transfer funds on the Internet, thereby effectively transforming their personal computers into ATMs. Many observers believe that online banking is the way to introduce people to e-money and smart cards.

Since the late 1990s, several banks have operated exclusively on the Internet. These "virtual banks" have no physical branch offices. Because few people are equipped to send funds to virtual banks via smart-card technology, the virtual banks have accepted deposits through physical delivery systems, such as the U.S. Postal Service or FedEx.

Regulatory Compliance

Banks have an interest in seeing the widespread use of online banking because of its significant potential for reducing costs and thus increasing profits. As in other areas of cyberspace, however, determining how laws apply to online banking activities can be difficult.

The Home Mortgage Disclosure Act[15] and the Community Reinvestment Act (CRA) of 1977,[16] for example, require a bank to define its market area and also to provide information to regulators about its deposits and loans. Under the CRA, banks establish market areas in communities contiguous to their branch offices. The banks map these areas, using boundaries defined by counties or standard metropolitan areas, and annually review the maps. The purpose of these requirements is to prevent discrimination in lending practices.

But how does a successful "cyberbank" delineate its community? If, for instance, Bank of Internet becomes a tremendous success, does it really have a physical community? Will regulators allow a written description of a cybercommunity for Internet customers? Such regulatory issues are new, challenging, and certain to become more complicated as Internet banking widens its scope internationally.

Privacy Protection

At the present time, it is not clear which, if any, laws apply to the security of e-money payment information and e-money issuers' financial records. This is partly because it is not clear whether e-money issuers fit within the traditional definition of a financial institution.

E-Money Payment Information The Federal Reserve has decided not to impose Regulation E, which governs certain electronic fund transfers, on e-money transactions. Federal laws prohibiting unauthorized access to electronic communications might apply, however. For example, the Electronic Communications Privacy Act of 1986[17] prohibits any person from knowingly divulging to any other person the contents of an electronic communication while that communication is in transmission or in electronic storage.

E-Money Issuers' Financial Records Under the Right to Financial Privacy Act of 1978,[18] before a financial institution may give financial information about you to a federal agency, you must explicitly consent. If you do not, a federal agency wishing to obtain your financial records must obtain a warrant. A digital cash issuer may be subject to this act if that issuer is deemed to be (1) a bank by virtue of its holding customer funds or (2) any entity that issues a physical card similar to a credit or debit card.

15. 12 U.S.C. Sections 2801–2810.
16. 12 U.S.C. Sections 2901–2908.
17. 18 U.S.C. Sections 2510–2521.
18. 12 U.S.C. Sections 3401 *et seq.*

A consumer uses a smart card to pay for lunch at a restaurant. Can the financial institution that issued the card disclose the consumer's personal information to a third party without the consumer's consent? Why or why not? (AP Photo/Eric Risberg)

.on the Web You can read the provisions of the Uniform Money Services Act and find out which states have adopted it by going to the Web site of the National Conference of Commissioners on Uniform State Laws at

http://www.nccusl.org,

and selecting the "Money Services Act" under the "Final Acts and Legislation" link.

Consumer Financial Data In 1999, Congress passed the Financial Services Modernization Act,[19] also known as the Gramm-Leach-Bliley Act, in an attempt to delineate how financial institutions can treat customer data. In general, the act and its rules[20] place restrictions and obligations on financial institutions to protect consumer data and privacy. Every financial institution must provide its customers with information on its privacy policies and practices. No financial institution can disclose nonpublic personal information about a consumer to an unaffiliated third party unless the act's disclosure and opt-out requirements are met.

The Uniform Money Services Act

Over the past few years, many states have enacted various regulations that apply to money services in a rather haphazard fashion. At the same time, e-money services that operate on the Internet—which, of course, cuts across jurisdictional lines—have been asking that these regulations be made more predictable.

In 2001, the National Conference of Commissioners on Uniform State Laws recommended to state legislatures a new law that would subject all money services businesses to the same regulations that apply to other, traditional financial service businesses. This law, which is known as the Uniform Money Services Act (UMSA), has been adopted in a few states.[21]

Traditional Money Services

Money service businesses (MSBs) have not been subject to regulation to the same extent as other financial service businesses. Unlike banks, MSBs do not accept deposits. They do, however, issue money orders, traveler's checks, and stored-value cards; exchange foreign currency; and cash checks. Immigrants often use these businesses to send money to their relatives in other countries. Because MSBs often do not have continuing relationships with their customers, their customers have sometimes evaded federal law with respect to large currency transactions or used the services to launder money (see Chapter 6). This has been particularly true with respect to financing terrorist activities.

The UMSA applies to persons engaged in money transmission, check cashing, or currency exchange. The uniform act requires an MSB involved in these activities to obtain a license from a state, to be examined by state officials, to report on its activities to the state, and to comply with certain record-keeping requirements. Each of these subjects has its provisions and exceptions. Safety and soundness measures, such as annual examinations, surety bonds (to guarantee financial soundness), and permissible investments, are also mandated by the act.

Internet-Based Money Services

Under the UMSA, Internet-based money services, and other types of e-money services, would be treated the same as other money services.[22] The drafters of the UMSA ensured that it would cover these services by referring to *monetary value*

19. 12 U.S.C. Sections 24a, 248b, 1820a, 1828b, 1831v–1831y, 1848a, 2908, 4809; 15 U.S.C. Sections 80b-10a, 6701, 6711–6717, 6731–6735, 6751–6766, 6781, 6801–6809, 6821–6827, 6901–6910; and others.

20. 12 C.F.R. Part 40.

21. To date, the UMSA has been adopted in Iowa, Vermont, and Washington State, and adoption legislation is currently pending in the U.S. Virgin Islands.

22. The UMSA does not apply to state governments, the federal government, securities dealers, banks, businesses that incidentally transport currency and instruments in the normal course of business, payday loan businesses, and others [UMSA 1–103].

instead of simply *money* [UMSA 1–102(c)(11)].

Internet-based monetary value systems subject to the new law may include:

1. *E-money and Internet payment mechanisms*—Money, or its substitute, that is stored as data on a chip or a personal computer so that it can be transferred over the Internet or an intranet.
2. *Internet scrip*—Monetary value that may be exchanged over the Internet but can also be redeemed for cash.
3. *Stored-value products*—Smart cards, prepaid cards, or value-added cards [UMSA 1–102(c)(21)].

REVIEWING CHECKS, THE BANKING SYSTEM, AND E-MONEY

RPM Pizza, Inc., issued a $96,000 check to Systems Marketing for an advertising campaign. A few days later, RPM decided not to go through with the deal and placed a written stop-payment order on the check. RPM and Systems had no further contact for many months. Three weeks after the stop-payment order expired, however, Toby Rierson, an employee at Systems, cashed the check. Bank One Cambridge, RPM's bank, paid the check with funds from RPM's account. Because of the amount of the check, and because the check was more than six months old (stale), the signature on the check should have been specially verified according to standard banking procedures and Bank One's own policies, but it was not. RPM filed a suit in a federal district court against Bank One to recover the amount of the check. Using the information presented in the chapter, answer the following questions.

1. How long is a written stop-payment order effective? What else could RPM have done to prevent this check from being cashed?
2. What would happen if it turned out that RPM did not have a legitimate reason for stopping payment on the check?
3. What are a bank's obligations with respect to stale checks? Should Bank One have contacted RPM before paying the check? Why or why not?
4. RPM claimed that Bank One violated its duty to act with ordinary care when it failed to verify the signature on the check. Do you agree? Why or why not?
5. Suppose that Toby Rierson, the employee at Systems who cashed the check, had altered the face amount of the check from $96,000 to $196,000 and Bank One had cashed it. How might this affect the outcome of the case? Which party normally would be responsible for the $100,000 difference (Bank One, RPM, or Systems)?

APPLICATION How to Use Stop-Payment Orders*

For a variety of reasons, a drawer should not misuse stop-payment orders. We look at some of those reasons here.

MONETARY COSTS AND RISKS

One reason is monetary: banks usually charge between $15 and $25 for a stop-payment order, so stopping payment is not cost-effective for a check written for a small amount. Another reason is the risk attached to the issuing of a stop-payment order for any drawer-customer. The bank is entitled to take a reasonable amount of time to put your stop-payment order into effect before it has liability for improper payment. Hence, the payee or another holder may be able to cash the check despite your stop-payment order if he or she acts quickly. Indeed, you could be writing out a stop-payment order in the bank lobby while the

* This *Application* is not meant to substitute for the services of an attorney who is licensed to practice law in your state.

(Continued)

APPLICATION How to Use Stop-Payment Orders—Continued

payee or holder cashes the check in the drive-in facility outside. In addition, even if a bank pays over a proper stop-payment order, the bank will be liable to the drawer-customer only for the amount of loss the drawer suffers from the improper payment.

When You Can Stop Payment

Remember that, to avoid liability, a drawer must have a legal reason for issuing a stop-payment order. You cannot stop payment on a check simply because you have had a change of heart about the wisdom of your purchase. Generally, you can safely stop payment if you clearly did not get what you paid for or were fraudulently induced to make a purchase. You can also stop payment if a "cooling-off" law governs the transaction—that is, if you legally have a few days in which to change your mind about a purchase. Any wrongful stop order subjects the *drawer* to liability to the payee or a holder, and this liability may include special damages that resulted from the order. When all is considered, it may be unwise to order a stop payment hastily on a check because of a minor dispute with the payee.

Checklist for Stop-Payment Orders

1. Compare the stop-payment fee with the disputed sum to make sure it is worthwhile to issue a stop-payment order.
2. Make sure that your bank will honor your stop-payment order before the payee cashes the check.
3. Make sure that you have a legal reason for issuing the stop-payment order.

KEY TERMS

cashier's check 602
certified check 603
check 602
clearinghouse 620
collecting bank 617
depositary bank 617
digital cash 626
electronic fund transfer (EFT) 623
e-money 626
Federal Reserve System 620
intermediary bank 617
overdraft 605
payor bank 617
Regulation E 624
smart card 626
stale check 606
stop-payment order 606
stored-value card 626
traveler's check 603

CHAPTER SUMMARY Checks, the Banking System, and E-Money

Checks (See pages 602–604.)	1. *Cashier's check*—A check drawn by a bank on itself (the bank is both the drawer and the drawee) and purchased by a customer. In effect, the bank lends its credit to the purchaser of the check, thus making the funds available for immediate use in banking circles. 2. *Traveler's check*—An instrument on which a financial institution is both the drawer and the drawee. The purchaser must provide his or her signature as a countersignature for a traveler's check to become a negotiable instrument. 3. *Certified check*—A check for which the drawee bank certifies in writing that it will set aside funds in the drawer's account to ensure payment of the check on presentation. On certification, the drawer and all prior indorsers are completely discharged from liability on the check.
The Bank-Customer Relationship (See pages 604–605.)	1. *Creditor-debtor relationship*—The bank and its customer have a creditor-debtor relationship (the bank is the debtor because it holds the customer's funds on deposit).

CHAPTER SUMMARY Checks, the Banking System, and E-Money—Continued

The Bank-Customer Relationship—Continued	2. *Agency relationship*—Because a bank must act in accordance with the customer's orders in regard to the customer's deposited money, an agency relationship also arises—the bank is the agent for the customer, who is the principal. 3. *Contractual relationship*—The bank's relationship with its customer is also contractual; both the bank and the customer assume certain contractual duties when a customer opens a bank account.
Bank's Duty to Honor Checks (See pages 605–615.)	Generally, a bank has a duty to honor its customers' checks, provided that the customers have sufficient funds on deposit to cover the checks [UCC 4–401(a)]. The bank is liable to its customers for actual damages proved to be due to wrongful dishonor. The bank's duty to honor its customers' checks is not absolute. See the *Concept Summary* on page 616 for a detailed list of the rights and liabilities of the bank and the customer in various situations, such as overdrafts and forged signatures.
Bank's Duty to Accept Deposits (See pages 615–623.)	A bank has a duty to accept deposits made by its customers into their accounts. Funds represented by checks deposited must be made available to customers according to a schedule mandated by the Expedited Funds Availability Act of 1987 and Regulation CC. A bank also has a duty to collect payment on any checks deposited by its customers. When checks deposited by customers are drawn on other banks, as they often are, the check-collection process comes into play (summarized next). 1. *Definitions of banks*—UCC 4–105 provides the following definitions of banks involved in the collection process: a. Depositary bank—The first bank to accept a check for payment. b. Payor bank—The bank on which a check is drawn. c. Collecting bank—Any bank except the payor bank that handles a check during the collection process. d. Intermediary bank—Any bank except the payor bank or the depositary bank to which an item is transferred in the course of the collection process. 2. *Check collection between customers of the same bank*—A check payable by the depositary bank that receives it is an "on-us item"; if the bank does not dishonor the check by the opening of the second banking day following its receipt, the check is considered paid [UCC 4–215(e)(2)]. 3. *Check collection between customers of different banks*—Each bank in the collection process must pass the check on to the next appropriate bank before midnight of the next banking day following its receipt [UCC 4–108, 4–202(b), 4–302]. 4. *How the Federal Reserve System clears checks*—The Federal Reserve System facilitates the check-clearing process by serving as a clearinghouse for checks. 5. *Electronic check presentment*—When checks are presented electronically, items may be encoded with information (such as the amount of the check) that is read and processed by other banks' computers. In some situations, a check may be retained at its place of deposit, and only its image or information describing it is presented for payment under a Federal Reserve agreement, clearinghouse rule, or other agreement [UCC 4–110].
Electronic Fund Transfers (See pages 623–626.)	1. *Types of EFT systems*— a. Automated teller machines (ATMs). b. Point-of-sale systems.

(Continued)

* * * Lema [also] contends that the provisions of the Deposit Agreement are ambiguous as to whether they were intended to modify the UCC * * * . [W]e conclude that they are not ambiguous, as asserted by Lema. The Deposit Agreement clearly states that unless prohibited by applicable law, the Bank has the right "to charge back to [Lema's] account the amount of any item deposited to [his] account or cashed for [him] which was initially paid by the payor bank and which is later returned to us due to [a] * * * claim of alteration * * * ."

The Agreement also does not terminate the Bank's rights of charge back and reimbursement, as does the UCC, once settlement becomes final and so alters the effect of Section 4–214, as permitted in the UCC. * * *

Moreover, *the Deposit Agreement is in accord with the UCC's policy of shielding transferees of items from the risk of loss created by, for instance, an unauthorized alteration.* Section 4–207(a)(3) of the UCC, for example, provides that, when a bank customer transfers an item and receives consideration, the customer warrants to the transferee that, among other things, "[t]he item has not been altered." Although Lema did not himself transfer the altered check to the Bank, the Deposit Agreement follows the general policy of this Section by providing protection for a transferee, in this case the Bank, that receives an altered item. [Emphasis added.]

* * * *

JUDGMENT * * * AFFIRMED.

DISSENTING OPINION

Dissenting opinion by *HARRELL*, J. [Judge] * * * .

* * * *

* * * I disagree * * * with the conclusion of the Majority that the Deposit Agreement functions to change the legal consequences which otherwise would flow from the provisions of the [UCC]. On the contrary, the plain meaning of the unambiguous language of the [Deposit Agreement] clause in question, clause 4(e), indicates that, far from altering the [UCC] by agreement, the terms used incorporate the [UCC] in its entirety into the Agreement.

* * * *

* * * [W]e must interpret the first clause of 4(e) as reading "Unless prohibited by applicable law [which, by definition, includes the provisions of Articles 3 and 4] * * * ." Because [Article] 4 is the applicable law, and the right of charge-back granted to the Bank contained in clause 4(e) is conditioned upon such charge-back not being prohibited by the applicable law, then if a section of [Article] 4 prohibits such a charge-back, that section of [Article] 4 controls the right of the Bank to charge-back the customer's account. Section 4–214 is such a section, and states in relevant part that "rights to revoke, charge-back, and obtain a refund terminate if and when a settlement for the item received by the bank is or becomes final" * * * , as opposed to provisional.

The question comes down to whether the credit to Lema's account was provisional or final. * * * Bank of America produced no evidence as to whether its release of funds was provisional or final. * * *

* * * Bank of America is the party asserting its rights under the Deposit Agreement and, thus, Bank of America has the burden of establishing its right to do so, which includes producing evidence establishing that the release of funds to Lema's account was provisional, and that final settlement had not occurred prior to the date of the charge-back. * * * Bank of America failed to meet its burden here.

* * * [T]he judgment of the [state intermediate appellate court], in my opinion, should be reversed, and the judgment of the trial court affirmed.

QUESTIONS FOR ANALYSIS

1 Law. How did the majority in this case answer the question stated at the beginning of this feature? What was the reasoning behind the response?

2 Law. Did the dissent appear to disagree with the majority in the application of the principle of freedom of contract? With what part of the majority's holding did the dissent disagree? Why?

3 Ethics. Is it fair for the court to hold Lema liable for the full amount of the altered check even though he did not sign or authorize the check? Why or why not?

4 Economic Dimensions. What is the significance of the holding in this case for a small business?

5 Implications for the Business Owner. Is the power to alter the provisions of the UCC unlimited? If not, what are the limits?

UNIT FIVE

DEBTOR-CREDITOR RELATIONSHIPS

UNIT CONTENTS

CHAPTER 25

Secured Transactions

"Article 9 is clearly the most novel and probably the most important article of the Code . . . and covers the entire range of transactions in which the debts are secured by personal property."

Walter D. Malcolm, 1904–1979
(President of the National Conference of Commissioners on Uniform State Laws, 1963–1966)

CHAPTER OUTLINE

- THE TERMINOLOGY OF SECURED TRANSACTIONS
- CREATING AND PERFECTING A SECURITY INTEREST
- THE SCOPE OF A SECURITY INTEREST
- PRIORITIES
- RIGHTS AND DUTIES OF DEBTORS AND CREDITORS
- DEFAULT

LEARNING OBJECTIVES

After reading this chapter, you should be able to answer the following questions:

1. What is a security interest? Who is a secured party? What is a security agreement? What is a financing statement?
2. What three requirements must be met to create an enforceable security interest?
3. What is the most common method of perfecting a security interest under Article 9?
4. If two secured parties have perfected security interests in the collateral of the debtor, which party has priority to the collateral on the debtor's default?
5. What rights does a secured creditor have on the debtor's default?

SECURED TRANSACTION
Any transaction in which the payment of a debt is guaranteed, or secured, by personal property owned by the debtor or in which the debtor has a legal interest.

Whenever the payment of a debt is guaranteed, or *secured,* by personal property owned by the debtor or in which the debtor has a legal interest, the transaction becomes known as a **secured transaction.** The concept of the secured transaction is as basic to modern business practice as the concept of credit. Logically, sellers and lenders do not want to risk nonpayment, so they usually will not sell goods or lend funds unless the payment is somehow guaranteed. Indeed, business as we know it could not exist without laws permitting and governing secured transactions.

Article 9 of the Uniform Commercial Code (UCC) governs secured transactions as applied to personal property, fixtures by contract, accounts, instruments, commercial assignments of $1,000 or more, *chattel paper* (any writing evidencing a debt secured by personal property), agricultural liens, and what are called general intangibles (such as patents and copyrights). Article 9 does not cover other creditor devices, such as landlord's liens, mechanic's liens, real estate mortgages, and the like [UCC 9–109]. The significance of Article 9 is related in this chapter's *Landmark in the Law* feature on the following two pages. In 1999, the National Conference of Commissioners on Uniform State Laws promulgated a revised version of Article 9. Because the revised version, which was later amended, has now been adopted by all of the states, we base this chapter's discussion of secured transactions entirely on the provisions of the revised version.

In this chapter, we first look at the terminology of secured transactions. We then discuss how the rights and duties of creditors and debtors are created and enforced under Article 9. As will become evident, the law of secured transactions tends to favor the rights of creditors; but, to a lesser extent, it offers debtors some protections, too.

SECURED PARTY
A lender, seller, or any other person in whose favor there is a security interest, including a person to whom accounts or chattel paper has been sold.

DEBTOR
Under Article 9 of the UCC, a debtor is any party who owes payment or performance of a secured obligation, whether or not the party actually owns or has rights in the collateral.

SECURITY INTEREST
Any interest in personal property or fixtures that secures payment or performance of an obligation.

SECURITY AGREEMENT
An agreement that creates or provides for a security interest between the debtor and a secured party.

COLLATERAL
Under Article 9 of the UCC, the property subject to a security interest, including accounts and chattel paper that have been sold.

FINANCING STATEMENT
A document prepared by a secured creditor, and filed with the appropriate state or local official, to give notice to the public that the creditor has a security interest in collateral belonging to the debtor named in the statement.

The Terminology of Secured Transactions

The UCC's terminology is now uniformly adopted in all documents used in situations involving secured transactions. A brief summary of the UCC's definitions of terms relating to secured transactions follows.

1. A **secured party** is any creditor who has a *security interest* in the *debtor's collateral.* This creditor can be a seller, a lender, a cosigner, and even a buyer of accounts or chattel paper [UCC 9–102(a)(72)].
2. A **debtor** is the "person" who *owes payment* or other performance of a secured obligation [UCC 9–102(a)(28)].
3. A **security interest** is the *interest* in the collateral (personal property, fixtures, and so forth) that *secures payment or performance of an obligation* [UCC 1–201(37)].
4. A **security agreement** is an *agreement* that *creates* or provides for a *security interest* [UCC 9–102(a)(73)].
5. **Collateral** is the *subject* of the *security interest* [UCC 9–102(a)(12)].
6. A **financing statement**—referred to as the UCC-1 form—is the *instrument normally filed* to give *public notice* to *third parties* of the *secured party's security interest* [UCC 9–102(a)(39)].

These basic definitions form the concept under which a debtor-creditor relationship becomes a secured-transaction relationship (see Exhibit 25–1).

EXHIBIT 25–1 SECURED TRANSACTIONS—CONCEPT AND TERMINOLOGY

In a security agreement, a debtor and a creditor agree that the creditor will have a security interest in collateral in which the debtor has rights. In essence, the collateral secures the loan and ensures the creditor of payment should the debtor default.

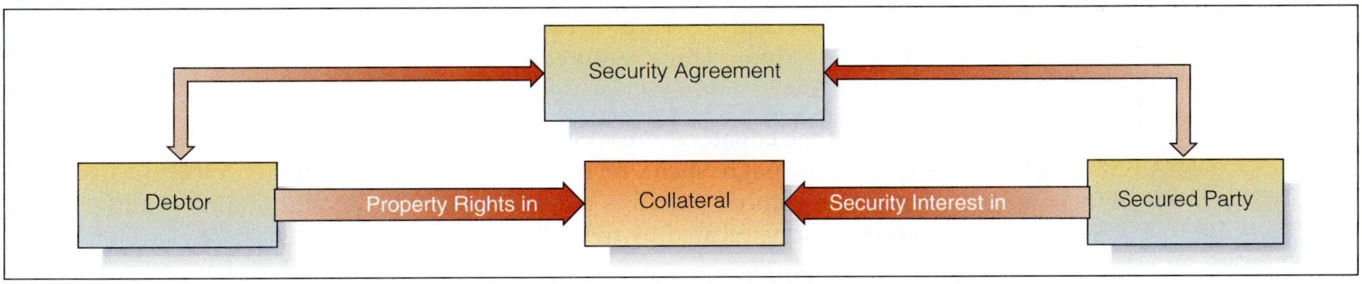

LANDMARK IN THE LAW

Article 9 Security Interest

Prior to the drafting of Article 9 of the Uniform Commercial Code and its adoption by the states, secured transactions were governed by a patchwork of security devices. The following summary of these devices will help you to understand the significance and landmark status of Article 9.

SECURITY DEVICES PRIOR TO ARTICLE 9 The security devices in use prior to the adoption of Article 9 were replete with variations that, according to many, made no logical sense. These devices included chattel mortgages, trust receipts, conditional sales contracts, assignments of accounts, and pledges. Additionally, each device had its own jargon. Depending on the device used, for example, a debtor could be called variously a pledgor, a mortgagor, a conditional vendee, an assignor, or a borrower.

One of the earliest security devices, historically, is the pledge. A *pledge* is a possessory security interest in which the secured party holds or controls possession of the property involved, called the *collateral,* to secure the payment or performance of the secured obligation. The pledge has existed since at least the fourth or fifth century. The pledge concept also gave rise to a device for obtaining a security interest in goods that could not be conveniently moved from the debtor's property. In such a situation, the creditor would have an independent warehouser establish a warehouse on the debtor's premises to obtain possession of the goods. This was called a *field warehouse* and dates from about 1900.

ARTICLE 9 STREAMLINED SECURED-TRANSACTIONS LAW The pledge and many other types of security devices were all designed to protect creditors' interests. Nonetheless, creditors still faced several legal problems. For example, in many states, a security interest could not be taken in inventory or stock in trade,

Creating and Perfecting a Security Interest

DEFAULT
The failure to observe a promise or discharge an obligation. The term is commonly used to mean the failure to pay a debt when it is due.

A creditor has two main concerns if the debtor **defaults** (fails to pay the debt as promised): (1) satisfaction of the debt through the possession and (usually) sale of the collateral and (2) priority over any other creditors or buyers who may have rights in the same collateral. We look here at how these two concerns are met through the creation and perfection of a security interest.

on the Web To find Article 9 of the UCC as adopted by a particular state, go to the Web site of Cornell University's Law School at **http://www.law.cornell.edu/ucc/ucc.table.html**.

CREATING A SECURITY INTEREST

To become a secured party, the creditor must obtain a security interest in the collateral of the debtor. Three requirements must be met for a creditor to have an enforceable security interest:

1. Either (a) the collateral must be in the possession of the secured party in accordance with an agreement, or (b) there must be a written or authenticated security agreement that describes the collateral subject to the security interest and is signed or authenticated by the debtor.
2. The secured party must give something of value to the debtor.

LANDMARK IN THE LAW—Continued

such as cars for a car dealer or chocolate for a candy manufacturer. Sometimes, highly technical limitations were placed on the use of a particular security device. If a court determined that a particular security device was not appropriate for a given transaction, it might void the security interest.

The drafters of Article 9 concluded that two elements were common to all security devices: (1) the objective of conferring on a creditor or secured party priority in certain property (the collateral) against the risk of the debtor's nonpayment of the debt or the debtor's insolvency or bankruptcy and (2) a means of notifying other creditors of this prior security interest. With these two elements in mind, the drafters created a new, simplified security device with a single set of terms to cover all situations. What is this security device called? It is called, simply, an Article 9 security interest.

APPLICATION TO TODAY'S BUSINESS WORLD

Although the law of secured transactions is still far from simple, it is now—thanks to the drafters of Article 9—far more rational and uniform than it was in the days prior to the UCC. The revised Article 9, which became effective in 2001, further streamlined the law concerning secured transactions by, among other things, simplifying the filing process and allowing documents for secured transactions to be filed electronically with the appropriate government officials.

RELEVANT WEB SITES

To locate information on the Web concerning Article 9 of the UCC, go to this text's Web site at **http://blt.westbuslaw.com**, *select "Chapter 25," and click on "URLs for Landmarks."*

3 The debtor must have "rights" in the collateral.

ATTACHMENT
In a secured transaction, the process by which a secured creditor's interest "attaches" to the property of another (collateral) and the creditor's security interest becomes enforceable.

Once these requirements have been met, the creditor's rights are said to *attach* to the collateral. **Attachment** gives the creditor an enforceable security interest in the collateral [UCC 9–203].[1]

Written or Authenticated Security Agreement When the collateral is *not* in the possession of the secured party, the security agreement must be either written or authenticated, and it must describe the collateral. Note here that *authentication* includes any agreement or signature inscribed on a tangible medium or stored in an electronic or other medium (called a *record*) that is retrievable [UCC 9–102(a)(7)(69)]. If the security agreement is in writing or authenticated, only the debtor's signature or authentication is required to create the security interest. The reason authentication is acceptable is to provide for electronic filing (the filing process will be discussed later).

1. Note that in the context of judicial liens, discussed in Chapter 26, the term *attachment* has a different meaning. In that context, it refers to a court-ordered seizure and taking into custody of property prior to the securing of a court judgment for a past-due debt.

A security agreement must contain a description of the collateral that reasonably identifies it. Generally, such words as "all the debtor's personal property" or "all the debtor's assets" would *not* constitute a sufficient description [UCC 9–108(c)]. See Exhibit 25–2 for a sample security agreement.

Secured Party Must Give Value The secured party must give to the debtor something of value. Some examples would be a binding commitment to extend credit, as security for the satisfaction of a preexisting debt, or consideration to support a simple contract [UCC 1–201(44)]. Normally, the value given by a secured party is in the form of a direct loan or a commitment to sell goods on credit.

Debtor Must Have Rights in the Collateral The debtor must have rights in the collateral; that is, the debtor must have some ownership interest or right to obtain possession of that collateral. The debtor's rights can represent either a current or a future legal interest in the collateral. For example, a retail seller-debtor can give a secured

EXHIBIT 25–2 AN EXAMPLE OF A SIMPLE SECURITY AGREEMENT

____
Date

____
Name No. and Street City County State

(hereinafter called "Debtor") hereby grants to ______________________________
Name

____
No. and Street City County State

(hereinafter called "Secured Party") a security interest in the following property (hereinafter called the "Collateral"): ______________________________

to secure payment and performance of obligations identified or set out as follows (hereinafter called the "Obligations"): ______________________________

Default in payment or performance of any of the Obligations or default under any agreement evidencing any of the Obligations is a default under this agreement. Upon such default, Secured Party may declare all Obligations immediately due and payable and shall have the remedies of a secured party under section(s) __________ of the Uniform Commercial Code.

Signed in (duplicate) triplicate.

Debtor	Secured Party
By____________________	By____________________

If a tractor used for harvesting became collateral for a secured loan, how would the collateral be classified? (Digital Vision)

party a security interest not only in existing inventory owned by the retailer but also in *future* inventory to be acquired by the retailer.

One common misconception about having rights in the collateral is that the debtor must have title. This is not a requirement. A beneficial interest in a trust (*trusts* will be discussed in Chapter 45), when title to the trust property is held by the trustee, may be made the subject of a security interest for a loan made to the beneficiary by a secured party (a creditor).

Classifications and Definitions of Collateral

Where or how to perfect a security interest (*perfection* will be discussed shortly) sometimes depends on the classification or definition of the collateral. Collateral is generally divided into two classifications: *tangible collateral* (collateral that can be seen, felt, touched, and so on) and *intangible collateral* (collateral that consists of or generates rights). Exhibit 25–3 on the following two pages summarizes the various classifications of collateral and the methods of perfecting a security interest in collateral falling within each of those classifications.[2]

Perfecting a Security Interest

PERFECTION
The legal process by which secured parties protect themselves against the claims of third parties who may wish to have their debts satisfied out of the same collateral; usually accomplished by filing a financing statement with the appropriate government official.

Perfection is the legal process by which secured parties protect themselves against the claims of third parties who may wish to have their debts satisfied out of the same collateral. Usually, perfection is accomplished by filing a financing statement with the office of the appropriate government official. In some circumstances, however, a security interest becomes perfected without the filing of a financing statement. (See the *Application* feature at the end of this chapter for additional information on perfecting your security interest.)

Perfection by Filing The most common means of perfection is by filing a *financing statement*—a document that gives public notice to third parties of the secured party's security interest—with the office of the appropriate government official. The security agreement itself can also be filed to perfect the security interest. The financing statement must provide the names of the debtor and the secured party and indicate the collateral covered by the financing statement. A uniform financing statement form as shown in Exhibit 25–4 on page 646 is now used in all states [see UCC 9–521].

Communication of the financing statement to the appropriate filing office, together with the correct filing fee, or the acceptance of the financing statement by the filing officer constitutes a filing [UCC 9–516(a)]. The word *communication* means that the filing can be accomplished electronically [UCC 9–102(a)(18)]. Once completed, filings are indexed in the name of the debtor so that they can be located by subsequent searchers. A financing statement may be filed even before a security agreement is made or a security interest attaches [UCC 9–502(d)].

The Debtor's Name. The UCC requires that a financing statement be filed under the name of the debtor [UCC 9–502(a)(1)]. Because most states use electronic filing systems, UCC 9–503 sets out some detailed rules for determining when the debtor's name as it appears on a financing statement is sufficient. For corporations, which

2. There are additional classifications, such as agricultural liens, investment property, and commercial tort claims. For definitions of these types of collateral, see UCC 9–102(a)(5), (a)(13), and (a)(49).

EXHIBIT 25–3 TYPES OF COLLATERAL AND METHODS OF PERFECTION

TYPE OF COLLATERAL	DEFINITION	METHOD OF PERFECTION
TANGIBLE	All things that are movable at the time the security interest attaches (such as livestock) or that are attached to the land, including timber to be cut and growing crops.	
1. Consumer Goods [UCC 9–301, 9–303, 9–309(1), 9–310(a), 9–313(a)]	Goods used or bought primarily for personal, family, or household purposes—for example, household furniture [UCC 9–102(a)(23)].	For purchase-money security interest, attachment (that is, the creation of a security interest) is sufficient; for boats, motor vehicles, and trailers, filing or compliance with a certificate-of-title statute is required; for other consumer goods, general rules of filing or possession apply.
2. Equipment [UCC 9–301, 9–310(a), 9–313(a)]	Goods bought for or used primarily in business (and not part of inventory or farm products)—for example, a delivery truck [UCC 9–102(a)(33)].	Filing or (rarely) possession by secured party.
3. Farm Products [UCC 9–301, 9–310(a), 9–313(a)]	Crops (including aquatic goods), livestock, or supplies produced in a farming operation—for example, ginned cotton, milk, eggs, and maple syrup [UCC 9–102(a)(34)].	Filing or (rarely) possession by secured party.
4. Inventory [UCC 9–301, 9–310(a), 9–313(a)]	Goods held by a person for sale or under a contract of service or lease; raw materials held for production and work in progress [UCC 9–102(a)(48)].	Filing or (rarely) possession by secured party.
5. Accessions [UCC 9–301, 9–310(a), 9–313(a)]	Personal property that is so attached, installed, or fixed to other personal property (goods) that it becomes a part of these goods—for example, a compact disc player installed in an automobile [UCC 9–102(a)(1)].	Filing or (rarely) possession by secured party (same as personal property being attached).
INTANGIBLE	Nonphysical property that exists only in connection with something else.	
1. Chattel Paper [UCC 9–301, 9–310(a), 9–312(a), 9–313(a), 9–314(a)]	A writing or writings (records) that evidence both a monetary obligation and a security interest in goods and software used in goods. For example, a security agreement or a security agreement and promissory note. *Note:* If the record or records consist of information stored in an electronic medium, the collateral is called *electronic chattel paper.* If the information is inscribed on a tangible medium, it is called *tangible chattel paper* [UCC 9–102(a)(11), (a)(31), and (a)(78)].	Filing or possession or control by secured party.
2. Instruments [UCC 9–301, 9–309(4), 9–310(a), 9–312(a) and (e), 9–313(a)]	A negotiable instrument, such as a check, note, certificate of deposit, or draft, or other writing that evidences a right to the payment of money and is not a security agreement or lease but rather a type that can ordinarily be transferred (after indorsement, if necessary) by delivery [UCC 9–102(a)(47)].	Except for temporary perfected status, filing or possession. For the sale of promissory notes, perfection can be by attachment (automatically on the creation of the security interest).

EXHIBIT 25–3 TYPES OF COLLATERAL AND METHODS OF PERFECTION—CONTINUED

TYPE OF COLLATERAL	DEFINITION	METHOD OF PERFECTION
3. Accounts [UCC 9–301, 9–309(2) and (5), 9–310(a)]	Any right to receive payment for the following: (a) any property, real or personal, sold, leased, licensed, assigned, or otherwise disposed of, including intellectual licensed property; (b) services rendered or to be rendered, such as contract rights; (c) policies of insurance; (d) secondary obligations incurred; (e) use of a credit card; (f) winnings of a government-sponsored or government-authorized lottery or other game of chance; and (g) health-care insurance receivables, defined as an interest or claim under a policy of insurance to payment for health-care goods or services provided [UCC 9–102(a)(2) and (a)(46)].	Filing required except for certain assignments that can be perfected by attachment (automatically on the creation of the security interest).
4. Deposit Accounts [UCC 9–104, 9–304, 9–312(b), 9–314(a)]	Any demand, time, savings, passbook, or similar account maintained with a bank [UCC 9–102(a)(29)].	Perfection by control, such as when the secured party is the bank in which the account is maintained or when the parties have agreed that the secured party can direct the disposition of funds in a particular account.
5. General Intangibles [UCC 9–301, 9–309(3), 9–310(a) and (b)(8)]	Any personal property (or debtor's obligation to pay money on such) other than that defined above [UCC 9–102(a)(42)], including software that is independent from a computer or a good [UCC 9–102(a)(44), (a)(61), and (a)(75)].	Filing only (for copyrights, with the U.S. Copyright Office), except a sale of a payment intangible by attachment (automatically on the creation of the security interest).

are part of "registered organizations," the debtor's name on the financing statement must be "the name of the debtor indicated on the public record of the debtor's jurisdiction of organization" [UCC 9–503(a)(1)]. Slight variations in names normally will not be considered misleading if a search of the filing office's records, using a standard computer search engine routinely used by that office, would disclose the filings [UCC 9–506(c)]. Note that if the debtor is identified by the correct name at the time of the filing of a financing statement, the secured party's interest retains its priority even if the debtor later changes his or her name.

If the debtor is a trust or a trustee with respect to property held in trust, the filed financing statement must disclose this information and must provide the trust's name as specified in its official documents [UCC 9–503(a)(3)]. In other cases, the filed financing statement must disclose "the individual or organizational name of the debtor" [UCC 9–503(a)(4)(A)]. As used here, the word *organization* includes unincorporated associations, such as clubs and some churches, as well as joint ventures and general partnerships, even when these organizations are created without obtaining any formal certificate of formation.

In general, providing only the debtor's trade name (or a fictitious name) in a financing statement is not sufficient for perfection [UCC 9–503(c)]. ■ EXAMPLE 25.1 Assume that a loan is being made to a sole proprietorship owned by Peter Jones. The trade, or fictitious, name is Pete's Plumbing. A financing statement cannot use the trade name Pete's Plumbing; rather, it has to be filed under the name of the actual debtor—in this instance, Peter Jones. ■ The reason for this rule is that a sole

EXHIBIT 25–4 THE UNIFORM FINANCING STATEMENT

UCC FINANCING STATEMENT

FOLLOW INSTRUCTIONS (front and back) CAREFULLY

A. NAME & PHONE OF CONTACT AT FILER (optional)

B. SEND ACKNOWLEDGEMENT TO: (Name and Address)

THE ABOVE SPACE IS FOR FILING OFFICE USE ONLY

1. DEBTOR'S EXACT FULL LEGAL NAME - Insert only one debtor name (1a or 1b) - do not abbreviate or combine names

1a. ORGANIZATION'S NAME

OR

1b. INDIVIDUAL'S LAST NAME	FIRST NAME	MIDDLE NAME		SUFFIX
1c. MAILING ADDRESS	CITY	STATE	POSTAL CODE	COUNTRY

1d. TAX ID# SSN OR EIN	ADDL INFO RE ORGANIZATION DEBTOR	1e. TYPE OF ORGANIZATION	1f. JURISDICTION OR ORGANIZATION	1g. ORGANIZATIONAL ID #, if any
				☐ NONE

2. ADDITIONAL DEBTOR'S EXACT FULL LEGAL NAME - Insert only one debtor name (2a or 2b) - do not abbreviate or combine names

2a. ORGANIZATION'S NAME

OR

2b. INDIVIDUAL'S LAST NAME	FIRST NAME	MIDDLE NAME		SUFFIX
2c. MAILING ADDRESS	CITY	STATE	POSTAL CODE	COUNTRY

2d. TAX ID# SSN OR EIN	ADDL INFO RE ORGANIZATION DEBTOR	1e. TYPE OF ORGANIZATION	1f. JURISDICTION OR ORGANIZATION	1g. ORGANIZATIONAL ID #, if any
				☐ NONE

3. SECURED PARTY'S NAME - (or NAME of TOTAL ASSIGNOR S/P) Insert only one secured party name (3a or 3b)

3a. ORGANIZATION'S NAME

OR

3b. INDIVIDUAL'S LAST NAME	FIRST NAME	MIDDLE NAME		SUFFIX
3c. MAILING ADDRESS	CITY	STATE	POSTAL CODE	COUNTRY

4. This FINANCING STATEMENT covers the following collateral:

5. ALTERNATIVE DESIGNATION (if applicable) ☐ LESSEE/LESSOR ☐ CONSIGNEE/CONSIGNOR ☐ BAILEE/BAILOR ☐ SELLER/BUYER ☐ AG. LIEN ☐ NON-UCC FILING

6. ☐ This FINANCING STATEMENT is to be filed [for record] (or recorded) in the REAL ESTATE RECORDS. Attach Addendum (if applicable) 7. Check to REQUEST SEARCH REPORT(S) on Debtor(s) (ADDITIONAL FEE) (optional) ☐ All Debtors ☐ Debtor 1 ☐ Debtor 2

OPTIONAL FILER REFERENCE DATA

NATIONAL UCC FINANCING STATEMENT (FORM UCC1) REV. 07/29/98)

proprietorship is not a legal entity distinct from the person who owns it. The rule also furthers an important goal of Article 9: to ensure that the debtor's name on a financing statement is one that prospective lenders can locate and recognize in future searches.

Changes in the Debtor's Name. A problem arises when the debtor subject to a filed perfected security interest changes her or his (or its) name. What happens if a subsequent creditor extends credit to the debtor and perfects its security interest under the debtor's new name? Obviously, a search by this subsequent creditor for filed security interests under the debtor's changed name may not disclose the previously filed security interest.

The UCC's revised Article 9 attempts to prevent potential conflicts caused by changes in the debtor's name if the debtor goes into default. First, UCC 9–503 states specifically what constitutes the "sufficiency" of the debtor's name in a financing statement. Second, if the debtor's name is insufficient, the filing is seriously misleading *unless* a search of records by the filing officer's search engine using the debtor's correct name would disclose the security interest [UCC 9–506(b) and (c)]. Third, even if the change of name renders the financing statement misleading, the financing statement is effective as a perfection of a security interest in collateral acquired by the debtor before *or* within four months after the name change. Unless an amendment is filed within this four-month period, collateral acquired by the debtor after the four-month period is unperfected [UCC 9–507(b) and (c)].

The following case illustrates some of the complications that can arise when a debtor has used more than one name to do business and two creditors assert claims to the same collateral under those different names.

CASE 25.1 Cabool State Bank v. Radio Shack, Inc.

Missouri Court of Appeals,
Southern District, Division One, 2002.
65 S.W.3d 613.
http://www.osca.state.mo.us[a]

BACKGROUND AND FACTS In June 1995, Michael and Debra Boudreaux, doing business as D & J Enterprises, Inc., bought from Van Pamperien a retail electronics store operated under a franchise from Radio Shack, Inc. To pay for the business, the Boudreauxes borrowed money from Cabool State Bank in Springfield, Missouri. The loan documents included a financing statement. On the statement's signature lines, the only capacity identified for the Boudreauxes' signatures was that of "Debtors." Elsewhere on the form, the bank listed "D & J Enterprises, Inc., Radio Shack, Dealer, Debra K. Boudreaux, Michael C. Boudreaux" as "Debtors." The statement covered, in part, the store inventory. Before the end of the year, the Boudreauxes changed the name of their business to Tri-B Enterprises, Inc. In January 1998, the store closed. The next month, Radio Shack terminated the franchise and, despite the lack of a security interest, took possession of the inventory, claiming the Boudreauxes and Tri-B owed Radio Shack $6,394.73. The bank filed a suit in a Missouri state court against Radio Shack, claiming a perfected security interest in the inventory with priority over Radio Shack's claim. The court entered a judgment for $15,529.43 in the bank's favor. Radio Shack appealed to a state intermediate appellate court.

a. In the "Court of Appeals" pull-down menu, select "Southern District" and click on "Go!" On that page, click on "Opinions and Orders." Scroll to "01/30/2002" and click on the name of the case to access the opinion. The Missouri Judiciary maintains this Web site.

IN THE WORDS OF THE COURT . . .

Kenneth W. *SHRUM,* Presiding Judge.

* * * *

* * * Radio Shack argues that the so-called change of name was seriously misleading * * *, the inventory that Radio Shack took from the store was acquired exclusively by Tri-B more than four months after the so-called name change; Bank never filed a new financing statement within four months of the so-called name change, and therefore, Bank's original * * * filings were ineffective to perfect a security interest in the inventory against Radio Shack.

* * * *

(Continued)

CASE 25.1—Continued

First and foremost, the argument thus advanced is based on flagrant mischaracterizations about what the record shows. Contrary to Radio Shack's * * * assertions that after November 1995 it only did business with Tri-B and the inventory taken from the closed store had been sold exclusively to the corporate entity, Radio Shack *stipulated* it had sold the subject inventory to Tri-B Enterprises *and* Boudreauxes, and it took the inventory *from both parties*—not just Tri-B Enterprises—after the store closed. Radio Shack confirmed that it recognized and treated Michael [Boudreaux], in his individual capacity, as having an ownership interest in the franchise and dealership after November 1995 when it stipulated that Tri-B *and* Boudreauxes "ceased business operations in January 1998[,]" and "[o]n February 25, 1998, Mr. Boudreaux *and* Tri-B * * * were given official notice * * * that the [franchise] agreement * * * was terminated." * * *

* * * [T]he record does show, without contradiction or conflict, that (1) Boudreauxes bought the original inventory in their individual names, (2) Boudreauxes gave Bank a security interest in the original inventory and "all inventory purchased or replaced," (3) Bank perfected its security interest in existing and future inventory owned by Boudreauxes by filing * * * financing statements that listed Boudreauxes and D & J Enterprises, Inc., as "Debtors," (4) Radio Shack had actual knowledge of the loan transaction between Bank and Boudreauxes, and (5) the subject inventory was sold to both the Boudreauxes and Tri-B. * * *

* * * From the outset, Bank listed Boudreauxes (who admittedly had an ownership interest in the inventory) as "Debtors" on the [UCC] filings. Because the financing statement was filed under the true name of at least one debtor/owner, there was no possibility the Bank's financing statement could seriously have misled Radio Shack.

DECISION AND REMEDY The state intermediate appellate court affirmed the judgment of the lower court. Radio Shack was not misled by the debtors' change of their business name because the financing statement was filed under the "true name" of at least one of the debtors with whom Radio Shack admitted doing business. Radio Shack also had actual knowledge of the bank loan.

WHY IS THIS CASE IMPORTANT? *In today's business climate, debtors frequently change the names under which they do business. The key to determining if a security interest has been perfected in such situations is whether the financing statement that was filed adequately notifies other potential creditors that a security interest exists. As this case illustrates, if a search of the records using the debtor's correct name would disclose the interest, that is generally sufficient.*

Description of the Collateral. The UCC requires that both the security agreement and the financing statement contain a description of the collateral in which the secured party has a security interest. The security agreement must describe the collateral because no security interest in goods can exist unless the parties agree on which goods are subject to the security interest. The financing statement must also describe the collateral because the purpose of filing the statement is to give public notice of the fact that certain goods of the debtor are subject to a security interest. Other parties who might later wish to lend money to the debtor or buy the collateral can thus learn of the security interest by checking with the state or local office in which a financing statement for that type of collateral would be filed. For land-related security interests, a legal description of the realty is also required [UCC 9–502(b)].

Sometimes, the descriptions in the two documents vary, with the description in the security agreement being more precise than the description in the financing statement, which is allowed to be more general. ■ EXAMPLE 25.2 A security agreement for a commercial loan to a manufacturer may list all of the manufacturer's equipment subject to the loan by serial number, whereas the financing statement may simply state "all equipment owned or hereafter acquired." ■ The UCC permits broad, general descriptions in the financing statement, such as "all assets" or "all personal property." Generally, therefore, whenever the description in a financing statement accurately describes the agreement between the secured party and the debtor, the description is sufficient [UCC 9–504].

Where to File. In most states, a financing statement must be filed centrally in the appropriate state office, such as the office of the secretary of state, in the state where the debtor is located. Filing in the county where the collateral is located is required only when the collateral consists of timber to be cut, fixtures, or collateral to be extracted—such as oil, coal, gas, and minerals [UCC 9–301(3) and (4), 9–502(b)].

The state office in which a financing statement should be filed depends on the *debtor's location,* not the location of the collateral (as was required under the unrevised Article 9) [UCC 9–301]. The debtor's location is determined as follows [UCC 9–307]:

1. For *individual debtors,* it is the state of the debtor's principal residence.
2. For an entity created by a filing (such as a corporation), it is in the state of filing. For example, if a debtor is incorporated in Maryland and has its chief executive office in New York, a secured party would file the financing statement in Maryland—the state of the debtor's organizational formation.
3. For all other entities, it is the state where the business is located or, if more than one, the state where the chief executive office is located.

Consequences of an Improper Filing. Any improper filing renders the secured party unperfected and reduces the secured party's claim in bankruptcy to that of an unsecured creditor. For instance, if the debtor's name on the financing statement is inaccurate or if the collateral is not sufficiently described in the financing statement, the filing may not be effective.

Perfection without Filing In two types of situations, security interests can be perfected without filing a financing statement. The first occurs when the collateral is transferred into the possession of the secured party. The second occurs when the security interest is one of a limited number (thirteen) under the UCC that can be perfected on attachment (without a filing and without having to possess the goods) [UCC 9–309]. The phrase *perfected on attachment* means that these security interests are automatically perfected at the time of their creation. Two of the more common security interests that are perfected on attachment are a *purchase-money security interest* in consumer goods (defined and explained below) and an assignment of a beneficial interest in a decedent's estate [UCC 9–309(1) and (13)].

PLEDGE
A common law security device (retained in Article 9 of the UCC) in which personal property is transferred into the possession of the creditor as security for the payment of a debt and retained by the creditor until the debt is paid.

Perfection by Possession. Under the common law, as discussed earlier in this chapter's *Landmark in the Law* feature, one of the most common means of obtaining financing was to **pledge** certain collateral as security for the debt and transfer the collateral into the creditor's possession. When the debt was paid, the collateral was returned to the debtor. Although the debtor usually entered into a written security agreement, an oral security agreement was also enforceable as long as the secured party possessed the collateral. Article 9 of the UCC retained the common law pledge and the principle that the security agreement need not be in writing to be enforceable if the collateral is transferred to the secured party [UCC 9–310, 9–312(b), 9–313].

For most collateral, possession by the secured party is impractical because it denies the debtor the right to use or derive income from the property to pay off the debt. ■ EXAMPLE 25.3 Suppose that a farmer takes out a loan to finance the purchase of a piece of heavy farm equipment needed to harvest crops and uses the equipment as collateral. Clearly, the purpose of the purchase would be defeated if the farmer transferred the collateral into the creditor's possession. ■ Certain items, however, such as stocks, bonds, instruments (negotiable), and jewelry, are commonly transferred into the creditor's possession when they are used as collateral for loans.

"I will pay you some, and, as most debtors do, promise you infinitely."

WILLIAM SHAKESPEARE, 1564–1616 (English dramatist and poet)

Perfection by Attachment—The Purchase-Money Security Interest in Consumer Goods. Under the UCC, thirteen types of security interests are perfected automatically at the time they are created [UCC 9–309]. The most common of these is the **purchase-money security interest (PMSI)** in consumer goods. A PMSI is created when a person buys consumer goods (items bought primarily for personal, family, or household purposes) and the seller or lender agrees to extend credit for part or all of the purchase price of the goods. The entity that extends the credit and obtains the PMSI can be either the seller (a store, for example) or a financial institution that lends the buyer the funds with which to purchase the goods [UCC 9–102(a)(2)].

PURCHASE-MONEY SECURITY INTEREST (PMSI) A security interest that arises when a seller or lender extends credit for part or all of the purchase price of goods purchased by a buyer.

CONTINUATION STATEMENT A statement that, if filed within six months prior to the expiration date of the original financing statement, continues the perfection of the original security interest for another five years. The perfection of a security interest can be continued in the same manner indefinitely.

A PMSI in consumer goods is perfected automatically at the time of a credit sale—that is, at the time the PMSI is created. The seller in this situation need do nothing more to perfect her or his interest. ■ EXAMPLE 25.4 Suppose that Jamie wants to purchase a new large-screen television from ABC Television, Inc. The purchase price is $2,500. Not being able to pay the entire amount in cash, Jamie signs a purchase agreement to pay $1,000 down and $100 per month until the balance plus interest is fully paid. ABC is to retain a security interest in the purchased goods until full payment has been made. Because the security interest was created as part of the purchase agreement, it is a PMSI. ■

An important exception to this rule of automatic perfection under Article 9 deals with certain types of security interests that are subject to other federal or state laws, which may require additional steps to be perfected [UCC 9–311]. For example, if a consumer purchases an automobile, trailer, or boat, the secured party will need to file a certificate of title with the appropriate state authority to perfect the PMSI.

If a couple purchases a plasma TV on an installment plan, what kind of security interest would be created? (Digital Vision)

Effective Time Duration of Perfection A financing statement is effective for five years from the date of filing [UCC 9–515)]. If a **continuation statement** is filed within six months *prior to* the expiration date, the effectiveness of the original statement is continued for another five years, starting with the expiration date of the first five-year period [UCC 9–515(d) and (e)]. The effectiveness of the statement can be continued in the same manner indefinitely. Any attempt to file a continuation statement outside the six-month window will render the continuation ineffective, and the perfection will lapse at the end of the five-year period.

If a financing statement lapses, the security interest that had been perfected by the filing now becomes unperfected. A purchaser for value can acquire the collateral as if the security interest had never been perfected [UCC 9–515(c)].

The Scope of a Security Interest

In addition to covering collateral already in the debtor's possession, a security agreement can cover various other types of property, including the proceeds of the sale of collateral, after-acquired property, and future advances.

PROCEEDS

PROCEEDS
Under Article 9 of the UCC, whatever is received when the collateral is sold or otherwise disposed of, such as by exchange.

Proceeds include whatever is received when collateral is sold or disposed of in some other way [UCC 9–102(a)(64)]. A secured party's security interest in the collateral includes a security interest in the proceeds of the sale of that collateral. ■ EXAMPLE 25.5 Suppose that a bank has a perfected security interest in the inventory of a retail seller of heavy farm machinery. The retailer sells a tractor out of this inventory to a farmer, who is by definition a *buyer in the ordinary course of business* (this term will be discussed later in the chapter). The farmer agrees, in a security agreement, to make monthly payments to the retailer for a period of twenty-four months. If the retailer should go into default on the loan from the bank, the bank is entitled to the remaining payments the farmer owes to the retailer as proceeds. ■

A security interest in proceeds perfects automatically on the *perfection* of the secured party's security interest in the original collateral and remains perfected for twenty days after receipt of the proceeds by the debtor. One way to extend the twenty-day automatic perfection period is to provide for such extended coverage in the original security agreement [UCC 9–315(c) and (d)]. This is typically done when the collateral is the type that is likely to be sold, such as a retailer's inventory—for example, of computers or DVD players. The UCC also permits a security interest in identifiable cash proceeds to remain perfected after twenty days [UCC 9–315(d)(2)].

AFTER-ACQUIRED PROPERTY

AFTER-ACQUIRED PROPERTY
Property that is acquired by the debtor after the execution of a security agreement.

After-acquired property is property that the debtor acquired after the execution of the security agreement. The security agreement may provide for a security interest in after-acquired property [UCC 9–204(1)]. This is particularly useful for inventory financing arrangements because a secured party whose security interest is in existing inventory knows that the debtor will sell that inventory, thereby reducing the collateral subject to the security interest.

Generally, the debtor will purchase new inventory to replace the inventory sold. The secured party wants this newly acquired inventory to be subject to the original security interest. Thus, the after-acquired property clause continues the secured party's claim to any inventory acquired thereafter. This is not to say that the original security interest will be superior to the rights of all other creditors with regard to this after-acquired inventory, as will be discussed later.

■ EXAMPLE 25.6 Amato buys factory equipment from Bronson on credit, giving as security an interest in all of her equipment—both what she is buying and what she already owns. The security interest with Bronson contains an after-acquired property clause. Six months later, Amato pays cash to another seller of factory equipment for more equipment. Six months after that, Amato goes out of business before she has paid off her debt to Bronson. Bronson has a security interest in all of Amato's equipment, even the equipment bought from the other seller. ■

FUTURE ADVANCES

Often, a debtor will arrange with a bank to have a *continuing line of credit* under which the debtor can borrow funds intermittently. Advances against lines of credit can be subject to a properly perfected security interest in certain collateral. The security agreement may provide that any future advances made against that line of credit are also subject to the security interest in the same collateral [UCC 9–204(c)]. Future advances do not have to be of the same type or otherwise related to the original advance to benefit from this type of cross-collateralization.[3] (Cross-collateralization occurs when an asset that is not the subject of a loan is used to secure that loan.)

■ EXAMPLE 25.7 Stroh is the owner of a small manufacturing plant with equipment valued at $1 million. He has an immediate need for $50,000 of working capital, so he obtains a loan from Midwestern Bank and signs a security agreement, putting up all of his equipment as security. The bank properly perfects its security interest. The security agreement provides that Stroh can borrow up to $500,000 in the future, using the same equipment as collateral for any future advances. In this situation, Midwestern Bank does not have to execute a new security agreement and perfect a security interest in the collateral each time an advance is made, up to a cumulative total of $500,000. For priority purposes, each advance is perfected as of the date of the original perfection. ■

THE FLOATING-LIEN CONCEPT

A security agreement that provides for a security interest in proceeds, in after-acquired property, or in collateral subject to future advances by the secured party (or in all three) is often characterized as a **floating lien.** This type of security interest continues in the collateral or proceeds even if the collateral is sold, exchanged, or disposed of in some other way.

FLOATING LIEN
A security interest in proceeds, after-acquired property, or collateral subject to future advances by the secured party (or all three); a security interest in collateral that is retained even when the collateral changes in character, classification, or location.

A Floating Lien in Inventory Floating liens commonly arise in the financing of inventories. A creditor is not interested in specific pieces of inventory, which are constantly changing, so the lien "floats" from one item to another, as the inventory changes.

■ EXAMPLE 25.8 Suppose that Cascade Sports, Inc., a corporation chartered in Oregon that operates as a cross-country ski dealer, has a line of credit with Portland First Bank to finance an inventory of cross-country skis. Cascade and Portland First enter into a security agreement that provides for coverage of proceeds, after-acquired inventory, present inventory, and future advances. This security interest in inventory is perfected by filing centrally (with the office of the secretary of state in Oregon). One day, Cascade sells a new pair of the latest cross-country skis and receives a used pair in trade. That same day, Cascade purchases two new pairs of cross-country skis from a local manufacturer for cash. Later that day, Cascade borrows $8,000 from Portland First Bank under the security agreement to meet its payroll.

This woman owns a store that sells used sporting equipment. As a creditor, why would you want a floating lien in a debtor's inventory? (Layne Kennedy/Corbis)

Portland First gets a perfected security interest in the used pair of skis under the proceeds clause, has a perfected security interest in the two new pairs of skis purchased from the local manufacturer under the after-acquired property clause, and has the new amount of funds advanced to Cascade secured on all of the above collateral by the future-advances clause. All of this is accomplished under the original perfected security interest. The various items in the inventory have changed, but Portland First still has a perfected security interest in Cascade's inventory. Hence, it has a floating lien on the inventory. ■

A Floating Lien in a Shifting Stock of Goods The concept of the floating lien can also apply to a shifting stock of goods. The lien can start with raw materials; follow them as they become finished goods and inventories; and continue as the goods are sold and are turned into accounts receivable, chattel paper, or cash.

3. See official Comment 5 to UCC 9–204.

Priorities

The importance of perfection to a secured party cannot be overemphasized, particularly when another party is claiming an interest in the same collateral covered by the perfected secured party's security interest.

THE GENERAL RULE

The general rule is that a perfected secured party's interest has priority over the interests of the following parties [UCC 9–317, 9–322]:

1. An unsecured creditor.
2. An unperfected secured party.
3. A subsequent lien creditor, such as a judgment creditor who acquires a lien on the collateral by *execution and levy*—a process discussed later in this chapter.
4. A trustee in bankruptcy (see Chapter 27)—at least, the perfected secured party has priority to the proceeds from the sale of the collateral by the trustee.
5. Most buyers who *do not* purchase the collateral in the ordinary course of a seller's business.

In addition, whether a secured party's security interest is perfected or unperfected may have serious consequences for the secured party if the debtor defaults on the debt or files for bankruptcy. For example, what if the debtor has borrowed money from two different creditors, using the same property as collateral for both loans? If the debtor defaults on both loans, which of the two creditors has first rights to the collateral? In this situation, the creditor with a perfected security interest will prevail.

BUYERS OF THE COLLATERAL

Sometimes, the conflict is between a perfected secured party and a buyer of the collateral. The question then arises as to which party has priority to the collateral.

Types of Buyers The UCC recognizes five types of buyers whose interest in purchased goods could conflict with those of a perfected secured party on the debtor's default. These five types are as follows (see Exhibit 25–5 on page 654 for details):

1. Buyers in the ordinary course of business—this type of buyer will be discussed in detail shortly.
2. Buyers *not* in the ordinary course of business of consumer goods.
3. Buyers of chattel paper [UCC 9–330].
4. Buyers of instruments, documents, or securities [UCC 9–330(d), 9–331(a)].
5. Buyers of farm products.[4]

Buyers in the Ordinary Course of Business Because buyers should not be required to find out if there is an outstanding security interest in, for example, a merchant's

4. Under the Food Security Act of 1985, buyers in the ordinary course of business include buyers of farm products from a farmer. Under this act, these buyers are protected from prior perfected security interests unless the secured parties perfected centrally by a special form called an *effective financing statement* (EFS) or the buyers received proper notice of the secured party's security interest.

inventory, the UCC also provides that a person who buys "in the ordinary course of business" will take the goods free from any security interest created by the seller in the purchased collateral. This is so even if the security interest is perfected and *even if the buyer knows of its existence* [UCC 9–320(a)].[5] The UCC defines a *buyer in the ordinary course of business* as any person who in good faith, and without knowledge that the sale is in violation of the ownership rights or security interest of a third party in the goods, buys in ordinary course from a person in the business of selling goods of that kind [UCC 1–201(9)].

5. Remember that, generally, there are three methods of perfection: by filing, by possession, and by attachment.

EXHIBIT 25–5 PRIORITY OF CLAIMS TO A DEBTOR'S COLLATERAL

PARTIES	PRIORITY
Unperfected Secured Party	An unperfected secured party prevails over unsecured creditors and creditors who have obtained judgments against the debtor but who have not begun the legal process to collect on those judgments [UCC 9–201(a)].
Purchaser of Debtor's Collateral	1. *Goods purchased in the ordinary course of the seller's business*—Buyer prevails over a secured party's security interest, even if perfected and even if the buyer knows of the security interest [UCC 9–320(a)]. 2. *Consumer goods purchased outside the ordinary course of business*—Buyer prevails over a secured party's interest, even if perfected by attachment, providing buyer purchased as follows: a. For value. b. Without actual knowledge of the security interest. c. For use as a consumer good. d. Prior to secured party's perfection by *filing* [UCC 9–320(b)]. 3. *Buyers of chattel paper*—Buyer prevails if the buyer: a. Gave new value in making the purchase. b. Took possession in the ordinary course of the buyer's business. c. Took without knowledge of the security interest [UCC 9–330]. 4. *Buyers of instruments, documents, or securities*—Buyers who are holders in due course, holders to whom negotiable documents have been duly negotiated, or bona fide purchasers of securities have priority over a previously perfected security interest [UCC 9–330(d), 9–331(a)]. 5. *Buyers of farm products*—Buyers from a farmer take free and clear of perfected security interests unless, where permitted, a secured party files centrally an effective financing statement (EFS) or the buyer receives proper notice of the security interest before the sale.
Perfected Secured Parties to the Same Collateral	1. *The general rule*—Between two perfected secured parties in the same collateral, the general rule is that first in time of perfection is first in right to the collateral [UCC 9–322(a)(1)]. 2. *Exception for purchase-money security interest (PMSI)*—A PMSI, even if second in time of perfection, has priority providing that the following conditions are met: a. Inventory—A PMSI has priority if it is perfected and proper written or authenticated notice is given to the other security-interest holder *on* or *before* the time the debtor takes possession [UCC 9–324(b)]. b. Other collateral—A PMSI has priority, providing it is perfected within twenty days after the debtor takes possession [UCC 9–324(a)]. c. Software—Applies to a PMSI in software only if used in goods subject to a PMSI. If the goods are inventory, priority is determined the same as for inventory; if they are not, priority is determined as for goods other than inventory [UCC 9–103(c), 9–324(f)].

■ **EXAMPLE 25.9** On August 1, West Bank has a perfected security interest in all of ABC Television's existing inventory and any inventory thereafter acquired. On September 1, Carla, a student at Central University, purchases one of the television sets in ABC's inventory. On December 1, ABC goes into default. Can West Bank repossess the TV set sold to Carla? The answer is no, because Carla is a buyer in the ordinary course of business (ABC is in the business of selling goods of that kind) and takes free and clear of West Bank's perfected security interest. ■

CREDITORS OR SECURED PARTIES

KEEP IN MIND Secured creditors—perfected or not—have priority over unsecured creditors.

Generally, the following UCC rules apply when more than one creditor claims rights in the same collateral:

1. *Conflicting perfected security interests.* When two or more secured parties have perfected security interests in the same collateral, generally the first to perfect (file or take possession of the collateral) has priority, unless the state's statute provides otherwise [UCC 9–322(a)(1)].
2. *Conflicting unperfected security interests.* When two conflicting security interests are unperfected, the first to attach has priority [UCC 9–322(a)(3)].
3. *Conflicting perfected security interests in commingled or processed goods.* When goods to which two or more perfected security interests attach are so manufactured or commingled that they lose their identities into a product or mass, the perfected parties' security interests attach to the new product or mass "according to the ratio that the cost of goods to which each interest originally attached bears to the cost of the total product or mass" [UCC 9–336].

Under some circumstances, on the debtor's default, the perfection of a security interest will not protect a secured party against certain other third parties having claims to the collateral. We have already discussed the priority of certain types of buyers over a perfected secured party. In addition, the UCC provides that in some situations a properly perfected PMSI[6] will prevail over another security interest in after-acquired collateral, even though the other was perfected first.

An Exception to the First-in-Time Rule—The PMSI An important exception to the first-in-time rule deals with certain types of collateral, such as equipment, in which one of the perfected security parties has a PMSI [UCC 9–324(a)]. ■ **EXAMPLE 25.10** Suppose that Smith borrows funds from West Bank, signing a security agreement in which she puts up all of her present and after-acquired equipment as security. On May 1, West Bank perfects this security interest (which is not a PMSI). On July 1, Smith purchases a new piece of equipment from XYZ Company on credit, signing a security agreement.

XYZ Company thus has a PMSI in the new equipment. The delivery date for the new equipment is August 1. If Smith defaults on her payments to both West Bank and XYZ, which party—West Bank or XYZ—has priority to the new piece of equipment? Generally, West Bank would have priority because its interest perfected first in time. In this situation, however, XYZ has a PMSI, and if it perfects its interest by filing before Smith takes possession on August 1, or within twenty days after that date, XYZ has priority. ■

6. Recall that, with some exceptions (such as motor vehicles), a PMSI in consumer goods is automatically perfected—no filing is necessary.

Another Exception to the First-in-Time Rule—Security Interest in Inventory Another important exception to the first-in-time rule has to do with security interests in inventory [UCC 9–324(b)]. ■ EXAMPLE 25.11 On May 1, ABC borrows funds from West Bank. ABC signs a security agreement, putting up all of its present inventory and any thereafter acquired as collateral. West Bank perfects its non-PMSI on that date. On June 10, ABC buys new inventory from Martin, Inc., a manufacturer, to use for its Fourth of July sale. ABC makes a down payment for the new inventory and signs a security agreement giving Martin a PMSI in the new inventory as collateral for the remaining debt. Martin delivers the inventory to ABC on June 28. Due to a hurricane in the area, ABC's Fourth of July sale is a disaster, and most of its inventory remains unsold. In August, ABC defaults on its payments to both West Bank and Martin.

Does West Bank or Martin have priority to the new inventory delivered on June 28? If Martin has not perfected its security interest by June 28, West Bank's after-acquired collateral clause has priority because it was the first to be perfected. If, however, Martin has perfected *and* gives proper notice of its security interest to West Bank before ABC takes possession of the goods on June 28, Martin has priority. ■

The following case illustrates how the first-in-time rule and its exceptions apply to determine the priority of conflicting security interests on a debtor's default.

CASE 25.2 In re Rebel Rents, Inc.

United States Bankruptcy Court,
Central District of California, 2004.
307 Bankr. 171.

BACKGROUND AND FACTS Rebel Rents, Inc., was the largest independent equipment rental company in Southern California. Rebel offered a wide variety of equipment for sale or lease to construction companies, industrial firms, commercial businesses, and homeowners. In September 2000, Rebel bought certain equipment from Snorkel International, Inc., to use as inventory. Textron Financial Corporation agreed to finance the purchase, for which Rebel granted Textron a security interest in the equipment and its proceeds. On December 29, General Electric Capital Corporation (GECC) agreed to loan Rebel up to $25 million, for which Rebel granted GECC a security interest in substantially all of Rebel's assets, including its inventory and proceeds. On January 5, 2001, GECC filed a financing statement with the California secretary of state to perfect its interest. Textron filed its financing statement on January 16. Rebel filed a bankruptcy petition with a federal bankruptcy court in September 2002. Between that date and September 2003, Rebel obtained $430,661 from leasing the Snorkel equipment. Pursuant to an order of the court, Rebel surrendered the Snorkel equipment to Textron. Textron asserted that it was also owed the income from the recent leases.

IN THE WORDS OF THE COURT . . .
PETER H. CARROLL, Bankruptcy Judge.

* * * *

* * * *[Under the bankruptcy laws,] the secured creditor [must] establish the validity, priority and extent of its interest in property.* * * * [A] party seeking to establish the "extent" of its interest in property under [the bankruptcy laws] must satisfy [the following] two-prong test. [Emphasis added.]

> First, as a preliminary matter, the party must prove that it holds a perfected security interest in post-petition revenues to which its liens [security interests] still rightly attach. Second, a party must prove the amount of money to which its liens attach.

In this case, Textron failed to meet its burden * * * to establish a valid, duly perfected lien on rental income attributable to the Equipment. Textron produced evi-

CASE 25.2—Continued

dence that Rebel generated revenue of $430,661 from leases of the Equipment between September 22, 2002 through September 19, 2003. However, Textron submitted no direct evidence in support of the motion establishing the validity, extent and priority of its lien on such revenue. Through confirmation of [Rebel's bankruptcy] Plan, Textron repeatedly pointed to its Finance Plan, Wholesale Security Agreement, Rental Inventory Addendum, and financing statement filed on January 16, 2001, as evidence of its secured claim in this case. * * *

* * * Textron's Finance Plan, Wholesale Security Agreement, Rental Inventory Addendum, and financing statement fail to establish that Textron's lien had priority over GECC's lien on the Equipment rental income. Under California law, conflicting security interests rank according to the priority in time of filing or perfection. A purchase-money lender's security interest in equipment is entitled to priority over conflicting interests in the same collateral only if the purchase-money security interest is perfected at the time the debtor receives possession of the collateral * * *.

There is no evidence that Textron perfected its security interest [at the time] Rebel received possession of the Equipment. Indeed, the documents reveal that Textron's security interest [was] attached on September 14, 2000, but was not perfected until January 16, 2001. Given that GECC's financing statement was filed on January 5, 2001, and preceded the filing of Textron's financing statement by eleven days, GECC's security interest was senior to Textron's and entitled to priority over Textron's security in the same collateral.

* * * *

In summary, Textron has failed * * * to establish the validity, extent and priority of its lien on the $430,661 in Equipment lease revenues claimed as cash collateral. * * * Textron's security interest * * * on "proceeds" [does not] defeat GECC's senior lien on rental income attributable to Rebel's lease of the Equipment to its customers. * * * Because Rebel had no duty to segregate the Equipment lease revenue as Textron's cash collateral * * * , Textron's motion is denied.

DECISION AND REMEDY The court held that GECC's security interest had priority over Textron's interest in Rebel's income. Conflicting security interests rank according to the priority in time of filing or perfection. Textron's security interest was attached on September 14, 2000, but was not perfected until January 16, 2001. GECC's financing statement was filed on January 5, 2001, preceding the filing of Textron's financing statement by eleven days.[a]

a. Because the security interests in this case were established before the effective date of the revised version of Article 9, the court applied the previous statute, but the result would likely have been the same under the revised version.

FOR CRITICAL ANALYSIS—Social Consideration *What could Textron have done differently to avoid the result in this case?*

Rights and Duties of Debtors and Creditors

The security agreement itself determines most of the rights and duties of the debtor and the secured party. The UCC, however, imposes some rights and duties that are applicable in the absence of a valid security agreement that states the contrary.

Information Requests

Under UCC 9–523(a), a secured party has the option, when making the filing, of furnishing a *copy* of the financing statement being filed to the filing officer and requesting that the filing officer make a note of the file number, the date, and the hour of the original filing on the copy. The filing officer must send this copy to the person designated by the secured party or to the debtor, if the debtor makes the request. Under UCC 9–523(c) and (d), a filing officer must also give information to a person who is contemplating obtaining a security interest from a prospective debtor. The filing officer must issue a certificate that provides information on possible perfected financing statements with respect to the named debtor. The filing officer will charge a fee for the certification and for any information copies provided [UCC 9–525(d)].

Release, Assignment, and Amendment

A secured party can release all or part of any collateral described in the filing, thereby terminating its security interest in that collateral. The release is recorded by filing a uniform amendment form [UCC 9–512, 9–521(b)]. A secured party can assign all or part of the security interest to a third party (the assignee). The assignee can become the secured party of record if the assignment is filed by use of a uniform amendment form [UCC 9–514, 9–521(a)].

If the debtor and secured parties so agree, the filing can be amended—by adding new collateral if authorized by the debtor, for example—by filing a uniform amendment form that indicates by file number the initial financing statement [UCC 9–512(a)]. The amendment does not extend the time period of perfection. If, however, the amendment adds collateral, the perfection date (for priority purposes) for the new collateral begins only on the date of the filing of the amendment [UCC 9–512(b) and (c)].

Confirmation or Accounting Request by Debtor

The debtor may believe that the unpaid debt amount or the listing of the collateral subject to the security interest is inaccurate. The debtor has the right to request a confirmation of his or her view of the unpaid debt or listing of collateral. The secured party must either approve or correct this confirmation request [UCC 9–210].

The secured party must comply with the debtor's confirmation request by authenticating and sending to the debtor an accounting within fourteen days after the request is received. Otherwise, the secured party will be held liable for any loss suffered by the debtor, plus $500 [UCC 9–210, 9–625(f)].

The debtor is entitled to one request without charge every six months. For any additional requests, the secured party is entitled to the payment of a statutory fee of up to $25 per request [UCC 9–210(f)].

Termination Statement

When the debtor has fully paid the debt, if the secured party perfected the security interest by filing, the debtor is entitled to have a termination statement filed. Such a statement demonstrates to the public that the filed perfected security interest has been terminated [UCC 9–513].

Whenever consumer goods are involved, the secured party *must* file a termination statement (or, in the alternative, a release) within one month of the final payment or within twenty days of receipt of the debtor's authenticated demand, whichever is earlier [UCC 9–513(b)].

When the collateral is other than consumer goods, on an authenticated demand by the debtor, the secured party must either send a termination statement to the debtor or file such a statement within twenty days [UCC 9–513(c)]. Otherwise, the secured party is not required to file or send a termination statement. Whenever a secured party fails to file or send the termination statement as requested, the debtor can recover $500 plus any additional loss suffered [UCC 9–625(e)(4) and (f)].

Default

Article 9 defines the rights, duties, and remedies of the secured party and of the debtor on the debtor's default. Should the secured party fail to comply with her or his duties, the debtor is afforded particular rights and remedies.

"If you think nobody cares if you're alive, try missing a couple of car payments."

EARL WILSON, 1907–1987 (American journalist)

The topic of default is one of great concern to secured lenders and to the lawyers who draft security agreements. What constitutes default is not always clear. In fact, Article 9 does not define the term. Consequently, parties are encouraged in practice—and by the UCC—to include in their security agreements certain standards to be applied in determining when default has actually occurred. In so doing, parties can stipulate the conditions that will constitute a default [UCC 9–601, 9–603]. Often, these critical terms are shaped by the creditor in an attempt to provide the maximum protection possible. The ultimate terms, however, are not allowed to go beyond the limitations imposed by the good faith requirement and the unconscionability provisions of the UCC. Article 9's definition of good faith includes "honesty in fact and the observance of reasonable commercial standards of fair dealing" [UCC 9–102(a)(43)].

Although any breach of the terms of the security agreement can constitute default, default occurs most commonly when the debtor fails to meet the scheduled payments that the parties have agreed on or when the debtor becomes bankrupt.

BASIC REMEDIES

The rights and remedies under UCC 9–601(a)(b) are *cumulative* [UCC 9–601(c)]. Therefore, if a creditor is unsuccessful in enforcing rights by one method, he or she can pursue another method. Generally, a secured party's remedies can be divided into the two basic categories discussed next.

Repossession of the Collateral—The Self-Help Remedy On the debtor's default, a secured party can take peaceful possession of the collateral without the use of judicial process [UCC 9–609(b)]. This provision is often referred to as the "self-help" provision of Article 9. The UCC does not define *peaceful possession*, however. The general rule is that the collateral has been taken peacefully if the secured party took possession without committing (1) trespass onto realty, (2) assault and/or battery, or (3) breaking and entering. On taking possession, the secured party may either retain the collateral for satisfaction of the debt [UCC 9–620] or resell the goods and apply the proceeds toward the debt [UCC 9–610].

RECALL A trespass to land occurs when a person, without permission, enters onto another's land and is established as a trespasser.

Judicial Remedies A secured party can relinquish a security interest and use any judicial remedy available, such as proceeding to judgment on the underlying debt, followed by execution and levy. (**Execution** is the implementation of a court's decree or judgment. **Levy** is the obtaining of funds by legal process through the seizure and sale of nonsecured property, usually done after a writ of execution has been issued.) Execution and levy are rarely undertaken unless the collateral is no longer in existence or has declined so much in value that it is worth substantially less than the

EXECUTION
An action to carry into effect the directions in a court decree or judgment.

LEVY
The obtaining of money by legal process through the seizure and sale of nonsecured property, usually done after a writ of execution has been issued.

amount of the debt and the debtor has other assets available that may be legally seized to satisfy the debt [UCC 9–601(a)].[7]

DISPOSITION OF COLLATERAL

Once default has occurred and the secured party has obtained possession of the collateral, the secured party may either retain the collateral in full satisfaction of the debt or may sell, lease, or otherwise dispose of the collateral in any commercially reasonable manner and apply the proceeds toward satisfaction of the debt [UCC 9–602(7), 9–603, 9–610(a), 9–620]. Any sale is always subject to procedures established by state law.

Retention of Collateral by the Secured Party The UCC acknowledges that parties are sometimes better off if they do not sell the collateral. Therefore, a secured party may retain the collateral unless it consists of consumer goods subject to a PMSI and the debtor has paid 60 percent or more of the purchase price or debt—as will be discussed shortly [UCC 9–620(e)].

This general right, however, is subject to several conditions. The secured party must send notice of the proposal to the debtor if the debtor has not signed a statement renouncing or modifying her or his rights *after default* [UCC 9–620(a), 9–621]. If the collateral is consumer goods, the secured party does not need to give any other notice. In all other situations, the secured party must send notice to any other secured party from whom the secured party has received written or authenticated notice of a claim of interest in the collateral in question. The secured party must also send notice to any other junior lien claimant (one holding a lien that is subordinate to a prior lien) who has filed a statutory lien (such as a mechanic's lien—see Chapter 26) or a security interest in the collateral ten days before the debtor consented to the retention [UCC 9–621].

If, within twenty days after the notice is sent, the secured party receives an objection sent by a person entitled to receive notification, the secured party must sell or otherwise dispose of the collateral. The collateral must be disposed of in accordance with the provisions of UCC 9–602, 9–603, 9–610, and 9–613 (disposition procedures will be discussed shortly). If no such written objection is forthcoming, the secured party may retain the collateral in full or partial satisfaction of the debtor's obligation [UCC 9–620(a), 9–621].

It is clear that a creditor can retain collateral in full satisfaction of a debt. The issue in the following case was whether a creditor could retain the collateral in *partial* satisfaction of the debt.

7. Some assets are exempt from creditors' claims—see Chapter 26.

CASE 25.3 Banks Brothers Corp. v. Donovan Floors, Inc.

Wisconsin Court of Appeals, 2000.
2000 WI App 253,
239 Wis.2d 381,
620 N.W.2d 631.
http://www.wisbar.org/WisCtApp/index.html[a]

a. In the "Court or Agency" section, select "Court of Appeals." Under the year, choose "2000" and then click on "Go." Scroll to the name of the case and click on it to access the opinion. The State Bar of Wisconsin maintains this Web site.

BACKGROUND AND FACTS Donovan Floors, Inc., and Breakfall, Inc., two companies controlled by James and Jo-Ann Donovan, borrowed $245,000 from Bank One, Milwaukee, N.A. The companies gave Bank One security interests in their assets, and the Donovans gave the lender a mortgage on their home. When Donovan Floors and Breakfall defaulted on the debt in 1991, Bank One filed a suit in a Wisconsin state court against the debtors. The Donovans agreed to surrender to Bank One some of the

CASE 25.3—Continued

firms' assets and agreed to a foreclosure on the home. Bank One promised not to act on the agreement immediately to give the Donovans a chance to revitalize their business. In 1993, Bank One assigned the debt and its security interest to Banks Brothers Corporation. Banks, the Donovans, and the Donovans' firms (Donovan Floors and Breakfall) signed an agreement under which, among other things, Banks was given some of the firms' assets (three cars, a truck, and a van), and Breakfall was released from the debt while the others remained liable. A payment schedule was set up, but none of the payments were made. Six years later, Banks scheduled a sale of the house. The Donovans and Donovan Floors filed a suit in a Wisconsin state court against Banks, arguing that the creditor's retention of assets and release of Breakfall operated as a full satisfaction of the debt. The court denied the request, and the debtors appealed to a state intermediate appellate court.

IN THE WORDS OF THE COURT . . .

FINE, J. [Judge]

* * * *

* * * Wis. Stat. [Section] 409.505(2) [Wisconsin's version of unrevised UCC 9–505(2)] permits the secured creditor to "propose to retain the collateral in satisfaction of the obligation," and, if the secured creditor seeks to do that, the secured creditor must send to the debtor "[w]ritten notice of such proposal."[b] In such a case, the debt would be satisfied in full. Section 409.505(2), however, gives to the debtor the power to [renounce or modify] the rights that the debtor has under the subsection, so long as the agreement "renouncing or modifying" those rights is "signed" by the debtor "after default" on the debt. Thus, Banks argues, * * * [under the agreement] executed after default, between Banks, Donovan Floors, and the Donovans * * * the Donovans and Donovan Floors renounced and modified their right under [Section] 409.505(2) to complete satisfaction of the debt, and * * * agreed that the satisfaction of the debt would [relieve] Breakfall only. * * *

Somewhat surprisingly, there are no cases directly on point—that is, dealing with a situation where, as here, a secured creditor has satisfied a debt as to some but not all debtors, and where, after default, all the debtors agreed to that arrangement in a statement signed by them. Wis. Stat. [Section] 409.505(2), however, clearly grants to debtors the right to renounce or modify the normal *quid pro quo* [a Latin phrase that means "the exchange of one thing for another"] for what is, in essence, strict foreclosure under [Section] 409.505(2): full satisfaction of the debt. * * * Stated another way, in return for the relatively inexpensive and expeditious application of the secured property to the debt, the secured creditor forgoes the right to chase the debtor for any deficiency. After default on the debt, however, debtors may renounce that *quid pro quo* for something more valuable—time within which to reorganize a business with the hope of saving it. That is what was done here.

Understandably, the Donovans and Donovan Floors would love to have their cake (the chance to save their business given to them by Banks's agreement to hold off on its right to claim the assets pledged for the debt) and eat it also (keep those assets). But that is not the way Wis. Stat. [Section] 409.505(2) works. Banks had a right under that section to immediate strict foreclosure of all the pledged assets. It gave up that right in consideration for a partial payment on the debt and the concomitant partial satisfaction. The Donovans and Donovan Floors have no legal or moral ground to complain; they agreed to that arrangement, and did so in a statement signed after default. This makes the arrangement legal under [Section] 409.505(2).

b. The court noted that although this case involved a provision in effect before the revision of Article 9, under the revised article's UCC 9–620, the result would have been the same.

(Continued)

CASE 25.3—Continued

DECISION AND REMEDY The state intermediate appellate court affirmed the order of the lower court. Creditors can retain collateral in partial satisfaction of a debt.

FOR CRITICAL ANALYSIS—Economic Consideration *What might be the effect on a lender's willingness to loan money if the law allowed the lender to retain collateral only in* full *satisfaction of the debt?*

REMEMBER Conversion is a tort that consists of an act depriving an owner of personal property without the owner's permission.

Consumer Goods When the collateral is consumer goods with a PMSI and the debtor has paid 60 percent or more of the debt or the purchase price, the secured party must sell or otherwise dispose of the repossessed collateral within ninety days [UCC 9–620(e) and (f)]. Failure to comply opens the secured party to an action for conversion or other liability under UCC 9–625(b) and (c) unless the consumer-debtor signed a written statement *after default* renouncing or modifying the right to demand the sale of the goods [UCC 9–624].

Disposition Procedures A secured party who does not choose to retain the collateral or who is required to sell it must resort to the disposition procedures prescribed under UCC 9–602(7), 9–603, 9–610(a), and 9–613. The UCC allows a great deal of flexibility with regard to disposition. UCC 9–610(a) states that after default, a secured party may sell, lease, license, or otherwise dispose of any or all of the collateral in its present condition or following any commercially reasonable preparation or processing. While the secured party may purchase the collateral at a public sale, it may not do so at a private sale—unless the collateral is of a kind customarily sold on a recognized market or is the subject of widely distributed standard price quotations [UCC 9–610(c)].

The Sale Must Be Accomplished in a Commercially Reasonable Manner. One of the major limitations on the disposition of the collateral is that it must be accomplished in a commercially reasonable manner. UCC 9–610(b) states as follows:

> Every aspect of a disposition of collateral, including the method, manner, time, place, and other terms, must be commercially reasonable. If commercially reasonable, a secured party may dispose of collateral by public or private proceedings, by one or more contracts, as a unit or in parcels, and at any time and place and on any terms.

Notification Requirements. Unless the collateral is perishable or will decline rapidly in value or is a type customarily sold on a recognized market, a secured party must send to the debtor and other identified persons "a reasonable authenticated notification of disposition" [UCC 9–611(b) and (c)]. The debtor may waive the right to receive this notice, but only after default [UCC 9–624(a)].

Proceeds from the Disposition Proceeds from the disposition of collateral after default on the underlying debt are distributed in the following order:

1. Expenses incurred by the secured party in repossessing, storing, and reselling the collateral.
2. Balance of the debt owed to the secured party.
3. Junior (subordinate) lienholders who have made written or authenticated demands.
4. Unless the collateral consists of accounts, payment intangibles, promissory notes, or chattel paper, any surplus goes to the debtor [UCC 9–608(a), 9–615(a) and (e)].

Noncash Proceeds Whenever the secured party receives noncash proceeds from the disposition of collateral after default, the secured party must make a value determination and apply this value in a commercially reasonable manner [UCC 9–608(a)(3), 9–615(c)].

Deficiency Judgment Often, after proper disposition of the collateral, the secured party has not collected all that the debtor still owes. Unless otherwise agreed, the debtor is liable for any deficiency, and the creditor can obtain a **deficiency judgment** from a court to collect the deficiency. Note, however, that if the underlying transaction was, for example, a sale of accounts or of chattel paper, the debtor is entitled to any surplus or is liable for any deficiency only if the security agreement so provides [UCC 9–615(d) and (e)].

DEFICIENCY JUDGMENT
A judgment against a debtor for the amount of a debt remaining unpaid after the collateral has been repossessed and sold.

Whenever the secured party fails to conduct a disposition in a commercially reasonable manner or to give proper notice, the deficiency of the debtor is reduced to the extent that such failure affected the price received at the disposition [UCC 9–626(a)(3)].

ETHICAL ISSUE 25.1

How long should a secured party have to seek a deficiency judgment? Because of depreciation, the amount received from the sale of collateral is frequently less than the amount the debtor owes the secured party. As noted, the secured party can file suit against the debtor in an attempt to collect the balance due. Practically speaking, however, debtors who have defaulted on a loan rarely have the cash to pay any deficiency. Article 9 does not contain a statute of limitations provision, though. Thus, it is not clear how long secured parties have after default to file a deficiency suit against debtors. If a secured party waits until the debtor becomes solvent again, the court might not allow the suit. Is this fair?

Consider, for example, a case that came before the Vermont Supreme Court in 2003. Duane Ouimette had bought a car with an extended warranty from a dealership under a retail installment sales contract. The contract was assigned to DaimlerChrysler. When Ouimette failed to make the payments, DaimlerChrysler repossessed the car and sold it at an auction. After the car was sold, Ouimette still owed more than $10,000 on the loan. Five and a half years later, DaimlerChrysler sued to collect the deficiency judgment, arguing that the company should have six years to file a deficiency action. The court noted that Vermont had never addressed the issue of what limitation period should apply to deficiency suits. Because the contract involved the sale of a car, however, the court held that the four-year limitation period stated in Article 2 applied, and thus the creditor's suit was too late.[8] ■

Redemption Rights At any time before the secured party disposes of the collateral or enters into a contract for its disposition, or before the debtor's obligation has been discharged through the secured party's retention of the collateral, the debtor or any other secured party can exercise the right of *redemption* of the collateral. The debtor or other secured party can do this by tendering performance of all obligations secured by the collateral and by paying the expenses reasonably incurred by the secured party in retaking and maintaining the collateral [UCC 9–623].

8. *DaimlerChrysler Services North America, LLC v. Ouimette*, 830 A.2d 38 (Vt. 2003).

REVIEWING SECURED TRANSACTIONS

Paul Barton owned a small property management company, doing business as Brighton Homes. In October, Barton went on a spending spree. First, he bought a Bose surround-sound system for his home from KDM Electronics. The next day, he purchased a Wilderness Systems kayak and roof rack from Outdoor Outfitters, and the day after that he bought a new Toyota 4-Runner financed through Bridgeport Auto. Two weeks later, Barton purchased six new iMac computers for his office, also from KDM Electronics. Barton bought each of these items under installment sales contracts. Six months later, Barton's property management business went bankrupt, and he could not make the payments due on any of these purchases and thus defaulted on the loans. Using the information presented in the chapter, answer the following questions.

1. Explain how a security interest was likely created for each of Barton's purchases (the surround-sound system, the kayak and roof rack, the 4-Runner, and the six iMacs).
2. For which of these purchases would the creditor need to file a financing statement to perfect its security interest?
3. Suppose that Barton's contract for the office computers mentioned only the name Brighton Homes. What would be the consequences if KDM Electronics filed a financing statement that listed only Brighton Homes as the debtor's name?
4. Which of these purchases would qualify as a PMSI in consumer goods? Would the security interest in each of these goods be automatically perfected? Why or why not? What else might a creditor have to do to perfect the security interest?
5. Suppose that after KDM Electronics repossesses the surround-sound system, it decides to keep it rather than to sell it. Could KDM do this under Article 9? Explain.

APPLICATION How Do You Perfect a Security Interest?*

The importance of perfecting your security interest cannot be overemphasized, particularly when the debt is large and you wish to maximize the priority of your security interest in the debtor's collateral. Failure to perfect or to perfect properly may result in your becoming the equivalent of an unsecured creditor.

Perfection by Filing

The filing of a financing statement in the appropriate location, as discussed in this chapter, is the most common method of perfection. Generally, the moment the filing takes place, your priority is established over the other creditors—as well as over some purchasers of the collateral and a subsequent trustee in bankruptcy.

When you create a security agreement, describe the collateral in terms that are specific enough to put third parties on notice of your security interest in that collateral. If your description is insufficient or misleading, your security interest will not be perfected.

Transactions outside Normal Business Relationships

Sometimes, credit transactions occur outside normal business relationships. You may be asked, for example, to aid an associate, a relative, or a friend. At that moment, you should reflect on your need for security for any debt that will be owed to you.

If there is a need for security, then you should perfect your security interest, even if you believe this action is unnecessary because the debtor is a friend or a relative. That particular friendship or blood relationship is irrele-

* This *Application* is not meant to substitute for the services of an attorney who is licensed to practice law in your state.

APPLICATION How Do You Perfect a Security Interest?—Continued

vant should he or she ever enter into bankruptcy proceedings. Bankruptcy law does not allow friends or relatives to be paid ahead of nonfriends or nonrelatives. You will end up standing in line with the other unsecured creditors if you have not perfected your security interest in the collateral. The best way to protect your security interest by perfection is to have your friend, relative, or associate transfer to your possession the collateral—stocks, bonds, jewelry, or whatever. By possessing such collateral, you can keep the transaction private but still have security for the loan.

CHECKLIST FOR PERFECTING YOUR SECURITY INTEREST

1. File a financing statement promptly.
2. Describe the collateral sufficiently—sometimes, it is better to err by giving too much detail than by giving too little.
3. Even with friends, relatives, or associates, be sure to perfect your security interest, perhaps by having the debtor transfer the collateral to your possession.

KEY TERMS

after-acquired property 651
attachment 641
collateral 639
continuation statement 650
debtor 639
default 640
deficiency judgment 663
execution 659
financing statement 639
floating lien 652
levy 659
perfection 643
pledge 649
proceeds 651
purchase-money security interest (PMSI) 650
secured party 639
secured transaction 638
security agreement 639
security interest 639

CHAPTER SUMMARY Secured Transactions

Creating a Security Interest (See pages 640–643.)	1. Unless the creditor has possession of the collateral, there must be a written or authenticated security agreement that is signed or authenticated by the debtor and describes the collateral subject to the security interest. 2. The secured party must give value to the debtor. 3. The debtor must have rights in the collateral—some ownership interest or right to obtain possession of the specified collateral.
Perfecting a Security Interest (See pages 643–650.)	1. *Perfection by filing*—The most common method of perfection is by filing a financing statement containing the names of the secured party and the debtor and indicating the collateral covered by the financing statement. a. Communication of the financing statement to the appropriate filing office, together with the correct filing fee, constitutes a filing. b. The financing statement must be filed under the name of the debtor; fictitious (trade) names normally are not accepted. c. The classification of collateral determines whether filing is necessary and where to file (see Exhibit 25–3 on pages 644 and 645).

(Continued)

CHAPTER SUMMARY Secured Transactions—Continued

Perfecting a Security Interest—Continued (See pages 643–650.)	2. *Perfection without filing—* a. By transfer of collateral—The debtor can transfer possession of the collateral to the secured party. A *pledge* is an example of this type of transfer. b. By attachment, such as the attachment of a purchase-money security interest (PMSI) in consumer goods—If the secured party has a PMSI in consumer goods (goods bought or used by the debtor for personal, family, or household purposes), the secured party's security interest is perfected automatically. In all, thirteen types of security interests can be perfected by attachment.
The Scope of a Security Interest (See pages 651–652.)	A security agreement can cover the following types of property: 1. *Collateral in the present possession or control of the debtor.* 2. *Proceeds from a sale, exchange, or disposition of secured collateral.* 3. *After-acquired property—*A security agreement may provide that property acquired after the execution of the security agreement will also be secured by the agreement. This provision often accompanies security agreements covering a debtor's inventory. 4. *Future advances—*A security agreement may provide that any future advances made against a line of credit will be subject to the initial security interest in the same collateral.
Priority of Claims to a Debtor's Collateral (See pages 653–657.)	See Exhibit 25–5 on page 654.
Rights and Duties of Debtors and Creditors (See pages 657–659.)	1. *Information request—*On request by any person, the filing officer must send a statement listing the file number, the date, and the hour of the filing of financing statements and other documents covering collateral of a particular debtor; a fee is charged. 2. *Release, assignment, and amendment—*A secured party may (a) release part or all of the collateral described in a filed financing statement, thus ending the creditor's security interest; (b) assign part or all of the security interest to another party; and (c) amend a filed financing statement. 3. *Confirmation or accounting request by debtor—*If a debtor believes that the unpaid debt amount or the listing of the collateral subject to the security interest is inaccurate, the debtor has the right to request a confirmation of his or her view of the unpaid debt or listing of collateral. The secured party must authenticate and send to the debtor an accounting within fourteen days after the request is received. Only one request without charge is permitted per six-month period. 4. *Termination statement—*When a debt is paid, the secured party generally must send a *termination statement* to the debtor or file such a statement with the filing officer to whom the original financing statement was given. Failure to comply results in the secured party's liability to the debtor for $500 plus any loss suffered by the debtor. a. If the financing statement covers consumer goods, the termination statement must be filed by the secured party within one month after the debt is paid, or if the debtor makes an authenticated demand, it must be filed within twenty days of the demand or one month after the debt is paid—whichever is earlier. b. In all other cases, the termination statement must be filed or furnished to the debtor within twenty days after an authenticated demand is made by the debtor.
Default (See pages 659–663.)	On the debtor's default, the secured party may do either of the following: 1. Take possession (peacefully or by court order) of the collateral covered by the security agreement and then pursue one of two alternatives:

CHAPTER SUMMARY Secured Transactions—Continued

Default—Continued	a. Retain the collateral (unless the secured party has a PMSI in consumer goods and the debtor has paid 60 percent or more of the selling price or loan), in which case the secured party must— (1) Give notice to the debtor if the debtor has not signed a statement renouncing or modifying his or her rights after default. With consumer goods, no other notice is necessary. (2) Send notice to any other secured party who has given written or authenticated notice of a claim to the same collateral or who has filed a security interest or a statutory lien ten days before the debtor consented to the retention. If an objection is received within twenty days from the debtor or any other secured party given notice, the creditor must dispose of the collateral according to the requirements of UCC 9–602, 9–603, 9–610, and 9–613. Otherwise, the creditor may retain the collateral in full or partial satisfaction of the debt. b. Dispose of the collateral in accordance with the requirements of UCC 9–602(7), 9–603, 9–610(a), and 9–613, in which case the secured party must— (1) Dispose of (sell, lease, or license) the goods in a commercially reasonable manner. (2) Notify the debtor and (except in sales of consumer goods) other identified persons, including those who have given notice of claims to the collateral to be sold (unless the collateral is perishable or will decline rapidly in value). (3) Apply the proceeds in the following order: (a) Expenses incurred by the secured party in repossessing, storing, and reselling the collateral. (b) The balance of the debt owed to the secured party. (c) Junior lienholders who have made written or authenticated demands. (d) Surplus to the debtor (unless the collateral consists of accounts, payment intangibles, promissory notes, or chattel paper). 2. Relinquish the security interest and use any judicial remedy available, such as proceeding to judgment on the underlying debt, followed by execution and levy on the nonexempt assets of the debtor.

FOR REVIEW

Answers for the even-numbered questions in this For Review *section can be found on this text's accompanying Web site at* http://blt.westbuslaw.com. *Select "Chapter 25" and click on "For Review."*

1. What is a security interest? Who is a secured party? What is a security agreement? What is a financing statement?
2. What three requirements must be met to create an enforceable security interest?
3. What is the most common method of perfecting a security interest under Article 9?
4. If two secured parties have perfected security interests in the collateral of the debtor, which party has priority to the collateral on the debtor's default?
5. What rights does a secured creditor have on the debtor's default?

attempts to secure a short-term loan from University Bank. The bank agrees to make a loan if Sabrina will have someone financially responsible guarantee the loan payments. Abigail, a well-known businessperson and a friend of Sabrina's family, calls the bank and agrees to pay the loan if Sabrina cannot. Because of Abigail's reputation, the bank makes the loan. Sabrina makes several payments on the loan, but because of illness she is not able to work for one month. She requests that University Bank extend the loan for three months. The bank agrees and raises the interest rate for the extended period. Abigail has not been notified of the extension (and therefore has not consented to it). One month later, Sabrina drops out of school. All attempts to collect from Sabrina have failed. University Bank wants to hold Abigail liable. Will the bank succeed? Explain.

26–4. Liens. Sylvia takes her car to Caleb's Auto Repair Shop. A sign in the window states that all repairs must be paid for in cash unless credit is approved in advance. Sylvia and Caleb agree that Caleb will repair Sylvia's car engine and put in a new transmission. No mention is made of credit. Because Caleb is not sure how much engine repair will be necessary, he refuses to give Sylvia an estimate. He repairs the engine and puts in a new transmission. When Sylvia comes to pick up her car, she learns that the bill is $995. Sylvia is furious, refuses to pay Caleb that amount, and demands possession of her car. Caleb demands payment. Discuss the rights of the parties in this matter.

26–5. Creditors' Remedies. Orkin owns a relatively old home valued at $45,000. He notices that the bathtubs and fixtures in both bathrooms are leaking and need to be replaced. He contracts with Pike to replace the bathtubs and fixtures. Pike replaces them and submits her bill of $4,000 to Orkin. Because of financial difficulties, Orkin does not pay the bill. Orkin's only asset is his home, which under state law is exempt up to $40,000 as a homestead. Discuss fully Pike's remedies in this situation.

26–6. Garnishment. Harmony Unlimited, Inc., obtained a judgment against John Chivetta and his company, JMC Enterprises. At the time of the judgment, John lacked sufficient funds to pay. Just before Harmony obtained the judgment, John had transferred $126,000 to his mother, Nettie, who had signed a promissory note. The note for $126,000 was payable on demand, carried no interest, and contained a provision that barred John from obtaining a money judgment against his mother. Nettie paid some of John's bills after the transfer of the $126,000 from her son to her. Harmony served a garnishment summons on Nettie, claiming that she was a party to a fraudulent scheme by her son to conceal his assets and was holding funds that belonged to her son. Nettie argued that Harmony's rights against her could not be any greater than John's rights against her and that because John could not obtain a judgment against her for the funds, Harmony could not do so either. Discuss Harmony's right of garnishment against Nettie. [*Harmony Unlimited, Inc. v. Chivetta,* 743 S.W.2d 884 (Mo.App. 1987)]

26–7. Guaranty. In 1988, Jamieson-Chippewa Investment Co. entered into a five-year commercial lease with TDM Pharmacy, Inc., for certain premises in Ellisville, Missouri, on which TDM intended to operate a small drugstore. Dennis and Tereasa McClintock ran the pharmacy business. The lease granted TDM three additional five-year options to renew. The lease was signed by TDM and by the McClintocks individually as guarantors. The lease did not state that the guaranty was continuing. In fact, there were no words of guaranty in the lease other than the single word "Guarantors" on the signature page. In 1993, Dennis McClintock, acting as the president of TDM, exercised TDM's option to renew the lease for one term. Three years later, when the pharmacy failed, TDM defaulted on the lease. Jamieson-Chippewa filed a suit in a Missouri state court against the McClintocks for the rent for the rest of the term, based on their guaranty. The McClintocks filed a motion for summary judgment, contending that they had not guaranteed any rent payments beyond the initial five-year term. How should the court rule? Why? [*Jamieson-Chippewa Investment Co. v. McClintock,* 996 S.W.2d 84 (Mo.App.E.D. 1999)]

26–8. Right of Subrogation. Levinson and Johnson, who had both signed a promissory note, did not pay the note when it was due. Instead, American Thermex, Inc., a corporation in which Johnson had a controlling interest, voluntarily paid the note. American Thermex later brought suit against Levinson, seeking reimbursement for the payment. American Thermex argued, among other things, that because it had paid the note, it had the legal right of subrogation against the note's co-maker, Levinson. Will the court agree that American Thermex has a legal right of subrogation? Why or why not? [*Levinson v. American Thermex, Inc.,* 196 Ga.App. 291, 396 S.E.2d 252 (1990)]

CASE PROBLEM WITH SAMPLE ANSWER

26–9. Susan Guinta is a real estate salesperson. Smythe Cramer Co. obtained in an Ohio state court a garnishment order to attach Guinta's personal earnings. The order was served on Russell Realtors to attach sales commissions that Russell owed to Guinta. Russell objected, arguing that commissions are not personal earnings and are therefore exempt from attachment under a garnishment of personal earnings. An Ohio statute defines *personal earnings* as "money, or any other consideration or thing of value, that is paid or due to a person in exchange for work, labor, or personal services provided by the person to an employer." An employer is "a person who is required to withhold taxes out of payments of personal earnings made to a judgment debtor." Russell does not withhold taxes from its salespersons' commissions. Under a federal statute, earnings means "compensation paid or payable for personal services, whether denominated as wages, salary, commission, bonus, or otherwise." Where the federal definition is more restrictive and results in a smaller garnishment, that definition is controlling. Property other than personal earnings may be subject to garnishment without limits. How should the court rule regarding Russell's objection? Why? [*Smythe Cramer Co. v. Guinta,* 762 N.E.2d 1083 (Ohio Mun. 2001)]

After you have answered this problem, compare your answer with the sample answer given on the Web site that accompanies this text. Go to http://blt.westbuslaw.com, select "Chapter 26," and click on "Case Problem with Sample Answer."

FOR CRITICAL ANALYSIS

26–10. Do you think that the law fairly balances the rights of creditors and those of debtors? Explain.

INTERNET EXERCISES

Go to the *Business Law Today* home page at http://blt.westbuslaw.com, select "Chapter 26," and click on "Internet Exercises." There you will find the following Internet research exercises that you can perform to learn more about topics covered in this chapter.

Activity 26–1: LEGAL PERSPECTIVE—Debtor-Creditor Relations

Activity 26–2: MANAGEMENT PERSPECTIVE—Mechanic's Liens

BEFORE THE TEST

Go to the *Business Law Today* home page at http://blt.westbuslaw.com, select "Chapter 26," and click on "Interactive Quizzes." You will find a number of interactive questions relating to this chapter.

CHAPTER 27

Bankruptcy

"Systems of bankruptcy are designed to relieve the honest debtor from the weight of indebtedness which has become oppressive and to permit him to have a fresh start in business or commercial life, freed from the obligation and responsibilities which may have resulted from business misfortunes."

William R. Day, 1849–1923
(Associate justice of the
United States Supreme Court, 1903–1922)

CHAPTER OUTLINE

- BANKRUPTCY PROCEEDINGS
- CHAPTER 7—LIQUIDATION
- CHAPTER 11—REORGANIZATION
- BANKRUPTCY RELIEF UNDER CHAPTER 13 AND CHAPTER 12

LEARNING OBJECTIVES

After reading this chapter, you should be able to answer the following questions:

1. In a bankruptcy proceeding, what constitutes the debtor's estate in property? What property is exempt from the estate under federal bankruptcy law?
2. What is a trustee? What does a trustee do?
3. Are all creditors' claims allowed in a bankruptcy proceeding? In what order are unsecured creditors' claims paid?
4. What is the difference between an exception to discharge and an objection to discharge?
5. In a Chapter 11 reorganization, what is the role of the debtor in possession?

Historically, debtors had few rights. Today, in contrast, debtors have numerous rights. Some of these rights were discussed in Chapters 25 and 26. In this chapter, we look at another significant right of debtors: the right to petition for bankruptcy relief under federal law. Article I, Section 8, of the U.S. Constitution gave Congress the power to establish "uniform Laws on the subject of Bankruptcies throughout the United States."

Bankruptcy law in the United States has two goals—to protect a debtor by giving him or her a fresh start, free from creditors' claims, and to ensure equitable treatment to creditors who are competing for a debtor's assets. Federal bankruptcy legislation was first enacted in 1898 and has undergone several modifications since that time.

For information and news on bankruptcy reform legislation, go to the site maintained by Bankruptcy Media at **http://www.bankruptcyfinder.com/bankruptcyreformnews.html**.

Bankruptcy law prior to 2005 was based on the Bankruptcy Reform Act of 1978, as amended—hereinafter called the Bankruptcy Code, or more simply, the Code (not to be confused with the Uniform Commercial Code, which is also sometimes called the Code). In 2005, Congress enacted a new Bankruptcy Reform Act.[1] As you will read throughout this chapter, the 2005 act significantly overhauled certain provisions of the Bankruptcy Code—for the first time in twenty-five years. Because of its significance for creditors and debtors alike, we present the Bankruptcy Reform Act as this chapter's *Landmark in the Law* feature on pages 688 and 689.

Bankruptcy Proceedings

Bankruptcy proceedings are held in federal bankruptcy courts, which are under the authority of the U.S. district courts, and rulings from bankruptcy courts can be appealed to the district courts. Although bankruptcy law is federal law, state laws on secured transactions, liens, judgments, and exemptions also play a role in federal bankruptcy proceedings.

Bankruptcy Courts

Essentially, a bankruptcy court fulfills the role of an administrative court for the federal district court concerning matters in bankruptcy. The bankruptcy court holds proceedings dealing with the procedures required to administer the estate of the debtor in bankruptcy. A bankruptcy court can conduct a jury trial if the appropriate district court has authorized it and the parties to the bankruptcy consent. Bankruptcy court judges are federally appointed for fourteen-year terms. The 2005 Bankruptcy Reform Act included a section entitled the Bankruptcy Judgeship Act of 2005, which enlarged the number of bankruptcy judges by twenty-eight (four for the Delaware District).

Types of Bankruptcy Relief

LIQUIDATION
The sale of all the nonexempt assets of a debtor and the distribution of the proceeds to the debtor's creditors. Chapter 7 of the Bankruptcy Code provides for liquidation bankruptcy proceedings.

Title 11 of the *United States Code* encompasses the Bankruptcy Code, which has eight chapters. Chapters 1, 3, and 5 of the Code contain general definitional provisions, as well as provisions governing case administration, creditors, the debtor, and the estate. These three chapters apply generally to all kinds of bankruptcies. The next five chapters of the Code set forth the different types of relief that debtors may seek. Chapter 7 provides for **liquidation** proceedings (the selling of all nonexempt assets and the distribution of the proceeds to the debtor's creditors). Chapter 9 governs the adjustment of a municipality's debts. Chapter 11 governs reorganizations. Chapters 12 and 13 provide for the adjustment of debts by parties with regular incomes (family farmers and family fishermen under Chapter 12 and individuals under Chapter 13).[2] A debtor

1. The full title of the act is the Bankruptcy Abuse Prevention and Consumer Protection Act of 2005, Pub. L. No. 109-8, 119 Stat. 23 (April 20, 2005).
2. There are no Chapters 2, 4, 6, 8, or 10 in Title 11. Such "gaps" are not uncommon in the *United States Code.* This is because chapter numbers (or other subdivisional unit numbers) are sometimes reserved for future use when a statute is enacted. (A gap may also appear if a law has been repealed.)

LANDMARK IN THE LAW

The Bankruptcy Reform Act of 2005

When Congress enacted the Bankruptcy Reform Act of 1978, many claimed that the new act made it too easy for debtors to file for bankruptcy protection. The Bankruptcy Reform Act of 2005 was passed, in part, in response to businesses' concerns about the rise in personal bankruptcy filings. Certainly, the facts cannot be denied: from 1978 to 2005, personal bankruptcy filings increased ninefold, reaching a peak of 1,613,097 in the year ending June 30, 2003. By the early 2000s, various business groups—including credit-card companies, banks, and firms providing loans for automobile purchases—were claiming that the bankruptcy process was being abused and that reform was necessary. As Mallory Duncan of the National Retail Federation put it, bankruptcy had gone from being a "stigma" to being a "financial planning tool" for many.[a]

The bulk of the act became effective 180 days after being signed by the president on April 20, 2005. Thus, the new provisions took effect in October 2005. Bankruptcy petitions that were filed before the act became effective continued to be administered and governed by the 1978 Reform Act, as amended.

MORE REPAYMENT PLANS, FEWER LIQUIDATION BANKRUPTCIES One of the major goals of the Bankruptcy Reform Act of 2005 is to require consumers to pay as many of their debts as they possibly can instead of having those debts fully discharged in bankruptcy. Prior to the new law, only about 20 percent of personal bankruptcies were filed under Chapter 13 of the Bankruptcy Code. As you will read later in this chapter, this chapter of the Bankruptcy Code involves establishing a repayment plan under which a debtor pays off as many of his or her debts as possible over a maximum period of five years. The remaining bankruptcies were filed under Chapter 7 of the Code, which permits debtors, with some exceptions, to have all of their debts discharged in bankruptcy.

The distinction has been important for all creditors. Given that most individuals who declare personal bankruptcy have few durable assets, filing for bankruptcy protection under Chapter 7 essentially means that creditors lose out. Under the new law, in contrast, whenever a debtor has an annual income in excess of the mean income in that debtor's state of residence, the debtor may be forced into a Chapter 13 repayment plan.

a. As cited in Nedra Pickler, "Bush Signs Big Rewrite of Bankruptcy Law," *The Los Angeles Times*, April 20, 2005.

(except for a municipality) need not be insolvent[3] to file for bankruptcy relief under any chapter of the Bankruptcy Code. Anyone obligated to a creditor can declare bankruptcy.

SPECIAL TREATMENT OF CONSUMER-DEBTORS

To fully inform a consumer-debtor of the various types of relief available, the Code requires that the clerk of the court provide certain information to all consumer-debtors prior to the commencement of a bankruptcy filing. (Recall from Chapter 26

3. The inability to pay debts as they become due is known as *equitable* insolvency. A *balance sheet* insolvency, which exists when a debtor's liabilities exceed assets, is not the test. Thus, it is possible for debtors to voluntarily petition for bankruptcy or to be thrown into involuntary bankruptcy even though their assets far exceed their liabilities. This may occur when a debtor's cash flow problems become severe.

LANDMARK IN THE LAW—Continued

OTHER SIGNIFICANT PROVISIONS OF THE ACT One of the provisions of the Bankruptcy Reform Act of 2005 involves the homestead exemption. Prior to the passage of the bankruptcy reform legislation, some states allowed debtors petitioning for bankruptcy to exempt all of the equity (the market value minus the outstanding mortgage owed) in their homes during bankruptcy proceedings. The 2005 act leaves these exemptions in place but puts some limits on their use. The 2005 act also includes a number of other changes. For example, one provision requires credit-card companies to make fuller disclosures about their interest rates and payment schedules. Another provision gives child-support obligations priority over other debts and allows enforcement agencies to continue efforts to collect child-support payments. Additionally, the act expands protections for family farmers and provides more protection for personal information about customers owned by businesses undergoing bankruptcy.

APPLICATION TO TODAY'S BUSINESS WORLD

The Bankruptcy Reform Act of 2005 subjects a large class of individuals in the United States to increased financial risk. Supporters of the law hope that it will curb abuse by deterring financially troubled debtors from looking at bankruptcy as a mere "planning tool" instead of as a last resort. Certainly, fewer debtors will be allowed to have their debts discharged in Chapter 7 liquidation proceedings. At the same time, the 2005 act will make it more difficult for debtors to obtain a "fresh start" financially—one of the major goals of bankruptcy law in the United States. Under the 2005 act, more debtors will be forced to file under Chapter 13. Additionally, the act has made the bankruptcy process more time consuming and costly because of its more extensive documentation and certification requirements.

RELEVANT WEB SITES

To locate information on the Web concerning the 2005 bankruptcy reform legislation, go to this text's Web site at **http://blt.westbuslaw.com**, *select "Chapter 27," and click on "URLs for Landmarks."*

that a consumer-debtor is a debtor whose debts result primarily from the purchase of goods for personal, family, or household use.) First, the clerk must give consumer-debtors written notice of the general purpose, benefits, and costs of each chapter of the Bankruptcy Code under which they might proceed. Second, under the 2005 act, the clerk must provide consumer-debtors with informational materials on the types of services available from credit counseling agencies.

In this chapter, we deal first with liquidation proceedings under Chapter 7 of the Code. We then examine the procedures required for Chapter 11 reorganizations and Chapter 12 and 13 plans. (The latter three chapters of the Code are known as "rehabilitation" chapters.)

Chapter 7—Liquidation

TRUSTEE
One who holds title to property for the use or benefit of another.

DISCHARGE
In bankruptcy proceedings, the extinction of the debtor's dischargeable debts.

PETITION IN BANKRUPTCY
A document filed with a bankruptcy court to initiate bankruptcy proceedings. The official forms required for a petition in bankruptcy must be completed accurately, sworn to under oath, and signed by the debtor.

U.S. TRUSTEE
A government official who performs certain administrative tasks that a bankruptcy judge would otherwise have to perform.

Liquidation under Chapter 7 of the Bankruptcy Code is generally the most familiar type of bankruptcy proceeding and is often referred to as an *ordinary*, or *straight, bankruptcy*. Put simply, a debtor in a liquidation bankruptcy turns all assets over to a **trustee.** The trustee sells the nonexempt assets and distributes the proceeds to creditors. With certain exceptions, the remaining debts are then **discharged** (extinguished), and the debtor is relieved of the obligation to pay the debts.

Any "person"—defined as including individuals, partnerships, and corporations[4]—may be a debtor in a liquidation proceeding. Railroads, insurance companies, banks, savings and loan associations, investment companies licensed by the Small Business Administration, and credit unions cannot be debtors in a liquidation bankruptcy, however. Other chapters of the Bankruptcy Code or federal or state statutes apply to them.

A straight bankruptcy may be commenced by the filing of either a voluntary or an involuntary **petition in bankruptcy**—the document that is filed with a bankruptcy court to initiate bankruptcy proceedings. If a debtor files the petition, it is a *voluntary bankruptcy*. If one or more creditors file a petition to force the debtor into bankruptcy, it is called an *involuntary bankruptcy*. We discuss both voluntary and involuntary bankruptcy proceedings under Chapter 7 in the following subsections.

VOLUNTARY BANKRUPTCY

To bring a voluntary petition in bankruptcy, the debtor files official forms designated for that purpose in the bankruptcy court. The Bankruptcy Reform Act of 2005 specifies that before debtors can file a petition, they must receive credit counseling from an approved nonprofit agency within the 180-day period preceding the date of filing. The act provides detailed criteria for the **U.S. Trustee** (a government official who performs appointment and other administrative tasks that a bankruptcy judge would otherwise have to perform) to approve nonprofit budget and counseling agencies and requires that a list of approved agencies be made publicly available.[5] A debtor filing a Chapter 7 petition must include a certificate proving that he or she received an individual or group briefing from an approved counseling agency within the last 180 days (roughly six months).

The Code requires a consumer-debtor who has opted for liquidation bankruptcy proceedings to confirm the accuracy of the petition's contents. The debtor must also state in the petition, at the time of filing, that he or she understands the relief available under other chapters of the Code and has chosen to proceed under Chapter 7. If an attorney is representing the consumer-debtor, the attorney must file an affidavit stating that she or he has informed the debtor of the relief available under each chapter of the Bankruptcy Code. In addition, the 2005 act requires the attorney to reasonably attempt to verify the accuracy of the consumer-debtor's petition and schedules (described below). Failure to do so is considered perjury.

Chapter 7 Schedules The voluntary petition must contain the following schedules:

1. A list of both secured and unsecured creditors, their addresses, and the amount of debt owed to each.

4. The definition of *corporation* includes unincorporated companies and associations. It also covers labor unions.

5. The Bankruptcy Reform Act of 2005 also required the director of the Executive Office for the U.S. Trustees to develop a curriculum for financial-management training and create materials that can be used to educate individual debtors on how to better manage their finances.

2. A statement of the financial affairs of the debtor.
3. A list of all property owned by the debtor, including property that the debtor claims is exempt.
4. A list of current income and expenses.
5. A certificate from an approved credit counseling agency (as discussed previously).
6. Proof of payments received from employers within sixty days prior to the filing of the petition.
7. A statement of the amount of monthly income, itemized to show how the amount is calculated.
8. A copy of the debtor's federal income tax return (or a transcript of such a return) for the most recent year ending immediately before the filing of the petition.

As previously noted, the official forms must be completed accurately, sworn to under oath, and signed by the debtor. To conceal assets or knowingly supply false information on these schedules is a crime under the bankruptcy laws.

Additional Information May Be Required. At the request of the court, the U.S. Trustee, or any party in interest, the debtor must file tax returns at the end of each tax year while the case is pending and provide copies to the court. This requirement also applies to Chapter 11 and 13 bankruptcies (discussed later in this chapter). Also, if requested by the U.S. Trustee or bankruptcy trustee, the debtor must provide a photo document establishing his or her identity (such as a driver's license or passport) or other personal identifying information.

Time Period for Filing Schedules. With the exception of tax returns, failure to file the required schedules within forty-five days after the filing of the petition (unless an extension of up to forty-five days is granted) will result in an automatic dismissal of the petition. The debtor has up to seven days before the date of the first creditors' meeting to provide a copy of the most recent tax returns to the trustee.

Substantial Abuse Prior to 2005, a bankruptcy court could dismiss a Chapter 7 petition for relief (discharge of debts) if the use of Chapter 7 would constitute a "substantial abuse" of that chapter. The Bankruptcy Reform Act of 2005 established a new system of "means testing" (based on the debtor's income) to determine whether a debtor's petition is presumed to be a "substantial abuse" of Chapter 7.

When Abuse Will Be Presumed. If the debtor's family income is greater than the median family income in the state in which the petition is filed, the trustee or any party in interest (such as a creditor) can bring a motion to dismiss the Chapter 7 petition. State median incomes vary from state to state and are calculated and reported by the U.S. Bureau of the Census.[6]

The debtor's current monthly income is calculated using the last six months' average income, less certain "allowed expenses" reflecting the basic needs of the debtor.[7] The monthly amount is then multiplied by twelve. If the resulting income exceeds the

6. For example, in 2004 the median family income in Kentucky was $53,319, and in West Virginia it was $49,470, according to statistics prepared by the Bureau of the Census and reported for each state annually in the *Federal Register.*

7. Section 707 of the Bankruptcy Reform Act of 2005 describes the means test and provides a detailed listing of the expenses allowed under the act.

state median income by $6,000 or more,[8] abuse is presumed, and the trustee or any creditor can file a motion to dismiss the petition. A debtor can rebut (refute) the presumption of abuse "by demonstrating special circumstances that justify additional expenses or adjustments of current monthly income for which there is no reasonable alternative." (One example might be anticipated medical costs not covered by health insurance.) These additional expenses or adjustments must be itemized and their accuracy attested to under oath by the debtor.

.on the Web For an overview of bankruptcy law and procedures with links to relevant code sections and cases, go to **http://www.law.cornell.edu/topics/bankruptcy.html**.

When Abuse Will Not Be Presumed. If the debtor's income is below the state median (or if the debtor has successfully rebutted the means-test presumption), abuse will not be presumed. In these situations, the court may still find substantial abuse, but the creditors will not have standing (see Chapter 3) to file a motion to dismiss. Basically, this leaves intact the prior law on substantial abuse, allowing the court to consider such factors as the debtor's bad faith or circumstances indicating substantial abuse. The following case illustrates how a court determined whether granting a Chapter 7 discharge to the debtor would constitute substantial abuse by applying the "totality-of-the-circumstances" test. Although the case was decided before the 2005 reforms were enacted, a court could take the same approach under the new law (if, for example, the means test did not require substantial abuse to be presumed).

8. This amount ($6,000) is the equivalent of $100 per month for five years, indicating that the debtor could pay at least $100 per month under a Chapter 13 five-year repayment plan.

CASE 27.1 In re Lamanna

United States Court of Appeals,
First Circuit, 1998.
153 F.3d 1.
http://www.law.emory.edu/1circuit[a]

BACKGROUND AND FACTS In 1996, Richard Lamanna was living with his parents. For this reason, his monthly expenses were only $580. His monthly income was $1,350.96, leaving a difference of $770.96, the amount of his disposable income.[b] He had no plans to move out of his parents' house. During four weeks in October and November, he charged $9,994.45 on credit cards. In February 1997, when his total unsecured debt was $15,911.96, he filed a voluntary petition in a federal bankruptcy court to declare bankruptcy under Chapter 7 of the Bankruptcy Code. The court noted that Lamanna was capable of paying all of his debts under a Chapter 13 repayment plan and dismissed the case. The U.S. Bankruptcy Appellate Panel (BAP)[c] for the First Circuit affirmed the dismissal, and Lamanna appealed to the U.S. Court of Appeals for the First Circuit. Lamanna argued in part that if he did not live with his parents, he would not have as much disposable income, and that thus he was being penalized for living with his parents.

a. In the "Listing by Month of Decision" section, click on "August" in the row for "1998" cases. When the list of cases appears, click on the case name to access the opinion. This Web site is maintained by Emory University School of Law.

b. *Disposable income* is income "not reasonably necessary to be expended for the maintenance or support of the debtor or a dependent of the debtor," according to 11 U.S.C. Section 1325(b)(2).

c. A *bankruptcy appellate panel* has jurisdiction, with the consent of the parties, to hear appeals from final judgments, orders, and decrees of bankruptcy judges.

IN THE WORDS OF THE COURT . . .

LYNCH, Circuit Judge.

* * * *

The question of whether allowing Lamanna's bankruptcy petition would constitute "substantial abuse" of Chapter 7 under Section 707(b) contains two compo-

CASE 27.1—Continued

nents: first, the proper test by which "substantial abuse" is measured; second, whether, applying that test, the BAP [Bankruptcy Appellate Panel] correctly decided the issue. * * *

* * * *

* * * Although tests employed by various courts of appeals do not employ precisely the same language, they share common elements. First and foremost, it is agreed that *a consumer debtor's ability to repay his debts out of future disposable income is strong evidence of "substantial abuse."* * * * In determining whether to apply Section 707(b) to an individual debtor, * * * a court should ascertain from the totality of the circumstances whether he is merely seeking an advantage over his creditors, or is "honest," * * * and whether he is "needy" in the sense that his financial predicament warrants the discharge of his debts in exchange for liquidation of his assets. * * * [T]he "totality of the circumstances" test demands a comprehensive review of the debtor's current and potential financial situation. [Emphasis added.]

* * * *

Applying the "totality of the circumstances" test to Lamanna's case results in affirmance of the dismissal of his Chapter 7 petition for "substantial abuse." Lamanna's schedules showed that he has sufficient disposable income to repay his debts under a Chapter 13 repayment plan in three to five years. There is no evidence that Lamanna's living situation was unstable or likely to change in the near future. There is no evidence of other factors that cast doubt on the stability of Lamanna's future income and expenses. Although Lamanna's expenses are particularly low because he lives with his parents, this state of affairs, as the BAP noted, "is not artificial; it is actual." The court properly based its decision on the current and foreseeable facts. If Lamanna's circumstances dramatically change, he is free to seek relief anew.

Lamanna's argument that the court penalized him for living with his parents (and thus having exceptionally low monthly expenses) boils down to the notion that Section 707 requires the bankruptcy court to impute a minimum cost of living to a debtor and then measure the debtor's actual income against the higher of the imputed minimum and the debtor's actual expenses. Section 707 does not contain such an implicit requirement, and this court will not write such a requirement into the statute.

DECISION AND REMEDY The U.S. Court of Appeals for the First Circuit affirmed the decision of the lower court and held that granting Lamanna's petition would constitute substantial abuse of Chapter 7. The appellate court looked at the "totality of the circumstances" to reach its conclusion.

FOR CRITICAL ANALYSIS—Economic Consideration *A finding of substantial abuse can be based on either a debtor's lack of honesty or his or her ability to pay outstanding debts after meeting necessary living expenses. What are some of the factors that might be considered in deciding whether a debtor is "needy"?*

Additional Grounds for Dismissal As noted, a debtor's voluntary petition for Chapter 7 relief may be dismissed for substantial abuse or for failing to provide the necessary documents (such as schedules and tax returns) within the specified time. In addition, a motion to dismiss a Chapter 7 filing might be granted in two other situations under the Bankruptcy Reform Act of 2005. First, if the debtor has been convicted of a violent crime or a drug-trafficking offense, the victim can file a motion to dismiss the voluntary petition.[9] Second, if the debtor fails to pay post-petition domestic-support obligations (which include child and spousal support), the court may dismiss the debtor's Chapter 7 petition.

ORDER FOR RELIEF
A court's grant of assistance to a complainant. In bankruptcy proceedings, the order relieves the debtor of the immediate obligation to pay the debts listed in the bankruptcy petition.

Order for Relief If the voluntary petition for bankruptcy is found to be proper, the filing of the petition will itself constitute an **order for relief.** (An order for relief is a court's grant of assistance to a complainant.) Once a consumer-debtor's voluntary petition has been filed, the clerk of the court or other appointee must give the trustee and creditors notice of the order for relief by mail not more than twenty days after entry of the order. A husband and wife may file jointly for bankruptcy under a single petition.

Involuntary Bankruptcy

An involuntary bankruptcy occurs when the debtor's creditors force the debtor into bankruptcy proceedings. An involuntary case cannot be commenced against a farmer[10] or a charitable institution. For an involuntary action to be filed against other debtors, the following requirements must be met: If the debtor has twelve or more creditors, three or more of these creditors having unsecured claims totaling at least $12,300 must join in the petition. If a debtor has fewer than twelve creditors, one or more creditors having a claim of $12,300 may file.

If the debtor challenges the involuntary petition, a hearing will be held, and the bankruptcy court will enter an order for relief if it finds either of the following:

1. The debtor is generally not paying debts as they become due.
2. A general receiver, assignee, or custodian took possession of, or was appointed to take charge of, substantially all of the debtor's property within 120 days before the filing of the petition.

If the court grants an order for relief, the debtor will be required to supply the same information in the bankruptcy schedules as in a voluntary bankruptcy.

An involuntary petition should not be used as an everyday debt-collection device, and the Code provides penalties for the filing of frivolous petitions against debtors. Judgment may be granted against the petitioning creditors for the costs and attorneys' fees incurred by the debtor in defending against an involuntary petition that is dismissed by the court. If the petition was filed in bad faith, damages can be awarded for injury to the debtor's reputation. Punitive damages may also be awarded.

Automatic Stay

AUTOMATIC STAY
In bankruptcy proceedings, the suspension of virtually all litigation and other action by creditors against the debtor or the debtor's property. The stay is effective the moment the debtor files a petition in bankruptcy.

The moment a petition, either voluntary or involuntary, is filed, an **automatic stay,** or suspension, of virtually all actions by creditors against the debtor or the debtor's property normally goes into effect. In other words, once a petition has been filed, creditors cannot contact the debtor by phone or mail or start any legal proceedings to recover debts or to repossess property. A secured creditor or other party in interest, however, may petition the bankruptcy court for relief from the automatic stay. The Code provides that if a creditor knowingly violates the automatic stay (a willful violation), any

9. Note that the court may not dismiss a case on this ground if the debtor's bankruptcy is necessary to satisfy a claim for a domestic-support obligation.
10. The definition of *farmer* includes persons who receive more than 50 percent of their gross income from farming operations, such as tilling the soil, dairy farming, ranching, or the production or raising of crops, poultry, or livestock. Corporations and partnerships may qualify under certain conditions.

party injured, including the debtor, is entitled to recover actual damages, costs, and attorneys' fees and may be entitled to recover punitive damages as well.

Underlying the Code's automatic-stay provision for a secured creditor is a concept known as *adequate protection*. The adequate protection doctrine, among other things, protects secured creditors from losing their security as a result of the automatic stay. The bankruptcy court can provide adequate protection by requiring the debtor or trustee to make periodic cash payments or a one-time cash payment (or to provide additional collateral or replacement liens) to the extent that the stay may actually cause the value of the property to decrease. Alternatively, the court may grant other relief that protects the secured party's interest in the property, such as a guaranty by a solvent third party to cover losses suffered by the secured party as a result of the stay.

Exceptions to the Automatic Stay The 2005 Bankruptcy Reform Act provides several exceptions to the automatic stay. A new exception is created for domestic-support obligations, which include any debt owed to or recoverable by a spouse, former spouse, child of the debtor, a child's parent or guardian, or a governmental unit. In addition, proceedings against the debtor related to divorce, child custody or visitation, domestic violence, and support enforcement are not stayed. Also excepted are investigations by a securities regulatory agency, the creation or perfection of statutory liens for property taxes or special assessments on real property, eviction actions on judgments obtained prior to filing the petition, and withholding from the debtor's wages for repayment of a retirement account loan.

Limitations on the Automatic Stay Under the new Code, if a creditor or other party in interest requests relief from the stay, the stay will automatically terminate sixty days after the request, unless the court grants an extension[11] or the parties agree otherwise. Also, the automatic stay on secured debts (see Chapter 25) will terminate thirty days after the petition is filed if the debtor had filed a bankruptcy petition that was dismissed within the prior year. (This is true unless the dismissal was based on the means test and the current petition was filed under a different chapter.) Any party in interest can request the court to extend the stay by showing that the filing is in good faith.

If two or more bankruptcy petitions were dismissed during the prior year, the Code presumes bad faith, and the automatic stay does not go into effect until the court determines that the filing was made in good faith. In addition, if the petition is subsequently dismissed because the debtor failed to file the required documents within thirty days of filing, for example, the stay is terminated. Finally, the automatic stay on secured property terminates forty-five days after the creditors' meeting (to be discussed shortly) unless the debtor redeems or reaffirms certain debts (*reaffirmation* will be discussed later in this chapter). In other words, the debtor cannot keep the secured property (such as a financed automobile), even if she or he continues to make payments on it, without reinstating the rights of the secured party to collect on the debt.

PROPERTY OF THE ESTATE

On the commencement of a liquidation proceeding under Chapter 7, an *estate in property* is created. The estate consists of all the debtor's interests in property currently held, wherever located, together with community property, property transferred in a

11. The court might grant an extension, for example, on a motion by the trustee that the property is of value to the estate.

transaction voidable by the trustee, proceeds and profits from the property of the estate, and certain after-acquired property. Interests in certain property—such as gifts, inheritances, property settlements (from divorce), and life insurance death proceeds—to which the debtor becomes entitled *within 180 days after filing* may also become part of the estate. Under the 2005 act, withholdings for employee benefit plan contributions are excluded from the estate. Generally, though, the filing of a bankruptcy petition fixes a dividing line: property acquired prior to the filing of the petition becomes property of the estate, and property acquired after the filing of the petition, except as just noted, remains the debtor's.

Creditors' Meeting and Claims

Within a reasonable time after the order for relief has been granted (not less than twenty days or more than forty days), the trustee must call a meeting of the creditors listed in the schedules filed by the debtor. The bankruptcy judge does not attend this meeting.

Debtor's Presence Required The debtor is required to attend the meeting (unless excused by the court) and to submit to examination under oath by the creditors and the trustee. Failing to appear when required or making false statements under oath may result in the debtor's being denied a discharge in bankruptcy. At the meeting, the trustee ensures that the debtor is aware of the potential consequences of bankruptcy and of his or her ability to file for bankruptcy under a different chapter of the Bankruptcy Code.

Creditors' Claims To be entitled to receive a portion of the debtor's estate, each creditor normally files a *proof of claim* with the bankruptcy court clerk within ninety days of the creditors' meeting.[12] The proof of claim lists the creditor's name and address, as well as the amount that the creditor asserts is owed to the creditor by the debtor. A creditor need not file a proof of claim if the debtor's schedules list the creditor's claim as liquidated (exactly determined) and the creditor does not dispute the amount of the claim. A proof of claim is necessary if there is any dispute concerning the claim. If a creditor fails to file a proof of claim, the bankruptcy court or trustee may file the proof of claim on the creditor's behalf but is not obligated to do so.

Generally, any legal obligation of the debtor is a claim (except claims for breach of employment contracts or real estate leases for terms longer than one year). When a claim is disputed, or unliquidated, the bankruptcy court will set the value of the claim. Any creditor holding a debtor's obligation can file a claim against the debtor's estate. These claims are automatically allowed unless contested by the trustee, the debtor, or another creditor. A creditor who files a false claim commits a crime.

Exemptions

The trustee takes control over the debtor's property, but an individual debtor is entitled to exempt certain property from the bankruptcy. The Bankruptcy Code exempts the following property:[13]

1. Up to $18,450 in equity in the debtor's residence and burial plot (the homestead exemption).

12. This ninety-day rule applies in Chapter 12 and Chapter 13 bankruptcies as well.

13. The dollar amounts stated in the Bankruptcy Code are adjusted automatically every three years on April 1 based on changes in the Consumer Price Index. The adjusted amounts are rounded to the nearest $25. The amounts stated in this chapter are in accordance with those computed on April 1, 2004.

*A mother and her daughter look over a collection of antiques and collectibles on display at a public auction. The auction is part of a company's liquidation bankruptcy proceeding. What other types of property might be included in the debtor's estate in property? (AP Photo/Christoper Record/*The Charlotte Observer)

2 Interest in a motor vehicle up to $2,950.

3 Interest, up to $475 for a particular item, in household goods and furnishings, wearing apparel, appliances, books, animals, crops, and musical instruments (the aggregate total of all items is limited, however, to $9,850).

4 Interest in jewelry up to $1,225.

5 Interest in any other property up to $975, plus any unused part of the $18,450 homestead exemption up to $9,250.

6 Interest in any tools of the debtor's trade up to $1,850.

7 Any unmatured life insurance contract owned by the debtor.

8 Certain interests in accrued dividends and interest under life insurance contracts owned by the debtor, not to exceed $9,850.

9 Professionally prescribed health aids.

10 The right to receive Social Security and certain welfare benefits, alimony and support, certain retirement funds and pensions, and education savings accounts held for specific periods of time.

11 The right to receive certain personal-injury and other awards up to $18,450.

Individual states have the power to pass legislation precluding debtors from using the federal exemptions within the state; a majority of the states have done this (see Chapter 26). In those states, debtors may use only state, not federal, exemptions. In the rest of the states, an individual debtor (or a husband and wife filing jointly) may choose either the exemptions provided under state law or the federal exemptions.[14]

Note also that the 2005 Bankruptcy Reform Act clarified specifically what is included in "household goods and furnishings" (referred to in number 3 in the above list). For example, the category includes one computer, one radio, one television, one videocassette recorder, educational materials or equipment primarily for use by minor dependent children, and furniture that is used exclusively by a minor dependent (or by an elderly or disabled dependent). Other items—such as works of art; electronic entertainment equipment with a fair market value of over $500; antiques and jewelry (except wedding rings) valued at more than $500; and motor vehicles, tractors, lawn mowers, watercraft, and aircraft—are not included in household goods.

The Homestead Exemption

The 2005 Bankruptcy Reform Act significantly changed the law for those debtors seeking to use state homestead exemption statutes (which were discussed in Chapter 26). In six states, among them Florida and Texas, homestead exemptions allow debtors petitioning for bankruptcy to shield unlimited amounts of equity in their homes from creditors. The prior Bankruptcy Code required that the debtor must have been domiciled in the state for at least six months to apply any of the state exemptions. Under the 2005 act, however, the domicile period is now two years. In other words, the debtor must have lived in the state for two years prior to filing the petition to be able to use the state homestead exemption.

14. State exemptions may or may not be limited with regard to value. Under state exemption laws, a debtor may enjoy an unlimited value exemption on a motor vehicle, for example, even though the federal bankruptcy scheme exempts a vehicle only up to a value of $2,950. A state's law may also define the property coming within an exemption differently than the federal law or may exclude, or except, specific items from an exemption, making it unavailable to a debtor who fits within the exception.

In addition, if the homestead is acquired within three and a half years preceding the date of filing, the maximum equity exempted is $125,000, even if the state law would permit a higher amount. (This does not apply to equity that has been rolled over during the specified period from the sale of a previous homestead in the same state.) Also, if the debtor owes a debt arising from a violation of securities law or if the debtor committed certain criminal or tortious acts in the previous five years that indicate the filing was substantial abuse, the debtor may not exempt any amount of equity.[15]

The Trustee

Promptly after the order for relief in the liquidation proceeding has been entered, an interim, or provisional, trustee is appointed by the U.S. Trustee. The interim, or provisional, trustee presides over the debtor's property until the first meeting of creditors. At this first meeting, either a permanent trustee is elected, or the interim trustee becomes the permanent trustee.

The basic duty of the trustee is to collect the debtor's available estate and reduce it to cash for distribution, preserving the interests of both the debtor and unsecured creditors. This requires that the trustee be accountable for administering the debtor's estate. To enable the trustee to accomplish this duty, the Code gives the trustee certain powers, stated in both general and specific terms. These powers must be exercised within two years of the order for relief.

New Duties under the 2005 Act The Bankruptcy Reform Act of 2005 imposes new duties on trustees (and bankruptcy administrators) with regard to means testing all debtors who file Chapter 7 petitions. Under the new law, the U.S. Trustee or bankruptcy administrator is required to promptly review all materials filed by the debtor. Not later than ten days after the first meeting of the creditors, the trustee must file a statement as to whether the case is presumed to be an abuse under the means test. The trustee must then provide a copy of this statement concerning abuse to all creditors within five days. Not later than forty days after the first creditors' meeting, the trustee must either file a motion to dismiss the petition (or convert it to a Chapter 13 case) or file a statement setting forth the reasons why the motion would not be appropriate.

Under the 2005 act, the trustee also has new duties designed to protect domestic-support creditors (those to whom a domestic-support obligation is owed). The trustee is required to provide written notice of the bankruptcy to the claim holder (a former spouse who is owed child support, for example). The notice must also include certain information, such as the debtor's address, the name and address of the debtor's last known employer, and the address and phone number of the state child-support enforcement agency. (Note that these requirements are not limited to Chapter 7 bankruptcies, and the trustee may have additional duties in other types of bankruptcy to collect assets for distribution to the domestic-support creditor.)

The Trustee's Powers The general powers of the trustee are described by the statement that the trustee occupies a position *equivalent* in rights to that of certain other parties. ■ EXAMPLE 27.1 The trustee has the same rights as a *lien creditor* who could

15. Specifically, the debtor may not claim the homestead exemption if the debtor has committed any criminal act, intentional tort, or willful or reckless misconduct that caused serious physical injury or death to another individual in the preceding five years. Also, if the debtor has been convicted of a felony, he or she may not be able to claim the exemption.

have obtained a judicial lien on the debtor's property or who could have levied execution on the debtor's property. This means that a trustee has priority over an unperfected secured party to the debtor's property. ■ This right of a trustee, equivalent to that of a lien creditor, is known as the *strong-arm power.* A trustee also has power equivalent to that of a *bona fide purchaser* of real property from the debtor.

Nevertheless, in most states a creditor with a purchase-money security interest may prevail against a trustee if the creditor files within ten days (twenty days, in many states) of the debtor's receipt of the collateral, even if the bankruptcy petition is filed before the creditor perfects. ■ EXAMPLE 27.2 Baker loaned Newbury $20,000 on January 1, taking a security interest in the machinery that Newbury purchased with the $20,000 and that was delivered on that same date. On January 27, before Baker had perfected her security interest, Newbury filed for bankruptcy. The trustee can invalidate Baker's security interest because it was unperfected when Newbury filed the bankruptcy petition. Baker can assert a claim only as an unsecured creditor. But if Newbury had filed for bankruptcy on January 7, and Baker had perfected her security interest on January 8, she would have prevailed, because she would have perfected her purchase-money security interest within ten days of Newbury's receipt of the machinery. ■

The Right to Possession of the Debtor's Property The trustee has the power to require persons holding the debtor's property at the time the petition is filed to deliver the property to the trustee. A trustee usually does not take actual possession of a debtor's property. Instead, a trustee's possession is constructive. ■ EXAMPLE 27.3 Suppose that a trustee needs to obtain control of a debtor's business inventory. The trustee might change the locks on the doors to the business and hire a security guard. ■

Avoidance Powers The trustee also has specific powers of *avoidance*—that is, the trustee can set aside a sale or other transfer of the debtor's property, taking it back as a part of the debtor's estate. These powers include any voidable rights available to the debtor, preferences, certain statutory liens, and fraudulent transfers by the debtor. Each of these powers is discussed in more detail below.

The debtor shares most of the trustee's avoidance powers. Thus, if the trustee does not take action to enforce one of the rights mentioned above, the debtor in a liquidation bankruptcy can nevertheless enforce that right.[16]

Note that under the 2005 act, the trustee no longer has the power to avoid any transfer that was a bona fide payment of a domestic-support debt.

Voidable Rights A trustee steps into the shoes of the debtor. Thus, any reason that a debtor can use to obtain the return of her or his property can be used by the trustee as well. These grounds include fraud, duress, incapacity, and mutual mistake.

■ EXAMPLE 27.4 Ben sells his boat to Tara. Tara gives Ben a check, knowing that she has insufficient funds in her bank account to cover the check. Tara has committed fraud. Ben has the right to avoid that transfer and recover the boat from Tara. Once an order for relief under Chapter 7 of the Code has been entered for Ben, the trustee can exercise the same right to recover the boat from Tara, and the boat becomes a part of the debtor's estate. ■

---

16. Under a Chapter 11 bankruptcy (to be discussed later), for which no trustee other than the debtor generally exists, the debtor has the same avoidance powers as a trustee under Chapter 7. Under Chapters 12 and 13 (also to be discussed later), a trustee must be appointed.

PREFERENCE
In bankruptcy proceedings, property transfers or payments made by the debtor that favor (give preference to) one creditor over others. The bankruptcy trustee is allowed to recover payments made both voluntarily and involuntarily to one creditor in preference over another.

Preferences A debtor is not permitted to transfer property or to make a payment that favors—or gives a **preference** to—one creditor over others. The trustee is allowed to recover payments made both voluntarily and involuntarily to one creditor in preference over another. If a *preferred creditor* (one who has received a preferential transfer from the debtor) has sold the property to an innocent third party, the trustee cannot recover the property from the innocent party. The preferred creditor, however, generally can be held accountable for the value of the property.

To have made a preferential payment that can be recovered, an *insolvent* debtor generally must have transferred property, for a *preexisting* debt, within *ninety days* prior to the filing of the petition in bankruptcy. The transfer must give the creditor more than the creditor would have received as a result of the bankruptcy proceedings. The trustee need not prove insolvency, as the Code provides that the debtor is presumed to be insolvent during this ninety-day period.

Preferences to Insiders. Sometimes, the creditor receiving the preference is an *insider*—an individual, a partner, a partnership, a corporation, or an officer or a director of a corporation (or a relative of one of these) who has a close relationship with the debtor. In this situation, the avoidance power of the trustee is extended to transfers made within *one year* before filing; however, the *presumption* of insolvency is confined to the ninety-day period. Therefore, the trustee must prove that the debtor was insolvent at the time of a transfer that occurred prior to the ninety-day period.

Transfers That Do Not Constitute Preferences. Not all transfers are preferences. To be a preference, the transfer must be made for something other than current consideration. Most courts generally assume that payment for services rendered within ten to fifteen days prior to the payment of the current consideration is not a preference. If a creditor receives payment in the ordinary course of business from an individual or business debtor, such as payment of last month's telephone bill, the payment cannot be recovered by the trustee in bankruptcy. To be recoverable, a preference must be a transfer for an antecedent (preexisting) debt, such as a year-old printing bill. In addition, the Code permits a consumer-debtor to transfer any property to a creditor up to a total value of $5,000, without the transfer's constituting a preference (this amount was increased from $600 to $5,000 by the 2005 act). Payment of domestic-support debts does not constitute a preference. Also, transfers that were made as part of an alternative repayment schedule negotiated by an approved credit counseling agency are not preferences.

Liens on Debtor's Property The trustee has the power to avoid certain statutory liens against the debtor's property, such as a landlord's lien for unpaid rent. The trustee can avoid statutory liens that first became effective against the debtor when the bankruptcy petition was filed or when the debtor became insolvent. The trustee can also avoid any lien against a bona fide purchaser that was not perfected or enforceable on the date of the bankruptcy filing. Under the 2005 act, the trustee cannot avoid certain warehouser's liens (see Chapter 43), however.

Fraudulent Transfers The trustee may avoid fraudulent transfers or obligations if they were made within two years of the filing of the petition or if they were made with actual intent to hinder, delay, or defraud a creditor. Transfers made for less than a reasonably equivalent consideration are also vulnerable if by making them, the debtor became insolvent, was left engaged in business with an unreasonably small amount of capital, or intended to incur debts that he or she could not pay. When a fraudulent transfer is made outside the Code's two-year limit, creditors may seek alternative relief under state laws. State laws often allow creditors to recover for transfers made up to three years prior to the filing of a petition.

DISTRIBUTION OF PROPERTY

The Code provides specific rules for the distribution of the debtor's property to secured and unsecured creditors. (We will examine these distributions shortly.) If any amount remains after the priority classes of creditors have been satisfied, it is turned over to the debtor. Exhibit 27–1 illustrates graphically the collection and distribution of property in most voluntary bankruptcies.

.on the Web To read a brief primer on the distribution of property in a Chapter 7 bankruptcy, go to **http://www.lawdog.com/bkrcy/lib2a8.htm**.

In a bankruptcy case in which the debtor has no assets,[17] creditors are notified of the debtor's petition for bankruptcy but are instructed not to file a claim. In such a case, the unsecured creditors will receive no payment, and most, if not all, of these debts will be discharged.

Distribution to Secured Creditors The rights of perfected secured creditors were discussed in Chapter 25. The Code provides that a consumer-debtor, either within thirty days of filing a liquidation petition or before the date of the first meeting of the creditors (whichever is first), must file with the clerk a statement of intention with respect to the secured collateral. The statement must indicate whether the debtor will redeem the collateral (make a single payment equal to the current value of the property), reaffirm the debt (continue making payments on the debt), or surrender the property to the secured party.[18] The trustee is obligated to enforce the debtor's statement within forty-five days after the meeting of the creditors. As noted previously, failure of the debtor to redeem or reaffirm within forty-five days terminates the automatic stay.

---

17. This type of bankruptcy is called a "no-asset" case.
18. Also, if applicable, the debtor must specify whether the collateral will be claimed as exempt property.

EXHIBIT 27–1 COLLECTION AND DISTRIBUTION OF PROPERTY IN MOST VOLUNTARY BANKRUPTCIES

This exhibit illustrates the property that might be collected in a debtor's voluntary bankruptcy and how it might be distributed to creditors. Involuntary bankruptcies and some voluntary bankruptcies could include additional types of property and other creditors.

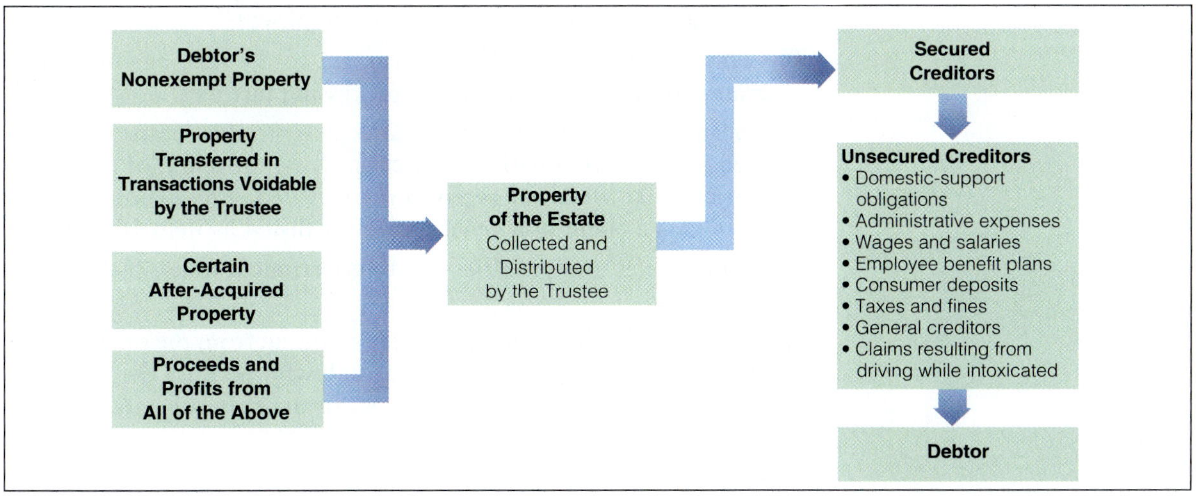

If the collateral is surrendered to the perfected secured party, the secured creditor can enforce the security interest either by accepting the property in full satisfaction of the debt or by foreclosing on the collateral and using the proceeds to pay off the debt. Thus, the perfected secured party has priority over unsecured parties as to the proceeds from the disposition of the collateral. Indeed, the Code provides that if the value of the collateral exceeds the perfected secured party's claim and if the security agreement so provides, the secured party also has priority as to the proceeds in an amount that will cover reasonable fees and costs incurred because of the debtor's default. Fees include reasonable attorneys' fees. Any excess over this amount is used by the trustee to satisfy the claims of unsecured creditors. Should the collateral be insufficient to cover the secured debt owed, the secured creditor becomes an unsecured creditor for the difference.

Distribution to Unsecured Creditors Bankruptcy law establishes an order of priority for classes of debts owed to *unsecured* creditors, and they are paid in the order of their priority. Each class must be fully paid before the next class is entitled to any of the remaining proceeds. If there are insufficient proceeds to pay fully all the creditors in a class, the proceeds are distributed *proportionately* to the creditors in that class, and classes lower in priority receive nothing. The new bankruptcy law elevated domestic-support obligations to the highest priority of unsecured claims. The order of priority among classes of unsecured creditors is as follows:

1. Claims for domestic-support obligations, such as child support and alimony (subject to the priority of the administrative costs that the trustee incurred in administering assets to pay the obligations).
2. Administrative expenses including court costs, trustee fees, and attorneys' fees.
3. In an involuntary bankruptcy, expenses incurred by the debtor in the ordinary course of business from the date of the filing of the petition up to the appointment of the trustee or the court's issuance of an order for relief.
4. Unpaid wages, salaries, and commissions earned within ninety days prior to the filing of the petition, limited to $4,925 per claimant. Any claim in excess of $4,925 or earned before the ninety-day period is treated as a claim of a general creditor (listed as item 10 below).
5. Unsecured claims for contributions to be made to employee benefit plans, limited to services performed during the 180-day period prior to the filing of the bankruptcy petition and $4,925 per employee.
6. Claims by farmers and fishermen, up to $4,925, against debtor-operators of grain storage or fish storage or processing facilities.
7. Consumer deposits of up to $2,225 given to the debtor before the petition was filed in connection with the purchase, lease, or rental of property or purchase of services that were not received or provided. Any claim in excess of $2,225 is treated as a claim of a general creditor (listed as item 10 below).
8. Certain taxes and penalties due to government units, such as income and property taxes.
9. Claims for death or personal injury resulting from the operation of a motor vehicle or vessel if such operation was unlawful because the debtor was intoxicated as a result of using alcohol, a drug, or another substance. (This provision was added by the 2005 act.)
10. Claims of general creditors.

DISCHARGE

From the debtor's point of view, the primary purpose of liquidation is to obtain a fresh start through a discharge of debts.[19] As mentioned earlier, once the debtor's assets have been distributed to creditors as permitted by the Code, the debtor's remaining debts are then discharged, meaning that the debtor is not obligated to pay them. Certain debts, however, are not dischargeable in bankruptcy. Also, certain debtors may not qualify to have all debts discharged in bankruptcy. These situations are discussed below.

Exceptions to Discharge Discharge of a debt may be denied because of the nature of the claim or the conduct of the debtor. Claims that are not dischargeable in a liquidation bankruptcy include the following:

1. Claims for back taxes accruing within two years prior to bankruptcy.
2. Claims for amounts borrowed by the debtor to pay federal taxes or any nondischargeable taxes.
3. Claims against property or funds obtained by the debtor under false pretenses or by false representations.
4. Claims by creditors who were not notified and did not know of the bankruptcy; these claims did not appear on the schedules the debtor was required to file.
5. Claims based on fraud or misuse of funds by the debtor while he or she was acting in a fiduciary capacity or claims involving the debtor's embezzlement or larceny.
6. Domestic-support obligations and property settlements as provided for in a separation agreement or divorce decree.
7. Claims for amounts due on a retirement account loan.
8. Claims based on willful or malicious conduct by the debtor toward another or the property of another.
9. Certain government fines and penalties, which under the 2005 act also include penalties imposed under federal election laws.
10. Certain student loans or obligations to repay funds received as an educational benefit, scholarship, or stipend—unless payment of the loans imposes an undue hardship on the debtor and the debtor's dependents.
11. Consumer debts of more than $500 for luxury goods or services owed to a single creditor incurred within ninety days of the order for relief. (Prior to the passage of the 2005 act, the amount was $1,150 and the period was sixty days.) This denial of discharge is a rebuttable presumption (that is, the denial may be challenged by the debtor), however, and any debts reasonably incurred to support the debtor or dependents are not classified as luxuries.
12. Cash advances totaling more than $750 that are extensions of open-end consumer credit obtained by the debtor within seventy days of the order for relief. (The prior law allowed $1,150 in cash advances that were obtained within sixty days.) A denial of discharge of these debts is also a rebuttable presumption.
13. Judgments or consent decrees against a debtor as a result of the debtor's operation of a motor vehicle or any vessel or aircraft while intoxicated.

---

19. Discharges are granted under Chapter 7 only to individuals, not to corporations or partnerships. The latter may use Chapter 11, or they may terminate their existence under state law.

CHAPTER 28

Agency Relationships in Business

"[It] is a universal principle in the law of agency, that the powers of the agent are to be exercised for the benefit of the principal only, and not of the agent or of third parties."

Joseph Story, 1779–1845
(Associate justice of the
United States Supreme Court, 1811–1844)

CHAPTER OUTLINE

- AGENCY RELATIONSHIPS
- HOW AGENCY RELATIONSHIPS ARE FORMED
- DUTIES OF AGENTS AND PRINCIPALS
- AGENT'S AUTHORITY
- LIABILITY IN AGENCY RELATIONSHIPS
- HOW AGENCY RELATIONSHIPS ARE TERMINATED

LEARNING OBJECTIVES

After reading this chapter, you should be able to answer the following questions:

1. What is the difference between an employee and an independent contractor?
2. How do agency relationships arise?
3. What duties do agents and principals owe to each other?
4. When is a principal liable for the agent's actions with respect to third parties? When is the agent liable?
5. What are some of the ways in which an agency relationship can be terminated?

AGENCY
A relationship between two parties in which one party (the agent) agrees to represent or act for the other (the principal).

One of the most common, important, and pervasive legal relationships is that of **agency.** As discussed in Chapter 23, in an agency relationship between two parties, one of the parties, called the *agent,* agrees to represent or act for the other, called the *principal.* The principal has the right to control the agent's conduct in matters entrusted to the agent, and the agent must exercise his or her powers "for the benefit of the principal only," as Justice Joseph Story indicated in the chapter-opening quotation. By using agents, a principal can conduct multiple business operations simultaneously in various locations. Thus, for example, contracts that bind the principal can be made at different places with different persons at the same time.

Agency relationships permeate the business world. Indeed, agency law is essential to the existence and operation of a corporate entity, because only through its agents can a corporation function and enter into contracts. A familiar example of an agent is a corporate officer who serves in a representative capacity for the owners of the corporation. In this capacity, the officer has the authority to bind the principal (the corporation) to a contract.

Agency Relationships

Section 1(1) of the *Restatement (Second) of Agency*[1] defines agency as "the fiduciary relation which results from the manifestation of consent by one person to another that the other shall act in his [or her] behalf and subject to his [or her] control, and consent by the other so to act." In other words, in a principal-agent relationship, the parties have agreed that the agent will act *on behalf and instead of* the principal in negotiating and transacting business with third parties.

FIDUCIARY
As a noun, a person having a duty created by his or her undertaking to act primarily for another's benefit in matters connected with the undertaking. As an adjective, a relationship founded on trust and confidence.

The term **fiduciary** is at the heart of agency law. The term can be used both as a noun and as an adjective. When used as a noun, it refers to a person having a duty created by her or his undertaking to act primarily for another's benefit in matters connected with the undertaking. When used as an adjective, as in "fiduciary relationship," it means that the relationship involves trust and confidence.

Agency relationships commonly exist between employers and employees. Agency relationships may sometimes also exist between employers and independent contractors who are hired to perform special tasks or services.

EMPLOYER-EMPLOYEE RELATIONSHIPS

Normally, all employees who deal with third parties are deemed to be agents. A salesperson in a department store, for instance, is an agent of the store's owner (the principal) and acts on the owner's behalf. Any sale of goods made by the salesperson to a customer is binding on the principal. Similarly, most representations of fact made by the salesperson with respect to the goods sold are binding on the principal.

.on the Web For information on the *Restatements of the Law,* including planned revisions, go to the American Law Institute's Web site at **http://www.ali.org**.

Because employees who deal with third parties are normally deemed to be agents of their employers, agency law and employment law overlap considerably. Agency relationships, though, as will become apparent, can exist outside an employer-employee relationship and thus have a broader reach than employment laws do. Additionally, bear in mind that agency law is based on the common law. In the employment realm, many common law doctrines have been displaced by statutory law and government regulations governing employment relationships.

Employment laws (state and federal) apply only to the employer-employee relationship. Statutes governing Social Security, withholding taxes, workers' compensation, unemployment compensation, workplace safety, employment discrimination, and the like (see Chapters 40 and 41) are applicable only if employer-employee status exists. *These laws do not apply to an independent contractor.*

EMPLOYER–INDEPENDENT CONTRACTOR RELATIONSHIPS

Independent contractors are not employees because, by definition, those who hire them have no control over the details of their physical performance. Section 2 of the *Restatement (Second) of Agency* defines an **independent contractor** as follows:

INDEPENDENT CONTRACTOR
One who works for, and receives payment from, an employer but whose working conditions and methods are not controlled by the employer. An independent contractor is not an employee but may be an agent.

> [An independent contractor is] a person who contracts with another to do something for him [or her] but who is not controlled by the other nor subject to the other's right to

1. The *Restatement (Second) of Agency* is an authoritative summary of the law of agency and is often referred to by jurists in their decisions and opinions.

control with respect to his [or her] physical conduct in the performance of the undertaking. *He [or she] may or may not be an agent.* [Emphasis added.]

Building contractors and subcontractors are independent contractors; a property owner does not control the acts of either of these professionals. Truck drivers who own their equipment and hire themselves out on a per-job basis are independent contractors, but truck drivers who drive company trucks on a regular basis are usually employees.

The relationship between a person or firm and an independent contractor may or may not involve an agency relationship. To illustrate: An owner of real estate who hires a real estate broker to negotiate a sale of the property not only has contracted with an independent contractor (the real estate broker) but also has established an agency relationship for the specific purpose of assisting in the sale of the property. Another example is an insurance agent, who is both an independent contractor and an agent of the insurance company for which she or he sells policies. (Note that an insurance *broker,* in contrast, normally is an agent of the person obtaining insurance and not of the insurance company.)

DETERMINING EMPLOYEE STATUS

The courts are frequently asked to determine whether a particular worker is an employee or an independent contractor. How a court decides this issue can have a significant effect on the rights and liabilities of the parties.

A businessperson (an independent contractor) sits on the floor working on his laptop computer in a computer server facility. What are some significant differences between employees and independent contractors? (Thinkstock Photo)

Criteria Used by the Courts In determining whether a worker has the status of an employee or an independent contractor, the courts often consider the following questions:

1. How much control can the employer exercise over the details of the work? (If an employer can exercise considerable control over the details of the work, this would indicate employee status. This is perhaps the most important factor weighed by the courts in determining employee status.)
2. Is the worker engaged in an occupation or business distinct from that of the employer? (If so, this points to independent-contractor status, not employee status.)
3. Is the work usually done under the employer's direction or by a specialist without supervision? (If the work is usually done under the employer's direction, this would indicate employee status.)
4. Does the employer supply the tools at the place of work? (If so, this would indicate employee status.)
5. For how long is the person employed? (If the person is employed for a long period of time, this would indicate employee status.)
6. What is the method of payment—by time period or at the completion of the job? (Payment by time period, such as once every two weeks or once a month, would indicate employee status.)
7. What degree of skill is required of the worker? (If little skill is required, this may indicate employee status.)

Sometimes, it is beneficial for workers to have employee status—to take advantage of laws protecting employees, for example. In contrast, independent-contractor status can sometimes be an advantage—for copyright ownership purposes, for example, as you will read shortly.

ETHICAL ISSUE 28.1

Why should it be left to the courts to determine who is or is not an independent contractor? Not surprisingly, many employers prefer to designate certain workers as independent contractors rather than as employees. As long as an employee agrees to be classified as an independent contractor, why should a court interfere in this decision? The answer is, at least in part, that issues of fairness may be involved, and the common law of agency, as developed and applied by the courts, implicitly recognizes these issues. After all, if a worker is an independent contractor, the worker must pay all Social Security taxes, instead of sharing them with his or her employer. Additionally, the worker will not be entitled to employer-provided benefits—such as pension plans, stock option plans, and group insurance coverage—that are often available to employees. Furthermore, the worker will not receive the legal protections afforded to employees under such laws as those regulating safety in the workplace or those protecting employees from discrimination. But what can a worker do, if an employer states that the worker is being hired as an independent contractor? Generally, in this situation the worker has only two options: either accept the arrangement or forfeit the job.[2] ■

Criteria Used by the IRS Often, the criteria for determining employee status are established by a statute or an administrative agency regulation. Businesspersons should be aware that the Internal Revenue Service (IRS) has established its own criteria for determining whether a worker is an independent contractor or an employee. Although the IRS once considered twenty factors in determining a worker's status, guidelines effective in 1997 encourage IRS examiners to focus on just one of those factors—the degree of control the business exercises over the worker.

The IRS tends to closely scrutinize a firm's classification of its workers because, as mentioned, employers can avoid certain tax liabilities by hiring independent contractors instead of employees. Even when a firm classifies a worker as an independent contractor, if the IRS decides that the worker is actually an employee, then the employer will be responsible for paying any applicable Social Security, withholding, and unemployment taxes.

In contrast, when a worker is a corporate officer, the exercise of control may be the opposite of the usual situation involving an employer and an employee. In that circumstance, the question may concern the degree of control that the officer (the employee) exercises over the corporation (the employer). In the following case, the issue was whether a corporate officer was an employee of the corporation.

2. See the *Question of Ethics* problem at the end of this chapter for a case brought by Microsoft Corporation's employees who were required to work as independent contractors instead of employees.

CASE 28.1 Nu-Look Design, Inc. v. Commissioner of Internal Revenue

United States Court of Appeals,
Third Circuit, 2004.
356 F.3d 290.

BACKGROUND AND FACTS Nu-Look Design, Inc., is a home-improvement company that provides carpentry, siding installation, and general residential construction services. During 1996, 1997, and 1998, Ronald Stark was Nu-Look's president, manager, and sole shareholder. He solicited business for the company, performed the bookkeeping, handled the firm's finances, and hired and supervised its workers. Instead of paying Stark a salary or wages, Nu-Look distributed its income to him "as Mr. Stark's needs arose." Nu-Look reported on its tax returns

(Continued)

CASE 28.1—Continued

for those years net income of $10,866.14, $14,216.37, and $7,103.60, respectively. Stark reported the same amounts as income on his tax returns. In 2001, the Internal Revenue Service (IRS) classified Stark as Nu-Look's employee and assessed federal employment taxes for 1996, 1997, and 1998. Nu-Look filed a suit in the U.S. Tax Court against the commissioner of the IRS, seeking relief from this liability. Nu-Look contended in part that Stark was not an employee because Nu-Look did not control Stark—Stark controlled Nu-Look. The court ruled against the firm, which appealed to the U.S. Court of Appeals for the Third Circuit.

IN THE WORDS OF THE COURT . . .

SMITH, Circuit Judge.

This appeal challenges the determination by the United States Tax Court that the Internal Revenue Service ("IRS") appropriately classified Ronald A. Stark, who was an officer and the sole shareholder of Nu-Look Design, Inc. ("Nu-Look"), as an employee of Nu-Look. That determination resulted in Nu-Look's liability for certain employment taxes under the Federal Insurance Contributions Act ("FICA") and the Federal Unemployment Tax Act ("FUTA"). * * *

* * * *

Nu-Look contends that the Tax Court erred in determining that Stark was an employee under the FICA and the FUTA. We begin by looking to the statutory language. Where the statutory language is plain and unambiguous, further inquiry is not required * * * .

Both the FICA and the FUTA impose taxes on employers based on the wages paid to individuals in their employ. "Wages," as defined by both Acts, includes, with certain exceptions not applicable here, "all remuneration for employment * * * *." Employment is "any service of whatever nature, performed* * * * *by an employee for the person employing him* * * * *." Employee is defined by the FICA [to include]* * * * *any officer of a corporation* * * * . Under the FUTA, the term employee, with certain exceptions not relevant here, has the same meaning * * * . [Under the IRS regulations] there is an exception for an "officer of a corporation who as such does not perform any services or performs only minor services and who neither receives nor is entitled to receive, directly or indirectly, any remuneration." [Emphasis added.]

* * * *

Mindful of these statutory provisions and Stark's status as a corporate officer, the Tax Court appropriately focused on the nature of the services Stark rendered and whether the distributions Nu-Look paid were remuneration for those services. It found that Stark performed more than minor services and that the distributions Stark received were, in fact, remuneration for his services. Those findings led the Tax Court to conclude that Stark was an employee for purposes of the FICA and the FUTA.

We agree. The record establishes that Stark was a corporate officer and that he single-handedly managed Nu-Look's entire operation. The services that Stark rendered for Nu-Look were, therefore, substantial and the Tax Court appropriately concluded that Stark was an employee * * * .

* * * *

In sum, we conclude that Stark was properly classified by the IRS as an employee of Nu-Look and that Nu-Look lacked a reasonable basis for failing to treat Stark as an employee. We will affirm the decision of the Tax Court that Nu-Look is liable for certain employment taxes under the FICA and the FUTA for calendar years 1996, 1997 and 1998.

CASE 28.1—Continued

DECISION AND REMEDY The U.S. Court of Appeals for the Third Circuit affirmed the ruling of the lower court. For federal tax purposes, Stark was to be considered an employee of Nu-Look, in light of the nature of the services that he rendered to the company and the income that the firm distributed to him as payment for those services.

WHY IS THIS CASE IMPORTANT? *Businesspersons should be aware that the mere designation of a person as either an independent contractor or a corporate officer does not mean the employer can avoid tax liability. The courts and the IRS look behind the label to ascertain the true relationship between the worker and the business entity.*

Employee Status and "Works for Hire" Under the Copyright Act of 1976, any copyrighted work created by an employee within the scope of her or his employment at the request of the employer is a "work for hire," and the employer owns the copyright to the work. When an employer hires an independent contractor—a freelance artist, writer, or computer programmer, for example—the independent contractor owns the copyright *unless* the parties agree in writing that the work is a "work for hire" and the work falls into one of nine specific categories, including audiovisual and other works.

■ EXAMPLE 28.1 Graham marketed CD-ROM discs containing compilations of software programs that are available free to the public. Graham hired James to create a file-retrieval program that allowed users to access the software on the CDs. James built into the final version of the program a notice stating that he was the author of the program and owned the copyright. Graham removed the notice. When James sold the program to another CD-ROM publisher, Graham filed a suit claiming that James's program was a "work for hire" and that Graham owned the copyright for the file-retrieval program. The court, however, decided that James—who was a skilled computer programmer who controlled the manner and method of his work—was an independent contractor and not an employee for hire. Thus, James owned the copyright for the file-retrieval program.[3] ■

How Agency Relationships Are Formed

Agency relationships normally are consensual; that is, they come about by voluntary consent and agreement between the parties. Generally, the agreement need not be in writing,[4] and consideration is not required.

A principal must have contractual capacity. A person who cannot legally enter into contracts directly should not be allowed to do so indirectly through an agent. Because an agent derives the authority to enter into contracts from the principal and because a contract made by an agent is legally viewed as a contract of the principal, it is immaterial whether the agent personally has the legal capacity to make that contract. Thus, a minor can be an agent but in some states cannot be a principal appointing an agent.[5] (When a minor is permitted to be a principal, however, any resulting

---

3. *Graham v. James,* 144 F.3d 229 (2d Cir. 1998).

4. There are two main exceptions to the statement that agency agreements need not be in writing: (1) Whenever agency authority empowers the agent to enter into a contract that the Statute of Frauds requires to be in writing, the agent's authority from the principal must likewise be in writing (this is called the *equal dignity rule,* which will be discussed later in this chapter). (2) A power of attorney, which confers authority to an agent, must be in writing.

5. Some courts have granted exceptions to allow a minor to appoint an agent for the limited purpose of contracting for the minor's necessities of life. See *Casey v. Kastel,* 237 N.Y. 305, 142 N.E. 671 (1924).

contracts will be voidable by the minor principal but not by the adult third party.) In sum, any person can be an agent, regardless of whether he or she has the capacity to contract. Even a person who is legally incompetent can be appointed an agent.

An agency relationship can be created for any legal purpose. An agency relationship that is created for an illegal purpose or that is contrary to public policy is unenforceable. ■ EXAMPLE 28.2 Suppose that Sharp (as principal) contracts with Blesh (as agent) to sell illegal narcotics. This agency relationship is unenforceable because selling illegal narcotics is a felony and is contrary to public policy. ■ It is also illegal for medical doctors and other licensed professionals to employ unlicensed agents to perform professional actions.

.on the Web An excellent source for information on agency, including court cases involving agency concepts, is the Legal Information Institute (LII) at Cornell University. You can access the LII's Web page on this topic at

http://www.law.cornell.edu/topics/agency.html.

Generally, an agency relationship can arise in four ways: by agreement of the parties, by ratification, by estoppel, and by operation of law. We look here at each of these possibilities, and they are summarized in the *Concept Summary* on the facing page.

AGENCY BY AGREEMENT

Most agency relationships are based on an express or implied agreement that the agent will act for the principal and that the principal agrees to have the agent so act. An agency agreement can take the form of an express written contract. ■ EXAMPLE 28.3 Renato enters into a written agreement with Troy, a real estate agent, to sell Renato's house. An agency relationship exists between Renato and Troy for the sale of the house and is detailed in a document that both parties sign. ■

Many express agency agreements are oral. ■ EXAMPLE 28.4 Suppose that Renato asks Cary, a gardener, to contract with others for the care of his lawn on a regular basis. Cary agrees. In this situation, an agency relationship exists between Renato and Cary for the lawn care. ■

RATIFICATION
The act of accepting and giving legal force to an obligation that previously was not enforceable.

An agency agreement can also be implied by conduct. ■ EXAMPLE 28.5 A hotel expressly allows only Boris Koontz to park cars, but Boris has no employment contract there. The hotel's manager tells Boris when to work, as well as where and how to park the cars. The hotel's conduct amounts to a manifestation of its willingness to have Boris park its customers' cars, and Boris can infer from the hotel's conduct that he has authority to act as a parking valet. It can be inferred that Boris is an agent-employee for the hotel, his purpose being to provide valet parking services for hotel guests. ■

A restaurant offers valet parking services. Can it be inferred that the parking attendant shown here is an agent of the restaurant? Why or why not? (Michael Newman/PhotoEdit)

AGENCY BY RATIFICATION

On occasion, a person who is in fact not an agent (or who is an agent acting outside the scope of her or his authority) may make a contract on behalf of another (a principal). If the principal approves or affirms that contract by word or by action, an agency relationship is created by **ratification.** Ratification is a question of intent, and intent can be expressed by either words or conduct. The basic requirements for ratification are discussed later in this chapter.

AGENCY BY ESTOPPEL

When a principal causes a third person to believe that another person is his or her agent, and the third person deals with the supposed agent, the principal is "estopped to deny" the agency relationship. In such a situation, the principal's actions create the *appearance* of an agency that does not in fact exist. The third person must prove that she or he *reasonably* believed that an agency relationship

CONCEPT SUMMARY How Agency Relationships Are Formed

METHOD OF FORMATION	DESCRIPTION
By Agreement	Agency relationship is formed through express consent (oral or written) or implied by conduct.
By Ratification	Principal either by act or by agreement ratifies conduct of a person who is not in fact an agent.
By Estoppel	Principal causes a third person to believe that another person is the principal's agent, and the third person acts to his or her detriment in reasonable reliance on that belief.
By Operation of Law	Agency relationship is based on a social duty (such as the need to support family members) or formed in emergency situations when the agent is unable to contact the principal.

existed, though.[6] Facts and circumstances must show that an ordinary, prudent person familiar with business practice and custom would have been justified in concluding that the agent had authority.

A proprietor reviews the inventory in her clothing store. Under what circumstances might a clothing importer be considered to act as an agent for the store? (Comstock Images)

■ EXAMPLE 28.6 Suppose that Andrew accompanies Grant, a seed sales representative, to call on a customer, Steve, the proprietor of the General Seed Store. Andrew has done independent sales work but has never signed an employment agreement with Grant. Grant boasts to Steve that he wishes he had three more assistants "just like Andrew." By making this representation, Grant creates the impression that Andrew is his agent and has authority to solicit orders. Steve has reason to believe from Grant's statements that Andrew is an agent for Grant. Steve then places seed orders with Andrew. If Grant does not correct the impression that Andrew is an agent, Grant will be bound to fill the orders just as if Andrew were really his agent. Grant's representation to Steve created the impression that Andrew was Grant's agent and had authority to solicit orders. ■

The acts or declarations of a purported *agent* in and of themselves do not create an agency by estoppel. Rather, it is the deeds or statements of the *principal* that create an agency by estoppel. ■ EXAMPLE 28.7 If Andrew walks into Steve's store and claims to be Grant's agent, when in fact he is not, and Grant has no knowledge of Andrew's representations, Grant will not be bound to any deal struck by Andrew and Steve. Andrew's acts and declarations alone do not create an agency by estoppel. ■

AGENCY BY OPERATION OF LAW

The courts may find an agency relationship in the absence of a formal agreement in other situations as well. This can occur in family relationships. For instance, suppose that one spouse purchases certain basic necessaries and charges them to the other spouse's charge account. The courts will often rule that the latter is liable for payment for the necessaries, either because of a social policy of promoting the general welfare of the spouse or because of a legal duty to supply necessaries to family members.

6. These concepts also apply when a person who is in fact an agent undertakes an action that is beyond the scope of her or his authority, as will be discussed later in this chapter.

liable. Employers can face liability for an agent's intentional torts in some situations, though, including those discussed next.

Acts Committed within the Scope of Employment. The doctrine of *respondeat superior* applies to intentional torts as well as to negligence. Thus, an employer can be held indirectly liable for the intentional torts of an employee that are committed within the course and scope of employment. For instance, an employer is liable when an employee (such as a "bouncer" at a nightclub or a security guard at a department store) commits the tort of assault and battery or false imprisonment while acting within the scope of employment.

An employer may also be liable for permitting an employee to engage in reckless actions that can injure others. ■ EXAMPLE 28.18 An employer observes an employee smoking while filling containerized trucks with highly flammable liquids. Failure to stop the employee will cause the employer to be liable for any injuries that result if a truck explodes. ■

Acts of Misrepresentation by an Agent. A principal is exposed to tort liability whenever a third person sustains a loss due to an agent's misrepresentation. The principal's liability depends on whether the agent was actually or apparently authorized to make representations and whether such representations were made within the scope of the agency. The principal is always directly responsible for an agent's misrepresentation made within the scope of the agent's authority. When a principal has placed an agent in a position of apparent authority—making it possible for the agent to defraud a third party—the principal may also be liable for the agent's fraudulent acts.

■ EXAMPLE 28.19 Assume that Bassett is a demonstrator for Moore's products. Moore sends Bassett to a home show to demonstrate the products and to answer questions from consumers. Moore has given Bassett authority to make statements about the products. If Bassett makes only true representations, all is fine; but if she makes false claims, Moore will be liable for any injuries or damages sustained by third parties in reliance on Bassett's false representations. ■

Liability for Independent Contractor's Torts Generally, an employer is not liable for physical harm caused to a third person by the negligent act of an independent contractor in the performance of the contract. This is because the employer does not have *the right to control* the details of an independent contractor's performance. Exceptions to this rule are made in certain situations, though, such as when unusually hazardous activities are involved. Typical examples of such activities include blasting operations, the transportation of highly volatile chemicals, or the use of poisonous gases. In these situations, an employer cannot be shielded from liability merely by using an independent contractor. Strict liability is imposed on the employer-principal as a matter of law. Also, in some states, strict liability may be imposed by statute.

Liability for Agent's Crimes An agent is liable for his or her own crimes. A principal or employer is not liable for an agent's crime even if the crime was committed within the scope of authority or employment—unless the principal participated by conspiracy or other action. In some jurisdictions, under specific statutes, a principal may be liable for an agent's violation, in the course and scope of employment, of regulations, such as those governing sanitation, prices, weights, and the sale of liquor.

INTERNATIONAL PERSPECTIVE

Islamic Law and *Respondeat Superior*

The doctrine of *respondeat superior* is well established in the legal systems of the United States and most Western countries. As you have already read, under this doctrine employers can be held liable for the acts of their agents, including employees. Middle Eastern countries, in contrast, do not follow this practice. Islamic law, as codified in the *sharia,* holds to a strict belief that responsibility for human actions lies with the individual and cannot be vicariously extended to others. This belief and other concepts of Islamic law are based on the writings of Muhammad, a seventh-century prophet whose revelations formed the basis of the Islamic religion and, by extension, the *sharia*. Muhammad's prophecies are documented in the Koran (Qur'an), which is the principal source of the *sharia*.

FOR CRITICAL ANALYSIS

How would U.S. society be affected if employers could not be held vicariously liable for their employees' torts?

How Agency Relationships Are Terminated

Agency law is similar to contract law in that both an agency and a contract can be terminated by an act of the parties or by operation of law. Once the relationship between the principal and the agent has ended, the agent no longer has the right to bind the principal. For an agent's apparent authority to be terminated, though, third persons may also need to be notified that the agency has been terminated.

Termination by Act of the Parties

An agency may be terminated by act of the parties in several ways, including those discussed here.

Lapse of Time An agency agreement may specify the time period during which the agency relationship will exist. If so, the agency ends when that time period expires. For instance, if the parties agree that the agency will begin on January 1, 2006, and end on December 31, 2007, the agency is automatically terminated on December 31, 2007. If no definite time is stated, then the agency continues for a reasonable time and can be terminated at will by either party. What constitutes a "reasonable time" depends, of course, on the circumstances and the nature of the agency relationship.

Purpose Achieved An agent can be employed to accomplish a particular objective, such as the purchase of stock for a cattle rancher. In that situation, the agency automatically ends after the cattle have been purchased. If more than one agent is employed to accomplish the same purpose, such as the sale of real estate, the first agent to complete the sale automatically terminates the agency relationship for all the others.

Occurrence of a Specific Event An agency can be created to terminate on the happening of a certain event. If Posner appoints Rubik to handle her business affairs while she is away, the agency automatically terminates when Posner returns.

Mutual Agreement Recall from the chapters on contract law that parties can cancel (rescind) a contract by mutually agreeing to terminate the contractual relationship. The same holds true in agency law regardless of whether the agency contract is in writing or whether it is for a specific duration.

Termination by One Party As a general rule, either party can terminate the agency relationship. The agent's act is called a *renunciation of authority.* The principal's act is referred to as a *revocation of authority.* Although both parties have the *power* to terminate the agency, they may not possess the *right.*

Wrongful termination can subject the canceling party to a suit for damages. ■ EXAMPLE 28.20 Rawlins has a one-year employment contract with Munro to act as an agent in return for $35,000. Munro can discharge Rawlins before the contract period expires (Munro has the *power* to breach the contract). Munro, though, will be liable to Rawlins for money damages because Munro has no *right* to breach the contract. ■

A special rule applies in an *agency coupled with an interest.* This type of agency is not an agency in the usual sense because it is created for the agent's benefit instead of for the principal's benefit. ■ EXAMPLE 28.21 Julie borrows $5,000 from Rob, giving Rob some of her jewelry and signing a letter giving Rob the power to sell the jewelry as her agent if she fails to repay the loan. After receiving the $5,000 from Rob, Julie attempts to revoke Rob's authority to sell the jewelry as her agent. Julie would not succeed in this attempt because a principal cannot revoke an agency created for the agent's benefit. ■

Notice of Termination When an agency has been terminated by act of the parties, it is the principal's duty to inform any third parties who know of the existence of the agency that it has been terminated (although notice of the termination may be given by others).

Agent's Authority Continues until Notified. An agent's authority continues until the agent receives some notice of termination. Notice to third parties follows the general rule that an agent's *apparent authority* continues until the third party receives notice (from any source) that such authority has been terminated. If the principal knows that a third party has dealt with the agent, the principal should notify that person directly. For third parties who have heard about the agency but have not yet dealt with the agent, *constructive notice* is sufficient.[16]

Form of Notice. No particular form is required for notice of agency termination to be effective. The principal can notify the agent directly, or the agent can learn of the termination through some other means. ■ EXAMPLE 28.22 Manning bids on a shipment of steel, and Stone is hired as an agent to arrange transportation of the shipment. When Stone learns that Manning has lost the bid, Stone's authority to make the transportation arrangement terminates. ■

If the agent's authority is written, it must be revoked in writing, and the writing must be shown to all people who saw the original writing that established the agency relationship. Sometimes, a written authorization (such as a power of attorney) contains an expiration date. The passage of the expiration date is sufficient notice of termination for third parties.

16. *Constructive notice* is information or knowledge of a fact imputed by law to a person if he or she could have discovered the fact by proper diligence. Constructive notice is often accomplished by newspaper publication.

TERMINATION BY OPERATION OF LAW

Termination of an agency by operation of law occurs in the circumstances discussed here. Note that when an agency terminates by operation of law, there is no duty to notify third persons.

Death or Insanity The general rule is that the death or mental incompetence of either the principal or the agent automatically and immediately terminates the ordinary agency relationship. Knowledge of the death is not required. ■ EXAMPLE 28.23 Suppose that Geer sends Pyron to China to purchase a rare painting. Before Pyron makes the purchase, Geer dies. Pyron's agent status is terminated at the moment of Geer's death, even though Pyron does not know that Geer has died. ■ Some states, however, have enacted statutes changing this common law rule to make knowledge of the principal's death a requirement for agency termination.

An agent's transactions that occur after the death of the principal are not binding on the principal's estate.[17] ■ EXAMPLE 28.24 Assume that Carson is hired by Perry to collect a debt from Thomas (a third party). Perry dies, but Carson, not knowing of Perry's death, still collects the funds from Thomas. Thomas's payment to Carson is no longer legally sufficient to discharge the debt to Perry because Carson's authority to collect ended on Perry's death. If Carson absconds with the funds, Thomas is still liable for the debt to Perry's estate. ■

Impossibility When the specific subject matter of an agency is destroyed or lost, the agency terminates. ■ EXAMPLE 28.25 Bullard employs Gonzalez to sell Bullard's house. Prior to any sale, the house is destroyed by fire. In this situation, Gonzalez's agency and authority to sell Bullard's house terminate. ■ Similarly, when it is impossible for the agent to perform the agency lawfully because of war or a change in the law, the agency terminates.

Changed Circumstances When an event occurs that has such an unusual effect on the subject matter of the agency that the agent can reasonably infer that the principal will not want the agency to continue, the agency terminates. ■ EXAMPLE 28.26 Roberts hires Mullen to sell a tract of land for $20,000. Subsequently, Mullen learns that there is oil under the land and that the land is worth $1 million. The agency and Mullen's authority to sell the land for $20,000 are terminated. ■

Bankruptcy If either the principal or the agent petitions for bankruptcy, the agency is *usually* terminated. In certain circumstances, as when the agent's financial status is irrelevant to the purpose of the agency, the agency relationship may continue. Insolvency (defined as the inability to pay debts when they become due or when liabilities exceed assets), as distinguished from bankruptcy, does not necessarily terminate the relationship.

War When the principal's country and the agent's country are at war with each other, the agency is terminated. In this situation, the agency is automatically suspended or terminated because there is no way to enforce the legal rights and obligations of the parties.

---

17. The Uniform Commercial Code (UCC) provides an exception to this rule in banking under which the bank, as the agent of the customer, can continue to exercise specific types of authority even after the customer has died or become mentally incompetent unless it has knowledge of the death or incompetence [UCC 4–405]. Even with knowledge of the customer's death, the bank has authority for ten days following the customer's death to honor checks in the absence of a stop-payment order.

REVIEWING AGENCY RELATIONSHIPS IN BUSINESS

James Blatt hired Marilyn Scott to sell insurance for the Massachusetts Mutual Life Insurance Company. Their contract stated, "Nothing in this contract shall be construed as creating the relationship of employer and employee." The contract was terminable at will by either party. Scott financed her own office and staff, was paid according to performance, had no taxes withheld from her checks, and could legally sell products of Massachusetts Mutual's competitors. But when Blatt learned that Scott was simultaneously selling insurance for Perpetual Life Insurance Corporation, one of Massachusetts Mutual's fiercest competitors, Blatt withheld client contact information from Scott that would have assisted her insurance sales for Massachusetts Mutual. Scott complained to Blatt that he was inhibiting her ability to sell insurance for Massachusetts Mutual. Blatt subsequently terminated their contract. Scott filed a suit in a New York state court against Blatt and Massachusetts Mutual. Scott claimed that she had lost sales for Massachusetts Mutual—and her commissions—as a result of Blatt's withholding contact information from her. Using the information presented in the chapter, answer the following questions.

1. Who is the principal and who is the agent in this scenario? By which method was an agency relationship formed between Scott and Blatt?
2. What criteria would the court consider to determine whether Scott was an employee or an independent contractor?
3. How would the Internal Revenue Service decide Scott's employee status?
4. What four duties did Blatt owe Scott in their agency relationship? Which, if any, of those duties has been breached?
5. What five duties did Scott owe Blatt? Did Scott breach any of her duties by selling insurance for Perpetual Life? Explain.

APPLICATION How Can an Employer Use Independent Contractors?*

As an employer, you may at some time consider hiring an independent contractor. Hiring workers as independent contractors instead of as employees may help you reduce both your potential tort liability and your tax liability.

Minimizing Potential Tort Liability

One reason for using an independent contractor is that doing so may reduce your susceptibility to tort liability. If, however, an independent contractor's words or conduct leads another party to believe that the independent contractor is your employee, you may not escape liability for the contractor's tort.

To minimize the possibility of being legally liable for negligence on the part of an independent contractor, you should inquire about the contractor's qualifications before hiring him or her. The degree to which you should investigate depends, of course, on the nature of the work. A more thorough investigation is necessary when the contractor's activities present a potential danger to the public (as in delivering explosives).

Generally, it is a good idea to have the independent contractor assume, in a written contract, liability for harms caused to third parties by the contractor's negligence. You should also require the independent contractor to purchase liability insurance to cover the costs of potential lawsuits for harms caused to third persons by the independent contractor's hazardous activities or negligence.

Reducing Tax Liability

Another reason for hiring independent contractors is that you need not pay or deduct Social Security and unemployment taxes on their behalf. The independent contractor is the party responsible for paying these taxes. Additionally,

* This *Application* is not meant to substitute for the services of an attorney who is licensed to practice law in your state.

APPLICATION How Can an Employer Use Independent Contractors?—Continued

the independent contractor is not eligible for any retirement or medical plans or other fringe benefits that you provide for yourself and your employees, and this is a cost saving to you.

A word of caution, though: simply designating a person as an independent contractor does not make her or him one. Under Internal Revenue Service (IRS) rules, individuals will be treated as employees if they are "in fact" employees, regardless of how you have classified them. For example, the IRS will not treat an office assistant as an independent contractor simply because you designate him or her as such. If the IRS determines that you exercise significant control over the assistant, the IRS may decide that the assistant is, in fact, an employee.

If you improperly designate an employee as an independent contractor, the penalty may be high. Usually, you will be liable for back Social Security and unemployment taxes, plus interest and penalties. When in doubt, seek professional assistance in such matters.

CHECKLIST FOR THE EMPLOYER

1. Check the qualifications of any independent contractor you plan to use to reduce the possibility that you might be legally liable for the contractor's negligence.
2. It is best to require in any contract with an independent contractor that the contractor assume liability for harm to a third person caused by the contractor's negligence.
3. Require that independent contractors working for you carry liability insurance. Examine the policy to make sure that it is current, particularly when the contractor will be undertaking actions that are more than normally hazardous to the public.
4. Make sure that independent contractors do not represent themselves as your employees to the rest of the world.
5. Regularly inspect the work of the independent contractor to make sure that it is being performed in accordance with contract specifications. Such supervision on your part will not change the worker's status as an independent contractor.

KEY TERMS

CHAPTER SUMMARY Agency Relationships in Business

Agency Relationships (See pages 725–729.)	In a *principal-agent* relationship, an agent acts on behalf of and instead of the principal in dealing with third parties. An employee who deals with third parties is normally an agent. An independent contractor is not an employee, and the employer has no control over the details of physical performance. An independent contractor may or may not be an agent.
How Agency Relationships Are Formed (See pages 729–732.)	Agency relationships may be formed by agreement, by ratification, by estoppel, and by operation of law—see the *Concept Summary* on page 731.

(Continued)

CHAPTER SUMMARY Agency Relationships in Business—Continued

Duties of Agents and Principals (See pages 732–735.)	1. *Duties of the agent*— a. Performance—The agent must use reasonable diligence and skill in performing her or his duties or use the special skills that the agent has represented to the principal that the agent possesses. b. Notification—The agent is required to notify the principal of all matters that come to his or her attention concerning the subject matter of the agency. c. Loyalty—The agent has a duty to act solely for the benefit of the principal and not in the interest of the agent or a third party. d. Obedience—The agent must follow all lawful and clearly stated instructions of the principal. e. Accounting—The agent has a duty to make available to the principal records of all property and money received and paid out on behalf of the principal. 2. *Duties of the principal*— a. Compensation—Except in a gratuitous agency relationship, the principal must pay the agreed-on value (or reasonable value) for an agent's services. b. Reimbursement and indemnification—The principal must reimburse the agent for all sums of money disbursed at the request of the principal and for all sums of money the agent disburses for necessary expenses in the course of reasonable performance of his or her agency duties. c. Cooperation—A principal must cooperate with and assist an agent in performing her or his duties. d. Safe working conditions—A principal must provide safe working conditions for the agent-employee.
Agent's Authority (See pages 735–739.)	1. *Express authority*—Can be oral or in writing. Authorization must be in writing if the agent is to execute a contract that must be in writing. 2. *Implied authority*—Authority customarily associated with the position of the agent or authority that is deemed necessary for the agent to carry out expressly authorized tasks. 3. *Apparent authority*—Exists when the principal, by word or action, causes a third party reasonably to believe that an agent has authority to act, even though the agent has no express or implied authority. 4. *Ratification*—The affirmation by the principal of an agent's unauthorized action or promise. For the ratification to be effective, the principal must be aware of all material facts.
Liability in Agency Relationships (See pages 739–746.)	1. *Liability for contracts*—If the principal's identity is disclosed or partially disclosed at the time the agent forms a contract with a third party, the principal is liable to the third party under the contract if the agent acted within the scope of his or her authority. If the principal's identity is undisclosed at the time of contract formation, the agent is personally liable to the third party, but if the agent acted within the scope of his or her authority, the principal is also bound by the contract. 2. *Liability for agent's negligence*—Under the doctrine of *respondeat superior,* the principal is liable for any harm caused to another through the agent's torts if the agent was acting within the scope of her or his employment at the time the harmful act occurred. 3. *Liability for agent's intentional torts*—Usually, employers are not liable for the intentional torts that their agents commit, *unless:* a. The acts are committed within the scope of employment and thus the doctrine of *respondeat superior* applies.

CHAPTER SUMMARY Agency Relationships in Business—Continued

Liability in Agency Relationships—Continued	b. The employer allowed an employee to engage in reckless acts that caused injury to another. c. The agent's misrepresentation causes a third party to sustain damage and the agent had either actual or apparent authority to act. 4. *Liability for independent contractor's torts*—A principal is not liable for harm caused by an independent contractor's negligence, unless hazardous activities are involved (in which situation the principal is strictly liable for any resulting harm) or other exceptions apply. 5. *Liability for agent's crimes*—An agent is responsible for his or her own crimes, even if the crimes were committed while the agent was acting within the scope of authority or employment. A principal will be liable for an agent's crime only if the principal participated by conspiracy or other action or (in some jurisdictions) if the agent violated certain government regulations in the course of employment.
How Agency Relationships Are Terminated (See pages 747–749.)	1. *By act of the parties*— a. Lapse of time (when the parties specified a definite time for the duration of the agency when it was established). b. Purpose achieved. c. Occurrence of a specific event. d. Mutual rescission (requires mutual consent of principal and agent). e. Termination by act of either the principal (revocation) or the agent (renunciation). (A principal cannot revoke an agency coupled with an interest.) f. Notice to third parties is required when an agency is terminated by act of the parties. Direct notice is required for those who have previously dealt with the agency; constructive notice will suffice for all other third parties. 2. *By operation of law*— a. Death or mental incompetence of either the principal or the agent (except when an agency is coupled with an interest). b. Impossibility (when the purpose of the agency cannot be achieved because of an event beyond the parties' control). c. Changed circumstances (in which it would be inequitable to require that the agency be continued). d. Bankruptcy of the principal or the agent, or war between the principal's and agent's countries. e. Notice to third parties is not required when an agency is terminated by operation of law.

FOR REVIEW

Answers for the even-numbered questions in this For Review *section can be found on this text's accompanying Web site at* http://blt.westbuslaw.com. *Select "Chapter 28" and click on "For Review."*

1. What is the difference between an employee and an independent contractor?
2. How do agency relationships arise?
3. What duties do agents and principals owe to each other?
4. When is a principal liable for the agent's actions with respect to third parties? When is the agent liable?
5. What are some of the ways in which an agency relationship can be terminated?

QUESTIONS AND CASE PROBLEMS

28–1. Ratification by Principal. Springer was a political candidate running for congressional office. He was operating on a tight budget and instructed his campaign staff not to purchase any campaign materials without his explicit authorization. In spite of these instructions, one of his campaign workers ordered Dubychek Printing Co. to print some promotional materials for Springer's campaign. When the printed materials were received, Springer did not return them but instead used them during his campaign. When Dubychek failed to obtain payment from Springer for the materials, he sued for recovery of the price. Springer contended that he was not liable on the sales contract because he had not authorized his agent to purchase the printing services. Dubychek argued that the campaign worker was Springer's agent and that the worker had authority to make the printing contract. Additionally, Dubychek claimed that even if the purchase was unauthorized, Springer's use of the materials constituted ratification of his agent's unauthorized purchase. Is Dubychek correct? Explain.

28–2. Employee versus Independent Contractor. Stephen Hemmerling was a driver for the Happy Cab Co. Hemmerling paid certain fixed expenses and abided by a variety of rules relating to the use of the cab, the hours that could be worked, and the solicitation of fares, among other things. Rates were set by the state. Happy Cab did not withhold taxes from Hemmerling's pay. While driving the cab, Hemmerling was injured in an accident and filed a claim against Happy Cab in a Nebraska state court for workers' compensation benefits. Such benefits are not available to independent contractors. On what basis might the court hold that Hemmerling is an employee? Explain.

28–3. Liability for Employee's Acts. Federated Financial Reserve Corp. leases consumer and business equipment. As part of its credit approval and debt-collection practices, Federated hires credit collectors, whom it authorizes to obtain credit reports on its customers. Janice Caylor, a Federated collector, used this authority to obtain a report on Karen Jones, who was not a Federated customer but who was the ex-wife of Caylor's roommate, Randy Lind. When Jones discovered that Lind had her address and how he had obtained it, she filed a suit in a federal district court against Federated and others. Jones claimed in part that they had violated the Fair Credit Reporting Act, the goal of which is to protect consumers from the improper use of credit reports. Under what theory might an employer be held liable for an agent-employee's violation of a statute? Does that theory apply in this case? Explain. [*Jones v. Federated Financial Reserve Corp.*, 144 F.3d 961 (6th Cir. 1998)]

28–4. Agent's Duties to Principal. Ana Barreto and Flavia Gugliuzzi asked Ruth Bennett, a real estate salesperson who worked for Smith Bell Real Estate, to list for sale their house in the Pleasant Valley area of Underhill, Vermont. Diana Carter, a California resident, visited the house as a potential buyer. Bennett worked under the supervision of David Crane, an officer of Smith Bell. Crane knew, but did not disclose to Bennett or Carter, that the house was subject to frequent and severe winds, that a window had blown in years earlier, and that other houses in the area had suffered wind damage. Crane knew of this because he lived in the Pleasant Valley area, had sold a number of nearby properties, and had been Underhill's zoning officer. Many valley residents, including Crane, had wind gauges on their homes to measure and compare wind speeds with their neighbors. Carter bought the house, and several months later, high winds blew in a number of windows and otherwise damaged the property. Carter filed a suit in a Vermont state court against Smith Bell and others, alleging fraud. She argued in part that Crane's knowledge of the winds was imputable to Smith Bell. Smith Bell responded that Crane's knowledge was obtained outside the scope of employment. What is the rule regarding how much of an agent's knowledge a principal is assumed to know? How should the court rule in this case? Why? [*Carter v. Gugliuzzi*, 716 A.2d 17 (Vt. 1998)]

CASE PROBLEM WITH SAMPLE ANSWER

28–5. Ford Motor Credit Co. is a subsidiary of Ford Motor Co. with its own offices, officers, and directors. Ford Credit buys contracts and leases of automobiles entered into by dealers and consumers. Ford Credit also provides inventory financing for dealers' purchases of Ford and non-Ford vehicles and makes loans to Ford and non-Ford dealers. Dealers and consumers are not required to finance their purchases or leases of Ford vehicles through Ford Credit. Ford Motor is not a party to the agreements between Ford Credit and its customers and does not directly receive any payments under those agreements. Also, Ford Credit is not subject to any agreement with Ford Motor "restricting or conditioning" its ability to finance the dealers' inventories or the consumers' purchases or leases of vehicles. A number of plaintiffs filed a product liability suit in a Missouri state court against Ford Motor. Ford Motor claimed that the court did not have venue. The plaintiffs asserted that Ford Credit, which had an office in the jurisdiction, acted as Ford's "agent for the transaction of its usual and customary business" there. Is Ford Credit an agent of Ford Motor? Discuss. [*State ex rel. Ford Motor Co. v. Bacon*, 63 S.W.3d 641 (Mo. 2002)]

After you have answered this problem, compare your answer with the sample answer given on the Web site that accompanies this text. Go to http://blt.westbuslaw.com, select "Chapter 28," and click on "Case Problem with Sample Answer."

28–6. Liability for Independent Contractor's Torts. Greif Brothers Corp., a steel drum manufacturer, owned and operated a manufacturing plant in Youngstown, Ohio. In 1987, Lowell Wilson, the plant superintendent, hired Youngstown Security Patrol, Inc. (YSP), a security company, to guard Greif property and "deter thieves and vandals." Some YSP security guards, as

Wilson knew, carried firearms. Eric Bator, a YSP security guard, was not certified as an armed guard but nevertheless took his gun, in a briefcase, to work. While working at the Greif plant on August 12, 1991, Bator fired his gun at Derrell Pusey, in the belief that Pusey was an intruder. The bullet struck and killed Pusey. Pusey's mother filed a suit in an Ohio state court against Greif and others, alleging in part that her son's death was the result of YSP's negligence, for which Greif was responsible. Greif filed a motion for a directed verdict. What is the plaintiff's best argument that Greif is responsible for YSP's actions? What is Greif's best defense? Explain. [*Pusey v. Bator,* 94 Ohio St.3d 275, 762 N.E.2d 968 (2002)]

28–7. Principal's Duties to Agent. Josef Boehm was an officer and the majority shareholder of Alaska Industrial Hardware, Inc. (AIH), in Anchorage, Alaska. In August 2001, Lincolnshire Management, Inc., in New York, created AIH Acquisition Corp. to buy AIH. The three firms signed a "commitment letter" to negotiate "a definitive stock purchase agreement" (SPA). In September, Harold Snow and Ronald Braley began to work, on Boehm's behalf, with Vincent Coyle, an agent for AIH Acquisition, to produce an SPA. They exchanged many drafts and dozens of e-mails. Finally, in February 2002, Braley told Coyle that Boehm would sign the SPA "early next week." That did not occur, however, and at the end of March, after more negotiations and drafts, Boehm demanded more money. AIH Acquisition agreed and, following more work by the agents, another SPA was drafted. In April, the parties met in Anchorage. Boehm still refused to sign. AIH Acquisition and others filed a suit in a federal district court against AIH. Did Boehm violate any of the duties that principals owe to their agents? If so, which duty, and how was it violated? Explain. [*AIH Acquisition Corp. v. Alaska Industrial Hardware, Inc.,* __ F.Supp.2d __ (S.D.N.Y. 2004)]

A QUESTION OF ETHICS

28–8. In 1990, the Internal Revenue Service (IRS) determined that a number of independent contractors working for Microsoft Corp. were actually employees of the company for tax purposes. The IRS arrived at this conclusion based on the significant control that Microsoft exercised over the independent contractors' work performance. As a result of the IRS's findings, Microsoft was ordered to pay back payroll taxes for hundreds of independent contractors who should have been classified as employees. Rather than contest the ruling, Microsoft required most of the workers in question, as well as a number of its other independent contractors, to become associated with employment agencies and work for Microsoft as temporary workers ("temps") or lose the opportunity to work for Microsoft. Workers who refused to register with employment agencies, as well as some who did register, sued Microsoft. The workers alleged that they were actually employees of the company and, as such, entitled to participate in Microsoft's stock option plan for employees. Microsoft countered that it need not provide such benefits because each of the workers had signed an independent-contractor agreement specifically stating that the worker was responsible for his or her own benefits. In view of these facts, consider the following questions. [*Vizcaino v. U.S. District Court for the Western District of Washington,* 173 F.3d 713 (9th Cir. 1999)]

1. If the decision were up to you, how would you rule in this case? Why?
2. Normally, when a company hires temporary workers from an employment agency, the agency—not the employer—is responsible for paying Social Security taxes and other withholding taxes. Yet the U.S. Court of Appeals for the Ninth Circuit held that being an employee of a temporary employment agency did not preclude the employee from having the status of a common law employee of Microsoft at the same time. Is this fair to the employer? Why or why not?
3. Generally, do you believe that Microsoft was trying to "skirt the law"—and its ethical responsibilities—by requiring its employees to sign up as "temps"?
4. Each of the employees involved in this case had signed an independent-contractor agreement. In view of this fact, is this decision fair to Microsoft? Why or why not?

FOR CRITICAL ANALYSIS

28–9. What policy is served by the law that employers do not have copyright ownership in works created by independent contractors (unless there is a written "work for hire" agreement)?

VIDEO QUESTION

28–10. Go to this text's Web site at **http://blt.westbuslaw.com** and select "Chapter 28." Click on "Video Questions" and view the video titled *Fast Times.* Then answer the following questions.

1. Recall from the video that Brad (Judge Reinhold) is told to deliver an order of Captain Hook Fish and Chips to IBM. Is Brad an employee or an independent contractor? Why?
2. Assume that Brad is an employee and agent of Captain Hook Fish and Chips. What duties does he owe Captain Hook Fish and Chips? What duties does Captain Hook Fish and Chips, as principal, owe to Brad?
3. In the video, Brad throws part of his uniform and several bags of the food that he is supposed to deliver out of his car window while driving. If Brad is an agent-employee and his actions cause injury to a person or property, can Captain Hook Fish and Chips be held liable? Why or why not? What should Captain Hook argue to avoid liability for Brad's actions?

substantiating these figures. To protect franchisees against arbitrary or bad faith terminations, the law might also require that certain procedures be followed in terminating a franchising relationship. State deceptive trade practices acts may also prohibit certain types of actions on the part of franchisors.

In response to the need for a uniform franchise law, the National Conference of Commissioners on Uniform State Laws drafted a model law that standardizes the various state franchise regulations. Because the uniform law represents a compromise of so many diverse interests, it has met with little success in being adopted as law by the various states.

A franchisee's claims against a franchisor under a state franchise disclosure law were at issue in the following case.

CASE 29.1 Bixby's Food Systems, Inc. v. McKay

United States District Court,
Northern District of Illinois, 2002.
193 F.Supp.2d 1053.

BACKGROUND AND FACTS In 1994, Phillip and Jan McKay met Ken Miyamoto, the president of Bixby's Food Systems, Inc., a franchisor of bagel restaurants. Miyamoto told the McKays that, among other things, the estimated start-up costs for a Bixby's franchise were between $143,000 and $198,000, that "existing bagel stores were doing annual sales in excess of $1,000,000.00, and that Bixby's franchises would exceed these revenue figures." In April 1995, at a meeting attended by the McKays, Miyamoto said that prospective franchisees had signed and paid for 340 development agreements; in actuality, however, no more than 15 had been executed. (A *development agreement* gave a prospective franchisee the right to buy a certain number of franchises within a given geographic area.) One week later, the McKays agreed to open a Bixby's store in Geneva, Illinois. Their initial costs, including a lease of space for the store, exceeded $400,000. After opening, their sales ranged from $25,000 to $30,000 per month. After eight months, Bixby's terminated their franchise agreement for failure to pay certain fees and filed a suit in a federal district court against the McKays for alleged violations of the agreement. The McKays filed a counterclaim against Miyamoto, alleging in part violations of the Illinois Franchise Disclosure Act (IFDA). The McKays filed a motion for summary judgment on these claims.

IN THE WORDS OF THE COURT . . .
NOLAN, United States Magistrate Judge.

* * * *

* * * [The Illinois Franchise Disclosure Act (IFDA)] provides that:

> [i]n connection with the offer or sale of any franchise made in this State, it is unlawful for any person, directly or indirectly, to * * * make any untrue statement of a material fact * * * .

The McKays list several untrue statements of material fact made by Miyamoto during the process of the franchise sale [including that] he knew the investment figures [he provided] were false * * * but he assured the McKays that the [figures] were accurate * * * . The McKays claim that they relied on these * * * representations * * * .

In addition, the McKays claim that Miyamoto violated [the IFDA] when he represented at the franchisees' April 11, 1995 meeting that Bixby's had 340 executed development agreements * * * . The McKays relied on these representations when they executed their franchise agreement * * * .

To be actionable under the IFDA, the misrepresentation must be an untrue statement of a material fact. * * *

A statement expressing an opinion or that relates to future or contingent events rather than to present facts, however, ordinarily does not constitute an actionable

CASE 29.1—Continued

misrepresentation * * * . For example, predictions of future sales or profitability are not considered representations of preexisting material facts. [Emphasis added.]

The McKays have not shown that, contrary to the general rule, Miyamoto's statements about future events, costs, and profitability are actionable misrepresentations under the IFDA, so summary judgment cannot be granted based upon those statements. * * *

The McKays have, however, conclusively shown that in April 1995, Miyamoto falsely claimed that Bixby's had 340 signed and paid-for development agreements when no more than fifteen development agreements had in fact been executed. Miyamoto's untrue statement was material to the McKays' decision to execute the Bixby's franchise agreement a week later. The McKays have demonstrated that there is no genuine dispute that Miyamoto made an untrue statement of a material fact in connection with the offer or sale of any franchise made in this State, and therefore summary judgment should be granted as to the McKays' claim under * * * the IFDA.

DECISION AND REMEDY The court granted the McKays' motion for summary judgment on the claim that Miyamoto violated the Illinois Franchise Disclosure Act when he falsely represented that Bixby's had 340 signed and paid-for development agreements. This was "an untrue statement of a material fact in connection with the offer or sale of any franchise," a violation of state law.

FOR CRITICAL ANALYSIS—Economic Consideration *Generally, what steps can a prospective franchisee take to ensure that a franchisor's statements as to future sales or profitability are reasonable estimates?*

The Franchise Contract

The franchise relationship is defined by a contract between the franchisor and the franchisee. The franchise contract specifies the terms and conditions of the franchise and spells out the rights and duties of the franchisor and the franchisee. If either party fails to perform the contractual duties, that party may be subject to a lawsuit for breach of contract. Generally, statutes and case law governing franchising tend to emphasize the importance of good faith and fair dealing in franchise relationships.

> **on the Web** A good source for information on the purchase and sale of franchises is Franchising.org, which is online at **http://www.franchising.org**.

Because each type of franchise relationship has its own characteristics, it is difficult to describe the broad range of details a franchising contract may include. In the remaining pages of this chapter, we look at some of the major issues that typically are addressed in a franchise contract. The *Application* feature at the end of this chapter further describes some steps a franchisee can take to avoid problems common in franchise agreements.

Payment for the Franchise

The franchisee ordinarily pays an initial fee or lump-sum price for the franchise license (the privilege of being granted a franchise). This fee is separate from the various products that the franchisee purchases from or through the franchisor. In some industries, the franchisor relies heavily on the initial sale of the franchise for realizing a profit. In other industries, the continued dealing between the parties brings profit to both. In most situations, the franchisor will receive a stated percentage of the annual sales or annual volume of business done by the franchisee. The franchise agreement may also require the franchisee to pay a percentage of advertising costs and certain administrative expenses.

CASE 29.2

Wisconsin Supre
273 Wis.App. 10
682 N.W.2d 328.

BACKGROUND AN national franchisor of fa Rasmussen, Inc. (DRI), i terms of their franchise Arby's specifications for business. DRI hired Catl Arby's restaurant in 199 Harvey Pierce, a local c privileges after a convic

implied. A franchisee must be given reasonable time to wind up the business—that is, to do the accounting and return the copyright or trademark or any other property of the franchisor.

Wrongful Termination

Because a franchisor's termination of a franchise often has adverse consequences for the franchisee, much franchise litigation involves claims of wrongful termination. Generally, the termination provisions of contracts are more favorable to the franchisor. This means that the franchisee, who normally invests a substantial amount of time and funds to make the franchise operation successful, may receive little or nothing for the business on termination. The franchisor owns the trademark and hence the business.

It is in this area that statutory and case law become important. The federal and state laws discussed earlier attempt, among other things, to protect franchisees from the arbitrary or unfair termination of their franchises by the franchisors. Generally, both statutory and case law emphasize the importance of good faith and fair dealing in terminating a franchise relationship.

The Importance of Good Faith and Fair Dealing

In determining whether a franchisor has acted in good faith when terminating a franchise agreement, the courts generally try to balance the rights of both parties. If a court perceives that a franchisor has arbitrarily or unfairly terminated a franchise, the franchisee will be provided with a remedy for wrongful termination. If a franchisor's decision to terminate a franchise was made in the normal course of the franchisor's business operations, however, and reasonable notice of termination was given to the franchisee, normally a court will not consider such a termination wrongful.

At issue in the following case was whether General Motors Corporation, Chrysler Corporation, and Toyota Motor Sales, U.S.A., Inc., acted wrongfully in terminating their franchises with a motor vehicle dealer in Ohio.

CASE 29.3 General Motors Corp. v. Monte Zinn Chevrolet Co.

Ohio Court of Appeals,
Tenth District, 2000.
136 Ohio App.3d 157,
736 N.E.2d 62.

BACKGROUND AND FACTS Monte Zinn operated Ohio motor vehicle dealerships, as Monte Zinn Chevrolet Company and Monte Zinn Motor Company, under separate franchise agreements with General Motors Corporation (GMC), Chrysler Corporation, and Toyota Motor Sales, U.S.A., Inc. Each agreement permitted the franchisor to terminate the dealership if the dealer was convicted of a felony. In 1995, Zinn pleaded guilty to committing a felony by violating federal statutes proscribing fraud and conspiracy to commit fraud in relation to his dealerships. He was sentenced to two years' probation and ordered to pay a fine and a special assessment. Each franchisor terminated its Zinn companies' franchise. The Zinn companies protested to the Ohio Motor Vehicle Dealers Board, a state agency that oversees motor vehicle franchises in Ohio. The board ruled in favor of the Zinn companies. The franchisors filed a suit in an Ohio state court against the Zinn companies, and the court reversed the board's order. The Zinn companies appealed to a state intermediate appellate court.

IN THE WORDS OF THE COURT . . .
BOWMAN, Judge.

* * * *

* * * [A] felony conviction for fraud committed by a dealer/operator undermines the trust between the manufacturer and the dealer, and between the public

CASE 29.3—Continued

and the dealer. * * * [F]rom 1991 to 1995, appellants' [the Zinn companies'] overall sales effectiveness had been in the bottom half of Chevrolet dealers in their service area and consistently ranked in the bottom twenty percent of all dealers in customer service and satisfaction. * * * [A]ppellants, the dealerships, as corporate entities, had made few investments into the dealership and * * * the property and facilities were personally owned by Zinn. These findings of fact all weigh in favor of finding good cause to terminate the franchise. The board's conclusion that General Motors had not met its burden of demonstrating good cause is not supported by the facts * * * .

Similarly, * * * [as to the Chrysler franchise,] appellants had been sizably undercapitalized every year from 1991; * * * between 1992 and 1996, their new vehicle sales volume increased at less than half the rate as the zone level and actually decreased between 1995 and 1996; and * * * appellants performed poorly in service-related areas compared to the zone average and * * * their scores on owner loyalty were below both zone and national averages. * * * Thus, in light of the * * * fact[s], which weigh heavily in favor of termination, the board's order to the contrary is not supported by reliable, probative [tending to prove], and substantial evidence, and is error as a matter of law.

Finally, as to the Toyota [franchise], in addition to the circumstances underlying the conviction, * * * Toyota's felony-termination clause was very important to Toyota * * * [;] it uniformly terminated dealerships following felony convictions * * * . Zinn personally owned the dealership facilities and would continue to retain them after termination of the franchise, and * * * other Toyota dealers could provide adequate service if appellants' franchises were terminated. In light of the absence of other findings of fact that weigh against finding good cause, the board's order is not supported by reliable, probative, and substantial evidence.

DECISION AND REMEDY The state intermediate appellate court affirmed the lower court's decision that the franchisors had good cause to terminate the franchises under the circumstances.

FOR CRITICAL ANALYSIS—Social Consideration *Should franchisors conduct background checks on prospective franchisees? Why or why not? Discuss whether a background check would have prevented the problems the franchisors encountered in this case.*

REVIEWING SOLE PROPRIETORSHIPS AND FRANCHISES

Carlos Del Rey decided to open a Mexican fast-food restaurant and signed a franchise contract with a national chain called *La Grande Enchilada*. The contract required the franchisee to strictly follow the franchisor's operating manual and stated that failure to do so would be grounds for terminating the franchise contract. The manual set forth detailed operating procedures and safety standards, and provided that a *La Grande* representative would inspect the restaurant monthly to ensure compliance. Nine months after Del Rey began operating his restaurant, a spark from the grill ignited an oily towel in the kitchen. No one was injured, but by the time firefighters were able to put out the fire, the kitchen had sustained extensive damage. The cook told the fire department that the

(Continued)

the bank for repaying the loan. Lukas could also be held liable to the bank in many states. Lukas has impliedly consented to the misrepresentation and will normally be estopped from denying that she is a partner of Sorento. She will be regarded as if she were in fact a partner in Sorento's business insofar as this loan is concerned. ■

Partnership Operation

The rights and duties of partners are governed largely by the specific terms of their partnership agreement. In the absence of provisions to the contrary in the partnership agreement, the law imposes the rights and duties discussed here. The character and nature of the partnership business generally influence the application of these rights and duties.

Rights of Partners

The rights of partners in a partnership relate to the following areas: management, interest in the partnership, compensation, inspection of books, accounting, and property.

Management Rights In a general partnership, all partners have equal rights in managing the partnership [UPA 401(f)]. Unless the partners agree otherwise, each partner has one vote in management matters *regardless of the proportional size of his or her interest in the firm.* Often, in a large partnership, partners will agree to delegate daily management responsibilities to a management committee made up of one or more of the partners.

The majority rule controls decisions in ordinary matters connected with partnership business, unless otherwise specified in the agreement. Decisions that significantly affect the nature of the partnership or that are not apparently for carrying on the ordinary course of the partnership business, or business of the kind, however, require the *unanimous* consent of the partners [UPA 301(2), 401(i), and 401(j)]. Unanimous consent is likely to be required for a decision to undertake any of the following actions:[2]

1. To alter the essential nature of the firm's business as expressed in the partnership agreement or to alter the capital structure of the partnership.
2. To admit new partners or to enter a wholly new business.
3. To assign partnership property to a trust for the benefit of creditors.
4. To dispose of the partnership's goodwill.
5. To confess judgment against the partnership or to submit partnership claims to arbitration. (A **confession of judgment** is the act of a debtor in permitting a judgment to be entered against him or her by a creditor, for an agreed sum, without the institution of legal proceedings.)
6. To undertake any act that would make further conduct of partnership business impossible.
7. To amend the articles of the partnership agreement.

CONFESSION OF JUDGMENT
The act or agreement of a debtor in permitting a judgment to be entered against him or her by a creditor, for an agreed sum, without the institution of legal proceedings.

2. The previous version of the UPA specifically listed most of these actions as requiring unanimous consent. The current version of the UPA omitted the list entirely to allow the courts more flexibility. The Official Comments explain that most of these acts, except for submitting a claim to arbitration, will likely remain outside the apparent authority of a partner.

Interest in the Partnership Each partner is entitled to the proportion of business profits and losses that is designated in the partnership agreement. If the agreement does not apportion profits (indicate how the profits will be shared), the UPA provides that profits will be shared equally. If the agreement does not apportion losses, losses will be shared in the same ratio as profits [UPA 401(b)].

■ EXAMPLE 30.4 The partnership agreement for Rico and Brent provides for capital contributions of $60,000 from Rico and $40,000 from Brent, but it is silent as to how Rico and Brent will share profits or losses. In this situation, Rico and Brent will share both profits and losses equally. If their partnership agreement provided for profits to be shared in the same ratio as capital contributions, however, 60 percent of the profits would go to Rico, and 40 percent of the profits would go to Brent. If their partnership agreement was silent as to losses, losses would be shared in the same ratio as profits (60 percent to 40 percent). ■

Compensation Devoting time, skill, and energy to partnership business is a partner's duty and generally is not a compensable service. Rather, as mentioned, a partner's income from the partnership takes the form of a distribution of profits according to the partner's share in the business. Partners can, of course, agree otherwise. For example, the managing partner of a law firm often receives a salary in addition to her or his share of profits for performing special administrative duties, such as managing the office or personnel.

UPA 401(h) provides that a partner is entitled to compensation for services in winding up partnership affairs (and reimbursement for expenses incurred in the process) above and apart from his or her share in the partnership profits.

Businesspersons examine accounting records. Are there any restrictions on the right of a partner to inspect his or her firm's books and records? Why or why not? (Jose L. Palaez/Getty Images)

Inspection of Books Partnership books and records must be kept accessible to all partners. Each partner has the right to receive (and each partner has the corresponding duty to produce) full and complete information concerning the conduct of all aspects of partnership business [UPA 403]. Each firm keeps books for recording and preserving such information. Partners contribute the information, and a bookkeeper or an accountant typically has the duty to preserve it. The books must be kept at the firm's principal business office and cannot be removed without the consent of all of the partners. Every partner, whether active or inactive, is entitled to inspect all books and records on demand and can make copies of the materials. The personal representative of a deceased partner's estate has the same right of access to partnership books and records that the decedent would have had [UPA 403].

Actions against the Partnership and among the Partners An accounting of partnership assets or profits is required to determine the value of each partner's share in the partnership. An accounting can be performed voluntarily, or it can be compelled by court order. Under UPA 405(b), a partner has the right to bring an action for an accounting during the term of the partnership, as well as on the firm's dissolution and winding up.[3] A partner also has the right to bring an action against the partnership or another partner, with or without a formal accounting, in the following situations:

1. To enforce the partner's rights under the partnership agreement.

3. Under the previous version of the UPA, a partner could bring an action for an accounting in any one of the following situations: the partnership agreement provided for it, the partner was wrongfully excluded from the business or its property or books, another partner was in breach of his or her fiduciary duty, or other circumstances rendered it "just and reasonable."

2. To enforce the partner's rights under the UPA.
3. To enforce the partner's rights and interests arising independently of the partnership relationship.

Property Rights A partner has the following three basic property rights:

1. An interest in the partnership.
2. A right in partnership property.
3. A right to participate in the management of the partnership, as previously discussed [UPA 401(f)].

Partner's Interest in the Firm. A partner's interest in the firm is a personal asset consisting of a proportionate share of the profits earned [UPA 502] and a return of capital on the partnership's termination. A partner's interest is subject to assignment or to a judgment creditor's lien (a lien obtained through the judicial process). Judgment creditors can attach a partner's interest by petitioning the court that entered the judgment to grant the creditors a **charging order.** This order entitles the judgment creditors to the profits of the partner and to any assets available to the partner on dissolution [UPA 504]. Neither an assignment nor a court's charging order entitling a judgment creditor to receive a share of the partner's funds will cause the dissolution of the firm [UPA 503].

CHARGING ORDER
In partnership law, an order granted by a court to a judgment creditor that entitles the creditor to attach profits or assets of a partner on the dissolution of the partnership.

Partnership Property. Property acquired by a partnership is the property of the partnership and not of the partners individually [UPA 203]. Property acquired *in the name of* the partnership or a partner is partnership property if the person's capacity as a partner or the existence of the partnership is indicated in the instrument transferring title. If the transferring instrument refers to neither of these, the property is still presumed to be partnership property when it is acquired with partnership funds [UPA 204].[4]

In all other circumstances, the property is presumed to be the property of an individual partner, even if it is used in the partnership business. Ultimately, in those situations, it is the intention of the partners that determines whether property belongs to the partnership or to a partner in his or her individual capacity [UPA 204(d)].

A partner may use or possess partnership property only on behalf of the partnership [UPA 401(g)]. A partner is not a co-owner of partnership property and has no interest in the property that can be transferred, either voluntarily or involuntarily [UPA 501]. In other words, partnership property is owned by the partnership as an entity and not by the individual partners.[5]

Duties and Liabilities of Partners

The duties and liabilities of partners are basically derived from agency law. Each partner is an agent of every other partner and acts as both a principal and an agent in any business transaction within the scope of the partnership agreement. Each

4. Partnership property was defined in the previous version of the UPA as "all property originally brought into the partnership's stock or subsequently acquired, by purchase or otherwise, on account of the partnership" [UPA 8(1)]. This definition, unlike the current UPA, did not provide any guidance concerning when property is "acquired by" a partnership.

5. Under the previous version of the UPA, partners were *tenants in partnership.* This meant that every partner was a co-owner with all other partners of the partnership property. The current UPA does not recognize this concept.

partner is also a general agent of the partnership in carrying out the usual business of the firm "or business of the kind carried on by the partnership" [UPA 301(1)].[6] Thus, every act of a partner concerning partnership business and "business of the kind," and every contract signed in the partnership's name, bind the firm. The UPA affirms general principles of agency law that pertain to the authority of a partner to bind a partnership in contract or tort.

We examine here the fiduciary duties of partners, the authority of partners, the joint and several liability that characterizes partnerships, and the limitations imposed on the liability of incoming partners for preexisting partnership debts.

Fiduciary Duties The only fiduciary duties a partner owes to the partnership and the other partners are the duty of loyalty and the duty of care, according to UPA 404(a). A partner's duty of loyalty is limited to accounting to the partnership for "any property, profit, or benefit" derived by the partner in the conduct of the partnership business or from a use of its property, and to refrain from dealing with the firm as an adverse party or competing with it in the conduct of the partnership business [UPA 404(b)]. A partner's duty of care is limited to refraining from "grossly negligent or reckless conduct, intentional misconduct, or a knowing violation of law" [UPA 404(c)].[7]

These duties may not be waived or eliminated in the partnership agreement, and in fulfilling them each partner must act consistently with the obligation of good faith and fair dealing, which applies to all contracts, including partnership agreements [UPA 103(b) and 404(d)].

A partner may pursue his or her own interests, however, without automatically violating these duties [UPA 404(e)]. For example, a partner who owns a shopping mall may vote against a partnership proposal to open a competing mall. Of course, the duties end on a partner's dissociation from the partnership (discussed later in this chapter) when the partner is free to, among other things, appropriate any new business opportunity for his or her own benefit [UPA 603(b)].

Authority of Partners The UPA affirms general principles of agency law that pertain to the authority of a partner to bind a partnership in contract. Under the same principles, a partner may also subject a partnership to liability in tort. When a partner is apparently carrying on partnership business or business of the kind with third parties in the usual way, both the partner and the firm share liability. The partnership will not be liable, however, if the third parties know that the partner has no such authority.

■ **EXAMPLE 30.5** Patricia, a partner in the partnership of Heise, Green, and Stevens, applies for a loan on behalf of the partnership without authorization from the other partners. The bank manager knows that Patricia has no authority. If the bank manager grants the loan, Patricia will be personally bound, but the firm will not be liable. ■

Under UPA 105 and 303, a partnership may file in a designated state office a "statement of partnership authority" to limit the capacity of a partner to act as the firm's agent or transfer property on its behalf. Any limit on a partner's authority, however, does not affect a third party who does not know about the statement,

6. It was not clear under the previous version of the UPA that a partner's apparent authority included acts in carrying on in the ordinary course "business of the kind carried on by the partnership," not just the business of the particular partnership in question.

7. The previous version of the UPA touched only briefly on the duty of loyalty and left the details of the partners' fiduciary duties to be developed under the law of agency.

Differences from Partnerships Joint ventures differ from partnerships in several important ways. The members of a joint venture have less implied and apparent authority than the partners in a partnership. As discussed in Chapter 30, each partner is treated as an agent of the other partners. Because the activities of a joint venture are more limited than the business of a partnership, the members of a joint venture are presumed to have less power to bind their co-venturers. In addition, unlike the death of a partner, the death of a joint venturer ordinarily does not terminate a joint venture. A joint venture normally terminates when the project or the transaction for which it was formed has been completed, though the members can specify how long the relationship will last.

CONTRAST A partnership involves a continuing relationship of the partners. A joint venture is often a one-time association.

Syndicates

SYNDICATE
An investment group of persons or firms brought together for the purpose of financing a project that they would not or could not undertake independently.

A group of individuals or firms that get together to finance a particular project, such as the building of a shopping center or the purchase of a professional basketball franchise, is called a **syndicate** or an *investment group*. The form of such groups varies considerably. A syndicate may exist as a corporation or as a general or limited partnership. In some instances, the members merely purchase and own property jointly but have no legally recognized business arrangement.

Joint Stock Companies

JOINT STOCK COMPANY
A hybrid form of business organization that combines characteristics of a corporation and a partnership. Usually, a joint stock company is regarded as a partnership for tax and other legal purposes.

A **joint stock company** is a true hybrid of a partnership and a corporation. It has many characteristics of a corporation in that (1) its ownership is represented by transferable shares of stock, (2) it is usually managed by directors and officers of the company or association, and (3) it can have a perpetual existence. Most of its other features, however, are more characteristic of a partnership, and it is usually treated like a partnership. As with a partnership, a joint stock company is formed by agreement (not statute), property is usually held in the names of the members, shareholders have personal liability, and the company generally is not treated as a legal entity for purposes of a lawsuit. In a joint stock company, however, shareholders are not considered to be agents of each other, as would be the case if the company were a true partnership (see Chapter 30).

Business Trusts

BUSINESS TRUST
A form of business organization in which investors (trust beneficiaries) transfer cash or property to trustees in exchange for trust certificates that represent their investment shares. The certificate holders share in the trust's profits but have limited liability.

A **business trust** is created by a written trust agreement that sets forth the interests of the beneficiaries and the obligations and powers of the trustees. With a business trust, legal ownership and management of the property of the business stay with one or more of the trustees, and the profits are distributed to the beneficiaries.

The business trust was started in Massachusetts in an attempt to obtain the limited liability advantage of corporate status while avoiding certain restrictions on a corporation's ownership and ability to develop real property. A business trust resembles a corporation in many respects. Beneficiaries of the trust, for example, are not personally responsible for the debts or obligations of the business trust. In fact, in a number of states, business trusts must pay corporate taxes.

Cooperatives

COOPERATIVE
An association, which may or may not be incorporated, that is organized to provide an economic service to its members. Unincorporated cooperatives are often treated like partnerships for tax and other legal purposes. Examples of cooperatives include consumer purchasing cooperatives, credit cooperatives, and farmers' cooperatives.

A **cooperative** is an association, which may or may not be incorporated, that is organized to provide an economic service to its members (or shareholders). Most cooperatives are organized under state statutes for cooperatives, general business incorporation statutes, or limited liability company (LLC) statutes. Generally, an incorporated cooperative will distribute dividends, or profits, to its owners on the basis of their transactions with the cooperative rather than on the basis of the amount of capital they contributed. Members of incorporated cooperatives have limited liability, as do shareholders of corporations and members of LLCs. Cooperatives that are unincorporated are often treated like partnerships. The members have joint liability for the cooperative's acts.

This form of business is generally adopted by groups of individuals who wish to pool their resources to gain some advantage in the marketplace. Consumer purchasing co-ops are formed to obtain lower prices through quantity discounts. Seller marketing co-ops are formed to control the market and thereby obtain higher sales prices from consumers. Co-ops range in size from small, local, consumer cooperatives to national businesses such as Ace Hardware and Land O' Lakes, the well-known producer of dairy products.

REVIEWING LIMITED LIABILITY COMPANIES AND SPECIAL BUSINESS FORMS

The city of Papagos, Arizona, had a deteriorating bridge in need of repair on a prominent public roadway. The city posted notices seeking proposals for an artistic bridge design and reconstruction. Davidson Masonry, LLC, which was owned and managed by Carl Davidson and his wife, Marilyn Rowe, decided to submit a bid for a decorative concrete project that incorporated artistic metalwork. They contacted Shana Lafayette, a local sculptor who specialized in large-scale metal designs, to help them design the bridge. The city selected their bridge design and awarded them the contract for a commission of $184,000. Davidson Masonry and Lafayette then entered into an agreement to work together on the bridge project. Davidson Masonry agreed to install and pay for concrete and structural work, and Lafayette agreed to install the metalwork at her expense. They agreed that overall profits would be split, with 25 percent to Lafayette and 75 percent to Davidson Masonry. Lafayette designed numerous metal sculptures of salmon that were incorporated into colorful decorative concrete forms designed by Rowe, while Davidson performed the structural engineering. The group worked together successfully until the project was completed. Using the information presented in the chapter, answer the following questions.

1. Would Davidson Masonry automatically be taxed as a partnership or a corporation?
2. What are the advantages and disadvantages of the limited liability company business form?
3. Is Davidson Masonry member managed or manager managed?
4. Would the project agreement between Davidson Masonry and Lafayette be considered a cooperative, a business trust, a joint stock company, a syndicate, or a joint venture? Explain.
5. What principles that apply to partnerships would not apply to the business arrangement between Davidson Masonry and Lafayette?

APPLICATION How Do You Choose between LLCs and LLPs?*

One of the most important decisions that an entrepreneur makes is the selection of the form in which to do business. To make the best decision, a businessperson should understand all aspects of the various forms, including legal, tax, licensing, and business considerations. It is also important that all of the participants in the business understand their actual relationship, regardless of the organizational structure.

* This *Application* is not meant to substitute for the services of an attorney who is licensed to practice law in your state.

(Continued)

APPLICATION How Do You Choose between LLCs and LLPs?—Continued

Number of Participants

During the last decade or so, new forms of business organizations, including limited liability partnerships (LLPs—discussed in Chapter 30) and limited liability companies (LLCs), have been added to the options for business entities. An initial consideration in choosing between these forms is the number of participants. An LLP must have two or more partners, but in many states, an LLC can have a single member (owner).

Liability Considerations

The members of an LLC are not liable for the obligations of the organization. The liability of the partners in an LLP varies from state to state. About half of the states exempt the partners from liability for any obligation of the firm. In some states, the partners are individually liable for the contractual obligations of the firm but are not liable for obligations arising from the torts of others. In either situation, each partner may be on his or her own with respect to liability unless the other partners decide to help.

Distributions from the Firm

Members and partners are generally paid by allowing them to withdraw funds from the firm against their share of the profits. In many states, a member of an LLC must repay so-called wrongful distributions even if she or he did not know that the distributions were wrongful. Under most LLP statutes, by contrast, the partners must repay only distributions that were fraudulent.

Management Structure

Both LLPs and LLCs can set up whatever management structure the participants desire. Also, all unincorporated business organizations, including LLPs and LLCs, are treated as partnerships for federal income tax purposes (unless an LLC elects to be treated as a corporation[a]). This means that the firms are not taxed at the entity level. Their income is passed through to the partners or members who must report it on their individual income tax returns. Some states impose additional taxes on LLCs.

a. The chief benefits of electing corporate status for tax purposes are that the members generally are not subject to self-employment taxes and that fringe benefits may be provided to employee-members on a tax-reduced basis. The tax laws are complicated, however, and a professional should be consulted about the details.

The Nature of the Business

The business in which a firm engages is another factor to consider in choosing a business form. For example, with a few exceptions, professionals, such as accountants, attorneys, and physicians, may organize as either an LLP or an LLC in any state. In many states, however, the ownership of an entity that engages in a certain profession and the liability of the owners are prescribed by state law.

Financial and Personal Relationships

Despite their importance, the legal consequences of choosing a business form are often secondary to the financial and personal relationships among the participants. Work effort, motivation, ability, and other personal attributes can be significant factors, as may fundamental business concerns such as the expenses and debts of the firm. Other practical factors to consider include the willingness of others to do business with an LLP or an LLC. A supplier, for example, may not be willing to extend credit to a firm whose partners or members will not accept personal liability for the debt.

Checklist for Choosing a Limited Liability Business Form

1. Determine the number of participants, the forms a state allows, and the limits on liability the state provides for the participants.
2. Evaluate the tax considerations.
3. Consider the business in which the firm engages, or will engage, and any restrictions imposed on that type of business.
4. Weigh such practical concerns as the financial and personal relationships among the participants and the willingness of others to do business with a particular organizational form.

KEY TERMS

articles of organization 807
business trust 816
cooperative 816
joint stock company 816
joint venture 813
limited liability company (LLC) 804
member 805
operating agreement 809
syndicate 816

CHAPTER SUMMARY Limited Liability Companies and Special Business Forms

Limited Liability Companies (LLCs) (See pages 805–813.)	1. *Formation*—Articles of organization must be filed with the appropriate state office—usually the office of the secretary of state—setting forth the name of the business, its principal address, the names of the owners (called *members*), and other relevant information. 2. *Advantages and disadvantages of the LLC*—Advantages of the LLC include limited liability, the option to be taxed as a partnership or as a corporation, and flexibility in deciding how the business will be managed and operated. Disadvantages relate mainly to the absence of uniformity in state LLC statutes and the lack of case law dealing with LLCs. 3. *Operating agreement*—When an LLC is formed, the members decide, in an operating agreement, how the business will be managed and what rules will apply to the organization. 4. *Management*—An LLC may be managed by members only, by some members and some nonmembers, or by nonmembers only.
Special Business Forms (See pages 813–817.)	1. *Joint venture*—An organization created by two or more persons in contemplation of a limited activity or a single transaction; similar to a partnership in many respects. 2. *Syndicate*—An investment group that undertakes to finance a particular project; may exist as a corporation or as a general or limited partnership. 3. *Joint stock company*—A business form similar to a corporation in some respects (transferable shares of stock, management by directors and officers, perpetual existence) but otherwise resembling a partnership. 4. *Business trust*—A business form created by a written trust agreement that sets forth the interests of the beneficiaries and the obligations and powers of the trustee(s); similar to a corporation in many respects. Beneficiaries are not personally liable for the debts or obligations of the business trust. 5. *Cooperative*—An association organized to provide an economic service, without profit, to its members; may take the form of a corporation or a partnership.

FOR REVIEW

Answers for the even-numbered questions in this For Review *section can be found on this text's accompanying Web site at* http://blt.westbuslaw.com. *Select "Chapter 31" and click on "For Review."*

1. What advantages do limited liability companies offer to businesspersons that are not offered by sole proprietorships or partnerships?
2. How are limited liability companies formed, and who decides how they will be managed and operated?
3. What are the two options for managing limited liability companies?
4. What is a joint venture? How is it similar to a partnership? How is it different?
5. What are the essential characteristics of joint stock companies, syndicates, business trusts, and cooperatives, respectively?

Sometimes, there is a defect in complying with statutory mandates—for example, the corporation charter may have expired. Under these circumstances, the corporation may have *de facto* (actual) status, meaning that the corporation in fact exists, even if not rightfully or lawfully. A corporation with *de facto* status cannot be challenged by third persons (except for the state). The following elements are required for *de facto* status:

1. There must be a state statute under which the corporation can be validly incorporated.
2. The parties must have made a good faith attempt to comply with the statute.
3. The enterprise must already have undertaken to do business as a corporation.

CORPORATION BY ESTOPPEL

If an association that is neither an actual corporation nor a *de facto* or *de jure* corporation holds itself out as being a corporation, it normally will be estopped from denying corporate status in a lawsuit by a third party. This usually occurs when a third party contracts with an association that claims to be a corporation but does not hold a certificate of incorporation. When the third party brings suit naming the so-called corporation as the defendant, the association may not escape liability on the ground that no corporation exists. When justice requires, the courts treat an alleged corporation as if it were an actual corporation for the purpose of determining the rights and liabilities involved in a particular situation. Corporation by estoppel is thus determined by the situation. It does not extend recognition of corporate status beyond the resolution of the problem at hand.

DISREGARDING THE CORPORATE ENTITY

PIERCING THE CORPORATE VEIL
An action in which a court disregards the corporate entity and holds the shareholders personally liable for corporate debts and obligations.

Occasionally, the owners use a corporate entity to perpetrate a fraud, circumvent the law, or in some other way accomplish an illegitimate objective. In these situations, the court will ignore the corporate structure by **piercing the corporate veil** and exposing the shareholders to personal liability. Generally, when the corporate privilege is abused for personal benefit or when the corporate business is treated so carelessly that the corporation and the controlling shareholder are no longer separate entities, the court will require the owner to assume personal liability to creditors for the corporation's debts.

In short, when the facts show that great injustice would result from the use of a corporation to avoid individual responsibility, a court of equity will look behind the corporate structure to the individual stockholder. The following are some of the factors that frequently cause the courts to pierce the corporate veil:

COMMINGLE
To mix together; to put funds or goods together into one mass so that they are so mixed that they no longer have separate identities. In corporate law, if personal and corporate interests are commingled to the extent that the corporation has no separate identity, a court may "pierce the corporate veil" and expose the shareholders to personal liability.

1. A party is tricked or misled into dealing with the corporation rather than the individual.
2. The corporation is set up never to make a profit or always to be insolvent, or it is too "thinly" capitalized—that is, it has insufficient capital at the time of formation to meet its prospective debts or potential liabilities.
3. Statutory corporate formalities, such as holding required corporation meetings, are not followed.
4. Personal and corporate interests are **commingled** (mixed together) to such an extent that the corporation has no separate identity.

THE COMMINGLING OF PERSONAL AND CORPORATE ASSETS

To elaborate on the fourth factor in the preceding list, consider a close corporation that is formed according to law by a single person or by a few family members. In such a situation, the separate status of the corporate entity and the sole stockholder (or family-member stockholders) must be carefully preserved. Certain practices invite trouble for the one-person or family-owned corporation: the commingling of corporate and personal funds, the failure to hold board of directors' meetings and record the minutes, or the shareholders' continuous personal use of corporate property (for example, vehicles).

In the following case, in response to a creditor's motion before a court to "pierce the corporate veil," the plaintiffs argued that "this is not a fraud, this is a family business."

CASE 32.3 Dimmitt & Owens Financial, Inc. v. Superior Sports Products, Inc.

United States District Court,
Northern District of Illinois, 2002.
196 F.Supp.2d 731.

BACKGROUND AND FACTS To import sportfishing products for wholesale distribution in North America, Donald Park incorporated Superior Sports Products, Inc. (SSP), in September 1996. Park's mother, Chong Hyok Park, was SSP's president at its incorporation, but she did not participate in its operations. Donald Park handled most of its activities out of his apartment in Schaumburg, Illinois, drawing funds from SSP when he needed to pay personal expenses. There were no employees. To engage in the same business, Superior Sports International, Inc. (SSII), was formed in February 1997, and Superior Source, Inc. (SSI), in October 1997. Chong was the president and sole shareholder of SSII, which had no employees and operated out of her home in Ontario, Canada. SSI was formed with Chong's friends, but it conducted only one sale as a wholesaler and was dissolved. None of the corporations issued stock or paid dividends, maintained corporate records, or followed other corporate formalities. All of the corporations, none of which made a profit, were financed by occasional loans by Park or his parents. This capital proved to be inadequate. In January 1998, Donald Park—representing himself as president of SSP, vice president of SSII, and manager of SSI when he was none of these—applied for, and obtained, loans from Dimmitt & Owens Financial, Inc. When the loans were not paid, Dimmitt filed a suit in a federal district court against SSP, SSII, SSI, and Donald Park, seeking in part a summary judgment to impose personal liability on Park.

IN THE WORDS OF THE COURT . . .
CASTILLO, District Judge.

* * * *

Illinois courts apply a two-prong test to determine whether to pierce the corporate veil: (1) there must be such unity of interest and ownership that the separate personalities of the corporation and the individual or other corporation no longer exist; and (2) circumstances must be that such an adherence to the fiction of separate corporate existence would sanction a fraud or promote injustice. [Emphasis added.]

* * * *

With respect to the first prong, in order to find sufficient unity of interest and ownership to warrant piercing the corporate veil, Illinois courts consider numerous factors including: (1) inadequate capitalization; (2) failure to issue stock; (3) failure to observe corporate formalities; (4) nonpayment of dividends; (5) insolvency of the

(Continued)

CASE 32.3—Continued

debtor corporation; (6) nonfunctioning of the other officers or directors; (7) absence of corporate records; (8) commingling of funds; (9) diversion of assets from the corporation by or to a shareholder; (10) failure to maintain arm's length relationships among related entities; and (11) whether the corporation is a mere facade for the operation of the dominant shareholders. * * *

* * * *

* * * [E]ach of these factors was present, to a large degree, in the instant [this] case. Therefore, with respect to the first prong, Plaintiffs have produced enough evidence supporting their argument that [Donald] Park exercised great personal control over the existing corporations thereby creating the sufficient unity of interest and ownership between Park and the corporations to warrant piercing the corporate veil.

* * * *

In addition to establishing sufficient unity of interest to justify piercing the corporate veil, Dimmitt [the finance company] must allege facts sufficiently demonstrating that adherence to the corporate formalities would promote injustice or fraud. * * * Here, Park misrepresented himself in obtaining financial assistance from Dimmitt. * * *

* * * [S]uch misrepresentations equal something akin to fraud or deception. Additionally, we find that there is a compelling public interest that individuals should not execute contracts while misrepresenting themselves and escape personal liability when monies, advanced on the basis of such contracts, disappear without a proper accounting for their disappearance.

DECISION AND REMEDY The court granted Dimmitt's motion and issued a summary judgment in the creditor's favor, holding that piercing the corporate veil was justified. The commingling of personal and corporate funds, among other misconduct, demonstrated that Park would be unjustly enriched, to Dimmitt's detriment, if Park were shielded from personal liability by his corporation, SSP.

FOR CRITICAL ANALYSIS—Social Consideration *If Park had not made the misrepresentations as to his positions with the corporations, would the "other misconduct" noted by the court have been enough to justify piercing the corporate veil in this case? Why or why not?*

Corporate Financing

SECURITIES
Generally, stock certificates, bonds, notes, debentures, warrants, or other documents given as evidence of an ownership interest in a corporation or as a promise of repayment by a corporation.

STOCK
An equity (ownership) interest in a corporation, measured in units of shares.

BOND
A certificate that evidences a corporate (or government) debt. It is a security that involves no ownership interest in the issuing entity.

Part of the process of corporate formation involves corporate financing. Corporations are financed by the issuance and sale of corporate securities. **Securities** (stocks and bonds) evidence the right to participate in earnings and the distribution of corporate property or the obligation to pay funds.

Stocks, or *equity securities*, represent the purchase of ownership in the business firm. **Bonds** (debentures), or *debt securities*, represent the borrowing of funds by firms (and governments). Of course, not all debt is in the form of debt securities. For example, some debt is in the form of accounts payable and notes payable. Accounts and notes payable are typically short-term debts. Bonds are simply a way for the corporation to split up its long-term debt so that it can market it more easily.

Bonds

Bonds are issued by business firms and by governments at all levels as evidence of the funds they are borrowing from investors. Bonds normally have a designated *maturity date*—the date when the principal, or face, amount of the bond is returned to the investor. They are sometimes referred to as *fixed-income securities* because their owners (that is, the creditors) receive fixed-dollar interest payments, usually semiannually, during the period of time prior to maturity.

BOND INDENTURE
A contract between the issuer of a bond and the bondholder.

Because debt financing represents a legal obligation on the part of the corporation, various features and terms of a particular bond issue are specified in a lending agreement called a **bond indenture.** A corporate trustee, often a commercial bank trust department, represents the collective well-being of all bondholders in ensuring that the corporation meets the terms of the bond issue. The bond indenture specifies the maturity date of the bond and the pattern of interest payments until maturity. The different types of corporate bonds are described in Exhibit 32–2.

STOCKS

Issuing stocks is another way that corporations can obtain financing. The ways in which stocks differ from bonds are summarized in Exhibit 32–3 on the next page. Basically, as mentioned, stocks represent ownership in a business firm, whereas bonds represent borrowing by the firm.

Exhibit 32–4 on page 847 summarizes the types of stocks issued by corporations. We look now at the two major types of stock—*common stock* and *preferred stock.*

COMMON STOCK
Shares of ownership in a corporation that give the owner of the stock a proportionate interest in the corporation with regard to control, earnings, and net assets. Shares of common stock are lowest in priority with respect to payment of dividends and distribution of the corporation's assets on dissolution.

Common Stock The true ownership of a corporation is represented by **common stock.** Common stock provides a proportionate interest in the corporation with regard to (1) control, (2) earnings, and (3) net assets. A shareholder's interest is generally in proportion to the number of shares he or she owns out of the total number of shares issued.

Voting rights in a corporation apply to the election of the firm's board of directors and to any proposed changes in the ownership structure of the firm. For example, a holder of common stock generally has the right to vote in a decision on a proposed merger, as mergers can change the proportion of ownership. State corporation law specifies the types of actions for which shareholder approval must be obtained.

Firms are not obligated to return a principal amount per share to each holder of common stock because no firm can ensure that the market price per share of its

EXHIBIT 32–2 TYPES OF CORPORATE BONDS

Debenture Bonds	Bonds for which no specific assets of the corporation are pledged as backing. Rather, they are backed by the general credit rating of the corporation, plus any assets that can be seized if the corporation allows the debentures to go into default.
Mortgage Bonds	Bonds that pledge specific property. If the corporation defaults on the bonds, the bondholders can take the property.
Convertible Bonds	Bonds that can be exchanged for a specified number of shares of common stock under certain conditions.
Callable Bonds	Bonds that may be called in and the principal repaid at specified times or under conditions specified in the bond indenture when the bond is issued.

EXHIBIT 32–3 HOW DO STOCKS AND BONDS DIFFER?

STOCKS	BONDS
1. Stocks represent ownership.	1. Bonds represent debt.
2. Stocks (common) do not have a fixed dividend rate.	2. Interest on bonds must always be paid, whether or not any profit is earned.
3. Stockholders can elect the board of directors, which controls the corporation.	3. Bondholders usually have no voice in, or control over, management of the corporation.
4. Stocks do not have a maturity date; the corporation usually does not repay the stockholder.	4. Bonds have a maturity date, when the corporation is to repay the bondholder the face value of the bond.
5. All corporations issue or offer to sell stocks. This is the usual definition of a corporation.	5. Corporations do not necessarily issue bonds.
6. Stockholders have a claim against the property and income of a corporation after all creditors' claims have been met.	6. Bondholders have a claim against the property and income of a corporation that must be met before the claims of stockholders.

common stock will not decline over time. The issuing firm also does not have to guarantee a dividend; indeed, some corporations never pay dividends.

Holders of common stock are investors who assume a *residual* position in the overall financial structure of a business. In terms of receiving payment for their investments, they are last in line. They are entitled to the earnings that are left after preferred stockholders, bondholders, suppliers, employees, and other groups have been paid. Once those groups are paid, however, the owners of common stock may be entitled to *all* the remaining earnings as dividends. (The board of directors normally is not under any duty to declare the remaining earnings as dividends, however.)

PREFERRED STOCK
Classes of stock that have priority over common stock as to both payment of dividends and distribution of assets on the corporation's dissolution.

Preferred Stock **Preferred stock** is stock with *preferences*. Usually, this means that holders of preferred stock have priority over holders of common stock as to dividends and as to payment on dissolution of the corporation. Holders of preferred stock may or may not have the right to vote.

Preferred stock is not included among the liabilities of a business because it is equity. Like other equity securities, preferred shares have no fixed maturity date on which the firm must pay them off. Although firms occasionally buy back preferred stock, they are not legally obligated to do so. A sample cumulative convertible preferred-stock certificate is shown in Exhibit 32–5 on page 848.

Holders of preferred stock are investors who have assumed a rather cautious position in their relationship to the corporation. They have a stronger position than common shareholders with respect to dividends and claims on assets, but as a result, they will not share in the full prosperity of the firm if it grows successfully over time. This is because the value of preferred shares will not rise as rapidly as that of common shares during a period of financial success. Preferred stockholders do receive

EXHIBIT 32–4 TYPES OF STOCKS

Common Stock	Voting shares that represent ownership interest in a corporation. Common stock has the lowest priority with respect to payment of dividends and distribution of assets on the corporation's dissolution.
Preferred Stock	Shares of stock that have priority over common-stock shares as to payment of dividends and distribution of assets on dissolution. Dividend payments are usually a fixed percentage of the face value of the share.
Cumulative Preferred Stock	Required dividends not paid in a given year must be paid in a subsequent year before any common-stock dividends are paid.
Participating Preferred Stock	Stock entitling the owner to receive the preferred-stock dividend and additional dividends if the corporation has paid dividends on common stock.
Convertible Preferred Stock	Stock entitling the owners to convert their shares into a specified number of common shares either in the issuing corporation or, sometimes, in another corporation.
Redeemable, or Callable, Preferred Stock	Preferred shares issued with the express condition that the issuing corporation has the right to repurchase the shares as specified.

fixed dividends periodically, however, and they may benefit to some extent from changes in the market price of the shares.

The return and the risk for preferred stock lie somewhere between those for bonds and those for common stock. Preferred stock is more similar to bonds than to common stock, even though preferred stock appears in the ownership section of the firm's balance sheet. As a result, preferred stock is often categorized with corporate bonds as a fixed-income security, even though the legal status is not the same.

"There are two times in a man's life when he should not speculate: When he can't afford it and when he can."

SAMUEL CLEMENS (MARK TWAIN), 1835–1910 (American author and humorist)

LOCATING POTENTIAL INVESTORS ONLINE

Today, the Internet allows promoters and others to access, easily and inexpensively, a large number of potential investors. A number of online "matching services" are available to match potential investors with companies or future companies that are seeking investors. A corporate promoter or a small company seeking capital investment can pay a fee to one of these services, which will then include a description of the company in a list that it makes available to investors, also for a fee.

Although matching services are not new, what is new is that service providers are now online and many of them have significantly expanded the geographic scope of their operations. Some services specialize in matching entrepreneurs in specific industries with potential investors. Other services focus on matching start-up companies with foreign investors or restrict their services to firms in a certain region, such as the Pacific Northwest.

Online matching services enable entrepreneurs to reach a wide group of potential investors quickly and with relatively little effort. They can also provide other kinds of assistance to businesspersons, such as help with creating an effective business plan or tips on how to manage financial issues.

EXHIBIT 32-5 CUMULATIVE CONVERTIBLE PREFERRED-STOCK CERTIFICATE

MORE THAN 100 SHARES

Number 640-0000

Shares

$1.75 CUMULATIVE CONVERTIBLE PREFERENCE STOCK

INCORPORATED UNDER THE LAWS OF THE STATE OF DELAWARE

GENERAL MILLS, INC.

THIS CERTIFICATE IS TRANSFERABLE IN COLUMBUS, GA. OR IN NEW YORK, N.Y.

See reverse for certain definitions

SPECIMEN

This Certifies that *is the owner of*

FULL-PAID AND NON-ASSESSABLE SHARES, OF THE $1.75 CUMULATIVE CONVERTIBLE PREFERENCE STOCK, WITHOUT PAR VALUE, OF

General Mills, Inc. transferable on the books of the Corporation by the holder hereof in person or by duly authorized attorney …

In Witness Whereof, the Corporation has caused this Certificate to be signed by its duly authorized officers and its Corporate Seal to be hereto affixed.

Dated

PRESIDENT

SECRETARY

REGISTERED:
THE CHASE MANHATTAN BANK (NATIONAL ASSOCIATION), REGISTRAR

By

AUTHORIZED SIGNATURE

COUNTERSIGNED:
FIRST NATIONAL CITY BANK, TRANSFER AGENT

By

AUTHORIZED OFFICER.

DELAWARE 1928

REVIEWING CORPORATE FORMATION AND FINANCING

William Sharp was the sole shareholder and manager of Chickasaw Club, Inc., an S corporation that operated a popular nightclub of the same name in Columbus, Georgia. Sharp maintained a corporate checking account, but paid the club's employees, suppliers, and entertainers in cash out of the club's proceeds. Sharp owned the property on which the club was located and rented it to the club, but made mortgage payments out of the club's proceeds and often paid other personal expenses with Chickasaw corporate funds. At 12:45 A.M. on July 31, 2005, eighteen-year-old Aubrey Lynn Pursley, who was already intoxicated, entered the Chickasaw Club. A city ordinance prohibited individuals under the age of twenty-one from entering nightclubs, but Chickasaw employees did not check Pursley's identification to verify her age. Pursley drank more alcohol at Chickasaw and was visibly intoxicated when she left the club at 3:00 A.M. with a beer in her hand. Shortly afterward, Pursley lost control of her car, struck a tree, and was killed. Joseph Dancause, Pursley's stepfather, filed a tort lawsuit in a Georgia state court against Chickasaw Club, Inc., and William Sharp, seeking damages. Using the information presented in the chapter, answer the following questions.

1. Under what theory might a court in this case make an exception to the limited liability of shareholders and hold Sharp personally liable for the damages? What factors would be relevant to the court's decision?
2. Suppose that Chickasaw's articles of incorporation failed to describe the corporation's purpose or management structure as required by state law. Would a court be likely to rule that Sharp is personally liable to Dancause on that basis?
3. Suppose that the club extended credit to its regular patrons in an effort maintain a loyal clientele, although neither the articles of incorporation nor the corporate bylaws authorized this practice. Would the corporation likely have the power to engage in this activity? Explain.
4. How would the court classify the Chickasaw Club corporation—domestic or foreign, public or private?
5. Suppose that Chickasaw Club, Inc., wants to obtain additional funds. Discuss the options available.

APPLICATION How to Incorporate Online*

Today, just about anybody can form a corporation for any lawful purpose in any state. The requirements differ from state to state. You do not have to form your corporation in the state where you live or the state where you are doing business, however. In fact, many individuals obtain their corporate charters from the state of Delaware because it has the fewest legal restrictions on corporate formation and operation. Traditionally, Delaware has also been the state most often chosen for "mail-order incorporation." Today, instead of incorporating by mail, entrepreneurs have the option of incorporating in the state of their choice via online companies that offer incorporation services.

* This *Application* is not meant to substitute for the services of an attorney who is licensed to practice law in your state.

FINDING INFORMATION ON INCORPORATION REQUIREMENTS

Nearly every state has a Web site at which you can find the individual state's requirements for incorporation. (To locate your state's Web site, go to **http://www.statelocalgov.net**.) Most state sites post guidelines or instructions on forming corporations (and other business entities), fee schedules, and frequently asked questions (FAQs). Many also provide downloadable corporate forms.

In addition, hundreds of companies now provide incorporation services via the Internet, and you can obtain a great deal of information at their Web sites. For example, at the Web site of The Company Corporation (TCC) of Delaware (**http://www.incorporate.com**), you can read about the

(Continued)

CASE 33.1 MM Companies, Inc. v. Liquid Audio, Inc.

Delaware Supreme Court, 2003.
813 A.2d 1118.

COMPANY PROFILE *Liquid Audio, Inc. (**http://www.liquidaudio.com**), is a Delaware corporation with its principal place of business in Redwood City, California. Liquid Audio provides software and services for the delivery of music over the Internet. Formed in 1996, Liquid Audio offered the first digital music–commerce system featuring copy protection and copyright management, as well as the first and largest digital music–distribution network. Liquid Audio's catalogue of secure music downloads is one of the world's largest.*

BACKGROUND AND FACTS MM Companies, Inc., a Delaware corporation with its principal place of business in New York City, owned 7 percent of Liquid Audio's stock. In October 2001, MM sent a letter to Liquid Audio's board of directors offering to buy all of the company's stock for about $3 per share. The board rejected the offer. Liquid Audio's bylaws provide for a board of five directors divided into three classes. One class is elected each year. The next election, at which two directors would be chosen, was set for September 2002. By mid-August, it appeared that MM's nominees, Seymour Holtzman and James Mitarotonda, would win the election. The board amended the bylaws to increase the number of directors to seven and appointed Judith Frank and James Somes to fill the new positions. In September, MM's nominees were elected to the board, but their influence was diminished because there were now seven directors. MM filed a suit in a Delaware state court against Liquid Audio and others, challenging the board's actions. The court ruled in favor of the defendants. MM appealed to the Delaware Supreme Court.

IN THE WORDS OF THE COURT . . .
HOLLAND, Justice:

* * * *

The most fundamental principles of corporate governance are a function of the allocation of power within a corporation between its stockholders and its board of directors. The stockholders' power is the right to vote on specific matters, in particular, in an election of directors. The power of managing the corporate enterprise is vested in the shareholders' duly elected board representatives. * * *

Maintaining a proper balance in the allocation of power between the stockholders' right to elect directors and the board of directors' right to manage the corporation is dependent upon the stockholders' unimpeded right to vote effectively in an election of directors. * * * [Emphasis added.]

* * * *

When the *primary purpose* of a board of directors' [action] is to interfere with or impede the effective exercise of the shareholder franchise in a contested election for directors, the board must first demonstrate a compelling justification for such action as a condition precedent to any judicial consideration of reasonableness and proportionality. * * * [S]uch * * * actions by a board need not actually prevent the shareholders from attaining any success in seating one or more nominees in a contested election for directors and the election contest need not involve a challenge for outright control of the board of directors. * * * [T]he * * * actions of the board only need to be taken for the primary purpose of interfering with or impeding the effectiveness of the stockholder vote in a contested election for directors.

* * * *

* * * [In this case, the directors] amended the bylaws to provide for a board of seven and appointed two additional members of the Board for the primary purpose of diminishing the influence of MM's two nominees * * *. That * * * action * * * compromised the essential role of corporate democracy in maintaining the proper allocation of power between the shareholders and the Board, because that action was taken in the context of a contested election for successor directors. Since the * * * Defendants did

CASE 33.1—Continued

not demonstrate a compelling justification for that * * * action, the bylaw amendment that expanded the size of the Liquid Audio board, and permitted the appointment of two new members on the eve of a contested election, should have been invalidated.

DECISION AND REMEDY The Delaware Supreme Court reversed the judgment of the lower court and remanded the case for further proceedings. The state supreme court concluded that the board's amending the bylaws to increase the number of directors and filling the new positions with appointments was invalid, because the board acted primarily to impede the shareholders' right to vote in an impending election for successor directors.

FOR CRITICAL ANALYSIS—Political Consideration *How could MM's newly elected nominees, or any two directors, affect the decisions of a five-member board?*

Board of Directors' Meetings

The board of directors conducts business by holding formal meetings with recorded minutes. The dates of regular meetings are usually established in the articles or bylaws or by board resolution, and no further notice is customarily required. Special meetings can be called, with notice sent to all directors. What happens if the directors do not receive proper notice? Does lack of sufficient notice of a special board meeting invalidate the resolutions adopted by the board of directors at that meeting? See this chapter's *Adapting the Law to the Online Environment* feature on the next page for a discussion of a case involving this issue.

QUORUM
The number of members of a decision-making body that must be present before business may be transacted.

Quorum requirements can vary among jurisdictions. (A **quorum** is the minimum number of members of a body of officials or other group that must be present in order for business to be validly transacted.) Many states leave the decision as to quorum requirements to the corporate articles or bylaws. In the absence of specific state statutes, most states provide that a quorum is a majority of the number of directors authorized in the articles or bylaws. Voting is done in person (unlike voting at shareholders' meetings, which can be done by proxy, as discussed later in this chapter).[1] The rule is one vote per director. Ordinary matters generally require a simple majority vote; certain extraordinary issues may require a greater-than-majority vote.

Rights of Directors

A director of a corporation has a number of rights, including the rights of participation, inspection, compensation, and indemnification.

.on the Web You can find definitions for terms used in corporate law, as well as court decisions and articles on corporate law topics, at **http://www.law.com**.

Participation and Inspection A corporate director must have certain rights to function properly in that position. The main right is one of participation—meaning that the director must be notified of board of directors' meetings so as to participate in them. As pointed out earlier in this chapter, the dates of regular board meetings are usually established by the bylaws or by board resolution, and no notice of these meetings is required. If special meetings are called, however, notice is required unless waived by the director.

A director must have access to all of the corporate books and records to make decisions and to exercise the necessary supervision over corporate officers and employees. This right of inspection is virtually absolute and cannot be restricted.

Compensation and Indemnification Historically, directors have had no inherent right to compensation for their services, but have often received nominal sums as

---

1. Except in Louisiana, which allows a director to vote by proxy under certain circumstances.

ADAPTING THE LAW TO THE ONLINE ENVIRONMENT

The Timing of Directors' Actions in an Electronic Age

As mentioned elsewhere, corporate directors can hold special board meetings to deal with extraordinary matters, provided that they give proper notice to all members of the board. If a special meeting is called without giving sufficient notice to all of the directors, are the resolutions made at that meeting invalid? If so, can the directors validate these resolutions by holding a second special board meeting with proper notice? In today's electronic age, matters of timing can be complicated and can affect a variety of other issues, including the effective date of a director's resignation and the validity of a resolution appointing a new director. These were the central issues presented by *In re Piranha, Inc.*[a]

THE ISSUE OF PROPER NOTICE

In May 2001, Edward Sample, the chairman of the board of directors of Piranha, Inc., called a special meeting for May 25 to consider restructuring Piranha's management in response to serious financial problems. The four members of the board of directors at that time were Sample, Richard Berger, Larry Greybill, and Michael Steele. Berger objected to the lack of notice of the May 25 meeting and refused to attend, claiming that the meeting was invalid. The other directors held the meeting without him and, among other things, voted to accept the resignations of two of the directors, Greybill and Steele, and appoint a new director, Mike Churchill.

After the meeting, Greybill submitted his written resignation, but Steele did not, fearing that Berger might be correct about the lack of notice rendering the meeting invalid. Nonetheless, the corporation's legal counsel filed a form with the Securities and Exchange Commission (SEC) on May 25 indicating the changes made to the board of directors. The SEC form stated that Steele *had* resigned as director and contained Steele's electronic signature.

THE SECOND MEETING

By early June, Piranha's legal counsel concluded that insufficient notice had probably rendered the May 25 meeting—and the resolutions made at that meeting—invalid. The attorneys informed the directors that, to effect the changes to the board, they would need to call another special meeting and provide sufficient notice. A second special meeting was held on June 15 with proper notice (to Berger, Sample, and Steele), and Churchill was voted in as a director. Steele, now confident that Churchill was validly appointed as a director, submitted his written resignation the following day.

Berger, however, contended that Churchill was not truly a corporate director because Steele had no right to vote at the second board meeting. At issue was whether the SEC filing of May 25 bearing Steele's electronic signature meant that Steele had effectively resigned on that date. If Churchill was not a valid director, then his subsequent vote that the corporation should file for bankruptcy would be invalid.[b]

THE COURT'S CONCLUSION

Ultimately, a federal appellate court held that Steele's electronic signature on the SEC filing did not operate as his formal resignation. Under the Uniform Electronic Transactions Act (UETA—see Chapter 17), a signature may not be denied legal effect solely because it is in an electronic form. Section 107(a) of the UETA, however, also allows a person to disavow the signature. Here, Steele claimed that he did not authorize his signature on the form submitted to the SEC. Therefore, the court found that Steele had not resigned until he submitted his written resignation following the second meeting. Thus, Churchill was a corporate director and could vote for the corporation to file for bankruptcy.

FOR CRITICAL ANALYSIS

What would the legal consequences have been if Berger had attended the first special board meeting despite the lack of sufficient notice? (Hint: See the section on the rights of directors in this chapter.)

a. 2003 WL 22922263 (5th Cir. 2003).

b. After the June 15 meeting, the directors voted that the corporation should file a petition for bankruptcy. Berger originally filed an action requesting that the court dismiss the bankruptcy petition because Churchill was not a valid director at the time of the vote. The bankruptcy court rejected this contention, and Berger appealed, resulting in the decision discussed here.

honoraria (an *honorarium* is an amount of money paid to someone, usually a professional, for providing a service, such as a consultation or a speech). In many corporations, directors are also chief corporate officers (president or chief executive officer, for example) and receive compensation in their managerial positions. Most directors also gain through indirect benefits, such as business contacts and prestige, and other rewards, such as stock options. There is a trend toward providing more than nominal compensation for directors, especially in large corporations where the time, work, effort, and risk involved can impose enormous burdens. Many states permit the corporate articles or bylaws to authorize compensation for directors, and in some instances the board can set its own compensation unless the articles or bylaws provide otherwise.

Corporate directors may become involved in lawsuits by virtue of their positions and their actions as directors. Most states (and RMBCA 8.51) permit a corporation to indemnify (guarantee reimbursement to) a director for legal costs, fees, and judgments involved in defending corporation-related suits. Many states specifically permit a corporation to purchase liability insurance for the directors and officers to cover indemnification. When the statutes are silent on this matter, the power to purchase such insurance is usually considered to be part of the corporation's implied power.

Directors' Management Responsibilities

Directors have responsibility for all policymaking decisions necessary to the management of corporate affairs. Just as shareholders cannot act individually to bind the corporation, the directors must act as a body in carrying out routine corporate business. The general areas of responsibility of the board of directors include the following:

1. Declaration and payment of corporate dividends to shareholders.
2. Authorization for major corporate policy decisions—for example, the initiation of proceedings for the sale or lease of corporate assets outside the regular course of business, the determination of new product lines, and the overseeing of major contract negotiations and major management-labor negotiations.
3. Appointment, supervision, and removal of corporate officers and other managerial employees and the determination of their compensation.
4. Financial decisions, such as the decision to issue authorized shares and bonds.

In most states, the board of directors can delegate some of its functions to an executive committee or to corporate officers. In doing so, the board is not relieved of its overall responsibility for directing the affairs of the corporation, but corporate officers and managerial personnel are empowered to make decisions relating to ordinary, daily corporate affairs within well-defined guidelines.

Role of Corporate Officers and Executives

CONTRAST Shareholders own a corporation and directors make policy decisions, but officers who run the daily business of the corporation often have significant decision-making power.

Corporate officers and other executive employees are hired by the board of directors or, in rare instances, by the shareholders. In addition to carrying out the duties articulated in the bylaws, corporate and managerial officers act as agents of the corporation, and the ordinary rules of agency (discussed in Chapter 28) normally apply to their employment. The qualifications required of officers and executive employees are determined at the discretion of the corporation and are included in the articles or bylaws. In most states, a person can hold more than one office and can be both an officer and a director of the corporation.

Corporate executives discuss the business of their firm. How do the rights and duties of corporate officers differ from those of corporate directors? (John Terence Turner/Getty Images)

Corporate officers and other high-level managers are employees of the company, so their rights are defined by employment contracts. The board of directors, though, normally can remove corporate officers at any time with or without cause and regardless of the terms of the employment contracts—although in so doing, the corporation may be liable for breach of contract. The duties of corporate officers are the same as those of directors because both groups are involved in decision making and are in similar positions of control. Hence, officers are viewed as having the same fiduciary duties of care and loyalty in their conduct of corporate affairs as directors have, a subject to which we now turn.

Duties and Liabilities of Directors and Officers

Directors and officers are deemed *fiduciaries* of the corporation because their relationship with the corporation and its shareholders is one of trust and confidence. As fiduciaries, directors and officers owe ethical—and legal—duties to the corporation and to the shareholders. These fiduciary duties include the duty of care and the duty of loyalty.

Duty of Care

Directors and officers must exercise due care in performing their duties. The standard of *due care* has been variously described in judicial decisions and codified in many corporation codes. Generally, a director or officer is expected to act in good faith, to exercise the care that an ordinarily prudent person would exercise in similar circumstances, and to act in what he or she considers to be the best interests of the corporation.[2] Directors and officers who have not exercised the required duty of care can be held liable for the harms suffered by the corporation as a result of their negligence. (Directors and officers also have a duty not to destroy evidence in the event of a lawsuit involving the corporation. The *Application* feature at the end of this chapter discusses how due care can be exercised to preserve electronic evidence by creating an e-document-retention policy.)

Duty to Make Informed and Reasonable Decisions Directors and officers are expected to be informed on corporate matters. To be informed, the director or officer must do what is necessary to become informed: attend presentations, ask for information from those who have it, read reports, and review other written materials such as contracts. In other words, directors and officers must carefully study a situation and its alternatives before making a decision. Depending on the nature of the business, directors and officers are often expected to act in accordance with their own knowledge and training. Nevertheless, most states (and Section 8.30 of the RMBCA) allow a director to make decisions in reliance on information furnished by competent officers or employees, professionals such as attorneys and accountants, or even an executive committee of the board without being accused of acting in bad faith or failing to exercise due care if such information turns out to be faulty.

Directors are also expected to make reasonable decisions. For example, a director should not accept a **tender offer** with only a moment's consideration and on the sole basis of the price per share that is being offered. A tender offer, sometimes referred to as a "takeover bid," is an offer to purchase shares in the company that is made by another company directly to the shareholders.

TENDER OFFER
An offer to purchase shares made by one company directly to the shareholders of another (target) company; often referred to as a "takeover bid."

Duty to Exercise Reasonable Supervision Directors are also expected to exercise a reasonable amount of supervision when they delegate work to corporate officers and employees. ■ **EXAMPLE 33.1** Suppose that a corporate bank director fails to attend any

2. RMBCA 8.30.

board of directors' meetings for five years. In addition, the director never inspects any of the corporate books or records and generally fails to supervise the efforts of the bank president and the loan committee. Meanwhile, the bank president, who is a corporate officer, makes various improper loans and permits large overdrafts. In this situation, the corporate director may be held liable to the corporation for losses resulting from the unsupervised actions of the bank president and the loan committee. ■

Dissenting Directors Directors are expected to attend board of directors' meetings, and their votes should be entered into the minutes of the meetings. Unless a dissent is entered, the director is presumed to have assented. Directors who dissent are rarely held individually liable for mismanagement of the corporation. For this reason, a director who is absent from a given meeting sometimes registers with the secretary of the board a dissent to actions taken at the meeting.

DUTY OF LOYALTY

Loyalty can be defined as faithfulness to one's obligations and duties. In the corporate context, the duty of loyalty requires directors and officers to subordinate their personal interests to the welfare of the corporation. Among other things, this means that directors may not use corporate funds or confidential corporate information for personal advantage. They must also refrain from self-dealing. For instance, a director should not oppose a tender offer that is in the corporation's best interest simply because its acceptance may cost the director her or his position. Cases dealing with fiduciary duty may involve one or more of the following:

1. Competing with the corporation.
2. Usurping (taking advantage of) a corporate opportunity.
3. Having an interest that conflicts with the interest of the corporation.
4. Engaging in insider trading (using information that is not public to make a profit trading securities, as will be discussed in Chapter 35).
5. Authorizing a corporate transaction that is detrimental to minority shareholders.

An officer or director usurps a corporate opportunity when she or he, for personal gain, takes advantage of a business opportunity that is financially within the corporation's reach and would be to the firm's practical advantage. The availability of cash to repay a corporation's debts can represent a "corporate opportunity." Does the use of that cash to repay a loan to a director constitute a "usurping" of that opportunity? That was the question in the following case.

CASE 33.2 In re Cumberland Farms, Inc.

United States Court of Appeals,
First Circuit, 2002.
284 F.3d 216.

BACKGROUND AND FACTS Cumberland Farms, Inc., a close corporation owned by the Haseotes family, operated a chain of gas stations. Demetrios Haseotes became the chief executive officer and chairman of the board of directors of Cumberland in 1960. In the 1970s, to provide Cumberland with a more secure gasoline supply, Haseotes acquired a refinery in Newfoundland, Canada. Because some states do not allow a company that operates a refinery to sell petroleum products retail, Haseotes chose to own the refinery through his own separate businesses, including Cumberland Crude Processing, Inc. (CCP). To operate the refinery, CCP borrowed more than $70 million from Cumberland, under an agreement that required the payment of that loan first. Haseotes also loaned money to CCP. When cash was available, Haseotes had CCP repay $5.75 million to him, without telling the Cumberland board.

(Continued)

CASE 33.2—Continued

CCP defaulted on its debt to Cumberland, which filed a bankruptcy petition in 1992. Haseotes filed a claim for $3 million against the firm, which asserted a claim for $5.75 million against him. Cumberland argued that Haseotes breached his duty of loyalty when he had CCP pay its debt to him while ignoring its debt to Cumberland. The court disallowed Haseotes's claim. On appeal, a federal district court affirmed this ruling. Haseotes appealed to the U.S. Court of Appeals for the First Circuit.

IN THE WORDS OF THE COURT . . .

LIPEZ, Circuit Judge.

* * * *

As a member of Cumberland's board of directors, Haseotes owed the corporation a fiduciary duty of loyalty and fair dealing. * * * *[D]irectors must act with absolute fidelity to the corporation and must place their duties to the corporation above every other financial or business obligation.* [Emphasis added.]

The fiduciary duty is especially exacting where the corporation is closely held. In a close corporation like Cumberland, the relationship among the stockholders must be one of trust, confidence and absolute loyalty if the enterprise is to succeed. * * * Disloyalty and self-seeking conduct on the part of any stockholder will engender bickering, corporate stalemates, and, perhaps, efforts to achieve dissolution.

* * * *

* * * When a corporate director learns of an opportunity that could benefit the corporation, she must inform the disinterested shareholders of all the material details of the opportunity so that they may decide whether the corporation can and should take advantage of it. It is inherently unfair for the director to deny the corporation that choice and instead take the opportunity for herself. * * * [T]he nondisclosure of a corporate opportunity is, *in itself,* unfair to a corporation and a breach of fiduciary duty.

* * * *

Here, any funds that became available in CCP provided an opportunity to pay down CCP's * * * debt to Cumberland. That opportunity was more than conceivably advantageous to Cumberland; it was desperately needed. Moreover, * * * [the loan] agreement explicitly required Haseotes to apply any available money toward Cumberland's loan before paying down CCP's debt to himself * * * . Yet, instead of attempting to repay Cumberland's loan, Haseotes had CCP pay more than $5 million on the loan from [him] * * * .

* * * *

* * * In such circumstances, Haseotes was obligated to seek approval from Cumberland's board before acting. * * *

* * * *

* * * [Haseotes] argues that disclosure was unnecessary because the other members of Cumberland's board knew that money was available in CCP, and that Haseotes was using it to repay the loan from [him]. * * * [H]owever, * * * Cumberland's directors were *not* aware of the opportunity for repayment.

DECISION AND REMEDY The U.S. Court of Appeals for the First Circuit affirmed the lower court's judgment. Haseotes breached his duty of loyalty to Cumberland when, without informing Cumberland's board that money had become available in CCP, he had CCP apply the money toward its debt to himself rather than to its debt to Cumberland.

WHY IS THIS CASE IMPORTANT? *As the judge in this case explained, the duty of loyalty is often considered to be more demanding for the directors and officers of a closely held corporation.*

Conflicts of Interest

The duty of loyalty also requires officers and directors to fully disclose to the board of directors any potential conflict of interest that might arise in any corporate transaction. The various state statutes contain different standards, but a contract will generally *not* be voidable if all of the following are true: if the contract was fair and reasonable to the corporation at the time it was made, if there was a full disclosure of the interest of the officers or directors involved in the transaction, and if the contract was approved by a majority of the disinterested directors or shareholders.

■ Example 33.2 Southwood Corporation needs office space. Lambert Alden, one of its five directors, owns the building adjoining the corporation's main office building. He negotiates a lease with Southwood for the space, making a full disclosure to Southwood and the other four board directors. The lease arrangement is fair and reasonable, and it is unanimously approved by the corporation's board of directors. In this situation, Alden has not breached his duty of loyalty to the corporation, and the contract is thus valid. If it were otherwise, directors would be prevented from ever giving financial assistance to the corporations they serve. ■

ETHICAL ISSUE 33.1

What happens to the duty of loyalty when a director sits on the boards of two corporations? Corporate directors often have many business affiliations, and they may even sit on the board of more than one corporation. (Of course, directors generally are precluded from sitting on the boards of directors of competing companies.) The duty of loyalty can become cloudy when corporate directors sit on the board of more than one corporation. Because of the potential for abuse in transactions negotiated between corporations whose boards have some members in common, courts tend to scrutinize such actions closely.

For example, suppose that four individuals own a total of 70 percent of the shares of Company A and 100 percent of the shares of Company B. All four of these shareholders sit on the boards of directors of both corporations. Company A decides to purchase all of Company B's stock for $6 million, when in fact it is worth only $3 million. The shareholder-directors of both firms have not breached their duty to Company B because the $6 million price is beneficial to that company. A court would likely hold that the directors breached their duty to the other shareholders of Company A (who owned the remaining 30 percent of Company A's shares), however, because these other shareholders had nothing to gain by the transaction and much to lose by Company A's purchase of Company B at an inflated price.[3] ■

Liability of Directors and Officers

Directors and officers are exposed to liability on many fronts. Corporate directors and officers may be held liable for the crimes and torts committed by themselves or by corporate employees under their supervision, as discussed in Chapter 6 and Chapter 28, respectively. Additionally, shareholders may perceive that the corporate directors are not acting in the best interests of the corporation and may sue the directors, in what is called a *shareholder's derivative suit,* on behalf of the corporation. (This type of action is discussed later in this chapter, in the context of shareholders' rights.)

The Business Judgment Rule A corporate director or officer may be able to avoid liability to the corporation or to its shareholders for poor business judgments under

3. See, for example, *Gries Sports Enterprises, Inc. v. Cleveland Browns Football Co.,* 26 Ohio St.3d 15, 496 N.E.2d 959 (1986).

BUSINESS JUDGMENT RULE A rule that immunizes corporate management from liability for actions that result in corporate losses or damages if the actions are undertaken in good faith and are within both the power of the corporation and the authority of management to make.

the **business judgment rule.** Directors and officers are expected to exercise due care and to use their best judgment in guiding corporate management, but they are not insurers of business success. Honest mistakes of judgment and poor business decisions on their part do not make them liable to the corporation for resulting damages.

The business judgment rule generally immunizes directors and officers from liability for the consequences of a decision that is within managerial authority, as long as the decision complies with management's fiduciary duties and as long as acting on the decision is within the powers of the corporation. Consequently, if there is a reasonable basis for a business decision, it is unlikely that a court will interfere with that decision, even if the corporation suffers as a result.

Requirements for the Rule to Apply To benefit from the business judgment rule, directors and officers must act in good faith, in what they consider to be the best interests of the corporation, and with the care that an ordinarily prudent person in a similar position would exercise in like circumstances. This requires an informed decision, with a rational basis, and with no conflict between the decision maker's personal interests and the interests of the corporation.

Role of Shareholders

The acquisition of a share of stock makes a person an owner and shareholder in a corporation. Shareholders thus own the corporation. Although they have no legal title to corporate property, such as buildings and equipment, they do have an equitable (ownership) interest in the firm.

As a general rule, shareholders have no responsibility for the daily management of the corporation, although they are ultimately responsible for choosing the board of directors, which does have such control. Ordinarily, corporate officers and other employees owe no direct duty to individual shareholders. Their duty is to the corporation as a whole. A director, however, is in a fiduciary relationship to the corporation and therefore serves the interests of the shareholders. Ordinarily, there is no legal relationship between shareholders and creditors of the corporation. Shareholders can, in fact, be creditors of the corporation and thus have the same rights of recovery against the corporation as any other creditor.

BE AWARE Shareholders normally are not agents of the corporation.

In this section, we look at the powers and voting rights of shareholders, which are generally established in the articles of incorporation and under the state's general corporation law.

Shareholders' Powers

Shareholders must approve fundamental changes affecting the corporation before the changes can be implemented. Hence, shareholders are empowered to amend the articles of incorporation (charter) and bylaws, approve a merger or the dissolution of the corporation, and approve the sale of all or substantially all of the corporation's assets. Some of these powers are subject to prior board approval.

Members of the board of directors are elected and removed by a vote of the shareholders. The first board of directors is either named in the articles of incorporation or chosen by the incorporators to serve until the first shareholders' meeting. From that time on, the selection and retention of directors are exclusively shareholder functions.

Directors usually serve their full terms; if they are unsatisfactory, they are simply not reelected. Shareholders have the inherent power, however, to remove a director

Shareholders meet to vote on corporate issues. What issues must be put before shareholders for their vote? (Bill Stryker)

from office *for cause* (breach of duty or misconduct) by a majority vote.[4] Some state statutes (and some corporate charters) even permit removal of directors without cause by the vote of a majority of the holders of outstanding shares entitled to vote.

SHAREHOLDERS' MEETINGS

Shareholders' meetings must occur at least annually. In addition, special meetings can be called to deal with urgent matters.

Notice of Meetings Each shareholder must receive written notice of the date, time, and place of a shareholders' meeting.[5] The notice must be received within a reasonable length of time prior to the date of the meeting. Notice of a special meeting must include a statement of the purpose of the meeting, and business transacted at the meeting is limited to that purpose.

Proxies Because it is usually not practical for owners of only a few shares of stock of publicly traded corporations to attend shareholders' meetings, such shareholders normally give third parties written authorization to vote their shares at the meeting. This authorization is called a **proxy** (from the Latin *procurare,* "to manage, take care of"). Proxies are often solicited by management, but any person can solicit proxies to concentrate voting power. Proxies have been used by a group of shareholders as a device for taking over a corporation (corporate takeovers will be discussed in Chapter 34). Proxies are normally revocable (that is, they can be withdrawn), unless they are specifically designated as irrevocable. Under RMBCA 7.22(c), proxies last for eleven months, unless the proxy agreement provides for a longer period.

PROXY
In corporate law, a written agreement between a stockholder and another party under which the stockholder authorizes the other party to vote the stockholder's shares in a certain manner.

Proxy Materials and Shareholder Proposals When shareholders want to change a company policy, they can put their idea up for a shareholder vote. They can do this by submitting a shareholder proposal to the board of directors and asking the board to include the proposal in the proxy materials that are sent to all shareholders before meetings.

The Securities and Exchange Commission (SEC), which regulates the purchase and sale of securities (see Chapter 35), has special provisions relating to proxies and shareholder proposals. SEC Rule 14a-8 requires that when a company sends proxy materials to its shareholders, the company must also include whatever proposals will be considered at the meeting and provide shareholders with the opportunity to vote on the proposals by marking and returning their proxy cards. SEC Rule 14a-8 provides that all shareholders who own stock worth at least $1,000 are eligible to submit proposals for inclusion in corporate proxy materials. Only those proposals that relate to significant policy considerations rather than ordinary business operations must be included.

.on the Web For information on the SEC's rulings, including rulings on proxy materials, go to **http://www.sec.gov/rules/final.shtml**.

SHAREHOLDER VOTING

Shareholders exercise ownership control through the power of their votes. Each shareholder is entitled to one vote per share, although the voting techniques that will be discussed shortly all enhance the power of the shareholder's vote. The articles

4. A director can often demand court review of removal for cause.

5. The shareholder can waive the requirement of written notice by signing a waiver form. In some states, a shareholder who does not receive written notice, but who learns of the meeting and attends without protesting the lack of notice, is said to have waived notice by such conduct. State statutes and corporate bylaws typically set forth the time within which notice must be sent, what methods can be used, and what the notice must contain.

of incorporation can exclude or limit voting rights, particularly for certain classes of shares. For example, owners of preferred shares are usually denied the right to vote [RMBCA 7.21].

BE CAREFUL Once a quorum is present, a vote can be taken even if some shareholders leave without casting their votes.

Quorum Requirements For shareholders to conduct business at a meeting, a quorum must be present. Generally, a quorum exists when shareholders holding more than 50 percent of the outstanding shares are present. Corporate business matters are presented in the form of *resolutions,* which shareholders vote to approve or disapprove. Some state statutes have set specific voting requirements, and corporations' articles or bylaws must abide by these statutory requirements. In some states, obtaining the unanimous written consent of shareholders is a permissible alternative to holding a shareholders' meeting [RMBCA 7.25].

Once a quorum is present, voting can proceed. A majority vote of the shares represented at the meeting is usually required to pass resolutions. ■ EXAMPLE 33.3 Assume that Novo Pictures, Inc., has 10,000 outstanding shares of voting stock. Its articles of incorporation set the quorum at 50 percent of outstanding shares and provide that a majority vote of the shares present is necessary to pass resolutions concerning ordinary matters. Therefore, for this firm, a quorum of shareholders representing 5,000 outstanding shares must be present at a shareholders' meeting to conduct business. If exactly 5,000 shares are represented at the meeting, a vote of at least 2,501 of those shares is needed to pass a resolution. If 6,000 shares are represented, a vote of 3,001 will be required, and so on. ■

At times, more than a simple majority vote will be required either by a state statute or by the corporate charter. Extraordinary corporate matters, such as a merger, consolidation, or dissolution of the corporation (see Chapter 34), require a higher percentage of all corporate shares entitled to vote [RMBCA 7.27].

Voting Lists The corporation prepares voting lists prior to each meeting of the shareholders. Only persons whose names appear on the corporation's shareholder records as owners are ordinarily entitled to vote.[6] The voting list contains the name and address of each shareholder as shown on the corporate records on a given cutoff date, or record date. (Under RMBCA 7.07, the record date may be as much as seventy days before the meeting.) The voting list also includes the number of voting shares held by each owner. The list is usually kept at the corporate headquarters and is available for shareholder inspection [RMBCA 7.20].

Cumulative Voting Most states permit or even require shareholders to elect directors by *cumulative voting,* a method of voting designed to allow minority shareholders representation on the board of directors.[7] With cumulative voting, the number of board members to be elected is multiplied by the number of voting shares a shareholder owns. The result equals the number of votes the shareholder has, and this total can be cast for one or more nominees for director. All nominees stand for election at the same time. When cumulative voting is not required either by statute or under the articles, the entire board can be elected by a simple majority of shares at a shareholders' meeting.

Cumulative voting can best be understood by an example. ■ EXAMPLE 33.4 Suppose that a corporation has 10,000 shares issued and outstanding. One group of

6. When the legal owner is bankrupt, incompetent, deceased, or in some other way under a legal disability, his or her vote can be cast by a person designated by law to control and manage the owner's property.

7. See, for example, California Corporate Code Section 708. Under RMBCA 7.28, however, no cumulative voting rights exist unless the articles of incorporation so provide.

shareholders (the minority shareholders) holds only 3,000 shares, and the other group of shareholders (the majority shareholders) holds the other 7,000 shares. Three members of the board are to be elected. The majority shareholders' nominees are Acevedo, Barkley, and Craycik. The minority shareholders' nominee is Drake. Can Drake be elected by the minority shareholders?

If cumulative voting is allowed, the answer is yes. The minority shareholders have 9,000 votes among them (the number of directors to be elected times the number of shares held by the minority shareholders equals 3 times 3,000, which equals 9,000 votes). All of these votes can be cast to elect Drake. The majority shareholders have 21,000 votes (3 times 7,000 equals 21,000 votes), but these votes have to be distributed among their three nominees. The principle of cumulative voting is that no matter how the majority shareholders cast their 21,000 votes, they will not be able to elect all three directors if the minority shareholders cast all of their 9,000 votes for Drake, as illustrated in Exhibit 33–1. ■

Other Voting Techniques Before a shareholders' meeting, a group of shareholders can agree in writing to vote their shares together in a specified manner. Such agreements, called *shareholder voting agreements,* are usually held to be valid and enforceable. A shareholder can also appoint a voting agent and vote by proxy. As mentioned previously, a proxy is a written authorization to cast the shareholder's vote, and a person can solicit proxies from a number of shareholders in an attempt to concentrate voting power.

VOTING TRUST
An agreement (trust contract) under which legal title to shares of corporate stock is transferred to a trustee who is authorized by the shareholders to vote the shares on their behalf.

Another technique is for shareholders to enter into a **voting trust,** which is an agreement (a trust contract) under which legal title (record ownership on the corporate books) is transferred to a trustee who is responsible for voting the shares. The agreement can specify how the trustee is to vote, or it can allow the trustee to use his or her discretion. The trustee takes physical possession of the stock certificate and in return gives the shareholder a voting trust certificate. The shareholder retains all of the rights of ownership (for example, the right to receive dividend payments) except for the power to vote the shares.

Rights of Shareholders

Shareholders possess numerous rights. A significant right—the right to vote their shares—has already been discussed. We now look at some additional rights of shareholders.

EXHIBIT 33–1 RESULTS OF CUMULATIVE VOTING

This exhibit illustrates how cumulative voting gives minority shareholders a greater chance of electing a director of their choice. By casting all of their 9,000 votes for one candidate (Drake), the minority shareholders will succeed in electing Drake to the board of directors.

BALLOT	MAJORITY SHAREHOLDERS' VOTES			MINORITY SHAREHOLDERS' VOTES	DIRECTORS ELECTED
	Acevedo	Barkley	Craycik	Drake	
1	10,000	10,000	1,000	9,000	Acevedo/Barkley/Drake
2	9,001	9,000	2,999	9,000	Acevedo/Barkley/Drake
3	6,000	7,000	8,000	9,000	Barkley/Craycik/Drake

APPLICATION Creating an E-Document Retention Policy—Continued

Procedure, which govern civil litigation procedures (see Chapter 3), a defendant in a lawsuit must disclose all relevant electronic data compilations and documents, as well as all relevant paper documents.

Although certain documents or data might free a company of any liability arising from a claim, others might serve to substantiate a civil claim or criminal charge. It is also possible that information contained in a document—an interoffice e-mail memo, for example (or even a memo referring to that memo)—could be used to convince a jury that the company or its directors or officers had condoned a certain action that they later denied condoning.

WHICH E-DOCUMENTS SHOULD BE RETAINED?

How does a company decide which e-documents should be retained and which should be destroyed? By law, corporations are required to keep certain types of documents, such as those specified in the *Code of Federal Regulations* and in regulations issued by government agencies, such as the Occupational Safety and Health Administration. Generally, any records that the company is not legally required to keep or that the company is sure it will have no legal need for should be removed from the files and destroyed. A partnership agreement, for example, should be kept. A memo about last year's company picnic, however, should be removed from the files and destroyed; obviously, it is just taking up storage space.

MODIFICATIONS MAY BE NECESSARY DURING AN INVESTIGATION

If the company becomes the target of an investigation, it usually must modify its document-retention policy until the investigation has been completed. Company officers, after receiving a subpoena to produce specific types of documents, should instruct the appropriate employees not to destroy relevant papers or e-documents that would otherwise be disposed of as part of the company's normal document-retention program.

Generally, to avoid being charged with obstruction of justice, company officials must always exercise good faith in deciding which documents should or should not be destroyed when attempting to comply with a subpoena. The specter of criminal prosecution would appear to encourage the retention of even those documents that are only remotely related to the dispute—at least until it has been resolved.

CHECKLIST FOR AN E-DOCUMENT RETENTION POLICY

1. Let employees know not only which e-documents should be retained and deleted but also which types of documents should not be created in the first place.
2. Find out which documents must be retained under the *Code of Federal Regulations* and under other government agency regulations to which your corporation is subject.
3. Retain other e-documents only if their retention is in the corporation's interest.
4. If certain corporate documents are subpoenaed, modify your document-retention policy to retain any document that is even remotely related to the dispute until the legal action has been resolved.

KEY TERMS

business judgment rule 866
no-par share 874
par-value share 874
preemptive right 870
proxy 867
quorum 859
receiver 873
right of first refusal 872
shareholder's derivative suit 873
stock certificate 870
stock warrant 871
tender offer 862
voting trust 869
watered stock 874

CHAPTER SUMMARY Corporate Directors, Officers, and Shareholders

Role of Directors (See pages 857–861.)	1. *Directors' qualifications*—Few qualifications are required; a director can be a shareholder but is not required to be. 2. *Election of directors*—The first board of directors is usually appointed by the incorporators; thereafter, directors are elected by the shareholders. Directors usually serve a one-year term, although the term can be longer and staggered terms are permitted under most state statutes. 3. *Board of directors' meetings*—The board of directors conducts business by holding formal meetings with recorded minutes. The date of regular meetings is usually established in the corporate articles or bylaws; special meetings can be called, with notice sent to all directors. Quorum requirements vary from state to state; usually, a quorum is a majority of the corporate directors. Voting must usually be done in person, and in ordinary matters only a majority vote is required. 4. *Rights of directors*—Directors' rights include the rights of participation, inspection, compensation, and indemnification. Compensation is usually specified in the corporate articles or bylaws. 5. *Directors' management responsibilities*—Directors are responsible for declaring and paying corporate dividends to shareholders; authorizing major corporate decisions; appointing, supervising, and removing corporate officers and other managerial employees; determining employees' compensation; making financial decisions necessary to the management of corporate affairs; and issuing authorized shares and bonds. Directors may delegate some of their responsibilities to executive committees and corporate officers and executives.
Role of Corporate Officers and Executives (See page 861–862.)	Corporate officers and other executive employees are normally hired by the board of directors. As employees, the rights of corporate officers and executives are defined by employment contracts. The duties of corporate officers are the same as those of directors.
Duties and Liabilities of Directors and Officers (See pages 862–866.)	1. *Duty of care*—Directors and officers are obligated to act in good faith, to use prudent business judgment in the conduct of corporate affairs, and to act in the corporation's best interests. If a director fails to exercise this duty of care, he or she can be answerable to the corporation and to the shareholders for breaching the duty. 2. *Duty of loyalty*—Directors and officers have a fiduciary duty to subordinate their own interests to those of the corporation in matters relating to the corporation. 3. *Conflicts of interest*—To fulfill their duty of loyalty, directors and officers must make a full disclosure of any potential conflicts between their personal interests and those of the corporation. 4. *Liability of directors and officers*—Corporate directors and officers are personally liable for their own torts and crimes; additionally, they may be held personally liable for the torts and crimes committed by corporate personnel under their direct supervision (see Chapters 6 and 32). 5. *The business judgment rule*—This rule immunizes directors and officers from liability when they acted in good faith, in the best interests of the corporation, and exercised due care. For the rule to apply, the directors and officers must have made an informed, reasonable, and loyal decision.
Role of Shareholders (See pages 866–869.)	1. *Shareholders' powers*—Shareholders' powers include the approval of all fundamental changes affecting the corporation and the election of the board of directors. 2. *Shareholders' meetings*—Shareholders' meetings must occur at least annually; special meetings can be called when necessary. Notice of the date, time, and place of the meeting (and its purpose, if it is specially called) must be sent to shareholders. Shareholders may vote by proxy (authorizing someone else to vote their shares) and may submit proposals to be included in the company's proxy materials sent to shareholders before meetings.

(Continued)

CHAPTER SUMMARY Corporate Directors, Officers, and Shareholders—Continued

Role of Shareholders—Continued (See pages 866–869.)	3. *Shareholder voting*—Shareholder voting requirements and procedures are as follows: a. A minimum number of shareholders (a quorum—generally, more than 50 percent of shares held) must be present at a meeting for business to be conducted; resolutions are passed (usually) by simple majority vote. b. The corporation must prepare voting lists of shareholders of record prior to each shareholders' meeting. c. Cumulative voting may or may not be required or permitted. Cumulative voting gives minority shareholders a better chance to be represented on the board of directors. d. A shareholder voting agreement (an agreement of shareholders to vote their shares together) is usually held to be valid and enforceable. e. A shareholder may appoint a proxy (substitute) to vote her or his shares. f. A shareholder may enter into a voting trust agreement by which title (record ownership) of his or her shares is given to a trustee, and the trustee votes the shares in accordance with the trust agreement.
Rights of Shareholders (See pages 869–873.)	Shareholders have numerous rights, which may include the following: 1. The right to a stock certificate, preemptive rights, and the right to stock warrants (depending on the corporate charter). 2. The right to obtain a dividend (at the discretion of the directors). 3. Voting rights. 4. The right to inspect the corporate records. 5. The right to transfer shares (this right may be restricted in close corporations). 6. The right to a share of corporate assets when the corporation is dissolved. 7. The right to sue on behalf of the corporation (bring a shareholder's derivative suit) when the directors fail to do so.
Liability of Shareholders (See pages 873–875.)	Shareholders may be liable for the retention of illegal dividends, for breach of a stock-subscription agreement, and for the value of watered stock.
Duties of Majority Shareholders (See pages 875–877.)	In certain situations, majority shareholders may be regarded as having a fiduciary duty to minority shareholders and will be liable if that duty is breached.

FOR REVIEW

Answers for the even-numbered questions in this For Review *section can be found on this text's accompanying Web site at* http://blt.westbuslaw.com. *Select "Chapter 33" and click on "For Review."*

1 What are the duties of corporate directors and officers?

2 Directors are expected to use their best judgment in managing the corporation. What must directors do to avoid liability for honest mistakes of judgment and poor business decisions?

3 What is a voting proxy? What is cumulative voting?

4 If a group of shareholders perceives that the corporation has suffered a wrong and the directors refuse to take action, can the shareholders compel the directors to act? If so, how?

5 From what sources may dividends be paid legally? In what circumstances is a dividend illegal? What happens if a dividend is illegally paid?

QUESTIONS AND CASE PROBLEMS

33–1. Voting Techniques. Algonquin Corp. has issued and has outstanding 100,000 shares of common stock. Four stockholders own 60,000 of these shares, and for the past six years they have nominated a slate of people for membership on the board, all of whom have been elected. Sergio and twenty other shareholders, owning 20,000 shares, are dissatisfied with corporate management and want a representative on the board who shares their views. Explain under what circumstances Sergio and the minority shareholders can elect their representative to the board.

33–2. Duties of Directors. Starboard, Inc., has a board of directors consisting of three members (Ellsworth, Green, and Morino) and approximately five hundred shareholders. At a regular meeting of the board, the board selects Tyson as president of the corporation by a two-to-one vote, with Ellsworth dissenting. The minutes of the meeting do not register Ellsworth's dissenting vote. Later, during an audit, it is discovered that Tyson is a former convict and has openly embezzled $500,000 from Starboard. This loss is not covered by insurance. The corporation wants to hold directors Ellsworth, Green, and Morino liable. Ellsworth claims no liability. Discuss the personal liability of the directors to the corporation.

33–3. Liability of Shareholders. Mallard has made a preincorporation subscription agreement to purchase 500 shares of a newly formed corporation. The shares have a par value of $100 per share. The corporation is formed, and it accepts Mallard's subscription. Mallard transfers a piece of land he owns to the corporation as payment for 250 of the shares, and the corporation issues 250 shares for it. Mallard pays for the other 250 shares with cash. One year later, with the corporation in serious financial difficulty, the board declares and pays a $5-per-share dividend. It is now learned that the land transferred by Mallard had a market value of $18,000. Discuss any liability that shareholder Mallard has to the corporation or to the creditors of the corporation.

33–4. Duty of Loyalty. Mackinac Cellular Corp. offered to sell Robert Broz a license to operate a cellular phone system in Michigan. Broz was a director of Cellular Information Systems, Inc. (CIS). CIS, as a result of bankruptcy proceedings, was in the process of selling its cellular holdings. Broz did not formally present the opportunity to the CIS board, but he told some of the firm's officers and directors, who replied that CIS was not interested. At the time, PriCellular, Inc., a firm that was interested in the Michigan license, was attempting to buy CIS. Without telling PriCellular, Broz bought the license himself. After PriCellular took over CIS, the company filed a suit in a Delaware state court against Broz, alleging that he had usurped a corporate opportunity. For what reasons might a court decide that Broz had done nothing wrong? Discuss. [*Broz v. Cellular Information Systems, Inc.,* 673 A.2d 148 (Del. 1996)]

33–5. Business Judgment Rule. Charles Pace and Maria Fuentez were shareholders of Houston Industries, Inc. (HII), and employees of Houston Lighting & Power, a subsidiary of HII, when they lost their jobs because of a company-wide reduction in its workforce. Pace, as a shareholder, three times wrote to HII, demanding that the board of directors terminate certain HII directors and officers and file a suit to recover damages for breach of fiduciary duty. Three times, the directors referred the charges to board committees and an outside law firm, which found that the facts did not support the charges. The board also received input from federal regulatory authorities about the facts behind some of the charges. The board notified Pace that it was refusing his demands. In response, Pace and Fuentez filed a shareholder's derivative suit in a Texas state court against Don Jordan and the other HII directors, contending that the board's investigation was inadequate. The defendants filed a motion for summary judgment, arguing that the suit was barred by the business judgment rule. Are the defendants right? How should the court rule? Why? [*Pace v. Jordan,* 999 S.W.2d 615 (Tex.App.—Houston [1 Dist.] 1999)]

CASE PROBLEM WITH SAMPLE ANSWER

33–6. Atlas Food Systems & Services, Inc., based in South Carolina, was a food vending service that provided refreshments to factories and other businesses. Atlas was a closely held corporation. John Kiriakides was a minority shareholder of Atlas. Alex Kiriakides was the majority shareholder. Throughout most of Atlas's history, Alex was the chairman of the board, which included John as a director. In 1995, while John was the president of the firm, the board and shareholders decided to convert Atlas to an S corporation. A few months later, however, Alex, without calling a vote, decided that the firm would not convert. In 1996, a dispute arose over Atlas's contract to buy certain property. John and others decided not to buy it. Without consulting anyone, Alex elected to go through with the sale. Within a few days, Alex refused to allow John to stay on as president. Two months later, Atlas offered to buy John's interest in the firm for almost $2 million. John refused, believing the offer was too low. John filed a suit in a South Carolina state court against Atlas and Alex, seeking, among other things, to force a buyout of John's shares. On what basis might the court grant John's request? Discuss. [*Kiriakides v. Atlas Food Systems & Services, Inc.,* 541 S.E.2d 257 (S.C. 2001)]

After you have answered this problem, compare your answer with the sample answer given on the Web site that accompanies this text. Go to http://blt.westbuslaw.com, select "Chapter 33," and click on "Case Problem with Sample Answer."

33–7. Inspection Rights. Craig Johnson founded Distributed Solutions, Inc. (DSI), in 1991 to make software and provide consulting services, including payroll services, for small companies.

A marquee for Harrah's hotel and casino is seen across the Strip from Caesars Palace in Las Vegas, Nevada. In 2004, Harrah's agreed to buy Caesars for about $5.2 billion, creating the world's largest casino operator. What are the various ways in which one corporation can extend its operations by combining with another corporation? (Reuters/Ethan Miller/Landov)

The results of a consolidation are essentially the same as the results of a merger. C is recognized as a new corporation and a single entity; A and B cease to exist. C inherits all of the rights, privileges, and powers previously held by A and B. Title to any property and assets owned by A and B passes to C without formal transfer. C assumes liability for all of the debts and obligations owed by A and B. The *articles of consolidation,* which state the terms of the consolidation, take the place of A's and B's original corporate articles and are thereafter regarded as C's corporate articles. ■

PROCEDURE FOR MERGER OR CONSOLIDATION

All states have statutes authorizing mergers and consolidations for domestic (in-state) corporations, and most states allow the combination of domestic and foreign (out-of-state) corporations. Although the procedures vary somewhat among jurisdictions, the basic requirements for a merger or a consolidation are as follows:

1. The board of directors of *each* corporation involved must approve a merger or consolidation plan.
2. The shareholders of *each* corporation must approve the plan, by vote, at a shareholders' meeting. Most state statutes require the approval of two-thirds of the outstanding shares of voting stock, although some states require only a simple majority, and others require a four-fifths vote. Frequently, statutes require that each class of stock approve the merger; thus, the holders of nonvoting stock must also approve. A corporation's bylaws can provide for a stricter requirement.
3. Once approved by all of the directors and shareholders, the plan (articles of merger or consolidation) is filed, usually with the secretary of state.
4. When state formalities are satisfied, the state issues a certificate of merger to the surviving corporation or a certificate of consolidation to the newly consolidated corporation.

Section 11.04 of the Revised Model Business Corporation Act (RMBCA) provides for a simplified procedure for the merger of a substantially owned subsidiary corporation into its parent corporation. Under these provisions, a **short-form merger**—also referred to as a **parent-subsidiary merger**—can be accomplished *without the approval of the shareholders* of either corporation. The short-form merger can be used only when the parent corporation owns at least 90 percent of the outstanding shares of each class of stock of the subsidiary corporation. The simplified procedure requires that a plan for the merger be approved by the board of directors of the parent corporation before it is filed with the state. A copy of the merger plan must be sent to each shareholder of record of the subsidiary corporation.

SHORT-FORM MERGER
A merger between a subsidiary corporation and a parent corporation that owns at least 90 percent of the outstanding shares of each class of stock issued by the subsidiary corporation. Short-form mergers can be accomplished without the approval of the shareholders of either corporation.

PARENT-SUBSIDIARY MERGER
A merger of companies in which one company (the parent corporation) owns most of the stock of the other corporation (the subsidiary corporation). A parent-subsidiary merger (short-form merger) can use a simplified procedure when the parent corporation owns at least 90 percent of the outstanding shares of each class of stock of the subsidiary corporation.

SHAREHOLDER APPROVAL

As mentioned, except in a short-form merger, the shareholders of both corporations must approve a merger or consolidation plan. Shareholders invest in a corporation with the expectation that the board of directors will manage the enterprise and make decisions on ordinary business matters. For extraordinary matters, however, the authorization of both the shareholders and the board of directors is required. In addition, state corporation statutes often require shareholder approval for various other types of extraordinary transactions, such as the sale, lease, or exchange of all or substantially all corporate assets outside the corporation's regular course of business. Amendments to the articles of incorporation and the dissolution of the corporation also generally require shareholder approval.

REMEMBER State statutes, articles of incorporation, and corporate bylaws can require the approval of more than a majority of shares for some extraordinary matters.

Hence, when any extraordinary matter arises, the corporation must proceed as authorized by law to obtain the approval of the shareholders and the board of directors. Sometimes, a transaction can be structured in such a way that shareholder approval is not required, but if the shareholders challenge the transaction, a court will use its equity powers to require such approval. To determine the nature of the transaction, the court will look to its consequences as well as its form.

Appraisal Rights

APPRAISAL RIGHT The right of a dissenting shareholder, who objects to an extraordinary transaction of the corporation (such as a merger or a consolidation), to have his or her shares appraised and to be paid the fair value of those shares by the corporation.

What if a shareholder disapproves of a merger or a consolidation but is outvoted by the other shareholders? The law recognizes that a dissenting shareholder should not be forced to become an unwilling shareholder in a corporation that is new or different from the one in which the shareholder originally invested. The shareholder has the right to dissent and may be entitled to be paid the fair value for the number of shares held on the date of the merger or consolidation. This right is referred to as the shareholder's **appraisal right.**

Appraisal rights are available only when a state statute specifically provides for them. State laws vary on whether appraisal rights are available in close corporations. Appraisal rights normally extend to regular mergers, consolidations, short-form mergers, and sales of substantially all of the corporate assets not in the ordinary course of business.

In a short-form merger, is the exercise of an appraisal right a minority shareholder's only remedy when he or she dissents from the merger? That was the question in the following case.

CASE 34.1 Glassman v. Unocal Exploration Corp.

Delaware Supreme Court, 2001.
777 A.2d 242.

BACKGROUND AND FACTS Unocal Corporation is an earth resources company primarily engaged in the exploration for, and production of, crude oil and natural gas. Unocal owned approximately 96 percent of the stock of Unocal Exploration Corporation (UXC), an oil and gas company operating in the Gulf of Mexico. In 1991, low natural gas prices caused a drop in both companies' revenues and earnings. Unocal decided that by merging with UXC, it could reduce expenses and save money. The boards of directors of the two firms appointed special committees to consider a short-form merger. The UXC committee agreed to a merger exchange ratio of about half a share of Unocal stock for each UXC share. Glassman and other UXC minority shareholders filed a suit in a Delaware state court against Unocal, alleging in part that the firm had breached its fiduciary duty of "entire fairness and full disclosure." The court held that the only remedy in connection with this short-form merger was the minority's appraisal right. The plaintiffs appealed to the Delaware Supreme Court.

IN THE WORDS OF THE COURT . . .
BERGER, Justice.

* * * *

* * * In its current form, * * * 8 [Delaware Code Section] 253 provides in relevant part:

> (a) In any case in which at least 90 percent of the outstanding shares of each class of the stock of a corporation * * * is owned by another corporation * * *, the corporation having such stock ownership may * * * merge the other corporation * * * into itself * * * by executing, acknowledging and filing * * * a certificate of such ownership

(Continued)

CASE 34.1—Continued

> and merger setting forth a copy of the resolution of its board of directors to so merge and the date of the adoption; provided, however, that in case the parent corporation shall not own all the outstanding stock of * * * the subsidiary corporation[,] * * * the resolution * * * shall state the terms and conditions of the merger * * * .
>
> * * * *
>
> (d) In the event that all of the stock of a subsidiary Delaware corporation * * * is not owned by the parent corporation immediately prior to the merger, the stockholders of the subsidiary Delaware corporation party to the merger shall have appraisal rights * * * .
>
> * * * *

* * * In a short-form merger, there is no agreement of merger negotiated by two companies; there is only a unilateral act—a decision by the parent company that its 90% owned subsidiary shall no longer exist as a separate entity. The minority stockholders receive no advance notice of the merger; their directors do not consider or approve it; and there is no vote. *Those who object are given the right to obtain fair value for their shares through appraisal.* [Emphasis added.]

* * * If * * * the corporate fiduciary sets up negotiating committees, hires independent financial and legal experts, etc., then it will have lost the very benefit provided by the statute—a simple, fast and inexpensive process for accomplishing a merger. * * *

Thus, we * * * hold that, absent fraud or illegality, appraisal is the exclusive remedy available to a minority stockholder who objects to a short-form merger.

DECISION AND REMEDY The Delaware Supreme Court affirmed the decision of the lower court, holding that appraisal was the exclusive remedy for a minority stockholder dissatisfied with a short-form merger.

FOR CRITICAL ANALYSIS—Ethical Consideration *Does the court's holding in this case mean that a parent corporation does not have a duty of full disclosure in a short-form merger? Explain why or why not.*

Appraisal Rights—Procedures Shareholders may lose their appraisal rights if they do not follow precisely the elaborate statutory procedures. Whenever they lose the right to an appraisal, dissenting shareholders must go along with the transaction despite their objections. The dissenting shareholders usually are required to file a written notice of dissent prior to the vote of the shareholders on the proposed transaction. This notice of dissent basically serves as a notice to all shareholders of the costs that dissenting shareholders may impose should the merger or consolidation be approved. In addition, after approval, the dissenting shareholders must make a written demand for payment and for the fair value of their shares.

Appraisal Rights and Shareholder Status In some jurisdictions, once dissenting shareholders elect appraisal rights under a statute, the shareholders lose their shareholder status. Without that status, the shareholders cannot vote, receive dividends, or sue to enjoin whatever action prompted their dissent. In some of those jurisdictions, statutes provide or courts have held that shareholder status may be reinstated during the appraisal process (for example, if a shareholder decides to withdraw from the process and the corporation approves). In other jurisdictions, shareholder status may not be reinstated until the appraisal is concluded. Even if an individual loses his or her shareholder status, courts may allow the individual to sue on the ground of fraud or other illegal conduct associated with the merger.

Valuation of Shares Valuation of shares is often a point of contention between a dissenting shareholder and the corporation. RMBCA 13.01 provides that the "fair value of shares" normally is the value on the day prior to the date on which the vote was taken. The corporation must make a written offer to purchase a dissenting shareholder's stock; also, a current balance sheet and income statement for the corporation should accompany the offer. If the shareholder and the corporation do not agree on the fair value, a court will determine it.

on the Web A searchable database of court cases dealing with corporate litigation, including lawsuits stemming from purchases of corporate assets, is available at **http://corporate-law.widener.edu**.

Purchase of Assets

When a corporation acquires all or substantially all of the assets of another corporation by direct purchase, the purchasing, or *acquiring*, corporation simply extends its ownership and control over more physical assets. Because no change in the legal entity occurs, the acquiring corporation is not required to obtain shareholder approval for the purchase.[3]

Although the acquiring corporation may not be required to obtain the shareholders' approval, both the U.S. Department of Justice and the Federal Trade Commission have issued guidelines that significantly constrain and often prohibit mergers that could result from a purchase of assets. These guidelines are part of the federal antitrust laws to enforce Section 7 of the Clayton Act (discussed in Chapter 37).

Sales of Corporate Assets

Note that the corporation that is *selling* all its assets is substantially changing its business position and perhaps its ability to carry out its corporate purposes. For that reason, the corporation whose assets are being sold must obtain the approval of both the board of directors and the shareholders. In most states and under RMBCA 13.02, a dissenting shareholder of the selling corporation can demand appraisal rights. (Occasionally, disputes arise over whether "all of the assets" being sold included certain property or property rights. For an example of one such dispute, see this chapter's *Adapting the Law to the Online Environment* feature on the next page.)

Potential Liability in Purchases of Assets

Generally, a corporation that purchases the assets of another corporation is not responsible for the liabilities of the selling corporation. Exceptions to this rule are made in the following circumstances:

RECALL In a merger or consolidation, the surviving corporation inherits the disappearing corporation's rights *and* obligations.

1. When the purchasing corporation impliedly or expressly assumes the seller's liabilities.
2. When the sale amounts to what is in fact a merger or consolidation.
3. When the purchaser continues the seller's business and retains the same personnel (same shareholders, directors, and officers).
4. When the sale is fraudulently executed to escape liability.

In any of these situations, the acquiring corporation will be held to have assumed both the assets and the liabilities of the selling corporation.

---

3. If the acquiring corporation plans to pay for the assets with its own corporate stock and not enough authorized unissued shares are available, the shareholders must vote to approve the issuance of additional shares by amendment of the corporate articles. Additionally, acquiring corporations whose stock is traded in a national stock exchange can be required to obtain their own shareholders' approval if they plan to issue a significant number of shares, such as a number equal to 20 percent or more of the outstanding shares.

ADAPTING THE LAW TO THE ONLINE ENVIRONMENT

Who Owns the Web Site?

Most contracts to purchase the assets of another corporation are performed with little difficulty. At times, however, a dispute may arise over some matter connected with the transaction. In one case, for example, the dispute had to do with ownership rights in a Web site. The case arose after 1-800-Postcards, Inc. (1-800), purchased the assets of Popsmear, Inc., which owned and operated a Web-based postcard-advertising business. The Web site address for Popsmear's business was **http://www.1800Postcards.com**. According to the purchase agreement, Popsmear's trademark rights were included in "all of the assets" being sold by Popsmear to 1-800.

THE PROBLEM WITH THE WEB SITE

Problems arose, however, when the sole owner and shareholder of Popsmear, James Morel, changed the password to the Web site. This meant that 1-800 was unable to make any administrative changes to the Web site or to create and change its e-mail boxes. When 1-800 objected to Morel's action, Morel contended that he personally, and not Popsmear, was the registered owner of the domain name and, as such, had a right to change the password. 1-800 then sued Morel for fraud and breach of contract and asked the court for a preliminary injunction against Morel's changing of the password. After all, argued 1-800, by making it impossible for 1-800 to control the Web site, Morel, in effect, had been "selling nothing" when Popsmear sold 1-800 its "trademark rights."

DID THE ASSETS BEING SOLD INCLUDE THE DOMAIN NAME RIGHTS?

In determining whether to grant the preliminary injunction, the court had to decide whether the sale of assets included the domain name rights. The question was complicated by the fact that Morel was the registered owner of the domain name. The court, however, held that this "nuance" was of little significance because both Morel and Popsmear were parties to the purchase agreement. The court also emphasized that the parties "quite likely understood that the domain name registration for the Web site was among the 'assets of the business' irrespective of whether record title was in [Popsmear] or its sole shareholder, Morel." Concluding that 1-800 would likely succeed in its case against Morel and Popsmear, the court granted 1-800's request for a preliminary injunction.[a]

FOR CRITICAL ANALYSIS

Would the court have reached the same conclusion if Morel had not been a party to the purchase agreement? Why or why not?

a. *1-800-Postcards, Inc. v. Morel,* 153 F.Supp.2d 359 (S.D.N.Y. 2001).

In the following case, the court was asked to determine to what extent a corporation that bought the assets of another firm was responsible for the liability of the seller.

CASE 34.2 Lee-Thomas, Inc. v. Hallmark Cards, Inc.

United States Court of Appeals,
Eighth Circuit, 2002.
275 F.3d 702.
http://www.findlaw.com/casecode/courts/8th.html[a]

BACKGROUND AND FACTS In the 1970s, Lee-Thomas, Inc., bought the assets of Patty Woodard, a manufacturer of women's clothing. Hallmark Cards, Inc., through its subsidiary Halls Merchandising, Inc., operates Halls, a department store in Kansas City, Missouri, that sells clothing and other merchandise. Deborah Reithmeyer bought a vintage Patty Woodard blouse from the store. Alleging that the blouse was defective, Reithmeyer filed a suit in a Missouri state court against Hallmark, on a theory of product liability (see Chapter 21). Hallmark contended that Lee-Thomas was obligated to defend or pay the expenses of defending against the suit.

a. In the "Party Name Search" box, type "Lee-Thomas" and click on "search." In the result, click on the name of the case to access the opinion.

CASE 34.2—Continued

When Lee-Thomas refused, Hallmark settled the suit for $50,000 and filed a suit in a federal district court against Lee-Thomas, seeking the amount of the settlement, fees, and other costs. The court issued a summary judgment in Hallmark's favor. Lee-Thomas appealed to the U.S. Court of Appeals for the Eighth Circuit.

IN THE WORDS OF THE COURT . . .

NANGLE, Senior District Judge.

* * * *

Appellant [Lee-Thomas] argues that the district court erred by finding that it is liable for the products liability claims as a successor-in-interest [one who follows another in the ownership or control of property] to Patty Woodard. This argument hinges on the district court's interpretation of the Agreement which facilitated the asset purchase transaction. Section 2.1 of the Agreement states as follows:

> *Assumption of Liabilities.* * * * [B]uyer *shall assume all the liabilities of the seller* existing on the date of the closing, *and liabilities arising solely out of the business conducted by seller prior to the closing* and shall indemnify seller from the same and from all costs or expenses associated therewith, in the same manner and to the same degree as if buyer had purchased all the outstanding * * * stock of seller at the closing.

* * * [I]t was Appellant's understanding that under Section 2.1 "Lee-Thomas would assume expenses and debts accrued from all costs of conducting business generally * * * not liabilities from extraordinary events such as tort claims." * * * Appellant further argues that because the Agreement does not specifically mention "product liability claims" or "unknown" or "contingent" claims, the district court erred by finding that the assumption of liability provision covers a products liability claim which arose over twenty years after the Agreement took effect. We conclude that neither of these contentions has any merit because we find that the Agreement's assumption of liability provision unambiguously requires Appellant to assume Patty Woodard's liabilities with respect to the products liability suit.

* * * *

Because the Agreement is not reasonably susceptible to [appellant's] interpretation, we find that the district court correctly granted Hallmark's summary judgment motion. Under Section 2.1 of the Agreement, Appellant agreed to indemnify Patty Woodard for all "liabilities arising solely out of the business conducted by the seller prior to the closing." Liabilities based on the sale of defective products sold by Patty Woodard prior to closing clearly fall within this category.

DECISION AND REMEDY The U.S. Court of Appeals for the Eighth Circuit affirmed the lower court's judgment. Under the unambiguous asset-purchase agreement between Lee-Thomas and Patty Woodard, the buyer, Lee-Thomas, assumed all of its predecessor's liabilities arising out of the business, including claims for defective products.

FOR CRITICAL ANALYSIS—Economic Consideration *Why would a company, when purchasing the assets of another firm, ever agree to assume the liabilities of that firm as well?*

Takeovers

TARGET CORPORATION
The corporation to be acquired in a corporate takeover; a corporation to whose shareholders a tender offer is submitted.

An alternative to the purchase of another corporation's assets is the purchase of a substantial number of the voting shares of its stock. This enables the acquiring corporation to control the **target corporation** (the corporation being acquired). The

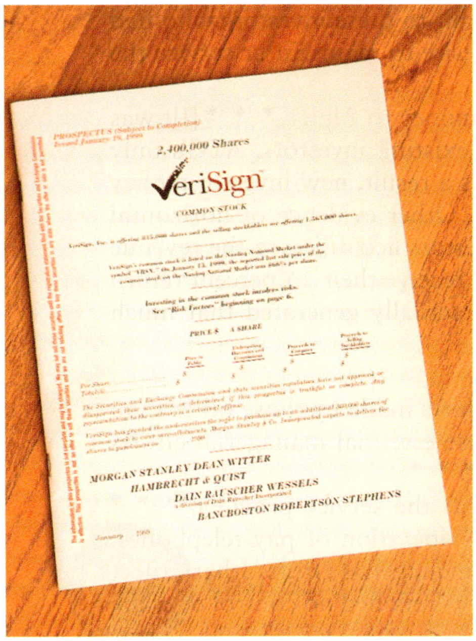

A registration statement discusses a security that is being offered to the public. What are the major contents of a registration statement? (David Young-Wolff/PhotoEdit)

3. A description of the management of the corporation and its security holdings; remuneration; and other benefits, including pensions and stock options. Any interests of directors or officers in any material transactions with the corporation must be disclosed.
4. A financial statement certified by an independent public accounting firm.
5. A description of pending lawsuits.

Other Requirements Before filing the registration statement and the prospectus with the SEC, the corporation is allowed to obtain an *underwriter*—a company that agrees to purchase the new issue of securities for resale to the public. There is a twenty-day waiting period (which can be accelerated by the SEC) after registration before the securities can be sold. During this period, oral offers between interested investors and the issuing corporation concerning the purchase and sale of the proposed securities may take place, and very limited written advertising is allowed. At this time, the so-called **red herring** prospectus may be distributed. The name comes from the red legend printed across the prospectus stating that the registration has been filed but has not become effective.

After the waiting period, the registered securities can be legally bought and sold. Written advertising is allowed in the form of a **tombstone ad,** so named because historically the format resembled a tombstone. Such ads simply tell the investor where and how to obtain a prospectus. Normally, any other type of advertising is prohibited until the registration becomes effective.

RED HERRING
A preliminary prospectus that can be distributed to potential investors after the registration statement (for a securities offering) has been filed with the Securities and Exchange Commission. The name derives from the red legend printed across the prospectus stating that the registration has been filed but has not become effective.

TOMBSTONE AD
An advertisement, historically in a format resembling a tombstone, of a securities offering. The ad tells potential investors where and how they may obtain a prospectus.

DON'T FORGET The purpose of the Securities Act of 1933 is disclosure—the SEC does not consider whether a security is worth the investment price.

EXEMPT SECURITIES

A number of specific securities are exempt from the registration requirements of the Securities Act of 1933. These securities—which can also generally be resold without being registered—include the following:[6]

1. All bank securities sold prior to July 27, 1933.
2. Commercial paper (such as negotiable instruments), if the maturity date does not exceed nine months.
3. Securities of charitable organizations.
4. Securities resulting from a corporate reorganization that are issued for exchange with the issuer's existing security holders and certificates that are issued by trustees, receivers, or debtors in possession under the bankruptcy laws (bankruptcy laws were discussed in Chapter 27).
5. Securities issued exclusively for exchange with the issuer's existing security holders, provided no commission is paid (for example, stock dividends and stock splits).
6. Securities issued to finance the acquisition of railroad equipment.
7. Any insurance, endowment, or annuity contract issued by a state-regulated insurance company.
8. Government-issued securities.
9. Securities issued by banks, savings and loan associations, farmers' cooperatives, and similar institutions subject to supervision by governmental authorities.

6. 15 U.S.C. Section 77c.

10 In consideration of the "small amount involved,"[7] an issuer's offer of up to $5 million in securities in any twelve-month period.

For the last exemption, under Regulation A,[8] the issuer must file with the SEC a notice of the issue and an offering circular, which must also be provided to investors before the sale. This is a much simpler and less expensive process than the procedures associated with full registration. Companies are allowed to "test the waters" for potential interest before preparing the offering circular. To *test the waters* means to determine potential interest without actually selling any securities or requiring any commitment on the part of those who express interest. Small-business issuers (companies with annual revenues of less than $25 million) can also use an integrated registration and reporting system that uses simpler forms than the full registration system.

Exhibit 35–1 summarizes the securities and transactions (discussed next) that are exempt from the registration requirements under the Securities Act of 1933 and SEC regulations.

BE AWARE The issuer of an exempt security does not have to disclose the same information that other issuers do.

7. 15 U.S.C. Section 77c(b).
8. 17 C.F.R. Sections 230.251–230.263.

EXHIBIT 35–1 EXEMPTIONS UNDER THE 1933 SECURITIES ACT

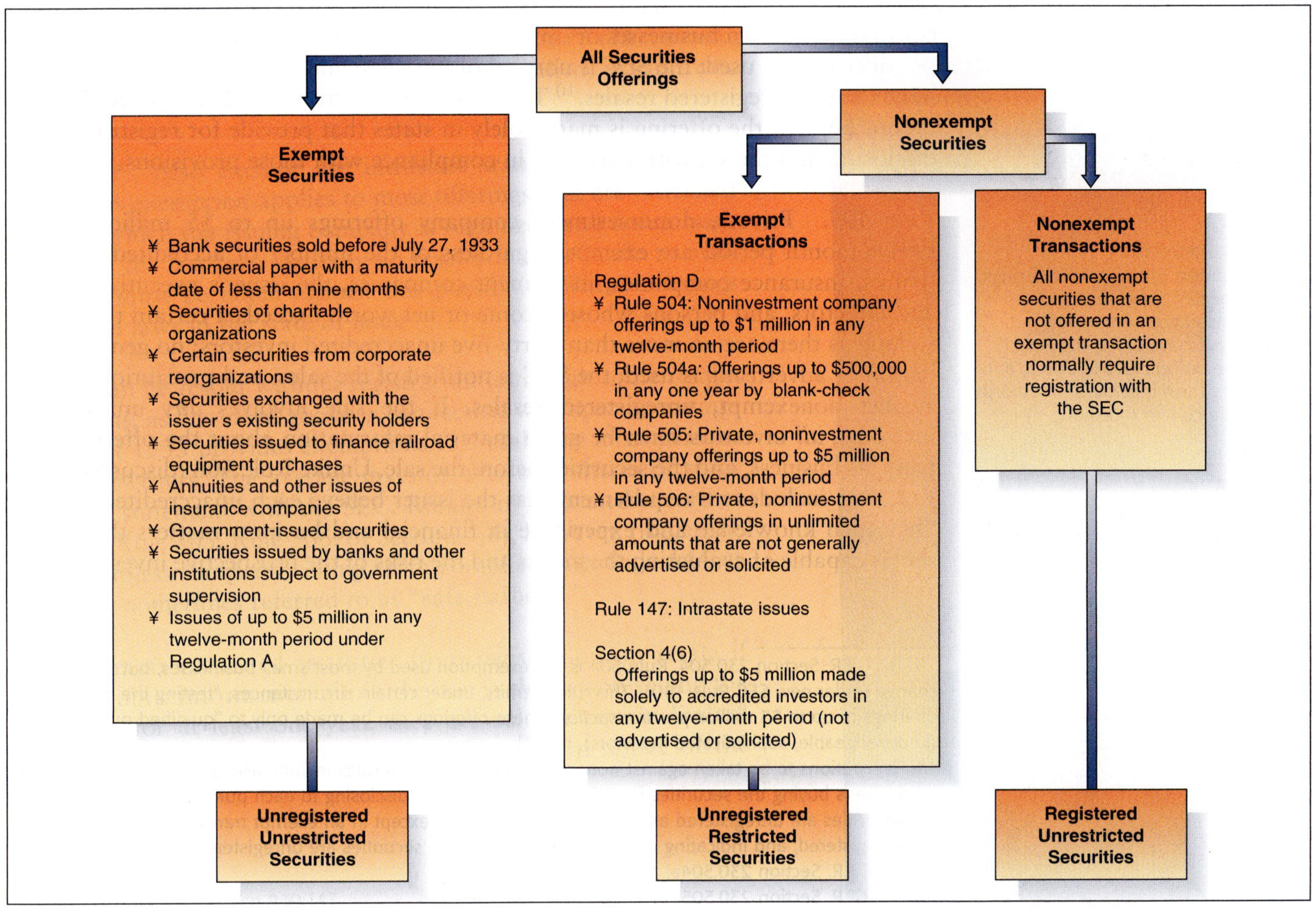

The Center for Corporate Law at the University of Cincinnati College of Law examines all of the acts discussed in this chapter. Go to

http://www.law.uc.edu/CCL.

ACCREDITED INVESTORS
In the context of securities offerings, "sophisticated" investors, such as banks, insurance companies, investment companies, the issuer's executive officers and directors, and persons whose income or net worth exceeds a certain threshold.

it is quite old. In the online world, however, the process can occur much more quickly and efficiently.

■ EXAMPLE 35.3 The most famous case in this area involved Jonathan Lebed, a fifteen-year-old stock trader and Internet user from New Jersey. Lebed was the first minor ever charged with securities fraud by the SEC, but it is unlikely that he will be the last. The SEC charged that Lebed bought thinly traded stocks. After purchasing a stock, he would flood stock-related chat rooms, particularly at Yahoo's finance boards, with messages touting the stock's virtues. He used numerous false names so that no one would know that a single person was posting the messages. He would say that the stock was the most "undervalued stock in history" and that its price would jump by 1,000 percent "very soon." When other investors would then buy the stock, the price would go up quickly, and Lebed would sell out. The SEC forced the teenager to repay almost $300,000 in gains plus interest. He was allowed, however, to keep about $500,000 of the profits he made by trading small-company stocks that he also touted on the Internet. ■

The SEC has been bringing an increasing number of cases against those who manipulate stock prices in this way. Consider that in 1995, such fraud resulted in only six SEC cases. By 2004, the SEC had brought over two hundred actions against online perpetrators of fraudulent stock-price manipulation.

REVIEWING INVESTOR PROTECTION AND CORPORATE GOVERNANCE

Dale Emerson served as the chief financial officer for Reliant Electric Company, a distributor of electricity serving portions of Montana and North Dakota. Reliant was in the final stages of planning a takeover of Dakota Gasworks, Inc., a natural gas distributor that operated solely within North Dakota. Emerson went on a weekend fishing trip with his uncle, Ernest Wallace. Emerson mentioned to Wallace that he had been putting in a lot of extra hours at the office planning a takeover of Dakota Gasworks. On returning from the fishing trip, Wallace met with a broker from Chambers Investments and purchased $20,000 of Reliant stock. Three weeks later, Reliant made a tender offer to Dakota Gasworks stockholders and purchased 57 percent of Dakota Gasworks stock. Over the next two weeks, the price of Reliant stock rose 72 percent before leveling out. Wallace then sold his Reliant stock for a gross profit of $14,400. Using the information presented in the chapter, answer the following questions.

1. Would registration with the SEC be required for Dakota Gasworks securities? Why or why not? List three types of transactions that would qualify as exempt from SEC registration.
2. Did Emerson violate any of the laws discussed in this chapter? Why or why not? Did he violate any legal duty? If so, to whom did he owe a duty?
3. Which securities law or laws might Wallace have violated? According to what theory? Explain.
4. Under the Sarbanes-Oxley Act of 2002, who would be required to certify the accuracy of financial statements filed with the SEC? What penalty could be imposed for wrongful certification?
5. Suppose that Reliant's directors chose to offer its stock for sale via the Internet. What would be some advantages of this procedure? How might an investor go about accessing information about Reliant's stock via the Internet?

KEY TERMS

CHAPTER SUMMARY Investor Protection and Corporate Governance

Securities Act of 1933 (See pages 909–917.)	Prohibits fraud and stabilizes the securities industry by requiring disclosure of all essential information relating to the issuance of stocks to the investing public. 1. *Registration requirements*—Securities, unless exempt, must be registered with the SEC before being offered to the public through the mails or any facility of interstate commerce (including securities exchanges). The *registration statement* must include detailed financial information about the issuing corporation; the intended use of the proceeds of the securities being issued; and certain disclosures, such as interests of directors or officers and pending lawsuits. 2. *Prospectus*—A *prospectus* must be provided to investors, describing the security being sold, the issuing corporation, and the risk attaching to the security. 3. *Exemptions*—The SEC has exempted certain offerings from the requirements of the Securities Act of 1933. Exemptions may be determined on the basis of the size of the issue, whether the offering is private or public, and whether advertising is involved. Exemptions are summarized in Exhibit 35–1 on page 913.
Securities Exchange Act of 1934 (See pages 917–925.)	Provides for the regulation and registration of securities exchanges, brokers, dealers, and national securities associations (such as the NASD). Maintains a continuous disclosure system for all corporations with securities on the securities exchanges and for those companies that have assets in excess of $10 million and five hundred or more shareholders (Section 12 companies). 1. *SEC Rule 10b-5 [under Section 10(b) of the 1934 act]*— a. Applies to insider trading by corporate officers, directors, majority shareholders, and any persons receiving information not available to the public who base their trading on this information. b. Liability for violations can be civil or criminal. c. May be violated by failing to disclose "material facts" that must be disclosed under this rule. d. Applies in virtually all cases concerning the trading of securities—a firm's securities do not have to be registered under the 1933 act for the 1934 act to apply. e. Liability may be based on the tipper/tippee theory or the misappropriation theory. f. Applies only when the requisites of federal jurisdiction (such as use of the mails, stock exchange facilities, or any facility of interstate commerce) are present. 2. *Insider trading [under Section 16(b) of the 1934 act]*—To prevent corporate officers and directors from taking advantage of inside information (information not available to the investing public), the 1934 act requires officers, directors, and shareholders owning 10 percent or more of the issued stock of a corporation to turn over to the corporation all short-term profits (called short-swing profits) realized from the purchase and sale or sale and purchase of corporate stock within any six-month period.

(Continued)

EXHIBIT 36–3 SELECTED INDEPENDENT REGULATORY AGENCIES

NAME AND DATE FORMED	PRINCIPAL DUTIES
Federal Reserve System Board of Governors (Fed) (1913)	Determines policy with respect to interest rates, credit availability, and the money supply.
Federal Trade Commission (FTC) (1914)	Prevents businesses from engaging in unfair trade practices; stops the formation of monopolies in the business sector; protects consumer rights.
Securities and Exchange Commission (SEC) (1934)	Regulates the nation's stock exchanges, in which shares of stock are bought and sold; enforces the securities laws, which require full disclosure of the financial profiles of companies that wish to sell stock and bonds to the public.
Federal Communications Commission (FCC) (1934)	Regulates all communications by telegraph, cable, telephone, radio, satellite, and television.
National Labor Relations Board (NLRB) (1935)	Protects employees' rights to join unions and bargain collectively with employers; attempts to prevent unfair labor practices by both employers and unions.
Equal Employment Opportunity Commission (EEOC) (1964)	Works to eliminate discrimination in employment based on religion, gender, race, color, disability, national origin, or age; investigates claims of discrimination.
Environmental Protection Agency (EPA) (1970)	Undertakes programs aimed at reducing air and water pollution; works with state and local agencies to help fight environmental hazards. (It has been suggested recently that its status be elevated to that of a department.)
Nuclear Regulatory Commission (NRC) (1975)	Ensures that electricity-generating nuclear reactors in the United States are built and operated safely; regularly inspects operations of such reactors.

executing its specified powers. The courts interpret these passages, under what is known as the **delegation doctrine,** as granting Congress the power to establish administrative agencies that can create rules for implementing those laws.

DELEGATION DOCTRINE
A doctrine based on Article I, Section 8, of the U.S. Constitution, which has been construed to allow Congress to delegate some of its power to make and implement laws to administrative agencies.

BUREAUCRACY
The organizational structure, consisting of government bureaus and agencies, through which the government implements and enforces the laws.

The three branches of government exercise certain controls over agency powers and functions, as is discussed later in this chapter, but in many ways administrative agencies function independently. For this reason, administrative agencies, which constitute the **bureaucracy,** are sometimes referred to as the "fourth branch" of the American government.

Administrative Process

The three functions mentioned previously—rulemaking, enforcement, and adjudication—make up what is called the administrative process. **Administrative process** involves the administration of law by administrative agencies, in contrast to **judicial process,** which involves the administration of law by the courts.

ADMINISTRATIVE PROCESS
The procedure used by administrative agencies in the administration of law.

JUDICIAL PROCESS
The procedures relating to, or connected with, the administration of justice through the judicial system.

The Administrative Procedure Act (APA) of 1946[3] imposes procedural requirements that all federal agencies must follow in their rulemaking, adjudication, and other functions. The APA is such an integral part of the administrative process that we examine its application as we go through the basic functions carried out by administrative agencies.

3. 5 U.S.C. Sections 551–706.

RULEMAKING

RULEMAKING
The actions undertaken by administrative agencies when formally adopting new regulations or amending old ones. Under the Administrative Procedure Act, rulemaking includes notifying the public of proposed rules or changes and receiving and considering the public's comments.

A major function of an administrative agency is **rulemaking**—the formulation of new regulations. In an agency's enabling legislation, Congress confers the agency's power to make rules. ■ EXAMPLE 36.2 The Occupational Safety and Health Act of 1970 authorized the Occupational Health and Safety Administration (OSHA) to develop and issue rules governing safety in the workplace. In 1991, OSHA deemed it in the public interest to issue a new rule regulating the health-care industry to prevent the spread of such diseases as acquired immune deficiency syndrome (AIDS). OSHA created a rule specifying various standards—on how contaminated instruments should be handled, for example—with which employers in that industry must comply. ■

In formulating rules, administrative agencies follow specific rulemaking procedures required under the APA. We look here at the most common rulemaking procedure, called **notice-and-comment rulemaking.** This procedure involves three basic steps: notice of the proposed rulemaking, a comment period, and the final rule.

NOTICE-AND-COMMENT RULEMAKING
A procedure in agency rulemaking that requires (1) notice, (2) opportunity for comment, and (3) a published draft of the final rule.

Notice of the Proposed Rulemaking When a federal agency decides to create a new rule, the agency publishes a notice of the proposed rulemaking proceedings in the *Federal Register,* a daily publication of the executive branch that prints government orders, rules, and regulations. The notice states where and when the proceedings will be held, the agency's legal authority for making the rule (usually its enabling legislation), and the terms or subject matter of the proposed rule.

Comment Period Following the publication of the notice of the proposed rulemaking proceedings, the agency must allow ample time for persons to comment on the proposed rule. The purpose of this comment period is to give interested parties the opportunity to express their views on the proposed rule in an effort to influence agency policy. The comments may be in writing or, if a hearing is held, may be given orally. The agency need not respond to all comments, but it must respond to any significant comments that bear directly on the proposed rule. The agency responds by either modifying its final rule or explaining, in a statement accompanying the final rule, why it did not make any changes. In some circumstances, particularly when the procedure being used in a specific instance is less formal, an agency may accept comments after the comment period is closed. The agency should summarize these *ex parte* (private, off-the-record) comments for possible review.

"In some respects matters of procedure constitute the very essence of ordered liberty under the Constitution."

WILEY B. RUTLEDGE,
1894–1949
(Associate justice of the United States Supreme Court, 1943–1949)

The Final Rule After the agency reviews the comments, it drafts the final rule and publishes it in the *Federal Register.* The final rule is later compiled with the rules and regulations of other federal administrative agencies in the Code of Federal Regulations (CFR). Final rules have binding legal effect unless the courts later overturn them.

The court in the following case considered whether to enforce rules that were issued outside of the rulemaking procedure.

CASE 36.1 Hemp Industries Association v. Drug Enforcement Administration

United States Court of Appeals,
Ninth Circuit, 2004.
357 F.3d 1012.

BACKGROUND AND FACTS The members of the Hemp Industries Association (HIA) import and distribute sterilized hemp seed and oil and cake derived from hemp seed, and make and sell food and cosmetic products made from hemp seed and oil. These products contain only nonpsychoactive trace amounts of tetrahydrocannabinols (THC).[a] On

a. A *nonpsychoactive substance* is one that does not affect a person's mind or behavior. Nonpsychoactive hemp is derived from industrial hemp plants grown in Canada and in Europe, the flowers of which contain only a trace amount of the THC contained in marijuana varieties grown for psychoactive use.

(Continued)

CASE 36.1—Continued

October 9, 2001, the U.S. Drug Enforcement Administration (DEA) published an interpretive rule declaring that "any product that contains any amount of THC is a Schedule I controlled substance."[b] On the same day, the DEA proposed two legislative rules. One rule—DEA-205F—amended the listing of THC in "Schedule I" to include natural, as well as synthetic, THC. The second rule—DEA-206F—exempted from control nonpsychoactive hemp products that contain trace amounts of THC not intended to enter the human body. On March 21, 2003, without following formal rulemaking procedures, the DEA declared that these rules were final. This effectively banned the possession and sale of the food products of the HIA's members. The HIA petitioned the U.S. Court of Appeals for the Ninth Circuit to review the rules, asserting that they could not be enforced.

b. A *controlled substance* is a drug whose availability is restricted by law.

IN THE WORDS OF THE COURT . . .

BETTY B. FLETCHER, Circuit Judge.

* * * *

* * * Appellants * * * argue that DEA-205F is a scheduling action—placing nonpsychoactive hemp in Schedule I for the first time—that fails to follow the procedures for such actions required by the Controlled Substances Act ("CSA"). * * *

* * * *

Under 21 U.S.C. [Section] 811(a) [of the CSA]:

> the Attorney General may by rule—
> (1) add to * * * a schedule * * * any drug or other substance if he—
> * * *
>
> (B) makes with respect to such drug or other substance the findings prescribed by subsection (b) of [S]ection 812 of this title * * * .

Rules of the Attorney General under this subsection shall be made on the record after opportunity for a hearing pursuant to the rulemaking procedures prescribed by [the Administrative Procedure Act (APA).]

* * * *Formal rulemaking requires hearings on the record, and [the APA] invites parties to submit proposed findings and oppose the stated bases of tentative agency decisions, and requires the agency to issue formal rulings on each finding, conclusion, or exception on the record.* We will not reproduce the entirety of the [APA] here; it suffices to say that the DEA did not and does not claim to have followed formal rulemaking procedures. [Emphasis added.]

In addition, the DEA did not comply with [Section] 811(a)(1)(B), because the findings required by [Section] 812(b) were not made. Section 812(b) states:

> (b) Placement on schedules; findings required. * * * [A] drug or other substance may not be placed in any schedule unless the findings required for such schedule are made with respect to such drug or other substance.

* * * *

The DEA does not purport to have met the requirements for placement of nonpsychoactive hemp on Schedule I * * * . Instead, the DEA argues that naturally occurring THC in those parts of the hemp plant excluded from the definition of "marijuana" have always been included under the listing for "THC" * * * .

* * * *

Two CSA provisions are relevant to determining whether Appellants' hemp products were banned before [DEA-205F and DEA-206F]: the definition of THC and the definition of marijuana. Both are unambiguous * * * : Appellants' products do not contain the "synthetic" "substances or derivatives" that are covered by the definition of THC, and nonpsychoactive hemp is explicitly excluded from the definition of marijuana.

* * * *

CASE 36.1—Continued

Under 21 U.S.C. [Section] 802(16) [of the CSA]:

> The term "marihuana" means all parts of the plant Cannabis sativa L. * * * . Such term does not include the mature stalks of such plant, fiber produced from such stalks, oil or cake made from the seeds of such plant, any other compound, manufacture, salt, derivative, mixture, or preparation of such mature stalks (except the resin extracted therefrom), fiber, oil, or cake, or the sterilized seed of such plant which is incapable of germination.

The nonpsychoactive hemp in Appellants' products is derived from the "mature stalks" or is "oil and cake made from the seeds" of the *Cannabis* plant, and therefore fits within the plainly stated exception to the CSA definition of marijuana.

* * * Congress knew what it was doing, and its intent to exclude nonpsychoactive hemp from regulation is entirely clear.

DECISION AND REMEDY The U.S. Court of Appeals for the Ninth Circuit held that DEA-205F and DEA-206F "are inconsistent with the unambiguous meaning of the CSA definitions of marijuana and THC," and that the DEA did not follow the proper administrative procedures required to schedule a substance. The court issued an injunction against the enforcement of the rules with respect to nonpsychoactive hemp or products containing it.

FOR CRITICAL ANALYSIS—Social Consideration *Suppose that the statutory definitions of THC and marijuana covered naturally occurring THC and nonpsychoactive hemp. Would the result in this case have been different?*

INVESTIGATION

Administrative agencies conduct investigations of the entities that they regulate. Agencies investigate a wide range of activities, including coal mining, automobile manufacturing, and the industrial discharge of pollutants into the environment. A typical agency investigation occurs during the rulemaking process to obtain information about a certain individual, firm, or industry. The purpose of such an investigation is to avoid issuing a rule that is arbitrary and capricious and instead to issue a rule based on a consideration of relevant factors. After final rules are issued, agencies conduct investigations to monitor compliance with those rules. A typical agency investigation of this kind might begin when a citizen reports a possible violation.

.on the Web The Internet Law Library contains links to federal and state regulatory materials, including the Code of Federal Regulations. This page can be found at **http://www.lawguru.com/ilawlib**.

Inspections and Tests Many agencies gather information through on-site inspections. Sometimes, inspecting an office, a factory, or some other business facility is the only way to obtain the evidence needed to prove a regulatory violation. At other times, an inspection or test is used in place of a formal hearing to show the need to correct or prevent an undesirable condition. Administrative inspections and tests cover a wide range of activities, including safety inspections of underground coal mines, safety tests of commercial equipment and automobiles, and environmental monitoring of factory emissions. An agency may also ask a firm or individual to submit certain documents or records to the agency for examination.

Normally, business firms comply with agency requests to inspect facilities or business records because it is in any firm's interest to maintain a good relationship with regulatory bodies. In some instances, however, such as when a firm thinks an agency's request is unreasonable and may be detrimental to the firm's interest, the firm may refuse to comply with the request. In such situations, an agency may resort to the use of a subpoena or a search warrant.

Subpoenas There are two basic types of subpoenas. The subpoena *ad testificandum* ("to testify") is an ordinary subpoena. It is a writ, or order, compelling a witness to appear at an agency hearing. The subpoena *duces tecum* ("bring it with you") compels an individual or organization to hand over books, papers, records, or documents to the agency. An administrative agency may use either type of subpoena to obtain testimony or documents.

There are limits on what an agency can demand. To determine whether an agency is abusing its discretion in its pursuit of information as part of an investigation, a court may consider such factors as the following:

1. The purpose of the investigation. An investigation must have a legitimate purpose. An improper purpose is, for example, harassment. An agency may not issue an administrative subpoena to inspect business records if the agency's motive is to harass or pressure the business into settling an unrelated matter.
2. The relevancy of the information being sought. Information is relevant if it reveals that the law is being violated or if it assures the agency that the law is not being violated.
3. The specificity of the demand for testimony or documents. A subpoena must, for example, adequately describe the material being sought.
4. The burden of the demand on the party from whom the information is sought. In responding to a request for information, a party must bear the costs of, for example, copying the documents that must be handed over, but a business is generally protected from revealing such information as trade secrets.

In addition, a subpoena might not be enforced when the subject matter of an investigation is not within the authority of the agency to investigate. The issue in the following case was whether the subject matter of certain subpoenas issued by the Federal Trade Commission had exceeded the agency's statutory authority.

CASE 36.2 Federal Trade Commission v. Ken Roberts Co.

United States Court of Appeals,
District of Columbia Circuit, 2001.
276 F.3d 583.

BACKGROUND AND FACTS Ken Roberts Company, Ken Roberts Institute, Inc., United States Chart Company, and Ted Warren Corporation (collectively, Roberts) sell instructional materials that claim to teach would-be investors how to make money investing. In 1999, the Federal Trade Commission (FTC) began investigating whether a variety of online businesses were engaged in deceptive marketing practices in violation of the Federal Trade Commission Act. Aiming at high-risk, high-yield investment activity and suspicious Internet advertising, the FTC soon focused on Roberts. The FTC issued subpoenas that required Roberts to produce documents and answer written questions relating to the companies' business practices. Roberts refused to respond to most of the requests. The FTC asked a federal district court to enforce the subpoenas. When the court ordered Roberts to comply, Roberts appealed to the U.S. Court of Appeals for the District of Columbia Circuit. Roberts argued that its companies were subject only to other federal agencies, whose authority under, in part, the Investment Advisers Act (IAA) preempted the FTC's authority to investigate Roberts's practices.

IN THE WORDS OF THE COURT . . .

HARRY T. EDWARDS, Circuit Judge:

* * * *

Subpoena enforcement power is not limitless * * * . *[A] subpoena is proper only where the inquiry is within the authority of the agency, the demand is not too indefinite and the information sought is reasonably relevant.* Accordingly, there is no

CASE 36.2—Continued

doubt that a court asked to enforce a subpoena will refuse to do so if the subpoena exceeds an express statutory limitation on the agency's investigative powers. Thus, a court must assure itself that the subject matter of the investigation is within the statutory jurisdiction of the subpoena-issuing agency. * * * [Emphasis added.]

* * * *

On its own terms, the FTC Act gives the FTC ample authority to investigate and, if deceptive practices are uncovered, to regulate appellants' advertising practices. Therefore, the FTC is entitled to have its subpoenas enforced unless some other source of law patently [clearly] undermines these broad powers. * * *

* * * *

[Appellants], whose businesses involve securities * * *, assert that the comprehensive scope of the Investment Advisers Act of 1940 preempts the FTC's jurisdiction to regulate the fraudulent practices of "investment advisers" such as themselves. * * *

* * * [T]he IAA contains no express exclusive jurisdiction provision. * * * [But] where intended by Congress, a precisely drawn, detailed statute preempts more general remedies. This can occur either where the two enactments are in irreconcilable conflict or where the latter was clearly meant to serve as a substitute for the former. Appellants contend that the antifraud provision of the IAA, which prohibits investment advisers from engaging "in any transaction, practice, or course of business which operates as a fraud or deceit upon any client or prospective client," stands as just such a specific remedy that displaces the more general coverage of the FTC Act.

* * * *

Because we live in an age of overlapping and concurring regulatory jurisdiction, a court must proceed with the utmost caution before concluding that one agency may not regulate merely because another may. In this case, while it may be true that the IAA and the FTC Act employ different verbal formulae to describe their antifraud standards, it hardly follows that they therefore impose conflicting or incompatible obligations. Undoubtedly, entities in appellants' position can—and of course should—refrain from engaging in both "unfair and deceptive acts or practices" *and* "any transaction, practice, or course of business which operates as a fraud or deceit upon a client or prospective client." The proscriptions of the IAA are not diminished or confused merely because investment advisers must also avoid that which the FTC Act proscribes. And, because these statutes are capable of co-existence, it becomes the *duty* of this court to regard each as effective—at least absent clear congressional intent to the contrary.

Appellants can point to nothing in the background or history of the IAA that demonstrates (or even hints at) a congressional intent to preempt the antifraud jurisdiction of the FTC over those covered by the new statute. Nor does the subsequent case law interpreting these statutes contain such declarations.

DECISION AND REMEDY The U.S. Court of Appeals for the District of Columbia Circuit affirmed the lower court's decision. The appellate court held that the FTC was entitled to the enforcement of its subpoenas against Roberts. The Investment Advisers Act does not preempt the FTC's authority to investigate possibly deceptive advertising and marketing practices merely because those practices relate to the investment business.

FOR CRITICAL ANALYSIS—Social Consideration *The FTC has never undertaken to adjudicate deceptive conduct in the sale and purchase of securities (stocks and bonds). On this basis, should it be concluded that the agency does not have that power?*

LEGISLATIVE CONTROLS

Congress also exercises authority over agency powers. Through enabling legislation, Congress gives power to an agency. Of course, an agency cannot exceed the power that Congress delegates to it. Through subsequent legislation, Congress can take away that power or even abolish an agency altogether. Legislative authority is required to fund an agency, and enabling legislation usually sets certain time and monetary limits relating to the funding of particular programs. Congress can always revise these limits.

In addition to its power to create and fund agencies, Congress has the authority to investigate the implementation of its laws and the agencies that it has created. Individual legislators may also affect agency policy through their casework activities, which involve attempts to help their constituents deal with agencies.

Congress also has the power to "freeze" the enforcement of most federal regulations before the regulations take effect. Under the Small Business Regulatory Enforcement Fairness Act of 1996,[5] all federal agencies must submit final rules to Congress before the rules become effective. If, within sixty days, Congress passes a joint resolution of disapproval concerning a rule, enforcement of the regulation is frozen while the rule is reviewed by congressional committees.

Other legislative checks on agency actions include the Administrative Procedure Act, discussed earlier in this chapter, and the laws discussed in the next section.

Public Accountability

"Law . . . is a human institution, created by human agents to serve human ends."

HARLAN F. STONE,
1872–1946
(Chief justice of the United States Supreme Court, 1941–1946)

As a result of growing public concern over the powers exercised by administrative agencies, Congress passed several laws to make agencies more accountable through public scrutiny. We discuss here the most significant of these laws.

FREEDOM OF INFORMATION ACT

Enacted in 1966, the Freedom of Information Act (FOIA)[6] requires the federal government to disclose certain records to any person on request, even without any reason being given for the request. The FOIA exempts certain types of records. For other records, though, a request that complies with the FOIA procedures need only contain a reasonable description of the information sought. An agency's failure to comply with such a request can be challenged in a federal district court. The media, industry trade associations, public-interest groups, and even companies seeking information about competitors rely on these FOIA provisions to obtain information from government agencies.

GOVERNMENT IN THE SUNSHINE ACT

Congress passed the Government in the Sunshine Act,[7] or open meeting law, in 1976. It requires that "every portion of every meeting of an agency" be open to "public observation." The act also requires procedures to ensure that the public is provided with adequate advance notice of the agency's scheduled meeting and agenda. Like the FOIA, the Sunshine Act contains certain exceptions. Closed meetings are permitted when (1) the subject of the meeting concerns accusing any person of a crime, (2) open

5. 5 U.S.C. Sections 801–808.
6. 5 U.S.C. Section 552.
7. 5 U.S.C. Section 552b.

meetings would frustrate implementation of future agency actions, or (3) the subject of the meeting involves matters relating to future litigation or rulemaking. Courts interpret these exceptions to allow open access whenever possible.

REGULATORY FLEXIBILITY ACT

Concern over the effects of regulation on the efficiency of businesses, particularly smaller ones, led Congress to pass the Regulatory Flexibility Act in 1980.[8] Under this act, whenever a new regulation will have a "significant impact upon a substantial number of small entities," the agency must conduct a regulatory flexibility analysis. The analysis must measure the cost that the rule would impose on small businesses and must consider less burdensome alternatives. The act also contains provisions to alert small businesses about forthcoming regulations. The act relieved small businesses of some record-keeping burdens, especially with regard to hazardous waste management.

SMALL BUSINESS REGULATORY ENFORCEMENT FAIRNESS ACT

As mentioned above, the Small Business Regulatory Enforcement Fairness Act (SBREFA) of 1996 allows Congress to review new federal regulations for at least sixty days before they take effect. This period gives opponents of the rules time to present their arguments to Congress.

The SBREFA also authorizes the courts to enforce the Regulatory Flexibility Act. This helps to ensure that federal agencies, such as the Internal Revenue Service, consider ways to reduce the economic impact of new regulations on small businesses. Federal agencies are required to prepare guides that explain in plain English how small businesses can comply with federal regulations.

At the Small Business Administration, the SBREFA set up the National Enforcement Ombudsman to receive comments from small businesses about their dealings with federal agencies. Based on these comments, Regional Small Business Fairness Boards rate the agencies and publicize their findings.

Finally, the SBREFA allows small businesses to recover their expenses and legal fees from the government when an agency makes demands for fines or penalties that a court considers excessive.

State Administrative Agencies

Although much of this chapter deals with federal administrative agencies, state agencies also play a significant role in regulating activities within the states. Many of the factors that encouraged the proliferation of federal agencies also fostered the growing presence of state agencies. For example, reasons for the growth of administrative agencies at all levels of government include the inability of Congress and state legislatures to oversee the actual implementation of their laws and the greater technical competence of the agencies.

.on the Web The State Web Locator provides links to information on state administrative agencies. The State Web Locator can be found at **http://www.infoctr.edu/swl**.

Commonly, a state creates an agency as a parallel to a federal agency to provide similar services on a more localized basis. For example, a state department of public welfare shoulders some of the same responsibilities at the state level as the Social Security Administration does at the federal level. A state pollution-control agency parallels the federal Environmental Protection Agency. Not all federal agencies have

8. 5 U.S.C. Sections 601–612.

parallel state agencies, however. For example, the Central Intelligence Agency has no parallel agency at the state level.

If the actions of parallel state and federal agencies conflict, the actions of the federal agency will prevail. ■ **Example 36.5** The Federal Aviation Administration (FAA) specifies the hours during which airplanes may land at and depart from airports. A California state agency issues inconsistent regulations governing the same activities. In a proceeding initiated by Interstate Distribution Corporation, an air transport company, to challenge the state rules, the FAA regulations would be held to prevail. ■ The priority of federal law over conflicting state laws is based on the supremacy clause of the U.S. Constitution. This clause, which is found in Article VI of the Constitution, states that the Constitution and "the Laws of the United States which shall be made in Pursuance thereof . . . shall be the supreme Law of the Land."

REVIEWING ADMINISTRATIVE LAW

Assume that the Securities and Exchange Commission (SEC) has a rule that it will enforce statutory provisions prohibiting insider trading only when the insiders make monetary profits for themselves. Then the SEC makes a new rule, declaring that it has the statutory authority to bring an enforcement action against an individual even if she or he does not personally profit from the insider trading. In making the new rule, the SEC does not conduct a rulemaking proceeding but simply announces its new decision. A stockbrokerage firm objects and says that the new rule was unlawfully developed without opportunity for public comment. The brokerage firm challenges the rule in an action that ultimately is reviewed by a federal appellate court. Using the information presented in the chapter, answer the following questions.

1. Is the SEC an executive agency or an independent regulatory agency? What is the difference between these two types of government agencies? Does this difference have any bearing on the outcome of this case? Explain.
2. Should the SEC's new rule be invalidated under the Administrative Procedure Act? Why or why not?
3. Generally, what issues will a court consider when reviewing an agency action?

KEY TERMS

adjudication 954
administrative process 948
bureaucracy 948
delegation doctrine 948
enabling legislation 945
final order 955
initial order 955
judicial process 948
legislative rule 947
notice-and-comment rulemaking 949
rulemaking 949

CHAPTER SUMMARY Administrative Law

Agency Creation and Powers (See pages 945–948.)	1. Under the U.S. Constitution, Congress can delegate the task of implementing its laws to government agencies. By delegating the task, Congress can indirectly monitor an area in which it has passed legislation without becoming bogged down in details relating to enforcement of the legislation.

CHAPTER SUMMARY Administrative Law—Continued

Agency Creation and Powers—Continued	2. Administrative agencies are created by enabling legislation, which usually specifies the name, composition, and powers of the agency. 3. Administrative agencies exercise enforcement, rulemaking, and adjudicatory powers.
Administrative Process—Rulemaking (See pages 949–951.)	1. Agencies are authorized to create new regulations—their rulemaking function. This power is conferred on an agency in the enabling legislation. 2. Agencies can create legislative rules, which are as important as formal acts of Congress. 3. Notice-and-comment rulemaking is the most common rulemaking procedure. It begins with the publication of the proposed regulation in the *Federal Register.* Publication of the notice is followed by a comment period to allow private parties to comment on the proposed rule.
Administrative Process—Investigation (See pages 951–954.)	1. Administrative agencies investigate the entities that they regulate. Investigations are conducted during the rulemaking process to obtain information and after rules are issued to monitor compliance. 2. The most important investigative tools available to an agency are the following: a. *Inspections and tests*—Used to gather information and to correct or prevent undesirable conditions. b. *Subpoenas*—Orders that direct individuals to appear at a hearing or to hand over specified documents. 3. Limits on administrative investigations include the following: a. The investigation must be for a legitimate purpose. b. The information sought must be relevant, and the investigative demands must be specific and not unreasonably burdensome. c. The Fourth Amendment protects companies and individuals from unreasonable searches and seizures by requiring search warrants in most instances.
Administrative Process—Adjudication (See pages 954–955.)	1. After a preliminary investigation, an agency may initiate an administrative action against an individual or organization by filing a complaint. Most such actions are resolved at this stage before they go through the formal adjudicatory process. 2. If there is no settlement, the case is presented to an administrative law judge (ALJ) in a proceeding similar to a trial. 3. After a case is concluded, the ALJ renders an initial order, which can be appealed by either party to the board or commission that governs the agency and ultimately to a federal appeals court. If no appeal is taken or the case is not reviewed, then the order becomes the final order of the agency. The charged party may be ordered to pay damages or to stop carrying on some specified activity.
Limitations on Agency Powers (See pages 955–958.)	1. *Judicial controls*—Administrative agencies are subject to the judicial review of the courts. For example, a court may review whether an agency has exceeded the scope of its enabling legislation or has properly interpreted the laws. 2. *Executive controls*—The president can control administrative agencies through appointments of federal officers and through vetoes of legislation creating or affecting agency powers. 3. *Legislative controls*—Congress can give power to an agency, take it away, increase or decrease the agency's funding, or abolish the agency. The Administrative Procedure Act of 1946 also limits agencies.

(Continued)

CHAPTER SUMMARY Administrative Law—Continued

Public Accountability (See pages 958–959.)	Congress has passed several laws to make agencies more accountable through public scrutiny. These laws include the *Freedom of Information Act of 1966,* the *Government in the Sunshine Act of 1976,* the *Regulatory Flexibility Act of 1980,* and the *Small Business Regulatory Enforcement Fairness Act of 1996.*
State Administrative Agencies (See pages 959–960.)	States create agencies that parallel federal agencies to provide similar services on a more localized basis. If the actions of parallel state and federal agencies conflict, the actions of the federal agency will prevail.

FOR REVIEW

Answers for the even-numbered questions in this For Review *section can be found on this text's accompanying Web site at* http://blt.westbuslaw.com. *Select "Chapter 36" and click on "For Review."*

1. How are federal administrative agencies created?
2. What are the three operations that make up the basic functions of most administrative agencies?
3. What sequence of events must normally occur before an agency rule becomes law?
4. How do administrative agencies enforce their rules?
5. How do the three branches of government limit the power of administrative agencies?

QUESTIONS AND CASE PROBLEMS

36–1. Rulemaking Procedures. Assume that the Food and Drug Administration (FDA), using proper procedures, adopts a rule describing its future investigations. This new rule covers all future cases in which the FDA wants to regulate food additives. Under the new rule, the FDA says that it will not regulate food additives without giving food companies an opportunity to cross-examine witnesses. Some time later, the FDA wants to regulate methylisocyanate, a food additive. In doing so, the FDA undertakes an informal rulemaking procedure, without cross-examination, and regulates methylisocyanate. Producers protest, saying that the FDA promised cross-examination. The FDA responds that the Administrative Procedure Act does not require such cross-examination and that it can freely withdraw the promise made in its new rule. If the producers challenge the FDA in a court, on what basis would the court rule in their favor?

36–2. Rulemaking and Adjudication Powers. For decades, the Federal Trade Commission (FTC) resolved fair trade and advertising disputes through individual adjudications. In the 1960s, the FTC began promulgating rules that defined fair and unfair trade practices. In cases involving violations of these rules, the due process rights of participants were more limited and did not include cross-examination. This was because, although anyone found violating a rule would receive a full adjudication, the legitimacy of the rule itself could not be challenged in the adjudication. Any party charged with violating a rule was almost certain to lose the adjudication. Affected parties complained to a court, arguing that their rights before the FTC were unduly limited by the new rules. What will the court examine to determine whether to uphold the new rules?

36–3. Executive Controls. In 1982, the president of the United States appointed Matthew Chabal, Jr., to the position of U.S. marshal. U.S. marshals are assigned to the federal courts. In the fall of 1985, Chabal received an unsatisfactory annual performance rating, and he was fired shortly thereafter by the president. Given that U.S. marshals are assigned to the federal courts, are these appointees members of the executive branch? Did the president have the right to fire Chabal without consulting Congress about the decision? [*Chabal v. Reagan,* 841 F.2d 1216 (3d Cir. 1988)]

36–4. Investigation. In 1990, Maureen Droge began working for United Air Lines, Inc. (UAL), as a flight attendant. In 1995, she was assigned to Paris, France, where she became pregnant. Because UAL does not allow its flight attendants to fly during their third trimester of pregnancy, Droge was placed on involuntary leave. She applied for temporary disability benefits through the French social security system, but her request was denied because UAL does not contribute to the French system on behalf of its U.S.-based flight attendants. Droge filed a charge of discrimination with the U.S. Equal Employment Opportunity Commission (EEOC), alleging that UAL had discriminated against her and other Americans. The EEOC issued a subpoena, asking UAL to detail all benefits received by all UAL employees living outside the United States. UAL refused to provide the information, in part on the grounds that it was irrelevant and compliance would be unduly burdensome. The EEOC filed a suit in a federal district court against UAL. Should the court enforce the subpoena? Why or why not? [*Equal Employment Opportunity Commission v. United Air Lines, Inc.,* 287 F.3d 643 (7th Cir. 2002)]

36–5. *Ex Parte* Comments. In 1976, the Environmental Protection Agency (EPA) proposed a rule establishing new standards for coal-fired steam generators. The agency gave notice and received comments in the manner prescribed by the Administrative Procedure Act. After the public comments had been received, the EPA received informal comments from members of Congress and other federal officials. In 1979, the EPA published its final standards. Several environmental groups protested these standards, arguing that they were too lax. As part of this protest, the groups complained that political influence from Congress and other federal officials had encouraged the EPA to relax the proposed standards. The groups went on to argue that the *ex parte* comments of the government officials were themselves illegal or that the comments should at least have been summarized in the record. What will the court decide? Discuss fully. [*Sierra Club v. Costle,* 657 F.2d 298 (D.C.Cir. 1981)]

36–6. Judicial Review. American Message Centers (AMC) provides answering services to retailers. Calls to a retailer are automatically forwarded to AMC, which pays for the calls. AMC obtains telephone service at a discount from major carriers, including Sprint. Sprint's tariff (a public document setting out rates and rules relating to Sprint's services) states that the "subscriber shall be responsible for the payment of all charges for service." When AMC learned that computer hackers had obtained the access code for AMC's lines and had made long-distance calls costing nearly $160,000, it asked Sprint to absorb the charges. Sprint refused. AMC filed a complaint with the Federal Communications Commission (FCC), claiming in part that Sprint's tariff was vague and ambiguous, in violation of the Communications Act of 1934 and FCC rules. These laws require that a carrier's tariff "clearly and definitely" specify any "exceptions or conditions which in any way affect the rates named in the tariff." The FCC rejected AMC's complaint. AMC appealed the FCC's decision to a federal appellate court, claiming that the FCC's decision to reject AMC's complaint was arbitrary and capricious. What should the court decide? Discuss fully. [*American Message Centers v. Federal Communications Commission,* 50 F.3d 35 (D.C.Cir. 1995)]

36–7. Arbitrary and Capricious Test. Lion Raisins, Inc., is a family-owned, family-operated business that grows and markets raisins to private enterprises. In the 1990s, Lion also successfully bid on more than fifteen contracts awarded by the U.S. Department of Agriculture (USDA). In May 1999, a USDA investigation reported that Lion appeared to have falsified inspectors' signatures, given false moisture content, and changed the grade of raisins on three USDA raisin certificates issued between 1996 and 1998. Lion was subsequently awarded five more USDA contracts. Then, in November 2000, the company was the low bidder on two new USDA contracts for school lunch programs. In January 2001, however, the USDA awarded these contracts to other bidders and, on the basis of the May 1999 report, suspended Lion from participating in government contracts for one year. Lion filed a suit in the U.S. Court of Federal Claims against the USDA, seeking, in part, lost profits on the school lunch contracts on the ground that the USDA's suspension was arbitrary and capricious. On what reasoning might the court grant a summary judgment in Lion's favor? [*Lion Raisins, Inc. v. United States,* 51 Fed.Cl. 238 (2001)]

CASE PROBLEM WITH SAMPLE ANSWER

36–8. Riverdale Mills Corp. makes plastic-coated steel wire products in Northbridge, Massachusetts. Riverdale uses a water-based cleaning process that generates acidic and alkaline wastewater. To meet federal clean-water requirements, Riverdale has a system within its plant to treat the water. It then flows through a pipe that opens into a manhole-covered test pit outside the plant in full view of Riverdale's employees. Three hundred feet away, the pipe merges into the public sewer system. In October 1997, the U.S. Environmental Protection Agency (EPA) sent Justin Pimpare and Daniel Granz to inspect the plant. Without a search warrant and without Riverdale's express consent, the agents took samples from the test pit. Based on the samples, Riverdale and James Knott, the company's owner, were charged with criminal violations of the federal Clean Water Act. The defendants filed a suit in a federal district court against the EPA agents and others, alleging violations of the Fourth Amendment. What right does the Fourth Amendment provide in this context? This right is based on a "reasonable expectation of privacy." Should the agents be held liable? Why or why not? [*Riverdale Mills Corp. v. Pimpare,* 392 F.3d 55 (1st Cir. 2004)]

After you have answered this problem, compare your answer with the sample answer given on the Web site that accompanies this text. Go to http://blt.westbuslaw.com, select "Chapter 36," and click on "Case Problem with Sample Answer."

A QUESTION OF ETHICS

36–9. The Marine Mammal Protection Act was enacted in 1972 to reduce incidental killing and injury of marine mammals during commercial fishing operations. Under the act, commercial fishing vessels are required to allow an employee of the National Oceanic and Atmospheric Administration (NOAA) to accompany the vessels to conduct research and observe operations. In December 1986, after NOAA had adopted a new policy of recruiting female as well as male observers, NOAA notified Caribbean Marine Services Co. that female observers would be assigned to accompany two of the company's fishing vessels on their next voyages. The owners and crew members of the ships (the plaintiffs) moved for an injunction against the implementation of the NOAA directive. The plaintiffs contended that the presence of a female onboard a fishing vessel would be very awkward, because the female would have to share the crew's quarters, and crew members enjoyed little or no privacy with respect to bodily functions. Further, they alleged that the presence of a female would be disruptive to fishing operations, because some of the crew members were "crude" men with little formal education who might harass or sexually assault a female observer, and the officers would therefore have to devote time to protecting the female from the crew. Finally, the plaintiffs argued that the presence of a female observer could destroy morale and distract the crew, thus affecting the crew's efficiency and decreasing the vessel's profits. [*Caribbean Marine Services Co. v. Baldrige,* 844 F.2d 668 (9th Cir. 1988)]

1. In general, do you think that the public policy of promoting equal employment opportunity should override the concerns of the vessel owners and crew? If you were the judge, would you grant the injunction? Why or why not?
2. The plaintiffs pointed out that fishing voyages could last three months or longer. Would the length of a particular voyage affect your answer to the preceding question?
3. The plaintiffs contended that even if the indignity of sharing bunk rooms and toilet facilities with a female observer could be overcome, the observer's very presence in the common areas of the vessel, such as the dining area, would unconstitutionally infringe on the crew members' right to privacy in these areas. Evaluate this claim.

FOR CRITICAL ANALYSIS

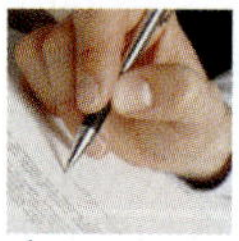

36–10. Does Congress delegate too much power to federal administrative agencies? Do the courts defer too much to Congress in its grant of power to those agencies? What are the alternatives to the agencies that we encounter in every facet of our lives?

INTERNET EXERCISES

Go to the *Business Law Today* home page at **http://blt.westbuslaw.com**, select "Chapter 36," and click on "Internet Exercises." There you will find the following Internet research exercises that you can perform to learn more about topics covered in this chapter.

Activity 36–1: LEGAL PERSPECTIVE—The Freedom of Information Act

Activity 36–2: MANAGEMENT PERSPECTIVE—Agency Inspections

BEFORE THE TEST

Go to the *Business Law Today* home page at **http://blt.westbuslaw.com**, select "Chapter 36," and click on "Interactive Quizzes." You will find a number of interactive questions relating to this chapter.

CHAPTER 37
Antitrust Law

"Free competition is worth more to society than it costs."

Oliver Wendell Holmes, Jr., 1841–1935
(Associate justice of the United States Supreme Court, 1902–1932)

CHAPTER OUTLINE

LEARNING OBJECTIVES

After reading this chapter, you should be able to answer the following questions:

1. What is a monopoly? What is market power? How do these concepts relate to each other?
2. What type of activity is prohibited by Section 1 of the Sherman Act? What type of activity is prohibited by Section 2 of the Sherman Act?
3. What are the four major provisions of the Clayton Act, and what types of activities do these provisions prohibit?
4. What agencies of the federal government enforce the federal antitrust laws?
5. What are four activities that are exempt from the antitrust laws?

Today's antitrust laws are the direct descendants of common law actions intended to limit *restraints on trade* (agreements between firms that have the effect of reducing competition in the marketplace). Such actions date to the fifteenth century in England. In the United States, concern over monopolistic practices arose following the Civil War with the growth of large corporate enterprises and their attempts to reduce or eliminate competition. In an attempt to thwart competition, they legally tied themselves together in business trusts. As discussed in Chapter 31, a *business trust* is a form of business organization in which trustees hold title to property for the benefit of others. The most powerful of these trusts, the Standard Oil trust, is examined in this chapter's *Landmark in the Law* feature on the following page.

the United States or injure other U.S. exporters. The Export Trading Company Act of 1982 broadened the Webb-Pomerene Act by permitting the Department of Justice to certify properly qualified export trading companies. Any activity within the scope described by the certificate is exempt from public prosecution under the antitrust laws.

5 *Professional baseball.* In 1922, the United States Supreme Court held that professional baseball was not within the reach of federal antitrust laws because it did not involve "interstate commerce."[17] Some of the effects of this decision, however, were modified by the Curt Flood Act of 1998. Essentially, the act allows players the option of suing team owners for anticompetitive practices if, for example, the owners collude to "blacklist" players, hold down players' salaries, or force players to play for specific teams.[18]

6 *Oil marketing.* The Interstate Oil Compact of 1935 allows states to determine quotas on oil that will be marketed in interstate commerce.

7 *Cooperative research and production.* Cooperative research among small-business firms is exempt under the Small Business Act of 1958, as amended. Research or production of a product, process, or service by joint ventures consisting of competitors is exempt under special federal legislation, including the National Cooperative Research Act of 1984 and the National Cooperative Production Amendments of 1993.

8 *Joint efforts by businesspersons to obtain legislative or executive action.* This is often referred to as the *Noerr-Pennington* doctrine.[19] For example, DVD producers may jointly lobby Congress to change the copyright laws without being held liable for attempting to restrain trade. Though selfish rather than purely public-minded conduct is permitted, there is an exception: an action will not be protected if it is clear that the action is "objectively baseless in the sense that no reasonable [person] could reasonably expect success on the merits" and it is an attempt to make anticompetitive use of government processes.[20]

9 *Other exemptions.* Other activities exempt from antitrust laws include activities approved by the president in furtherance of the defense of our nation (under the Defense Production Act of 1950, as amended); state actions, when the state policy is clearly articulated and the policy is actively supervised by the state;[21] and activities of regulated industries (such as the communication and banking industries) when federal commissions, boards, or agencies (such as the Federal Communications Commission and the Federal Maritime Commission) have primary regulatory authority.

NOTE State actions include the regulation of public utilities, whose rates may be set by the states in which they do business.

The following case concerns the first exemption in the above list.

17. *Federal Baseball Club of Baltimore, Inc. v. National League of Professional Baseball Clubs,* 259 U.S. 200, 42 S.Ct. 465, 66 L.Ed. 898 (1922).

18. In 2003, a federal appellate court held that because baseball was exempt from federal antitrust laws, it was also exempt from the reach of state antitrust laws due to the supremacy clause. *Major League Baseball v. Crist,* 331 F.3d 1177 (11th Cir. 2003).

19. See *United Mine Workers of America v. Pennington,* 381 U.S. 657, 85 S.Ct. 1585, 14 L.Ed.2d 626 (1965); and *Eastern Railroad Presidents Conference v. Noerr Motor Freight, Inc.,* 365 U.S. 127, 81 S.Ct. 523, 5 L.Ed.2d 464 (1961).

20. *Professional Real Estate Investors, Inc. v. Columbia Pictures Industries, Inc.,* 508 U.S. 49, 113 S.Ct. 1920, 123 L.Ed.2d 611 (1993).

21. See *Parker v. Brown,* 317 U.S. 341, 63 S.Ct. 307, 87 L.Ed. 315 (1943).

CASE 37.3 Clarett v. National Football League

United States Court of Appeals,
Second Circuit, 2004.
369 F.3d 124.

BACKGROUND AND FACTS Maurice Clarett was a star football player attending Ohio State University (OSU). In his freshman year, Clarett led his team to an undefeated season. The season was capped by a double-overtime victory over the University of Miami in the Fiesta Bowl, OSU's first national championship in thirty-four years. Clarett's goal was to play in the National Football League (NFL) in the fall of 2004. The NFL, an unincorporated association of thirty-two member clubs, consistently outperforms all other professional sports leagues, in both revenues and television ratings, representing an unparalleled opportunity for an aspiring football player in terms of salary and level of competition. The only thing preventing Clarett from achieving his goal was an NFL rule that limited eligibility to players three seasons removed from their high school graduation. Clarett filed a suit in a federal district court against the NFL, claiming that the rule was an illegal restraint of trade. Clarett argued that by adopting the rule, the NFL teams had agreed to exclude a broad class of players from the NFL labor market. The court issued a summary judgment in Clarett's favor. The NFL appealed to the U.S. Court of Appeals for the Second Circuit.

IN THE WORDS OF THE COURT . . .
SOTOMAYOR, Circuit Judge.

* * * *

* * * *[T]o accommodate the collective bargaining process, certain concerted activity among and between labor and employers [is] held to be beyond the reach of the antitrust laws.* * * * [Emphasis added.]

* * * *

Although the NFL has maintained draft eligibility rules in one form or another for much of its history, the inception of a collective bargaining relationship between the NFL and its players union some thirty years ago irrevocably altered the governing legal regime. * * * [P]rospective players no longer have the right to negotiate directly with the NFL teams over the terms and conditions of their employment. That responsibility is instead committed to the NFL and the players union to accomplish through the collective bargaining process, and throughout that process the NFL and the players union are to have the freedom to craft creative solutions to their differences in light of the economic imperatives of their industry. Furthermore, the NFL teams are permitted to engage in joint conduct with respect to the terms and conditions of players' employment as a multi-employer bargaining unit without risking antitrust liability. * * *

* * * *

Clarett's argument that antitrust law should permit him to circumvent this scheme established by federal labor law starts with the contention that the eligibility rules do not constitute a mandatory subject of collective bargaining and thus cannot fall within the protection of the * * * exemption. * * * [H]owever, we find that the eligibility rules are mandatory bargaining subjects. Though tailored to the unique circumstances of a professional sports league, the eligibility rules for the draft represent a quite literal condition for initial employment and for that reason alone might constitute a mandatory bargaining subject. But moreover, the eligibility rules constitute a mandatory bargaining subject because they have tangible effects on the wages and working conditions of current NFL players. *Because the unusual economic imperatives of professional sports raise numerous problems with little or no precedent in standard industrial relations,* * * * *many of the arrangements in professional sports that, at first glance, might not appear to deal with wages or working conditions are indeed mandatory bargaining subjects.* * * * [Emphasis added.]

CASE 37.3—Continued

Furthermore, by reducing competition in the market for entering players, the eligibility rules also affect the job security of veteran players. Because the size of NFL teams is capped, the eligibility rules diminish a veteran player's risk of being replaced by either a drafted rookie or a player who enters the draft and, though not drafted, is then hired as a rookie free agent. Consequently, * * * we find that to regard the NFL's eligibility rules as merely permissive bargaining subjects would ignore the reality of collective bargaining in sports.

DECISION AND REMEDY The U.S. Court of Appeals for the Second Circuit reversed the judgment of the lower court and remanded the case for the entry of a judgment in favor of the NFL. The appellate court vacated the order designating Clarett eligible to participate in the year's NFL draft.

FOR CRITICAL ANALYSIS—Social Consideration *Why are the NFL's member clubs permitted to agree that a player will not be hired until three full football seasons after the player's high school graduation?*

REVIEWING ANTITRUST LAW

The Internet Corporation for Assigned Names and Numbers (ICANN) is a nonprofit entity organizing Internet domain names. It is governed by a board of directors elected by various groups with commercial interests in the Internet. One of ICANN's functions is to authorize an entity as a registry for certain "top level domains" (TLDs). ICANN entered into an agreement with VeriSign to serve as registry for the ".com" TLD to provide registry services in accordance with ICANN's specifications. VeriSign complained that ICANN was restricting the services that it could make available as a registrar and blocking new services, imposing unnecessary conditions on those services, and setting prices at which the services were offered. VeriSign claimed that ICANN's control of the registry services for domain names violated Section 1 of the Sherman Act.

1. Should ICANN's actions be judged under the rule of reason or deemed a *per se* violation of Section 1 of the Sherman Act?
2. Should ICANN's actions be viewed as a horizontal or a vertical restraint of trade?
3. Does it matter that ICANN's leadership is chosen by those with a commercial interest in the Internet?
4. If judged under the rule of reason, what might be ICANN's defense for having a standardized set of registry services that must be used?

KEY TERMS

antitrust law 967
attempted monopolization 977
divestiture 981
exclusive-dealing contract 978
group boycott 971
horizontal merger 979
horizontal restraint 970
market concentration 979
market power 968
market-share test 974
monopolization 974
monopoly 967
monopoly power 968
per se violation 968
predatory pricing 974
price discrimination 978
price-fixing agreement 970
resale price maintenance agreement 973
rule of reason 968
treble damages 981
tying arrangement 979
vertical merger 980
vertical restraint 972
vertically integrated firm 972

CHAPTER SUMMARY Antitrust Law

The Sherman Antitrust Act (1890) (See pages 967–977.)	1. *Major provisions*— a. Section 1—Prohibits contracts, combinations, and conspiracies in restraint of trade. (1) Horizontal restraints subject to Section 1 include price-fixing agreements, group boycotts (joint refusals to deal), horizontal market divisions, and trade association agreements. (2) Vertical restraints subject to Section 1 include territorial or customer restrictions, resale price maintenance agreements, and refusals to deal. b. Section 2—Prohibits monopolies and attempts to monopolize. 2. *Jurisdictional requirements*—The Sherman Act applies only to activities that have a significant impact on interstate commerce. 3. *Interpretive rules*— a. *Per se* rule—Applied to restraints on trade that are so inherently anticompetitive that they cannot be justified and are deemed illegal as a matter of law. b. Rule of reason—Applied when an anticompetitive agreement may be justified by legitimate benefits. Under the rule of reason, the lawfulness of a trade restraint will be determined by the purpose and effects of the restraint.
The Clayton Act (1914) (See pages 978–980.)	The major provisions are as follows: 1. *Section 2*—As amended in 1936 by the Robinson-Patman Act, prohibits price discrimination that substantially lessens competition and prohibits a seller engaged in interstate commerce from selling to two or more buyers goods of similar grade and quality at different prices when the result is a substantial lessening of competition or the creation of a competitive injury. 2. *Section 3*—Prohibits exclusionary practices, such as exclusive-dealing contracts and tying arrangements, when the effect may be to substantially lessen competition. 3. *Section 7*—Prohibits mergers when the effect may be to substantially lessen competition or to tend to create a monopoly. a. Horizontal mergers—The acquisition by merger or consolidation of a competing firm engaged in the same relevant market. Will be unlawful only if the merger results in the merging firms' holding a disproportionate share of the market, resulting in a substantial lessening of competition, and if the merger does not enhance consumer welfare by increasing efficiency of production or marketing. b. Vertical mergers—The acquisition by a seller of one of its buyers or vice versa. Will be unlawful if the merger prevents competitors of either merging firm from competing in a segment of the market that otherwise would be open to them, resulting in a substantial lessening of competition. 4. *Section 8*—Prohibits interlocking directorates.
Enforcement of Antitrust Laws (See pages 980–981.)	Federal agencies that enforce antitrust laws are the Department of Justice and the Federal Trade Commission, which was established by the Federal Trade Commission Act of 1914. Private parties who have been injured as a result of violations of the Sherman Act or Clayton Act may also bring civil suits. In recent years, many private parties have filed such suits largely because, if successful, they may be awarded treble damages and attorneys' fees.
Exemptions from Antitrust Laws (See pages 981–984.)	1. Labor unions (under Section 6 of the Clayton Act of 1914). 2. Agricultural associations and fisheries (under Section 6 of the Clayton Act of 1914, the Capper-Volstead Act of 1922, and the Fisheries Cooperative Marketing Act of 1976).

(Continued)

CHAPTER SUMMARY Antitrust Law—Continued

Exemptions from Antitrust Laws—Continued (See pages 981–984.)	3. Insurance when state regulation exists (under the McCarran-Ferguson Act of 1945). 4. Export trading companies (under the Webb-Pomerene Act of 1918 and the Export Trading Company Act of 1982). 5. Professional baseball (by a 1922 judicial decision, although modified by a 1998 federal statute). 6. Oil marketing (under the Interstate Oil Compact of 1935). 7. Cooperative research and production (under various acts, including the Small Business Act of 1958, as amended, the National Cooperative Research Act of 1984, and the National Cooperative Production Amendments of 1993). 8. Joint efforts by businesspersons to obtain legislative or executive action (under the *Noerr-Pennington* doctrine). 9. Other activities, including certain national defense activities, state actions, and activities of certain regulated industries.

FOR REVIEW

Answers for the even-numbered questions in this For Review *section can be found on this text's accompanying Web site at* http://blt.westbuslaw.com. *Select "Chapter 37" and click on "For Review."*

1. What is a monopoly? What is market power? How do these concepts relate to each other?
2. What type of activity is prohibited by Section 1 of the Sherman Act? What type of activity is prohibited by Section 2 of the Sherman Act?
3. What are the four major provisions of the Clayton Act, and what types of activities do these provisions prohibit?
4. What agencies of the federal government enforce the federal antitrust laws?
5. What are four activities that are exempt from the antitrust laws?

QUESTIONS AND CASE PROBLEMS

37–1. Sherman Act. An agreement that is blatantly and substantially anticompetitive is deemed a *per se* violation of Section 1 of the Sherman Act. Under what rule is an agreement analyzed if it appears to be anticompetitive but is not a *per se* violation? In making this analysis, what factors will a court consider?

37–2. Antitrust Laws. Allitron, Inc., and Donovan, Ltd., are interstate competitors selling similar appliances, principally in the states of Illinois, Indiana, Kentucky, and Ohio. Allitron and Donovan agree that Allitron will no longer sell in Ohio and Indiana and that Donovan will no longer sell in Kentucky and Illinois. Have Allitron and Donovan violated any antitrust laws? If so, which law? Explain.

37–3. Horizontal Restraints. Jorge's Appliance Corp. was a new retail seller of appliances in Sunrise City. Because of its innovative sales techniques and financing, Jorge's caused the appliance department of No-Glow Department Store, a large chain store with a great deal of buying power, to lose a substantial amount of sales. No-Glow told a number of appliance manufacturers that if they continued to sell to Jorge's, No-Glow would discontinue its large volume of purchases from them. The manufacturers immediately stopped selling appliances to Jorge's. Jorge's filed suit against No-Glow and the manufacturers, claiming that their actions constituted an antitrust violation. No-Glow and the manufacturers were able to prove that Jorge's was a small retailer with a small portion of the market. They claimed that because the relevant market was not substantially affected, they were not guilty of restraint of trade. Discuss fully whether there was an antitrust violation.

37–4. Exclusionary Practices. Instant Foto Corp. is a manufacturer of photography film. At the present time, Instant Foto has approximately 50 percent of the market. Instant Foto advertises that the purchase price for its film includes photo processing by Instant Foto Corp. Instant Foto claims that its film processing is specially designed to improve the quality of photos taken with Instant Foto film. Is Instant Foto's combination of film and film processing an antitrust violation? Explain.

37–5. Tying Arrangement. Public Interest Corp. (PIC) owned and operated the television station WTMV-TV in Lakeland, Florida. MCA Television, Ltd., owns and licenses syndicated television programs. The parties entered into a licensing contract with respect to several television shows. MCA conditioned the license on PIC's agreeing to take another show, *Harry and the Hendersons*. PIC agreed to this arrangement, although it would not have chosen to license *Harry* if it had not had to do so to secure the licenses for the other shows. More than two years into the contract, a dispute arose over PIC's payments, and negotiations failed to resolve the dispute. In a letter, MCA suspended PIC's broadcast rights for all of its shows and stated that "[a]ny telecasts of MCA programming by WTMV-TV . . . will be deemed unauthorized and shall constitute an infringement of MCA's copyrights." PIC nonetheless continued broadcasting MCA's programs, with the exception of *Harry*. MCA filed a suit in a federal district court against PIC, alleging breach of contract and copyright infringement. PIC filed a counterclaim, contending in part that MCA's deal was an illegal tying arrangement. Is PIC correct? Explain. [*MCA Television, Ltd. v. Public Interest Corp.*, 171 F.3d 1265 (11th Cir. 1999)]

CASE PROBLEM WITH SAMPLE ANSWER

37–6. In 1995, to make personal computers (PCs) easier to use, Intel Corp. and other companies developed a standard, called the Universal Serial Bus (USB) specification, to enable peripherals (printers and other hardware) to be easily attached to PCs. Intel and others formed the Universal Serial Bus Implementers Forum (USB-IF) to promote USB technology and products. Intel, however, makes relatively few USB products and does not make any USB interconnect devices. Multivideo Labs, Inc. (MVL), designed and distributed Active Extension Cables (AECs) to connect peripheral devices to each other or to a PC. The AECs were not USB compliant, a fact that Intel employees told other USB-IF members. Asserting that this caused a "general cooling of the market" for AECs, MVL filed a suit in a federal district court against Intel, claiming in part attempted monopolization in violation of the Sherman Act. Intel filed a motion for summary judgment. How should the court rule, and why? [*Multivideo Labs, Inc. v. Intel Corp.*, __ F.Supp.2d __ (S.D.N.Y. 2000)]

After you have answered this problem, compare your answer with the sample answer given on the Web site that accompanies this text. Go to <u>http://blt.westbuslaw.com</u>, select "Chapter 37," and click on "Case Problem with Sample Answer."

37–7. Monopolization. Moist snuff is a smokeless tobacco product sold in small round cans from racks, which include point-of-sale (POS) ads. POS ads are critical because tobacco advertising is restricted and the number of people who use smokeless tobacco products is relatively small. In the moist snuff market in the United States, there are only four competitors, including U.S. Tobacco Co. and its affiliates (USTC) and Conwood Co. In 1990, USTC, which held 87 percent of the market, began to convince major retailers, including Wal-Mart Stores, Inc., to use USTC's "exclusive racks" to display its products and those of all other snuff makers. USTC agents would then destroy competitors' racks. USTC also began to provide retailers with false sales data to convince them to maintain its poor-selling items and drop competitors' less expensive products. Conwood's Wal-Mart market share fell from 12 percent to 6.5 percent. In stores in which USTC did not have rack exclusivity, however, Conwood's market share increased to 25 percent. Conwood filed a suit in a federal district court against USTC, alleging in part that USTC used its monopoly power to exclude competitors from the moist snuff market. Should the court rule in Conwood's favor? What is USTC's best defense? Discuss. [*Conwood Co., L.P. v. U.S. Tobacco Co.*, 290 F.3d 768 (6th Cir. 2002)]

37–8. Sherman Act. Dentsply International, Inc., is one of a dozen manufacturers of artificial teeth for dentures and other restorative devices. Dentsply sells its teeth to twenty-three dealers of dental products. The dealers supply the teeth to dental laboratories, which fabricate dentures for sale to dentists. There are hundreds of other dealers who compete with each other on the basis of price and service. Some manufacturers sell directly to the laboratories. There are also thousands of laboratories that compete with each other on the basis of price and service. Because of advances in dental medicine, however, artificial tooth manufacturing is marked by low growth potential, and Dentsply dominates the industry. Dentsply's market share is greater than 75 percent and is about fifteen times larger than that of its next-closest competitor. Dentsply prohibits its dealers from marketing competitors' teeth unless they were selling the teeth before 1993. The federal government filed a suit in a federal district court against Dentsply, alleging in part a violation of Section 2 of the Sherman Act. What must the government show to succeed in its suit? Are those elements present in this case? What should the court rule? Explain. [*United States v. Dentsply International, Inc.*, 399 F.3d 181 (3d Cir. 2005)]

A QUESTION OF ETHICS

37–9. A group of lawyers in the District of Columbia regularly acted as court-appointed attorneys for indigent defendants in District of Columbia criminal cases. At a meeting of the Superior Court Trial Lawyers Association (SCTLA), the attorneys agreed to stop providing this representation until the district increased their compensation. Their subsequent boycott had a severe impact on the district's criminal justice system, and the District of Columbia gave in to the lawyers' demands for higher pay. After the lawyers had returned to work, the Federal Trade Commission filed a complaint against the SCTLA and four of its officers and, after an investigation, ruled that the SCTLA's activities constituted an illegal group boycott in violation of antitrust laws. [*Federal Trade Commission v. Superior Court Trial Lawyers Association,* 493 U.S. 411, 110 S.Ct. 768, 107 L.Ed.2d 851 (1990)]

1. The SCTLA obviously was aware of the negative impact its decision would have on the district's criminal justice system. Given this fact, do you think the lawyers behaved ethically?
2. On appeal, the SCTLA claimed that its boycott was undertaken to publicize that the attorneys were underpaid and that the boycott thus constituted an expression protected by the First Amendment. Do you agree with this argument?
3. Labor unions have the right to strike when negotiations between labor and management fail to result in agreement. Is it fair to prohibit members of the SCTLA from "striking" against their employer, the District of Columbia, simply because the SCTLA is a professional organization and not a labor union?

FOR CRITICAL ANALYSIS

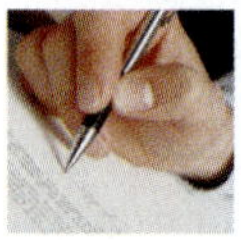

37–10. Critics of antitrust law claim that in the long run, competitive market forces will eliminate private monopolies unless they are fostered by government regulation. Do you agree? Why or why not?

INTERNET EXERCISES

Go to the *Business Law Today* home page at **http://blt.westbuslaw.com**, select "Chapter 37," and click on "Internet Exercises." There you will find the following Internet research exercises that you can perform to learn more about topics covered in this chapter.

Activity 37–1: LEGAL PERSPECTIVE—The Standard Oil Trust

Activity 37–2: MANAGEMENT PERSPECTIVE—Avoiding Antitrust Problems

BEFORE THE TEST

Go to the *Business Law Today* home page at **http://blt.westbuslaw.com**, select "Chapter 37," and click on "Interactive Quizzes." You will find a number of interactive questions relating to this chapter.

CHAPTER 38

Consumer Law

"Subject to specific constitutional limitations, when the legislature has spoken, the public interest has been declared in terms well nigh conclusive."

William O. Douglas, 1898–1980
(Associate justice of the United States Supreme Court, 1939–1975)

CHAPTER OUTLINE

- ADVERTISING
- LABELING AND PACKAGING
- SALES
- HEALTH AND SAFETY PROTECTION
- CREDIT PROTECTION
- STATE CONSUMER PROTECTION LAWS

LEARNING OBJECTIVES

After reading this chapter, you should be able to answer the following questions:

1. When will advertising be deemed deceptive?
2. What special rules apply to telephone solicitation?
3. What is Regulation Z, and to what type of transactions does it apply?
4. How does the Federal Food, Drug and Cosmetic Act protect consumers?
5. What are the major federal statutes providing for consumer protection in credit transactions?

The "public interest" referred to by Justice William O. Douglas in the chapter-opening quotation was evident during the 1960s and 1970s in what has come to be known as the consumer movement. Some have labeled the 1960s and 1970s "the age of the consumer" because so much legislation was passed to protect consumers against purportedly unsafe products and unfair practices of sellers. Since the 1980s, the impetus driving the consumer movement has lessened, to a great extent because so many of its goals have been achieved. *Consumer law* consists of all of the statutes, administrative agency rules, and judicial decisions that serve to protect the interests of consumers.

In the first part of this chapter, we examine some of the sources and some of the major issues of consumer protection. Sources of consumer protection exist at all levels of government. At the federal level, a number of laws have been passed to define the duties of sellers and the rights of consumers. Federal administrative agencies, such as the Federal Trade Commission (FTC), also provide an important source of consumer protection. Nearly every agency and department of the federal government has an office of consumer affairs, and most states have one or more such offices, including the offices of state attorneys general, to assist consumers.

Because of the wide variation among state consumer protection laws, our primary focus here will be on federal legislation—specifically, on legislation governing deceptive advertising, telemarketing and electronic advertising, labeling and packaging, sales, health protection, product safety, and credit protection. Realize, though, that state laws often provide more sweeping and significant protections for the consumer than do federal laws. State consumer protection laws will be discussed at the end of this chapter.

Advertising

One of the earliest—and still one of the most important—federal consumer protection laws is the Federal Trade Commission Act of 1914 (mentioned in Chapter 37). The act created the FTC to carry out the broadly stated goal of preventing unfair and deceptive trade practices, including deceptive advertising, within the meaning of Section 5 of the act. We look here at deceptive advertising and at laws regulating telemarketing and electronic advertising.

Deceptive Advertising

DECEPTIVE ADVERTISING Advertising that misleads consumers, either by unjustified claims concerning a product's performance or by the omission of a material fact concerning the product's composition or performance.

Generally, **deceptive advertising** occurs if a reasonable consumer would be misled by the advertising claim. Vague generalities and obvious exaggerations are permissible. These claims are known as *puffery.* Recall from Chapter 21 that puffery consists of statements about a product that a reasonable person would not believe to be true. When a claim takes on the appearance of literal authenticity, however, it may create problems. Advertising that *appears* to be based on factual evidence but in fact is scientifically untrue will be deemed deceptive. A classic example occurred in a 1944 case in which the claim that a skin cream would restore youthful qualities to aged skin was deemed deceptive.[1]

Some advertisements contain "half-truths," meaning that the presented information is true but incomplete and, therefore, leads consumers to a false conclusion. ■ EXAMPLE 38.1 The makers of Campbell's soups advertised that "most" Campbell's soups were low in fat and cholesterol and thus were helpful in fighting heart disease. What the ad did not say was that Campbell's soups were high in sodium, and high-sodium diets may increase the risk of heart disease. The FTC ruled that Campbell's claims were thus deceptive. ■ Advertising that contains an endorsement by a celebrity may be deemed deceptive if the celebrity does not actually use the product.

BAIT-AND-SWITCH ADVERTISING Advertising a product at a very attractive price (the "bait") and then, once the consumer is in the store, saying that the advertised product is either not available or is of poor quality; the customer is then urged to purchase ("switched" to) a more expensive item.

Bait-and-Switch Advertising The FTC has issued rules that govern specific advertising techniques. One of the most important rules is contained in the FTC's "Guides on Bait Advertising."[2] The rule is designed to prevent **bait-and-switch advertising**—that is, advertising a very low price for a particular item that will likely be unavailable to the consumer and then encouraging him or her to purchase a more expensive item. The low price is the "bait" to lure the consumer into the store. The salesper-

1. *Charles of the Ritz Distributing Corp. v. Federal Trade Commission,* 143 F.2d 676 (2d Cir. 1944).
2. 16 C.F.R. Section 288.

son is instructed to "switch" the consumer to a different, more expensive item. According to the FTC guidelines, bait-and-switch advertising occurs if the seller refuses to show the advertised item, fails to have reasonable quantities of it available, fails to promise to deliver the advertised item within a reasonable time, or discourages employees from selling the item.

.on the Web A government-sponsored Web site that contains reports on consumer issues, including issues relating to online deceptive advertising and other forms of online fraud, can be accessed at **http://www.consumer.gov**.

Online Deceptive Advertising Deceptive advertising may occur in the online environment as well. For several years, the FTC has actively monitored online advertising and has identified hundreds of Web sites that have made false or deceptive advertising claims for products ranging from medical treatments for various diseases to exercise equipment and weight-loss aids.

In 2000, the FTC issued new guidelines to help online businesses comply with existing laws prohibiting deceptive advertising.[3] The guidelines did not set forth new rules but rather described how existing laws apply to online advertising. Generally, the rules emphasize that any ads—online or offline—must be truthful and not misleading and that any claims made in any ads must be substantiated. Additionally, ads cannot be unfair, defined in the guidelines as "caus[ing] or . . . likely to cause substantial consumer injury that consumers could not reasonably avoid and that is not outweighed by the benefit to consumers or competition."

REMEMBER Changes in technology often require changes in the law.

The guidelines also call for "clear and conspicuous" disclosure of any qualifying or limiting information. The FTC suggests that advertisers should assume that consumers will not read an entire Web page. Therefore, to satisfy the "clear and conspicuous" requirement, advertisers should place the disclosure as close as possible to the claim being qualified or include the disclosure within the claim itself. If such placement is not feasible, the next-best placement is on a section of the page to which a consumer can easily scroll. Generally, hyperlinks to a disclosure are recommended only for lengthy disclosures or for disclosures that must be repeated in a variety of locations on the Web page.

.on the Web You can find current articles concerning consumer issues at the Alexander Law Firm's "Consumer Law Page." Go to **http://consumerlawpage.com/intro.html**.

FTC Actions against Deceptive Advertising The FTC receives complaints from many sources, including competitors of alleged violators, consumers, consumer organizations, trade associations, Better Business Bureaus, government organizations, and state and local officials. If enough consumers complain and the complaints are widespread, the FTC will investigate the problem. If the FTC concludes that a given advertisement is unfair or deceptive, it sends a formal complaint to the alleged offender. The company may agree to settle the complaint without further proceedings; if not, the FTC can conduct a hearing before an administrative law judge (discussed in Chapter 36) in which the company can present its defense.

If the FTC succeeds in proving that an advertisement is unfair or deceptive, it usually issues a **cease-and-desist order** requiring that the challenged advertising be stopped. It might also require **counteradvertising** in which the company advertises anew—in print, on radio, and on television—to inform the public about the earlier misinformation.

CEASE-AND-DESIST ORDER
An administrative or judicial order prohibiting a person or business firm from conducting activities that an agency or court has deemed illegal.

COUNTERADVERTISING
New advertising that is undertaken pursuant to a Federal Trade Commission order for the purpose of correcting earlier false claims that were made about a product.

TELEMARKETING AND ELECTRONIC ADVERTISING

The pervasive use of the telephone to market goods and services to homes and businesses led to the passage in 1991 of the Telephone Consumer Protection Act (TCPA).[4] The act prohibits telephone solicitation using an automatic telephone

3. *Advertising and Marketing on the Internet: Rules of the Road,* September 2000.
4. 47 U.S.C. Sections 227 *et seq.*

What federal act prohibits telemarketers from using an automatic telephone dialing system, and what agency enforces that act? (Corbis. All rights reserved.)

dialing system or a prerecorded voice. Most states also have laws regulating telephone solicitation. The TCPA also makes it illegal to transmit ads via fax without first obtaining the recipient's permission. (Similar issues have arisen with respect to junk e-mail, called "spam"—see Chapter 4.)

The act is enforced by the Federal Communications Commission and also provides for a private right of action. Consumers can recover any actual monetary loss resulting from a violation of the act or receive $500 in damages for each violation, whichever is greater. If a court finds that a defendant willfully or knowingly violated the act, the court has the discretion to treble (triple) the damages awarded.

The Telemarketing and Consumer Fraud and Abuse Prevention Act[5] of 1994 directed the FTC to establish rules governing telemarketing and to bring actions against fraudulent telemarketers. The FTC's Telemarketing Sales Rule[6] of 1995 requires a telemarketer, before making a sales pitch, to inform the recipient that the call is a sales call and to identify the seller's name and the product being sold. The rule makes it illegal for telemarketers to misrepresent information (including facts about their goods or services and earnings potential, for example). Additionally, telemarketers must inform the people they call of the total cost of the goods being sold, any restrictions on obtaining or using the goods, and whether a sale will be considered final and nonrefundable. A telemarketer must also remove a consumer's name from its list of potential contacts if the consumer so requests. A 2002 amendment to the Telemarketing Sales Rule established a national "Do Not Call" registry, which became effective in October 2003. Telemarketers must refrain from calling those consumers who have placed their names on the list.

Today's consumers are increasingly concerned about eating genetically modified crops and the potential presence of pesticides, hormones, and mad cow disease in foods. Many consumers have thus switched to buying organic foods. How might an organic label be deceptive to consumers? Do ordinary consumers understand what is required for a food to be labeled "organic"? Why or why not? (PhotoDisc)

Labeling and Packaging

A number of federal and state laws deal specifically with the information given on labels and packages. The rules are designed to ensure that labels provide accurate information about the product and to warn about possible dangers from its use or misuse. In general, labels must be accurate and must use words that are understood by the ordinary consumer. For example, a box of cereal cannot be labeled "giant" if that would exaggerate the amount of cereal contained in the box. In some instances, labels must specify the raw materials used in the product, such as the percentage of cotton, nylon, or other fibers used in a garment. In other instances, the products must carry a warning. Cigarette packages and advertising, for example, must include one of several warnings about the health hazards associated with smoking.[7] Some cigar manufacturers have also agreed to voluntarily put similar warnings on cigar packages and labels.

Food Labeling

The Fair Packaging and Labeling Act requires that product labels identify (1) the product; (2) the net quantity of the contents and, if the number of servings is stated, the size of a serving; (3) the manufacturer; and (4) the packager or distributor.[8] The act also provides for additional requirements concerning descriptions on packages, savings claims, components of nonfood products, and standards for the partial filling of packages.

5. 15 U.S.C. Sections 6101–6108.
6. 16 C.F.R. Sections 310.1–310.8.
7. 15 U.S.C. Sections 1331 *et seq.*
8. 15 U.S.C. Sections 4401–4408.

Food products must bear labels detailing the food's nutrition content, including how much fat the food contains and what kind of fat it is. The Department of Health and Human Services, as well as the FTC, enforces these rules. The Nutrition Labeling and Education Act of 1990 requires standard nutrition facts (including fat content) on food labels; regulates the use of such terms as *fresh* and *low fat;* and, subject to the federal Food and Drug Administration's approval, authorizes certain health claims.

OTHER FEDERAL STATUTES

Federal laws regulating the labeling and packaging of products include the Wool Products Labeling Act of 1939,[9] the Fur Products Labeling Act of 1951,[10] the Flammable Fabrics Act of 1953,[11] the Fair Packaging and Labeling Act of 1966,[12] the Comprehensive Smokeless Tobacco Health Education Act of 1986,[13] and the Nutrition Labeling and Education Act of 1990.[14] The Comprehensive Smokeless Tobacco Health Education Act, for example, requires that producers, packagers, and importers of smokeless tobacco label their product with one of several warnings about the health hazards associated with the use of smokeless tobacco; the warnings are similar to those required on cigarette packages.

Sales

A number of statutes protect consumers by requiring the disclosure of certain terms in sales transactions and providing rules governing home or door-to-door sales, mail-order transactions, referral sales, and unsolicited merchandise. The Federal Reserve Board of Governors, for example, has issued **Regulation Z,** which governs credit provisions associated with sales contracts. Many states have also passed laws providing remedies to consumers in home sales. Furthermore, states have provided a number of consumer protection measures, such as implied warranties, through the adoption of the Uniform Commercial Code. In some states, the Uniform Consumer Credit Code's requirements, including disclosure requirements, also protect consumers in credit transactions.

REGULATION Z
A set of rules promulgated by the Federal Reserve Board of Governors to implement the provisions of the Truth-in-Lending Act.

DOOR-TO-DOOR SALES

The laws of most states single out door-to-door sales for special treatment in part because of the nature of the sales transaction. Repeat purchases are less likely than in stores, so the seller has less incentive to cultivate the goodwill of the purchaser. Furthermore, the seller is unlikely to present alternative products and their prices. Thus, a number of states have passed **"cooling-off" laws** that permit the buyers of goods sold door to door to cancel their contracts within a specified period of time, usually two to three days after the sale.

"COOLING-OFF" LAWS
Laws that allow buyers a period of time, such as three days, in which to cancel door-to-door sales contracts.

An FTC regulation also requires sellers to give consumers three days to cancel any door-to-door sale. Because this rule applies in addition to the relevant state

9. 15 U.S.C. Section 68.
10. 15 U.S.C. Section 69.
11. 15 U.S.C. Section 1191.
12. 15 U.S.C. Sections 1451 *et seq.*
13. 15 U.S.C. Sections 4401–4408.
14. 21 U.S.C. Section 343-1.

To learn more about the FTC's Cooling-Off Rule, go to

http://www.ftc.gov/bcp/conline/pubs/buying/cooling.htm.

statutes, consumers are given the benefits of both the FTC rule and their own state statutes. In addition, the FTC rule requires that consumers be notified in Spanish of this right if the oral negotiations for the sale were in that language.

Telephone and Mail-Order Sales

The nation's Better Business Bureaus receive more complaints about sales made by telephone or mail order than about any other transactions. Many mail-order houses are far removed from the buyers who order from them, making it difficult for a consumer to bring a complaint against a seller. To a certain extent, consumers are protected under federal laws prohibiting mail fraud, which were discussed in Chapter 6, and under state consumer protection laws that parallel and supplement the federal laws.

The FTC's Mail or Telephone Order Merchandise Rule of 1993, which amended the FTC's Mail Order Rule of 1975,[15] provides specific protections for consumers who purchase goods via phone lines or through the mails. The 1993 rule extended the 1975 rule to include sales in which orders are transmitted using computers, fax machines, or any similar means involving telephone lines. Among other things, the rule requires mail-order merchants to ship orders within the time promised in their catalogues or advertisements, to notify consumers when orders cannot be shipped on time, and to issue a refund within a specified period of time when a consumer cancels an order.

In addition, the Postal Reorganization Act of 1970[16] provides that unsolicited merchandise sent by U.S. mail may be retained, used, discarded, or disposed of in any manner the recipient deems appropriate, without the recipient's incurring any obligation to the sender.

Online Sales

In recent years, the Internet has become a vehicle for a wide variety of business-to-consumer (B2C) sales transactions. Most mail-order houses now have a Web presence, and other Web sites offer consumers an increasing array of goods, ranging from airline tickets to books to xylophones. Protecting consumers from fraudulent and deceptive sales practices conducted via the Internet has proved to be a challenging task. Nonetheless, the FTC and other federal agencies have brought a number of enforcement actions against those who perpetrate online fraud. Additionally, the laws mentioned earlier, such as the federal statute prohibiting wire fraud, apply to online transactions.

Some states have amended their consumer protection statutes to cover Internet transactions as well. For example, the California legislature revised its Business and Professional Code to include transactions conducted over the Internet or by "any other electronic means of communication." Previously, that code covered only telephone, mail-order catalogue, radio, and television sales. Now any entity selling over the Internet in California must explicitly create an on-screen notice indicating its refund and return policies, where its business is physically located, its legal name, and a number of other details. Various states are also setting up information sites to help consumers protect themselves.

15. 16 C.F.R. Sections 435.1–435.2.
16. 39 U.S.C. Section 3009.

Health and Safety Protection

The laws discussed earlier regarding the labeling and packaging of products go a long way toward promoting consumer health and safety. There is a significant distinction, however, between regulating the information dispensed about a product and regulating the actual content of the product. The classic example is tobacco products. Producers of tobacco products are required to warn consumers about the hazards associated with the use of their products. Yet the sale of tobacco products has not yet been subject to significant restrictions or banned outright despite their obvious hazards. We now examine various laws that regulate the actual products made available to consumers.

Food and Drugs

The first federal legislation regulating food and drugs was enacted in 1906 as the Pure Food and Drugs Act.[17] That law, as amended in 1938, exists now as the Federal Food, Drug and Cosmetic Act (FFDCA).[18] The act protects consumers against adulterated and misbranded foods and drugs. More recent amendments to the act added other substantive and procedural requirements. In its present form, the act establishes food standards, specifies safe levels of potentially hazardous food additives, and sets classifications of food and food advertising.

BE AWARE The Food and Drug Administration is authorized to obtain, among other things, orders for the recall and seizure of certain products.

Most of these statutory requirements are monitored and enforced by the Food and Drug Administration (FDA). Under an extensive set of procedures established by the FDA, drugs must be shown to be effective as well as safe before they may be marketed to the public, and the use of some food additives suspected of being carcinogenic is prohibited. A 1976 amendment to the FFDCA[19] authorizes the FDA to regulate medical devices, such as pacemakers and other health devices or equipment, and to withdraw from the market any such device that is mislabeled.

Consumer Product Safety

Legislation regulating the safety of consumer products began in 1953 with the enactment of the Flammable Fabrics Act, which prohibits the sale of highly flammable clothing or materials. Over the next two decades, Congress enacted legislation regarding the design or composition of specific classes of products. Then, in 1972,

17. 21 U.S.C. Sections 1–5, 7–15.
18. 21 U.S.C. Section 301.
19. 21 U.S.C. Sections 352(o), 360(j), 360(k), and 360c–360k.

These stuffed teddy bears were recalled because the plastic beads inside the toy could come out and create a choking hazard for young children. Which area of consumer protection law governs such a recall? (Photo by the Consumer Product Safety Commission/Getty Images)

Congress enacted the Consumer Product Safety Act,[20] which created a comprehensive scheme of regulation over matters concerning consumer safety. The act also established the Consumer Product Safety Commission (CPSC) and gave it far-reaching authority over consumer safety.

The CPSC conducts research on the safety of individual products and maintains a clearinghouse on the risks associated with various products. The Consumer Product Safety Act authorizes the CPSC to set standards for consumer products and to ban the manufacture and sale of any product that the commission deems to be potentially hazardous to consumers. The CPSC also has authority to remove from the market any products it believes to be imminently hazardous and to require manufacturers to report on any products already sold or intended for sale if the products have proved to be hazardous. Additionally, the CPSC administers other product-safety legislation, such as the Child Protection and Toy Safety Act of 1969[21] and the Federal Hazardous Substances Act of 1960.[22] The CPSC's authority is sufficiently broad to allow it to ban any product that the commission believes poses merely an "unreasonable risk" to the consumer.

The Consumer Product Safety Act imposes notification requirements on distributors of consumer products. Distributors must immediately notify the CPSC when they receive information that a product "contains a defect which . . . creates a substantial risk to the public" or "an unreasonable risk of serious injury or death." The following case illustrates the consequences of failing to fulfill this requirement.

20. 15 U.S.C. Section 2051.
21. 15 U.S.C. Section 1262(e).
22. 15 U.S.C. Sections 1261–1273.

CASE 38.1 United States v. Mirama Enterprises, Inc.

United States District Court,
Southern District of California, 2002.
185 F.Supp.2d 1148.

BACKGROUND AND FACTS Mirama Enterprises, Inc., began operations in 1996 and today does business as Aroma Housewares Company. From 1996 until 1998, Aroma distributed a juice extractor, or juicer, made by a company in Taiwan, to retail stores throughout the United States. In early January 1998, Aroma received a complaint from a consumer whose juicer had broken. In February, consumer Richard Norton wrote Aroma to report that his juicer had shattered. In capital letters, Norton stated that the juicer

> SUDDENLY EXPLODED, THROWING WITH GREAT VIOLENCE PIECES OF THE CLEAR PLASTIC COVER AND SHREDS OF THE RAZOR-SHARP SEPARATOR SCREEN AS FAR AS EIGHT FEET IN MY KITCHEN. * * *

Over the next months, Aroma received twenty-three complaints about exploding juicers, some of which had caused injuries. One consumer, Jan Griffin, concluded her complaint by saying, "I feel that this juicer should be recalled, as it is very unsafe. The injuries that I suffered could have been a lot worse." In August, consumer Sylvia Mendoza filed a suit against Aroma, alleging injuries caused by a shattering juicer. On November 16, Aroma filed a report with the CPSC, which recalled the juicer on June 30, 1999. The federal government filed a suit against Mirama, seeking damages for its alleged failure to notify the CPSC of the danger earlier. The federal government then filed a motion for summary judgment.

IN THE WORDS OF THE COURT . . .

KEEP, District Judge.

* * * *

[The] reporting requirement was imposed upon consumer product manufacturers to protect the public health and safety—the sooner the [Consumer Product Safety]

CASE 38.1—Continued

Commission knows of a potential problem, the sooner it can investigate and take necessary action. This notification requirement was statutorily imposed upon manufacturers * * * because they are often the first to receive information about hazardous consumer products. * * *

The thrust of the Act is clearly for firms to quickly inform the Commission as soon as they might "reasonably believe" that their product, through defect or otherwise, poses a significant threat to consumers. Upon receipt of "first information," a company is required to report *within 24 hours* to the Commission. Companies are advised that they should not await complete or accurate risk estimates before reporting * * * . While a firm may investigate to determine whether the information is reportable, a firm should not take more than 10 days unless it can demonstrate that such additional time is reasonable. * * * [Emphasis added.]

* * * The issue is whether, prior to [its reporting] date, Aroma received information which "reasonably supported" the conclusion that the juicer either * * * contained a "defect" which created a "substantial product hazard," such that it "created a substantial risk to the public," or created an "unreasonable risk of serious injury or death."

* * * *

The Court finds that Aroma was in receipt of overwhelming evidence such that a reasonable person could conclude that the juicer contained a defect which created a substantial risk to the public. The Court will not set forth again the litany of phone calls and letters with which scared, angry, and often injured consumers bombarded the company. The Court finds particularly noteworthy, however, several items in particular. * * * [I]n a period of approximately only one month, Aroma received three telephone calls and two letters recounting exploding juicers, flying pieces of razor-sharp metal, and one emergency room visit. Hence, by at least early March, Aroma had enough information for a reasonable person to conclude that the juicer contained a defect, whether in the actual unit or in the instructions and warnings, that created a substantial risk to the public.

DECISION AND REMEDY The court granted the plaintiff's motion for summary judgment. The defendant had sufficient knowledge from consumer complaints that the juicer contained "a defect which . . . creates a substantial risk to the public" to report to the CPSC as early as March 1998.

WHY IS THIS CASE IMPORTANT? *This case emphasizes that the law imposes a strict requirement on all businesses that sell goods to notify the CPSC immediately of any reports indicating that a product poses a substantial risk to the public.*

Credit Protection

Considering the extensive use of credit by U.S. consumers, credit protection is one of the most important aspects of consumer protection legislation. A key statute regulating the credit and credit-card industries is the Truth-in-Lending Act (TILA), the name commonly given to Title 1 of the Consumer Credit Protection Act (CCPA),[23] which was passed by Congress in 1968.

23. 15 U.S.C. Sections 1601–1693r. The act was amended in 1980 by the Truth-in-Lending Simplification and Reform Act.

access the ITC product warehouse, and other "upgrades." The Federal Trade Commission filed a suit in a federal district court against end70 and Zamora, seeking an injunction and other relief. Are the defendants' claims "deceptive advertising"? If so, what might the court order the defendants to do to correct any misrepresentations? [*Federal Trade Commission v. end70 Corp.*, __ F.Supp.2d __ (N.D.Tex. 2003)]

A QUESTION OF ETHICS

38–8. Renee Purtle bought a 1986 Chevrolet Blazer from Eldridge Auto Sales, Inc. To finance the purchase through Eldridge, Purtle filled out a credit application on which she misrepresented her employment status. Based on the misrepresentation, Eldridge extended credit. In the credit contract, Eldridge did not disclose the finance charge, the annual percentage rate, or the total sales price or use the term *amount financed,* as the Truth-in-Lending Act (TILA) and its regulations require. Purtle defaulted on the loan, and Eldridge repossessed the vehicle. Purtle filed a suit in a federal district court against Eldridge, alleging violations of the TILA. The court awarded Purtle $1,000 in damages, plus attorneys' fees and costs. Eldridge appealed, arguing in part that Purtle was not entitled to damages because she had committed fraud on her credit application. Considering these facts, answer the following questions. [*Purtle v. Eldridge Auto Sales, Inc.*, 91 F.3d 797 (6th Cir. 1996)]

1. How will the appellate court rule in this case? Why?
2. The trial court awarded Purtle money damages for the car dealer's violation of the TILA even though Purtle had lied about her job on the credit application. Do you think it is fair for the court to reward a plaintiff who has committed fraud? What should the court do?
3. The plaintiff in this case also defaulted on the loan. Generally, should a person who defaults on a loan be prohibited from suing the creditor for violating the TILA? Why or why not?

FOR CRITICAL ANALYSIS

38–9. As discussed in the text, many states have enacted laws that go even further than federal law to protect the interests of consumers. These laws vary tremendously from state to state. Generally, do you think it is fair that citizens of one state receive more protection than citizens of another state? What about fairness to sellers, who may be prohibited from engaging in a practice in one state that is perfectly legal in another? Should all consumer protection statutes be legislated federally? Why or why not?

VIDEO QUESTION

DIGITAL VIDEO LIBRARY WEST LEGAL STUDIES IN BUSINESS

38–10. Go to this text's Web site at **http://blt.westbuslaw.com** and select "Chapter 38." Click on "Video Questions" and view the video titled *Advertising Communication Law: Bait and Switch.* Then answer the following questions.

1. Is the auto dealership's advertisement for the truck in the video deceptive? Why or why not?
2. Is the advertisement for the truck an offer to which the dealership is bound? Does it matter if Betty detrimentally relied on the advertisement?
3. Is Tony committed to buying Betty's trade-in truck for $3,000 because that is what he told her over the phone?

INTERNET EXERCISES

Go to the *Business Law Today* home page at **http://blt.westbuslaw.com**, select "Chapter 38," and click on "Internet Exercises." There you will find the following Internet research exercises that you can perform to learn more about topics covered in this chapter.

Activity 38–1: LEGAL PERSPECTIVE—The Food and Drug Administration

Activity 38–2: MANAGEMENT PERSPECTIVE—Internet Advertising and Marketing

BEFORE THE TEST

Go to the *Business Law Today* home page at **http://blt.westbuslaw.com**, select "Chapter 38," and click on "Interactive Quizzes." You will find a number of interactive questions relating to this chapter.

CHAPTER 39
Environmental Law

"Man, however much he may like to pretend the contrary, is part of nature."

Rachel Carson, 1907–1964
(American writer and conservationist)

CHAPTER OUTLINE

LEARNING OBJECTIVES

After reading this chapter, you should be able to answer the following questions:

1. Under what common law theories can polluters be held liable?
2. What is an environmental impact statement, and who must file one?
3. What does the Environmental Protection Agency do?
4. What major federal statutes regulate air and water pollution?
5. What is Superfund? To what categories of persons does liability under Superfund extend?

Concern over the degradation of the environment has increased over time in response to the environmental effects of population growth, urbanization, and industrialization. Environmental protection is not without a price, however. For many businesses, the costs of complying with environmental regulations are high, and for some they are too high. A constant tension exists between the desirability of increasing profits and productivity and the need to protect the environment.

To a great extent, environmental law consists of statutes passed by federal, state, or local governments and regulations issued by administrative agencies. Before examining statutory and regulatory environmental laws, however, we look at the remedies available under the common law against environmental pollution.

Common Law Actions

Common law remedies against environmental pollution originated centuries ago in England. Those responsible for operations that created dirt, smoke, noxious odors, noise, or toxic substances were sometimes held liable under common law theories of nuisance or negligence. Today, injured individuals continue to rely on the common law to obtain damages and injunctions against business polluters.

NUISANCE

NUISANCE
A common law doctrine under which persons may be held liable for using their property in a manner that unreasonably interferes with others' rights to use or enjoy their own property.

Under the common law doctrine of **nuisance,** persons may be held liable if they use their property in a manner that unreasonably interferes with others' rights to use or enjoy their own property. In these situations, the courts commonly balance the equities between the harm caused by the pollution and the costs of stopping it.

Courts have often denied injunctive relief on the ground that the hardships that would be imposed on the polluter and on the community are relatively greater than the hardships suffered by the plaintiff. ■ EXAMPLE 39.1 A factory that causes neighboring landowners to suffer from smoke, dirt, and vibrations may be left in operation if it is the core of a local economy. The injured parties may be awarded only money damages. These damages may include compensation for the decrease in the value of the neighbors' property that results from the factory's operation. ■

A property owner may be given relief from pollution if he or she can identify a distinct harm separate from that affecting the general public. This harm is referred to as a "private" nuisance. Under the common law, citizens were denied standing (access to the courts—see Chapter 3) unless they suffered a harm distinct from the harm suffered by the public at large. Some states still require this. ■ EXAMPLE 39.2 A group of individuals who made their living by commercial fishing in a major river in New York sued for damages and to obtain an injunction against a company that was polluting the river. The court found that the plaintiffs had standing because they were particularly harmed by the pollution in the river.[1] ■ A public authority (such as a state's attorney general), though, can sue to abate a "public" nuisance.

NEGLIGENCE AND STRICT LIABILITY

TOXIC TORT
A civil wrong arising from exposure to a toxic substance, such as asbestos, radiation, or hazardous waste.

An injured party may sue a business polluter in tort under the negligence and strict liability theories discussed in Chapter 4. The basis for a negligence action is the business's alleged failure to use reasonable care toward the party whose injury was foreseeable and, of course, caused by the lack of reasonable care. For example, employees might sue an employer whose failure to use proper pollution controls contaminated the air and caused the employees to suffer respiratory illnesses. A developing area of tort law involves **toxic torts**—civil wrongs arising from exposure to a toxic substance, such as asbestos, radiation, or hazardous waste.

Businesses that engage in ultrahazardous activities—such as the transportation of radioactive materials—are strictly liable for whatever injuries the activities cause. In a strict liability action, the injured party does not need to prove that the business failed to exercise reasonable care.

1. *Lee v. General Electric Co.,* 538 N.Y.S.2d 844, 145 A.D.2d 291 (1989).

Federal, State, and Local Regulation

All levels of government in the United States regulate some aspect of the environment. In this section, we look at some of the ways in which the federal, state, and local governments control business activities and land use in the interests of environmental preservation and protection.

FEDERAL REGULATION

Congress has enacted a number of statutes to control the impact of human activities on the environment. Some of these laws have been passed to improve the quality of air and water. Some of them specifically regulate toxic chemicals, including pesticides, herbicides, and hazardous wastes.

Environmental Regulatory Agencies Much of the body of federal law governing business activities consists of the regulations issued and enforced by administrative agencies. The most well known of the agencies regulating environmental law is, of course, the Environmental Protection Agency (EPA), which was created in 1970 to coordinate federal environmental responsibilities. Other federal agencies with authority to regulate specific environmental matters include the Department of the Interior, the Department of Defense, the Department of Labor, the Food and Drug Administration, and the Nuclear Regulatory Commission. These regulatory agencies—and all other agencies of the federal government—must take environmental factors into consideration when making significant decisions.

Most federal environmental laws provide that citizens can sue to enforce environmental regulations if government agencies fail to do so—or if agencies go too far in their enforcement actions. Typically, a threshold hurdle in such suits is meeting the requirements for standing to sue.

State and local regulatory agencies also play a significant role in implementing federal environmental legislation. Typically, the federal government relies on state and local governments to enforce federal environmental statutes and regulations such as those regulating air quality.

ENVIRONMENTAL IMPACT STATEMENT (EIS)
A statement required by the National Environmental Policy Act for any major federal action that will significantly affect the quality of the environment. The statement must analyze the action's impact on the environment and explore alternative actions that might be taken.

Environmental Impact Statements The National Environmental Policy Act (NEPA) of 1969[2] requires that an **environmental impact statement (EIS)** be prepared for every major federal action that significantly affects the quality of the environment. An EIS must analyze (1) the impact on the environment that the action will have, (2) any adverse effects on the environment and alternative actions that might be taken, and (3) irreversible effects the action might generate.

An action qualifies as "major" if it involves a substantial commitment of resources (monetary or otherwise). An action is "federal" if a federal agency has the power to control it. Construction by a private developer of a ski resort on federal land, for example, may require an EIS.[3] Building or operating a nuclear plant, which requires a federal permit,[4] would require an EIS, as would constructing a dam as part of a federal project.[5] If an agency decides that an EIS is unnecessary, it must issue a statement supporting this conclusion. EISs have become instruments for private citizens,

2. 42 U.S.C. Sections 4321–4370d.
3. *Robertson v. Methow Valley Citizens' Council,* 490 U.S. 332, 109 S.Ct. 1835, 104 L.Ed.2d 351 (1989).
4. *Calvert Cliffs Coordinating Committee v. Atomic Energy Commission,* 449 F.2d 1109 (D.C. Cir. 1971).
5. *Marsh v. Oregon Natural Resources Council,* 490 U.S. 360, 109 S.Ct. 1851, 104 L.Ed.2d 377 (1989).

"All property in thi
held under the impli
that the owner's use
not be injurious to t
community."
J
(Assoc
United State

Joint and Several Liability under Superfund Liability under Superfund is usually joint and several—that is, a person who generated *only a fraction of the hazardous waste* disposed of at the site may nevertheless be liable for *all* of the clean-up costs. CERCLA authorizes a party who has incurred clean-up costs to bring a "contribution action" against any other person who is liable or potentially liable for a percentage of the costs, however.

REVIEWING ENVIRONMENTAL LAW

In the late 1980s, various residents of Lake Caliopa, Minnesota, began noticing an unusually high number of lung ailments among their population. A group of concerned local citizens pooled their resources and commissioned a study of the frequency of these health conditions per capita as compared to national averages. The study concluded that Lake Caliopa had four to seven times the usual frequency of asthma, bronchitis, and emphysema when compared to national data. During the study period, citizens began expressing concerns about the large volumes of smog emitted by the Cotton Design apparel manufacturing plant on the outskirts of town. The plant had opened its production facility two miles east of town beside the Tawakoni River in 1977 and employed seventy full-time workers by 1991. Just downstream on the Tawakoni River, the city of Lake Caliopa operated a public water works facility, which supplied all city residents with water. In August 1991, the Minnesota Pollution Control Agency required Cotton Design to install new equipment to control air and water pollution. In May 1992, thirty citizens brought a class-action lawsuit in a Minnesota state court against Cotton Design for various respiratory ailments allegedly caused or compounded by smog from Cotton Design's factory. Using the information presented in the chapter, answer the following questions.

1. Under the common law, what would each plaintiff be required to identify in order to be given relief by the court?
2. Are air-quality regulations typically overseen by federal, state, or local governments? Which agency establishes these regulations?
3. The equipment to control air pollution has to meet what standard for limiting air pollution from Cotton Design? To what requirements relating to water pollution would Cotton Design be subject?
4. In what ways can the Environmental Protection Agency regulate organizations, such as Cotton Design, that use toxic substances?

KEY TERMS

environmental impact statement (EIS) 1011
nuisance 1010
potentially responsible party (PRP) 1019
toxic tort 1010
wetlands 1016

CHAPTER SUMMARY Environmental Law

Common Law Actions (See page 1010.)	1. *Nuisance*—A common law doctrine under which actions against pollution-causing activities may be brought. An action is permissible only if an individual suffers a harm separate and distinct from that of the general public.

CHAPTER SUMMARY Environmental Law—Continued

Common Law Actions—Continued	2. *Negligence and strict liability*—Parties may recover damages for injuries sustained as a result of a firm's pollution-causing activities if it can be demonstrated that the harm was a foreseeable result of the firm's failure to exercise reasonable care (negligence); businesses engaging in ultrahazardous activities are liable for whatever injuries the activities cause, regardless of whether the firms exercise reasonable care.
Federal, State, and Local Regulation (See pages 1011–1020.)	Activities affecting the environment are controlled at the local and state levels through regulations relating to land use, the disposal and recycling of garbage and waste, and pollution-causing activities in general. Federal regulation involves the following: 1. *Environmental protection agencies*—The most well known of the agencies regulating environmental law is the federal Environmental Protection Agency (EPA), which was created in 1970 to coordinate federal environmental programs. The EPA administers most federal environmental policies and statutes. 2. *Assessing environmental impact*—The National Environmental Policy Act of 1969 imposes environmental responsibilities on all federal agencies and requires the preparation of an environmental impact statement (EIS) for every major federal action. An EIS must analyze the action's impact on the environment, its adverse effects and possible alternatives, and its irreversible effects on environmental quality. 3. *Important areas regulated by the federal government*—Important areas regulated by the federal government include the following: a. Air pollution—Regulated under the authority of the Clean Air Act of 1963 and its amendments, particularly those of 1970, 1977, and 1990. b. Water pollution—Regulated under the authority of the Rivers and Harbors Appropriation Act of 1899, as amended, and the Federal Water Pollution Control Act of 1948, as amended by the Clean Water Act of 1972. c. Toxic chemicals and hazardous waste—Pesticides and herbicides, toxic substances, and hazardous waste are regulated under the authority of the Federal Insecticide, Fungicide, and Rodenticide Act of 1947, the Toxic Substances Control Act of 1976, and the Resource Conservation and Recovery Act of 1976, respectively. The Comprehensive Environmental Response, Compensation, and Liability Act (CERCLA) of 1980, as amended, regulates the clean-up of hazardous waste–disposal sites.

FOR REVIEW

Answers for the even-numbered questions in this For Review *section can be found on this text's accompanying Web site at* http://blt.westbuslaw.com. *Select "Chapter 39" and click on "For Review."*

1. Under what common law theories can polluters be held liable?
2. What is an environmental impact statement, and who must file one?
3. What does the Environmental Protection Agency do?
4. What major federal statutes regulate air and water pollution?
5. What is Superfund? To what categories of persons does liability under Superfund extend?

QUESTIONS AND CASE PROBLEMS

39–1. Clean Air Act. Current scientific knowledge indicates that there is no safe level of exposure to a cancer-causing agent. In theory, even one molecule of such a substance has the potential for causing cancer. Section 112 of the Clean Air Act requires that all cancer-causing substances be regulated to ensure a margin of safety. Some environmental groups have argued that all emissions of such substances must be eliminated if a margin of safety is to be reached. Such a total elimination would likely shut down many major U.S. industries. Should the Environmental Protection Agency totally eliminate all emissions of cancer-causing chemicals? Discuss.

39–2. Water Pollution. Fruitade, Inc., is a processor of a soft drink called Freshen Up. Fruitade uses returnable bottles and employs a special acid to clean its bottles for further beverage processing. The acid is diluted with water and then allowed to pass into a navigable stream. Fruitade crushes its broken bottles and also throws the crushed glass into the stream. Discuss fully any environmental laws that Fruitade has violated.

39–3. Common Law Actions. Moonbay is a home-building corporation that primarily develops retirement communities. Farmtex owns a number of feedlots in Sunny Valley. Moonbay purchased 20,000 acres of farmland in the same area and began building and selling homes on this acreage. In the meantime, Farmtex continued to expand its feedlot business, and eventually only 500 feet separated the two operations. Because of the odor and flies from the feedlots, Moonbay found it difficult to sell the homes in its development. Moonbay wants to enjoin Farmtex from operating its feedlots in the vicinity of the retirement home development. Under what common law theory would Moonbay file this action? Has Farmtex violated any federal environmental laws? Discuss.

39–4. Strict Liability. Cities Service Co. operated a phosphate rock mine that included large settling ponds for the extraction of phosphate. A dam outside of one of these ponds broke, sending a billion gallons of phosphate slime into the nearby Peace River. This killed fish and caused other damage. The state of Florida sued Cities Service under a theory of strict liability for damages. Given these facts, should Cities Service be liable? [*Cities Service Co. v. State,* 312 So.2d 799 (Fla.App. 1975)]

39–5. Clean Water Act. Attique Ahmad owned the Spin-N-Market, a convenience store and gas station. The gas pumps were fed by underground tanks, one of which had a leak at its top that allowed water to enter. Ahmad emptied the tank by pumping its contents into a storm drain and a sewer system. Through the storm drain, gasoline flowed into a creek, forcing the city to clean the water. Through the sewer system, gasoline flowed into a sewage treatment plant, forcing the city to evacuate the plant and two nearby schools. Ahmad was charged with discharging a pollutant without a permit, which is a criminal violation of the Clean Water Act. The act provides that a person who "knowingly violates" the act commits a felony. Ahmad claimed that he had believed he was discharging only water. Did Ahmad commit a felony? Why or why not? Discuss fully. [*United States v. Ahmad,* 101 F.3d 386 (5th Cir. 1996)]

39–6. Environmental Impact Statement. Greers Ferry Lake is in Arkansas, and its shoreline is under the management of the U.S. Army Corps of Engineers, which is part of the U.S. Department of Defense (DOD). The Corps's 2000 Shoreline Management Plan (SMP) rezoned numerous areas along the lake, authorized the Corps to issue permits for the construction of new boat docks in the rezoned areas, increased by 300 percent the area around habitable structures that could be cleared of vegetation, and instituted a Wildlife Enhancement Permit to allow limited modifications of the shoreline. In relation to the SMP's adoption, the Corps issued a Finding of No Significant Impact, which declared that no environmental impact statement (EIS) was necessary. The Corps issued thirty-two boat dock construction permits under the SMP before Save Greers Ferry Lake, Inc., filed a suit in a federal district court against the DOD, asking the court to, among other things, stop the Corps from acting under the SMP and order it to prepare an EIS. What are the requirements for an EIS? Is an EIS needed in this case? Explain. [*Save Greers Ferry Lake, Inc. v. Department of Defense,* 255 F.3d 498 (8th Cir. 2001)]

39–7. CERCLA. Beginning in 1926, Marietta Dyestuffs Co. operated an industrial facility in Marietta, Ohio, to make dyes and other chemicals. In 1944, Dyestuffs became part of American Home Products Corp. (AHP), which sold the Marietta facility to American Cyanamid Co. in 1946. In 1950, AHP sold the rest of the Dyestuffs assets and all of its stock to Goodrich Co., which immediately liquidated the acquired corporation. Goodrich continued to operate the dissolved corporation's business, however. Cyanamid continued to make chemicals at the Marietta facility, and in 1993, it created Cytec Industries, Inc., which expressly assumed all environmental liabilities associated with Cyanamid's ownership and operation of the facility. Cytec spent nearly $25 million on clean-up costs and filed a suit in a federal district court against Goodrich to recover, under CERCLA, a portion of the costs attributable to the clean-up of hazardous wastes that may have been discarded at the site between 1926 and 1946. Cytec filed a motion for summary judgment in its favor. Should the court grant Cytec's motion? Explain. [*Cytec Industries, Inc. v. B. F. Goodrich Co.,* 196 F.Supp.2d 644 (S.D. Ohio 2002)]

CASE PROBLEM WITH SAMPLE ANSWER

39–8. William Gurley was the president and majority stockholder in Gurley Refining Co. (GRC). GRC bought used oil, treated it, and sold it. The refining process created a by-product residue of oily waste. GRC disposed of this waste by dumping it at, among other locations, a landfill in West Memphis, Arkansas. In February 1992, after detecting hazardous chemicals at the site, the Environmental Protection Agency (EPA) asked Gurley about his assets, the generators of the material disposed of at the landfill, site operations, and the structure of GRC. Gurley refused to respond, except to suggest that the EPA ask GRC. In October, the EPA placed the site on its clean-up list and again asked Gurley for information. When he still refused to respond, the EPA filed a suit in a federal district court against him, asking the court to impose a civil penalty. In February 1999, Gurley finally answered the EPA's questions. Under CERCLA, a court may impose a civil penalty "not to exceed $25,000 for each day of noncompliance against any person who unreasonably fails to comply" with an information request. Should the court assess a penalty in this case? Why or why not? [*United States v. Gurley,* 384 F.3d 316 (6th Cir. 2004)]

After you have answered this problem, compare your answer with the sample answer given on the Web site that accompanies this text. Go to http://blt.westbuslaw.com, select "Chapter 39," and click on "Case Problem with Sample Answer."

A QUESTION OF ETHICS

39–9. The Endangered Species Act of 1973 makes it unlawful for any person to "take" endangered or threatened species. The act defines *take* to mean "harass, harm, pursue," "wound," or "kill." The secretary of the interior (Bruce Babbitt) issued a regulation that further defined *harm* to include "significant habitat modification or degradation where it actually kills or injures wildlife." A group of businesses and individuals involved in the timber industry brought an action against the secretary of the interior and others. The group complained that the application of the "harm" regulation to the red-cockaded woodpecker and the northern spotted owl had injured the group economically by preventing logging operations (habitat modification) in Pacific Northwest forests containing these species. The group challenged the regulation's validity, contending that Congress had not intended the word *take* to include habitat modification. The case ultimately reached the United States Supreme Court, which held that the secretary had reasonably construed Congress's intent when he defined *harm* to include habitat modification. [*Babbitt v. Sweet Home Chapter of Communities for a Great Oregon,* 515 U.S. 687, 115 S.Ct. 2407, 132 L.Ed.2d 597 (1995)]

1. Traditionally, the term *take* has been used to refer to the capture or killing of wildlife, usually for private gain. Is the secretary's regulation prohibiting habitat modification consistent with this definition?
2. One of the issues in this case was whether Congress intended to protect existing generations of species or future generations. How do the terms *take* and *habitat modification* relate to this issue?
3. Three dissenting Supreme Court justices contended that construing the act as prohibiting habitat modification "imposes unfairness to the point of financial ruin—not just upon the rich, but upon the simplest farmer who finds his land conscripted to national zoological use." Should private parties be required to bear the burden of preserving habitats for wildlife?
4. Generally, should the economic welfare of private parties be taken into consideration in the creation and application of environmental statutes and regulations?

FOR CRITICAL ANALYSIS

39–10. It has been estimated that for every dollar spent cleaning up hazardous waste sites, administrative agencies spend seven dollars in overhead. Can you think of any way to trim the administrative costs associated with the clean-up of contaminated sites?

INTERNET EXERCISES

Go to the *Business Law Today* home page at http://blt.westbuslaw.com, select "Chapter 39," and click on "Internet Exercises." There you will find the following Internet research exercises that you can perform to learn more about topics covered in this chapter.

Activity 39–1: LEGAL PERSPECTIVE—Nuisance Law

Activity 39–2: MANAGEMENT PERSPECTIVE—Complying with Environmental Regulation

Activity 39–3: ETHICAL PERSPECTIVE—Environmental Justice

BEFORE THE TEST

Go to the *Business Law Today* home page at http://blt.westbuslaw.com, select "Chapter 39," and click on "Interactive Quizzes." You will find a number of interactive questions relating to this chapter.

CHAPTER 40

Employment and Labor Law

"Show me the country in which there are no strikes, and I'll show you the country in which there is no liberty."

Samuel Gompers, 1850–1924
(American labor leader)

CHAPTER OUTLINE

- EMPLOYMENT AT WILL
- WAGE-HOUR LAWS
- LABOR UNIONS
- WORKER HEALTH AND SAFETY
- INCOME SECURITY
- FAMILY AND MEDICAL LEAVE
- EMPLOYEE PRIVACY RIGHTS

LEARNING OBJECTIVES

After reading this chapter, you should be able to answer the following questions:

1. What is the employment-at-will doctrine? When and why are exceptions to this doctrine made?
2. What federal statute governs working hours and wages? What federal statutes govern labor unions and collective bargaining?
3. What federal act was enacted to protect the health and safety of employees? What are workers' compensation laws?
4. Under the Family and Medical Leave Act of 1993, under what circumstances may an employee take family or medical leave?
5. Does electronic performance monitoring violate employees' privacy rights? What other types of activities undertaken by employers might violate the privacy rights of employees?

Until the early 1900s, most employer-employee relationships were governed by the common law. Today, the workplace is regulated extensively by statutes and administrative agency regulations. Recall from Chapter 1 that common law doctrines apply only to areas *not* covered by statutory law. Common law doctrines have thus been displaced to a large extent by statutory law.

In the 1930s, during the Great Depression, both state and federal governments began to regulate employment relationships. Legislation during the 1930s and subsequent decades established the right of employees to form labor unions. At the heart of labor rights is the right to unionize and bargain with management for improved working conditions, salaries, and benefits. The ultimate weapon of labor is, of course, the strike. As noted in the chapter-opening quotation, the labor leader

Samuel Gompers concluded that without the right to strike, there could be no liberty. A succession of other laws during and since the 1930s provided further protection for employees. Today's employers must comply with a myriad of laws and regulations to ensure that employee rights are protected.

In this chapter, we look at the most significant laws regulating employment relationships. We deal with other important laws regulating the workplace—those that prohibit employment discrimination—in the next chapter.

Employment at Will

EMPLOYMENT AT WILL
A common law doctrine under which either party may terminate an employment relationship at any time for any reason, unless a contract specifies otherwise.

Traditionally, employment relationships have generally been governed by the common law doctrine of **employment at will.** Other common law rules governing employment relationships—including rules under contract, tort, and agency law—have already been discussed at length in previous chapters of this text.

Given that many employees (those who deal with third parties) are normally deemed agents of an employer, agency concepts are especially relevant in the employment context. The distinction under agency law between employee status and independent-contractor status is also relevant to employment relationships. Generally, the laws discussed in this chapter and in Chapter 41 apply only to the employer-employee relationship; they do not apply to independent contractors.

Under the employment-at-will doctrine, either party may terminate the employment relationship at any time and for any reason, unless doing so would violate the provisions of an employment contract. The majority of U.S. workers continue to have the legal status of "employees at will." In other words, this common law doctrine is still in widespread use, and only one state (Montana) does not apply the doctrine. Nonetheless, as mentioned in the chapter introduction, federal and state statutes governing employment relationships prevent the doctrine from being applied in a number of circumstances. Today, an employer is not permitted to fire an employee if to do so would violate a federal or state employment statute, such as one prohibiting employment termination for discriminatory reasons (see Chapter 41).

Exceptions to the Employment-at-Will Doctrine

Under the employment-at-will doctrine, as mentioned, an employer may hire and fire employees at will (regardless of the employees' performance) without liability, unless doing so violates the terms of an employment contract or statutory law. Because of the harsh effects of the employment-at-will doctrine for employees, the courts have carved out various exceptions to the doctrine. These exceptions are based on contract theory, tort theory, and public policy.

Exceptions Based on Contract Theory Some courts have held that an *implied* employment contract exists between an employer and an employee. If an employee is fired outside the terms of the implied contract, he or she may succeed in an action for breach of contract even though no written employment contract exists. ■ EXAMPLE 40.1 Suppose that an employer's manual or personnel bulletin states that, as a matter of policy, workers will be dismissed only for good cause. If the employee is aware of this policy and continues to work for the employer, a court may find that there is an implied contract based on the terms stated in the manual or bulletin.[1] ■ Generally, the key consideration in determining whether an employment manual creates an implied contractual obligation is the employee's reasonable expectations.

1. See, for example, *Pepe v. Rival Co.,* 85 F.Supp.2d 349 (D.N.J. 1999).

REMEMBER An implied contract may exist if a party furnishes a service expecting to be paid, and the other party, who knows (or should know) of this expectation, has a chance to reject the service and does not.

An employer's oral promises to employees regarding discharge policy may also be considered part of an implied contract. If the employer fires a worker in a manner contrary to what was promised, a court may hold that the employer has violated the implied contract and is liable for damages. Most state courts will judge a claimed breach of implied employment contract by traditional contract standards. In some cases, courts have held that an implied employment contract exists even though employees agreed in writing to be employees at will.[2]

Courts in a few states have gone further and held that all employment contracts contain an implied covenant of good faith. This means that both sides promise to abide by the contract in good faith. If an employer fires an employee for an arbitrary or unjustified reason, the employee can claim that the covenant of good faith was breached and the contract violated.

Exceptions Based on Tort Theory In a few situations, the discharge of an employee may give rise to an action for wrongful discharge under tort theories. Abusive discharge procedures may result in a suit for intentional infliction of emotional distress or defamation, and some courts have permitted workers to sue their employers under the tort theory of fraud. ■ EXAMPLE 40.2 Suppose that an employer induces a prospective employee to leave a lucrative job and move to another state by offering "a long-term job with a thriving business." In fact, the employer is having significant financial problems. Also, the employer is planning a merger that will result in the elimination of the position offered to the prospective employee. If the employee takes the job in reliance on the employer's representations and is fired shortly thereafter, the employee may be able to bring an action against the employer for fraud.[3] ■

Exceptions Based on Public Policy The most widespread common law exception to the employment-at-will doctrine is made on the basis of public policy. Courts may apply this exception when an employer fires a worker for reasons that violate a fundamental public policy of the jurisdiction. Generally, the courts require that the public policy involved be expressed clearly in the statutory law governing the jurisdiction. ■ EXAMPLE 40.3 As you will read later in this chapter, employers with fifty or more employees are required by the Family and Medical Leave Act (FMLA) to give employees up to twelve weeks of unpaid family or medical leave per year. Mila's employer, however, has only forty employees and is thus not covered by the federal law. Nonetheless, if Mila is fired from her job because she takes three weeks of unpaid family leave to help her son through a difficult surgery, a court may deem that the employer's actions violated the public policy expressed in the FMLA. ■

WHISTLEBLOWING An employee's disclosure to government authorities, upper-level managers, or the press that the employer is engaged in unsafe or illegal activities.

Sometimes, an employer will direct employees to perform an illegal act and fire them if they refuse to do so. At other times, employers will fire or discipline employees who "blow the whistle" on the employer's wrongdoing. **Whistleblowing** occurs when an employee tells government authorities, upper-level managers, or the press that her or his employer is engaged in some unsafe or illegal activity. Whistleblowers on occasion have been protected from wrongful discharge for reasons of public policy. For example, a bank was held to have wrongfully discharged an employee who pressured the employer to comply with state and federal consumer credit laws.[4]

---

2. See, for example, *Kuest v. Regent Assisted Living, Inc.,* 111 Wash.App. 36, 43 P.3d 23 (2002).
3. See, for example, *Lazar v. Superior Court of Los Angeles County,* 12 Cal.4th 631, 909 P.2d 981, 49 Cal.Rptr.2d 377 (1996); and *McConkey v. Aon Corp.,* 804 A.2d 572 (N.J.Super.A.D. 2002).
4. *Harless v. First National Bank in Fairmont,* 162 W.Va. 116, 246 S.E.2d 270 (1978).

Today, whistleblowers have some protection under statutory law. Most states have enacted so-called whistleblower statutes that protect a whistleblower from subsequent retaliation by the employer. On the federal level, the Whistleblower Protection Act of 1989[5] protects federal employees who blow the whistle on their employers from retaliatory actions. Whistleblower statutes may also offer an incentive to disclose information by providing the whistleblower with a monetary reward. For instance, under the federal False Claims Reform Act of 1986,[6] a whistleblower who has disclosed information relating to a fraud perpetrated against the U.S. government will receive between 15 and 25 percent of the proceeds if the government brings a suit against the wrongdoer.

ETHICAL ISSUE 40.1

Is it fair for whistleblowing statutes to reward employees who participated in the fraud? Many whistleblowing statutes reward employees who report their employer's wrongdoing with a percentage of the funds recovered after a lawsuit. In other words, employees have a strong financial incentive to disclose their employers' wrongful behavior. Is this practice fair? What happens if the employee was somehow involved in the employer's wrongdoing? Should the employee still receive a share of the proceeds?

Consider, for example, the largest Medicaid fraud settlement in U.S. history, involving a deal between Bayer Corporation and Kaiser Permanente, a health-care organization. As one of Bayer's biggest customers, Kaiser demanded a discount price on Cipro, an antibiotic manufactured by Bayer. By law, however, Bayer could not sell the antibiotic to Kaiser for less than it sold Cipro to the federal government for use in the Medicaid program. (Medicaid helps needy and low-income persons pay for necessary medical services.) If Bayer lowered the price of Cipro to Kaiser, it would have to refund millions of dollars to Medicaid. Therefore, Bayer "privately labeled" the antibiotic using a different name and sold it to Kaiser at a 40 percent discount. Ironically, the person who blew the whistle on the fraudulent scheme—George Couto—was the marketing manager who negotiated the private labeling deal with Kaiser. Although Couto did not initiate the labeling scheme and had suspected that it was illegal, he was instrumental in its success. Even though Couto had been a prime mover in the fraudulent scheme on behalf of Bayer, he was awarded 24 percent of the government's share of the $257 million settlement.[7] ■

WRONGFUL DISCHARGE

Whenever an employer discharges an employee in violation of an employment contract or a statute protecting employees, the employee may bring an action for **wrongful discharge.** Even if an employer's actions do not violate any provisions in an employment contract or a statute, the employer may still be subject to liability under a common law doctrine, such as a tort theory or agency.

WRONGFUL DISCHARGE
An employer's termination of an employee's employment in violation of the law.

Wage-Hour Laws

In the 1930s, Congress enacted several laws regulating the wages and working hours of employees. In 1931, Congress passed the Davis-Bacon Act,[8] which requires contractors and subcontractors working on government construction projects to pay

5. 5 U.S.C. Section 1201.
6. 31 U.S.C. Sections 3729–3733. This act amended the False Claims Act of 1863.
7. Peter Aronson, "A Rogue to Catch a Rogue," *The National Law Journal,* August 18–25, 2003.
8. 40 U.S.C. Sections 276a–276a-5.

establish a pension plan. When a plan exists, however, ERISA establishes standards for its management.

VESTING
The creation of an absolute or unconditional right or power.

A key provision of ERISA concerns vesting. **Vesting** gives an employee a legal right to receive pension benefits at some future date when he or she stops working. Before ERISA was enacted, some employees who had worked for companies for as long as thirty years received no pension benefits when their employment terminated, because those benefits had not vested. ERISA establishes complex vesting rules. Generally, however, all employee contributions to pension plans vest immediately, and employee rights to employer contributions to a plan vest after five years of employment.

In an attempt to prevent mismanagement of pension funds, ERISA has established rules on how they must be invested. Pension managers must be cautious in their investments and refrain from investing more than 10 percent of the fund in securities of the employer. ERISA also contains detailed record-keeping and reporting requirements.

Unemployment Insurance

To ease the financial impact of unemployment, the United States has a system of unemployment insurance. The Federal Unemployment Tax Act (FUTA) of 1935[24] created a state-administered system that provides unemployment compensation to eligible individuals. Under this system, employers pay into a fund, and the proceeds are paid out to qualified unemployed workers. The FUTA and state laws require employers that fall under the provisions of the act to pay unemployment taxes at regular intervals.

WATCH OUT If an employer does not pay unemployment taxes, a state government can place a lien (claim) on the employer's property to secure the debt. (Liens were discussed in Chapter 26.)

To be eligible for unemployment compensation, a worker must be willing and able to work and be actively seeking employment. Workers who have been fired for misconduct or who have voluntarily left their jobs are not eligible for benefits. To leave a job voluntarily is to leave it without good cause. In the following case, an unemployed worker left his job. The question was whether he left the job for good cause and was therefore eligible for unemployment benefits.

24. 26 U.S.C. Sections 3301–3310.

CASE 40.2 Lewis v. Director, Employment Security Department

Court of Appeals of Arkansas,
Division I, 2004.
141 S.W.3d 896.
http://courts.state.ar.us/opinions/ca2004a.htm[a]

BACKGROUND AND FACTS The jobs in the warehouse unit of Ace Hardware Corporation in Arkansas are divided between two departments: break order and full case. Break-order positions involve lifting no more than fifty pounds. The full-case department fills heavier orders (up to five thousand pounds). Employees who complete orders in less time than Ace allows earn incentive pay. Employees believe that incentive pay is lower in the full-case department. Jobs are awarded on a seniority basis: new hires start in the full-case department but bid for other positions as soon as possible. Jimmy Lewis had worked for Ace since 1984, primarily in the break-order department. Ace had a high turnover in the full-case department, however, and whenever additional workers were needed, Ace reassigned Lewis. In 1998, Lewis began to complain regularly to his superiors about the reassignments. He offered to train others to fill the position, but his managers declined. In 2003, Lewis quit and applied for unemployment benefits. Ace questioned Lewis's entitlement. An Arkansas state employment tribunal ruled in Lewis's favor, a state review board reversed the ruling, and Lewis appealed to a state intermediate appellate court.

a. Click on "January 21, 2004." On the next page, scroll to the name of the case and click on the appropriate link to access the opinion. The Arkansas Judiciary maintains this Web site.

CASE 40.2—Continued

IN THE WORDS OF THE COURT . . .

WENDELL L. GRIFFEN, Judge.

* * * *

An individual shall be disqualified for unemployment benefits if he or she left his or her last work voluntarily and without good cause connected with the work. Good cause is a cause that would reasonably impel an average, able-bodied, qualified worker to give up his or her employment. *Good cause is dependent not only on the reaction of the average employee, but also on the good faith of the employee involved, which includes the presence of a genuine desire to work and to be self-supporting.* In addition, in order to receive unemployment benefits, an employee must make reasonable efforts to preserve his or her job rights. [Emphasis added.]

We hold that the [Arkansas Board of Review] erred in finding that appellant [Lewis] did not leave his work for good cause. The Board concluded that Ace had a legitimate, business-related reason for not training women to work in the full-case department, in that if women were required to call for assistance to lift the heavier objects, that would compound Ace's staffing problems. However, Ace made no such assertion. By Ace's own admission, the only reason that it failed to train other workers was because appellant was already trained and it was easier to reassign him. Appellant testified that some orders in the full-case department weighed as much as 5,000 pounds. Thus, presumably even men who are reassigned to the full-case department will be required to call for the assistance of a forklift to handle such heavy material.

While an employer has managerial discretion, it may not use that discretion in a discriminatory manner. Even if we agree that Ace had a legitimate, business-related reason for not training *women* to work in the full-case department, it advanced no such reason for not training other *men* to work in that department. We cannot ignore that Ace's staffing problems were self-created and that its reassignment policy seems to violate its own rules regarding seniority upon which its employees rely. [Emphasis added.]

Appellant left his job when he realized that Ace was never going to permanently address the underlying situation that caused his reassignment to the full-case department: in spite of the fact that employees regularly bid out of the full-case department, causing staffing shortages in that department, Ace refused to train other existing workers to fill those shortages. *An element in determining good cause is whether the employee took appropriate steps to prevent mistreatment from continuing.* Appellant had worked for Ace for nearly twenty years. After five years of complaining to all levels of management about being reassigned to a position that, in his experience, caused him to lose pay, after offering to assist with training other employees, and after having management violate its own seniority rules and take virtually no action to provide a permanent remedy, appellant quit. We agree with appellant that his circumstances would reasonably impel an average, able-bodied, qualified worker to give up his or her employment. [Emphasis added.]

DECISION AND REMEDY The state intermediate appellate court reversed the review board's decision and remanded the case for an order to award benefits. The court held that Lewis left his job for good cause and was therefore entitled to unemployment benefits.

FOR CRITICAL ANALYSIS—Social Consideration *The court in the* Lewis *case based its decision in part on the employee's reaction to the situation on the job. What other factors should be considered in deciding whether a worker had "good cause" to quit?*

COBRA

Federal legislation also addresses the issue of health insurance for workers whose jobs have been terminated—and who are thus no longer eligible for group health-insurance plans. The Consolidated Omnibus Budget Reconciliation Act (COBRA) of 1985[25] prohibits the elimination of a worker's medical, optical, or dental insurance on the voluntary or involuntary termination of the worker's employment. The act applies to most workers who have either lost their jobs or had their hours decreased so that they are no longer eligible for coverage under the employer's health plan. Only workers fired for gross misconduct are excluded from protection.

The worker has sixty days (beginning with the date that the group coverage would stop) to decide whether to continue with the employer's group insurance plan. If the worker chooses to discontinue the coverage, the employer has no further obligation. If the worker chooses to continue coverage, though, the employer is obligated to keep the policy active for up to eighteen months. If the worker is disabled, the employer must extend coverage for up to twenty-nine months. The coverage provided must be the same as that enjoyed by the worker prior to the termination or reduction of work. If family members were originally included, for example, COBRA prohibits their exclusion. To receive continued benefits, however, the worker may be required to pay all of the premiums, as well as a 2 percent administrative charge.

Employers, with some exceptions, must comply with COBRA if they employ twenty or more workers and provide a benefit plan to those workers. An employer must inform an employee of COBRA's provisions when that worker faces termination or a reduction of hours that would affect his or her eligibility for coverage under the plan. The employer need not provide benefit coverage if the employer eliminates its group benefit plan or if the worker becomes eligible for Medicare, becomes covered under a spouse's health plan, becomes insured under a different plan (with a new employer, for example), or fails to pay the premium. An employer that does not comply with COBRA risks substantial penalties, such as a tax of up to 10 percent of the annual cost of the group plan or $500,000, whichever is less.

"It is the job of the legislature to follow the spirit of the nation, provided it is not contrary to the principles of government."

CHARLES-LOUIS DE SECONDAT,
BARON DE MONTESQUIEU,
1689–1755
(French philosopher and jurist)

Family and Medical Leave

In 1993, Congress passed the Family and Medical Leave Act (FMLA)[26] to allow employees to take time off from work for family or medical reasons. A majority of the states also have legislation allowing for a leave from employment for family or medical reasons, and many employers maintain private family-leave plans for their workers.

.on the Web An excellent Web site for information on employee benefits—including the full text of relevant statutes, such as the FMLA and COBRA, as well as case law and current articles—is BenefitsLink.com. Go to **http://www.benefitslink.com/index.shtml**.

COVERAGE AND APPLICABILITY OF THE FMLA

The FMLA requires employers who have fifty or more employees to provide employees with up to twelve weeks of unpaid family or medical leave during any twelve-month period. Generally, an employee may take family leave to care for a newborn baby, an adopted child, or a foster child and take medical leave when the employee or the employee's spouse, child, or parent has a "serious health condition" requiring care.[27] The employer must continue the worker's health-care coverage and guarantee

25. 29 U.S.C. Sections 1161–1169.
26. 29 U.S.C. Sections 2601, 2611–2619, 2651–2654.
27. The foster care must be state sanctioned before such an arrangement falls within the coverage of the FMLA.

employment in the same position or a comparable position when the employee returns to work. An important exception to the FMLA, however, allows the employer to avoid reinstating a *key employee*—defined as an employee whose pay falls within the top 10 percent of the firm's workforce. Also, the act does not apply to part-time or newly hired employees (those who have worked for less than one year).

Employees suffering from certain chronic health conditions, such as asthma, diabetes, and pregnancy, may take FMLA leave for their own incapacities that require absences of less than three days. ■ EXAMPLE 40.6 Estel, an employee who has asthma, suffers from periodic episodes of illness. According to regulations issued by the Department of Labor, employees with such conditions are covered by the FMLA. Thus, Estel may take a medical leave. ■

The FMLA expressly covers private and public (government) employees. Nevertheless, some states argued that public employees could not sue their state employers in federal courts to enforce their FMLA rights unless the states consented to be sued.[28] This argument came before the United States Supreme Court in the following case.

28. Under the Eleventh Amendment to the U.S. Constitution, a state is immune from suit in a federal court unless the state agrees to be sued.

CASE 40.3 Nevada Department of Human Resources v. Hibbs

Supreme Court of the United States, 2003.
538 U.S. 721,
123 S.Ct. 1972,
155 L.Ed.2d 953.

BACKGROUND AND FACTS William Hibbs worked for the Nevada Department of Human Resources. In April 1997, Hibbs asked for time off under the FMLA to care for his sick wife, who was recovering from a car accident and neck surgery. The department granted Hibbs's request, allowing him to use the leave intermittently, as needed, beginning in May. Hibbs did this until August 5, after which he did not return to work. In October, the department told Hibbs that he had exhausted his FMLA leave, that no further leave would be granted, and that he must return to work by November 12. When he did not return, he was discharged. Hibbs filed a suit in a federal district court against the department. The court held that the Eleventh Amendment to the U.S. Constitution barred the suit. On Hibbs's appeal, the U.S. Court of Appeals for the Ninth Circuit reversed this holding. The department appealed to the United States Supreme Court.

IN THE WORDS OF THE COURT . . .

Chief Justice *REHNQUIST* delivered the opinion of the Court.

* * * *

[After the enactment of Title VII of the Civil Rights Act of 1964] state gender discrimination did not cease. * * * According to evidence that was before Congress when it enacted the FMLA, States continue[d] to rely on invalid gender stereotypes in the employment context, specifically in the administration of leave benefits. * * *

* * * *

Congress * * * heard testimony that "[p]arental leave for fathers * * * is rare. Even * * * [w]here child-care leave policies do exist, men, *both in the public and private sectors,* receive notoriously discriminatory treatment in their requests for such leave." Many States offered women extended "maternity" leave that far exceeded the typical 4- to 8-week period of physical disability due to pregnancy and childbirth, but very few States granted men a parallel benefit: Fifteen States provided women up to

(Continued)

CASE 40.3—Continued

one year of extended maternity leave, while only four provided men with the same. This and other differential leave policies were not attributable to any differential physical needs of men and women, but rather to the pervasive sex-role stereotype that caring for family members is women's work.

* * * *

* * * Because employers continued to regard the family as the woman's domain, they often denied men similar accommodations or discouraged them from taking leave. These mutually reinforcing stereotypes created a self-fulfilling cycle of discrimination that forced women to continue to assume the role of primary family caregiver, and fostered employers' stereotypical views about women's commitment to work and their value as employees. * * *

We believe that Congress's chosen remedy, the family-care leave provision of the FMLA, is congruent [corresponds to] and [is] proportional to the targeted violation. * * *

By creating an across-the-board, routine employment benefit for all eligible employees, Congress sought to ensure that family-care leave would no longer be stigmatized as an inordinate drain on the workplace caused by female employees, and that employers could not evade leave obligations simply by hiring men. By setting a minimum standard of family leave for *all* eligible employees, irrespective of gender, the FMLA attacks the formerly state-sanctioned stereotype that only women are responsible for family caregiving, thereby reducing employers' incentives to engage in discrimination by basing hiring and promotion decisions on stereotypes.

DECISION AND REMEDY The United States Supreme Court affirmed the lower court's decision, concluding that the FMLA corresponds to and is proportional to the discrimination that Congress intended the FMLA to address. Thus, the FMLA, which expressly covers public employees, can serve as the basis for a suit against a state employer regardless of whether the state consents to the suit.

FOR CRITICAL ANALYSIS—Cultural Consideration *How might a law foster discrimination even when the law is not obviously discriminatory?*

VIOLATIONS OF THE FMLA

An employer who violates the FMLA may be held liable for damages to compensate an employee for unpaid wages (or salary), lost benefits, denied compensation, and actual monetary losses (such as the cost of providing for care of the family member) up to an amount equivalent to the employee's wages for twelve weeks. Supervisors may also be subject to personal liability, as employers, for violations of the act.[29] A court may require the employer to reinstate the employee in her or his job or to grant a promotion that had been denied. A successful plaintiff is entitled to court costs; attorneys' fees; and, in cases involving bad faith on the part of the employer, double damages.

Regulations issued by the Department of Labor (DOL) impose additional sanctions on employers who fail to notify employees when an absence will be counted against leave authorized under the act. Under one such rule, if an employer failed to provide notice, then the employee's absence would not count as a portion of the leave time available under the FMLA. ■ **EXAMPLE 40.7** An employee had been absent

29. See, for example, *Rupnow v. TRC, Inc.*, 999 F.Supp. 1047 (N.D. Ohio 1998).

A boy leans against his pregnant mother's belly. The mother hopes to take time off from her full-time corporate job when the baby is born. What is required for the Family and Medical Leave Act (FMLA) to apply to her employer? If the employer is covered by the FMLA, how much family leave does the act authorize? (PhotoDisc)

"We are rapidly entering the age of no privacy, where everyone is open to surveillance at all times; where there are no secrets."
WILLIAM O. DOUGLAS, 1898–1980 (Associate justice of the United States Supreme Court, 1939–1975)

from work for thirty weeks while undergoing treatment for cancer. The employer had not designated any of the employee's time off as FMLA leave. Thus, under the DOL's regulation, the employee was entitled to an additional leave of twelve weeks. ■ In 2002, however, the United States Supreme Court invalidated this rule. The Court reasoned that it would be unjust for an employee to obtain additional protected leave as a windfall.[30]

Employee Privacy Rights

In the last twenty-five years, concerns about the privacy rights of employees have arisen in response to the sometimes invasive tactics used by employers to monitor and screen workers. Perhaps the greatest privacy concern in today's employment arena has to do with electronic performance monitoring. Clearly, employers need to protect themselves from liability for their employees' online activities. They also have a legitimate interest in monitoring the productivity of their workers. At the same time, employees expect to have a certain zone of privacy in the workplace. Indeed, many lawsuits have involved allegations that employers' intrusive monitoring practices violate employees' privacy rights.

ELECTRONIC MONITORING IN THE WORKPLACE

A variety of specially designed software products have made it easier for an employer to track employees' Internet use. Software now allows an employer to track virtually every move made by an employee using the Internet, including the specific Web sites visited and the time spent surfing the Web. Filtering software, which was discussed in Chapter 2, can also be used to prevent employees from accessing certain Web sites, such as sites containing pornographic or sexually explicit images. Other filtering software may be used to screen incoming e-mail for viruses and block junk mail (spam).

Although the use of filtering software by public employers (government agencies) has led to charges that blocking access to Web sites violates employees' rights to free speech, this issue does not arise in private businesses. This is because the First Amendment's protection of free speech applies only to *government* restraints on speech, and not normally to restraints imposed in the private sector.

Laws Protecting Employee Privacy Rights A number of laws protect privacy rights. We look here at laws that apply in the employment context.

Protection under Constitutional and Tort Law. Recall from Chapter 2 that the U.S. Constitution does not contain a provision that explicitly guarantees a right to privacy. A personal right to privacy, however, has been inferred from other constitutional guarantees provided by the First, Third, Fourth, Fifth, and Ninth Amendments to the Constitution. Tort law (see Chapter 4), state constitutions, and a number of state and federal statutes also provide for privacy rights.

The Electronic Communications Privacy Act. The major statute with which employers must comply is the Electronic Communications Privacy Act (ECPA) of 1986.[31] This act amended existing federal wiretapping law to cover electronic forms

30. *Ragsdale v. Wolverine World Wide, Inc.*, 535 U.S. 81, 122 S.Ct. 1155, 152 L.Ed.2d 167 (2002).
31. 18 U.S.C. Sections 2510–2521.

federal appellate court held that these reasons were likely just excuses and that the real reason was discriminatory intent.[4] ■

ETHICAL ISSUE 41.1

Are English-only policies in the workplace a form of national-origin discrimination? As the U.S. population becomes more multilingual, so does the workforce. In response to this development, many employers have instituted English-only policies in their workplaces, particularly in states with large immigrant populations, such as Texas and California. Are English-only policies fair to workers who do not speak English? Do they violate Title VII's prohibition against discrimination on the basis of race or national origin, as workers in a number of lawsuits have alleged? Generally, the courts have shown a fair degree of tolerance with respect to English-only rules, especially when an employer can show that there is a legitimate business reason for the rules, such as improved communication among employees or worker safety. Some courts, however, tend to regard with suspicion policies that require that English be spoken not only during work time but also on breaks, lunch hours, and the like. For example, one federal district court held that a Texas firm had engaged in disparate-treatment discrimination based on national origin by requiring that English be spoken exclusively in the workplace, including during breaks, except when employees were communicating with customers who could not speak English.[5] ■

Discrimination Based on Religion

Title VII of the Civil Rights Act of 1964 also prohibits government employers, private employers, and unions from discriminating against persons because of their religion. An employer must "reasonably accommodate" the religious practices of its employees, unless to do so would cause undue hardship to the employer's business. For example, if an employee's religion prohibits him or her from working on a certain day of the week or at a certain type of job, the employer must make a reasonable attempt to accommodate these religious requirements. Employers must reasonably accommodate an employee's religious belief even if the belief is not based on the tenets or dogma of a particular church, sect, or denomination. The only requirement is that the belief be sincerely held by the employee.[6]

"A sign that says 'men only' looks very different on a bathroom door than a courthouse door."

THURGOOD MARSHALL, 1908–1993
(Associate justice of the United States Supreme Court, 1967–1991)

Discrimination Based on Gender

Under Title VII, as well as other federal acts, employers are forbidden to discriminate against employees on the basis of gender. Employers are prohibited from classifying jobs as male or female and from advertising in help-wanted columns that are designated male or female unless the employer can prove that the gender of the applicant is essential to the job. Furthermore, employers cannot have separate male and female seniority lists. Generally, to succeed in a suit for gender discrimination, a plaintiff must demonstrate that gender was a determining factor in the employer's decision to hire, fire, or promote her or him. Typically, this involves looking at all of the surrounding circumstances.

---

4. *McCullough v. Real Foods, Inc.,* 140 F.3d 1123 (8th Cir. 1998). The federal district court had granted summary judgment for the employer in this case. The Eighth Circuit Court of Appeals reversed the district court's decision and remanded the case for trial.
5. *EEOC v. Premier Operator Services, Inc.,* 113 F.Supp.2d 1066 (N.D.Tex. 2000).
6. *Frazee v. Illinois Department of Employment Security,* 489 U.S. 829, 109 S.Ct. 1514, 103 L.Ed.2d 914 (1989).

The Pregnancy Discrimination Act of 1978,[7] which amended Title VII, expanded the definition of gender discrimination to include discrimination based on pregnancy. Women affected by pregnancy, childbirth, or related medical conditions must be treated—for all employment-related purposes, including the receipt of benefits under employee benefit programs—the same as other persons not so affected but similar in ability to work.

Sometimes employees claim that they were "constructively discharged" from their jobs. **Constructive discharge** occurs when the employer causes the employee's working conditions to be so intolerable that a reasonable person in the employee's position would feel compelled to quit. Title VII encompasses employer liability for constructive discharge.[8] In the case that follows, the question was whether the employer should have been aware of the employee's mistreatment and unbearable working conditions and done something about them.

CONSTRUCTIVE DISCHARGE
A termination of employment brought about by making the employee's working conditions so intolerable that the employee reasonably feels compelled to leave.

7. 42 U.S.C. Section 2000e(k).
8. *Pennsylvania State Police v. Suders,* 542 U.S. 129, 124 S.Ct. 2342, 159 L.Ed.2d 204 (2004).

CASE 41.1 Conway-Jepsen v. Small Business Administration

United States District Court,
District of Montana, 2004.
303 F.Supp.2d 1155.

BACKGROUND AND FACTS In August 1992, Jo Alice Mospan took charge of the Helena, Montana, office of the U.S. Small Business Administration (SBA) as the district director. At the time, there were no other females above a certain pay level in the Helena office, and most of the senior employees and supervisors were male. Mospan was an "in-your-face" micromanager, frequently disciplining employees. In Helena, her purportedly express purpose was to harass and ultimately rid the office of certain male employees so that they could be replaced by females. In 1993, Mospan recruited Mary Conway-Jepsen from the SBA office in Santa Ana, California. Conway-Jepsen soon learned what Mospan was doing, told her that it was wrong, and refused to cooperate. Mospan retaliated. Among other things, she overloaded Conway-Jepsen with irrelevant assignments, took counterproductive actions to her projects, and set her up to make mistakes. Conway-Jepsen's physician recommended that she quit her job. She applied for a transfer, but when none was forthcoming, she resigned in August 1997. By 2000, all of the targeted males were also gone. Conway-Jepsen filed a suit in a federal district court against the SBA, claiming a violation of Title VII.

IN THE WORDS OF THE COURT . . .
LOVELL, Senior District Judge.

* * * *

Title VII prohibits an employer from discriminating against any employee because he or she has opposed * * * *an unlawful employment practice* * * * . In order to prove retaliation, Plaintiff must show that (1) she opposed an unlawful employment practice, (2) she suffered an adverse employment action, and (3) a causal connection existed between the adverse employment action and the protected activity or opposition. * * * [Emphasis added.]

Among the unlawful employment practices forbidden by Title VII is the rule that *employers must not* * * * *discharge any individual, or otherwise* * * * *discriminate against any individual with respect to his compensation, terms, conditions, or privileges of employment, because of such individual's race, color, religion, sex, or national origin.* * * * [Emphasis added.]

(Continued)

CASE 41.1—Continued

* * * *

In order to meet her burden of proving that she was constructively discharged, Plaintiff must show that a reasonable person in her position would have felt compelled to resign because of intolerable working conditions. * * *

In addition, Plaintiff must show that the intolerable working conditions were created by the very conduct that constituted a violation of Title VII (in this case, e.g., the retaliation) and that her resignation resulted from the intolerable working conditions.

* * * *

At all pertinent times herein, Mospan was the duly appointed and acting agent and [district director] of Helena SBA, acting within the scope and course of her authority and employment so to act, and Defendant is answerable for actionable wrongs committed by [its] agent Mospan against Plaintiff in violation of Title VII. Defendant knew or should have known of the hostile working conditions at Helena SBA, yet failed to prevent or remedy these conditions.

* * * [T]he Court concludes that Plaintiff reasonably found her hostile working conditions intolerable, that the intolerable working conditions were created by conduct that constituted a violation of Title VII, and that Plaintiff's resignation resulted from the hostile and intolerable working conditions. The Court concludes that Plaintiff was a diligent and competent SBA employee who was constructively discharged from her position by Mospan's lengthy, continuous, and pervasive pattern of retaliatory treatment for the reason that she had objected to employment practices which were unlawful under Title VII.

* * * *

* * * Plaintiff believes that Mospan ruined her career, and the Court views this belief as justifiable under all the circumstances. * * * The Court finds that Mospan continued to retaliate against Plaintiff after Plaintiff's resignation by interfering with Plaintiff's ability to obtain [further] work in Montana. * * *

DECISION AND REMEDY The court concluded that Conway-Jepsen was constructively discharged in violation of Title VII. The hostile working conditions at the Helena SBA office were created by conduct in violation of Title VII, Conway-Jepsen reasonably found the conditions intolerable, and her resignation resulted from these conditions. On her behalf, the court awarded back pay, job reinstatement, compensatory damages, and attorneys' fees.

WHY IS THIS CASE IMPORTANT? *Employers should be aware that if a manager or supervisor creates intolerable working conditions because of his or her own personal bias, the employer could be held liable under Title VII.*

Sexual Harassment

SEXUAL HARASSMENT
In the employment context, the demanding of sexual favors in return for job promotions or other benefits, or language or conduct that is so sexually offensive that it creates a hostile working environment.

Title VII also protects employees against **sexual harassment** in the workplace. Sexual harassment has often been classified as either *quid pro quo* harassment or hostile-environment harassment. *Quid pro quo* harassment[9] occurs when sexual favors are demanded in return for job opportunities, promotions, salary increases, and the like. According to the United States Supreme Court, hostile-environment harassment occurs when "the workplace is permeated with discriminatory intimi-

9. *Quid pro quo* is a Latin phrase that is often translated to mean "something in exchange for something else."

"Justice is better than chivalry if we cannot have both."

ALICE STONE BLACKWELL, 1857–1950 (American suffragist and editor)

dation, ridicule, and insult, that is sufficiently severe or pervasive to alter the conditions of the victim's employment and create an abusive working environment."[10]

Generally, the courts apply this Supreme Court guideline on a case-by-case basis. Some courts have held that just one incident of sexually offensive conduct—such as a sexist remark by a co-worker or a photo on an employer's desk of his bikini-clad wife—can create a hostile environment.[11] According to some employment specialists, employers should assume that hostile-environment harassment has occurred if an employee claims that it has.

Harassment by Supervisors What if an employee is harassed by a manager or supervisor of a large firm, and the firm itself (the "employer") is not aware of the harassment? Should the employer be held liable for the harassment nonetheless? For some time, the courts were in disagreement on this issue. Typically, employers were held liable for Title VII violations by the firm's managerial or supervisory personnel in *quid pro quo* harassment cases regardless of whether the employer knew about the harassment. In hostile-environment cases, the majority of courts tended to hold employers liable only if the employer knew or should have known of the harassment and failed to take prompt remedial action.

Tangible Employment Action. For an employer to be held liable for a supervisor's sexual harassment, the supervisor must have taken a tangible employment action against the employee. A *tangible employment action* is a significant change in employment status, such as firing or failing to promote an employee, reassigning the employee to a position with significantly different responsibilities, or effecting a significant change in employment benefits.

Only a supervisor, or another person acting with the authority of the employer, can cause this sort of injury. A co-worker can sexually harass another employee, and anyone who has regular contact with an employee can inflict psychological injuries by offensive conduct. A co-worker cannot dock another's pay, demote her or him, or set conditions for continued employment, though.

■ EXAMPLE 41.3 Jin was a sales agent at Metropolitan Life Insurance Company (MetLife). Morabito was Jin's supervisor. Morabito made sexual remarks to Jin, offensively touched her, and forced her to engage in sexual acts by threatening to fire her and physically harm her if she did not submit to his demands. When Jin sued MetLife for sexual harassment, the jury found that she was not subjected to a tangible employment action. A federal appellate court reversed, however. The court reasoned that Morabito had used his authority as a supervisor to impose on Jin the added job requirement that she submit to sexual abuse to keep her job.[12] ■

Supreme Court Guidelines. In 1998, in two separate cases, the United States Supreme Court issued some significant guidelines relating to the liability of employers for their supervisors' harassment of employees in the workplace. In *Faragher v. City of Boca Raton,*[13] the Court held that an employer (a city) could be held liable for a supervisor's harassment of employees even though the employer was unaware

---

10. *Harris v. Forklift Systems,* 510 U.S. 17, 114 S.Ct. 367, 126 L.Ed.2d 295 (1993).

11. For other examples, see *Radtke v. Everett,* 442 Mich. 368, 501 N.W.2d 155 (1993); and *Nadeau v. Rainbow Rugs, Inc.,* 675 A.2d 973 (Me. 1996).

12. *Jin v. Metropolitan Life Insurance Co.,* 295 F.3d 335 (2d Cir. 2002), republished at 310 F.3d 84 (2d Cir. 2002).

13. 524 U.S. 775, 118 S.Ct. 2275, 141 L.Ed.2d 662 (1998).

of the behavior. The Court reached this conclusion primarily because, although the city had a written policy against sexual harassment, the policy had not been distributed to city employees. Additionally, the city had not established any procedures that could be followed by employees who felt that they were victims of sexual harassment. In *Burlington Industries, Inc. v. Ellerth,*[14] the Court ruled that a company could be held liable for the harassment of an employee by one of its vice presidents even though the employee suffered no adverse job consequences.

In these two cases, the Court set forth some guidelines on workplace harassment that are helpful to employers and employees alike. On the one hand, employees benefit by the ruling that employers may be held liable for their supervisors' harassment even though the employers were unaware of the actions and even though the employees suffered no adverse job consequences. On the other hand, the Court made it clear in both decisions that employers have an affirmative defense against liability for their supervisors' harassment of employees if the employers can show the following:

1. That they have taken "reasonable care to prevent and correct promptly any sexually harassing behavior" (by establishing effective harassment policies and complaint procedures, for example).
2. That the employees suing for harassment failed to follow these policies and procedures.

.on the Web The New York State Governor's Office of Employee Relations maintains an interactive site on sexual harassment and how to prevent sexual harassment in the workplace. Go to

http://www.goer.state.ny.us/Train/onlinelearning/SH/intro.html.

Harassment by Co-Workers and Nonemployees Often, employees alleging harassment complain that the actions of co-workers, not supervisors, are responsible for creating a hostile working environment. In such cases, the employee may still have a cause of action against the employer. Normally, though, the employer will be held liable only if the employer knew, or should have known, about the harassment and failed to take immediate remedial action. (For a further discussion of the importance of taking immediate and *effective* remedial action in response to complaints of sexual harassment, see this chapter's *Management Perspective* feature.)

Employers may also be liable for harassment by *nonemployees* in certain circumstances. ■ **EXAMPLE 41.4** If a restaurant owner or manager knows that a certain customer repeatedly harasses a waitress and permits the harassment to continue, the restaurant owner may be liable under Title VII even though the customer is not an employee of the restaurant. The issue turns on the control that the employer exerts over a nonemployee. In one case, an owner of a Pizza Hut franchise was held liable for the harassment of a waitress by two male customers because no steps were taken to prevent the harassment.[15] ■

Same-Gender Harassment The courts have also had to address the issue of whether men who are harassed by other men, or women who are harassed by other women, are protected by laws that prohibit gender-based discrimination in the workplace. For example, what if the male president of a firm demands sexual favors from a male employee? Does this action qualify as sexual harassment? For some time, the courts were widely split on this issue. In 1998, in *Oncale v. Sundowner Offshore Services, Inc.,*[16] the Supreme Court resolved the issue by holding that Title VII protection extends to situations in which individuals are harassed by members of the same gender.

14. 524 U.S. 742, 118 S.Ct. 2257, 141 L.Ed.2d 633 (1998).
15. *Lockard v. Pizza Hut, Inc.,* 162 F.3d 1062 (10th Cir. 1998).
16. 523 U.S. 75, 118 S.Ct. 998, 140 L.Ed.2d 207 (1998).

MANAGEMENT PERSPECTIVE

Responding to Sexual Harassment in the Workplace

MANAGEMENT FACES A LEGAL ISSUE

As discussed elsewhere in this chapter, in two cases decided in 1998, the United States Supreme Court issued guidelines concerning the liability of employers for their supervisors' harassment of employees in the workplace. Generally, these guidelines allow employers to avoid liability if they take reasonable steps to prevent sexual harassment in the workplace and take prompt remedial action to correct sexually harassing behavior. Although these cases involved harassment of workers by supervisors, the principles expressed in the rulings have also been applied to harassment by co-workers. One question remains, though: When an employee complains of an incident of sexual harassment, what steps must the employer take to satisfy the requirement of "prompt remedial action"? The answer to this question has important implications for today's business owners and managers.

WHAT THE COURTS SAY

Generally, when it can be shown that a worker was sexually harassed (by either a supervisor *or* a co-worker), management must make sure that whatever action it takes will effectively prevent similar incidents of harassment in the future. Consider the outcome of two cases dealing with just this issue. One case, decided by the Supreme Court of Hawaii, involved a plaintiff—a female worker in a restaurant—who had experienced a short, isolated instance of unwanted contact from a male co-worker (the co-worker had squeezed her buttock for approximately one second). She asked him to stop and then asked a manager, who had witnessed the incident, to ask the co-worker to not do it again. The manager did so immediately. A few weeks later, the co-worker again squeezed the plaintiff's buttock for a second or so. Management immediately suspended the co-worker and terminated him shortly thereafter. The trial court granted the employer's motion for summary judgment, concluding that the manager's response was sufficient to avoid liability. The Hawaii Supreme Court, however, reversed the trial court's decision and remanded the case for trial. The state supreme court held that reasonable minds could differ as to whether the manager's response was reasonably calculated to end the harassment. The court noted that the co-worker was given only an oral warning, which, the manager later admitted to the plaintiff, the co-worker did not take seriously. Second, the co-worker was not threatened with a future written reprimand, nor was he informed that he could be suspended or terminated if his behavior continued (even though he was, in fact, later terminated, when the harassment continued).[a]

In the other case, the plaintiff, Jamie McCurdy, worked as a radio dispatcher for the Arkansas State Police. After a police sergeant allegedly groped her breast, touched her hair, and made suggestive sexual comments to her, she immediately reported the incident to her supervisor. Shortly thereafter, supervisory officers investigated the incident and ultimately demoted the sergeant and transferred him to a different location. In this case, a federal appellate court concluded that these actions were sufficient to justify the lower court's grant of summary judgment for the employer.[b]

IMPLICATIONS FOR MANAGERS

These cases both illustrate that a key factor in a court's determination of employer liability for harassment in the workplace is the *effectiveness* of the response. Is the employer's response effective in the sense that it will help to prevent incidents of harassment? To avoid liability, managers would be wise to give more than just oral warnings to offending employees and to take definite preventive steps. These steps range from removing the offending supervisor or co-worker from a complainant's work area to terminating the offender.

a. *Arquero v. Hilton Hawaiian Village, L.L.C.*, 104 Hawaii 423, 91 P.3d 505 (2004).

b. *McCurdy v. Arkansas State Police*, 375 F.3d 762 (8th Cir. 2004).

Nevertheless, it can be difficult to prove that the harassment in same-gender harassment cases is "based on sex." ■ EXAMPLE 41.5 Suppose that a gay man is harassed by another man at the workplace. The harasser is not a homosexual and does not treat all men with hostility—just this one man. Does the victim in this situation have a cause of action under Title VII? A court may find that this does not qualify as sexual harassment under Title VII because the harasser's conduct was because of the employee's sexual orientation, not "because of sex."[17] ■

ONLINE HARASSMENT

Employees' online activities can create a hostile working environment in many ways. Racial jokes, ethnic slurs, or other comments contained in e-mail may become the basis for a claim of hostile-environment harassment or other forms of discrimination. A worker who sees sexually explicit images on a co-worker's computer screen may find the images offensive and claim that they create a hostile working environment.

Avoiding Liability through Prompt Remedial Action Generally, employers may be able to avoid liability for online harassment if they take prompt remedial action. ■ EXAMPLE 41.6 In *Daniels v. WorldCom, Inc.*,[18] Angela Daniels, an employee of Robert Half International under contract to WorldCom, Inc., received racially harassing e-mailed jokes from another employee. After receiving the jokes, Daniels complained to WorldCom managers. Shortly afterward, the company issued a warning to the offending employee about the proper use of the e-mail system and held two meetings to discuss company policy on the use of the system. In Daniels's suit against WorldCom for racial discrimination, a federal district court concluded that the employer was not liable for its employee's racially harassing e-mails because the employer took prompt remedial action. ■

An Ongoing Challenge Employers who have taken steps to avoid online harassment in the workplace continue to face challenging problems. Clearly, if they do not take effective steps to curb such harassment, they may face liability for violating Title VII. At the same time, if they monitor their employees' communications, they may face liability under other laws—for invading their employees' privacy, for instance.

Additionally, an employee who is fired for misusing the employer's computer system to, say, e-mail pornographic images to co-workers or others may claim that he or she was wrongfully discharged. Finally, there are constitutional rights to be considered. In one case, a court held that religious speech that unintentionally creates a hostile environment is constitutionally protected.[19]

REMEDIES UNDER TITLE VII

Employer liability under Title VII may be extensive. If the plaintiff successfully proves that unlawful discrimination occurred, he or she may be awarded reinstatement, back pay, retroactive promotions, and damages. Compensatory damages are available only in cases of intentional discrimination. Punitive damages may be

---

17. See, for example, *McCown v. St. John's Health System*, 349 F.3d 540 (8th Cir. 2003); and *Rene v. MGM Grand Hotel, Inc.*, 305 F.3d 1061 (9th Cir. 2002).
18. 1998 WL 91261 (N.D.Tex. 1998).
19. *Meltebeke v. B.O.L.I.*, 903 P.2d 351 (Or. 1995).

recovered against a private employer only if the employer acted with malice or reckless indifference to an individual's rights. The statute limits the total amount of compensatory and punitive damages that the plaintiff can recover from specific employers—ranging from $50,000 against employers with one hundred or fewer employees to $300,000 against employers with more than five hundred employees.

on the Web The Illinois state bar site provides information on remedies for employment discrimination at **http://www.illinoisbar.org/LawEd/johnston.htm**.

Equal Pay Act of 1963

The Equal Pay Act of 1963 was enacted as an amendment to the Fair Labor Standards Act of 1938. Basically, the act prohibits gender-based discrimination in the wages paid for similar work on jobs that require the same amount of skill, effort, and responsibility. For the act's equal pay requirements to apply, the male and female employees must work at the same establishment.

A person alleging wage discrimination in violation of the Equal Pay Act may sue her or his employer. To determine whether the Equal Pay Act has been violated, a court will look to the primary duties of the two jobs. It is job content rather than job description that controls in all cases. The jobs of a barber and a beautician, for example, are considered essentially "equal." So, too, are those of a tailor and a seamstress. Nevertheless, an employer will *not* be found liable for violating the act if it can show that the wage differential for equal work was based on (1) a seniority system, (2) a merit system, (3) a system that pays according to quality or quantity of production, or (4) any factor other than gender. Small differences in job content, however, do not justify higher pay for one gender. The Equal Pay Act is administered by the EEOC.

Discrimination Based on Age

Age discrimination is potentially the most widespread form of discrimination, because anyone—regardless of race, color, national origin, or gender—could be a victim at some point in life. The Age Discrimination in Employment Act (ADEA) of 1967, as amended, prohibits employment discrimination on the basis of age against individuals forty years of age or older. The act also prohibits mandatory retirement for nonmanagerial workers. For the act to apply, an employer must have twenty or more employees, and the employer's business activities must affect interstate commerce. The EEOC administers the ADEA, but the act also permits private causes of action against employers for age discrimination.

PROCEDURES UNDER THE ADEA

REMEMBER The Fourteenth Amendment prohibits any state from denying to any person "the equal protection of the laws." This prohibition applies to the *federal* government through the due process clause of the Fifth Amendment.

The burden-shifting procedure under the ADEA is similar to that under Title VII. If a plaintiff can establish that she or he (1) was a member of the protected age group, (2) was qualified for the position from which she or he was discharged, and (3) was discharged under circumstances that give rise to an inference of discrimination, the plaintiff has established a *prima facie* case of unlawful age discrimination. The burden then shifts to the employer, who must articulate a legitimate reason for the discrimination. If the plaintiff can prove that the employer's reason is only a pretext (excuse) and that the plaintiff's age was a determining factor in the employer's decision, the employer will be held liable under the ADEA.

CASE 42.2—Continued

DECISION AND REMEDY The Supreme Court of New Jersey affirmed the judgment of the lower court. A new trial was ordered because the jury had been given erroneous instructions in the applicable law. The law in New Jersey (and other states) provides that to recover in a legal malpractice case, a plaintiff needs to show only that the lawyer's negligence was a substantial factor in causing the harm.

FOR CRITICAL ANALYSIS—Social Consideration *Should lawyers be subject to higher legal and ethical standards than other professionals?*

Professionals' Liability for Fraud

Actual fraud and constructive fraud present two different circumstances under which an accountant may be found liable. Recall from Chapter 12 that fraud, or misrepresentation, consists of the following elements:

1. A misrepresentation of a material fact has occurred.
2. There exists an intent to deceive.
3. The innocent party has justifiably relied on the misrepresentation.
4. For damages, the innocent party must have been injured.

A professional may be held liable for *actual fraud* when he or she intentionally misstates a material fact to mislead his or her client and the client justifiably relies on the misstated fact to his or her injury. A material fact is one that a reasonable person would consider important in deciding whether to act. In contrast, a professional may be held liable for *constructive fraud* whether or not he or she acted with fraudulent intent. ■ EXAMPLE 42.2 In conducting an audit of National Computing Company (NCC), Paula, the auditor, accepts the explanations of Ron, an NCC officer, regarding certain financial irregularities, despite evidence that contradicts those explanations and indicates that the irregularities may be illegal. Paula's conduct could be characterized as an intentional failure to perform a duty in reckless disregard of the consequences of such a failure. This would constitute gross negligence and could be held to be constructive fraud. ■ Both actual and constructive fraud are potential sources of legal liability under which a client can bring an action against an accountant or other professional.

Auditors' Liability to Third Parties

Traditionally, an accountant or other professional did not owe any duty to a third person with whom he or she had no direct contractual relationship—that is, to any person not in *privity of contract* with the professional. A professional's duty was only to his or her client. Violations of statutory laws, fraud, and other intentional or reckless acts of wrongdoing were the only exceptions to this general rule.

Today, numerous third parties—including investors, shareholders, creditors, corporate managers and directors, regulatory agencies, and others—rely on professional opinions, such as those of auditors, when making decisions. In view of this extensive reliance, many courts have all but abandoned the privity requirement in regard to accountants' liability to third parties.

In this section, we focus primarily on the potential liability of auditors to third parties. Understanding an auditor's common law liability to third parties is critical, because often, when a business fails, its independent auditor (accountant) may be one of the few potentially solvent defendants. The majority of courts now hold that auditors can be held liable to third parties for negligence, but the standard for the imposition of this liability varies. There are generally three different views of accountants' liability to third parties, each of which we discuss below.

THE *ULTRAMARES* RULE

The traditional rule regarding an accountant's liability to third parties was enunciated by Chief Judge Benjamin Cardozo in *Ultramares Corp. v. Touche,* a case decided in 1931.[2] In *Ultramares,* Fred Stern & Company (Stern) hired the public accounting firm of Touche, Niven & Company (Touche) to review Stern's financial records and prepare a balance sheet for the year ending December 31, 1923.[3] Touche prepared the balance sheet and supplied Stern with thirty-two certified copies. According to the certified balance sheet, Stern had a net worth (assets less liabilities) of $1,070,715.26. In reality, however, Stern was insolvent—the company's records had been falsified by Stern's insiders to reflect a positive net worth. In reliance on the certified balance sheets, a lender, Ultramares Corporation, loaned substantial amounts to Stern. After Stern was declared bankrupt, Ultramares brought an action against Touche for negligence in an attempt to recover damages.

The New York Court of Appeals (that state's highest court) refused to impose liability on the accountants and concluded that they owed a duty of care only to those persons for whose "primary benefit" the statements were intended. In this case, Stern was the only person for whose primary benefit the statements were intended. The court held that in the absence of privity or a relationship "so close as to approach that of privity," a party could not recover from an accountant.

The court's requirement of privity or near privity has since been referred to as the *Ultramares* rule, or the New York rule. The rule was restated and somewhat modified in a 1985 New York case, *Credit Alliance Corp. v. Arthur Andersen & Co.*[4] In that case, the court held that if a third party has a sufficiently close relationship or nexus (link or connection) with an accountant, then the *Ultramares* privity requirement may be satisfied even if no accountant-client relationship is established. The rule enunciated in *Credit Alliance* is often referred to as the "near privity" rule. Only a minority of states have adopted this rule of accountants' liability to third parties.

Under this rule, does an accountant who is aware that a nonclient might rely on the accountant's work owe the nonclient a duty of care, when preparing reports on that party's financial status for his or her manager? Does the accountant have a duty to advise the nonclient on other financial transactions? These were the questions in the following case.

---

2. 255 N.Y. 170, 174 N.E. 441 (1931).
3. A balance sheet is often relied on by banks, creditors, stockholders, purchasers, or sellers as a basis for making decisions relating to a company's business.
4. 65 N.Y.2d 536, 483 N.E.2d 110 (1985): A "relationship sufficiently intimate to be equated with privity" is sufficient for a third party to sue another's accountant for negligence.

CASE 42.3 Reznor v. J. Artist Management, Inc.

United States District Court,
Southern District of New York, 2005.
365 F.Supp.2d 565.

BACKGROUND AND FACTS Michael Trent Reznor met John Malm, Jr., a part-time promoter of local rock bands, in Cleveland, Ohio, in 1985. Malm became Reznor's manager and formed J. Artist Management, Inc. (JAM). Reznor became the lead singer in the band Nine Inch Nails (NIN), which performed its first show in 1988. Reznor and Malm signed a management agreement, under which JAM was to receive 20 percent of Reznor's gross compensation. Over the next few years, Reznor and Malm created other companies to sell NIN's merchandise

(Continued)

CASE 42.3—Continued

and perform various services. In 1996, Malm hired accountant Richard Szekelyi and his firm, Navigent Group, to provide financial consulting services to JAM and the jointly owned companies. Szekelyi did not provide services to Reznor personally, but his duties included examining Reznor's financial records. Szekelyi discovered that the accounting among the parties was flawed, with Malm, for example, receiving tax benefits that should have gone to Reznor. According to Szekelyi, by 2003, Reznor owed JAM $1.56 million, and the jointly owned companies owed Reznor $5.5 million, which (as later became clear) was unlikely to be repaid. Reznor fired Malm and filed a suit in a federal district court against JAM and others, including Szekelyi and Navigent.

IN THE WORDS OF THE COURT . . .
JED S. RAKOFF, U.S.D.J. [United States District Judge]

* * * *

* * * [C]o-defendants Szekelyi and Navigent Group (hereinafter, collectively "Szekelyi") seek summary judgment on Reznor's claims against them of negligence, breach of fiduciary duty, and malpractice. There is little distinction between these claims, all of which allege that Szekelyi did not meet the standards of the accounting profession in the performance of professional duties to Reznor.

Since Reznor was not Szekelyi's client, Szekelyi would be liable to Reznor for malpractice only where he was aware that the nonclient would rely on his work for a particular purpose. Szekelyi's presentations to Reznor in 2002 and 2003 meet this standard, and so Szekelyi is liable for any malpractice he may have committed in preparing and presenting these reports of Reznor's financial status. However, there is no evidence that Szekelyi breached any standard of care in preparing and presenting these reports. Reznor does not allege any inaccuracies in these reports; rather, after establishing that Szekelyi owed a duty of care with respect to these reports, he argues that Szekelyi failed to counsel Reznor adequately concerning certain other transactions. Because Szekelyi was not Reznor's accountant or business manager, he owed Reznor in his individual capacity no such duty with respect to other transactions. [Emphasis added.]

* * * Szekelyi (and Navigent) also move for summary judgment with respect to Reznor's claims against them alleging fraud and aiding and abetting fraud. *An accountant can be liable to a nonclient for fraud if he has knowledge of the falsity of his client's statements or acts in reckless disregard of such falsity where the circumstances should cast doubt on the information's veracity [truth] and where the accountant is aware of the plaintiff's reasonable reliance on him.* Here, Reznor alleges that Szekelyi assisted Malm in secretly and illegally diverting Reznor's money into the jointly held companies. However, there is no evidence that, even if Malm were defrauding Reznor by misleading him as to which accounts the loans were coming from, Szekelyi knew or should have known of any impropriety. Indeed, there is no evidence that Szekelyi did anything but attempt to correct the only clearly flawed accounting in evidence, *i.e.,* the improper tax treatment * * * . Accordingly, summary judgment must be granted on the fraud claims, which also means that, given the above-described grant of summary judgment on the other claims against Szekelyi and Navigent, summary judgment is granted as to *all* counts against Szekelyi and Navigent Group. [Emphasis added.]

DECISION AND REMEDY The court granted the motion of Szekelyi and Navigent for summary judgment, and dismissed them from the case. Szekelyi did not breach any standard of care in preparing and presenting reports of Reznor's financial status, nor did he fail to counsel Reznor adequately concerning other transactions.

CASE 42.3—Continued

"Because Szekelyi was not Reznor's accountant or business manager, he owed Reznor in his individual capacity no such duty."

WHY IS THIS CASE IMPORTANT? *The circumstances here give support to the warning that a person should take steps to become aware of the legal consequences of her or his agreements. The rock star at the center of this case might have avoided the negative impact of the result if he had sought the advice of an attorney before entering into the contract at issue.*

THE *RESTATEMENT* RULE

In the past several years, the *Ultramares* rule has been severely criticized. Auditors perform much of their work for use by persons who are not parties to the contract. Thus, it is asserted that they owe a duty to these third parties. Consequently, there has been an erosion of the *Ultramares* rule, and accountants have been exposed to potential liability to third parties.

The majority of courts have adopted the position taken by the *Restatement (Second) of Torts,* which states that accountants are subject to liability for negligence not only to their clients but also to *foreseen,* or *known,* users—or classes of users—of their reports or financial statements. Under Section 552(2) of the *Restatement (Second) of Torts,* an accountant's liability extends to those persons for whose benefit and guidance the accountant "intends to supply the information or knows that the recipient intends to supply it" and to those persons whom the accountant "intends the information to influence or knows that the recipient so intends." ■ EXAMPLE 42.3 Steve, an accountant, prepares a financial statement for Tech Software, Inc., a client, knowing that the client will submit that statement to First National Bank to secure a loan. If Steve makes negligent misstatements or omissions in the statement, he may be held liable by the bank because he knew that the bank would rely on his work product when deciding whether to make the loan. ■

LIABILITY TO REASONABLY FORESEEABLE USERS

A small minority of courts hold accountants liable to any users whose reliance on an accountant's statements or reports was *reasonably foreseeable.* This standard has been criticized as extending liability too far. ■ EXAMPLE 42.4 In *Raritan River Steel Co. v. Cherry, Bekaert & Holland,* the North Carolina Supreme Court stated that "in fairness accountants should not be liable in circumstances where they are unaware of the use to which their opinions will be put. Instead, their liability should be commensurate with those persons or classes of persons whom they know will rely on their work. With such knowledge the auditor can, through purchase of liability insurance, setting fees, and adopting other protective measures appropriate to the risk, prepare accordingly."[5] ■

It is the view of the majority of the courts that the *Restatement*'s approach is the more reasonable one because it allows accountants to control their exposure to liability. Liability is "fixed by the accountants' particular knowledge at the moment the audit is published," not by the foreseeability of the harm that might occur to a third party after the report is released.[6]

---

5. 322 N.C. 200, 367 S.E.2d 609 (1988).
6. *Bethlehem Steel Corp. v. Ernst & Whinney,* 822 S.W.2d 592 (1991).

Even the California courts, which for several years relied on reasonable foreseeability as the standard for determining an auditor's liability to third parties, have changed their position. In a 1992 case, the California Supreme Court held that an accountant "owes no general duty of care regarding the conduct of an audit to persons other than the client." The court went on to say that if third parties rely on an auditor's opinion, "there is no liability even though the [auditor] should reasonably have foreseen such a possibility."[7]

LIABILITY OF ATTORNEYS TO THIRD PARTIES

Like accountants, attorneys may be held liable under the common law to third parties who rely on legal opinions to their detriment. Generally, an attorney is not liable to a nonclient unless there is fraud (or malicious conduct) by the attorney. The liability principles stated in Section 552 of the *Restatement (Second) of Torts,* however, may apply to attorneys just as they may apply to accountants.

The Sarbanes-Oxley Act of 2002

As previously mentioned, in 2002 Congress enacted the Sarbanes-Oxley Act, which became effective on August 29, 2002. The act imposes a number of strict requirements on both domestic and foreign public accounting firms that provide auditing services to companies ("issuers") whose securities are sold to public investors. The act defines the term *issuer* as a company that has securities that are registered under Section 12 of the Securities Exchange Act of 1934; that is required to file reports under Section 15(d) of the 1934 act; or that files—or has filed—a registration statement that has not yet become effective under the Securities Act of 1933.

THE PUBLIC COMPANY ACCOUNTING OVERSIGHT BOARD

Among other things, the Sarbanes-Oxley Act calls for an increased degree of government oversight over public accounting practices. To this end, the act created the Public Company Accounting Oversight Board, which reports to the Securities and Exchange Commission. The board consists of a chair and four other members. The purpose of the board is to oversee the audit of public companies that are subject to securities laws in order to protect public investors and to ensure that public accounting firms comply with the provisions of the Sarbanes-Oxley Act.

APPLICABILITY TO PUBLIC ACCOUNTING FIRMS

Titles I and II of the act set forth the key provisions relating to the duties of the new oversight board and the requirements relating to public accounting firms—defined by the act as firms and associated persons that are "engaged in the practice of public accounting or preparing or issuing audit reports." These provisions are summarized in Exhibit 42–1. (Provisions of the act that are more directly concerned with corporate fraud and the responsibilities of corporate officers and directors were described in Chapter 35.)

WORKING PAPERS
The various documents used and developed by an accountant during an audit. Working papers include notes, computations, memoranda, copies, and other papers that make up the work product of an accountant's services to a client.

REQUIREMENTS FOR MAINTAINING WORKING PAPERS

Performing an audit for a client involves an accumulation of **working papers**—the various documents used and developed during the audit. These include notes, computations, memoranda, copies, and other papers that make up the work product of

7. *Bily v. Arthur Young & Co.,* 3 Cal.4th 370, 834 P.2d 745, 11 Cal.Rptr.2d 51 (1992).

EXHIBIT 42–1 KEY PROVISIONS OF THE SARBANES-OXLEY ACT OF 2002 RELATING TO PUBLIC ACCOUNTING FIRMS

DUTIES OF THE PUBLIC COMPANY ACCOUNTING OVERSIGHT BOARD

Title I of the Sarbanes-Oxley Act of 2002 states that the duties of the Public Company Accounting Oversight Board are as follows:

- Generally, to oversee the audit of companies ("issuers") whose securities are sold to public investors in order to protect the interests of investors and further the public interest.
- To register public accounting firms that prepare audit reports for issuers. (A nonregistered firm is prohibited from preparing, or participating in the preparation of, an audit report with respect to an issuer.)
- To establish or adopt standards relating to the preparation of audit reports for issuers.
- To enforce compliance with the Sarbanes-Oxley Act by inspecting registered public accounting firms (RPAFs) and by investigating and disciplining, by appropriate sanctions, firms that violate the act's provisions. (Sanctions range from a temporary or permanent suspension to civil penalties that can be as high as $15 million for intentional violations.)
- To perform any other duties necessary or appropriate to promote high professional standards among RPAFs and improve the quality of audit services offered by those firms.

AUDITOR INDEPENDENCE

To help ensure that auditors remain independent of the firms that they audit, Title II of the Sarbanes-Oxley Act does the following:

- Makes it unlawful for RPAFs to perform both audit and nonaudit services for the same company at the same time. Nonaudit services include the following:
  1. Bookkeeping or other services related to the accounting records or financial statements of the audit client.
  2. Financial information systems design and implementation.
  3. Appraisal or valuation services.
  4. Fairness opinions.
  5. Management functions.
  6. Broker or dealer, investment adviser, or investment banking services.
- Requires preapproval for most auditing services from the issuer's audit committee.
- Requires audit partner rotation by prohibiting RPAFs from providing audit services to an issuer if either the lead audit partner or the audit partner responsible for reviewing the audit has provided such services to the issuer in each of the prior five years.
- Requires RPAFs to make timely reports to the audit committees of the issuers. The report must indicate all critical accounting policies and practices to be used; all alternative treatments of financial information within generally accepted accounting principles that have been discussed with the issuer's management officials, the ramifications of the use of such alternative treatments, and the treatment preferred by the auditor; and other material written communications between the auditor and the issuer's management.
- Makes it unlawful for an RPAF to provide auditing services to an issuer if the issuer's chief executive officer, chief financial officer, chief accounting officer, or controller was previously employed by the auditor and participated in any capacity in the audit of the issuer during the one-year period preceding the date that the audit began.

DOCUMENT RETENTION AND DESTRUCTION

- The Sarbanes-Oxley Act provides that anyone who destroys, alters, or falsifies records with the intent to obstruct or influence a federal investigation or in relation to bankruptcy proceedings can be criminally prosecuted and sentenced to a fine, imprisonment for up to twenty years, or both.
- The act also requires accountants who audit or review publicly traded companies to retain all working papers related to the audit or review for a period of five years (now amended to seven years). Violators can be sentenced to a fine, imprisonment for up to ten years, or both.

an accountant's services to a client. Under the common law, which in this instance has been codified in a number of states, working papers remain the accountant's property. It is important for accountants to retain such records in the event that they need to defend against lawsuits for negligence or other actions in which their competence is challenged. But because an accountant's working papers reflect the client's financial situation, the client has a right to access them. (On a client's request, an accountant must return to the client any of the client's records or journals, and failure to do so may result in liability.)

Under Section 802(a)(1) of the Sarbanes-Oxley Act, accountants must maintain working papers relating to an audit or review for five years (which has been amended to seven years since the passage of the act) from the end of the fiscal period in which the audit or review was concluded. A knowing violation of this requirement will subject the accountant to a fine, imprisonment for up to ten years, or both.

Potential Statutory Liability of Accountants

Both civil and criminal liability may be imposed on accountants under the Securities Act of 1933, the Securities Exchange Act of 1934, and the Private Securities Litigation Reform Act of 1995.[8]

LIABILITY UNDER THE SECURITIES ACT OF 1933

The Securities Act of 1933 requires registration statements to be filed with the Securities and Exchange Commission (SEC) prior to an offering of securities (see Chapter 35).[9] Accountants frequently prepare and certify (attest to the accuracy of) the issuer's financial statements that are included in the registration statement.

Liability under Section 11 Section 11 of the Securities Act of 1933 imposes civil liability on accountants for misstatements and omissions of material facts in registration statements. Therefore, an accountant may be found liable if he or she prepared any financial statements included in the registration statement that "contained an untrue statement of a material fact or omitted to state a material fact required to be stated therein or necessary to make the statements therein not misleading."[10]

Liability to Purchasers of Securities. Under Section 11, an accountant's liability for a misstatement or omission of a material fact in a registration statement extends to anyone who acquires a security covered by the registration statement. A purchaser of a security need only demonstrate that he or she has suffered a loss on the security. Proof of reliance on the materially false statement or misleading omission is not ordinarily required. Nor is there a requirement of privity between the accountant and the security purchasers.

DUE DILIGENCE
A required standard of care that certain professionals, such as accountants, must meet to avoid liability for securities violations.

The Due Diligence Standard. Section 11 imposes a duty on accountants to use **due diligence** in the preparation of financial statements included in the filed registration statements. After a purchaser has proved a loss on the security, the accountant bears the burden of showing that he or she exercised due diligence in the preparation of the financial statements. To avoid liability, the accountant must show that he or she had, "after reasonable investigation, reasonable grounds to believe and did believe, at the time such part of the registration statement became effective, that the statements

8. Other potential sources of civil and criminal liability that may be imposed on accountants and other professionals include provisions of the Racketeer Influenced and Corrupt Organizations Act (RICO). RICO is discussed in Chapter 6.

9. Many securities and transactions are expressly exempted from the 1933 act.

10. 15 U.S.C. Section 77k(a).

therein were true and that there was no omission of a material fact required to be stated therein or necessary to make the statements therein not misleading."[11] Further, the failure to follow GAAP and GAAS is also proof of a lack of due diligence.

In particular, the due diligence standard places a burden on accountants to verify information furnished by a corporation's officers and directors. The burden of proving due diligence requires an accountant to demonstrate that he or she is free from negligence or fraud. Merely asking questions is not always sufficient to satisfy the requirement of due diligence. ■ EXAMPLE 42.5 In *Escott v. BarChris Construction Corp.*,[12] accountants were held liable for failing to detect danger signals in documents furnished by corporate officers that, under GAAS, required further investigation under the circumstances. ■

Defenses to Liability. Besides proving that he or she has acted with due diligence, an accountant can raise the following defenses to Section 11 liability:

1. There were no misstatements or omissions.
2. The misstatements or omissions were not of material facts.
3. The misstatements or omissions had no causal connection to the plaintiff's loss.
4. The plaintiff purchaser invested in the securities knowing of the misstatements or omissions.

Liability under Section 12(2) Section 12(2) of the Securities Act of 1933 imposes civil liability for fraud in relation to offerings or sales of securities.[13] Liability is based on the communication to an investor, whether orally or in the written prospectus,[14] of an untrue statement or the omission of a material fact.

Penalties and Sanctions for Violations Those who purchase securities and suffer harm as a result of a false or omitted statement, or some other violation, may bring a suit in a federal court to recover their losses and other damages. The U.S. Department of Justice brings criminal actions against those who commit willful violations. The penalties include fines up to $10,000, imprisonment up to five years, or both. The SEC is authorized to seek an injunction against a willful violator to prevent further violations. The SEC can also ask a court to grant other relief, such as an order to a violator to refund profits derived from an illegal transaction.

LIABILITY UNDER THE SECURITIES EXCHANGE ACT OF 1934

Under Sections 18 and 10(b) of the Securities Exchange Act of 1934 and Rule 10b-5 of the Securities and Exchange Commission, an accountant may be found liable for fraud. A plaintiff has a substantially heavier burden of proof under the 1934 act than under the 1933 act. Unlike the 1933 act, the 1934 act provides that an accountant need not prove due diligence to escape liability.

Liability under Section 18 Section 18 of the 1934 act imposes civil liability on an accountant who makes or causes to be made in any application, report, or document

11. 15 U.S.C. Section 77k(b)(3).
12. 283 F.Supp. 643 (S.D.N.Y. 1968).
13. 15 U.S.C. Section 77*l*.
14. As discussed in Chapter 32, a prospectus contains financial disclosures about the corporation for the benefit of potential investors.

QUESTIONS AND CASE PROBLEMS

42–1. *Ultramares* Rule. Larkin, Inc., retains Howard Perkins to manage its books and prepare its financial statements. Perkins, a certified public accountant, lives in Indiana and practices there. After twenty years, Perkins has become a bit bored with generally accepted accounting principles and has become creative in his accounting methods. Now, though, Perkins has a problem, as he is being sued by Molly Tucker, one of Larkin's creditors. Tucker alleges that Perkins either knew or should have known that Larkin's financial statements would be distributed to various individuals. Furthermore, she asserts that these financial statements were negligently prepared and seriously inaccurate. What are the consequences of Perkins's failure to adopt generally accepted accounting principles? Under the traditional *Ultramares* rule, can Tucker recover damages from Perkins? Explain.

42–2. Accountant's Liability to Third Parties and Public Policy. The accounting firm of Goldman, Walters, Johnson & Co. prepared financial statements for Lucy's Fashions, Inc. After reviewing the various financial statements, Happydays State Bank agreed to loan Lucy's Fashions $35,000 for expansion. When Lucy's Fashions declared bankruptcy under Chapter 11 six months later, Happydays State Bank promptly filed an action against Goldman, Walters, Johnson & Co., alleging negligent preparation of financial statements. Assuming that the court has abandoned the *Ultramares* approach, what is the result? What are the policy reasons for holding accountants liable to third parties with whom they are not in privity?

42–3. Accountant's Liability under Rule 10b-5. In early 1995, Bennett, Inc., offered a substantial number of new common shares to the public. Harvey Helms had a long-standing interest in Bennett because his grandfather had once been president of the company. On receiving a prospectus prepared and distributed by Bennett, Helms was dismayed by the pessimism it embodied. Helms decided to delay purchasing stock in the company. Later, Helms asserted that the prospectus prepared by the accountants was overly pessimistic and contained materially misleading statements. Discuss fully how successful Helms would be in bringing a cause of action under Rule 10b-5 against the accountants of Bennett, Inc.

42–4. Negligence. Robert Potts was a partner at the accounting firm of Touche Ross and its successor, Deloitte & Touche. Potts was the concurring partner for 1988 and 1989 audits of Kahler Corp., which owned and managed the University Park Hotel. According to the American Institute of Certified Public Accountants, a *concurring partner* assures that an audited company's financial statements conform with generally accepted accounting principles (GAAP) and generally accepted auditing standards. In 1988 and 1989, the hotel lost money, but Kahler showed a gain in 1988 by accounting for the hotel as an asset held for sale. Under GAAP, certain conditions must be met to account for property as an asset held for sale. Despite evidence that Kahler did not meet the conditions, Potts approved the audits. Potts also agreed to Kahler's valuation of the hotel, despite evidence that it was worth less than Kahler said. The Securities and Exchange Commission filed a complaint against Potts, alleging that he had acted negligently. Will the court agree? Why or why not? [*Potts v. SEC,* 151 F.3d 810 (8th Cir. 1998)]

42–5. Accountant's Liability to Third Parties. In June 1993, Sparkomatic Corp. agreed to negotiate a sale of its Kenco Engineering division to Williams Controls, Inc. At the end of July, Sparkomatic asked its accountants, Parente, Randolph, Orlando, Carey & Associates, to audit Kenco's financial statements for the previous three years and to certify interim and closing balance sheets to be included with the sale's closing documents. All of the parties knew that these documents would serve as a basis for setting the sale price. Within a few days, Williams signed an "Asset Purchase Agreement" that promised access to Parente's records with respect to Kenco. The sale closed in mid-August. In September, Williams was given the financial statements for Kenco's previous three years and the interim and closing balance sheets, all of which were certified by Parente. Williams's accountant found no errors in the closing balance sheet but did not review any of the other documents. The parties set a final purchase price. Later, however, Williams filed a suit in a federal district court against Parente, claiming negligent misrepresentation, among other things, in connection with Parente's preparation of the financial documents. Parente responded with a motion for summary judgment, asserting that the parties lacked privity. Under the *Restatement (Second) of Torts,* Section 552, how should the court rule? Explain. [*Williams Controls, Inc. v. Parente, Randolph, Orlando, Carey & Associates,* 39 F.Supp.2d 517 (M.D.Pa. 1999)]

CASE PROBLEM WITH SAMPLE ANSWER

42–6. In October 1993, Marilyn Greenen, a licensed certified public accountant (CPA), began working at the Port of Vancouver, Washington (the Port), as an account manager. She was not directly engaged in public accounting at the Port, but she oversaw the preparation of financial statements and supervised employees with accounting duties. At the start of her employment, she enrolled her husband for benefits under the Port's medical plan. Her marriage was dissolved in November, but she did not notify the Port of the change. In May 1998 and April 1999, the Port confronted her about the divorce, but she did not update her insurance information. After she was terminated, she reimbursed the Port for the additional premiums it had paid for unauthorized coverage for her former spouse. The Washington State Board of Accountancy imposed sanctions on Greenen for "dishonesty and misleading representations" while, in the words of an applicable state statute, "representing oneself as a CPA." Greenen asked a Washington state court to review the case. What might be an appropriate sanction in this case? What might be Greenen's best argument against the board's action?

On what reasoning might the court uphold the decision? [*Greenen v. Washington State Board of Accountancy,* 824 Wash.App. 126, 110 P.3d 224 (Div. 2 2005)]

After you have answered this problem, compare your answer with the sample answer given on the Web site that accompanies this text. Go to http://blt.westbuslaw.com, select "Chapter 42," and click on "Case Problem with Sample Answer."

42–7. Accountant's Liability. In 1995, JTD Health Systems, Inc., hired Tammy Heiby as accounting coordinator. Apparently overwhelmed by the duties of the position, Heiby failed to make payroll tax payments to the Internal Revenue Service (IRS) in 1995 and 1996. Heiby tried to hide this omission by falsifying journal entries and manually writing three checks out of sequence, totaling $1.7 million and payable to a bank, from JTD's cash account (to dispose of excess funds that should have been paid in taxes). JTD hired Pricewaterhouse Coopers, LLP, to review JTD's internal accounting procedures and audit its financial statements for 1995. Coopers's inexperienced auditor was aware that the cash account had not been balanced in months and knew about the checks but never questioned them. The auditor instead mistakenly explained that the unbalanced account was due to changes in Medicaid/Medicare procedures and recommended no further investigation. In 1996, the IRS asked JTD to remit the unpaid taxes, plus interest and penalties. JTD filed a suit in an Ohio state court against Coopers, alleging common law negligence and breach of contract. Should Coopers be held liable to JTD on these grounds? Why or why not? [*JTD Health Systems, Inc. v. Pricewaterhouse Coopers, LLP,* 141 Ohio App.3d 280, 750 N.E.2d 1177 (Ohio App. 3 Dist. 2001)]

42–8. Accountant's Liability under the Private Securities Litigation Reform Act. Solucorp Industries, Ltd., a corporation headquartered in New York, develops and markets products for use in environmental clean-ups. Solucorp's financial statements for the six months ending December 31, 1997, recognized $1.09 million in license fees payable by Smart International, Ltd. The fees comprised about 50 percent of Solucorp's revenue for the period. At the time, however, the parties had a license agreement only "in principle," and Smart had made only one payment of $150,000. Glenn Ohlhauser, an accountant asked to audit the statements, objected to the inclusion of the fees. In February 1998, Solucorp showed Ohlhauser a license agreement backdated to September 1997 but refused to provide any financial information about Smart. Ohlhauser issued an unqualified opinion on the 1997 statements, which were included with forms filed with the Securities and Exchange Commission (SEC). The SEC sued Ohlhauser. What might be the basis in the Private Securities Litigation Reform Act for the SEC's suit? What might be Ohlhauser's defense? Discuss. [*Securities and Exchange Commission v. Solucorp Industries, Ltd.,* 197 F.Supp.2d 4 (S.D.N.Y. 2002)]

FOR CRITICAL ANALYSIS

42–9. In cases in which third parties suffer losses in reliance on negligent misrepresentation in accountants' financial reports, the courts apply different standards to assess liability. Some courts impose liability only when there is privity between the accountant and the party who seeks recovery. Other courts impose liability under a foreseeability rule. What do you see as the implications of imposing liability on accountants for losses suffered by third parties on the basis of foreseeability rather than privity?

VIDEO QUESTION

42–10. Go to this text's Web site at http://blt.westbuslaw.com and select "Chapter 42." Click on "Video Questions" and view the video titled *Accountant's Liability.* Then answer the following questions.

1. Should Ray prepare a financial statement that values a list of assets provided by the advertising firm without verifying that the firm actually owns these assets?
2. Discuss whether Ray is in privity with the company interested in buying Laura's advertising firm.
3. Under the *Ultramares* rule, to whom does Ray owe a duty?
4. Assume that Laura did not tell Ray that she intended to give the financial statement to the potential acquirer. Would this fact change Ray's liability under the *Ultramares* rule? Explain.

INTERNET EXERCISES

Go to the *Business Law Today* home page at http://blt.westbuslaw.com, select "Chapter 42," and click on "Internet Exercises." There you will find the following Internet research exercises that you can perform to learn more about topics covered in this chapter.

Activity 42–1: LEGAL PERSPECTIVE—The Sarbanes-Oxley Act of 2002

Activity 42–2: MANAGEMENT PERSPECTIVE—Avoiding Legal Liability

BEFORE THE TEST

Go to the *Business Law Today* home page at http://blt.westbuslaw.com, select "Chapter 42," and click on "Interactive Quizzes." You will find a number of interactive questions relating to this chapter.

Tennessee v. Lane

The Americans with Disabilities Act (ADA) of 1990 is discussed in Chapter 41. The ADA provides, among other things, that "no qualified individual with a disability shall, by reason of such disability, be excluded from participation in or be denied the benefits of the services, programs or activities of a public entity, or be subjected to discrimination by any such entity." In this extended case study, we examine Tennessee v. Lane,[1] *a decision that focuses on whether access to the courts, and the services they provide, falls under the promise of the ADA and whether the ADA gives citizens the right to bring an action for damages if a state does not fulfill that promise. The specific question in this case is whether that provision of the ADA is a legitimate exercise of Congress's authority under the Fourteenth Amendment to the U.S. Constitution (see Chapter 2).*

1. 541 U.S. 509, 124 S.Ct. 1978, 158 L.Ed.2d 820, 2004 WL 1085482 (2004). This opinion may be accessed online at http://www.findlaw.com/casecode/supreme.html. In the "Browsing" section, click on "2004 Decisions." On the resulting page, click on the name of the case to access the opinion.

CASE BACKGROUND

George Lane is a paraplegic. In 1996, he was ordered to appear in the Polk County courthouse in Benton, Tennessee, to respond to a charge of driving with a revoked driver's license. Because there is no elevator in the building, to make the appearance he was forced to crawl up two flights of stairs. When Lane was ordered to appear a second time, he refused to crawl. He also refused an offer to be carried. The state arrested and jailed him for failing to make the second appearance.

Lane and Beverly Jones, a court reporter who is also a paraplegic, filed a suit in a federal district court against Tennessee and some of its counties, claiming violations of the ADA. Jones alleged that she could not gain access to a number of county courthouses and, as a result, had lost both work and an opportunity to participate in the judicial process. The plaintiffs asked for damages and other relief.

Tennessee filed a motion to dismiss, which the court denied. The state appealed to the U.S. Court of Appeals for the Sixth Circuit, which affirmed the lower court's decision and remanded the case for further proceedings. The state appealed to the United States Supreme Court.

MAJORITY OPINION

Justice STEVENS delivered the opinion of the Court.

* * * *

* * * Congress enacted [the ADA] against a backdrop of pervasive unequal treatment in the administration of state services and programs, including systematic deprivations of fundamental rights. For example, as of 1979, most States * * * categorically disqualified "idiots" from voting, without regard to individual capacity. The majority of these laws remain on the books, and have been the subject of legal challenge as recently as 2001. Similarly, a number of States have prohibited and continue to prohibit persons with disabilities from engaging in activities such as marrying and serving as jurors. The historical experience that [the ADA] reflects is also documented in this Court's cases, which have identified unconstitutional treatment of disabled persons by state agencies in a variety of settings * * * .

* * * *

With respect to the particular services at issue in this case, Congress learned that many individuals, in many States across the country, were being excluded from courthouses and court proceedings by reason of their disabilities. * * * [S]ome 76% of public services and programs housed in state-owned buildings were inaccessible to and unusable by persons with disabilities * * * . [E]xamples of the exclusion of persons with disabilities from state judicial services and programs include[d] exclusion of persons with visual impairments and hearing impairments from jury service, failure of state and local governments to provide interpretive services for the hearing impaired, failure to permit the testimony of adults with developmental disabilities in abuse cases, and failure to make courtrooms accessible to witnesses with physical disabilities.

* * * *

Congress's chosen remedy for the pattern of exclusion and discrimination described above, [the ADA's] requirement of program accessibility, is congruent [consistent with] and proportional to its object of enforcing the right of access to the courts. * * *

* * * *

This duty to accommodate is perfectly consistent with the well-established due process principle that, within the limits of practicability, a State must afford to all individuals a meaningful opportunity to be heard in its courts. Our cases have recognized a number of affirmative obligations that flow from this principle: the duty to waive filing fees in certain family-law and criminal cases, the duty to provide transcripts to criminal defendants seeking review of their convictions, and the duty to provide counsel to certain criminal defendants. Each of these cases makes clear that *ordinary considerations of cost and convenience alone cannot justify a State's failure to provide individuals with a meaningful right of access to the courts.* Judged against this backdrop, [the ADA's] affirmative obligation to accommodate persons with disabilities in the administration of justice cannot be said to be so out of proportion to a supposed remedial or preventive object that it cannot be understood as responsive to, or designed to prevent, unconstitutional behavior. It is, rather, a reasonable prophylactic measure, reasonably targeted to a legitimate end. [Emphasis added.]

For these reasons, we conclude that [the ADA], as it applies to the class of cases implicating the fundamental right of access to the courts, constitutes a valid exercise of Congress' * * * authority to enforce the guarantees of the Fourteenth Amendment. The judgment of the Court of Appeals is therefore affirmed.[2]

2. The lower court's decision on remand was not yet available at the time this book went to press, but it may be by the time you read this. You may be able to locate the remanded decision online. See this text's inside front cover for URLs for online court decisions.

DISSENTING OPINION

Chief Justice REHNQUIST * * * dissenting.

* * * *

* * * The bulk of the [majority's] evidence concerns discrimination by nonstate governments, rather than the States themselves. * * * Most of the brief anecdotes do not involve States at all, and those that do are not sufficiently detailed to determine whether the instances of unequal treatment were irrational, and thus unconstitutional * * * .

With respect to the due process "access to the courts" rights on which the [majority] ultimately relies, Congress' failure to identify a pattern of actual constitutional violations by the States is even more striking. Indeed, there is *nothing* in the [ADA's] legislative record or statutory findings to indicate that disabled persons were systematically denied the right to be present at criminal trials, denied the meaningful opportunity to be heard in civil cases, unconstitutionally excluded from jury service, or denied the right to attend criminal trials.

* * * *

Even if the anecdotal evidence and conclusory statements relied on by the majority could be properly considered, the mere existence of an architecturally "inaccessible" courthouse—[that is,] one a disabled person cannot utilize without assistance—does not state a constitutional violation. A violation of due process occurs only when a person is actually denied the constitutional right to access a given judicial proceeding. We have never held that a person has a *constitutional* right to make his way into a courtroom without any external assistance. Indeed, the fact that the State may need to assist an individual to attend a hearing has no bearing on whether the individual successfully exercises his due process right to be present at the proceeding. Nor does an "inaccessible" courthouse violate the [Fourteenth Amendment] unless it is irrational for the State not to alter the courthouse to make it "accessible." But financial considerations almost always furnish a rational basis for a State to decline to make those alterations. Thus, evidence regarding inaccessible courthouses * * * is not evidence of constitutional violations * * * .

* * * *

For the foregoing reasons, I respectfully dissent.

QUESTIONS FOR ANALYSIS

1. **Law.** What did the majority conclude on the central issue in this case, and what support did it provide for its decision?
2. **Law.** What was the dissent's argument with regard to this question?
3. **Political Consideration.** Should the ADA be applied differently to cases involving disabilities than other laws are applied to cases involving other bases of discrimination? Why or why not?
4. **Economic Dimensions.** How are the states affected by the decision in this case, and what are the limits to that effect?
5. **Implications for the States.** What does the ruling in this case say to the state governments?

bailable property. Was the letter bailable property? Discuss fully. [*Liddle v. Salem School District No. 600,* 249 Ill.App.3d 768, 619 N.E.2d 530, 188 Ill.Dec. 905 (1993)]

43–4. Gratuitous Bailments. Raul Covarrubias, David Haro, and Javier Aguirre immigrated to the United States from Colima, Mexico, to find jobs and help their families. When they learned that Francisco Alcaraz-Garcia planned to travel to Colima, they asked him to deliver various sums, totaling more than $25,000, to their families. During customs inspections at the border, Alcaraz told officers of the U.S. Customs Service that he was not carrying more than $10,000. In fact, he carried more than $35,000. He was charged with—and convicted of—criminal currency and customs violations, and the government seized most of the cash. Covarrubias, Haro, and Aguirre filed a petition for the return of their money, arguing that Alcaraz was a gratuitous bailee and that they still had title to the money. Are they right? Explain fully. [*United States v. Alcaraz-Garcia,* 79 F.3d 769 (9th Cir. 1996)]

43–5. Gift *Inter Vivos*. Thomas Stafford owned four promissory notes. Payments on the notes were deposited into a bank account in the names of Stafford and his daughter, June Zink, "as joint tenants with right of survivorship." Stafford kept control of the notes and would not allow Zink to spend any of the proceeds. He also kept the interest on the account. On one note, Stafford indorsed "Pay to the order of Thomas J. Stafford or June S. Zink, or the survivor." The payee on each of the other notes was "Thomas J. Stafford and June S. Zink, or the survivor." When Stafford died, Zink took possession of the notes, claiming that she had been a joint tenant of the notes with her father. Stafford's son, also Thomas, filed a suit in a Virginia state court against Zink, claiming that the notes were partly his. The son argued that their father had not made a valid gift *inter vivos* of the notes to Zink. In whose favor will the court rule? Why? [*Zink v. Stafford,* 509 S.E.2d 833 (Va. 1999)]

CASE PROBLEM WITH SAMPLE ANSWER

43–6. A. D. Lock owned Lock Hospitality, Inc., which in turn owned the Best Western Motel in Conway, Arkansas. Joe Terry and David Stocks were preparing the motel for renovation. As they were removing the ceiling tiles in Room 118, with Lock present in the room, they noticed a dusty cardboard box near the heating and air-supply vent where it had apparently been concealed. Terry climbed a ladder to reach the box, opened it, and handed it to Stocks. The box was filled with more than $38,000 in old currency. Lock took possession of the box and its contents. Terry and Stocks filed a suit in an Arkansas state court against Lock and his corporation to obtain the money. Should the money be characterized as lost, mislaid, or abandoned property? To whom should the court award it? Explain. [*Terry v. Lock,* 37 S.W.3d 202 (Ark. 2001)]

After you have answered this problem, compare your answer with the sample answer given on the Web site that accompanies this text. Go to http://blt.westbuslaw.com, select "Chapter 43," and click on "Case Problem with Sample Answer."

43–7. Concurrent Ownership. Vincent Slavin was a partner at Cantor Fitzgerald Securities in the World Trade Center (WTC) in New York City. In 1998, Slavin and Anna Baez became engaged and began living together. They placed both of their names on three accounts at Chase Manhattan Bank according to the bank's terms, which provided that "accounts with multiple owners are joint, payable to either owner or the survivor." Slavin arranged for the direct deposit of his salary and commissions into one of the accounts. On September 11, 2001, Slavin died when two planes piloted by terrorists crashed into the WTC towers, causing their collapse. At the time, the balance in the three accounts was $656,944.36. On September 14, Cantor Fitzgerald deposited an additional $58,264.73 into the direct-deposit account. Baez soon withdrew the entire amount from all of the accounts. Mary Jelnek, Slavin's mother, filed a suit in a New York state court against Baez to determine the ownership of the funds that had been in the accounts. In what form of ownership were the accounts held? Who is entitled to which of the funds, and why? [*In re Jelnek,* 3 Misc.3d 725, 777 N.Y.S.2d 871 (Sur. 2004)]

FOR CRITICAL ANALYSIS

43–8. Suppose that a certificate of deposit (CD) owned by two joint tenants (with the right of survivorship) is given by one of the joint tenants as security for a loan (without the other joint tenant's knowledge). Further suppose that the joint tenant dies after defaulting on the loan. Who has superior rights in the CD, the creditor or the other surviving joint tenant?

VIDEO QUESTION

43–9. Go to this text's Web site at http://blt.westbuslaw.com and select "Chapter 43." Click on "Video Questions" and view the video titled *Personal Property and Bailments.* Then answer the following questions.

1. What type of bailment is discussed in the video?
2. What were Vinny's duties with regard to the rug-cleaning machine? What standard of care should apply?
3. Did Vinny exercise the appropriate degree of care? Why or why not? How would a court decide this issue?

INTERNET EXERCISES

Go to the *Business Law Today* home page at **http://blt.westbuslaw.com**, select "Chapter 43," and click on "Internet Exercises." There you will find the following Internet research exercises that you can perform to learn more about topics covered in this chapter.

Activity 43–1: LEGAL PERSPECTIVE—Lost Property

Activity 43–2: MANAGEMENT PERSPECTIVE—Bailments

BEFORE THE TEST

Go to the *Business Law Today* home page at **http://blt.westbuslaw.com**, select "Chapter 43," and click on "Interactive Quizzes." You will find a number of interactive questions relating to this chapter.

"The right of property is the most sacred of all the rights of citizenship."
Jean-Jacques Rousseau, 1712–1778
(French writer and philosopher)

CHAPTER 44
Real Property

CHAPTER OUTLINE

LEARNING OBJECTIVES

After reading this chapter, you should be able to answer the following questions:

1. What can a person who holds property in fee simple absolute do with the property? Can a person who holds property as a life estate do the same?
2. What are the requirements for acquiring property by adverse possession?
3. What limitations may be imposed on the rights of property owners?
4. What is a leasehold estate? What types of leasehold estates, or tenancies, can be created when real property is leased?
5. What are the respective duties of the landlord and tenant concerning the use and maintenance of leased property? Is the tenant responsible for all damages that he or she causes?

From earliest times, property has provided a means for survival. Primitive peoples lived off the fruits of the land, eating the vegetation and wildlife. Later, as the wildlife was domesticated and the vegetation cultivated, property provided pasturage and farmland. In the twelfth and thirteenth centuries in Europe, the power of feudal lords was determined by the amount of land they held; the more land, the more powerful they were. After the age of feudalism passed, property continued to be an indicator of family wealth and social position. In the Western world, an individual's right to his or her property has become, in the words of Jean-Jacques Rousseau, one of the "most sacred of all the rights of citizenship."

In this chapter, we first examine the nature of real property. We then look at the various ways in which real property can be owned and at how ownership rights in real property are transferred from one person to another. We conclude the chapter with a discussion of leased property and landlord-tenant relationships.

The Nature of Real Property

Real property consists of land and the buildings, plants, and trees that are on it. Real property also includes subsurface and air rights, as well as personal property that has become permanently attached to real property. Whereas personal property is movable, real property—also called *real estate* or *realty*—is immovable.

LAND

Land includes the soil on the surface of the earth and the natural or artificial structures that are attached to it. It further includes all the waters contained on or under the surface and much, but not necessarily all, of the airspace above it. The exterior boundaries of land extend down to the center of the earth and up to the farthest reaches of the atmosphere (subject to certain qualifications).

.on the Web For links to numerous online legal sources relating to real property, go to

http://www.findlaw.com/01topics/index.html

and click on "Property Law & Real Estate."

AIR AND SUBSURFACE RIGHTS

The owner of real property has rights to the airspace above the land, as well as to the soil and minerals underneath it. Limitations on either air rights or subsurface rights normally have to be indicated on the document that transfers title at the time of purchase. When no such limitations, or *encumbrances*, are noted, a purchaser can normally expect to have an unlimited right to possession of the property.

Air Rights Early cases involving air rights dealt with such matters as whether a telephone wire could be run across a person's property when the wire did not touch any of the property[1] and whether a bullet shot over a person's land constituted trespass.[2] Today, disputes concerning air rights may involve the right of commercial and private planes to fly over property and the right of individuals and governments to seed clouds and produce rain artificially. Flights over private land normally do not violate the property owners' rights unless the flights are low and frequent enough to cause a direct interference with the enjoyment and use of the land.[3] Leaning walls or buildings and projecting eave spouts or roofs may also violate the air rights of an adjoining property owner.

A plane flies low over a residential area. Are the property owners' rights violated by such a low-flying plane? Why or why not? (Jonathan Nourok/PhotoEdit)

1. *Butler v. Frontier Telephone Co.,* 186 N.Y. 486, 79 N.E. 716 (1906).
2. *Herrin v. Sutherland,* 74 Mont. 587, 241 P. 328 (1925). Shooting over a person's land constitutes trespass.
3. *United States v. Causby,* 328 U.S. 256, 66 S.Ct. 1062, 90 L.Ed. 1206 (1946).

"The meek shall inherit the earth, but not the mineral rights."

J. PAUL GETTY, 1892–1976 (American entrepreneur and industrialist)

Subsurface Rights In many states, land ownership may be separated, in that the surface of a piece of land and the subsurface may have different owners. Subsurface rights can be extremely valuable, as these rights include the ownership of minerals, oil, and natural gas. But subsurface rights would be of little value if the owner could not use the surface to exercise those rights. Hence, a subsurface owner will have a right (called a *profit*, discussed later in this chapter) to go onto the surface of the land to, for example, discover and mine minerals.

PLANT LIFE AND VEGETATION

Plant life, both natural and cultivated, is also considered to be real property. In many instances, the natural vegetation, such as trees, adds greatly to the value of the realty. When a parcel of land is sold and the land has growing crops on it, the sale includes the crops, unless otherwise specified in the sales contract. When crops are sold by themselves, however, they are considered to be personal property or goods. Consequently, the sale of crops is a sale of goods and thus is governed by the Uniform Commercial Code (UCC) rather than by real property law.[4]

FIXTURES

FIXTURE
A thing that was once personal property but has become attached to real property in such a way that it takes on the characteristics of real property and becomes part of that real property.

Certain personal property can become so closely associated with the real property to which it is attached that the law views it as real property. Such property is known as a **fixture**—a thing *affixed* to realty, meaning that it is attached to the real property by roots; embedded in it; permanently situated on it; or permanently attached by means of cement, plaster, bolts, nails, or screws. The fixture can be physically attached to real property, be attached to another fixture, or even be without any actual physical attachment to the land (such as a statue). As long as the owner intends the property to be a fixture, normally it will be a fixture.

Fixtures are included in the sale of land if the sales contract does not provide otherwise. The sale of a house includes the land and the house and the garage on the land, as well as the cabinets, plumbing, and windows. Because these are permanently affixed to the property, they are considered to be a part of it. Certain items, such as drapes and window-unit air conditioners, are difficult to classify. Thus, a contract for the sale of a house or commercial realty should indicate which items of this sort are included in the sale.

At issue in the following case was whether an agricultural irrigation system qualified as a fixture.

4. See UCC 2–107(2).

CASE 44.1 In re Sand & Sage Farm & Ranch, Inc.

United States Bankruptcy Court,
District of Kansas, 2001.
266 Bankr. 507.

BACKGROUND AND FACTS In 1988, Randolf and Sandra Ardery bought an eighty-acre tract in Edwards County, Kansas. On the land was an eight-tower center-pivot irrigation system. The system consisted of an underground well and pump connected to a pipe that ran to the pivot where the water line was attached to a further system of pipes and sprinklers suspended from the towers, extending over the land in a circular fashion. The system's engine and gearhead were bolted to a concrete slab above the pump and well and were attached to the pipe. To secure a loan to buy the land, the Arderys granted to Farmers State Bank a mortgage that covered "all buildings, improvements, and fixtures." In 1996, the

CASE 44.1—Continued

Arderys, and their firm Sand & Sage Farm & Ranch, Inc., granted Ag Services of America a security interest in the farm's "equipment." Nothing in the security agreement or financing statement referred to fixtures.[a] In 2000, the Arderys and Sand & Sage filed for bankruptcy in a federal bankruptcy court and asked for permission to sell the land, with the irrigation system, to Bohn Enterprises, Limited Partnership. Ag Services claimed that it had priority to the proceeds covering the value of the irrigation system. The bank responded that it had priority because the system was a "fixture."

a. Security agreements and financing statements were discussed in Chapter 25.

IN THE WORDS OF THE COURT . . .

ROBERT E. NUGENT, Bankruptcy Judge.

* * * *

* * * [There is] a three-step judicial test for determining whether personalty attached to real estate is legally a fixture. Paraphrased, the steps are:

(i) how firmly the goods are attached or the ease of their removal (annexation);
(ii) the relationship of the parties involved (intent); and
(iii) how operation of the goods is related to the use of the land (adaptation).

Of the three factors, intent is the controlling factor and is deduced largely from the property-owner's acts and the surrounding circumstances. [Emphasis added.]

* * * *

* * * [The irrigation system] is firmly attached to the realty. The irrigation pipes are connected to the center pivot which is bolted to a cement slab in the center of the irrigation property and connected to the underground well and pump by wires and pipes. Further, the system is not easily removable. The towers must be disassembled in sections and transported separately, and disassembly and removal of the engine, gearhead and pump would be time-consuming and require the assistance of experienced people. It would also be expensive * * * .

The relationships between the parties involved in each transaction also suggest the shared intent that the irrigation system be a fixture. In 1988, * * * Ardery [bought the land] with the irrigation system included. Ardery, in turn, mortgaged the land, and the fixtures, to the Bank [whose officer] testified that he considered the conveyance of the mortgage to include the system as that was the Bank's custom and practice in Edwards County. Ardery and Bohn clearly intend the system to pass with the land in the sale now before the Court. * * *

The irrigation system is suitably adapted to the land. There can be little dispute concerning the need for pivot irrigation in the semi-arid conditions of southwestern Kansas. All witnesses agreed, and it is well within this Court's common experience, that irrigated units of land are substantially more productive of crops than dryland acres. This alone demonstrates the relation between the operation of the goods and use of the land.

DECISION AND REMEDY The court concluded that the system was a fixture. The bank was entitled to the proceeds from its sale.

WHY IS THIS CASE IMPORTANT? *When dealing with real property, it is crucial that the parties to a contract specifically list which fixtures they intend to be subjected to a security interest or included in a sale or transfer. In the end, it is far simpler and less expensive to itemize fixtures in a contract than to engage in litigation.*

Ownership Interests in Real Property

"Few . . . men own their property. The property owns them."
ROBERT G. INGERSOLL, 1833–1899 (American politician and lecturer)

Ownership of property is an abstract concept that cannot exist independently of the legal system. No one can actually possess or *hold* a piece of land, the air above it, the earth below it, and all the water contained on it. The legal system therefore recognizes certain rights and duties that constitute ownership interests in real property.

Recall from Chapter 43 that property ownership is often viewed as a bundle of rights. One who possesses the entire bundle of rights is said to hold the property in *fee simple*, which is the most complete form of ownership. When only some of the rights in the bundle are transferred to another person, the effect is to limit the ownership rights of both the transferor of the rights and the recipient.

Ownership in Fee Simple

FEE SIMPLE ABSOLUTE
An ownership interest in land in which the owner has the greatest possible aggregation of rights, privileges, and power. Ownership in fee simple absolute is limited absolutely to a person and her or his heirs.

In a **fee simple absolute,** the owner has the greatest aggregation of rights, privileges, and power possible. The owner can give the property away, sell the property, or transfer the property by will to another. Also, the owner has the rights of *exclusive* possession and use of the property. The fee simple is limited to a person and his or her heirs and is assigned forever without limitation or condition.

The rights that accompany a fee simple include the right to use the land for whatever purpose the owner sees fit. Of course, other laws, including laws that prevent the owner from unreasonably interfering with another person's land and applicable zoning and environmental laws, may limit the owner's ability to use the property in certain ways. A fee simple is potentially infinite in duration and can be disposed of by deed (the instrument used to transfer property, which will be discussed later in this chapter) or by will. When there is no will, the fee simple passes to the owner's legal heirs.

Life Estates

LIFE ESTATE
An interest in land that exists only for the duration of the life of some person, usually the holder of the estate.

CONVEYANCE
The transfer of a title to land from one person to another by deed; a document (such as a deed) by which an interest in land is transferred from one person to another.

A **life estate** is an estate that lasts for the life of some specified individual. A **conveyance,** or transfer of real property, "to A for his life" creates a life estate.[5] In a life estate, the life tenant's ownership rights cease to exist on the life tenant's death. The life tenant has the right to use the land, provided that he or she commits no waste (injury to the land). In other words, the life tenant cannot use the land in a manner that would adversely affect its value. The life tenant is entitled to any rents generated by the land and can harvest crops from the land. If mines and oil wells are already on the land, the life tenant is entitled to any royalties and can extract minerals and oil from it, but he or she cannot exploit the land by creating new wells or mines.

The life tenant has the right to mortgage the life estate and can create liens, *easements* (discussed below), and leases, but none can extend beyond the life of the tenant. In addition, with few exceptions, the owner of a life estate has an exclusive right to possession during her or his life. Along with these rights, the life tenant also has some duties—to keep the property in repair and to pay property taxes. In short, the owner of the life estate has the same rights as a fee simple owner except that the life tenant must maintain the value of the property during her or his tenancy.

5. A less common type of life estate is created by the conveyance "to A for the life of B." This is known as an estate *pur autre vie,* or an estate for the duration of the life of another.

NONPOSSESSORY INTERESTS

In contrast to the types of property interests just described, some interests in land do not include any rights to possess the property. These interests, known as *nonpossessory interests,* include easements, profits, and licenses.

EASEMENT
A nonpossessory right to use another's property in a manner established by either express or implied agreement.

PROFIT
In real property law, the right to enter on and remove things from the property of another (for example, the right to enter onto a person's land and remove sand and gravel therefrom).

An **easement** is the right of a person to make limited use of another person's real property without taking anything from the property. An easement, for instance, can be the right to walk or drive across another's property. In contrast, a **profit**[6] is the right to go onto land in possession of another and take away some part of the land itself or some product of the land. ■ EXAMPLE 44.1 Akmed owns Sandy View. Akmed gives Carmen the right to go there to remove all the sand and gravel that she needs for her cement business. Carmen has a profit. ■

Easements and profits can be classified as either *appurtenant* or *in gross.* Because easements and profits are similar and the same rules apply to both, we discuss them together.

Easement or Profit Appurtenant With an easement or profit appurtenant, the owner of one piece of land has a right to go onto (or to remove things from) an *adjacent* piece of land owned by another. The easement is intended to benefit the first piece of land and runs with that land when the land is transferred. ■ EXAMPLE 44.2 Suppose Acosta has a right to drive his car across Green's land, which is adjacent to Acosta's land. This right-of-way over Green's property is an easement appurtenant to Acosta's property and can be used only by Acosta. Acosta can convey the easement when he conveys his property, though. ■

CONTRAST An easement appurtenant requires two adjacent pieces of land owned by two different persons, but an easement in gross needs only one piece of land owned by someone other than the owner of the easement.

Easement or Profit in Gross In an easement or profit *in gross,* the right to use or take things from another's land exists even though the owner of the easement or profit does not own an adjacent tract of land. The easement is intended to benefit a particular person, not a particular piece of land, and cannot be transferred. Only one parcel of land is required for an easement or profit in gross. ■ EXAMPLE 44.3 Avery owns a parcel of land with a marble quarry. Avery conveys to Classic Stone Corporation the right to come onto her land and remove up to five hundred pounds of marble per day. Classic Stone owns a profit in gross and cannot transfer this right to another. ■ Similarly, when a utility company is granted an easement to run its power lines across another's property, it obtains an easement in gross.

Creation of an Easement or Profit Easements and profits can be created by deed or will, by contract, by implication, by necessity, or by prescription. Creation by *deed or will* simply involves the delivery of a deed or a disposition in a will by the owner of an easement or profit stating that her or his rights have been granted to the grantee (the person receiving the easement or profit). Two parties can create an easement by *contract* in which they agree that one party has the right to an easement or profit on a portion of the other party's land.

An easement or profit may arise by *implication* when the circumstances surrounding the division of a parcel of property imply its creation. ■ EXAMPLE 44.4 Barrow divides a parcel of land that has only one well for drinking water. If Barrow conveys the half without a well to Jarad, a profit by implication arises because Jarad needs drinking water. ■

6. The term *profit,* as used here, does not refer to the "profits" made by a business firm. Rather, it means a gain or an advantage.

An easement may also be created by *necessity.* An easement by necessity does not require a division of property for its existence. A person who rents an apartment, for example, has an easement by necessity in the private road leading up to it.

Easements and profits by *prescription* are created in essentially the same way as title to property is obtained by *adverse possession* (discussed later in this chapter). Easements, however, are nonpossessory and involve only the use of the land, whereas adverse possession occurs when one possesses someone else's land and eventually acquires title. An easement by prescription arises when one person exercises an easement, such as a right-of-way, on another person's land without the landowner's consent, and the use is apparent and continues for the length of time required by the applicable statute of limitations.

Effect of a Sale of Property When a parcel of land that is *benefited* by an easement or profit appurtenant is sold, the property carries the easement or profit along with it. Thus, in Example 44.2, if Acosta sells his property to Thomas and includes the appurtenant right-of-way across Green's property in the deed to Thomas, Thomas will own both the property and the easement that benefits it.

When a parcel of land that has the *burden* of an easement or profit appurtenant is sold, the new owner must recognize its existence only if he or she knew or should have known of it or if it was recorded in the appropriate county office. ■ EXAMPLE 44.5 Acosta records his easement across Green's property in the appropriate county office. Green then conveys his land. The new owner of Green's property will have to allow Acosta, or any subsequent owner of Acosta's property, to continue to use the path across the land formerly owned by Green. ■

Termination of an Easement or Profit An easement or profit can be terminated or extinguished in several ways. The simplest way is to deed it back to the owner of the land that is burdened by it. Another way is to abandon it and create evidence of intent to relinquish the right to use it. Mere nonuse will not extinguish an easement or profit *unless the nonuse is accompanied by the intent to abandon.* Also, if the owner of an easement or profit becomes the owner of the property burdened by it, then it is merged into the property.

LICENSE
A revocable right or privilege of a person to come onto another person's land.

License A **license** is the revocable right of a person to come onto another person's land. It is a personal privilege that arises from the consent of the owner of the land and can be revoked by the owner. A ticket to attend a movie at a theater is an example of a license. ■ EXAMPLE 44.6 The owner of a Broadway theater issues Alena a ticket to see a play. If Alena is refused entry into the theater because she is improperly dressed, she has no right to force her way into the theater. The ticket is only a revocable license, not a conveyance of an interest in property. ■

Transfer of Ownership

Ownership of real property can pass from one person to another in several ways. Commonly, ownership interests in land are transferred by sale, and the terms of the transfer are specified in a real estate sales contract. Often, real estate brokers or agents who are licensed by the state assist the buyers and sellers during the sales transaction. Real property ownership can also be transferred by gift, by will or inheritance (see Chapter 45), by adverse possession, or by eminent domain. When ownership rights in real property are transferred, the type of interest being transferred and the conditions of the transfer normally are set forth in a *deed* executed by the person who is conveying the property.

Deeds

DEED
A document by which title to property (usually real property) is passed.

Possession and title to land are passed from person to person by means of a **deed**—the instrument of conveyance of real property. A deed is a writing signed by an owner of real property that transfers title to another. Deeds must meet certain requirements. Unlike a contract, a deed does not have to be supported by legally sufficient consideration. Gifts of real property are common, and they require deeds even though there is no consideration for the gift. The necessary components of a valid deed are the following:

1. The names of the *grantor* (the giver or seller) and the *grantee* (donee or buyer).
2. Words evidencing an intent to convey the property (for example, "I hereby bargain, sell, grant, or give").
3. A legally sufficient description of the land.
4. The grantor's (and usually her or his spouse's) signature.
5. Delivery of the deed.

WARRANTY DEED
A deed in which the grantor assures (warrants to) the grantee that the grantor has title to the property conveyed in the deed, that there are no encumbrances on the property other than what the grantor has represented, and that the grantee will enjoy quiet possession of the property; a deed that provides the greatest amount of protection for the grantee.

Warranty Deeds Different types of deeds provide different degrees of protection against defects of title. A **warranty deed** makes the greatest number of warranties and thus provides the greatest protection against defects of title. A sample warranty deed is shown in Exhibit 44–1 on the following page.

In most states, special language is required to create a general warranty deed. Typically, the deed must include a written promise to protect the buyer against all claims of ownership of the property. A general warranty deed makes the grantor liable for all defects of title occurring while he or she (the grantor) and the previous titleholders held the property.

The Usual Covenants. Warranty deeds commonly include a number of *covenants,* or promises, that the grantor makes to the grantee. A *covenant of seisin*[7] and a *covenant of the right to convey* warrant that the seller has title to, and the power to convey, the property described in the deed. A *covenant against encumbrances* is a promise that the property being sold or conveyed is not subject to any outstanding rights or interests of third parties, except as explicitly stated. Examples of common encumbrances include mortgages, liens, profits, easements, and private deed restrictions on the use of the land.

A *covenant of quiet enjoyment* guarantees that the buyer will not be disturbed in her or his possession of the land by the seller or any third persons. ■ EXAMPLE 44.7 Assume that Julio sells a two-acre lot and office building by warranty deed. Subsequently, a third person shows up who has better title than Julio had and forces the buyer off the property. Here, the covenant of quiet enjoyment has been breached, and the buyer can sue Julio to recover the purchase price of the land plus any other damages incurred as a result. ■

If a contract calls for a "warranty deed" without specifying the covenants to be included in the deed, or if a deed states that the seller is providing the "usual covenants," most courts will infer that all of the covenants mentioned above are included.

7. Pronounced *see*-zuhn.

Should the government be permitted to take undeveloped coastal property from private citizens for public use without compensation? Why or why not? (Vic Bider/PhotoEdit)

EMINENT DOMAIN

Even ownership in real property in fee simple absolute is limited by a superior ownership. Just as in medieval England the king was the ultimate landowner, so in the United States the government has an ultimate ownership right in all land. This right is called **eminent domain,** and it allows the government to take land for public use. Eminent domain gives the government the right to acquire possession of real property in the manner directed by the U.S. Constitution and the laws of the state whenever the public interest requires it. Property may be taken only for public use, not for private benefit.

EMINENT DOMAIN
The power of a government to take land for public use from private citizens for just compensation.

CONDEMNATION
The process of taking private property for public use through the government's power of eminent domain.

TAKING
The taking of private property by the government for public use. The government may not take private property for public use without "just compensation."

The power of eminent domain is generally invoked through **condemnation** proceedings (and the power of eminent domain is sometimes referred to as the *condemnation power* of government). When a new public highway is to be built, for instance, the government must decide where to build it and how much land to condemn. After the government determines that a particular parcel of land is necessary for public use, it will first offer to buy the property. If the owner refuses the offer, the government brings a judicial (condemnation) proceeding to obtain title to the land. Then, in another proceeding, the court determines the *fair value* of the land, which is usually approximately equal to its market value.

When the government takes land owned by a private party for public use, it is referred to as a **taking,** and the government must compensate the private party. Under the so-called *takings clause* of the Fifth Amendment to the U.S. Constitution, the government may not take private property for public use without "just compensation." State constitutions contain similar provisions. Can the power of eminent domain be used to further economic development? That was the question in the following case.

Featured Case

CASE 44.2 Kelo v. City of New London, Connecticut

Supreme Court of the United States, 2005.
__ U.S. __,
125 S.Ct. 2655,
162 L.Ed.2d 439.
http://www.findlaw.com/casecode/supreme.html[a]

a. In the "Browsing" section, click on "2005 Decisions." In the result, click on the name of the case to access the opinion.

MAJORITY OPINION

Justice *STEVENS* delivered the opinion of the Court.

* * * *

The city of New London (hereinafter City) sits at the junction of the Thames River and the Long Island Sound in southeastern Connecticut. Decades of economic decline led a state agency in 1990 to designate the City a

CASE 44.2—Continued

"distressed municipality." In 1996, the Federal Government closed the Naval Undersea Warfare Center, which had been located in the Fort Trumbull area of the City and had employed over 1,500 people. In 1998, the City's unemployment rate was nearly double that of the State, and its population of just under 24,000 residents was at its lowest since 1920.

These conditions prompted state and local officials to target New London, and particularly its Fort Trumbull area, for economic revitalization. * * * In February [1998] the pharmaceutical company Pfizer, Inc., announced that it would build a $300 million research facility on a site immediately adjacent to Fort Trumbull; local planners hoped that Pfizer would draw new business to the area, thereby serving as a catalyst to the area's rejuvenation. * * *

* * * *

The city council approved [a] plan in January 2000 [to redevelop the area that once housed the federal facility]. The [City] successfully negotiated the purchase of most of the real estate in the 90-acre area, but its negotiations with [some of the property owners] failed. As a consequence, in November 2000, the [City] initiated * * * condemnation proceedings * * * .

* * * *

* * * Susette Kelo has lived in the Fort Trumbull area since 1997. She has made extensive improvements to her house, which she prizes for its water view. * * *

In December 2000 [Kelo and others] brought this action in [a Connecticut state] Court [against the City and others]. They claimed, among other things, that the taking of their properties would violate the "public use" restriction in the [U.S. Constitution's] Fifth Amendment. * * * [T]he * * * Court [issued a ruling partly in favor of both sides].

* * * [B]oth sides took appeals to the Supreme Court of Connecticut. That court held * * * that all of the City's proposed takings were valid. * * *

* * * *

We granted *certiorari* to determine whether a city's decision to take property for the purpose of economic development satisfies the "public use" requirement of the Fifth Amendment.

* * * *

* * * [T]his Court long ago rejected any literal requirement that condemned property be put into use for the general public. Indeed, while many state courts in the mid–19th century endorsed "use by the public" as the proper definition of public use, that narrow view steadily eroded over time. Not only was the "use by the public" test difficult to administer (*e.g.*, what proportion of the public need have access to the property? at what price?), but it proved to be impractical given the diverse and always evolving needs of society. Accordingly, * * * this Court * * * embraced the broader and more natural interpretation of public use as "public purpose." * * *

The disposition of this case therefore turns on the question whether the City's development plan serves a "public purpose." Without exception, our cases have defined that concept broadly, reflecting our long-standing policy of deference to legislative judgments in this field.

* * * *

Viewed as a whole, our jurisprudence has recognized that the needs of society have varied between different parts of the Nation, just as they have evolved over time in response to changed circumstances. Our earliest cases in particular embodied a strong theme of federalism, emphasizing the great respect that we owe to state legislatures and state courts in discerning local public needs. For more than a century, our public use jurisprudence has wisely eschewed rigid formulas and intrusive scrutiny in favor of affording legislatures broad latitude in determining what public needs justify the use of the takings power.

* * * *

Those who govern the City were not confronted with the need to remove blight in the Fort Trumbull area, but their determination that the area was sufficiently distressed to justify a program of economic rejuvenation is entitled to our deference. The City has carefully formulated an economic development plan that it believes will provide appreciable benefits to the community, including—but by no means limited to—new jobs and increased tax revenue. As with other exercises in urban planning and development, the City is endeavoring to coordinate a variety of commercial, residential, and recreational uses of land, with the hope that they will form a whole greater than the sum of its parts. To effectuate this plan, the City has invoked a state statute that specifically authorizes the use of eminent domain to promote economic development. Given the comprehensive character of the plan, the thorough deliberation that preceded its adoption, and the limited scope of our review, it is appropriate for us * * * to resolve the challenges of the individual owners, not on a piecemeal basis, but rather in light of the entire plan. Because that plan unquestionably serves a public purpose, the takings challenged here satisfy the public use requirement of the Fifth Amendment.

* * * *

(Continued)

CASE 44.2—Continued

The judgment of the Supreme Court of Connecticut is affirmed.

It is so ordered.

DISSENTING OPINION

Justice *O'CONNOR* * * *, dissenting.

* * * *

* * * In [a previous case in which private property was condemned over the objection of the owner] the extraordinary, pre-condemnation use of the targeted property inflicted affirmative harm on society * * * through blight resulting from extreme poverty * * * . And * * * the relevant legislative body had found that eliminating the existing property use was necessary to remedy the harm. Thus a public purpose was realized when the harmful use was eliminated. Because [the] taking *directly* achieved a public benefit, it did not matter that the property was turned over to private use. Here, in contrast, New London does not claim that Susette Kelo's * * * well-maintained [home is] the source of any social harm. Indeed, it could not so claim without adopting the absurd argument that any single-family home that might be razed to make way for an apartment building, or any church that might be replaced with a retail store, or any small business that might be more lucrative if it were instead part of a national franchise, is inherently harmful to society and thus within the government's power to condemn.

* * * *

* * * [Under the majority's ruling, the] specter of condemnation hangs over all property. Nothing is to prevent the State from replacing any Motel 6 with a Ritz-Carlton, any home with a shopping mall, or any farm with a factory.

* * * *

Any property may now be taken for the benefit of another private party, but the fallout from this decision will not be random. The beneficiaries are likely to be those citizens with disproportionate influence and power in the political process, including large corporations and development firms. As for the victims, the government now has license to transfer property from those with fewer resources to those with more. The Founders cannot have intended this perverse result. * * *

I would hold that the takings * * * are unconstitutional, reverse the judgment of the Supreme Court of Connecticut, and remand for further proceedings.

TEST YOUR COMPREHENSION: CASE DETAILS

1. What was the plaintiffs' claim against the city in this dispute?
2. Did the state courts rule in favor of the plaintiffs on their claim?
3. Why did the United States Supreme Court grant *certiorari* in this case?
4. What did the Court hold with respect to the principal issue?
5. How did the dissent characterize the impact of the majority's decision?

Leasehold Estates

LEASEHOLD ESTATE An estate in realty held by a tenant under a lease. In every leasehold estate, the tenant has a qualified right to possess and/or use the land.

A **leasehold estate** is created when a real property owner (lessor, or landlord) agrees to convey the right to possess and use the property to a lessee (tenant) for a certain period of time. In every leasehold estate, the tenant has a *qualified* right to exclusive possession (qualified by the right of the landlord to enter on the premises to assure that waste is not being committed). The tenant can use the land—for example, by harvesting crops—but cannot injure it by such activities as cutting down timber for sale or extracting oil.

The respective rights and duties of the landlord and tenant that arise under a lease agreement will be discussed shortly. Here we look at the types of leasehold estates, or tenancies, that can be created when real property is leased.

Tenancy for Years

TENANCY FOR YEARS A type of tenancy under which property is leased for a specified period of time, such as a month, a year, or a period of years.

A **tenancy for years** is created by an express contract by which property is leased for a specified period of time, such as a day, a month, a year, or a period of years. Signing a one-year lease to occupy an apartment, for instance, creates a tenancy for years. At the end of the period specified in the lease, the lease ends (without notice), and possession of the apartment returns to the lessor. If the tenant dies during the period of the lease, the lease interest passes to the tenant's heirs as personal property. Often, leases include renewal or extension provisions.

Periodic Tenancy

PERIODIC TENANCY
A lease interest in land for an indefinite period involving payment of rent at fixed intervals, such as week to week, month to month, or year to year.

A **periodic tenancy** is created by a lease that does not specify how long it is to last but does specify that rent is to be paid at certain intervals. This type of tenancy is automatically renewed for another rental period unless properly terminated. ■ Example 44.9 Kayla enters a lease with Capital Properties. The lease states, "Rent is due on the tenth day of every month." This provision creates a periodic tenancy from month to month. ■ This type of tenancy can also extend from week to week or from year to year.

Under the common law, to terminate a periodic tenancy, the landlord or tenant must give at least one period's notice to the other party. If the tenancy extends from month to month, for example, one month's notice must be given prior to the last month's rent payment. State statutes may require a different period for notice of termination in a periodic tenancy, however.

Tenancy at Will

TENANCY AT WILL
A type of tenancy that either party can terminate without notice; usually arises when a tenant who has been under a tenancy for years retains possession, with the landlord's consent, after the tenancy for years has terminated.

Suppose that a landlord rents an apartment to a tenant "for as long as both agree." In such a situation, the tenant receives a leasehold estate known as a **tenancy at will.** Under the common law, either party can terminate the tenancy without notice (that is, "at will"). This type of estate usually arises when a tenant who has been under a tenancy for years retains possession after the termination date of that tenancy with the landlord's consent. Before the tenancy has been converted into a periodic tenancy (by the periodic payment of rent), it is a tenancy at will, terminable by either party without notice. Once the tenancy is treated as a periodic tenancy, notice of termination must conform to the requirements already discussed for that type of tenancy. The death of either party or the voluntary commission of waste by the tenant will terminate a tenancy at will.

Tenancy at Sufferance

TENANCY AT SUFFERANCE
A type of tenancy under which a tenant who, after rightfully being in possession of leased premises, continues (wrongfully) to occupy the property after the lease has been terminated. The tenant has no rights to possess the property and occupies it only because the person entitled to evict the tenant has not done so.

The mere possession of land without right is called a **tenancy at sufferance.** A tenancy at sufferance is not a true tenancy because it is created when a tenant *wrongfully* retains possession of property. Whenever a tenancy for years or a periodic tenancy ends and the tenant continues to retain possession of the premises without the owner's permission, a tenancy at sufferance is created.

Landlord-Tenant Relationships

In the past several decades, landlord-tenant relationships have become much more complex, as has the law governing them. Generally, the law has come to apply contract doctrines, such as those relating to implied warranties and unconscionability, to the landlord-tenant relationship. Increasingly, landlord-tenant relationships have become subject to specific state and local statutes and ordinances as well. In 1972, in an effort to create more uniformity in the law governing landlord-tenant relationships, the National Conference of Commissioners on Uniform State Laws issued the Uniform Residential Landlord and Tenant Act (URLTA). More than one-third of the states have adopted variations of the URLTA.

on the Web You can find online links to most uniform laws, including the URLTA, at **http://www.lawsource.com.**

A landlord-tenant relationship is established by a lease contract. A lease contract may be oral or written. In most states, statutes mandate that leases be in writing for some tenancies (such as those exceeding one year). Generally, to ensure the validity of a lease agreement, it should be in writing and do the following:

1. Express an intent to establish the relationship.
2. Provide for the transfer of the property's possession to the tenant at the beginning of the term.
3. Provide for the landlord's *reversionary* (future) interest, which entitles the property owner to retake possession at the end of the term.
4. Describe the property—for example, give its street address.
5. Indicate the length of the term, the amount of the rent, and how and when it is to be paid.

ILLEGALITY

State or local law often dictates permissible lease terms. For example, a state law might prohibit gambling houses. Thus, if a landlord and tenant intend that the leased premises be used only to house an illegal betting operation, their lease is unenforceable.

A property owner cannot legally discriminate against prospective tenants on the basis of race, color, national origin, religion, gender, or disability. In addition, a tenant cannot legally promise to do something counter to laws prohibiting discrimination. A tenant, for example, cannot legally promise to do business only with members of a particular race.

RIGHTS AND DUTIES

The rights and duties of landlords and tenants generally pertain to four broad areas of concern—the possession, use, maintenance, and, of course, rent of leased property.

Possession A landlord is obligated to give a tenant possession of the property that the tenant has agreed to lease. Many states follow the "English" rule, which requires the landlord to provide actual *physical possession* to the tenant (making sure that the previous tenant has vacated). Other states follow the "American" rule, which requires the landlord to transfer only the *legal right to possession* (thus, the new tenant is responsible for removing a previous tenant). After obtaining possession, the tenant retains the property exclusively until the lease expires, unless the lease states otherwise.

.on the Web Many Web sites now provide information on laws and other information relating to landlord-tenant relationships. One of them is TenantNet™ at **http://www.tenant.net**.

The covenant of quiet enjoyment mentioned previously also applies to leased premises. Under this covenant, the landlord promises that during the lease term, neither the landlord nor anyone having a superior title to the property will disturb the tenant's use and enjoyment of the property. This covenant forms the essence of the landlord-tenant relationship, and if it is breached, the tenant can terminate the lease and sue for damages.

If the landlord deprives the tenant of possession of the leased property or interferes with the tenant's use or enjoyment of it, an **eviction** occurs. An eviction occurs, for instance, when the landlord changes the lock and refuses to give the tenant a new key. A **constructive eviction** occurs when the landlord wrongfully performs or fails to perform any of the duties the lease requires, thereby making the tenant's further use and enjoyment of the property exceedingly difficult or impossible. Examples of constructive eviction include a landlord's failure to provide heat in the winter, light, or other essential utilities.

EVICTION
A landlord's act of depriving a tenant of possession of the leased premises.

CONSTRUCTIVE EVICTION
A form of eviction that occurs when a landlord fails to perform adequately any of the undertakings (such as providing heat in the winter) required by the lease, thereby making the tenant's further use and enjoyment of the property exceedingly difficult or impossible.

Use and Maintenance of the Premises If the parties do not limit by agreement the uses to which the property may be put, the tenant may make any use of it, as long as the use is legal and reasonably relates to the purpose for which the property is adapted or ordinarily used and does not injure the landlord's interest.

The tenant is responsible for any damage to the premises that he or she causes, intentionally or negligently, and may be held liable for the cost of returning the property to the physical condition it was in at the lease's inception. Also, the tenant is not entitled to create a *nuisance* by substantially interfering with others' quiet enjoyment of their property rights (the tort of nuisance was discussed in Chapter 39). Unless the parties have agreed otherwise, the tenant is not responsible for ordinary wear and tear and the property's consequent depreciation in value.

In some jurisdictions, landlords of residential property are required by statute to maintain the premises in good repair. Landlords must also comply with any applicable state statutes and city ordinances regarding maintenance and repair of buildings.

IMPLIED WARRANTY OF HABITABILITY
An implied promise by a landlord that rented residential premises are fit for human habitation—that is, in a condition that is safe and suitable for people to live in.

Implied Warranty of Habitability The **implied warranty of habitability** requires a landlord who leases residential property to furnish premises that are in a habitable condition—that is, in a condition that is safe and suitable for people to live in. Also, the landlord must make repairs to maintain the premises in that condition for the lease's duration. Some state legislatures have enacted this warranty into law. In other jurisdictions, courts have based the warranty on the existence of a landlord's statutory duty to keep leased premises in good repair, or they have simply applied it as a matter of public policy. Generally, this warranty applies to major, or *substantial,* physical defects that the landlord knows or should know about and has had a reasonable time to repair—for example, a large hole in the roof.

NOTE Options that may be available to a tenant on a landlord's breach of the implied warranty of habitability include repairing the defect and deducting the amount from the rent, canceling the lease, and suing for damages.

Rent *Rent* is the tenant's payment to the landlord for the tenant's occupancy or use of the landlord's real property. Usually, the tenant must pay the rent even if she or he refuses to occupy the property or moves out, as long as the refusal or the move is unjustified and the lease is in force. Under the common law, if the leased premises were destroyed by fire or flood, the tenant still had to pay rent. Today, however, most state's statutes provide that if an apartment building burns down, tenants are not required to continue to pay rent.

In some situations, such as when a landlord breaches the implied warranty of habitability, a tenant may be allowed to withhold rent as a remedy. When rent withholding is authorized under a statute, the tenant must usually put the amount withheld into an *escrow account.* This account is held in the name of the depositor (the tenant) and an *escrow agent* (usually the court or a government agency), and the funds are returnable to the depositor if the third person (the landlord) fails to make the premises habitable. Generally, the tenant may withhold an amount equal to the amount by which the defect rendering the premises unlivable reduces the property's rental value. How much that is may be determined in different ways, and a tenant who withholds more than is legally permissible is liable to the landlord for the excessive amount withheld.

Transferring Rights to Leased Property

Either the landlord or the tenant may wish to transfer her or his rights to the leased property during the term of the lease. If complete title to the leased property is transferred, the tenant becomes the tenant of the new owner. The new owner may collect subsequent rent but must abide by the terms of the existing lease agreement.

The tenant's transfer of his or her entire interest in the leased property to a third person is an *assignment of the lease.* Many leases require that the assignment have the landlord's written consent. An assignment that lacks consent can be avoided (nullified) by the landlord. State statutes may specify that the landlord may not unreasonably withhold such consent, though. Also, a landlord who knowingly

FOR REVIEW

Answers for the even-numbered questions in this For Review *section can be found on this text's accompanying Web site at* http://blt.westbuslaw.com. *Select "Chapter 44" and click on "For Review."*

1. What can a person who holds property in fee simple absolute do with the property? Can a person who holds property as a life estate do the same?
2. What are the requirements for acquiring property by adverse possession?
3. What limitations may be imposed on the rights of property owners?
4. What is a leasehold estate? What types of leasehold estates, or tenancies, can be created when real property is leased?
5. What are the respective duties of the landlord and tenant concerning the use and maintenance of leased property? Is the tenant responsible for all damages that he or she causes?

QUESTIONS AND CASE PROBLEMS

44–1. Property Ownership. Twenty-two years ago Lorenz was a wanderer. At that time, he decided to settle down on an unoccupied, three-acre parcel of land that he did not own. People in the area told him that they had no idea who owned the property. Lorenz built a house on the land, got married, and raised three children while living there. He fenced in the land, installed a gate with a sign above it that read "Lorenz's Homestead," and had trespassers removed. Lorenz is now confronted by Joe Reese, who has a deed in his name as owner of the property. Reese, claiming ownership of the land, orders Lorenz and his family off the property. Discuss who has the better "title" to the property.

44–2. Deeds. Wiley and Gemma are neighbors. Wiley's lot is extremely large, and his present and future use of it will not involve the entire area. Gemma wants to build a single-car garage and driveway along the present lot boundary. Because of ordinances requiring buildings to be set back fifteen feet from an adjoining property line, and because of the placement of her existing structures, Gemma cannot build the garage. Gemma contracts to purchase ten feet of Wiley's property along their boundary line for $3,000. Wiley is willing to sell but will give Gemma only a quitclaim deed, whereas Gemma wants a warranty deed. Discuss the differences between these deeds as they would affect the rights of the parties if the title to this ten feet of land later proves to be defective.

44–3. Taking. Richard and Jaquelyn Jackson owned property in a residential subdivision near an airport operated by the Metropolitan Knoxville Airport Authority in Blount County, Tennessee. The Airport Authority considered extending a runway near the subdivision and undertook a study that found that the noise, vibration, and pollution from aircraft using the extension would render the Jacksons' property incompatible with residential use. The airport built the extension, bringing about the predicted results, and the Jacksons filed a suit against the Airport Authority, alleging a taking of their property. The Airport Authority responded that there was no taking because there were no direct flights over the Jacksons' property. In whose favor will the court rule, and why? [*Jackson v. Metropolitan Knoxville Airport Authority,* 922 S.W.2d 860 (Tenn. 1996)]

44–4. Warranty of Habitability. Three-year-old Nkenge Lynch fell from the window of her third-floor apartment and suffered serious and permanent injuries. There were no window stops or guards on the window. The use of window stops, even if installed, is optional with the tenant. Stanley James owned the apartment building. Zsa Zsa Kinsey, Nkenge's mother, filed a suit on Nkenge's behalf in a Massachusetts state court against James, alleging in part a breach of an implied warranty of habitability. The plaintiff did not argue that the absence of stops or guards made the apartment unfit for human habitation. Instead, she asserted that their absence "endangered and materially impaired her health and safety" and, therefore, the failure to install them was a breach of warranty. Should the court rule that the absence of window stops breached a warranty of habitability? Should the court mandate that landlords provide window guards? Why or why not? [*Lynch v. James,* 44 Mass.App.Ct. 448, 692 N.E.2d 81 (1998)]

44–5. Adverse Possession. In 1972, Ted Pafundi bought a quarry in West Pawlet, Vermont, from his neighbor, Marguerite Scott. The deed vaguely described the eastern boundary of the quarry as "the westerly boundary of the lands of" the neighboring property owners. Pafundi quarried green slate from the west wall until his death in 1979, when his son Gary began to work the east wall until *his* death in 1989. Gary's daughter Connie then took over operations. All of the Pafundis used the floor of the quarry as their base of operations. In 1992, N.A.S. Holdings, Inc., bought the neighboring property. A survey revealed that virtually the entire quarry was within the boundaries of N.A.S.'s property and that twenty years earlier, Ted had actually bought only a small strip of land on the west side. When N.A.S. attempted to begin quarrying, Connie blocked the access. N.A.S. filed a suit in a Vermont state court against Connie, seeking to establish title. Connie argued that she had title to the quarry through adverse possession under a state statute with a possessory period of fifteen years. What are the elements to acquire title by adverse possession? Are they satisfied in this case? In whose favor should the court rule, and why? [*N.A.S. Holdings, Inc. v. Pafundi,* 736 A.2d 780 (Vt. 1999)]

CASE PROBLEM WITH SAMPLE ANSWER

44–6. Jennifer Tribble leased an apartment from Spring Isle II, a limited partnership. The written lease agreement provided that if Tribble was forced to move because of a job transfer or because she accepted a new job, she could vacate on sixty days' notice and owe only an extra two months' rent plus no more than a $650 rerenting fee. The initial term was for one year, and the parties renewed the lease for a second one-year term. The security deposit was $900. State law allowed a landlord to withhold a security deposit for the nonpayment of rent but required timely notice stating valid reasons for the withholding or the tenant would be entitled to twice the amount of the deposit as damages. One month into the second term, Tribble notified Spring Isle in writing that she had accepted a new job and would move out within a week. She paid the extra rent required by the lease, but not the rerental fee, and vacated the apartment. Spring Isle wrote her a letter, stating that it was keeping the entire security deposit until the apartment was rerented or the lease term ended, whichever came first. Spring Isle later filed a suit in a Wisconsin state court against Tribble, claiming that she owed, among other things, the rest of the rent until the apartment had been rented again and the costs of rerenting. Tribble responded that withholding the security deposit was improper and that she was entitled to "any penalties." Does Tribble owe Spring Isle anything? Does Spring Isle owe Tribble anything? Explain. [*Spring Isle II v. Tribble,* 610 N.W.2d 229 (Wis.App. 2000)]

After you have answered this problem, compare your answer with the sample answer given on the Web site that accompanies this text. Go to http://blt.westbuslaw.com, select "Chapter 44," and click on "Case Problem with Sample Answer."

44–7. Commercial Lease Terms. Metropolitan Life Insurance Co. leased space in its Trail Plaza Shopping Center in Florida to Winn-Dixie Stores, Inc., to operate a supermarket. Under the lease, the landlord agreed not to permit "any [other] property located within the shopping center to be used for or occupied by any business dealing in or which shall keep in stock or sell for off-premises consumption any staple or fancy groceries" in more than "500 square feet of sales area." In 1999, Metropolitan leased 22,000 square feet of space in Trail Plaza to 99 Cent Stuff-Trail Plaza, LLC, under a lease that prohibited it from selling "groceries" in more than 500 square feet of "sales area." Shortly after 99 Cent Stuff opened, it began selling food and other products, including soap, matches, and paper napkins. Alleging that these sales violated the parties' leases, Winn-Dixie filed a suit in a Florida state court against 99 Cent Stuff and others. The defendants argued in part that the groceries provision covered only food and the 500-square-foot restriction included only shelf space, not store aisles. How should these lease terms be interpreted? Should the court grant an injunction in Winn-Dixie's favor? Explain. [*Winn-Dixie Stores, Inc. v. 99 Cent Stuff-Trail Plaza, LLC,* 811 So.2d 719 (Fla.App. 3 Dist. 2002)]

44–8. Easements. The Wallens family owned a cabin on Lummi Island in the state of Washington. A driveway ran from the cabin across their property to South Nugent Road. In 1952, Floyd Massey bought the adjacent lot and built a cabin. To gain access to his property, he used a bulldozer to extend the driveway, without the Wallenses' permission but also without their objection. In 1975, the Wallenses sold their property to Wright Fish Co. Massey continued to use and maintain the driveway without permission or objection. In 1984, Massey sold his property to Robert Drake. Drake and his employees continued to use and maintain the driveway without permission or objection, although Drake knew it was located largely on Wright's property. In 1997, Wright sold its lot to Robert Smersh. The next year, Smersh told Drake to stop using the driveway. Drake filed a suit in a Washington state court against Smersh, claiming an easement by prescription (which is created by meeting the same requirements as adverse possession). Does Drake's use of the driveway meet all of the requirements? What should the court rule? Explain. [*Drake v. Smersh,* 122 Wash.App. 147, 89 P.3d 726 (Div. 1 2004)]

A QUESTION OF ETHICS

44–9. John and Terry Hoffius own property in Jackson, Michigan, which they rent. Kristal McCready and Keith Kerr responded to the Hoffiuses' ad about the property. The Hoffiuses refused to rent to McCready and Kerr, however, when they learned that the two were single and intended to live together. John Hoffius told all prospective tenants that unmarried cohabitation violated his religious beliefs. McCready and others filed a suit in a Michigan state court against the Hoffiuses. They alleged in part that the Hoffiuses' actions violated the plaintiffs' civil rights under a state law that prohibits discrimination on the basis of "marital status." The Hoffiuses responded in part that forcing them to rent to unmarried couples in violation of the Hoffiuses' religious beliefs would be unconstitutional. [*McCready v. Hoffius,* 586 N.W.2d 723 (Mich. 1998)]

1. Did the defendants violate the plaintiffs' civil rights? Explain.
2. Should a court, in the interest of preventing discrimination in housing, compel a landlord to violate his or her conscience? In other words, whose rights should prevail in this case? Why?
3. Is there an objective rule that determines when civil rights or religious freedom, or any two similarly important principles, should prevail? If so, what is it? If not, should there be?

FOR CRITICAL ANALYSIS

44–10. Real property law dates back hundreds of years. What changes have occurred in society, including business and technological changes, that have affected the development and application of real property law? (Hint: Was airspace an issue three hundred years ago?)

INTERNET EXERCISES

Go to the *Business Law Today* home page at **http://blt.westbuslaw.com**, select "Chapter 44," and click on "Internet Exercises." There you will find the following Internet research exercises that you can perform to learn more about topics covered in this chapter.

Activity 44–1: LEGAL PERSPECTIVE—Eminent Domain

Activity 44–2: MANAGEMENT PERSPECTIVE—Fair Housing

Activity 44–3: SOCIAL PERSPECTIVE—The Rights of Tenants

BEFORE THE TEST

Go to the *Business Law Today* home page at **http://blt.westbuslaw.com**, select "Chapter 44," and click on "Interactive Quizzes." You will find a number of interactive questions relating to this chapter.

"Insurance is part charity and part business, but all common sense."

Calvin Coolidge, 1872–1933
(Thirtieth president of the United States, 1923–1929)

CHAPTER 45

Insurance, Wills, and Trusts

CHAPTER OUTLINE

- INSURANCE
- WILLS
- TRUSTS

LEARNING OBJECTIVES

After reading this chapter, you should be able to answer the following questions:

1. What is an insurable interest? When must an insurable interest exist—at the time the insurance policy is obtained, at the time the loss occurs, or both?
2. Is an insurance broker the agent of the insurance applicant or the agent of the insurer?
3. What are the basic requirements for executing a will? How may a will be revoked?
4. What is the difference between a *per stirpes* distribution and a *per capita* distribution of an estate to the grandchildren of the deceased?
5. What are the four essential elements of a trust? What is the difference between an express trust and an implied trust?

Most individuals insure both real and personal property (as well as their lives). As Calvin Coolidge asserted in the chapter-opening quotation, insurance is "all common sense"—by insuring our property, we protect ourselves against damage and loss.

The first part of this chapter focuses on insurance, which is a foremost concern of all property owners. We then examine how property is transferred on the death of its owner. Certainly, the laws of succession of property are a necessary corollary to the concept of private ownership of property. Our laws require that on death, title to the property of a decedent (one who has recently died) must be delivered in full somewhere. In this chapter, we see that this can be done by will, through trusts, or through state laws prescribing distribution of property among heirs or next of kin.

INSURANCE
A contract in which, for a stipulated consideration, one party agrees to compensate the other for loss on a specific subject by a specified peril.

RISK
A prediction concerning potential loss based on known and unknown factors.

RISK MANAGEMENT
Planning that is undertaken to protect one's interest should some event threaten to undermine its security. In the context of insurance, risk management involves transferring certain risks from the insured to the insurance company.

Insurance

Insurance is a contract by which an insurance company (the insurer) promises to pay a certain amount or give something of value to another (either the insured or the beneficiary) in the event that the insured is injured, dies, or sustains damage to her or his property as a result of particular, stated contingencies. Basically, insurance is an arrangement for *transferring and allocating risk*. In many cases, **risk** can be described as a prediction concerning potential loss based on known and unknown factors. Insurance, however, involves much more than a game of chance.

Risk management normally involves the transfer of certain risks from the individual to the insurance company by a contractual agreement. The insurance contract and its provisions will be examined shortly. First, however, we look at the different types of insurance that can be obtained, insurance terminology, and the concept of insurable interest.

A New York building that was damaged by debris from the collapse of the World Trade Center in 2001. What impact has the risk of terrorist acts had on insurance? (Michael Rieger/FEMA News Photo)

CLASSIFICATIONS OF INSURANCE

Insurance is classified according to the nature of the risk involved. For instance, fire insurance, casualty insurance, life insurance, and title insurance apply to different types of risk. Furthermore, policies of these types protect different persons and interests. This is reasonable because the types of losses that are expected and that are foreseeable or unforeseeable vary with the nature of the activity. Exhibit 45–1 on pages 1152 and 1153 presents a list of insurance classifications.

All-risk insurance is property insurance that covers damage resulting from all risks not specifically excluded. Typical exclusions are war, pollution, earthquakes, and floods. After September 11, 2001, insurance companies commonly added acts of terrorism to the list of exclusions. Separate terrorism insurance is available, though. The question in the following case was whether an agreement that required a business to carry all-risk insurance and "other reasonable insurance" included coverage against terrorism.

CASE 45.1 Omni Berkshire Corp. v. Wells Fargo Bank, N.A.

United States District Court,
Southern District of New York, 2004.
307 F.Supp.2d 534.

BACKGROUND AND FACTS Omni Berkshire Corporation and its business affiliates own or operate hotels in the United States, Canada, and Mexico. In 1998, Omni borrowed $250 million from Secore Financial Corporation. The loan was secured by five of Omni's hotels, worth collectively about $349 million. The loan agreement required Omni to obtain and maintain certain

CASE 45.1—Continued

insurance, including all-risk insurance on the hotels and "such other reasonable insurance" as the lender might request. In 1998, Omni's all-risk policy provided that "damage done by terrorists * * * is insured." When Omni renewed the policy in 2002, however, it excluded coverage for acts of terrorism. Wells Fargo Bank, N.A., which collected the payments on the loan, told Omni that insurance against terrorist acts was required to comply with the agreement. Omni learned that $60 million in terrorism coverage for the five hotels for one year could be purchased for $316,000—63 percent of the cost of an all-risk policy. Omni filed a suit in a federal district court against Wells Fargo, seeking an order that it was *not* required to obtain insurance against terrorism.

IN THE WORDS OF THE COURT . . .

CHIN, District Judge.

* * * *

The first issue is whether Omni was required, by virtue of the "all risk" clause of the Agreement, to purchase terrorism coverage after insurance companies started excluding acts of terrorism from "all risk" policies after 9/11. I hold that it was not.

* * * *

* * * The Agreement does not spell out the parameters of the required "all risk" insurance, and the Agreement itself makes no reference to terrorism or terrorism insurance. Accordingly, to ascertain the intent of the parties, I may look not only to the language of the Agreement but to extrinsic evidence.

There is little in terms of extrinsic evidence. As the parties agree, in 1998, when the Agreement was executed, all risk policies covered acts of terrorism because terrorism was not specifically excluded. When the parties negotiated the Agreement, terrorism insurance was a "non-issue," and there was no discussion of terrorism insurance. Hence, there is no direct evidence of what the parties intended * * * .

Nonetheless, there is some circumstantial evidence as to what the parties intended. The parties did not define "all risk" insurance at least in part because there was, and still is, a general understanding in the insurance industry as to the meaning of "all risk" insurance. It was commonly understood that the standard "all risk" policy had evolved over time and that it could continue to evolve over time. * * *

Under these circumstances, if the parties had intended to require Omni to maintain for the life of the Agreement "all risk" insurance in the form that existed in August 1998 [it included terrorism insurance], they surely would have said so. * * * That the parties did not include such or similar language suggests that the parties intended to require only what the industry generally accepted—knowing that the generally accepted all risk policy might evolve over time.

* * * *

* * * [T]he issue remains whether Wells Fargo acted reasonably in requiring Omni to purchase terrorism coverage under the "other insurance" clause of the Agreement. I conclude that Wells Fargo acted reasonably * * * .

First, Wells Fargo's concern that Omni's hotels are at risk is, unfortunately, reasonable. In the World Trade Center attacks on 9/11, one hotel was destroyed and two others were damaged. * * *

Second, the record contains substantial proof that the owners of many hotels and other commercial properties have purchased terrorism insurance. * * *

Third, the cost of the $60 million in coverage * * * is reasonable * * * .

Fourth, the additional insurance would benefit not only Wells Fargo but Omni as well. * * *

* * * *

(Continued)

CASE 45.1—Continued

> * * * [I]n the post–9/11 world when so much more is at risk, it was reasonable for Wells Fargo to request * * * that Omni provide an additional $60 million in insurance coverage to account for the loss of terrorism coverage created when the insurance industry decided to exclude terrorism from all risk policies.

DECISION AND REMEDY The court held that a business is required to carry terrorism insurance under an agreement that requires all-risk insurance and "such other reasonable insurance" as the lender might request. The court dismissed Omni's complaint and ordered it to obtain terrorism insurance. If Omni failed to do so, the court authorized Wells Fargo to obtain a policy and charge the expense to Omni.

WHY IS THIS CASE IMPORTANT? *The decision in this case marked the first time that terrorism insurance was classified and required as "other reasonable insurance."*

POLICY
In insurance law, a contract between the insurer and the insured in which, for a stipulated consideration, the insurer agrees to compensate the insured for loss on a specific subject by a specified peril.

INSURANCE TERMINOLOGY

An insurance contract is called a **policy;** the consideration paid to the insurer is called a *premium;* and the insurance company is sometimes called an *underwriter.* The parties to an insurance policy are the *insurer* (the insurance company) and the *insured* (the person covered by its provisions or the holder of the policy).

EXHIBIT 45–1 INSURANCE CLASSIFICATIONS

TYPE OF INSURANCE	COVERAGE
Accident	Covers expenses, losses, and suffering incurred by the insured because of accidents causing physical injury and any consequent disability; sometimes includes a specified payment to heirs of the insured if death results from an accident.
All-risk	Covers all losses that the insured may incur except those resulting from fraud on the part of the insured.
Automobile	May cover damage to automobiles resulting from specified hazards or occurrences (such as fire, vandalism, theft, or collision); normally provides protection against liability for personal injuries and property damage resulting from the operation of the vehicle.
Casualty	Protects against losses incurred by the insured as a result of being held liable for personal injuries or property damage sustained by others.
Credit	Pays to a creditor the balance of a debt on the disability, death, insolvency, or bankruptcy of the debtor; often offered by lending institutions.
Decreasing-term life	Provides life insurance; requires uniform payments over the life (term) of the policy, but with a decreasing face value (amount of coverage).
Employer's liability	Insures employers against liability for injuries or losses sustained by employees during the course of their employment; covers claims not covered under workers' compensation insurance.
Fidelity or guaranty	Provides indemnity against losses in trade or losses caused by the dishonesty of employees, the insolvency of debtors, or breaches of contract.
Fire	Covers losses incurred by the insured as a result of fire.
Floater	Covers movable property, as long as the property is within the territorial boundaries specified in the contract.
Group	Provides individual life, medical, or disability insurance coverage but is obtainable through a group of persons, usually employees; the policy premium is paid either entirely by the employer or partially by the employer and partially by the employee.

Insurance contracts are usually obtained through an *agent,* who ordinarily works for the insurance company, or through a *broker,* who is ordinarily an *independent contractor.* When a broker deals with an applicant for insurance, the broker is, in effect, the applicant's agent and not an agent of the insurance company. In contrast, an insurance agent is an agent of the insurance company, not of the applicant. As a general rule, the insurance company is bound by the acts of its insurance agents when they act within the agency relationship (discussed in Chapter 28). In most situations, state law determines the status of all parties writing or obtaining insurance.

ETHICAL ISSUE 45.1

Does an insurance agent have a duty to advise insurance applicants about coverage? When a person applies for insurance coverage through an insurance company's agent, is the agent obligated to advise that person as to what coverage he or she should obtain? If the agent does not advise a client about certain types of coverage, has the agent breached a duty to the applicant? For example, suppose that a couple applies for auto insurance, and the insurance agent does not advise them that they should sign up for uninsured motorist coverage. Later, the couple is involved in an accident with an uninsured motorist, and the insurance company refuses to compensate them for their injuries and losses. The couple claims that the insurance agent was negligent in not

EXHIBIT 45–1 INSURANCE CLASSIFICATIONS—CONTINUED

TYPE OF INSURANCE	COVERAGE
Health	Covers expenses incurred by the insured as a result of physical injury or illness and other expenses relating to health and life maintenance.
Homeowners'	Protects homeowners against some or all risks of loss to their residences and the residences' contents or liability arising from the use of the property.
Key-person	Protects a business in the event of the death or disability of a key employee.
Liability	Protects against liability imposed on the insured as a result of injuries to the person or property of another.
Life	Covers the death of the policyholder. On the death of the insured, an amount specified in the policy is paid by the insurer to the insured's beneficiary.
Major medical	Protects the insured against major hospital, medical, or surgical expenses.
Malpractice	Protects professionals (physicians, lawyers, and others) against malpractice claims brought against them by their patients or clients; a form of liability insurance.
Marine	Covers movable property (including ships, freight, and cargo) against certain perils or navigation risks during a specific voyage or time period.
Mortgage	Covers a mortgage loan; the insurer pays the balance of the mortgage to the creditor on the death or disability of the debtor.
No-fault auto	Covers personal injuries and (sometimes) property damage resulting from automobile accidents. The insured submits his or her claims to his or her own insurance company, regardless of who was at fault. A person may sue the party at fault or that party's insurer only when an accident results in serious medical injury and consequent high medical costs. Governed by state "no-fault" statutes.
Term life	Provides life insurance for a specified period of time (term) with no cash surrender value; usually renewable.
Title	Protects against any defects in title to real property and any losses incurred as a result of existing claims against or liens on the property at the time of purchase.

advising them to sign up for uninsured motorist coverage. Was the agent negligent? No. As mentioned earlier, an insurance agent is an agent of the insurer, not the insured. As such, the agent owes fiduciary duties to the insurer (the insurance company), but not to the insured. The agent's only duties to the insured are contractual in nature.

While some may think that this rule is unfair to insurance applicants, who may know less about the need for certain types of insurance coverage than the agent does, a contrary rule might create even more unfairness. An insurance agent could be held liable for failure to advise a client of every possible insurance option, and the insured would be relieved of any burden to take care of his or her own financial needs and expectations. Also, as one court noted, if the state legislature does not require such coverage, why should the courts require insurance companies to offer or explain available optional coverage?[1] ■

INSURABLE INTEREST

INSURABLE INTEREST An interest either in a person's life or well-being or in property that is sufficiently substantial that insuring against injury to (or the death of) the person or against damage to the property does not amount to a mere wagering (betting) contract.

A person can insure anything in which she or he has an **insurable interest.** Without this insurable interest, there is no enforceable contract, and a transaction to purchase insurance coverage would have to be treated as a wager. In regard to real and personal property, an insurable interest exists when the insured derives a pecuniary benefit (a benefit consisting of or relating to money) from the preservation and continued existence of the property. Put another way, one has an insurable interest in property when one would sustain a financial loss from its destruction. In regard to life insurance, a person must have a reasonable expectation of benefit from the continued life of another in order to have an insurable interest in that person's life. The benefit may be pecuniary (as with so-called *key-person insurance,* which insures the lives of important employees, usually in small companies), or it may be founded on the relationship between the parties (by blood or affinity).

For property insurance, the insurable interest must exist at the time the loss occurs but need not exist when the policy is purchased. In contrast, for life insurance, the insurable interest must exist at the time the policy is obtained. The existence of an insurable interest is a primary concern in determining liability under an insurance policy.

THE INSURANCE CONTRACT

NOTE The federal government has the power to regulate the insurance industry under the commerce clause of the U.S. Constitution. Instead of exercising this power itself, Congress allows the states to regulate insurance.

An insurance contract is governed by the general principles of contract law, although the insurance industry is heavily regulated by each state. Several aspects of the insurance contract will be treated here.

Application The filled-in application form for insurance is usually attached to the policy and made a part of the insurance contract. Thus, an insurance applicant is bound by any false statements that appear in the application (subject to certain exceptions). Because the insurance company evaluates the risk factors based on the information included in the insurance application, misstatements or misrepresentations can void a policy, especially if the insurance company can show that it would not have extended insurance if it had known the true facts.

Effective Date The effective date of an insurance contract—that is, the date on which the insurance coverage begins—is important. In some instances, the insurance applicant is not protected until a formal written policy is issued. In other situations,

1. *Jones v. Kennedy,* 108 S.W.3d 203 (Mo.App. 2003).

the applicant is protected between the time the application is received and the time the insurance company either accepts or rejects it. Four facts should be kept in mind:

1. A broker is merely the agent of an applicant. Therefore, until the broker obtains a policy, the applicant normally is not insured.
2. A person who seeks insurance from an insurance company's agent will usually be protected from the moment the application is made, provided that some form of premium has been paid. Between the time the application is received and either rejected or accepted, the applicant is covered (possibly subject to a medical examination). Usually, the agent will write a memorandum, or **binder,** indicating that a policy is pending and stating its essential terms.

BINDER
A written, temporary insurance policy.

3. If the parties agree that the policy will be issued and delivered at a later time, the contract is not effective until the policy is issued and delivered or sent to the applicant, depending on the agreement. Thus, any loss sustained between the time of application and the delivery of the policy is not covered.
4. The parties may agree that a life insurance policy will be binding at the time the insured pays the first premium, or the policy may be expressly contingent on the applicant's passing a physical examination. If the applicant pays the premium and passes the examination, the policy coverage is continuously in effect. If the applicant pays the premium but dies before having the physical examination, then in order to collect, the applicant's estate must show that the applicant *would have passed* the examination had he or she not died.

Coinsurance Clauses Often, when taking out fire insurance policies, property owners insure their property for less than full value because most fires do not result in a total loss. To encourage owners to insure their property for an amount as close to full value as possible, fire insurance policies commonly include a coinsurance clause. Typically, a *coinsurance clause* provides that if the owner insures the property up to a specified percentage—usually 80 percent—of its value, she or he will recover any loss up to the face amount of the policy. If the insurance is for less than the fixed percentage, the owner is responsible for a proportionate share of the loss.

Coinsurance applies only in instances of partial loss. ■ EXAMPLE 45.1 If the owner of property valued at \$100,000 takes out a policy in the amount of \$40,000 and suffers a loss of \$30,000, the recovery will be \$15,000. The formula for calculating the recovery amount is as follows:

$$\frac{\text{amount of insurance (\$40,000)}}{\text{coinsurance percentage (80\%)} \times \text{property value (\$100,000)}} = \begin{array}{c}\text{recovery percentage}\\ \text{(50\%)}\end{array}$$

$$\text{recovery percentage (50\%)} \times \text{amount of loss (\$30,000)} = \text{recovery amount (\$15,000)}$$

If the owner had taken out a policy in the amount of \$80,000, then, according to the same formula, the full loss would have been recovered up to the face value of the policy. ■

Other Provisions and Clauses Some other important provisions and clauses contained in insurance contracts are listed and defined in Exhibit 45–2 on the next page. The courts are aware that most people do not have the special training necessary to understand the intricate terminology used in insurance policies. Thus, the words used in an insurance contract have their ordinary meanings. They are interpreted by the courts in light of the nature of the coverage involved.

EXHIBIT 45–2 INSURANCE CONTRACT PROVISIONS AND CLAUSES

Incontestability clause	An incontestability clause provides that after a policy has been in force for a specified length of time—usually two or three years—the insurer cannot contest statements made in the application.
Appraisal clause	Insurance policies frequently provide that if the parties cannot agree on the amount of a loss covered under the policy or the value of the property lost, an appraisal, or estimate, by an impartial and qualified third party can be demanded.
Arbitration clause	Many insurance policies include clauses that call for arbitration of disputes that may arise between the insurer and the insured concerning the settlement of claims.
Antilapse clause	An antilapse clause provides that the policy will not automatically lapse if no payment is made on the date due. Ordinarily, under such a provision, the insured has a *grace period* of thirty or thirty-one days within which to pay an overdue premium before the policy is canceled.
Multiple insurance	Many insurance policies include a clause providing that if the insured has multiple insurance policies that cover the same property and the amount of coverage exceeds the loss, the loss will be shared proportionately by the insurance companies.

When there is an ambiguity in the policy, the provision generally is interpreted against the insurance company. Also when it is unclear whether an insurance contract actually exists because the written policy has not been delivered, the uncertainty normally is resolved against the insurance company. The court presumes that the policy is in effect unless the company can show otherwise. Similarly, an insurer must make sure that the insured is adequately notified of any change in coverage under an existing policy.

Cancellation The insured can cancel a policy at any time, and the insurer can cancel under certain circumstances. When an insurance company can cancel its insurance contract, the policy or a state statute usually requires that the insurer give advance written notice of the cancellation to the insured.[2] The same requirement applies when only part of a policy is canceled. Any premium paid in advance may be refundable on the policy's cancellation. The insured may also be entitled to a life insurance policy's cash surrender value.

The insurer may cancel an insurance policy for various reasons, depending on the type of insurance. For example, automobile insurance can be canceled for nonpayment of premiums or suspension of the insured's driver's license. Property insurance can be canceled for nonpayment of premiums or for other reasons, including the insured's fraud or misrepresentation, conviction for a crime that

.on the Web The Web site of the Insurance Information Institute provides a wealth of news and information on insurance-related issues, including statistical data, a glossary of insurance terms, and various PowerPoint presentations. Go to

http://www.iii.org.

2. In at least one case, the court held that a diskette containing a computerized document, which could be printed out as "hard copy," was sufficient to constitute "written notice" of cancellation. See *Clyburn v. Allstate Insurance Co.,* 826 F.Supp. 955 (D.S.C. 1993).

increases the hazard insured against, or gross negligence that increases the hazard insured against. Life and health policies can be canceled because of false statements made by the insured in the application, but cancellation can only take place before the effective date of an incontestability clause. An insurer cannot cancel—or refuse to renew—a policy for discriminatory reasons or other reasons that violate public policy, or because the insured has appeared as a witness in a case against the company.

Good Faith Obligations Both parties to an insurance contract are responsible for the obligation they assume under the contract (contract law was discussed in Chapters 8 through 17). In addition, both the insured and the insurer have an implied duty to act in good faith.

Good faith requires the party who is applying for insurance to reveal everything necessary for the insurer to evaluate the risk. In other words, the applicant must disclose all material facts, including all facts that an insurer would consider in determining whether to charge a higher premium or to refuse to issue a policy altogether.

Once the insurer has accepted the risk, and some event occurs that gives rise to a claim, the insurer has a duty to investigate to determine the facts. When a policy provides insurance against third party claims, the insurer is obligated to make reasonable efforts to settle such a claim. If a settlement cannot be reached, then regardless of the claim's merit, the insurer must defend any suit against the insured. Usually, a policy provides that in this situation the insured must cooperate. A policy provision may expressly require the insured to attend hearings and trials, to help in obtaining evidence and witnesses, and to assist in reaching a settlement.

The question in the following case was whether the insurer acted in bad faith in investigating and paying an insured's claim.

CASE 45.2 Columbia National Insurance Co. v. Freeman

Supreme Court of Arkansas, 2002.
347 Ark. 423,
64 S.W.3d 720.
http://courts.state.ar.us/opinions/opinions.html[a]

BACKGROUND AND FACTS Gary and Peggy Freeman owned and operated Circle F Trading Company, a western wear and general store, in Arkansas. The Freemans were insured against losses to the building, its contents, continuing business expenses, and other coverage, under a policy with Columbia National Insurance Company. In October 1997, a fire damaged Circle F's building and destroyed its inventory. The Freemans filed a claim with Columbia, providing an appraisal of the lost merchandise at $107,905.13 and a list of their continuing business expenses. Columbia obtained a second appraisal of $71,231.69 and attempted to find Circle F a building to serve as a temporary office. In December, Columbia paid the Freemans $77,892.28 for inventory, supplies, and lost income. No payment was made for continuing business expenses, and no office was provided. The parties agreed on an amount of $32,725 to cover the cost of the damage to the building, but Columbia offered to pay only 80 percent of this amount. Circle F never reopened. The Freemans filed a suit in an Arkansas state court against Columbia, alleging, among other things, bad faith. A jury returned a verdict for the Freemans, awarding $170,000 in compensatory damages and $200,000 in punitive damages. Columbia filed a motion for a directed verdict, which the court denied. Columbia appealed to the Arkansas Supreme Court.

a. In the "Search Cases by Party Name" section, enter "Freeman" in the "Party Name" box and select "Search by Date Range." For the date range, choose "From January 2002" and "To February 2002," and click on "Search." From the list of results, click on the name of the case to access the opinion. The Arkansas judiciary maintains this Web site.

(Continued)

CASE 45.2—Continued

IN THE WORDS OF THE COURT . . .

RAY THORNTON, Justice.

* * * *

* * * An insurance company commits the tort of bad faith when it affirmatively engages in dishonest, malicious, or oppressive conduct in order to avoid a just obligation to its insured. *We have defined "bad faith" as dishonest, malicious, or oppressive conduct carried out with a state of mind characterized by hatred, ill will, or a spirit of revenge. Mere negligence or bad judgment is insufficient* * * * . [Emphasis added.]

* * * *

* * * First, appellees [the Freemans] argue that appellant acted in bad faith when it failed to pay appellees' ongoing business expenses. These expenses included utility bills and appellees' mortgage payment. Bill Green, an insurance adjuster who worked for appellant, was responsible for providing appellees money to cover their ongoing business expenses. He testified that he asked appellees to provide him documentation of the ongoing business expenses before he could pay the expenses. Mr. Freeman and Mrs. Freeman each testified that they had made the requested copies of the bills and mailed the documentation to Mr. Green. Mr. Green testified that the only documentation he received from appellees was a handwritten list of bills * * * . There was sufficient evidence for the jury, without resorting to suspicion or conjecture, to determine whether adequate documentation had been provided, and to support a finding that failure to cover appellees' ongoing business expenses, to which they were entitled, was an act of bad faith.

Next, appellees contend that appellant acted in bad faith when it failed to provide appellees with a temporary location for their business. Sufficient evidence was admitted to present to the jury the question of whether appellant's agent agreed to provide a trailer for appellees to use, researched the cost of providing such a service, and then failed to go forward with the agreement.

Additionally, appellees argue that appellant was acting in bad faith when it * * * agreed * * * upon the sum of $32,725 for the cost of repairing the building but * * * tendered only eighty percent of the amount agreed upon. There was sufficient evidence of such an agreement to submit to the jury the question of whether an agreement was entered into by the parties and then breached by appellant.

* * * *

Finally, appellees argue that appellant acted with bad faith when it requested that two appraisals be performed on appellees' inventory and chose to pay appellees based on the lower of the two appraisals.

DECISION AND REMEDY The Arkansas Supreme Court affirmed the lower court's judgment. The state supreme court concluded that there was substantial evidence to support the jury's verdict that Columbia's actions constituted oppressive conduct carried out with a state of mind characterized by ill will.

FOR CRITICAL ANALYSIS—Social Consideration *Suppose that after an investigation, Columbia had simply refused to pay the Freemans' claim. Would the result in this case have been the same? Why or why not?*

Defenses against Payment An insurance company can raise any of the defenses that would be valid in any ordinary action on a contract, as well as some defenses that do not apply in ordinary contract actions. If the insurance company can show that the policy was procured by fraud or misrepresentation, it may have a valid defense for not paying on a claim. (The insurance company may also have the right to disaffirm or rescind an insurance contract.) An absolute defense exists if the insurer can show that the insured lacked an insurable interest—thus rendering the policy void from the beginning. Improper actions, such as those that are against public policy or are otherwise illegal, can also give the insurance company a defense against the payment of a claim or allow it to rescind the contract.

An insurance company can be prevented from asserting some defenses that are normally available, however. ■ EXAMPLE 45.2 Suppose that a company tells an insured that information requested on a form is optional, and the insured provides it anyway. The company cannot use the information to avoid its contractual obligation under the insurance contract. Similarly, an insurance company normally cannot escape payment on the death of an insured on the ground that the person's age was stated incorrectly on the application. ■

WILL
An instrument directing what is to be done with the testator's property on his or her death, made by the testator and revocable during his or her lifetime. No interests in the testator's property pass until the testator dies.

TESTATE
Having left a will at death.

INTESTATE
As a noun, one who has died without having created a valid will; as an adjective, the state of having died without a will.

INTESTACY LAWS
State statutes that specify how property will be distributed when a person dies intestate (without a valid will); also called statutes of descent and distribution.

TESTATOR
One who makes and executes a will.

EXECUTOR
A person appointed by a testator in a will to see that her or his will is administered appropriately.

ADMINISTRATOR
One who is appointed by a court to handle the probate (disposition) of a person's estate if that person dies intestate (without a valid will) or if the executor named in the will cannot serve.

DEVISE
To make a gift of real property by will.

BEQUEST
A gift by will of personal property (from the verb *to bequeath*).

LEGACY
A gift of personal property under a will.

DEVISEE
One designated in a will to receive a gift of real property.

LEGATEE
One designated in a will to receive a gift of personal property.

Wills

Private ownership of property leads logically to both the protection of that property by insurance coverage while the owner is alive and the transfer of that property on the death of the owner to those designated in the owner's will. A **will** is the final declaration of how a person desires to have her or his property disposed of after death. It is a formal instrument that must follow exactly the requirements of state law to be effective. A will is referred to as a *testamentary disposition* of property, and one who dies after having made a valid will is said to have died **testate.**

A will can serve other purposes besides the distribution of property. It can appoint a guardian for minor children or incapacitated adults. It can also appoint a personal representative to settle the affairs of the deceased.

A person who dies without having created a valid will is said to have died **intestate.** In this situation, state **intestacy laws** prescribe the distribution of the property among heirs or next of kin. If no heirs or kin can be found, title to the property will be transferred to the state.

Terminology of Wills

A person who makes out a will is known as a **testator** (from the Latin *testari,* "to make a will"). The court responsible for administering any legal problems surrounding a will is called a *probate court,* as mentioned in Chapter 3. When a person dies, a personal representative administers the estate and settles finally all of the decedent's (deceased person's) affairs. An **executor** is a personal representative named in the will; an **administrator** is a personal representative appointed by the court for a decedent who dies without a will. The court will also appoint an administrator if the will does not name an executor or if the named person lacks the capacity to serve as an executor.

A gift of real estate by will is generally called a **devise,** and a gift of personal property by will is called a **bequest,** or **legacy.** The recipient of a gift by will is a **devisee** or a **legatee,** depending on whether the gift was a devise or a legacy.

Types of Gifts

Gifts by will can be specific, general, or residuary. A *specific* devise or bequest (legacy) describes particular property (such as "Eastwood Estate" or "my gold pocket watch") that can be distinguished from all the rest of the testator's property. A *general* devise or bequest (legacy) uses less restrictive terminology. For example, "I devise all my lands" is a general devise. A general bequest often specifies a sum of money instead of a particular item of property, such as a watch or an automobile. For example, "I give to my nephew, Carleton, $30,000" is a general bequest.

Estate planning—preparing for the transfer of assets to others on one's death—involves a number of tools, including wills and trusts. These and other devices that can be used in estate planning are described by the American Academy of Estate Planning Attorneys on its Web site at **http://www.aaepa.com**.

If the assets of an estate are insufficient to pay in full all general bequests provided for in the will, an *abatement* takes place, meaning the legatees receive reduced benefits. ■ EXAMPLE 45.3 Yusuf's will leaves "$15,000 each to my children, Tamara and Kwame." On Yusuf's death, only $10,000 is available to honor these bequests. By abatement, each child will receive $5,000. ■ If bequests are more complicated, abatement may be more complex. The testator's intent, as expressed in the will, controls.

Sometimes, a will provides that any assets remaining after the estate's debts have been paid and specific gifts have been made—called the *residuary* (or *residuum*)—are to be distributed in a specific way, such as to the testator's spouse or descendants. Such a clause, called a *residuary clause,* is often used when the exact amount to be distributed cannot be determined until all of the other gifts and payouts have been made. If the testator has not indicated what party or parties should receive the residuary of the estate, the residuary passes according to state laws of intestacy.

PROBATE PROCEDURES

PROBATE
The process of proving and validating a will and settling all matters pertaining to an estate.

Laws governing wills come into play when a will is probated. To **probate** a will means to establish its validity and to carry the administration of the estate through a court process. Probate laws vary from state to state. In 1969, however, the American Bar Association and the National Conference of Commissioners on Uniform State Laws approved the Uniform Probate Code (UPC). The UPC codifies general principles and procedures for the resolution of conflicts in settling estates and relaxes some of the requirements for a valid will contained in earlier state laws. Nearly all of the states have adopted some part of the UPC. Nevertheless, succession and inheritance laws still vary widely among the states, so one should always check the laws of the particular state involved.[3] Typically, probate procedures differ, depending on the size of the decedent's estate.

"If you want to see a man's true character, watch him divide an estate."

BENJAMIN FRANKLIN, 1706–1790
(American diplomat, author, and scientist)

Informal Probate For smaller estates, most state statutes provide for the distribution of assets without formal probate proceedings. Faster and less expensive methods are then used. For example, property can be transferred by *affidavit* (a written statement taken before a person who has authority to affirm it), and problems or questions can be handled during an administrative hearing. In addition, some state statutes provide that title to cars, savings and checking accounts, and certain other property can be passed merely by filling out forms.

To learn more about wills and probate procedures, you can access the Uniform Probate Code online at **http://www.law.cornell.edu/uniform/probate.html**.

A majority of states also provide for *family settlement agreements,* which are private agreements among the beneficiaries. Once a will is admitted to probate, the family members can agree to settle among themselves the distribution of the decedent's assets. Although a family settlement agreement speeds the settlement process, a court order is still needed to protect the estate from future creditors and to clear title to the assets involved. The use of these and other types of summary procedures in estate administration can save time and expense.

Formal Probate For larger estates, formal probate proceedings normally are undertaken, and the probate court supervises every aspect of the settlement of the decedent's estate. Additionally, in some situations—such as when a guardian for minor children or for an incompetent person must be appointed and a trust has been created to protect the minor or the incompetent person—more formal probate pro-

3. For example, California law differs substantially from the UPC.

cedures cannot be avoided. Formal probate proceedings may take several months to complete, and as a result, a sizable portion of the decedent's assets (up to perhaps 10 percent) may go toward payment of court costs and fees charged by attorneys and personal representatives.

WILL SUBSTITUTES
Various documents that attempt to dispose of an estate in the same or similar manner as a will, such as trusts or life insurance plans.

Property Transfers outside the Probate Process In the ordinary situation, a person can employ various **will substitutes** to avoid the cost of probate—for example, *inter vivos* trusts (discussed later in this chapter), life insurance policies or Individual Retirement Accounts (IRAs) with named beneficiaries, or joint-tenancy arrangements. Not all methods are suitable for every estate, but there are alternatives to complete probate administration.

REQUIREMENTS FOR A VALID WILL

A will must comply with statutory formalities designed to ensure that the testator understood his or her actions at the time the will was made. These formalities are intended to help prevent fraud. Unless they are followed, the will is declared void, and the decedent's property is distributed according to the laws of intestacy of that state. The requirements are not uniform among jurisdictions. Most states, however, uphold certain basic requirements for executing a will. We now look at these requirements.

RECALL In most states, the age of majority for contractual purposes is also eighteen years.

Testamentary Capacity and Intent For a will to be valid, the testator must have testamentary capacity—that is, the testator must be of legal age and sound mind *at the time the will is made.* The legal age for executing a will varies, but in most states and under the UPC, the minimum age is eighteen years [UPC 2–501]. Thus, the will of a twenty-one-year-old decedent written when the person was sixteen is invalid if, under state law, the legal age for executing a will is eighteen.

HOLOGRAPHIC WILL
A will written entirely in the signer's handwriting and usually not witnessed.

The concept of "being of sound mind" refers to the testator's ability to formulate and to comprehend a personal plan for the disposition of property. Generally, a testator must (1) intend the document to be his or her last will and testament, (2) comprehend the kind and character of the property being distributed, and (3) comprehend and remember the "natural objects of his or her bounty" (usually, family members and persons for whom the testator has affection).

A valid will is one that represents the maker's intention to transfer and distribute her or his property. When it can be shown that the decedent's plan of distribution was the result of fraud or of undue influence, the will is declared invalid. The court may sometimes infer undue influence if the testator ignored blood relatives and named as beneficiary a nonrelative who was in constant close contact with the testator and in a position to influence the making of the will.

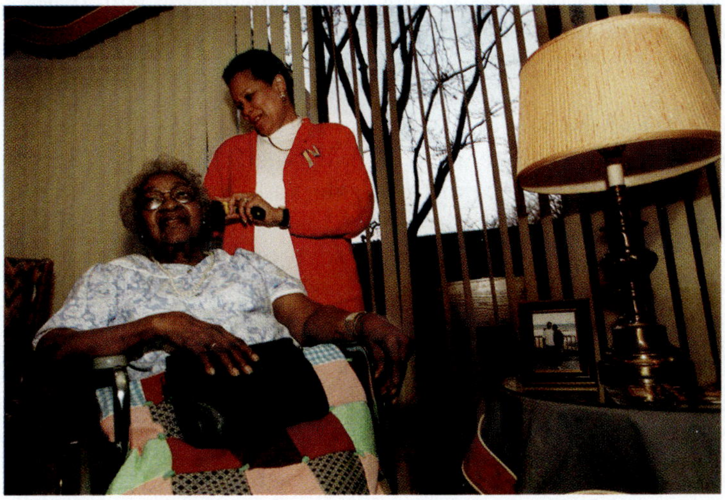

Suppose this elderly woman drafts a will that excludes her children and leaves the entire estate to her caregiver. Why might a court hold such a will to be invalid? (AP Photo/Elizabeth Ellis)

Writing Requirements Generally, a will must be in writing. The writing itself can be informal as long as it substantially complies with the statutory requirements. In some states, a will can be handwritten in crayon or ink. It can be written on a sheet or scrap of paper, on a paper bag, or on a piece of cloth. A will that is completely in the handwriting of the testator is called a **holographic will** (sometimes referred to as an *olographic will*).

NUNCUPATIVE WILL
An oral will (often called a deathbed will) made before witnesses; usually limited to transfers of personal property.

A **nuncupative will** is an oral will made before witnesses. Most states do not permit such wills. Where authorized by statute, nuncupative wills are generally valid only if made during the last illness of the testator and are therefore sometimes referred to as *deathbed wills*. Normally, only personal property can be transferred by a nuncupative will. Statutes frequently permit soldiers and sailors to make nuncupative wills when on active duty.

Signature Requirements It is a fundamental requirement that the testator's signature appear, generally at the end of the will. Each jurisdiction dictates by statute and court decision what constitutes a signature. Initials, an X or other mark, and words such as "Mom" have all been upheld as valid when it was shown that the testators *intended* them to be signatures.

Witness Requirements A will normally must be attested (sworn to) by two, and sometimes three, witnesses. The number of witnesses, their qualifications, and the manner in which the witnessing must be done are generally set out in a statute. A witness can be required to be disinterested—that is, not a beneficiary under the will. The UPC, however, provides that a will is valid even if it is attested by an interested witness [UPC 2–505]. There are no age requirements for witnesses, but they must be mentally competent.

The purpose of witnesses is to verify that the testator actually executed (signed) the will and had the requisite intent and capacity at the time. A witness does not have to read the contents of the will. Usually, the testator and all witnesses must sign in the sight or the presence of one another, but there are exceptions.[4] The UPC does not require all parties to sign in the presence of one another and deems it sufficient if the testator acknowledges her or his signature to the witnesses [UPC 2–502].

.on the Web To find the wills of many famous people, including Benjamin Franklin and Elvis Presley, go to **http://www.geocities.com/Athens/Acropolis/6537/wills.htm**.

Publication Requirements A will is *published* by an oral declaration by the maker to the witnesses that the document they are about to sign is his or her "last will and testament." Publication is becoming an unnecessary formality in most states, and it is not required under the UPC.

REVOCATION OF WILLS

An executed will is revocable by the maker at any time during the maker's lifetime. The maker may revoke a will by a physical act, such as tearing up the will, or by a subsequent writing. Wills can also be revoked by operation of law. Revocation can be partial or complete, and it must follow certain strict formalities.

Revocation by a Physical Act of the Maker A testator may revoke a will by intentionally burning, tearing, canceling, obliterating, or otherwise destroying it, or by having someone else do so in the presence of the maker and at the maker's direction.[5] In some states, partial revocation by physical act of the maker is recognized. Thus, those portions of a will lined out or torn away are dropped, and the remaining parts of the will are valid. In no circumstances, however, can a provision be crossed out and an additional or substitute provision written in. Such altered portions require reexecution (re-signing) and reattestation (rewitnessing).

4. See, for example, *Slack v. Truitt,* 368 Md. 2, 791 A.2d 129 (2000).

5. The destruction cannot be inadvertent. The maker's intent to revoke must be shown. Consequently, when a will has been burned or torn accidentally, the maker should normally have a new document created to avoid any suggestion that the maker intended to revoke the will.

To revoke a will by physical act, it is necessary to follow the mandates of a state statute exactly. When a state statute prescribes the specific methods for revoking a will by physical act, only those methods can be used to revoke the will.

CODICIL
A written supplement or modification to a will. A codicil must be executed with the same formalities as a will.

Revocation by a Subsequent Writing A will may also be wholly or partially revoked by a **codicil,** a written instrument separate from the will that amends or revokes provisions in the will. A codicil eliminates the necessity of redrafting an entire will merely to add to it or amend it. A codicil can also be used to revoke an entire will. The codicil must be executed with the same formalities required for a will, and it must refer expressly to the will. In effect, it updates a will because the will is "incorporated by reference" into the codicil.

A new will (second will) can be executed that may or may not revoke the first or a prior will, depending on the language used. To revoke a prior will, the second will must use language specifically revoking other wills, such as, "This will hereby revokes all prior wills." If the second will is otherwise valid and properly executed, it will revoke all prior wills. If the express *declaration of revocation* is missing, then both wills are read together. If any of the dispositions made in the second will are inconsistent with the prior will, the second will controls.

Revocation by Operation of Law Revocation by *operation of law* occurs when marriage, divorce or annulment, or the birth of a child takes place after a will has been executed. In most states, when a testator marries after executing a will that does not include the new spouse, on the testator's death the spouse can still receive the amount he or she would have taken had the testator died intestate (how an intestate's property is distributed under state laws will be discussed shortly). In effect, the will is revoked to the point of providing the spouse with an intestate share. The rest of the estate is passed under the will [UPC 2–301, 2–508]. If, however, the new spouse is otherwise provided for in the will (or by transfer of property outside the will), he or she will not be given an intestate amount.

At common law and under the UPC, divorce does not necessarily revoke the entire will. A divorce or an annulment occurring after a will has been executed will revoke those dispositions of property made under the will to the former spouse [UPC 2–508].

If a child is born after a will has been executed and if it appears that the deceased parent would have made a provision for the child, the child is entitled to receive whatever portion of the estate she or he is allowed under state laws providing for the distribution of an intestate's property. Most state laws allow a child to receive some portion of a parent's estate if no provision is made in the parent's will, unless it appears from the terms of the will that the testator intended to disinherit the child. Under the UPC, the rule is the same.

INTESTACY LAWS

"You cannot live without the lawyers, and certainly you cannot die without them."
JOSEPH H. CHOATE, 1832–1917
(American lawyer and diplomat)

As mentioned, state intestacy laws determine how property will be distributed when a person dies intestate (without a valid will). These statutes are more formally known as *statutes of descent and distribution.* Intestacy laws attempt to carry out the likely intent and wishes of the decedent. These laws assume that deceased persons would have intended that their natural heirs (spouses, children, grandchildren, or other family members) inherit their property. Therefore, intestacy statutes set out rules and priorities under which these heirs inherit the property. If no heirs exist, the state will assume ownership of the property. The rules of descent vary widely from state to state.

Surviving Spouse and Children Usually, state statutes provide that first the debts of the decedent must be satisfied out of the estate; then the remaining assets pass to the surviving spouse and to the children. A surviving spouse usually receives only a share of the estate—one-half if there is also a surviving child and one-third if there are two or more children. Only if no children or grandchildren survive the decedent will a surviving spouse succeed to the entire estate.

■ EXAMPLE 45.4 Assume that Allen dies intestate and is survived by his wife, Della, and his children, Duane and Tara. Allen's property passes according to intestacy laws. After Allen's outstanding debts are paid, Della will receive the homestead (either in fee simple or as a life estate) and ordinarily a one-third interest in all other property. The remaining real and personal property will pass to Duane and Tara in equal portions. ■ Under most state intestacy laws and under the UPC, in-laws do not share in an estate. If a child dies before his or her parents, the child's spouse will not receive an inheritance on the parents' death. For example, if Duane died before his father (Allen), Duane's spouse would not inherit Duane's share of Allen's estate.

When there is no surviving spouse or child, the order of inheritance is grandchildren, then brothers and sisters, and, in some states, parents of the decedent. These relatives are usually called *lineal descendants.* If there are no lineal descendants, then *collateral heirs*—nieces, nephews, aunts, and uncles of the decedent—make up the next group to share. If there are no survivors in any of these groups, most statutes provide for the property to be distributed among the next of kin of the collateral heirs.

Stepchildren, Adopted Children, and Illegitimate Children Under intestacy laws, stepchildren are not considered kin. Legally adopted children, however, are recognized as lawful heirs of their adoptive parents. Statutes vary from state to state in regard to the inheritance rights of illegitimate children. Generally, an illegitimate child is treated as the child of the mother and can inherit from her and her relatives. The child is usually not regarded as the legal child of the father with the right of inheritance unless paternity was established through some legal proceeding prior to the father's death.

Distribution to Grandchildren When an intestate is survived by descendants of deceased children, a question arises as to what share these descendants (that is, grandchildren of the intestate) will receive. One method of dividing an intestate's estate is ***per stirpes.*** Under this method, within a class or group of distributees (for example, grandchildren), the children of any one descendant take the share that their deceased parent *would have been* entitled to inherit.

PER STIRPES
A Latin term meaning "by the roots." In the law governing estate distribution, a method of distributing an intestate's estate so that each heir in a certain class (such as grandchildren) takes the share to which her or his deceased ancestor (such as a mother or father) would have been entitled.

PER CAPITA
A Latin term meaning "per person." In the law governing estate distribution, a method of distributing the property of an intestate's estate so that each heir in a certain class (such as grandchildren) receives an equal share.

■ EXAMPLE 45.5 Assume that Michael, a widower, has two children, Scott and Jonathan. Scott has two children (Becky and Holly), and Jonathan has one child (Paul). Scott and Jonathan die before their father, and then Michael dies. If Michael's estate is distributed *per stirpes,* Becky and Holly each receive one-fourth of the estate (dividing Scott's one-half share). Paul receives one-half of the estate (taking Jonathan's one-half share). ■

An estate may also be distributed on a ***per capita*** basis, which means that each person in a class or group takes an equal share of the estate. If Michael's estate is distributed *per capita,* Becky, Holly, and Paul each receive a one-third share.

Trusts

TRUST
An arrangement in which title to property is held by one person (a trustee) for the benefit of another (a beneficiary).

A **trust** is any arrangement through which property is transferred from one person to a trustee to be administered for the transferor's or another party's benefit. It can also be defined as a right of property, real or personal, held by one party for the benefit of another. A trust can be created for any purpose that is not illegal or against public policy. Its essential elements are as follows:

1. A designated beneficiary.
2. A designated trustee.
3. A fund sufficiently identified to enable title to pass to the trustee.
4. Actual delivery by the settlor or grantor (the person creating the trust) to the trustee with the intention of passing title.

"Put not your trust in money, but put your money in trust."
OLIVER WENDELL HOLMES, JR.,
1841–1935
(Associate justice of the United States Supreme Court, 1902–1932)

■ EXAMPLE 45.6 If James conveys his farm to the First Bank of Minnesota to be held for the benefit of his daughters, he has created a trust. James is the settlor, the First Bank of Minnesota is the trustee, and James's daughters are the beneficiaries. ■ Numerous types of trusts can be established. In this section, we look at some of the major types of trusts and their characteristics.

EXPRESS TRUSTS

An express trust is created or declared in explicit terms, usually in writing. Express trusts fall into two categories: *inter vivos* (living) trusts and *testamentary* trusts (trusts provided for in a last will and testament).

***INTER VIVOS* TRUST**
A trust created by the grantor (settlor) and effective during the grantor's lifetime; a trust not established by a will.

An ***inter vivos* trust** is executed by a grantor during her or his lifetime. The grantor (settlor) executes a *trust deed*, and legal title to the trust property passes to the named trustee. The trustee has a duty to administer the property as directed by the grantor for the benefit and in the interest of the beneficiaries. The trustee must preserve the trust property, make it productive, and, if required by the terms of the trust agreement, pay income to the beneficiaries, all in accordance with the terms of the trust. Once the *inter vivos* trust is created, the grantor has, in effect, given over the property for the benefit of the beneficiaries. Often, setting up this type of trust offers tax-related benefits.

TESTAMENTARY TRUST
A trust that is created by will and therefore does not take effect until the death of the testator.

A **testamentary trust** is created by a will to come into existence on the settlor's death. Although a testamentary trust has a trustee who maintains legal title to the trust property, the trustee's actions are subject to judicial approval. This trustee can be named in the will or be appointed by the court. Thus, a testamentary trust does not fail because a trustee has not been named in the will. The legal responsibilities of the trustee are the same as in an *inter vivos* trust. If the will setting up a testamentary trust is invalid, the trust will also be invalid. The property that was supposed to be in the trust will then pass according to intestacy laws, not according to the terms of the trust.

IMPLIED TRUSTS

Sometimes, a trust will be imposed (implied) by law, even in the absence of an express trust. Implied trusts include resulting trusts and constructive trusts.

RESULTING TRUST
An implied trust arising from the conduct of the parties. A trust in which a party holds the actual legal title to another's property but only for that person's benefit.

A **resulting trust** arises from the conduct of the parties. Here, the trust results, or is created, when circumstances raise an inference that the party holding legal title to the property does so for the benefit of another. ■ EXAMPLE 45.7 Suppose that

Garrison wants to put one acre of land she owns on the market for sale. Because she is going out of the country for two years and would not be able to deed the property to a buyer during that period, Garrison conveys the property to her good friend Oswald. Oswald will attempt to sell the property while Garrison is gone. Because the intent of the transaction in which Garrison conveyed the property to Oswald is neither a sale nor a gift, the property will be held in trust (a resulting trust) by Oswald for the benefit of Garrison. Therefore, on Garrison's return, Oswald will be required either to deed back the property to Garrison or, if the property has been sold, to turn over the proceeds (held in trust) to her. Here, the trust arises (*results from*) the *apparent intention* of the parties. ■

CONSTRUCTIVE TRUST
An equitable trust that is imposed in the interests of fairness and justice when someone wrongfully holds legal title to property. A court may require the owner to hold the property in trust for the person or persons who rightfully should own the property.

A **constructive trust** is an equitable trust imposed by a court in the interests of fairness and justice. In a constructive trust, the owner is declared to be a trustee for the parties who are, in equity, actually entitled to the benefits that flow from the trust. If someone wrongfully holds legal title to property—because the property was obtained through fraud or in breach of a legal duty, for example—a court may impose a constructive trust. ■ EXAMPLE 45.8 Arturo and Spring are partners in buying, developing, and selling real estate. Arturo learns through a staff member of the partnership that two hundred acres of land will soon come on the market and that the staff member will recommend that the partnership purchase the land. Arturo purchases the property secretly in his own name, thus violating his fiduciary relationship. When these facts are discovered, a court will determine that Arturo must hold the property in trust for the partnership. ■

SPECIAL TYPES OF TRUSTS

CHARITABLE TRUST
A trust in which the property held by the trustee must be used for a charitable purpose, such as the advancement of health, education, or religion.

SPENDTHRIFT TRUST
A trust created to protect the beneficiary from spending all the funds to which she or he is entitled. Only a certain portion of the total amount is given to the beneficiary at any one time, and most states prohibit creditors from attaching assets of the trust.

TOTTEN TRUST
A trust created by the deposit of a person's own funds in his or her own name as a trustee for another. It is a tentative trust, revocable at will until the depositor dies or completes the gift in his or her lifetime by some unequivocal act or declaration.

Certain trusts are created for special purposes. Three of these trusts that warrant discussion are charitable, spendthrift, and Totten trusts. A **charitable trust** is designed for the benefit of a segment of the public or of the public in general. Usually, to be deemed a charitable trust, a trust must be created for charitable, educational, religious, or scientific purposes.

A **spendthrift trust** is created to provide for the maintenance of a beneficiary by preventing him or her from being careless with the bestowed funds. Unlike other trusts, the beneficiary in a spendthrift trust is not permitted to transfer or assign his or her right to the trust's principal or future payments from the trust. Essentially, the beneficiary can draw only a certain portion of the total amount to which he or she is entitled at any one time. The majority of states allow spendthrift trust provisions that prohibit creditors from attaching such trusts.

A **Totten trust**[6] is created when one person deposits funds in her or his own name as a trustee for another. This trust is tentative in that it is revocable at will until the depositor dies or completes the gift in her or his lifetime by some unequivocal act or declaration (for example, delivery of the funds to the intended beneficiary). If the depositor dies before the beneficiary dies and if the depositor has not revoked the trust expressly or impliedly, a presumption arises that an absolute (a binding, irrevocable) trust has been created for the benefit of the beneficiary. At the death of the depositor, the beneficiary obtains property rights to the balance on hand.

6. This type of trust derives its unusual name from *In re Totten,* 179 N.Y. 112, 71 N.E. 748 (1904).

REVIEWING INSURANCE, WILLS, AND TRUSTS

Provident Insurance, Inc., issued an insurance policy to a company providing an employee, Steve Matlin, with life and disability insurance. Soon thereafter, Matlin was diagnosed with "panic disorder and phobia of returning to work." He lost his job and sought disability coverage. Provident denied coverage, doubting the diagnosis of disability. Matlin and his employer sued Provident. During pretrial discovery, the insurer learned that Matlin had stated on the policy application that he had never been treated for any "emotional, mental, nervous, urinary, or digestive disorder" or any kind of heart disease. In fact, before Matlin filled out the application he had visited a physician for chest pains and general anxiety, and the physician had prescribed an antidepressant and recommended that Matlin stop smoking. Using the information presented in the chapter, answer the following questions.

1. Did Matlin commit a misrepresentation on his policy application?
2. If there is any ambiguity on the application, should it be resolved in favor of the insured or the insurer?
3. Assuming that the policy is valid, does Matlin's situation fall within the terms of the disability policy?
4. Suppose that Matlin had not lost his job but died in a car accident. He had designated his wife, Lisa, as his sole beneficiary. Could Lisa collect on the life insurance policy outside the probate process?

KEY TERMS

administrator 1159
bequest 1159
binder 1155
charitable trust 1166
codicil 1163
constructive trust 1166
devise 1159
devisee 1159
executor 1159
holographic will 1161
insurable interest 1154
insurance 1150
inter vivos trust 1165
intestacy laws 1159
intestate 1159
legacy 1159
legatee 1159
nuncupative will 1162
per capita 1164
per stirpes 1164
policy 1152
probate 1160
resulting trust 1165
risk 1150
risk management 1150
spendthrift trust 1166
testamentary trust 1165
testate 1159
testator 1159
Totten trust 1166
trust 1165
will 1159
will substitutes 1161

CHAPTER SUMMARY Insurance, Wills, and Trusts

	INSURANCE
Classifications (See pages 1150–1152.)	See Exhibit 45–1 on pages 1152 and 1153.
Terminology (See pages 1152–1154.)	1. *Policy*—The insurance contract. 2. *Premium*—The consideration paid to the insurer for a policy.

(Continued)

CHAPTER SUMMARY Insurance, Wills, and Trusts—Continued

Terminology—Continued (See pages 1152–1154.)	3. *Underwriter*—The insurance company. 4. *Parties*—Include the insurer (the insurance company), the insured (the person covered by insurance), an agent (a representative of the insurance company) or a broker (ordinarily an independent contractor), and a beneficiary (a person to receive proceeds under the policy).
Insurable Interest (See page 1154.)	An insurable interest exists whenever an individual or entity benefits from the preservation of the health or life of the insured or the property to be insured. For life insurance, an insurable interest must exist at the time the policy is issued. For property insurance, an insurable interest must exist at the time of the loss.
The Insurance Contract (See pages 1154–1159.)	1. *Laws governing*—The general principles of contract law are applied; the insurance industry is also heavily regulated by the states. 2. *Application*—An insurance applicant is bound by any false statements that appear in the application (subject to certain exceptions), which is part of the insurance contract. Misstatements or misrepresentations may be grounds for voiding the policy. 3. *Effective date*—Coverage on an insurance policy can begin when a *binder* (a written memorandum indicating that a formal policy is pending and stating its essential terms) is written; when the policy is issued; at the time of contract formation; or depending on the terms of the contract, when certain conditions are met. 4. *Provisions and clauses*—See Exhibit 45–2 on page 1156. Words will be given their ordinary meanings, and any ambiguity in the policy will be interpreted against the insurance company. When the written policy has not been delivered and it is unclear whether an insurance contract actually exists, the uncertainty will be resolved against the insurance company. The court will presume that the policy is in effect unless the company can show otherwise. 5. *Defenses against payment to the insured*—Defenses include misrepresentation, fraud, or violation of warranties by the applicant.
	WILLS
Terminology (See page 1159.)	1. *Intestate*—One who dies without a valid will. 2. *Testator*—A person who makes out a will. 3. *Personal representative*—A person appointed in a will or by a court to settle the affairs of a decedent. A personal representative named in the will is an *executor;* a personal representative appointed by the court for an intestate decedent is an *administrator.* 4. *Devise*—A gift of real estate by will; may be general or specific. The recipient of a devise is a *devisee.* 5. *Bequest, or legacy*—A gift of personal property by will; may be general or specific. The recipient of a bequest (legacy) is a *legatee.*
Probate Procedures (See pages 1160–1161.)	To probate a will means to establish its validity and to carry the administration of the estate through a court process. Probate laws vary from state to state. Probate procedures may be informal or formal, depending on the size of the estate and other factors, such as whether a guardian for minor children must be appointed.
Requirements for a Valid Will (See pages 1161–1162.)	1. The testator must have testamentary capacity (be of legal age and sound mind at the time the will is made). 2. A will must be in writing (except for nuncupative wills). A holographic will is completely in the handwriting of the testator. 3. A will must be signed by the testator; what constitutes a signature varies from jurisdiction to jurisdiction.

CHAPTER SUMMARY Insurance, Wills, and Trusts—Continued

Requirements for a Valid Will—Continued	4. A nonholographic will (an attested will) must be witnessed in the manner prescribed by state statute. 5. A will may have to be *published*—that is, the testator may be required to announce to witnesses that this is his or her "last will and testament"; not required under the UPC.
Revocation of Wills (See pages 1162–1163.)	1. *By physical act of the maker*—Tearing up, canceling, obliterating, or deliberately destroying part or all of a will. 2. *By subsequent writing*— a. Codicil—A formal, separate document to amend or revoke an existing will. b. Second will or new will—A new, properly executed will expressly revoking the existing will. 3. *By operation of law*— a. Marriage—Generally revokes part of a will written before the marriage. b. Divorce or annulment—Revokes dispositions of property made under a will to a former spouse. c. Subsequently born child—It is *implied* that the child is entitled to receive the portion of the estate granted under intestacy distribution laws.
Intestacy Laws (See pages 1163–1164.)	1. Intestacy laws vary widely from state to state. Usually, the law provides that the surviving spouse and children inherit the property of the decedent (after the decedent's debts are paid). The spouse usually inherits the entire estate if there are no children, one-half of the estate if there is one child, and one-third of the estate if there are two or more children. 2. If there is no surviving spouse or child, then, in order, lineal descendants (grandchildren, brothers and sisters, and—in some states—parents of the decedent) inherit. If there are no lineal descendants, then collateral heirs (nieces, nephews, aunts, and uncles of the decedent) inherit.
	TRUSTS
Definition (See page 1165.)	A trust is any arrangement through which property is transferred from one person to a trustee to be administered for another party's benefit. The essential elements of a trust are (1) a designated beneficiary, (2) a designated trustee, (3) a fund sufficiently identified to enable title to pass to the trustee, and (4) actual delivery to the trustee with the intention of passing title.
Express Trusts (See page 1165.)	Express trusts are created by explicit terms, usually in writing, and fall into two categories: 1. *Inter vivos trust*—A trust executed by a grantor during her or his lifetime. 2. *Testamentary trust*—A trust created by will and coming into existence on the death of the grantor.
Implied Trusts (See pages 1165–1166.)	Implied trusts, which are imposed by law in the interests of fairness and justice, include the following: 1. *Resulting trust*—Arises from the conduct of the parties when an *apparent* intention to create a trust is present. 2. *Constructive trust*—Arises by operation of law whenever a transaction takes place in which the person who takes title to property is in equity not entitled to enjoy the beneficial interest therein.
Special Types of Trusts (See page 1166.)	1. *Charitable trust*—A trust designed for the benefit of a public group or the public in general. 2. *Spendthrift trust*—A trust created to provide for the maintenance of a beneficiary by allowing the beneficiary to receive only a certain portion of the total amount at any one time. 3. *Totten trust*—A trust created when one person deposits funds in his or her own name as a trustee for another.

FOR REVIEW

Answers for the even-numbered questions in this For Review *section can be found on this text's accompanying Web site at* http://blt.westbuslaw.com. *Select "Chapter 45" and click on "For Review."*

1. What is an insurable interest? When must an insurable interest exist—at the time the insurance policy is obtained, at the time the loss occurs, or both?
2. Is an insurance broker the agent of the insurance applicant or the agent of the insurer?
3. What are the basic requirements for executing a will? How may a will be revoked?
4. What is the difference between a *per stirpes* distribution and a *per capita* distribution of an estate to the grandchildren of the deceased?
5. What are the four essential elements of a trust? What is the difference between an express trust and an implied trust?

QUESTIONS AND CASE PROBLEMS

45–1. Timing of Insurance Coverage. On October 10, Joleen Vora applied for a $50,000 life insurance policy with Magnum Life Insurance Co.; she named her husband, Jay, as the beneficiary. Joleen paid the insurance company the first year's policy premium on making the application. Two days later, before she had a chance to take the physical examination required by the insurance company and before the policy was issued, Joleen was killed in an automobile accident. Jay submitted a claim to the insurance company for the $50,000. Can Jay collect? Explain.

45–2. Estate Distribution. Benjamin is a widower who has two married children, Edward and Patricia. Patricia has two children, Perry and Paul. Edward has no children. Benjamin dies, and his typewritten will leaves all his property equally to his children, Edward and Patricia, and provides that should a child predecease him, the grandchildren are to take *per stirpes*. The will was witnessed by Patricia and by Benjamin's lawyer and was signed by Benjamin in their presence. Patricia has predeceased Benjamin. Edward claims the will is invalid.

(a) Discuss whether the will is valid.
(b) Discuss the distribution of Benjamin's estate if the will is invalid.
(c) Discuss the distribution of Benjamin's estate if the will is valid.

45–3. Revocation. William Laneer urged his son, also William, to join the family business. The son, who was made partner, became suspicious of the handling of the business's finances. He filed a suit against the business and reported it to the Internal Revenue Service. The elder Laneer then executed a will that disinherited his son, giving him one dollar and leaving the balance of the estate equally to his four daughters, including Bellinda Barrera. Until his death more than twenty years later, Laneer harbored ill feelings toward his son. After Laneer's death, his original copy of the will could not be found. A photocopy was found in his safe-deposit box, however, and his lawyer's original copy was entered for probate in an Arkansas state court. Barrera, who wanted her brother William to share an equal portion of the inheritance, filed a petition to contest the will. Barrera claimed, among other things, that Laneer had revoked the will and that was why his original copy of the will could not be found. Was the will revoked? If so, to whom would the estate be distributed? [*Barrera v. Vanpelt*, 332 Ark. 482, 965 S.W.2d 780 (1998)]

45–4. Insurer's Defenses. In 1990, the city of Worcester, Massachusetts, adopted an ordinance that required rooming houses to be equipped with automatic sprinkler systems no later than September 25, 1995. In Worcester, James and Mark Duffy owned a forty-eight-room lodging house with two retail stores on the first floor. In 1994, the Duffys applied with General Star Indemnity Co. for an insurance policy to cover the premises. The application indicated that the premises had a sprinkler system. General issued a policy that required, among other safety features, a sprinkler system. Within a month, the premises were inspected on behalf of General. On the inspection form forwarded to the insurer, the inspector inserted only a hyphen next to the word *sprinkler* in the list of safety systems. In July 1995, when the premises sustained over $100,000 in fire damage, General learned that there was no sprinkler system. The insurer filed a suit in a federal district court against the Duffys to rescind the policy, alleging misrepresentation in their insurance application about the presence of sprinklers. How should the court rule, and why? [*General Star Indemnity Co. v. Duffy*, 191 F.3d 55 (1st Cir. 1999)]

CASE PROBLEM WITH SAMPLE ANSWER

45–5. Valley Furniture & Interiors, Inc., bought an insurance policy from Transportation Insurance Co. (TIC). The policy provided coverage of $50,000 for each occurrence of property loss caused by employee dishonesty. An "occurrence" was defined as "a single act or series of related acts." Valley allowed its employees to take pay advances and to buy discounted merchandise, with the advances and the cost of the merchandise deducted from their paychecks. The payroll manager was to notify the payroll company to make the deductions. Over a period of six years, without notifying the payroll company, the payroll manager issued advances to other employees and herself and bought merchandise for herself, in amounts totaling more than $200,000. Valley filed claims with TIC for three "occurrences" of employee theft. TIC considered the acts a "series of related acts" and paid only $50,000. Valley filed a suit in a Washington state court against TIC, alleging, in part, breach of contract. What is the standard for interpreting an insurance clause? How should this court interpret "series of related acts"? Why? [*Valley Furniture & Interiors, Inc. v. Transportation Insurance Co.,* 107 Wash.App. 104, 26 P.3d 952 (Div. 1 2001)]

After you have answered this problem, compare your answer with the sample answer given on the Web site that accompanies this text. Go to http://blt.westbuslaw.com, select "Chapter 45," and click on "Case Problem with Sample Answer."

45–6. Intestacy Laws. In January 1993, three and a half years after Lauren and Warren Woodward were married, they were informed that Warren had leukemia. At the time, the couple had no children, and the doctors told the Woodwards that the leukemia treatment might leave Mr. Woodward sterile. The couple arranged for Mr. Woodward's sperm to be collected and placed in a sperm bank for later use. In October 1993, Warren Woodward died. Two years later, Lauren Woodward gave birth to twin girls who had been conceived through artificial insemination using Mr. Woodward's sperm. The following year, Mrs. Woodward applied for Social Security survivor benefits for the two children. The Social Security Administration (SSA) rejected her on the ground that she had not established that the twins were the husband's children within the meaning of the Social Security Act of 1935. Mrs. Woodward then filed a paternity action in Massachusetts, and the probate court determined that Warren Woodward was the twins' father. Mrs. Woodward resubmitted her application to the SSA but was again refused survivor benefits for the twins. She then filed an action in a federal district court to determine the inheritance rights, under Massachusetts intestacy law, of children conceived from the sperm of a deceased individual and his surviving spouse. How should the court resolve this case? Should children conceived after a parent's death (by means of artificial insemination or *in vitro* fertilization) still inherit under intestate succession laws? Why or why not? [*Woodward v. Commissioner of Social Security,* 435 Mass. 536, 760 N.E.2d 257 (2002)]

45–7. Wills. In 1944, Benjamin Feinberg bought a plot in Beth Israel Cemetery in Plattsburgh, New York. A mausoleum was built on the plot to contain six crypts. In 1954, Feinberg's spouse died and was interred in one of the crypts. Feinberg, his only son, one of his two daughters, and the daughter's son, Julian Bergman, began using the mausoleum regularly as a place of prayer and meditation. When Feinberg died, he was interred in the mausoleum. His two daughters were interred in two of the remaining crypts on their deaths. Feinberg's son died in 2001 and was interred in the fifth crypt. His widow, Laurie, then changed the locks on the mausoleum and refused access to Julian, who filed a suit in a New York state court against her to obtain a key. Feinberg and all of his children died testate, but none of them made a specific bequest of their interest in the plot to anyone. Each person's will included a residuary clause, however. Who owns the plot, who has access to it, and why? [*Bergman v. Feinberg,* 6 A.D.3d 1031, 776 N.Y.S.2d 611 (3 Dept. 2004)]

FOR CRITICAL ANALYSIS

45–8. Statistics show that the extent of risk assumed by insurance companies varies depending on the gender of the insured. Many people contend that laws prohibiting gender-based insurance rates are thus fundamentally unfair. Do you agree with this contention? Why or why not?

VIDEO QUESTION

45–9. Go to this text's Web site at http://blt.westbuslaw.com and select "Chapter 45." Click on "Video Questions" and view the video titled *Double Indemnity.* Then answer the following questions.

1. Recall from the video that Mrs. Dietrichson (Barbara Stanwyck) is attempting to take out an "accident insurance" policy (similar to life insurance) on her husband without his knowledge. Does Mrs. Dietrichson have an insurable interest in the life of her husband? Why or why not?
2. Why would Walter (Fred MacMurray), the insurance agent, refuse to sell Mrs. Dietrichson an insurance policy covering her husband's life without her husband's knowledge?
3. Suppose that Mrs. Dietrichson contacts a different insurance agent and does not tell the agent that she wants to obtain insurance on her husband without his knowledge. Instead, she asks the agent to leave an insurance application for her husband to sign. Without her husband's knowledge, Mrs. Dietrichson then fills out the application for insurance, which includes a two-year incontestability clause, and forges Mr. Dietrichson's signature. Mr. Dietrichson dies three years after the policy is issued. Will the insurance company be obligated to pay on the policy? Why or why not?

INTERNET EXERCISES

Go to the *Business Law Today* home page at **http://blt.westbuslaw.com**, select "Chapter 45," and click on "Internet Exercises." There you will find the following Internet research exercises that you can perform to learn more about topics covered in this chapter.

Activity 45–1: SOCIAL PERSPECTIVE—Disappearing Decisions

Activity 45–2: LEGAL PERSPECTIVE—Wills and Trusts

Activity 45–3: MANAGEMENT PERSPECTIVE—Risk Management in Cyberspace

BEFORE THE TEST

Go to the *Business Law Today* home page at **http://blt.westbuslaw.com**, select "Chapter 45," and click on "Interactive Quizzes." You will find a number of interactive questions relating to this chapter.

Ace Equipment Sales, Inc. v. Buccino

Real property ownership and the rights of property owners are discussed in Chapter 44. Water rights, called riparian rights, *constitute a distinct property interest. The owner of land that borders a waterway, such as a river or stream, generally has the right to the reasonable and beneficial use of water on his or her land. Similar to subsurface rights (to minerals and oil, for example), riparian rights follow ownership of the land, but can be conveyed separately and often become a valuable component of real property rights. The following case explores a number of issues concerning water rights. Does an owner of the real property abutting a body of water have the right to use the water for swimming, boating, fishing, and other recreational purposes? Does it matter who owns the land under the water, or how the body of water was created? Does it make any difference whether a deed does, or does not, specifically grant the abutting owner a right to recreational uses, as opposed to industrial or other uses? What if the abutting owner is responsible for maintaining the level of the water through the operation of a dam? No Connecticut court had decided these questions prior to the case of* Ace Equipment Sales, Inc. v. Buccino.[1] *In this extended case study, we focus on the* Ace *case and examine these issues.*

1. 82 Conn.App. 573, 848 A.2d 474 (2004).

CASE BACKGROUND

Conat Brook is connected to the Willimantic River in Willington, Connecticut. Before the 1950s, Gardiner Hall, Jr., Company, the owner of the surrounding land, built a dam and spillway to impound Conat's waters and create Hall's Pond, a twenty-acre body of water.

By the 1990s, Ace Equipment Sales, Inc., owned the land under the pond, and Ace, Willington Fish and Game Club, LLC (WFGC, LLC), and Thomas and Irma Buccino owned all of the land abutting the pond. According to their deed, the Buccinos had a right to use the pond's water to operate a mill and factory. The Buccinos were also obligated to maintain the dam.

WFGC, LLC, and Willington Fish and Game Club, Inc. (WFGC, Inc.), stocked the pond with fish and used it for recreational fishing. With the Buccinos' permission, Hall's Pond Fly Fishing Club, Inc., and others began to use the Buccinos' property to access the pond for swimming, boating, fishing, and other recreation.

Ace, WFGC, LLC, and WFGC, Inc., filed a suit in a Connecticut state court against the Buccinos and their invitees. The plaintiffs alleged that they had the exclusive right to use the pond for recreation because they owned the land under it. The court issued a summary judgment in favor of the defendants and ordered the plaintiffs to remove any obstructions to the defendants' access. The plaintiffs appealed to a state intermediate appellate court.

MAJORITY OPINION

DUPONT, J. [Judge]

* * * *

Owners of property abutting a water surface are often called riparian owners * * * . In Connecticut, a riparian right to use non-navigable water does not create ownership of the water, but rather allows the use of the water for bathing and other recreational uses.

I

* * * *

Riparian rights exist as inherent rights incident to ownership of land contiguous to or traversed by a watercourse, and each riparian owner has an equal right with other such owners to make reasonable use of it for recreational purposes. * * * [Emphasis added.]

* * * *

If title extends only to the edge of a private watercourse but does not include the water, the titleholder has a right to use the surface in common with other riparian owners in any way that is not a trespass on the bottom of the water and can object to any obstruction of the water by another that interferes with his use.

* * * *

The [lower] court correctly held that * * * the defendants have the right to use the pond for reasonable recreational purposes in common with the owners of the bed of the pond.

II

* * * *

Both natural and artificial lakes have been used historically in Connecticut to generate power to run mills.

* * * The owner of land on which a dam is constructed may use the water for any purpose, provided he does not thereby interfere with the rights of other proprietors either above or below him. * * *

We agree with the trial court that there is no distinction to be made between a natural and an artificial body of water and the riparian rights that accrue * * * . We conclude that the recreational riparian rights of the Buccinos, who must maintain the dam to achieve the resultant impoundment of water, are not obliterated [destroyed] because the pond may have been artificial when created.

III

* * * *

Water rights appurtenant [attached] to abutting land pass by conveyance [transfer] of the land even though the deed does not specifically mention water rights. If the language of an easement, for example, to use water for industrial purposes, is broad enough to permit any reasonable use of a pond created by a dam, it may be used for recreational purposes *even though at the time of the creation of the easement, the parties probably contemplated that the major purpose would be to furnish water to a sawmill for power.* [Emphasis added.]

The Buccinos' deed gave them "the right * * * to take and use water from [the] pond through [a] penstock [a gate or sluice for controlling a flow of water] and the further right to take and use water from said pond that may be necessary for industrial purposes and operations in the mill and factory buildings." * * *

The deed also states that "(t)he right to draw the pond down below the natural water mark is not granted." Thus, when the grantor of the Buccinos wanted to exclude a right, it explicitly did so. There is no such exclusion in the deed for riparian rights. We interpret the entire language of the deed broadly and conclude that the deed does not impliedly preclude the defendants from using the pond for recreational as well as industrial purposes.

* * * *

The judgment is affirmed.

DISSENTING OPINION

SCHALLER, J., dissenting.

In determining that the trial court properly rendered summary judgment in favor of the defendants, Thomas Buccino and Irma Buccino, the majority concludes that the ownership of the subaqueous land was not a material fact. * * * I respectfully disagree * * * . I believe that, under the circumstances of this case, the appropriate doctrine is [a] * * * rule which has been adopted by numerous other state appellate courts * * * . I believe that [this] rule * * * produces a more sensible and fair result in situations like the present one.

* * * [Under this rule] the general public has no rights to the recreational use of a private lake, such rights being exclusive in the owner of the bed. * * * And * * * small inland lakes are susceptible of private ownership, at least to the extent that the owner or owners of the bed have the sole rights to the recreational uses of the waters.

* * * *

* * * [Under this rule] in the case of a non-navigable lake or pond where the land under the water is owned by others, no riparian rights attach to the property bordering on the water, and an attempt to exercise any such rights by invading the water is as much a trespass as if an unauthorized entry were made upon the dry land of another.

* * * *

* * * Because the construction of a man-made water body often involves the expenditure of substantial sums of money and the expense is not, as a rule, divided proportionately among the various abutting owners, the individual making the expenditure is justified in expecting that superior privileges will inure to him in return for his investment. In contrast, the abutting owners to a natural water body probably invest proportionally equal amounts for the increased value of the water front property. * * *

* * * *

* * * Accordingly, * * * I conclude that summary judgment was inappropriate in this case, and I would remand it for further proceedings.

QUESTIONS FOR ANALYSIS

1 Law. How does the majority answer the questions set out in the introduction to this case?

2 Law. What rule does the dissent favor, and why?

3 Social Consideration. Under the decision in the *Ace* case, what are the rights of the owner of the bed of a body of water abutted by public land, such as a public park or road?

4 Economic Dimensions. Does the majority's decision make bodies of water more available for different kinds of uses, or is the dissent's position more favorable for the use and development of bodies of water? Why?

5 Implications for the Property Owner. What impact might the ruling in this case have on waterfront property owners?

UNIT NINE

THE INTERNATIONAL LEGAL ENVIRONMENT

UNIT CONTENTS

CHAPTER 46

International Law in a Global Economy

"Our interests are those of the open door—a door of friendship and mutual advantage. This is the only door we care to enter."

Woodrow Wilson, 1856–1924
(Twenty-eighth president of the United States, 1913–1921)

CHAPTER OUTLINE

LEARNING OBJECTIVES

After reading this chapter, you should be able to answer the following questions:

1. What is the principle of comity, and why do courts deciding disputes involving a foreign law or judicial decree apply this principle?
2. What is the act of state doctrine? In what circumstances is this doctrine applied?
3. Under the Foreign Sovereign Immunities Act of 1976, on what bases might a foreign state be considered subject to the jurisdiction of U.S. courts?
4. In what circumstances will U.S. antitrust laws be applied extraterritorially?
5. Do U.S. laws prohibiting employment discrimination apply in all circumstances to U.S. employees working for U.S. employers abroad?

International business transactions are not unique to the modern world. Indeed, as suggested by President Woodrow Wilson's statement in the chapter-opening quotation, people have always found that they can benefit from exchanging goods with others. What is new in our day is the dramatic growth in world trade and the emergence of a global business community. Because the exchange of goods, services, and ideas on a global level is now routine, students of business law should be familiar with the laws pertaining to international business transactions. In this chapter, we first examine the legal context of international business transactions. We then look at some selected areas relating to business activities in a global context, including international sales contracts, civil dispute resolution, letters of credit, and investment protection. We conclude the chapter with a discussion of the application of certain U.S. laws in a transnational setting.

International Principles and Doctrines

INTERNATIONAL LAW
The law that governs relations among nations. International customs and treaties are important sources of international law.

NATIONAL LAW
Laws that pertain to a particular nation (as opposed to international law).

Recall from our discussion in Chapter 1 that **international law** can be defined as a body of law—formed as a result of international customs, treaties, and organizations—that governs relations among or between nations. **National law,** in contrast, is the law of a particular nation, such as Brazil, Germany, Japan, or the United States. Here, we look at some legal principles and doctrines of international law that have evolved over time and that the courts of various nations have employed—to a greater or lesser extent—to resolve or reduce conflicts that involve a foreign element. The three important legal principles and doctrines discussed in the following subsections are based primarily on courtesy and respect and are applied in the interests of maintaining harmonious relations among nations.

The Principle of Comity

COMITY
The principle by which one nation defers and gives effect to the laws and judicial decrees of another nation. This recognition is based primarily on respect.

Under what is known as the principle of **comity,** one nation will defer and give effect to the laws and judicial decrees of another country, as long as those laws and judicial decrees are consistent with the law and public policy of the accommodating nation. ■ EXAMPLE 46.1 Assume that a Swedish seller and a U.S. buyer have formed a contract, which the buyer breaches. The seller sues the buyer in a Swedish court, which awards damages. The buyer's assets, however, are in the United States and cannot be reached unless the judgment is enforced by a U.S. court of law. In this situation, if a U.S. court determines that the procedures and laws applied in the Swedish court were consistent with U.S. national law and policy, that court will likely defer to (and enforce) the foreign court's judgment. ■

Normally, the principle of comity is extended to foreign bankruptcy proceedings. The question in the following case was whether a U.S. court is required to determine the ownership of a disputed asset before a bankruptcy case goes forward in a foreign court.

CASE 46.1 JP Morgan Chase Bank v. Altos Hornos de Mexico, S.A. de C.V.

United States District Court,
Southern District of New York, 2004.
__ F.Supp.2d __.

BACKGROUND AND FACTS In April 1997, Altos Hornos de Mexico, S.A. de C.V., Mexico's largest liquid steel producer, borrowed $330 million from twenty-eight banks, including JP Morgan Chase Bank (JPMCB). JPMCB was the loan's "facility agent," distributing payments among the lenders through a "collection account" set up in the loan documents. As a term of the loan, Altos Hornos told three of its customers to pay into the collection account. The loan documents contained forum-selection and choice-of-law clauses in favor of New York. In May 1999, after significant losses in the global steel market, Altos Hornos filed a petition with a Mexican court to be declared in *suspensión de pagos* (suspension of payments, or SOP, which, under Mexican bankruptcy law, is similar to a Chapter 11 reorganization under U.S. bankruptcy law—see Chapter 27). The court granted the petition. In June and August, Altos Hornos's three customers paid $4.7 million into JPMCB's collection account. Altos Hornos asked the SOP court to order JPMCB to reimburse the funds for distribution in the SOP proceeding. Meanwhile, JPMCB filed a suit in a federal district court against Altos Hornos, seeking a declaration that these funds did not belong to the borrower. Altos Hornos filed a motion to dismiss this suit.

IN THE WORDS OF THE COURT . . .
BAER, J. [Judge]

* * * *

Under the principle of comity, American courts defer to proceedings in foreign countries so long as the foreign court had proper jurisdiction and enforcement does

(Continued)

CASE 46.1—Continued

not prejudice the rights of the United States citizens or violate domestic public policy. We have repeatedly noted the importance of extending comity to foreign bankruptcy proceedings. Since the equitable and orderly distribution of a debtor's property requires assembling all claims against the limited assets in a single proceeding, American courts regularly defer to such actions. The decision whether or not to extend comity is generally a matter of discretion. * * * "Comity," in the legal sense, is neither a matter of absolute obligation, on the one hand, nor of mere courtesy and good will, upon the other. *But it is the recognition which one nation allows within its territory to the legislative, executive, or judicial acts of another nation, having due regard both to international duty and convenience, and to the rights of its own citizens, or of other persons who are under the protection of its laws.* [Emphasis added.]

* * * *

As to whether under Mexican law U.S. courts can, should, or must resolve the issue [in this case] JPMCB posits the thought that under Mexican law the ownership of this property is more appropriately resolved by a U.S. court, given that * * * the SOP court lacks jurisdiction * * * .

* * * [T]his argument is what psychiatrists might characterize as rationalization. Article 126 of the Mexican bankruptcy law establishes the scope of claims that must be heard by the bankruptcy court. It provides as follows:

> All pending suits against the bankrupt shall be tried jointly with the bankruptcy proceedings, except * * * [t]hose dealing with secured claims or collateral.

Assuming that JPMCB is correct that the assets in the Collection Account are assets that deal with secured claims or collateral and thus fall within the exception * * * the SOP court has jurisdiction. * * *

* * * *

* * * I do not believe that there is anything in Mexican law that would require the issue of ownership of the Collection Account to be resolved in a Mexican court; nor is there any principle in Mexican law that would be offended by this Court's resolution of the issue. In short, Mexican law appears to be quite agnostic on this issue—it does not dictate one way or the other where the dispute must be decided.

* * * *

JPMCB contends that the forum-selection and choice-of-law clause * * * operate[s] to prevent Altos Hornos from objecting to jurisdiction here. * * *

It is settled law that the presence of such a forum-selection and choice-of-law clause does not preclude comity where it is otherwise warranted. * * * [C]onsiderations associated with comity trump the parties' express wishes. That the parties here appear to have stated their intentions * * * does not change the fact that there are important considerations that may not have concerned the parties [at the time of their contract] but which must concern this Court now—for example, Altos Hornos's other creditors and the importance of a unified administration rather than a piecemeal administration of its estate in the SOP proceeding.

DECISION AND REMEDY The court held that it was not required to resolve the question of the ownership of a bank account before its possible owner's bankruptcy proceeding in a Mexican court. The court dismissed JPMCB's complaint on the basis of comity.

FOR CRITICAL ANALYSIS—Social Consideration *Why might a Mexican court be better able to determine the ownership of the funds in the collection account in this case?*

THE ACT OF STATE DOCTRINE

ACT OF STATE DOCTRINE
A doctrine providing that the judicial branch of one country will not examine the validity of public acts committed by a recognized foreign government within its own territory.

The **act of state doctrine** is a judicially created doctrine that provides that the judicial branch of one country will not examine the validity of public acts committed by a recognized foreign government within its own territory. This doctrine is premised on the theory that the judicial branch should not "pass upon the validity of foreign acts when to do so would vex the harmony of our international relations with that foreign nation."[1]

The act of state doctrine can have important consequences for individuals and firms doing business with, and investing in, other countries. For example, this doctrine is frequently employed in situations involving expropriation or confiscation. **Expropriation** occurs when a government seizes a privately owned business or privately owned goods for a proper public purpose and awards just compensation. When a government seizes private property for an illegal purpose or without just compensation, the taking is referred to as a **confiscation.** The line between these two forms of taking is sometimes blurred because of differing interpretations of what is illegal and what constitutes just compensation.

EXPROPRIATION
The seizure by a government of a privately owned business or personal property for a proper public purpose and with just compensation.

CONFISCATION
A government's taking of a privately owned business or personal property without a proper public purpose or an award of just compensation.

When applicable, both the act of state doctrine and the doctrine of *sovereign immunity* (to be discussed next) tend to immunize (protect) foreign governments from the jurisdiction of U.S. courts. This means that firms or individuals who own property overseas often have diminished legal protection against government actions in the countries in which they operate.

THE DOCTRINE OF SOVEREIGN IMMUNITY

SOVEREIGN IMMUNITY
A doctrine that immunizes foreign nations from the jurisdiction of U.S. courts when certain conditions are satisfied.

When certain conditions are satisfied, the doctrine of **sovereign immunity** immunizes foreign nations from the jurisdiction of U.S. courts. In 1976, Congress codified this rule in the Foreign Sovereign Immunities Act (FSIA).[2] The FSIA exclusively governs the circumstances in which an action may be brought in the United States against a foreign nation, including attempts to attach a foreign nation's property.

Section 1605 of the FSIA sets forth the major exceptions to the jurisdictional immunity of a foreign state or country. A foreign state is not immune from the jurisdiction of U.S. courts when the state has "waived its immunity either explicitly or by implication" or when the action is taken "in connection with a commercial activity carried on in the United States by the foreign state" or having "a direct effect in the United States."[3]

The question frequently arises as to whether an entity falls within the category of a foreign state. The question of what is a commercial activity has also been the subject of dispute. Under Section 1603 of the FSIA, a *foreign state* includes both a political subdivision of a foreign state and an instrumentality of a foreign state. Section 1603 broadly defines a *commercial activity* as a commercial activity that is carried out by a foreign state within the United States, but it does not describe the particulars of what constitutes a commercial activity. Thus, the courts are left to decide whether a particular activity is governmental or commercial in nature. In the following case, the United States Supreme Court considered whether the principles of the FSIA should apply to a dispute dating back to World War II, before the FSIA had been enacted.

1. *Libra Bank, Ltd. v. Banco Nacional de Costa Rica, S.A.,* 570 F.Supp. 870 (S.D.N.Y. 1983).
2. 28 U.S.C. Sections 1602–1611.
3. See, for example, *Keller v. Central Bank of Nigeria,* 277 F.3d 811 (6th Cir. 2002), in which the court held that failure to pay promised funds to a Cleveland account was an action having a direct effect in the United States.

Featured Case

CASE 46.2 Republic of Austria v. Altmann

Supreme Court of the United States, 2004.
541 U.S. 677,
124 S.Ct. 2240,
159 L.Ed.2d 1.
http://www.findlaw.com/casecode/supreme.html[a]

MAJORITY OPINION

Justice *STEVENS* delivered the opinion of the Court.

In 1998 an Austrian journalist, granted access to the Austrian Gallery's archives [in Vienna, Austria], discovered evidence that certain valuable works in the Gallery's collection had not been donated by their rightful owners but had been seized by the Nazis or expropriated by the Austrian Republic after World War II. The journalist provided some of that evidence to respondent [Maria Altmann], who in turn filed this action [in a U.S. federal district court] to recover possession of six Gustav Klimt paintings. Prior to the Nazi invasion of Austria [in 1938], the paintings had hung in the palatial Vienna home of respondent's uncle, Ferdinand Bloch-Bauer, a Czechoslovakian Jew and patron of the arts. Respondent claims ownership of the paintings under a will executed by her uncle after he fled Austria in 1938. [In the will, he left his estate to Altmann, another niece, and Robert Bentley, a nephew.] She alleges that the Gallery obtained possession of the paintings through wrongful conduct in the years during and after World War II.

The defendants (petitioners here)—the Republic of Austria and the Austrian Gallery (Gallery), an instrumentality of the Republic—filed a motion to dismiss the complaint asserting, among other defenses, a claim of sovereign immunity. [Respondent argued that petitioners are not entitled to immunity because the FSIA exempts from immunity all cases involving "rights in property taken in violation of international law."] The District Court denied the [defendants'] motion, and the [U.S.] Court of Appeals [for the Ninth Circuit] affirmed. We granted *certiorari* limited to the question whether the Foreign Sovereign Immunities Act of 1976 (FSIA or Act) * * * applies to claims that, like respondent's, are based on conduct that occurred before the Act's enactment * * *.

* * * *

To begin with, the preamble of the FSIA expresses Congress' understanding that the Act would apply to all postenactment claims of sovereign immunity. That section provides:

> Claims of foreign states to immunity should henceforth be decided by courts of the United States and of the States in conformity with the principles set forth in this chapter.

* * * [T]his language is unambiguous: Immunity "claims"—not actions protected by immunity, but assertions of immunity to suits arising from those actions—are the relevant conduct regulated by the Act; those claims are "henceforth" to be decided by the courts. * * * [T]his language suggests Congress intended courts to resolve *all* such claims "in conformity with the principles set forth" in the Act, regardless of when the underlying conduct occurred.

The FSIA's overall structure strongly supports this conclusion. Many of the Act's provisions unquestionably apply to cases arising out of conduct that occurred before 1976. * * * [F]or example, * * * whether an entity qualifies as an "instrumentality" of a "foreign state" for purposes of the FSIA's grant of immunity depends on the relationship between the entity and the state at the time suit is brought rather than when the conduct occurred. * * * [T]here has never been any doubt that the Act's procedural provisions relating to venue, removal, execution, and attachment apply to all pending cases. Thus, the FSIA's preamble indicates that it applies "henceforth," and its body includes numerous provisions that unquestionably apply to claims based on pre-1976 conduct. In this context, it would be anomalous to presume that an isolated provision (such as the expropriation exception on which respondent relies) is of purely prospective application absent any statutory language to that effect.

Finally, applying the FSIA to all pending cases regardless of when the underlying conduct occurred is most consistent with two of the Act's principal purposes: clarifying the rules that judges should apply in resolving sovereign immunity claims and eliminating political participation in the resolution of such claims. * * * [T]o accomplish these purposes, Congress established a comprehensive framework for resolving any claim of sovereign immunity: * * * the text and structure of the FSIA demonstrate Congress' intention that the FSIA be the sole basis for obtaining jurisdiction over a foreign state in our courts. * * * Section 1604 bars federal and state courts from exercising jurisdiction when a foreign state *is* enti-

a. In the "Browsing" section, click on "2004 Decisions." In the result, click on the name of the case to access the opinion.

CASE 46.2—Continued

tled to immunity, and Section 1330(a) confers jurisdiction on district courts to hear suits brought by United States citizens and by aliens when a foreign state is *not* entitled to immunity. * * *

* * * Quite obviously, Congress' purposes in enacting such a comprehensive jurisdictional scheme would be frustrated if, in postenactment cases concerning preenactment conduct, courts were to continue to follow the same ambiguous and politically charged standards that the FSIA replaced.

* * * [W]e affirm the [Court of Appeals'] judgment because the Act * * * clearly applies to conduct, like petitioners' alleged wrongdoing, that occurred prior to 1976 * * *.

* * * *

The judgment of the Court of Appeals is affirmed.

It is so ordered.

DISSENTING OPINION

Justice *KENNEDY* * * *, dissenting.

This is an important decision for interpreting the Foreign Sovereign Immunities Act of 1976 (FSIA or Act). As the Court's careful opinion illustrates, the case is difficult. In my respectful view, however, its decision is incorrect.

* * * To reach its conclusion the Court must weaken the reasoning and diminish the force of the rule against the retroactivity of statutes, a rule of fairness based on respect for expectations; the Court abruptly tells foreign nations this important principle of American law is unavailable to them in our courts * * *.

* * * *

The question is whether the courts, by applying the statutory principles the FSIA announced, will impose a retroactive effect in a case involving conduct that occurred over 50 years ago, and nearly 30 years before the FSIA's enactment. It is our general rule not to apply a statute if its application will impose a retroactive effect on the litigants. This * * * is an old and well-established principle. It is a principle in the English common law, as ancient as the law itself, that a statute * * * is not to have a [retroactive] effect. The principle stems from fundamental fairness concerns.

The single acknowledged exception to the rule against retroactivity is when the statute itself, by a clear statement, requires it.

The FSIA does not meet this exception because it contains no clear statement requiring retroactive effect. * * *

In an awkward twist, however, the Court * * * maintains that the "[Act's] language is unambiguous" and that it "suggests Congress intended courts to resolve *all* [foreign sovereign immunity] claims 'in conformity with the principles set forth' in the Act, regardless of when the underlying conduct occurred." If the statute were in fact this clear, the exception would apply. * * * If the Court really thinks the statute is unambiguous, it should rest on that premise.

* * * *

If one of the Act's principles were that "the Act shall govern all claims, whenever filed, and involving conduct that occurred whenever in time," the provision would command retroactive application. A statement like this, however, cannot be found in the FSIA. The statute says only that it must be applied "henceforth." That says no more than that the principles immediately apply from the point of the Act's effective date on * * *. A statement that a statute will become effective on a certain date does not even arguably suggest that it has any application to conduct that occurred at an earlier date.

TEST YOUR COMPREHENSION: CASE DETAILS

1. How did this case come before the United States Supreme Court?
2. What did the United States Supreme Court hold in this case, and why?
3. How did the dissent view the majority's decision?
4. What are the "fundamental fairness concerns" cited by the dissent?
5. What is the next step for this case in its journey through the courts?

Doing Business Internationally

A U.S. domestic firm can engage in international business transactions in a number of ways. The simplest way is to seek out foreign markets for domestically produced products or services. In other words, U.S. firms can look abroad for **export** markets for their goods and services. Alternatively, a U.S. firm can establish foreign production

EXPORT
To sell products to buyers located in other countries.

facilities so as to be closer to the foreign market or markets in which its products are sold. A domestic firm can also obtain revenues by licensing its technology to an existing foreign company or by selling franchises to overseas entities.

.on the Web If you are interested in learning more about what is involved in exporting goods to other countries, go to the state of New Mexico's Web page on "How to Export" at

http://www.edd.state.nm.us/TRADE/HOWTO/howto.html.

EXPORTING

Exporting can take two forms: direct exporting and indirect exporting. In *direct exporting,* a U.S. company signs a sales contract with a foreign purchaser that provides for the conditions of shipment and payment for the goods. (How payments are made in international transactions is discussed later in this chapter.) If sufficient business develops in a foreign country, a U.S. corporation may set up a specialized marketing organization in that foreign market by appointing a foreign agent or a foreign distributor. This is called *indirect exporting.*

When a U.S. firm desires to limit its involvement in an international market, it will typically establish an *agency relationship* with a foreign firm. In an agency relationship (discussed in Chapter 28), one person (the agent) agrees to act on behalf of another (the principal). The foreign agent is thereby empowered to enter into contracts in the agent's country on behalf of the U.S. principal.

When a substantial market exists in a foreign country, a U.S. firm may wish to appoint a distributor located in that country. The U.S. firm and the distributor enter into a **distribution agreement,** which is a contract between the seller and the distributor setting out the terms and conditions of the distributorship—for example, price, currency of payment, availability of supplies, and method of payment. The terms and conditions primarily involve contract law. Disputes concerning distribution agreements may involve jurisdictional or other issues (discussed in detail later in this chapter). In addition, some **exclusive distributorships**—in which distributors agree to distribute only the sellers' goods—have raised antitrust problems.

DISTRIBUTION AGREEMENT
A contract between a seller and a distributor of the seller's products setting out the terms and conditions of the distributorship.

EXCLUSIVE DISTRIBUTORSHIP
A distributorship in which the seller and the distributor of the seller's products agree that the distributor has the exclusive right to distribute the seller's products in a certain geographic area.

MANUFACTURING ABROAD

An alternative to direct or indirect exporting is the establishment of foreign manufacturing facilities. Typically, U.S. firms establish manufacturing plants abroad if they believe that doing so will reduce their costs—particularly for labor, shipping, and raw materials—and enable them to compete more effectively in foreign markets. A U.S. firm can manufacture goods in other countries in several ways. They include licensing and franchising, as well as investing in a wholly owned subsidiary or a joint venture.

Licensing A U.S. firm can obtain business from abroad by licensing a foreign manufacturing company to use its copyrighted, patented, or trademarked intellectual property or trade secrets. Like any other licensing agreement (see Chapters 5 and 17), a licensing agreement with a foreign-based firm calls for a payment of royalties on some basis—such as so many cents per unit produced or a certain percentage of profits from units sold in a particular geographic territory.

Franchising Franchising is a well-known form of licensing. Recall from Chapter 29 that in a franchise arrangement the owner of a trademark, trade name, or copyright (the franchisor) licenses another (the franchisee) to use the trademark, trade name, or copyright under certain conditions or limitations in the selling of goods or services. In return, the franchisee pays a fee, which is usually based on a per-

A woman in Taiwan holds a Barbie doll that was manufactured in Taiwan. Why would a U.S. corporation, such as Mattel, Inc., outsource its manufacturing jobs to a foreign firm? (AP Photo/ Wally Santana)

centage of gross or net sales. Examples of international franchises include Holiday Inn and Hertz.

Investing in a Wholly Owned Subsidiary or a Joint Venture Another way to expand into a foreign market is to establish a wholly owned subsidiary firm in a foreign country. When a wholly owned subsidiary is established, the parent company, which remains in the United States, retains complete ownership of all the facilities in the foreign country, as well as complete authority and control over all phases of the operation. A U.S. firm can also expand into international markets through a joint venture. In a joint venture, the U.S. company owns only part of the operation; the rest is owned either by local owners in the foreign country or by another foreign entity. All of the firms involved in a joint venture share responsibilities, as well as profits and liabilities.

Commercial Contracts in an International Setting

Like all commercial contracts, an international contract should be in writing. For an example of an actual international sales contract, refer back to the foldout contract in Chapter 18.

.on the Web For information on the legal requirements of doing business abroad, a good source is the Internet Law Library's collection of laws of other nations. Go to **http://www.lawguru.com/ilawlib/index.html**.

Contract Clauses

Language and legal differences among nations can create special problems for parties to international contracts when disputes arise. It is possible to avoid these problems by including in a contract special provisions designating the official language of the contract, the legal forum (court or place) in which disputes under the contract will be settled, and the substantive law that will be applied in settling any disputes. Parties to international contracts should also indicate in their contracts what acts or events will excuse the parties from performance under the contract and whether disputes under the contract will be arbitrated or litigated.

Choice of Language A deal struck between a U.S. company and a company in another country normally involves two languages. Typically, many phrases in one language are not readily translatable into another. Consequently, the complex contractual terms involved may not be understood by one party in the other party's language. To make sure that no disputes arise out of this language problem, an international sales contract should have a **choice-of-language clause** designating the official language by which the contract will be interpreted in the event of disagreement.

CHOICE-OF-LANGUAGE CLAUSE
A clause in a contract designating the official language by which the contract will be interpreted in the event of a future disagreement over the contract's terms.

Choice of Forum When parties from several countries are involved, litigation may be pursued in courts in different nations. There are no universally accepted rules as to which court has jurisdiction over particular subject matter or parties to a dispute. Consequently, parties to an international transaction should always include in the contract a **forum-selection clause** indicating what court, jurisdiction, or tribunal will decide any disputes arising under the contract. It is especially important to indicate the specific court that will have jurisdiction. The forum does not necessarily have to be within the geographic boundaries of the home nation of either party. The following case involved a question about the application of a forum-selection clause.

FORUM-SELECTION CLAUSE
A provision in a contract designating the court, jurisdiction, or tribunal that will decide any disputes arising under the contract.

CASE 46.3 Garware Polyester, Ltd. v. Intermax Trading Corp.

United States District Court,
Southern District of New York, 2001.
__ F.Supp.2d __.

BACKGROUND AND FACTS Garware Polyester, Ltd., based in Mumbai, India, develops and makes plastics and high-tech polyester film. In 1987, Intermax Trading Corporation, based in New York, became Garware's North American sales agent. Over the next decade, the parties executed four written agreements, collectively referred to as the "Agency Agreements." Each agreement provided, "The courts at Bombay [India] alone will have jurisdiction to try out suits in respect of any claim or dispute arising out of or under this agreement or in any way relating to the same." Intermax sold Garware products on a commission basis. In some transactions, Intermax arranged for customers to order products directly from Garware. In other transactions, Intermax sold Garware products through warehouse sales by which Intermax bought products from Garware, warehoused them in the United States, and resold them. When Intermax fell behind in its payments, Garware filed a suit in a U.S. district court to collect on the unpaid invoices. Garware argued that the forum-selection clause did not apply to the invoices in dispute because they involved the warehouse sales, which, Garware claimed, were not part of, and did not relate to, the Agency Agreements.

IN THE WORDS OF THE COURT . . .

CHIN, D.J. [District Judge]

* * * *

* * * [F]orum selection clauses eliminate uncertainty in international commerce and insure that the parties are not unexpectedly subjected to hostile forums and laws. Moreover, international comity dictates that American courts enforce these sorts of clauses out of respect for the integrity and respect of foreign tribunals. *The presumptive validity of forum selection clauses may only be overcome by a strong showing that the clause is unreasonable under the circumstances.* [Emphasis added.]

* * * *

* * * A forum selection clause should not be defeated by artful pleading of claims not based on the contract containing the clause if those claims grow out of the contractual relationship, or if the gist of those claims is a breach of that relationship. * * *

Here, the "gist" of Garware's claim is a breach of the Agency Agreements. The warehouse sales in question were made by Intermax for the purpose of selling Garware product in the contractually defined territory. The Agency Agreements specifically relate to Intermax's role as Garware's "selling agents for promoting sales of GARFILM * * * in the United States of America * * * ." Thus, if these sales are not squarely within the scope of the Agency Agreements, they are, at the very least, related to the Agreements. Further, the parties' course of dealing supports the conclusion that the parties themselves believed the Agency Agreements included warehouse sales: as required by the Agreements, Garware paid commissions to Intermax on these sales.

DECISION AND REMEDY The court held that each of the Agency Agreements contained a valid and enforceable forum-selection clause, which applied to this suit. The court dismissed the case for improper venue.

WHY IS THIS CASE IMPORTANT? *As this case illustrates, when the underlying transaction is international, courts generally presume that forum-selection clauses are valid because such clauses eliminate uncertainty in international commerce. It takes a strong showing that the clause was unreasonable under the circumstances to overcome this presumptive validity.*

CHOICE-OF-LAW CLAUSE
A clause in a contract designating the law (such as the law of a particular state or nation) that will govern the contract.

Choice of Law A contractual provision designating the applicable law—such as the law of Germany or England or California—is called a **choice-of-law clause.** Every international contract typically includes a choice-of-law clause. At common law (and in European civil law systems), parties are allowed to choose the law that will govern their contractual relationship, provided that the law chosen is the law of a jurisdiction that has a substantial relationship to the parties and to the international business transaction.

Under Section 1–105 of the Uniform Commercial Code, parties may choose the law that will govern the contract as long as the choice is "reasonable." Article 6 of the United Nations Convention on Contracts for the International Sale of Goods (discussed in Chapter 18), however, imposes no limitation on the parties' choice of what law will govern the contract. The 1986 Hague Convention on the Law Applicable to Contracts for the International Sale of Goods—often referred to as the Choice-of-Law Convention—allows unlimited autonomy in the choice of law. The Hague Convention indicates that whenever a contract does not specify a choice of law, the governing law is that of the country in which the *seller's* place of business is located.

***FORCE MAJEURE* CLAUSE**
A provision in a contract stipulating that certain unforeseen events—such as war, political upheavals, or acts of God—will excuse a party from liability for nonperformance of contractual obligations.

***Force Majeure* Clause** Every contract, particularly those involving international transactions, should have a ***force majeure* clause.** *Force majeure* is a French term meaning "impossible or irresistible force"—sometimes loosely identified as "an act of God." In international business contracts, *force majeure* clauses commonly stipulate that in addition to acts of God, a number of other eventualities (such as government orders or embargoes, for example) may excuse a party from liability for nonperformance.

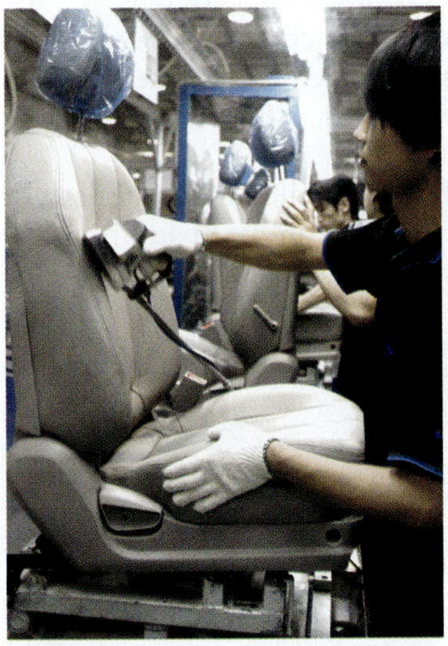
Workers at a manufacturing plant owned by a U.S. company in Beijing, China. What contract clauses would affect where and how these foreign workers are able to resolve disputes with their U.S. employer? (Ricky Wong/ Bloomberg News*/Landov)*

CIVIL DISPUTE RESOLUTION

International contracts frequently include arbitration clauses. By means of such clauses, the parties agree in advance to be bound by the decision of a specified third party in the event of a dispute, as discussed in Chapter 3. The third party may be a neutral entity (such as the International Chamber of Commerce), a panel of individuals representing both parties' interests, or some other group or organization. (For an example of an arbitration clause in an international contract, refer to the foldout exhibit in Chapter 18.) The United Nations Convention on the Recognition and Enforcement of Foreign Arbitral Awards (often referred to as the New York Convention) assists in the enforcement of arbitration clauses, as do provisions in specific treaties among nations. The New York Convention has been implemented in nearly one hundred countries, including the United States.

If a sales contract does not include an arbitration clause, litigation may occur. If the contract contains forum-selection and choice-of-law clauses, the lawsuit will be heard by a court in the specified forum and decided according to that forum's law. If no forum and choice of law have been specified, however, legal proceedings will be more complex and attended by much more uncertainty. For instance, litigation may take place in two or more countries, with each country applying its own choice-of-law rules to determine the substantive law that will be applied to the particular transactions.

Also, even if a plaintiff wins a favorable judgment in a lawsuit litigated in the plaintiff's country, there is no way to predict whether courts in the defendant's country will enforce the judgment.

Making Payment on International Transactions

Currency differences between nations and the geographic distance between parties to international sales contracts add a degree of complexity to international sales that does not exist in the domestic market. Because international contracts involve greater financial risks, special care should be taken in drafting these contracts to specify both the currency in which payment is to be made and the method of payment.

MONETARY SYSTEMS

Although our national currency, the U.S. dollar, is one of the primary forms of international currency, any U.S. firm undertaking business transactions abroad must be prepared to deal with one or more other currencies. Currencies are convertible when they can be freely exchanged one for the other at some specified market rate in a **foreign exchange market.** Foreign exchange markets comprise a worldwide system for the buying and selling of foreign currencies. At any point in time, the foreign exchange rate is set by the forces of supply and demand in unrestricted foreign exchange markets. The foreign exchange rate is simply the price of a unit of one country's currency in terms of another country's currency. For example, if today's exchange rate is one hundred Japanese yen for one dollar, that means that anybody with one hundred yen can obtain one dollar, and vice versa.

FOREIGN EXCHANGE MARKET
A worldwide system in which foreign currencies are bought and sold.

Frequently, a U.S. company can rely on its domestic bank to take care of all international transfers of funds. Commercial banks often transfer funds internationally through their **correspondent banks** in other countries. ■ EXAMPLE 46.2 Suppose that a customer of Citibank wishes to pay a bill in euros to a company in Paris. Citibank can draw a bank check payable in euros on its account in Crédit Lyonnais, a Paris correspondent bank, and then send the check to the French company to which its customer owes the funds. Alternatively, Citibank's customer can request a wire transfer of the funds to the French company. Citibank instructs Crédit Lyonnais by wire to pay the necessary amount in euros. ■

CORRESPONDENT BANK
A bank in which another bank has an account (and vice versa) for the purpose of facilitating fund transfers.

The Clearinghouse Interbank Payment System (CHIPS) handles about 90 percent of both national and international interbank transfers of U.S. funds. In addition, the Society for Worldwide International Financial Telecommunications (SWIFT) is a communication system that provides banks with messages concerning international transactions.

LETTERS OF CREDIT

Because buyers and sellers engaged in international business transactions are frequently separated by thousands of miles, special precautions are often taken to ensure performance under the contract. Sellers want to avoid delivering goods for which they might not be paid. Buyers desire the assurance that sellers will not be paid until there is evidence that the goods have been shipped. Thus, **letters of credit** are frequently used to facilitate international business transactions.

LETTER OF CREDIT
A written instrument, usually issued by a bank on behalf of a customer or other person, in which the issuer promises to honor drafts or other demands for payment by third persons in accordance with the terms of the instrument.

In a simple letter-of-credit transaction, the *issuer* (a bank) agrees to issue a letter of credit and to ascertain whether the *beneficiary* (seller) performs certain acts. In return, the *account party* (buyer) promises to reimburse the issuer for the amount paid to the beneficiary. The transaction may also involve an *advising bank* that transmits information and a *paying bank* that expedites payment under the letter of credit.

Under a letter of credit, the issuer is bound to pay the beneficiary (seller) when the beneficiary has complied with the terms and conditions of the letter of credit.

The beneficiary looks to the issuer, not to the account party (buyer), when it presents the documents required by the letter of credit. Typically, the letter of credit will require that the beneficiary deliver a *bill of lading* to the issuing bank to prove that shipment has been made. A letter of credit assures the beneficiary (seller) of payment and at the same time assures the account party (buyer) that payment will not be made until the beneficiary has complied with the terms and conditions of the letter of credit.

The Value of a Letter of Credit The basic principle behind letters of credit is that payment is made against the documents presented by the beneficiary and not against the facts that the documents purport to reflect. Thus, in a letter-of-credit transaction, the issuer does not police the underlying contract; a letter of credit is independent of the underlying contract between the buyer and the seller. Eliminating the need for banks (issuers) to inquire into whether actual contractual conditions have been satisfied greatly reduces the costs of letters of credit. Moreover, the use of a letter of credit protects both buyers and sellers.

DON'T FORGET A letter of credit is independent of the underlying contract between the buyer and the seller.

Compliance with a Letter of Credit A letter-of-credit transaction generally involves at least three separate and distinct contracts: the contract between the account party (buyer) and the beneficiary (seller); the contract between the issuer (bank) and the account party (buyer); and, finally, the letter of credit itself, which involves the issuer (bank) and the beneficiary (seller). These contracts are separate and distinct, and the issuer's obligations under the letter of credit do not concern the underlying contract between the buyer and the seller. Rather, it is the issuer's duty to ascertain whether the documents presented by the beneficiary (seller) comply with the terms of the letter of credit.

If the documents presented by the beneficiary comply with the terms of the letter of credit, the issuer (bank) must honor the letter of credit. If the issuing bank refuses to pay the beneficiary (seller) even though the beneficiary has complied with all the requirements, the beneficiary can bring an action to enforce payment. Sometimes, however, it can be difficult to determine exactly what a letter of credit requires. Traditionally, courts required strict compliance with the terms of a letter of credit, but in recent years, some courts have moved to a standard of *reasonable* compliance.

Regulation of Specific Business Activities

Doing business abroad can affect the economies, foreign policies, domestic policies, and other national interests of the countries involved. For this reason, nations impose laws to restrict or facilitate international business. Controls may also be imposed by international agreements. We discuss here how different types of international activities are regulated.

Investing

Firms that invest in foreign nations face the risk that the foreign government may take possession of the investment property. Expropriation, as already mentioned, occurs when property is taken and the owner is paid just compensation for what is taken. Expropriation does not violate generally observed principles of international law. Such principles are normally violated, however, when a government confiscates property without compensation (or without adequate compensation). Few remedies are available for confiscation of property by a foreign government. Claims are often resolved by lump-sum settlements after negotiations between the United States and the taking nation.

To counter the deterrent effect that the possibility of confiscation may have on potential investors, many countries guarantee that foreign investors will be compensated if their property is taken. A guaranty can take the form of national constitutional or statutory laws or provisions in international treaties. As further protection for foreign investments, some countries provide insurance for their citizens' investments abroad.

EXPORT CONTROLS

NOTE Most countries restrict exports for the same reasons: to protect national security, to further foreign policy objectives, to prevent the spread of nuclear weapons, and to preserve scarce commodities.

The U.S. Constitution provides in Article I, Section 9, that "No Tax or Duty shall be laid on Articles exported from any State." Thus, Congress cannot impose any export taxes. Congress can, however, use a variety of other devices to control exports. Congress may set export quotas on various items, such as grain being sold abroad. Under the Export Administration Act of 1979,[4] the flow of technologically advanced products and technical data can be restricted. In recent years, the U.S. Department of Commerce has made a controversial attempt to restrict the export of encryption software.

While restricting certain exports, the United States (and other nations) also use devices such as export incentives and subsidies to stimulate other exports and thereby aid domestic businesses. The Revenue Act of 1971,[5] for instance, gave tax benefits to firms marketing their products overseas through certain foreign sales corporations by exempting income produced by the exports. Under the Export Trading Company Act of 1982,[6] U.S. banks are encouraged to invest in export trading companies, which are formed when exporting firms join together to export a line of goods. The Export-Import Bank of the United States provides financial assistance, consisting primarily of credit guaranties given to commercial banks that in turn lend funds to U.S. exporting companies.

"The notion dies hard that in some sort of way exports are patriotic but imports are immoral."

LORD HARLECH (DAVID ORMSLEY GORE), 1918–1985 (English writer)

IMPORT CONTROLS

All nations have restrictions on imports, and the United States is no exception. Restrictions include strict prohibitions, quotas, and tariffs. Under the Trading with the Enemy Act of 1917,[7] for instance, no goods may be imported from nations that have been designated enemies of the United States. Other laws prohibit the importation of illegal drugs, books that urge insurrection against the United States, and agricultural products that pose dangers to domestic crops or animals.

QUOTA
A set limit on the amount of goods that can be imported.

TARIFF
A tax on imported goods.

Quotas and Tariffs Limits on the amounts of goods that can be imported are known as **quotas.** At one time, the United States had legal quotas on the number of automobiles that could be imported from Japan. Today, Japan "voluntarily" restricts the number of automobiles exported to the United States. **Tariffs** are taxes on imports. A tariff is usually a percentage of the value of the import, but it can be a flat rate per unit (for example, per barrel of oil). Tariffs raise the prices of goods, causing some consumers to purchase less expensive, domestically manufactured goods.

4. 50 U.S.C. Sections 2401–2420.
5. 26 U.S.C. Sections 991–994.
6. 15 U.S.C. Sections 4001, 4003.
7. 12 U.S.C. Section 95a.

DUMPING
The selling of goods in a foreign country at a price below the price charged for the same goods in the domestic market.

Dumping The United States has specific laws directed at what it sees as unfair international trade practices. **Dumping,** for example, is the sale of imported goods at "less than fair value." "Fair value" is usually determined by the price of those goods in the exporting country. Foreign firms that engage in dumping in the United States hope to undersell U.S. businesses to obtain a larger share of the U.S. market. To prevent this, an extra tariff—known as an *antidumping duty*—may be assessed on the imports.

NORMAL TRADE RELATIONS (NTR) STATUS
A status granted in an international treaty by a provision stating that the citizens of the contracting nations may enjoy the privileges accorded by either party to citizens of its NTR nations. Generally, this status is designed to establish equality of international treatment.

Minimizing Trade Barriers Restrictions on imports are also known as *trade barriers.* The elimination of trade barriers is sometimes seen as essential to the world's economic well-being. Most of the world's leading trading nations are members of the World Trade Organization (WTO), which was established in 1995. To minimize trade barriers among nations, each member country of the WTO is required to grant **normal trade relations (NTR) status** (formerly known as *most-favored-nation status*) to other member countries. This means each member is obligated to treat other members at least as well as it treats the country that receives its most favorable treatment with regard to imports or exports.

Various regional trade agreements and associations also help to minimize trade barriers between nations. The European Union (EU), for example, is working to minimize or remove barriers to trade among its member countries. The EU is a single integrated trading unit made up of twenty-five European nations. Another important regional trade agreement is the North American Free Trade Agreement (NAFTA). NAFTA, which became effective on January 1, 1994, created a regional trading unit consisting of Mexico, the United States, and Canada. The primary goal of NAFTA is to eliminate tariffs among these three countries on substantially all goods over a period of fifteen to twenty years.

Bribing Foreign Officials

Giving cash or in-kind benefits to foreign government officials to obtain business contracts and other favors is often considered normal practice. To reduce such bribery by representatives of U.S. corporations, Congress enacted the Foreign Corrupt Practices Act in 1977.[8] This act and its implications for American businesspersons engaged in international business transactions were discussed in Chapter 7.

U.S. Laws in a Global Context

The internationalization of business raises questions about the extraterritorial application of a nation's laws—that is, the effect of the country's laws outside its boundaries. To what extent do U.S. domestic laws apply to other nations' businesses? To what extent do U.S. domestic laws apply to U.S. firms doing business abroad? Here, we discuss these questions in the context of U.S. antitrust law. We also look at the extraterritorial application of U.S. laws prohibiting employment discrimination.

U.S. Antitrust Laws

U.S. antitrust laws (discussed in Chapter 37) have a wide application. They may *subject* persons in foreign nations to their provisions, as well as *protect* foreign consumers and competitors from violations committed by U.S. citizens. Consequently, *foreign persons,* a term that by definition includes foreign governments, may sue under U.S. antitrust laws in U.S. courts.

8. 15 U.S.C. Sections 78m–78ff.

Section 1 of the Sherman Act provides for the extraterritorial effect of the U.S. antitrust laws. The United States is a major proponent of free competition in the global economy. Thus, any conspiracy that has a *substantial effect* on U.S. commerce is within the reach of the Sherman Act. The law applies even if the violation occurs outside the United States, and foreign governments as well as persons can be sued for violations.

Before U.S. courts will exercise jurisdiction and apply antitrust laws, however, it must be shown that the alleged violation had a substantial effect on U.S. commerce. U.S. jurisdiction is automatically invoked when a *per se* violation occurs.[9] An example of a *per se* violation is a price-fixing contract.

ANTIDISCRIMINATION LAWS

As explained in Chapter 41, federal laws in the United States prohibit discrimination on the basis of race, color, national origin, religion, gender, age, and disability. These laws, as they affect employment relationships, generally apply extraterritorially. Since 1984, for example, the Age Discrimination in Employment Act of 1967 has covered U.S. employees working abroad for U.S. employers. The Americans with Disabilities Act of 1990, which requires employers to accommodate the needs of workers with disabilities, also applies to U.S. nationals working abroad for U.S. firms. Title VII of the Civil Rights Act of 1964 also applies to all U.S. employees working for U.S. employers abroad. Generally, U.S. employers must abide by U.S. antidiscrimination laws unless to do so would violate the laws of the country where their workplaces are located. This "foreign laws exception" allows employers to avoid being subjected to conflicting laws.

9. Certain types of restrictive contracts, such as price-fixing agreements, are deemed inherently anticompetitive and thus in restraint of trade as a matter of law. Such a restrictive contract constitutes a *per se* violation of the antitrust laws. See Chapter 37.

REVIEWING INTERNATIONAL LAW IN A GLOBAL ECONOMY

Robco, Inc., was a Florida arms dealer. The armed forces of Honduras contracted to purchase weapons from Robco over a six-year period. After the government was replaced and a democracy installed, the Honduran government sought to reduce the size of its military, and its relationship with Robco deteriorated. Honduras refused to go through with the contract and purchase the inventory of arms, which Robco could sell only at a much lower price. Robco filed a suit in a federal district court in the United States to recover damages for this breach of contract by the government of Honduras. Using the information presented in the chapter, answer the following questions.

1. Should the Foreign Sovereign Immunities Act (FSIA) preclude this lawsuit?
2. What exception to the FSIA might apply?
3. If a contract enforcement action had been filed in Honduras, what doctrine of deference would that implicate?
4. Should the act of state doctrine bar this lawsuit?

KEY TERMS

act of state doctrine 1179
choice-of-language clause 1183
choice-of-law clause 1185
comity 1177
confiscation 1179
correspondent bank 1186
distribution agreement 1182
dumping 1189
exclusive distributorship 1182
export 1181
expropriation 1179
force majeure clause 1185
foreign exchange market 1186
forum-selection clause 1183
international law 1177
letter of credit 1186
national law 1177
normal trade relations (NTR) status 1189
quota 1188
sovereign immunity 1179
tariff 1188

CHAPTER SUMMARY International Law in a Global Economy

International Principles and Doctrines (See pages 1177–1181.)	1. *The principle of comity*—Under this principle, nations give effect to the laws and judicial decrees of other nations for reasons of courtesy and international harmony. 2. *The act of state doctrine*—A doctrine under which U.S. courts avoid passing judgment on the validity of public acts committed by a recognized foreign government within its own territory. 3. *The doctrine of sovereign immunity*—When certain conditions are satisfied, foreign nations are immune from U.S. jurisdiction under the Foreign Sovereign Immunities Act of 1976. Exceptions are made (a) when a foreign state has "waived its immunity either explicitly or by implication" or (b) when the action is based on a "commercial activity carried on in the United States by the foreign state."
Doing Business Internationally (See pages 1181–1183.)	Ways in which U.S. domestic firms engage in international business transactions include (a) exporting, which may involve foreign agents or distributors, and (b) manufacturing abroad through licensing arrangements, franchising operations, wholly owned subsidiaries, or joint ventures.
Commercial Contracts in an International Setting (See pages 1183–1185.)	International business contracts often include choice-of-language, forum-selection, and choice-of-law clauses to reduce the uncertainties associated with interpreting the language of the agreement and dealing with legal differences. Most domestic and international contracts include *force majeure* clauses. They commonly stipulate that certain events, such as floods, fires, accidents, labor strikes, and government orders, may excuse a party from liability for nonperformance of the contract. Arbitration clauses are also frequently found in international contracts.
Making Payment on International Transactions (See pages 1186–1187.)	1. *Currency conversion*—Because nations have different monetary systems, payment on international contracts requires currency conversion at a rate specified in a foreign exchange market. 2. *Correspondent banking*—Correspondent banks facilitate the transfer of funds from a buyer in one country to a seller in another. 3. *Letters of credit*—Letters of credit facilitate international transactions by ensuring payment to sellers and assuring buyers that payment will not be made until the sellers have complied with the terms of the letters of credit. Typically, compliance occurs when a bill of lading is delivered to the issuing bank.
Regulation of Specific Business Activities (See pages 1187–1189.)	National laws regulate foreign investments, exporting, and importing. The World Trade Organization attempts to minimize trade barriers among nations, as do regional trade agreements and associations, including the European Union and the North American Free Trade Agreement.

(Continued)

CHAPTER SUMMARY International Law in a Global Economy—Continued

U.S. Laws in a Global Context (See pages 1189–1190.)	1. *Antitrust laws*—U.S. antitrust laws may be applied beyond the borders of the United States. Any conspiracy that has a substantial effect on commerce within the United States may be subject to the Sherman Act, even if the violation occurs outside the United States. 2. *Antidiscrimination laws*—The major U.S. laws prohibiting employment discrimination, including Title VII of the Civil Rights Act of 1964, the Age Discrimination in Employment Act of 1967, and the Americans with Disabilities Act of 1990, cover U.S. employees working abroad for U.S. firms—*unless* to apply the U.S. laws would violate the laws of the host country.

FOR REVIEW

Answers for the even-numbered questions in this For Review *section can be found on this text's accompanying Web site at* http://blt.westbuslaw.com. *Select "Chapter 46" and click on "For Review."*

1. What is the principle of comity, and why do courts deciding disputes involving a foreign law or judicial decree apply this principle?
2. What is the act of state doctrine? In what circumstances is this doctrine applied?
3. Under the Foreign Sovereign Immunities Act of 1976, on what bases might a foreign state be considered subject to the jurisdiction of U.S. courts?
4. In what circumstances will U.S. antitrust laws be applied extraterritorially?
5. Do U.S. laws prohibiting employment discrimination apply in all circumstances to U.S. employees working for U.S. employers abroad?

QUESTIONS AND CASE PROBLEMS

46–1. Letters of Credit. The Swiss Credit Bank issued a letter of credit in favor of Antex Industries to cover the sale of 92,000 electronic integrated circuits manufactured by Electronic Arrays. The letter of credit specified that the chips would be transported to Tokyo by ship. Antex shipped the circuits by air. Payment on the letter of credit was dishonored because the shipment by air did not fulfill the precise terms of the letter of credit. Should a court compel payment? Explain.

46–2. Antitrust Claims. Billy Lamb and Carmon Willis (the plaintiffs) were tobacco growers in Kentucky. Phillip Morris, Inc., and B.A.T. Industries, PLC, routinely purchased tobacco not only from Kentucky growers but also from producers in several foreign countries. In 1982, subsidiaries of Phillip Morris and B.A.T. (the defendants) entered into an agreement with La Fundacion Del Niño (the Children's Foundation) of Caracas, Venezuela, headed by the wife of the president of Venezuela. The agreement provided that the two subsidiaries would donate a total of approximately $12.5 million to the Children's Foundation, and in exchange, the subsidiaries would obtain price controls on Venezuelan tobacco, elimination of controls on retail cigarette prices in Venezuela, tax deductions for the donations, and assurances that existing tax rates applicable to tobacco companies would not be increased. The plaintiffs brought an action, alleging that the Venezuelan arrangement was an inducement designed to restrain trade in violation of U.S. antitrust laws. Such an arrangement, the plaintiffs contended, would result in the artificial depression of tobacco prices to the detriment of domestic tobacco growers, while ensuring lucrative retail prices for tobacco products sold abroad. The trial court held that the plaintiffs' claim was barred by the act of state doctrine. What will result on appeal? Discuss. [*Lamb v. Phillip Morris, Inc.,* 915 F.2d 1024 (6th Cir. 1990)]

46–3. Discrimination Claims. Radio Free Europe and Radio Liberty (RFE/RL), a U.S. corporation doing business in Germany, employs more than three hundred U.S. citizens at its principal place of business in Munich, Germany. The concept of mandatory retirement is deeply embedded in German labor policy, and a contract formed in 1982 between RFE/RL and a German labor union contained a clause that required workers to be retired when they reach the age of sixty-five. When William Mahoney and other U.S. employees (the plaintiffs) reached the age of sixty-five, RFE/RL terminated their employment as required under its contract with the labor union. The plaintiffs sued RFE/RL for discriminating against them on the basis of age, in violation of the Age Discrimination in Employment Act of 1967. Will the plaintiffs succeed in their suit? Discuss fully. [*Mahoney v. RFE/RL, Inc.,* 47 F.3d 447 (D.C. Cir. 1995)]

46–4. Sovereign Immunity. Nuovo Pignone, Inc., is an Italian company that designs and manufactures turbine systems. Nuovo sold a turbine system to Cabinda Gulf Oil Co. (CABGOC). The system was manufactured, tested, and inspected in Italy; then it was sent to Louisiana for mounting on a platform by CABGOC's contractor. Nuovo sent a representative to consult on the mounting. The platform went to a CABGOC site off the coast of West Africa. Marcus Pere, an instrument technician at the site, was killed when a turbine within the system exploded. Pere's widow filed a suit in a U.S. district court against Nuovo and others. Nuovo claimed sovereign immunity on the ground that its majority shareholder at the time of the explosion was Ente Nazionale Idrocaburi, which was created by the government of Italy to lead its oil and gas exploration and development. Is Nuovo exempt from suit under the doctrine of sovereign immunity? Is it subject to suit under the "commercial activity" exception? Why or why not? [*Pere v. Nuovo Pignone, Inc.,* 150 F.3d 477 (5th Cir. 1998)]

46–5. Dumping. In response to a petition filed on behalf of the U.S. pineapple industry, the U.S. Commerce Department initiated an investigation of canned pineapple imported from Thailand. The investigation concerned Thai producers of the canned fruit, including the Thai Pineapple Public Co. The Thai producers also turned out products, such as pineapple juice and juice concentrate, outside the scope of the investigation. These products use separate parts of the same fresh pineapple, so they share raw material costs. To determine fair value and antidumping duties, the Commerce Department had to calculate the Thai producers' cost of production and, in so doing, had to allocate a portion of the shared fruit costs to the canned fruit. These allocations were based on the producers' own financial records, which were consistent with Thai generally accepted accounting principles. The result was a determination that more than 90 percent of the canned fruit sales were below the cost of production. The producers filed a suit in the U.S. Court of International Trade against the federal government, challenging this allocation. The producers argued that their records did not reflect actual production costs, which instead should be based on the weight of fresh fruit used to make the products. Did the Commerce Department act reasonably in determining the cost of production? Why or why not? [*Thai Pineapple Public Co. v. United States,* 187 F.3d 1362 (Fed.Cir. 1999)]

CASE PROBLEM WITH SAMPLE ANSWER

46–6. Tonoga, Ltd., doing business as Taconic Plastics, Ltd., is a manufacturer incorporated in Ireland with its principal place of business in New York. In 1997, Taconic entered into a contract with a German construction company to supply special material for a tent project designed to shelter religious pilgrims visiting holy sites in Saudi Arabia. Most of the material was made in, and shipped from, New York. The company did not pay Taconic and eventually filed for bankruptcy. Another German firm, Werner Voss Architects and Engineers, acting as an agent for the government of Saudi Arabia, guaranteed the payments due Taconic to induce it to complete the project. When it did not receive the final payment, Taconic filed a suit in a U.S. district court against the government of Saudi Arabia, claiming a breach of the guaranty and seeking to collect, in part, about $3 million. The defendant filed a motion to dismiss based, in part, on the doctrine of sovereign immunity. Under what circumstances does this doctrine apply? What are its exceptions? Should this suit be dismissed under the "commercial activity" exception? Explain. [*Tonoga, Ltd. v. Ministry of Public Works and Housing of Kingdom of Saudi Arabia,* 135 F.Supp.2d 350 (N.D.N.Y. 2001)]

After you have answered this problem, compare your answer with the sample answer given on the Web site that accompanies this text. Go to http://blt.westbuslaw.com, select "Chapter 46," and click on "Case Problem with Sample Answer."

46–7. Imports. DaimlerChrysler Corp. makes and markets motor vehicles. DaimlerChrysler assembled the 1993 and 1994 model years of its trucks at plants in Mexico. Assembly involved sheet metal components sent from the United States. DaimlerChrysler subjected some of the parts to a complicated treatment process, which included applying coats of paint to prevent corrosion, impart color, and protect the finish. Under U.S. law, goods that are assembled abroad using U.S.-made parts can be imported tariff free. A U.S. *statute* provides that painting is "incidental" to assembly and does not affect the status of the goods. A U.S. *regulation,* however, states that "painting primarily intended to enhance the appearance of an article or to impart distinctive features or characteristics" is not incidental. The U.S. Customs Service levied a tariff on the trucks. DaimlerChrysler filed a suit in the U.S. Court of International Trade, challenging the levy. Should the court rule in DaimlerChrysler's favor? Why or why not? [*DaimlerChrysler Corp. v. United States,* 361 F.3d 1378 (Fed.Cir. 2004)]

FOR CRITICAL ANALYSIS

46–8. Business cartels and monopolies that are legal in some countries may engage in practices that violate U.S. antitrust laws. In view of this fact, what are some of the implications of applying U.S. antitrust laws extraterritorially?

VIDEO QUESTION

DIGITAL VIDEO LIBRARY
WEST LEGAL STUDIES IN BUSINESS

46–9. Go to this text's Web site at http://blt.westbuslaw.com and select "Chapter 46." Click on "Video Questions" and view the video titled *International Letter of Credit.* Then answer the following questions.

1. Do banks always require the same documents to be presented in letter-of-credit transactions? If not, who dictates what documents will be required in the letter of credit?
2. At what point does the seller receive payment in a letter-of-credit transaction?
3. What assurances does a letter of credit provide to the buyer and the seller involved in the transaction?

INTERNET EXERCISES

Go to the *Business Law Today* home page at **http://blt.westbuslaw.com**, select "Chapter 46," and click on "Internet Exercises." There you will find the following Internet research exercises that you can perform to learn more about topics covered in this chapter.

Activity 46–1: LEGAL PERSPECTIVE—The World Trade Organization

Activity 46–2: MANAGEMENT PERSPECTIVE—Overseas Business Opportunities

BEFORE THE TEST

Go to the *Business Law Today* home page at **http://blt.westbuslaw.com**, select "Chapter 46," and click on "Interactive Quizzes." You will find a number of interactive questions relating to this chapter.

Dole Food Co. v. Patrickson

Chapter 46 discusses the Foreign Sovereign Immunities Act of 1976 (FSIA). Under the FSIA, foreign states, or nations, can claim certain rights in suits against them in U.S. courts, including in some circumstances immunity from the litigation. A corporate entity that is an "instrumentality" of a foreign state, as defined in the FSIA, may also avail itself of some of these rights. (Corporations and their characteristics are covered in Chapters 32 through 35.) In this extended case study, we review Dole Food Co. v. Patrickson,[1] *a case focusing on this definition. The specific question was whether a corporate subsidiary can claim to be an instrumentality of a foreign state if the state does not own a majority of the shares of the subsidiary's stock, but does own a majority of the shares of the corporate parent.*

CASE BACKGROUND

In 1851, Dole Food Company was founded in Hawaii. Dole is the world's largest producer and seller of fresh fruit, fresh vegetables, and fresh-cut flowers and markets a growing line of packaged foods. The firm does business in more than 90 countries, employing globally more than 33,000 full-time permanent employees and 24,000 full-time seasonal or temporary employees.

In 1997, Gerardo Patrickson and other farmworkers who worked in banana fields in Costa Rica, Ecuador, Guatemala, and Panama filed a suit in a Hawaii state court against Dole and others, seeking damages for injuries from exposure to dibromochloropropane, a chemical used as an agricultural pesticide. Dole impleaded[2] two Israeli firms—Dead Sea Bromine Company and Bromine Compounds, Ltd. (the Dead Sea companies)—that allegedly made the pesticides.

The Dead Sea companies asked a U.S. district court to hear the suit on the ground that they were instrumentalities of a foreign state as defined in the FSIA. The court denied this request, but held that it had jurisdiction on other grounds and dismissed the suit. The workers appealed to the U.S. Court of Appeals for the Ninth Circuit, which reversed the dismissal but agreed that the Dead Sea companies were not instrumentalities of a foreign state as defined in the FSIA. The Dead Sea companies appealed to the United States Supreme Court.

1. 538 U.S. 468, 123 S.Ct. 1655, 155 L.Ed.2d 843 (2004). This opinion may be accessed online at http://straylight.law.cornell.edu/supct/search/index.html. Enter "Dole Food Company" in the "Search" box, and select "All Decisions." Scroll to the name of the case and click on it to access the opinion.

2. *Implead* is to bring a new party into a suit between others, with the allegation that the new party is liable for part of the claim to the party that impleaded it.

MAJORITY OPINION

Justice *KENNEDY* delivered the opinion of the Court.

* * * *

The State of Israel did not have direct ownership of shares in either of the Dead Sea Companies at any time pertinent to this suit. Rather, these companies were, at various times, separated from the State of Israel by one or more intermediate corporate tiers. For example, from 1984–1985, Israel wholly owned a company called Israeli Chemicals, Ltd.; which owned a majority of shares in another company called Dead Sea Works, Ltd.; which owned a majority of shares in Dead Sea Bromine Co., Ltd.; which owned a majority of shares in Bromine Compounds, Ltd.

* * * *

* * * The Dead Sea Companies urge us to ignore corporate formalities and use the colloquial [everyday] sense of that term. They ask whether, in common parlance, Israel would be said to own the Dead Sea Companies. *We reject this analysis. In issues of corporate law, structure often matters.* It is evident from the [FSIA's] text that Congress was aware of settled principles of corporate law and legislated within that context. The language of [Section] 1603(b)(2) refers to ownership of "shares," showing that *Congress intended statutory coverage to turn on formal corporate ownership.* Likewise, [Section] 1603(b)(1), another component of the definition of instrumentality, refers to a "separate legal person, corporate or otherwise." * * * [Emphasis added.]

A basic tenet [rule] of American corporate law is that the corporation and its shareholders are distinct entities. An individual shareholder, by virtue of his ownership of compensation." A taking occurs when an ordinance denies an owner economically viable use of his or her property. In this case, the plaintiffs alleged that they lost customers because of the ordinance. The court reasoned that the ordinance's only effect on the plaintiffs' businesses is to restrict the areas in which customers can smoke and the conditions under which smoking is permitted. This might "require some financial investment, but an ordinance does not effect a taking merely because compliance with it requires the expenditure of money." Besides, the owners could elect to make other uses of their property. As for the preemption issue, a state statute takes precedence over a local ordinance when they conflict. In this case, a statute prohibits smoking in certain locations, but "it does not contain the slightest hint that the legislature intended to create a positive right to smoke in all public places where it did not expressly forbid smoking. Nothing in the [statute] is inconsistent with a local jurisdiction's decision to impose greater limits on public smoking."

Review of Sample Court Case

Here we provide a review of the briefed version to indicate the kind of information that is contained in each section.

CITATION The name of the case is *D.A.B.E., Inc. v. City of Toledo*. D.A.B.E. is the plaintiff; Toledo is the defendant. The U.S. Court of Appeals for the Sixth Circuit decided this case in 2005. The citation states that this case can be found in volume 393 the *Federal Reporter, Third Series,* on page 692.

FACTS The *Facts* section identifies the plaintiff and the defendant, describes the events leading up to this suit, the allegations made by the plaintiff in the initial suit, and (because this case is an appellate court decision) the lower court's ruling and the party appealing this ruling. The appellant's contention on appeal is also sometimes included here.

ISSUE The *Issue* section presents the central issue (or issues) decided by the court. In this case, the U.S. Court of Appeals for the Sixth Circuit considers whether the ordinance constitutes a taking in violation of the Fifth Amendment and whether a state statute preempts (or supersedes) the city ordinance.

DECISION The *Decision* section includes the court's decision on the issues before it. The decision reflects the opinion of the judge or justice hearing the case. Decisions by appellate courts are frequently phrased in reference to the lower court's decision; that is, the appellate court may "affirm" the lower court's ruling or "reverse" it. Here, the court determined that the ordinance did not effect a taking because it did not prevent the plaintiffs' beneficial use of their property. The statute did not preempt the ordinance because the legislature did not indicate an intent to prohibit a city from restricting smoking in places excluded from the statute. The court affirmed the lower court's ruling.

REASON The *Reason* section includes references to the relevant laws and legal principles that the court applied in arriving at its conclusion in the case. The relevant law here included the Fifth Amendment, the state indoor smoking statute, and the principles derived from judicial interpretations and applications of those laws. This section also explains the court's application of the law to the facts in this case.

Analyzing Case Problems

In addition to learning how to brief cases, students of business law and the legal environment also find it helpful to know how to analyze case problems. Part of the study of business law and the legal environment usually involves analyzing case problems, such as those included in this text at the end of each chapter.

For each case problem in this book, we provide the relevant background and facts of the lawsuit and the issue before the court. When you are assigned one of these problems, your job will be to determine how the court should decide the issue, and why. In other words, you will need to engage in legal analysis and reasoning. Here we offer some suggestions on how to make this task less daunting. We begin by presenting a sample problem:

> While Janet Lawson, a famous pianist, was shopping in Quality Market, she slipped and fell on a wet floor in one of the aisles. The floor had recently been mopped by one of the store's employees, but there were no signs warning customers that the floor in that area was wet. As a result of the fall, Lawson injured her right arm and was unable to perform piano concerts for the next six months. Had she been able to perform the scheduled concerts, she would have earned approximately $60,000 over that period of time. Lawson sued Quality Market for this amount, plus another $10,000 in medical expenses. She claimed that the store's failure to warn customers of the wet floor constituted negligence and therefore the market was liable for her injuries. Will the court agree with Lawson? Discuss.

Understand the Facts

This may sound obvious, but before you can analyze or apply the relevant law to a specific set of facts, you must clearly understand those facts. In other words, you should read through the case problem carefully—more than once, if necessary—to make sure you understand the identity of the plaintiff(s) and defendant(s) in the case and the progression of events that led to the lawsuit.

In the sample case just given, the identity of the parties is fairly obvious. Janet Lawson is the one bringing the suit; therefore, she is the plaintiff. Quality Market, against whom she is bringing the suit, is the defendant. Some of the case problems you may work on have multiple plaintiffs or defendants. Often, it is helpful to use abbreviations for the parties. To indicate a reference to a plaintiff, for example, the *pi* symbol—π—is often used, and a defendant is denoted by a *delta*—Δ—a triangle.

The events leading to the lawsuit are also fairly straightforward. Lawson slipped and fell on a wet floor, and she contends that Quality Market should be liable for her injuries because it was negligent in not posting a sign warning customers of the wet floor.

When you are working on case problems, realize that the facts should be accepted as they are given. For example, in our sample problem, it should be accepted that the floor was wet and that there was no sign. In other words, avoid making conjectures, such as "Maybe the floor wasn't too wet," or "Maybe an employee was getting a sign to put up," or "Maybe someone stole the sign." Questioning the facts as they are presented only adds confusion to your analysis.

Legal Analysis and Reasoning

Once you understand the facts given in the case problem, you can begin to analyze the case. The **IRAC method** is a helpful tool to use in the legal analysis and reasoning process. IRAC is an acronym for Issue, Rule, Application, Conclusion. Applying this method to our sample problem would involve the following steps:

1. First, you need to decide what legal **issue** is involved in the case. In our sample case, the basic issue is whether Quality Market's failure to warn customers of the wet floor constituted negligence. As discussed in Chapter 4, negligence is a *tort*—a civil wrong. In a tort lawsuit, the plaintiff seeks to be compensated for another's wrongful act. A defendant will be deemed negligent if he or she breached a duty of care owed to the plaintiff and the breach of that duty caused the plaintiff to suffer harm.
2. Once you have identified the issue, the next step is to determine what **rule of law** applies to the issue. To make this determination, you will want to review carefully the text of the chapter in which the problem appears to find the relevant rule of law. Our sample case involves the tort of negligence, covered in Chapter 7. The applicable rule of law is the tort law principle that business owners owe a duty to exercise reasonable care to protect their customers ("business invitees"). Reasonable care, in this context, includes either removing—or warning customers of—*foreseeable* risks about which the owner *knew* or *should have known*. Business owners need not warn customers of "open and obvious" risks, however. If a business owner breaches this duty of care (fails to exercise the appropriate degree of care toward customers), and the breach of duty causes a customer to be injured, the business owner will be liable to the customer for the customer's injuries.
3. The next—and usually the most difficult—step in analyzing case problems is the **application** of the relevant rule of law to the specific facts of the case you are studying. In our sample problem, applying the tort law principle just discussed presents few difficulties. An employee of the store had mopped the floor in the aisle where Lawson slipped and fell, but no sign was present indicating that the floor was wet. That a customer might fall on a wet floor is clearly a foreseeable risk. Therefore, the failure to warn customers about the wet floor was a breach of the duty of care owed by the business owner to the store's customers.
4. Once you have completed step 3 in the IRAC method, you should be ready to draw your **conclusion.** In our sample case, Quality Market is liable to Lawson for her injuries, because the market's breach of its duty of care caused Lawson's injuries.

The fact patterns in the case problems presented in this text are not always as simple as those presented in our sample problem. Often, for example, there may be more than one plaintiff or defendant. There also may be more than one issue involved in a case and more than one applicable rule of law. Furthermore, in some case problems the facts may indicate that the general rule of law should not apply. For example, suppose a store employee advised Lawson not to walk on the floor in the aisle because it was wet, but Lawson decided to walk on it anyway. This fact could alter the outcome of the case because the store could then raise the defense of assumption of risk (see Chapter 4). Nonetheless, a careful review of the chapter should always provide you with the knowledge you need to analyze the problem thoroughly and arrive at accurate conclusions.

APPENDIX B

The Constitution of the United States

Preamble

We the People of the United States, in Order to form a more perfect Union, establish Justice, insure domestic Tranquility, provide for the common defence, promote the general Welfare, and secure the Blessings of Liberty to ourselves and our Posterity, do ordain and establish this Constitution for the United States of America.

Article I

Section 1. All legislative Powers herein granted shall be vested in a Congress of the United States, which shall consist of a Senate and House of Representatives.

Section 2. The House of Representatives shall be composed of Members chosen every second Year by the People of the several States, and the Electors in each State shall have the Qualifications requisite for Electors of the most numerous Branch of the State Legislature.

No Person shall be a Representative who shall not have attained to the Age of twenty five Years, and been seven Years a Citizen of the United States, and who shall not, when elected, be an Inhabitant of that State in which he shall be chosen.

Representatives and direct Taxes shall be apportioned among the several States which may be included within this Union, according to their respective Numbers, which shall be determined by adding to the whole Number of free Persons, including those bound to Service for a Term of Years, and excluding Indians not taxed, three fifths of all other Persons. The actual Enumeration shall be made within three Years after the first Meeting of the Congress of the United States, and within every subsequent Term of ten Years, in such Manner as they shall by Law direct. The Number of Representatives shall not exceed one for every thirty Thousand, but each State shall have at Least one Representative; and until such enumeration shall be made, the State of New Hampshire shall be entitled to chuse three, Massachusetts eight, Rhode Island and Providence Plantations one, Connecticut five, New York six, New Jersey four, Pennsylvania eight, Delaware one, Maryland six, Virginia ten, North Carolina five, South Carolina five, and Georgia three.

When vacancies happen in the Representation from any State, the Executive Authority thereof shall issue Writs of Election to fill such Vacancies.

The House of Representatives shall chuse their Speaker and other Officers; and shall have the sole Power of Impeachment.

Section 3. The Senate of the United States shall be composed of two Senators from each State, chosen by the Legislature thereof, for six Years; and each Senator shall have one Vote.

Immediately after they shall be assembled in Consequence of the first Election, they shall be divided as equally as may be into three Classes. The Seats of the Senators of the first Class shall be vacated at the Expiration of the second Year, of the second Class at the Expiration of the fourth Year, and of the third Class at the Expiration of the sixth Year, so that one third may be chosen every second Year; and if Vacancies happen by Resignation, or otherwise, during the Recess of the Legislature of any State, the Executive thereof may make temporary Appointments until the next Meeting of the Legislature, which shall then fill such Vacancies.

No Person shall be a Senator who shall not have attained to the Age of thirty Years, and been nine Years a Citizen of the United States, and who shall not, when elected, be an Inhabitant of that State for which he shall be chosen.

The Vice President of the United States shall be President of the Senate, but shall have no Vote, unless they be equally divided.

The Senate shall chuse their other Officers, and also a President pro tempore, in the Absence of the Vice President, or when he shall exercise the Office of President of the United States.

The Senate shall have the sole Power to try all Impeachments. When sitting for that Purpose, they shall be on Oath or Affirmation. When the President of the United States is tried, the Chief Justice shall preside: And no Person shall be convicted without the Concurrence of two thirds of the Members present.

Judgment in Cases of Impeachment shall not extend further than to removal from Office, and disqualification to hold and enjoy any Office of honor, Trust, or Profit under the United States: but the Party convicted shall nevertheless be liable and subject to Indictment, Trial, Judgment, and Punishment, according to Law.

Section 4. The Times, Places and Manner of holding Elections for Senators and Representatives, shall be prescribed in each State by the Legislature thereof; but the Congress may at any time by Law make or alter such Regulations, except as to the Places of chusing Senators.

The Congress shall assemble at least once in every Year, and such Meeting shall be on the first Monday in December, unless they shall by Law appoint a different Day.

Section 5. Each House shall be the Judge of the Elections, Returns, and Qualifications of its own Members, and a Majority of each shall constitute a Quorum to do Business; but a smaller Number may adjourn from day to day, and may be authorized to compel the Attendance of absent Members, in such Manner, and under such Penalties as each House may provide.

Each House may determine the Rules of its Proceedings, punish its Members for disorderly Behavior, and, with the Concurrence of two thirds, expel a Member.

Each House shall keep a Journal of its Proceedings, and from time to time publish the same, excepting such Parts as may in their Judgment require Secrecy; and the Yeas and Nays of the Members of either House on any question shall, at the Desire of one fifth of those Present, be entered on the Journal.

Neither House, during the Session of Congress, shall, without the Consent of the other, adjourn for more than three days, nor to any other Place than that in which the two Houses shall be sitting.

Section 6. The Senators and Representatives shall receive a Compensation for their Services, to be ascertained by Law, and paid out of the Treasury of the United States. They shall in all Cases, except Treason, Felony and Breach of the Peace, be privileged from Arrest during their Attendance at the Session of their respective Houses, and in going to and returning from the same; and for any Speech or Debate in either House, they shall not be questioned in any other Place.

No Senator or Representative shall, during the Time for which he was elected, be appointed to any civil Office under the Authority of the United States, which shall have been created, or the Emoluments whereof shall have been increased during such time; and no Person holding any Office under the United States, shall be a Member of either House during his Continuance in Office.

Section 7. All Bills for raising Revenue shall originate in the House of Representatives; but the Senate may propose or concur with Amendments as on other Bills.

Every Bill which shall have passed the House of Representatives and the Senate, shall, before it become a Law, be presented to the President of the United States; If he approve he shall sign it, but if not he shall return it, with his Objections to the House in which it shall have originated, who shall enter the Objections at large on their Journal, and proceed to reconsider it. If after such Reconsideration two thirds of that House shall agree to pass the Bill, it shall be sent together with the Objections, to the other House, by which it shall likewise be reconsidered, and if approved by two thirds of that House, it shall become a Law. But in all such Cases the Votes of both Houses shall be determined by Yeas and Nays, and the Names of the Persons voting for and against the Bill shall be entered on the Journal of each House respectively. If any Bill shall not be returned by the President within ten Days (Sundays excepted) after it shall have been presented to him, the Same shall be a Law, in like Manner as if he had signed it, unless the Congress by their Adjournment prevent its Return in which Case it shall not be a Law.

Every Order, Resolution, or Vote, to which the Concurrence of the Senate and House of Representatives may be necessary (except on a question of Adjournment) shall be presented to the President of the United States; and before the Same shall take Effect, shall be approved by him, or being disapproved by him, shall be repassed by two thirds of the Senate and House of Representatives, according to the Rules and Limitations prescribed in the Case of a Bill.

Section 8. The Congress shall have Power To lay and collect Taxes, Duties, Imposts and Excises, to pay the Debts and provide for the common Defence and general Welfare of the United States; but all Duties, Imposts and Excises shall be uniform throughout the United States;

To borrow Money on the credit of the United States;

To regulate Commerce with foreign Nations, and among the several States, and with the Indian Tribes;

To establish an uniform Rule of Naturalization, and uniform Laws on the subject of Bankruptcies throughout the United States;

To coin Money, regulate the Value thereof, and of foreign Coin, and fix the Standard of Weights and Measures;

To provide for the Punishment of counterfeiting the Securities and current Coin of the United States;

To establish Post Offices and post Roads;

To promote the Progress of Science and useful Arts, by securing for limited Times to Authors and Inventors the exclusive Right to their respective Writings and Discoveries;

To constitute Tribunals inferior to the supreme Court;

To define and punish Piracies and Felonies committed on the high Seas, and Offenses against the Law of Nations;

To declare War, grant Letters of Marque and Reprisal, and make Rules concerning Captures on Land and Water;

To raise and support Armies, but no Appropriation of Money to that Use shall be for a longer Term than two Years;

To provide and maintain a Navy;

To make Rules for the Government and Regulation of the land and naval Forces;

To provide for calling forth the Militia to execute the Laws of the Union, suppress Insurrections and repel Invasions;

To provide for organizing, arming, and disciplining, the Militia, and for governing such Part of them as may be employed in the Service of the United States, reserving to the States respectively, the Appointment of the Officers, and the Authority of training the Militia according to the discipline prescribed by Congress;

To exercise exclusive Legislation in all Cases whatsoever, over such District (not exceeding ten Miles square) as may, by Cession of particular States, and the Acceptance of Congress, become the Seat of the Government of the United States, and to exercise like Authority over all Places purchased by the Consent of the Legislature of the State in which the Same shall be, for the Erection of Forts, Magazines, Arsenals, dock-Yards, and other needful Buildings;—And

To make all Laws which shall be necessary and proper for carrying into Execution the foregoing Powers, and all other Powers vested by this Constitution in the Government of the United States, or in any Department or Officer thereof.

Section 9. The Migration or Importation of such Persons as any of the States now existing shall think proper to admit, shall not be prohibited by the Congress prior to the Year one thousand eight hundred and eight, but a Tax or duty may be imposed on such Importation, not exceeding ten dollars for each Person.

The privilege of the Writ of Habeas Corpus shall not be suspended, unless when in Cases of Rebellion or Invasion the public Safety may require it.

No Bill of Attainder or ex post facto Law shall be passed.

No Capitation, or other direct, Tax shall be laid, unless in Proportion to the Census or Enumeration herein before directed to be taken.

No Tax or Duty shall be laid on Articles exported from any State.

No Preference shall be given by any Regulation of Commerce or Revenue to the Ports of one State over those of another: nor shall Vessels bound to, or from, one State be obliged to enter, clear, or pay Duties in another.

No Money shall be drawn from the Treasury, but in Consequence of Appropriations made by Law; and a regular Statement and Account of the Receipts and Expenditures of all public Money shall be published from time to time.

No Title of Nobility shall be granted by the United States: And no Person holding any Office of Profit or Trust under them, shall, without the Consent of the Congress, accept of any present, Emolument, Office, or Title, of any kind whatever, from any King, Prince, or foreign State.

Section 10. No State shall enter into any Treaty, Alliance, or Confederation; grant Letters of Marque and Reprisal; coin Money; emit Bills of Credit; make any Thing but gold and silver Coin a Tender in Payment of Debts; pass any Bill of Attainder, ex post facto Law, or Law impairing the Obligation of Contracts, or grant any Title of Nobility.

No State shall, without the Consent of the Congress, lay any Imposts or Duties on Imports or Exports, except what may be absolutely necessary for executing its inspection Laws: and the net Produce of all Duties and Imposts, laid by any State on Imports or Exports, shall be for the Use of the Treasury of the United States; and all such Laws shall be subject to the Revision and Controul of the Congress.

No State shall, without the Consent of Congress, lay any Duty of Tonnage, keep Troops, or Ships of War in time of Peace, enter into any Agreement or Compact with another State, or with a foreign Power, or engage in War, unless actually invaded, or in such imminent Danger as will not admit of delay.

Article II

Section 1. The executive Power shall be vested in a President of the United States of America. He shall hold his Office during the Term of four Years, and, together with the Vice President, chosen for the same Term, be elected, as follows:

Each State shall appoint, in such Manner as the Legislature thereof may direct, a Number of Electors, equal to the whole Number of Senators and Representatives to which the State may be entitled in the Congress; but no Senator or Representative, or Person holding an Office of Trust or Profit under the United States, shall be appointed an Elector.

The Electors shall meet in their respective States, and vote by Ballot for two Persons, of whom one at least shall not be an Inhabitant of the same State with themselves. And they shall make a List of all the Persons voted for, and of the Number of Votes for each; which List they shall sign and certify, and transmit sealed to the Seat of the Government of the United States, directed to the President of the Senate. The President of the Senate shall, in the Presence of the Senate and House of Representatives, open all the Certificates, and the Votes shall then be counted. The Person having the greatest Number of Votes shall be the President, if such Number be a Majority of the whole Number of Electors appointed; and if there be more than one who have such Majority, and have an equal Number of Votes, then the House of Representatives shall immediately chuse by Ballot one of them for President; and if no Person have a Majority, then from the five highest on the List the said House shall in like Manner chuse the President. But in chusing the President, the Votes shall be taken by States, the Representation from each State having one Vote; A quorum for this Purpose shall consist of a Member or Members from two thirds of the States, and a Majority of all the States shall be necessary to a Choice. In every Case, after the Choice of the President, the Person having the greater Number of Votes of the Electors shall be the Vice President. But if there should remain two or more who have equal Votes, the Senate shall chuse from them by Ballot the Vice President.

The Congress may determine the Time of chusing the Electors, and the Day on which they shall give their Votes; which Day shall be the same throughout the United States.

No person except a natural born Citizen, or a Citizen of the United States, at the time of the Adoption of this Constitution, shall be eligible to the Office of President; neither shall any Person be eligible to that Office who shall not have attained to the Age of thirty five Years, and been fourteen Years a Resident within the United States.

In Case of the Removal of the President from Office, or of his Death, Resignation or Inability to discharge the Powers and Duties of the said Office, the same shall devolve on the Vice President, and the Congress may by Law provide for the Case of Removal, Death, Resignation or Inability, both of the President and Vice President, declaring what Officer shall then act as President, and such Officer shall act accordingly, until the Disability be removed, or a President shall be elected.

The President shall, at stated Times, receive for his Services, a Compensation, which shall neither be increased nor diminished during the Period for which he shall have been elected, and he shall not receive within that Period any other Emolument from the United States, or any of them.

Before he enter on the Execution of his Office, he shall take the following Oath or Affirmation: "I do solemnly swear (or affirm) that I will faithfully execute the Office of President of the United States, and will to the best of my Ability, preserve, protect and defend the Constitution of the United States."

Section 2. The President shall be Commander in Chief of the Army and Navy of the United States, and of the Militia of the several States, when called into the actual Service of the United States; he may require the Opinion, in writing, of the principal Officer in each of the executive Departments, upon any Subject relating to the Duties of their respective Offices, and he shall have Power to grant Reprieves and Pardons for Offenses against the United States, except in Cases of Impeachment.

He shall have Power, by and with the Advice and Consent of the Senate to make Treaties, provided two thirds of the Senators present concur; and he shall nominate, and by and with the Advice and Consent of the Senate, shall appoint Ambassadors, other public Ministers and Consuls, Judges of the supreme Court, and all other Officers of the United States, whose Appointments are not herein otherwise provided for, and which shall be established by Law; but the Congress may by Law vest the Appointment of such inferior Officers, as they think proper, in the President alone, in the Courts of Law, or in the Heads of Departments.

The President shall have Power to fill up all Vacancies that may happen during the Recess of the Senate, by granting Commissions which shall expire at the End of their next Session.

Section 3. He shall from time to time give to the Congress Information of the State of the Union, and recommend to their Consideration such Measures as he shall judge necessary and expedient; he may, on extraordinary Occasions, convene both Houses, or either of them, and in Case of Disagreement between them, with Respect to the Time of Adjournment, he may adjourn them to such Time as he shall think proper; he shall receive Ambassadors and other public Ministers; he shall take Care that the Laws be faithfully executed, and shall Commission all the Officers of the United States.

Section 4. The President, Vice President and all civil Officers of the United States, shall be removed from Office on Impeachment for, and Conviction of, Treason, Bribery, or other high Crimes and Misdemeanors.

ARTICLE III

Section 1. The judicial Power of the United States, shall be vested in one supreme Court, and in such inferior Courts as the Congress may from time to time ordain and establish. The Judges, both of the supreme and inferior Courts, shall hold their Offices during good Behaviour, and shall, at stated Times, receive for their Services a Compensation, which shall not be diminished during their Continuance in Office.

Section 2. The judicial Power shall extend to all Cases, in Law and Equity, arising under this Constitution, the Laws of the United States, and Treaties made, or which shall be made, under their Authority;—to all Cases affecting Ambassadors, other public Ministers and Consuls;—to all Cases of admiralty and maritime Jurisdiction;—to Controversies to which the United States shall be a Party;—to Controversies between two or more States;—between a State and Citizens of another State;—between Citizens of different States;—between Citizens of the same State claiming Lands under Grants of different States, and between a State, or the Citizens thereof, and foreign States, Citizens or Subjects.

In all Cases affecting Ambassadors, other public Ministers and Consuls, and those in which a State shall be a Party, the supreme Court shall have original Jurisdiction. In all the other Cases before mentioned, the supreme Court shall have appellate Jurisdiction, both as to Law and Fact, with such Exceptions, and under such Regulations as the Congress shall make.

The Trial of all Crimes, except in Cases of Impeachment, shall be by Jury; and such Trial shall be held in the State where the said Crimes shall have been committed; but when not committed within any State, the Trial shall be at such Place or Places as the Congress may by Law have directed.

Section 3. Treason against the United States, shall consist only in levying War against them, or, in adhering to their Enemies, giving them Aid and Comfort. No Person shall be convicted of Treason unless on the Testimony of two Witnesses to the same overt Act, or on Confession in open Court.

The Congress shall have Power to declare the Punishment of Treason, but no Attainder of Treason shall work Corruption of Blood, or Forfeiture except during the Life of the Person attainted.

Article IV

Section 1. Full Faith and Credit shall be given in each State to the public Acts, Records, and judicial Proceedings of every other State. And the Congress may by general Laws prescribe the Manner in which such Acts, Records and Proceedings shall be proved, and the Effect thereof.

Section 2. The Citizens of each State shall be entitled to all Privileges and Immunities of Citizens in the several States.

A Person charged in any State with Treason, Felony, or other Crime, who shall flee from Justice, and be found in another State, shall on Demand of the executive Authority of the State from which he fled, be delivered up, to be removed to the State having Jurisdiction of the Crime.

No Person held to Service or Labour in one State, under the Laws thereof, escaping into another, shall, in Consequence of any Law or Regulation therein, be discharged from such Service or Labour, but shall be delivered up on Claim of the Party to whom such Service or Labour may be due.

Section 3. New States may be admitted by the Congress into this Union; but no new State shall be formed or erected within the Jurisdiction of any other State; nor any State be formed by the Junction of two or more States, or Parts of States, without the Consent of the Legislatures of the States concerned as well as of the Congress.

The Congress shall have Power to dispose of and make all needful Rules and Regulations respecting the Territory or other Property belonging to the United States; and nothing in this Constitution shall be so construed as to Prejudice any Claims of the United States, or of any particular State.

Section 4. The United States shall guarantee to every State in this Union a Republican Form of Government, and shall protect each of them against Invasion; and on Application of the Legislature, or of the Executive (when the Legislature cannot be convened) against domestic Violence.

Article V

The Congress, whenever two thirds of both Houses shall deem it necessary, shall propose Amendments to this Constitution, or, on the Application of the Legislatures of two thirds of the several States, shall call a Convention for proposing Amendments, which, in either Case, shall be valid to all Intents and Purposes, as part of this Constitution, when ratified by the Legislatures of three fourths of the several States, or by Conventions in three fourths thereof, as the one or the other Mode of Ratification may be proposed by the Congress; Provided that no Amendment which may be made prior to the Year One thousand eight hundred and eight shall in any Manner affect the first and fourth Clauses in the Ninth Section of the first Article; and that no State, without its Consent, shall be deprived of its equal Suffrage in the Senate.

Article VI

All Debts contracted and Engagements entered into, before the Adoption of this Constitution shall be as valid against the United States under this Constitution, as under the Confederation.

This Constitution, and the Laws of the United States which shall be made in Pursuance thereof; and all Treaties made, or which shall be made, under the Authority of the United States, shall be the supreme Law of the Land; and the Judges in every State shall be bound thereby, any Thing in the Constitution or Laws of any State to the Contrary notwithstanding.

The Senators and Representatives before mentioned, and the Members of the several State Legislatures, and all executive and judicial Officers, both of the United States and of the several States, shall be bound by Oath or Affirmation, to support this Constitution; but no religious Test shall ever be required as a Qualification to any Office or public Trust under the United States.

Article VII

The Ratification of the Conventions of nine States shall be sufficient for the Establishment of this Constitution between the States so ratifying the Same.

Amendment I [1791]

Congress shall make no law respecting an establishment of religion, or prohibiting the free exercise thereof; or abridging the freedom of speech, or of the press; or the right of the people peaceably to assembly, and to petition the Government for a redress of grievances.

Amendment II [1791]

A well regulated Militia, being necessary to the security of a free State, the right of the people to keep and bear Arms, shall not be infringed.

Amendment III [1791]

No Soldier shall, in time of peace be quartered in any house, without the consent of the Owner, nor in time of war, but in a manner to be prescribed by law.

Amendment IV [1791]

The right of the people to be secure in their persons, houses, papers, and effects, against unreasonable searches and seizures, shall not be violated, and no Warrants shall issue, but upon probable cause, supported by Oath or affirmation, and particularly describing the place to be searched, and the persons or things to be seized.

Amendment V [1791]

No person shall be held to answer for a capital, or otherwise infamous crime, unless on a presentment or indictment of a Grand Jury, except in cases arising in the land or naval forces, or in the Militia, when in actual service in time of War or public danger; nor shall any person be subject for the same offence to be twice put in jeopardy of life or limb; nor shall be compelled in any criminal case to be a witness against himself, nor be deprived of life, liberty, or property, without due process of law; nor shall private property be taken for public use, without just compensation.

Amendment VI [1791]

In all criminal prosecutions, the accused shall enjoy the right to a speedy and public trial, by an impartial jury of the State and district wherein the crime shall have been committed, which district shall have been previously ascertained by law, and to be informed of the nature and cause of the accusation; to be confronted with the witnesses against him; to have compulsory process for obtaining witnesses in his favor, and to have the Assistance of Counsel for his defence.

Amendment VII [1791]

In Suits at common law, where the value in controversy shall exceed twenty dollars, the right of trial by jury shall be preserved, and no fact tried by jury, shall be otherwise re-examined in any Court of the United States, than according to the rules of the common law.

Amendment VIII [1791]

Excessive bail shall not be required, nor excessive fines imposed, nor cruel and unusual punishments inflicted.

Amendment IX [1791]

The enumeration in the Constitution, of certain rights, shall not be construed to deny or disparage others retained by the people.

Amendment X [1791]

The powers not delegated to the United States by the Constitution, nor prohibited by it to the States, are reserved to the States respectively, or to the people.

Amendment XI [1798]

The Judicial power of the United States shall not be construed to extend to any suit in law or equity, commenced or prosecuted against one of the United States by Citizens of another State, or by Citizens or Subjects of any Foreign State.

Amendment XII [1804]

The Electors shall meet in their respective states, and vote by ballot for President and Vice-President, one of whom, at least, shall not be an inhabitant of the same state with themselves; they shall name in their ballots the person voted for as President, and in distinct ballots the person voted for as Vice-President, and they shall make distinct lists of all persons voted for as President, and of all persons voted for as Vice-President, and of the number of votes for each, which lists they shall sign and certify, and transmit sealed to the seat of the government of the United States, directed to the President of the Senate;—The President of the Senate shall, in the presence of the Senate and House of Representatives, open all the certificates and the votes shall then be counted;—The person having the greatest number of votes for President, shall be the President, if such number be a majority of the whole number of Electors appointed; and if no person have such majority, then from the persons having the highest numbers not exceeding three on the list of those voted for as President, the House of Representatives shall choose immediately, by ballot, the President. But in choosing the President, the votes shall be taken by states, the representation from each state having one vote; a quorum for this purpose shall consist of a member or members from two-thirds of the states, and a majority of all states shall be necessary to a choice. And if the House of Representatives shall not choose a President whenever the right of choice shall devolve upon them, before the fourth day of March next following, then the Vice-President shall act as President, as in the case of the death or other constitutional disability of the President.—The person having the greatest number of votes as Vice-President, shall be the Vice-President, if such number be a majority of the whole number of Electors appointed, and if no person have a majority, then from the two highest numbers on the list, the Senate shall choose the Vice-President; a quorum for the purpose shall consist of two-thirds of the whole number of Senators, and a majority of the whole number shall be necessary to a choice. But no person constitutionally ineligible to the office of President shall be eligible to that of Vice-President of the United States.

Amendment XIII [1865]

Section 1. Neither slavery nor involuntary servitude, except as a punishment for crime whereof the party shall have been duly convicted, shall exist within the United States, or any place subject to their jurisdiction.

Section 2. Congress shall have power to enforce this article by appropriate legislation.

Amendment XIV [1868]

Section 1. All persons born or naturalized in the United States, and subject to the jurisdiction thereof, are citizens of the United States and of the State wherein they reside. No State shall make or enforce any law which shall abridge the privileges or immunities of citizens of the United States; nor shall any State deprive any person of life, liberty, or property, without due process of law; nor deny to any person within its jurisdiction the equal protection of the laws.

Section 2. Representatives shall be apportioned among the several States according to their respective numbers, counting the whole number of persons in each State, excluding Indians not taxed. But when the right to vote at any election for the choice of electors for President and Vice President of the United States, Representatives in Congress, the Executive and Judicial officers of a State, or the members of the Legislature thereof, is denied to any of the male inhabitants of such State, being twenty-one years of age, and citizens of the United States, or in any way abridged, except for participation in rebellion, or other crime, the basis of representation therein shall be reduced in the proportion which the number of such male citizens shall bear to the whole number of male citizens twenty-one years of age in such State.

Section 3. No person shall be a Senator or Representative in Congress, or elector of President and Vice President, or hold any office, civil or military, under the United States, or under any State, who having previously taken an oath, as a member of Congress, or as an officer of the United States, or as a member of any State legislature, or as an executive or judicial officer of any State, to support the Constitution of the United States, shall have engaged in insurrection or rebellion against the same, or given aid or comfort to the enemies thereof. But Congress may by a vote of two-thirds of each House, remove such disability.

Section 4. The validity of the public debt of the United States, authorized by law, including debts incurred for payment of pensions and bounties for services in suppressing insurrection or rebellion, shall not be questioned. But neither the United States nor any State shall assume or pay any debt or obligation incurred in aid of insurrection or rebellion against the United States, or any claim for the loss or emancipation of any slave; but all such debts, obligations and claims shall be held illegal and void.

Section 5. The Congress shall have power to enforce, by appropriate legislation, the provisions of this article.

Amendment XV [1870]

Section 1. The right of citizens of the United States to vote shall not be denied or abridged by the United States or by any State on account of race, color, or previous condition of servitude.

Section 2. The Congress shall have power to enforce this article by appropriate legislation.

Amendment XVI [1913]

The Congress shall have power to lay and collect taxes on incomes, from whatever source derived, without apportionment among the several States, and without regard to any census or enumeration.

Amendment XVII [1913]

Section 1. The Senate of the United States shall be composed of two Senators from each State, elected by the people thereof, for six years; and each Senator shall have one vote. The electors in each State shall have the qualifications requisite for electors of the most numerous branch of the State legislatures.

Section 2. When vacancies happen in the representation of any State in the Senate, the executive authority of such State shall issue writs of election to fill such vacancies: *Provided,* That the legislature of any State may empower the executive thereof to make temporary appointments until the people fill the vacancies by election as the legislature may direct.

Section 3. This amendment shall not be so construed as to affect the election or term of any Senator chosen before it becomes valid as part of the Constitution.

Amendment XVIII [1919]

Section 1. After one year from the ratification of this article the manufacture, sale, or transportation of intoxicating liquors within, the importation thereof into, or the exportation thereof from the United States and all territory subject to the jurisdiction thereof for beverage purposes is hereby prohibited.

Section 2. The Congress and the several States shall have concurrent power to enforce this article by appropriate legislation.

Section 3. This article shall be inoperative unless it shall have been ratified as an amendment to the Constitution by the legislatures of the several States, as provided in the Constitution, within seven years from the date of the submission hereof to the States by the Congress.

Amendment XIX [1920]

Section 1. The right of citizens of the United States to vote shall not be denied or abridged by the United States or by any State on account of sex.

Section 2. Congress shall have power to enforce this article by appropriate legislation.

Amendment XX [1933]

Section 1. The terms of the President and Vice President shall end at noon on the 20th day of January, and the terms of Senators and Representatives at noon on the 3d day of January, of the years in which such terms would have ended if this article had not been ratified; and the terms of their successors shall then begin.

Section 2. The Congress shall assemble at least once in every year, and such meeting shall begin at noon on the 3d day of January, unless they shall by law appoint a different day.

Section 3. If, at the time fixed for the beginning of the term of the President, the President elect shall have died, the Vice President elect shall become President. If the President shall not have been chosen before the time fixed for the beginning of his term, or if the President elect shall have failed to qualify, then the Vice President elect shall act as President until a President shall have qualified; and the Congress may by law provide for the case wherein neither a President elect nor a Vice President elect shall have qualified, declaring who shall then act as President, or the manner in which one who is to act shall be selected, and such person shall act accordingly until a President or Vice President shall have qualified.

Section 4. The Congress may by law provide for the case of the death of any of the persons from whom the House of Representatives may choose a President whenever the right of choice shall have devolved upon them, and for the case of the death of any of the persons from whom the Senate may choose a Vice President whenever the right of choice shall have devolved upon them.

Section 5. Sections 1 and 2 shall take effect on the 15th day of October following the ratification of this article.

Section 6. This article shall be inoperative unless it shall have been ratified as an amendment to the Constitution by the legislatures of three-fourths of the several States within seven years from the date of its submission.

Amendment XXI [1933]

Section 1. The eighteenth article of amendment to the Constitution of the United States is hereby repealed.

Section 2. The transportation or importation into any State, Territory, or possession of the United States for delivery or use therein of intoxicating liquors, in violation of the laws thereof, is hereby prohibited.

Section 3. This article shall be inoperative unless it shall have been ratified as an amendment to the Constitution by conventions in the several States, as provided in the Constitution, within seven years from the date of the submission hereof to the States by the Congress.

Amendment XXII [1951]

Section 1. No person shall be elected to the office of the President more than twice, and no person who has held the office of President, or acted as President, for more than two years of a term to which some other person was elected President shall be elected to the office of President more than once. But this Article shall not apply to any person holding the office of President when this Article was proposed by the Congress, and shall not prevent any person who may be holding the office of President, or acting as President, during the term within which this Article becomes operative from holding the office of President or acting as President during the remainder of such term.

Section 2. This article shall be inoperative unless it shall have been ratified as an amendment to the Constitution by the legislatures of three-fourths of the several States within seven years from the date of its submission to the States by the Congress.

Amendment XXIII [1961]

Section 1. The District constituting the seat of Government of the United States shall appoint in such manner as the Congress may direct:

A number of electors of President and Vice President equal to the whole number of Senators and Representatives in Congress to which the District would be entitled if it were a State, but in no event more than the least populous state; they shall be in addition to those appointed by the states, but they shall be considered, for the purposes of the election of President and Vice President, to be electors appointed by a state; and they shall meet in the District and perform such duties as provided by the twelfth article of amendment.

Section 2. The Congress shall have power to enforce this article by appropriate legislation.

Amendment XXIV [1964]

Section 1. The right of citizens of the United States to vote in any primary or other election for President or Vice President, for electors for President or Vice President, or for Senator or Representative in Congress, shall not be denied or abridged by the United States, or any State by reason of failure to pay any poll tax or other tax.

Section 2. The Congress shall have power to enforce this article by appropriate legislation.

Amendment XXV [1967]

Section 1. In case of the removal of the President from office or of his death or resignation, the Vice President shall become President.

Section 2. Whenever there is a vacancy in the office of the Vice President, the President shall nominate a Vice President who shall take office upon confirmation by a majority vote of both Houses of Congress.

Section 3. Whenever the President transmits to the President pro tempore of the Senate and the Speaker of the House of Representatives his written declaration that he is unable to discharge the powers and duties of his office, and until he transmits to them a written declaration to the contrary, such powers and duties shall be discharged by the Vice President as Acting President.

Section 4. Whenever the Vice President and a majority of either the principal officers of the executive departments or of such other body as Congress may by law provide, transmit to the President pro tempore of the Senate and the Speaker of the House of Representatives their written declaration that the President is unable to discharge the powers and duties of his office, the Vice President shall immediately assume the powers and duties of the office as Acting President.

Thereafter, when the President transmits to the President pro tempore of the Senate and the Speaker of the House of Representatives his written declaration that no inability exists, he shall resume the powers and duties of his office unless the Vice President and a majority of either the principal officers of the executive department or of such other body as Congress may by law provide, transmit within four days to the President pro tempore of the Senate and the Speaker of the House of Representatives their written declaration that the President is unable to discharge the powers and duties of his office. Thereupon Congress shall decide the issue, assembling within forty-eight hours for that purpose if not in session. If the Congress, within twenty-one days after receipt of the latter written declaration, or, if Congress is not in session, within twenty-one days after Congress is required to assemble, determines by two-thirds vote of both Houses that the President is unable to discharge the powers and duties of his office, the Vice President shall continue to discharge the same as Acting President; otherwise, the President shall resume the powers and duties of his office.

Amendment XXVI [1971]

Section 1. The right of citizens of the United States, who are eighteen years of age or older, to vote shall not be denied or abridged by the United States or by any State on account of age.

Section 2. The Congress shall have power to enforce this article by appropriate legislation.

Amendment XXVII [1992]

No law, varying the compensation for the services of the Senators and Representatives, shall take effect, until an election of Representatives shall have intervened.

APPENDIX C

Uniform Commercial Code (Excerpts)

(Adopted in fifty-two jurisdictions; all fifty States, although Louisiana has adopted only Articles 1, 3, 4, 7, 8, and 9; the District of Columbia; and the Virgin Islands.)

The Code consists of the following articles:

Art.

1. General Provisions
2. Sales

2A. Leases

3. Negotiable Instruments
4. Bank Deposits and Collections

4A. Funds Transfers

5. Letters of Credit
6. Repealer of Article 6—Bulk Transfers and [Revised] Article 6—Bulk Sales
7. Warehouse Receipts, Bills of Lading and Other Documents of Title
8. Investment Securities
9. Secured Transactions
10. Effective Date and Repealer
11. Effective Date and Transition Provisions

Article 1
GENERAL PROVISIONS

Part 1 Short Title, Construction, Application and Subject Matter of the Act

§ 1–101. Short Title.

This Act shall be known and may be cited as Uniform Commercial Code.

§ 1–102. Purposes; Rules of Construction; Variation by Agreement.

(1) This Act shall be liberally construed and applied to promote its underlying purposes and policies.

(2) Underlying purposes and policies of this Act are

(a) to simplify, clarify and modernize the law governing commercial transactions;

(b) to permit the continued expansion of commercial practices through custom, usage and agreement of the parties;

(c) to make uniform the law among the various jurisdictions.

(3) The effect of provisions of this Act may be varied by agreement, except as otherwise provided in this Act and except that the obligations of good faith, diligence, reasonableness and care prescribed by this Act may not be disclaimed by agreement but the parties may by agreement determine the standards by which the performance of such obligations is to be measured if such standards are not manifestly unreasonable.

(4) The presence in certain provisions of this Act of the words "unless otherwise agreed" or words of similar import does not imply that the effect of other provisions may not be varied by agreement under subsection (3).

(5) In this Act unless the context otherwise requires

(a) words in the singular number include the plural, and in the plural include the singular;

(b) words of the masculine gender include the feminine and the neuter, and when the sense so indicates words of the neuter gender may refer to any gender.

§ 1–103. Supplementary General Principles of Law Applicable.

Unless displaced by the particular provisions of this Act, the principles of law and equity, including the law merchant and the law relative to capacity to contract, principal and agent, estoppel, fraud, misrepresentation, duress, coercion, mistake, bankruptcy, or other validating or invalidating cause shall supplement its provisions.

§ 1–104. Construction Against Implicit Repeal.

This Act being a general act intended as a unified coverage of its subject matter, no part of it shall be deemed to be impliedly repealed by subsequent legislation if such construction can reasonably be avoided.

§ 1–105. Territorial Application of the Act; Parties' Power to Choose Applicable Law.

(1) Except as provided hereafter in this section, when a transaction bears a reasonable relation to this state and also to another state or nation the parties may agree that the law either of this state or of such other state or nation shall govern their rights and duties. Failing such agreement this Act applies to transactions bearing an appropriate relation to this state.

(2) Where one of the following provisions of this Act specifies the applicable law, that provision governs and a contrary agreement is effective only to the extent permitted by the law (including the conflict of laws rules) so specified:

Rights of creditors against sold goods. Section 2–402.

Applicability of the Article on Leases. Sections 2A–105 and 2A–106.

Applicability of the Article on Bank Deposits and Collections. Section 4–102.

Governing law in the Article on Funds Transfers. Section 4A–507.

Letters of Credit, Section 5–116.

Bulk sales subject to the Article on Bulk Sales. Section 6–103.

Applicability of the Article on Investment Securities. Section 8–106.

Law governing perfection, the effect of perfection or non-perfection, and the priority of security interests and agricultural liens. Sections 9–301 through 9–307.

As amended in 1972, 1987, 1988, 1989, 1994, 1995, and 1999.

§ 1–106. Remedies to Be Liberally Administered.

(1) The remedies provided by this Act shall be liberally administered to the end that the aggrieved party may be put in as good a position as if the other party had fully performed but neither consequential or special nor penal damages may be had except as specifically provided in this Act or by other rule of law.

(2) Any right or obligation declared by this Act is enforceable by action unless the provision declaring it specifies a different and limited effect.

§ 1–107. Waiver or Renunciation of Claim or Right After Breach.

Any claim or right arising out of an alleged breach can be discharged in whole or in part without consideration by a written waiver or renunciation signed and delivered by the aggrieved party.

§ 1–108. Severability.

If any provision or clause of this Act or application thereof to any person or circumstances is held invalid, such invalidity shall not affect other provisions or applications of the Act which can be given effect without the invalid provision or application, and to this end the provisions of this Act are declared to be severable.

§ 1–109. Section Captions.

Section captions are parts of this Act.

Part 2 General Definitions and Principles of Interpretation

§ 1–201. General Definitions.

Subject to additional definitions contained in the subsequent Articles of this Act which are applicable to specific Articles or Parts thereof, and unless the context otherwise requires, in this Act:

(1) "Action" in the sense of a judicial proceeding includes recoupment, counterclaim, set-off, suit in equity and any other proceedings in which rights are determined.

(2) "Aggrieved party" means a party entitled to resort to a remedy.

(3) "Agreement" means the bargain of the parties in fact as found in their language or by implication from other circumstances including course of dealing or usage of trade or course of performance as provided in this Act (Sections 1–205 and 2–208). Whether an agreement has legal consequences is determined by the provisions of this Act, if applicable; otherwise by the law of contracts (Section 1–103). (Compare "Contract".)

(4) "Bank" means any person engaged in the business of banking.

(5) "Bearer" means the person in possession of an instrument, document of title, or certificated security payable to bearer or indorsed in blank.

(6) "Bill of lading" means a document evidencing the receipt of goods for shipment issued by a person engaged in the business of transporting or forwarding goods, and includes an airbill. "Airbill" means a document serving for air transportation as a bill of lading does for marine or rail transportation, and includes an air consignment note or air waybill.

(7) "Branch" includes a separately incorporated foreign branch of a bank.

(8) "Burden of establishing" a fact means the burden of persuading the triers of fact that the existence of the fact is more probable than its non-existence.

(9) "Buyer in ordinary course of business" means a person that buys goods in good faith, without knowledge that the sale violates the rights of another person in the goods, and in the ordinary course from a person, other than a pawnbroker, in the business of selling goods of that kind. A person buys goods in the ordinary course if the sale to the person comports with the usual or customary practices in the kind of business in which the seller is engaged or with the seller's own usual or customary practices. A person that sells oil, gas, or other minerals at the wellhead or minehead is a person in the business of selling goods of that kind. A buyer in ordinary course of business may buy for cash, by exchange of other property, or on secured or unsecured credit, and may acquire goods or documents of title under a pre-existing contract for sale. Only a buyer that takes possession of the goods or has a right to recover the goods from the seller under Article 2 may be a buyer in ordinary course of business. A person that acquires goods in a transfer in bulk or as security for or in total or partial satisfaction of a money debt is not a buyer in ordinary course of business.

(10) "Conspicuous": A term or clause is conspicuous when it is so written that a reasonable person against whom it is to operate ought to have noticed it. A printed heading in capitals (as: NON-NEGOTIABLE BILL OF LADING) is conspicuous. Language in the body of a form is "conspicuous" if it is in larger or other contrasting type or color. But in a telegram any stated term is "conspicuous". Whether a term or clause is "conspicuous" or not is for decision by the court.

(11) "Contract" means the total legal obligation which results from the parties' agreement as affected by this Act and any other applicable rules of law. (Compare "Agreement".)

(12) "Creditor" includes a general creditor, a secured creditor, a lien creditor and any representative of creditors, including an assignee for the benefit of creditors, a trustee in bankruptcy, a receiver in equity and an executor or administrator of an insolvent debtor's or assignor's estate.

(13) "Defendant" includes a person in the position of defendant in a cross-action or counterclaim.

(14) "Delivery" with respect to instruments, documents of title, chattel paper, or certificated securities means voluntary transfer of possession.

(15) "Document of title" includes bill of lading, dock warrant, dock receipt, warehouse receipt or order for the delivery of goods, and also any other document which in the regular course of business or financing is treated as adequately evidencing that the person in possession of it is entitled to receive, hold and dispose of the document and the goods it covers. To be a document of title a document must purport to be issued by or addressed to a bailee and purport to cover goods in the bailee's possession which are either identified or are fungible portions of an identified mass.

(16) "Fault" means wrongful act, omission or breach.

(17) "Fungible" with respect to goods or securities means goods or securities of which any unit is, by nature or usage of trade, the equivalent of any other like unit. Goods which are not fungible shall be deemed fungible for the purposes of this Act to the extent that under a particular agreement or document unlike units are treated as equivalents.

(18) "Genuine" means free of forgery or counterfeiting.

(19) "Good faith" means honesty in fact in the conduct or transaction concerned.

(20) "Holder" with respect to a negotiable instrument, means the person in possession if the instrument is payable to bearer or, in the cases of an instrument payable to an identified person, if the identified person is in possession. "Holder" with respect to a document of title means the person in possession if the goods are deliverable to bearer or to the order of the person in possession.

(21) To "honor" is to pay or to accept and pay, or where a credit so engages to purchase or discount a draft complying with the terms of the credit.

(22) "Insolvency proceedings" includes any assignment for the benefit of creditors or other proceedings intended to liquidate or rehabilitate the estate of the person involved.

(23) A person is "insolvent" who either has ceased to pay his debts in the ordinary course of business or cannot pay his debts as they become due or is insolvent within the meaning of the federal bankruptcy law.

(24) "Money" means a medium of exchange authorized or adopted by a domestic or foreign government and includes a monetary unit of account established by an intergovernmental organization or by agreement between two or more nations.

(25) A person has "notice" of a fact when

(a) he has actual knowledge of it; or

(b) he has received a notice or notification of it; or

(c) from all the facts and circumstances known to him at the time in question he has reason to know that it exists.

A person "knows" or has "knowledge" of a fact when he has actual knowledge of it. "Discover" or "learn" or a word or phrase of similar import refers to knowledge rather than to reason to know. The time and circumstances under which a notice or notification may cease to be effective are not determined by this Act.

(26) A person "notifies" or "gives" a notice or notification to another by taking such steps as may be reasonably required to

inform the other in ordinary course whether or not such other actually comes to know of it. A person "receives" a notice or notification when

(a) it comes to his attention; or

(b) it is duly delivered at the place of business through which the contract was made or at any other place held out by him as the place for receipt of such communications.

(27) Notice, knowledge or a notice or notification received by an organization is effective for a particular transaction from the time when it is brought to the attention of the individual conducting that transaction, and in any event from the time when it would have been brought to his attention if the organization had exercised due diligence. An organization exercises due diligence if it maintains reasonable routines for communicating significant information to the person conducting the transaction and there is reasonable compliance with the routines. Due diligence does not require an individual acting for the organization to communicate information unless such communication is part of his regular duties or unless he has reason to know of the transaction and that the transaction would be materially affected by the information.

(28) "Organization" includes a corporation, government or governmental subdivision or agency, business trust, estate, trust, partnership or association, two or more persons having a joint or common interest, or any other legal or commercial entity.

(29) "Party", as distinct from "third party", means a person who has engaged in a transaction or made an agreement within this Act.

(30) "Person" includes an individual or an organization (See Section 1–102).

(31) "Presumption" or "presumed" means that the trier of fact must find the existence of the fact presumed unless and until evidence is introduced which would support a finding of its non-existence.

(32) "Purchase" includes taking by sale, discount, negotiation, mortgage, pledge, lien, issue or re-issue, gift or any other voluntary transaction creating an interest in property.

(33) "Purchaser" means a person who takes by purchase.

(34) "Remedy" means any remedial right to which an aggrieved party is entitled with or without resort to a tribunal.

(35) "Representative" includes an agent, an officer of a corporation or association, and a trustee, executor or administrator of an estate, or any other person empowered to act for another.

(36) "Rights" includes remedies.

(37) "Security interest" means an interest in personal property or fixtures which secures payment or performance of an obligation. The term also includes any interest of a consignor and a buyer of accounts, chattel paper, a payment intangible, or a promissory note in a transaction that is subject to Article 9. The special property interest of a buyer of goods on identification of those goods to a contract for sale under Section 2–401 is not a "security interest", but a buyer may also acquire a "security interest" by complying with Article 9. Except as otherwise provided in Section 2–505, the right of a seller or lessor of goods under Article 2 or 2A to retain or acquire possession of the goods is not a "security interest", but a seller or lessor may also acquire a "security interest" by complying with Article 9. The retention or reservation of title by a seller of goods notwithstanding shipment or delivery to the buyer (Section 2–401) is limited in effect to a reservation of a "security interest".

Whether a transaction creates a lease or security interest is determined by the facts of each case; however, a transaction creates a security interest if the consideration the lessee is to pay the lessor for the right to possession and use of the goods is an obligation for the term of the lease not subject to termination by the lessee, and

(a) the original term of the lease is equal to or greater than the remaining economic life of the goods,

(b) the lessee is bound to renew the lease for the remaining economic life of the goods or is bound to become the owner of the goods,

(c) the lessee has an option to renew the lease for the remaining economic life of the goods for no additional consideration or nominal additional consideration upon compliance with the lease agreement, or

(d) the lessee has an option to become the owner of the goods for no additional consideration or nominal additional consideration upon compliance with the lease agreement.

A transaction does not create a security interest merely because it provides that

(a) the present value of the consideration the lessee is obligated to pay the lessor for the right to possession and use of the goods is substantially equal to or is greater than the fair market value of the goods at the time the lease is entered into,

(b) the lessee assumes risk of loss of the goods, or agrees to pay taxes, insurance, filing, recording, or registration fees, or service or maintenance costs with respect to the goods,

(c) the lessee has an option to renew the lease or to become the owner of the goods,

(d) the lessee has an option to renew the lease for a fixed rent that is equal to or greater than the reasonably predictable fair market rent for the use of the goods for the term of the renewal at the time the option is to be performed, or

(e) the lessee has an option to become the owner of the goods for a fixed price that is equal to or greater than the reasonably predictable fair market value of the goods at the time the option is to be performed.

For purposes of this subsection (37):

(x) Additional consideration is not nominal if (i) when the option to renew the lease is granted to the lessee the rent is stated to be the fair market rent for the use of the goods for the term of the renewal determined at the time the option is to be performed, or (ii) when the option to become the owner of the goods is granted to the lessee the price is stated to be the fair market value of the goods determined at the time the option is to be performed. Additional consideration is nominal if it is less than the lessee's reasonably predictable cost of performing under the lease agreement if the option is not exercised;

(y) "Reasonably predictable" and "remaining economic life of the goods" are to be determined with reference to the facts and circumstances at the time the transaction is entered into; and

(z) "Present value" means the amount as of a date certain of one or more sums payable in the future, discounted to the date certain. The discount is determined by the interest rate specified by the parties if the rate is not manifestly unreasonable at the time the transaction is entered into; otherwise, the discount is determined by a commercially reasonable rate that takes into account the facts and circumstances of each case at the time the transaction was entered into.

(38) "Send" in connection with any writing or notice means to deposit in the mail or deliver for transmission by any other usual means of communication with postage or cost of transmission provided for and properly addressed and in the case of an instrument to an address specified thereon or otherwise agreed, or if there be none to any address reasonable under the circumstances. The receipt of any writing or notice within the time at which it would have arrived if properly sent has the effect of a proper sending.

(39) "Signed" includes any symbol executed or adopted by a party with present intention to authenticate a writing.

(40) "Surety" includes guarantor.

(41) "Telegram" includes a message transmitted by radio, teletype, cable, any mechanical method of transmission, or the like.

(42) "Term" means that portion of an agreement which relates to a particular matter.

(43) "Unauthorized" signature means one made without actual, implied or apparent authority and includes a forgery.

(44) "Value". Except as otherwise provided with respect to negotiable instruments and bank collections (Sections 3–303, 4–210 and 4–211) a person gives "value" for rights if he acquires them

(a) in return for a binding commitment to extend credit or for the extension of immediately available credit whether or not drawn upon and whether or not a chargeback is provided for in the event of difficulties in collection; or

(b) as security for or in total or partial satisfaction of a preexisting claim; or

(c) by accepting delivery pursuant to a preexisting contract for purchase; or

(d) generally, in return for any consideration sufficient to support a simple contract.

(45) "Warehouse receipt" means a receipt issued by a person engaged in the business of storing goods for hire.

(46) "Written" or "writing" includes printing, typewriting or any other intentional reduction to tangible form.

§ 1–202. **Prima Facie Evidence by Third Party Documents.**

A document in due form purporting to be a bill of lading, policy or certificate of insurance, official weigher's or inspector's certificate, consular invoice, or any other document authorized or required by the contract to be issued by a third party shall be prima facie evidence of its own authenticity and genuineness and of the facts stated in the document by the third party.

§ 1–203. **Obligation of Good Faith.**

Every contract or duty within this Act imposes an obligation of good faith in its performance or enforcement.

§ 1–204. **Time; Reasonable Time; "Seasonably".**

(1) Whenever this Act requires any action to be taken within a reasonable time, any time which is not manifestly unreasonable may be fixed by agreement.

(2) What is a reasonable time for taking any action depends on the nature, purpose and circumstances of such action.

(3) An action is taken "seasonably" when it is taken at or within the time agreed or if no time is agreed at or within a reasonable time.

§ 1–205. **Course of Dealing and Usage of Trade.**

(1) A course of dealing is a sequence of previous conduct between the parties to a particular transaction which is fairly to be regarded as establishing a common basis of understanding for interpreting their expressions and other conduct.

(2) A usage of trade is any practice or method of dealing having such regularity of observance in a place, vocation or trade as to justify an expectation that it will be observed with respect to the transaction in question. The existence and scope of such a usage are to be proved as facts. If it is established that such a usage is embodied in a written trade code or similar writing the interpretation of the writing is for the court.

(3) A course of dealing between parties and any usage of trade in the vocation or trade in which they are engaged or of which they are or should be aware give particular meaning to and supplement or qualify terms of an agreement.

(4) The express terms of an agreement and an applicable course of dealing or usage of trade shall be construed wherever reasonable as consistent with each other; but when such construction is unreasonable express terms control both course of dealing and usage of trade and course of dealing controls usage trade.

(5) An applicable usage of trade in the place where any part of performance is to occur shall be used in interpreting the agreement as to that part of the performance.

(6) Evidence of a relevant usage of trade offered by one party is not admissible unless and until he has given the other party such notice as the court finds sufficient to prevent unfair surprise to the latter.

§ 1–206. Statute of Frauds for Kinds of Personal Property Not Otherwise Covered.

(1) Except in the cases described in subsection (2) of this section a contract for the sale of personal property is not enforceable by way of action or defense beyond five thousand dollars in amount or value of remedy unless there is some writing which indicates that a contract for sale has been made between the parties at a defined or stated price, reasonably identifies the subject matter, and is signed by the party against whom enforcement is sought or by his authorized agent.

(2) Subsection (1) of this section does not apply to contracts for the sale of goods (Section 2–201) nor of securities (Section 8–113) nor to security agreements (Section 9–203).

As amended in 1994.

§ 1–207. Performance or Acceptance Under Reservation of Rights.

(1) A party who with explicit reservation of rights performs or promises performance or assents to performance in a manner demanded or offered by the other party does not thereby prejudice the rights reserved. Such words as "without prejudice", "under protest" or the like are sufficient.

(2) Subsection (1) does not apply to an accord and satisfaction.

As amended in 1990.

§ 1–208. Option to Accelerate at Will.

A term providing that one party or his successor in interest may accelerate payment or performance or require collateral or additional collateral "at will" or "when he deems himself insecure" or in words of similar import shall be construed to mean that he shall have power to do so only if he in good faith believes that the prospect of payment or performance is impaired. The burden of establishing lack of good faith is on the party against whom the power has been exercised.

§ 1–209. Subordinated Obligations.

An obligation may be issued as subordinated to payment of another obligation of the person obligated, or a creditor may subordinate his right to payment of an obligation by agreement with either the person obligated or another creditor of the person obligated. Such a subordination does not create a security interest as against either the common debtor or a subordinated creditor. This section shall be construed as declaring the law as it existed prior to the enactment of this section and not as modifying it. Added 1966.

Note: *This new section is proposed as an optional provision to make it clear that a subordination agreement does not create a security interest unless so intended.*

Article 2
SALES

Part 1 Short Title, General Construction and Subject Matter

§ 2–101. Short Title.

This Article shall be known and may be cited as Uniform Commercial Code—Sales.

§ 2–102. Scope; Certain Security and Other Transactions Excluded From This Article.

Unless the context otherwise requires, this Article applies to transactions in goods; it does not apply to any transaction which although in the form of an unconditional contract to sell or present sale is intended to operate only as a security transaction nor does this Article impair or repeal any statute regulating sales to consumers, farmers or other specified classes of buyers.

§ 2–103. Definitions and Index of Definitions.

(1) In this Article unless the context otherwise requires

(a) "Buyer" means a person who buys or contracts to buy goods.

(b) "Good faith" in the case of a merchant means honesty in fact and the observance of reasonable commercial standards of fair dealing in the trade.

(c) "Receipt" of goods means taking physical possession of them.

(d) "Seller" means a person who sells or contracts to sell goods.

(2) Other definitions applying to this Article or to specified Parts thereof, and the sections in which they appear are:

"Acceptance". Section 2–606.
"Banker's credit". Section 2–325.
"Between merchants". Section 2–104.
"Cancellation". Section 2–106(4).
"Commercial unit". Section 2–105.
"Confirmed credit". Section 2–325.
"Conforming to contract". Section 2–106.
"Contract for sale". Section 2–106.
"Cover". Section 2–712.
"Entrusting". Section 2–403.
"Financing agency". Section 2–104.
"Future goods". Section 2–105.
"Goods". Section 2–105.
"Identification". Section 2–501.
"Installment contract". Section 2–612.
"Letter of Credit". Section 2–325.
"Lot". Section 2–105.
"Merchant". Section 2–104.
"Overseas". Section 2–323.
"Person in position of seller". Section 2–707.

"Present sale". Section 2–106.
"Sale". Section 2–106.
"Sale on approval". Section 2–326.
"Sale or return". Section 2–326.
"Termination". Section 2–106.

(3) The following definitions in other Articles apply to this Article:

"Check". Section 3–104.
"Consignee". Section 7–102.
"Consignor". Section 7–102.
"Consumer goods". Section 9–109.
"Dishonor". Section 3–507.
"Draft". Section 3–104.

(4) In addition Article 1 contains general definitions and principles of construction and interpretation applicable throughout this Article.

As amended in 1994 and 1999.

§ 2–104. Definitions: "Merchant"; "Between Merchants"; "Financing Agency".

(1) "Merchant" means a person who deals in goods of the kind or otherwise by his occupation holds himself out as having knowledge or skill peculiar to the practices or goods involved in the transaction or to whom such knowledge or skill may be attributed by his employment of an agent or broker or other intermediary who by his occupation holds himself out as having such knowledge or skill.

(2) "Financing agency" means a bank, finance company or other person who in the ordinary course of business makes advances against goods or documents of title or who by arrangement with either the seller or the buyer intervenes in ordinary course to make or collect payment due or claimed under the contract for sale, as by purchasing or paying the seller's draft or making advances against it or by merely taking it for collection whether or not documents of title accompany the draft. "Financing agency" includes also a bank or other person who similarly intervenes between persons who are in the position of seller and buyer in respect to the goods (Section 2–707).

(3) "Between merchants" means in any transaction with respect to which both parties are chargeable with the knowledge or skill of merchants.

§ 2–105. Definitions: Transferability; "Goods"; "Future" Goods; "Lot"; "Commercial Unit".

(1) "Goods" means all things (including specially manufactured goods) which are movable at the time of identification to the contract for sale other than the money in which the price is to be paid, investment securities (Article 8) and things in action. "Goods" also includes the unborn young of animals and growing crops and other identified things attached to realty as described in the section on goods to be severed from realty (Section 2–107).

(2) Goods must be both existing and identified before any interest in them can pass. Goods which are not both existing and identified are "future" goods. A purported present sale of future goods or of any interest therein operates as a contract to sell.

(3) There may be a sale of a part interest in existing identified goods.

(4) An undivided share in an identified bulk of fungible goods is sufficiently identified to be sold although the quantity of the bulk is not determined. Any agreed proportion of such a bulk or any quantity thereof agreed upon by number, weight or other measure may to the extent of the seller's interest in the bulk be sold to the buyer who then becomes an owner in common.

(5) "Lot" means a parcel or a single article which is the subject matter of a separate sale or delivery, whether or not it is sufficient to perform the contract.

(6) "Commercial unit" means such a unit of goods as by commercial usage is a single whole for purposes of sale and division of which materially impairs its character or value on the market or in use. A commercial unit may be a single article (as a machine) or a set of articles (as a suite of furniture or an assortment of sizes) or a quantity (as a bale, gross, or carload) or any other unit treated in use or in the relevant market as a single whole.

§ 2–106. Definitions: "Contract"; "Agreement"; "Contract for Sale"; "Sale"; "Present Sale"; "Conforming" to Contract; "Termination"; "Cancellation".

(1) In this Article unless the context otherwise requires "contract" and "agreement" are limited to those relating to the present or future sale of goods. "Contract for sale" includes both a present sale of goods and a contract to sell goods at a future time. A "sale" consists in the passing of title from the seller to the buyer for a price (Section 2–401). A "present sale" means a sale which is accomplished by the making of the contract.

(2) Goods or conduct including any part of a performance are "conforming" or conform to the contract when they are in accordance with the obligations under the contract.

(3) "Termination" occurs when either party pursuant to a power created by agreement or law puts an end to the contract otherwise than for its breach. On "termination" all obligations which are still executory on both sides are discharged but any right based on prior breach or performance survives.

(4) "Cancellation" occurs when either party puts an end to the contract for breach by the other and its effect is the same as that of "termination" except that the cancelling party also retains any remedy for breach of the whole contract or any unperformed balance.

§ 2–107. Goods to Be Severed From Realty: Recording.

(1) A contract for the sale of minerals or the like (including oil and gas) or a structure or its materials to be removed from realty is a contract for the sale of goods within this Article if they are to be severed by the seller but until severance a purported present sale thereof which is not effective as a transfer of an interest in land is effective only as a contract to sell.

(2) A contract for the sale apart from the land of growing crops or other things attached to realty and capable of severance with-

out material harm thereto but not described in subsection (1) or of timber to be cut is a contract for the sale of goods within this Article whether the subject matter is to be severed by the buyer or by the seller even though it forms part of the realty at the time of contracting, and the parties can by identification effect a present sale before severance.

(3) The provisions of this section are subject to any third party rights provided by the law relating to realty records, and the contract for sale may be executed and recorded as a document transferring an interest in land and shall then constitute notice to third parties of the buyer's rights under the contract for sale.

As amended in 1972.

Part 2 Form, Formation and Readjustment of Contract

§ 2–201. Formal Requirements; Statute of Frauds.

(1) Except as otherwise provided in this section a contract for the sale of goods for the price of $500 or more is not enforceable by way of action or defense unless there is some writing sufficient to indicate that a contract for sale has been made between the parties and signed by the party against whom enforcement is sought or by his authorized agent or broker. A writing is not insufficient because it omits or incorrectly states a term agreed upon but the contract is not enforceable under this paragraph beyond the quantity of goods shown in such writing.

(2) Between merchants if within a reasonable time a writing in confirmation of the contract and sufficient against the sender is received and the party receiving it has reason to know its contents, its satisfies the requirements of subsection (1) against such party unless written notice of objection to its contents is given within ten days after it is received.

(3) A contract which does not satisfy the requirements of subsection (1) but which is valid in other respects is enforceable

(a) if the goods are to be specially manufactured for the buyer and are not suitable for sale to others in the ordinary course of the seller's business and the seller, before notice of repudiation is received and under circumstances which reasonably indicate that the goods are for the buyer, has made either a substantial beginning of their manufacture or commitments for their procurement; or

(b) if the party against whom enforcement is sought admits in his pleading, testimony or otherwise in court that a contract for sale was made, but the contract is not enforceable under this provision beyond the quantity of goods admitted; or

(c) with respect to goods for which payment has been made and accepted or which have been received and accepted (Sec. 2–606).

§ 2–202. Final Written Expression: Parol or Extrinsic Evidence.

Terms with respect to which the confirmatory memoranda of the parties agree or which are otherwise set forth in a writing intended by the parties as a final expression of their agreement with respect to such terms as are included therein may not be contradicted by evidence of any prior agreement or of a contemporaneous oral agreement but may be explained or supplemented

(a) by course of dealing or usage of trade (Section 1–205) or by course of performance (Section 2–208); and

(b) by evidence of consistent additional terms unless the court finds the writing to have been intended also as a complete and exclusive statement of the terms of the agreement.

§ 2–203. Seals Inoperative.

The affixing of a seal to a writing evidencing a contract for sale or an offer to buy or sell goods does not constitute the writing a sealed instrument and the law with respect to sealed instruments does not apply to such a contract or offer.

§ 2–204. Formation in General.

(1) A contract for sale of goods may be made in any manner sufficient to show agreement, including conduct by both parties which recognizes the existence of such a contract.

(2) An agreement sufficient to constitute a contract for sale may be found even though the moment of its making is undetermined.

(3) Even though one or more terms are left open a contract for sale does not fail for indefiniteness if the parties have intended to make a contract and there is a reasonably certain basis for giving an appropriate remedy.

§ 2–205. Firm Offers.

An offer by a merchant to buy or sell goods in a signed writing which by its terms gives assurance that it will be held open is not revocable, for lack of consideration, during the time stated or if no time is stated for a reasonable time, but in no event may such period of irrevocability exceed three months; but any such term of assurance on a form supplied by the offeree must be separately signed by the offeror.

§ 2–206. Offer and Acceptance in Formation of Contract.

(1) Unless other unambiguously indicated by the language or circumstances

(a) an offer to make a contract shall be construed as inviting acceptance in any manner and by any medium reasonable in the circumstances;

(b) an order or other offer to buy goods for prompt or current shipment shall be construed as inviting acceptance either by a prompt promise to ship or by the prompt or current shipment of conforming or nonconforming goods, but such a shipment of non-conforming goods does not constitute an acceptance if the seller seasonably notifies the buyer that the shipment is offered only as an accommodation to the buyer.

(2) Where the beginning of a requested performance is a reasonable mode of acceptance an offeror who is not notified of

acceptance within a reasonable time may treat the offer as having lapsed before acceptance.

§ 2–207. Additional Terms in Acceptance or Confirmation.

(1) A definite and seasonable expression of acceptance or a written confirmation which is sent within a reasonable time operates as an acceptance even though it states terms additional to or different from those offered or agreed upon, unless acceptance is expressly made conditional on assent to the additional or different terms.

(2) The additional terms are to be construed as proposals for addition to the contract. Between merchants such terms become part of the contract unless:

(a) the offer expressly limits acceptance to the terms of the offer;

(b) they materially alter it; or

(c) notification of objection to them has already been given or is given within a reasonable time after notice of them is received.

(3) Conduct by both parties which recognizes the existence of a contract is sufficient to establish a contract for sale although the writings of the parties do not otherwise establish a contract. In such case the terms of the particular contract consist of those terms on which the writings of the parties agree, together with any supplementary terms incorporated under any other provisions of this Act.

§ 2–208. Course of Performance or Practical Construction.

(1) Where the contract for sale involves repeated occasions for performance by either party with knowledge of the nature of the performance and opportunity for objection to it by the other, any course of performance accepted or acquiesced in without objection shall be relevant to determine the meaning of the agreement.

(2) The express terms of the agreement and any such course of performance, as well as any course of dealing and usage of trade, shall be construed whenever reasonable as consistent with each other; but when such construction is unreasonable, express terms shall control course of performance and course of performance shall control both course of dealing and usage of trade (Section 1–205).

(3) Subject to the provisions of the next section on modification and waiver, such course of performance shall be relevant to show a waiver or modification of any term inconsistent with such course of performance.

§ 2–209. Modification, Rescission and Waiver.

(1) An agreement modifying a contract within this Article needs no consideration to be binding.

(2) A signed agreement which excludes modification or rescission except by a signed writing cannot be otherwise modified or rescinded, but except as between merchants such a requirement on a form supplied by the merchant must be separately signed by the other party.

(3) The requirements of the statute of frauds section of this Article (Section 2–201) must be satisfied if the contract as modified is within its provisions.

(4) Although an attempt at modification or rescission does not satisfy the requirements of subsection (2) or (3) it can operate as a waiver.

(5) A party who has made a waiver affecting an executory portion of the contract may retract the waiver by reasonable notification received by the other party that strict performance will be required of any term waived, unless the retraction would be unjust in view of a material change of position in reliance on the waiver.

§ 2–210. Delegation of Performance; Assignment of Rights.

(1) A party may perform his duty through a delegate unless otherwise agreed or unless the other party has a substantial interest in having his original promisor perform or control the acts required by the contract. No delegation of performance relieves the party delegating of any duty to perform or any liability for breach.

(2) Except as otherwise provided in Section 9–406, unless otherwise agreed, all rights of either seller or buyer can be assigned except where the assignment would materially change the duty of the other party, or increase materially the burden or risk imposed on him by his contract, or impair materially his chance of obtaining return performance. A right to damages for breach of the whole contract or a right arising out of the assignor's due performance of his entire obligation can be assigned despite agreement otherwise.

(3) The creation, attachment, perfection, or enforcement of a security interest in the seller's interest under a contract is not a transfer that materially changes the duty of or increases materially the burden or risk imposed on the buyer or impairs materially the buyer's chance of obtaining return performance within the purview of subsection (2) unless, and then only to the extent that, enforcement actually results in a delegation of material performance of the seller. Even in that event, the creation, attachment, perfection, and enforcement of the security interest remain effective, but (i) the seller is liable to the buyer for damages caused by the delegation to the extent that the damages could not reasonably by prevented by the buyer, and (ii) a court having jurisdiction may grant other appropriate relief, including cancellation of the contract for sale or an injunction against enforcement of the security interest or consummation of the enforcement.

(4) Unless the circumstnaces indicate the contrary a prohibition of assignment of "the contract" is to be construed as barring only the delegation to the assigness of the assignor's performance.

(5) An assignment of "the contract" or of "all my rights under the contract" or an assignment in similar general terms is an assignment of rights and unless the language or the circumstances (as in an assignment for security) indicate the contrary, it is a delegation of performance of the duties of the assignor and its acceptance by the assignee constitutes a promise by him

to perform those duties. This promise is enforceable by either the assignor or the other party to the original contract.

(6) The other party may treat any assignment which delegates performance as creating reasonable grounds for insecurity and may without prejudice to his rights against the assignor demand assurances from the assignee (Section 2–609).

As amended in 1999.

Part 3 General Obligation and Construction of Contract

§ 2–301. General Obligations of Parties.

The obligation of the seller is to transfer and deliver and that of the buyer is to accept and pay in accordance with the contract.

§ 2–302. Unconscionable Contract or Clause.

(1) If the court as a matter of law finds the contract or any clause of the contract to have been unconscionable at the time it was made the court may refuse to enforce the contract, or it may enforce the remainder of the contract without the unconscionable clause, or it may so limit the application of any unconscionable clause as to avoid any unconscionable result.

(2) When it is claimed or appears to the court that the contract or any clause thereof may be unconscionable the parties shall be afforded a reasonable opportunity to present evidence as to its commercial setting, purpose and effect to aid the court in making the determination.

§ 2–303. Allocations or Division of Risks.

Where this Article allocates a risk or a burden as between the parties "unless otherwise agreed", the agreement may not only shift the allocation but may also divide the risk or burden.

§ 2–304. Price Payable in Money, Goods, Realty, or Otherwise.

(1) The price can be made payable in money or otherwise. If it is payable in whole or in part in goods each party is a seller of the goods which he is to transfer.

(2) Even though all or part of the price is payable in an interest in realty the transfer of the goods and the seller's obligations with reference to them are subject to this Article, but not the transfer of the interest in realty or the transferor's obligations in connection therewith.

§ 2–305. Open Price Term.

(1) The parties if they so intend can conclude a contract for sale even though the price is not settled. In such a case the price is a reasonable price at the time for delivery if

(a) nothing is said as to price; or

(b) the price is left to be agreed by the parties and they fail to agree; or

(c) the price is to be fixed in terms of some agreed market or other standard as set or recorded by a third person or agency and it is not so set or recorded.

(2) A price to be fixed by the seller or by the buyer means a price for him to fix in good faith.

(3) When a price left to be fixed otherwise than by agreement of the parties fails to be fixed through fault of one party the other may at his option treat the contract as cancelled or himself fix a reasonable price.

(4) Where, however, the parties intend not to be bound unless the price be fixed or agreed and it is not fixed or agreed there is no contract. In such a case the buyer must return any goods already received or if unable so to do must pay their reasonable value at the time of delivery and the seller must return any portion of the price paid on account.

§ 2–306. Output, Requirements and Exclusive Dealings.

(1) A term which measures the quantity by the output of the seller or the requirements of the buyer means such actual output or requirements as may occur in good faith, except that no quantity unreasonably disproportionate to any stated estimate or in the absence of a stated estimate to any normal or otherwise comparable prior output or requirements may be tendered or demanded.

(2) A lawful agreement by either the seller or the buyer for exclusive dealing in the kind of goods concerned imposes unless otherwise agreed an obligation by the seller to use best efforts to supply the goods and by the buyer to use best efforts to promote their sale.

§ 2–307. Delivery in Single Lot or Several Lots.

Unless otherwise agreed all goods called for by a contract for sale must be tendered in a single delivery and payment is due only on such tender but where the circumstances give either party the right to make or demand delivery in lots the price if it can be apportioned may be demanded for each lot.

§ 2–308. Absence of Specified Place for Delivery.

Unless otherwise agreed

(a) the place for delivery of goods is the seller's place of business or if he has none his residence; but

(b) in a contract for sale of identified goods which to the knowledge of the parties at the time of contracting are in some other place, that place is the place for their delivery; and

(c) documents of title may be delivered through customary banking channels.

§ 2–309. Absence of Specific Time Provisions; Notice of Termination.

(1) The time for shipment or delivery or any other action under a contract if not provided in this Article or agreed upon shall be a reasonable time.

(2) Where the contract provides for successive performances but is indefinite in duration it is valid for a reasonable time but unless otherwise agreed may be terminated at any time by either party.

(3) Termination of a contract by one party except on the happening of an agreed event requires that reasonable notification be received by the other party and an agreement dispensing with notification is invalid if its operation would be unconscionable.

§ 2–310. Open Time for Payment or Running of Credit; Authority to Ship Under Reservation.

Unless otherwise agreed

(a) payment is due at the time and place at which the buyer is to receive the goods even though the place of shipment is the place of delivery; and

(b) if the seller is authorized to send the goods he may ship them under reservation, and may tender the documents of title, but the buyer may inspect the goods after their arrival before payment is due unless such inspection is inconsistent with the terms of the contract (Section 2–513); and

(c) if delivery is authorized and made by way of documents of title otherwise than by subsection (b) then payment is due at the time and place at which the buyer is to receive the documents regardless of where the goods are to be received; and

(d) where the seller is required or authorized to ship the goods on credit the credit period runs from the time of shipment but post-dating the invoice or delaying its dispatch will correspondingly delay the starting of the credit period.

§ 2–311. Options and Cooperation Respecting Performance.

(1) An agreement for sale which is otherwise sufficiently definite (subsection (3) of Section 2–204) to be a contract is not made invalid by the fact that it leaves particulars of performance to be specified by one of the parties. Any such specification must be made in good faith and within limits set by commercial reasonableness.

(2) Unless otherwise agreed specifications relating to assortment of the goods are at the buyer's option and except as otherwise provided in subsections (1)(c) and (3) of Section 2–319 specifications or arrangements relating to shipment are at the seller's option.

(3) Where such specification would materially affect the other party's performance but is not seasonably made or where one party's cooperation is necessary to the agreed performance of the other but is not seasonably forthcoming, the other party in addition to all other remedies

(a) is excused for any resulting delay in his own performance; and

(b) may also either proceed to perform in any reasonable manner or after the time for a material part of his own performance treat the failure to specify or to cooperate as a breach by failure to deliver or accept the goods.

§ 2–312. Warranty of Title and Against Infringement; Buyer's Obligation Against Infringement.

(1) Subject to subsection (2) there is in a contract for sale a warranty by the seller that

(a) the title conveyed shall be good, and its transfer rightful; and

(b) the goods shall be delivered free from any security interest or other lien or encumbrance of which the buyer at the time of contracting has no knowledge.

(2) A warranty under subsection (1) will be excluded or modified only by specific language or by circumstances which give the buyer reason to know that the person selling does not claim title in himself or that he is purporting to sell only such right or title as he or a third person may have.

(3) Unless otherwise agreed a seller who is a merchant regularly dealing in goods of the kind warrants that the goods shall be delivered free of the rightful claim of any third person by way of infringement or the like but a buyer who furnishes specifications to the seller must hold the seller harmless against any such claim which arises out of compliance with the specifications.

§ 2–313. Express Warranties by Affirmation, Promise, Description, Sample.

(1) Express warranties by the seller are created as follows:

(a) Any affirmation of fact or promise made by the seller to the buyer which relates to the goods and becomes part of the basis of the bargain creates an express warranty that the goods shall conform to the affirmation or promise.

(b) Any description of the goods which is made part of the basis of the bargain creates an express warranty that the goods shall conform to the description.

(c) Any sample or model which is made part of the basis of the bargain creates an express warranty that the whole of the goods shall conform to the sample or model.

(2) It is not necessary to the creation of an express warranty that the seller use formal words such as "warrant" or "guarantee" or that he have a specific intention to make a warranty, but an affirmation merely of the value of the goods or a statement purporting to be merely the seller's opinion or commendation of the goods does not create a warranty.

§ 2–314. Implied Warranty: Merchantability; Usage of Trade.

(1) Unless excluded or modified (Section 2–316), a warranty that the goods shall be merchantable is implied in a contract for their sale if the seller is a merchant with respect to goods of that kind. Under this section the serving for value of food or drink to be consumed either on the premises or elsewhere is a sale.

(2) Goods to be merchantable must be at least such as

(a) pass without objection in the trade under the contract description; and

(b) in the case of fungible goods, are of fair average quality within the description; and

(c) are fit for the ordinary purposes for which such goods are used; and

(d) run, within the variations permitted by the agreement, of even kind, quality and quantity within each unit and among all units involved; and

(e) are adequately contained, packaged, and labeled as the agreement may require; and

(f) conform to the promises or affirmations of fact made on the container or label if any.

(3) Unless excluded or modified (Section 2–316) other implied warranties may arise from course of dealing or usage of trade.

§ 2–315. Implied Warranty: Fitness for Particular Purpose.

Where the seller at the time of contracting has reason to know any particular purpose for which the goods are required and that the buyer is relying on the seller's skill or judgment to select or furnish suitable goods, there is unless excluded or modified under the next section an implied warranty that the goods shall be fit for such purpose.

§ 2–316. Exclusion or Modification of Warranties.

(1) Words or conduct relevant to the creation of an express warranty and words or conduct tending to negate or limit warranty shall be construed wherever reasonable as consistent with each other; but subject to the provisions of this Article on parol or extrinsic evidence (Section 2–202) negation or limitation is inoperative to the extent that such construction is unreasonable.

(2) Subject to subsection (3), to exclude or modify the implied warranty of merchantability or any part of it the language must mention merchantability and in case of a writing must be conspicuous, and to exclude or modify any implied warranty of fitness the exclusion must be by a writing and conspicuous. Language to exclude all implied warranties of fitness is sufficient if it states, for example, that "There are no warranties which extend beyond the description on the face hereof."

(3) Notwithstanding subsection (2)

(a) unless the circumstances indicate otherwise, all implied warranties are excluded by expressions like "as is", "with all faults" or other language which in common understanding calls the buyer's attention to the exclusion of warranties and makes plain that there is no implied warranty; and

(b) when the buyer before entering into the contract has examined the goods or the sample or model as fully as he desired or has refused to examine the goods there is no implied warranty with regard to defects which an examination ought in the circumstances to have revealed to him; and

(c) an implied warranty can also be excluded or modified by course of dealing or course of performance or usage of trade.

(4) Remedies for breach of warranty can be limited in accordance with the provisions of this Article on liquidation or limitation of damages and on contractual modification of remedy (Sections 2–718 and 2–719).

§ 2–317. Cumulation and Conflict of Warranties Express or Implied.

Warranties whether express or implied shall be construed as consistent with each other and as cumulative, but if such construction is unreasonable the intention of the parties shall determine which warranty is dominant. In ascertaining that intention the following rules apply:

(a) Exact or technical specifications displace an inconsistent sample or model or general language of description.

(b) A sample from an existing bulk displaces inconsistent general language of description.

(c) Express warranties displace inconsistent implied warranties other than an implied warranty of fitness for a particular purpose.

§ 2–318. Third Party Beneficiaries of Warranties Express or Implied.

Note: If this Act is introduced in the Congress of the United States this section should be omitted. (States to select one alternative.)

Alternative A

A seller's warranty whether express or implied extends to any natural person who is in the family or household of his buyer or who is a guest in his home if it is reasonable to expect that such person may use, consume or be affected by the goods and who is injured in person by breach of the warranty. A seller may not exclude or limit the operation of this section.

Alternative B

A seller's warranty whether express or implied extends to any natural person who may reasonably be expected to use, consume or be affected by the goods and who is injured in person by breach of the warranty. A seller may not exclude or limit the operation of this section.

Alternative C

A seller's warranty whether express or implied extends to any person who may reasonably be expected to use, consume or be affected by the goods and who is injured by breach of the warranty. A seller may not exclude or limit the operation of this section with respect to injury to the person of an individual to whom the warranty extends.

As amended 1966.

§ 2–319. F.O.B. and F.A.S. Terms.

(1) Unless otherwise agreed the term F.O.B. (which means "free on board") at a named place, even though used only in connection with the stated price, is a delivery term under which

(a) when the term is F.O.B. the place of shipment, the seller must at that place ship the goods in the manner provided in this Article (Section 2–504) and bear the expense and risk of putting them into the possession of the carrier; or

(b) when the term is F.O.B. the place of destination, the seller must at his own expense and risk transport the goods to that place and there tender delivery of them in the manner provided in this Article (Section 2–503);

(c) when under either (a) or (b) the term is also F.O.B. vessel, car or other vehicle, the seller must in addition at his own expense and risk load the goods on board. If the term is F.O.B. vessel the buyer must name the vessel and in an appropriate case the seller must comply with the provisions of this Article on the form of bill of lading (Section 2–323).

(2) Unless otherwise agreed the term F.A.S. vessel (which means "free alongside") at a named port, even though used only in connection with the stated price, is a delivery term under which the seller must

(a) at his own expense and risk deliver the goods alongside the vessel in the manner usual in that port or on a dock designated and provided by the buyer; and

(b) obtain and tender a receipt for the goods in exchange for which the carrier is under a duty to issue a bill of lading.

(3) Unless otherwise agreed in any case falling within subsection (1)(a) or (c) or subsection (2) the buyer must seasonably give any needed instructions for making delivery, including when the term is F.A.S. or F.O.B. the loading berth of the vessel and in an appropriate case its name and sailing date. The seller may treat the failure of needed instructions as a failure of cooperation under this Article (Section 2–311). He may also at his option move the goods in any reasonable manner preparatory to delivery or shipment.

(4) Under the term F.O.B. vessel or F.A.S. unless otherwise agreed the buyer must make payment against tender of the required documents and the seller may not tender nor the buyer demand delivery of the goods in substitution for the documents.

§ 2–320. C.I.F. and C. & F. Terms.

(1) The term C.I.F. means that the price includes in a lump sum the cost of the goods and the insurance and freight to the named destination. The term C. & F. or C.F. means that the price so includes cost and freight to the named destination.

(2) Unless otherwise agreed and even though used only in connection with the stated price and destination, the term C.I.F. destination or its equivalent requires the seller at his own expense and risk to

(a) put the goods into the possession of a carrier at the port for shipment and obtain a negotiable bill or bills of lading covering the entire transportation to the named destination; and

(b) load the goods and obtain a receipt from the carrier (which may be contained in the bill of lading) showing that the freight has been paid or provided for; and

(c) obtain a policy or certificate of insurance, including any war risk insurance, of a kind and on terms then current at the port of shipment in the usual amount, in the currency of the contract, shown to cover the same goods covered by the bill of lading and providing for payment of loss to the order of the buyer or for the account of whom it may concern; but the seller may add to the price the amount of the premium for any such war risk insurance; and

(d) prepare an invoice of the goods and procure any other documents required to effect shipment or to comply with the contract; and

(e) forward and tender with commercial promptness all the documents in due form and with any indorsement necessary to perfect the buyer's rights.

(3) Unless otherwise agreed the term C. & F. or its equivalent has the same effect and imposes upon the seller the same obligations and risks as a C.I.F. term except the obligation as to insurance.

(4) Under the term C.I.F. or C. & F. unless otherwise agreed the buyer must make payment against tender of the required documents and the seller may not tender nor the buyer demand delivery of the goods in substitution for the documents.

§ 2–321. C.I.F. or C. & F.: "Net Landed Weights"; "Payment on Arrival"; Warranty of Condition on Arrival.

Under a contract containing a term C.I.F. or C. & F.

(1) Where the price is based on or is to be adjusted according to "net landed weights", "delivered weights", "out turn" quantity or quality or the like, unless otherwise agreed the seller must reasonably estimate the price. The payment due on tender of the documents called for by the contract is the amount so estimated, but after final adjustment of the price a settlement must be made with commercial promptness.

(2) An agreement described in subsection (1) or any warranty of quality or condition of the goods on arrival places upon the seller the risk of ordinary deterioration, shrinkage and the like in transportation but has no effect on the place or time of identification to the contract for sale or delivery or on the passing of the risk of loss.

(3) Unless otherwise agreed where the contract provides for payment on or after arrival of the goods the seller must before payment allow such preliminary inspection as is feasible; but if the goods are lost delivery of the documents and payment are due when the goods should have arrived.

§ 2–322. Delivery "Ex-Ship".

(1) Unless otherwise agreed a term for delivery of goods "ex-ship" (which means from the carrying vessel) or in equivalent language is not restricted to a particular ship and requires delivery from a ship which has reached a place at the named port of destination where goods of the kind are usually discharged.

(2) Under such a term unless otherwise agreed

(a) the seller must discharge all liens arising out of the carriage and furnish the buyer with a direction which puts the carrier under a duty to deliver the goods; and

(b) the risk of loss does not pass to the buyer until the goods leave the ship's tackle or are otherwise properly unloaded.

§ 2–323. Form of Bill of Lading Required in Overseas Shipment; "Overseas".

(1) Where the contract contemplates overseas shipment and contains a term C.I.F. or C. & F. or F.O.B. vessel, the seller unless otherwise agreed must obtain a negotiable bill of lading stating that the goods have been loaded on board or, in the case of a term C.I.F. or C. & F., received for shipment.

(2) Where in a case within subsection (1) a bill of lading has been issued in a set of parts, unless otherwise agreed if the documents are not to be sent from abroad the buyer may demand tender of the full set; otherwise only one part of the bill of lading need be tendered. Even if the agreement expressly requires a full set

(a) due tender of a single part is acceptable within the provisions of this Article on cure of improper delivery (subsection (1) of Section 2–508); and

(b) even though the full set is demanded, if the documents are sent from abroad the person tendering an incomplete set may nevertheless require payment upon furnishing an indemnity which the buyer in good faith deems adequate.

(3) A shipment by water or by air or a contract contemplating such shipment is "overseas" insofar as by usage of trade or agreement it is subject to the commercial, financing or shipping practices characteristic of international deep water commerce.

§ 2–324. "No Arrival, No Sale" Term.

Under a term "no arrival, no sale" or terms of like meaning, unless otherwise agreed,

(a) the seller must properly ship conforming goods and if they arrive by any means he must tender them on arrival but he assumes no obligation that the goods will arrive unless he has caused the non-arrival; and

(b) where without fault of the seller the goods are in part lost or have so deteriorated as no longer to conform to the contract or arrive after the contract time, the buyer may proceed as if there had been casualty to identified goods (Section 2–613).

§ 2–325. "Letter of Credit" Term; "Confirmed Credit".

(1) Failure of the buyer seasonably to furnish an agreed letter of credit is a breach of the contract for sale.

(2) The delivery to seller of a proper letter of credit suspends the buyer's obligation to pay. If the letter of credit is dishonored, the seller may on seasonable notification to the buyer require payment directly from him.

(3) Unless otherwise agreed the term "letter of credit" or "banker's credit" in a contract for sale means an irrevocable credit issued by a financing agency of good repute and, where the shipment is overseas, of good international repute. The term "confirmed credit" means that the credit must also carry the direct obligation of such an agency which does business in the seller's financial market.

§ 2–326. Sale on Approval and Sale or Return; Rights of Creditors.

(1) Unless otherwise agreed, if delivered goods may be returned by the buyer even though they conform to the contract, the transaction is

(a) a "sale on approval" if the goods are delivered primarily for use, and

(b) a "sale or return" if the goods are delivered primarily for resale.

(2) Goods held on approval are not subject to the claims of the buyer's creditors until acceptance; goods held on sale or return are subject to such claims while in the buyer's possession.

(3) Any "or return" term of a contract for sale is to be treated as a separate contract for sale within the statute of frauds section of this Article (Section 2–201) and as contradicting the sale aspect of the contract within the provisions of this Article or on parol or extrinsic evidence (Section 2–202).

As amended in 1999.

§ 2–327. Special Incidents of Sale on Approval and Sale or Return.

(1) Under a sale on approval unless otherwise agreed

(a) although the goods are identified to the contract the risk of loss and the title do not pass to the buyer until acceptance; and

(b) use of the goods consistent with the purpose of trial is not acceptance but failure seasonably to notify the seller of election to return the goods is acceptance, and if the goods conform to the contract acceptance of any part is acceptance of the whole; and

(c) after due notification of election to return, the return is at the seller's risk and expense but a merchant buyer must follow any reasonable instructions.

(2) Under a sale or return unless otherwise agreed

(a) the option to return extends to the whole or any commercial unit of the goods while in substantially their original condition, but must be exercised seasonably; and

(b) the return is at the buyer's risk and expense.

§ 2–328. Sale by Auction.

(1) In a sale by auction if goods are put up in lots each lot is the subject of a separate sale.

(2) A sale by auction is complete when the auctioneer so announces by the fall of the hammer or in other customary manner. Where a bid is made while the hammer is falling in acceptance of a prior bid the auctioneer may in his discretion reopen the bidding or declare the goods sold under the bid on which the hammer was falling.

(3) Such a sale is with reserve unless the goods are in explicit terms put up without reserve. In an auction with reserve the auctioneer may withdraw the goods at any time until he

announces completion of the sale. In an auction without reserve, after the auctioneer calls for bids on an article or lot, that article or lot cannot be withdrawn unless no bid is made within a reasonable time. In either case a bidder may retract his bid until the auctioneer's announcement of completion of the sale, but a bidder's retraction does not revive any previous bid.

(4) If the auctioneer knowingly receives a bid on the seller's behalf or the seller makes or procures such as bid, and notice has not been given that liberty for such bidding is reserved, the buyer may at his option avoid the sale or take the goods at the price of the last good faith bid prior to the completion of the sale. This subsection shall not apply to any bid at a forced sale.

Part 4 Title, Creditors and Good Faith Purchasers

§ 2–401. Passing of Title; Reservation for Security; Limited Application of This Section.

Each provision of this Article with regard to the rights, obligations and remedies of the seller, the buyer, purchasers or other third parties applies irrespective of title to the goods except where the provision refers to such title. Insofar as situations are not covered by the other provisions of this Article and matters concerning title became material the following rules apply:

(1) Title to goods cannot pass under a contract for sale prior to their identification to the contract (Section 2–501), and unless otherwise explicitly agreed the buyer acquires by their identification a special property as limited by this Act. Any retention or reservation by the seller of the title (property) in goods shipped or delivered to the buyer is limited in effect to a reservation of a security interest. Subject to these provisions and to the provisions of the Article on Secured Transactions (Article 9), title to goods passes from the seller to the buyer in any manner and on any conditions explicitly agreed on by the parties.

(2) Unless otherwise explicitly agreed title passes to the buyer at the time and place at which the seller completes his performance with reference to the physical delivery of the goods, despite any reservation of a security interest and even though a document of title is to be delivered at a different time or place; and in particular and despite any reservation of a security interest by the bill of lading

(a) if the contract requires or authorizes the seller to send the goods to the buyer but does not require him to deliver them at destination, title passes to the buyer at the time and place of shipment; but

(b) if the contract requires delivery at destination, title passes on tender there.

(3) Unless otherwise explicitly agreed where delivery is to be made without moving the goods,

(a) if the seller is to deliver a document of title, title passes at the time when and the place where he delivers such documents; or

(b) if the goods are at the time of contracting already identified and no documents are to be delivered, title passes at the time and place of contracting.

(4) A rejection or other refusal by the buyer to receive or retain the goods, whether or not justified, or a justified revocation of acceptance revests title to the goods in the seller. Such revesting occurs by operation of law and is not a "sale".

§ 2–402. Rights of Seller's Creditors Against Sold Goods.

(1) Except as provided in subsections (2) and (3), rights of unsecured creditors of the seller with respect to goods which have been identified to a contract for sale are subject to the buyer's rights to recover the goods under this Article (Sections 2–502 and 2–716).

(2) A creditor of the seller may treat a sale or an identification of goods to a contract for sale as void if as against him a retention of possession by the seller is fraudulent under any rule of law of the state where the goods are situated, except that retention of possession in good faith and current course of trade by a merchant-seller for a commercially reasonable time after a sale or identification is not fraudulent.

(3) Nothing in this Article shall be deemed to impair the rights of creditors of the seller

(a) under the provisions of the Article on Secured Transactions (Article 9); or

(b) where identification to the contract or delivery is made not in current course of trade but in satisfaction of or as security for a pre-existing claim for money, security or the like and is made under circumstances which under any rule of law of the state where the goods are situated would apart from this Article constitute the transaction a fraudulent transfer or voidable preference.

§ 2–403. Power to Transfer; Good Faith Purchase of Goods; "Entrusting".

(1) A purchaser of goods acquires all title which his transferor had or had power to transfer except that a purchaser of a limited interest acquires rights only to the extent of the interest purchased. A person with voidable title has power to transfer a good title to a good faith purchaser for value. When goods have been delivered under a transaction of purchase the purchaser has such power even though

(a) the transferor was deceived as to the identity of the purchaser, or

(b) the delivery was in exchange for a check which is later dishonored, or

(c) it was agreed that the transaction was to be a "cash sale", or

(d) the delivery was procured through fraud punishable as larcenous under the criminal law.

(2) Any entrusting of possession of goods to a merchant who deals in goods of that kind gives him power to transfer all rights of the entruster to a buyer in ordinary course of business.

(3) "Entrusting" includes any delivery and any acquiescence in retention of possession regardless of any condition expressed

between the parties to the delivery or acquiescence and regardless of whether the procurement of the entrusting or the possessor's disposition of the goods have been such as to be larcenous under the criminal law.

(4) The rights of other purchasers of goods and of lien creditors are governed by the Articles on Secured Transactions (Article 9), Bulk Transfers (Article 6) and Documents of Title (Article 7).

As amended in 1988.

Part 5 Performance

§ 2–501. Insurable Interest in Goods; Manner of Identification of Goods.

(1) The buyer obtains a special property and an insurable interest in goods by identification of existing goods as goods to which the contract refers even though the goods so identified are nonconforming and he has an option to return or reject them. Such identification can be made at any time and in any manner explicitly agreed to by the parties. In the absence of explicit agreement identification occurs

(a) when the contract is made if it is for the sale of goods already existing and identified;

(b) if the contract is for the sale of future goods other than those described in paragraph (c), when goods are shipped, marked or otherwise designated by the seller as goods to which the contract refers;

(c) when the crops are planted or otherwise become growing crops or the young are conceived if the contract is for the sale of unborn young to be born within twelve months after contracting or for the sale of crops to be harvested within twelve months or the next normal harvest season after contracting whichever is longer.

(2) The seller retains an insurable interest in goods so long as title to or any security interest in the goods remains in him and where the identification is by the seller alone he may until default or insolvency or notification to the buyer that the identification is final substitute other goods for those identified.

(3) Nothing in this section impairs any insurable interest recognized under any other statute or rule of law.

§ 2–502. Buyer's Right to Goods on Seller's Insolvency.

(1) Subject to subsections (2) and (3) and even though the goods have not been shipped a buyer who has paid a part or all of the price of goods in which he has a special property under the provisions of the immediately preceding section may on making and keeping good a tender of any unpaid portion of their price recover them from the seller if:

(a) in the case of goods bought for personal, family, or household purposes, the seller repudiates or fails to deliver as required by the contract; or

(b) in all cases, the seller becomes insolvent within ten days after receipt of the first installment on their price.

(2) The buyer's right to recover the goods under subsection (1)(a) vests upon acquisition of a special property, even if the seller had not then repudiated or failed to deliver.

(3) If the identification creating his special property has been made by the buyer he acquires the right to recover the goods only if they conform to the contract for sale.

As amended in 1999.

§ 2–503. Manner of Seller's Tender of Delivery.

(1) Tender of delivery requires that the seller put and hold conforming goods at the buyer's disposition and give the buyer any notification reasonably necessary to enable him to take delivery. The manner, time and place for tender are determined by the agreement and this Article, and in particular

(a) tender must be at a reasonable hour, and if it is of goods they must be kept available for the period reasonably necessary to enable the buyer to take possession; but

(b) unless otherwise agreed the buyer must furnish facilities reasonably suited to the receipt of the goods.

(2) Where the case is within the next section respecting shipment tender requires that the seller comply with its provisions.

(3) Where the seller is required to deliver at a particular destination tender requires that he comply with subsection (1) and also in any appropriate case tender documents as described in subsections (4) and (5) of this section.

(4) Where goods are in the possession of a bailee and are to be delivered without being moved

(a) tender requires that the seller either tender a negotiable document of title covering such goods or procure acknowledgment by the bailee of the buyer's right to possession of the goods; but

(b) tender to the buyer of a non-negotiable document of title or of a written direction to the bailee to deliver is sufficient tender unless the buyer seasonably objects, and receipt by the bailee of notification of the buyer's rights fixes those rights as against the bailee and all third persons; but risk of loss of the goods and of any failure by the bailee to honor the non-negotiable document of title or to obey the direction remains on the seller until the buyer has had a reasonable time to present the document or direction, and a refusal by the bailee to honor the document or to obey the direction defeats the tender.

(5) Where the contract requires the seller to deliver documents

(a) he must tender all such documents in correct form, except as provided in this Article with respect to bills of lading in a set (subsection (2) of Section 2–323); and

(b) tender through customary banking channels is sufficient and dishonor of a draft accompanying the documents constitutes non-acceptance or rejection.

§ 2–504. Shipment by Seller.

Where the seller is required or authorized to send the goods to the buyer and the contract does not require him to deliver them at a particular destination, then unless otherwise agreed he must

(a) put the goods in the possession of such a carrier and make such a contract for their transportation as may be reasonable having regard to the nature of the goods and other circumstances of the case; and

(b) obtain and promptly deliver or tender in due form any document necessary to enable the buyer to obtain possession of the goods or otherwise required by the agreement or by usage of trade; and

(c) promptly notify the buyer of the shipment.

Failure to notify the buyer under paragraph (c) or to make a proper contract under paragraph (a) is a ground for rejection only if material delay or loss ensues.

§ 2–505. Seller's Shipment under Reservation.

(1) Where the seller has identified goods to the contract by or before shipment:

(a) his procurement of a negotiable bill of lading to his own order or otherwise reserves in him a security interest in the goods. His procurement of the bill to the order of a financing agency or of the buyer indicates in addition only the seller's expectation of transferring that interest to the person named.

(b) a non-negotiable bill of lading to himself or his nominee reserves possession of the goods as security but except in a case of conditional delivery (subsection (2) of Section 2–507) a non-negotiable bill of lading naming the buyer as consignee reserves no security interest even though the seller retains possession of the bill of lading.

(2) When shipment by the seller with reservation of a security interest is in violation of the contract for sale it constitutes an improper contract for transportation within the preceding section but impairs neither the rights given to the buyer by shipment and identification of the goods to the contract nor the seller's powers as a holder of a negotiable document.

§ 2–506. Rights of Financing Agency.

(1) A financing agency by paying or purchasing for value a draft which relates to a shipment of goods acquires to the extent of the payment or purchase and in addition to its own rights under the draft and any document of title securing it any rights of the shipper in the goods including the right to stop delivery and the shipper's right to have the draft honored by the buyer.

(2) The right to reimbursement of a financing agency which has in good faith honored or purchased the draft under commitment to or authority from the buyer is not impaired by subsequent discovery of defects with reference to any relevant document which was apparently regular on its face.

§ 2–507. Effect of Seller's Tender; Delivery on Condition.

(1) Tender of delivery is a condition to the buyer's duty to accept the goods and, unless otherwise agreed, to his duty to pay for them. Tender entitles the seller to acceptance of the goods and to payment according to the contract.

(2) Where payment is due and demanded on the delivery to the buyer of goods or documents of title, his right as against the seller to retain or dispose of them is conditional upon his making the payment due.

§ 2–508. Cure by Seller of Improper Tender or Delivery; Replacement.

(1) Where any tender or delivery by the seller is rejected because non-conforming and the time for performance has not yet expired, the seller may seasonably notify the buyer of his intention to cure and may then within the contract time make a conforming delivery.

(2) Where the buyer rejects a non-conforming tender which the seller had reasonable grounds to believe would be acceptable with or without money allowance the seller may if he seasonably notifies the buyer have a further reasonable time to substitute a conforming tender.

§ 2–509. Risk of Loss in the Absence of Breach.

(1) Where the contract requires or authorizes the seller to ship the goods by carrier

(a) if it does not require him to deliver them at a particular destination, the risk of loss passes to the buyer when the goods are duly delivered to the carrier even though the shipment is under reservation (Section 2–505); but

(b) if it does require him to deliver them at a particular destination and the goods are there duly tendered while in the possession of the carrier, the risk of loss passes to the buyer when the goods are there duly so tendered as to enable the buyer to take delivery.

(2) Where the goods are held by a bailee to be delivered without being moved, the risk of loss passes to the buyer

(a) on his receipt of a negotiable document of title covering the goods; or

(b) on acknowledgment by the bailee of the buyer's right to possession of the goods; or

(c) after his receipt of a non-negotiable document of title or other written direction to deliver, as provided in subsection (4)(b) of Section 2–503.

(3) In any case not within subsection (1) or (2), the risk of loss passes to the buyer on his receipt of the goods if the seller is a merchant; otherwise the risk passes to the buyer on tender of delivery.

(4) The provisions of this section are subject to contrary agreement of the parties and to the provisions of this Article on sale on approval (Section 2–327) and on effect of breach on risk of loss (Section 2–510).

§ 2–510. Effect of Breach on Risk of Loss.

(1) Where a tender or delivery of goods so fails to conform to the contract as to give a right of rejection the risk of their loss remains on the seller until cure or acceptance.

(2) Where the buyer rightfully revokes acceptance he may to the extent of any deficiency in his effective insurance coverage treat the risk of loss as having rested on the seller from the beginning.

(3) Where the buyer as to conforming goods already identified to the contract for sale repudiates or is otherwise in breach before risk of their loss has passed to him, the seller may to the extent of any deficiency in his effective insurance coverage treat the risk of loss as resting on the buyer for a commercially reasonable time.

§ 2–511. Tender of Payment by Buyer; Payment by Check.

(1) Unless otherwise agreed tender of payment is a condition to the seller's duty to tender and complete any delivery.

(2) Tender of payment is sufficient when made by any means or in any manner current in the ordinary course of business unless the seller demands payment in legal tender and gives any extension of time reasonably necessary to procure it.

(3) Subject to the provisions of this Act on the effect of an instrument on an obligation (Section 3–310), payment by check is conditional and is defeated as between the parties by dishonor of the check on due presentment.

As amended in 1994.

§ 2–512. Payment by Buyer Before Inspection.

(1) Where the contract requires payment before inspection non-conformity of the goods does not excuse the buyer from so making payment unless

(a) the non-conformity appears without inspection; or

(b) despite tender of the required documents the circumstances would justify injunction against honor under this Act (Section 5–109(b)).

(2) Payment pursuant to subsection (1) does not constitute an acceptance of goods or impair the buyer's right to inspect or any of his remedies.

As amended in 1995.

§ 2–513. Buyer's Right to Inspection of Goods.

(1) Unless otherwise agreed and subject to subsection (3), where goods are tendered or delivered or identified to the contract for sale, the buyer has a right before payment or acceptance to inspect them at any reasonable place and time and in any reasonable manner. When the seller is required or authorized to send the goods to the buyer, the inspection may be after their arrival.

(2) Expenses of inspection must be borne by the buyer but may be recovered from the seller if the goods do not conform and are rejected.

(3) Unless otherwise agreed and subject to the provisions of this Article on C.I.F. contracts (subsection (3) of Section 2–321), the buyer is not entitled to inspect the goods before payment of the price when the contract provides

(a) for delivery "C.O.D." or on other like terms; or

(b) for payment against documents of title, except where such payment is due only after the goods are to become available for inspection.

(4) A place or method of inspection fixed by the parties is presumed to be exclusive but unless otherwise expressly agreed it does not postpone identification or shift the place for delivery or for passing the risk of loss. If compliance becomes impossible, inspection shall be as provided in this section unless the place or method fixed was clearly intended as an indispensable condition failure of which avoids the contract.

§ 2–514. When Documents Deliverable on Acceptance; When on Payment.

Unless otherwise agreed documents against which a draft is drawn are to be delivered to the drawee on acceptance of the draft if it is payable more than three days after presentment; otherwise, only on payment.

§ 2–515. Preserving Evidence of Goods in Dispute.

In furtherance of the adjustment of any claim or dispute

(a) either party on reasonable notification to the other and for the purpose of ascertaining the facts and preserving evidence has the right to inspect, test and sample the goods including such of them as may be in the possession or control of the other; and

(b) the parties may agree to a third party inspection or survey to determine the conformity or condition of the goods and may agree that the findings shall be binding upon them in any subsequent litigation or adjustment.

Part 6 Breach, Repudiation and Excuse

§ 2–601. Buyer's Rights on Improper Delivery.

Subject to the provisions of this Article on breach in installment contracts (Section 2–612) and unless otherwise agreed under the sections on contractual limitations of remedy (Sections 2–718 and 2–719), if the goods or the tender of delivery fail in any respect to conform to the contract, the buyer may

(a) reject the whole; or

(b) accept the whole; or

(c) accept any commercial unit or units and reject the rest.

§ 2–602. Manner and Effect of Rightful Rejection.

(1) Rejection of goods must be within a reasonable time after their delivery or tender. It is ineffective unless the buyer seasonably notifies the seller.

(2) Subject to the provisions of the two following sections on rejected goods (Sections 2–603 and 2–604),

(a) after rejection any exercise of ownership by the buyer with respect to any commercial unit is wrongful as against the seller; and

(b) if the buyer has before rejection taken physical possession of goods in which he does not have a security interest under the provisions of this Article (subsection (3) of Section 2–711), he is under a duty after rejection to hold them with reasonable care at the seller's disposition for a time sufficient to permit the seller to remove them; but

(c) the buyer has no further obligations with regard to goods rightfully rejected.

(3) The seller's rights with respect to goods wrongfully rejected are governed by the provisions of this Article on Seller's remedies in general (Section 2–703).

§ 2–603. Merchant Buyer's Duties as to Rightfully Rejected Goods.

(1) Subject to any security interest in the buyer (subsection (3) of Section 2–711), when the seller has no agent or place of business at the market of rejection a merchant buyer is under a duty after rejection of goods in his possession or control to follow any reasonable instructions received from the seller with respect to the goods and in the absence of such instructions to make reasonable efforts to sell them for the seller's account if they are perishable or threaten to decline in value speedily. Instructions are not reasonable if on demand indemnity for expenses is not forthcoming.

(2) When the buyer sells goods under subsection (1), he is entitled to reimbursement from the seller or out of the proceeds for reasonable expenses of caring for and selling them, and if the expenses include no selling commission then to such commission as is usual in the trade or if there is none to a reasonable sum not exceeding ten per cent on the gross proceeds.

(3) In complying with this section the buyer is held only to good faith and good faith conduct hereunder is neither acceptance nor conversion nor the basis of an action for damages.

§ 2–604. Buyer's Options as to Salvage of Rightfully Rejected Goods.

Subject to the provisions of the immediately preceding section on perishables if the seller gives no instructions within a reasonable time after notification of rejection the buyer may store the rejected goods for the seller's account or reship them to him or resell them for the seller's account with reimbursement as provided in the preceding section. Such action is not acceptance or conversion.

§ 2–605. Waiver of Buyer's Objections by Failure to Particularize.

(1) The buyer's failure to state in connection with rejection a particular defect which is ascertainable by reasonable inspection precludes him from relying on the unstated defect to justify rejection or to establish breach

(a) where the seller could have cured it if stated seasonably; or

(b) between merchants when the seller has after rejection made a request in writing for a full and final written statement of all defects on which the buyer proposes to rely.

(2) Payment against documents made without reservation of rights precludes recovery of the payment for defects apparent on the face of the documents.

§ 2–606. What Constitutes Acceptance of Goods.

(1) Acceptance of goods occurs when the buyer

(a) after a reasonable opportunity to inspect the goods signifies to the seller that the goods are conforming or that he will take or retain them in spite of their nonconformity; or

(b) fails to make an effective rejection (subsection (1) of Section 2–602), but such acceptance does not occur until the buyer has had a reasonable opportunity to inspect them; or

(c) does any act inconsistent with the seller's ownership; but if such act is wrongful as against the seller it is an acceptance only if ratified by him.

(2) Acceptance of a part of any commercial unit is acceptance of that entire unit.

§ 2–607. Effect of Acceptance; Notice of Breach; Burden of Establishing Breach After Acceptance; Notice of Claim or Litigation to Person Answerable Over.

(1) The buyer must pay at the contract rate for any goods accepted.

(2) Acceptance of goods by the buyer precludes rejection of the goods accepted and if made with knowledge of a non-conformity cannot be revoked because of it unless the acceptance was on the reasonable assumption that the non-conformity would be seasonably cured but acceptance does not of itself impair any other remedy provided by this Article for non-conformity.

(3) Where a tender has been accepted

(a) the buyer must within a reasonable time after he discovers or should have discovered any breach notify the seller of breach or be barred from any remedy; and

(b) if the claim is one for infringement or the like (subsection (3) of Section 2–312) and the buyer is sued as a result of such a breach he must so notify the seller within a reasonable time after he receives notice of the litigation or be barred from any remedy over for liability established by the litigation.

(4) The burden is on the buyer to establish any breach with respect to the goods accepted.

(5) Where the buyer is sued for breach of a warranty or other obligation for which his seller is answerable over

(a) he may give his seller written notice of the litigation. If the notice states that the seller may come in and defend and that if the seller does not do so he will be bound in any action against him by his buyer by any determination of fact common to the two litigations, then unless the seller after seasonable receipt of the notice does come in and defend he is so bound.

(b) if the claim is one for infringement or the like (subsection (3) of Section 2–312) the original seller may demand in writing that his buyer turn over to him control of the litigation including settlement or else be barred from any remedy over and if he also agrees to bear all expense and to satisfy any adverse judgment, then unless the buyer after seasonable receipt of the demand does turn over control the buyer is so barred.

(6) The provisions of subsections (3), (4) and (5) apply to any obligation of a buyer to hold the seller harmless against infringement or the like (subsection (3) of Section 2–312).

§ 2–608. Revocation of Acceptance in Whole or in Part.

(1) The buyer may revoke his acceptance of a lot or commercial unit whose non-conformity substantially impairs its value to him if he has accepted it

(a) on the reasonable assumption that its nonconformity would be cured and it has not been seasonably cured; or

(b) without discovery of such non-conformity if his acceptance was reasonably induced either by the difficulty of discovery before acceptance or by the seller's assurances.

(2) Revocation of acceptance must occur within a reasonable time after the buyer discovers or should have discovered the ground for it and before any substantial change in condition of the goods which is not caused by their own defects. It is not effective until the buyer notifies the seller of it.

(3) A buyer who so revokes has the same rights and duties with regard to the goods involved as if he had rejected them.

§ 2–609. Right to Adequate Assurance of Performance.

(1) A contract for sale imposes an obligation on each party that the other's expectation of receiving due performance will not be impaired. When reasonable grounds for insecurity arise with respect to the performance of either party the other may in writing demand adequate assurance of due performance and until he receives such assurance may if commercially reasonable suspend any performance for which he has not already received the agreed return.

(2) Between merchants the reasonableness of grounds for insecurity and the adequacy of any assurance offered shall be determined according to commercial standards.

(3) Acceptance of any improper delivery or payment does not prejudice the party's right to demand adequate assurance of future performance.

(4) After receipt of a justified demand failure to provide within a reasonable time not exceeding thirty days such assurance of due performance as is adequate under the circumstances of the particular case is a repudiation of the contract.

§ 2–610. Anticipatory Repudiation.

When either party repudiates the contract with respect to a performance not yet due the loss of which will substantially impair the value of the contract to the other, the aggrieved party may

(a) for a commercially reasonable time await performance by the repudiating party; or

(b) resort to any remedy for breach (Section 2–703 or Section 2–711), even though he has notified the repudiating party that he would await the latter's performance and has urged retraction; and

(c) in either case suspend his own performance or proceed in accordance with the provisions of this Article on the seller's right to identify goods to the contract notwithstanding breach or to salvage unfinished goods (Section 2–704).

§ 2–611. Retraction of Anticipatory Repudiation.

(1) Until the repudiating party's next performance is due he can retract his repudiation unless the aggrieved party has since the repudiation cancelled or materially changed his position or otherwise indicated that he considers the repudiation final.

(2) Retraction may be by any method which clearly indicates to the aggrieved party that the repudiating party intends to perform, but must include any assurance justifiably demanded under the provisions of this Article (Section 2–609).

(3) Retraction reinstates the repudiating party's rights under the contract with due excuse and allowance to the aggrieved party for any delay occasioned by the repudiation.

§ 2–612. "Installment Contract"; Breach.

(1) An "installment contract" is one which requires or authorizes the delivery of goods in separate lots to be separately accepted, even though the contract contains a clause "each delivery is a separate contract" or its equivalent.

(2) The buyer may reject any installment which is non-conforming if the non-conformity substantially impairs the value of that installment and cannot be cured or if the non-conformity is a defect in the required documents; but if the non-conformity does not fall within subsection (3) and the seller gives adequate assurance of its cure the buyer must accept that installment.

(3) Whenever non-conformity or default with respect to one or more installments substantially impairs the value of the whole contract there is a breach of the whole. But the aggrieved party reinstates the contract if he accepts a non-conforming installment without seasonably notifying of cancellation or if he brings an action with respect only to past installments or demands performance as to future installments.

§ 2–613. Casualty to Identified Goods.

Where the contract requires for its performance goods identified when the contract is made, and the goods suffer casualty without fault of either party before the risk of loss passes to the buyer, or in a proper case under a "no arrival, no sale" term (Section 2–324) then

(a) if the loss is total the contract is avoided; and

(b) if the loss is partial or the goods have so deteriorated as no longer to conform to the contract the buyer may nevertheless demand inspection and at his option either treat the contract as voided or accept the goods with due allowance from the contract price for the deterioration or the deficiency in quantity but without further right against the seller.

§ 2–614. Substituted Performance.

(1) Where without fault of either party the agreed berthing, loading, or unloading facilities fail or an agreed type of carrier becomes unavailable or the agreed manner of delivery otherwise becomes commercially impracticable but a commercially reasonable substitute is available, such substitute performance must be tendered and accepted.

(2) If the agreed means or manner of payment fails because of domestic or foreign governmental regulation, the seller may withhold or stop delivery unless the buyer provides a means or manner of payment which is commercially a substantial equivalent. If delivery has already been taken, payment by the means or in the manner provided by the regulation discharges the buyer's obligation unless the regulation is discriminatory, oppressive or predatory.

§ 2–615. Excuse by Failure of Presupposed Conditions.

Except so far as a seller may have assumed a greater obligation and subject to the preceding section on substituted performance:

(a) Delay in delivery or non-delivery in whole or in part by a seller who complies with paragraphs (b) and (c) is not a breach of his duty under a contract for sale if performance as agreed has been made impracticable by the occurrence of a contingency the nonoccurrence of which was a basic assumption on which the contract was made or by compliance in good faith with any applicable foreign or domestic governmental regulation or order whether or not it later proves to be invalid.

(b) Where the causes mentioned in paragraph (a) affect only a part of the seller's capacity to perform, he must allocate production and deliveries among his customers but may at his option include regular customers not then under contract as well as his own requirements for further manufacture. He may so allocate in any manner which is fair and reasonable.

(c) The seller must notify the buyer seasonably that there will be delay or non-delivery and, when allocation is required under paragraph (b), of the estimated quota thus made available for the buyer.

§ 2–616. Procedure on Notice Claiming Excuse.

(1) Where the buyer receives notification of a material or indefinite delay or an allocation justified under the preceding section he may by written notification to the seller as to any delivery concerned, and where the prospective deficiency substantially impairs the value of the whole contract under the provisions of this Article relating to breach of installment contracts (Section 2–612), then also as to the whole,

(a) terminate and thereby discharge any unexecuted portion of the contract; or

(b) modify the contract by agreeing to take his available quota in substitution.

(2) If after receipt of such notification from the seller the buyer fails so to modify the contract within a reasonable time not exceeding thirty days the contract lapses with respect to any deliveries affected.

(3) The provisions of this section may not be negated by agreement except in so far as the seller has assumed a greater obligation under the preceding section.

Part 7 Remedies

§ 2–701. Remedies for Breach of Collateral Contracts Not Impaired.

Remedies for breach of any obligation or promise collateral or ancillary to a contract for sale are not impaired by the provisions of this Article.

§ 2–702. Seller's Remedies on Discovery of Buyer's Insolvency.

(1) Where the seller discovers the buyer to be insolvent he may refuse delivery except for cash including payment for all goods theretofore delivered under the contract, and stop delivery under this Article (Section 2–705).

(2) Where the seller discovers that the buyer has received goods on credit while insolvent he may reclaim the goods upon demand made within ten days after the receipt, but if misrepresentation of solvency has been made to the particular seller in writing within three months before delivery the ten day limitation does not apply. Except as provided in this subsection the seller may not base a right to reclaim goods on the buyer's fraudulent or innocent misrepresentation of solvency or of intent to pay.

(3) The seller's right to reclaim under subsection (2) is subject to the rights of a buyer in ordinary course or other good faith purchaser under this Article (Section 2–403). Successful reclamation of goods excludes all other remedies with respect to them.

§ 2–703. Seller's Remedies in General.

Where the buyer wrongfully rejects or revokes acceptance of goods or fails to make a payment due on or before delivery or repudiates with respect to a part or the whole, then with respect to any goods directly affected and, if the breach is of the whole contract (Section 2–612), then also with respect to the whole undelivered balance, the aggrieved seller may

(a) withhold delivery of such goods;

(b) stop delivery by any bailee as hereafter provided (Section 2–705);

(c) proceed under the next section respecting goods still unidentified to the contract;

(d) resell and recover damages as hereafter provided (Section 2–706);

(e) recover damages for non-acceptance (Section 2–708) or in a proper case the price (Section 2–709);

(f) cancel.

§ 2–704. Seller's Right to Identify Goods to the Contract Notwithstanding Breach or to Salvage Unfinished Goods.

(1) An aggrieved seller under the preceding section may

(a) identify to the contract conforming goods not already identified if at the time he learned of the breach they are in his possession or control;

(b) treat as the subject of resale goods which have demonstrably been intended for the particular contract even though those goods are unfinished.

(2) Where the goods are unfinished an aggrieved seller may in the exercise of reasonable commercial judgment for the purposes of avoiding loss and of effective realization either complete the manufacture and wholly identify the goods to the contract or cease manufacture and resell for scrap or salvage value or proceed in any other reasonable manner.

§ 2–705. Seller's Stoppage of Delivery in Transit or Otherwise.

(1) The seller may stop delivery of goods in the possession of a carrier or other bailee when he discovers the buyer to be insolvent (Section 2–702) and may stop delivery of carload, truckload, planeload or larger shipments of express or freight when the buyer repudiates or fails to make a payment due before delivery or if for any other reason the seller has a right to withhold or reclaim the goods.

(2) As against such buyer the seller may stop delivery until

(a) receipt of the goods by the buyer; or

(b) acknowledgment to the buyer by any bailee of the goods except a carrier that the bailee holds the goods for the buyer; or

(c) such acknowledgment to the buyer by a carrier by reshipment or as warehouseman; or

(d) negotiation to the buyer of any negotiable document of title covering the goods.

(3) (a) To stop delivery the seller must so notify as to enable the bailee by reasonable diligence to prevent delivery of the goods.

(b) After such notification the bailee must hold and deliver the goods according to the directions of the seller but the seller is liable to the bailee for any ensuing charges or damages.

(c) If a negotiable document of title has been issued for goods the bailee is not obliged to obey a notification to stop until surrender of the document.

(d) A carrier who has issued a non-negotiable bill of lading is not obliged to obey a notification to stop received from a person other than the consignor.

§ 2–706. Seller's Resale Including Contract for Resale.

(1) Under the conditions stated in Section 2–703 on seller's remedies, the seller may resell the goods concerned or the undelivered balance thereof. Where the resale is made in good faith and in a commercially reasonable manner the seller may recover the difference between the resale price and the contract price together with any incidental damages allowed under the provisions of this Article (Section 2–710), but less expenses saved in consequence of the buyer's breach.

(2) Except as otherwise provided in subsection (3) or unless otherwise agreed resale may be at public or private sale including sale by way of one or more contracts to sell or of identification to an existing contract of the seller. Sale may be as a unit or in parcels and at any time and place and on any terms but every aspect of the sale including the method, manner, time, place and terms must be commercially reasonable. The resale must be reasonably identified as referring to the broken contract, but it is not necessary that the goods be in existence or that any or all of them have been identified to the contract before the breach.

(3) Where the resale is at private sale the seller must give the buyer reasonable notification of his intention to resell.

(4) Where the resale is at public sale

(a) only identified goods can be sold except where there is a recognized market for a public sale of futures in goods of the kind; and

(b) it must be made at a usual place or market for public sale if one is reasonably available and except in the case of goods which are perishable or threaten to decline in value speedily the seller must give the buyer reasonable notice of the time and place of the resale; and

(c) if the goods are not to be within the view of those attending the sale the notification of sale must state the place where the goods are located and provide for their reasonable inspection by prospective bidders; and

(d) the seller may buy.

(5) A purchaser who buys in good faith at a resale takes the goods free of any rights of the original buyer even though the seller fails to comply with one or more of the requirements of this section.

(6) The seller is not accountable to the buyer for any profit made on any resale. A person in the position of a seller (Section 2–707) or a buyer who has rightfully rejected or justifiably revoked acceptance must account for any excess over the amount of his security interest, as hereinafter defined (subsection (3) of Section 2–711).

§ 2–707. "Person in the Position of a Seller".

(1) A "person in the position of a seller" includes as against a principal an agent who has paid or become responsible for the price of goods on behalf of his principal or anyone who otherwise holds a security interest or other right in goods similar to that of a seller.

(2) A person in the position of a seller may as provided in this Article withhold or stop delivery (Section 2–705) and resell (Section 2–706) and recover incidental damages (Section 2–710).

§ 2–708. Seller's Damages for Non-Acceptance or Repudiation.

(1) Subject to subsection (2) and to the provisions of this Article with respect to proof of market price (Section 2–723), the measure of damages for non-acceptance or repudiation by the buyer is the difference between the market price at the time and place for tender and the unpaid contract price together with any incidental damages provided in this Article (Section 2–710), but less expenses saved in consequence of the buyer's breach.

(2) If the measure of damages provided in subsection (1) is inadequate to put the seller in as good a position as performance would have done then the measure of damages is the profit (including reasonable overhead) which the seller would have made from full performance by the buyer, together with any incidental damages provided in this Article (Section 2–710), due allowance for costs reasonably incurred and due credit for payments or proceeds of resale.

§ 2–709. Action for the Price.

(1) When the buyer fails to pay the price as it becomes due the seller may recover, together with any incidental damages under the next section, the price

(a) of goods accepted or of conforming goods lost or damaged within a commercially reasonable time after risk of their loss has passed to the buyer; and

(b) of goods identified to the contract if the seller is unable after reasonable effort to resell them at a reasonable price or the circumstances reasonably indicate that such effort will be unavailing.

(2) Where the seller sues for the price he must hold for the buyer any goods which have been identified to the contract and are still in his control except that if resale becomes possible he may resell them at any time prior to the collection of the judgment. The net proceeds of any such resale must be credited to the buyer and payment of the judgment entitles him to any goods not resold.

(3) After the buyer has wrongfully rejected or revoked acceptance of the goods or has failed to make a payment due or has repudiated (Section 2–610), a seller who is held not entitled to the price under this section shall nevertheless be awarded damages for non-acceptance under the preceding section.

§ 2–710. Seller's Incidental Damages.

Incidental damages to an aggrieved seller include any commercially reasonable charges, expenses or commissions incurred in stopping delivery, in the transportation, care and custody of goods after the buyer's breach, in connection with return or resale of the goods or otherwise resulting from the breach.

§ 2–711. Buyer's Remedies in General; Buyer's Security Interest in Rejected Goods.

(1) Where the seller fails to make delivery or repudiates or the buyer rightfully rejects or justifiably revokes acceptance then with respect to any goods involved, and with respect to the whole if the breach goes to the whole contract (Section 2–612), the buyer may cancel and whether or not he has done so may in addition to recovering so much of the price as has been paid

(a) "cover" and have damages under the next section as to all the goods affected whether or not they have been identified to the contract; or

(b) recover damages for non-delivery as provided in this Article (Section 2–713).

(2) Where the seller fails to deliver or repudiates the buyer may also

(a) if the goods have been identified recover them as provided in this Article (Section 2–502); or

(b) in a proper case obtain specific performance or replevy the goods as provided in this Article (Section 2–716).

(3) On rightful rejection or justifiable revocation of acceptance a buyer has a security interest in goods in his possession or control for any payments made on their price and any expenses reasonably incurred in their inspection, receipt, transportation, care and custody and may hold such goods and resell them in like manner as an aggrieved seller (Section 2–706).

§ 2–712. "Cover"; Buyer's Procurement of Substitute Goods.

(1) After a breach within the preceding section the buyer may "cover" by making in good faith and without unreasonable delay any reasonable purchase of or contract to purchase goods in substitution for those due from the seller.

(2) The buyer may recover from the seller as damages the difference between the cost of cover and the contract price together with any incidental or consequential damages as hereinafter defined (Section 2–715), but less expenses saved in consequence of the seller's breach.

(3) Failure of the buyer to effect cover within this section does not bar him from any other remedy.

§ 2–713. Buyer's Damages for Non-Delivery or Repudiation.

(1) Subject to the provisions of this Article with respect to proof of market price (Section 2–723), the measure of damages for non-delivery or repudiation by the seller is the difference between the market price at the time when the buyer learned of the breach and the contract price together with any incidental and consequential damages provided in this Article (Section 2–715), but less expenses saved in consequence of the seller's breach.

(2) Market price is to be determined as of the place for tender or, in cases of rejection after arrival or revocation of acceptance, as of the place of arrival.

§ 2–714. Buyer's Damages for Breach in Regard to Accepted Goods.

(1) Where the buyer has accepted goods and given notification (subsection (3) of Section 2–607) he may recover as damages for any non-conformity of tender the loss resulting in the ordinary course of events from the seller's breach as determined in any manner which is reasonable.

(2) The measure of damages for breach of warranty is the difference at the time and place of acceptance between the value of the goods accepted and the value they would have had if they had been as warranted, unless special circumstances show proximate damages of a different amount.

(3) In a proper case any incidental and consequential damages under the next section may also be recovered.

§ 2–715. Buyer's Incidental and Consequential Damages.

(1) Incidental damages resulting from the seller's breach include expenses reasonably incurred in inspection, receipt, transportation and care and custody of goods rightfully rejected, any commercially reasonable charges, expenses or commissions in connection with effecting cover and any other reasonable expense incident to the delay or other breach.

(2) Consequential damages resulting from the seller's breach include

(a) any loss resulting from general or particular requirements and needs of which the seller at the time of contracting had reason to know and which could not reasonably be prevented by cover or otherwise; and

(b) injury to person or property proximately resulting from any breach of warranty.

§ 2–716. Buyer's Right to Specific Performance or Replevin.

(1) Specific performance may be decreed where the goods are unique or in other proper circumstances.

(2) The decree for specific performance may include such terms and conditions as to payment of the price, damages, or other relief as the court may deem just.

(3) The buyer has a right of replevin for goods identified to the contract if after reasonable effort he is unable to effect cover for such goods or the circumstances reasonably indicate that such effort will be unavailing or if the goods have been shipped under reservation and satisfaction of the security interest in them has been made or tendered. In the case of goods bought for personal, family, or household purposes, the buyer's right of replevin vests upon acquisition of a special property, even if the seller had not then repudiated or failed to deliver.

As amended in 1999.

§ 2–717. Deduction of Damages From the Price.

The buyer on notifying the seller of his intention to do so may deduct all or any part of the damages resulting from any breach of the contract from any part of the price still due under the same contract.

§ 2–718. Liquidation or Limitation of Damages; Deposits.

(1) Damages for breach by either party may be liquidated in the agreement but only at an amount which is reasonable in the light of the anticipated or actual harm caused by the breach, the difficulties of proof of loss, and the inconvenience or nonfeasibility of otherwise obtaining an adequate remedy. A term fixing unreasonably large liquidated damages is void as a penalty.

(2) Where the seller justifiably withholds delivery of goods because of the buyer's breach, the buyer is entitled to restitution of any amount by which the sum of his payments exceeds

(a) the amount to which the seller is entitled by virtue of terms liquidating the seller's damages in accordance with subsection (1), or

(b) in the absence of such terms, twenty per cent of the value of the total performance for which the buyer is obligated under the contract or $500, whichever is smaller.

(3) The buyer's right to restitution under subsection (2) is subject to offset to the extent that the seller establishes

(a) a right to recover damages under the provisions of this Article other than subsection (1), and

(b) the amount or value of any benefits received by the buyer directly or indirectly by reason of the contract.

(4) Where a seller has received payment in goods their reasonable value or the proceeds of their resale shall be treated as payments for the purposes of subsection (2); but if the seller has notice of the buyer's breach before reselling goods received in part performance, his resale is subject to the conditions laid down in this Article on resale by an aggrieved seller (Section 2–706).

§ 2–719. Contractual Modification or Limitation of Remedy.

(1) Subject to the provisions of subsections (2) and (3) of this section and of the preceding section on liquidation and limitation of damages,

(a) the agreement may provide for remedies in addition to or in substitution for those provided in this Article and may limit or alter the measure of damages recoverable under this Article, as by limiting the buyer's remedies to return of the goods and repayment of the price or to repair and replacement of nonconforming goods or parts; and

(b) resort to a remedy as provided is optional unless the remedy is expressly agreed to be exclusive, in which case it is the sole remedy.

(2) Where circumstances cause an exclusive or limited remedy to fail of its essential purpose, remedy may be had as provided in this Act.

(3) Consequential damages may be limited or excluded unless the limitation or exclusion is unconscionable. Limitation of consequential damages for injury to the person in the case of consumer goods is prima facie unconscionable but limitation of damages where the loss is commercial is not.

§ 2–720. Effect of "Cancellation" or "Rescission" on Claims for Antecedent Breach.

Unless the contrary intention clearly appears, expressions of "cancellation" or "rescission" of the contract or the like shall not be construed as a renunciation or discharge of any claim in damages for an antecedent breach.

2–313A or 2–313B extends to any person that may reasonably be expected to use, consume or be affected by the goods and that is injured by breach of the warranty, remedial promise or obligation. A seller may not exclude or limit the operation of this section with respect to injury to the person of an individual to whom the warranty, remedial promise or obligation extends.

* * * *

Part 5 Performance

* * * *

§ 2–502. Buyer's Right to Goods on Seller's Insolvency.

(1) Subject to subsections (2) and (3) and even though the goods have not been shipped a buyer that has paid a part or all of the price of goods in which the buyer has a special property under the provisions of the immediately preceding section may on making and keeping good a tender of any unpaid portion of their price recover them from the seller if:

(a) in the case of goods bought by a consumer, the seller repudiates or fails to deliver as required by the contract; or

(b) in all cases, the seller becomes insolvent within ten days after receipt of the first installment on their price.

(2) The buyer's right to recover the goods under subsection (1) vests upon acquisition of a special property, even if the seller had not then repudiated or failed to deliver.

(3) If the identification creating the special property has been made by the buyer, the buyer acquires the right to recover the goods only if they conform to the contract for sale.

* * * *

§ 2–508. Cure by Seller of Improper Tender or Delivery; Replacement.

(1) Where the buyer rejects goods or a tender of delivery under Section 2–601 or 2–612 or, except in a consumer contract, justifiably revokes acceptance under Section 2–608(1)(b) and the agreed time for performance has not expired, a seller that has performed in good faith, upon seasonable notice to the buyer and at the seller's own expense, may cure the breach of contract by making a conforming tender of delivery within the agreed time. The seller shall compensate the buyer for all of the buyer's reasonable expenses caused by the seller's breach of contract and subsequent cure.

(2) Where the buyer rejects goods or a tender of delivery under Section 2–601 or 2–612 or except in a consumer contract justifiably revokes acceptance under Section 2–608(1)(b) and the agreed time for performance has expired, a seller that has performed in good faith, upon seasonable notice to the buyer and at the seller's own expense, may cure the breach of contract, if the cure is appropriate and timely under the circumstances, by making a tender of conforming goods. The seller shall compensate the buyer for all of the buyer's reasonable expenses caused by the seller's breach of contract and subsequent cure.

§ 2–509. Risk of Loss in the Absence of Breach.

(1) Where the contract requires or authorizes the seller to ship the goods by carrier

(a) if it does not require the seller to deliver them at a particular destination, the risk of loss passes to the buyer when the goods are delivered to the carrier even though the shipment is under reservation (Section 2–505); but

(b) if it does require the seller to deliver them at a particular destination and the goods are there tendered while in the possession of the carrier, the risk of loss passes to the buyer when the goods are there so tendered as to enable the buyer to take delivery.

(2) Where the goods are held by a bailee to be delivered without being moved, the risk of loss passes to the buyer

(a) on the buyer's receipt of a negotiable document of title covering the goods; or

(b) on acknowledgment by the bailee to the buyer of the buyer's right to possession of the goods; or

(c) after the buyer's receipt of a non-negotiable document of title or other direction to deliver in a record, as provided in subsection (4)(b) of Section 2–503.

(3) In any case not within subsection (1) or (2), the risk of loss passes to the buyer on the buyer's receipt of the goods.

(4) The provisions of this section are subject to contrary agreement of the parties and to the provisions of this Article on sale on approval (Section 2–327) and on effect of breach on risk of loss (Section 2–510).

* * * *

§ 2–513. Buyer's Right to Inspection of Goods.

* * * *

(3) Unless otherwise agreed, the buyer is not entitled to inspect the goods before payment of the price when the contract provides

(a) for delivery on terms that under applicable course of performance, course of dealing, or usage of trade are interpreted to preclude inspection before payment; or

(b) for payment against documents of title, except where such payment is due only after the goods are to become available for inspection.

* * * *

Part 6 Breach, Repudiation and Excuse

* * * *

§ 2–605. Waiver of Buyer's Objections by Failure to Particularize.

(1) The buyer's failure to state in connection with rejection a particular defect or in connection with revocation of acceptance a

defect that justifies revocation precludes the buyer from relying on the unstated defect to justify rejection or revocation of acceptance if the defect is ascertainable by reasonable inspection

(a) where the seller had a right to cure the defect and could have cured it if stated seasonably; or

(b) between merchants when the seller has after rejection made a request in a record for a full and final statement in record form of all defects on which the buyer proposes to rely.

(2) A buyer's payment against documents tendered to the buyer made without reservation of rights precludes recovery of the payment for defects apparent on the face of the documents.

* * * *

§ 2–607. Effect of Acceptance; Notice of Breach; Burden of Establishing Breach After Acceptance; Notice of Claim or Litigation to Person Answerable Over.

* * * *

(3) Where a tender has been accepted

(a) the buyer must within a reasonable time after the buyer discovers or should have discovered any breach notify the seller. However, failure to give timely notice bars the buyer from a remedy only to the extent that the seller is prejudiced by the failure and

(b) if the claim is one for infringement or the like (subsection (3) of Section 2–312) and the buyer is sued as a result of such a breach the buyer must so notify the seller within a reasonable time after the buyer receives notice of the litigation or be barred from any remedy over for liability established by the litigation.

* * * *

§ 2–608. Revocation of Acceptance in Whole or in Part.

* * * *

(4) If a buyer uses the goods after a rightful rejection or justifiable revocation of acceptance, the following rules apply:

(a) Any use by the buyer which is unreasonable under the circumstances is wrongful as against the seller and is an acceptance only if ratified by the seller.

(b) Any use of the goods which is reasonable under the circumstances is not wrongful as against the seller and is not an acceptance, but in an appropriate case the buyer shall be obligated to the seller for the value of the use to the buyer.

* * * *

§ 2–612. "Installment Contract"; Breach.

* * * *

(2) The buyer may reject any installment which is non-conforming if the non-conformity substantially impairs the value of that installment to the buyer or if the non-conformity is a defect in the required documents; but if the non-conformity does not fall within subsection (3) and the seller gives adequate assurance of its cure the buyer must accept that installment.

(3) Whenever non-conformity or default with respect to one or more installments substantially impairs the value of the whole contract there is a breach of the whole. But the aggrieved party reinstates the contract if the party accepts a non-conforming installment without seasonably notifying of cancellation or if the party brings an action with respect only to past installments or demands performance as to future installments.

* * * *

Part 7 Remedies

§ 2–702. Seller's Remedies on Discovery of Buyer's Insolvency.

* * * *

(2) Where the seller discovers that the buyer has received goods on credit while insolvent the seller may reclaim the goods upon demand made within a reasonable time after the buyer's receipt of the goods. Except as provided in this subsection the seller may not base a right to reclaim goods on the buyer's fraudulent or innocent misrepresentation of solvency or of intent to pay.

* * * *

§ 2–703. Seller's Remedies in General.

(1) A breach of contract by the buyer includes the buyer's wrongful rejection or wrongful attempt to revoke acceptance of goods, wrongful failure to perform a contractual obligation, failure to make a payment when due, and repudiation.

(2) If the buyer is in breach of contract the seller, to the extent provided for by this Act or other law, may:

(a) withhold delivery of the goods;

(b) stop delivery of the goods under Section 2–705;

(c) proceed under Section 2–704 with respect to goods unidentified to the contract or unfinished;

(d) reclaim the goods under Section 2–507(2) or 2–702(2);

(e) require payment directly from the buyer under Section 2–325(c);

(f) cancel;

(g) resell and recover damages under Section 2–706;

(h) recover damages for nonacceptance or repudiation under Section 2–708(1);

(i) recover lost profits under Section 2–708(2);

(j) recover the price under Section 2–709;

(k) obtain specific performance under Section 2–716;

(l) recover liquidated damages under Section 2–718;

(m) in other cases, recover damages in any manner that is reasonable under the circumstances.

(3) If a buyer becomes insolvent, the seller may:

(a) withhold delivery under Section 2–702(1);

(b) stop delivery of the goods under Section 2–705;

(c) reclaim the goods under Section 2–702(2).

* * * *

§ 2–705. Seller's Stoppage of Delivery in Transit or Otherwise.

(1) The seller may stop delivery of goods in the possession of a carrier or other bailee when the seller discovers the buyer to be insolvent (Section 2–702) or when the buyer repudiates or fails to make a payment due before delivery or if for any other reason the seller has a right to withhold or reclaim the goods.

* * * *

§ 2–706. Seller's Resale Including Contract for Resale.

(1) In an appropriate case involving breach by the buyer, the seller may resell the goods concerned or the undelivered balance thereof. Where the resale is made in good faith and in a commercially reasonable manner the seller may recover the difference between the contract price and the resale price together with any incidental or consequential damages allowed under the provisions of this Article (Section 2–710), but less expenses saved in consequence of the buyer's breach.

* * * *

§ 2–708. Seller's Damages for Non-Acceptance or Repudiation.

(1) Subject to subsection (2) and to the provisions of this Article with respect to proof of market price (Section 2–723)

(a) the measure of damages for non-acceptance by the buyer is the difference between the contract price and the market price at the time and place for tender together with any incidental or consequential damages provided in this Article (Section 2–710), but less expenses saved in consequence of the buyer's breach; and

(b) the measure of damages for repudiation by the buyer is the difference between the contract price and the market price at the place for tender at the expiration of a commercially reasonable time after the seller learned of the repudiation, but no later than the time stated in paragraph (a), together with any incidental or consequential damages provided in this Article (Section 2–710), but less expenses saved in consequence of the buyer's breach.

(2) If the measure of damages provided in subsection (1) or in Section 2–706 is inadequate to put the seller in as good a position as performance would have done then the measure of damages is the profit (including reasonable overhead) which the seller would have made from full performance by the buyer, together with any incidental or consequential damages provided in this Article (Section 2–710).

§ 2–709. Action for the Price.

(1) When the buyer fails to pay the price as it becomes due the seller may recover, together with any incidental or consequential damages under the next section, the price

(a) of goods accepted or of conforming goods lost or damaged within a commercially reasonable time after risk of their loss has passed to the buyer; and

(b) of goods identified to the contract if the seller is unable after reasonable effort to resell them at a reasonable price or the circumstances reasonably indicate that such effort will be unavailing.

* * * *

§ 2–710. Seller's Incidental and Consequential Damages.

(1) Incidental damages to an aggrieved seller include any commercially reasonable charges, expenses or commissions incurred in stopping delivery, in the transportation, care and custody of goods after the buyer's breach, in connection with return or resale of the goods or otherwise resulting from the breach.

(2) Consequential damages resulting from the buyer's breach include any loss resulting from general or particular requirements and needs of which the buyer at the time of contracting had reason to know and which could not reasonably be prevented by resale or otherwise.

(3) In a consumer contract, a seller may not recover consequential damages from a consumer.

* * * *

§ 2–711. Buyer's Remedies in General; Buyer's Security Interest in Rejected Goods.

(1) A breach of contract by the seller includes the seller's wrongful failure to deliver or to perform a contractual obligation, making of a nonconforming tender of delivery or performance, and repudiation.

(2) If a seller is in breach of contract under subsection (1) the buyer, to the extent provided for by this Act or other law, may:

(a) in the case of rightful cancellation, rightful rejection or justifiable revocation of acceptance recover so much of the price as has been paid;

(b) deduct damages from any part of the price still due under Section 2–717;

(c) cancel;

(d) cover and have damages under Section 2–712 as to all goods affected whether or not they have been identified to the contract;

(e) recover damages for non-delivery or repudiation under Section 2–713;

(f) recover damages for breach with regard to accepted goods or breach with regard to a remedial promise under Section 2–714;

the holder in the name stated in the instrument or in the holder's name or both, but signature in both names may be required by a person paying or taking the instrument for value or collection.

§ 3–205. Special Indorsement; Blank Indorsement; Anomalous Indorsement.

(a) If an indorsement is made by the holder of an instrument, whether payable to an identified person or payable to bearer, and the indorsement identifies a person to whom it makes the instrument payable, it is a "special indorsement." When specially indorsed, an instrument becomes payable to the identified person and may be negotiated only by the indorsement of that person. The principles stated in Section 3–110 apply to special indorsements.

(b) If an indorsement is made by the holder of an instrument and it is not a special indorsement, it is a "blank indorsement." When indorsed in blank, an instrument becomes payable to bearer and may be negotiated by transfer of possession alone until specially indorsed.

(c) The holder may convert a blank indorsement that consists only of a signature into a special indorsement by writing, above the signature of the indorser, words identifying the person to whom the instrument is made payable.

(d) "Anomalous indorsement" means an indorsement made by a person who is not the holder of the instrument. An anomalous indorsement does not affect the manner in which the instrument may be negotiated.

§ 3–206. Restrictive Indorsement.

(a) An indorsement limiting payment to a particular person or otherwise prohibiting further transfer or negotiation of the instrument is not effective to prevent further transfer or negotiation of the instrument.

(b) An indorsement stating a condition to the right of the indorsee to receive payment does not affect the right of the indorsee to enforce the instrument. A person paying the instrument or taking it for value or collection may disregard the condition, and the rights and liabilities of that person are not affected by whether the condition has been fulfilled.

(c) If an instrument bears an indorsement (i) described in Section 4–201(b), or (ii) in blank or to a particular bank using the words "for deposit," "for collection," or other words indicating a purpose of having the instrument collected by a bank for the indorser or for a particular account, the following rules apply:

(1) A person, other than a bank, who purchases the instrument when so indorsed converts the instrument unless the amount paid for the instrument is received by the indorser or applied consistently with the indorsement.

(2) A depositary bank that purchases the instrument or takes it for collection when so indorsed converts the instrument unless the amount paid by the bank with respect to the instrument is received by the indorser or applied consistently with the indorsement.

(3) A payor bank that is also the depositary bank or that takes the instrument for immediate payment over the counter from a person other than a collecting bank converts the instrument unless the proceeds of the instrument are received by the indorser or applied consistently with the indorsement.

(4) Except as otherwise provided in paragraph (3), a payor bank or intermediary bank may disregard the indorsement and is not liable if the proceeds of the instrument are not received by the indorser or applied consistently with the indorsement.

(d) Except for an indorsement covered by subsection (c), if an instrument bears an indorsement using words to the effect that payment is to be made to the indorsee as agent, trustee, or other fiduciary for the benefit of the indorser or another person, the following rules apply:

(1) Unless there is notice of breach of fiduciary duty as provided in Section 3–307, a person who purchases the instrument from the indorsee or takes the instrument from the indorsee for collection or payment may pay the proceeds of payment or the value given for the instrument to the indorsee without regard to whether the indorsee violates a fiduciary duty to the indorser.

(2) A subsequent transferee of the instrument or person who pays the instrument is neither given notice nor otherwise affected by the restriction in the indorsement unless the transferee or payor knows that the fiduciary dealt with the instrument or its proceeds in breach of fiduciary duty.

(e) The presence on an instrument of an indorsement to which this section applies does not prevent a purchaser of the instrument from becoming a holder in due course of the instrument unless the purchaser is a converter under subsection (c) or has notice or knowledge of breach of fiduciary duty as stated in subsection (d).

(f) In an action to enforce the obligation of a party to pay the instrument, the obligor has a defense if payment would violate an indorsement to which this section applies and the payment is not permitted by this section.

§ 3–207. Reacquisition.

Reacquisition of an instrument occurs if it is transferred to a former holder, by negotiation or otherwise. A former holder who reacquires the instrument may cancel indorsements made after the reacquirer first became a holder of the instrument. If the cancellation causes the instrument to be payable to the reacquirer or to bearer, the reacquirer may negotiate the instrument. An indorser whose indorsement is canceled is discharged, and the discharge is effective against any subsequent holder.

Part 3 Enforcement of Instruments

§ 3–301. Person Entitled to Enforce Instrument.

"Person entitled to enforce" an instrument means (i) the holder of the instrument, (ii) a nonholder in possession of the instrument who has the rights of a holder, or (iii) a person not in possession of the instrument who is entitled to enforce the instrument pursuant to Section 3–309 or 3–418(d). A person may be a person entitled to enforce the instrument even though the person is not the owner of the instrument or is in wrongful possession of the instrument.

§ 3–302. Holder in Due Course.

(a) Subject to subsection (c) and Section 3–106(d), "holder in due course" means the holder of an instrument if:

(1) the instrument when issued or negotiated to the holder does not bear such apparent evidence of forgery or alteration or is not otherwise so irregular or incomplete as to call into question its authenticity; and

(2) the holder took the instrument (i) for value, (ii) in good faith, (iii) without notice that the instrument is overdue or has been dishonored or that there is an uncured default with respect to payment of another instrument issued as part of the same series, (iv) without notice that the instrument contains an unauthorized signature or has been altered, (v) without notice of any claim to the instrument described in Section 3–306, and (vi) without notice that any party has a defense or claim in recoupment described in Section 3–305(a).

(b) Notice of discharge of a party, other than discharge in an insolvency proceeding, is not notice of a defense under subsection (a), but discharge is effective against a person who became a holder in due course with notice of the discharge. Public filing or recording of a document does not of itself constitute notice of a defense, claim in recoupment, or claim to the instrument.

(c) Except to the extent a transferor or predecessor in interest has rights as a holder in due course, a person does not acquire rights of a holder in due course of an instrument taken (i) by legal process or by purchase in an execution, bankruptcy, or creditor's sale or similar proceeding, (ii) by purchase as part of a bulk transaction not in ordinary course of business of the transferor, or (iii) as the successor in interest to an estate or other organization.

(d) If, under Section 3–303(a)(1), the promise of performance that is the consideration for an instrument has been partially performed, the holder may assert rights as a holder in due course of the instrument only to the fraction of the amount payable under the instrument equal to the value of the partial performance divided by the value of the promised performance.

(e) If (i) the person entitled to enforce an instrument has only a security interest in the instrument and (ii) the person obliged to pay the instrument has a defense, claim in recoupment, or claim to the instrument that may be asserted against the person who granted the security interest, the person entitled to enforce the instrument may assert rights as a holder in due course only to an amount payable under the instrument which, at the time of enforcement of the instrument, does not exceed the amount of the unpaid obligation secured.

(f) To be effective, notice must be received at a time and in a manner that gives a reasonable opportunity to act on it.

(g) This section is subject to any law limiting status as a holder in due course in particular classes of transactions.

§ 3–303. Value and Consideration.

(a) An instrument is issued or transferred for value if:

(1) the instrument is issued or transferred for a promise of performance, to the extent the promise has been performed;

(2) the transferee acquires a security interest or other lien in the instrument other than a lien obtained by judicial proceeding;

(3) the instrument is issued or transferred as payment of, or as security for, an antecedent claim against any person, whether or not the claim is due;

(4) the instrument is issued or transferred in exchange for a negotiable instrument; or

(5) the instrument is issued or transferred in exchange for the incurring of an irrevocable obligation to a third party by the person taking the instrument.

(b) "Consideration" means any consideration sufficient to support a simple contract. The drawer or maker of an instrument has a defense if the instrument is issued without consideration. If an instrument is issued for a promise of performance, the issuer has a defense to the extent performance of the promise is due and the promise has not been performed. If an instrument is issued for value as stated in subsection (a), the instrument is also issued for consideration.

§ 3–304. Overdue Instrument.

(a) An instrument payable on demand becomes overdue at the earliest of the following times:

(1) on the day after the day demand for payment is duly made;

(2) if the instrument is a check, 90 days after its date; or

(3) if the instrument is not a check, when the instrument has been outstanding for a period of time after its date which is unreasonably long under the circumstances of the particular case in light of the nature of the instrument and usage of the trade.

(b) With respect to an instrument payable at a definite time the following rules apply:

(1) If the principal is payable in installments and a due date has not been accelerated, the instrument becomes overdue upon default under the instrument for nonpayment of an installment, and the instrument remains overdue until the default is cured.

(2) If the principal is not payable in installments and the due date has not been accelerated, the instrument becomes overdue on the day after the due date.

(3) If a due date with respect to principal has been accelerated, the instrument becomes overdue on the day after the accelerated due date.

(c) Unless the due date of principal has been accelerated, an instrument does not become overdue if there is default in payment of interest but no default in payment of principal.

§ 3–305. Defenses and Claims in Recoupment.

(a) Except as stated in subsection (b), the right to enforce the obligation of a party to pay an instrument is subject to the following:

(1) a defense of the obligor based on (i) infancy of the obligor to the extent it is a defense to a simple contract, (ii) duress, lack of legal capacity, or illegality of the transaction which, under other law, nullifies the obligation of the obligor, (iii) fraud that induced the obligor to sign the instrument with neither knowledge nor reasonable opportunity to learn of its character or its essential terms, or (iv) discharge of the obligor in insolvency proceedings;

(2) a defense of the obligor stated in another section of this Article or a defense of the obligor that would be available if the person entitled to enforce the instrument were enforcing a right to payment under a simple contract; and

(3) a claim in recoupment of the obligor against the original payee of the instrument if the claim arose from the transaction that gave rise to the instrument; but the claim of the obligor may be asserted against a transferee of the instrument only to reduce the amount owing on the instrument at the time the action is brought.

(b) The right of a holder in due course to enforce the obligation of a party to pay the instrument is subject to defenses of the obligor stated in subsection (a)(1), but is not subject to defenses of the obligor stated in subsection (a)(2) or claims in recoupment stated in subsection (a)(3) against a person other than the holder.

(c) Except as stated in subsection (d), in an action to enforce the obligation of a party to pay the instrument, the obligor may not assert against the person entitled to enforce the instrument a defense, claim in recoupment, or claim to the instrument (Section 3–306) of another person, but the other person's claim to the instrument may be asserted by the obligor if the other person is joined in the action and personally asserts the claim against the person entitled to enforce the instrument. An obligor is not obliged to pay the instrument if the person seeking enforcement of the instrument does not have rights of a holder in due course and the obligor proves that the instrument is a lost or stolen instrument.

(d) In an action to enforce the obligation of an accommodation party to pay an instrument, the accommodation party may assert against the person entitled to enforce the instrument any defense or claim in recoupment under subsection (a) that the accommodated party could assert against the person entitled to enforce the instrument, except the defenses of discharge in insolvency proceedings, infancy, and lack of legal capacity.

§ 3–306. Claims to an Instrument.

A person taking an instrument, other than a person having rights of a holder in due course, is subject to a claim of a property or possessory right in the instrument or its proceeds, including a claim to rescind a negotiation and to recover the instrument or its proceeds. A person having rights of a holder in due course takes free of the claim to the instrument.

§ 3–307. Notice of Breach of Fiduciary Duty.

(a) In this section:

(1) "Fiduciary" means an agent, trustee, partner, corporate officer or director, or other representative owing a fiduciary duty with respect to an instrument.

(2) "Represented person" means the principal, beneficiary, partnership, corporation, or other person to whom the duty stated in paragraph (1) is owed.

(b) If (i) an instrument is taken from a fiduciary for payment or collection or for value, (ii) the taker has knowledge of the fiduciary status of the fiduciary, and (iii) the represented person makes a claim to the instrument or its proceeds on the basis that the transaction of the fiduciary is a breach of fiduciary duty, the following rules apply:

(1) Notice of breach of fiduciary duty by the fiduciary is notice of the claim of the represented person.

(2) In the case of an instrument payable to the represented person or the fiduciary as such, the taker has notice of the breach of fiduciary duty if the instrument is (i) taken in payment of or as security for a debt known by the taker to be the personal debt of the fiduciary, (ii) taken in a transaction known by the taker to be for the personal benefit of the fiduciary, or (iii) deposited to an account other than an account of the fiduciary, as such, or an account of the represented person.

(3) If an instrument is issued by the represented person or the fiduciary as such, and made payable to the fiduciary personally, the taker does not have notice of the breach of fiduciary duty unless the taker knows of the breach of fiduciary duty.

(4) If an instrument is issued by the represented person or the fiduciary as such, to the taker as payee, the taker has notice of the breach of fiduciary duty if the instrument is (i) taken in payment of or as security for a debt known by the taker to be the personal debt of the fiduciary, (ii) taken in a transaction known by the taker to be for the personal benefit of the fiduciary, or (iii) deposited to an account other than an account of the fiduciary, as such, or an account of the represented person.

§ 3–308. Proof of Signatures and Status as Holder in Due Course.

(a) In an action with respect to an instrument, the authenticity of, and authority to make, each signature on the instrument is admitted unless specifically denied in the pleadings. If the validity of a signature is denied in the pleadings, the burden of establishing validity is on the person claiming validity, but the signature is presumed to be authentic and authorized unless the action is to enforce the liability of the purported signer and the signer is dead or incompetent at the time of trial of the issue of validity of the signature. If an action to enforce the instrument is brought against a person as the undisclosed principal of a person who signed the instrument as a party to the instrument, the plaintiff has the burden of establishing that the defendant is liable on the instrument as a represented person under Section 3–402(a).

(b) If the validity of signatures is admitted or proved and there is compliance with subsection (a), a plaintiff producing the instrument is entitled to payment if the plaintiff proves entitlement to enforce the instrument under Section 3–301, unless the defendant proves a defense or claim in recoupment. If a defense or claim in recoupment is proved, the right to payment of the plaintiff is subject to the defense or claim, except to the extent the plaintiff proves that the plaintiff has rights of a holder in due course which are not subject to the defense or claim.

§ 3–309. Enforcement of Lost, Destroyed, or Stolen Instrument.

(a) A person not in possession of an instrument is entitled to enforce the instrument if (i) the person was in possession of the instrument and entitled to enforce it when loss of possession occurred, (ii) the loss of possession was not the result of a transfer by the person or a lawful seizure, and (iii) the person cannot reasonably obtain possession of the instrument because the instrument was destroyed, its whereabouts cannot be determined, or it is in the wrongful possession of an unknown person or a person that cannot be found or is not amenable to service of process.

(b) A person seeking enforcement of an instrument under subsection (a) must prove the terms of the instrument and the person's right to enforce the instrument. If that proof is made, Section 3–308 applies to the case as if the person seeking enforcement had produced the instrument. The court may not enter judgment in favor of the person seeking enforcement unless it finds that the person required to pay the instrument is adequately protected against loss that might occur by reason of a claim by another person to enforce the instrument. Adequate protection may be provided by any reasonable means.

§ 3–310. Effect of Instrument on Obligation for Which Taken.

(a) Unless otherwise agreed, if a certified check, cashier's check, or teller's check is taken for an obligation, the obligation is discharged to the same extent discharge would result if an amount of money equal to the amount of the instrument were taken in payment of the obligation. Discharge of the obligation does not affect any liability that the obligor may have as an indorser of the instrument.

(b) Unless otherwise agreed and except as provided in subsection (a), if a note or an uncertified check is taken for an obligation, the obligation is suspended to the same extent the obligation would be discharged if an amount of money equal to the amount of the instrument were taken, and the following rules apply:

(1) In the case of an uncertified check, suspension of the obligation continues until dishonor of the check or until it is paid or certified. Payment or certification of the check results in discharge of the obligation to the extent of the amount of the check.

(2) In the case of a note, suspension of the obligation continues until dishonor of the note or until it is paid. Payment of the note results in discharge of the obligation to the extent of the payment.

(3) Except as provided in paragraph (4), if the check or note is dishonored and the obligee of the obligation for which the instrument was taken is the person entitled to enforce the instrument, the obligee may enforce either the instrument or the obligation. In the case of an instrument of a third person which is negotiated to the obligee by the obligor, discharge of the obligor on the instrument also discharges the obligation.

(4) If the person entitled to enforce the instrument taken for an obligation is a person other than the obligee, the obligee may not enforce the obligation to the extent the obligation is suspended. If the obligee is the person entitled to enforce the instrument but no longer has possession of it because it was lost, stolen, or destroyed, the obligation may not be enforced to the extent of the amount payable on the instrument, and to that extent the obligee's rights against the obligor are limited to enforcement of the instrument.

(c) If an instrument other than one described in subsection (a) or (b) is taken for an obligation, the effect is (i) that stated in subsection (a) if the instrument is one on which a bank is liable as maker or acceptor, or (ii) that stated in subsection (b) in any other case.

§ 3–311. Accord and Satisfaction by Use of Instrument.

(a) If a person against whom a claim is asserted proves that (i) that person in good faith tendered an instrument to the claimant as full satisfaction of the claim, (ii) the amount of the claim was unliquidated or subject to a bona fide dispute, and (iii) the claimant obtained payment of the instrument, the following subsections apply.

(b) Unless subsection (c) applies, the claim is discharged if the person against whom the claim is asserted proves that the instrument or an accompanying written communication contained a conspicuous statement to the effect that the instrument was tendered as full satisfaction of the claim.

(c) Subject to subsection (d), a claim is not discharged under subsection (b) if either of the following applies:

(1) The claimant, if an organization, proves that (i) within a reasonable time before the tender, the claimant sent a conspicuous statement to the person against whom the claim is asserted that communications concerning disputed debts, including an instrument tendered as full satisfaction of a debt, are to be sent to a designated person, office, or place, and (ii) the instrument or accompanying communication was not received by that designated person, office, or place.

(2) The claimant, whether or not an organization, proves that within 90 days after payment of the instrument, the claimant tendered repayment of the amount of the instrument to the person against whom the claim is asserted. This

paragraph does not apply if the claimant is an organization that sent a statement complying with paragraph (1)(i).

(d) A claim is discharged if the person against whom the claim is asserted proves that within a reasonable time before collection of the instrument was initiated, the claimant, or an agent of the claimant having direct responsibility with respect to the disputed obligation, knew that the instrument was tendered in full satisfaction of the claim.

§ 3–312. Lost, Destroyed, or Stolen Cashier's Check, Teller's Check, or Certified Check.*

(a) In this section:

(1) "Check" means a cashier's check, teller's check, or certified check.

(2) "Claimant" means a person who claims the right to receive the amount of a cashier's check, teller's check, or certified check that was lost, destroyed, or stolen.

(3) "Declaration of loss" means a written statement, made under penalty of perjury, to the effect that (i) the declarer lost possession of a check, (ii) the declarer is the drawer or payee of the check, in the case of a certified check, or the remitter or payee of the check, in the case of a cashier's check or teller's check, (iii) the loss of possession was not the result of a transfer by the declarer or a lawful seizure, and (iv) the declarer cannot reasonably obtain possession of the check because the check was destroyed, its whereabouts cannot be determined, or it is in the wrongful possession of an unknown person or a person that cannot be found or is not amenable to service of process.

(4) "Obligated bank" means the issuer of a cashier's check or teller's check or the acceptor of a certified check.

(b) A claimant may assert a claim to the amount of a check by a communication to the obligated bank describing the check with reasonable certainty and requesting payment of the amount of the check, if (i) the claimant is the drawer or payee of a certified check or the remitter or payee of a cashier's check or teller's check, (ii) the communication contains or is accompanied by a declaration of loss of the claimant with respect to the check, (iii) the communication is received at a time and in a manner affording the bank a reasonable time to act on it before the check is paid, and (iv) the claimant provides reasonable identification if requested by the obligated bank. Delivery of a declaration of loss is a warranty of the truth of the statements made in the declaration. If a claim is asserted in compliance with this subsection, the following rules apply:

(1) The claim becomes enforceable at the later of (i) the time the claim is asserted, or (ii) the 90th day following the date of the check, in the case of a cashier's check or teller's check, or the 90th day following the date of the acceptance, in the case of a certified check.

(2) Until the claim becomes enforceable, it has no legal effect and the obligated bank may pay the check or, in the case of a teller's check, may permit the drawee to pay the check. Payment to a person entitled to enforce the check discharges all liability of the obligated bank with respect to the check.

(3) If the claim becomes enforceable before the check is presented for payment, the obligated bank is not obliged to pay the check.

(4) When the claim becomes enforceable, the obligated bank becomes obliged to pay the amount of the check to the claimant if payment of the check has not been made to a person entitled to enforce the check. Subject to Section 4–302(a)(1), payment to the claimant discharges all liability of the obligated bank with respect to the check.

(c) If the obligated bank pays the amount of a check to a claimant under subsection (b)(4) and the check is presented for payment by a person having rights of a holder in due course, the claimant is obliged to (i) refund the payment to the obligated bank if the check is paid, or (ii) pay the amount of the check to the person having rights of a holder in due course if the check is dishonored.

(d) If a claimant has the right to assert a claim under subsection (b) and is also a person entitled to enforce a cashier's check, teller's check, or certified check which is lost, destroyed, or stolen, the claimant may assert rights with respect to the check either under this section or Section 3–309.

Added in 1991.

*[Section 3–312 was not adopted as part of the 1990 Official Text of Revised Article 3. It was officially approved and recommended for enactment in all states in August 1991 by the National Conference of Commissioners on Uniform State Laws.]

Part 4 Liability of Parties

§ 3–401. Signature.

(a) A person is not liable on an instrument unless (i) the person signed the instrument, or (ii) the person is represented by an agent or representative who signed the instrument and the signature is binding on the represented person under Section 3–402.

(b) A signature may be made (i) manually or by means of a device or machine, and (ii) by the use of any name, including a trade or assumed name, or by a word, mark, or symbol executed or adopted by a person with present intention to authenticate a writing.

§ 3–402. Signature by Representative.

(a) If a person acting, or purporting to act, as a representative signs an instrument by signing either the name of the represented person or the name of the signer, the represented person is bound by the signature to the same extent the represented person would be bound if the signature were on a simple contract. If the represented person is bound, the signature of the representative is the "authorized signature of the represented person" and the represented person is liable on the instrument, whether or not identified in the instrument.

(b) If a representative signs the name of the representative to an instrument and the signature is an authorized signature of the represented person, the following rules apply:

(1) If the form of the signature shows unambiguously that the signature is made on behalf of the represented person who is identified in the instrument, the representative is not liable on the instrument.

(2) Subject to subsection (c), if (i) the form of the signature does not show unambiguously that the signature is made in a representative capacity or (ii) the represented person is not identified in the instrument, the representative is liable on the instrument to a holder in due course that took the instrument without notice that the representative was not intended to be liable on the instrument. With respect to any other person, the representative is liable on the instrument unless the representative proves that the original parties did not intend the representative to be liable on the instrument.

(c) If a representative signs the name of the representative as drawer of a check without indication of the representative status and the check is payable from an account of the represented person who is identified on the check, the signer is not liable on the check if the signature is an authorized signature of the represented person.

§ 3–403. Unauthorized Signature.

(a) Unless otherwise provided in this Article or Article 4, an unauthorized signature is ineffective except as the signature of the unauthorized signer in favor of a person who in good faith pays the instrument or takes it for value. An unauthorized signature may be ratified for all purposes of this Article.

(b) If the signature of more than one person is required to constitute the authorized signature of an organization, the signature of the organization is unauthorized if one of the required signatures is lacking.

(c) The civil or criminal liability of a person who makes an unauthorized signature is not affected by any provision of this Article which makes the unauthorized signature effective for the purposes of this Article.

§ 3–404. Impostors; Fictitious Payees.

(a) If an impostor, by use of the mails or otherwise, induces the issuer of an instrument to issue the instrument to the impostor, or to a person acting in concert with the impostor, by impersonating the payee of the instrument or a person authorized to act for the payee, an indorsement of the instrument by any person in the name of the payee is effective as the indorsement of the payee in favor of a person who, in good faith, pays the instrument or takes it for value or for collection.

(b) If (i) a person whose intent determines to whom an instrument is payable (Section 3–110(a) or (b)) does not intend the person identified as payee to have any interest in the instrument, or (ii) the person identified as payee of an instrument is a fictitious person, the following rules apply until the instrument is negotiated by special indorsement:

(1) Any person in possession of the instrument is its holder.

(2) An indorsement by any person in the name of the payee stated in the instrument is effective as the indorsement of the payee in favor of a person who, in good faith, pays the instrument or takes it for value or for collection.

(c) Under subsection (a) or (b), an indorsement is made in the name of a payee if (i) it is made in a name substantially similar to that of the payee or (ii) the instrument, whether or not indorsed, is deposited in a depositary bank to an account in a name substantially similar to that of the payee.

(d) With respect to an instrument to which subsection (a) or (b) applies, if a person paying the instrument or taking it for value or for collection fails to exercise ordinary care in paying or taking the instrument and that failure substantially contributes to loss resulting from payment of the instrument, the person bearing the loss may recover from the person failing to exercise ordinary care to the extent the failure to exercise ordinary care contributed to the loss.

§ 3–405. Employer's Responsibility for Fraudulent Indorsement by Employee.

(a) In this section:

(1) "Employee" includes an independent contractor and employee of an independent contractor retained by the employer.

(2) "Fraudulent indorsement" means (i) in the case of an instrument payable to the employer, a forged indorsement purporting to be that of the employer, or (ii) in the case of an instrument with respect to which the employer is the issuer, a forged indorsement purporting to be that of the person identified as payee.

(3) "Responsibility" with respect to instruments means authority (i) to sign or indorse instruments on behalf of the employer, (ii) to process instruments received by the employer for bookkeeping purposes, for deposit to an account, or for other disposition, (iii) to prepare or process instruments for issue in the name of the employer, (iv) to supply information determining the names or addresses of payees of instruments to be issued in the name of the employer, (v) to control the disposition of instruments to be issued in the name of the employer, or (vi) to act otherwise with respect to instruments in a responsible capacity. "Responsibility" does not include authority that merely allows an employee to have access to instruments or blank or incomplete instrument forms that are being stored or transported or are part of incoming or outgoing mail, or similar access.

(b) For the purpose of determining the rights and liabilities of a person who, in good faith, pays an instrument or takes it for value or for collection, if an employer entrusted an employee with responsibility with respect to the instrument and the employee or a person acting in concert with the employee makes a fraudulent indorsement of the instrument, the indorsement is effective as the indorsement of the person to whom the instrument is payable if it is made in the name of that person. If the person paying the instrument or taking it for value or for collection fails to exercise ordinary care in paying or taking the instrument and that failure substantially contributes to loss resulting from the fraud, the person bearing the loss may recover from the person failing to exercise ordinary care to the extent the failure to exercise ordinary care contributed to the loss.

(c) Under subsection (b), an indorsement is made in the name of the person to whom an instrument is payable if (i) it is made in a name substantially similar to the name of that person or (ii) the instrument, whether or not indorsed, is deposited in a depositary bank to an account in a name substantially similar to the name of that person.

§ 3–406. Negligence Contributing to Forged Signature or Alteration of Instrument.

(a) A person whose failure to exercise ordinary care substantially contributes to an alteration of an instrument or to the making of a forged signature on an instrument is precluded from asserting the alteration or the forgery against a person who, in good faith, pays the instrument or takes it for value or for collection.

(b) Under subsection (a), if the person asserting the preclusion fails to exercise ordinary care in paying or taking the instrument and that failure substantially contributes to loss, the loss is allocated between the person precluded and the person asserting the preclusion according to the extent to which the failure of each to exercise ordinary care contributed to the loss.

(c) Under subsection (a), the burden of proving failure to exercise ordinary care is on the person asserting the preclusion. Under subsection (b), the burden of proving failure to exercise ordinary care is on the person precluded.

§ 3–407. Alteration.

(a) "Alteration" means (i) an unauthorized change in an instrument that purports to modify in any respect the obligation of a party, or (ii) an unauthorized addition of words or numbers or other change to an incomplete instrument relating to the obligation of a party.

(b) Except as provided in subsection (c), an alteration fraudulently made discharges a party whose obligation is affected by the alteration unless that party assents or is precluded from asserting the alteration. No other alteration discharges a party, and the instrument may be enforced according to its original terms.

(c) A payor bank or drawee paying a fraudulently altered instrument or a person taking it for value, in good faith and without notice of the alteration, may enforce rights with respect to the instrument (i) according to its original terms, or (ii) in the case of an incomplete instrument altered by unauthorized completion, according to its terms as completed.

§ 3–408. Drawee Not Liable on Unaccepted Draft.

A check or other draft does not of itself operate as an assignment of funds in the hands of the drawee available for its payment, and the drawee is not liable on the instrument until the drawee accepts it.

§ 3–409. Acceptance of Draft; Certified Check.

(a) "Acceptance" means the drawee's signed agreement to pay a draft as presented. It must be written on the draft and may consist of the drawee's signature alone. Acceptance may be made at any time and becomes effective when notification pursuant to instructions is given or the accepted draft is delivered for the purpose of giving rights on the acceptance to any person.

(b) A draft may be accepted although it has not been signed by the drawer, is otherwise incomplete, is overdue, or has been dishonored.

(c) If a draft is payable at a fixed period after sight and the acceptor fails to date the acceptance, the holder may complete the acceptance by supplying a date in good faith.

(d) "Certified check" means a check accepted by the bank on which it is drawn. Acceptance may be made as stated in subsection (a) or by a writing on the check which indicates that the check is certified. The drawee of a check has no obligation to certify the check, and refusal to certify is not dishonor of the check.

§ 3–410. Acceptance Varying Draft.

(a) If the terms of a drawee's acceptance vary from the terms of the draft as presented, the holder may refuse the acceptance and treat the draft as dishonored. In that case, the drawee may cancel the acceptance.

(b) The terms of a draft are not varied by an acceptance to pay at a particular bank or place in the United States, unless the acceptance states that the draft is to be paid only at that bank or place.

(c) If the holder assents to an acceptance varying the terms of a draft, the obligation of each drawer and indorser that does not expressly assent to the acceptance is discharged.

§ 3–411. Refusal to Pay Cashier's Checks, Teller's Checks, and Certified Checks.

(a) In this section, "obligated bank" means the acceptor of a certified check or the issuer of a cashier's check or teller's check bought from the issuer.

(b) If the obligated bank wrongfully (i) refuses to pay a cashier's check or certified check, (ii) stops payment of a teller's check, or (iii) refuses to pay a dishonored teller's check, the person asserting the right to enforce the check is entitled to compensation for expenses and loss of interest resulting from the nonpayment and may recover consequential damages if the obligated bank refuses to pay after receiving notice of particular circumstances giving rise to the damages.

(c) Expenses or consequential damages under subsection (b) are not recoverable if the refusal of the obligated bank to pay occurs because (i) the bank suspends payments, (ii) the obligated bank asserts a claim or defense of the bank that it has reasonable grounds to believe is available against the person entitled to enforce the instrument, (iii) the obligated bank has a reasonable doubt whether the person demanding payment is the person entitled to enforce the instrument, or (iv) payment is prohibited by law.

§ 3–412. Obligation of Issuer of Note or Cashier's Check.

The issuer of a note or cashier's check or other draft drawn on the drawer is obliged to pay the instrument (i) according to its terms at the time it was issued or, if not issued, at the time it first came into possession of a holder, or (ii) if the issuer signed an incomplete instrument, according to its terms when completed, to the extent stated in Sections 3–115 and 3–407. The obligation is owed to a person entitled to enforce the instrument or to an indorser who paid the instrument under Section 3–415.

§ 3–413. Obligation of Acceptor.

(a) The acceptor of a draft is obliged to pay the draft (i) according to its terms at the time it was accepted, even though the acceptance states that the draft is payable "as originally drawn" or equivalent terms, (ii) if the acceptance varies the terms of the draft, according to the terms of the draft as varied, or (iii) if the acceptance is of a draft that is an incomplete instrument, according to its terms when completed, to the extent stated in Sections 3–115 and 3–407. The obligation is owed to a person entitled to enforce the draft or to the drawer or an indorser who paid the draft under Section 3–414 or 3–415.

(b) If the certification of a check or other acceptance of a draft states the amount certified or accepted, the obligation of the acceptor is that amount. If (i) the certification or acceptance does not state an amount, (ii) the amount of the instrument is subsequently raised, and (iii) the instrument is then negotiated to a holder in due course, the obligation of the acceptor is the amount of the instrument at the time it was taken by the holder in due course.

§ 3–414. Obligation of Drawer.

(a) This section does not apply to cashier's checks or other drafts drawn on the drawer.

(b) If an unaccepted draft is dishonored, the drawer is obliged to pay the draft (i) according to its terms at the time it was issued or, if not issued, at the time it first came into possession of a holder, or (ii) if the drawer signed an incomplete instrument, according to its terms when completed, to the extent stated in Sections 3–115 and 3–407. The obligation is owed to a person entitled to enforce the draft or to an indorser who paid the draft under Section 3–415.

(c) If a draft is accepted by a bank, the drawer is discharged, regardless of when or by whom acceptance was obtained.

(d) If a draft is accepted and the acceptor is not a bank, the obligation of the drawer to pay the draft if the draft is dishonored by the acceptor is the same as the obligation of an indorser under Section 3–415(a) and (c).

(e) If a draft states that it is drawn "without recourse" or otherwise disclaims liability of the drawer to pay the draft, the drawer is not liable under subsection (b) to pay the draft if the draft is not a check. A disclaimer of the liability stated in subsection (b) is not effective if the draft is a check.

(f) If (i) a check is not presented for payment or given to a depositary bank for collection within 30 days after its date, (ii) the drawee suspends payments after expiration of the 30-day period without paying the check, and (iii) because of the suspension of payments, the drawer is deprived of funds maintained with the drawee to cover payment of the check, the drawer to the extent deprived of funds may discharge its obligation to pay the check by assigning to the person entitled to enforce the check the rights of the drawer against the drawee with respect to the funds.

§ 3–415. Obligation of Indorser.

(a) Subject to subsections (b), (c), and (d) and to Section 3–419(d), if an instrument is dishonored, an indorser is obliged to pay the amount due on the instrument (i) according to the terms of the instrument at the time it was indorsed, or (ii) if the indorser indorsed an incomplete instrument, according to its terms when completed, to the extent stated in Sections 3–115 and 3–407. The obligation of the indorser is owed to a person entitled to enforce the instrument or to a subsequent indorser who paid the instrument under this section.

(b) If an indorsement states that it is made "without recourse" or otherwise disclaims liability of the indorser, the indorser is not liable under subsection (a) to pay the instrument.

(c) If notice of dishonor of an instrument is required by Section 3–503 and notice of dishonor complying with that section is not given to an indorser, the liability of the indorser under subsection (a) is discharged.

(d) If a draft is accepted by a bank after an indorsement is made, the liability of the indorser under subsection (a) is discharged.

(e) If an indorser of a check is liable under subsection (a) and the check is not presented for payment, or given to a depositary bank for collection, within 30 days after the day the indorsement was made, the liability of the indorser under subsection (a) is discharged.

As amended in 1993.

§ 3–416. Transfer Warranties.

(a) A person who transfers an instrument for consideration warrants to the transferee and, if the transfer is by indorsement, to any subsequent transferee that:

(1) the warrantor is a person entitled to enforce the instrument;

(2) all signatures on the instrument are authentic and authorized;

(3) the instrument has not been altered;

(4) the instrument is not subject to a defense or claim in recoupment of any party which can be asserted against the warrantor; and

(5) the warrantor has no knowledge of any insolvency proceeding commenced with respect to the maker or acceptor or, in the case of an unaccepted draft, the drawer.

(b) A person to whom the warranties under subsection (a) are made and who took the instrument in good faith may recover from the warrantor as damages for breach of warranty an amount equal to the loss suffered as a result of the breach, but not more than the amount of the instrument plus expenses and loss of interest incurred as a result of the breach.

(c) The warranties stated in subsection (a) cannot be disclaimed with respect to checks. Unless notice of a claim for breach of warranty is given to the warrantor within 30 days after the claimant has reason to know of the breach and the identity of the warrantor, the liability of the warrantor under subsection (b) is discharged to the extent of any loss caused by the delay in giving notice of the claim.

(d) A [cause of action] for breach of warranty under this section accrues when the claimant has reason to know of the breach.

§ 3–417. **Presentment Warranties.**

(a) If an unaccepted draft is presented to the drawee for payment or acceptance and the drawee pays or accepts the draft, (i) the person obtaining payment or acceptance, at the time of presentment, and (ii) a previous transferor of the draft, at the time of transfer, warrant to the drawee making payment or accepting the draft in good faith that:

(1) the warrantor is, or was, at the time the warrantor transferred the draft, a person entitled to enforce the draft or authorized to obtain payment or acceptance of the draft on behalf of a person entitled to enforce the draft;

(2) the draft has not been altered; and

(3) the warrantor has no knowledge that the signature of the drawer of the draft is unauthorized.

(b) A drawee making payment may recover from any warrantor damages for breach of warranty equal to the amount paid by the drawee less the amount the drawee received or is entitled to receive from the drawer because of the payment. In addition, the drawee is entitled to compensation for expenses and loss of interest resulting from the breach. The right of the drawee to recover damages under this subsection is not affected by any failure of the drawee to exercise ordinary care in making payment. If the drawee accepts the draft, breach of warranty is a defense to the obligation of the acceptor. If the acceptor makes payment with respect to the draft, the acceptor is entitled to recover from any warrantor for breach of warranty the amounts stated in this subsection.

(c) If a drawee asserts a claim for breach of warranty under subsection (a) based on an unauthorized indorsement of the draft or an alteration of the draft, the warrantor may defend by proving that the indorsement is effective under Section 3–404 or 3–405 or the drawer is precluded under Section 3–406 or 4–406 from asserting against the drawee the unauthorized indorsement or alteration.

(d) If (i) a dishonored draft is presented for payment to the drawer or an indorser or (ii) any other instrument is presented for payment to a party obliged to pay the instrument, and (iii) payment is received, the following rules apply:

(1) The person obtaining payment and a prior transferor of the instrument warrant to the person making payment in good faith that the warrantor is, or was, at the time the warrantor transferred the instrument, a person entitled to enforce the instrument or authorized to obtain payment on behalf of a person entitled to enforce the instrument.

(2) The person making payment may recover from any warrantor for breach of warranty an amount equal to the amount paid plus expenses and loss of interest resulting from the breach.

(e) The warranties stated in subsections (a) and (d) cannot be disclaimed with respect to checks. Unless notice of a claim for breach of warranty is given to the warrantor within 30 days after the claimant has reason to know of the breach and the identity of the warrantor, the liability of the warrantor under subsection (b) or (d) is discharged to the extent of any loss caused by the delay in giving notice of the claim.

(f) A [cause of action] for breach of warranty under this section accrues when the claimant has reason to know of the breach.

§ 3–418. **Payment or Acceptance by Mistake.**

(a) Except as provided in subsection (c), if the drawee of a draft pays or accepts the draft and the drawee acted on the mistaken belief that (i) payment of the draft had not been stopped pursuant to Section 4–403 or (ii) the signature of the drawer of the draft was authorized, the drawee may recover the amount of the draft from the person to whom or for whose benefit payment was made or, in the case of acceptance, may revoke the acceptance. Rights of the drawee under this subsection are not affected by failure of the drawee to exercise ordinary care in paying or accepting the draft.

(b) Except as provided in subsection (c), if an instrument has been paid or accepted by mistake and the case is not covered by subsection (a), the person paying or accepting may, to the extent permitted by the law governing mistake and restitution, (i) recover the payment from the person to whom or for whose benefit payment was made or (ii) in the case of acceptance, may revoke the acceptance.

(c) The remedies provided by subsection (a) or (b) may not be asserted against a person who took the instrument in good faith and for value or who in good faith changed position in reliance on the payment or acceptance. This subsection does not limit remedies provided by Section 3–417 or 4–407.

(d) Notwithstanding Section 4–215, if an instrument is paid or accepted by mistake and the payor or acceptor recovers payment or revokes acceptance under subsection (a) or (b), the instrument is deemed not to have been paid or accepted and is treated as dishonored, and the person from whom payment is recovered has rights as a person entitled to enforce the dishonored instrument.

§ 3–419. Instruments Signed for Accommodation.

(a) If an instrument is issued for value given for the benefit of a party to the instrument ("accommodated party") and another party to the instrument ("accommodation party") signs the instrument for the purpose of incurring liability on the instrument without being a direct beneficiary of the value given for the instrument, the instrument is signed by the accommodation party "for accommodation."

(b) An accommodation party may sign the instrument as maker, drawer, acceptor, or indorser and, subject to subsection (d), is obliged to pay the instrument in the capacity in which the accommodation party signs. The obligation of an accommodation party may be enforced notwithstanding any statute of frauds and whether or not the accommodation party receives consideration for the accommodation.

(c) A person signing an instrument is presumed to be an accommodation party and there is notice that the instrument is signed for accommodation if the signature is an anomalous indorsement or is accompanied by words indicating that the signer is acting as surety or guarantor with respect to the obligation of another party to the instrument. Except as provided in Section 3–605, the obligation of an accommodation party to pay the instrument is not affected by the fact that the person enforcing the obligation had notice when the instrument was taken by that person that the accommodation party signed the instrument for accommodation.

(d) If the signature of a party to an instrument is accompanied by words indicating unambiguously that the party is guaranteeing collection rather than payment of the obligation of another party to the instrument, the signer is obliged to pay the amount due on the instrument to a person entitled to enforce the instrument only if (i) execution of judgment against the other party has been returned unsatisfied, (ii) the other party is insolvent or in an insolvency proceeding, (iii) the other party cannot be served with process, or (iv) it is otherwise apparent that payment cannot be obtained from the other party.

(e) An accommodation party who pays the instrument is entitled to reimbursement from the accommodated party and is entitled to enforce the instrument against the accommodated party. An accommodated party who pays the instrument has no right of recourse against, and is not entitled to contribution from, an accommodation party.

§ 3–420. Conversion of Instrument.

(a) The law applicable to conversion of personal property applies to instruments. An instrument is also converted if it is taken by transfer, other than a negotiation, from a person not entitled to enforce the instrument or a bank makes or obtains payment with respect to the instrument for a person not entitled to enforce the instrument or receive payment. An action for conversion of an instrument may not be brought by (i) the issuer or acceptor of the instrument or (ii) a payee or indorsee who did not receive delivery of the instrument either directly or through delivery to an agent or a co-payee.

(b) In an action under subsection (a), the measure of liability is presumed to be the amount payable on the instrument, but recovery may not exceed the amount of the plaintiff's interest in the instrument.

(c) A representative, other than a depositary bank, who has in good faith dealt with an instrument or its proceeds on behalf of one who was not the person entitled to enforce the instrument is not liable in conversion to that person beyond the amount of any proceeds that it has not paid out.

Part 5 Dishonor

§ 3–501. Presentment.

(a) "Presentment" means a demand made by or on behalf of a person entitled to enforce an instrument (i) to pay the instrument made to the drawee or a party obliged to pay the instrument or, in the case of a note or accepted draft payable at a bank, to the bank, or (ii) to accept a draft made to the drawee.

(b) The following rules are subject to Article 4, agreement of the parties, and clearing-house rules and the like:

(1) Presentment may be made at the place of payment of the instrument and must be made at the place of payment if the instrument is payable at a bank in the United States; may be made by any commercially reasonable means, including an oral, written, or electronic communication; is effective when the demand for payment or acceptance is received by the person to whom presentment is made; and is effective if made to any one of two or more makers, acceptors, drawees, or other payors.

(2) Upon demand of the person to whom presentment is made, the person making presentment must (i) exhibit the instrument, (ii) give reasonable identification and, if presentment is made on behalf of another person, reasonable evidence of authority to do so, and (. . .) sign a receipt on the instrument for any payment made or surrender the instrument if full payment is made.

(3) Without dishonoring the instrument, the party to whom presentment is made may (i) return the instrument for lack of a necessary indorsement, or (ii) refuse payment or acceptance for failure of the presentment to comply with the terms of the instrument, an agreement of the parties, or other applicable law or rule.

(4) The party to whom presentment is made may treat presentment as occurring on the next business day after the day of presentment if the party to whom presentment is made has established a cut-off hour not earlier than 2 P.M. for the receipt and processing of instruments presented for payment or acceptance and presentment is made after the cut-off hour.

§ 3–502. Dishonor.

(a) Dishonor of a note is governed by the following rules:

(1) If the note is payable on demand, the note is dishonored if presentment is duly made to the maker and the note is not paid on the day of presentment.

(2) If the note is not payable on demand and is payable at or through a bank or the terms of the note require presentment, the note is dishonored if presentment is duly made and the note is not paid on the day it becomes payable or the day of presentment, whichever is later.

(3) If the note is not payable on demand and paragraph (2) does not apply, the note is dishonored if it is not paid on the day it becomes payable.

(b) Dishonor of an unaccepted draft other than a documentary draft is governed by the following rules:

(1) If a check is duly presented for payment to the payor bank otherwise than for immediate payment over the counter, the check is dishonored if the payor bank makes timely return of the check or sends timely notice of dishonor or nonpayment under Section 4–301 or 4–302, or becomes accountable for the amount of the check under Section 4–302.

(2) If a draft is payable on demand and paragraph (1) does not apply, the draft is dishonored if presentment for payment is duly made to the drawee and the draft is not paid on the day of presentment.

(3) If a draft is payable on a date stated in the draft, the draft is dishonored if (i) presentment for payment is duly made to the drawee and payment is not made on the day the draft becomes payable or the day of presentment, whichever is later, or (ii) presentment for acceptance is duly made before the day the draft becomes payable and the draft is not accepted on the day of presentment.

(4) If a draft is payable on elapse of a period of time after sight or acceptance, the draft is dishonored if presentment for acceptance is duly made and the draft is not accepted on the day of presentment.

(c) Dishonor of an unaccepted documentary draft occurs according to the rules stated in subsection (b)(2), (3), and (4), except that payment or acceptance may be delayed without dishonor until no later than the close of the third business day of the drawee following the day on which payment or acceptance is required by those paragraphs.

(d) Dishonor of an accepted draft is governed by the following rules:

(1) If the draft is payable on demand, the draft is dishonored if presentment for payment is duly made to the acceptor and the draft is not paid on the day of presentment.

(2) If the draft is not payable on demand, the draft is dishonored if presentment for payment is duly made to the acceptor and payment is not made on the day it becomes payable or the day of presentment, whichever is later.

(e) In any case in which presentment is otherwise required for dishonor under this section and presentment is excused under Section 3–504, dishonor occurs without presentment if the instrument is not duly accepted or paid.

(f) If a draft is dishonored because timely acceptance of the draft was not made and the person entitled to demand acceptance consents to a late acceptance, from the time of acceptance the draft is treated as never having been dishonored.

§ 3–503. Notice of Dishonor.

(a) The obligation of an indorser stated in Section 3–415(a) and the obligation of a drawer stated in Section 3–414(d) may not be enforced unless (i) the indorser or drawer is given notice of dishonor of the instrument complying with this section or (ii) notice of dishonor is excused under Section 3–504(b).

(b) Notice of dishonor may be given by any person; may be given by any commercially reasonable means, including an oral, written, or electronic communication; and is sufficient if it reasonably identifies the instrument and indicates that the instrument has been dishonored or has not been paid or accepted. Return of an instrument given to a bank for collection is sufficient notice of dishonor.

(c) Subject to Section 3–504(c), with respect to an instrument taken for collection by a collecting bank, notice of dishonor must be given (i) by the bank before midnight of the next banking day following the banking day on which the bank receives notice of dishonor of the instrument, or (ii) by any other person within 30 days following the day on which the person receives notice of dishonor. With respect to any other instrument, notice of dishonor must be given within 30 days following the day on which dishonor occurs.

§ 3–504. Excused Presentment and Notice of Dishonor.

(a) Presentment for payment or acceptance of an instrument is excused if (i) the person entitled to present the instrument cannot with reasonable diligence make presentment, (ii) the maker or acceptor has repudiated an obligation to pay the instrument or is dead or in insolvency proceedings, (iii) by the terms of the instrument presentment is not necessary to enforce the obligation of indorsers or the drawer, (iv) the drawer or indorser whose obligation is being enforced has waived presentment or otherwise has no reason to expect or right to require that the instrument be paid or accepted, or (v) the drawer instructed the drawee not to pay or accept the draft or the drawee was not obligated to the drawer to pay the draft.

(b) Notice of dishonor is excused if (i) by the terms of the instrument notice of dishonor is not necessary to enforce the obligation of a party to pay the instrument, or (ii) the party whose obligation is being enforced waived notice of dishonor. A waiver of presentment is also a waiver of notice of dishonor.

(c) Delay in giving notice of dishonor is excused if the delay was caused by circumstances beyond the control of the person giving the notice and the person giving the notice exercised reasonable diligence after the cause of the delay ceased to operate.

§ 3–505. Evidence of Dishonor.

(a) The following are admissible as evidence and create a presumption of dishonor and of any notice of dishonor stated:

(1) a document regular in form as provided in subsection (b) which purports to be a protest;

(2) a purported stamp or writing of the drawee, payor bank, or presenting bank on or accompanying the instrument stating that acceptance or payment has been refused unless reasons for the refusal are stated and the reasons are not consistent with dishonor;

(3) a book or record of the drawee, payor bank, or collecting bank, kept in the usual course of business which shows dishonor, even if there is no evidence of who made the entry.

(b) A protest is a certificate of dishonor made by a United States consul or vice consul, or a notary public or other person authorized to administer oaths by the law of the place where dishonor occurs. It may be made upon information satisfactory to that person. The protest must identify the instrument and certify either that presentment has been made or, if not made, the reason why it was not made, and that the instrument has been dishonored by nonacceptance or nonpayment. The protest may also certify that notice of dishonor has been given to some or all parties.

Part 6 Discharge and Payment

§ 3–601. Discharge and Effect of Discharge.

(a) The obligation of a party to pay the instrument is discharged as stated in this Article or by an act or agreement with the party which would discharge an obligation to pay money under a simple contract.

(b) Discharge of the obligation of a party is not effective against a person acquiring rights of a holder in due course of the instrument without notice of the discharge.

§ 3–602. Payment.

(a) Subject to subsection (b), an instrument is paid to the extent payment is made (i) by or on behalf of a party obliged to pay the instrument, and (ii) to a person entitled to enforce the instrument. To the extent of the payment, the obligation of the party obliged to pay the instrument is discharged even though payment is made with knowledge of a claim to the instrument under Section 3–306 by another person.

(b) The obligation of a party to pay the instrument is not discharged under subsection (a) if:

(1) a claim to the instrument under Section 3–306 is enforceable against the party receiving payment and (i) payment is made with knowledge by the payor that payment is prohibited by injunction or similar process of a court of competent jurisdiction, or (ii) in the case of an instrument other than a cashier's check, teller's check, or certified check, the party making payment accepted, from the person having a claim to the instrument, indemnity against loss resulting from refusal to pay the person entitled to enforce the instrument; or

(2) the person making payment knows that the instrument is a stolen instrument and pays a person it knows is in wrongful possession of the instrument.

§ 3–603. Tender of Payment.

(a) If tender of payment of an obligation to pay an instrument is made to a person entitled to enforce the instrument, the effect of tender is governed by principles of law applicable to tender of payment under a simple contract.

(b) If tender of payment of an obligation to pay an instrument is made to a person entitled to enforce the instrument and the tender is refused, there is discharge, to the extent of the amount of the tender, of the obligation of an indorser or accommodation party having a right of recourse with respect to the obligation to which the tender relates.

(c) If tender of payment of an amount due on an instrument is made to a person entitled to enforce the instrument, the obligation of the obligor to pay interest after the due date on the amount tendered is discharged. If presentment is required with respect to an instrument and the obligor is able and ready to pay on the due date at every place of payment stated in the instrument, the obligor is deemed to have made tender of payment on the due date to the person entitled to enforce the instrument.

§ 3–604. Discharge by Cancellation or Renunciation.

(a) A person entitled to enforce an instrument, with or without consideration, may discharge the obligation of a party to pay the instrument (i) by an intentional voluntary act, such as surrender of the instrument to the party, destruction, mutilation, or cancellation of the instrument, cancellation or striking out of the party's signature, or the addition of words to the instrument indicating discharge, or (ii) by agreeing not to sue or otherwise renouncing rights against the party by a signed writing.

(b) Cancellation or striking out of an indorsement pursuant to subsection (a) does not affect the status and rights of a party derived from the indorsement.

§ 3–605. Discharge of Indorsers and Accommodation Parties.

(a) In this section, the term "indorser" includes a drawer having the obligation described in Section 3–414(d).

(b) Discharge, under Section 3–604, of the obligation of a party to pay an instrument does not discharge the obligation of an indorser or accommodation party having a right of recourse against the discharged party.

(c) If a person entitled to enforce an instrument agrees, with or without consideration, to an extension of the due date of the obligation of a party to pay the instrument, the extension discharges an indorser or accommodation party having a right of recourse against the party whose obligation is extended to the extent the indorser or accommodation party proves that the extension caused loss to the indorser or accommodation party with respect to the right of recourse.

(d) If a person entitled to enforce an instrument agrees, with or without consideration, to a material modification of the obligation of a party other than an extension of the due date, the modification discharges the obligation of an indorser or accommodation party having a right of recourse against the person whose obligation is modified to the extent the modification causes loss to the indorser or accommodation party with respect to the right of recourse. The loss suffered by the indorser or accommodation party as a result of the modification is equal to the amount of the right of recourse unless the person enforcing the instrument proves that no loss was caused by the modification or that the loss caused by the modification was an amount less than the amount of the right of recourse.

(e) If the obligation of a party to pay an instrument is secured by an interest in collateral and a person entitled to enforce the instrument impairs the value of the interest in collateral, the obligation of an indorser or accommodation party having a right of recourse against the obligor is discharged to the extent of the impairment. The value of an interest in collateral is impaired to the extent (i) the value of the interest is reduced to an amount less than the amount of the right of recourse of the party asserting discharge, or (ii) the reduction in value of the interest causes an increase in the amount by which the amount of the right of recourse exceeds the value of the interest. The burden of proving impairment is on the party asserting discharge.

(f) If the obligation of a party is secured by an interest in collateral not provided by an accommodation party and a person entitled to enforce the instrument impairs the value of the interest in collateral, the obligation of any party who is jointly and severally liable with respect to the secured obligation is discharged to the extent the impairment causes the party asserting discharge to pay more than that party would have been obliged to pay, taking into account rights of contribution, if impairment had not occurred. If the party asserting discharge is an accommodation party not entitled to discharge under subsection (e), the party is deemed to have a right to contribution based on joint and several liability rather than a right to reimbursement. The burden of proving impairment is on the party asserting discharge.

(g) Under subsection (e) or (f), impairing value of an interest in collateral includes (i) failure to obtain or maintain perfection or recordation of the interest in collateral, (ii) release of collateral without substitution of collateral of equal value, (iii) failure to perform a duty to preserve the value of collateral owed, under Article 9 or other law, to a debtor or surety or other person secondarily liable, or (iv) failure to comply with applicable law in disposing of collateral.

(h) An accommodation party is not discharged under subsection (c), (d), or (e) unless the person entitled to enforce the instrument knows of the accommodation or has notice under Section 3–419(c) that the instrument was signed for accommodation.

(i) A party is not discharged under this section if (i) the party asserting discharge consents to the event or conduct that is the basis of the discharge, or (ii) the instrument or a separate agreement of the party provides for waiver of discharge under this section either specifically or by general language indicating that parties waive defenses based on suretyship or impairment of collateral.

ADDENDUM TO REVISED ARTICLE 3

Notes to Legislative Counsel

1. If revised Article 3 is adopted in your state, the reference in Section 2–511 to Section 3–802 should be changed to Section 3–310.

2. If revised Article 3 is adopted in your state and the Uniform Fiduciaries Act is also in effect in your state, you may want to consider amending Uniform Fiduciaries Act § 9 to conform to Section 3–307(b)(2)(iii) and (4)(iii). See Official Comment 3 to Section 3–307.

Revised Article 4
BANK DEPOSITS AND COLLECTIONS

Part 1 General Provisions and Definitions

§ 4–101. Short Title.

This Article may be cited as Uniform Commercial Code—Bank Deposits and Collections.

As amended in 1990.

§ 4–102. Applicability.

(a) To the extent that items within this Article are also within Articles 3 and 8, they are subject to those Articles. If there is conflict, this Article governs Article 3, but Article 8 governs this Article.

(b) The liability of a bank for action or non-action with respect to an item handled by it for purposes of presentment, payment, or collection is governed by the law of the place where the bank is located. In the case of action or non-action by or at a branch or separate office of a bank, its liability is governed by the law of the place where the branch or separate office is located.

§ 4–103. Variation by Agreement; Measure of Damages; Action Constituting Ordinary Care.

(a) The effect of the provisions of this Article may be varied by agreement, but the parties to the agreement cannot disclaim a bank's responsibility for its lack of good faith or failure to exercise ordinary care or limit the measure of damages for the lack or failure. However, the parties may determine by agreement the standards by which the bank's responsibility is to be measured if those standards are not manifestly unreasonable.

(b) Federal Reserve regulations and operating circulars, clearinghouse rules, and the like have the effect of agreements under subsection (a), whether or not specifically assented to by all parties interested in items handled.

(c) Action or non-action approved by this Article or pursuant to Federal Reserve regulations or operating circulars is the exercise of ordinary care and, in the absence of special instructions, action or non-action consistent with clearing-house rules and the like or with a general banking usage not disapproved by this Article, is prima facie the exercise of ordinary care.

(d) The specification or approval of certain procedures by this Article is not disapproval of other procedures that may be reasonable under the circumstances.

(e) The measure of damages for failure to exercise ordinary care in handling an item is the amount of the item reduced by an amount that could not have been realized by the exercise of ordinary care. If there is also bad faith it includes any other damages the party suffered as a proximate consequence.

As amended in 1990.

§ 4–104. Definitions and Index of Definitions.

(a) In this Article, unless the context otherwise requires:

(1) "Account" means any deposit or credit account with a bank, including a demand, time, savings, passbook, share draft, or like account, other than an account evidenced by a certificate of deposit;

(2) "Afternoon" means the period of a day between noon and midnight;

(3) "Banking day" means the part of a day on which a bank is open to the public for carrying on substantially all of its banking functions;

(4) "Clearing house" means an association of banks or other payors regularly clearing items;

(5) "Customer" means a person having an account with a bank or for whom a bank has agreed to collect items, including a bank that maintains an account at another bank;

(6) "Documentary draft" means a draft to be presented for acceptance or payment if specified documents, certificated securities (Section 8–102) or instructions for uncertificated securities (Section 8–102), or other certificates, statements, or the like are to be received by the drawee or other payor before acceptance or payment of the draft;

(7) "Draft" means a draft as defined in Section 3–104 or an item, other than an instrument, that is an order;

(8) "Drawee" means a person ordered in a draft to make payment;

(9) "Item" means an instrument or a promise or order to pay money handled by a bank for collection or payment. The term does not include a payment order governed by Article 4A or a credit or debit card slip;

(10) "Midnight deadline" with respect to a bank is midnight on its next banking day following the banking day on which it receives the relevant item or notice or from which the time for taking action commences to run, whichever is later;

(11) "Settle" means to pay in cash, by clearing-house settlement, in a charge or credit or by remittance, or otherwise as agreed. A settlement may be either provisional or final;

(12) "Suspends payments" with respect to a bank means that it has been closed by order of the supervisory authorities, that a public officer has been appointed to take it over, or that it ceases or refuses to make payments in the ordinary course of business.

(b) [Other definitions' section references deleted.]

(c) [Other definitions' section references deleted.]

(d) In addition, Article 1 contains general definitions and principles of construction and interpretation applicable throughout this Article.

§ 4–105. "Bank"; "Depositary Bank"; "Payor Bank"; "Intermediary Bank"; "Collecting Bank"; "Presenting Bank".

In this Article:

(1) "Bank" means a person engaged in the business of banking, including a savings bank, savings and loan association, credit union, or trust company;

(2) "Depositary bank" means the first bank to take an item even though it is also the payor bank, unless the item is presented for immediate payment over the counter;

(3) "Payor bank" means a bank that is the drawee of a draft;

(4) "Intermediary bank" means a bank to which an item is transferred in course of collection except the depositary or payor bank;

(5) "Collecting bank" means a bank handling an item for collection except the payor bank;

(6) "Presenting bank" means a bank presenting an item except a payor bank.

§ 4–106. Payable Through or Payable at Bank: Collecting Bank.

(a) If an item states that it is "payable through" a bank identified in the item, (i) the item designates the bank as a collecting bank and does not by itself authorize the bank to pay the item, and (ii) the item may be presented for payment only by or through the bank.

Alternative A

(b) If an item states that it is "payable at" a bank identified in the item, the item is equivalent to a draft drawn on the bank.

Alternative B

(b) If an item states that it is "payable at" a bank identified in the item, (i) the item designates the bank as a collecting bank and does not by itself authorize the bank to pay the item, and (ii) the item may be presented for payment only by or through the bank.

(c) If a draft names a nonbank drawee and it is unclear whether a bank named in the draft is a co-drawee or a collecting bank, the bank is a collecting bank.

As added in 1990.

§ 4–107. Separate Office of Bank.

A branch or separate office of a bank is a separate bank for the purpose of computing the time within which and determining the place at or to which action may be taken or notices or orders shall be given under this Article and under Article 3.

As amended in 1962 and 1990.

§ 4–108. Time of Receipt of Items.

(a) For the purpose of allowing time to process items, prove balances, and make the necessary entries on its books to determine its position for the day, a bank may fix an afternoon hour of 2 P.M. or later as a cutoff hour for the handling of money and items and the making of entries on its books.

(b) An item or deposit of money received on any day after a cutoff hour so fixed or after the close of the banking day may be treated as being received at the opening of the next banking day.

As amended in 1990.

§ 4–109. Delays.

(a) Unless otherwise instructed, a collecting bank in a good faith effort to secure payment of a specific item drawn on a payor other than a bank, and with or without the approval of any person involved, may waive, modify, or extend time limits imposed or permitted by this [act] for a period not exceeding two additional banking days without discharge of drawers or indorsers or liability to its transferor or a prior party.

(b) Delay by a collecting bank or payor bank beyond time limits prescribed or permitted by this [act] or by instructions is excused if (i) the delay is caused by interruption of communication or computer facilities, suspension of payments by another bank, war, emergency conditions, failure of equipment, or other circumstances beyond the control of the bank, and (ii) the bank exercises such diligence as the circumstances require.

§ 4–110. Electronic Presentment.

(a) "Agreement for electronic presentment" means an agreement, clearing-house rule, or Federal Reserve regulation or operating circular, providing that presentment of an item may be made by transmission of an image of an item or information describing the item ("presentment notice") rather than delivery of the item itself. The agreement may provide for procedures governing retention, presentment, payment, dishonor, and other matters concerning items subject to the agreement.

(b) Presentment of an item pursuant to an agreement for presentment is made when the presentment notice is received.

(c) If presentment is made by presentment notice, a reference to "item" or "check" in this Article means the presentment notice unless the context otherwise indicates.

As added in 1990.

§ 4–111. Statute of Limitations.

An action to enforce an obligation, duty, or right arising under this Article must be commenced within three years after the [cause of action] accrues.

As added in 1990.

Part 2 Collection of Items: Depositary and Collecting Banks

§ 4–201. Status of Collecting Bank as Agent and Provisional Status of Credits; Applicability of Article; Item Indorsed "Pay Any Bank".

(a) Unless a contrary intent clearly appears and before the time that a settlement given by a collecting bank for an item is or becomes final, the bank, with respect to an item, is an agent or sub-agent of the owner of the item and any settlement given for the item is provisional. This provision applies regardless of the form of indorsement or lack of indorsement and even though credit given for the item is subject to immediate withdrawal as of right or is in fact withdrawn; but the continuance of ownership of an item by its owner and any rights of the owner to proceeds of the item are subject to rights of a collecting bank, such as those resulting from outstanding advances on the item and rights of recoupment or setoff. If an item is handled by banks for purposes of presentment, payment, collection, or return, the relevant provisions of this Article apply even though action of the parties clearly establishes that a particular bank has purchased the item and is the owner of it.

(b) After an item has been indorsed with the words "pay any bank" or the like, only a bank may acquire the rights of a holder until the item has been:

(1) returned to the customer initiating collection; or

(2) specially indorsed by a bank to a person who is not a bank.

As amended in 1990.

§ 4–202. Responsibility for Collection or Return; When Action Timely.

(a) A collecting bank must exercise ordinary care in:

(1) presenting an item or sending it for presentment;

(2) sending notice of dishonor or nonpayment or returning an item other than a documentary draft to the bank's transferor after learning that the item has not been paid or accepted, as the case may be;

(3) settling for an item when the bank receives final settlement; and

(4) notifying its transferor of any loss or delay in transit within a reasonable time after discovery thereof.

(b) A collecting bank exercises ordinary care under subsection (a) by taking proper action before its midnight deadline following receipt of an item, notice, or settlement. Taking proper action within a reasonably longer time may constitute the exercise of ordinary care, but the bank has the burden of establishing timeliness.

(c) Subject to subsection (a)(1), a bank is not liable for the insolvency, neglect, misconduct, mistake, or default of another bank or person or for loss or destruction of an item in the possession of others or in transit.

As amended in 1990.

§ 4–203. Effect of Instructions.

Subject to Article 3 concerning conversion of instruments (Section 3–420) and restrictive indorsements (Section 3–206), only a collecting bank's transferor can give instructions that affect the bank or constitute notice to it, and a collecting bank is not liable to prior parties for any action taken pursuant to the instructions or in accordance with any agreement with its transferor.

§ 4–204. Methods of Sending and Presenting; Sending Directly to Payor Bank.

(a) A collecting bank shall send items by a reasonably prompt method, taking into consideration relevant instructions, the nature of the item, the number of those items on hand, the cost of collection involved, and the method generally used by it or others to present those items.

(b) A collecting bank may send:

(1) an item directly to the payor bank;

(2) an item to a nonbank payor if authorized by its transferor; and

(3) an item other than documentary drafts to a nonbank payor, if authorized by Federal Reserve regulation or operating circular, clearing-house rule, or the like.

(c) Presentment may be made by a presenting bank at a place where the payor bank or other payor has requested that presentment be made.

As amended in 1990.

§ 4–205. Depositary Bank Holder of Unindorsed Item.

If a customer delivers an item to a depositary bank for collection:

(1) the depositary bank becomes a holder of the item at the time it receives the item for collection if the customer at the time of delivery was a holder of the item, whether or not the customer indorses the item, and, if the bank satisfies the other requirements of Section 3–302, it is a holder in due course; and

(2) the depositary bank warrants to collecting banks, the payor bank or other payor, and the drawer that the amount of the item was paid to the customer or deposited to the customer's account.

As amended in 1990.

§ 4–206. Transfer Between Banks.

Any agreed method that identifies the transferor bank is sufficient for the item's further transfer to another bank.

As amended in 1990.

§ 4–207. Transfer Warranties.

(a) A customer or collecting bank that transfers an item and receives a settlement or other consideration warrants to the transferee and to any subsequent collecting bank that:

(1) the warrantor is a person entitled to enforce the item;

(2) all signatures on the item are authentic and authorized;

(3) the item has not been altered;

(4) the item is not subject to a defense or claim in recoupment (Section 3–305(a)) of any party that can be asserted against the warrantor; and

(5) the warrantor has no knowledge of any insolvency proceeding commenced with respect to the maker or acceptor or, in the case of an unaccepted draft, the drawer.

(b) If an item is dishonored, a customer or collecting bank transferring the item and receiving settlement or other consideration is obliged to pay the amount due on the item (i) according to the terms of the item at the time it was transferred, or (ii) if the transfer was of an incomplete item, according to its terms when completed as stated in Sections 3–115 and 3–407. The obligation of a transferor is owed to the transferee and to any subsequent collecting bank that takes the item in good faith. A transferor cannot disclaim its obligation under this subsection by an indorsement stating that it is made "without recourse" or otherwise disclaiming liability.

(c) A person to whom the warranties under subsection (a) are made and who took the item in good faith may recover from the warrantor as damages for breach of warranty an amount equal to the loss suffered as a result of the breach, but not more than the amount of the item plus expenses and loss of interest incurred as a result of the breach.

(d) The warranties stated in subsection (a) cannot be disclaimed with respect to checks. Unless notice of a claim for breach of warranty is given to the warrantor within 30 days after the claimant has reason to know of the breach and the identity of the warrantor, the warrantor is discharged to the extent of any loss caused by the delay in giving notice of the claim.

(e) A cause of action for breach of warranty under this section accrues when the claimant has reason to know of the breach.

As amended in 1990.

§ 4–208. Presentment Warranties.

(a) If an unaccepted draft is presented to the drawee for payment or acceptance and the drawee pays or accepts the draft, (i) the person obtaining payment or acceptance, at the time of presentment, and (ii) a previous transferor of the draft, at the time of transfer, warrant to the drawee that pays or accepts the draft in good faith that:

(1) the warrantor is, or was, at the time the warrantor transferred the draft, a person entitled to enforce the draft or authorized to obtain payment or acceptance of the draft on behalf of a person entitled to enforce the draft;

(2) the draft has not been altered; and

(3) the warrantor has no knowledge that the signature of the purported drawer of the draft is unauthorized.

(b) A drawee making payment may recover from a warrantor damages for breach of warranty equal to the amount paid by the drawee less the amount the drawee received or is entitled to receive from the drawer because of the payment. In addition, the drawee is entitled to compensation for expenses and loss of interest resulting from the breach. The right of the drawee to recover damages under this subsection is not affected by any failure of the drawee to exercise ordinary care in making payment. If the drawee accepts the draft (i) breach of warranty is a defense to the obligation of the acceptor, and (ii) if the acceptor makes payment with respect to the draft, the acceptor is entitled to recover from a warrantor for breach of warranty the amounts stated in this subsection.

(c) If a drawee asserts a claim for breach of warranty under subsection (a) based on an unauthorized indorsement of the draft or an alteration of the draft, the warrantor may defend by proving that the indorsement is effective under Section 3–404 or 3–405 or the drawer is precluded under Section 3–406 or 4–406 from asserting against the drawee the unauthorized indorsement or alteration.

(d) If (i) a dishonored draft is presented for payment to the drawer or an indorser or (ii) any other item is presented for payment to a party obliged to pay the item, and the item is paid, the person obtaining payment and a prior transferor of the item warrant to the person making payment in good faith that the warrantor is, or was, at the time the warrantor transferred the item, a person entitled to enforce the item or authorized to obtain payment on behalf of a person entitled to enforce the item. The person making payment may recover from any warrantor for breach of warranty an amount equal to the amount paid plus expenses and loss of interest resulting from the breach.

(e) The warranties stated in subsections (a) and (d) cannot be disclaimed with respect to checks. Unless notice of a claim for breach of warranty is given to the warrantor within 30 days after the claimant has reason to know of the breach and the identity of the warrantor, the warrantor is discharged to the extent of any loss caused by the delay in giving notice of the claim.

(f) A cause of action for breach of warranty under this section accrues when the claimant has reason to know of the breach.

As amended in 1990.

§ 4–209. Encoding and Retention Warranties.

(a) A person who encodes information on or with respect to an item after issue warrants to any subsequent collecting bank and to the payor bank or other payor that the information is correctly encoded. If the customer of a depositary bank encodes, that bank also makes the warranty.

(b) A person who undertakes to retain an item pursuant to an agreement for electronic presentment warrants to any subsequent collecting bank and to the payor bank or other payor that retention and presentment of the item comply with the agreement. If a customer of a depositary bank undertakes to retain an item, that bank also makes this warranty.

(c) A person to whom warranties are made under this section and who took the item in good faith may recover from the warrantor as damages for breach of warranty an amount equal to the loss suffered as a result of the breach, plus expenses and loss of interest incurred as a result of the breach.

As added in 1990.

§ 4–210. Security Interest of Collecting Bank in Items, Accompanying Documents and Proceeds.

(a) A collecting bank has a security interest in an item and any accompanying documents or the proceeds of either:

(1) in case of an item deposited in an account, to the extent to which credit given for the item has been withdrawn or applied;

(2) in case of an item for which it has given credit available for withdrawal as of right, to the extent of the credit given, whether or not the credit is drawn upon or there is a right of charge-back; or

(3) if it makes an advance on or against the item.

(b) If credit given for several items received at one time or pursuant to a single agreement is withdrawn or applied in part, the security interest remains upon all the items, any accompanying documents or the proceeds of either. For the purpose of this section, credits first given are first withdrawn.

(c) Receipt by a collecting bank of a final settlement for an item is a realization on its security interest in the item, accompanying documents, and proceeds. So long as the bank does not receive final settlement for the item or give up possession of the item or accompanying documents for purposes other than collection, the security interest continues to that extent and is subject to Article 9, but:

(1) no security agreement is necessary to make the security interest enforceable (Section 9–203(1)(a));

(2) no filing is required to perfect the security interest; and

(3) the security interest has priority over conflicting perfected security interests in the item, accompanying documents, or proceeds.

As amended in 1990 and 1999.

§ 4–211. When Bank Gives Value for Purposes of Holder in Due Course.

For purposes of determining its status as a holder in due course, a bank has given value to the extent it has a security interest in an item, if the bank otherwise complies with the requirements of Section 3–302 on what constitutes a holder in due course.

As amended in 1990.

§ 4–212. Presentment by Notice of Item Not Payable by, Through, or at Bank; Liability of Drawer or Indorser.

(a) Unless otherwise instructed, a collecting bank may present an item not payable by, through, or at a bank by sending to the party to accept or pay a written notice that the bank holds the item for acceptance or payment. The notice must be sent in time to be received on or before the day when presentment is due and the bank must meet any requirement of the party to accept or pay under Section 3–501 by the close of the bank's next banking day after it knows of the requirement.

(b) If presentment is made by notice and payment, acceptance, or request for compliance with a requirement under Section 3–501 is not received by the close of business on the day after maturity or, in the case of demand items, by the close of business on the third banking day after notice was sent, the presenting bank may treat the item as dishonored and charge any drawer or indorser by sending it notice of the facts.

As amended in 1990.

§ 4–213. Medium and Time of Settlement by Bank.

(a) With respect to settlement by a bank, the medium and time of settlement may be prescribed by Federal Reserve regulations or circulars, clearing-house rules, and the like, or agreement. In the absence of such prescription:

(1) the medium of settlement is cash or credit to an account in a Federal Reserve bank of or specified by the person to receive settlement; and

(2) the time of settlement is:

(i) with respect to tender of settlement by cash, a cashier's check, or teller's check, when the cash or check is sent or delivered;

(ii) with respect to tender of settlement by credit in an account in a Federal Reserve Bank, when the credit is made;

(iii) with respect to tender of settlement by a credit or debit to an account in a bank, when the credit or debit is made or, in the case of tender of settlement by authority to charge an account, when the authority is sent or delivered; or

(iv) with respect to tender of settlement by a funds transfer, when payment is made pursuant to Section 4A–406(a) to the person receiving settlement.

(b) If the tender of settlement is not by a medium authorized by subsection (a) or the time of settlement is not fixed by subsection (a), no settlement occurs until the tender of settlement is accepted by the person receiving settlement.

(c) If settlement for an item is made by cashier's check or teller's check and the person receiving settlement, before its midnight deadline:

(1) presents or forwards the check for collection, settlement is final when the check is finally paid; or

(2) fails to present or forward the check for collection, settlement is final at the midnight deadline of the person receiving settlement.

(d) If settlement for an item is made by giving authority to charge the account of the bank giving settlement in the bank receiving settlement, settlement is final when the charge is made by the bank receiving settlement if there are funds available in the account for the amount of the item.

As amended in 1990.

§ 4–214. Right of Charge-Back or Refund; Liability of Collecting Bank: Return of Item.

(a) If a collecting bank has made provisional settlement with its customer for an item and fails by reason of dishonor, suspension of payments by a bank, or otherwise to receive settlement for the item which is or becomes final, the bank may revoke the settlement given by it, charge back the amount of any credit given for the item to its customer's account, or obtain refund from its customer, whether or not it is able to return the item, if by its midnight deadline or within a longer reasonable time after it learns the facts it returns the item or sends notification of the facts. If the return or notice is delayed beyond the bank's midnight deadline or a longer reasonable time after it learns the facts, the bank may revoke the settlement, charge back the credit, or obtain refund from its customer, but it is liable for any loss resulting from the delay. These rights to revoke, charge back, and obtain refund terminate if and when a settlement for the item received by the bank is or becomes final.

(b) A collecting bank returns an item when it is sent or delivered to the bank's customer or transferor or pursuant to its instructions.

(c) A depositary bank that is also the payor may charge back the amount of an item to its customer's account or obtain refund in accordance with the section governing return of an item received by a payor bank for credit on its books (Section 4–301).

(d) The right to charge back is not affected by:

(1) previous use of a credit given for the item; or

(2) failure by any bank to exercise ordinary care with respect to the item, but a bank so failing remains liable.

(e) A failure to charge back or claim refund does not affect other rights of the bank against the customer or any other party.

(f) If credit is given in dollars as the equivalent of the value of an item payable in foreign money, the dollar amount of any charge-back or refund must be calculated on the basis of the bank-offered spot rate for the foreign money prevailing on the day when the person entitled to the charge-back or refund learns that it will not receive payment in ordinary course.

As amended in 1990.

§ 4–215. Final Payment of Item by Payor Bank; When Provisional Debits and Credits Become Final; When Certain Credits Become Available for Withdrawal.

(a) An item is finally paid by a payor bank when the bank has first done any of the following:

(1) paid the item in cash;

(2) settled for the item without having a right to revoke the settlement under statute, clearing-house rule, or agreement; or

(3) made a provisional settlement for the item and failed to revoke the settlement in the time and manner permitted by statute, clearing-house rule, or agreement.

(b) If provisional settlement for an item does not become final, the item is not finally paid.

(c) If provisional settlement for an item between the presenting and payor banks is made through a clearing house or by debits or credits in an account between them, then to the extent that provisional debits or credits for the item are entered in accounts between the presenting and payor banks or between the presenting and successive prior collecting banks seriatim, they become final upon final payment of the item by the payor bank.

(d) If a collecting bank receives a settlement for an item which is or becomes final, the bank is accountable to its customer for the amount of the item and any provisional credit given for the item in an account with its customer becomes final.

(e) Subject to (i) applicable law stating a time for availability of funds and (ii) any right of the bank to apply the credit to an obligation of the customer, credit given by a bank for an item in a customer's account becomes available for withdrawal as of right:

(1) if the bank has received a provisional settlement for the item, when the settlement becomes final and the bank has had a reasonable time to receive return of the item and the item has not been received within that time;

(2) if the bank is both the depositary bank and the payor bank, and the item is finally paid, at the opening of the bank's second banking day following receipt of the item.

(f) Subject to applicable law stating a time for availability of funds and any right of a bank to apply a deposit to an obligation of the depositor, a deposit of money becomes available for withdrawal as of right at the opening of the bank's next banking day after receipt of the deposit.

As amended in 1990.

§ 4–216. Insolvency and Preference.

(a) If an item is in or comes into the possession of a payor or collecting bank that suspends payment and the item has not been finally paid, the item must be returned by the receiver, trustee, or agent in charge of the closed bank to the presenting bank or the closed bank's customer.

(b) If a payor bank finally pays an item and suspends payments without making a settlement for the item with its customer or the presenting bank which settlement is or becomes final, the owner of the item has a preferred claim against the payor bank.

(c) If a payor bank gives or a collecting bank gives or receives a provisional settlement for an item and thereafter suspends payments, the suspension does not prevent or interfere with the settlement's becoming final if the finality occurs automatically upon the lapse of certain time or the happening of certain events.

(d) If a collecting bank receives from subsequent parties settlement for an item, which settlement is or becomes final and the bank suspends payments without making a settlement for the item with its customer which settlement is or becomes final, the owner of the item has a preferred claim against the collecting bank.

As amended in 1990.

Part 3 Collection of Items: Payor Banks

§ 4–301. Deferred Posting; Recovery of Payment by Return of Items; Time of Dishonor; Return of Items by Payor Bank.

(a) If a payor bank settles for a demand item other than a documentary draft presented otherwise than for immediate payment over the counter before midnight of the banking day of receipt, the payor bank may revoke the settlement and recover the settlement if, before it has made final payment and before its midnight deadline, it

(1) returns the item; or

(2) sends written notice of dishonor or nonpayment if the item is unavailable for return.

(b) If a demand item is received by a payor bank for credit on its books, it may return the item or send notice of dishonor and may revoke any credit given or recover the amount thereof withdrawn by its customer, if it acts within the time limit and in the manner specified in subsection (a).

(c) Unless previous notice of dishonor has been sent, an item is dishonored at the time when for purposes of dishonor it is returned or notice sent in accordance with this section.

(d) An item is returned:

(1) as to an item presented through a clearing house, when it is delivered to the presenting or last collecting bank or to the clearing house or is sent or delivered in accordance with clearing-house rules; or

(2) in all other cases, when it is sent or delivered to the bank's customer or transferor or pursuant to instructions.

As amended in 1990.

§ 4–302. Payor Bank's Responsibility for Late Return of Item.

(a) If an item is presented to and received by a payor bank, the bank is accountable for the amount of:

(1) a demand item, other than a documentary draft, whether properly payable or not, if the bank, in any case in which it is not also the depositary bank, retains the item beyond midnight of the banking day of receipt without settling for it or, whether or not it is also the depositary bank, does not pay or return the item or send notice of dishonor until after its midnight deadline; or

(2) any other properly payable item unless, within the time allowed for acceptance or payment of that item, the bank either accepts or pays the item or returns it and accompanying documents.

(b) The liability of a payor bank to pay an item pursuant to subsection (a) is subject to defenses based on breach of a presentment warranty (Section 4–208) or proof that the person seeking enforcement of the liability presented or transferred the item for the purpose of defrauding the payor bank.

As amended in 1990.

§ 4–303. When Items Subject to Notice, Stop-Payment Order, Legal Process, or Setoff; Order in Which Items May Be Charged or Certified.

(a) Any knowledge, notice, or stop-payment order received by, legal process served upon, or setoff exercised by a payor bank comes too late to terminate, suspend, or modify the bank's right or duty to pay an item or to charge its customer's account for the item if the knowledge, notice, stop-payment order, or legal process is received or served and a reasonable time for the bank to act thereon expires or the setoff is exercised after the earliest of the following:

(1) the bank accepts or certifies the item;

(2) the bank pays the item in cash;

(3) the bank settles for the item without having a right to revoke the settlement under statute, clearing-house rule, or agreement;

(4) the bank becomes accountable for the amount of the item under Section 4–302 dealing with the payor bank's responsibility for late return of items; or

(5) with respect to checks, a cutoff hour no earlier than one hour after the opening of the next banking day after the banking day on which the bank received the check and no later than the close of that next banking day or, if no cutoff hour is fixed, the close of the next banking day after the banking day on which the bank received the check.

(b) Subject to subsection (a), items may be accepted, paid, certified, or charged to the indicated account of its customer in any order.

As amended in 1990.

Part 4 Relationship Between Payor Bank and Its Customer

§ 4–401. When Bank May Charge Customer's Account.

(a) A bank may charge against the account of a customer an item that is properly payable from the account even though the charge creates an overdraft. An item is properly payable if it is authorized by the customer and is in accordance with any agreement between the customer and bank.

(b) A customer is not liable for the amount of an overdraft if the customer neither signed the item nor benefited from the proceeds of the item.

(c) A bank may charge against the account of a customer a check that is otherwise properly payable from the account, even though payment was made before the date of the check, unless the customer has given notice to the bank of the postdating describing the check with reasonable certainty. The notice is effective for the period stated in Section 4–403(b) for stop-payment orders, and must be received at such time and in such manner as to afford the bank a reasonable opportunity to act on it before the bank takes any action with respect to the check described in Section 4–303. If a bank charges against the account of a customer a check before the date stated in the notice of postdating, the bank is liable for damages for the loss resulting from its act. The loss may include damages for dishonor of subsequent items under Section 4–402.

(d) A bank that in good faith makes payment to a holder may charge the indicated account of its customer according to:

(1) the original terms of the altered item; or

(2) the terms of the completed item, even though the bank knows the item has been completed unless the bank has notice that the completion was improper.

As amended in 1990.

§ 4–402. Bank's Liability to Customer for Wrongful Dishonor; Time of Determining Insufficiency of Account.

(a) Except as otherwise provided in this Article, a payor bank wrongfully dishonors an item if it dishonors an item that is properly payable, but a bank may dishonor an item that would create an overdraft unless it has agreed to pay the overdraft.

(b) A payor bank is liable to its customer for damages proximately caused by the wrongful dishonor of an item. Liability is limited to actual damages proved and may include damages for an arrest or prosecution of the customer or other consequential damages. Whether any consequential damages are proximately caused by the wrongful dishonor is a question of fact to be determined in each case.

(c) A payor bank's determination of the customer's account balance on which a decision to dishonor for insufficiency of available funds is based may be made at any time between the time the item is received by the payor bank and the time that the payor bank returns the item or gives notice in lieu of return, and no more than one determination need be made. If, at the election of the payor bank, a subsequent balance determination is made for the purpose of reevaluating the bank's decision to dishonor the item, the account balance at that time is determinative of whether a dishonor for insufficiency of available funds is wrongful.

As amended in 1990.

§ 4–403. Customer's Right to Stop Payment; Burden of Proof of Loss.

(a) A customer or any person authorized to draw on the account if there is more than one person may stop payment of any item drawn on the customer's account or close the account by an order to the bank describing the item or account with reasonable certainty received at a time and in a manner that affords the bank a reasonable opportunity to act on it before any action by the bank with respect to the item described in Section 4–303. If the signature of more than one person is required to draw on an account, any of these persons may stop payment or close the account.

(b) A stop-payment order is effective for six months, but it lapses after 14 calendar days if the original order was oral and was not confirmed in writing within that period. A stop-payment order may be renewed for additional six-month periods by a writing given to the bank within a period during which the stop-payment order is effective.

(c) The burden of establishing the fact and amount of loss resulting from the payment of an item contrary to a stop-payment order or order to close an account is on the customer. The loss from payment of an item contrary to a stop-payment order may include damages for dishonor of subsequent items under Section 4–402.

As amended in 1990.

§ 4–404. Bank Not Obliged to Pay Check More Than Six Months Old.

A bank is under no obligation to a customer having a checking account to pay a check, other than a certified check, which is presented more than six months after its date, but it may charge its customer's account for a payment made thereafter in good faith.

§ 4–405. Death or Incompetence of Customer.

(a) A payor or collecting bank's authority to accept, pay, or collect an item or to account for proceeds of its collection, if otherwise effective, is not rendered ineffective by incompetence of a customer of either bank existing at the time the item is issued or its collection is undertaken if the bank does not know of an adjudication of incompetence. Neither death nor incompetence of a customer revokes the authority to accept, pay, collect, or account until the bank knows of the fact of death or of an adjudication of incompetence and has reasonable opportunity to act on it.

(b) Even with knowledge, a bank may for 10 days after the date of death pay or certify checks drawn on or before the date unless ordered to stop payment by a person claiming an interest in the account.

As amended in 1990.

§ 4–406. Customer's Duty to Discover and Report Unauthorized Signature or Alteration.

(a) A bank that sends or makes available to a customer a statement of account showing payment of items for the account shall either return or make available to the customer the items paid or provide information in the statement of account sufficient to allow the customer reasonably to identify the items paid. The statement of account provides sufficient information if the item is described by item number, amount, and date of payment.

(b) If the items are not returned to the customer, the person retaining the items shall either retain the items or, if the items are destroyed, maintain the capacity to furnish legible copies of the items until the expiration of seven years after receipt of the items. A customer may request an item from the bank that paid the item, and that bank must provide in a reasonable time either the item or, if the item has been destroyed or is not otherwise obtainable, a legible copy of the item.

(c) If a bank sends or makes available a statement of account or items pursuant to subsection (a), the customer must exercise reasonable promptness in examining the statement or the items to determine whether any payment was not authorized because of an alteration of an item or because a purported signature by or on behalf of the customer was not authorized. If, based on the statement or items provided, the customer should reasonably have discovered the unauthorized payment, the customer must promptly notify the bank of the relevant facts.

(d) If the bank proves that the customer failed, with respect to an item, to comply with the duties imposed on the customer by subsection (c), the customer is precluded from asserting against the bank:

(1) the customer's unauthorized signature or any alteration on the item, if the bank also proves that it suffered a loss by reason of the failure; and

(2) the customer's unauthorized signature or alteration by the same wrongdoer on any other item paid in good faith by the bank if the payment was made before the bank received notice from the customer of the unauthorized signature or alteration and after the customer had been afforded a reasonable period of time, not exceeding 30 days, in which to examine the item or statement of account and notify the bank.

(e) If subsection (d) applies and the customer proves that the bank failed to exercise ordinary care in paying the item and that the failure substantially contributed to loss, the loss is allocated between the customer precluded and the bank asserting the preclusion according to the extent to which the failure of the customer to comply with subsection (c) and the failure of the bank to exercise ordinary care contributed to the loss. If the customer proves that the bank did not pay the item in good faith, the preclusion under subsection (d) does not apply.

(f) Without regard to care or lack of care of either the customer or the bank, a customer who does not within one year after the statement or items are made available to the customer (subsection (a)) discover and report the customer's unauthorized signature on or any alteration on the item is precluded from asserting against the bank the unauthorized signature or alteration. If there is a preclusion under this subsection, the payor bank may not recover for breach or warranty under Section 4–208 with respect to the unauthorized signature or alteration to which the preclusion applies.

As amended in 1990.

§ 4–407. Payor Bank's Right to Subrogation on Improper Payment.

If a payor has paid an item over the order of the drawer or maker to stop payment, or after an account has been closed, or otherwise under circumstances giving a basis for objection by the drawer or maker, to prevent unjust enrichment and only to the extent necessary to prevent loss to the bank by reason of its payment of the item, the payor bank is subrogated to the rights

(1) of any holder in due course on the item against the drawer or maker;

(2) of the payee or any other holder of the item against the drawer or maker either on the item or under the transaction out of which the item arose; and

(3) of the drawer or maker against the payee or any other holder of the item with respect to the transaction out of which the item arose.

As amended in 1990.

Part 5 Collection of Documentary Drafts

§ 4–501. Handling of Documentary Drafts; Duty to Send for Presentment and to Notify Customer of Dishonor.

A bank that takes a documentary draft for collection shall present or send the draft and accompanying documents for presentment and, upon learning that the draft has not been paid or accepted in due course, shall seasonably notify its customer of the fact even though it may have discounted or bought the draft or extended credit available for withdrawal as of right.

As amended in 1990.

§ 4–502. Presentment of "On Arrival" Drafts.

If a draft or the relevant instructions require presentment "on arrival", "when goods arrive" or the like, the collecting bank need not present until in its judgment a reasonable time for arrival of the goods has expired. Refusal to pay or accept because the goods have not arrived is not dishonor; the bank must notify its transferor of the refusal but need not present the draft again until it is instructed to do so or learns of the arrival of the goods.

§ 4–503. Responsibility of Presenting Bank for Documents and Goods; Report of Reasons for Dishonor; Referee in Case of Need.

Unless otherwise instructed and except as provided in Article 5, a bank presenting a documentary draft:

(1) must deliver the documents to the drawee on acceptance of the draft if it is payable more than three days after presentment, otherwise, only on payment; and

(2) upon dishonor, either in the case of presentment for acceptance or presentment for payment, may seek and follow instructions from any referee in case of need designated in the draft or, if the presenting bank does not choose to utilize the referee's services, it must use diligence and good faith to ascertain the reason for dishonor, must notify its transferor of the dishonor and of the results of its effort to ascertain the reasons therefor, and must request instructions.

However, the presenting bank is under no obligation with respect to goods represented by the documents except to follow any reasonable instructions seasonably received; it has a right to reimbursement for any expense incurred in following instructions and to prepayment of or indemnity for those expenses.

As amended in 1990.

§ 4–504. Privilege of Presenting Bank to Deal With Goods; Security Interest for Expenses.

(a) A presenting bank that, following the dishonor of a documentary draft, has seasonably requested instructions but does not receive them within a reasonable time may store, sell, or otherwise deal with the goods in any reasonable manner.

(b) For its reasonable expenses incurred by action under subsection (a) the presenting bank has a lien upon the goods or their proceeds, which may be foreclosed in the same manner as an unpaid seller's lien.

As amended in 1990.

Article 4A
FUNDS TRANSFERS

Part 1 Subject Matter and Definitions

§ 4A–101. Short Title.

This Article may be cited as Uniform Commercial Code—Funds Transfers.

§ 4A–102. Subject Matter.

Except as otherwise provided in Section 4A–108, this Article applies to funds transfers defined in Section 4A–104.

§ 4A–103. Payment Order–Definitions.

(a) In this Article:

(1) "Payment order" means an instruction of a sender to a receiving bank, transmitted orally, electronically, or in writing, to pay, or to cause another bank to pay, a fixed or determinable amount of money to a beneficiary if:

(i) the instruction does not state a condition to payment to the beneficiary other than time of payment,

(ii) the receiving bank is to be reimbursed by debiting an account of, or otherwise receiving payment from, the sender, and

(iii) the instruction is transmitted by the sender directly to the receiving bank or to an agent, funds-transfer system, or communication system for transmittal to the receiving bank.

(2) "Beneficiary" means the person to be paid by the beneficiary's bank.

(3) "Beneficiary's bank" means the bank identified in a payment order in which an account of the beneficiary is to be credited pursuant to the order or which otherwise is to make payment to the beneficiary if the order does not provide for payment to an account.

(4) "Receiving bank" means the bank to which the sender's instruction is addressed.

(5) "Sender" means the person giving the instruction to the receiving bank.

(b) If an instruction complying with subsection (a)(1) is to make more than one payment to a beneficiary, the instruction is a separate payment order with respect to each payment.

(c) A payment order is issued when it is sent to the receiving bank.

§ 4A–104. Funds Transfer–Definitions.

In this Article:

(a) "Funds transfer" means the series of transactions, beginning with the originator's payment order, made for the purpose of making payment to the beneficiary of the order. The term includes any payment order issued by the originator's bank or an intermediary bank intended to carry out the originator's payment order. A funds transfer is completed by acceptance by the beneficiary's bank of a payment order for the benefit of the beneficiary of the originator's payment order.

(b) "Intermediary bank" means a receiving bank other than the originator's bank or the beneficiary's bank.

(c) "Originator" means the sender of the first payment order in a funds transfer.

(d) "Originator's bank" means (i) the receiving bank to which the payment order of the originator is issued if the originator is not a bank, or (ii) the originator if the originator is a bank.

§ 4A–105. Other Definitions.

(a) In this Article:

(1) "Authorized account" means a deposit account of a customer in a bank designated by the customer as a source of payment of payment orders issued by the customer to the bank. If a customer does not so designate an account, any account of the customer is an authorized account if payment of a payment order from that account is not inconsistent with a restriction on the use of that account.

(2) "Bank" means a person engaged in the business of banking and includes a savings bank, savings and loan association, credit union, and trust company. A branch or separate office of a bank is a separate bank for purposes of this Article.

(3) "Customer" means a person, including a bank, having an account with a bank or from whom a bank has agreed to receive payment orders.

(4) "Funds-transfer business day" of a receiving bank means the part of a day during which the receiving bank is open for the receipt, processing, and transmittal of payment orders and cancellations and amendments of payment orders.

(5) "Funds-transfer system" means a wire transfer network, automated clearing house, or other communication system of a clearing house or other association of banks through which a payment order by a bank may be transmitted to the bank to which the order is addressed.

(6) "Good faith" means honesty in fact and the observance of reasonable commercial standards of fair dealing.

(7) "Prove" with respect to a fact means to meet the burden of establishing the fact (Section 1–201(8)).

(b) Other definitions applying to this Article and the sections in which they appear are:

"Acceptance"	Section 4A–209
"Beneficiary"	Section 4A–103
"Beneficiary's bank"	Section 4A–103
"Executed"	Section 4A–301
"Execution date"	Section 4A–301
"Funds transfer"	Section 4A–104
"Funds-transfer system rule"	Section 4A–501
"Intermediary bank"	Section 4A–104
"Originator"	Section 4A–104
"Originator's bank"	Section 4A–104
"Payment by beneficiary's bank to beneficiary"	Section 4A–405
"Payment by originator to beneficiary"	Section 4A–406
"Payment by sender to receiving bank"	Section 4A–403
"Payment date"	Section 4A–401
"Payment order"	Section 4A–103
"Receiving bank"	Section 4A–103
"Security procedure"	Section 4A–201
"Sender"	Section 4A–103

(c) The following definitions in Article 4 apply to this Article:

"Clearing house"	Section 4–104
"Item"	Section 4–104
"Suspends payments"	Section 4–104

(d) In addition, Article 1 contains general definitions and principles of construction and interpretation applicable throughout this Article.

§ 4A–106. Time Payment Order Is Received.

(a) The time of receipt of a payment order or communication cancelling or amending a payment order is determined by the rules applicable to receipt of a notice stated in Section 1–201(27). A receiving bank may fix a cut-off time or times on a funds-transfer business day for the receipt and processing of payment orders and communications cancelling or amending payment orders. Different cut-off times may apply to payment orders, cancellations, or amendments, or to different categories of payment orders, cancellations, or amendments. A cut-off time may apply to senders generally or different cut-off times may apply to different senders or categories of payment orders. If a payment order or communication cancelling or amending a payment order is received after the close of a funds-transfer business day or after the appropriate cut-off time on a funds-transfer business day, the receiving bank may treat the payment order or communication as received at the opening of the next funds-transfer business day.

(b) If this Article refers to an execution date or payment date or states a day on which a receiving bank is required to take action, and the date or day does not fall on a funds-transfer business day, the next day that is a funds-transfer business day is treated as the date or day stated, unless the contrary is stated in this Article.

§ 4A–107. Federal Reserve Regulations and Operating Circulars.

Regulations of the Board of Governors of the Federal Reserve System and operating circulars of the Federal Reserve Banks supersede any inconsistent provision of this Article to the extent of the inconsistency.

§ 4A–108. Exclusion of Consumer Transactions Governed by Federal Law.

This Article does not apply to a funds transfer any part of which is governed by the Electronic Fund Transfer Act of 1978 (Title XX, Public Law 95–630, 92 Stat. 3728, 15 U.S.C. § 1693 et seq.) as amended from time to time.

Part 2 Issue and Acceptance of Payment Order

§ 4A–201. Security Procedure.

"Security procedure" means a procedure established by agreement of a customer and a receiving bank for the purpose of (i) verifying that a payment order or communication amending or cancelling a payment order is that of the customer, or (ii) detecting error in the transmission or the content of the payment order or communication. A security procedure may require the use of algorithms or other codes, identifying words or numbers, encryption, callback procedures, or similar security devices. Comparison of a signature on a payment order or communication with an authorized specimen signature of the customer is not by itself a security procedure.

§ 4A–202. Authorized and Verified Payment Orders.

(a) A payment order received by the receiving bank is the authorized order of the person identified as sender if that person authorized the order or is otherwise bound by it under the law of agency.

(b) If a bank and its customer have agreed that the authenticity of payment orders issued to the bank in the name of the customer as sender will be verified pursuant to a security procedure, a payment order received by the receiving bank is effective as the order of the customer, whether or not authorized, if (i) the security procedure is a commercially reasonable method of providing security against unauthorized payment orders, and (ii) the bank proves that it accepted the payment order in good faith and in compliance with the security procedure and any written agreement or instruction of the customer restricting acceptance of payment orders issued in the name of the customer. The bank is not required to follow an instruction that violates a written agreement with the customer or notice of which is not received at a time and in a manner affording the bank a reasonable opportunity to act on it before the payment order is accepted.

(c) Commercial reasonableness of a security procedure is a question of law to be determined by considering the wishes of the customer expressed to the bank, the circumstances of the customer known to the bank, including the size, type, and frequency of payment orders normally issued by the customer to the bank, alternative security procedures offered to the customer, and security procedures in general use by customers and receiving banks similarly situated. A security procedure is deemed to be commercially reasonable if (i) the security procedure was chosen by the customer after the bank offered, and the customer refused, a security procedure that was commercially reasonable for that customer, and (ii) the customer expressly agreed in writing to be bound by any payment order, whether or not authorized, issued in its name and accepted by the bank in compliance with the security procedure chosen by the customer.

(d) The term "sender" in this Article includes the customer in whose name a payment order is issued if the order is the authorized order of the customer under subsection (a), or it is effective as the order of the customer under subsection (b).

(e) This section applies to amendments and cancellations of payment orders to the same extent it applies to payment orders.

(f) Except as provided in this section and in Section 4A–203(a)(1), rights and obligations arising under this section or Section 4A–203 may not be varied by agreement.

§ 4A–203. Unenforceability of Certain Verified Payment Orders.

(a) If an accepted payment order is not, under Section 4A–202(a), an authorized order of a customer identified as sender, but is effective as an order of the customer pursuant to Section 4A–202(b), the following rules apply:

(1) By express written agreement, the receiving bank may limit the extent to which it is entitled to enforce or retain payment of the payment order.

(2) The receiving bank is not entitled to enforce or retain payment of the payment order if the customer proves that the order was not caused, directly or indirectly, by a person (i) entrusted at any time with duties to act for the customer with respect to payment orders or the security procedure, or (ii) who obtained access to transmitting facilities of the customer or who obtained, from a source controlled by the customer and without authority of the receiving bank, information facilitating breach of the security procedure, regardless of how the information was obtained or whether the customer was at fault. Information includes any access device, computer software, or the like.

(b) This section applies to amendments of payment orders to the same extent it applies to payment orders.

§ 4A–204. Refund of Payment and Duty of Customer to Report with Respect to Unauthorized Payment Order.

(a) If a receiving bank accepts a payment order issued in the name of its customer as sender which is (i) not authorized and not effective as the order of the customer under Section 4A–202, or (ii) not enforceable, in whole or in part, against the customer under Section 4A–203, the bank shall refund any payment of the payment order received from the customer to the extent the bank is not entitled to enforce payment and shall pay interest on the refundable amount calculated from the date the bank received payment to the date of the refund. However, the customer is not entitled to interest from the bank on the amount to be refunded if the customer fails to exercise ordinary care to determine that the order was not authorized by the customer and to notify the bank of the relevant facts within a reasonable time not exceeding 90 days after the date the customer received notification from the bank that the order was accepted or that the customer's account was debited with respect to the order. The bank is not entitled to any recovery from the customer on account of a failure by the customer to give notification as stated in this section.

(b) Reasonable time under subsection (a) may be fixed by agreement as stated in Section 1–204(1), but the obligation of a receiving bank to refund payment as stated in subsection (a) may not otherwise be varied by agreement.

§ 4A–205. Erroneous Payment Orders.

(a) If an accepted payment order was transmitted pursuant to a security procedure for the detection of error and the payment order (i) erroneously instructed payment to a beneficiary not intended by the sender, (ii) erroneously instructed payment in an amount greater than the amount intended by the sender, or (iii) was an erroneously transmitted duplicate of a payment order previously sent by the sender, the following rules apply:

(1) If the sender proves that the sender or a person acting on behalf of the sender pursuant to Section 4A–206 complied with the security procedure and that the error would have been detected if the receiving bank had also complied, the sender is not obliged to pay the order to the extent stated in paragraphs (2) and (3).

(2) If the funds transfer is completed on the basis of an erroneous payment order described in clause (i) or (iii) of subsection (a), the sender is not obliged to pay the order and the receiving bank is entitled to recover from the beneficiary any amount paid to the beneficiary to the extent allowed by the law governing mistake and restitution.

(3) If the funds transfer is completed on the basis of a payment order described in clause (ii) of subsection (a), the sender is not obliged to pay the order to the extent the amount received by the beneficiary is greater than the amount intended by the sender. In that case, the receiving bank is entitled to recover from the beneficiary the excess amount received to the extent allowed by the law governing mistake and restitution.

(b) If (i) the sender of an erroneous payment order described in subsection (a) is not obliged to pay all or part of the order, and (ii) the sender receives notification from the receiving bank that the order was accepted by the bank or that the sender's account was debited with respect to the order, the sender has a duty to exercise ordinary care, on the basis of information available to the sender, to discover the error with respect to the order and to advise the bank of the relevant facts within a reasonable time, not exceeding 90 days, after the bank's notification was received by the sender. If the bank proves that the sender failed to perform that duty, the sender is liable to the bank for the loss the bank proves it incurred as a result of the failure, but the liability of the sender may not exceed the amount of the sender's order.

(c) This section applies to amendments to payment orders to the same extent it applies to payment orders.

§ 4A–206. Transmission of Payment Order through Funds-Transfer or Other Communication System.

(a) If a payment order addressed to a receiving bank is transmitted to a funds-transfer system or other third party communication system for transmittal to the bank, the system is deemed to be an agent of the sender for the purpose of transmitting the payment order to the bank. If there is a discrepancy between the terms of the payment order transmitted to the system and the terms of the payment order transmitted by the system to the bank, the terms of the payment order of the sender are those transmitted by the system. This section does not apply to a funds-transfer system of the Federal Reserve Banks.

(b) This section applies to cancellations and amendments to payment orders to the same extent it applies to payment orders.

§ 4A–207. Misdescription of Beneficiary.

(a) Subject to subsection (b), if, in a payment order received by the beneficiary's bank, the name, bank account number, or other identification of the beneficiary refers to a nonexistent or unidentifiable person or account, no person has rights as a beneficiary of the order and acceptance of the order cannot occur.

(b) If a payment order received by the beneficiary's bank identifies the beneficiary both by name and by an identifying or bank account number and the name and number identify different persons, the following rules apply:

(1) Except as otherwise provided in subsection (c), if the beneficiary's bank does not know that the name and number refer to different persons, it may rely on the number as the proper identification of the beneficiary of the order. The beneficiary's bank need not determine whether the name and number refer to the same person.

(2) If the beneficiary's bank pays the person identified by name or knows that the name and number identify different persons, no person has rights as beneficiary except the person paid by the beneficiary's bank if that person was entitled to

(2) if the proceeds are not goods, to the extent that the secured party identifies the proceeds by a method of tracing, including application of equitable principles, that is permitted under law other than this article with respect to commingled property of the type involved.

(c) A security interest in proceeds is a perfected security interest if the security interest in the original collateral was perfected.

(d) A perfected security interest in proceeds becomes unperfected on the 21st day after the security interest attaches to the proceeds unless:

(1) the following conditions are satisfied:

(A) a filed financing statement covers the original collateral;

(B) the proceeds are collateral in which a security interest may be perfected by filing in the office in which the financing statement has been filed; and

(C) the proceeds are not acquired with cash proceeds;

(2) the proceeds are identifiable cash proceeds; or

(3) the security interest in the proceeds is perfected other than under subsection (c) when the security interest attaches to the proceeds or within 20 days thereafter.

(e) If a filed financing statement covers the original collateral, a security interest in proceeds which remains perfected under subsection (d)(1) becomes unperfected at the later of:

(1) when the effectiveness of the filed financing statement lapses under Section 9–515 or is terminated under Section 9–513; or

(2) the 21st day after the security interest attaches to the proceeds.

§ 9–316. Continued Perfection of Security Interest Following Change in Governing Law.

(a) A security interest perfected pursuant to the law of the jurisdiction designated in Section 9–301(1) or 9–305(c) remains perfected until the earliest of:

(1) the time perfection would have ceased under the law of that jurisdiction;

(2) the expiration of four months after a change of the debtor's location to another jurisdiction; or

(3) the expiration of one year after a transfer of collateral to a person that thereby becomes a debtor and is located in another jurisdiction.

(b) If a security interest described in subsection (a) becomes perfected under the law of the other jurisdiction before the earliest time or event described in that subsection, it remains perfected thereafter. If the security interest does not become perfected under the law of the other jurisdiction before the earliest time or event, it becomes unperfected and is deemed never to have been perfected as against a purchaser of the collateral for value.

(c) A possessory security interest in collateral, other than goods covered by a certificate of title and as-extracted collateral consisting of goods, remains continuously perfected if:

(1) the collateral is located in one jurisdiction and subject to a security interest perfected under the law of that jurisdiction;

(2) thereafter the collateral is brought into another jurisdiction; and

(3) upon entry into the other jurisdiction, the security interest is perfected under the law of the other jurisdiction.

(d) Except as otherwise provided in subsection (e), a security interest in goods covered by a certificate of title which is perfected by any method under the law of another jurisdiction when the goods become covered by a certificate of title from this State remains perfected until the security interest would have become unperfected under the law of the other jurisdiction had the goods not become so covered.

(e) A security interest described in subsection (d) becomes unperfected as against a purchaser of the goods for value and is deemed never to have been perfected as against a purchaser of the goods for value if the applicable requirements for perfection under Section 9–311(b) or 9–313 are not satisfied before the earlier of:

(1) the time the security interest would have become unperfected under the law of the other jurisdiction had the goods not become covered by a certificate of title from this State; or

(2) the expiration of four months after the goods had become so covered.

(f) A security interest in deposit accounts, letter-of-credit rights, or investment property which is perfected under the law of the bank's jurisdiction, the issuer's jurisdiction, a nominated person's jurisdiction, the securities intermediary's jurisdiction, or the commodity intermediary's jurisdiction, as applicable, remains perfected until the earlier of:

(1) the time the security interest would have become unperfected under the law of that jurisdiction; or

(2) the expiration of four months after a change of the applicable jurisdiction to another jurisdiction.

(g) If a security interest described in subsection (f) becomes perfected under the law of the other jurisdiction before the earlier of the time or the end of the period described in that subsection, it remains perfected thereafter. If the security interest does not become perfected under the law of the other jurisdiction before the earlier of that time or the end of that period, it becomes unperfected and is deemed never to have been perfected as against a purchaser of the collateral for value.

[Subpart 3. Priority]

§ 9–317. Interests That Take Priority over or Take Free of Security Interest or Agricultural Lien.

(a) A security interest or agricultural lien is subordinate to the rights of:

(1) a person entitled to priority under Section 9–322; and

(2) except as otherwise provided in subsection (e), a person that becomes a lien creditor before the earlier of the time:

(A) the security interest or agricultural lien is perfected; or

(B) one of the conditions specified in Section 9–203(b)(3) is met and a financing statement covering the collateral is filed.

(b) Except as otherwise provided in subsection (e), a buyer, other than a secured party, of tangible chattel paper, documents, goods, instruments, or a security certificate takes free of a security interest or agricultural lien if the buyer gives value and receives delivery of the collateral without knowledge of the security interest or agricultural lien and before it is perfected.

(c) Except as otherwise provided in subsection (e), a lessee of goods takes free of a security interest or agricultural lien if the lessee gives value and receives delivery of the collateral without knowledge of the security interest or agricultural lien and before it is perfected.

(d) A licensee of a general intangible or a buyer, other than a secured party, of accounts, electronic chattel paper, general intangibles, or investment property other than a certificated security takes free of a security interest if the licensee or buyer gives value without knowledge of the security interest and before it is perfected.

(e) Except as otherwise provided in Sections 9–320 and 9–321, if a person files a financing statement with respect to a purchase-money security interest before or within 20 days after the debtor receives delivery of the collateral, the security interest takes priority over the rights of a buyer, lessee, or lien creditor which arise between the time the security interest attaches and the time of filing.

As amended in 2000.

§ 9–318. No Interest Retained in Right to Payment That Is Sold; Rights and Title of Seller of Account or Chattel Paper with Respect to Creditors and Purchasers.

(a) A debtor that has sold an account, chattel paper, payment intangible, or promissory note does not retain a legal or equitable interest in the collateral sold.

(b) For purposes of determining the rights of creditors of, and purchasers for value of an account or chattel paper from, a debtor that has sold an account or chattel paper, while the buyer's security interest is unperfected, the debtor is deemed to have rights and title to the account or chattel paper identical to those the debtor sold.

§ 9–319. Rights and Title of Consignee with Respect to Creditors and Purchasers.

(a) Except as otherwise provided in subsection (b), for purposes of determining the rights of creditors of, and purchasers for value of goods from, a consignee, while the goods are in the possession of the consignee, the consignee is deemed to have rights and title to the goods identical to those the consignor had or had power to transfer.

(b) For purposes of determining the rights of a creditor of a consignee, law other than this article determines the rights and title of a consignee while goods are in the consignee's possession if, under this part, a perfected security interest held by the consignor would have priority over the rights of the creditor.

§ 9–320. Buyer of Goods.

(a) Except as otherwise provided in subsection (e), a buyer in ordinary course of business, other than a person buying farm products from a person engaged in farming operations, takes free of a security interest created by the buyer's seller, even if the security interest is perfected and the buyer knows of its existence.

(b) Except as otherwise provided in subsection (e), a buyer of goods from a person who used or bought the goods for use primarily for personal, family, or household purposes takes free of a security interest, even if perfected, if the buyer buys:

(1) without knowledge of the security interest;

(2) for value;

(3) primarily for the buyer's personal, family, or household purposes; and

(4) before the filing of a financing statement covering the goods.

(c) To the extent that it affects the priority of a security interest over a buyer of goods under subsection (b), the period of effectiveness of a filing made in the jurisdiction in which the seller is located is governed by Section 9–316(a) and (b).

(d) A buyer in ordinary course of business buying oil, gas, or other minerals at the wellhead or minehead or after extraction takes free of an interest arising out of an encumbrance.

(e) Subsections (a) and (b) do not affect a security interest in goods in the possession of the secured party under Section 9–313.

§ 9–321. Licensee of General Intangible and Lessee of Goods in Ordinary Course of Business.

(a) In this section, "licensee in ordinary course of business" means a person that becomes a licensee of a general intangible in good faith, without knowledge that the license violates the rights of another person in the general intangible, and in the ordinary course from a person in the business of licensing general intangibles of that kind. A person becomes a licensee in the ordinary course if the license to the person comports with the usual or customary practices in the kind of business in which the licensor is engaged or with the licensor's own usual or customary practices.

(b) A licensee in ordinary course of business takes its rights under a nonexclusive license free of a security interest in the general intangible created by the licensor, even if the security interest is perfected and the licensee knows of its existence.

(c) A lessee in ordinary course of business takes its leasehold interest free of a security interest in the goods created by the lessor, even if the security interest is perfected and the lessee knows of its existence.

§ 9–322. **Priorities among Conflicting Security Interests in and Agricultural Liens on Same Collateral.**

(a) Except as otherwise provided in this section, priority among conflicting security interests and agricultural liens in the same collateral is determined according to the following rules:

(1) Conflicting perfected security interests and agricultural liens rank according to priority in time of filing or perfection. Priority dates from the earlier of the time a filing covering the collateral is first made or the security interest or agricultural lien is first perfected, if there is no period thereafter when there is neither filing nor perfection.

(2) A perfected security interest or agricultural lien has priority over a conflicting unperfected security interest or agricultural lien.

(3) The first security interest or agricultural lien to attach or become effective has priority if conflicting security interests and agricultural liens are unperfected.

(b) For the purposes of subsection (a)(1):

(1) the time of filing or perfection as to a security interest in collateral is also the time of filing or perfection as to a security interest in proceeds; and

(2) the time of filing or perfection as to a security interest in collateral supported by a supporting obligation is also the time of filing or perfection as to a security interest in the supporting obligation.

(c) Except as otherwise provided in subsection (f), a security interest in collateral which qualifies for priority over a conflicting security interest under Section 9–327, 9–328, 9–329, 9–330, or 9–331 also has priority over a conflicting security interest in:

(1) any supporting obligation for the collateral; and

(2) proceeds of the collateral if:

(A) the security interest in proceeds is perfected;

(B) the proceeds are cash proceeds or of the same type as the collateral; and

(C) in the case of proceeds that are proceeds of proceeds, all intervening proceeds are cash proceeds, proceeds of the same type as the collateral, or an account relating to the collateral.

(d) Subject to subsection (e) and except as otherwise provided in subsection (f), if a security interest in chattel paper, deposit accounts, negotiable documents, instruments, investment property, or letter-of-credit rights is perfected by a method other than filing, conflicting perfected security interests in proceeds of the collateral rank according to priority in time of filing.

(e) Subsection (d) applies only if the proceeds of the collateral are not cash proceeds, chattel paper, negotiable documents, instruments, investment property, or letter-of-credit rights.

(f) Subsections (a) through (e) are subject to:

(1) subsection (g) and the other provisions of this part;

(2) Section 4–210 with respect to a security interest of a collecting bank;

(3) Section 5–118 with respect to a security interest of an issuer or nominated person; and

(4) Section 9–110 with respect to a security interest arising under Article 2 or 2A.

(g) A perfected agricultural lien on collateral has priority over a conflicting security interest in or agricultural lien on the same collateral if the statute creating the agricultural lien so provides.

§ 9–323. **Future Advances.**

(a) Except as otherwise provided in subsection (c), for purposes of determining the priority of a perfected security interest under Section 9–322(a)(1), perfection of the security interest dates from the time an advance is made to the extent that the security interest secures an advance that:

(1) is made while the security interest is perfected only:

(A) under Section 9–309 when it attaches; or

(B) temporarily under Section 9–312(e), (f), or (g); and

(2) is not made pursuant to a commitment entered into before or while the security interest is perfected by a method other than under Section 9–309 or 9–312(e), (f), or (g).

(b) Except as otherwise provided in subsection (c), a security interest is subordinate to the rights of a person that becomes a lien creditor to the extent that the security interest secures an advance made more than 45 days after the person becomes a lien creditor unless the advance is made:

(1) without knowledge of the lien; or

(2) pursuant to a commitment entered into without knowledge of the lien.

(c) Subsections (a) and (b) do not apply to a security interest held by a secured party that is a buyer of accounts, chattel paper, payment intangibles, or promissory notes or a consignor.

(d) Except as otherwise provided in subsection (e), a buyer of goods other than a buyer in ordinary course of business takes free of a security interest to the extent that it secures advances made after the earlier of:

(1) the time the secured party acquires knowledge of the buyer's purchase; or

(2) 45 days after the purchase.

(e) Subsection (d) does not apply if the advance is made pursuant to a commitment entered into without knowledge of the buyer's purchase and before the expiration of the 45-day period.

(f) Except as otherwise provided in subsection (g), a lessee of goods, other than a lessee in ordinary course of business, takes the leasehold interest free of a security interest to the extent that it secures advances made after the earlier of:

(1) the time the secured party acquires knowledge of the lease; or

(2) 45 days after the lease contract becomes enforceable.

(g) Subsection (f) does not apply if the advance is made pursuant to a commitment entered into without knowledge of the lease and before the expiration of the 45-day period.

As amended in 1999.

§ 9–324. Priority of Purchase-Money Security Interests.

(a) Except as otherwise provided in subsection (g), a perfected purchase-money security interest in goods other than inventory or livestock has priority over a conflicting security interest in the same goods, and, except as otherwise provided in Section 9–327, a perfected security interest in its identifiable proceeds also has priority, if the purchase-money security interest is perfected when the debtor receives possession of the collateral or within 20 days thereafter.

(b) Subject to subsection (c) and except as otherwise provided in subsection (g), a perfected purchase-money security interest in inventory has priority over a conflicting security interest in the same inventory, has priority over a conflicting security interest in chattel paper or an instrument constituting proceeds of the inventory and in proceeds of the chattel paper, if so provided in Section 9–330, and, except as otherwise provided in Section 9–327, also has priority in identifiable cash proceeds of the inventory to the extent the identifiable cash proceeds are received on or before the delivery of the inventory to a buyer, if:

(1) the purchase-money security interest is perfected when the debtor receives possession of the inventory;

(2) the purchase-money secured party sends an authenticated notification to the holder of the conflicting security interest;

(3) the holder of the conflicting security interest receives the notification within five years before the debtor receives possession of the inventory; and

(4) the notification states that the person sending the notification has or expects to acquire a purchase-money security interest in inventory of the debtor and describes the inventory.

(c) Subsections (b)(2) through (4) apply only if the holder of the conflicting security interest had filed a financing statement covering the same types of inventory:

(1) if the purchase-money security interest is perfected by filing, before the date of the filing; or

(2) if the purchase-money security interest is temporarily perfected without filing or possession under Section 9–312(f), before the beginning of the 20-day period thereunder.

(d) Subject to subsection (e) and except as otherwise provided in subsection (g), a perfected purchase-money security interest in livestock that are farm products has priority over a conflicting security interest in the same livestock, and, except as otherwise provided in Section 9–327, a perfected security interest in their identifiable proceeds and identifiable products in their unmanufactured states also has priority, if:

(1) the purchase-money security interest is perfected when the debtor receives possession of the livestock;

(2) the purchase-money secured party sends an authenticated notification to the holder of the conflicting security interest;

(3) the holder of the conflicting security interest receives the notification within six months before the debtor receives possession of the livestock; and

(4) the notification states that the person sending the notification has or expects to acquire a purchase-money security interest in livestock of the debtor and describes the livestock.

(e) Subsections (d)(2) through (4) apply only if the holder of the conflicting security interest had filed a financing statement covering the same types of livestock:

(1) if the purchase-money security interest is perfected by filing, before the date of the filing; or

(2) if the purchase-money security interest is temporarily perfected without filing or possession under Section 9–312(f), before the beginning of the 20-day period thereunder.

(f) Except as otherwise provided in subsection (g), a perfected purchase-money security interest in software has priority over a conflicting security interest in the same collateral, and, except as otherwise provided in Section 9–327, a perfected security interest in its identifiable proceeds also has priority, to the extent that the purchase-money security interest in the goods in which the software was acquired for use has priority in the goods and proceeds of the goods under this section.

(g) If more than one security interest qualifies for priority in the same collateral under subsection (a), (b), (d), or (f):

(1) a security interest securing an obligation incurred as all or part of the price of the collateral has priority over a security interest securing an obligation incurred for value given to enable the debtor to acquire rights in or the use of collateral; and

(2) in all other cases, Section 9–322(a) applies to the qualifying security interests.

§ 9–325. Priority of Security Interests in Transferred Collateral.

(a) Except as otherwise provided in subsection (b), a security interest created by a debtor is subordinate to a security interest in the same collateral created by another person if:

(1) the debtor acquired the collateral subject to the security interest created by the other person;

(2) the security interest created by the other person was perfected when the debtor acquired the collateral; and

(3) there is no period thereafter when the security interest is unperfected.

(b) Subsection (a) subordinates a security interest only if the security interest:

(1) otherwise would have priority solely under Section 9–322(a) or 9–324; or

(2) arose solely under Section 2–711(3) or 2A–508(5).

§ 9–326. Priority of Security Interests Created by New Debtor.

(a) Subject to subsection (b), a security interest created by a new debtor which is perfected by a filed financing statement that is effective solely under Section 9–508 in collateral in which a new debtor has or acquires rights is subordinate to a security interest in the same collateral which is perfected other than by a filed financing statement that is effective solely under Section 9–508.

(b) The other provisions of this part determine the priority among conflicting security interests in the same collateral perfected by filed financing statements that are effective solely under Section 9–508. However, if the security agreements to which a new debtor became bound as debtor were not entered into by the same original debtor, the conflicting security interests rank according to priority in time of the new debtor's having become bound.

§ 9–327. Priority of Security Interests in Deposit Account.

The following rules govern priority among conflicting security interests in the same deposit account:

(1) A security interest held by a secured party having control of the deposit account under Section 9–104 has priority over a conflicting security interest held by a secured party that does not have control.

(2) Except as otherwise provided in paragraphs (3) and (4), security interests perfected by control under Section 9–314 rank according to priority in time of obtaining control.

(3) Except as otherwise provided in paragraph (4), a security interest held by the bank with which the deposit account is maintained has priority over a conflicting security interest held by another secured party.

(4) A security interest perfected by control under Section 9–104(a)(3) has priority over a security interest held by the bank with which the deposit account is maintained.

§ 9–328. Priority of Security Interests in Investment Property.

The following rules govern priority among conflicting security interests in the same investment property:

(1) A security interest held by a secured party having control of investment property under Section 9–106 has priority over a security interest held by a secured party that does not have control of the investment property.

(2) Except as otherwise provided in paragraphs (3) and (4), conflicting security interests held by secured parties each of which has control under Section 9–106 rank according to priority in time of:

(A) if the collateral is a security, obtaining control;

(B) if the collateral is a security entitlement carried in a securities account and:

(i) if the secured party obtained control under Section 8–106(d)(1), the secured party's becoming the person for which the securities account is maintained;

(ii) if the secured party obtained control under Section 8–106(d)(2), the securities intermediary's agreement to comply with the secured party's entitlement orders with respect to security entitlements carried or to be carried in the securities account; or

(iii) if the secured party obtained control through another person under Section 8–106(d)(3), the time on which priority would be based under this paragraph if the other person were the secured party; or

(C) if the collateral is a commodity contract carried with a commodity intermediary, the satisfaction of the requirement for control specified in Section 9–106(b)(2) with respect to commodity contracts carried or to be carried with the commodity intermediary.

(3) A security interest held by a securities intermediary in a security entitlement or a securities account maintained with the securities intermediary has priority over a conflicting security interest held by another secured party.

(4) A security interest held by a commodity intermediary in a commodity contract or a commodity account maintained with the commodity intermediary has priority over a conflicting security interest held by another secured party.

(5) A security interest in a certificated security in registered form which is perfected by taking delivery under Section 9–313(a) and not by control under Section 9–314 has priority over a conflicting security interest perfected by a method other than control.

(6) Conflicting security interests created by a broker, securities intermediary, or commodity intermediary which are perfected without control under Section 9–106 rank equally.

(7) In all other cases, priority among conflicting security interests in investment property is governed by Sections 9–322 and 9–323.

§ 9–329. Priority of Security Interests in Letter-of-Credit Right.

The following rules govern priority among conflicting security interests in the same letter-of-credit right:

(1) A security interest held by a secured party having control of the letter-of-credit right under Section 9–107 has priority to the extent of its control over a conflicting security interest held by a secured party that does not have control.

(2) Security interests perfected by control under Section 9–314 rank according to priority in time of obtaining control.

§ 9–330. Priority of Purchaser of Chattel Paper or Instrument.

(a) A purchaser of chattel paper has priority over a security interest in the chattel paper which is claimed merely as proceeds of inventory subject to a security interest if:

(1) in good faith and in the ordinary course of the purchaser's business, the purchaser gives new value and takes possession of the chattel paper or obtains control of the chattel paper under Section 9–105; and

(2) the chattel paper does not indicate that it has been assigned to an identified assignee other than the purchaser.

(b) A purchaser of chattel paper has priority over a security interest in the chattel paper which is claimed other than merely as proceeds of inventory subject to a security interest if the purchaser gives new value and takes possession of the chattel paper or obtains control of the chattel paper under Section 9–105 in good faith, in the ordinary course of the purchaser's business, and without knowledge that the purchase violates the rights of the secured party.

(c) Except as otherwise provided in Section 9–327, a purchaser having priority in chattel paper under subsection (a) or (b) also has priority in proceeds of the chattel paper to the extent that:

(1) Section 9–322 provides for priority in the proceeds; or

(2) the proceeds consist of the specific goods covered by the chattel paper or cash proceeds of the specific goods, even if the purchaser's security interest in the proceeds is unperfected.

(d) Except as otherwise provided in Section 9–331(a), a purchaser of an instrument has priority over a security interest in the instrument perfected by a method other than possession if the purchaser gives value and takes possession of the instrument in good faith and without knowledge that the purchase violates the rights of the secured party.

(e) For purposes of subsections (a) and (b), the holder of a purchase-money security interest in inventory gives new value for chattel paper constituting proceeds of the inventory.

(f) For purposes of subsections (b) and (d), if chattel paper or an instrument indicates that it has been assigned to an identified secured party other than the purchaser, a purchaser of the chattel paper or instrument has knowledge that the purchase violates the rights of the secured party.

§ 9–331. **Priority of Rights of Purchasers of Instruments, Documents, and Securities under Other Articles; Priority of Interests in Financial Assets and Security Entitlements under Article 8.**

(a) This article does not limit the rights of a holder in due course of a negotiable instrument, a holder to which a negotiable document of title has been duly negotiated, or a protected purchaser of a security. These holders or purchasers take priority over an earlier security interest, even if perfected, to the extent provided in Articles 3, 7, and 8.

(b) This article does not limit the rights of or impose liability on a person to the extent that the person is protected against the assertion of a claim under Article 8.

(c) Filing under this article does not constitute notice of a claim or defense to the holders, or purchasers, or persons described in subsections (a) and (b).

§ 9–332. **Transfer of Money; Transfer of Funds from Deposit Account.**

(a) A transferee of money takes the money free of a security interest unless the transferee acts in collusion with the debtor in violating the rights of the secured party.

(b) A transferee of funds from a deposit account takes the funds free of a security interest in the deposit account unless the transferee acts in collusion with the debtor in violating the rights of the secured party.

§ 9–333. **Priority of Certain Liens Arising by Operation of Law.**

(a) In this section, "possessory lien" means an interest, other than a security interest or an agricultural lien:

(1) which secures payment or performance of an obligation for services or materials furnished with respect to goods by a person in the ordinary course of the person's business;

(2) which is created by statute or rule of law in favor of the person; and

(3) whose effectiveness depends on the person's possession of the goods.

(b) A possessory lien on goods has priority over a security interest in the goods unless the lien is created by a statute that expressly provides otherwise.

§ 9–334. **Priority of Security Interests in Fixtures and Crops.**

(a) A security interest under this article may be created in goods that are fixtures or may continue in goods that become fixtures. A security interest does not exist under this article in ordinary building materials incorporated into an improvement on land.

(b) This article does not prevent creation of an encumbrance upon fixtures under real property law.

(c) In cases not governed by subsections (d) through (h), a security interest in fixtures is subordinate to a conflicting interest of an encumbrancer or owner of the related real property other than the debtor.

(d) Except as otherwise provided in subsection (h), a perfected security interest in fixtures has priority over a conflicting interest of an encumbrancer or owner of the real property if the debtor has an interest of record in or is in possession of the real property and:

(1) the security interest is a purchase-money security interest;

(2) the interest of the encumbrancer or owner arises before the goods become fixtures; and

(3) the security interest is perfected by a fixture filing before the goods become fixtures or within 20 days thereafter.

(e) A perfected security interest in fixtures has priority over a conflicting interest of an encumbrancer or owner of the real property if:

(1) the debtor has an interest of record in the real property or is in possession of the real property and the security interest:

(A) is perfected by a fixture filing before the interest of the encumbrancer or owner is of record; and

(B) has priority over any conflicting interest of a predecessor in title of the encumbrancer or owner;

(2) before the goods become fixtures, the security interest is perfected by any method permitted by this article and the fixtures are readily removable:

(A) factory or office machines;

(B) equipment that is not primarily used or leased for use in the operation of the real property; or

(C) replacements of domestic appliances that are consumer goods;

(3) the conflicting interest is a lien on the real property obtained by legal or equitable proceedings after the security interest was perfected by any method permitted by this article; or

(4) the security interest is:

(A) created in a manufactured home in a manufactured-home transaction; and

(B) perfected pursuant to a statute described in Section 9–311(a)(2).

(f) A security interest in fixtures, whether or not perfected, has priority over a conflicting interest of an encumbrancer or owner of the real property if:

(1) the encumbrancer or owner has, in an authenticated record, consented to the security interest or disclaimed an interest in the goods as fixtures; or

(2) the debtor has a right to remove the goods as against the encumbrancer or owner.

(g) The priority of the security interest under paragraph (f)(2) continues for a reasonable time if the debtor's right to remove the goods as against the encumbrancer or owner terminates.

(h) A mortgage is a construction mortgage to the extent that it secures an obligation incurred for the construction of an improvement on land, including the acquisition cost of the land, if a recorded record of the mortgage so indicates. Except as otherwise provided in subsections (e) and (f), a security interest in fixtures is subordinate to a construction mortgage if a record of the mortgage is recorded before the goods become fixtures and the goods become fixtures before the completion of the construction. A mortgage has this priority to the same extent as a construction mortgage to the extent that it is given to refinance a construction mortgage.

(i) A perfected security interest in crops growing on real property has priority over a conflicting interest of an encumbrancer or owner of the real property if the debtor has an interest of record in or is in possession of the real property.

(j) Subsection (i) prevails over any inconsistent provisions of the following statutes:

[List here any statutes containing provisions inconsistent with subsection (i).]

Legislative Note: States that amend statutes to remove provisions inconsistent with subsection (i) need not enact subsection (j).

§ 9–335. Accessions.

(a) A security interest may be created in an accession and continues in collateral that becomes an accession.

(b) If a security interest is perfected when the collateral becomes an accession, the security interest remains perfected in the collateral.

(c) Except as otherwise provided in subsection (d), the other provisions of this part determine the priority of a security interest in an accession.

(d) A security interest in an accession is subordinate to a security interest in the whole which is perfected by compliance with the requirements of a certificate-of-title statute under Section 9–311(b).

(e) After default, subject to Part 6, a secured party may remove an accession from other goods if the security interest in the accession has priority over the claims of every person having an interest in the whole.

(f) A secured party that removes an accession from other goods under subsection (e) shall promptly reimburse any holder of a security interest or other lien on, or owner of, the whole or of the other goods, other than the debtor, for the cost of repair of any physical injury to the whole or the other goods. The secured party need not reimburse the holder or owner for any diminution in value of the whole or the other goods caused by the absence of the accession removed or by any necessity for replacing it. A person entitled to reimbursement may refuse permission to remove until the secured party gives adequate assurance for the performance of the obligation to reimburse.

§ 9–336. Commingled Goods.

(a) In this section, "commingled goods" means goods that are physically united with other goods in such a manner that their identity is lost in a product or mass.

(b) A security interest does not exist in commingled goods as such. However, a security interest may attach to a product or mass that results when goods become commingled goods.

(c) If collateral becomes commingled goods, a security interest attaches to the product or mass.

(d) If a security interest in collateral is perfected before the collateral becomes commingled goods, the security interest that attaches to the product or mass under subsection (c) is perfected.

(e) Except as otherwise provided in subsection (f), the other provisions of this part determine the priority of a security interest that attaches to the product or mass under subsection (c).

(f) If more than one security interest attaches to the product or mass under subsection (c), the following rules determine priority:

(1) A security interest that is perfected under subsection (d) has priority over a security interest that is unperfected at the time the collateral becomes commingled goods.

(2) If more than one security interest is perfected under subsection (d), the security interests rank equally in proportion to the value of the collateral at the time it became commingled goods.

§ 9–337. Priority of Security Interests in Goods Covered by Certificate of Title.

If, while a security interest in goods is perfected by any method under the law of another jurisdiction, this State issues a certificate of title that does not show that the goods are subject to the security interest or contain a statement that they may be subject to security interests not shown on the certificate:

(1) a buyer of the goods, other than a person in the business of selling goods of that kind, takes free of the security interest if the buyer gives value and receives delivery of the goods after issuance of the certificate and without knowledge of the security interest; and

(2) the security interest is subordinate to a conflicting security interest in the goods that attaches, and is perfected under Section 9–311(b), after issuance of the certificate and without the conflicting secured party's knowledge of the security interest.

§ 9–338. Priority of Security Interest or Agricultural Lien Perfected by Filed Financing Statement Providing Certain Incorrect Information.

If a security interest or agricultural lien is perfected by a filed financing statement providing information described in Section 9–516(b)(5) which is incorrect at the time the financing statement is filed:

(1) the security interest or agricultural lien is subordinate to a conflicting perfected security interest in the collateral to the extent that the holder of the conflicting security interest gives value in reasonable reliance upon the incorrect information; and

(2) a purchaser, other than a secured party, of the collateral takes free of the security interest or agricultural lien to the extent that, in reasonable reliance upon the incorrect information, the purchaser gives value and, in the case of chattel paper, documents, goods, instruments, or a security certificate, receives delivery of the collateral.

§ 9–339. Priority Subject to Subordination.

This article does not preclude subordination by agreement by a person entitled to priority.

[Subpart 4. Rights of Bank]

§ 9–340. Effectiveness of Right of Recoupment or Set-Off against Deposit Account.

(a) Except as otherwise provided in subsection (c), a bank with which a deposit account is maintained may exercise any right of recoupment or set-off against a secured party that holds a security interest in the deposit account.

(b) Except as otherwise provided in subsection (c), the application of this article to a security interest in a deposit account does not affect a right of recoupment or set-off of the secured party as to a deposit account maintained with the secured party.

(c) The exercise by a bank of a set-off against a deposit account is ineffective against a secured party that holds a security interest in the deposit account which is perfected by control under Section 9–104(a)(3), if the set-off is based on a claim against the debtor.

§ 9–341. Bank's Rights and Duties with Respect to Deposit Account.

Except as otherwise provided in Section 9–340(c), and unless the bank otherwise agrees in an authenticated record, a bank's rights and duties with respect to a deposit account maintained with the bank are not terminated, suspended, or modified by:

(1) the creation, attachment, or perfection of a security interest in the deposit account;

(2) the bank's knowledge of the security interest; or

(3) the bank's receipt of instructions from the secured party.

§ 9–342. Bank's Right to Refuse to Enter into or Disclose Existence of Control Agreement.

This article does not require a bank to enter into an agreement of the kind described in Section 9–104(a)(2), even if its customer so requests or directs. A bank that has entered into such an agreement is not required to confirm the existence of the agreement to another person unless requested to do so by its customer.

Part 4 Rights of Third Parties

§ 9–401. Alienability of Debtor's Rights.

(a) Except as otherwise provided in subsection (b) and Sections 9–406, 9–407, 9–408, and 9–409, whether a debtor's rights in collateral may be voluntarily or involuntarily transferred is governed by law other than this article.

(b) An agreement between the debtor and secured party which prohibits a transfer of the debtor's rights in collateral or makes the transfer a default does not prevent the transfer from taking effect.

§ 9–402. Secured Party Not Obligated on Contract of Debtor or in Tort.

The existence of a security interest, agricultural lien, or authority given to a debtor to dispose of or use collateral, without more, does not subject a secured party to liability in contract or tort for the debtor's acts or omissions.

§ 9–403. Agreement Not to Assert Defenses against Assignee.

(a) In this section, "value" has the meaning provided in Section 3–303(a).

(b) Except as otherwise provided in this section, an agreement between an account debtor and an assignor not to assert against an assignee any claim or defense that the account debtor may have against the assignor is enforceable by an assignee that takes an assignment:

(1) for value;

(2) in good faith;

(3) without notice of a claim of a property or possessory right to the property assigned; and

(4) without notice of a defense or claim in recoupment of the type that may be asserted against a person entitled to enforce a negotiable instrument under Section 3–305(a).

(c) Subsection (b) does not apply to defenses of a type that may be asserted against a holder in due course of a negotiable instrument under Section 3–305(b).

(d) In a consumer transaction, if a record evidences the account debtor's obligation, law other than this article requires that the record include a statement to the effect that the rights of an assignee are subject to claims or defenses that the account debtor could assert against the original obligee, and the record does not include such a statement:

(1) the record has the same effect as if the record included such a statement; and

(2) the account debtor may assert against an assignee those claims and defenses that would have been available if the record included such a statement.

(e) This section is subject to law other than this article which establishes a different rule for an account debtor who is an individual and who incurred the obligation primarily for personal, family, or household purposes.

(f) Except as otherwise provided in subsection (d), this section does not displace law other than this article which gives effect to an agreement by an account debtor not to assert a claim or defense against an assignee.

§ 9–404. Rights Acquired by Assignee; Claims and Defenses against Assignee.

(a) Unless an account debtor has made an enforceable agreement not to assert defenses or claims, and subject to subsections (b) through (e), the rights of an assignee are subject to:

(1) all terms of the agreement between the account debtor and assignor and any defense or claim in recoupment arising from the transaction that gave rise to the contract; and

(2) any other defense or claim of the account debtor against the assignor which accrues before the account debtor receives a notification of the assignment authenticated by the assignor or the assignee.

(b) Subject to subsection (c) and except as otherwise provided in subsection (d), the claim of an account debtor against an assignor may be asserted against an assignee under subsection (a) only to reduce the amount the account debtor owes.

(c) This section is subject to law other than this article which establishes a different rule for an account debtor who is an individual and who incurred the obligation primarily for personal, family, or household purposes.

(d) In a consumer transaction, if a record evidences the account debtor's obligation, law other than this article requires that the record include a statement to the effect that the account debtor's recovery against an assignee with respect to claims and defenses against the assignor may not exceed amounts paid by the account debtor under the record, and the record does not include such a statement, the extent to which a claim of an account debtor against the assignor may be asserted against an assignee is determined as if the record included such a statement.

(e) This section does not apply to an assignment of a health-care-insurance receivable.

§ 9–405. Modification of Assigned Contract.

(a) A modification of or substitution for an assigned contract is effective against an assignee if made in good faith. The assignee acquires corresponding rights under the modified or substituted contract. The assignment may provide that the modification or substitution is a breach of contract by the assignor. This subsection is subject to subsections (b) through (d).

(b) Subsection (a) applies to the extent that:

(1) the right to payment or a part thereof under an assigned contract has not been fully earned by performance; or

(2) the right to payment or a part thereof has been fully earned by performance and the account debtor has not received notification of the assignment under Section 9–406(a).

(c) This section is subject to law other than this article which establishes a different rule for an account debtor who is an individual and who incurred the obligation primarily for personal, family, or household purposes.

(d) This section does not apply to an assignment of a health-care-insurance receivable.

§ 9–406. Discharge of Account Debtor; Notification of Assignment; Identification and Proof of Assignment; Restrictions on Assignment of Accounts, Chattel Paper, Payment Intangibles, and Promissory Notes Ineffective.

(a) Subject to subsections (b) through (i), an account debtor on an account, chattel paper, or a payment intangible may discharge its obligation by paying the assignor until, but not after, the account debtor receives a notification, authenticated by the assignor or the assignee, that the amount due or to become due has been assigned and that payment is to be made to the assignee. After receipt of the notification, the account debtor may discharge its obligation by paying the assignee and may not discharge the obligation by paying the assignor.

(b) Subject to subsection (h), notification is ineffective under subsection (a):

(1) if it does not reasonably identify the rights assigned;

(2) to the extent that an agreement between an account debtor and a seller of a payment intangible limits the account debtor's duty to pay a person other than the seller and the limitation is effective under law other than this article; or

(3) at the option of an account debtor, if the notification notifies the account debtor to make less than the full amount of any installment or other periodic payment to the assignee, even if:

(A) only a portion of the account, chattel paper, or payment intangible has been assigned to that assignee;

(B) a portion has been assigned to another assignee; or

(C) the account debtor knows that the assignment to that assignee is limited.

(c) Subject to subsection (h), if requested by the account debtor, an assignee shall seasonably furnish reasonable proof that the assignment has been made. Unless the assignee complies, the account debtor may discharge its obligation by paying the assignor, even if the account debtor has received a notification under subsection (a).

(d) Except as otherwise provided in subsection (e) and Sections 2A–303 and 9–407, and subject to subsection (h), a term in an agreement between an account debtor and an assignor or in a promissory note is ineffective to the extent that it:

(1) prohibits, restricts, or requires the consent of the account debtor or person obligated on the promissory note to the assignment or transfer of, or the creation, attachment, perfection, or enforcement of a security interest in, the account, chattel paper, payment intangible, or promissory note; or

(2) provides that the assignment or transfer or the creation, attachment, perfection, or enforcement of the security interest may give rise to a default, breach, right of recoupment, claim, defense, termination, right of termination, or remedy under the account, chattel paper, payment intangible, or promissory note.

(e) Subsection (d) does not apply to the sale of a payment intangible or promissory note.

(f) Except as otherwise provided in Sections 2A–303 and 9–407 and subject to subsections (h) and (i), a rule of law, statute, or regulation that prohibits, restricts, or requires the consent of a government, governmental body or official, or account debtor to the assignment or transfer of, or creation of a security interest in, an account or chattel paper is ineffective to the extent that the rule of law, statute, or regulation:

(1) prohibits, restricts, or requires the consent of the government, governmental body or official, or account debtor to the assignment or transfer of, or the creation, attachment, perfection, or enforcement of a security interest in the account or chattel paper; or

(2) provides that the assignment or transfer or the creation, attachment, perfection, or enforcement of the security interest may give rise to a default, breach, right of recoupment, claim, defense, termination, right of termination, or remedy under the account or chattel paper.

(g) Subject to subsection (h), an account debtor may not waive or vary its option under subsection (b)(3).

(h) This section is subject to law other than this article which establishes a different rule for an account debtor who is an individual and who incurred the obligation primarily for personal, family, or household purposes.

(i) This section does not apply to an assignment of a health-care-insurance receivable.

(j) This section prevails over any inconsistent provisions of the following statutes, rules, and regulations:

[List here any statutes, rules, and regulations containing provisions inconsistent with this section.]

Legislative Note: States that amend statutes, rules, and regulations to remove provisions inconsistent with this section need not enact subsection (j).

As amended in 1999 and 2000.

§ 9–407. Restrictions on Creation or Enforcement of Security Interest in Leasehold Interest or in Lessor's Residual Interest.

(a) Except as otherwise provided in subsection (b), a term in a lease agreement is ineffective to the extent that it:

(1) prohibits, restricts, or requires the consent of a party to the lease to the assignment or transfer of, or the creation, attachment, perfection, or enforcement of a security interest in an interest of a party under the lease contract or in the lessor's residual interest in the goods; or

(2) provides that the assignment or transfer or the creation, attachment, perfection, or enforcement of the security interest may give rise to a default, breach, right of recoupment, claim, defense, termination, right of termination, or remedy under the lease.

(b) Except as otherwise provided in Section 2A–303(7), a term described in subsection (a)(2) is effective to the extent that there is:

(1) a transfer by the lessee of the lessee's right of possession or use of the goods in violation of the term; or

(2) a delegation of a material performance of either party to the lease contract in violation of the term.

(c) The creation, attachment, perfection, or enforcement of a security interest in the lessor's interest under the lease contract or the lessor's residual interest in the goods is not a transfer that materially impairs the lessee's prospect of obtaining return performance or materially changes the duty of or materially increases the burden or risk imposed on the lessee within the purview of Section 2A–303(4) unless, and then only to the extent that, enforcement actually results in a delegation of material performance of the lessor.

As amended in 1999.

§ 9–408. Restrictions on Assignment of Promissory Notes, Health-Care-Insurance Receivables, and Certain General Intangibles Ineffective.

(a) Except as otherwise provided in subsection (b), a term in a promissory note or in an agreement between an account debtor and a debtor which relates to a health-care-insurance receivable or a general intangible, including a contract, permit, license, or franchise, and which term prohibits, restricts, or requires the consent of the person obligated on the promissory note or the account debtor to, the assignment or transfer of, or creation, attachment, or perfection of a security interest in, the promissory note, health-care-insurance receivable, or general intangible, is ineffective to the extent that the term:

(1) would impair the creation, attachment, or perfection of a security interest; or

(2) provides that the assignment or transfer or the creation, attachment, or perfection of the security interest may give rise to a default, breach, right of recoupment, claim, defense, termination, right of termination, or remedy under the promissory note, health-care-insurance receivable, or general intangible.

(b) Subsection (a) applies to a security interest in a payment intangible or promissory note only if the security interest arises out of a sale of the payment intangible or promissory note.

(c) A rule of law, statute, or regulation that prohibits, restricts, or requires the consent of a government, governmental body or official, person obligated on a promissory note, or account debtor to the assignment or transfer of, or creation of a security interest in, a promissory note, health-care-insurance receivable, or general intangible, including a contract, permit, license, or franchise between an account debtor and a debtor, is ineffective to the extent that the rule of law, statute, or regulation:

(1) would impair the creation, attachment, or perfection of a security interest; or

(2) provides that the assignment or transfer or the creation, attachment, or perfection of the security interest may give rise to a default, breach, right of recoupment, claim, defense, termination, right of termination, or remedy under the promissory note, health-care-insurance receivable, or general intangible.

(d) To the extent that a term in a promissory note or in an agreement between an account debtor and a debtor which relates to a health-care-insurance receivable or general intangible or a rule of law, statute, or regulation described in subsection (c) would be effective under law other than this article but is ineffective under subsection (a) or (c), the creation, attachment, or perfection of a security interest in the promissory note, health-care-insurance receivable, or general intangible:

(1) is not enforceable against the person obligated on the promissory note or the account debtor;

(2) does not impose a duty or obligation on the person obligated on the promissory note or the account debtor;

(3) does not require the person obligated on the promissory note or the account debtor to recognize the security interest, pay or render performance to the secured party, or accept payment or performance from the secured party;

(4) does not entitle the secured party to use or assign the debtor's rights under the promissory note, health-care-insurance receivable, or general intangible, including any related information or materials furnished to the debtor in the transaction giving rise to the promissory note, health-care-insurance receivable, or general intangible;

(5) does not entitle the secured party to use, assign, possess, or have access to any trade secrets or confidential information of the person obligated on the promissory note or the account debtor; and

(6) does not entitle the secured party to enforce the security interest in the promissory note, health-care-insurance receivable, or general intangible.

(e) This section prevails over any inconsistent provisions of the following statutes, rules, and regulations:

[List here any statutes, rules, and regulations containing provisions inconsistent with this section.]

Legislative Note: States that amend statutes, rules, and regulations to remove provisions inconsistent with this section need not enact subsection (e).

As amended in 1999.

§ 9–409. Restrictions on Assignment of Letter-of-Credit Rights Ineffective.

(a) A term in a letter of credit or a rule of law, statute, regulation, custom, or practice applicable to the letter of credit which prohibits, restricts, or requires the consent of an applicant, issuer, or nominated person to a beneficiary's assignment of or creation of a security interest in a letter-of-credit right is ineffective to the extent that the term or rule of law, statute, regulation, custom, or practice:

(1) would impair the creation, attachment, or perfection of a security interest in the letter-of-credit right; or

(2) provides that the assignment or the creation, attachment, or perfection of the security interest may give rise to a default, breach, right of recoupment, claim, defense, termination, right of termination, or remedy under the letter-of-credit right.

(b) To the extent that a term in a letter of credit is ineffective under subsection (a) but would be effective under law other than this article or a custom or practice applicable to the letter of credit, to the transfer of a right to draw or otherwise demand performance under the letter of credit, or to the assignment of a right to proceeds of the letter of credit, the creation, attachment, or perfection of a security interest in the letter-of-credit right:

(1) is not enforceable against the applicant, issuer, nominated person, or transferee beneficiary;

(2) imposes no duties or obligations on the applicant, issuer, nominated person, or transferee beneficiary; and

(3) does not require the applicant, issuer, nominated person, or transferee beneficiary to recognize the security interest, pay or render performance to the secured party, or accept payment or other performance from the secured party.

As amended in 1999.

Part 5 Filing

[Subpart 1. Filing Office; Contents and Effectiveness of Financing Statement]

§ 9–501. **Filing Office.**

(a) Except as otherwise provided in subsection (b), if the local law of this State governs perfection of a security interest or agricultural lien, the office in which to file a financing statement to perfect the security interest or agricultural lien is:

(1) the office designated for the filing or recording of a record of a mortgage on the related real property, if:

(A) the collateral is as-extracted collateral or timber to be cut; or

(B) the financing statement is filed as a fixture filing and the collateral is goods that are or are to become fixtures; or

(2) the office of [ ] [or any office duly authorized by [ ]], in all other cases, including a case in which the collateral is goods that are or are to become fixtures and the financing statement is not filed as a fixture filing.

(b) The office in which to file a financing statement to perfect a security interest in collateral, including fixtures, of a transmitting utility is the office of [ ]. The financing statement also constitutes a fixture filing as to the collateral indicated in the financing statement which is or is to become fixtures.

Legislative Note: The State should designate the filing office where the brackets appear. The filing office may be that of a governmental official (e.g., the Secretary of State) or a private party that maintains the State's filing system.

§ 9–502. **Contents of Financing Statement; Record of Mortgage as Financing Statement; Time of Filing Financing Statement.**

(a) Subject to subsection (b), a financing statement is sufficient only if it:

(1) provides the name of the debtor;

(2) provides the name of the secured party or a representative of the secured party; and

(3) indicates the collateral covered by the financing statement.

(b) Except as otherwise provided in Section 9–501(b), to be sufficient, a financing statement that covers as-extracted collateral or timber to be cut, or which is filed as a fixture filing and covers goods that are or are to become fixtures, must satisfy subsection (a) and also:

(1) indicate that it covers this type of collateral;

(2) indicate that it is to be filed [for record] in the real property records;

(3) provide a description of the real property to which the collateral is related [sufficient to give constructive notice of a mortgage under the law of this State if the description were contained in a record of the mortgage of the real property]; and

(4) if the debtor does not have an interest of record in the real property, provide the name of a record owner.

(c) A record of a mortgage is effective, from the date of recording, as a financing statement filed as a fixture filing or as a financing statement covering as-extracted collateral or timber to be cut only if:

(1) the record indicates the goods or accounts that it covers;

(2) the goods are or are to become fixtures related to the real property described in the record or the collateral is related to the real property described in the record and is as-extracted collateral or timber to be cut;

(3) the record satisfies the requirements for a financing statement in this section other than an indication that it is to be filed in the real property records; and

(4) the record is [duly] recorded.

(d) A financing statement may be filed before a security agreement is made or a security interest otherwise attaches.

Legislative Note: Language in brackets is optional. Where the State has any special recording system for real property other than the usual grantor-grantee index (as, for instance, a tract system or a title registration or Torrens system) local adaptations of subsection (b) and Section 9–519(d) and (e) may be necessary. See, e.g., Mass. Gen. Laws Chapter 106, Section 9–410.

§ 9–503. **Name of Debtor and Secured Party.**

(a) A financing statement sufficiently provides the name of the debtor:

(1) if the debtor is a registered organization, only if the financing statement provides the name of the debtor indicated on the public record of the debtor's jurisdiction of organization which shows the debtor to have been organized;

(2) if the debtor is a decedent's estate, only if the financing statement provides the name of the decedent and indicates that the debtor is an estate;

(3) if the debtor is a trust or a trustee acting with respect to property held in trust, only if the financing statement:

(A) provides the name specified for the trust in its organic documents or, if no name is specified, provides the name of the settlor and additional information sufficient to distinguish the debtor from other trusts having one or more of the same settlors; and

(B) indicates, in the debtor's name or otherwise, that the debtor is a trust or is a trustee acting with respect to property held in trust; and

(4) in other cases:

(A) if the debtor has a name, only if it provides the individual or organizational name of the debtor; and

(B) if the debtor does not have a name, only if it provides the names of the partners, members, associates, or other persons comprising the debtor.

(b) A financing statement that provides the name of the debtor in accordance with subsection (a) is not rendered ineffective by the absence of:

(1) a trade name or other name of the debtor; or

(2) unless required under subsection (a)(4)(B), names of partners, members, associates, or other persons comprising the debtor.

(c) A financing statement that provides only the debtor's trade name does not sufficiently provide the name of the debtor.

(d) Failure to indicate the representative capacity of a secured party or representative of a secured party does not affect the sufficiency of a financing statement.

(e) A financing statement may provide the name of more than one debtor and the name of more than one secured party.

§ 9–504. Indication of Collateral.

A financing statement sufficiently indicates the collateral that it covers if the financing statement provides:

(1) a description of the collateral pursuant to Section 9–108; or

(2) an indication that the financing statement covers all assets or all personal property.

As amended in 1999.

§ 9–505. Filing and Compliance with Other Statutes and Treaties for Consignments, Leases, Other Bailments, and Other Transactions.

(a) A consignor, lessor, or other bailor of goods, a licensor, or a buyer of a payment intangible or promissory note may file a financing statement, or may comply with a statute or treaty described in Section 9–311(a), using the terms "consignor", "consignee", "lessor", "lessee", "bailor", "bailee", "licensor", "licensee", "owner", "registered owner", "buyer", "seller", or words of similar import, instead of the terms "secured party" and "debtor".

(b) This part applies to the filing of a financing statement under subsection (a) and, as appropriate, to compliance that is equivalent to filing a financing statement under Section 9–311(b), but the filing or compliance is not of itself a factor in determining whether the collateral secures an obligation. If it is determined for another reason that the collateral secures an obligation, a security interest held by the consignor, lessor, bailor, licensor, owner, or buyer which attaches to the collateral is perfected by the filing or compliance.

§ 9–506. Effect of Errors or Omissions.

(a) A financing statement substantially satisfying the requirements of this part is effective, even if it has minor errors or omissions, unless the errors or omissions make the financing statement seriously misleading.

(b) Except as otherwise provided in subsection (c), a financing statement that fails sufficiently to provide the name of the debtor in accordance with Section 9–503(a) is seriously misleading.

(c) If a search of the records of the filing office under the debtor's correct name, using the filing office's standard search logic, if any, would disclose a financing statement that fails sufficiently to provide the name of the debtor in accordance with Section 9–503(a), the name provided does not make the financing statement seriously misleading.

(d) For purposes of Section 9–508(b), the "debtor's correct name" in subsection (c) means the correct name of the new debtor.

§ 9–507. Effect of Certain Events on Effectiveness of Financing Statement.

(a) A filed financing statement remains effective with respect to collateral that is sold, exchanged, leased, licensed, or otherwise disposed of and in which a security interest or agricultural lien continues, even if the secured party knows of or consents to the disposition.

(b) Except as otherwise provided in subsection (c) and Section 9–508, a financing statement is not rendered ineffective if, after the financing statement is filed, the information provided in the financing statement becomes seriously misleading under Section 9–506.

(c) If a debtor so changes its name that a filed financing statement becomes seriously misleading under Section 9–506:

(1) the financing statement is effective to perfect a security interest in collateral acquired by the debtor before, or within four months after, the change; and

(2) the financing statement is not effective to perfect a security interest in collateral acquired by the debtor more than four months after the change, unless an amendment to the financing statement which renders the financing statement not seriously misleading is filed within four months after the change.

§ 9–508. Effectiveness of Financing Statement If New Debtor Becomes Bound by Security Agreement.

(a) Except as otherwise provided in this section, a filed financing statement naming an original debtor is effective to perfect a security interest in collateral in which a new debtor has or acquires rights to the extent that the financing statement would have been effective had the original debtor acquired rights in the collateral.

(b) If the difference between the name of the original debtor and that of the new debtor causes a filed financing statement that is effective under subsection (a) to be seriously misleading under Section 9–506:

(1) the financing statement is effective to perfect a security interest in collateral acquired by the new debtor before, and within four months after, the new debtor becomes bound under Section 9B–203(d); and

(2) the financing statement is not effective to perfect a security interest in collateral acquired by the new debtor more than four months after the new debtor becomes bound under Section 9–203(d) unless an initial financing statement providing the name of the new debtor is filed before the expiration of that time.

(c) This section does not apply to collateral as to which a filed financing statement remains effective against the new debtor under Section 9–507(a).

§ 9–509. Persons Entitled to File a Record.

(a) A person may file an initial financing statement, amendment that adds collateral covered by a financing statement, or amendment that adds a debtor to a financing statement only if:

(1) the debtor authorizes the filing in an authenticated record or pursuant to subsection (b) or (c); or

(2) the person holds an agricultural lien that has become effective at the time of filing and the financing statement covers only collateral in which the person holds an agricultural lien.

(b) By authenticating or becoming bound as debtor by a security agreement, a debtor or new debtor authorizes the filing of an initial financing statement, and an amendment, covering:

(1) the collateral described in the security agreement; and

(2) property that becomes collateral under Section 9–315(a)(2), whether or not the security agreement expressly covers proceeds.

(c) By acquiring collateral in which a security interest or agricultural lien continues under Section 9–315(a)(1), a debtor authorizes the filing of an initial financing statement, and an amendment, covering the collateral and property that becomes collateral under Section 9–315(a)(2).

(d) A person may file an amendment other than an amendment that adds collateral covered by a financing statement or an amendment that adds a debtor to a financing statement only if:

(1) the secured party of record authorizes the filing; or

(2) the amendment is a termination statement for a financing statement as to which the secured party of record has failed to file or send a termination statement as required by Section 9–513(a) or (c), the debtor authorizes the filing, and the termination statement indicates that the debtor authorized it to be filed.

(e) If there is more than one secured party of record for a financing statement, each secured party of record may authorize the filing of an amendment under subsection (d).

As amended in 2000.

§ 9–510. Effectiveness of Filed Record.

(a) A filed record is effective only to the extent that it was filed by a person that may file it under Section 9–509.

(b) A record authorized by one secured party of record does not affect the financing statement with respect to another secured party of record.

(c) A continuation statement that is not filed within the six-month period prescribed by Section 9–515(d) is ineffective.

§ 9–511. Secured Party of Record.

(a) A secured party of record with respect to a financing statement is a person whose name is provided as the name of the secured party or a representative of the secured party in an initial financing statement that has been filed. If an initial financing statement is filed under Section 9–514(a), the assignee named in the initial financing statement is the secured party of record with respect to the financing statement.

(b) If an amendment of a financing statement which provides the name of a person as a secured party or a representative of a secured party is filed, the person named in the amendment is a secured party of record. If an amendment is filed under Section 9–514(b), the assignee named in the amendment is a secured party of record.

(c) A person remains a secured party of record until the filing of an amendment of the financing statement which deletes the person.

§ 9–512. Amendment of Financing Statement.

[Alternative A]

(a) Subject to Section 9–509, a person may add or delete collateral covered by, continue or terminate the effectiveness of, or, subject to subsection (e), otherwise amend the information provided in, a financing statement by filing an amendment that:

(1) identifies, by its file number, the initial financing statement to which the amendment relates; and

(2) if the amendment relates to an initial financing statement filed [or recorded] in a filing office described in Section 9–501(a)(1), provides the information specified in Section 9–502(b).

[Alternative B]

(a) Subject to Section 9–509, a person may add or delete collateral covered by, continue or terminate the effectiveness of, or, subject to subsection (e), otherwise amend the information provided in, a financing statement by filing an amendment that:

(1) identifies, by its file number, the initial financing statement to which the amendment relates; and

(2) if the amendment relates to an initial financing statement filed [or recorded] in a filing office described in Section 9–501(a)(1), provides the date [and time] that the initial financing statement was filed [or recorded] and the information specified in Section 9–502(b).

[End of Alternatives]

(b) Except as otherwise provided in Section 9–515, the filing of an amendment does not extend the period of effectiveness of the financing statement.

(c) A financing statement that is amended by an amendment that adds collateral is effective as to the added collateral only from the date of the filing of the amendment.

(d) A financing statement that is amended by an amendment that adds a debtor is effective as to the added debtor only from the date of the filing of the amendment.

(e) An amendment is ineffective to the extent it:

(1) purports to delete all debtors and fails to provide the name of a debtor to be covered by the financing statement; or

(2) purports to delete all secured parties of record and fails to provide the name of a new secured party of record.

Legislative Note: States whose real-estate filing offices require additional information in amendments and cannot search their records by both the name of the debtor and the file number should enact Alternative B to Sections 9–512(a), 9–518(b), 9–519(f), and 9–522(a).

§ 9–513. Termination Statement.

(a) A secured party shall cause the secured party of record for a financing statement to file a termination statement for the financing statement if the financing statement covers consumer goods and:

(1) there is no obligation secured by the collateral covered by the financing statement and no commitment to make an advance, incur an obligation, or otherwise give value; or

(2) the debtor did not authorize the filing of the initial financing statement.

(b) To comply with subsection (a), a secured party shall cause the secured party of record to file the termination statement:

(1) within one month after there is no obligation secured by the collateral covered by the financing statement and no commitment to make an advance, incur an obligation, or otherwise give value; or

(2) if earlier, within 20 days after the secured party receives an authenticated demand from a debtor.

(c) In cases not governed by subsection (a), within 20 days after a secured party receives an authenticated demand from a debtor, the secured party shall cause the secured party of record for a financing statement to send to the debtor a termination statement for the financing statement or file the termination statement in the filing office if:

(1) except in the case of a financing statement covering accounts or chattel paper that has been sold or goods that are the subject of a consignment, there is no obligation secured by the collateral covered by the financing statement and no commitment to make an advance, incur an obligation, or otherwise give value;

(2) the financing statement covers accounts or chattel paper that has been sold but as to which the account debtor or other person obligated has discharged its obligation;

(3) the financing statement covers goods that were the subject of a consignment to the debtor but are not in the debtor's possession; or

(4) the debtor did not authorize the filing of the initial financing statement.

(d) Except as otherwise provided in Section 9–510, upon the filing of a termination statement with the filing office, the financing statement to which the termination statement relates ceases to be effective. Except as otherwise provided in Section 9–510, for purposes of Sections 9–519(g), 9–522(a), and 9–523(c), the filing with the filing office of a termination statement relating to a financing statement that indicates that the debtor is a transmitting utility also causes the effectiveness of the financing statement to lapse.

As amended in 2000.

§ 9–514. Assignment of Powers of Secured Party of Record.

(a) Except as otherwise provided in subsection (c), an initial financing statement may reflect an assignment of all of the secured party's power to authorize an amendment to the financing statement by providing the name and mailing address of the assignee as the name and address of the secured party.

(b) Except as otherwise provided in subsection (c), a secured party of record may assign of record all or part of its power to authorize an amendment to a financing statement by filing in the filing office an amendment of the financing statement which:

(1) identifies, by its file number, the initial financing statement to which it relates;

(2) provides the name of the assignor; and

(3) provides the name and mailing address of the assignee.

(c) An assignment of record of a security interest in a fixture covered by a record of a mortgage which is effective as a financing statement filed as a fixture filing under Section 9–502(c) may be made only by an assignment of record of the mortgage in the manner provided by law of this State other than [the Uniform Commercial Code].

§ 9–515. Duration and Effectiveness of Financing Statement; Effect of Lapsed Financing Statement.

(a) Except as otherwise provided in subsections (b), (e), (f), and (g), a filed financing statement is effective for a period of five years after the date of filing.

(b) Except as otherwise provided in subsections (e), (f), and (g), an initial financing statement filed in connection with a public-finance transaction or manufactured-home transaction is effective for a period of 30 years after the date of filing if it indicates that it is filed in connection with a public-finance transaction or manufactured-home transaction.

(c) The effectiveness of a filed financing statement lapses on the expiration of the period of its effectiveness unless before the lapse a continuation statement is filed pursuant to subsection (d). Upon lapse, a financing statement ceases to be effective and any security interest or agricultural lien that was perfected by the financing statement becomes unperfected, unless the security interest is perfected otherwise. If the security interest or agricultural lien becomes unperfected upon lapse, it is deemed never to have been perfected as against a purchaser of the collateral for value.

(d) A continuation statement may be filed only within six months before the expiration of the five-year period specified in subsection (a) or the 30-year period specified in subsection (b), whichever is applicable.

(e) Except as otherwise provided in Section 9–510, upon timely filing of a continuation statement, the effectiveness of the initial financing statement continues for a period of five years commencing on the day on which the financing statement would have become ineffective in the absence of the filing. Upon the expiration of the five-year period, the financing statement lapses in the same manner as provided in subsection (c), unless, before the lapse, another continuation statement is filed pursuant to subsection (d). Succeeding continuation statements may be filed in the same manner to continue the effectiveness of the initial financing statement.

(f) If a debtor is a transmitting utility and a filed financing statement so indicates, the financing statement is effective until a termination statement is filed.

(g) A record of a mortgage that is effective as a financing statement filed as a fixture filing under Section 9–502(c) remains effective as a financing statement filed as a fixture filing until the mortgage is released or satisfied of record or its effectiveness otherwise terminates as to the real property.

§ 9–516. What Constitutes Filing; Effectiveness of Filing.

(a) Except as otherwise provided in subsection (b), communication of a record to a filing office and tender of the filing fee or acceptance of the record by the filing office constitutes filing.

(b) Filing does not occur with respect to a record that a filing office refuses to accept because:

(1) the record is not communicated by a method or medium of communication authorized by the filing office;

(2) an amount equal to or greater than the applicable filing fee is not tendered;

(3) the filing office is unable to index the record because:

(A) in the case of an initial financing statement, the record does not provide a name for the debtor;

(B) in the case of an amendment or correction statement, the record:

(i) does not identify the initial financing statement as required by Section 9–512 or 9–518, as applicable; or

(ii) identifies an initial financing statement whose effectiveness has lapsed under Section 9–515;

(C) in the case of an initial financing statement that provides the name of a debtor identified as an individual or an amendment that provides a name of a debtor identified as an individual which was not previously provided in the financing statement to which the record relates, the record does not identify the debtor's last name; or

(D) in the case of a record filed [or recorded] in the filing office described in Section 9–501(a)(1), the record does not provide a sufficient description of the real property to which it relates;

(4) in the case of an initial financing statement or an amendment that adds a secured party of record, the record does not provide a name and mailing address for the secured party of record;

(5) in the case of an initial financing statement or an amendment that provides a name of a debtor which was not previously provided in the financing statement to which the amendment relates, the record does not:

(A) provide a mailing address for the debtor;

(B) indicate whether the debtor is an individual or an organization; or

(C) if the financing statement indicates that the debtor is an organization, provide:

(i) a type of organization for the debtor;

(ii) a jurisdiction of organization for the debtor; or

(iii) an organizational identification number for the debtor or indicate that the debtor has none;

(6) in the case of an assignment reflected in an initial financing statement under Section 9–514(a) or an amendment filed under Section 9–514(b), the record does not provide a name and mailing address for the assignee; or

(7) in the case of a continuation statement, the record is not filed within the six-month period prescribed by Section 9–515(d).

(c) For purposes of subsection (b):

(1) a record does not provide information if the filing office is unable to read or decipher the information; and

(2) a record that does not indicate that it is an amendment or identify an initial financing statement to which it relates, as required by Section 9–512, 9–514, or 9–518, is an initial financing statement.

(d) A record that is communicated to the filing office with tender of the filing fee, but which the filing office refuses to accept for a reason other than one set forth in subsection (b), is effective as a filed record except as against a purchaser of the collateral which gives value in reasonable reliance upon the absence of the record from the files.

§ 9–517. Effect of Indexing Errors.

The failure of the filing office to index a record correctly does not affect the effectiveness of the filed record.

§ 9–518. Claim Concerning Inaccurate or Wrongfully Filed Record.

(a) A person may file in the filing office a correction statement with respect to a record indexed there under the person's name if the person believes that the record is inaccurate or was wrongfully filed.

[Alternative A]

(b) A correction statement must:

(1) identify the record to which it relates by the file number assigned to the initial financing statement to which the record relates;

(2) indicate that it is a correction statement; and

(3) provide the basis for the person's belief that the record is inaccurate and indicate the manner in which the person believes the record should be amended to cure any inaccuracy or provide the basis for the person's belief that the record was wrongfully filed.

[Alternative B]

(b) A correction statement must:

(1) identify the record to which it relates by:

(A) the file number assigned to the initial financing statement to which the record relates; and

(B) if the correction statement relates to a record filed [or recorded] in a filing office described in Section 9–501(a)(1), the date [and time] that the initial financing statement was filed [or recorded] and the information specified in Section 9–502(b);

(2) indicate that it is a correction statement; and

(3) provide the basis for the person's belief that the record is inaccurate and indicate the manner in which the person believes the record should be amended to cure any inaccuracy or provide the basis for the person's belief that the record was wrongfully filed.

[End of Alternatives]

(c) The filing of a correction statement does not affect the effectiveness of an initial financing statement or other filed record.

Legislative Note: States whose real-estate filing offices require additional information in amendments and cannot search their records by both the name of the debtor and the file number should enact Alternative B to Sections 9–512(a), 9–518(b), 9–519(f), and 9–522(a).

[Subpart 2. Duties and Operation of Filing Office]

§ 9–519. Numbering, Maintaining, and Indexing Records; Communicating Information Provided in Records.

(a) For each record filed in a filing office, the filing office shall:

(1) assign a unique number to the filed record;

(2) create a record that bears the number assigned to the filed record and the date and time of filing;

(3) maintain the filed record for public inspection; and

(4) index the filed record in accordance with subsections (c), (d), and (e).

(b) A file number [assigned after January 1, 2002,] must include a digit that:

(1) is mathematically derived from or related to the other digits of the file number; and

(2) aids the filing office in determining whether a number communicated as the file number includes a single-digit or transpositional error.

(c) Except as otherwise provided in subsections (d) and (e), the filing office shall:

(1) index an initial financing statement according to the name of the debtor and index all filed records relating to the initial financing statement in a manner that associates with one another an initial financing statement and all filed records relating to the initial financing statement; and

(2) index a record that provides a name of a debtor which was not previously provided in the financing statement to which the record relates also according to the name that was not previously provided.

(d) If a financing statement is filed as a fixture filing or covers as-extracted collateral or timber to be cut, [it must be filed for record and] the filing office shall index it:

(1) under the names of the debtor and of each owner of record shown on the financing statement as if they were the mortgagors under a mortgage of the real property described; and

(2) to the extent that the law of this State provides for indexing of records of mortgages under the name of the mortgagee, under the name of the secured party as if the secured party were the mortgagee thereunder, or, if indexing is by description, as if the financing statement were a record of a mortgage of the real property described.

(e) If a financing statement is filed as a fixture filing or covers as-extracted collateral or timber to be cut, the filing office shall index an assignment filed under Section 9–514(a) or an amendment filed under Section 9–514(b):

(1) under the name of the assignor as grantor; and

(2) to the extent that the law of this State provides for indexing a record of the assignment of a mortgage under the name of the assignee, under the name of the assignee.

[Alternative A]

(f) The filing office shall maintain a capability:

(1) to retrieve a record by the name of the debtor and by the file number assigned to the initial financing statement to which the record relates; and

(2) to associate and retrieve with one another an initial financing statement and each filed record relating to the initial financing statement.

[Alternative B]

(f) The filing office shall maintain a capability:

(1) to retrieve a record by the name of the debtor and:

(A) if the filing office is described in Section 9–501(a)(1), by the file number assigned to the initial financing statement to which the record relates and the date [and time] that the record was filed [or recorded]; or

(B) if the filing office is described in Section 9–501(a)(2), by the file number assigned to the initial financing statement to which the record relates; and

(2) to associate and retrieve with one another an initial financing statement and each filed record relating to the initial financing statement.

[End of Alternatives]

(g) The filing office may not remove a debtor's name from the index until one year after the effectiveness of a financing statement naming the debtor lapses under Section 9–515 with respect to all secured parties of record.

(h) The filing office shall perform the acts required by subsections (a) through (e) at the time and in the manner prescribed by filing-office rule, but not later than two business days after the filing office receives the record in question.

[(i) Subsection[s] [(b)] [and] [(h)] do[es] not apply to a filing office described in Section 9–501(a)(1).]

Legislative Notes:

1. States whose filing offices currently assign file numbers that include a verification number, commonly known as a "check digit," or can implement this requirement before the effective date of this Article should omit the bracketed language in subsection (b).

2. In States in which writings will not appear in the real property records and indices unless actually recorded the bracketed language in subsection (d) should be used.

3. States whose real-estate filing offices require additional information in amendments and cannot search their records by both the name of the debtor and the file number should enact Alternative B to Sections 9–512(a), 9–518(b), 9–519(f), and 9–522(a).

4. A State that elects not to require real-estate filing offices to comply with either or both of subsections (b) and (h) may adopt an applicable variation of subsection (i) and add "Except as otherwise provided in subsection (i)," to the appropriate subsection or subsections.

§ 9–520. Acceptance and Refusal to Accept Record.

(a) A filing office shall refuse to accept a record for filing for a reason set forth in Section 9–516(b) and may refuse to accept a record for filing only for a reason set forth in Section 9–516(b).

(b) If a filing office refuses to accept a record for filing, it shall communicate to the person that presented the record the fact of and reason for the refusal and the date and time the record would have been filed had the filing office accepted it. The communication must be made at the time and in the manner prescribed by filing-office rule but [, in the case of a filing office described in Section 9–501(a)(2),] in no event more than two business days after the filing office receives the record.

(c) A filed financing statement satisfying Section 9–502(a) and (b) is effective, even if the filing office is required to refuse to accept it for filing under subsection (a). However, Section 9–338 applies to a filed financing statement providing information described in Section 9–516(b)(5) which is incorrect at the time the financing statement is filed.

(d) If a record communicated to a filing office provides information that relates to more than one debtor, this part applies as to each debtor separately.

Legislative Note: A State that elects not to require real-property filing offices to comply with subsection (b) should include the bracketed language.

§ 9–521. Uniform Form of Written Financing Statement and Amendment.

(a) A filing office that accepts written records may not refuse to accept a written initial financing statement in the following form and format except for a reason set forth in Section 9–516(b):

[NATIONAL UCC FINANCING STATEMENT (FORM UCC1)(REV. 7/29/98)]

[NATIONAL UCC FINANCING STATEMENT ADDENDUM (FORM UCC1Ad)(REV. 07/29/98)]

(b) A filing office that accepts written records may not refuse to accept a written record in the following form and format except for a reason set forth in Section 9–516(b):

[NATIONAL UCC FINANCING STATEMENT AMENDMENT (FORM UCC3)(REV. 07/29/98)]

[NATIONAL UCC FINANCING STATEMENT AMENDMENT ADDENDUM (FORM UCC3Ad)(REV. 07/29/98)]

§ 9–522. Maintenance and Destruction of Records.

[Alternative A]

(a) The filing office shall maintain a record of the information provided in a filed financing statement for at least one year after the effectiveness of the financing statement has lapsed under Section 9–515 with respect to all secured parties of record. The record must be retrievable by using the name of the debtor and by using the file number assigned to the initial financing statement to which the record relates.

[Alternative B]

(a) The filing office shall maintain a record of the information provided in a filed financing statement for at least one year after the effectiveness of the financing statement has lapsed under Section 9–515 with respect to all secured parties of record. The record must be retrievable by using the name of the debtor and:

filing would satisfy the applicable requirements for perfection under this [Act].

(c) This [Act] does not render ineffective an effective financing statement that, before this [Act] takes effect, is filed and satisfies the applicable requirements for perfection under the law of the jurisdiction governing perfection as provided in [former Section 9–103]. However, except as otherwise provided in subsections (d) and (e) and Section 9–706, the financing statement ceases to be effective at the earlier of:

(1) the time the financing statement would have ceased to be effective under the law of the jurisdiction in which it is filed; or

(2) June 30, 2006.

(d) The filing of a continuation statement after this [Act] takes effect does not continue the effectiveness of the financing statement filed before this [Act] takes effect. However, upon the timely filing of a continuation statement after this [Act] takes effect and in accordance with the law of the jurisdiction governing perfection as provided in Part 3, the effectiveness of a financing statement filed in the same office in that jurisdiction before this [Act] takes effect continues for the period provided by the law of that jurisdiction.

(e) Subsection (c)(2) applies to a financing statement that, before this [Act] takes effect, is filed against a transmitting utility and satisfies the applicable requirements for perfection under the law of the jurisdiction governing perfection as provided in [former Section 9–103] only to the extent that Part 3 provides that the law of a jurisdiction other than the jurisdiction in which the financing statement is filed governs perfection of a security interest in collateral covered by the financing statement.

(f) A financing statement that includes a financing statement filed before this [Act] takes effect and a continuation statement filed after this [Act] takes effect is effective only to the extent that it satisfies the requirements of Part 5 for an initial financing statement.

§ 9–706. **When Initial Financing Statement Suffices to Continue Effectiveness of Financing Statement.**

(a) The filing of an initial financing statement in the office specified in Section 9–501 continues the effectiveness of a financing statement filed before this [Act] takes effect if:

(1) the filing of an initial financing statement in that office would be effective to perfect a security interest under this [Act];

(2) the pre-effective-date financing statement was filed in an office in another State or another office in this State; and

(3) the initial financing statement satisfies subsection (c).

(b) The filing of an initial financing statement under subsection (a) continues the effectiveness of the pre-effective-date financing statement:

(1) if the initial financing statement is filed before this [Act] takes effect, for the period provided in [former Section 9–403] with respect to a financing statement; and

(2) if the initial financing statement is filed after this [Act] takes effect, for the period provided in Section 9–515 with respect to an initial financing statement.

(c) To be effective for purposes of subsection (a), an initial financing statement must:

(1) satisfy the requirements of Part 5 for an initial financing statement;

(2) identify the pre-effective-date financing statement by indicating the office in which the financing statement was filed and providing the dates of filing and file numbers, if any, of the financing statement and of the most recent continuation statement filed with respect to the financing statement; and

(3) indicate that the pre-effective-date financing statement remains effective.

§ 9–707. **Amendment of Pre-Effective-Date Financing Statement.**

(a) In this section, "Pre-effective-date financing statement" means a financing statement filed before this [Act] takes effect.

(b) After this [Act] takes effect, a person may add or delete collateral covered by, continue or terminate the effectiveness of, or otherwise amend the information provided in, a pre-effective-date financing statement only in accordance with the law of the jurisdiction governing perfection as provided in Part 3. However, the effectiveness of a pre-effective-date financing statement also may be terminated in accordance with the law of the jurisdiction in which the financing statement is filed.

(c) Except as otherwise provided in subsection (d), if the law of this State governs perfection of a security interest, the information in a pre-effective-date financing statement may be amended after this [Act] takes effect only if:

(1) the pre-effective-date financing statement and an amendment are filed in the office specified in Section 9–501;

(2) an amendment is filed in the office specified in Section 9–501 concurrently with, or after the filing in that office of, an initial financing statement that satisfies Section 9–706(c); or

(3) an initial financing statement that provides the information as amended and satisfies Section 9–706(c) is filed in the office specified in Section 9–501.

(d) If the law of this State governs perfection of a security interest, the effectiveness of a pre-effective-date financing statement may be continued only under Section 9–705(d) and (f) or 9–706.

(e) Whether or not the law of this State governs perfection of a security interest, the effectiveness of a pre-effective-date financing statement filed in this State may be terminated after this [Act] takes effect by filing a termination statement in the office in which the pre-effective-date financing statement is filed, unless an initial financing statement that satisfies Section 9–706(c) has been filed in the office specified by the law of the jurisdiction governing perfection as provided in Part 3 as the office in which to file a financing statement.

As amended in 2000.

§ 9–708. Persons Entitled to File Initial Financing Statement or Continuation Statement.

A person may file an initial financing statement or a continuation statement under this part if:

(1) the secured party of record authorizes the filing; and

(2) the filing is necessary under this part:

(A) to continue the effectiveness of a financing statement filed before this [Act] takes effect; or

(B) to perfect or continue the perfection of a security interest.

As amended in 2000.

§ 9–709. Priority.

(a) This [Act] determines the priority of conflicting claims to collateral. However, if the relative priorities of the claims were established before this [Act] takes effect, [former Article 9] determines priority.

(b) For purposes of Section 9–322(a), the priority of a security interest that becomes enforceable under Section 9–203 of this [Act] dates from the time this [Act] takes effect if the security interest is perfected under this [Act] by the filing of a financing statement before this [Act] takes effect which would not have been effective to perfect the security interest under [former Article 9]. This subsection does not apply to conflicting security interests each of which is perfected by the filing of such a financing statement.

As amended in 2000.

APPENDIX D

Uniform Partnership Act (Excerpts)

(The Uniform Partnership Act was amended in 1997 to provide limited liability for partners in a limited liability partnership. Over half the states, including District of Columbia, Puerto Rico, and the U.S. Virgin Islands, have adopted this latest version of the UPA.)

Article 1
GENERAL PROVISIONS

SECTION 101. Definitions In this [Act]:

* * * *

(6) "Partnership" means an association of two or more persons to carry on as co-owners a business for profit formed under Section 202, predecessor law, or comparable law of another jurisdiction.

(7) "Partnership agreement" means the agreement, whether written, oral, or implied, among the partners concerning the partnership, including amendments to the partnership agreement.

(8) "Partnership at will" means a partnership in which the partners have not agreed to remain partners until the expiration of a definite term or the completion of a particular undertaking.

(9) "Partnership interest" or "partner's interest in the partnership" means all of a partner's interests in the partnership, including the partner's transferable interest and all management and other rights.

(10) "Person" means an individual, corporation, business trust, estate, trust, partnership, association, joint venture, government, governmental subdivision, agency, or instrumentality, or any other legal or commercial entity.

* * * *

SECTION 103. Effect of Partnership Agreement; Nonwaivable Provisions.

(a) Except as otherwise provided in subsection (b), relations among the partners and between the partners and the partnership are governed by the partnership agreement. To the extent the partnership agreement does not otherwise provide, this [Act] governs relations among the partners and between the partners and the partnership.

(b) The partnership agreement may not:

(1) vary the rights and duties under Section 105 except to eliminate the duty to provide copies of statements to all of the partners;

(2) unreasonably restrict the right of access to books and records under Section 403(b);

(3) eliminate the duty of loyalty under Section 404(b) or 603(b)(3), but:

(i) the partnership agreement may identify specific types or categories of activities that do not violate the duty of loyalty, if not manifestly unreasonable; or

(ii) all of the partners or a number or percentage specified in the partnership agreement may authorize or ratify, after full disclosure of all material facts, a specific act or transaction that otherwise would violate the duty of loyalty;

(4) unreasonably reduce the duty of care under Section 404(c) or 603(b)(3);

(5) eliminate the obligation of good faith and fair dealing under Section 404(d), but the partnership agreement may prescribe the standards by which the performance of the obligation is to be measured, if the standards are not manifestly unreasonable;

(6) vary the power to dissociate as a partner under Section 602(a), except to require the notice under Section 601(1) to be in writing;

(7) vary the right of a court to expel a partner in the events specified in Section 601(5);

* * * *

SECTION 105. Execution, Filing, and Recording of Statements.

(a) A statement may be filed in the office of [the Secretary of State]. A certified copy of a statement that is filed in an office in another State may be filed in the office of [the Secretary of State]. Either filing has the effect provided in this [Act] with respect to partnership property located in or transactions that occur in this State.

(b) A certified copy of a statement that has been filed in the office of the [Secretary of State] and recorded in the office for recording transfers of real property has the effect provided for recorded statements in this [Act]. A recorded statement that is not a certified copy of a statement filed in the office of the [Secretary of State] does not have the effect provided for recorded statements in this [Act].

* * * *

SECTION 106. Governing Law.

(a) Except as otherwise provided in subsection (b), the law of the jurisdiction in which a partnership has its chief executive office governs relations among the partners and between the partners and the partnership.

(b) The law of this State governs relations among the partners and between the partners and the partnership and the liability of partners for an obligation of a limited liability partnership.

* * * *

Article 2
NATURE OF PARTNERSHIP

SECTION 201. Partnership as Entity.

(a) A partnership is an entity distinct from its partners.

(b) A limited liability partnership continues to be the same entity that existed before the filing of a statement of qualification under Section 1001.

SECTION 202. Formation of Partnership.

* * * *

(c) In determining whether a partnership is formed, the following rules apply:

(1) Joint tenancy, tenancy in common, tenancy by the entireties, joint property, common property, or part ownership does not by itself establish a partnership, even if the co-owners share profits made by the use of the property.

(2) The sharing of gross returns does not by itself establish a partnership, even if the persons sharing them have a joint or common right or interest in property from which the returns are derived.

(3) A person who receives a share of the profits of a business is presumed to be a partner in the business, unless the profits were received in payment:

(i) of a debt by installments or otherwise;

(ii) for services as an independent contractor or of wages or other compensation to an employee;

(iii) of rent;

(iv) of an annuity or other retirement or health benefit to a beneficiary, representative, or designee of a deceased or retired partner;

(v) of interest or other charge on a loan, even if the amount of payment varies with the profits of the business, including a direct or indirect present or future ownership of the collateral, or rights to income, proceeds, or increase in value derived from the collateral; or

(vi) for the sale of the goodwill of a business or other property by installments or otherwise.

SECTION 203. Partnership Property.

Property acquired by a partnership is property of the partnership and not of the partners individually.

SECTION 204. When Property is Partnership Property.

* * * *

(d) Property acquired in the name of one or more of the partners, without an indication in the instrument transferring title to the property of the person's capacity as a partner or of the existence of a partnership and without use of partnership assets, is presumed to be separate property, even if used for partnership purposes.

Article 3
RELATIONS OF PARTNERS TO PERSONS DEALING WITH PARTNERSHIP

SECTION 301. Partner Agent of Partnership.

Subject to the effect of a statement of partnership authority under Section 303:

(1) Each partner is an agent of the partnership for the purpose of its business. An act of a partner, including the execution of an instrument in the partnership name, for apparently carrying on in the ordinary course the partnership business or business of the kind carried on by the partnership binds the partnership, unless the partner had no authority to act for the partnership in the particular matter and the person with whom the partner was dealing knew or had received a notification that the partner lacked authority.

(2) An act of a partner which is not apparently for carrying on in the ordinary course the partnership business or business of the kind carried on by the partnership binds the partnership only if the act was authorized by the other partners.

* * * *

SECTION 303. Statement of Partnership Authority.

(a) A partnership may file a statement of partnership authority, which:

(1) must include:

(i) the name of the partnership;

(ii) the street address of its chief executive office and of one office in this State, if there is one;

(iii) the names and mailing addresses of all of the partners or of an agent appointed and maintained by the partnership for the purpose of subsection (b); and

(iv) the names of the partners authorized to execute an instrument transferring real property held in the name of the partnership; and

(2) may state the authority, or limitations on the authority, of some or all of the partners to enter into other transactions on behalf of the partnership and any other matter.

* * * *

(d) Except as otherwise provided in subsection (g), a filed statement of partnership authority supplements the authority of a partner to enter into transactions on behalf of the partnership as follows:

(1) Except for transfers of real property, a grant of authority contained in a filed statement of partnership authority is conclusive in favor of a person who gives value without knowledge to the contrary, so long as and to the extent that a limitation on that authority is not then contained in another filed statement. A filed cancellation of a limitation on authority revives the previous grant of authority.

(2) A grant of authority to transfer real property held in the name of the partnership contained in a certified copy of a filed statement of partnership authority recorded in the office for recording transfers of that real property is conclusive in favor of a person who gives value without knowledge to the contrary, so long as and to the extent that a certified copy of a filed statement containing a limitation on that authority is not then of record in the office for recording transfers of that real property. The recording in the office for recording transfers of that real property of a certified copy of a filed cancellation of a limitation on authority revives the previous grant of authority.

(e) A person not a partner is deemed to know of a limitation on the authority of a partner to transfer real property held in the name of the partnership if a certified copy of the filed statement containing the limitation on authority is of record in the office for recording transfers of that real property.

(f) Except as otherwise provided in subsections (d) and (e) and Sections 704 and 805, a person not a partner is not deemed to know of a limitation on the authority of a partner merely because the limitation is contained in a filed statement.

* * * *

SECTION 305. Partnership Liable for Partner's Actionable Conduct.

(a) A partnership is liable for loss or injury caused to a person, or for a penalty incurred, as a result of a wrongful act or omission, or other actionable conduct, of a partner acting in the ordinary course of business of the partnership or with authority of the partnership.

(b) If, in the course of the partnership's business or while acting with authority of the partnership, a partner receives or causes the partnership to receive money or property of a person not a partner, and the money or property is misapplied by a partner, the partnership is liable for the loss.

SECTION 306. Partner's Liability.

(a) Except as otherwise provided in subsections (b) and (c), all partners are liable jointly and severally for all obligations of the partnership unless otherwise agreed by the claimant or provided by law.

(b) A person admitted as a partner into an existing partnership is not personally liable for any partnership obligation incurred before the person's admission as a partner.

(c) An obligation of a partnership incurred while the partnership is a limited liability partnership, whether arising in contract, tort, or otherwise, is solely the obligation of the partnership. A partner is not personally liable, directly or indirectly, by way of contribution or otherwise, for such an obligation solely by reason of being or so acting as a partner. This subsection applies notwithstanding anything inconsistent in the partnership agreement that existed immediately before the vote required to become a limited liability partnership under Section 1001(b).

SECTION 307. Actions by and Against Partnership and Partners.

(a) A partnership may sue and be sued in the name of the partnership.

* * * *

(d) A judgment creditor of a partner may not levy execution against the assets of the partner to satisfy a judgment based on a claim against the partnership unless the partner is personally liable for the claim under Section 306 and:

(1) a judgment based on the same claim has been obtained against the partnership and a writ of execution on the judgment has been returned unsatisfied in whole or in part;

(2) the partnership is a debtor in bankruptcy;

(3) the partner has agreed that the creditor need not exhaust partnership assets;

(4) a court grants permission to the judgment creditor to levy execution against the assets of a partner based on a finding that partnership assets subject to execution are clearly insufficient to satisfy the judgment, that exhaustion of partnership assets is excessively burdensome, or that the grant of permission is an appropriate exercise of the court's equitable powers; or

(5) liability is imposed on the partner by law or contract independent of the existence of the partnership.

(e) This section applies to any partnership liability or obligation resulting from a representation by a partner or purported partner under Section 308.

SECTION 308. Liability of Purported Partner.

(a) If a person, by words or conduct, purports to be a partner, or consents to being represented by another as a partner, in a partnership or with one or more persons not partners, the purported partner is liable to a person to whom the representation is made, if that person, relying on the representation, enters into a transaction with the actual or purported partnership. If the representation, either by the purported partner or by a person with the purported partner's consent, is made in a public manner, the purported partner is liable to a person who relies upon the purported partnership even if the purported partner is not aware of being held out as a partner to the claimant. If partnership liability results, the purported partner is liable with respect to that liability as if the purported partner were a partner. If no partnership liability results, the purported partner is liable with respect to that liability jointly and severally with any other person consenting to the representation.

(b) If a person is thus represented to be a partner in an existing partnership, or with one or more persons not partners, the purported partner is an agent of persons consenting to the representation to bind them to the same extent and in the same manner as if the purported partner were a partner, with respect to persons who enter into transactions in reliance upon the representation. If all of the partners of the existing partnership consent to the representation, a partnership act or obligation results. If fewer than all of the partners of the existing partnership consent to the representation, the person acting and the partners consenting to the representation are jointly and severally liable.

* * * *

Article 4
RELATIONS OF PARTNERS TO EACH OTHER AND TO PARTNERSHIP

SECTION 401. Partner's Rights and Duties.

* * * *

(b) Each partner is entitled to an equal share of the partnership profits and is chargeable with a share of the partnership losses in proportion to the partner's share of the profits.

* * * *

(f) Each partner has equal rights in the management and conduct of the partnership business.

(g) A partner may use or possess partnership property only on behalf of the partnership.

(h) A partner is not entitled to remuneration for services performed for the partnership, except for reasonable compensation for services rendered in winding up the business of the partnership.

(i) A person may become a partner only with the consent of all of the partners.

(j) A difference arising as to a matter in the ordinary course of business of a partnership may be decided by a majority of the partners. An act outside the ordinary course of business of a partnership and an amendment to the partnership agreement may be undertaken only with the consent of all of the partners.

* * * *

SECTION 403. Partner's Rights and Duties with Respect to Information.

(a) A partnership shall keep its books and records, if any, at its chief executive office.

(b) A partnership shall provide partners and their agents and attorneys access to its books and records. It shall provide former partners and their agents and attorneys access to books and records pertaining to the period during which they were partners. The right of access provides the opportunity to inspect and copy books and records during ordinary business hours. A partnership may impose a reasonable charge, covering the costs of labor and material, for copies of documents furnished.

* * * *

SECTION 404. General Standards of Partner's Conduct.

(a) The only fiduciary duties a partner owes to the partnership and the other partners are the duty of loyalty and the duty of care set forth in subsections (b) and (c).

(b) A partner's duty of loyalty to the partnership and the other partners is limited to the following:

(1) to account to the partnership and hold as trustee for it any property, profit, or benefit derived by the partner in the conduct and winding up of the partnership business or

APPENDIX E

Revised Model Business Corporation Act (Excerpts)

Chapter 2. INCORPORATION

§ 2.01 Incorporators

One or more persons may act as the incorporator or incorporators of a corporation by delivering articles of incorporation to the secretary of state for filing.

§ 2.02 Articles of Incorporation

(a) The articles of incorporation must set forth:

(1) a corporate name * * * ;

(2) the number of shares the corporation is authorized to issue;

(3) the street address of the corporation's initial registered office and the name of its initial registered agent at that office; and

(4) the name and address of each incorporator.

(b) The articles of incorporation may set forth:

(1) the names and addresses of the individuals who are to serve as the initial directors;

(2) provisions not inconsistent with law regarding:

(i) the purpose or purposes for which the corporation is organized;

(ii) managing the business and regulating the affairs of the corporation;

(iii) defining, limiting, and regulating the powers of the corporation, its board of directors, and shareholders;

(iv) a par value for authorized shares or classes of shares;

(v) the imposition of personal liability on shareholders for the debts of the corporation to a specified extent and upon specified conditions;

(3) any provision that under this Act is required or permitted to be set forth in the bylaws; and

(4) a provision eliminating or limiting the liability of a director to the corporation or its shareholders for money damages for any action taken, or any failure to take any action, as a director, except liability for (A) the amount of a financial benefit received by a director to which he is not entitled; (B) an intentional infliction of harm on the corporation or the shareholders; (C) [unlawful distributions]; or (D) an intentional violation of criminal law.

(c) The articles of incorporation need not set forth any of the corporate powers enumerated in this Act.

§ 2.03 Incorporation

(a) Unless a delayed effective date is specified, the corporate existence begins when the articles of incorporation are filed.

(b) The secretary of state's filing of the articles of incorporation is conclusive proof that the incorporators satisfied all conditions precedent to incorporation except in a proceeding by the state to cancel or revoke the incorporation or involuntarily dissolve the corporation.

§ 2.04 Liability for Preincorporation Transactions

All persons purporting to act as or on behalf of a corporation, knowing there was no incorporation under this Act, are jointly and severally liable for all liabilities created while so acting.

§ 2.05 Organization of Corporation

(a) After incorporation:

(1) if initial directors are named in the articles of incorporation, the initial directors shall hold an organizational meeting, at the call of a majority of the directors, to complete the organization of the corporation by appointing officers, adopting bylaws, and carrying on any other business brought before the meeting;

(2) if initial directors are not named in the articles, the incorporator or incorporators shall hold an organizational meeting at the call of a majority of the incorporators:

(i) to elect directors and complete the organization of the corporation; or

(ii) to elect a board of directors who shall complete the organization of the corporation.

(b) Action required or permitted by this Act to be taken by incorporators at an organizational meeting may be taken without a meeting if the action taken is evidenced by one or more written consents describing the action taken and signed by each incorporator.

(c) An organizational meeting may be held in or out of this state.

* * * *

Chapter 3. PURPOSES AND POWERS

§ 3.01 Purposes

(a) Every corporation incorporated under this Act has the purpose of engaging in any lawful business unless a more limited purpose is set forth in the articles of incorporation.

(b) A corporation engaging in a business that is subject to regulation under another statute of this state may incorporate under this Act only if permitted by, and subject to all limitations of, the other statute.

§ 3.02 General Powers

Unless its articles of incorporation provide otherwise, every corporation has perpetual duration and succession in its corporate name and has the same powers as an individual to do all things necessary or convenient to carry out its business and affairs, including without limitation power:

(1) to sue and be sued, complain and defend in its corporate name;

(2) to have a corporate seal, which may be altered at will, and to use it, or a facsimile of it, by impressing or affixing it or in any other manner reproducing it;

(3) to make and amend bylaws, not inconsistent with its articles of incorporation or with the laws of this state, for managing the business and regulating the affairs of the corporation;

(4) to purchase, receive, lease, or otherwise acquire, and own, hold, improve, use, and otherwise deal with, real or personal property, or any legal or equitable interest in property, wherever located;

(5) to sell, convey, mortgage, pledge, lease, exchange, and otherwise dispose of all or any part of its property;

(6) to purchase, receive, subscribe for, or otherwise acquire; own, hold, vote, use, sell, mortgage, lend, pledge, or otherwise dispose of; and deal in and with shares or other interests in, or obligations of, any other entity;

(7) to make contracts and guarantees, incur liabilities, borrow money, issue its notes, bonds, and other obligations (which may be convertible into or include the option to purchase other securities of the corporation), and secure any of its obligations by mortgage or pledge of any of its property, franchises, or income;

(8) to lend money, invest and reinvest its funds, and receive and hold real and personal property as security for repayment;

(9) to be a promoter, partner, member, associate, or manager of any partnership, joint venture, trust, or other entity;

(10) to conduct its business, locate offices, and exercise the powers granted by this Act within or without this state;

(11) to elect directors and appoint officers, employees, and agents of the corporation, define their duties, fix their compensation, and lend them money and credit;

(12) to pay pensions and establish pension plans, pension trusts, profit sharing plans, share bonus plans, share option plans, and benefit or incentive plans for any or all of its current or former directors, officers, employees, and agents;

(13) to make donations for the public welfare or for charitable, scientific, or educational purposes;

(14) to transact any lawful business that will aid governmental policy;

(15) to make payments or donations, or do any other act, not inconsistent with law, that furthers the business and affairs of the corporation.

* * * *

Chapter 5. OFFICE AND AGENT

§ 5.01 Registered Office and Registered Agent

Each corporation must continuously maintain in this state:

(1) a registered office that may be the same as any of its places of business; and

(2) a registered agent, who may be:

(i) an individual who resides in this state and whose business office is identical with the registered office;

(ii) a domestic corporation or not-for-profit domestic corporation whose business office is identical with the registered office; or

(iii) a foreign corporation or not-for-profit foreign corporation authorized to transact business in this state whose business office is identical with the registered office.

* * * *

§ 5.04 Service on Corporation

(a) A corporation's registered agent is the corporation's agent for service of process, notice, or demand required or permitted by law to be served on the corporation.

(b) If a corporation has no registered agent, or the agent cannot with reasonable diligence be served, the corporation may be served by registered or certified mail, return receipt requested, addressed to the secretary of the corporation at its principal office. Service is perfected under this subsection at the earliest of:

(1) the date the corporation receives the mail;

(2) the date shown on the return receipt, if signed on behalf of the corporation; or

(3) five days after its deposit in the United States Mail, if mailed postpaid and correctly addressed.

(c) This section does not prescribe the only means, or necessarily the required means, of serving a corporation.

Chapter 6. SHARES AND DISTRIBUTIONS

* * * *

Subchapter B. Issuance of Shares

* * * *

§ 6.21 Issuance of Shares

(a) The powers granted in this section to the board of directors may be reserved to the shareholders by the articles of incorporation.

(b) The board of directors may authorize shares to be issued for consideration consisting of any tangible or intangible property or benefit to the corporation, including cash, promissory notes, services performed, contracts for services to be performed, or other securities of the corporation.

(c) Before the corporation issues shares, the board of directors must determine that the consideration received or to be received for shares to be issued is adequate. That determination by the board of directors is conclusive insofar as the adequacy of consideration for the issuance of shares relates to whether the shares are validly issued, fully paid, and nonassessable.

(d) When the corporation receives the consideration for which the board of directors authorized the issuance of shares, the shares issued therefor are fully paid and nonassessable.

(e) The corporation may place in escrow shares issued for a contract for future services or benefits or a promissory note, or make other arrangements to restrict the transfer of the shares, and may credit distributions in respect of the shares against their purchase price, until the services are performed, the note is paid, or the benefits received. If the services are not performed, the note is not paid, or the benefits are not received, the shares escrowed or restricted and the distributions credited may be cancelled in whole or part.

* * * *

§ 6.27 Restriction on Transfer or Registration of Shares and Other Securities

(a) The articles of incorporation, bylaws, an agreement among shareholders, or an agreement between shareholders and the corporation may impose restrictions on the transfer or registration of transfer of shares of the corporation. A restriction does not affect shares issued before the restriction was adopted unless the holders of the shares are parties to the restriction agreement or voted in favor of the restriction.

(b) A restriction on the transfer or registration of transfer of shares is valid and enforceable against the holder or a transferee of the holder if the restriction is authorized by this section and its existence is noted conspicuously on the front or back of the certificate or is contained in the information statement [sent to the shareholder]. Unless so noted, a restriction is not enforceable against a person without knowledge of the restriction.

(c) A restriction on the transfer or registration of transfer of shares is authorized:

(1) to maintain the corporation's status when it is dependent on the number or identity of its shareholders;

(2) to preserve exemptions under federal or state securities law;

(3) for any other reasonable purpose.

(d) A restriction on the transfer or registration of transfer of shares may:

(1) obligate the shareholder first to offer the corporation or other persons (separately, consecutively, or simultaneously) an opportunity to acquire the restricted shares;

(2) obligate the corporate or other persons (separately, consecutively, or simultaneously) to acquire the restricted shares;

(3) require the corporation, the holders of any class of its shares, or another person to approve the transfer of the restricted shares, if the requirement is not manifestly unreasonable;

(4) prohibit the transfer of the restricted shares to designated persons or classes of persons, if the prohibition is not manifestly unreasonable.

(e) For purposes of this section, "shares" includes a security convertible into or carrying a right to subscribe for or acquire shares.

* * * *

Chapter 7. SHAREHOLDERS

Subchapter A. Meetings

§ 7.01 Annual Meeting

(a) A corporation shall hold annually at a time stated in or fixed in accordance with the bylaws a meeting of shareholders.

(b) Annual shareholders' meetings may be held in or out of this state at the place stated in or fixed in accordance with the bylaws. If no place is stated in or fixed in accordance with the bylaws, annual meetings shall be held at the corporation's principal office.

(c) The failure to hold an annual meeting at the time stated in or fixed in accordance with a corporation's bylaws does not affect the validity of any corporate action.

* * * *

§ 7.05 Notice of Meeting

(a) A corporation shall notify shareholders of the date, time, and place of each annual and special shareholders' meeting no fewer than 10 nor more than 60 days before the meeting date. Unless this Act or the articles of incorporation require otherwise, the corporation is required to give notice only to shareholders entitled to vote at the meeting.

(b) Unless this Act or the articles of incorporation require otherwise, notice of an annual meeting need not include a description of the purpose or purposes for which the meeting is called.

(c) Notice of a special meeting must include a description of the purpose or purposes for which the meeting is called.

(d) If not otherwise fixed * * *, the record date for determining shareholders entitled to notice of and to vote at an annual or special shareholders' meeting is the day before the first notice is delivered to shareholders.

(e) Unless the bylaws require otherwise, if an annual or special shareholders' meeting is adjourned to a different date, time, or place, notice need not be given of the new date, time, or place if the new date, time, or place is announced at the meeting before adjournment. * * *

* * * *

§ 7.07 Record Date

(a) The bylaws may fix or provide the manner of fixing the record date for one or more voting groups in order to determine the shareholders entitled to notice of a shareholders' meeting, to demand a special meeting, to vote, or to take any other action. If the bylaws do not fix or provide for fixing a record date, the board of directors of the corporation may fix a future date as the record date.

(b) A record date fixed under this section may not be more than 70 days before the meeting or action requiring a determination of shareholders.

(c) A determination of shareholders entitled to notice of or to vote at a shareholders' meeting is effective for any adjournment of the meeting unless the board of directors fixes a new record date, which it must do if the meeting is adjourned to a date more than 120 days after the date fixed for the original meeting.

(d) If a court orders a meeting adjourned to a date more than 120 days after the date fixed for the original meeting, it may provide that the original record date continues in effect or it may fix a new record date.

Subchapter B. Voting

§ 7.20 Shareholders' List for Meeting

(a) After fixing a record date for a meeting, a corporation shall prepare an alphabetical list of the names of all its shareholders who are entitled to notice of a shareholders' meeting. The list must be arranged by voting group (and within each voting group by class or series of shares) and show the address of and number of shares held by each shareholder.

(b) The shareholders' list must be available for inspection by any shareholder, beginning two business days after notice of the meeting is given for which the list was prepared and continuing through the meeting, at the corporation's principal office or at a place identified in the meeting notice in the city where the meeting will be held. A shareholder, his agent, or attorney is entitled on written demand to inspect and, subject to the requirements of section 16.02(c), to copy the list, during regular business hours and at his expense, during the period it is available for inspection.

(c) The corporation shall make the shareholders' list available at the meeting, and any shareholder, his agent, or attorney is entitled to inspect the list at any time during the meeting or any adjournment.

(d) If the corporation refuses to allow a shareholder, his agent, or attorney to inspect the shareholders' list before or at the meeting (or copy the list as permitted by subsection (b)), the [name or describe] court of the county where a corporation's principal office (or, if none in this state, its registered office) is located, on application of the shareholder, may summarily order the inspection or copying at the corporation's expense and may postpone the meeting for which the list was prepared until the inspection or copying is complete.

(e) Refusal or failure to prepare or make available the shareholders' list does not affect the validity of action taken at the meeting.

* * * *

§ 7.22 Proxies

(a) A shareholder may vote his shares in person or by proxy.

(b) A shareholder may appoint a proxy to vote or otherwise act for him by signing an appointment form, either personally or by his attorney-in-fact.

(c) An appointment of a proxy is effective when received by the secretary or other officer or agent authorized to tabulate votes. An appointment is valid for 11 months unless a longer period is expressly provided in the appointment form.

* * * *

§ 7.28 Voting for Directors; Cumulative Voting

(a) Unless otherwise provided in the articles of incorporation, directors are elected by a plurality of the votes cast by the shares entitled to vote in the election at a meeting at which a quorum is present.

(b) Shareholders do not have a right to cumulate their votes for directors unless the articles of incorporation so provide.

(c) A statement included in the articles of incorporation that "[all] [a designated voting group of] shareholders are entitled to cumulate their votes for directors" (or words of similar import) means that the shareholders designated are entitled to multiply the number of votes they are entitled to cast by the number of directors for whom they are entitled to vote and cast the product for a single candidate or distribute the product among two or more candidates.

(d) Shares otherwise entitled to vote cumulatively may not be voted cumulatively at a particular meeting unless:

(1) the meeting notice or proxy statement accompanying the notice states conspicuously that cumulative voting is authorized; or

(2) a shareholder who has the right to cumulate his votes gives notice to the corporation not less than 48 hours before the time set for the meeting of his intent to cumulate his votes during the meeting, and if one shareholder gives this notice all other shareholders in the same voting group participating in the election are entitled to cumulate their votes without giving further notice.

* * * *

Subchapter D. Derivative Proceedings

* * * *

§ 7.41 Standing

A shareholder may not commence or maintain a derivative proceeding unless the shareholder:

(1) was a shareholder of the corporation at the time of the act or omission complained of or became a shareholder through transfer by operation of law from one who was a shareholder at that time; and

(2) fairly and adequately represents the interests of the corporation in enforcing the right of the corporation.

§ 7.42 Demand

No shareholder may commence a derivative proceeding until:

(1) a written demand has been made upon the corporation to take suitable action; and

(2) 90 days have expired from the date the demand was made unless the shareholder has earlier been notified that the demand has been rejected by the corporation or unless irreparable injury to the corporation would result by waiting for the expiration of the 90 day period.

* * * *

Chapter 8. DIRECTORS AND OFFICERS

Subchapter A. Board of Directors

* * * *

§ 8.02 Qualifications of Directors

The articles of incorporation or bylaws may prescribe qualifications for directors. A director need not be a resident of this state or a shareholder of the corporation unless the articles of incorporation or bylaws so prescribe.

§ 8.03 Number and Election of Directors

(a) A board of directors must consist of one or more individuals, with the number specified in or fixed in accordance with the articles of incorporation or bylaws.

(b) If a board of directors has power to fix or change the number of directors, the board may increase or decrease by 30 percent or less the number of directors last approved by the shareholders, but only the shareholders may increase or decrease by more than 30 percent the number of directors last approved by the shareholders.

(c) The articles of incorporation or bylaws may establish a variable range for the size of the board of directors by fixing a minimum and maximum number of directors. If a variable range is established, the number of directors may be fixed or changed from time to time, within the minimum and maximum, by the shareholders or the board of directors. After shares are issued, only the shareholders may change the range for the size of the board or change from a fixed to a variable-range size board or vice versa.

(d) Directors are elected at the first annual shareholders' meeting and at each annual meeting thereafter unless their terms are staggered under section 8.06.

* * * *

§ 8.08 Removal of Directors by Shareholders

(a) The shareholders may remove one or more directors with or without cause unless the articles of incorporation provide that directors may be removed only for cause.

(b) If a director is elected by a voting group of shareholders, only the shareholders of that voting group may participate in the vote to remove him.

(c) If cumulative voting is authorized, a director may not be removed if the number of votes sufficient to elect him under cumulative voting is voted against his removal. If cumulative voting is not authorized, a director may be removed only if the number of votes cast to remove him exceeds the number of votes cast not to remove him.

(d) A director may be removed by the shareholders only at a meeting called for the purpose of removing him and the meeting notice must state that the purpose, or one of the purposes, of the meeting is removal of the director.

* * * *

Subchapter B. Meetings and Action of the Board

§ 8.20 Meetings

(a) The board of directors may hold regular or special meetings in or out of this state.

(b) Unless the articles of incorporation or bylaws provide otherwise, the board of directors may permit any or all directors to participate in a regular or special meeting by, or conduct the meeting through the use of, any means of communication by which all directors participating may simultaneously hear each other during the meeting. A director participating in a meeting by this means is deemed to be present in person at the meeting.

* * * *

§ 8.22 Notice of Meeting

(a) Unless the articles of incorporation or bylaws provide otherwise, regular meetings of the board of directors may be held without notice of the date, time, place, or purpose of the meeting.

(b) Unless the articles of incorporation or bylaws provide for a longer or shorter period, special meetings of the board of directors must be preceded by at least two days' notice of the date, time, and place of the meeting. The notice need not describe the purpose of the special meeting unless required by the articles of incorporation or bylaws.

* * * *

§ 8.24 Quorum and Voting

(a) Unless the articles of incorporation or bylaws require a greater number, a quorum of a board of directors consists of:

(1) a majority of the fixed number of directors if the corporation has a fixed board size; or

(2) a majority of the number of directors prescribed, or if no number is prescribed the number in office immediately before the meeting begins, if the corporation has a variable-range size board.

(b) The articles of incorporation or bylaws may authorize a quorum of a board of directors to consist of no fewer than one-third of the fixed or prescribed number of directors determined under subsection (a).

(c) If a quorum is present when a vote is taken, the affirmative vote of a majority of directors present is the act of the board of directors unless the articles of incorporation or bylaws require the vote of a greater number of directors.

(d) A director who is present at a meeting of the board of directors or a committee of the board of directors when corporate action is taken is deemed to have assented to the action taken unless: (1) he objects at the beginning of the meeting (or promptly upon his arrival) to holding it or transacting business at the meeting; (2) his dissent or abstention from the action taken is entered in the minutes of the meeting; or (3) he delivers written notice of his dissent or abstention to the presiding officer of the meeting before its adjournment or to the corporation immediately after adjournment of the meeting. The right of dissent or abstention is not available to a director who votes in favor of the action taken.

* * * *

Subchapter C. Standards of Conduct

§ 8.30 General Standards for Directors

(a) A director shall discharge his duties as a director, including his duties as a member of a committee:

(1) in good faith;

(2) with the care an ordinarily prudent person in a like position would exercise under similar circumstances; and

(3) in a manner he reasonably believes to be in the best interests of the corporation.

(b) In discharging his duties a director is entitled to rely on information, opinions, reports, or statements, including financial statements and other financial data, if prepared or presented by:

(1) one or more officers or employees of the corporation whom the director reasonably believes to be reliable and competent in the matters presented;

(2) legal counsel, public accountants, or other persons as to matters the director reasonably believes are within the person's professional or expert competence; or

(3) a committee of the board of directors of which he is not a member if the director reasonably believes the committee merits confidence.

(c) A director is not acting in good faith if he has knowledge concerning the matter in question that makes reliance otherwise permitted by subsection (b) unwarranted.

(d) A director is not liable for any action taken as a director, or any failure to take any action, if he performed the duties of his office in compliance with this section.

* * * *

Subchapter D. Officers

* * * *

§ 8.41 Duties of Officers

Each officer has the authority and shall perform the duties set forth in the bylaws or, to the extent consistent with the bylaws, the duties prescribed by the board of directors or by direction of an officer authorized by the board of directors to prescribe the duties of other officers.

§ 8.42 Standards of Conduct for Officers

(a) An officer with discretionary authority shall discharge his duties under that authority:

(1) in good faith;

(2) with the care an ordinarily prudent person in a like position would exercise under similar circumstances; and

(3) in a manner he reasonably believes to be in the best interests of the corporation.

(b) In discharging his duties an officer is entitled to rely on information, opinions, reports, or statements, including financial statements and other financial data, if prepared or presented by:

(1) one or more officers or employees of the corporation whom the officer reasonably believes to be reliable and competent in the matters presented; or

(2) legal counsel, public accountants, or other persons as to matters the officer reasonably believes are within the person's professional or expert competence.

(c) An officer is not acting in good faith if he has knowledge concerning the matter in question that makes reliance otherwise permitted by subsection (b) unwarranted.

(d) An officer is not liable for any action taken as an officer, or any failure to take any action, if he performed the duties of his office in compliance with this section.

* * * *

Chapter 11. MERGER AND SHARE EXCHANGE

§ 11.01 Merger

(a) One or more corporations may merge into another corporation if the board of directors of each corporation adopts and its shareholders (if required * * *) approve a plan of merger.

(b) The plan of merger must set forth:

(1) the name of each corporation planning to merge and the name of the surviving corporation into which each other corporation plans to merge;

(2) the terms and conditions of the merger; and

(3) the manner and basis of converting the shares of each corporation into shares, obligations, or other securities of the surviving or any other corporation or into cash or other property in whole or part.

(c) The plan of merger may set forth:

(1) amendments to the articles of incorporation of the surviving corporation; and

(2) other provisions relating to the merger.

* * * *

§ 11.04 Merger of Subsidiary

(a) A parent corporation owning at least 90 percent of the outstanding shares of each class of a subsidiary corporation may merge the subsidiary into itself without approval of the shareholders of the parent or subsidiary.

(b) The board of directors of the parent shall adopt a plan of merger that sets forth:

(1) the names of the parent and subsidiary; and

(2) the manner and basis of converting the shares of the subsidiary into shares, obligations, or other securities of the parent or any other corporation or into cash or other property in whole or part.

(c) The parent shall mail a copy or summary of the plan of merger to each shareholder of the subsidiary who does not waive the mailing requirement in writing.

(d) The parent may not deliver articles of merger to the secretary of state for filing until at least 30 days after the date it mailed a copy of the plan of merger to each shareholder of the subsidiary who did not waive the mailing requirement.

(e) Articles of merger under this section may not contain amendments to the articles of incorporation of the parent corporation (except for amendments enumerated in section 10.02).

* * * *

§ 11.06 Effect of Merger or Share Exchange

(a) When a merger takes effect:

(1) every other corporation party to the merger merges into the surviving corporation and the separate existence of every corporation except the surviving corporation ceases;

(2) the title to all real estate and other property owned by each corporation party to the merger is vested in the surviving corporation without reversion or impairment;

(3) the surviving corporation has all liabilities of each corporation party to the merger;

(4) a proceeding pending against any corporation party to the merger may be continued as if the merger did not occur or the surviving corporation may be substituted in the proceeding for the corporation whose existence ceased;

(5) the articles of incorporation of the surviving corporation are amended to the extent provided in the plan of merger; and

(6) the shares of each corporation party to the merger that are to be converted into shares, obligations, or other securities of the surviving or any other corporation or into cash or other property are converted and the former holders of the shares are entitled only to the rights provided in the articles of merger or to their rights under chapter 13.

(b) When a share exchange takes effect, the shares of each acquired corporation are exchanged as provided in the plan, and the former holders of the shares are entitled only to the exchange rights provided in the articles of share exchange or to their rights under chapter 13.

* * * *

Chapter 13. DISSENTERS' RIGHTS

Subchapter A. Right to Dissent and Obtain Payment for Shares

* * * *

§ 13.02 Right to Dissent

(a) A shareholder is entitled to dissent from, and obtain payment of the fair value of his shares in the event of, any of the following corporate actions:

(1) consummation of a plan of merger to which the corporation is a party (i) if shareholder approval is required for the merger by [statute] or the articles of incorporation and the shareholder is entitled to vote on the merger or (ii) if the corporation is a subsidiary that is merged with its parent under section 11.04;

(2) consummation of a plan of share exchange to which the corporation is a party as the corporation whose shares will be acquired, if the shareholder is entitled to vote on the plan;

(3) consummation of a sale or exchange of all, or substantially all, of the property of the corporation other than in the usual and regular course of business, if the shareholder is entitled to vote on the sale or exchange, including a sale in dissolution, but not including a sale pursuant to court order or a sale for cash pursuant to a plan by which all or substantially all of the net proceeds of the sale will be distributed to the shareholders within one year after the date of sale;

(4) an amendment of the articles of incorporation that materially and adversely affects rights in respect of a dissenter's shares because it:

(i) alters or abolishes a preferential right of the shares;

(ii) creates, alters, or abolishes a right in respect of redemption, including a provision respecting a sinking fund for the redemption or repurchase, of the shares;

(iii) alters or abolishes a preemptive right of the holder of the shares to acquire shares or other securities;

(iv) excludes or limits the right of the shares to vote on any matter, or to cumulate votes, other than a limitation by dilution through issuance of shares or other securities with similar voting rights; or

(v) reduces the number of shares owned by the shareholder to a fraction of a share if the fractional share so created is to be acquired for cash * * * ; or

(5) any corporate action taken pursuant to a shareholder vote to the extent the articles of incorporation, bylaws, or a resolution of the board of directors provides that voting or nonvoting shareholders are entitled to dissent and obtain payment for their shares.

(b) A shareholder entitled to dissent and obtain payment for his shares under this chapter may not challenge the corporate action creating his entitlement unless the action is unlawful or fraudulent with respect to the shareholder or the corporation.

* * * *

Subchapter B. Procedure for Exercise of Dissenters' Rights

* * * *

§ 13.21 Notice of Intent to Demand Payment

(a) If proposed corporate action creating dissenters' rights under section 13.02 is submitted to a vote at a shareholders' meeting, a shareholder who wishes to assert dissenters' rights (1) must deliver to the corporation before the vote is taken written notice of his intent to demand payment for his shares if the proposed action is effectuated and (2) must not vote his shares in favor of the proposed action.

(b) A shareholder who does not satisfy the requirements of subsection (a) is not entitled to payment for his shares under this chapter.

* * * *

§ 13.25 Payment

(a) * * * [A]s soon as the proposed corporate action is taken, or upon receipt of a payment demand, the corporation shall pay each dissenter * * * the amount the corporation estimates to be the fair value of his shares, plus accrued interest.

* * * *

§ 13.28 Procedure If Shareholder Dissatisfied with Payment or Offer

(a) A dissenter may notify the corporation in writing of his own estimate of the fair value of his shares and amount of interest due, and demand payment of his estimate (less any payment under section 13.25) * * * if:

(1) the dissenter believes that the amount paid under section 13.25 * * * is less than the fair value of his shares or that the interest due is incorrectly calculated;

(2) the corporation fails to make payment under section 13.25 within 60 days after the date set for demanding payment; or

(3) the corporation, having failed to take the proposed action, does not return the deposited certificates or release the transfer restrictions imposed on uncertificated shares within 60 days after the date set for demanding payment.

(b) A dissenter waives his right to demand payment under this section unless he notifies the corporation of his demand in writing under subsection (a) within 30 days after the corporation made or offered payment for his shares.

* * * *

Chapter 14. DISSOLUTION

Subchapter A. Voluntary Dissolution

* * * *

§ 14.02 Dissolution by Board of Directors and Shareholders

(a) A corporation's board of directors may propose dissolution for submission to the shareholders.

(b) For a proposal to dissolve to be adopted:

(1) the board of directors must recommend dissolution to the shareholders unless the board of directors determines that because of conflict of interest or other special circumstances

it should make no recommendation and communicates the basis for its determination to the shareholders; and

(2) the shareholders entitled to vote must approve the proposal to dissolve as provided in subsection (e).

(c) The board of directors may condition its submission of the proposal for dissolution on any basis.

(d) The corporation shall notify each shareholder, whether or not entitled to vote, of the proposed shareholders' meeting in accordance with section 7.05. The notice must also state that the purpose, or one of the purposes, of the meeting is to consider dissolving the corporation.

(e) Unless the articles of incorporation or the board of directors (acting pursuant to subsection (c)) require a greater vote or a vote by voting groups, the proposal to dissolve to be adopted must be approved by a majority of all the votes entitled to be cast on that proposal.

* * * *

§ 14.05 Effect of Dissolution

(a) A dissolved corporation continues its corporate existence but may not carry on any business except that appropriate to wind up and liquidate its business and affairs, including:

(1) collecting its assets;

(2) disposing of its properties that will not be distributed in kind to its shareholders;

(3) discharging or making provision for discharging its liabilities;

(4) distributing its remaining property among its shareholders according to their interests; and

(5) doing every other act necessary to wind up and liquidate its business and affairs.

(b) Dissolution of a corporation does not:

(1) transfer title to the corporation's property;

(2) prevent transfer of its shares or securities, although the authorization to dissolve may provide for closing the corporation's share transfer records;

(3) subject its directors or officers to standards of conduct different from those prescribed in chapter 8;

(4) change quorum or voting requirements for its board of directors or shareholders; change provisions for selection, resignation, or removal of its directors or officers or both; or change provisions for amending its bylaws;

(5) prevent commencement of a proceeding by or against the corporation in its corporate name;

(6) abate or suspend a proceeding pending by or against the corporation on the effective date of dissolution; or

(7) terminate the authority of the registered agent of the corporation.

* * * *

Subchapter C. Judicial Dissolution

§ 14.30 Grounds for Judicial Dissolution

The [name or describe court or courts] may dissolve a corporation:

(1) in a proceeding by the attorney general if it is established that:

(i) the corporation obtained its articles of incorporation through fraud; or

(ii) the corporation has continued to exceed or abuse the authority conferred upon it by law;

(2) in a proceeding by a shareholder if it is established that:

(i) the directors are deadlocked in the management of the corporate affairs, the shareholders are unable to break the deadlock, and irreparable injury to the corporation is threatened or being suffered, or the business and affairs of the corporation can no longer be conducted to the advantage of the shareholders generally, because of the deadlock;

(ii) the directors or those in control of the corporation have acted, are acting, or will act in a manner that is illegal, oppressive, or fraudulent;

(iii) the shareholders are deadlocked in voting power and have failed, for a period that includes at least two consecutive annual meeting dates, to elect successors to directors whose terms have expired; or

(iv) the corporate assets are being misapplied or wasted;

(3) in a proceeding by a creditor if it is established that:

(i) the creditor's claim has been reduced to judgment, the execution on the judgment returned unsatisfied, and the corporation is insolvent; or

(ii) the corporation has admitted in writing that the creditor's claim is due and owing and the corporation is insolvent; or

(4) in a proceeding by the corporation to have its voluntary dissolution continued under court supervision.

* * * *

Chapter 16. RECORDS AND REPORTS

Subchapter A. Records

§ 16.01 Corporate Records

(a) A corporation shall keep as permanent records minutes of all meetings of its shareholders and board of directors, a record of all actions taken by the shareholders or board of directors without a meeting, and a record of all actions taken by a committee of the board of directors in place of the board of directors on behalf of the corporation.

(b) A corporation shall maintain appropriate accounting records.

(c) A corporation or its agent shall maintain a record of its shareholders, in a form that permits preparation of a list of the names and addresses of all shareholders, in alphabetical order by class of shares showing the number and class of shares held by each.

(d) A corporation shall maintain its records in written form or in another form capable of conversion into written form within a reasonable time.

(e) A corporation shall keep a copy of the following records at its principal office:

(1) its articles or restated articles of incorporation and all amendments to them currently in effect;

(2) its bylaws or restated bylaws and all amendments to them currently in effect;

(3) resolutions adopted by its board of directors creating one or more classes or series of shares, and fixing their relative rights, preferences, and limitations, if shares issued pursuant to those resolutions are outstanding;

(4) the minutes of all shareholders' meetings, and records of all action taken by shareholders without a meeting, for the past three years;

(5) all written communications to shareholders generally within the past three years, including the financial statements furnished for the past three years * * * ;

(6) a list of the names and business addresses of its current directors and officers; and

(7) its most recent annual report delivered to the secretary of state * * *.

§ 16.02 Inspection of Records by Shareholders

(a) Subject to section 16.03(c), a shareholder of a corporation is entitled to inspect and copy, during regular business hours at the corporation's principal office, any of the records of the corporation described in section 16.01(e) if he gives the corporation written notice of his demand at least five business days before the date on which he wishes to inspect and copy.

(b) A shareholder of a corporation is entitled to inspect and copy, during regular business hours at a reasonable location specified by the corporation, any of the following records of the corporation if the shareholder meets the requirements of subsection (c) and gives the corporation written notice of his demand at least five business days before the date on which he wishes to inspect and copy:

(1) excerpts from minutes of any meeting of the board of directors, records of any action of a committee of the board of directors while acting in place of the board of directors on behalf of the corporation, minutes of any meeting of the shareholders, and records of action taken by the shareholders or board of directors without a meeting, to the extent not subject to inspection under section 16.02(a);

(2) accounting records of the corporation; and

(3) the record of shareholders.

(c) A shareholder may inspect and copy the records identified in subsection (b) only if:

(1) his demand is made in good faith and for a proper purpose;

(2) he describes with reasonable particularity his purpose and the records he desires to inspect; and

(3) the records are directly connected with his purpose.

(d) The right of inspection granted by this section may not be abolished or limited by a corporation's articles of incorporation or bylaws.

(e) This section does not affect:

(1) the right of a shareholder to inspect records under section 7.20 or, if the shareholder is in litigation with the corporation, to the same extent as any other litigant;

(2) the power of a court, independently of this Act, to compel the production of corporate records for examination.

(f) For purposes of this section, "shareholder" includes a beneficial owner whose shares are held in a voting trust or by a nominee on his behalf.

(3) an amendment to the articles of organization under Section 204;

(4) the compromise of an obligation to make a contribution under Section 402(b);

(5) the compromise, as among members, of an obligation of a member to make a contribution or return money or other property paid or distributed in violation of this [Act];

(6) the making of interim distributions under Section 405(a), including the redemption of an interest;

(7) the admission of a new member;

(8) the use of the company's property to redeem an interest subject to a charging order;

(9) the consent to dissolve the company under Section 801(b)(2);

(10) a waiver of the right to have the company's business wound up and the company terminated under Section 802(b);

(11) the consent of members to merge with another entity under Section 904(c)(1); and

(12) the sale, lease, exchange, or other disposal of all, or substantially all, of the company's property with or without goodwill.

(d) Action requiring the consent of members or managers under this [Act] may be taken without a meeting.

(e) A member or manager may appoint a proxy to vote or otherwise act for the member or manager by signing an appointment instrument, either personally or by the member's or manager's attorney-in-fact.

* * * *

APPENDIX G

Restatement (Second) of Torts (Excerpts)

Section 402 A. Special liability of seller of product for physical harm to user or consumer.

(1) One who sells any product in a defective condition unreasonably dangerous to the consumer or to his property is subject to liability for physical harm thereby caused to the ultimate user or consumer, or to his property, if

(a) the seller is engaged in the business of selling such a product, and

(b) it is expected to and does reach the user or consumer without substantial change in the condition in which it is sold.

(2) The rule stated in Subsection (1) applies although

(a) the seller has exercised all possible care in the preparation and sale of his product, and

(b) the user or consumer has not bought the product from or entered into any contractual relation with the seller.

Section 402 B. Misrepresentation by seller of chattels to consumer.

One engaged in the business of selling chattels who, by advertising, labels, or otherwise, makes to the public a misrepresentation of a material fact concerning the character or quality of a chattel sold by him is subject to liability for physical harm to a consumer of the chattel caused by justifiable reliance upon the misrepresentation, even though

(a) it is not made fraudulently or negligently, and

(b) the consumer has not bought the chattel from or entered into any contractual relations with the seller.

APPENDIX H

Restatement (Third) of Torts (Excerpts)

Section 2. CATEGORIES OF PRODUCT DEFECT

A product is defective when, at the time of sale or distribution, it contains a manufacturing defect, is defective in design, or is defective because of inadequate instructions or warnings. A product:

(a) contains a manufacturing defect when the product departs from its intended design even though all possible care was exercised in the preparation and marketing of the product;

(b) is defective in design when the foreseeable risks of harm posed by the product could have been reduced or avoided by the adoption of a reasonable alternative design by the seller or other distributor, or a predecessor in the commercial chain of distribution, and the omission of the alternative design renders the product not reasonably safe;

(c) is defective because of inadequate instructions or warnings when the foreseeable risks of harm posed by the product could have been reduced or avoided by the provision of reasonable instructions or warnings by the seller or other distributor, or a predecessor in the commercial chain of distribution, and the omission of the instructions or warnings renders the product not reasonably safe.

* * * *

Section 10. LIABILITY OF COMMERCIAL PRODUCT SELLER OR DISTRIBUTOR FOR HARM CAUSED BY POST-SALE FAILURE TO WARN

(a) One engaged in the business of selling or otherwise distributing products is subject to liability for harm to persons or property caused by the seller's failure to provide a warning after the time of sale or distribution of a product if a reasonable person in the seller's position would provide such a warning.

(b) A reasonable person in the seller's position would provide a warning after the time of sale if:

(1) the seller knows or reasonably should know that the product poses a substantial risk of harm to persons or property; and

(2) those to whom a warning might be provided can be identified and can reasonably be assumed to be unaware of the risk of harm; and

(3) a warning can be effectively communicated to and acted on by those to whom a warning might be provided; and

(4) the risk of harm is sufficiently great to justify the burden of providing a warning.

* * * *

Section 17. APPORTIONMENT OF RESPONSIBILITY BETWEEN OR AMONG PLAINTIFF, SELLERS AND DISTRIBUTORS OF DEFECTIVE PRODUCTS, AND OTHERS

(a) A plaintiff's recovery of damages for harm caused by a product defect may be reduced if the conduct of the plaintiff combines with the product defect to cause the harm and the plaintiff's conduct fails to conform to generally applicable rules establishing appropriate standards of care.

(b) The manner and extent of the reduction under Subsection (a) and the apportionment of plaintiff's recovery among multiple defendants are governed by generally applicable rules apportioning responsibility.

APPENDIX I

Sherman Antitrust Act of 1890 (Excerpts)

Section. 1 Every contract, combination in the form of trust or otherwise, or conspiracy, in restraint of trade or commerce among the several States, or with foreign nations, is hereby declared to be illegal. Every person who shall make any such contract or engage in any such combination or conspiracy shall be deemed guilty of a felony, and, on conviction thereof, shall be punished by fine not exceeding one million dollars if a corporation, or, if any other person, one hundred thousand dollars or by imprisonment not exceeding three years, or by both said punishments in the discretion of the court.

Section 2. Every person who shall monopolize, or attempt to monopolize, or conspire with any other person or persons, to monopolize any part of the trade or commerce among the several States, or with foreign nations, shall be deemed guilty of a felony, and, on conviction thereof, shall be punished by fine not exceeding one million dollars if a corporation, or, if any other person, one hundred thousand dollars or by imprisonment not exceeding three years, or by both said punishments, in the discretion of the court.

APPENDIX J

Securities Act of 1933 (Excerpts)

Definitions

Section 2. When used in this title, unless the context requires—

(1) The term "security" means any note, stock, treasury stock, bond, debenture, evidence of indebtedness, certificate of interest or participation in any profit-sharing agreement, collateral-trust certificate, preorganization certificate or subscription, transferable share, investment contract, voting-trust certificate, certificate of deposit for a security, fractional undivided interest in oil, gas, or other mineral rights, any put, call, straddle, option, or privilege on any security, certificate of deposit, or group or index of securities (including any interest therein or based on the value thereof), or any put, call, straddle, option, or privilege entered into on a national securities exchange relating to foreign currency, or, in general, any interest or participation in, temporary or interim certificate for, receipt for, guarantee of, or warrant or right to subscribe to or purchase, any of the foregoing.

Exempted Securities

Section 3. (a) Except as hereinafter expressly provided the provisions of this title shall not apply to any of the following classes of securities:

* * * *

(2) Any security issued or guaranteed by the United States or any territory thereof, or by the District of Columbia, or by any State of the United States, or by any political subdivision of a State or Territory, or by any public instrumentality of one or more States or Territories, or by any person controlled or supervised by and acting as an instrumentality of the Government of the United States pursuant to authority granted by the Congress of the United States; or any certificate of deposit for any of the foregoing; or any security issued or guaranteed by any bank; or any security issued by or representing an interest in or a direct obligation of a Federal Reserve Bank. * * *

(3) Any note, draft, bill of exchange, or banker's acceptance which arises out of a current transaction or the proceeds of which have been or are to be used for current transactions, and which has a maturity at the time of issuance of not exceeding nine months, exclusive of days of grace, or any renewal thereof the maturity of which is likewise limited;

(4) Any security issued by a person organized and operated exclusively for religious, educational, benevolent, fraternal, charitable, or reformatory purposes and not for pecuniary profit, and no part of the net earnings of which inures to the benefit of any person, private stockholder, or individual;

* * * *

(11) Any security which is a part of an issue offered and sold only to persons resident within a single State or Territory, where the issuer of such security is a person resident and doing business within, or, if a corporation, incorporated by and doing business within, such State or Territory.

(b) The Commission may from time to time by its rules and regulations and subject to such terms and conditions as may be described therein, add any class of securities to the securities exempted as provided in this section, if it finds that the enforcement of this title with respect to such securities is not necessary in the public interest and for the protection of investors by reason of the small amount involved or the limited character of the public offering; but no issue of securities shall be exempted under this subsection where the aggregate amount at which such issue is offered to the public exceeds $5,000,000.

Exempted Transactions

Section 4. The provisions of section 5 shall not apply to—

(1) transactions by any person other than an issuer, underwriter, or dealer.

(2) transactions by an issuer not involving any public offering.

(3) transactions by a dealer (including an underwriter no longer acting as an underwriter in respect of the security involved in such transactions), except—

(A) transactions taking place prior to the expiration of forty days after the first date upon which the security was bona fide offered to the public by the issuer or by or through an underwriter.

(B) transactions in a security as to which a registration statement has been filed taking place prior to the expiration of forty days after the effective date of such registration statement or prior to the expiration of forty days after the first date upon which the security was bona fide offered to the public by the issuer or by or through an underwriter after such effective date, whichever is later (excluding in the computation of such forty days any time during which a stop order issued under section 8 is in effect as to the security), or such shorter period as the Commission may specify by rules and regulations or order, and

(C) transactions as to the securities constituting the whole or a part of an unsold allotment to or subscription by such dealer as a participant in the distribution of such securities by the issuer or by or through an underwriter.

With respect to transactions referred to in clause (B), if securities of the issuer have not previously been sold pursuant to an earlier effective registration statement the applicable period, instead of forty days, shall be ninety days, or such shorter period as the Commission may specify by rules and regulations or order.

(4) brokers' transactions, executed upon customers' orders on any exchange or in the over-the-counter market but not the solicitation of such orders.

* * * *

(6) transactions involving offers or sales by an issuer solely to one or more accredited investors, if the aggregate offering price of an issue of securities offered in reliance on this paragraph does not exceed the amount allowed under Section 3(b) of this title, if there is no advertising or public solicitation in connection with the transaction by the issuer or anyone acting on the issuer's behalf, and if the issuer files such notice with the Commission as the Commission shall prescribe.

Prohibitions Relating to Interstate Commerce and the Mails

Section 5. (a) Unless a registration statement is in effect as to a security, it shall be unlawful for any person, directly or indirectly—

(1) to make use of any means or instruments of transportation or communication in interstate commerce or of the mails to sell such security through the use or medium of any prospectus or otherwise; or

(2) to carry or cause to be carried through the mails or in interstate commerce, by any means or instruments of transportation, any such security for the purpose of sale or for delivery after sale.

(b) It shall be unlawful for any person, directly or indirectly—

(1) to make use of any means or instruments of transportation or communication in interstate commerce or of the mails to carry or transmit any prospectus relating to any security with respect to which a registration statement has been filed under this title, unless such prospectus meets the requirements of section 10, or

(2) to carry or to cause to be carried through the mails or in interstate commerce any such security for the purpose of sale or for delivery after sale, unless accompanied or preceded by a prospectus that meets the requirements of subsection (a) of section 10.

(c) It shall be unlawful for any person, directly, or indirectly, to make use of any means or instruments of transportation or communication in interstate commerce or of the mails to offer to sell or offer to buy through the use or medium of any prospectus or otherwise any security, unless a registration statement has been filed as to such security, or while the registration statement is the subject of a refusal order or stop order or (prior to the effective date of the registration statement) any public proceeding of examination under section 8.

APPENDIX K

Securities Exchange Act of 1934 (Excerpts)

Definitions and Application of Title

Section 3. (a) When used in this title, unless the context otherwise requires—

* * * *

(4) The term "broker" means any person engaged in the business of effecting transactions in securities for the account of others, but does not include a bank.

(5) The term "dealer" means any person engaged in the business of buying and selling securities for his own account, through a broker or otherwise, but does not include a bank, or any person insofar as he buys or sells securities for his own account, either individually or in some fiduciary capacity, but not as part of a regular business.

* * * *

(7) The term "director" means any director of a corporation or any person performing similar functions with respect to any organization, whether incorporated or unincorporated.

(8) The term "issuer" means any person who issues or proposes to issue any security; except that with respect to certificates of deposit for securities, voting-trust certificates, or collateral-trust certificates, or with respect to certificates of interest or shares in an unincorporated investment trust not having a board of directors or the fixed, restricted management, or unit type, the term "issuer" means the person or persons performing the acts and assuming the duties of depositor or manager pursuant to the provisions of the trust or other agreement or instrument under which such securities are issued; and except that with respect to equipment-trust certificates or like securities, the term "issuer" means the person by whom the equipment or property is, or is to be, used.

(9) The term "person" means a natural person, company, government, or political subdivision, agency, or instrumentality of a government.

Regulation of the Use of Manipulative and Deceptive Devices

Section 10. It shall be unlawful for any person, directly or indirectly, by the use of any means or instrumentality of interstate commerce or of the mails, or of any facility of any national securities exchange—

(a) To effect a short sale, or to use or employ any stop-loss order in connection with the purchase or sale, of any security registered on a national securities exchange, in contravention of such rules and regulations as the Commission may prescribe as necessary or appropriate in the public interest or for the protection of investors.

(b) To use or employ, in connection with the purchase or sale of any security registered on a national securities exchange or any security not so registered, any manipulative or deceptive device or contrivance in contravention of such rules and regulations as the Commission may prescribe as necessary or appropriate in the public interest or for the protection of investors.

APPENDIX L

United Nations Convention on Contracts for the International Sale of Goods (Excerpts)

Part I. SPHERE OF APPLICATION AND GENERAL PROVISIONS

* * * *

Chapter II—General Provisions

* * * *

Article 8

(1) For the purposes of this Convention statements made by and other conduct of a party are to be interpreted according to his intent where the other party knew or could not have been unaware what that intent was.

(2) If the preceding paragraph is not applicable, statements made by and other conduct of a party are to be interpreted according to the understanding that a reasonable person of the same kind as the other party would have had in the same circumstances.

(3) In determining the intent of a party or the understanding a reasonable person would have had, due consideration is to be given to all relevant circumstances of the case including the negotiations, any practices which the parties have established between themselves, usages and any subsequent conduct of the parties.

Article 9

(1) The parties are bound by any usage to which they have agreed and by any practices which they have established between themselves.

(2) The parties are considered, unless otherwise agreed, to have impliedly made applicable to their contract or its formation a usage of which the parties knew or ought to have known and which in international trade is widely known to, and regularly observed by, parties to contracts of the type involved in the particular trade concerned.

* * * *

Article 11

A contract of sale need not be concluded in or evidenced by writing and is not subject to any other requirement as to form. It may be proved by any means, including witnesses.

* * * *

Part II. FORMATION OF THE CONTRACT

Article 14

(1) A proposal for concluding a contract addressed to one or more specific persons constitutes an offer if it is sufficiently definite and indicates the intention of the offeror to be bound in case of acceptance. A proposal is sufficiently definite if it indicates the goods and expressly or implicitly fixes or makes provision for determining the quantity and the price.

(2) A proposal other than one addressed to one or more specific persons is to be considered merely as an invitation to make offers, unless the contrary is clearly indicated by the person making the proposal.

Article 15

(1) An offer becomes effective when it reaches the offeree.

(2) An offer, even if it is irrevocable, may be withdrawn if the withdrawal reaches the offeree before or at the same time as the offer.

Article 16

(1) Until a contract is concluded an offer may be revoked if the revocation reaches the offeree before he has dispatched an acceptance.

(2) However, an offer cannot be revoked:

(a) If it indicates, whether by stating a fixed time for acceptance or otherwise, that it is irrevocable; or

(b) If it was reasonable for the offeree to rely on the offer as being irrevocable and the offeree has acted in reliance on the offer.

Article 17

An offer, even if it is irrevocable, is terminated when a rejection reaches the offeror.

Article 18

(1) A statement made by or other conduct of the offeree indicating assent to an offer is an acceptance. Silence or inactivity does not in itself amount to acceptance.

(2) An acceptance of an offer becomes effective at the moment the indication of assent reaches the offeror. An acceptance is not effective if the indication of assent does not reach the offeror within the time he has fixed or, if no time is fixed, within a reasonable time, due account being taken of the circumstances of the transaction, including the rapidity of the means of communication employed by the offeror. An oral offer must be accepted immediately unless the circumstances indicate otherwise.

(3) However, if, by virtue of the offer or as a result of practices which the parties have established between themselves or of usage, the offeree may indicate assent by performing an act, such as one relating to the dispatch of the goods or payment of the price, without notice to the offeror, the acceptance is effective at the moment the act is performed, provided that the act is performed within the period of time laid down in the preceding paragraph.

Article 19

(1) A reply to an offer which purports to be an acceptance but contains additions, limitations or other modifications is a rejection of the offer and constitutes a counter-offer.

(2) However, a reply to an offer which purports to be an acceptance but contains additional or different terms which do not materially alter the terms of the offer constitutes an acceptance, unless the offeror, without undue delay, objects orally to the discrepancy or dispatches a notice to that effect. If he does not so object, the terms of the contract are the terms of the offer with the modifications contained in the acceptance.

(3) Additional or different terms relating, among other things, to the price, payment, quality and quantity of the goods, place and time of delivery, extent of one party's liability to the other or the settlement of disputes are considered to alter the terms of the offer materially.

* * * *

Article 22

An acceptance may be withdrawn if the withdrawal reaches the offeror before or at the same time as the acceptance would have become effective.

* * * *

Part III. SALE OF GOODS

Chapter I—General Provisions

Article 25

A breach of contract committed by one of the parties is fundamental if it results in such detriment to the other party as substantially to deprive him of what he is entitled to expect under the contract, unless the party in breach did not foresee and a reasonable person of the same kind in the same circumstances would not have foreseen such a result.

* * * *

Article 28

If, in accordance with the provisions of this Convention, one party is entitled to require performance of any obligation by the other party, a court is not bound to enter a judgment for specific performance unless the court would do so under its own law in respect of similar contracts of sale not governed by this Convention.

Article 29

(1) A contract may be modified or terminated by the mere agreement of the parties.

(2) A contract in writing which contains a provision requiring any modification or termination by agreement to be in writing may not be otherwise modified or terminated by agreement. However, a party may be precluded by his conduct from asserting such a provision to the extent that the other party has relied on that conduct.

* * * *

Chapter II—Obligations of the Seller

* * * *

Section II. Conformity of the Goods and Third Party Claims

Article 35

(1) The seller must deliver goods which are of the quantity, quality and description required by the contract and which are contained or packaged in the manner required by the contract.

(2) Except where the parties have agreed otherwise, the goods do not conform with the contract unless they:

(a) Are fit for the purposes for which goods of the same description would ordinarily be used;

(b) Are fit for any particular purpose expressly or impliedly made known to the seller at the time of the conclusion of the contract, except where the circumstances show that the buyer did not rely, or that it was unreasonable for him to rely, on the seller's skill and judgment;

(c) Possess the qualities of goods which the seller has held out to the buyer as a sample or model;

(d) Are contained or packaged in the manner usual for such goods or, where there is no such manner, in a manner adequate to preserve and protect the goods.

(3) The seller is not liable under subparagraphs (a) to (d) of the preceding paragraph for any lack of conformity of the goods if

at the time of the conclusion of the contract the buyer knew or could not have been unaware of such lack of conformity.

* * * *

Article 64

(1) The seller may declare the contract avoided:

(a) If the failure by the buyer to perform any of his obligations under the contract or this Convention amounts to a fundamental breach of contract; or

(b) If the buyer does not, within the additional period of time fixed by the seller in accordance with paragraph (1) of article 63, perform his obligation to pay the price or take delivery of the goods, or if he declares that he will not do so within the period so fixed.

(2) However, in cases where the buyer has paid the price, the seller loses the right to declare the contract avoided unless he does so:

(a) In respect of late performance by the buyer, before the seller has become aware that performance has been rendered; or

(b) In respect of any breach other than late performance by the buyer, within a reasonable time:

(i) After the seller knew or ought to have known of the breach; or

(ii) After the expiration of any additional period of time fixed by the seller in accordance with paragraph (1) of article 63, or after the buyer has declared that he will not perform his obligations within such an additional period.

* * * *

Chapter IV—Passing of Risk

* * * *

Article 67

(1) If the contract of sale involves carriage of the goods and the seller is not bound to hand them over at a particular place, the risk passes to the buyer when the goods are handed over to the first carrier for transmission to the buyer in accordance with the contract of sale. If the seller is bound to hand the goods over to a carrier at a particular place, the risk does not pass to the buyer until the goods are handed over to the carrier at that place. The fact that the seller is authorized to retain documents controlling the disposition of the goods does not affect the passage of the risk.

(2) Nevertheless, the risk does not pass to the buyer until the goods are clearly identified to the contract, whether by markings on the goods, by shipping documents, by notice given to the buyer or otherwise.

* * * *

Chapter V—Provisions Common to the Obligations of the Seller and of the Buyer

Section I. Anticipatory Breach and Instalment Contracts

Article 71

(1) A party may suspend the performance of his obligations if, after the conclusion of the contract, it becomes apparent that the other party will not perform a substantial part of his obligations as a result of:

(a) A serious deficiency in his ability to perform or in his creditworthiness; or

(b) His conduct in preparing to perform or in performing the contract.

(2) If the seller has already dispatched the goods before the grounds described in the preceding paragraph become evident, he may prevent the handing over of the goods to the buyer even though the buyer holds a document which entitles him to obtain them. The present paragraph relates only to the rights in the goods as between the buyer and the seller.

(3) A party suspending performance, whether before or after dispatch of the goods, must immediately give notice of the suspension to the other party and must continue with performance if the other party provides adequate assurance of his performance.

Article 72

(1) If prior to the date for performance of the contract it is clear that one of the parties will commit a fundamental breach of contract, the other party may declare the contract avoided.

(2) If time allows, the party intending to declare the contract avoided must give reasonable notice to the other party in order to permit him to provide adequate assurance of his performance.

(3) The requirements of the preceding paragraph do not apply if the other party has declared that he will not perform his obligations.

Article 73

(1) In the case of a contract for delivery of goods by instalments, if the failure of one party to perform any of his obligations in respect of any instalment constitutes a fundamental breach of contract with respect to that instalment, the other party may declare the contract avoided with respect to that instalment.

(2) If one party's failure to perform any of his obligations in respect of any instalment gives the other party good grounds to conclude that a fundamental breach of contract will occur with respect to future instalments, he may declare the contract avoided for the future, provided that he does so within a reasonable time.

(3) A buyer who declares the contract avoided in respect of any delivery may, at the same time, declare it avoided in respect of deliveries already made or of future deliveries if, by reason of their interdependence, those deliveries could not be used for the purpose contemplated by the parties at the time of the conclusion of the contract.

Section II. Damages

Article 74

Damages for breach of contract by one party consist of a sum equal to the loss, including loss of profit, suffered by the other party as a consequence of the breach. Such damages may not exceed the loss which the party in breach foresaw or ought to have foreseen at the time of the conclusion of the contract, in the light of the facts and matters of which he then knew or ought to have known, as a possible consequence of the breach of contract.

Article 75

If the contract is avoided and if, in a reasonable manner and within a reasonable time after avoidance, the buyer has bought goods in replacement or the seller has resold the goods, the party claiming damages may recover the difference between the contract price and the price in the substitute transaction as well as any further damages recoverable under article 74.

Article 76

(1) If the contract is avoided and there is a current price for the goods, the party claiming damages may, if he has not made a purchase or resale under article 75, recover the difference between the price fixed by the contract and the current price at the time of avoidance as well as any further damages recoverable under article 74. If, however, the party claiming damages has avoided the contract after taking over the goods, the current price at the time of such taking over shall be applied instead of the current price at the time of avoidance.

(2) For the purposes of the preceding paragraph, the current price is the price prevailing at the place where delivery of the goods should have been made or, if there is no current price at that place, the price at such other place as serves as a reasonable substitute, making due allowance for differences in the cost of transporting the goods.

Article 77

A party who relies on a breach of contract must take such measures as are reasonable in the circumstances to mitigate the loss, including loss of profit, resulting from the breach. If he fails to take such measures, the party in breach may claim a reduction in the damages in the amount by which the loss should have been mitigated.

APPENDIX M

Digital Millennium Copyright Act of 1998 (Excerpts)

Sec. 1201. Circumvention of copyright protection systems

(a) VIOLATIONS REGARDING CIRCUMVENTION OF TECHNOLOGICAL MEASURES—(1)(A) No person shall circumvent a technological measure that effectively controls access to a work protected under this title. * * *

* * * *

(b) ADDITIONAL VIOLATIONS—(1) No person shall manufacture, import, offer to the public, provide, or otherwise traffic in any technology, product, service, device, component, or part thereof, that—

(A) is primarily designed or produced for the purpose of circumventing protection afforded by a technological measure that effectively protects a right of a copyright owner under this title in a work or a portion thereof;

(B) has only limited commercially significant purpose or use other than to circumvent protection afforded by a technological measure that effectively protects a right of a copyright owner under this title in a work or a portion thereof; or

(C) is marketed by that person or another acting in concert with that person with that person's knowledge for use in circumventing protection afforded by a technological measure that effectively protects a right of a copyright owner under this title in a work or a portion thereof.

* * * *

Sec. 1202. Integrity of copyright management information

(a) FALSE COPYRIGHT MANAGEMENT INFORMATION—No person shall knowingly and with the intent to induce, enable, facilitate, or conceal infringement—

(1) provide copyright management information that is false, or

(2) distribute or import for distribution copyright management information that is false.

(b) REMOVAL OR ALTERATION OF COPYRIGHT MANAGEMENT INFORMATION—No person shall, without the authority of the copyright owner or the law—

(1) intentionally remove or alter any copyright management information,

(2) distribute or import for distribution copyright management information knowing that the copyright management information has been removed or altered without authority of the copyright owner or the law, or

(3) distribute, import for distribution, or publicly perform works, copies of works, or phonorecords, knowing that copyright management information has been removed or altered without authority of the copyright owner or the law, knowing, or, with respect to civil remedies under section 1203, having reasonable grounds to know, that it will induce, enable, facilitate, or conceal an infringement of any right under this title.

(c) DEFINITION—As used in this section, the term "copyright management information" means any of the following information conveyed in connection with copies or phonorecords of a work or performances or displays of a work, including in digital form, except that such term does not include any personally identifying information about a user of a work or of a copy, phonorecord, performance, or display of a work:

(1) The title and other information identifying the work, including the information set forth on a notice of copyright.

(2) The name of, and other identifying information about, the author of a work.
(3) The name of, and other identifying information about, the copyright owner of the work, including the information set forth in a notice of copyright.
(4) With the exception of public performances of works by radio and television broadcast stations, the name of, and other identifying information about, a performer whose performance is fixed in a work other than an audiovisual work.
(5) With the exception of public performances of works by radio and television broadcast stations, in the case of an audiovisual work, the name of, and other identifying information about, a writer, performer, or director who is credited in the audiovisual work.
(6) Terms and conditions for use of the work.
(7) Identifying numbers or symbols referring to such information or links to such information.
(8) Such other information as the Register of Copyrights may prescribe by regulation, except that the Register of Copyrights may not require the provision of any information concerning the user of a copyrighted work.

* * * *

Sec. 512. Limitations on liability relating to material online

(a) TRANSITORY DIGITAL NETWORK COMMUNICATIONS—A service provider shall not be liable for monetary relief, or, except as provided in subsection (j), for injunctive or other equitable relief, for infringement of copyright by reason of the provider's transmitting, routing, or providing connections for, material through a system or network controlled or operated by or for the service provider, or by reason of the intermediate and transient storage of that material in the course of such transmitting, routing, or providing connections, if—

(1) the transmission of the material was initiated by or at the direction of a person other than the service provider;
(2) the transmission, routing, provision of connections, or storage is carried out through an automatic technical process without selection of the material by the service provider;
(3) the service provider does not select the recipients of the material except as an automatic response to the request of another person;
(4) no copy of the material made by the service provider in the course of such intermediate or transient storage is maintained on the system or network in a manner ordinarily accessible to anyone other than anticipated recipients, and no such copy is maintained on the system or network in a manner ordinarily accessible to such anticipated recipients for a longer period than is reasonably necessary for the transmission, routing, or provision of connections; and
(5) the material is transmitted through the system or network without modification of its content.

APPENDIX N

Uniform Electronic Transactions Act (Excerpts)

* * * *

Section 5. USE OF ELECTRONIC RECORDS AND ELECTRONIC SIGNATURES; VARIATION BY AGREEMENT.

(a) This [Act] does not require a record or signature to be created, generated, sent, communicated, received, stored, or otherwise processed or used by electronic means or in electronic form.

(b) This [Act] applies only to transactions between parties each of which has agreed to conduct transactions by electronic means. Whether the parties agree to conduct a transaction by electronic means is determined from the context and surrounding circumstances, including the parties' conduct.

(c) A party that agrees to conduct a transaction by electronic means may refuse to conduct other transactions by electronic means. The right granted by this subsection may not be waived by agreement.

(d) Except as otherwise provided in this [Act], the effect of any of its provisions may be varied by agreement. The presence in certain provisions of this [Act] of the words "unless otherwise agreed," or words of similar import, does not imply that the effect of other provisions may not be varied by agreement.

(e) Whether an electronic record or electronic signature has legal consequences is determined by this [Act] and other applicable law.

Section 6. CONSTRUCTION AND APPLICATION. This [Act] must be construed and applied:

(1) to facilitate electronic transactions consistent with other applicable law;

(2) to be consistent with reasonable practices concerning electronic transactions and with the continued expansion of those practices; and

(3) to effectuate its general purpose to make uniform the law with respect to the subject of this [Act] among States enacting it.

Section 7. LEGAL RECOGNITION OF ELECTRONIC RECORDS, ELECTRONIC SIGNATURES, AND ELECTRONIC CONTRACTS.

(a) A record or signature may not be denied legal effect or enforceability solely because it is in electronic form.

(b) A contract may not be denied legal effect or enforceability solely because an electronic record was used in its formation.

(c) If a law requires a record to be in writing, an electronic record satisfies the law.

(d) If a law requires a signature, an electronic signature satisfies the law.

* * * *

Section 10. EFFECT OF CHANGE OR ERROR. If a change or error in an electronic record occurs in a transmission between parties to a transaction, the following rules apply:

(1) If the parties have agreed to use a security procedure to detect changes or errors and one party has conformed to the procedure, but the other party has not, and the nonconforming party would have detected the change or error had that party also conformed, the conforming party may avoid the effect of the changed or erroneous electronic record.

(2) In an automated transaction involving an individual, the individual may avoid the effect of an electronic record that resulted from an error made by the individual in dealing with the electronic agent of another person if the electronic agent did not provide an opportunity for the prevention or correction of the error and, at the time the individual learns of the error, the individual:

(A) promptly notifies the other person of the error and that the individual did not intend to be bound by the electronic record received by the other person;

(B) takes reasonable steps, including steps that conform to the other person's reasonable instructions, to return to the other person or, if instructed by the other person, to destroy the consideration received, if any, as a result of the erroneous electronic record; and

(C) has not used or received any benefit or value from the consideration, if any, received from the other person.

(3) If neither paragraph (1) nor paragraph (2) applies, the change or error has the effect provided by other law, including the law of mistake, and the parties' contract, if any.

(4) Paragraphs (2) and (3) may not be varied by agreement.

APPENDIX O

Electronic Signatures in Global and National Commerce Act of 2000 (Excerpts)

SEC. 101. GENERAL RULE OF VALIDITY.

(a) IN GENERAL—Notwithstanding any statute, regulation, or other rule of law (other than this title and title II), with respect to any transaction in or affecting interstate or foreign commerce—

(1) a signature, contract, or other record relating to such transaction may not be denied legal effect, validity, or enforceability solely because it is in electronic form; and

(2) a contract relating to such transaction may not be denied legal effect, validity, or enforceability solely because an electronic signature or electronic record was used in its formation.

* * * *

(d) RETENTION OF CONTRACTS AND RECORDS—

(1) ACCURACY AND ACCESSIBILITY—If a statute, regulation, or other rule of law requires that a contract or other record relating to a transaction in or affecting interstate or foreign commerce be retained, that requirement is met by retaining an electronic record of the information in the contract or other record that—

(A) accurately reflects the information set forth in the contract or other record; and

(B) remains accessible to all persons who are entitled to access by statute, regulation, or rule of law, for the period required by such statute, regulation, or rule of law, in a form that is capable of being accurately reproduced for later reference, whether by transmission, printing, or otherwise.

(2) EXCEPTION—A requirement to retain a contract or other record in accordance with paragraph (1) does not apply to any information whose sole purpose is to enable the contract or other record to be sent, communicated, or received.

(3) ORIGINALS—If a statute, regulation, or other rule of law requires a contract or other record relating to a transaction in or affecting interstate or foreign commerce to be provided, available, or retained in its original form, or provides consequences if the contract or other record is not provided, available, or retained in its original form, that statute, regulation, or rule of law is satisfied by an electronic record that complies with paragraph (1).

(4) CHECKS—If a statute, regulation, or other rule of law requires the retention of a check, that requirement is satisfied by retention of an electronic record of the information on the front and back of the check in accordance with paragraph (1).

* * * *

(g) NOTARIZATION AND ACKNOWLEDGMENT—If a statute, regulation, or other rule of law requires a signature or record relating to a transaction in or affecting interstate or foreign commerce to be notarized, acknowledged, verified, or made under oath, that requirement is satisfied if the electronic signature of the person authorized to perform those acts, together with all other information required to be included by other applicable statute, regulation, or rule of law, is attached to or logically associated with the signature or record.

(h) ELECTRONIC AGENTS—A contract or other record relating to a transaction in or affecting interstate or foreign commerce may not be denied legal effect, validity, or enforceability solely because its formation, creation, or delivery involved the action of one or more electronic agents so long as the action of any such electronic agent is legally attributable to the person to be bound.

(i) INSURANCE—It is the specific intent of the Congress that this title and title II apply to the business of insurance.

(j) INSURANCE AGENTS AND BROKERS—An insurance agent or broker acting under the direction of a party that enters into a contract by means of an electronic record or electronic signature may not be held liable for any deficiency in the electronic procedures agreed to by the parties under that contract if—

(1) the agent or broker has not engaged in negligent, reckless, or intentional tortious conduct;
(2) the agent or broker was not involved in the development or establishment of such electronic procedures; and
(3) the agent or broker did not deviate from such procedures.

* * * *

SEC. 103. SPECIFIC EXCEPTIONS.

(a) EXCEPTED REQUIREMENTS—The provisions of section 101 shall not apply to a contract or other record to the extent it is governed by—

(1) a statute, regulation, or other rule of law governing the creation and execution of wills, codicils, or testamentary trusts;
(2) a State statute, regulation, or other rule of law governing adoption, divorce, or other matters of family law; or
(3) the Uniform Commercial Code, as in effect in any State, other than sections 1–107 and 1–206 and Articles 2 and 2A.

(b) ADDITIONAL EXCEPTIONS—The provisions of section 101 shall not apply to—

(1) court orders or notices, or official court documents (including briefs, pleadings, and other writings) required to be executed in connection with court proceedings;
(2) any notice of—
    (A) the cancellation or termination of utility services (including water, heat, and power);
    (B) default, acceleration, repossession, foreclosure, or eviction, or the right to cure, under a credit agreement secured by, or a rental agreement for, a primary residence of an individual;
    (C) the cancellation or termination of health insurance or benefits or life insurance benefits (excluding annuities); or
    (D) recall of a product, or material failure of a product, that risks endangering health or safety; or
(3) any document required to accompany any transportation or handling of hazardous materials, pesticides, or other toxic or dangerous materials.

APPENDIX P

Sarbanes-Oxley Act of 2002 (Excerpts and Explanatory Comments)

Note: The author's explanatory comments appear in italics following the excerpt from each section.

SECTION 302

Corporate responsibility for financial reports[1]

(a) Regulations required

The Commission shall, by rule, require, for each company filing periodic reports under section 13(a) or 15(d) of the Securities Exchange Act of 1934 (15 U.S.C. 78m, 78o(d)), that the principal executive officer or officers and the principal financial officer or officers, or persons performing similar functions, certify in each annual or quarterly report filed or submitted under either such section of such Act that—

(1) the signing officer has reviewed the report;

(2) based on the officer's knowledge, the report does not contain any untrue statement of a material fact or omit to state a material fact necessary in order to make the statements made, in light of the circumstances under which such statements were made, not misleading;

(3) based on such officer's knowledge, the financial statements, and other financial information included in the report, fairly present in all material respects the financial condition and results of operations of the issuer as of, and for, the periods presented in the report;

(4) the signing officers—

(A) are responsible for establishing and maintaining internal controls;

(B) have designed such internal controls to ensure that material information relating to the issuer and its consolidated subsidiaries is made known to such officers by others within those entities, particularly during the period in which the periodic reports are being prepared;

(C) have evaluated the effectiveness of the issuer's internal controls as of a date within 90 days prior to the report; and

(D) have presented in the report their conclusions about the effectiveness of their internal controls based on their evaluation as of that date;

(5) the signing officers have disclosed to the issuer's auditors and the audit committee of the board of directors (or persons fulfilling the equivalent function)—

(A) all significant deficiencies in the design or operation of internal controls which could adversely affect the issuer's ability to record, process, summarize, and report financial data and have identified for the issuer's auditors any material weaknesses in internal controls; and

(B) any fraud, whether or not material, that involves management or other employees who have a significant role in the issuer's internal controls; and

(6) the signing officers have indicated in the report whether or not there were significant changes in internal controls or in other factors that could significantly affect internal controls subsequent to the date of their evaluation, including any corrective actions with regard to significant deficiencies and material weaknesses.

(b) Foreign reincorporations have no effect

Nothing in this section shall be interpreted or applied in any way to allow any issuer to lessen the legal force of the statement required under this section, by an issuer having reincorporated

1. This section of the Sarbanes-Oxley Act is codified at 15 U.S.C. Section 7241.

or having engaged in any other transaction that resulted in the transfer of the corporate domicile or offices of the issuer from inside the United States to outside of the United States.

(c) Deadline

The rules required by subsection (a) of this section shall be effective not later than 30 days after July 30, 2002.

EXPLANATORY COMMENTS: *Section 302 requires the chief executive officer (CEO) and chief financial officer (CFO) of each public company to certify that they have reviewed the company's quarterly and annual reports to be filed with the Securities and Exchange Commission (SEC). The CEO and CFO must certify that, based on their knowledge, the reports do not contain any untrue statement of a material fact or any half-truth that would make the report misleading, and that the information contained in the reports fairly presents the company's financial condition.*

In addition, this section also requires the CEO and CFO to certify that they have created and designed an internal control system for their company and have recently evaluated that system to ensure that it is effectively providing them with relevant and accurate financial information. If the signing officers have found any significant deficiencies or weaknesses in the company's system or have discovered any evidence of fraud, they must have reported the situation, and any corrective actions they have taken, to the auditors and the audit committee.

SECTION 306

Insider trades during pension fund blackout periods[2]

(a) Prohibition of insider trading during pension fund blackout periods

(1) In general

Except to the extent otherwise provided by rule of the Commission pursuant to paragraph (3), it shall be unlawful for any director or executive officer of an issuer of any equity security (other than an exempted security), directly or indirectly, to purchase, sell, or otherwise acquire or transfer any equity security of the issuer (other than an exempted security) during any blackout period with respect to such equity security if such director or officer acquires such equity security in connection with his or her service or employment as a director or executive officer.

(2) Remedy

(A) In general

Any profit realized by a director or executive officer referred to in paragraph (1) from any purchase, sale, or other acquisition or transfer in violation of this subsection shall inure to and be recoverable by the issuer, irrespective of any intention on the part of such director or executive officer in entering into the transaction.

(B) Actions to recover profits

An action to recover profits in accordance with this subsection may be instituted at law or in equity in any court of competent jurisdiction by the issuer, or by the owner of any security of the issuer in the name and in behalf of the issuer if the issuer fails or refuses to bring such action within 60 days after the date of request, or fails diligently to prosecute the action thereafter, except that no such suit shall be brought more than 2 years after the date on which such profit was realized.

(3) Rulemaking authorized

The Commission shall, in consultation with the Secretary of Labor, issue rules to clarify the application of this subsection and to prevent evasion thereof. Such rules shall provide for the application of the requirements of paragraph (1) with respect to entities treated as a single employer with respect to an issuer under section 414(b), (c), (m), or (o) of Title 26 to the extent necessary to clarify the application of such requirements and to prevent evasion thereof. Such rules may also provide for appropriate exceptions from the requirements of this subsection, including exceptions for purchases pursuant to an automatic dividend reinvestment program or purchases or sales made pursuant to an advance election.

(4) Blackout period

For purposes of this subsection, the term "blackout period", with respect to the equity securities of any issuer—

(A) means any period of more than 3 consecutive business days during which the ability of not fewer than 50 percent of the participants or beneficiaries under all individual account plans maintained by the issuer to purchase, sell, or otherwise acquire or transfer an interest in any equity of such issuer held in such an individual account plan is temporarily suspended by the issuer or by a fiduciary of the plan; and

(B) does not include, under regulations which shall be prescribed by the Commission—

(i) a regularly scheduled period in which the participants and beneficiaries may not purchase, sell, or otherwise acquire or transfer an interest in any equity of such issuer, if such period is—

(I) incorporated into the individual account plan; and

(II) timely disclosed to employees before becoming participants under the individual account plan or as a subsequent amendment to the plan; or

(ii) any suspension described in subparagraph (A) that is imposed solely in connection with persons becoming participants or beneficiaries, or ceasing to be participants or beneficiaries, in an individual account plan by reason of a corporate merger, acquisition, divestiture, or similar transaction involving the plan or plan sponsor.

(5) Individual account plan

For purposes of this subsection, the term "individual account plan" has the meaning provided in section 1002(34) of Title 29, except that such term shall not include a one-participant retirement plan (within the meaning of section 1021(i)(8)(B) of Title 29).

2. Codified at 15 U.S.C. Section 7244.

(6) Notice to directors, executive officers, and the Commission

In any case in which a director or executive officer is subject to the requirements of this subsection in connection with a blackout period (as defined in paragraph (4)) with respect to any equity securities, the issuer of such equity securities shall timely notify such director or officer and the Securities and Exchange Commission of such blackout period.

* * * *

EXPLANATORY COMMENTS: *Corporate pension funds typically prohibit employees from trading shares of the corporation during periods when the pension fund is undergoing significant change. Prior to 2002, however, these blackout periods did not affect the corporation's executives, who frequently received shares of the corporate stock as part of their compensation. During the collapse of Enron, for example, its pension plan was scheduled to change administrators at a time when Enron's stock price was falling. Enron's employees therefore could not sell their shares while the price was dropping, but its executives could and did sell their stock, consequently avoiding some of the losses. Section 306 was Congress's solution to the basic unfairness of this situation. This section of the act required the SEC to issue rules that prohibit any director or executive officer from trading during pension fund blackout periods. (The SEC later issued these rules, entitled Regulation Blackout Trading Restriction, or Reg BTR.) Section 306 also provided shareholders with a right to file a shareholder's derivative suit against officers and directors who have profited from trading during these blackout periods (provided that the corporation has failed to bring a suit). The officer or director can be forced to return to the corporation any profits received, regardless of whether the director or officer acted with bad intent.*

SECTION 402

Periodical and other reports[3]

* * * *

(i) Accuracy of financial reports

Each financial report that contains financial statements, and that is required to be prepared in accordance with (or reconciled to) generally accepted accounting principles under this chapter and filed with the Commission shall reflect all material correcting adjustments that have been identified by a registered public accounting firm in accordance with generally accepted accounting principles and the rules and regulations of the Commission.

(j) Off-balance sheet transactions

Not later than 180 days after July 30, 2002, the Commission shall issue final rules providing that each annual and quarterly financial report required to be filed with the Commission shall disclose all material off-balance sheet transactions, arrangements, obligations (including contingent obligations), and other relationships of the issuer with unconsolidated entities or other persons, that may have a material current or future effect on financial condition, changes in financial condition, results of operations, liquidity, capital expenditures, capital resources, or significant components of revenues or expenses.

(k) Prohibition on personal loans to executives

(1) In general

It shall be unlawful for any issuer (as defined in section 7201 of this title), directly or indirectly, including through any subsidiary, to extend or maintain credit, to arrange for the extension of credit, or to renew an extension of credit, in the form of a personal loan to or for any director or executive officer (or equivalent thereof) of that issuer. An extension of credit maintained by the issuer on July 30, 2002, shall not be subject to the provisions of this subsection, provided that there is no material modification to any term of any such extension of credit or any renewal of any such extension of credit on or after July 30, 2002.

(2) Limitation

Paragraph (1) does not preclude any home improvement and manufactured home loans (as that term is defined in section 1464 of Title 12), consumer credit (as defined in section 1602 of this title), or any extension of credit under an open end credit plan (as defined in section 1602 of this title), or a charge card (as defined in section 1637(c)(4)(e) of this title), or any extension of credit by a broker or dealer registered under section 78o of this title to an employee of that broker or dealer to buy, trade, or carry securities, that is permitted under rules or regulations of the Board of Governors of the Federal Reserve System pursuant to section 78g of this title (other than an extension of credit that would be used to purchase the stock of that issuer), that is—

(A) made or provided in the ordinary course of the consumer credit business of such issuer;

(B) of a type that is generally made available by such issuer to the public; and

(C) made by such issuer on market terms, or terms that are no more favorable than those offered by the issuer to the general public for such extensions of credit.

(3) Rule of construction for certain loans

Paragraph (1) does not apply to any loan made or maintained by an insured depository institution (as defined in section 1813 of Title 12), if the loan is subject to the insider lending restrictions of section 375b of Title 12.

(l) Real time issuer disclosures

Each issuer reporting under subsection (a) of this section or section 78o(d) of this title shall disclose to the public on a rapid and current basis such additional information concerning material changes in the financial condition or operations of the issuer, in plain English, which may include trend and qualitative information and graphic presentations, as the Commission determines, by rule, is necessary or useful for the protection of investors and in the public interest.

---

3. This section of the Sarbanes-Oxley Act amended some of the provisions of the 1934 Securities Exchange Act and added the paragraphs reproduced here at 15 U.S.C. Section 78m.

EXPLANATORY COMMENTS: *Corporate executives during the Enron era typically received extremely large salaries, significant bonuses, and abundant stock options, even when the companies for which they worked were suffering. Executives were also routinely given personal loans from corporate funds, many of which were never paid back. The average large company during that period loaned almost $1 million a year to top executives, and some companies, including Tyco International and Adelphia Communications Corporation, loaned hundreds of millions of dollars to their executives every year. Section 402 amended the 1934 Securities Exchange Act to prohibit public companies from making personal loans to executive officers and directors. There are a few exceptions to this prohibition, such as home-improvement loans made in the ordinary course of business. Note also that while loans are forbidden, outright gifts are not. A corporation is free to give gifts to its executives, including cash, provided that these gifts are disclosed on its financial reports. The idea is that corporate directors will be deterred from making substantial gifts to their executives by the disclosure requirement—particularly if the corporation's financial condition is questionable—because making such gifts could be perceived as abusing their authority.*

SECTION 403

Directors, officers, and principal stockholders[4]

(a) Disclosures required

(1) Directors, officers, and principal stockholders required to file

Every person who is directly or indirectly the beneficial owner of more than 10 percent of any class of any equity security (other than an exempted security) which is registered pursuant to section 78l of this title, or who is a director or an officer of the issuer of such security, shall file the statements required by this subsection with the Commission (and, if such security is registered on a national securities exchange, also with the exchange).

(2) Time of filing

The statements required by this subsection shall be filed—

(A) at the time of the registration of such security on a national securities exchange or by the effective date of a registration statement filed pursuant to section 78l(g) of this title;

(B) within 10 days after he or she becomes such beneficial owner, director, or officer;

(C) if there has been a change in such ownership, or if such person shall have purchased or sold a security-based swap agreement (as defined in section 206(b) of the Gramm-Leach-Bliley Act (15 U.S.C. 78c note)) involving such equity security, before the end of the second business day following the day on which the subject transaction has been executed, or at such other time as the Commission shall establish, by rule, in any case in which the Commission determines that such 2-day period is not feasible.

(3) Contents of statements

A statement filed—

(A) under subparagraph (A) or (B) of paragraph (2) shall contain a statement of the amount of all equity securities of such issuer of which the filing person is the beneficial owner; and

(B) under subparagraph (C) of such paragraph shall indicate ownership by the filing person at the date of filing, any such changes in such ownership, and such purchases and sales of the security-based swap agreements as have occurred since the most recent such filing under such subparagraph.

(4) Electronic filing and availability

Beginning not later than 1 year after July 30, 2002—

(A) a statement filed under subparagraph (C) of paragraph (2) shall be filed electronically;

(B) the Commission shall provide each such statement on a publicly accessible Internet site not later than the end of the business day following that filing; and

(C) the issuer (if the issuer maintains a corporate website) shall provide that statement on that corporate website, not later than the end of the business day following that filing.

* * * *

EXPLANATORY COMMENTS: *This section dramatically shortens the time period provided in the Securities Exchange Act of 1934 for disclosing transactions by insiders. The prior law stated that most transactions had to be reported within ten days of the beginning of the following month, although certain transactions did not have to be reported until the following fiscal year (within the first forty-five days). Because some of the insider trading that occurred during the Enron fiasco did not have to be disclosed (and was therefore not discovered) until long after the transactions, Congress added this section to reduce the time period for making disclosures. Under Section 403, most transactions by insiders must be electronically filed with the SEC within two business days. Also, any company that maintains a Web site must post these SEC filings on its site by the end of the next business day. Congress enacted this section in the belief that if insiders are required to file reports of their transactions promptly with the SEC, companies will do more to police themselves and prevent insider trading.*

SECTION 404

Management assessment of internal controls[5]

(a) Rules required

4. This section of the Sarbanes-Oxley Act amended the disclosure provisions of the 1934 Securities Exchange Act, at 15 U.S.C. Section 78p.

5. Codified at 15 U.S.C. Section 7262.

The Commission shall prescribe rules requiring each annual report required by section 78m(a) or 78o(d) of this title to contain an internal control report, which shall—

(1) state the responsibility of management for establishing and maintaining an adequate internal control structure and procedures for financial reporting; and

(2) contain an assessment, as of the end of the most recent fiscal year of the issuer, of the effectiveness of the internal control structure and procedures of the issuer for financial reporting.

(b) Internal control evaluation and reporting

With respect to the internal control assessment required by subsection (a) of this section, each registered public accounting firm that prepares or issues the audit report for the issuer shall attest to, and report on, the assessment made by the management of the issuer. An attestation made under this subsection shall be made in accordance with standards for attestation engagements issued or adopted by the Board. Any such attestation shall not be the subject of a separate engagement.

EXPLANATORY COMMENTS: *This section was enacted to prevent corporate executives from claiming they were ignorant of significant errors in their companies' financial reports. For instance, several CEOs testified before Congress that they simply had no idea that the corporations' financial statements were off by billions of dollars. Congress therefore passed Section 404, which requires each annual report to contain a description and assessment of the company's internal control structure and financial reporting procedures. The section also requires that an audit be conducted of the internal control assessment, as well as the financial statements contained in the report. This section goes hand in hand with Section 302 (which, as discussed previously, requires various certifications attesting to the accuracy of the information in financial reports).*

Section 404 has been one of the more controversial and expensive provisions in the Sarbanes-Oxley Act because it requires companies to assess their own internal financial controls to make sure that their financial statements are reliable and accurate. A corporation might need to set up a disclosure committee and a coordinator, establish codes of conduct for accounting and financial personnel, create documentation procedures, provide training, and outline the individuals who are responsible for performing each of the procedures. Companies that were already well managed have not experienced substantial difficulty complying with this section. Other companies, however, have spent millions of dollars setting up, documenting, and evaluating their internal financial control systems. Although initially creating the internal financial control system is a onetime-only expense, the costs of maintaining and evaluating it are ongoing. Some corporations that spent considerable sums complying with Section 404 have been able to offset these costs by discovering and correcting inefficiencies or frauds within their systems. Nevertheless, it is unlikely that any corporation will find compliance with this section to be inexpensive.

SECTION 802 (A)

Destruction, alteration, or falsification of records in Federal investigations and bankruptcy[6]

Whoever knowingly alters, destroys, mutilates, conceals, covers up, falsifies, or makes a false entry in any record, document, or tangible object with the intent to impede, obstruct, or influence the investigation or proper administration of any matter within the jurisdiction of any department or agency of the United States or any case filed under title 11, or in relation to or contemplation of any such matter or case, shall be fined under this title, imprisoned not more than 20 years, or both.

Destruction of corporate audit records[7]

(a) (1) Any accountant who conducts an audit of an issuer of securities to which section 10A(a) of the Securities Exchange Act of 1934 (15 U.S.C. 78j-1(a)) applies, shall maintain all audit or review workpapers for a period of 5 years from the end of the fiscal period in which the audit or review was concluded.

(2) The Securities and Exchange Commission shall promulgate, within 180 days, after adequate notice and an opportunity for comment, such rules and regulations, as are reasonably necessary, relating to the retention of relevant records such as workpapers, documents that form the basis of an audit or review, memoranda, correspondence, communications, other documents, and records (including electronic records) which are created, sent, or received in connection with an audit or review and contain conclusions, opinions, analyses, or financial data relating to such an audit or review, which is conducted by any accountant who conducts an audit of an issuer of securities to which section 10A(a) of the Securities Exchange Act of 1934 (15 U.S.C. 78j-1(a)) applies. The Commission may, from time to time, amend or supplement the rules and regulations that it is required to promulgate under this section, after adequate notice and an opportunity for comment, in order to ensure that such rules and regulations adequately comport with the purposes of this section.

(b) Whoever knowingly and willfully violates subsection (a)(1), or any rule or regulation promulgated by the Securities and Exchange Commission under subsection (a)(2), shall be fined under this title, imprisoned not more than 10 years, or both.

(c) Nothing in this section shall be deemed to diminish or relieve any person of any other duty or obligation imposed by Federal or State law or regulation to maintain, or refrain from destroying, any document.

EXPLANATORY COMMENTS: *Section 802(a) enacted two new statutes that punish those who alter or destroy documents. The first statute is not specifically limited to securities fraud cases. It provides that anyone who alters, destroys, or falsifies records in federal investigations or bankruptcy may be criminally prosecuted and sentenced to a fine or to up to twenty years*

6. Codified at 15 U.S.C. Section 1519.

7. Codified at 15 U.S.C. Section 1520.

in prison, or both. The second statute requires auditors of public companies to keep all audit or review working papers for five years but expressly allows the SEC to amend or supplement these requirements as it sees fit. The SEC has, in fact, amended this section by issuing a rule that requires auditors who audit reporting companies to retain working papers for seven years from the conclusion of the review. Section 802(a) further provides that anyone who knowingly and willfully violates this statute is subject to criminal prosecution and can be sentenced to a fine, imprisoned for up to ten years, or both if convicted.

This portion of the Sarbanes-Oxley Act implicitly recognizes that persons who are under investigation often are tempted to respond by destroying or falsifying documents that might prove their complicity in wrongdoing. The severity of the punishment should provide a strong incentive for these individuals to resist the temptation.

SECTION 804

Time limitations on the commencement of civil actions arising under Acts of Congress[8]

(a) Except as otherwise provided by law, a civil action arising under an Act of Congress enacted after the date of the enactment of this section may not be commenced later than 4 years after the cause of action accrues.

(b) Notwithstanding subsection (a), a private right of action that involves a claim of fraud, deceit, manipulation, or contrivance in contravention of a regulatory requirement concerning the securities laws, as defined in section 3(a)(47) of the Securities Exchange Act of 1934 (15 U.S.C. 78c(a)(47)), may be brought not later than the earlier of—

(1) 2 years after the discovery of the facts constituting the violation; or

(2) 5 years after such violation.

EXPLANATORY COMMENTS: *Prior to the enactment of this section, Section 10(b) of the Securities Exchange Act of 1934 had no express statute of limitations. The courts generally required plaintiffs to have filed suit within one year from the date that they should (using due diligence) have discovered that a fraud had been committed but no later than three years after the fraud occurred. Section 804 extends this period by specifying that plaintiffs must file a lawsuit within two years after they discover (or should have discovered) a fraud but no later than five years after the fraud's occurrence. This provision has prevented the courts from dismissing numerous securities fraud lawsuits.*

SECTION 806

Civil action to protect against retaliation in fraud cases[9]

(a) Whistleblower protection for employees of publicly traded companies.—

No company with a class of securities registered under section 12 of the Securities Exchange Act of 1934 (15 U.S.C. 78l), or that is required to file reports under section 15(d) of the Securities Exchange Act of 1934 (15 U.S.C. 78o(d)), or any officer, employee, contractor, subcontractor, or agent of such company, may discharge, demote, suspend, threaten, harass, or in any other manner discriminate against an employee in the terms and conditions of employment because of any lawful act done by the employee—

(1) to provide information, cause information to be provided, or otherwise assist in an investigation regarding any conduct which the employee reasonably believes constitutes a violation of section 1341, 1343, 1344, or 1348, any rule or regulation of the Securities and Exchange Commission, or any provision of Federal law relating to fraud against shareholders, when the information or assistance is provided to or the investigation is conducted by—

(A) a Federal regulatory or law enforcement agency;

(B) any Member of Congress or any committee of Congress; or

(C) a person with supervisory authority over the employee (or such other person working for the employer who has the authority to investigate, discover, or terminate misconduct); or

(2) to file, cause to be filed, testify, participate in, or otherwise assist in a proceeding filed or about to be filed (with any knowledge of the employer) relating to an alleged violation of section 1341, 1343, 1344, or 1348, any rule or regulation of the Securities and Exchange Commission, or any provision of Federal law relating to fraud against shareholders.

(b) Enforcement action.—

(1) In general.—A person who alleges discharge or other discrimination by any person in violation of subsection (a) may seek relief under subsection (c), by—

(A) filing a complaint with the Secretary of Labor; or

(B) if the Secretary has not issued a final decision within 180 days of the filing of the complaint and there is no showing that such delay is due to the bad faith of the claimant, bringing an action at law or equity for de novo review in the appropriate district court of the United States, which shall have jurisdiction over such an action without regard to the amount in controversy.

(2) Procedure.—

(A) In general.—An action under paragraph (1)(A) shall be governed under the rules and procedures set forth in section 42121(b) of title 49, United States Code.

(B) Exception.—Notification made under section 42121(b)(1) of title 49, United States Code, shall be made to the person named in the complaint and to the employer.

(C) Burdens of proof.—An action brought under paragraph (1)(B) shall be governed by the legal burdens of

8. Codified at 28 U.S.C. Section 1658.
9. Codified at 18 U.S.C. Section 1514A.

proof set forth in section 42121(b) of title 49, United States Code.

(D) Statute of limitations.—An action under paragraph (1) shall be commenced not later than 90 days after the date on which the violation occurs.

(c) Remedies.—

(1) In general.—An employee prevailing in any action under subsection (b)(1) shall be entitled to all relief necessary to make the employee whole.

(2) Compensatory damages.—Relief for any action under paragraph (1) shall include—

(A) reinstatement with the same seniority status that the employee would have had, but for the discrimination;

(B) the amount of back pay, with interest; and

(C) compensation for any special damages sustained as a result of the discrimination, including litigation costs, expert witness fees, and reasonable attorney fees.

(d) Rights retained by employee.—Nothing in this section shall be deemed to diminish the rights, privileges, or remedies of any employee under any Federal or State law, or under any collective bargaining agreement.

EXPLANATORY COMMENTS: *Section 806 is one of several provisions that were included in the Sarbanes-Oxley Act to encourage and protect whistleblowers—that is, employees who report their employer's alleged violations of securities law to the authorities. This section applies to employees, agents, and independent contractors who work for publicly traded companies or testify about such a company during an investigation. It sets up an administrative procedure at the Department of Labor for individuals who claim that their employer retaliated against them (fired or demoted them, for example) for blowing the whistle on the employer's wrongful conduct. It also allows the award of civil damages—including back pay, reinstatement, special damages, attorneys' fees, and court costs—to employees who prove that they suffered retaliation. Since this provision was enacted, whistleblowers have filed numerous complaints with the Department of Labor under this section.*

SECTION 807

Securities fraud[10]

Whoever knowingly executes, or attempts to execute, a scheme or artifice—

(1) to defraud any person in connection with any security of an issuer with a class of securities registered under section 12 of the Securities Exchange Act of 1934 (15 U.S.C. 78l) or that is required to file reports under section 15(d) of the Securities Exchange Act of 1934 (15 U.S.C. 78o(d)); or

(2) to obtain, by means of false or fraudulent pretenses, representations, or promises, any money or property in connection with the purchase or sale of any security of an issuer with a class of securities registered under section 12 of the Securities Exchange Act of 1934 (15 U.S.C. 78l) or that is required to file reports under section 15(d) of the Securities Exchange Act of 1934 (15 U.S.C. 78o(d)); shall be fined under this title, or imprisoned not more than 25 years, or both.

EXPLANATORY COMMENTS: *Section 807 adds a new provision to the federal criminal code that addresses securities fraud. Prior to 2002, federal securities law had already made it a crime—under Section 10(b) of the Securities Exchange Act of 1934 and SEC Rule 10b-5, both of which are discussed in Chapter 41—to intentionally defraud someone in connection with a purchase or sale of securities, but the offense was not listed in the federal criminal code. Also, paragraph 2 of Section 807 goes beyond what is prohibited under securities law by making it a crime to obtain by means of false or fraudulent pretenses any money or property from the purchase or sale of securities. This new provision allows violators to be punished by up to twenty-five years in prison, a fine, or both.*

SECTION 906

Failure of corporate officers to certify financial reports[11]

(a) Certification of periodic financial reports.—Each periodic report containing financial statements filed by an issuer with the Securities Exchange Commission pursuant to section 13(a) or 15(d) of the Securities Exchange Act of 1934 (15 U.S.C. 78m(a) or 78o(d)) shall be accompanied by a written statement by the chief executive officer and chief financial officer (or equivalent thereof) of the issuer.

(b) Content.—The statement required under subsection (a) shall certify that the periodic report containing the financial statements fully complies with the requirements of section 13(a) or 15(d) of the Securities Exchange Act of 1934 (15 U.S.C. 78m or 78o(d)) and that information contained in the periodic report fairly presents, in all material respects, the financial condition and results of operations of the issuer.

(c) Criminal penalties.—Whoever—

(1) certifies any statement as set forth in subsections (a) and (b) of this section knowing that the periodic report accompanying the statement does not comport with all the requirements set forth in this section shall be fined not more than $1,000,000 or imprisoned not more than 10 years, or both; or

(2) willfully certifies any statement as set forth in subsections (a) and (b) of this section knowing that the periodic report accompanying the statement does not comport with all the requirements set forth in this section shall be fined not more than $5,000,000, or imprisoned not more than 20 years, or both.

10. Codified at 18 U.S.C. Section 1348.

11. Codified at 18 U.S.C. Section 1350.

EXPLANATORY COMMENTS: *As previously discussed, under Section 302 a corporation's CEO and CFO are required to certify that they believe the quarterly and annual reports their company files with the SEC are accurate and fairly present the company's financial condition. Section 906 adds "teeth" to these requirements by authorizing criminal penalties for those officers who intentionally certify inaccurate SEC filings. Knowing violations of the requirements are punishable by a fine of up to $1 million, ten years in prison, or both. Willful violators may be fined up to $5 million, sentenced to up to twenty years in prison, or both. Although the difference between a knowing and a willful violation is not entirely clear, the section is obviously intended to remind corporate officers of the serious consequences of certifying inaccurate reports to the SEC.*

GLOSSARY

A

Abandoned Property Property with which the owner has voluntarily parted, with no intention of recovering it.

Acceleration Clause A clause that allows a payee or other holder of a time instrument to demand payment of the entire amount due, with interest, if a certain event occurs, such as a default in the payment of an installment when due.

Acceptance A voluntary act by the offeree that shows assent, or agreement, to the terms of an offer; may consist of words or conduct.

Acceptor A drawee that is legally obligated to pay an instrument when the instrument is presented later for payment.

Access Contract A contract formed for the purpose of obtaining, by electronic means, access to another's database or information processing system.

Accession Addition of value to personal property through addition of labor or materials. In some situations, a person can acquire ownership rights in another's property through accession.

Accommodation Party A party who signs an instrument for the purpose of lending his or her name as credit to another party on the instrument.

Accord and Satisfaction A common means of settling a disputed claim, in which a debtor offers to pay a lesser amount than the creditor purports to be owed. The creditor's acceptance of the offer creates an accord (agreement), and when the accord is executed, satisfaction occurs.

Accredited Investor In the context of securities offerings, a "sophisticated" investor, such as a bank, an insurance company, an investment company, an executive officer or director of the issuing company, or any person whose income or net worth exceeds a certain threshold.

Act of State Doctrine A doctrine that provides that the judicial branch of one country will not examine the validity of public acts committed by a recognized foreign government within its own territory.

Actionable Capable of serving as the basis of a lawsuit. An actionable claim can be pursued in a lawsuit or other court action.

Actual Malice Real and demonstrable evil intent. In a defamation suit, a statement made about a public figure normally must be made with actual malice (with either knowledge of its falsity or a reckless disregard of the truth) for liability to be incurred.

Adequate Protection Doctrine In bankruptcy law, a doctrine that protects secured creditors from losing the value of their security as a result of the automatic stay on legal proceedings. The bankruptcy court can provide adequate protection by requiring the debtor or trustee to make cash payments to the creditor or to provide additional collateral or replacement liens in case the stay causes the property to lose value.

Adhesion Contract A "standard-form" contract, such as that between a large retailer and a consumer, in which the stronger party dictates the terms.

Adjudicate To render a judicial decision. In the administrative process, adjudication is the proceeding in which an administrative law judge hears and decides on issues that arise when an administrative agency charges a person or a firm with violating a law or regulation enforced by the agency.

Adjudication The act of rendering a judicial decision. In an administrative process, the proceeding in which an administrative law judge hears and decides on issues that arise when an administrative agency charges a person or a firm with violating a law or regulation enforced by the agency.

Administrative Agency A federal, state, or local government agency established to perform a specific function. Administrative agencies are authorized by legislative acts to make and enforce rules to administer and enforce the acts.

Administrative Law The body of law (in the form of rules, regulations, orders, and decisions) that administrative agencies create in order to carry out their duties and responsibilities.

Administrative Law Judge (ALJ) One who presides over an administrative agency hearing and has the power to administer oaths, take testimony, rule on questions of evidence, and make determinations of fact.

Administrative Process The procedure used by administrative agencies in the administration of law.
Administrator One who is appointed by a court to handle the probate (disposition) of a person's estate if that person dies intestate (without a valid will) or if the executor named in the will cannot serve.
Adverse Possession A means of acquiring title to real property by occupying it openly, without the consent of the owner, for a period of time specified by a state statute. The occupation must be actual, open, notorious, exclusive, and in opposition to all others, including the owner.
Affirmative Action Job-hiring policies that give special consideration to members of protected classes in an effort to overcome present effects of past discrimination.
After-Acquired Property Property acquired by the debtor after the execution of a security agreement.
Agency A relationship between two parties in which one party (the agent) agrees to represent or act for the other (the principal).
Agent A person who agrees to represent or act for another, called the principal.
Agreement A meeting of two or more minds in regard to the terms of a contract, usually broken down into two events—an offer and an acceptance.
Alien Corporation A designation in the United States for a corporation formed in another country but doing business in the United States.
Alienation The process of transferring land out of one's possession (thus "alienating" the land from oneself).
Allonge A piece of paper firmly attached to a negotiable instrument on which transferees can make indorsements if there is no room left on the instrument itself.
Alternative Dispute Resolution (ADR) The resolution of disputes through processes other than the traditional judicial process. Negotiation, mediation, and arbitration are examples of ADR methods.
Answer Procedurally, a defendant's response to the plaintiff's complaint.
Anticipatory Repudiation An assertion or action by a party indicating that he or she will not perform an obligation that the party is contractually obligated to perform at a future time.
Antitrust Laws Laws protecting commerce from unlawful restraints.
Appraisal Right The right of a dissenting shareholder who objects to an extraordinary transaction of the corporation (such as a merger or a consolidation) to have his or her shares appraised and to be paid the fair value of those shares by the corporation.
Appropriation In tort law, the use by one person of another person's name, likeness, or other identifying characteristic without permission and for the benefit of the user.
Arbitration A method of settling disputes outside of court by using the services of a neutral third party, who renders a decision that is most often legally binding.
Arbitration Clause A clause in a contract that provides that, in case of a dispute, the parties will submit the dispute to arbitration rather than litigate the dispute in court.
Arson The intentional burning of another's dwelling. Some statutes have expanded this to include any real property regardless of ownership and the destruction of property by other means—for example, by explosion.
Articles of Incorporation A document filed with the appropriate governmental agency, usually the secretary of state, when a business is incorporated. State statutes usually prescribe what kind of information must be contained in the articles of incorporation.
Articles of Organization A document filed with a designated state official by which a limited liability company is formed.
Articles of Partnership A written agreement that sets forth each partner's rights and obligations with respect to the partnership.
Artisan's Lien A possessory lien given to a person who has made improvements and added value to another person's personal property as security for payment for services performed.
Assault Any word or action intended to make another person fearful of immediate physical harm; a reasonably believable threat.
Assignee A party to whom the rights under a contract are transferred, or assigned.
Assignment The act of transferring to another all or part of one's rights arising under a contract.
Assignor A party who transfers (assigns) his or her rights under a contract to another party (called the assignee).
Assumption of Risk A doctrine whereby a plaintiff may not recover for injuries or damages suffered from risks he or she knew of and voluntarily assumed.
Attachment In a secured transaction, the process by which a secured creditor's interest "attaches" to the property of another (collateral) and the creditor's security interest becomes enforceable. In the context of judicial liens, a court-ordered seizure and taking into custody of property prior to the securing of a judgment for a past-due debt.
Attempted Monopolization Any actions by a firm to eliminate competition and gain monopoly power.
Authenticate To sign a record or, with the intent to sign a record, to execute or adopt an electronic sound, symbol, or the like to link with the record. A *record* is retrievable information inscribed on a tangible medium or stored in an electronic or other medium.
Automated Clearinghouse (ACH) An electronic banking system used to transfer payments and settle accounts.
Automatic Stay In bankruptcy proceedings, the suspension of virtually all litigation and other action by creditors against the debtor or the debtor's property. The stay is effective the moment the debtor files a petition in bankruptcy.
Award The amount of money awarded to a plaintiff in a civil lawsuit as damages.

B

B2B Transaction A business-to-business transaction conducted via the Internet; an online sale or lease of goods or services from one business party to another.
B2C Transaction A business-to-consumer transaction conducted via the Internet; an online sale or lease of goods or services from a business party to a consumer.
Bailee One to whom goods are entrusted by a bailor. Under the UCC, a party who, by a bill of lading, warehouse receipt, or other document of title, acknowledges possession of goods and/or contracts to deliver them.
Bailment A situation in which the personal property of one person (a bailor) is entrusted to another (a bailee), who is obligated to return the bailed property to the bailor or dispose of it as directed.
Bailor One who entrusts goods to a bailee.

Bait-and-Switch Advertising Advertising a product at a very attractive price (the "bait") and then, once the consumer is in the store, saying that the advertised product either is not available or is of poor quality; the customer is then urged to purchase ("switched" to) a more expensive item.
Bankruptcy Court A federal court of limited jurisdiction that handles only bankruptcy proceedings. Bankruptcy proceedings are governed by federal bankruptcy law.
Battery The unprivileged, intentional touching of another.
Beachhead Acquisition The gradual accumulation of a bloc of a target corporation's shares by an aggressor during an attempt to obtain control of the corporation.
Bearer A person in the possession of an instrument payable to bearer or indorsed in blank.
Bearer Instrument Any instrument that is not payable to a specific person, including instruments payable to the bearer or to "cash."
Bequest A gift of personal property by will (from the verb *to bequeath*).
Beyond a Reasonable Doubt The standard of proof used in criminal cases. If there is any reasonable doubt that a criminal defendant did not commit the crime with which she or he has been charged, then the verdict must be "not guilty."
Bilateral Contract A type of contract that arises when a promise is given in exchange for a return promise.
Bilateral Mistake Mistake that occurs when both parties to a contract are mistaken about the same material fact and the mistake is one that a reasonable person would make; either party can rescind the contract.
Bill of Rights The first ten amendments to the U.S. Constitution.
Binder A written, temporary insurance policy.
Binding Authority Any source of law that a court must follow when deciding a case. Binding authorities include constitutions, statutes, and regulations that govern the issue being decided, as well as court decisions that are controlling precedents within the jurisdiction.
Blank Indorsement An indorsement that specifies no particular indorsee and can consist of a mere signature. An order instrument that is indorsed in blank becomes a bearer instrument.
Blue Laws State or local laws that prohibit the performance of certain types of commercial activities on Sunday.
Blue Sky Laws State laws that regulate the offer and sale of securities.
Bona Fide Occupational Qualification (BFOQ) An identifiable characteristic reasonably necessary to the normal operation of a particular business. Such characteristics can include gender, national origin, and religion, but not race.
Bond A certificate that evidences a corporate (or government) debt. It is a security that involves no ownership interest in the issuing entity.
Bond Indenture A contract between the issuer of a bond and the bondholder.
Bounty Payment A reward given to a person or persons who perform a certain service—such as informing legal authorities of illegal actions.
Breach The failure to perform a legal obligation.
Breach of Contract The failure, without legal excuse, of a promisor to perform the obligations of a contract.
Brief A formal legal document submitted to an appellate court when a case is appealed. Each party's attorney submits a brief. The appellant's brief outlines the facts and issues of the case, the judge's rulings or jury's findings that should be reversed or modified, the applicable law, and the arguments on the client's behalf. The appellee's brief responds to the appellant's brief.
Browse-Wrap Terms Terms and conditions of use that are presented to an Internet user at the time certain products, such as software, are being downloaded but to which the user need not agree (by clicking "I agree," for example) before being able to install or use the product.
Bureaucracy The organizational structure, consisting of government bureaus and agencies, through which the government implements and enforces the laws.
Burglary The unlawful entry or breaking into a building with the intent to commit a felony. (Some state statutes expand this to include the intent to commit any crime.)
Business Ethics Ethics in a business context; a consensus of what constitutes right or wrong behavior in the world of business and the application of moral principles to situations that arise in a business setting.
Business Invitee A person, such as a customer or a client, who is invited onto business premises by the owner of those premises for business purposes.
Business Judgment Rule A rule that immunizes corporate management from liability for actions that result in corporate losses or damages if the actions are undertaken in good faith and are within both the power of the corporation and the authority of management to make.
Business Necessity A defense to allegations of employment discrimination in which the employer demonstrates that an employment practice that discriminates against members of a protected class is related to job performance.
Business Tort The wrongful interference with another's business rights.
Business Trust A form of business organization in which investors (trust beneficiaries) transfer cash or property to trustees in exchange for trust certificates that represent their investment shares. The certificate holders share in the trust's profits but have limited liability.
Buyout Price The amount payable to a partner on his or her dissociation from a partnership, based on the amount distributable to that partner if the firm were wound up on that date, and offset by any damages for wrongful dissociation.
Bylaws A set of governing rules adopted by a corporation or other association.

C

Case Law The rules of law announced in court decisions. Case law includes the aggregate of reported cases that interpret judicial precedents, statutes, regulations, and constitutional provisions.
Cashier's Check A check drawn by a bank on itself.
Categorical Imperative A concept developed by the philosopher Immanuel Kant as an ethical guideline for behavior. In deciding whether an action is right or wrong, or desirable or undesirable, a person should evaluate the action in terms of what would happen if everybody else in the same situation, or category, acted the same way.
Causation in Fact An act or omission without which an event would not have occurred.

Cease-and-Desist Order An administrative or judicial order prohibiting a person or business firm from conducting activities that an agency or court has deemed illegal.
Certificate of Deposit (CD) A note of a bank in which the bank acknowledges a receipt of money from a party and promises to repay the money, with interest, to the party on a certain date.
Certificate of Incorporation The primary document that evidences corporate existence (often referred to as the *corporate charter*).
Certificate of Limited Partnership A document filed with a designated state official by which a limited partnership is formed.
Certified Check A check that has been accepted in writing by the bank on which it is drawn. Essentially, the bank, by certifying (accepting) the check, promises to pay the check at the time the check is presented.
Charging Order In partnership law, an order granted by a court to a judgment creditor that entitles the creditor to attach profits or assets of a partner on the dissolution of the partnership.
Charitable Trust A trust in which the property held by the trustee must be used for a charitable purpose, such as the advancement of health, education, or religion.
Chattel All forms of personal property.
Check A draft drawn by a drawer ordering the drawee bank or financial institution to pay a certain amount of money to the holder on demand.
Checks and Balances The national government is composed of three separate branches: executive, legislative, and judicial. Each branch exercises a check on the actions of the others.
Choice-of-Language Clause A clause in a contract designating the official language by which the contract will be interpreted in the event of a future disagreement over the contract's terms.
Chose in Action A right that can be enforced in court to recover a debt or to obtain property or damages.
Citation A reference to a publication in which a legal authority—such as a statute or a court decision—or other source can be found. Law based on the U.S. Constitution and the constitutions of the various states.
Civil Law The branch of law dealing with the definition and enforcement of all private or public rights, as opposed to criminal matters.
Civil Law System A system of law derived from that of the Roman Empire and based on a code rather than case law; the predominant system of law in the nations of continental Europe and the nations that were once their colonies. In the United States, Louisiana, because of its historical ties to France, has in part a civil law system.
Clearinghouse A system or place where banks exchange checks and drafts drawn on each other and settle daily balances.
Click-On Agreement An agreement that arises when a buyer, engaging in a transaction on a computer, indicates his or her assent to be bound by the terms of an offer by clicking on a button that says, for example, "I agree"; sometimes referred to as a *click-on license* or a *click-wrap agreement*.
Close Corporation A corporation whose shareholders are limited to a small group of persons, often including only family members. The rights of shareholders of a close corporation usually are restricted regarding the transfer of shares to others.
Closed Shop A firm that requires union membership as a condition of employment. The closed shop was made illegal by the Labor-Management Relations Act of 1947.
Codicil A written supplement or modification to a will. A codicil must be executed with the same formalities as a will.
Collateral Under Article 9 of the UCC, the property subject to a security interest.
Collateral Promise A secondary promise that is ancillary, or subsidiary, to a principal transaction or primary contractual relationship, such as a promise made by a third party to pay the debts of a primary party to a contract if the latter fails to perform. A collateral promise normally must be in writing to be enforceable.
Collecting Bank Any bank handling an item for collection, except the payor bank.
Collective Bargaining The process by which labor and management negotiate the terms and conditions of employment, including working hours and workplace conditions.
Comity The principle by which one nation defers and gives effect to the laws and judicial decrees of another nation.
Commerce Clause The provision in Article I, Section 8, of the U.S. Constitution that gives Congress the power to regulate interstate commerce.
Commingle To mix together; to put funds or goods together into one mass so that the funds or goods are so mixed that they no longer have separate identities. In corporate law, if personal and corporate interests are commingled to the extent that the corporation has no separate identity, a court may "pierce the corporate veil" and expose the shareholders to personal liability.
Common Carrier An owner of a truck, railroad, airline, ship, or other vehicle that is licensed to offer transportation services to the public, generally in return for compensation.
Common Law That body of law developed from custom or judicial decisions in English and U.S. courts, not attributable to a legislature.
Common Stock Shares of ownership in a corporation that give the owner of the stock a proportionate interest in the corporation with regard to control, earnings, and net assets. Shares of common stock are lowest in priority with respect to payment of dividends and distribution of the corporation's assets on dissolution.
Community Property Co-ownership of property in which each spouse technically owns an undivided one-half interest in property acquired during the marriage. This form of joint ownership occurs in only ten states and Puerto Rico.
Comparative Negligence A theory in tort law under which the liability for injuries resulting from negligent acts is shared by all persons who were guilty of negligence (including the injured party), on the basis of each person's proportionate carelessness.
Compensatory Damages A money award equivalent to the actual value of injuries or damages sustained by the aggrieved party.
Complaint The pleading made by a plaintiff alleging wrongdoing on the part of the defendant; the document that, when filed with a court, initiates a lawsuit.
Computer Crime Any act that is directed against computers and computer parts, that uses computers as instruments of crime, or that involves computers and constitutes abuse.
Computer Information As defined by the Uniform Computer Information Transactions Act, "information in an electronic form obtained from or through use of a computer, or that is in digital or an equivalent form capable of being processed by a computer."
Concurrent Conditions Conditions that must occur or be performed at the same time; they are mutually dependent. No obligations arise until these conditions are simultaneously performed.

Concurrent Jurisdiction Jurisdiction that exists when two different courts have the power to hear a case. For example, some cases can be heard in either a federal or a state court.
Concurrent Ownership Joint ownership.
Condemnation The process of taking private property for public use through the government's power of eminent domain.
Condition A possible future event, the occurrence or nonoccurrence of which will trigger the performance of a legal obligation or terminate an existing obligation under a contract.
Condition Precedent In a contractual agreement, a condition that must be met before a party's promise becomes absolute.
Condition Subsequent In a contractual agreement, a condition that, if not fulfilled, operates to terminate a party's absolute promise to perform.
Confession of Judgment The act or agreement of a debtor in permitting a judgment to be entered against him or her by a creditor, for an agreed sum, without the institution of legal proceedings.
Confiscation A government's taking of a privately owned business or personal property without a proper public purpose or an award of just compensation.
Confusion The mixing together of goods belonging to two or more owners so that the separately owned goods cannot be identified.
Conglomerate Merger A merger between unrelated firms that are neither competitors nor customers or suppliers of each other.
Consent The voluntary agreement to a proposition or an act of another; a concurrence of wills.
Consequential Damages Special damages that compensate for a loss that does not flow directly or immediately from the party's breach but are a foreseeable result of that breach (for example, lost profits). For the plaintiff to collect special damages, the loss must have been reasonably foreseeable at the time the breach or injury occurred.
Consideration Generally, the value given in return for a promise. The consideration must be something of legally sufficient value, and there must be a bargained-for exchange.
Consignment A transaction in which an owner of goods (the consignor) delivers the goods to another (the consignee) for the consignee to sell. The consignee pays the consignor only for the goods that are sold by the consignee.
Consolidation A contractual and statutory process in which two or more corporations join to become a completely new corporation. The original corporations cease to exist, and the new corporation acquires all their assets and liabilities.
Constitutional Law Law based on the U.S. Constitution and the constitutions of the various states.
Constructive Delivery An act equivalent to the actual, physical delivery of property that cannot be physically delivered because of difficulty or impossibility; for example, the transfer of a key to a safe constructively delivers the contents of the safe.
Constructive Discharge A termination of employment brought about by making the employee's working conditions so intolerable that the employee reasonably feels compelled to leave.
Constructive Eviction A form of eviction that occurs when a landlord fails to perform adequately any of the undertakings (such as providing heat in the winter) required by the lease, thereby making the tenant's further use and enjoyment of the property exceedingly difficult or impossible.
Constructive Trust An equitable trust that is imposed in the interests of fairness and justice when someone wrongfully holds legal title to property. A court may require the owner to hold the property in trust for the person or persons who rightfully should own the property.
Consumer-Debtor An individual whose debts are primarily consumer debts (debts for purchases made primarily for personal or household use).
Continuation Statement A statement that, if filed within six months prior to the expiration date of the original financing statement, continues the perfection of the original security interest for another five years. The perfection of a security interest can be continued in the same manner indefinitely.
Contract An agreement that can be enforced in court; formed by two or more competent parties who agree, for consideration, to perform or to refrain from performing some legal act now or in the future.
Contractual Capacity The threshold mental capacity required by law for a party who enters into a contract to be bound by that contract.
Contributory Negligence A theory in tort law under which a complaining party's own negligence contributed to or caused his or her injuries. Contributory negligence is an absolute bar to recovery in a minority of jurisdictions.
Conversion The act of wrongfully taking or retaining possession of a person's personal property and placing it in the service of another.
Conveyance The transfer of a title to land from one person to another by deed; a document (such as a deed) by which an interest in land is transferred from one person to another.
"Cooling-Off" Laws Laws that allow buyers a period of time, such as three days, in which to cancel door-to-door sales contracts.
Cooperative An association, which may or may not be incorporated, that is organized to provide an economic service to its members. Unincorporated cooperatives are often treated like partnerships for tax and other legally related purposes.
Copyright The exclusive right of authors to publish, print, or sell an intellectual production for a statutory period of time. A copyright has the same monopolistic nature as a patent or trademark, but it differs in that it applies exclusively to works of art, literature, and other works of authorship (including computer programs).
Corporate Charter A document issued by a state agency or authority (usually the secretary of state) that grants a corporation legal existence and the right to function.
Corporate Social Responsibility The concept that corporations can and should act ethically and be accountable to society for their actions.
Corporation A legal entity formed in compliance with statutory requirements. The entity is distinct from its shareholder-owners.
Correspondent Bank A bank in which another bank has an account for the purpose of facilitating fund transfers.
Cost-Benefit Analysis A decision-making technique that involves weighing the costs of a given action against the benefits of that action.
Co-surety A joint surety; a person who assumes liability jointly with another surety for the payment of an obligation.
Counteradvertising Advertising undertaken pursuant to a Federal Trade Commission order for the purpose of correcting earlier false claims that were made about a product.
Counterclaim A claim made by a defendant in a civil lawsuit against the plaintiff. In effect, the defendant is suing the plaintiff.

Counteroffer An offeree's response to an offer in which the offeree rejects the original offer and at the same time makes a new offer.

Course of Dealing Prior conduct between parties to a contract that establishes a common basis for their understanding.

Course of Performance The conduct that occurs under the terms of a particular agreement; such conduct indicates what the parties to an agreement intended it to mean.

Covenant Not to Compete A contractual promise of one party to refrain from conducting business similar to that of another party for a certain period of time and within a specified geographic area. Courts commonly enforce such covenants if they are reasonable in terms of time and geographic area and part of, or supplemental to, an employment contract or a contract for the sale of a business.

Covenant Not to Sue An agreement to substitute a contractual obligation for some other type of legal action based on a valid claim.

Cover A buyer or lessee's purchase on the open market of goods to substitute for those promised but never delivered by the seller. Under the UCC, if the cost of cover exceeds the cost of the contract goods, the buyer or lessee can recover the difference, plus incidental and consequential damages.

Cram-Down Provision A provision of the Bankruptcy Code that allows a court to confirm a debtor's Chapter 11 reorganization plan even though only one class of creditors has accepted it.

Creditors' Composition Agreement An agreement between a debtor and his or her creditors in which the creditors agree to accept a sum less than that owed by the debtor in full satisfaction of the debt.

Crime A wrong against society proclaimed in a statute and punishable by society through fines and/or imprisonment—and, in some cases, death.

Criminal Law Law that defines and governs actions that constitute crimes. Generally, criminal law has to do with wrongful actions committed against society for which society demands redress.

Cure The right of a party who tenders nonconforming performance to correct that performance within the contract period [UCC 2–508(1)].

Cyber Crime A crime that occurs online, in the virtual community of the Internet, as opposed to the physical world.

Cyber Mark A trademark in cyberspace.

Cyber Tort A tort committed via the Internet.

Cyberlaw An informal term used to refer to all laws governing electronic communications and transactions, particularly those conducted via the Internet.

Cybernotary A legally recognized authority that can certify the validity of digital signatures.

Cybersquatting An act that occurs when a person registers a domain name that is the same as, or confusingly similar to, the trademark of another and offers to sell the domain name back to the trademark owner.

Cyberstalker A person who commits the crime of stalking in cyberspace. Generally, stalking consists of harassing a person and putting that person in reasonable fear for his or her safety or the safety of his or her immediate family.

Cyberterrorist A hacker whose purpose is to exploit a target computer to create a serious impact, such as corrupting a program to sabotage a business.

D

Damages Compensation sought as a remedy for a breach of contract or a tortious action.

Debit Card A plastic card that allows the bearer to transfer funds to a merchant's account, provided that the bearer authorizes the transfer by providing personal identification.

Debtor Under Article 9 of the UCC, any party who owes payment or performance of a secured obligation.

Debtor in Possession (DIP) In Chapter 11 bankruptcy proceedings, a debtor who is allowed to continue in possession of the estate in property (the business) and to continue business operations.

Deceptive Advertising Advertising that misleads consumers, either by making unjustified claims concerning a product's performance or by omitting a material fact concerning the product's composition or performance.

Deed A document by which title to property (usually real property) is passed.

Defalcation Embezzlement; the misappropriation of funds by a party, such as a corporate officer or a public official, in a fiduciary relationship with another.

Defamation Anything published or publicly spoken that causes injury to another's good name, reputation, or character.

Default The failure to observe a promise or discharge an obligation. The term is commonly used to mean the failure to pay a debt when it is due.

Default Judgment A judgment entered by a court against a defendant who has failed to appear in court to answer or defend against the plaintiff's claim.

Default Rules Rules that apply under the Uniform Computer Information Transactions Act only in the absence of an agreement between contracting parties indicating otherwise.

Defendant One against whom a lawsuit is brought; the accused person in a criminal proceeding.

Defense Reasons that a defendant offers in an action or suit as to why the plaintiff should not obtain what he or she is seeking.

Deficiency Judgment A judgment against a debtor for the amount of a debt remaining unpaid after collateral has been repossessed and sold.

Delegatee A party to whom contractual obligations are transferred, or delegated.

Delegation Doctrine A doctrine based on Article I, Section 8, of the U.S. Constitution, which has been construed to allow Congress to delegate some of its power to make and implement laws to administrative agencies.

Delegation of Duties The act of transferring to another all or part of one's duties arising under a contract.

Delegator A party who transfers (delegates) her or his obligations under a contract to another party (called the delegatee).

Depositary Bank The first bank to receive a check for payment.

Deposition The testimony of a party to a lawsuit or a witness taken under oath before a trial.

Destination Contract A contract in which the seller is required to ship the goods by carrier and to deliver the goods at a particular destination. The seller assumes liability for any losses or damage to the goods until they are tendered at the destination specified in the contract.

Devise A gift of real property by will.

Devisee One designated in a will to receive a gift of real property.

Digital Cash Any funds stored on microchips and other computer devices.
Disaffirmance The legal avoidance, or setting aside, of a contractual obligation.
Discharge The termination of an obligation. In contract law, discharge occurs when the parties have fully performed their contractual obligations or when events, conduct of the parties, or operation of the law releases the parties from performance. In bankruptcy proceedings, the term refers to the extinction of the debtor's dischargeable debts.
Disclosed Principal A principal whose identity is known to a third party at the time the agent makes a contract with the third party.
Discovery A phase in the litigation process during which the opposing parties obtain information from each other and from third parties prior to trial.
Disparagement of Property An economically injurious false statement made about another's product or property; includes the torts of slander of quality and slander of title.
Disparate-Impact Discrimination A form of employment discrimination that results from certain employer practices or procedures that, although not discriminatory on their face, have a discriminatory effect.
Disparate-Treatment Discrimination A form of employment discrimination that results when an employer intentionally discriminates against employees who are members of protected classes.
Dissociation The severance of the relationship between a partner and a partnership when the partner ceases to be associated with the carrying on of the partnership business.
Dissolution The formal disbanding of a partnership or a corporation. Dissolution of a partnership can take place by (1) acts of the partners, (2) operation of law, or (3) judicial decree. Dissolution of a corporation can take place by (1) an act of the state legislature, (2) agreement of the shareholders and the board of directors, (3) the expiration of a time period stated in the certificate of incorporation, or (4) court order.
Distributed Network A network that can be used by persons located (distributed) around the country or the globe to share computer files.
Distribution Agreement A contract between a seller and a distributor of the seller's products setting out the terms and conditions of the distributorship.
Diversity of Citizenship Under Article III, Section 2, of the Constitution, a basis for federal district court jurisdiction over a lawsuit between (1) citizens of different states, (2) a foreign country and citizens of a state or of different states, or (3) citizens of a state and citizens or subjects of a foreign country. The amount in controversy must be more than $75,000 before a federal district court can take jurisdiction in such cases.
Divestiture The act of selling one or more of a company's parts, such as a subsidiary or plant; often mandated by the courts in merger or monopolization cases.
Dividend A distribution to corporate shareholders of corporate profits or income, disbursed in proportion to the number of shares held.
Docket The list of cases entered on a court's calendar and thus scheduled to be heard by the court.
Document of Title Paper exchanged in the regular course of business that evidences the right to possession of goods (for example, a bill of lading or a warehouse receipt).
Domain Name The core part of an Internet address, or URL, such as "westlaw.com." The top level (the part of the name to the right of the period) represents the type of entity that operates the site ("com" is an abbreviation for "commercial"). The second level (the part of the name to the left of the period) is chosen by the entity.
Domestic Corporation In a given state, a corporation that does business in, and is organized under the laws of, that state.
Dominion Ownership rights in property, including the right to possess and control the property.
Double Jeopardy A situation occurring when a person is tried twice for the same criminal offense; prohibited by the Fifth Amendment to the Constitution.
Draft Any instrument (such as a check) drawn on a drawee that orders the drawee to pay a certain sum of money, usually to a third party (the payee), on demand or at a definite future time.
Dram Shop Act A state statute that imposes liability on the owners of bars and taverns, as well as those who serve alcoholic drinks to the public, for injuries resulting from accidents caused by intoxicated persons when the sellers or servers of alcoholic drinks contributed to the intoxication.
Drawee The party that is ordered to pay a draft or check. With a check, a bank or a financial institution is always the drawee.
Drawer The party that initiates a draft (writes a check, for example), thereby ordering the drawee to pay.
Due Diligence A required standard of care that certain professionals, such as accountants, must meet to avoid liability for securities violations.
Due Process Clause The provisions of the Fifth and Fourteenth Amendments to the Constitution that guarantee that no person shall be deprived of life, liberty, or property without due process of law. Similar clauses are found in most state constitutions.
Dumping The selling of goods in a foreign country at a price below the price charged for the same goods in the domestic market.
Duress Unlawful pressure brought to bear on a person, causing the person to perform an act that she or he would not otherwise have performed.
Duty of Care The duty of all persons, as established by tort law, to exercise a reasonable amount of care in their dealings with others. Failure to exercise due care, which is normally determined by the "reasonable person standard," constitutes the tort of negligence.

E

E-Agent According to the Uniform Computer Information Transactions Act, "a computer program, electronic or other automated means used to independently initiate an action or to respond to electronic messages or performances without review by an individual."
E-Contract A contract that is formed electronically.
E-Evidence A type of evidence that consists of computer-generated or electronically recorded information, including e-mail, voice mail, spreadsheets, word-processing documents, and other data.
E-Money Prepaid funds recorded on a computer or a card (such as a smart card or a stored-value card).
E-Signature Under the Uniform Electronic Transactions Act, a signature can be any electronic sound, symbol, or process attached to electronically stored information. This definition is intentionally broad in order to give legal effect to acts that people intend to be the equivalent of their written signatures.

Early Neutral Case Evaluation A form of alternative dispute resolution in which a neutral third party evaluates the strengths and weaknesses of the disputing parties' positions; the evaluator's opinion forms the basis for negotiating a settlement.
Easement A nonpossessory right to use another's property in a manner established by either express or implied agreement.
Electronic Fund Transfer (EFT) Transfer of funds by means of an electronic terminal, a telephone, a computer, or magnetic tape.
Emancipation In regard to minors, the act of being freed from parental control; occurs when a child's parent or legal guardian relinquishes the legal right to exercise control over the child. Normally, a minor who leaves home to support himself or herself is considered emancipated.
Embezzlement The fraudulent appropriation of funds or other property by a person to whom such items have been entrusted.
Eminent Domain The power of a government to take land for public use from private citizens for just compensation.
Employment at Will A common law doctrine under which either party can terminate an employment relationship at any time for any reason, unless a contract specifies otherwise.
Employment Contract A contract between an employer and an employee in which the terms and conditions of employment are stated.
Employment Discrimination Treating employees or job applicants unequally on the basis of race, color, national origin, religion, gender, age, or disability; prohibited by federal statutes.
Enabling Legislation Statutes enacted by Congress that authorize the creation of an administrative agency and specify the name, composition, and powers of the agency being created.
Entrapment In criminal law, a defense in which the defendant claims that he or she was induced by a public official—usually an undercover agent or police officer—to commit a crime that he or she would otherwise not have committed.
Entrepreneur One who initiates and assumes the financial risk of a new business enterprise and undertakes to provide or control its management.
Environmental Impact Statement (EIS) A statement required by the National Environmental Policy Act for any major federal action that will significantly affect the quality of the environment. The statement must analyze the action's impact on the environment and explore alternative actions that might be taken.
Equal Dignity Rule In most states, a rule stating that express authority given to an agent must be in writing if the contract to be made on behalf of the principal is required to be in writing.
Equal Protection Clause The provision in the Fourteenth Amendment to the Constitution that guarantees that no state will "deny to any person within its jurisdiction the equal protection of the laws." This clause mandates that the state governments treat similarly situated individuals in a similar manner.
Equitable Principles and Maxims General propositions or principles of law that have to do with fairness (equity).
Establishment Clause The provision in the First Amendment to the Constitution that prohibits Congress from creating any law "respecting an establishment of religion."
Estate in Property In bankruptcy proceedings, all of the debtor's legal and equitable interests in property currently held, wherever located, together with certain jointly owned property, property transferred in transactions voidable by the trustee, proceeds and profits from the property of the estate, and certain property interests to which the debtor becomes entitled within 180 days after filing for bankruptcy.
Estopped Barred, impeded, or precluded.
Estray Statute A statute defining finders' rights in property when the true owners are unknown.
Ethical Reasoning A reasoning process in which an individual links his or her moral convictions or ethical standards to the particular situation at hand.
Ethics Moral principles and values applied to social behavior.
Eviction A landlord's act of depriving a tenant of possession of the leased premises.
Exclusionary Rule In criminal procedure, a rule under which any evidence that is obtained in violation of the accused's constitutional rights guaranteed by the Fourth, Fifth, and Sixth Amendments, as well as any evidence derived from illegally obtained evidence, will not be admissible in court.
Exclusive-Dealing Contract An agreement under which a seller forbids a buyer to purchase products from the seller's competitors.
Exclusive Distributorship A distributorship in which the seller and the distributor of the seller's products agree that the distributor has the exclusive right to distribute the seller's products in a certain geographic area.
Exclusive Jurisdiction Jurisdiction that exists when a case can be heard only in a particular court or type of court.
Exculpatory Clause A clause that releases a contractual party from liability in the event of monetary or physical injury, no matter who is at fault.
Executed Contract A contract that has been completely performed by both parties.
Execution An action to carry into effect the directions in a court decree or judgment.
Executive Agency An administrative agency within the executive branch of government. At the federal level, executive agencies are those within the cabinet departments.
Executor A person appointed by a testator in a will to see that her or his will is administered appropriately.
Executory Contract A contract that has not as yet been fully performed.
Executory Interest A future interest, held by a person other than the grantor, that begins after the termination of the preceding estate.
Export To sell products to buyers located in other countries.
Express Contract A contract in which the terms of the agreement are stated in words, oral or written.
Express Warranty A seller's or lessor's oral or written promise or affirmation of fact, ancillary to an underlying sales or lease agreement, as to the quality, description, or performance of the goods being sold or leased.
Expropriation The seizure by a government of a privately owned business or personal property for a proper public purpose and with just compensation.
Extension Clause A clause in a time instrument that allows the instrument's date of maturity to be extended into the future.

F

Family Limited Liability Partnership (FLLP) A type of limited liability partnership owned by family members or fiduciaries of family members.

Federal Form of Government A system of government in which the states form a union and the sovereign power is divided between a central government and the member states.

Federal Question A question that pertains to the U.S. Constitution, acts of Congress, or treaties. A federal question provides a basis for federal jurisdiction.

Federal Reserve System A network of twelve district banks and related branches located around the country and headed by the Federal Reserve Board of Governors. Most banks in the United States have Federal Reserve accounts.

Fee Simple An absolute form of property ownership entitling the property owner to use, possess, or dispose of the property as he or she chooses during his or her lifetime. On death, the interest in the property passes to the owner's heirs.

Fee Simple Absolute An ownership interest in land in which the owner has the greatest possible aggregation of rights, privileges, and power. Ownership in fee simple absolute is limited absolutely to a person and his or her heirs.

Fee Simple Defeasible An ownership interest in real property that can be taken away (by the prior grantor) on the occurrence or nonoccurrence of a specified event.

Felony A crime—such as arson, murder, rape, or robbery—that carries the most severe sanctions, which range from one year in a state or federal prison to the death penalty.

Fictitious Payee A payee on a negotiable instrument whom the maker or drawer does not intend to have an interest in the instrument. Indorsements by fictitious payees are treated as authorized indorsements under Article 3 of the UCC.

Fiduciary As a noun, a person having a duty created by his or her undertaking to act primarily for another's benefit in matters connected with the undertaking. As an adjective, a relationship founded on trust and confidence.

Filtering Software A computer program that includes a pattern through which data are passed. When designed to block access to certain Web sites, the pattern blocks the retrieval of a site whose URL or key words are on a list within the program.

Final Order The final decision of an administrative agency on an issue. If no appeal is taken, or if the case is not reviewed or considered anew by the agency commission, the administrative law judge's initial order becomes the final order of the agency.

Financing Statement A document prepared by a secured creditor, and filed with the appropriate government official, to give notice to the public that the creditor has a security interest in collateral. The financing statement must contain the names and addresses of both the debtor and the secured party and describe the collateral by type or item.

Firm Offer An offer (by a merchant) that is irrevocable without consideration for a stated period of time or, if no definite period is stated, for a reasonable time (neither period to exceed three months). A firm offer by a merchant must be in writing and must be signed by the offeror.

Fixture A thing that was once personal property but has become attached to real property in such a way that it takes on the characteristics of real property and becomes part of that real property.

Floating Lien A security interest in proceeds, after-acquired property, or collateral (or all three) subject to future advances by the secured party; a security interest in collateral that is retained even when the collateral changes in character, classification, or location.

Forbearance The act of refraining from an action that one has a legal right to undertake.

***Force Majeure* Clause** A provision in a contract stipulating that certain unforeseen events—such as war, political upheavals, acts of God, or other events—will excuse a party from liability for nonperformance of contractual obligations.

Foreign Corporation In a given state, a corporation that does business in the state without being incorporated therein.

Foreign Exchange Market Part of a worldwide system in which foreign currencies are bought and sold.

Forgery The fraudulent making or altering of any writing in a way that changes the legal rights and liabilities of another.

Formal Contract A contract that by law requires a special form or method of creation to be enforceable.

Forum-Selection Clause A provision in a contract designating the court, jurisdiction, or tribunal that will decide any disputes arising under the contract.

Franchise Any arrangement in which the owner of a trademark, trade name, or copyright licenses another to use that trademark, trade name, or copyright in the selling of goods and services.

Franchisee One receiving a license to use another's (the franchisor's) trademark, trade name, or copyright in the sale of goods and services.

Franchisor One licensing another (the franchisee) to use the owner's trademark, trade name, or copyright in the sale of goods or services.

Fraudulent Misrepresentation Any misrepresentation, either by misstatement or by omission of a material fact, knowingly made with the intention of deceiving another and on which a reasonable person would and does rely to his or her detriment.

Free Exercise Clause The provision in the First Amendment to the Constitution that prohibits Congress from making any law "prohibiting the free exercise" of religion.

Fungible Goods Goods that are alike by physical nature, by agreement, or by trade usage. Examples of fungible goods are wheat, oil, and wine that are identical in type and quality. When owners of fungible goods hold the goods as tenants in common, title and risk can pass without actual separation of the goods being sold from the mass of fungible goods.

Future Interest An interest in real property in which the person who holds the interest does not currently possess the property but may possess it in the future.

G

Garnishment A legal process used by a creditor to collect a debt by seizing property of the debtor (such as wages) that is being held by a third party (such as the debtor's employer).

General Partner In a limited partnership, a partner who assumes responsibility for the management of the partnership and liability for all partnership debts.

Generally Accepted Accounting Principles (GAAP) The conventions, rules, and procedures that define accepted accounting practices at a particular time. The source of the principles is the Financial Accounting Standards Board.

Generally Accepted Auditing Standards (GAAS) Standards concerning an auditor's professional qualities and the judgment exercised by him or her in the performance of an audit and report. The source of the standards is the American Institute of Certified Public Accountants.

Gift Any voluntary transfer of property made without consideration, past or present.
Gift *Causa Mortis* A gift made in contemplation of death. If the donor does not die of the contemplated cause, the gift is revoked.
Gift *Inter Vivos* A gift made during one's lifetime and not in contemplation of imminent death, in contrast to a gift *causa mortis*.
Good Faith Purchaser A purchaser who buys without notice of any circumstance that would put a person of ordinary prudence on inquiry as to whether the seller has valid title to the goods being sold.
Good Samaritan Statute A state statute stipulating that persons who rescue or provide emergency services to others in peril—unless they do so recklessly, thus causing further harm—cannot be sued for negligence.
Grand Jury A group of citizens called to decide, after hearing the state's evidence, whether a reasonable basis (probable cause) exists for believing that a crime has been committed and whether a trial ought to be held. Grand juries usually include more jurors than ordinary trial juries.
Group Boycott The refusal to deal with a particular person or firm by a group of competitors.
Guarantor A person who agrees to satisfy the debt of another (the debtor) only after the principal debtor defaults; a guarantor's liability is thus secondary.

H

Hacker A person who uses one computer to break into another. Professional computer programmers refer to such persons as "crackers."
Historical School A school of legal thought that emphasizes the evolutionary process of law and that looks to the past to discover what the principles of contemporary law should be.
Holder Any person in the possession of an instrument drawn, issued, or indorsed to him or her, to his or her order, to bearer, or in blank.
Holder in Due Course (HDC) A holder who acquires a negotiable instrument for value; in good faith; and without notice that the instrument is overdue, that it has been dishonored, that any person has a defense against it or a claim to it, or that the instrument contains unauthorized signatures, has been altered, or is so irregular or incomplete as to call into question its authenticity.
Holographic Will A will written entirely in the signer's handwriting and usually not witnessed.
Homestead Exemption A law permitting a debtor to retain the family home, either in its entirety or up to a specified dollar amount, free from the claims of unsecured creditors or trustees in bankruptcy.
Horizontal Merger A merger between two firms that are competing in the same market.
Horizontal Restraint Any agreement that in some way restrains competition between rival firms competing in the same market.
Hot-Cargo Agreement An agreement in which employers voluntarily agree with unions not to handle, use, or deal in other employers' goods that were not produced by union employees.

I

Identification In a sale of goods, the express designation of the specific goods provided for in the contract.
Identity Theft Theft of another's identifying information—such as name, date of birth, and Social Security number—and use of the information to access the victim's financial resources.
Implied-in-Fact Contract A contract formed in whole or in part from the conduct of the parties (as opposed to an express contract).
Implied Warranty A warranty that arises by law by implication or inference from the nature of the transaction or the relative situations or circumstances of the parties.
Implied Warranty of Fitness for a Particular Purpose A warranty that goods sold or leased are fit for a particular purpose. The warranty arises when any seller or lessor knows the particular purpose for which a buyer or lessee will use the goods and knows that the buyer or lessee is relying on the skill and judgment of the seller or lessor to select suitable goods.
Implied Warranty of Habitability An implied promise by a landlord that rented residential premises are fit for human habitation—that is, in a condition that is safe and suitable for people to live in.
Implied Warranty of Merchantability A warranty that goods being sold or leased are reasonably fit for the ordinary purpose for which they are sold or leased, are properly packaged and labeled, and are of fair quality. The warranty automatically arises in every sale or lease of goods made by a merchant who deals in goods of the kind sold or leased.
Impossibility of Performance A doctrine under which a party to a contract is relieved of his or her duty to perform when performance becomes objectively impossible or totally impracticable (through no fault of either party).
Imposter One who, by use of the mail, telephone, or personal appearance, induces a maker or drawer to issue an instrument in the name of an impersonated payee. Indorsements by imposters are treated as authorized indorsements under Article 3 of the UCC.
Incidental Beneficiary A third party who incidentally benefits from a contract but whose benefit was not the reason the contract was formed; an incidental beneficiary has no rights in a contract and cannot sue to have the contract enforced.
Incidental Damages Losses reasonably associated with or related to actual damages resulting from a breach of contract.
Independent Contractor One who works for, and receives payment from, an employer but whose working conditions and methods are not controlled by the employer. An independent contractor is not an employee but may be an agent.
Independent Regulatory Agency An administrative agency that is not considered part of the government's executive branch and is not subject to the authority of the president. Independent agency officials cannot be removed without cause.
Indictment A charge by a grand jury that a reasonable basis (probable cause) exists for believing that a crime has been commited and that a trial should be held.
Indorsee The person to whom a negotiable instrument is transferred by indorsement.
Indorsement A signature placed on an instrument for the purpose of transferring one's ownership rights in the instrument.
Indorser A person who transfers an instrument by signing (indorsing) it and delivering it to another person.
Informal Contract A contract that does not require a special form to be valid.
Information A formal accusation or complaint (without an indictment) issued in certain types of actions (usually criminal actions involving lesser crimes) by a law officer, such as a magistrate.

Information Return A tax return submitted by a partnership that only reports the income and losses earned by the business. The partnership as an entity does not pay taxes on the income received by the partnership. A partner's profit from the partnership (whether distributed or not) is taxed as individual income to the individual partner.

Initial Order In the context of administrative law, an agency's disposition in a matter other than a rulemaking. An administrative law judge's initial order becomes final unless it is appealed.

Innkeeper's Lien A possessory lien placed on the luggage of hotel guests for hotel charges that remain unpaid.

Insider Trading The purchase or sale of securities on the basis of inside information (information that has not been made available to the public).

Insolvent Under the UCC, a term describing a person who ceases to pay "his [or her] debts in the ordinary course of business or cannot pay his [or her] debts as they become due or is insolvent within the meaning of federal bankruptcy law" [UCC 1–201(23)].

Installment Contract Under the UCC, a contract that requires or authorizes delivery in two or more separate lots to be accepted and paid for separately.

Insurable Interest In regard to insurance law, an interest either in a person's life or well-being or in property that is sufficiently substantial that insuring against injury to (or the death of) the person or against damage to the property does not amount to a mere wagering (betting) contract. In regard to the sale or lease of goods, a property interest in the goods that is sufficiently substantial to permit a party to insure against damage to the goods.

Insurance A contract in which, for a stipulated consideration, one party agrees to compensate the other for loss on a specific subject by a specified peril.

Intangible Property Property that cannot be seen or touched but exists only conceptually, such as corporate stocks and bonds, patents and copyrights, and ordinary contract rights. Article 2 of the UCC does not govern intangible property.

Integrated Contract A written contract that constitutes the final expression of the parties' agreement. If a contract is integrated, evidence extraneous to the contract that contradicts or alters the meaning of the contract in any way is inadmissible.

Intellectual Property Property resulting from intellectual, creative processes.

Intended Beneficiary A third party for whose benefit a contract is formed; an intended beneficiary can sue the promisor if such a contract is breached.

Intentional Tort A wrongful act knowingly committed.

***Inter Vivos* Trust** A trust created by the grantor (settlor) and effective during the grantor's lifetime; a trust not established by a will.

Intermediary Bank Any bank to which an item is transferred in the course of collection, except the depositary or payor bank.

International Law The law that governs relations among nations. National laws, customs, treaties, and international conferences and organizations are generally considered the most important sources of international law.

Interrogatories A series of written questions for which written answers are prepared, usually with the assistance of the party's attorney, and then signed under oath by a party to a lawsuit.

Intestacy Laws State statutes that specify how property will be distributed when a person dies intestate (without a valid will); also called statutes of descent and distribution.

Intestate As a noun, one who has died without having created a valid will; as an adjective, the state of having died without a will.

Investment Company A company that acts on behalf of many smaller shareholders by buying a large portfolio of securities and professionally managing that portfolio.

J

Joint and Several Liability In partnership law, a doctrine under which a plaintiff can sue, and collect a judgment from, one or more of the partners separately (severally, or individually) or all of the partners together (jointly). This is true even if one of the partners sued did not participate in, ratify, or know about whatever it was that gave rise to the cause of action.

Joint Liability Shared liability. In partnership law, partners incur joint liability for partnership obligations and debts. For example, if a third party sues a partner on a partnership debt, the partner has the right to insist that the other partners be sued with him or her.

Joint Stock Company A hybrid form of business organization that combines characteristics of a corporation and a partnership. Usually, the joint stock company is regarded as a partnership for tax and other legally related purposes.

Joint Tenancy Co-ownership of property in which each party owns an undivided interest that passes to the surviving joint tenant(s) at death.

Joint Venture A joint undertaking of a specific commercial enterprise by an association of persons or business entities. A joint venture normally is not a legal entity and is treated like a partnership for federal income tax purposes.

Judicial Process The procedures relating to, or connected with, the administration of justice through the judicial system.

Judicial Review The process by which a court decides on the constitutionality of legislative enactments and actions of the executive branch.

Jurisdiction The authority of a court to hear and decide a specific action.

Jurisprudence The science or philosophy of law.

Justiciable Controversy A controversy that is not hypothetical or academic but real and substantial; a requirement that must be satisfied before a court will hear a case.

L

Larceny The wrongful taking and carrying away of another person's personal property with the intent to permanently deprive the owner of the property. Some states classify larceny as either grand or petit, depending on the property's value.

Law A body of enforceable rules governing relationships among individuals and between individuals and their society.

Lease In real property law, a contract by which the owner of real property (the landlord, or lessor) grants to a person (the tenant, or lessee) an exclusive right to use and possess the property, usually for a specified period of time, in return for rent or some other form of payment.

Lease Agreement In regard to the lease of goods, an agreement in which one person (the lessor) agrees to transfer the right to the possession and use of property to another person (the lessee) in exchange for rental payments.

Leasehold Estate An estate in realty held by a tenant under a lease. In every leasehold estate, the tenant has a qualified right to possess and/or use the land.

Legacy A gift of personal property by will.

Legal Positivism A school of legal thought centered on the assumption that there is no law higher than the laws created by the government. Laws must be obeyed, even if they are unjust, to prevent anarchy.

Legal Realism A school of legal thought of the 1920s and 1930s that generally advocated a less abstract and more pragmatic approach to the law, an approach that takes into account customary practices and the circumstances in which transactions take place. The school left a lasting imprint on American jurisprudence.

Legatee One designated in a will to receive a gift of personal property.

Legislative Rule An administrative agency rule that carries the same weight as a congressionally enacted statute.

Lessee A person who acquires the right to the possession and use of another's goods in exchange for rental payments.

Lessor A person who sells the right to the possession and use of goods to another in exchange for rental payments.

Letter of Credit A written instrument, usually issued by a bank on behalf of a customer or other person, in which the issuer promises to honor drafts or other demands for payment by third persons in accordance with the terms of the instrument.

Leveraged Buyout (LBO) A corporate takeover financed by loans secured by the acquired corporation's assets or by the issuance of corporate bonds, resulting in a high debt load for the corporation.

Levy Obtaining money by legal process through the seizure and sale of property, usually done after a writ of execution has been issued.

Libel Defamation in writing or other form (such as videotape) having the quality of permanence.

License A revocable right or privilege of a person to come onto another person's land.

Lien A claim against specific property to satisfy a debt.

Life Estate An interest in land that exists only for the duration of the life of some person, usually the holder of the estate.

Limited Liability Company (LLC) A hybrid form of business enterprise that offers the limited liability of a corporation and the tax advantages of a partnership.

Limited Liability Limited Partnership (LLLP) A type of limited partnership in which the liability of all of the partners, including general partners, is limited to the amount of their investments.

Limited Liability Partnership (LLP) A business organizational form similar to the LLC but designed more for professionals who normally do business as partners in a partnership. The LLP is a pass-through entity for tax purposes, like a general partnership, but it limits the personal liability of the partners.

Limited Partner In a limited partnership, a partner who contributes capital to the partnership but who has no right to participate in the management and operation of the business. The limited partner assumes no liability for partnership debts beyond the capital contributed.

Limited Partnership A partnership consisting of one or more general partners (who manage the business and are liable to the full extent of their personal assets for debts of the partnership) and one or more limited partners (who contribute only assets and are liable only up to the extent of their contributions).

Liquidated Damages An amount, stipulated in the contract, to be paid in the event of a default or breach of contract. The amount must be a reasonable estimate of the damages that would result from breach in order for the court to enforce it.

Liquidation The sale of all the nonexempt assets of a debtor and the distribution of the proceeds to the debtor's creditors. Chapter 7 of the Bankruptcy Code provides for liquidation bankruptcy proceedings. In regard to corporations, the process by which corporate assets are converted into cash and distributed among creditors and shareholders according to specific rules of preference.

Litigation The process of resolving a dispute through the court system.

Long Arm Statute A state statute that permits a state to obtain personal jurisdiction over nonresident defendants. A defendant must have certain minimum contacts with that state for the statute to apply.

Lost property Property with which the owner has involuntarily parted and which he or she then cannot find or recover.

M

Mailbox Rule A rule providing that an acceptance of an offer becomes effective on dispatch (on being placed in an official mailbox), if mail is expressly or impliedly an authorized means of communication of acceptance to the offeror.

Maker One who promises to pay a fixed amount of money to the holder of a promissory note or a certificate of deposit (CD).

Malpractice Professional misconduct or lack of the requisite degree of skill as a professional. Negligence—the failure to exercise due care—on the part of a professional, such as a physician, is commonly referred to as malpractice.

Market Concentration The degree to which a small number of firms control a large percentage of a relevant market area.

Market Power The power of a firm to control the market price of its product. A monopoly has the greatest degree of market power.

Market-Share Test The primary measure of monopoly power. A firm's market share is the percentage of a market that the firm controls.

Marshalling Assets The arrangement or ranking of assets in a certain order toward the payment of debts. When two creditors have recourse to the same property of a debtor, but one also has recourse to other property of the debtor, that creditor must resort first to those assets of the debtor available only to him or her.

Mass-Market License An e-contract that is presented with a package of computer information in the form of a *click-on license* or a *shrink-wrap license.*

Material Fact A fact to which a reasonable person would attach importance in determining his or her course of action.

Mechanic's Lien A statutory lien on the real property of another, created to ensure payment for work performed and materials furnished in the repair or improvement of real property, such as a building.

Mediation A method of settling disputes outside of court by using the services of a neutral third party, who acts as a communicating agent between the parties and assists them in negotiating a settlement.

Member The term used to designate a person who has an ownership interest in a limited liability company.

Merchant A person engaged in the purchase and sale of goods. Under the UCC, a person who deals in goods of the kind involved in the sales contract, or who holds himself or herself out as having skill and knowledge peculiar to the practices or goods involved in the transaction, or who employs a merchant as an intermediary. For definitions, see UCC 2–104.

Merger A contractual and statutory process in which one corporation (the surviving corporation) acquires all of the assets and liabilities of another corporation (the merged corporation). The shareholders of the merged corporation either are paid for their shares or receive shares in the surviving corporation.

Meta Tag A key word in a document that can serve as an index reference to the document. On the Web, search engines return results based, in part, on the tags in Web documents.

Mini-Trial A private proceeding in which the parties to a dispute argue their positions in turn. A neutral third party may be present as an adviser and may render an opinion if the parties fail to reach an agreement.

Minimum Wage The lowest wage, either by government regulation or union contract, that an employer may pay an hourly worker.

Mirror Image Rule A common law rule that requires that the terms of the offeree's acceptance adhere exactly to the terms of the offeror's offer for a valid contract to be formed.

Misdemeanor A lesser crime than a felony, punishable by a fine or incarceration in jail for up to one year.

Mislaid Property Property with which the owner has voluntarily parted and which he or she then cannot find or recover.

Mitigation of Damages A rule requiring a plaintiff to have done whatever was reasonable to minimize the damages caused by the defendant.

Money Laundering Falsely reporting income that has been obtained through criminal activity as income obtained through a legitimate business enterprise—in effect, "laundering" the "dirty money."

Money Services Services provided by legal or commercial entities engaged in money transmission, the sale of payment instruments (such as money orders, traveler's checks, or stored-value cards), check cashing, or currency exchange.

Monopolization The possession of monopoly power in the relevant market and the willful acquisition or maintenance of that power, as distinguished from growth or development as a consequence of a superior product, business acumen, or historic accident.

Monopoly A term generally used to describe a market in which there is a single seller or a limited number of sellers.

Monopoly Power The ability of a monopoly to dictate what takes place in a given market.

Moral Minimum The minimum degree of ethical behavior expected of a business firm, which is usually defined as compliance with the law.

Mortgagee Under a mortgage agreement, a creditor who takes a security interest in a debtor's property.

Mortgagor Under a mortgage agreement, a debtor who gives a creditor a security interest in the debtor's property in return for a mortgage loan.

Motion for a Directed Verdict In a jury trial, a motion requesting the judge to take the decision out of the hands of the jury and direct a verdict for the party who filed the motion on the ground that the other party has not produced sufficient evidence to support her or his claim.

Motion for a New Trial A motion asserting that the trial was so fundamentally flawed (because of error, newly discovered evidence, prejudice, or other reason) that a new trial is necessary to prevent a miscarriage of justice.

Motion for Judgment *N.O.V.* A motion requesting the court to grant judgment in favor of the party making the motion on the ground that the jury verdict against him or her was unreasonable and erroneous.

Motion for Judgment on the Pleadings A motion by either party to a lawsuit at the close of the pleadings requesting the court to decide the issue solely on the pleadings without proceeding to trial. The motion will be granted only if no facts are in dispute.

Motion for Summary Judgment A motion requesting the court to enter a judgment without proceeding to trial. The motion can be based on evidence outside the pleadings and will be granted only if no facts are in dispute.

Motion to Dismiss A pleading in which a defendant asserts that the plaintiff's claim fails to state a cause of action (that is, has no basis in law) or that there are other grounds on which the suit should be dismissed.

Mutual Fund A type of investment company that continually buys and sells to investors shares of ownership in a portfolio.

N

National Law Law that pertains to a particular nation (as opposed to international law).

Natural Law A system of universal moral and ethical principles that are held to be inherent in human nature. The natural law school is the oldest and one of the most significant schools of legal thought.

Necessaries Necessities required for life, such as food, shelter, clothing, and medical attention; may include whatever is believed to be necessary to maintain a person's standard of living or financial and social status.

Negligence The failure to exercise the standard of care that a reasonable person would exercise in similar circumstances.

Negligence *Per Se* An action or failure to act in violation of a statutory requirement.

Negotiable Instrument A signed writing that contains an unconditional promise or order to pay an exact sum of money on demand or at an exact future time to a specific person or order or to bearer.

Negotiation A dispute-resolution method in which parties attempt to settle their dispute informally, with or without attorneys to represent them. The transfer of an instrument in such form that the transferee (the person to whom the instrument is transferred) becomes a holder.

Nominal Damages A small monetary award (often one dollar) granted to a plaintiff when no actual damage was suffered or when the plaintiff is unable to show such loss with sufficient certainty.

No-par Share A corporate share that has no face value—that is, no specific dollar amount is printed on its face.

Normal Trade Relations (NTR) Status A status granted in an international treaty by a provision stating that the citizens of the contracting nations may enjoy the privileges accorded by either party to citizens of its NTR nations. Generally, this status is designed to establish equality of international treatment.

Notary Public A public official authorized to attest to the authenticity of signatures.

Notice-and-Comment Rulemaking A procedure in agency rulemaking that requires (1) notice, (2) opportunity for comment, and (3) a published draft of the final rule.

Novation The substitution, by agreement, of a new contract for an old one, with the rights under the old one being terminated. Typically, novation involves the substitution of a new party for one of the original parties to the contract.

Nuisance A common law doctrine under which persons can be held liable for using their property in a way that unreasonably interferes with others' rights to use or enjoy their own property.

Nuncupative Will An oral will (often called a deathbed will) made before witnesses; usually limited to transfers of personal property.

O

Objective Theory of Contracts A theory under which the intent to form a contract will be judged by outward, objective facts as interpreted by a reasonable person, rather than by the party's own secret, subjective intentions.

Obligee One to whom an obligation is owed.

Obligor One who owes an obligation to another.

Offer A promise or commitment to perform or refrain from performing some specified act in the future.

Offeree A person to whom an offer is made.

Offeror A person who makes an offer.

Online Dispute Resolution (ODR) The resolution of disputes with the assistance of organizations that offer dispute-resolution services via the Internet.

Operating Agreement In a limited liability company, an agreement in which the members set forth the details of how the business will be managed and operated. State statutes typically give the members wide latitude in deciding for themselves the rules that will govern their organization.

Optimum Profits The amount of profits that a business can make and still act ethically, as opposed to maximum profits, defined as the amount of profits a firm can make if it is willing to disregard ethical concerns.

Option Contract A contract under which an offeror promises to hold an offer open for a specified period in return for consideration given by the offeree.

Order for Relief A court's grant of assistance to a complainant. In bankruptcy proceedings, the order relieves the debtor of the immediate obligation to pay the debts listed in the bankruptcy petition.

Order Instrument A negotiable instrument payable "to the order of an identified person" or "to an identified person or order."

Ordinance A regulation enacted by a city or county legislative body that becomes part of that state's statutory law.

Output Contract An agreement in which a seller agrees to sell and a buyer agrees to buy all or up to a stated amount of what the seller produces.

Overdraft A check that is written on a checking account in which there are insufficient funds to cover the check and that is paid by the bank.

P

Parent-Subsidiary Merger A merger of companies in which one company (the parent corporation) owns most of the stock of the other corporation (the subsidiary corporation). A parent-subsidiary merger (short-form merger) can use a simplified procedure when the parent corporation owns at least 90 percent of the outstanding shares of each class of stock of the subsidiary corporation.

Parol Evidence Rule A substantive rule of contracts, as well as a procedural rule of evidence, under which a court will not receive into evidence the parties' prior negotiations, prior agreements, or contemporaneous oral agreements if that evidence contradicts or varies the terms of the parties' written contract.

Partially Disclosed Principal A principal whose identity is unknown by a third person at the time the agent and the third person form a contract, but the third person knows that the agent is or may be acting for a principal.

Partnering Agreement An agreement between a seller and a buyer who frequently do business with each other on the terms and conditions that will apply to all subsequently formed electronic contracts.

Partnership An agreement by two or more persons to carry on, as co-owners, a business for profit.

Par-Value Share A corporate share that has a specific face value, or formal cash-in value, printed on it.

Pass-Through Entity A business entity that has no tax liability; the entity's income is passed through to the owners, and the owners pay taxes on the income.

Past Consideration An act done before the contract is made, which ordinarily, by itself, cannot be consideration for a later promise to pay for the act.

Patent A government grant that gives an inventor the exclusive right or privilege to make, use, or sell his or her invention for a limited time period.

Payee A person to whom an instrument is made payable.

Payor Bank The bank on which a check is drawn (the drawee bank).

Peer-to-Peer (P2P) Networking A technology that allows Internet users to access files on other users' computers.

Penalty An amount, stipulated in the contract, to be paid in the event of a default or breach of contract. When the amount is not a reasonable measure of damages, the court will not enforce it but will limit recovery to actual damages.

Per Capita A Latin term meaning "per person"; in the law governing estate distribution, a method of distributing the property of an intestate's estate in which all heirs in a certain class (such as grandchildren) receive equal shares.

***Per Se* Violation** A type of anticompetitive agreement—such as a horizontal price-fixing agreement—that is considered to be so injurious to the public that there is no need to determine whether it actually injures market competition; rather, it is in itself (*per se*) a violation of the Sherman Act.

Per Stirpes A Latin term meaning "by the roots"; in the law governing estate distribution, a method of distributing an intestate's estate in which, within a certain class (such as grandchildren), the children of any one descendant take the share to which their deceased ancestor (such as a mother or father) would have been entitled.

Perfection The legal process by which secured parties protect themselves against the claims of third parties who may wish to have their debts satisfied out of the same collateral; usually accomplished by filing a financing statement with the appropriate government official.

Performance In contract law, the fulfillment of one's duties arising under a contract with another; the normal way of discharging one's contractual obligations.

Periodic Tenancy A lease interest in land for an indefinite period involving payment of rent at fixed intervals, such as week to week, month to month, or year to year.
Personal Defense A defense that can be used to avoid payment to an ordinary holder of a negotiable instrument but not a holder in due course (HDC) or a holder with the rights of an HDC.
Personal Property Property that is movable; any property that is not real property.
Persuasive Authority Any legal authority or source of law that a court may look to for guidance but on which it need not rely in making its decision. Persuasive authorities include cases from other jurisdictions and secondary sources of law.
Petition in Bankruptcy A document filed with a bankruptcy court to initiate bankruptcy proceedings. The official forms required for a petition in bankruptcy must be completed accurately, sworn to under oath, and signed by the debtor.
Petty Offense In criminal law, the least serious kind of criminal offense, such as a traffic or building-code violation.
Piercing the Corporate Veil An action in which a court disregards the corporate entity and holds the shareholders personally liable for corporate debts and obligations.
Plaintiff One who initiates a lawsuit.
Plea Bargaining The process by which a criminal defendant and the prosecutor in a criminal case work out a mutually satisfactory disposition of the case, subject to court approval; usually involves the defendant's pleading guilty to a lesser offense in return for a lighter sentence.
Pleadings Statements made by the plaintiff and the defendant in a lawsuit that detail the facts, charges, and defenses involved in the litigation; the complaint and answer are part of the pleadings.
Pledge A common law security device (retained in Article 9 of the UCC) in which possession of personal property is turned over to the creditor as security for the payment of a debt and retained by the creditor until the debt is paid.
Police Powers Regulatory powers possessed by states as part of their inherent sovereignty. These powers may be exercised to protect or promote the public order, health, safety, morals, and general welfare.
Policy In insurance law, a contract between the insurer and the insured in which, for a stipulated consideration, the insurer agrees to compensate the insured for loss on a specific subject by a specified peril.
Positive Law The body of conventional, or written, law of a particular society at a particular point in time.
Potentially Responsible Party (PRP) A party liable for the costs of cleaning up a hazardous waste–disposal site under the Comprehensive Environmental Response, Compensation, and Liability Act (CERCLA). Any person who generated the hazardous waste, transported it, owned or operated the waste site at the time of disposal, or currently owns or operates the site may be responsible for some or all of the cleanup costs.
Power of Attorney A written document, which is usually notarized, authorizing another to act as one's agent; it can be special (permitting the agent to do specified acts only) or general (permitting the agent to transact all business for the principal).
Precedent A court decision that furnishes an example or authority for deciding subsequent cases involving identical or similar facts.
Predatory Behavior Business behavior that is undertaken with the intention of unlawfully driving competitors out of the market.
Predatory Pricing The pricing of a product below cost with the intent to drive competitors out of the market.
Predominant-Factor Test A test courts use to determine whether a contract is primarily for the sale of goods or for the sale of services.
Preemption A doctrine under which certain federal laws preempt, or take precedence over, conflicting state or local laws.
Preemptive Right The right of a shareholder to purchase newly issued shares of a corporation's stock, equal in percentage to shares already held, before the stock is offered to any outside buyers. Preemptive rights enable shareholders to maintain their proportionate ownership and voice in the corporation.
Preference In bankruptcy proceedings, property transfers or payments made by the debtor that favor (give preference to) one creditor over others. The bankruptcy trustee is allowed to recover payments made both voluntarily and involuntarily to one creditor in preference over another.
Preferred Stock Classes of stock that have priority over common stock as to both payment of dividends and distribution of assets on the corporation's dissolution.
Premium In insurance law, the price paid by the insured for insurance protection for a specified period of time.
Prenuptial Agreement An agreement made before marriage that defines each partner's ownership rights in the other partner's property. Prenuptial agreements must be in writing to be enforceable.
Presentment The act of presenting an instrument to the party liable on the instrument to collect payment; presentment also occurs when a person presents an instrument to a drawee for a required acceptance.
Presentment Warranties Any person who presents an instrument for payment or acceptance impliedly warrants that (1) he or she is entitled to enforce the instrument or authorized to obtain payment or acceptance on behalf of a person who is entitled, (2) the instrument has not been altered, and (3) he or she has no knowledge that the signature of the drawer is unauthorized.
Price Discrimination Setting prices in such a way that two competing buyers pay two different prices for identical products or services.
Price-Fixing Agreement An agreement between competitors to fix the prices of products or services at a certain level.
***Prima Facie* Case** A case in which the plaintiff has produced sufficient evidence supporting his or her claim that the case can go to a jury; a case in which the evidence is such that the plaintiff will win if the defendant produces no affirmative defense or evidence to disprove it.
Primary Source of Law A document that establishes the law on a particular issue, such as a constitution, a statute, an administrative rule, or a court decision.
Principal In agency law, a person who agrees to have another, called the agent, act on her or his behalf.
Principle of Rights The principle that human beings have certain fundamental rights (to life, freedom, and the pursuit of happiness, for example). Those who adhere to this "rights theory" believe that a key factor in determining whether a business decision is ethical is how that decision affects the rights of various groups.
Privilege In tort law, the ability to act contrary to another person's

right without that person's having legal redress for such acts. Privilege may be raised as a defense to defamation.

Privity of Contract The relationship that exists between the promisor and the promisee of a contract.

Probable Cause Reasonable grounds for believing that a person should be arrested or searched.

Probate The process of proving and validating a will and settling all matters pertaining to an estate.

Probate Court A state court of limited jurisdiction that conducts proceedings relating to the settlement of a deceased person's estate.

Procedural Law Law that establishes the methods of enforcing the rights established by substantive law.

Proceeds Under Article 9 of the UCC, whatever is received when the collateral is sold or otherwise disposed of, such as by exchange.

Product Liability The legal liability of manufacturers, sellers, and lessors of goods to consumers, users, and bystanders for injuries or damages that are caused by the goods.

Profit In real property law, the right to enter on and remove things from the property of another (for example, the right to enter onto a person's land and remove sand and gravel).

Promise A person's assurance that the person will or will not do something.

Promisee A person to whom a promise is made.

Promisor A person who makes a promise.

Promissory Estoppel A doctrine that applies when a promisor makes a clear and definite promise on which the promisee justifiably relies; such a promise is binding if justice will be better served by the enforcement of the promise.

Promissory Note A written promise made by one person (the maker) to pay a fixed amount of money to another person (the payee or a subsequent holder) on demand or on a specified date.

Promoter A person who takes the preliminary steps in organizing a corporation, including (usually) issuing a prospectus, procuring stock subscriptions, making contracts for necessary purchases and services, securing a corporate charter, and the like.

Property Legally protected rights and interests in anything with an ascertainable value that is subject to ownership.

Prospectus A document required by federal or state securities laws that describes the financial operations of the corporation, thus allowing investors to make informed decisions.

Protected Class A group of persons protected by specific laws because of the group's defining characteristics. Under laws prohibiting employment discrimination, these characteristics include race, color, religion, national origin, gender, age, and disability.

Proximate Cause Legal cause; exists when the connection between an act and an injury is strong enough to justify imposing liability.

Proxy In corporation law, a written agreement between a stockholder and another under which the stockholder authorizes the other to vote the stockholder's shares in a certain manner.

Proxy Fight A conflict between an individual, group, or firm attempting to take control of a corporation and the corporation's management for the votes of the shareholders.

Puffery A salesperson's exaggerated claims concerning the quality of property offered for sale. Such claims involve opinions rather than facts and are not considered to be legally binding promises or warranties.

Punitive Damages Money damages that may be awarded to a plaintiff to punish the defendant and deter future similar conduct.

Purchase-Money Security Interest (PMSI) A security interest that arises when a seller or lender extends credit for part or all of the purchase price of goods purchased by a buyer.

Q

Qualified Indorsement An indorsement in which the indorser disclaims any contract liability on the instrument; the notation "without recourse" is commonly used to create a qualified indorsement.

Quasi Contract A fictional contract imposed on parties by a court in the interests of fairness and justice; usually imposed to avoid the unjust enrichment of one party at the expense of another.

Quitclaim Deed A deed intended to pass any title, interest, or claim that the grantor may have in the property but not warranting that such title is valid. A quitclaim deed offers the least amount of protection against defects in the title.

Quorum The number of members of a decision-making body that must be present before business can be transacted.

Quota A set limit on the amount of goods that can be imported.

R

Ratification The act of accepting and giving legal force to an obligation that previously was not enforceable.

Reaffirmation Agreement An agreement between a debtor and a creditor in which the debtor voluntarily agrees to pay, or reaffirm, a debt dischargeable in bankruptcy. To be enforceable, the agreement must be made before the debtor is granted a discharge.

Real Property Land and everything attached to it, such as trees and buildings.

Reasonable Person Standard The standard of behavior expected of a hypothetical "reasonable person." The standard against which negligence is measured and that must be observed to avoid liability for negligence.

Receiver In a corporate dissolution, a court-appointed person who winds up corporate affairs and liquidates corporate assets.

Record According to the Uniform Electronic Transactions Act, information that is either inscribed on a tangible medium or stored in an electronic or other medium and that is retrievable. The Uniform Computer Information Transactions Act uses the term *record* instead of *writing*.

Recording Statutes Statutes that allow deeds, mortgages, and other real property transactions to be recorded so as to provide notice to future purchasers or creditors of an existing claim on the property.

Red Herring A preliminary prospectus that can be distributed to potential investors after the registration statement (for a securities offering) has been filed with the Securities and Exchange Commission. The name derives from the red legend printed across the prospectus stating that the registration has been filed but has not become effective.

Reformation A court-ordered correction of a written contract so that it reflects the true intentions of the parties.

Regulation E A set of rules issued by the Federal Reserve System's Board of Governors to protect users of elecronic fund transfer systems.

Regulation Z A set of rules promulgated by the Federal Reserve Board to implement the provisions of the Truth-in-Lending Act.

Release A contract in which one party forfeits the right to pursue a legal claim against the other party.

Remainder A future interest in property held by a person other than the original owner.

Remedy The relief given to an innocent party to enforce a right or compensate for the violation of a right.
Replevin An action to recover identified goods in the hands of a party who is wrongfully withholding them from the other party. Under the Uniform Commercial Code, this remedy is usually available only if the buyer or lessee is unable to cover.
Reply Procedurally, a plaintiff's response to a defendant's answer.
Requirements Contract An agreement in which a buyer agrees to purchase and a seller agrees to sell all or up to a stated amount of what the buyer needs or requires.
Res Ipsa Loquitur A doctrine under which negligence may be inferred simply because an event occurred, if it is the type of event that would not occur in the absence of negligence. Literally, the term means "the facts speak for themselves."
Resale Price Maintenance Agreement An agreement between a manufacturer and a retailer in which the manufacturer specifies what the retail price of its products must be.
Rescission A remedy whereby a contract is canceled and the parties are returned to the positions they occupied before the contract was made; may be effected through the mutual consent of the parties, by their conduct, or by court decree.
Respondeat Superior In Latin, "Let the master respond." A doctrine under which a principal or an employer is held liable for wrongful acts committed by agents or employees acting within the course and scope of their agency or employment.
Restitution An equitable remedy under which a person is restored to his or her original position prior to loss or injury.
Restrictive Indorsement An indorsement that requires the indorsee to comply with certain instructions regarding the funds involved. A restrictive indorsement does not prohibit the further negotiation of the instrument.
Resulting Trust An implied trust arising from the conduct of the parties. A trust in which a party holds the actual legal title to another's property but only for that person's benefit.
Retained Earnings The portion of a corporation's profits that has not been paid out as dividends to shareholders.
Reversionary Interest A future interest in property retained by the original owner.
Revocation In contract law, the withdrawal of an offer by an offeror; unless the offer is irrevocable, it can be revoked at any time prior to acceptance without liability.
Right of Contribution The right of a co-surety who pays more than his or her proportionate share on a debtor's default to recover the excess paid from other co-sureties.
Right of First Refusal The right to purchase personal or real property—such as corporate shares or real estate—before the property is offered for sale to others.
Right of Reimbursement The legal right of a person to be restored, repaid, or indemnified for costs, expenses, or losses incurred or expended on behalf of another.
Right of Subrogation The right of a person to stand in the place of (be substituted for) another, giving the substituted party the same legal rights the original party had.
Right-to-Work Law A state law providing that employees cannot be required to join a union as a condition of retaining employment.
Risk A prediction concerning potential loss based on known and unknown factors.
Risk Management Planning that is undertaken to protect one's interest should some event threaten to undermine its security. In the context of insurance, risk management involves transferring certain risks from the insured to the insurance company.
Robbery The act of forcefully and unlawfully taking personal property of any value from another; force or intimidation is usually necessary for an act of theft to be considered a robbery.
Rule of Four A rule of the United States Supreme Court under which the Court will not issue a writ of *certiorari* unless at least four justices approve of the decision to issue the writ.
Rule of Reason A test by which a court balances the positive effects (such as economic efficiency) of an agreement against its potentially anticompetitive effects. In antitrust litigation, many practices are analyzed under the rule of reason.
Rulemaking The actions undertaken by administrative agencies when formally adopting new regulations or amending old ones. Under the Administrative Procedure Act, rulemaking includes notifying the public of proposed rules or changes and receiving and considering the public's comments.

S

S Corporation A close business corporation that has met certain requirements as set out by the Internal Revenue Code and thus qualifies for special income tax treatment. Essentially, an S corporation is taxed the same as a partnership, but its owners enjoy the privilege of limited liability.
Sale The passing of title (evidence of ownership rights) to property from the seller to the buyer for a price.
Sale on Approval A type of conditional sale in which the buyer takes the goods on a trial basis. The sale becomes absolute only when the buyer approves of (or is satisfied with) the goods being sold.
Sale or Return A type of conditional sale in which title and possession pass from the seller to the buyer, but the buyer retains the option to return the goods during a specified period even though the goods conform to the contract.
Sales Contract A contract for the sale of goods under which the ownership of goods is transferred from a seller to a buyer for a price.
Scienter Knowledge by the misrepresenting party that material facts have been falsely represented or omitted with an intent to deceive.
Search Warrant An order granted by a public authority, such as a judge, that authorizes law enforcement personnel to search particular premises or property.
Seasonably Within a specified time period, or, if no period is specified, within a reasonable time.
SEC Rule 10b-5 A rule of the Securities and Exchange Commission (SEC) that makes it unlawful, in connection with the purchase or sale of any security, to make any untrue statement of a material fact or to omit a material fact if such omission causes the statement to be misleading.
Secondary Boycott A union's refusal to work for, purchase from, or handle the products of a secondary employer, with whom the union has no dispute, in order to force that employer to stop doing business with the primary employer, with whom the union has a labor dispute.
Secondary Source of Law A publication that summarizes or interprets the law, such as a legal encyclopedia, a legal treatise, or an article in a law review.

Secured Party A lender, seller, or any other creditor in whose favor there is a security interest.
Secured Transaction Any transaction in which the payment of a debt is guaranteed, or secured, by personal property owned by the debtor or in which the debtor has a legal interest.
Security Generally, a stock certificate, bond, note, debenture, warrant, or other document given as evidence of an ownership interest in a corporation or as a promise of repayment by a corporation.
Security Agreement An agreement that creates or provides for a security interest between the debtor and a secured party.
Security Interest Any interest "in personal property or fixtures which secures payment or performance of an obligation" [UCC 1–201(37)].
Self-Defense The legally recognized privilege to protect oneself or one's property against injury by another. The privilege of self-defense protects only acts that are reasonably necessary to protect oneself, one's property, or another person.
Self-Incrimination The giving of testimony that may subject the testifier to criminal prosecution. The Fifth Amendment to the Constitution protects against self-incrimination by providing that no person "shall be compelled in any criminal case to be a witness against himself."
Seniority System In regard to employment relationships, a system in which those who have worked longest for the company are first in line for promotions, salary increases, and other benefits and last to be laid off if the workforce must be reduced.
Service Mark A mark used in the sale or advertising of services to distinguish the services of one person or company from those of others.
Sexual Harassment In the employment context, (1) the granting of job promotions or other benefits in return for sexual favors or (2) language or conduct that is so sexually offensive that it creates a hostile working environment.
Shareholder's Derivative Suit A suit brought by a shareholder to enforce a corporate cause of action against a third person.
Shelter Principle The principle that a holder of a negotiable instrument who cannot qualify as a holder in due course (HDC), but who derives his or her title through an HDC, acquires the rights of an HDC.
Shipment Contract A contract in which the seller is required to ship the goods by carrier. The seller assumes liability for any losses or damage to the goods until they are delivered to the carrier. Generally, all contracts are assumed to be shipment contracts if nothing to the contrary is stated in the contract.
Short-Form Merger A merger between a subsidiary corporation and a parent corporation that owns at least 90 percent of the outstanding shares of each class of stock issued by the subsidiary corporation. Short-form mergers can be accomplished without the approval of the shareholders of either corporation.
Shrink-Wrap Agreement An agreement whose terms are expressed in a document located inside a box in which goods (usually software) are packaged; sometimes called a *shrink-wrap license.*
Signature Under the UCC, "any symbol executed or adopted by a party with a present intention to authenticate a writing."
Slander Defamation in oral form.
Slander of Quality (Trade Libel) The publication of false information about another's product, alleging that it is not what its seller claims.
Slander of Title The publication of a statement that denies or casts doubt on another's legal ownership of any property, causing financial loss to that property's owner.
Small Claims Court A special court in which parties litigate small claims (such as $5,000 or less). Attorneys are not required in small claims courts and, in some states, are not allowed to represent the parties.
Smart Card A card containing a microprocessor that permits storage of funds via security programming. The smart card can communicate with other computers and does not require online authorization for fund transfers.
Sociological School A school of legal thought that views the law as a tool for promoting justice in society.
Sole Proprietorship The simplest form of business, in which the owner is the business. The owner reports business income on his or her personal income tax return and is legally responsible for all debts and obligations incurred by the business.
Sovereign Immunity A doctrine that immunizes foreign nations from the jurisdiction of U.S. courts when certain conditions are satisfied.
Spam Bulk, unsolicited ("junk") e-mail.
Special Indorsement An indorsement that indicates the specific person to whom the indorser intends to make the instrument payable; that is, it names the indorsee.
Special Warranty Deed A deed in which the grantor only warrants that the grantor or seller held good title during his or her ownership of the property and does not warrant that there were no defects of title when the property was held by previous owners.
Specific Performance An equitable remedy requiring the breaching party to perform as promised under the contract; usually granted only when money damages would be an inadequate remedy and the subject matter of the contract is unique (for example, real property).
Spendthrift Trust A trust created to protect the beneficiary from spending all the funds to which she or he is entitled. Only a certain portion of the total amount is given to the beneficiary at any one time, and most states prohibit creditors from attaching assets of the trust.
Stale Check A check, other than a certified check, that is presented for payment more than six months after its date.
Standing to Sue The requirement that an individual must have a sufficient stake in a controversy before he or she can bring a lawsuit. The plaintiff must demonstrate that he or she has been either injured or threatened with injury.
Stare Decisis A common law doctrine under which judges are obligated to follow the precedents established in prior decisions.
Statute of Frauds A state statute under which certain types of contracts must be in writing to be enforceable.
Statute of Limitations A federal or state statute setting the maximum time period during which a certain action can be brought or certain rights enforced.
Statute of Repose Basically, a statute of limitations that is not dependent on the happening of a cause of action. Statutes of repose generally begin to run at an earlier date and run for a longer period of time than statutes of limitations.
Statutory Law The body of law enacted by legislative bodies (as opposed to constitutional law, administrative law, or case law).
Stock An equity (ownership) interest in a corporation, measured in units of shares.

Stock Certificate A certificate issued by a corporation evidencing the ownership of a specified number of shares in the corporation.
Stock Warrant A certificate that grants the owner the option to buy a given number of shares of stock, usually within a set time period.
Stop-Payment Order An order by a bank customer to his or her bank not to pay or certify a certain check.
Stored-Value Card A card bearing magnetically encoded data providing access to stored funds.
Strict Liability Liability regardless of fault.
Strike An action undertaken by unionized workers when collective bargaining fails; the workers leave their jobs, refuse to work, and (typically) picket the employer's workplace.
Sublease A lease executed by the lessee of real estate to a third person, conveying the same interest that the lessee enjoys but for a period shorter than the term of the original lease.
Substantive Law Law that defines, describes, regulates, and creates legal rights and obligations.
Summary Jury Trial (SJT) A method of settling disputes, used in many federal courts, in which a trial is held but the jury's verdict is not binding. The verdict acts only as a guide to both sides in reaching an agreement during the mandatory negotiations that immediately follow the trial.
Summons A document informing a defendant that a legal action has been commenced against him or her and that the defendant must appear in court on a certain date to answer the plaintiff's complaint. The document is delivered by a sheriff or any other authorized person.
Supremacy Clause The provision in Article VI of the Constitution that establishes the Constitution, laws, and treaties of the United States as "the supreme Law of the Land." Under this clause, state and local laws that directly conflict with federal law will be rendered invalid.
Surety A person, such as a cosigner on a note, who agrees to be primarily responsible for the debt of another.
Suretyship An express contract in which a third party to a debtor-creditor relationship (the surety) promises to be primarily responsible for the debtor's obligation.
Symbolic Speech Nonverbal expressions of beliefs. Symbolic speech, which includes gestures, movements, and articles of clothing, is given substantial protection by the courts.
Syndicate An investment group of persons or firms brought together for the purpose of financing a project that they would not or could not undertake independently.

T

Takeover Acquiring ownership or control of a corporation, usually by the purchase of voting shares or assets, a tender offer, or a merger.
Taking The taking of private property by the government for public use. Under the Fifth Amendment to the Constitution, the government may not take private property for public use without "just compensation."
Tangible Property Property that has physical existence and can be distinguished by the senses of touch, sight, and so on. A car is tangible property; a patent right is intangible property.
Target Corporation The corporation to be acquired in a corporate takeover; a corporation to whose shareholders a tender offer is submitted.
Tariff A tax on imported goods.
Technology Licensing Allowing another to use and profit from intellectual property (patents, copyrights, trademarks, innovative products or processes, and so on) for consideration. In the context of international business transactions, technology licensing is sometimes an attractive alternative to the establishment of foreign production facilities.
Tenancy at Sufferance A type of tenancy under which a tenant who, after rightfully being in possession of leased premises, continues (wrongfully) to occupy the property after the lease has been terminated. The tenant has no rights to possess the property and occupies it only because the person entitled to evict the tenant has not done so.
Tenancy at Will A type of tenancy under which either party can terminate the tenancy without notice; usually arises when a tenant who has been under a tenancy for years retains possession, with the landlord's consent, after the tenancy for years has terminated.
Tenancy by the Entirety Co-ownership of property by a husband and wife in which neither party can transfer his or her interest in the property without the consent of the other.
Tenancy for Years A type of tenancy under which property is leased for a specified period of time, such as a month, a year, or a period of years.
Tenancy in Common Co-ownership of property in which each party owns an undivided interest that passes to her or his heirs at death.
Tender An unconditional offer to perform an obligation by a person who is ready, willing, and able to do so.
Tender Offer An offer to purchase shares made by one company directly to the shareholders of another (target) company; often referred to as a takeover bid.
Testamentary Trust A trust that is created by will and therefore does not take effect until the death of the testator.
Testate Having left a will at death.
Testator One who makes and executes a will.
Third Party Beneficiary One for whose benefit a promise is made in a contract but who is not a party to the contract.
Tippee A person who receives inside information.
Tombstone Ad An advertisement, historically in a format resembling a tombstone, of a securities offering. The ad informs potential investors of where and how they can obtain a prospectus.
Tort A civil wrong not arising from a breach of contract. A breach of a legal duty that proximately causes harm or injury to another.
Tortfeasor One who commits a tort.
Totten Trust A trust created by the deposit of a person's own funds in his or her own name as a trustee for another. It is a tentative trust, revocable at will until the depositor dies or completes the gift in his or her lifetime by some unequivocal act or declaration.
Toxic Tort A civil wrong arising from exposure to a toxic substance, such as asbestos, radiation, or hazardous waste.
Trade Acceptance A draft drawn by a seller of goods ordering the buyer to pay a specified sum of money to the seller, usually at a stated time in the future. The buyer accepts the draft by signing the face of the draft, thus creating an enforceable obligation to pay the draft when it comes due. On a trade acceptance, the seller is both the drawer and the payee.
Trade Dress The image and overall appearance of a product—for example, the distinctive decor, menu, layout, and style of service of

a particular restaurant. Basically, trade dress is subject to the same protection as trademarks.

Trade Name A term that is used to indicate part or all of a business's name and that is directly related to the business's reputation and goodwill. Trade names are protected under the common law (and under trademark law, if the name is the same as the firm's trademarked property).

Trade Secrets Information or processes that give a business an advantage over competitors who do not know the information or processes.

Trademark A distinctive mark, motto, device, or emblem that a manufacturer stamps, prints, or otherwise affixes to the goods it produces so that they can be identified on the market and their origins made known. Once a trademark is established (under the common law or through registration), the owner is entitled to its exclusive use.

Transfer Warranties Implied warranties, made by any person who transfers an instrument for consideration to subsequent transferees and holders who take the instrument in good faith, that (1) the transferor is entitled to enforce the instrument, (2) all signatures are authentic and authorized, (3) the instrument has not been altered, (4) the instrument is not subject to a defense or claim of any party that can be asserted against the transferor, and (5) the transferor has no knowledge of any insolvency proceedings against the maker, the acceptor, or the drawer of the instrument.

Traveler's Check A check that is payable on demand, drawn on or payable through a financial institution, and designated as a traveler's check.

Treble Damages Damages that, by statute, are three times the amount that the fact finder determines is owed.

Trespass to Land The entry onto, above, or below the surface of land owned by another without the owner's permission or legal authorization.

Trespass to Personal Property The unlawful taking or harming of another's personal property; interference with another's right to the exclusive possession of his or her personal property.

Trust An arrangement in which title to property is held by one person (a trustee) for the benefit of another (a beneficiary).

Trust Indorsement An indorsement for the benefit of the indorser or a third person; also known as an *agency indorsement*. The indorsement results in legal title vesting in the original indorsee.

Tying Arrangement An agreement between a buyer and a seller under which the buyer of a specific product or service becomes obligated to purchase additional products or services from the seller.

U

U.S. Trustee A government official who performs certain administrative tasks that a bankruptcy judge would otherwise have to perform.

Ultra Vires A Latin term meaning "beyond the powers"; in corporate law, describes acts of a corporation that are beyond its express and implied powers to undertake.

Unconscionable Contract or Clause A contract or clause that is void on the basis of public policy because one party, as a result of disproportionate bargaining power, is forced to accept terms that are unfairly burdensome and that unfairly benefit the dominating party.

Underwriter In insurance law, the insurer, or the one assuming a risk in return for the payment of a premium.

Undisclosed Principal A principal whose identity is unknown by a third person at the time the agent and the third person form a contract, and the third person has no knowledge that the agent is acting for a principal.

Unenforceable Contract A valid contract rendered unenforceable by some statute or law.

Unilateral Contract A contract that results when an offer can be accepted only by the offeree's performance.

Unilateral Mistake Mistake that occurs when one party to a contract is mistaken as to a material fact; the contract normally is enforceable.

Union Shop A place of employment where all workers, once employed, must become union members within a specified period of time as a condition of their continued employment.

Universal Defense A defense that is valid against all holders of a negotiable instrument, including holders in due course (HDCs) and holders with the rights of HDCs.

Unreasonably Dangerous Product In product liability, a product that is defective to the point of threatening a consumer's health and safety. A product will be considered unreasonably dangerous if it is dangerous beyond the expectation of the ordinary consumer or if a less dangerous alternative was economically feasible for the manufacturer but the manufacturer failed to produce it.

Usage of Trade Any practice or method of dealing having such regularity of observance in a place, vocation, or trade as to justify an expectation that it will be observed with respect to the transaction in question.

Usury Charging an illegal rate of interest.

Utilitarianism An approach to ethical reasoning that evaluates behavior not on the basis of any absolute ethical or moral values but on the consequences of that behavior for those who will be affected by it. In utilitarian reasoning, a "good" decision is one that results in the greatest good for the greatest number of people affected by the decision.

V

Valid Contract A contract for which the elements necessary for contract formation (agreement, consideration, legal purpose, and contractual capacity) are present.

Venue The geographic district in which an action is tried and from which the jury is selected.

Vertical Merger The acquisition by a company at one level in a marketing chain of a company at a higher or lower level in the chain (such as its supplier or retailer).

Vertical Restraint Any restraint on trade created by agreements between firms at different levels in the manufacturing and distribution process.

Vertically Integrated Firm A firm that carries out two or more functional phases (manufacture, distribution, retailing, and so on) of a product.

Vesting Under ERISA, a pension plan becomes vested when an employee has a legal right to the benefits purchased with the employer's contributions, even if the employee is no longer working for this employer.

Vicarious Liability Legal responsibility placed on one person for the acts of another; indirect liability imposed on a supervisory party (such as an employer) for the actions of a subordinate (such as an employee) because of the relationship between the two parties.

Void Contract A contract having no legal force or binding effect.

Voidable Contract A contract that may be legally avoided (canceled, or annulled) at the option of one or both of the parties.

Voir Dire French verbs that mean, literally, "to see" and "to speak." In jury trials, the phrase refers to the process in which the attorneys question prospective jurors to determine whether they are biased or have any connection with a party to the action or with a prospective witness.

Voting Trust An agreement (trust contract) under which legal title to shares of corporate stock is transferred to a trustee who is authorized by the shareholders to vote the shares on their behalf.

W

Warranty Deed A deed in which the grantor assures (warrants to) the grantee that the grantor has title to the property conveyed in the deed, that there are no encumbrances on the property other than what the grantor has represented, and that the grantee will enjoy quiet possession of the property; this type of deed provides the greatest amount of protection for the grantee.

Watered Stock Shares of stock issued by a corporation for which the corporation receives, as payment, less than the fair market value of the shares.

Wetlands Water-saturated areas of land that support specific types of vegetation. Under the Clean Water Act, wetlands are protected areas that cannot be filled in or dredged by private contractors or parties without a permit.

Whistleblowing An employee's disclosure to a government official, upper-management authorities, or the press that the employer is engaged in unsafe or illegal activities.

White-Collar Crime Nonviolent crime committed by individuals or corporations to obtain a personal or business advantage.

Will An instrument directing what is to be done with the testator's property on his or her death, made by the testator and revocable during his or her lifetime. No interests in the testator's property pass until the testator dies.

Will Substitutes Various documents that attempt to dispose of an estate in the same or similar manner as a will, such as trusts or life insurance plans.

Winding Up In partnership law, the second of two stages in the termination of a partnership. Once the firm is dissolved, it continues to exist legally until the process of winding up all business affairs (collecting and distributing the firm's assets) is complete.

Workers' Compensation Laws State statutes establishing an administrative procedure for compensating workers for injuries that arise out of—or in the course of—their employment, regardless of fault.

Working Papers The various documents used and developed by an accountant during an audit. Working papers include notes, computations, memoranda, copies, and other papers that make up the work product of an accountant's services to a client.

Workout An out-of-court agreement between a debtor and his or her creditors in which the parties work out a payment plan or schedule under which the debtor's debts can be discharged.

Writ of Attachment A court's order, prior to a trial to collect a debt, directing the sheriff or other officer to seize nonexempt property of the debtor. If the creditor prevails at trial, the seized property can be sold to satisfy the judgment.

Writ of *Certiorari* A writ from a higher court asking the lower court for the record of a case.

Writ of Execution A court's order, after a judgment has been entered against the debtor, directing the sheriff to seize (levy) and sell nonexempt real or personal property of the debtor. The proceeds of the sale are used to pay off the judgment, accrued interest, and costs of the sale; any surplus is paid to the debtor.

Wrongful Discharge An employer's termination of an employee's employment in violation of the law.

G

H

I

J

K

INDEX

E

S

U

LANDMARK IN THE LAW

ADAPTING THE LAW TO THE ONLINE ENVIRONMENT

FEATURED CASE